Ecological Economics

Taking as its starting point the interdependence of human and natural systems this book provides a comprehensive introduction to the emerging field of ecological economics. The authors, who have written extensively on the economics of sustainability, build on insights from both mainstream economics and ecological sciences. It assumes no prior knowledge of economics and is well suited for use on interdisciplinary environmental science and management courses.

MICHAEL COMMON is Emeritus Professor at the Graduate School of Environmental Studies, University of Strathclyde and a member of the editorial board of the journal *Ecological Economics*. He is highly respected both for his teaching and as author of numerous journal and book publications on the economics of the environment since 1973.

SIGRID STAGL is a Senior Research Fellow at SPRU, University of Sussex. She is a member of the editorial board of the journal *Environmental Values* and is currently Vice-President of the European Society of Ecological Economics. She was awarded the first Ph.D in Ecological Economics worldwide.

Companion website: www.cambridge.org/common

Common and Stagl have written the definitive text to date for ecological/ environmental economics. It presents the standard theories of neoclassical economics and points the way toward a richer understanding of the relationship between the human economy and the natural world. The field of economics is undergoing a revolution that will fundamentally change economic theory and policy. Central to this revolution is the recognition by economists that economic behavior cannot be understood outside its social and environmental context. This text brings environmental economics into the twenty-first century and will be the standard in the field for years to come.'

JOHN GOWDY, Professor of Economics, Rensselaer Polytechnic Institute, and former President of the U.S. Society for Ecological Economics

'*Environmental* economics has existed as a powerful discipline for nearly 50 years. *Ecological* economics borrows heavily from it, and overlaps it significantly. But there are differences. Ecological economics perhaps invests more heavily in understanding ecological science, takes more note of discontinuities and non-linearities in ecological and economic systems, and pays less attention to notions of economic efficiency and outcomes determined by short-term human wants. Anyone wanting an explanation and exploration of these differences in a lucid and informative manner will want to own Mick Common and Sigrid Stagl's textbook. It is a very fine introduction.'

DAVID PEARCE, Emeritus Professor of Environmental Economics, University College London

'Clear presentations of the reasoning and facts underlying environmental science and economics, a steady focus on the high hopes of economists and the earthly fears of ecologists, and inspiring descriptions of how ecological economists are trying to make sense of life on earth. This is the book we have been waiting for.'

RICHARD B. NORGAARD, Professor of Energy and Resources, University of California, Berkeley, and former President of the International Society for Ecological Economics

'This book provides a coherent account of the major environmental challenges to economic and human progress of the twenty first century. It is clear, direct and easily understandable and conveys a powerful message that we ignore the sustainability and ecological aspects of the economy at out peril. I recommended it highly to all students and scholars of the emerging field.'

NEIL ADGER, Reader in Environmental Economics,
University of East Anglia.

'This book satisfies the urgent need for an introductory text on Ecological Economics that is informative but not overly detailed on environmental sciences, strong on and where necessary critical of economics, and representative in its coverage of new theory and methods.'

JEROEN C. J. M. VAN DEN BERGH, Professor of Environmental
Economics, Free University, Amsterdam

'With this excellent text, Mick Common and Sigrid Stagl have provided an authoritative introduction to ecological economics. It offers a very clear and comprehensive review of the concepts, methods and issues on which ecological economics focuses, with a wealth of examples and worked simulations. Assuming nothing more than the most basic knowledge of mathematics, the book develops the economic principles relevant to environmental policy; it also introduces the necessary understanding of the relevant natural scientific concepts and principles. These economic and scientific methods are then synthesised to analyse current environmental problems and to indicate policy approaches to their solution. With extensive referencing to the current literature, the book is an excellent basis for the study of ecological economics and environmental policy.'

JOHN PROOPS, Professor of Ecological Economics, Keele University, and
former President of the International Society for Ecological Economics

'Here it is – the book that fills the gap! It offers students a very good introduction to environmental management as the interdisciplinary challenge it is. It integrates core elements from natural and social sciences into a coherent text – a rare feature. In doing so it is really enlightening, well structured and enjoyable to read. Moreover, it is well organized for teaching purposes – even with a web page attached to it.'

ARILD VATN, Professor of Environmental Sciences, and
Vice-President of the European Society for Ecological Economics,
Norwegian University of Life Sciences

'This book offers an innovative and sophisticated approach to teaching ecological economics at the introductory level. For economics students, Common and Stagl provide a basic understanding of the biophysical foundations and environmental impacts of economic activity. For environmental studies students, the authors provide a grounded and yet accessible introduction to the concepts and methods of economics – especially as they relate to the interplay between economic growth, natural resource depletion, and the achievement of sustainable development. "Ecological Economics: An Introduction" could and should be used in core courses in academic programs aimed at integrating ecology and economics at the levels of research and praxis.'

RICHARD B. HOWARTH, Professor of Environmental Studies,
Dartmouth College

'This textbook is a brilliant guide to understanding the global environmental and distributional challenges we are facing. Common and Stagl master a truly transdisciplinary approach and take a fresh look at the structuring of the issues, resulting in a textbook that is both committed and balanced and which offers an alternative perspective to traditional environmental economics introductions. Furthermore, the educational presentation is very carefully prepared and clear, ideal for beginning students.'

INGE RØPKE, Associate Professor, Technical University of Denmark

'This is the most comprehensive and readable treatment of the complex transdisciplinary field of Ecological Economics to date. It will be a standard reference for students and practioners for years to come. When it has come to replace "Samuelson" as the standard textbook for introductory economics courses, we will know the world is on a path toward sustainability.'

ROBERT COSTANZA, Gund Professor of Ecological Economics and Director,
Gund Institute of Ecological Economics, The University of Vermont, and
former President of the International Society for Ecological Economics

'How refreshing to see an introductory economics textbook which begins by stating, "The pursuit of sustainable development . . . cannot be left to markets – there is an inescapable role for government"! This new text is the first I've seen which actually begins from the beginning, setting the economy in its environmental context and requiring no prior economics indoctrination (which then would need to be critiqued and expunged). It explains the rationale behind modelling and explores basic principles of ecology, thermodynamics and economics before discussing their many complex interrelationships with currency and style. The sections on policy and governance are sophisticated and comprehensive. This is an introduction to economics for the 21st century, economics as it must become if the profession – and the global economy itself – are to survive.'

PATRICIA E. PERKINS, Associate Professor, York University, Toronto

'This is the most coherent book introducing ecological economics to date. Other attempts have proven to be a mishmash to standard economics and alternative thinking which is often contradictory. Common and Stagl tackle what makes ecological economics distinct head on and provide the strongest textbook currently on the market. Their coverage of ethical issues upfront is particularly welcome. The text is clear and well written for the uninitiated.'

PROFESSOR CLIVE L. SPASH, Research Chair in Environmental & Rural
Economics, University of Aberdeen, and President of the
European Society for Ecological Economics

Ecological Economics
An Introduction

Mick Common and Sigrid Stagl

CAMBRIDGE
UNIVERSITY PRESS

CAMBRIDGE UNIVERSITY PRESS
Cambridge, New York, Melbourne, Madrid, Cape Town, Singapore, São Paulo

Cambridge University Press
The Edinburgh Building, Cambridge CB2 2RU, UK

Published in the United States of America by Cambridge University Press, New York

www.cambridge.org
Information on this title: www.cambridge.org/9780521016704

First published 2005

Printed in the United Kingdom at the University Press, Cambridge

A catalogue record for this book is available from the British Library

Library of Congress Cataloguing in Publication data

ISBN-13   978-0-521-81645-8 hardback
ISBN-10   0-521-81645-9 hardback
ISBN-13   978-0-521-01670-4 paperback
ISBN-10   0-521-01670-3 paperback

Contents

PART III   GOVERNANCE *359*

Figures

Tables

Boxes

Preface

We will explain what this text is about, who it is written for, and how it is organised in the Introduction, and in Chapter 1. In regard to subject matter, we can say here that ecological economics is the transdisciplinary study of the human economy as part of nature's economy. In modern terms, the idea that the human economy needs to be, and can be, studied in this way is a relatively new one. Institutionally, ecological economics can be said to date from the establishment of the International Society for Ecological Economics, ISEE, in 1989.

ISEE now has several thousand members throughout the world, and our first acknowledgement is of the intellectual stimulation and nourishment provided by fellow members of that organisation. Perusal of the contents of the journal *Ecological Economics*, or of the proceedings of one of the many conferences and workshops organised by ISEE and its affiliated regional societies, will make clear our debt here. It is impossible to fully acknowledge our debts to the many individuals, not all members of ISEE, who have contributed to the development of ecological economics. Some indications of some of these debts are given in the Further Reading sections at the end of each chapter.

A number of colleagues, not all members of ISEE, were kind enough to read various draft chapters and offer comments and advice. In naming Steve Dovers, Felix Fitzroy, John Gowdy, Greig Mill, Roger Perman, Charles Perrings and John Proops we thank them and absolve them from any blame for deficiencies due to our not following their advice. We have both also benefited from feedback from students at the universities in Australia, Austria, UK and the US at which we have used some of the material here when teaching ecological economics.

We would like to thank staff at Cambridge University Press for their work in producing this textbook, especially Chris Harrison and Pat Maurice for, respectively, commissioning it and organising and supervising production. Finally, we thank our partners – Branwen Common and Peter Kaufmann – for putting up with the disruptions to family life that writing a book always entails, and for their encouragement to persevere with what at times was a daunting task.

Introduction

WHO IS THIS BOOK FOR?

This textbook is written for students who are beginning a programme which is essentially concerned with the interdependence of the economy and the natural environment. We have called it *Ecological Economics: An Introduction* because that interdependence is what Ecological Economics is all about. However, programmes dealing with it also go under such labels as Environmental Management or Sustainable Development, and programmes in Environmental Science often include substantial components dealing with human systems and their effect on the environment.

Such interdisciplinary programmes are offered at both the undergraduate and postgraduate levels. This textbook is written primarily for beginning undergraduate students. However, where such programmes are at the postgraduate level, most beginning students are to some degree in the same position as beginning undergraduates – they have no previous background in one of the traditional disciplines involved. So, we think that this book should be useful to graduate as well as undergraduate students. For the former particularly, we have included Further Reading sections with each chapter which point to more advanced treatments.

While the book is mainly aimed at students beginning these kinds of programmes, we should say that in our view it would also serve very well as an introductory text in an economics programme. It is our view that all economists should appreciate that the material basis for economic activity is the natural environment, and have some idea about how that works in relation to human interests. Starting the study of economics here seems to us the proper way to ensure that they do.

Nowhere do we assume prior knowledge of ecology, economics or environmental science – it is an introductory text. Those who come to the book having previously studied in one of these areas can use the chapters selectively. Nor do we assume that readers have any background in mathematics beyond arithmetic and elementary algebra.

CONTENTS AND ORGANISATION

The book is organised into four parts. These are preceded by a chapter that introduces ecological economics, and the ideas of sustainability and sustainable development, which are themes that run through the book. This chapter also explains the relationship between ecological economics and 'ordinary' economics and how that is handled in the book.

Part I is called 'Interdependent Systems'. Chapters 2 to 4 provide necessary ideas and information from ecology and environmental science, look at the history of our species, and then set out a framework for thinking about the interdependence of the modern economy and its environment.

Part II, 'Economic Activity', Chapters 5 to 9, is focused mainly on the economy and on economics. It starts with an introduction to economic accounting, and then looks at economic growth and human well-being, on the one hand, and economic growth and the environment, on the other. Chapter 8 introduces the case for markets as the means to organise economic activity, while Chapter 9 examines limits to what markets can do in regard to the natural environment and sustainability.

The pursuit of sustainable development, which requires sustainability, cannot be left to markets – there is an inescapable role for government. This is what Part III, 'Governance', Chapters 10–11, is about. In considering government policy it is helpful to distinguish between policy targets and policy instruments. Chapter 10 deals with the former, Chapter 11 with the latter.

Many of the problems that ecological economics is concerned with, and which threaten sustainability, transcend the boundaries of the nation states that are the principal means by which the world is organised politically. Part IV, Chapters 12 to 14, is called 'The International Dimension'. Chapter 12 is about international trade and related institutions, and the final two chapters deal with two major threats to sustainability that are essentially global in nature – climate change in Chapter 13 and biodiversity loss in Chapter 14.

We see the book as the basis for a two-semester course, and for that purpose the chapters follow a logical progression. However, we realise that in many programmes it may not be possible to devote two semesters to ecological economics. Often, some of the material that is in this book will be covered in parallel, or subsequent, modules/units in the programme. The book is an introduction, and all of the topics that it covers could beneficially be revisited in more depth and rigour in a degree programme dealing with the interdependence of human and natural systems. The range of topics will vary depending on the specific degree programme.

The wide variety of such programmes, and of the backgrounds of students beginning them, makes it difficult to be prescriptive about how the book could be used for a one-semester course – it depends a lot on what other courses the programme includes. However, we do offer the following list of chapters as a suggestion which could be useful in a variety of contexts:

(1) An introduction to ecological economics
(2) The environment
(3) Humans in the environment – some history
(4) The economy in the environment – a conceptual framework
(6) Economic growth and human well-being
(7) Economic growth and the environment
(11) Policy instruments
(13) Climate change
(14) Biodiversity loss.

Chapter 4 is the key chapter, setting out a way of thinking about economy–environment interdependence. Chapter 2 covers some topics in environmental science necessary for a proper appreciation of the significance of that interdependence – those who have done, are doing, or will do basic environmental science in other units could skip this. Chapter 3 provides some historical perspective. Chapter 6 deals with human poverty and economic growth as the means to its alleviation, and Chapter 7 with the question of whether growth can be sustained given economy–environment interdependence. The climate change problem, Chapter 13, is perhaps the biggest global environmental problem, and exemplifies all of the dimensions of the global sustainable development problem. Biodiversity loss, Chapter 14, is similar in many respects, but this chapter is short and probably worth reading with Chapter 13. Chapter 11, on policy instruments, provides some background to the discussion of policy in these two chapters.

PEDAGOGICAL FEATURES

Each chapter begins with a clear statement of what it will cover, and ends with a summary and a list, with page references, of key words and their meanings. At the end of each chapter there is a Further Reading section, and a list of website addresses where relevant material can be found. The Further Reading references are mainly intended for those who wish to take things further, whether in terms of the depth of treatment or the technical level of treatment. References at a similar introductory level to this text are marked with an *.

If you flick through the pages of this book you may well form the impression that there are lots of numbers and lots of mathematics. We assure you that, while this is true, there is no reason for anybody who considers themselves not proficient mathematically to be concerned. There is use of arithmetic and simple algebra where that is the simplest and most efficient way of getting across the basic ideas at an introductory level – as it often is. But, be assured, there is nothing beyond arithmetic and simple algebra, and every time either is used it is explained very carefully. Most of the time, it is just arithmetic. In a few places, the algebra is simple but tedious and it has been put in an appendix. In some chapters we use simulations done using a spreadsheet on a pc. In such cases the repetitive arithmetic that the spreadsheet does is carefully explained. Simulations are a very useful tool in the study of all kinds of systems.

SPECIAL FEATURES

Each chapter contains many features designed to enhance student learning.
- Chapters open with a list of four to eight key areas covered in the chapter to focus student learning.
- Focus boxes enliven the material with real-world illustrations drawn from various sources.
- Keywords are highlighted in bold throughout the text. End-of-chapter lists of keywords facilitate review of important terms.
- End-of-chapter discussion questions stimulate discussion and debate inside and outside the classroom.
- End-of-chapter exercises encourage students to work with and apply the material, gaining increasing mastery of concepts, models and techniques of analysis.
- The book has a companion website.

COMPANION WEBSITE

Ecological economics is a developing field of transdisciplinary study, and sustainability and sustainable development issues are increasingly prominent in political debate and policy making. New publications, new data, new institutions and new policies are continuously appearing. Given this, there is a companion website to this book, which will be periodically updated to keep abreast of the latest developments. The companion website will also provide links to other related websites, which links will also be periodically updated. The address for this website is www.cambridge.org.common.

Part of this website will have restricted access for instructors. This contains transparencies for all graphs in the book, answers to end-of-chapter exercises and notes on discussion questions.

1

An introduction to ecological economics

The purpose of this short chapter is to introduce the subject matter and to explain the organisation of the book.

1.1 WHAT IS ECOLOGICAL ECONOMICS?

The Greek word 'oikos' is the origin of the 'eco' in both ecology and economics. Oikos means household. Ecology is the study of nature's housekeeping, and economics is the study of housekeeping in human societies. **Ecology** can be defined as the study of the relations of animals and plants to their organic and inorganic environments and **economics** as the study of how humans make their living, how they satisfy their needs and desires.

Ecological economics is the study of the relationships between human housekeeping and nature's housekeeping. Put another way, it is about the interactions between economic systems and ecological systems. Humans are a species of animal so that in a sense, on these definitions, the field of study for economics is a subset of that for ecology. However, humans are a special kind of animal, mainly distinguished by their capacity for social interaction between individuals, and their economic activity is now distinctly different from that of other animals. Rather than one being a subset of the other, economics and ecology are disciplines whose subject matters overlap, and, as shown in Figure 1.1, ecological economics is where they overlap. Figure 1.2 is a summary of the essentials of the interactions between economic and ecological systems. Whereas Figure 1.1 is about fields of study, Figure 1.2 concerns the systems of interest. In it the 'Economy' is the world's economies treated as a single system, and the 'Environment' is the whole natural environment, planet earth. The economy is located within the environment, and exchanges energy and matter with it. In making their living, humans extract various kinds of useful things – oil, iron ore, timber, etc., for example – from the environment. Humans also put back into the environment the various kinds of wastes that necessarily arise in the making of their living – sulphur dioxide and carbon dioxide from burning oil, for example. The environment for humans, planet Earth, itself has an environment, which is the rest of the universe. Our environment exchanges energy, but not matter, with its environment. Human economic activity has always involved the material and energy exchanges with the environment shown in Figure 1.2. It would be impossible for humans to satisfy their needs without interacting with nature. For most of human history, mainly because there were few humans, the

Figure 1.1
Locating
ecological
economics.

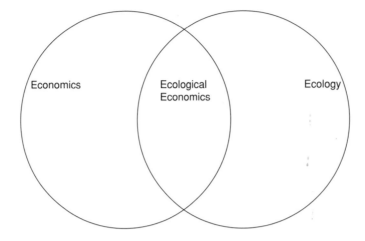

Figure 1.2 The
economy in the
environment.

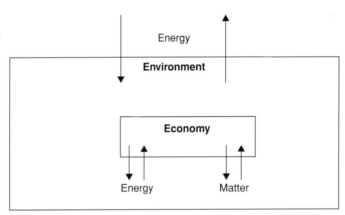

level of interaction did not much affect the functioning of the environment, except locally. However, in the last three centuries the magnitude of the interactions has been increasing rapidly. The global scale of human economic activity is now such that the levels of its extractions from and insertions into the environment do affect the way that it works. Changes in the way that the environment works affect its ability to provide services to human economic activity. The economy and the environment are interdependent – what happens in the economy affects the environment which affects the economy. Another way that we shall sometimes put this is to say that the economy and the environment are a joint system.

One example of this is the role of carbon dioxide in climate change. Fossil fuels are extracted from the environment and burned in the economy, resulting in the release into the atmosphere of carbon dioxide. Carbon dioxide is one of several 'greenhouse gases'. The exchanges of energy between the environment and its environment shown in Figure 1.2 are affected by the amounts of these gases present in the atmosphere – higher concentrations of these gases mean that the environment, planet earth, gets warmer. As a result of the increasing use of fossil fuels in the last two hundred years, the amount of carbon dioxide in the atmosphere has increased. The expert consensus is that this has warmed the planet, and will warm it further. The amount of warming to be expected, by say 2100, is not known with any precision. But, the expert consensus is that it will be enough to have serious impacts on human economic activity and the satisfaction of needs and desires. Beyond 2100, the impacts may be catastrophic.

1.2 A BRIEF HISTORY OF THE ENVIRONMENT IN ECONOMICS

One way to introduce ecological economics is to look at the way that the natural environment has figured in economics through that subject's history.

Economics as a distinct field of study began in 1776 when Adam Smith (1723–1790) published *The Wealth of Nations*. This wide-ranging enquiry into the nature and causes of economic progress is now famous mainly for Smith's doctrine of the 'invisible hand'. This is the idea that, in the right circumstances, the social good will be best served by leaving individuals free to pursue their own selfish interests. Smith was one of a group now known as 'the classical economists', whose ideas dominated economics until the last quarter of the nineteenth century. **Classical economics** was widely known as 'the dismal science'. This was because it took the view, particularly associated with Thomas Malthus (1766–1834), that the long-run prospects for improving living standards were poor. This view was based on the assumed fixity of the supply of agricultural land, together with the propensity of the human population to grow in size. The environment, for the classical economists, set limits to the expansion of economic activity, so that the long-run tendency would be for the wages of workers to be driven down to subsistence level.

As a prediction, this has not fared well. In fact, to date, it has been wrong. For the economies of western Europe and their offshoots, the main features of experience since the beginning of the nineteenth century have been population growth and rising living standards. The standard explanation as to why Malthus got it wrong is that he overlooked technological progress. He, and the other classical economists, did assume an unchanging technology, when in fact it was changing very rapidly in the wake of the industrial revolution. However, it should also be noted that the economies of western Europe were not operating with a fixed supply of agricultural land during this period – increasingly food was being imported into those economies from 'new' land in the Americas and Australasia, to which those economies exported population.

This predictive failure was one factor leading to the demise of classical economics. Starting around 1870 mainstream economics began to evolve from classical economics towards what is now called 'neoclassical economics'. By 1950, the ideas of the classical economists were taught to students of economics only as part of the history of the subject. While the natural environment, in the particular form of the availability of land, had been a major concern of the classical economists, **neoclassical economics**, *circa* 1950, largely ignored the relationships between human housekeeping and nature's housekeeping. In the 1950s and 1960s, economists developed theories of economic growth in which the natural environment simply did not figure. These theories implied that given proper economic management, living standards could go on rising indefinitely. The pursuit of economic growth became a dominant objective of economic policy. One important reason for this was that economic growth seemed to offer the prospect of alleviating poverty in a relatively painless way. Neoclassical economics is not at all 'dismal'.

Starting in the early 1970s, neoclassical economics began to show renewed interest in the natural environment and it now includes the two important specialisations, or sub-disciplines, of **environmental economics** and **natural resource economics** (sometimes just resource economics). In terms of Figure 1.2, environmental economics (mainly) concerns itself with the economy's insertions into the environment, and with problems of environmental pollution. Natural resource economics concerns itself (mainly) with the economy's extractions from the environment, and with problems associated with the use of 'natural resources'. Many university economics programmes now offer higher-level optional courses in one or both of these specialisations. The compulsory courses in most economics programmes do not pay much attention to economy–environment interactions. It is possible to qualify as an economist and to know very little about environmental and resource economics. While neoclassical economists do not ignore the natural environment, they do not think that an understanding of the connections between the economy and the environment, as sketched in Figure 1.2, is an essential part of an economist's education.

Ecological economists do think that such an understanding is an essential part of an economist's education. Ecological economics is based on the idea that the proper study of 'how humans make their living' has to include the study of the relations of the human animal to its 'organic and inorganic environment'. Whereas neoclassical economics treats the study of economy–environment interdependence as an optional extra, for ecological economics it is foundational. It *starts* with the fact that economic activity takes place within the environment. Figure 1.2 – we shall look at a more detailed version of this in Chapter 4 – is the point of departure for ecological economics.

Ecological economics is a relatively new, transdisciplinary, field of study. In the last three decades of the twentieth century it became increasingly apparent to many scientists that human economic activity was having damaging impacts on the natural environment, and that this had economically harmful implications for future generations. The establishment, in 1989, of the International Society for Ecological Economics was motivated by the conviction, on the part of a number of scholars from several disciplines, that studying economy–environment interdependence and its implications requires a transdisciplinary approach, embracing parts of the traditional fields of study of the sciences of economics and ecology.

We need to explain our use of the term transdisciplinary here, and how it differs from terms such as interdisciplinary and multidisciplinary. For the prefixes here, the dictionary consulted gave the following meanings:

> multi – many; more than two
> inter – among; between; mutual, mutually
> trans – across, over; beyond, on the far side of; through.

In connection with academic disciplines and research, the prefixes get used in slightly different ways by different people. However, the following captures what most people mean:

Multidisciplinary research tries to bring together knowledge from different disciplines – the problem is studied in several disciplines. Understanding of the problem is improved by the multidisciplinary approach, and the insights gained feed back into the development of the contributing disciplines.

Interdisciplinary research implies additionally that the disciplinary representatives are all involved in defining the problem, work to become familiar with the concepts and tools from the other disciplines, take on board results from the other disciplines, and that all are involved in presenting the results.

Transdisciplinary research is issue-oriented and interdisciplinary, and ideally involves stakeholders as well as scientists from relevant disciplines.

When we say that ecological economics is transdisciplinary, we do not simply mean that it is concerned with economic and ecological phenomena and draws on the disciplines of economics and ecology. It is and it does, but more is involved. The point of the 'trans' in relation to ecological economics is that there are phenomena and problems that cross, or are beyond, the disciplinary boundaries. Studying such phenomena and problems requires not just that an economist and an ecologist work on them together each using their own perspectives and tools. It requires a common perspective that 'transcends' those that are standard in the two disciplines. When working on economy–environment interdependence, the traditional perspective of economics needs to be modified to take on board the material basis for economic activity and the fact that humans are, whatever else as well, a species of animal. The traditional perspective of ecology needs to recognise the role of humanity as a species in the functioning of all ecosystems. With these shifts of perspective go the recognition of the usefulness of tools and methods of analysis historically seen as going with the other discipline.

Two more points. First, the proper study of economy–environment interdependence involves more than ecological economics as we have described it – many disciplines are highly relevant. However, we do consider that ecological economics is a useful starting point. Second, there are many phenomena and problems to do with economies and ecosystems that can be handled within the traditional disciplinary boundaries. If you only want to study the way the stock market works, you do not really need to take much from ecology: if you are concerned with only the food chains in a remote lake, you do not need to think much about economics. However, if you want to understand the global economy as a system for satisfying human needs and desires, or the operation of the global ecosystem in terms of the distribution and abundance of species, then you do need to cross boundaries.

Throughout the history of economics, as well as studying how humans actually do make their living, economists have offered advice on how they should make their living. One of the reasons that many are attracted to the study of economics is its prescriptive role. In the beginning, Adam Smith urged more reliance on markets and less state intervention in economic affairs than was actually the case at the time that he wrote. Since his time, the views of economists on many issues of public policy have always been an important input to political debate. Notoriously, economists do not, and have never, spoken with a single voice on any given policy issue. There are differences within the ranks of neoclassical economists, as well as between neoclassical and ecological economists. In order to prepare the ground for an introduction to the relationship between ecological and neoclassical economics, we need to look at the origins of differences on policy.

We will do that in section 1.5. First we need to explain the way we will use the terms 'economist(s)', 'neoclassical economist(s)' and 'ecological economist(s)' there, and throughout the rest of this text. There is much that the majority of neoclassical and the majority of ecological economists agree about. Where we are discussing something of this nature, we will refer to 'economists' or to 'economics' without any qualification. Where we are discussing something where there are significant differences we will refer to 'neoclassical economists/economics' or to 'ecological economists/economics' as appropriate.

1.3 SCIENCE AND ETHICS

In considering modes of study, a distinction is made between the 'positive' and the 'normative'. A positive study is purely descriptive, whereas a normative study includes prescriptive elements. A report on a positive study would consist entirely of statements about what is, or might be – it would be about facts and explanations. A report on a normative study would likely include such positive statements, but would also include normative statements about what ought to be – it would involve recommendations. A positive statement takes the form 'event A always follows action B'. A related normative statement would be 'event A is bad, and therefore action B should be avoided'. The recommendation here requires two elements – the factual link from B to A, and the classification of the outcome A as something bad. All recommendations, all policy advice, involve both positive and normative elements.

In principle, it is possible to establish the truth or falsity of positive statements in a way that would satisfy all interested parties. Suppose that Jack and Jill are the interested parties. Jack believes that A always follows B, but Jill does not. The disagreement can be resolved. Jack and Jill could, for example, observe many repetitions of action B and record the subsequent occurrence, or non-occurrence, of event A. If ever A did not occur, Jack would have to agree that the statement 'event A always follows action B' is incorrect. The situation is different with normative statements – they cannot be classified as true or false on a factual basis. If Jack and Jill disagree about whether A is a bad outcome, there is no experiment that can resolve that difference.

One definition of science is that it is the business of sorting positive statements into the categories of true and false. Some people would argue that any field of study that involves making recommendations is not a science. However, many people working in fields generally regarded as branches of science do make recommendations. There need not be a contradiction here. Many recommendations are really conditional advice. Thus, if it were established knowledge in some field that A does always follow B, a recommendation from a scientist working in that field could take the form: 'if you want A to happen, make B happen'. This is the sort of thing that medical scientists, for example, spend a lot of time doing – 'if you want to feel less pain, then take this medication'. Where, as in this case, the objective that is the basis for the recommendation – pain reduction – would be generally regarded as self-evidently desirable, this kind of statement by a scientist does not give rise to any problems. Often, the conditionality is so obvious and so uncontroversial, that it is not explicitly stated.

The recommendations that economists make can be regarded as conditional advice-type statements of this sort – 'if you want a healthy economy, then repeal the minimum wage legislation'. Although, the economist's and the doctor's statements both have an 'if . . . then . . .' structure, there are important differences between them. Whereas pain is experienced directly via the senses of an individual, 'economic health' is an abstraction defined with reference to many individuals. Exactly what a 'healthy economy' might be is itself something to be enquired into, and any definition must involve normative elements.

There are two sorts of reason why different economists come up with different recommendations – some disagreements have positive origins, some normative origins. Not all positive statements in economics have been definitively classified as true or false. Economists disagree as to how the economy actually works – some consider that minimum wage legislation increases unemployment, others that it does not. However, even if all economists agreed on the true/false classification of all possible positive statements about the workings of the economy, different recommendations could still follow from different appreciations of what 'economic health' is – economist Jack could consider it to require an unemployment below 3 per cent, while Jill could consider any level of unemployment below 10 per cent to be consistent with a healthy economy.

In so far as economists agree about recommendations, it is because they agree about both positive descriptions of how things work and normative criteria for assessing performance. At the level of studying individuals choosing between alternatives, we refer to the normative criteria that they use as 'preferences' or 'tastes'. Given that Jack could buy oranges or lemons, we say that what he actually buys is determined by his preferences as between oranges and lemons. In the context of analysing policy choices, we look at the normative criteria involved in terms of their basis in some ethical position. **Ethics**, or moral philosophy, is the study of the principles that ought to govern human conduct. One of its fundamental questions is: how do we decide whether or not an action is morally correct? There are two broad schools of thought.

According to deontological theories, moral correctness is a matter of fulfilling obligations, a matter of duty. According to consequentialist theories, moral correctness is to be judged in terms of the consequences that follow from an action. To illustrate the difference, consider the question: can it ever be right to tell a lie? The answer is 'no' on deontological criteria, 'yes' on consequential criteria. In the former case, it is argued that there is a universal duty to tell the truth. In the latter case, that there may be circumstances such that telling a lie produces a better outcome than telling the truth.

Utilitarianism is a particular variety of consequentialism. According to utilitarianism, the moral correctness of an action depends on the balance of pleasure and pain that it produces. Actions that increase the totality of pleasure or reduce the totality of pain are morally correct; actions that reduce the totality of pleasure or increase the totality of pain are morally incorrect. The term 'utility' refers to the situation of an individual in regard to the balance of pleasure and pain – pleasure is that which increases an individual's utility; pain is that which reduces an individual's utility. The term 'welfare' is used for the totality of utility across individuals, and according to utilitarianism morally correct actions are those that increase welfare. Utilitarianism is the ethical basis for economics.

There are three main questions for utilitarianism. First, whose utility counts? Second, how is utility assessed? Third, how is utility across individuals added up to get welfare? There are different varieties of utilitarianism according to the answers to these three questions. We will look at differences, and commonalities, between neoclassical and ecological economics in terms of these questions later in this chapter.

1.4 SUSTAINABILITY AND SUSTAINABLE DEVELOPMENT

The ideas of sustainability and sustainable development will figure very large in this book, as they are very important central ideas in ecological economics. **Sustainability** is:

maintaining the capacity of the joint economy–environment system to continue to satisfy the needs and desires of humans for a long time into the future

If the joint economy–environment system is operating as required for sustainability, it is in a sustainable mode of operation, otherwise it is unsustainable. As subsequent chapters will explain, the difference between sustainable and unsustainable configurations for the economy involves questions about both the scale and the composition, in terms of the sorts of extractions from and insertions into the environment, of economic activity. The scholars who set up the International Society for Ecological Economics in 1989 were largely motivated by the judgement that the way the world economy was operating was unsustainable. They were concerned by what they judged to be threats to sustainability, features of current economic activity that could undermine the capacity of the joint economy–environment system to continue to satisfy human needs and desires. Climate change is an example of a threat to sustainability.

The idea that it is important to 'maintain' a capacity implies that it is sufficient. In fact, in the second half of the twentieth century many scholars argued that the capacity of the joint economy–environment system to deliver human satisfactions needed to be increased rather than maintained. A major feature of the current human condition is the existence of mass poverty. The generally accepted remedy for poverty is economic growth, increasing the scale of economic activity. Here is a major problem. On the one hand, many judge that the current scale of global economic activity threatens sustainability: threatens to reduce the future capacity to satisfy human needs and desires. On the other hand, many argue that it is necessary to increase the scale of economic activity to alleviate poverty. Dealing with poverty now, it seems, is going to create future economic problems, via the environmental impacts arising from increasing the scale of current economic activity.

One of the most important and influential publications of the last part of the twentieth century was *Our common future*. This report by the World Commission on Environment and Development, WCED, was published in 1987, two years before the formation of the International Society for Ecological Economics. It is sometimes referred to as the 'Brundtland Report', Ms Brundtland having been the commission's chair. *Our common future* described both the extent of poverty and the various threats to sustainability. It argued that the circle could be squared, that the economic growth required to deal with poverty need not, via its environmental impacts, create future economic problems. What was needed, the **Brundtland Report** argued, was a new kind of economic growth that had much less environmental impact and which, rather than threatening sustainability, actually increased the joint economy–environment system's capacity to deliver human satisfactions. It argued that what was needed could be done, and called it **sustainable development**. It is:

a form of economic growth that would meet the needs and desires of the present without compromising the economy–environment system's capacity to meet them in the future.

1.5 THE RELATIONSHIP BETWEEN ECOLOGICAL AND NEOCLASSICAL ECONOMICS

In this section we want to look at the broad relationship between ecological and neoclassical economics in terms of the normative and positive elements of both.

The first question about utilitarianism that we noted was: whose utility counts? In economics, ecological and neoclassical, the answer is: all of the humans who are affected by the action. There is no reason, in principle, why utilitarianism could not take account of the pleasure/pain of all affected animals. Some moral philosophers belonging to the utilitarian school argue that in working out the balance as between pleasure and pain, all affected beings capable of feeling pain and pleasure should be accounted for. If this argument were accepted, welfare would depend on the utilities of all 'sentient' beings, not just on the utilities of humans. The suggested candidates for consideration along with humans have mainly been the higher mammals. Normative economics does not take account of the utilities of non-human beings. It is **anthropocentric** in that the effects of an action on non-human beings are taken into account only in so far as they produce pain or pleasure for human beings. If no humans feel (mental) pain on account of animal suffering caused by an action, then that suffering does not figure in the calculation of the pleasure/pain balance to be used to judge the action. If any human does feel pain, that pain, not the animal suffering, does figure in the pleasure/pain balance. Also, if any human feels pain on account of the damage to a non-sentiment entity, such as a building for example, then that should be accounted for in evaluating the action responsible for the damage and the pain.

In terms of the answer to this first question, there is no difference at all between ecological economics and neoclassical economics. Both are anthropocentric, as well as utilitarian. In regard to the second question – how is human pleasure/pain to be measured? – there are some differences. In neoclassical economics, each affected human individual is the sole judge of whether her utility has increased or

Figure 1.3
Ethical
positions of
neoclassical
and ecological
economics.

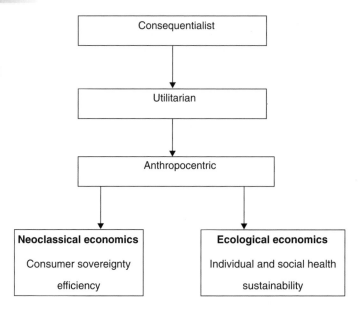

decreased. The change in an individual's utility is measured solely in terms of the preferences of that individual. Individual preferences are taken as given, and are not subject to any moral evaluation. This is sometimes referred to as the doctrine of 'consumer sovereignty'. Ecological economics does not ignore individual preferences, but it treats them neither as sovereign, nor as the only source of normative criteria.

In neoclassical economics, provided it can be assumed that an individual is in possession of all relevant information, there can be no ethical basis for seeking to change his preferences. There can be no basis for saying that a taste for cycling should be encouraged, while a taste for driving motor cars should be discouraged. In ecological economics, there can be an ethical basis for comparing, evaluating and seeking to change tastes. Ecological economists would be sympathetic to the argument that tastes should be educated in the direction of cycling and away from motoring on the grounds that more cycling and less motoring promotes individual and social health. They consider sustainability to be a requirement of social health. In ecological economics, sustainability requirements are a source of normative criteria. Figure 1.3 summarises the discussion thus far of the ethical underpinnings of neoclassical and ecological economics.

We now look at the third question about utilitarianism – how to add up increases and decreases in utility across affected human individuals so as to get welfare. To make things simple, assume that there are just two individuals, identified as A and B, and use U^A and U^B to represent their utility levels, and W to represent welfare. Then simple addition for welfare would be

$$W = U^A + U^B$$

The problem that some see here is that this way of getting from utilities to welfare takes no account of the relative positions of A and B. Suppose that A's utility is much higher than B's, and that the action being considered would increase A's utility by more than it decreased B's. According to simple addition this would increase welfare, and the action would be morally correct, though it makes the better-off even better-off and the worse-off even worse-off. This, to many utilitarians, does not seem fair.

They would argue that welfare should be defined as a weighted sum of individual utilities with more weight being given to the utility of those whose utility is low. Instead of simple addition, this argument is, proposed actions should be assessed using

$$W = (w_A \times U^A) + (w_B \times U^B)$$

where w_A and w_B are the weights to be assigned to the utilities of A and B respectively. This becomes simple addition if $w_A = w_B = 1$. For B with lower utility than A, the argument would be that w_B should be larger than w_A. Suppose that $w_A = 1$ and $w_B = 5$, for example. An action that increased A's utility and decreased B's would have to increase A's by five times as much as it decreased B's in order to be considered morally correct. The choice of the weights is itself an ethical issue. Ecological economists tend to be more inclined to argue for the use of weights that favour the less well-off than do neoclassical economists. They tend, that is, in judging alternative policies to be more concerned with the equity dimensions of the choice than neoclassical economists are. While neoclassical economists do not ignore **equity** issues, they focus more on policies to promote **efficiency**, a situation where it is not possible to increase one person's utility without reducing that of one or more other persons.

Sustainability and sustainable development are central concerns of ecological economics, which has been defined as the science of sustainability, but not of neoclassical economics. In part this is because of the differences in ethical positions just described, normative differences. But it is also because of differences about positive matters, questions of fact. Ecological economists judge that serious threats to sustainability exist, and they are somewhat sceptical about the feasibility of sustainable development. Neoclassical economists do not claim that there are no threats to sustainability, but they judge them to be less serious than do ecological economists, and they tend to believe that sustainable development will come about given some relatively minor policy changes. They have confidence in the ability of markets to drive technological and behavioural changes that will enable the capacity of the economy–environment system to satisfy humans to go on increasing. Ecological economists have less confidence in markets and technology. They tend to believe that solving the problem of poverty cannot be left to economic growth alone, but will require the redistribution of income and wealth from the better- to the worse-off.

Earlier, we said that positive statements are the business of science, and that differences over their validity can be resolved by appeal to evidence, as a matter of principle. This is a useful way to distinguish positive from normative statements, because differences over the latter cannot be so resolved, even as a matter of principle. But, without keeping firmly in mind the qualification 'as a matter of principle', the statement about positive statements can mislead. Science has not yet sorted all positive statements into true and false classes, and it never will. It has been very successful where controlled experiments are possible, much less where they are not. Many of the positive issues that divide ecological and neoclassical economists are not amenable to definitive resolution by controlled experiment.

Again, the example of climate change can be cited. Most scientists working in the field consider that the global climate is changing, and that this is due, mainly, to the release into the atmosphere of greenhouse gases by human activities such as burning coal, oil and gas. There are some scientists who dispute that the global climate really is changing. There are others who accept that the global climate is changing, but dispute that the cause is human activity. All agree that the atmospheric concentration of these gases is one of the things that influences climate, and that humans have been releasing increasing amounts of these gases into the atmosphere since 1750. The problem is that in the historical record all of the things that influence global climate have been changing, so even if everyone accepted that climate had been changing, it would not be possible to definitively establish whether or not that was due to human activities. Doing that would require a controlled experiment where human releases of the gases were held constant at the 1750 level, while all the other influences on climate behaved as they did in history since 1750. That is not possible.

The construction of a model is a response to this kind of problem. A **model** is a simplified version of the set of relationships which are thought to determine some phenomenon. In principle, a model can be stated in several ways – using language, constructing a physical system, drawing graphs, as a set of equations. Most usually, and most effectively, models are stated mathematically, as sets of equations. A model is a substitute for a controlled experiment. The investigator can turn relationships in the model on and off to see what difference it makes to the model outcome. This is exactly how climate scientists investigate the role of the various influences on the global climate – they run their model of that phenomenon with and without, for example, the history of human greenhouse gas emissions since 1750, so as to see what difference those emissions make.

The problem is, of course, that the model is a model. Ideally, it incorporates accurately all of the relationships that actually do have a role in determining the phenomenon being investigated. In practice, as in the climate change case, different investigators have different models because it is not definitively known which those relationships are. What happens is that an investigator reviews previous work in the field from which she selects the relationships that she judges to be the ones that a model needs to incorporate. The resulting model is then tested by seeing whether it can replicate to a reasonable degree of accuracy the behaviour of the phenomenon of interest as observed in the historical data. If it is judged that it does replicate history satisfactorily, then it is used to conduct 'what if?' investigations, experiments, by modifying the relationships that it includes. One type of 'what if?' experiment is forecasting – using the model to predict the behaviour of the phenomenon of interest conditional on assumptions about how the things at the other end – to it – of the included relationships behave.

In the last few paragraphs we have often used the word 'judgement', and sometimes 'belief'. Many of the positive issues that neoclassical and ecological economists disagree about are matters to be investigated by modelling rather than controlled experiment. While there are certain agreed conventions about how to decide whether or not a relationship has a role in determining some phenomenon – these are the rules of statistical inference – their application necessarily involves judgement. Two equally honest and skilled investigators can quite reasonably come up with different models for the same phenomenon. Similarly, the application of the conventions for deciding whether a model explains the phenomenon satisfactorily is a matter of judgement.

Many of the differences between neoclassical and ecological economics are differences about the models judged to be useful in explaining various economic and environmental phenomena, and, therefore, predicting what will happen to those phenomena. For example, a fundamental judgement of ecological economics is that a useful explanation – model – of the rapid growth in the average level of consumption of goods and services in the industrial economies in the last 200 years must include relationships describing economy–environment interdependence. Figure 1.2 presents a very simple version of such a model as a picture. Figure 4.1 will present a less simple version as a picture. Some such model of economy–environment interdependence is the starting point for ecological economics. The judgement in neoclassical economics is that these relationships are not an essential part of a useful model of economic growth. Their existence is not denied. It just does not figure in the core models by means of which students are introduced to the study of economics. As ecological economists, the authors of this book judge that to be a major failing on the part of neoclassical economics, which is why we have written an introductory ecological economics textbook.

That said, it also needs to be stated, and emphasised, that there are very many, important, positive questions where ecological and neoclassical economics are in agreement.

1.6 A GUIDED TOUR

There are four parts to this book. Part I, 'Interdependent Systems', explains properly the necessary interdependence of the economy and the environment sketched in outline terms in Figure 1.2. Chapter 2, 'The environment', reviews the basic environmental science necessary for an understanding of ecological economics. Chapter 3, 'Humans in the environment – some history', looks at the evolution of economy–environment interdependence in human history. Chapter 4, 'The economy in the environment – a conceptual framework', sets out our basic model of the current relationships between economic activity and the natural environment.

Part II, 'Economic Activity', focuses on the modern industrial economy and the means by which it is mainly organised, the market system. Chapter 5, 'Economic accounting', sets out the framework used for economic analysis, and explains how GDP and the like are measured and what they mean. GDP growth has been the dominant feature of the economic history of the last few hundred years. Chapter 6, 'Economic growth and human well-being', looks at explanations for the phenomenon and at the relationship between it and human well-being. Economic growth is widely seen as the only way to eliminate poverty. However, the facts of economy–environment interdependence have led many to ask whether the environment can accommodate further growth of global GDP. Chapter 7, 'Economic growth and the environment', uses the model of economic growth, and some other models, to look at whether sustainable development is feasible.

The market system, is now the dominant mode of economic organisation. Chapter 8, 'Exchange and markets', explains how markets work and how they make possible the realisation of the benefits – in terms of efficiency – that specialisation and exchange offer. Chapter 9, 'Limits to markets', explains why economic organisation cannot be left entirely to markets, why there is a role for government. As explained there, markets are often absent, or function badly, in relation to the regulation of economy–environment interdependencies as is required for sustainable development. If this is going to happen, it requires government to guide market forces in the necessary directions.

This is what Part III, 'Governance', is about. In thinking about what government does it is useful to distinguish between questions about ends and means. Chapter 10, 'Determining policy objectives', is about setting the ends at which policies should be directed so as promote sustainability – how much pollution should be allowed, for example. Chapter 11, 'Environmental policy instruments', is about the means by which the ends decided on should be pursued – how to control the activities of polluters, for example.

The sustainable development problem is a global problem in both its economic and its environmental dimensions, but there is no world government. Human society is organised around the institution of the nation state. Part IV, 'The International Dimension', is concerned with this mis-match and some of its implications. Chapter 12, 'A world of nation states', looks at trade between nations, at the ways in which some environmental problems cross national borders, and at the institutions that have been developed to address the, many, problems that require coordination and cooperation between nation states. The last two chapters – 13, 'Climate change' and 14, 'Biodiversity loss' – draw on the look at two major, and related, problems of this kind, which are major threats to the prospects of realising sustainable development.

Nowhere in the book is any prior knowledge assumed – it is an introductory text. You should be able to use this book successfully even if you have not previously studied either economics or ecology. No familiarity with environmental science is assumed. Nor is any mathematical ability beyond arithmetic assumed, a matter to which we return in a moment. Those who come to the book with some previous knowledge of some of the fields covered can be selective in their use of the various chapters. At the start of each chapter there is a statement of what it is going to cover, and at the end there is a summary and a list of keywords, with page references, and their meanings. These should help you to use the book effectively. At the end of each chapter there is a section on Further Reading, which is intended to guide those who want to take their study of ecological economics further.

You may well have flicked through the book by now and formed the impression that what looks like mathematics appears quite a lot. Your impression is quite right, but, even if you consider yourself somewhat weak as far as mathematics goes, you have no cause for concern. There is in this book quite extensive use of arithmetic and simple algebra, where that is the simplest and most efficient way of getting across the basic ideas at an introductory level – as it often is. But, be assured, there is nothing beyond arithmetic and simple algebra, and every time either is used it is explained very carefully. Most of the time, it is just arithmetic. The most advanced algebra used is the solving of (easy) pairs of simultaneous equations. In a few places, the algebra is simple but tedious and it has been put in an appendix.

In the text we often make use of simulations, and some of the exercises invite you to deepen your understanding by doing your own simulations. A **simulation**, as we will explain in detail when we get to the first one in the next chapter, is just doing repetitive arithmetic to study the time paths for variables determined by a model. This is a simple way to explore the properties of a model. It may sound hard and/or tedious, but it is not hard and need not be tedious. To do the arithmetic easily and accurately, all you need is a calculating machine that will – as well as add, subtract, multiply and divide – raise numbers to powers, and give logarithms and anti-logarithms. Doing the arithmetic this way is easy, but can be tedious. The way to avoid the tedium is by automating the arithmetic using the copy-and-paste formula facility of a spreadsheet, such as Excel™, for a PC. We will not go into the details of this – if you are not already familiar with such facilities, you will need a course or a book about Excel™, or whatever spreadsheet you are going to use. We will, however, for every simulation that we introduce, spell out the arithmetic that needs to be done. Once you get the hang of simulating models it is a very powerful way to learn about the properties of different kinds of systems.

Finally, we need to come back to the question of the relationship between ecological and neoclassical economics, and how we deal with it in this book. In the section of this chapter we looked, in general terms, at the relationship in its normative and its positive dimensions. We noted that in both dimensions there is much common ground, as well as areas where they diverge. Much of what you will learn from this book carries over into neoclassical economics. If, that is, you go on to study more advanced economics of a basically neoclassical kind you will not have to unlearn what you have learned from this book. What you have learned here should, however, give you a different, and often more critical, perspective there than would be the case had you not been introduced to economics via ecological economics.

The purpose of this book is to introduce you to ecological economics, not to develop a critique of neoclassical economics. On the other hand, exposure to different ideas, and the origins of the differences, is part of learning about economics as an active field of enquiry and debate, rather than just a repository of established truth. There is a choice to be made here, as economics teaches that there is almost everywhere. In this case it is between a very long, but comprehensive book, and a fairly long book that concentrates very much on telling the ecological economics story and largely neglects differentiating that story from the neoclassical story. We have chosen the latter option. We explicitly compare and contrast only when that is necessary for understanding ecological economics. For those who are interested we will provide references to works that do more of the compare and contrast sort of thing.

KEYWORDS

Anthropocentric (p. 9): centred on human beings.
Brundtland Report (p. 9): *Our Common Future* (1987) put the idea of sustainable development on the political agenda.

Classical economics (p. 3): the economic thinking of the first half of the nineteenth century.

Ecology (p. 1): the study of the relations of animals and plants to their organic and inorganic environments.

Ecological economics (p. 1): the study of the human economy as part of nature's economy.

Economics (p. 1): the study of how humans satisfy their needs and desires.

Efficiency (p. 11): a situation where nobody can be made to feel better-off except by making somebody else feel worse-off.

Environmental economics (p. 4): the specialisation within neoclassical economics that is concerned with the economy's insertions into the natural environment.

Equity (p. 11): the question of fairness.

Ethics (p. 7): the study of the principles that ought to govern human conduct.

Model (p. 12): a simplified version of the set of relationships which are thought to determine some phenomenon.

Neoclassical economics (p. 3): the currently dominant school of economics.

Natural resource economics (p. 4): the specialisation within neoclassical economics that is concerned with the economy's extractions from the natural environment.

Simulation (p. 15): numerical analysis of the properties of a model.

Sustainability (p. 8): maintaining the capacity of the joint economy–environment system to continue to satisfy the needs and desires of humans for a long time into the future.

Sustainable development (p. 9): economic growth that would meet the needs and aspirations of the present without compromising the ability to meet those of the future.

Utilitarianism (p. 7): the school of ethics according to which the moral correctness of an action depends on the balance of pleasure and pain that it produces.

FURTHER READING

This book is written as an introductory text, and it is assumed that many, but not all, readers will be going on to do, or concurrently be doing, other courses in economics, ecology, environmental science and management. The suggestions for further reading reflect these assumptions. Where a reading is marked with an asterisk: *, this indicates material that should prove useful to all readers, that could be regarded as a source of desirable supplementary reading in an introductory course centred on this book, that is at a similar level to this text. Otherwise, the suggestions take things further and/or move up a level in technical difficulty, and are there primarily for those not going to get exposed to more advanced material in other courses.

The standard text on the history of economics is Blaug (1985). It is really for specialists, and Barber (1967) and, especially, Heilbronner* (1991) are more accessible and cover the essentials. Crocker (1999) covers the rediscovery of the environment by neoclassical economics, while the first part of Costanza et al. (1997a) deals with the emergence of ecological economics. Important journals covering neoclassical economics work on the natural environment are: *Journal of Environmental Economics* and *Management, Environment and Resource Economics, Land Economics,* and *Environment and Development Economics. Ecological Economics* is the journal of the International Society for Ecological Economics.

Singer (1993) is a good introduction to ethics which considers environmental applications. Brennan* (2003) is a recent survey of philosophical writing on matters environmental. Glasser (1999) is a survey article on ethics and environmental policy. Sen (1987) looks at ethics in relation to economics. The journal *Environmental Values* publishes articles by people from a variety of academic disciplines on ethics and the environment. *Ecological Economics* often carries papers about ethics and philosophy, and the February/March 1998 issue (vol. 24, nos. 2 and 3) was a special issue on 'Economics, ethics and the environment'.

WEBSITES

The address of the website of the International Society for Ecological Economics, ISEE, is http://www.ecoeco.org. It has links to a number of other relevant sites. One of the features of the ISEE site is the ongoing assembly of an online encyclopedia of ecological economics, in which there is an entry on 'The early history of ecological economics and ISEE' written by Robert Costanza, one of the founders of ISEE.

DISCUSSION QUESTIONS

1.   Should sustainability be an objective of government policy?
2.   Is mathematics a science? Is history?
3.   Is utilitarianism that takes account of all sentient beings feasible?

PART I
INTERDEPENDENT SYSTEMS

Ecological economics starts from the fact that human and natural systems are interdependent. The environment is the material base for economic activity.

Chapter 2 will explain those aspects of the functioning of environmental systems that are particularly relevant to an understanding of economy–environment interdependence. The nature of that interdependence has changed a great deal in the course of human history, as is explained in Chapter 3. Chapter 4 develops a conceptual framework, a model, for the study of the way a modern economy interacts with its environment.

2

The environment

In this chapter you will:

- Learn about the ways in which the natural environment functions and sustains life;
- Look at the first and second laws of thermodynamics;
- Learn about energy and nutrient flows in ecosystems;
- See how the fossil fuels came into existence;
- Study population dynamics;
- Consider the concept of ecosystem resilience;
- Learn about global nutrient cycles;
- Look at evolutionary processes.

In the previous chapter we introduced the idea that the economy and the natural environment are interdependent systems, with the economy located within the environment. That idea is to be developed in the following chapters of Part I. This chapter looks at the functioning of the natural environment itself, largely ignoring the role of humanity. It is a simple, and brief, overview of the material from environmental science that is necessary for an understanding of ecological economics. Readers who are familiar with environmental science will find that they can get through the chapter quickly, though they probably should not skip it completely. For other readers, the Further Reading section at the end of the chapter offers some guidance on how to go further into the environmental science topics introduced here.

This chapter is organised as follows. First, in section 2.1, we look at the planet in terms of four interacting systems. Section 2.2 is about thermodynamics, the science of energy. Some appreciation of the essentials of thermodynamics is essential for understanding the way that the planet works, and particularly the nature of life on earth, which is dependent on energy. In section 2.3, we shall explore various aspects of the organisation of life on earth by considering ecosystems, which are systems of interaction among living organisms. Life requires matter as well as energy, and in section 2.4 we will look at some of the important cycles of matter through the planetary systems. The ways in which planetary systems, especially the living

Figure 2.1
Four
interacting
environmental
systems.

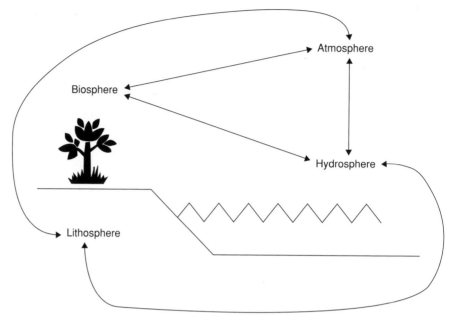

systems, work have changed through the history of the planet, and the chapter finishes, in section 2.5, by looking briefly at some aspects of that coevolutionary history.

2.1 PLANET EARTH

By 'the natural environment', or just 'the environment', we mean planet earth. It is one of nine planets in the solar system, and is, as far as we know, the only one that supports life. The system that is planet earth can itself be seen as comprising four main systems:

(1)   **Lithosphere** – the solid outer shell of the earth;
(2)   **Hydrosphere** – the water on or near the surface of the earth;
(3)   **Atmosphere** – the gases surrounding the earth's surface;
(4)   **Biosphere** – living organisms and their immediate environment.

As indicated in Figure 2.1, these systems all interact with one another. We will discuss some aspects of the interactions later in the chapter. Here, after saying something about the idea of a system, we will concentrate mainly on simple descriptions of the four systems considered separately.

2.1.1 Systems

A **system** is a set of components that interact with each other. The idea of a system necessarily entails the idea of an environment within which the system exists, and of a boundary between the system and its environment, as illustrated in Figure 2.2.

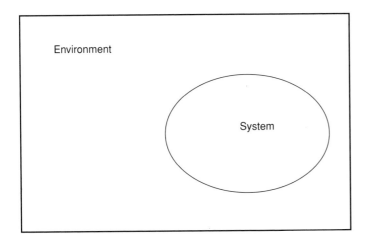

Figure 2.2
System and
environment.

In this context, the term 'environment' has nothing necessarily to do with the natural environment. It simply means what is outside the boundary of whatever system is under consideration.

A system must be distinguishable from its environment. There is no general and precise rule about what establishes distinguishability. The definition of a system and its environment cannot be reduced to a set of precise rules that apply in all circumstances. What is distinguished as a system will depend on what the purpose of the exercise is. For some purposes, it will make sense to treat planet earth as a system and consider it in relation to its environment. For others, it will make sense to treat, say, the hydrosphere as a system with its environment comprising the other three planetary systems.

One way of thinking about some standard academic disciplines is in terms of systems definitions and boundaries. Biology is concerned with things in the biosphere, hydrology with things in the hydrosphere, geology with things in the lithosphere, and so on. Systems analysis is a discipline which takes the position that there are insights to be gained from focussing on systems as such, rather than the particular natures of their component parts. A distinguishing characteristic of systems analysis is that it is as concerned with the nature of the interactions as it is with the nature of the components. One of the ways in which it is useful is that it turns out that there are patterns of interaction arising across quite different sorts of assemblages of components. The fact that there are such patterns means that knowledge gained about the behaviour of one system can be applied to the behaviour of a system with quite different components, if it can be established that the two systems have the same pattern of interactions. This sort of transfer can occur across the boundaries of conventionally defined disciplines. Lessons learned about system characteristics in, say, ecology, can be applicable in, say, economics.

2.1.2 The lithosphere

The lithosphere comprises the upper part of the mantle and the earth's crust. While the lithosphere as such is geologically important, especially in regard to volcanic activity, it is really the crust that is of interest here as this is the part of the lithosphere that interacts with other environmental systems. The crust comprises less than 1 per cent of the earth's mass, and about 0.5 per cent of its radius. Its thickness varies from 35 km to 5 km. The crust is made up of rocks which are composed of minerals. Over 2,000 minerals are known to exist. Just 8 of the 100 plus chemical elements known to exist account for over 99 per cent of the mass of the earth's crust. Oxygen accounts for 47 per cent, silicon 28 per cent, aluminium 8 per cent, iron 5 per cent.

Rocks are classified according to the way in which they were formed. Igneous rocks (e.g. granite) arise from the solidification of molten material, magma, originating in the earth's mantle. Sedimentary rocks (e.g. sandstone, limestone) come into being as the result of erosion, or as the result of dissolved material precipitating from water, or as the result of biological activity. Metamorphic rocks are the result of the alteration of some parent rock (e.g. marble from limestone) by extreme heat and/or pressure.

Rocks are, over geological time, created, modified and destroyed in cyclical processes driven by energy which comes from the cooling of the interior of the planet, radioactive processes, and the sun. The processes involved are, relative to the processes involved in the other three environmental systems distinguished here, very slow – they operate on timescales of millions of years. From the human perspective this is so slow as to be imperceptible, and for many purposes features of the lithosphere are taken as unchanging. From the human perspective, the lithosphere system is of direct economic interest mainly on account of the formation of exploitable mineral deposits, by geological processes, and soils, by climatic and biological processes.

2.1.3 The hydrosphere

The hydrosphere includes oceans, lakes, rivers and water vapour in the atmosphere. Approximately 70 per cent of the earth's surface is covered with water, and 10 per cent of the land is covered with ice. Of the total amount of water, about 97 per cent is stored in the oceans and 2 per cent in ice caps and glaciers. Water vapour in the atmosphere accounts for 0.0001 per cent, and lakes and rivers 0.009 per cent, of total water.

The basic general process involving water is the hydrological cycle. Driven by the energy of solar radiation, water evaporates from the oceans, lakes and rivers, and from soil, to become water vapour in the atmosphere. Precipitation returns water to the oceans directly when it falls on them, and indirectly when it falls upon land from which it reaches the oceans via rivers. The processes involved in the hydrosphere are much faster than those of the lithosphere. The average length of time that a water molecule remains in one of its stores varies from days, in the case of residence in the atmosphere as water vapour, to thousands of years, in the case of residence as salt water in the oceans.

Water is important for several, related, reasons. It is directly necessary for life: see the discussion of plants and animals in section 2.2 below. Many elements dissolve in water, and are thereby dispersed through the lithosphere and the atmosphere by the operation of the hydrological cycle. It therefore plays a key role in the major bio-element, or nutrient, cycles to be discussed in section 2.4 below. Water is strongly involved in most of the climatic and biological processes by means of which soils are produced from rocks.

2.1.4 The atmosphere

The atmosphere is predominantly a mixture of gases, though it also contains particulate matter. The most abundant gases are nitrogen, approximately 78 per cent of the total volume, and oxygen, 21 per cent. All the other gases, then, together comprise only 1 per cent of the atmosphere. This does not mean that these other gases are unimportant. For example, carbon dioxide (0.04 per cent of the total volume) and methane (0.0002 per cent) are 'greenhouse gases', variations in the amounts of which in the atmosphere affect the global climate system. It should also be noted that, given the size of the atmosphere, a small concentration of a gas goes with a large absolute amount in the atmosphere – the total amount of carbon dioxide in the earth's atmosphere is approximately 2,800 Gigatonnes. Box 2.1 explains that the prefix 'Giga' means thousands of millions.

The boundary between the earth's atmosphere and space is not a sharp one. But, in effect all of the atmosphere lies within 80,000 km of the surface of the earth, and 99 per cent within 50 km of the surface. The troposphere extends up to between 8 (at the poles) and 16 km (at the equator) above the surface of the earth, and contains about 75 per cent of the mass of the atmosphere, including about 90 per cent of the particulate matter and water vapour. It is the only part of the atmosphere where the temperature is above $0°C$, and is where weather patterns are mainly determined. The stratosphere is the region of the atmosphere immediately above the troposphere, and extends up to about 60 km above the surface of the earth. Although processes in the stratosphere are not so directly and closely related to circumstances at the earth's surface, they are still important. For example, the stratosphere is where the ozone that screens the earth's surface from the sun's ultraviolet radiation resides. That ultraviolet radiation is harmful to organisms, and life on earth would be impossible without the presence of the stratospheric ozone layer.

Atmospheric processes operate on timescales that are more similar to hydrological processes than they are to geological processes. The atmospheric residence times of the principal greenhouse gases, for example, vary from the order of 10 years for methane to that of the order of 100 years for carbon dioxide and nitrous oxide.

2.1.5 The biosphere

The biosphere is that part of the earth in which living things, i.e. biota, exist. It includes parts of the lithosphere, the hydrosphere and the atmosphere. The biosphere extends from the top of the troposphere to about 10 km below sea level. That is a maximum vertical extent of about 25 km. The radius of the earth is about 6,400 km, so the biosphere is a very thin layer of the earth – less than 0.4 per cent of the radius. In fact, only pollen grains and spores and a few species of insects and birds can exist at more than 6 km above sea level, so that most life on earth exists within a layer which is about 16 km deep.

The conditions that enable the biosphere to support life are: a supply of water; a supply of usable energy; a supply of air; a suitable temperature range; the presence of essential nutrients and trace elements. That these conditions exist is due to the fact that the biosphere is located where the systems which are the lithosphere, the hydrosphere and the atmosphere interact. These conditions, and hence life as we now know it, have not always existed on planet earth, as will be discussed in section 2.5.

The functioning of the biosphere will be considered in section 2.3. In order to be able to do that, we need to look at thermodynamics.

2.2 THERMODYNAMICS

Thermodynamics is the study of energy transformations. The laws of thermodynamics are fundamental to an understanding of the operation of environmental systems. It follows that they are also fundamental to an understanding of the operation of economic systems, and although this chapter is basically about the natural environment, in this section we will say something about the economic implications of the laws of thermodynamics.

2.2.1 Energy, heat and work

In order to state and explain the laws of thermodynamics, we need to begin with some definitions. Energy transformations involve work, heat and energy. **Energy** is the potential to do work or supply heat. Work is what is done when something is moved, and the amount done is the product of the force applied and the distance moved. The possible effects of heat on a substance are an increase in temperature, expansion, a change of state (melting of a solid/vaporisation of a liquid), or an increase in pressure. Energy, work and heat are all measured in the same units. In the SI system, the basic unit is the joule. In work terms one joule is the work done when one kilogram is moved one metre. It is also the heat required to raise the temperature of one cubic centimetre of water by $0.239°C$. For many purposes the joule is an inconveniently small unit. Box 2.1 gives standard prefixes used with joules, and other small measurement units, to specify larger units which are often more convenient. Box 2.1 also gives some conversion factors for SI and other systems.

Power is work per unit of time. The unit of power corresponding to the joule is the watt, which is one joule per second. As the potential to do work or supply heat, energy can take a variety of forms. Potential energy exists by virtue of position, as in the case of water in an elevated lake. Kinetic energy exists by virtue of motion, as in the case of flowing water. Radiant energy is given off by hot objects, as with the solar energy given off by the sun. Electrical energy is carried by a flow of charged particles in a conductor. Chemical energy is that given off in chemical reactions such as the combustion of coal.

2.2.2 First law of thermodynamics

The first law of thermodynamics says that energy can be converted from one form to another, but can be neither created nor destroyed. Consider a coal-fired electricity

Box 2.1 Energy measurement

The basic SI unit of measurement for energy (and heat and work) is the joule. It is a very small quantity – the work done when 1 kilogram (kg) is moved 1 metre (m). Energy, heat and work are therefore usually measured in units which are multiples of the joule. The same multiples can be used with other basic SI units, such as the gramme (g) for mass, the metre (m) for distance and the litre (l) for volume.

A simple standard mathematical notation is frequently used in defining and using these multiples. Consider the number 5 million, i.e. 5,000,000. One million is 1,000,000 which is equal to 100 multiplied by 100 multiplied by 100, i.e. $100 \times 100 \times 100$. One hundred is 10 multiplied by 10, i.e. 10×10, which is 10 squared or 10 raised to the power 2, written 10^2. So one million is equal to 10 multiplied by 10 six times, i.e. 1,000,000 equals $10 \times 10 \times 10 \times 10 \times 10 \times 10$, which is 10 raised to the power 6, written as 10^6. The number 5 million can be, and frequently would be, written as 5×10^6. In the same way, one thousand is 10 to the power 3, written as 10^3, and 5,000 could be written as 5×10^3, while one billion (one thousand million throughout this book) is 10 to the power 9 and 5 billion (5,000,000,000) could be written as 5×10^9.

The following table lists the word prefixes used for the standard multiples, the corresponding symbols or abbreviations, the size of the multiple in power of ten notation, and – to indicate the usefulness and economy of the power notation – the corresponding number in standard arithmetic form.

Prefix	Symbol	Multiple as power of 10	Multiple
hecto	h	10^2	100
kilo	k	10^3	1,000
mega	M	10^6	1,000,000
giga	G	10^9	1,000,000,000
tera	T	10^{12}	1,000,000,000,000
peta	P	10^{15}	1,000,000,000,000,000
exa	E	10^{18}	1,000,000,000,000,000,000

To give some sense of the orders of magnitude here, consider electricity supply from a coal-burning power station. The size of such a plant is usually discussed in terms of the maximum amount of power that it could send out. Recall that the basic unit for power is the watt, which is one joule per second. The size of a typical modern coal-fired electric power plant is 1,000 megawatts, or 1,000 Mw. If the plant ran at maximum power for 1 hour it would send out 1,000 megawatt hours, 1,000 Mwh, of electrical energy. For a thermal efficiency of 33 per cent, that would mean burning an amount of coal with chemical energy content 10800000 ($= 3,000 \times 60$ minutes $\times 60$ seconds) Mj, or 10,800 Gj, or 10.8 Tj. From the definition of a joule as the heat required to raise the temperature of one cubic centimetre of water by $0.239°C$, and assuming an ambient temperature of $15°C$, it would require 180,000 joules, or 0.18 Mj, to bring a 0.5 litre kettle of water to the boil. In one hour the power plant could boil 20 million such kettles (1,000 × 60 × 60 = 3,600,000 Mj, which divided by 0.18 is 20 × 10^6 kettles).

The use of measurement units based on the joule is now widespread in energy analysis, but it is by no means universal, and conversions as between the units used in different sources can be tedious. In the SI system there is another basic unit for energy/heat/work which is the calorie. One calorie is the heat required to raise the temperature of one gramme of water by one degree centigrade. It is approximately equal to 4.2 joules. The use of the calorie as the basic unit is particularly widespread in analysis of the chemical energy of food, and in discussions of weight-loss programmes. Again, as the calorie is a small amount, such analysis is usually reported in terms of kilocalories, often written as kcals, or sometimes as Cals. The amount of food energy required by a human adult varies with her size, the ambient temperature, and the activities engaged in. A widely used figure for an average human adult leading a moderately active live is 2,500 kcals per day. In terms of joules this is 2,500 × 1,000 × 4.2 = 10,500,000, which is often stated as 10 Mj per day, or 10 × 365 = 3,650 Mj per year.

Not all sources use SI units. Particularly, but not exclusively, in economic analysis involving energy originating in the USA the basic unit is the British Thermal Unit, BTU. One BTU is the amount of heat required to raise the temperature of one pound of water by one degree Fahrenheit. It is equal to 1,055 joules, and for many purposes the approximation of 1 BTU equals 1,000 j will suffice. The BTU is quite a small amount, and a widely used unit based on it is the Therm, which is 100,000 BTU, and, therefore, approximately equal to 100,000,000 joules, i.e. 100 Mj. A very large unit in this system of measurement is the Quad, which is 10^{15} BTU, approximately 10^{18} joules or 1 Ej (exajoule).

As will be discussed in later chapters, in the modern economy the fossil fuels – coal, oil and gas – are the dominant source of energy. In many sources, data on the fossil fuels are reported in the mass and volume units, rather than in energy units. Thus, coal is typically measured in metric tonnes, where one tonne is 1,000 kilograms, which is approximately 0.98 Imperial tons. Oil is frequently measured in units called 'barrels', which refers to the size of the barrels used to transport oil away from the world's first oil well, opened in the 1860s, in Pennsylvania. One barrel is 42 US gallons, approximately 35 Imperial gallons. Oil varies in weight. The number of barrels to a tonne of oil varies from approximately 6.5 to 8, with an average of about 7. Gas is often measured in cubic feet or cubic metres, and multiples thereof.

For many purposes it is useful to be able to compare, or add, across quantities of the different fossil fuels, and alternative energy sources such as nuclear power or wind power, in common, energy, units. This is sometimes done by expressing everything in terms of tonnes of coal, or oil, equivalent. More usually, and more usefully, nowadays the more common practice is to express everything in SI energy terms based on the joule. The following are conversion factors that can be used for this purpose:

Fuel	Quantity	Gj
Coal	1 tonne	29
Oil	1 tonne	42
Gas	1 tonne	55

These are approximate averages. Just as the weight of a barrel of crude oil varies a little according to where it comes from, so does the exact amount of heat released when it is burned. The same goes for coal and gas – the heat content of one tonne of, say, east-coast US coal is not exactly the same as the heat content of one tonne of coal mined in, say, Queensland in Australia. Whereas the average heat content of 1 tonne of UK coal is 26 Gj, the figure of 29 Gj given above is widely used for compiling data for international comparisons.

All this means that some caution is appropriate when working with energy data from different sources, as it is not necessarily the case that the same conversion factors have been used in all of the sources. On the other hand, where the data for the different fossil fuels comes in tonnes, converting it all into energy units using averages such as those given above will involve errors in any particular case. Given that the raw numbers are usually large, small differences in the conversion factors can give rise to non-trivial differences in the energy data produced.

To see what can be involved here, go back to the 1,000 Mw coal-fired electricity generating station considered above. We saw that operated at capacity for one hour it would burn 10,800 Gj of coal energy. If we use the UK average figure of 26 Gj per tonne, this is 415 tonnes of coal. If we use the international average of 29 Gj per tonne, this is 372 tonnes of coal.

generating plant. With combustion, all of the chemical energy in the coal is converted to other forms of energy – electrical in the desired output from the plant sent out over the grid, heat energy as waste heat carried away in cooling water or vented to the atmosphere, and chemical energy in the residual matter such as ash. Note that the electrical energy sent out is later transformed to work or heat in homes and factories. Although all of the chemical energy in the coal is conserved, from a human point of view some of the energy transformations are more useful than others. Seen as a source of electrical energy, the plant has a thermal efficiency of (considerably) less than one – the thermal efficiency is the ratio of the electrical energy to the chemical energy content of the burned coal. For modern large generating plants, thermal efficiency is of the order of 35 per cent. What are known as 'combined heat and power' plants use some of the heat that is wasted in a pure electricity generating plant to warm buildings or run production processes. In this way, more of the input chemical energy is converted to energy forms useful to humans, and in that sense the 'efficiency' of the plant is increased.

The first law of thermodynamics is a conservation law. It says that energy is conserved. There is a corresponding conservation law for matter. Matter can neither be created nor destroyed. This law of conservation of matter is sometimes known as the **materials balance principle**. We shall discuss it further at various points in this chapter and in Chapter 4.

Many of those who are concerned about the environment want to encourage people to go in for 'energy conservation'. But, the first law says that there is always

100 per cent energy conservation whatever people do. There is no real contradiction here, just an imprecise use of language on the part of those seeking to promote 'energy conservation'. What they actually want to encourage is people doing the things that they do now but in ways that require less heat and/or less work, and therefore less energy conversion.

There is another widespread use of words in regard to energy that is strictly inaccurate. Often, and especially in economics, people talk about energy 'consumption'. The first law says that energy cannot be consumed in the sense of being used up so that there is less of it than there was previously. What is meant by energy consumption is the conversion of energy from one form to another, and into work and heat. This strictly incorrect usage will often be followed in this book, as it is so widespread, and does not cause any real problems in the contexts where we shall follow it.

The first law of thermodynamics is about energy quantity. The other thermodynamic law that we need to consider, the second law, is about energy quality. Before looking at the second law, we need to look at the way that thermodynamics classifies systems.

2.2.3 Thermodynamic systems classification

Based on a differentiation between flows of energy and flows of matter across the system boundary, thermodynamics distinguishes three types of system:
(1)   An open system exchanges matter and energy with its environment;
(2)   A closed system exchanges only energy with its environment;
(3)   An isolated system exchanges neither matter nor energy with its environment.

If you refer back to Figure 1.1, you will see an example of a thermodynamically open system and an example of a thermodynamically closed system. Thermodynamically, the economy is an open system. It takes from and returns to its environment – which is 'the natural environment' or often just 'the environment' in this book – both matter and energy. The environment is a thermodynamically closed system. It receives from and returns to its environment – the rest of the universe – only energy.

Energy goes from the environment to the economy in many forms – radiation (sunshine), kinetic (flowing water, wind, waves), potential (water reservoirs) and chemical (plant and animal tissue, fossil fuels), for example. Energy goes from the economy to the environment mainly as waste heat and chemical energy in residues. Material flows across the economy–environment boundary take many forms, in both directions. Note that the law of conservation of matter means that the mass of flows across the boundary in each direction will be equal – in terms of total mass, extractions by the economy from the environment equal insertions by the economy into the environment. The composition of the extraction stream is, of course, different from that of the insertion stream. We shall return to this in Chapter 4.

It is not strictly true that 'the environment', i.e. planet earth, is a closed system in a thermodynamic sense. However, it exchanges much energy and very little matter with its environment, and is generally treated as a closed system. As regards matter, meteorites regularly and frequently (thousands each year) enter the environment, and have done so throughout the history of the planet. Meteorites vary in size, but most are very small and burn up in the atmosphere. Of those that have reached the surface, the largest that can still be seen weighs 60 tonnes. Exceptionally large meteorites may have had major impacts on the history of planet earth. A favoured explanation for the extinction of the dinosaurs, and hence the rise of the mammals, is the climatic change that followed the impact, 65 million years ago, of a meteorite 6 miles across. For most of the planet's history there has been no outgoing matter. In the last fifty years human beings have developed the capacity to send matter (as space vehicles of various kinds) out across the environment/universe boundary, but the amount involved has been very small. This is likely to remain the case for some time.

The energy flows crossing the boundary between our environment and its environment are very large, and have been so throughout the history of the planet. The incoming flow is solar radiation, of which approximately $2,500 \times 10^3$ Ej reaches the surface of the earth each year. As shown in Box 2.1, an Exajoule or Ej (approximately equal to a Quad), is a very big energy unit. Later we will compare this number for incident solar radiation with some other 'big' energy numbers of economic relevance.

All living organisms are open systems, which exchange energy and matter with their environments. We shall look at plants and animals as open systems in a little detail after considering the second law of thermodynamics.

Strictly, the only isolated system that exists is the entire universe. All other systems that could be delineated must be, at least, closed systems. However, thermodynamicists often use the idea of an isolated system for analytical purposes, and actual systems can be constructed in the laboratory that approximate to isolated systems in the same way as planet earth approximates to a closed system.

We can now state the first law in a slightly different way: the energy content of an isolated system is constant. This is a more precise way of stating the first law. It avoids a possible misunderstanding of it based on the way it was stated above. To say that energy can be neither created nor destroyed is not to say that the energy content of a system cannot change. It is only the energy content of an isolated system that cannot change. Open and closed systems can exchange energy with their environments, and it follows that their energy content can change. Consider again a coal-fired electricity generating plant, and let it with a given stock of coal on its premises be the, open, system. As the coal is burned and electricity (and waste) sent out, so the energy content of this system decreases, reaching a minimum when all the coal is burnt. The energy content of this system's environment increases by the same amount as the system's decreases. Once all of the initial stock of coal is burnt, bringing in more coal will increase the energy content of the system, and decrease that of its environment.

2.2.4 Second law of thermodynamics

It has been said that whereas the first law of thermodynamics is that you cannot get anything for nothing, the second law is that you will always pay over the odds anyway. According to the first law, that is, energy cannot be created, only converted from one form to another. As regards the second law, the point being made is that all conversions involve losses. This seems to contradict the first law, but does not. The loss is not in terms of energy quantity, but in terms of energy quality. All energy conversion processes involve some downgrading of the quality of energy. Quality here refers to the proportion of energy that is available for conversion.

The second law is known as 'the entropy law' because its most basic statement is: the **entropy** of an isolated system cannot decrease. What is entropy? One answer is that it is energy that is not available for conversion. Another is that it is a measure of disorder.

In order to explain how these answers are related, and hence the meaning and implications of the basic statement of the second law, we need to go back to the idea of energy as the potential to do work or supply heat. This implies that heat and work are related. Recall that they are measured in the same units. In the middle of the nineteenth century an engineer called Carnot formulated the relationship that governs the conversion of heat to work – the maximum amount of work that can be obtained from a quantity of heat depends on only the temperature of the heat source relative to its surroundings. The maximum proportion of the heat that can be turned into work is given by

$$E = (T - T_0) \div T$$

where T is the temperature of the heat source and T_0 is the temperature of its surroundings, where temperature is measured in degrees Absolute. This is

$$E = (T \div T) - (T_0 \div T) = 1 - (T_0 \div T)$$

which is 1 only if $T_0 = 0$. But a temperature of zero degrees Absolute (which is minus 273 degrees Centigrade) is impossible, so E must be less than 1. The Carnot efficiency of conversion must be less than one.

Matter in its various forms comprises assemblies of molecules. The molecules that comprise a lump of matter do not completely fill the space that the lump occupies. In the air that surrounds us, the average distance between molecules is about ten times the size of a molecule. In solids, the molecules are more tightly packed together – which is why one can sit on a chair but not on air. In all forms of matter, the molecules are constantly in random motion. The speed of the motion increases with temperature. Faster random motion means less order. Think of heating a suitable solid so that it passes from a solid to a liquid and then to a gaseous state. What is happening is that the amount of random motion is increasing, and goes through critical values so as to produce the transition from one state to another. More random motion is more disorder – a solid is more ordered than a liquid, which is more ordered than a gas. Entropy is a measure of disorder.

To see the connection between the two meanings of entropy, think about a given mass of gas expanding to fill the volume of its container which is increased by the gas pushing back a piston. Suppose that there is no temperature change involved. Looked at from the disorder point of view, the number of molecules is constant, so the distances between them increase, so the amount of random motion increases, so the entropy of the gas increases. Looked at from the energy point of view, the expansion of the gas must be accompanied by an influx of heat to compensate for the energy converted to work to push back the piston, so the entropy of the gas increases. From both points of view, the gas has higher entropy after it has expanded to fill the larger volume.

The second law can, then, be stated in two equivalent ways. It says that the unavailable energy in an isolated system cannot decrease. It says that disorder cannot decrease in an isolated system. Looked at either way, this seems like very bad news. It seems to be saying, and has been interpreted as saying, that things necessarily run down, becoming more disordered, less structured. However, it must be kept in mind that in this version, the entropy law *applies only to isolated systems*. The entropy of a closed or an open system does not necessarily increase, as such systems can import available energy and thereby reduce disorder. The entropy law does have implications for closed and open systems, but they do not include the implication that entropy always increases. One of the scientists who developed thermodynamics, Clausius, said that 'The entropy of the world grows to a maximum'. If by the 'world' he meant planet earth, and if he meant continuously and inevitably, he was wrong. So long as the sun continues to deliver solar radiation, the entropy of the system which is planet earth need not increase. What is true for any system is that in the absence of some input of energy, the system becomes more disorganised.

One implication of the entropy law for non-isolated systems, such as planet earth, is that all conversions of energy from one form to another are, in terms of available energy, less than 100 per cent efficient. It follows from this that all conversions of energy from one form to another are irreversible.

When these implications are put together with those of the first law of thermodynamics, they are extremely important for the study of economics. Were it not for the laws of thermodynamics, material economic production could be expanded indefinitely. That production involves doing work, moving and transforming materials. Doing work requires energy. If energy conversions were 100 per cent efficient and reversible, limited energy availability would not imply a limited capacity to do work. We will come back to various particular aspects of this in the other chapters in Part I. We now use what we have learned about thermodynamics to look at life, in the form of plants and animals.

2.2.5 Plants as open systems

Looked at from the point of view of thermodynamics, a living plant is an open system. It exchanges energy and matter with its environment. A living plant is a highly ordered system, in which disorder is not increasing because the plant is taking energy from its environment to maintain order, i.e. life. At death, the plant ceases to take energy from its environment, and a process of increasing disorder, decay, starts. Eventually, when the decay process is complete, the system that was the plant has become so disordered that it is indistinguishable from its environment.

Plants are a subset of the class of organisms known as 'autotrophs' or 'producers'. The distinguishing characteristic of autotrophs is that they use chlorophyll to make organic matter from inorganic matter, using energy. Most autotrophs are 'phototrophs' in that the energy used is solar radiation, and the process by which organic matter is made is **photosynthesis**. The word 'photosynthesis' means 'building by light'. As well as land and water plants, the class of phototrophs includes

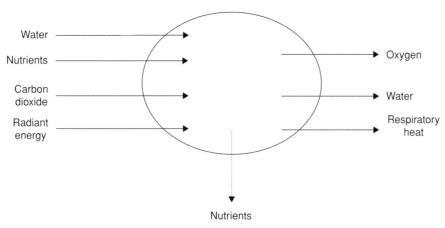

Figure 2.3
Living plant as
an open
system.

algae, plankton and bacteria – plankton, or phytoplankton, are actually plants with-out roots. We look at things in terms of land plants, but what is said about them also goes for the other phototrophs. Autotrophs that are not phototrophs are not very important in the big picture and will be ignored here (they include some bacteria and some algae).

Figure 2.3 shows the important features of a living plant as an open system. The inflows are water, carbon dioxide and radiant energy, i.e. solar radiation or sun-light. The photosynthetic process converts some of the radiant energy to chemical energy stored in the plant tissue, and some of the input energy is returned to the environment as heat. This return of heat is known as respiration, and reflects the energy required to run the photosynthetic process and for the maintenance of the plant system. Oxygen and water also cross the system boundary from the plant to the environment. The operation of the process of photosynthesis requires the presence of certain mineral elements, known as nutrients. These are taken up by the growing plant, from the soil and water, and incorporated into its tissue. When the plant dies and decays these nutrients are returned to the environment. Included in the nutrients necessary for the operation of the process of photosynthesis are: nitrogen, phosphorous, potassium, sulphur, copper, iron, zinc.

The rate at which plants produce plant tissue is known as **primary productivity**, and is usually measured in terms of energy per unit area per unit time – calories per square metre per year, say. Individual plant species, and assemblages of dif-ferent species of plants, can be compared in terms of their primary productivity. Gross primary productivity is the total amount of solar energy that is fixed by pho-tosynthesis, whereas net primary productivity is that less the amount of energy lost to the environment as respiration, and so the amount that is actually stored in the plant tissue. Net primary productivity is the measure of the energy that is potentially available to the animals that eat the plants in question.

Plant species vary in their primary productivity. For a given species, the pri-mary productivity of a particular population will vary with the environment. The environmental conditions most relevant are: the amount of light (solar radiation), the amount of water, availability of carbon dioxide, temperature, and nutrient availability. Scarcity relative to the plant's requirements in respect of any one of these factors will inhibit plant growth, and reduce primary productivity, and cannot be compensated for by the uptake of more of some other factor for which there is no scarcity. If, for example, the availability of water is inhibiting growth, the inhibition can only be overcome by making more water available – providing more nutrients or carbon dioxide will not solve a water supply problem. In the language of economics (see Chapter 8 on this), in terms of primary production by plants, the various inputs are complements rather than substitutes. Biologists talk in terms of limiting factors – if some input is scarce relative to requirements, it is a limiting factor on growth, no matter how abundant the others may be. At the extreme, the inhibition is so great that the plant cannot grow at all. Arid deserts are the most obvious examples of such extremes, where water is the limiting factor.

The efficiency with which plants convert incident solar energy into tissue varies from 2 per cent to 6 per cent. Much of the solar energy that reaches the surface of the earth does not fall upon plants, or upon places where plants might grow. It was noted above that each year approximately 2,500 Ej of solar energy arrives at the surface of the earth. Photosynthesis annually produces approximately 1.2 Ej of plant tissue, which is 0.05 per cent of the solar energy arriving at the earth's surface.

2.2.6 Animals as open systems

With the substitution of 'animal' for 'plant', the first paragraph of the last section serves as the first for this, as follows.

Looked at from the point of view of thermodynamics, a living animal is an open system. It exchanges energy and matter with its environment. A living animal is a highly ordered system, in which disorder is not increasing because the animal is taking energy from its environment to maintain order, i.e. life. At death, the animal ceases to take energy from its environment, and a process of increasing disorder, decay, starts. Eventually, when the decay process is complete, the system that was the animal has become so disordered that it is indistinguishable from its environment.

Viewed as open systems, there are two main differences between plants and animals. The first is in terms of the source and form of the input energy. For plants it is solar radiation. For animals, input energy is the chemical energy in the food that is taken in. The second is that, whereas plants take in carbon dioxide and give out oxygen, animals take in oxygen and give out carbon dioxide. An animal as an open system is depicted in Figure 2.4. Like plants, animals need inputs of water and nutrients. The latter are obtained, along with energy, from food input. Energy/heat goes from the animal system to its environment in two ways. The animal's faeces contain stored chemical energy in the undigested food. There is also, as with plants, respiratory heat. The animal's faeces also contain nutrients. These are also returned to the environment when the animal dies, and decomposition releases those that were stored in the animal tissue. Whereas plants are known as producers, animals are known as consumers, or 'heterotrophs'. Animals are classified according to the source of the food that they consume. Animals that consume plants as food are

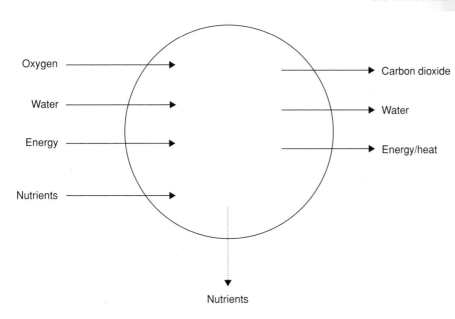

Figure 2.4
Living animal as
an open
system.

known as 'herbivores', or 'primary consumers', while animals that consume animals are 'carnivores', or 'secondary consumers'.

We saw that plants convert only a small proportion of the incident solar energy into chemical energy stored in plant tissue. Herbivores likewise convert only a small proportion of the chemical energy of plant tissue into animal tissue. Consumption efficiency is

$$CE = \frac{I}{P}$$

where P is the net primary productivity of the plant system and I is the amount of productivity ingested by the animal system. Assimilation efficiency is

$$AE = \frac{A}{I}$$

where A is the productivity actually assimilated by the herbivore system, the difference between A and I being accounted for by energy expelled with the faeces. Production efficiency is

$$PE = \frac{T}{A}$$

where T is the net productivity of the herbivore system, i.e. the chemical energy incorporated into animal tissue. The difference between T and A is due to heat respiration, which in the case of an animal system additionally arises when energy is converted to the work involved in the animal moving around. The overall efficiency, E, for the conversion of energy from storage in plant to storage in animal tissue is

Box 2.2 Animal food-gathering strategies

Of the food energy taken in, eaten or consumed, by an animal, some is assimilated and some leaves the animal in faeces and urine. Of the assimilated food energy, some is stored as new tissue and some is used in respiration and eventually dissipated as heat. Respiration is the work done to maintain the animal's structure. That work includes the gathering of the food that is the source of the energy taken in. Clearly, if the system that is an animal is to be viable, it must be the case that the energy taken in from food per unit time is greater than the energy expended in acquiring the food. In fact, the ratio:

$$\frac{C}{E} = \frac{\text{Energy consumed}}{\text{Energy expended}}$$

must be greater than some number greater than 1, because some of the energy consumed is not assimilated. If, say, 50 per cent of food eaten were assimilated, then a viable design for an animal system would require that C/E were greater than 2.

The table below gives data for six animals on the energy expended in feeding and the C/E ratio. Given that these are animals that exist, the fact that the minimum value for C/E is greater than one is not the point about these data – matters could not be otherwise. Rather, the point is that the range for the ratio is much narrower than the range for the rates of energy expenditure, E.

In the next chapter we will look at human food-provision methods in this way.

Animal	E calories per minute	$\dfrac{C}{E}$
Hummingbird	32.9	7–70
3 Hummingbird species	16.1–21.5	3.8–22.2
Finch	15.6	12.8
Bumblebee	0.32–0.46	4.4–20.2
Damselfly larva*	5×10^{-6}–5×10^{-5}	1.1–3.6
Black bass	2.2–3.0	3.8–10.3

* Note the use here, in $5 \times 10^{-6} - 5 \times 10^{-5}$, of an extension of the notation introduced in Box 2.1. 10^{-6} is $1/10^6 = 1/(10 \times 10 \times 10 \times 10 \times 10 \times 10) = 1 \div 1{,}000{,}000 = 0.000001$, so that $5 \times 10^{-6} = 0.000005$. Similarly, $5 \times 10^{-5} = 0.00005$.
Source: Lawton (1973).

then given by

$$E = CE \times AE \times PE$$

According to the plant species and the herbivore species, it is estimated that E varies between 5 per cent and 20 per cent.

Carnivores could be looked at in the same way, with P in the first, consumption efficiency, ratio being the productivity of the animal that gets eaten rather than of the plant that gets eaten.

The production efficiency of an animal, herbivore or carnivore, varies with the level of activity. Respiration is at its minimum when the animal is at rest, and increases with the level of activity. The continuance of life for the animal requires that, at least, as much energy is acquired from food as is required for respiration on account of movement and the maintenance of basic metabolic functions. More than that is required for non-adult animals so that growth in mass can occur. Reproduction also requires additional energy inputs. Different animal species have different strategies for food acquisition, which differ in their implications for energy input requirements. However, any viable strategy must have the characteristic that, on average and over a suitably defined period of time, energy acquired as food must be at least as great as energy expended in acquisition. Otherwise, the animal will die.

2.3 ECOSYSTEMS

An **ecosystem** is a system comprising living organisms, known as biota, and their non-living, or abiotic, environment, and all of the interactions between all of the biotic and abiotic components of the system. The delineation of the boundary of an ecosystem is a matter of judgement, and depends to some extent on the purpose at hand. Very detailed studies can be conducted of ecosystems of small spatial extent, such as, for example, a pond or a small woodland area. At the other extreme, the entire biosphere can be treated as a single ecosystem, and studied at a less detailed level. Both extremes have their uses in trying to understand how 'the environment' works. For some purposes, the world is divided into large areas of similar climate and plant life, which large ecosystems are referred to as 'biomes'.

At whatever scale they are defined, ecosystems have generic structural features in common. It is these common features that we shall be looking at here. We look first at the way energy and matter move through ecosystems.

2.3.1 Energy and nutrient flows

We have seen that both plants and animals are thermodynamically open systems. Plants and animals are involved in a feeding chain. For a very simple example, in an aquatic context, we can think of plankton (plant) which gets eaten by a crustacean (herbivore) which gets eaten by a herring (carnivore) which gets eaten by a human (top carnivore, in this chain). In practice, feeding chains do not have such simple structures. Usually, for example, an organism at one level is an input to more than one organism at the next higher level. Figure 2.5 shows, still in simplified form, a more realistic set of relationships between producers and consumers in a foodweb. The particular foodweb here is a woodland ecosystem in the UK. However, the basic solar energy → producers → consumers structure applies to all ecosystems, at whatever level, from the local to the global, they are delineated.

In looking at plants and animals as open systems, we noted that the photo-synthetic conversion of solar radiation to stored energy in plant tissue is (considerably) less than 100 per cent efficient, as is the conversion of plant tissue to animal tissue. There are, likewise, losses as we go from primary to secondary, and from secondary to tertiary, consumers. As a result, when we look at the structure of an ecosystem in terms of the chemical energy stored per unit time at the various levels of the foodweb, we get a **trophic pyramid** of the general form shown in Figure 2.6. 'Trophic' means 'of, having to do with, nutrition' – recall 'autotroph' for plant as producer, and 'heterotroph' for animal as consumer. In Figure 2.6 there are four 'trophic levels', corresponding to the four classes of organism whose nutrition is at issue.

The units of measurement at each level in Figure 2.6 are energy, stored in organic tissue, per unit area per unit time, say calories per square metre per year. Because, as discussed above, the consumption, assimilation and production efficiencies are all less than 100 per cent, for any ecosystem the amount of energy fixed in herbivore tissue over a given period of time must be less than the amount fixed in plant tissue. The same is true for the transition from any trophic level to the one above it, and hence the pyramid shape when we stack the energy stored by level as in

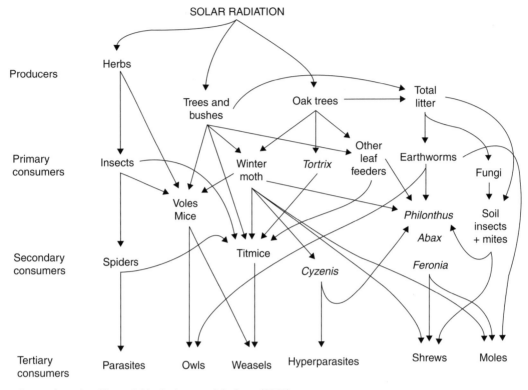

Source: based on Figure 9.1 in Jackson and Jackson (2000).

Figure 2.5 A foodweb for a woodland ecosystem.

Figure 2.6. Particular ecosystems vary from one another in the detail of their trophic pyramids, but all have the basic pyramid shape showing the necessary structure of the flow of energy through an ecosystem. The relative sizes of the rectangles in Figure 2.6 understate the narrowing of the pyramid that would be found in any actual ecosystem. The upper limit to the size of the rectangle at one level as a proportion of the size of the rectangle at the level below is estimated to be about 20 per cent. Assuming that upper limit holds at every stage, the size of the tertiary consumers' rectangle would be less than 1 per cent of the size of the rectangle

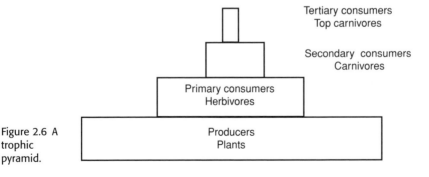

Figure 2.6 A trophic pyramid.

Table 2.1 Net primary productivities for selected biomes

Biome	Area 10^6 sq km	Net primary productivity per unit area tonnes per sq km per year		Net primary productivity World total 10^9 tonnes per year
		Range	*Mean*	
Tropical rainforest	17.0 (3.3)	1000–3500	2200	37.4 (22.0)
Temperate deciduous forest	7.0 (1.4)	600–2500	1200	8.4 (4.9)
Boreal forest	12.0 (2.4)	400–2000	800	9.6 (5.6)
Temperate grassland	9.0 (1.8)	200–1500	600	5.4 (3.2)
Tundra and alpine	8.0 (1.6)	10–400	140	1.1 (0.7)
Desert and semi-desert	18.0 (3.5)	10–250	90	1.6 (0.9)
Cultivated land	14.0 (2.7)	100–3500	650	9.1 (5.4)
Swamp and marsh	2.0 (0.4)	800–3500	2000	4.0 (2.4)
Total terrestrial	**149 (29.2)**		**773**	**115 (67.6)**
Open ocean	332.0 (65.1)	2–400	125	41.5 (24.4)
Continental shelf	26.6 (5.2)	200–600	360	9.6 (5.6)
Algal beds and reefs	0.6 (0.1)	500–4000	2500	1.6 (0.9)
Estuaries	1.4 (0.3)	2000–3500	1500	2.1 (1.2)
Total marine	**361 (70.8)**		**152**	**55.0 (32.4)**
Total	**510**		**333**	**170**

Source: based on Jackson and Jackson (2000), Table 9.4.

for plants – the energy stored in the tissue of top carnivores would be less than a hundredth of that stored in the system's plants.

Abundance at different trophic levels can also be looked at in terms of numbers of individuals per unit area, or in terms of biomass per unit area. Biomass is simply the weight of living material. In terms of either numbers or biomass, the same pyramid shape is generally obtained as when looking at trophic levels in energy terms.

The base for the trophic pyramid of an ecosystem is net primary productivity, the amount of energy fixed as plant tissue per unit time. It follows that the relative abundance of life of all kinds in different ecosystems is mainly determined by relative performance in terms of net primary productivity. Table 2.1 gives information about this for some selected **biomes**. The data of Table 2.1 directly refer to plant life, but the relativities that they reveal will also apply, broadly, to the abundance of animal life given its dependence on plant life. The biomes listed in Table 2.1 do not account for the whole of the earth's surface: figures for the missing biomes can be obtained from the source for Table 2.1, which also gives data on biomass. The second column gives the area of the biome in millions of square kilometres, and, in parenthesis, as a percentage of the total surface area of the earth. The productivity data in Table 2.1 are in terms of equivalent mass rather than energy units. The third column gives productivity per unit area, i.e. per square kilometre, in terms of the range across the biome and the mean for the biome as a whole. The fourth column gives the biome's total productivity, in billions of tonnes, as the product of its area and its mean productivity, and, in parenthesis, its percentage contribution to global productivity.

The main points to be noted from Table 2.1 are as follows. The marine biomes account for 70 per cent of the earth's surface, but only 32 per cent of its total net primary productivity. This is mainly due to the fact that the open oceans account for over 90 per cent of the marine surface area, but have relatively low per unit productivity. The mean productivity per unit area for the open oceans is about the same as that for the tundra/alpine terrestrial biome, and not much greater than that for desert and semi-desert. Note, however, that algal beds and reefs and estuaries have per unit area productivities similar to those for the most productive terrestrial biomes. In fact, the upper end of the range for algal beds and reefs, which refers to tropical rain coral reefs, is higher than the upper end of the range for any terrestrial biome.

As regards the terrestrial biomes, per unit area productivity generally declines with increasing distance from the equator, reflecting declining receipts of solar radiation. It is estimated that more than 70 per cent of total terrestrial net productivity occurs between latitudes 30 °N and 30 °S. Tropical rainforest has the highest mean productivity. Note that the upper limit of the range for cultivated land is the same as the upper limit for tropical rainforest, but that, because cultivated land spans a wide range of latitude, its mean is well below the mean for tropical forest. Although tropical rain forest accounts for only 3.3 per cent of the surface, it accounts for 22 per cent of total global productivity. Cultivated land accounts for 2.7 per cent of the surface and 5.4 per cent of productivity.

Ecosystems can, then, be analysed in terms of the way that energy flows through them. As we saw in the discussion above of plants and animals as open systems, energy is not the only thing that crosses the boundaries of plants and animals. Minerals, or nutrients, are necessary for plants and animals to process energy conversions, and cross the boundaries of systems which are individual organisms. However, if we take the ecosystem as the system to be analysed, there is an important difference between energy flows and the flows of nutrients. Essentially, there is a one-way flow of useful energy through an ecosystem, whereas nutrients cycle around an ecosystem. As we shall see when we consider planetary processes below, this is strictly true only if we are looking at an ecosystem which is the whole biosphere – for other delineations of ecosystems, minerals do cross their boundaries. However, the statement is approximately true for most of the boundaries that would define interesting ecosystems, and it does make an important point in a simple way, so we shall proceed for now as if it were true without qualification.

Figure 2.7 shows energy and nutrient movement in an ecosystem. Energy as solar radiation enters the system, and is converted to organic matter by producers, and thus passed to herbivores and carnivores, as discussed above, and to decomposers, to be considered shortly. The heat flows shown in Figure 2.7 go from the system to its environment: they are the products of respiration processes, and are not useful energy. The flow of useful energy is unidirectional: energy is not recycled. Decomposers are the organisms that operate the decomposition processes in an ecosystem, which processes are the means by which nutrients are recycled round the system. **Decomposition** is the breakdown of dead organic matter, which releases the inorganic nutrients that it contains, making it available to be taken up from

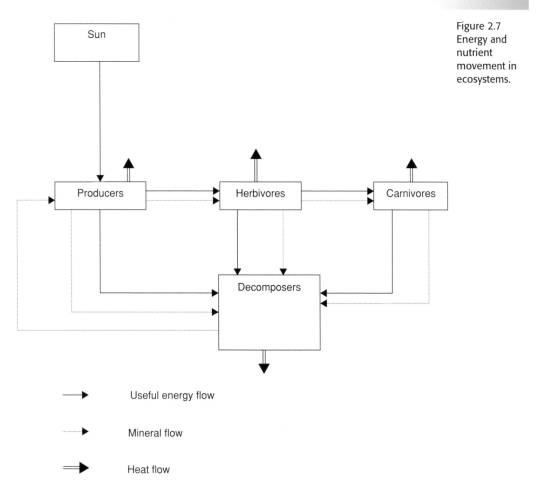

Figure 2.7
Energy and
nutrient
movement in
ecosystems.

→   Useful energy flow

⋯▶   Mineral flow

⇒   Heat flow

the soil by living plants. There are two classes of decomposers. Fungi and bacteria secrete digestive enzymes which break down the complex molecules of dead organic matter into simpler ones that they can utilise. These organisms are known as 'saprophytes'. The second class of decomposer organisms are animals, known as 'detritivores', that eat dead organic material. The material that these animals excrete is finer-textured than the material that they eat, which makes it easier for the fungi and bacteria to work on. Examples of detritivores are centipedes, earthworms, nematodes and woodlice.

The complete decomposition of dead organic material is rare. Soils contain small quantities of organic material known as 'humus'. The processes involved in decomposition are inhibited by low oxygen availability, low temperature and high acidity. Where such conditions apply, the result is the accumulation of dead organic material. This is the starting point for processes, operating over millions of years, that led to the existence of the fossil fuels. Since modern industrial economies are characterised by extensive use of fossil fuels, we now discuss their origins.

2.3.1.1 Origins of the fossil fuels

The **fossil fuels** are coal, oil and natural gas. All are organic in origin, and all are the product of solar radiation that reached the surface of the earth over long periods of time a long time ago.

Coal was once vegetation, and particularly peat. Peat is an organic deposit which accumulates when the rate of production of plant tissue by photosynthesis exceeds the rate at which it is decomposed. Such a situation is usually associated with wetland areas, and peat is now found mainly in the higher latitudes of the northern hemisphere. Peat builds up over thousands of years. Coal was formed when ancient peat deposits were buried beneath sediment layers and thus compressed. There are several classes of coal according to the amount of compression, and hence the remaining moisture content. In order of increasing compression/decreasing moisture the classes are: lignite, brown coal, bituminous coal, anthracite. Bituminous and anthracite coal was laid down in the Carboniferous period (360 to 280 million years ago), and lignite and brown coal during the Cretaceous period (140 to 60 million years ago).

Oil was once animal tissue. It is thought to have originated with the accumulation on the sea bottom of the bodies of very small sea creatures. Under some conditions, decomposition was incomplete and the organic molecules were converted into hydrocarbon molecules, some of which accumulated as oil in porous rock formations. Oil being lighter than the water that saturates porous rock, it migrates towards the surface of the earth. Liquid oil deposits arise where this process leads to accumulation in reservoirs of porous and permeable rock capped by impermeable rock, so further movement towards the earth's surface is impossible. Oil shale is shale containing preserved organic matter that has undergone some conversion to hydrocarbons, but which has not migrated to a reservoir for liquid oil. Tar sand is sandstone in which some of the pore spaces are filled with heavy hydrocarbons.

Natural gas consists mainly of methane, which is released as a by-product during the formation of oil, and natural gas deposits are usually found in association with oil deposits. Methane is also produced during the process by which coal is formed from peat, and is sometimes found in association with coal deposits. Natural gas is so called because for many years the gas that was burned in homes and factories was produced from coal. In the UK natural gas, from fields under the North Sea, displaced 'towngas' produced in 'gasworks' in the 1960s.

The foregoing account of the origins of the fossil fuels is the standard account, accepted by the overwhelming majority of geologists. For oil and natural gas, an alternative has been proposed. Whereas in the standard account, oil and natural gas have biological origins, in the alternative their origins are inorganic. According to this alternative theory, the majority of the earth's oil and gas is the result of the entrapment on this planet of some of the primordial hydrocarbons dispersed through the debris that became the solar system. If true, this could imply that the amounts of oil and natural gas existing on planet earth are much larger than is currently estimated. However, it would also be true that most of the 'additional' oil and natural gas would be extremely difficult to exploit, given foreseeable technology. In this book we shall accept the standard story, and largely ignore the alternative account and its implications.

Given the standard account of the origins of the fossil fuels, we can think of solar energy as being like a flow of money coming in as income, and then the fossil fuels are like a savings account into which deposits were made (by means of photosynthesis), a long time ago, from that income. The fossil fuels are saved-up past receipts of solar energy, where the saving was made possible because some solar energy was converted to plant tissue by the process of photosynthesis. Now, we saw, when looking at plants as thermodynamically open systems, that of the solar radiation that reaches the earth's surface only a small proportion is converted to plant tissue by photosynthesis. And, we have just seen that in the case of coal, the saving of that tissue occurred only in some circumstances and only over some periods of geological time – all of the coal was laid down in two geological epochs with a joint duration of 160 million years, which is less than 5 per cent of the geological history of the earth. Similar considerations apply to oil, and to natural gas on the standard account of their origins.

Given those origins, the amount of energy that is stored in the savings account that is the fossil fuels must be finite, and is really quite small. Each year approximately $2,500 \times 10^3$ Ej of solar radiation arrives at the surface of the earth. Of this, photosynthesis is estimated as fixing 1.2×10^3 Ej as primary productivity. A central estimate of the size of the stock of fossil fuels prior to the start of their depletion by humans is 315×10^3 Ej. That is equivalent to just 260 years' worth of global primary productivity, and much less than one year's worth of the solar radiation arriving at the surface of the earth.

Given that the fossil fuels are incompletely decomposed organic matter, it follows from our discussion of plants and animals as open systems that the fossil fuels must contain carbon. Coal, oil and gas vary in their carbon content. And, for any one of the fossil fuels the carbon content varies across deposits, so that the following figures are averages. Natural gas has the lowest carbon content at 14.6 kg per Gj (kilograms per Gigajoule). Oil is next lowest at 18.6 kg per Gj. Coal is the most carbon-intensive of the fossil fuels at 24.1 kg of carbon per Gj of energy content. Taking natural gas as the base with value one, the relative carbon intensities are 1.27 for oil and 1.65 for coal. On average, and approximately, deriving a given amount of work or heat from coal results in the release into the atmosphere of 65 per cent more carbon than would be the case if gas were used.

2.3.2 Population dynamics

The biotic components of an ecosystem are populations of plants and animals. A **population** is a group of individuals belonging to the same species which live in a given area at a given time. A **species** is a set of individuals who are capable of interbreeding. Organisms which are physiologically incapable of interbreeding (or which produce sterile offspring when they do interbreed) are members of different species. A population is, then, a reproductively isolated subset of a species. Its reproductive isolation is due to location, as opposed to physiology. Different ecosystems may contain organisms from the same species, but different ecosystems contain different populations. One way of looking at ecosystem behaviour over time is in terms of the behaviours over time – the dynamics – of the populations that make up the ecosystem.

Figure 2.8
Exponential
growth.

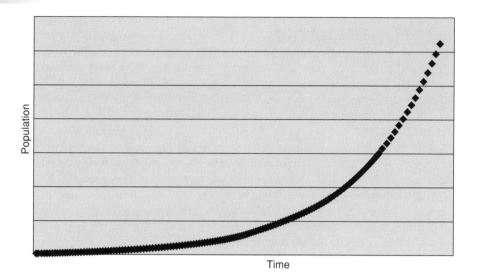

The actual dynamics of actual populations in actual ecosystems are determined by many factors, and disentangling the various processes at work can be very difficult. Ecologists try to understand the basic processes involved by constructing models, and by conducting controlled experiments in laboratories.

2.3.2.1 Exponential growth

A very simple model is **exponential growth**, where the proportional increase is the same in each time period, which means that the absolute increase keeps on getting bigger over time. Figure 2.8 shows a population growing exponentially. It is drawn using numbers from a simulation generated in an Excel^{TM} spreadsheet, as follows. The initial population size, 1, was entered in the cell A1. Then, the entry for cell A2 was generated using the formula palette as

$$A2 = A1^*1.05$$

which is the entry in A1 times 1.05, so that A2 is 5 per cent bigger than A1. Then, cell A2 was copied and pasted into cells A3 to A100. Because this is using relative rather than absolute cell references, the effect is that the entry in A3 is 1.05 times that in A2, the entry in A4 is 1.05 times that in A3, and so on and so on. Reading down the A cells gives exponential growth at the rate of 0.05 or 5 per cent.

Using some symbols, we can state the general exponential model in simple algebra. Let N_0 represent the population size at the beginning of the initial period, and the size at the beginning of the next period is

$$N_1 = (1+r) \times N_0$$

and for the one after that it is

$$N_2 = (1+r) \times N_1 = (1+r) \times [(1+r) \times N_0] = (1+r)^2 \times N_0$$

Table 2.2 Annual growth rates and doubling times

Growth rate %	Doubling time years
1	69.7
2	35.0
3	23.5
4	17.7
5	14.2
6	11.9
8	9.0
10	7.3

and so on and so on, so that generally

$$N_t = (1 + r)^t \times N_0$$

gives the population size at the start of period t, N_t, for exponential growth at the rate r from a starting level of N_0. For two adjacent periods this is

$$N_t = N_{t-1} + (r \times N_{t-1})$$

where N_{t-1} is size at the start of one period and N_t is size at the start of the next period. The absolute amount of growth is

$$N_t - N_{t-1} = r \times N_{t-1}$$

and proportionate growth is

$$\frac{N_t - N_{t-1}}{N_{t-1}} = r$$

In this model, N, the population size, is the variable that we are interested in the behaviour of, and r, the growth rate, is a parameter. A parameter is something that is constant in one simulation. Different simulations of the same model arise with different values for the parameter – Exercise 2.1 at the end of the chapter asks you to plot graphs of exponential growth for different growth rates. A model with just one parameter is a very simple model. In the next sub-section we will look at a population growth model with two parameters.

A useful way of expressing the implications of exponential growth is in terms of the 'doubling time'. This is the number of periods that it takes for whatever it is that is growing at a constant proportional rate to double in size. Table 2.2 shows some annual percentage growth rates and the approximate corresponding doubling times in years. The same numbers would apply for different periods of time used consistently. Thus, for a daily growth rate of 3 per cent the doubling time would be 23.5 days. Money left to earn interest in a savings account grows exponentially – according to Table 2.2 if you could get 5 per cent per year which you never took out of the account, your money would double within 15 years. We will look at this kind of compounding in Chapter 8. The Appendix at the end of the chapter here explains how the entries in Table 2.2 are obtained.

2.3.2.2 Density-dependent growth

It is, of course, impossible for a population to experience exponential growth indefinitely. The population's environment sets an upper limit to the size that it can attain because there is an upper limit to available solar radiation, for a plant population, or to available food, for an animal population. The maximum population size that the environment can support is called its 'carrying capacity'. Figure 2.9 shows a simple model of population dynamics where there is an upper limit to population size, which limit is known as the environment's **carrying capacity**. Initially the population grows exponentially, but as it increases in size so the growth rate

Figure 2.9
Density-
dependent
growth.

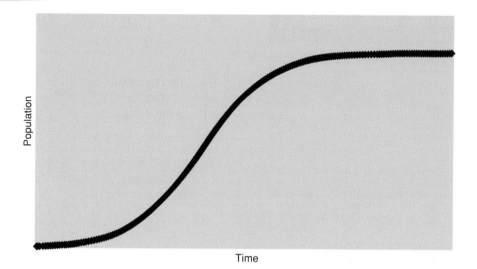

falls and goes towards zero as the population size approaches carrying capacity. This type of population dynamics is known as density-dependent growth because the growth rate depends on population size, which, given a particular environment, is equivalent to population density. Figure 2.9 actually shows an Excel^{TM}-generated plot of **logistic growth**, which is a particular kind of density-dependent growth. When we explained how Excel^{TM} was used to generate numbers for exponential growth at 5 per cent, instead of

$$A2 = A1^*1.05$$

we could have said

$$A2 = A1 + (0.05^*A1)$$

and got exactly the same results. In logistic growth, instead of a fixed number like 0.05, there is a number which varies with the difference between the size of the population and the carrying capacity of its environment. For the results graphed in Figure 2.9, the carrying capacity was 100, and the formula for A2 was

$$A2 = A1 + \left(0.1 \times \left(\frac{100 - A1}{100}\right)\right) \times A1$$

which in Excel^{TM} notation is

$$A1 = A1 + (0.1^*((100 - A1)/100)^*A1)$$

There is a growth rate 0.1 which is modified by a factor which is the proportion by which A1 falls short of the carrying capacity 100. For the simulation graphed in Figure 2.9, the entry in A1 is 1.

As for exponential growth, this formula is copied into cells A3 to A100, so that the entry in cell A3, for example, will be

$$A3 = A2 + \left(0.1 \times \left(\frac{100 - A2}{100}\right)\right) \times A2$$

or, in Excel^{TM} notation:

$$A3 = A2 + (0.1*((100 - A2)/100)*A2)$$

And so on, and so on. Going down the cells, 100 minus the entry for the cell above gets smaller, so the factor applied to the entry for the cell above to get this one gets smaller – the growth rate declines, and eventually it tends to zero.

Adding K for carrying capacity to the symbols introduced above for exponential growth, logistic growth can generally be represented as

$$N_t - N_{t-1} = r \times \left(\frac{K - N_{t-1}}{K} \right) \times N_{t-1}$$

where r and K are the parameters of the model. Comparing this with the general version of the exponential growth model

$$N_t - N_{t-1} = r \times N_{t-1}$$

you can see that a constant proportional growth rate r has been replaced by the proportional growth rate

$$r \times \left(\frac{K - N_{t-1}}{K} \right)$$

which varies with N_{t-1}, while r and K are fixed. In the logistic growth model r is referred to as the intrinsic growth rate, as it is the rate at which the population would grow (exponentially) if there were no environmental limits. When N_t is small, $(K - N_{t-1}) \div K$ is close to one, and the actual growth rate is close to the intrinsic growth rate r. As N_{t-1} increases towards the carrying capacity K, so $(K - N_{t-1}) \div K$ gets smaller and the actual growth rate decreases. For N_{t-1} equal to K, the numerator in $(K - N_{t-1}) \div K$ is zero so $(K - N_{t-1}) \div K$ is zero and the growth rate is zero.

2.3.2.3 Species types

Ecologists have found it useful to classify types of organism, species, in terms of the two parameters r, the intrinsic growth rate, and K, the carrying capacity, of the logistic growth model. They distinguish between r species, or strategists, and K species, or strategists. The idea is that species vary along a continuum with r species at one extreme and K species at the other. Most species exhibit some combination of the characteristics of a pure r and a pure K species.

The main characteristic of r strategists is a high value for r – given favourable conditions, they reproduce very rapidly. Another characteristic is that the population growth rate is not very sensitive to the population density, does not slow down very much as the carrying capacity is approached. As a result, there is a tendency for the population size to overshoot the carrying capacity, leading to a subsequent collapse. Individual members of r species tend to have relatively short lives, and to be small in size. For animals the length of time that offspring receive parental care is short. Examples of r species are annual plants and rabbits.

The main characteristic of K strategists is a low value for r, the intrinsic growth rate. Also, the actual population growth rate is more sensitive to the population density and K strategists tend to exist at population levels close to the carrying capacity of their environment. Individual members of K species tend to have relatively long lives, to be of large size, and, for animals, to provide extended parental care. Examples of K species are trees, elephants and humans.

2.3.2.4 Equilibrium and stability

The models presented above for exponential and logistic growth are examples of difference equations. A difference equation is an equation that gives the path taken by some variable over successive periods of time, as in Figures 2.8 and 2.9. There are many different types of difference equation.

One interesting question about the time path generated by a difference equation is whether there is an **equilibrium**, i.e. whether there is some level for the variable such that if it is attained the variable will, in the absence of shocks, remain at that level. With the exponential growth model, there is an equilibrium and it is zero. If you put 0 in the first cell when you simulate that model, all the subsequent cell values will be 0. Zero is also an equilibrium for the logistic growth model, as you can verify in the same way. However, this model has another equilibrium, which is K, the carrying capacity. You can verify this by putting the value for K in cell A1 when you do a simulation – see Exercise 2.2.

If an equilibrium exists, an interesting question about the time path generated by a difference equation is whether it has a tendency to return to an equilibrium if moved away from it by some external shock. This is the question of **stability**. Put another way, the question is: for an initial value which is not an equilibrium, will the variable move towards an equilibrium value? If there is more than one equilibrium, there is also the question of which the variable will move towards from a given initial value. These are questions about stability.

In the simulations for Figures 2.8 and 2.9 the initial values for the variable were not equilibrium values. In the exponential case, the equilibrium is 0 and the initial value is 1, and the variable grows away from 0. It is clear that this is what will happen for any starting level other than 0. Exponential growth is unstable – start it away from equilibrium and it will get further away from it.

In the logistic case of Figure 2.9, the population size moved over time towards carrying capacity, not towards 0. This is what will happen for any starting level other than zero. Logistic growth is stable with respect to the carrying-capacity equilibrium. Put another way, in the logistic growth model the carrying capacity is a stable equilibrium. Zero is an unstable equilibrium – start somewhere other than it, and the variable will move away from it.

Figure 2.10 shows simulations of some other types of population dynamics, where there are oscillations. In Figure 2.10(a) the size of the oscillations, known as the amplitude, is decreasing over time, and you can see that the variable is converging on an equilibrium, which is, then, a stable equilibrium. In Figure 2.10(c) the amplitude is increasing over time – there is an equilibrium, but it is unstable. Note that in this case the amplitude of the oscillations will eventually get so big that on the downswing the population size goes to zero and the population goes extinct. In Figure 2.10(b) the oscillations are of constant amplitude, and this pattern of behaviour is known as a 'limit cycle'.

(a)

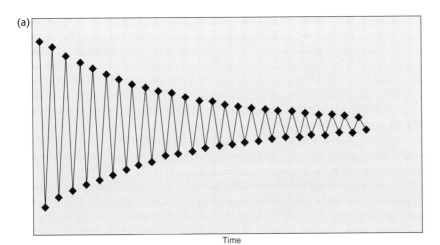

Time

(b)

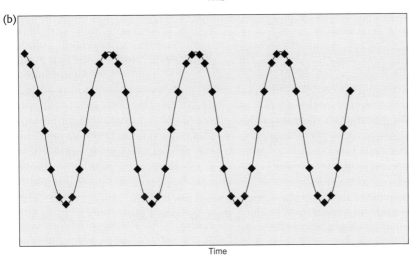

Time

(c)

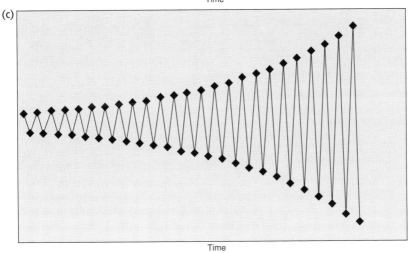

Time

Figure 2.10
Some types of
population
dynamics.

2.3.2.5 Population interactions

The difference equation models for the simulations shown in Figures 2.8 to 2.10 refer to the behaviour of just one population. In ecosystems there are many populations, of different species, that interact with one another and with the abiotic environment. Ecologists have constructed more complicated models in which two, or more, populations interact in various ways, and have also run experiments where populations interact with one another.

One standard example is the model of inter-species competition for limited food. Analysis of this model shows four possible sorts of outcome, depending on the numerical values taken by the parameters which describe the intrinsic growth rates for each of two populations from different species, what the carrying capacity of the environment would be for each population if it alone existed in it, and how the size of one population affects the growth of its competitor. The possible outcomes are:

(1)   There is no equilibrium in which both populations exist. Either population A completely out-competes population B, and B goes locally extinct, or vice versa.

(2)   There is an equilibrium in which both populations exist, and it is a stable equilibrium. Starting from population sizes that are not the equilibrium levels, both population sizes will converge on their equilibrium levels.

(3)   There is an equilibrium in which both populations exist, but it is an unstable equilibrium. Any disturbance to an equilibrium state will set in motion dynamic behaviour that involves the extinction of one of the populations.

Most, but not all, laboratory experiments with simple organisms in simple environments result in outcomes where only one of the competitive populations survives. The coexistence in field conditions of apparently competitive populations is generally taken to suggest either that the species are not fully competitive, that they are not both completely dependent on the same food supply, or that the supply of food is not actually a limiting factor.

Another standard example is the predator–prey model. In this model there is a prey population – rabbits say – that is the food for the predator population – foxes say. The solution in this model is that the sizes of both populations oscillate, with the turning points for the predator lagging behind those for the prey. The oscillations may be either damped or of constant amplitude. This type of behaviour can be produced in laboratory experiments, and is observed in the field.

2.3.3 System dynamics

An ecosystem is an assembly of many interacting populations, together with their abiotic environment. Even in a small localised ecosystem the population interactions will be many and complex, as illustrated by the foodweb shown in Figure 2.5. As well as studying the behaviour of the individual populations that comprise an ecosystem, ecologists study the dynamics of entire ecosystems. In doing that they focus on processes and functions of the system as a whole, as well as the characteristics of the component populations.

(a)

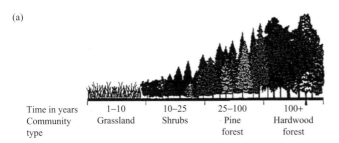

Time in years	1–10	10–25	25–100	100+
Community type	Grassland	Shrubs	Pine forest	Hardwood forest

(b)

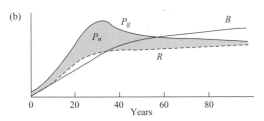

Key:　P_g - gross primary productivity
　　　P_n - net primary productivity
　　　R　- respiration
　　　B - biomass

Source: adapted from Folke (1999).

Figure 2.11
Forest
succession.

2.3.3.1 Succession

An important idea in much ecological thinking is **succession**. This refers to the way in which the species composition of an ecosystem occupying a particular area changes over time, converging on what is known as a 'climax state'. The process starts with an area with very little vegetation. This may be the result of natural events, such as fire or storm, or of human activity, such as clear-cut logging. Figure 2.11 illustrates the case where the process starts from the situation after clear-cut logging. The area is first colonised by annual plants, especially grasses, which are *r*-strategy species. This involves the expansion of remnant populations from the original state of the area, and/or invasion of the area by populations from outside. The species involved at this stage are also known as 'pioneer' or 'fugitive' species.

The pioneer species change the opportunities that the area offers to other species of plants and animals, and further colonisation takes place. The vegetation comes to be dominated by perennial plants, which in turn alter the opportunities available to various kinds of plants and animals, and eventually the area reaches a climax state in which it is dominated by *K*-strategy species such as, in this case, trees. Figure 2.11(a) shows an idealised forest succession in terms of the plants dominant at each stage: the animal species present, being dependent on plants for food, would also change as succession progressed. Figure 2.11(b) shows how primary productivity and biomass vary through the stages of this succession. The pattern shown there – biomass increasing to a stationary level at the climax state – is thought to be typical of successional processes in general. The climax state can be seen as the system equivalent of the equilibrium level for an individual population.

2.3.3.2 Species functions

From the perspective of the behaviour of the ecosystem as a whole, what is most interesting about the different species represented in it is the roles that they play in the functioning of the system as a whole. The functioning of the system has certain essential requirements – solar energy capture and decomposition are obvious examples. It appears that in any given ecosystem there is a subset of the total suite of species present that carries out the essential roles. Ecologists call such species 'keystone species'. A simple constructed example is as follows. Imagine an ecosystem in which solar energy capture is largely by a plant species which drops its seeds to the ground beneath. The seeds are dispersed by one particular species of bird which eats the seeds and then deposits them around the ecosystem in its faeces. In the absence of this species of bird, the plant species could not reproduce, and the ecosystem would suffer a major loss of its primary productivity, with major implications for the survival of other animal species. The bird species is, for this ecosystem, a **keystone species**.

It is tempting to infer from the existence of keystone species that the other, non-keystone, species in an ecosystem are functionally redundant. This inference would be incorrect. We will return to this question shortly, after introducing the concept of ecosystem resilience to which it relates. It can be noted here that while the identification of keystone species is in some cases fairly straightforward, in many circumstances it is very difficult and there is a great deal of ignorance about which are, and which are not, keystone species in most ecosystems. For example, given the necessity of nutrient recycling it is clear that the role played by the class of detritivores is essential in all ecosystems. However, there are in any ecosystem many detritivore species and it is not the case that those which are keystone in any particular ecosystem have been definitively identified.

Different species can perform the same role in different ecosystems. To continue with the seed dispersal by birds example: in ecosystem A plant species X is responsible for z per cent of solar capture and its seeds are dispersed by bird species I: in ecosystem B plant species Y is responsible for z percent of solar capture and its seeds are dispersed by bird species II. Different species playing the same role in different systems are known as 'ecological equivalents'.

Australia, which became a separate land mass 60 million years ago, provides striking evidence on ecological equivalents. Australia has never had any placental mammals. In the rest of the world, the placental mammals (mostly) out-competed and displaced other types of mammals, notably the marsupials. The Australian marsupials did not face that competition. As a result, there evolved in Australia a whole range of marsupial species – herbivores, carnivores and top carnivores – which play ecological roles that are played elsewhere by placental species of mammals. A different way of putting this is to say that in Australia marsupial species fill ecological niches that are elsewhere filled by placental species.

2.3.3.3 Resilience

An ecosystem is said to be resilient if it tends to maintain its functional integrity when subjected to some disturbance. A resilient system is one that, when subjected

(a) A resilient system

Figure 2.12
Resilience.

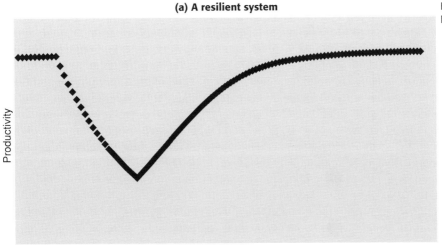

Time

(b) A non-resilient system

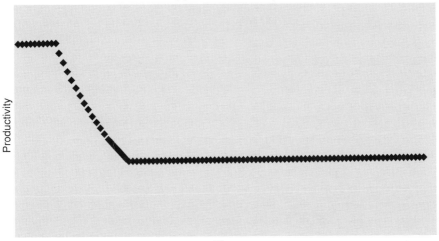

Time

to some shock, continues to exist and to function in the same essential ways. Note that it is not being said that resilience requires continued functioning in exactly the same way, nor is it being said that it requires that functions continue to be carried out by the same species. **Resilience** is, rather, consistent with some of the populations in the ecosystem going to zero.

How do we tell whether or not functional integrity is maintained? We need some kind of indicator. One candidate, which in fact ecologists do use quite widely, is primary productivity. Using this indicator, Figure 2.12 shows the difference between a resilient and a non-resilient system. In the former case, productivity recovers following some disturbance that reduces it. In the latter, it does not. To repeat the point made above, it is not necessarily the case that in the panel a situation

Figure 2.13
Another look
at resilience.

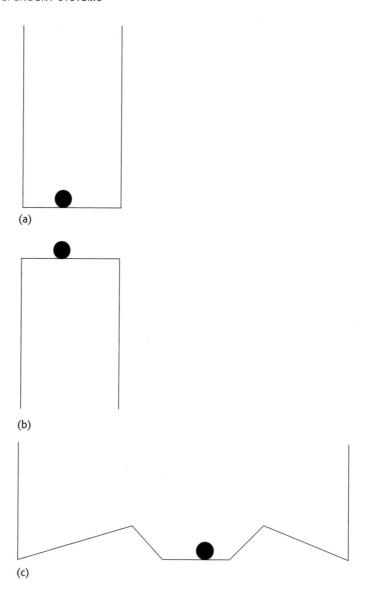

all of the populations in the system recover their former size. Some may 'go out of business'. The point is that the system as a whole 'stays in business' and that, given time, for the system as a whole 'business as normal', as reflected in primary productivity, is resumed.

Figure 2.13 provides another way of thinking about the idea of resilience, and introduces some further development of the concept. Again, Figure 2.13(a) refers to a resilient system, panel b to a system which is not resilient. Figure 2.13(a) shows a glass standing on a table in an upright position, with a ball in the bottom of it. Pick the glass up and shake it. The ball will roll around the bottom of the glass, within limits set by the sides of the glass. Put the glass back on the table and the ball will settle pretty much where it was before the disturbance. This corresponds to resilience – following a disturbance, the system returns to its original state. Figure 2.13(b) shows the glass upside down on the table, with the ball sitting on the outside of the bottom of the glass. Now the slightest disturbance will see the ball roll off the bottom of the glass, and down onto the table – there is no way back once this has happened. This corresponds to an extreme case of the form of non-resilience shown in Figure 2.12(b) – the system falls apart in the face of a disturbance.

Now look at Figure 2.13(c), where the bottom of the glass has been modified. Now, instead of being flat, it has a central circular depression around which the raised circumference has a slight downward slope out to the side of the glass. For a gentle shake, the ball will remain in the central depression, and the situation is as in Figure 2.13(a). A stronger shake will cause the ball to jump from the central depression onto the surrounding area. This behaviour is intermediate between that of Figure 2.13(a) and (b). It does not involve no change of state whatever the shock as in Figure 2.13(a), nor does it involve collapse for any disturbance as in Figure 2.13(b). Does this sort of situation get described as resilient or non-resilient? It gets described as non-resilient because the system does not revert to its original state, but remains in a different state after the disturbance. Going back to ecosystems, the idea that the only alternative to resilience is total collapse, as in Figure 2.13(b), is not correct. A non-resilient ecosystem will not necessarily collapse in the face of disturbance, but it will not regain its original state.

Resilience is a property of the system, rather than of its component parts. An obvious question is whether we can identify characteristics of ecosystems that promote resilience. If some systems are more resilient than others, why is that? This turns out to be, except in fairly general terms, a hard question to answer. One reason for this is that an ecosystem may be resilient with respect to one type of disturbance, but not to another – it may cope with fire but not with man-made pollution, for example. Similarly, a system may be resilient with respect to disturbance up to a certain level, but not beyond that – it may have a threshold level of disturbance beyond which it losses its resilience. In the present state of knowledge, the resilience or otherwise of an ecosystem is something that we can be sure about only after the occurrence of a disturbance, and then only that the system turned out to be resilient, or not, in the face of that particular disturbance.

Generally, many ecologists now take the view that species diversity promotes resilience. At one time it was generally agreed that more complex ecosystems were more stable in the sense that the sizes of the component populations fluctuated less, and that this promoted the ability of the system to persist in the face of disturbance. In that context, complexity was measured by the number of species in the system and the number of feeding links between them. The basic idea was that with many links, the removal of one link would do less damage. It is now understood that things are not that straightforward. It has been shown by mathematical modelling that increased complexity in this sense does not necessarily increase stability. It is now understood that resilience of the system is not directly and simply related to the stability of the component populations, and that ecosystems where there is low population stability can exhibit resilience.

A disturbance will threaten the functional integrity of an ecosystem to the extent that it threatens the existence of the keystone species. However, while the functions required for resilience are given and fixed, the identity of the species that carry out those functions need not be. The fact that the function of, say, seed dispersal is now carried out by species *x* does not, necessarily, mean that species *x* is the only species present in the system that could do the necessary seed dispersal. What are currently redundant species may be reservoirs of replacement keystone species, should disturbance severely reduce the ability of the current keystone species to carry out necessary functions. Also, currently redundant species may not be able themselves to exercise any necessary functions, but may be reservoirs of genetic material from which new species that can do that may evolve.

Ecologists admit to much ignorance regarding the nature and determination of resilience. But, among ecologists the majority view is that species diversity promotes resilience. That is one of the reasons why they, and other biological scientists, argue for the conservation of biological diversity. We return to this at various points in the rest of the book, and especially in Chapter 14.

2.4 NUTRIENT CYCLES

As already noted, as well as energy life requires the availability of certain chemical elements that get called **nutrients**. A nutrient is a chemical element taken up by an organism to maintain its functions. The 'macro nutrients', which collectively account for 99 per cent of human body mass, are: oxygen, hydrogen, carbon, nitrogen, calcium, phosphorous, sulphur, potassium, magnesium. Nutrients present in organisms in smaller quantities are called 'micro nutrients' and include sodium, iron, copper, zinc and iodine.

As seen when looking at ecosystems, nutrients cycle through the environment. Each nutrient has its own cycle which operates at the planetary level. The cycles involve both biotic and abiotic processes, and are for that reason sometimes referred to as 'biogeochemical'. Each cycle involves processes that connect it to other cycles. For reasons of space, we will look at just one cycle – the carbon cycle – here. Directions to descriptions of the other important cycles will be found in the Further Reading section at the end of the chapter. The carbon cycle illustrates the essentials of a nutrient cycle, and some familiarity with it is required for an understanding of the climate change problem.

2.4.1 The carbon cycle

There are basically two forms of carbon. The first is organic carbon, which is that found in living, and dead but not decomposed, organisms. Otherwise carbon is inorganic. Also, there are really two carbon cycles, a slow one and a fast one. Reference to 'the carbon cycle' is almost always a reference to the fast cycle, the slow one being so slow that for many purposes it can be ignored.

2.4.1.1 The slow cycle

The slow cycle is geological. More than 99 per cent of all terrestrial carbon is contained in the lithosphere. Most of this is inorganic carbon stored in sedimentary rock such as limestone: the organic carbon in the lithosphere is contained in fossil

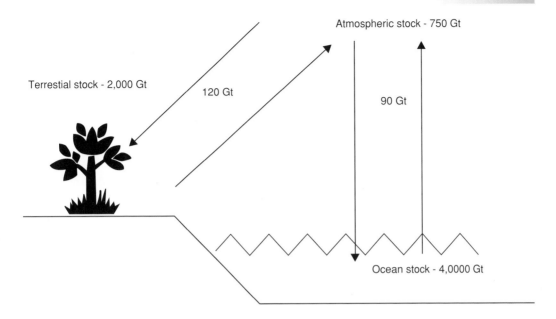

Figure 2.14 The carbon cycle.

fuel deposits – recall that fossil fuels are incompletely decomposed organic matter. In geological time there is cycling of the inorganic carbon between the earth's crust, the oceans and the atmosphere. The crustal store gets added to by a process that first has precipitation taking carbon out of the atmosphere and (eventually) into the ocean, where it sinks to the ocean bottom, or is taken up by marine organisms the decomposed remains of which eventually also sink to the bottom. In both of these ways, sediment accumulates, which is converted to rocks such as limestone. Movement in the opposite direction occurs when, due to tectonic movements, such sedimentary rocks are subjected to heat and pressure releasing carbon dioxide into the atmosphere in volcanic eruptions.

As regards the organic carbon in the lithosphere, until very recently – 200 years ago – any significant exchanges between the fossil fuel deposits and other carbon stores also operated over geological time. This has changed since man began the large-scale extraction and combustion of fossil fuels, which releases the carbon that they contain into the atmosphere.

2.4.1.2 The fast cycle

The operation of the fast cycle in the absence of anthropogenic influences (i.e. caused by humans) is shown in summary in Figure 2.14. The flows and stocks of carbon are measured in Gigatonnes (Gt). There are three stocks, or reservoirs, of carbon – the ocean stock, the atmospheric stock and the terrestrial stock. The size of the annual exchanges between the stocks, often referred to as 'fluxes', are shown by the numbers between the relevant arrows. As shown in Figure 2.14, the flows in each direction are equal. Strictly this is not the case, but it is true to a close approximation, and in the absence of anthropogenic influences the relative sizes of the stocks would change very slowly over time. It is the atmospheric stock that determines the concentration of carbon dioxide in the atmosphere, which concentration influences the global climate. It is for this reason that, although it is the smallest of the three, it is the stock upon which interest is currently mainly focused. Note that total annual exchanges between this stock and the other two are approximately one quarter of the stock size, whereas for the other two stocks the flux/stock ratio is much lower. This indicates that the size of the atmospheric stock would be relatively sensitive to changes in the fluxes.

The terrestrial stock is the carbon contained in the tissue of land biota, in soil litter and in peat. Of the total of 2,000 Gt of carbon shown in Figure 2.14, about one quarter is accounted for by the biota. The exchanges between this stock and the atmospheric stock are effected by the processes of photosynthesis and respiration described above when looking at plants and animals as open systems.

The oceanic stock is by far the largest of the three – it is approximately fifty times the size of the atmospheric stock. Exchanges between this stock and the atmospheric stock are effected by chemical processes which establish an equilibrium between the concentration of carbon dioxide in the surface layers of the oceans and the concentration in the air above that surface. Some of the carbon thus absorbed into the oceans is taken up into the tissue of plankton. When these die some of the carbon they contain is carried down to the ocean bottom where it is effectively removed from the fast carbon cycle. This is one of the reasons why the fast cycle exchanges between the atmosphere and the oceans are not exactly equal.

2.4.1.3 Anthropogenic influences

Estimates of the quantity of carbon contained in fossil fuel deposits are in the range 5,000–10,000 Gt. As noted above, until recently this store did not figure in the fast carbon cycle. Now, due to human activity, it does, and its influence on the fast, global carbon cycle is significant.

Humanity's use of the fossil fuels essentially began with the start of the industrial revolution in the late eighteenth century. At that time the amount of carbon in the atmosphere meant that the concentration of CO_2 was 280 ppmv, where ppmv stands for 'parts per million by volume', so that this is saying that CO_2 comprised 0.028 per cent of the global atmosphere. Such has been the growth of fossil fuel use since the industrial revolution – to be discussed further in Chapter 3 – that the atmospheric CO_2 concentration is now (2004) approximately 370 ppmv. The concentration has increased by more than 30 per cent in a little over 200 years. According to the best estimates, the present concentration level definitely has not been exceeded during the last 420,000 years, and it is likely that it has not been exceeded in the last 20 million years. The rate of increase in atmospheric carbon over the last century is unprecedented in the past 20,000 years, and is likely to be high by the standards of a much longer period of time.

In the decade 1990–1999, anthropogenic releases of CO_2 into the atmosphere expressed in terms of carbon averaged (central estimates throughout this paragraph and the next) 6.3 Gt per year. As well as fossil fuel combustion, the production of cement from limestone contributed to these emissions, but fossil fuels account for over 96 per cent of total emissions. Note that the interaction of the atmospheric store with the fossil fuel store is unlike the interaction of the atmospheric store with the others shown in Figure 2.15 in that it is one way – there is a flow from the fossil fuel store to the atmosphere but not in the reverse direction.

In the decade 1990–1999, the amount of CO_2 in the atmosphere expressed in terms of carbon increased at an average of 3.2 Gt per year. The atmospheric stock increased by less than anthropogenic emissions. This is because some of the CO_2 released into the atmosphere by human activity was removed from it by the exchanges with the terrestrial and ocean stocks shown in Figure 2.15. Of 6.3 Gt per annum the oceans accounted for a net uptake of 1.7 Gt per annum, and the land for a net uptake of 1.4 Gt per annum. The net uptake by the land store consists of two elements. Land use changes by humans – mainly deforestation – reduced the rate at which the terrestrial store took CO_2 from the atmosphere. On the other hand, what is known as the 'residual terrestrial sink' increased the rate at which CO_2 was removed from the atmosphere. The term 'residual terrestrial sink' refers to a residual amount of CO_2 removal from the atmosphere which it can be established was not effected by exchanges with the ocean, but which cannot yet be definitively assigned to identified exchanges with the land store. One possibly important element in the operation of the 'residual terrestrial sink' is CO_2 fertilisation, whereby the rate at which plants take up CO_2 increases with the CO_2 concentration. Accounting for CO_2 is not a precise science. There is much, at the level of detail, that is not known.

While this is true, the big picture is clear. Human activity is affecting the global carbon cycle in a readily detectable way. Basically, carbon is being moved from the fossil fuel deposit store to the atmosphere. The increasing atmospheric concentration of CO_2 is affecting the global climate system. Discussion of this will come up at a number of places in the rest of the book. It is the subject of Chapter 14.

2.5 EVOLUTION

Evolution is the process of change over time. All kinds of systems undergo evolution. In this section we will be concerned mainly with evolution in the natural environment, and especially with biological evolution. We will look at evolution in human systems, especially economic systems, in subsequent chapters.

2.5.1 Biological evolution

An individual organism can be looked at in terms of its genotypes and its phenotypes. The **genotypes** are the organism's genetic inheritance, which at birth define the boundaries for potential development of the organism. The maximum height, for example, that a human organism can attain during his or her life is set by the genes that it is endowed with by the parents. The **phenotypes** are the organism's observable characteristics. To continue the example, the actual height of the human is one of his or her phenotypes. Phenotypes are determined by the genotypes and the organism's environment. An individual human may be phenotypically short notwithstanding genotypical tallness, due to inadequate nourishment.

The mechanism that drives biological evolution is **natural selection**, which works as follows. The individuals that comprise a population – members of the same species coexisting as a reproductive unit – differ genotypically and phenotypically. The reproductive capacity of a population generally exceeds the carrying capacity of the environment, and there is competition among individuals for the inputs needed for survival. Those individuals that are most fit will be the ones that survive. Fitness is directly a matter of phenotype, but generally has an underlying genetic basis. Individuals that survive to reproductive age can pass their genes to offspring, individuals that do not cannot. Hence, the struggle for survival, and for reproduction, over time shapes the genetic make-up of the population, as well as its phenotypical structure. By means of natural selection, a population becomes better adapted to its environment. A mutation is a random error in the process by which an organism inherits its genes from its parents. Mutations are occurring all the time in all populations. In most cases they result in an organism which is genotypically less fit than its parents, but sometimes they result in a better-fitted organism. If the latter outcome is an individual that can reproduce, then the process of natural selection towards a population better fitted to its environment is advanced by that mutation.

Natural selection is the generally accepted explanation for the proliferation of species, which process is known as 'speciation'. The basic idea is that a population splits spatially into reproductively isolated groups, i.e. becomes two populations. To the extent that the environments of the two populations differ, they will be subject to different adaptive selection. Also, the effects of any 'successful' mutation are confined to the population in which it occurs. The two populations diverge both in terms of genotypes and phenotypes. If the divergence goes to the extent that the two populations would be incapable of interbreeding then **speciation** has occurred.

As described here, the process of speciation, which is what is generally understood by 'biological evolution', works through adaptation driving natural selection operating on genotypes. An individual organism's fitness is determined by its phenotypes, but what it passes on are genes, and adaptation works because of the link between genotypes and phenotypes. The generally accepted position is that there is an effect from genotype to phenotype, but not from phenotype to genotype. The response of an organism to the environment that it is exposed to during its life, cannot, that is, affect the genes that it passes to its offspring. Phenotypical adaptation by an individual organism confers no benefits on its offspring. While this is true for biological evolution, it is not necessarily true of evolution in other contexts. In the evolution of human culture, for example, parents can pass to their offspring information that they have acquired. We shall come back to this in Chapter 3.

A final point needs to be made in this very brief account of biological evolution. Natural selection is very often referred to as involving the 'survival of the fittest'. It would be more accurate if the phrase that has become so widespread had been 'survival of the fitter'. The point is that what gets selected is that which, from among what is available, is relatively the best fitted to the relevant environment. It is not the case that what gets selected is the best possible adaptation to the relevant environment. Natural selection can only operate on what is there.

2.5.2 Coevolution

Biological evolution is a complicated business. It is about organisms adapting to their environment. But the environment which is being adapted to is itself constantly changing. Indeed, adaptation itself drives environmental change, because for any population its 'environment' includes lots of other populations from other species, all of which are themselves subject to the pressures of natural selection. What is actually going on all of the time is 'coevolution'.

For a given population of a species, only a small part of the totality of the environment is directly relevant. The part of the environment with which interaction takes place is the population's niche. For example, a given species of bee has a niche which comprises a particular range of plants from among the many that occupy the space where they operate, while wolves have a niche which comprises many animal species, but still a lot less than the totality of the animal species in their territory. **Coevolution** refers to the fact that the niche for any one population is affected by evolutionary change involving other populations. For the bees new plants may appear, or existing ones vanish. A niche may be enlarged or reduced. Previously successful adaptation may be rendered obsolete, and a sufficient amount of niche reduction will lead to extinction. On the other hand, speciation will itself tend to create new niches, through, for example, new predation possibilities, thus promoting yet more speciation. Biological evolution has the potential to sustain itself through ongoing coevolution.

In fact, in the history of planet earth it appears that coevolution has involved non-living as well as living systems. The abiotic environment has affected the biotic, and the biotic has affected the abiotic. The nutrient cycles as they now exist are the result of coevolutionary processes involving non-living and living systems that took place many hundreds of millions of years ago. The atmosphere of the earth for the first few hundred million years after its formation contained no oxygen, but did contain a lot of carbon dioxide, as well as nitrogen, methane and ammonia. Given the presence in the atmosphere of a lot of carbon dioxide, it is supposed that the global temperature was then much higher than it is now.

The earth is thought to be about 4,500 million years old. For the first 1,000 million years there was no life on earth at all. It appeared, how is not really known, as a very primitive bacterial form, about 3,500 million years ago. The appearance of a form of life capable of utilising solar radiation came about 500 million years after that. These organisms took in carbon dioxide from the atmosphere and released oxygen into it. For the then existing organisms, oxygen was toxic. However, its rate of accumulation in the atmosphere was very slow. About 2,000 million years ago the first oxygen-tolerant photosynthesising organisms appeared. Had this not happened, the slow build-up of oxygen in the atmosphere would have extinguished life on earth. It did happen, and the composition of the atmosphere became more oxygen-rich, and eventually sufficiently so as to support animal life. With plants taking in carbon dioxide and releasing oxygen and animals taking in oxygen and releasing carbon dioxide, the carbon and oxygen cycles were linked. Simple forms of life, it appears, played a crucial role in creating the conditions for the existence of complex forms of life. The early simple forms are now almost completely extinct.

SUMMARY

This chapter has provided an introduction to some of the key ideas about how the natural environment works, focusing on those most relevant to ecological economics. The idea of a system is very important in the environmental sciences, and, as we shall see in subsequent chapters, in the social sciences as well. Thermodynamics is the study of energy conversions in systems. Living organisms are systems that perform energy conversions. An ecosystem is a collection of interacting populations of organisms, together with their abiotic environment. The biosphere is the global ecosystem considered in its entirety. The biosphere has evolved throughout 3,500 million years of the history of planet earth, and will continue to evolve. A major motivation for the study of ecological economics is the fact that the future evolution of the biosphere will be strongly influenced by human economic activity.

KEYWORDS

Biome (p. 39): a spatially large ecosystem defined by climatic and vegetative conditions.

Carrying capacity (p. 45): the maximum population size that a given environment can support.

Coevolution (p. 61): the process whereby the environment in which one population is evolving is itself changing due to the evolution of its constituent populations.

Decomposition (p. 40): the breakdown of dead organic matter into inorganic matter.

Ecosystem (p. 37): a system of living organisms and their non-living environment.

Energy (p. 26): the potential to supply heat or do work.

Entropy (p. 31): energy that is not available for conversion, a measure of disorder.

Equilibrium (p. 48): a population level that if attained will persist in the absence of disturbance.

Evolution (p. 59): the process of change over time.

Exponential growth (p. 44): growth at a constant proportional rate.

Fossil fuels (p. 42): energy sources of organic origin.

Genotypes (p. 59): an organism's genetic inheritance.

Keystone species (p. 52): species that carry out functions essential for ecosystem functioning.

Logistic growth (p. 46): a particular form of density-dependent growth with the growth rate declining as the population grows.

Materials balance principle (p. 28): matter can be neither created nor destroyed.

Natural selection (p. 60): genetic adaptation to the environment driven by relative reproductive success.

Nutrients (p. 56): chemical elements taken up by organisms to maintain their functioning.

Phenotypes (p. 59): an organism's observable characteristics.

Photosynthesis (p. 32): the process by which plants use solar radiation to convert inorganic to organic matter.

Population (p. 43): a group of individuals belonging to the same species living in a given area at a given time.

Primary productivity (p. 33): the rate at which plants create organic matter, usually measured as energy per unit area per unit time.

Resilience (p. 53): the maintenance by an ecosystem of its functional integrity when subjected to disturbance.

Speciation (p. 60): the emergence of new species.

Species (p. 43): a set of individuals who are capable of interbreeding.

Stability (p. 48): the tendency of a population size to return to its equilibrium following a disturbance.

Succession (p. 51): the way in which the species composition of an ecosystem occupying a particular area changes over time, converging on a climax state.

System (p. 22): a set of interacting components.

Thermodynamics (p. 26): the study of energy transformations.

Trophic pyramid (p. 37): the decline in biomass moving from plants to herbivores to carnivores.

APPENDIX: DOUBLING TIMES WITH EXPONENTIAL GROWTH

From

$$N_t = (1 + r)^t \times N_0$$

the doubling time is the t value that is the solution to

$$2 = (1 + r)^t \times 1$$

Dividing both sides by 1 gives

$$2 = (1 + r)^t$$

and taking natural logarithms on both sides this is

$$\ln 2 = t \times \ln(1 + r)$$

The natural logarithm of 2 is 0.6931, and so the doubling time is

$$t = \frac{0.6931}{\ln(1 + r)}$$

If you solve this for $r = 0.01$, etc. you will get the results shown in Table 2.2. The reason for working with natural logarithms rather than logarithms to the base 10 is that it so happens that this answer lines up with an approximation that is easy to remember – divide 70 by the growth rate expressed as a percentage. So, for r as 5 per cent, for example, the approximation is, in whole numbers, 14.

FURTHER READING

Jackson and Jackson (2000) and Park* (2001) are two standard environmental science texts that deal with all of the topics dealt with in this chapter at greater length. Both are at an introductory level: Jackson and Jackson assumes some prior knowledge of chemistry. Rogers and Feiss* (1998) is an introductory environmental science text that approaches the material from the perspective of human interests. Bowler (1992) is a history of the development of the environmental sciences.

Thermodynamics is difficult for the non-specialist, for whom many accounts of the first and second laws have been written. Chapman (1975), Ramage* (1983) and Slesser (1978) are well-written books, intended for the non-specialist general reader, on energy matters, which contain reasonably straightforward expositions of thermodynamics and its implications. Although 'old' they are not 'dated' except in so far as they come at 'the energy problem' from the perspective of limited supplies of fossil fuels rather than that of the climatic implications of the use of fossil fuels. They all consider the technological limits that arise: see also Ayres (1978), Chapman and Roberts (1983), Hall *et al.* (1986), and Ruth (1999). Faber *et al.* (1996), chs. 6 and 7 especially, deals with the first and second laws in relation to ecological economics. Georgescu-Roegen (1971) introduced thermodynamics to economists, and is one of the seminal works in the development of ecological economics: it is not an easy read. The energetic data in the chapter is, where not otherwise cited, based on data from Ramage* (1983) and Georgescu-Roegen (1976).

The alternative theory of the origins of the fossil fuels is set out in Gold (1999). If true it has important implications for our understanding of the origins of life on earth, and for assessment of the prospects of life on other planets. Cole (1996) is a non-technical account of the controversy surrounding Gold's ideas, which is also very interesting for what it says about the actual practice of science. Despite its obvious practical, as well as scientific, importance, and the expenditure of lots of money on 'definitive' tests of Gold's hypothesis, the controversy remains unresolved.

Krebs* (2001) is a successful ecology text that is comprehensive but assumes no prior knowledge of the subject. Folke (1999) is a brief overview of ecological principles as they relate to ecological economics, and provides useful references to the literature. Krebs deals with the basics of the mathematical modelling of population dynamics. Gilbert and Troitzsch (1999) provides an overview of simulation modelling and available software. Hannon and Ruth (1994) is an introduction to the use of the Stella^{RM} software package for the simulation of dynamic models. The (Excel^{TM}) simulations for Figure 2.10 here can be found on the companion website. Our typology of the sorts of behaviour that difference equations can produce omits chaos. For some ranges of the parameter values, simple non-linear difference equations produce outcomes with oscillations where the amplitude is neither constant, constantly increasing or constantly decreasing, but varies over time. Also, the pattern of variation changes with very small changes in the initial conditions. There is now a large literature on chaos and its implications – Hannon and Ruth (1994) provide simple models that produce chaos. Closely related to the work on chaos is work on complex systems – roughly speaking a complex system is one whose behaviour is not predictable from the behaviour of its component parts. Kauffman (1995) covers much of the ground from the perspective of a biologist actively involved in the work: Gleick (1988) and Waldrop (1994) are journalistic, but informative, accounts.

As set out here, the idea of resilience as a property of an ecosystem was introduced in Holling (1973). It is further developed in Holling (1986). The paper by Ludwig *et al.* (1997) is a clear, but technical, exposition of the basic mathematics of Holling resilience and how it relates to another concept of resilience that appears in the ecology literature.

Nutrient cycles are covered in Park* (2001), Jackson and Jackson (2000) and Krebs* (2001); see also Ayres (1999), which, with Jackson and Jackson, gives more details on the chemistry. The information given on the carbon cycle in the chapter is taken from Houghton (1997) and Houghton *et al.* (2001). Further references relating to the carbon cycle will appear at Chapter 13 which deals with the problem of climate change.

Biological evolution and coevolution are dealt with Park* (2001) and Krebs* (2001). Faber *et al.* (1996) take a general formulation of evolution to be one of the distinguishing conceptual foundations for ecological economics. Norgaard (1994) looks at economic development as a process of coevolution involving economic and environmental systems. Kauffman (1995) looks at the way that the mathematical developments noted above can be used to understand the evolution of complex systems in nature and society. The historical coevolution of living and non-living systems in the history of planet earth is the source of the 'Gaia hypothesis' advanced in Lovelock (1979) and Lovelock (1988).

WEBSITES

The Encyclopedia at the ISEE website, http://www.ecoeco.org, includes two short entries relevant to this chapter – one on 'Entropy' by S. Baumgärtner and one on 'Resilience defined' by C. S. Holling and B. Walker. Holling is originator of the idea of resilience as set out in the chapter here, which is sometimes referred to as 'resilience in the sense of Holling'.

EXERCISES

1. Set up a spreadsheet simulation for exponential growth to confirm the doubling time results of Table 2.2, and that 0 is an equilibrium.
2. Set up a spreadsheet simulation for logistic growth with $K = 100$, and plot growth over time for $r = 0.1$, $r = 0.25$ and $r = 0.5$. Confirm that 0 and 100 are equilibria.
3. Set up a spreadsheet simulation for

$$y_t = (3.7 \times y_{t-1}) \times (1 - y_{t-1})$$

and do simulations for initial values for y of 0.5 and 0.501. This is an example of chaos – the small shift from 0.5 to 0.501 produces a completely different time path.

3 Humans in the environment – some history

In this chapter you will:

- Learn about the broad outlines of human history;
- See how the size of the human population has grown during that history;
- And how the per capita use of energy has grown during that history;
- Learn about the major historical changes in the way humans feed themselves;
- See how the human species now dominates ecosystems.

H umans are an animal species with a remarkable capacity for culture. In this chapter we take a brief look at a broad view of our cultural evolution. We are particularly interested in the ways that we have used our environment to satisfy our needs and desires, and in the demands that we have made upon that environment.

3.1 HUMAN EVOLUTION

The details of the process by which the species that is modern humanity – *homo sapiens sapiens* – evolved biologically are matters of some dispute, and the accepted account changes over time as new research techniques are used and new evidence is discovered. However, it is the broad outline that we are concerned with, and this does, in general terms and with some lack of precision as to dates, seem reasonably clear.

Our species shares 98.4 per cent of its genetic endowment with chimpanzees: genetically we are closer to chimpanzees than they are to apes. The evolutionary divergence of humans and chimpanzees took place between 6 million and 8 million years ago. By 5 million years ago there were creatures walking around in the African savanna in much the same way as modern humans do. The oldest tools found in Africa date from at least 2.5 million years ago, and are thought to have been used by a species called *Homo habilis*. Members of that species were omnivorous, i.e. they ate both plant and animal food, as were the other *homo species*.

The species *Homo errectus* is thought to have appeared about 1.7 million years ago, and to have persisted until about 300,000 years ago. *Homo sapiens* appeared about 500,000 years ago. *Homo sapiens neanderthalensis* is known to have existed in Europe between 70,000 and 40,000 years ago. The Neanderthals were anatomically different from *Homo sapiens sapiens*, being short and stocky with brow ridges and large jaws. The earliest remains of *Homo sapiens sapiens* date from about 90,000 years ago in Africa. Such anatomically modern humans were in Europe by 40,000 years ago. As noted in Box 3.1, *Homo sapiens sapiens* is also known to have reached Australia by 40,000 years ago.

So, if we want to say that human history started with *Homo habilis* it is some 2.5 million long, while if we want to say that it started with *Homo sapiens sapiens* it is some 100,000 years long. If we take a generation to be 25 years then human history comprises 100,000 generations on the broad definition of human, 4,000 generations on the narrow definition.

The physical characteristics that distinguish humans from other primate species are upright posture, the structure of the hand, a relatively small amount of bodily hair, and a relatively large brain. Associated with these differences is an enormous difference in the capacity for **culture**, by which is meant social interaction between individuals and its consequences in terms of technologies, institutions, customs and the like. Culture is based on the ability to use symbols for communication. Humans have the physical ability to make a wide range of sounds, which combined with the ability to use symbols was the basis for the development of spoken language by means of which information could be passed from one individual to another. The ability to transmit information was further enhanced, relatively recently, by the invention of writing.

3.1.1 Cultural evolution

In Chapter 2 we saw that biological evolution works by natural selection operating on genotypes (section 2.5.1). An individual organism's fitness is determined by its phenotypes, but what it passes on are genes, and adaptation works because of the link between genotypes and phenotypes. In biological evolution there is an effect from genotype to phenotype, but not from phenotype to genotype. The response of an organism to the environment that it is exposed to during its life cannot, that is, affect the genes that it passes to its offspring. Phenotypical adaptation by an individual organism confers no benefits on its offspring.

This account of how evolution works is often referred to as 'Darwinian evolution', it being the explanation offered by Charles Darwin. It stands in distinction to 'Lamarckian evolution' named after the French biologist Jean Bapiste de Lamarck who, some fifty years before Darwin published his ideas, put forward an account of evolution in which characteristics acquired by parents were passed to their offspring. Thus, for example, according to Lamarck among a species eating leaves from bushes and trees, individuals habitually taking vegetation further from the ground would develop longer and stronger necks, an attribute that their offspring would inherit. And so, giraffes evolved. Clearly, evolution operating according to Lamarck could be, and would generally be expected to be, much faster than evolution operating according to Darwin. As far as biological evolution is concerned, Lamarck's ideas have been discredited and are in contradiction to the central tenets of modern biology.

However, evolution and natural selection do not operate solely in biology. Culture evolves, and the processes involved in cultural evolution can be Lamarckian. Using language human parents can pass to their children what they have learned. Cultural evolution can proceed much more quickly than biological evolution. The rate at which it proceeds is increasing over time. It is effectively unique to the human species, and it is the ability for cultural evolution that really sets that species apart from all others.

In discussing economic activity in subsequent chapters, the role and significance of the accumulation over time of various kinds – durable, human and social – of capital will be noted. Capital accumulation is central to economic history, and to the matter of sustainability. The accumulation of capital, in all of its forms, is one, major, aspect of human cultural evolution as a Lamarckian process. What one generation accumulates does not disappear with that generation, but is passed on to the next. With the invention of writing, and subsequent developments in information storage and retrieval, the efficacy of the process of transmitting accumulated knowledge from one generation to the next has been greatly enhanced.

3.2 THE HISTORY OF HUMAN NUMBERS

Figure 3.1 shows the history of human numbers since 12,000 BP, where BP stands for 'before the present', with the present being taken to be 2,000 AD. As this identification of the present indicates, we are interested here in the 'big picture', rather than matters of detail. For most of human history, our knowledge of how many humans there were is based on estimation and inference from various fragmentary sources – the first census in Britain was conducted in 1801. Until the last 100 years or so, we can have confidence only in the broad trends shown in Figure 3.1, which are widely agreed on. Figure 3.1 divides human history into three broad phases. Much the longest was the hunter-gatherer phase, which lasted from humanity's beginnings until around 12,000 BP. It is estimated that at that time there were some 4 million people. Even if we put humanity's beginnings as recently as 100,000 years BP, it is clear that human numbers must have grown very slowly during the hunter-gatherer phase. Given the scale at which Figure 3.1 has to be drawn to accommodate current human numbers, a line showing the size of the human population during the hunter-gatherer phase would be indistinguishable from the horizontal axis.

As will be discussed shortly, agriculture started around 12,000 BP, and with it the growth of human numbers accelerated. By 2,500 BP, that is BC 500, the human population was (rough estimate) 100 million. In Figure 3.1 there is a straight line from the horizontal axis at 12,000 BP to 0.1 billion at 2,500 BP. This is not intended to convey the idea that the growth in human numbers over this period was smooth and uninterrupted – it was not, but we are interested in the trend not the detailed history.

Around 2,500 BP, for reasons that are not clear, the growth rate increased, and by the time of the industrial revolution – 1800 AD, that is 200 BP – the global population had reached (less rough estimate) 0.9 billion. Again, the fact that Figure 3.1 shows a straight line from 2,500 to 200 BP does not reflect smooth growth – several

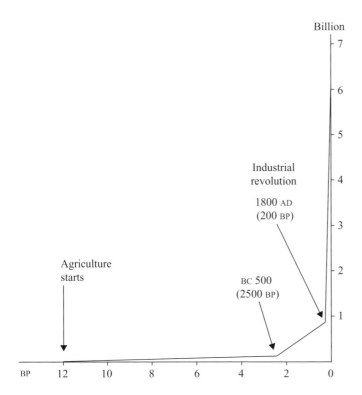

Figure 3.1
Human
population
growth.

periods in which human numbers declined, catastrophically in parts of the world, have been identified.

Since 200 BP the size of the human population has grown at a rate totally unprecedented in human history. At the time that this chapter was being written, early 2002, the most recent year for which data on global population size was available was 1999. In that year the estimated human population was 5.8627 billion, 5.8627×10^9. The estimated growth rate for 1975–1999 was 1.6 per cent per year. Applying this to the figure for 1999 gives 5.9565×10^9 for 2000. Given that the 1999 figure is necessarily less than totally precise, the appropriate way to state the size of the human population in 2000 is as 6 billion. Growth from 1 to 6 billion over 200 years corresponds to an average annual growth rate of 0.9 per cent. Over the period from 12,000 BP to 200 BP the average annual growth rate was 0.04 per cent.

3.3 HUNTER-GATHERERS

The hunting-and-gathering way of housekeeping is that for which our species is adapted by biological evolution, and that which it has practised for most of its history. Man as hunter-gatherer was a non-specialist omnivorous mammal. As compared with other mammal species, man is relatively non-specialist, i.e. able to subsist on a wide variety of plants and animals as food sources. However, the main point is that as hunter-gatherer, man operated in foodwebs – see Chapter 2 – in the same way as other animal species, and was competitor with some, predator on some, and prey for some. Human numbers were, in the hunter-gatherer phase, determined in the same ways as those of other species, and were ultimately constrained by the thermodynamics of the trophic pyramid – see Figure 2.6 in Chapter 2.

Humans as hunter-gatherers were a very successful species. The non-specialist omnivorous strategy for food acquisition is highly adaptable, and man had a unique capacity for culture. This influenced the particulars of food gathering through the ability to communicate, and thus operate effectively and flexibly in groups, and to use tools and weapons. As hunter-gatherers, humans occupied most of the world, and lived in habitats ranging from tropical rainforest to arctic tundra, though most lived in temperate to sub-tropical environments with moderate rainfall. Hunter-gatherers were usually nomadic with population densities ranging from 0.2 to 2 people km^2.

If human history starts with *Homo sapiens sapiens*, then humans have been hunter-gatherers for 88 per cent of their history: if we start human history with *Homo habilis*, the hunter-gatherer phase is over 99 per cent of human history.

The dominant image of hunter-gatherers has undergone some revision in the last hundred years or so. In the nineteenth century their way of life was widely regarded as 'nasty, brutish and short', and they were seen as primitives. Latterly, there is more of an inclination to regard them as 'noble savages' living in harmony with nature. There are many reasons for the change in perception. One is that we now have more information about the hunter-gatherer way of life, based, in part, on careful anthropological studies of the few examples of it that persisted into the twentieth century. Box 3.1 gives some information about the Australian aboriginals, a small number of whom were still largely unaffected by European contact well into the twentieth century.

It appears reasonable to conclude that for most of the hunter-gatherer societies that have existed in human history, most of the people for most of the time were well nourished, and did not have to spend most of their waking hours seeking food. While hunter-gatherers were generally healthy, their life expectancies were short by modern standards. There are two reasons for this. First, the lifestyle involved greater risk of injury. Apart from the risks associated with continual direct contact with the natural environment, some authorities consider that in many hunter-gatherer societies inter-group violence was endemic. Second, if injured, an individual was more likely to die, given the absence of any of the facilities and treatments of modern medicine.

One very important aspect of the role of culture in the hunting and gathering mode of human existence was the discovery of the controlled use of fire, based on the combustion of wood, an event which probably took place around 500,000 BP. Fire was used for cooking, which meant that previously unavailable food sources could be exploited. It was also used to provide warmth, to clear areas of forest cover so as to cause the growth of new vegetation of the kind that would attract desired prey, and to cause prey to move in desired directions.

The energy that an animal acquires in its food, and which is converted into work, growth and heat, is called **somatic energy**. When the human animal learned how to control fire, it began the exploitation of **extrasomatic energy**. It began, that

Box 3.1   The Australian aboriginals

The modern history of Australia dates from 1788 when the British established a penal colony at Sydney. In the preface to his book on the history of the aboriginals, the Australian historian Geoffrey Blainey describes the origins of the book as follows:

> The seeds of the book were lectures given to undergraduates. I used to begin a course on Australian economic history in the accepted manner with the European explorations of the eighteenth century until one day the archaeologist, John Mulvaney, in conversation enquired what I said about the earlier 99 per cent of time embraced by the human history of Australia. (p.v.)

The title of Blainey's book is *Triumph of the nomads*. This is intended to indicate the revisionist nature of the book. Blainey's central story is that, contrary to popular understanding, the 'early Australians had impressive achievements'.

Among these was survival over a long period of time. There are disagreements about exactly how long the aboriginals have been in Australia. It is clear that they definitely were there 40,000 years ago. Some have argued that they have been there for upwards of 70,000 years. The most widely accepted account of their origin is that they arrived in Australia from Asia about 50,000 years ago, when, because more of the world's water was in the form of ice, sea levels were much lower than they now are so that the sea-crossing to Australia was much shorter than it now is.

Throughout their history prior to the European invasion the Australian aboriginals were hunter-gatherers. The evidence of their economic activity comes from archaeology, from the accounts of Europeans involved in early contacts, and from anthropological studies in the twentieth century of some groups of aboriginals who, by virtue of occupying areas relatively unattractive to Europeans, were able to continue to live in the traditional ways. The evidence from these three sources is largely consistent.

Studies in Arnhem Land in the 1940s found that aboriginal diets were adequate by the standards then recommended for Americans, and that they were rich in protein. The amount of effort devoted to providing food was not great – four to five hours per day, including frequent rests. Not everyone sought food every day. Earlier observers had reported two to four hours per day on average for hunting and gathering. Little time was spent on making or maintaining tools and equipment, and there were no buildings to work on. Much time was spent on social life, on ceremonial activities, and on instructing the young. There was no clear-cut demarcation between work and leisure – in some of the aboriginal languages there are no words that distinguish work from play.

Most of the Europeans involved in early contacts with the aboriginals took the lack of agriculture to mean that they lived continually on the edge of starvation. This was not true as the more perceptive European observers noted. Captain James Cook, regarded by the British as the discoverer of Australia, wrote in his journal of the aboriginals whom he encountered that:

> they may appear to some to be the most wretched people on earth, but in reality they are far more happier [*sic*] than we Europeans. They live in a Tranquillity which is not disturb'd by the Inequality of Condition: The Earth and sea of their own accord furnishes them with all things necessary for life, they covet not Magnificent Houses, Household-stuff &c', they live in a warm and fine climate and enjoy a very wholesome Air, so that they have very little need of clothing . . . they think themselves provided with all the necessarys of Life and that they have no superfluities.   (quoted in Dingle, 1988: p. 28)

Blainey's assessment is that:

> If we specify the main ingredients of a good standard of living as food, health, shelter and warmth, the average aboriginal was probably as well off as the average European in 1800 . . . they were probably much better off than the poorest one-tenth. In the eastern half of Europe the comparison favours the aboriginals, and they probably lived in more comfort than nine-tenths of the population of eastern Europe   (Blainey, 1982: p. 225)

When James Cook claimed much of eastern Australia for the British crown it was treated as *terra nullius*, i.e. land which was not owned by anybody. This was because the aboriginals did not practise agriculture, and so from the European viewpoint could not be regarded as owners of the land from which they drew their sustenance. The same perspective saw the history of Australia in the nineteenth century as the story of European migrants making its land productive in a way that the aboriginal inhabitants had been unable to do. In fact, in the first half of the century the amount of food and material produced in Australia probably fell, as the size of the aboriginal population fell by more than the numbers of the invaders increased.

While the Australian aboriginals lived more lightly on the land than those who displaced them, it is not true that they had no impact on their environment. Their practice of 'fire stick farming' – using fire to promote the growth of new plant material so as to attract animals for easier hunting – is thought to have exercised selective pressure on plant species, and to be partially responsible for the vegetative state of some areas of the continent. Between 30,000 and 20,000 years ago, several species of large marsupials are known to have become extinct in Australia. It seems likely that aboriginal hunting was a contributory factor in at least some of these extinctions. It is generally thought that the major factor was climatic change.

Sources: Blainey (1982), Boyden *et al.* (1990), Dingle (1988).

is, to be able to exert more power than was available from its own muscles. The use of extrasomatic energy, a manifestation of culture, is a uniquely human mode of behaviour, which has had enormous influence on human evolution, as we shall see in subsequent sections of this chapter.

The **Human Energy Equivalent**, HEE, is a unit of measurement which is the amount of somatic energy required by a human individual. This amount varies across individuals and with circumstances. A convenient amount to use for the HEE is 10 Mj per day, which (see Box 2.1) is a round number version of what is required by an adult leading a moderately active life in favourable climatic conditions. It is estimated that the use of fire by an individual in hunter-gatherer societies was, on average and approximately, equivalent to the use of 1 HEE – per capita the use of fire was about equivalent to the amount of energy flowing through a human body. The total per capita use of energy was, that is, about 2 HEE.

3.4 THE TRANSITION TO AGRICULTURE

Agriculture is a fundamentally different food-acquisition strategy to hunting and gathering. The latter essentially involves taking what the environment offers, much as other animals do. Agriculture involves the domestication of some plants and animals, the manipulation of their reproductive behaviour, and the control of non-domesticated, 'wild', plants and animals so as to limit their competition with, or predation of, the domesticated species. It involves the deliberate alteration of the relative abundance of the various populations of plants and animals in the area farmed, so as to favour the domesticated populations. Agriculture is about disturbing mature ecosystems and then maintaining them in an early successional state. The intention is to increase the availability of the domesticated populations, and to reduce the presence of the non-domesticated, thus increasing the availability of food to the human population. For a given area, the point about agriculture as compared with the hunter-gatherer system of food production is that a larger proportion of the energy fixed by photosynthesis is appropriated by humans. As a result, whereas the hunter-gatherer system of food production could support 0.2 to 2 humans per square kilometre, the agricultural system could support 25 to 1,000 humans per square kilometre.

The emergence of agriculture is sometimes referred to as the **domestic transition** because it involved the domestication of some plants and animals, and also the domestication of humans in that they ceased to be nomads and took up a settled way of life. Another term sometimes used for this evolutionary development is **agricultural revolution**. While it is true that it totally changed the nature of human existence, the use of 'revolution' is misleading in two respects. First, it implies that we are dealing with something that happened quickly and abruptly. Second, it implies purposeful intent, that human hunter-gatherers perceived the broad implications of a switch to agriculture and decided to adopt it.

The transition to agriculture was neither quick nor abrupt. The first successful domestication efforts appear to have taken place around 12,000 BP in southwest Asia. Agriculture emerged also, and apparently independently, in China around 9,000 BP, and in Mesoamerica (Mexico), also around 9,000 BP. It spread from these centres slowly. While most of the plant species now farmed had been domesticated by 4,000 BP, as recently as 200 BP one continent, Australia, was still inhabited solely by hunter-gatherers. In much of western Europe most of the land was still covered by virgin forest in 2,000 BP.

Why did humans adopt agriculture? This is a very complicated question, to which there can be no simple definite answer. At one time the favoured general answer was that it was an early manifestation of purposeful human progress, that people saw the way to a better life and 'went for it'. Now the dominant view is that the transition started as adaptation to deterioration in the hunter-gatherer way of life, that people initially adopted agricultural practices because they needed to in order to survive. This pushes the question back a stage – how and why did hunting and gathering deteriorate as a food-gathering strategy? There are three broad sorts of answer to this question. They are not mutually exclusive – more than one may have been operative in some of the circumstances in which agricultural practices were adopted.

One explanation is in terms of climate change reducing the availability of species targeted by hunter-gatherers. Another is growth of a hunter-gatherer population beyond the size that the resources of the area inhabited could support, given that food-acquisition strategy. The third is displacement of a hunter-gatherer population, by a stronger incoming migrant human population, from its home range to an area less productive for it given the resources available in the new area and the technology of the displaced population. Note in this regard that because agriculture supports many more people per unit area, once agriculture had started, the populations practising it would have generally been much larger than populations of hunter-gatherers. Consequently in any contact and conflict between agriculturalists and hunter-gatherers, the former would generally be expected to prevail.

The emergence of agriculture created conditions for further cultural evolution. Enough food could be produced to support individuals not directly engaged in agriculture. This made urbanisation possible. The first towns appeared around 9,000 BP, and by 5,000 BP there existed what could reasonably be called cities – large numbers of people living in a built environment largely devoid of edible plants and animals, and totally reliant on food brought in from the surrounding farmland. Within such societies there was occupational specialisation, leading to social stratification. Urbanisation was totally absent from, and social stratification was generally very limited in, hunter-gatherer societies. Trade was a feature of some hunter-gatherer systems, but with the emergence of towns and cities and specialised production it grew greatly to become an important part of the agricultural system of food supply.

The agricultural phase of human history lasted about 12,000 years. The technology of energy use was evolving throughout this period. By its end the average human being was deploying some 3–4 HEE, so that in addition to his own muscle power he was using extrasomatic energy at the rate of 2–3 HEE. In addition to fire, still almost entirely based on biomass (mainly wood) combustion, the sources of extrasomatic energy were animal muscles, the wind and water. Animals – horses, oxen, donkeys – were used mainly for motive power in transport and agriculture. The wind was used to propel boats, to drive pumps for lifting water, and to drive mills for grinding corn. Water mills were also used for grinding corn, as well as powering early machinery for producing textiles and the like.

Comparing the energetic situation at the end of the agricultural phase of human history with that of the hunter-gatherer phase, the per capita use of energy had approximately doubled, and the population size had increased by a factor of about 200, so that total energy use by humans had increased by a factor of about 400.

The transition to agriculture enabled the human population to increase its appropriation of the product of photosynthesis, and hence to increase in size. The individual human condition in the agricultural phase of history varied with location and date. Also, the social stratification noted above meant that individual experiences in a given place at a given time differed more than was the case for hunter-gatherer societies. For most people for most of the time, it appears to be the case that agriculturalists worked at least as hard as hunter-gatherers for a diet that was less varied and less nutritious. The settled way of life and the higher population densities meant the appearance of the 'diseases of civilisation' – cholera, typhoid, the plague, smallpox, malaria, for example – especially in the urban centres. It appears that many agricultural societies were not far from famine conditions for much of the time. Dependence on a narrow range of crops often made them vulnerable to pests and changing climatic conditions. For most humans who lived as agriculturalists, life expectancy was probably not much longer than it had been for hunter-gatherers. Some of the more perceptive explorers from agricultural societies who came into contact with hunter-gatherers noted that the 'savages' were often better-off than the mass of the population at home – see Box 3.1 for an example.

The environmental impact of agriculture was much greater than it had been for the hunter-gatherer food production system. The distribution of plants and animals was shifted in favour of the human domesticates. Particularly in the temperate zone, large areas of forest were cleared to make way for crop production and animal grazing. Some agricultural systems had environmental impacts that undermined their productivity and led to their eventual collapse. The main problems were soil erosion and salinisation, both often associated with the removal of tree cover.

3.5 THE SECOND TRANSITION

Trees were not chopped down solely to clear land for agriculture. As noted above, extrasomatic energy use increased greatly during the agricultural phase of human history, and one major source was biomass, especially timber. Towards the end of the agricultural phase in western Europe, there was an energy crisis due to the shortage of timber. The adaptive response to this crisis was a major feature of the second great transition in human history, that from the agricultural to the industrial phase.

Just as the first transition is often referred to as the agricultural revolution, so the second is often referred to as the **industrial revolution**. Again, the use of the term 'revolution' is not entirely appropriate, though in this case the transition was quicker. Depending on what are taken to be the distinguishing characteristics of the industrial phase of human history, its earliest beginnings could be put somewhere between 1200 AD and 1800 AD. By 2000 AD, while in some parts of the world most people were still agriculturalists, the global economy was totally dominated by the industrial way of economic life. For reasons to be explained shortly, we take

1800 AD, 200 BP, as the date for the industrial revolution, as indicated in Figure 3.1. On that basis, the transition to the industrial way of economic life took just two centuries.

Most historians take the essential feature of the industrial revolution to be the adoption of a system of manufacturing using machines in factories. It is generally taken to have occurred in England in the eighteenth century. Earlier dates for the beginning of the industrial revolution are based on the idea that this development was only made possible by earlier technological and/or social innovations, such as, for example, the spread of the use of water power to drive a wide range of machines in thirteenth-century Europe. Many take another defining characteristic of the industrial revolution to be the use of coal to drive the machines in the factories, and to transport raw materials to and manufactures from the factories. This first happened in England in the second half of the eighteenth and the beginning of the nineteenth centuries, so we take 200 BP as the round numbers date for the start of the industrial revolution.

Coal use for domestic heating in England dated from the thirteenth century, and by the seventeenth it was used in some manufacturing activities. However, wood remained the dominant, and generally preferred, source of energy. The transition from wood to coal was driven by shortages of, and rising prices for, wood rather than by an appreciation of coal as a superior fuel. The increasing scarcity of wood was driven by population growth which increased the demand for fuel, and for construction materials. The consequent increasing demand for coal led to problems in its mining, particularly in pumping water from the deeper workings. This stimulated an interest in pumping technology which was largely responsible for the development of the steam engine. This and related technological innovations in machinery use were increasing the demand for iron, which in the first half of the eighteenth century was still produced using charcoal, a wood-based fuel. Given the increasing price of wood, machinery was also increasing in price.

The decisive step in the initiation of the industrial revolution in England appears to have been the discovery of how to use coal in iron making. In the latter part of the eighteenth century, coal largely replaced charcoal as the fuel used in iron making. The need to move coal, and to supply food to the rapidly growing urban areas, put great strain on the existing transport system based on horse-drawn vehicles of various kinds. In early nineteenth-century England the steam engine was successfully applied to the transportation of goods and people, and its use spread rapidly through the country during the first half of that century.

During the nineteenth century, Britain led the industrial revolution, and became the world's dominant economic power, importing food and raw materials and exporting coal and manufactured goods. The technological developments in transport that made this trade feasible were themselves based on coal and its use in iron and steel production – steamships and railways. Britain's coal production increased from about 10 million tons in 1800 to over 200 million tons in 1900. World coal consumption increased from about 15 million tons in 1800 to about 700 million in 1900. The exploitation of oil began in the second half of the nineteenth century, but coal remained the dominant fuel until well into the twentieth. Currently total world energy consumption is equivalent to about 10,000 million tons of coal per year.

The history of the last 200 years is not, of course, to be understood solely in terms of the consequences that flowed from the systematic and widespread use of fossil fuels. There were associated political, social, scientific and technological developments. While not all of these, in every detail, can be attributed to the transformation of the human position in respect of the ability to use energy, it is clear that without that transformation the history of the last 200 years would have been completely different to that which was actually experienced.

3.5.1 Energy slaves

It was noted above that by the end of the agricultural phase of human history, for the world as a whole, the average human used some 3–4 HEE, of which 2–3 were extrasomatic. By 1900 the average human used about 14 extrasomatic HEE. It is as if by 1900 the average human had at her command 14 human slaves. By the end of the twentieth century the average human used about 19 extrasomatic HEE – the equivalent of 19 human slaves. This global average for 1997 comes from a wide range for individual nations. In 1997, per capita extrasomatic energy use in the USA was 93 HEE, while in Bangladesh it was 4. In the USA the extrasomatic energy comes predominantly from the fossil fuels, while in Bangladesh it comes mainly from biomass.

Expressing extrasomatic HEE history in terms of human slaves is not fanciful. It makes concrete a very important reality. For most of the agricultural phase of human history large-scale construction projects, for example, involved actual human slaves – think of the pyramids of Egypt, or the Great Wall of China as famous examples. Slaves were essential to the functioning of the Roman Empire's transport system, for another example. Given the availability of fossil fuels and the machinery to use them, modern empires do not need human slaves to move and/or transform matter in bulk. At another level, the decline of the employment of household servants in modern industrial societies is largely attributable to the availability of electrical appliances that do a lot of the work involved in running a household.

Suppose that all the work done by extrasomatic energy in the world economy today were to be done by human slaves. For global per capita extrasomatic HEE take a round number of 20, which is approximately the global average – this is about one fifth of the figure for the USA, to whose standards of living most of the world's population aspires. In that case, doing the world's work would require an additional human population 20 times the size of the existing population. That would be, in round numbers, an extra 120 billion people. Nobody seriously argues that the planet could support that many human beings.

The period since the industrial revolution has seen, as shown in Figure 3.1, an enormous growth in human numbers, from 0.9 billion in 200 BP to 6 billion now. This has been associated with an enormous growth in the stock of capital in the form of buildings, machines, tools and equipment. This increase in the stock of durable capital is obviously related to the use of extrasomatic energy, which permits of higher levels of production in the economy, making more available for the accumulation of things as well as the consumption of things. Also, the use of much of this stock now requires the use of extrasomatic energy – to heat the buildings, run the machines, drive the vehicles.

The increased use of durable capital powered by extrasomatic energy has reduced the total amount of human labour time directly needed for a given level of production, and has particularly reduced the total amount of physically demanding work – such as digging, lifting and the like – that gets done. As compared with societies from the agricultural phase of human history, modern industrial societies have a larger excess of human resources over the amount required to work physically at the provision of basic human needs. Those extrasomatic energy slaves enable modern industrial societies to devote more of their human resources to scientific and technological research, to education, and to managing things efficiently. For those in work, hours of work in a modern industrial society are not much different from what they were in many agricultural societies. The point is rather the kinds of work that those in the labour force do, and the fact that the proportion of the population in the labour force is lower. In regard to the latter, whereas in many agricultural societies most children entered the labour force well before puberty, in modern industrial societies most will not enter it before the age of 18, and many will remain in education until early adulthood. Modern industrial societies have a much greater potential for high rates of human capital accumulation and cultural evolution than did agricultural societies.

3.5.2 Human numbers in the industrial phase of human history

The growth of human numbers since the industrial revolution reflects the effects of human capital accumulation. It has been largely driven by the growth in scientific knowledge and its application to the problems created by the higher human population densities consequent upon agriculture, and especially the diseases of civilisation associated with urbanisation. The representation of the path of human numbers in Figure 3.1 is intended to bring out the big picture over the broad sweep of human history. As regards what has happened in the industrial phase since 200 BP it is actually somewhat misleading.

To look in more detail at that period, it is necessary to distinguish between developments in what are now the rich industrial nations – the developed world – and the rest – what we now call the developing world. In the first 100 years of the industrial phase, most of the growth in human numbers took place in the developed world. Population growth there was almost entirely due to falling death rates together with constant birth rates. The falling death rates partly reflected improved standards of nutrition, due in part to world trade in food products, but was mainly due to progress in dealing with the causes of the diseases of civilisation – improved sanitation and the like. It should also be noted that during the nineteenth century and early twentieth century the land area occupied by these countries was effectively increasing, with the opening up to their populations of opportunities for migration, to the Americas especially. During this period, the medicinal and public health improvements taking place in the developed world had very little impact on the developing world.

This situation began to change somewhat in the first half of the twentieth century. By 1950 the world population was around 2 billion, of whom about 0.9 billion lived in the developed world, while 1.3 billion lived in the developing world. From 1950 to 1999, the population of the developed world increased to about 1.1 billion, while that of the developing world increased to about 4.8 billion. Basically what drove these developments is that, first, developed world medical and public health standards spread to the developing world, where death rates went down while birth rates remained at previous levels. Second, in the developed world birth rates dropped – in many developed economies by the end of the twentieth century they had dropped so far that they were below the level needed to prevent the population size going down.

At the end of the twentieth century, birth rates in much of the developing world were also declining. Nonetheless, the prospects for human numbers are that they will continue to increase for the next 50 years – current UN projections for 2050 span, in round numbers, the range 8 billion to 11 billion. The proportion of the human population living in the developing world as it now is will continue to increase.

3.6 ENERGY AND AGRICULTURE

The industrial revolution and its consequences profoundly affected agriculture, which in modern industrial economies is itself an industrial activity, in that it uses large amounts of extrasomatic energy.

Table 3.1 shows the inputs to and output from three representative systems of food production, where both inputs and output are measured in energy units – Mj per hectare per year. The data for hunting and gathering relate to the !Kung Bushmen whose way of life persisted in Africa into the twentieth century, and is based on studies conducted by anthropologists in the mid-twentieth century. By 'pre-industrial agriculture' is meant agriculture as it was practised during the agricultural phase of human history. The data in Table 3.1 actually relate to Chinese peasant farming in 1935–37. At that time the agricultural methods of Chinese peasant farmers were those that were used throughout the world in the agricultural phase of human history. The data for industrial agriculture are for rice-growing in the USA in the 1960s. By that date virtually all of agriculture in the developed world had been affected by the industrial revolution. In all three cases in Table 3.1, the accounting for energy inputs does not include the incident solar radiation on the land where food production takes place – per hectare per year this would be approximately the same amount across all three systems.

The hunting and gathering system for food acquisition uses as input only the somatic energy of the humans who practise it. Hence, for this system the ratio of output to input energy is the same as the ratio of output to human energy input. Recall that an adult human requires approximately 10 Mj of food input per day. For the hunter-gatherer system of Table 3.1 food production is about 3 Mj per hectare per year, which is 3,000 Mj per square kilometre per year, or about 8 Mj per square kilometre per day. As noted above, population densities for hunter-gatherers range from 0.2 to 2 people per square kilometre. These data for the !Kung Bushmen would put them near the middle of that range as they have a square kilometre yielding about 80 per cent of the food requirements for one adult.

Looking at the data for agriculture as practised prior to the industrial revolution, we see that much more labour is used per unit area, and that labour is not the only input used. The muscle power of domesticated animals is used. The 'machinery' that is used comprises hand tools and ploughs, and is powered by human and animal muscles: the entry of 230 Mj per hectare per year against machinery is an estimate of the share of the total energy used in the construction of such equipment accounted for by its use for one year on one hectare. As compared with the hunter-gatherer system, agriculture uses inputs several thousand times larger. There is a high pay-off in terms of output, so that that output to input ratio increases from about 8 to about 40 – a five-fold increase. The increase in the ratio of output to human labour input is six-fold, due to the use of simple machinery and animal muscle power. The ability of agriculture to support much higher populations per unit area than hunting and gathering is clear from these data.

Table 3.1   Energy accounts for food production

	Hunting and gathering	Pre-industrial agriculture	Industrial agriculture
Labour	0.37	5650	20
Animals		960	
Machinery		230	18590
Fertiliser			11660
Pesticides			1090
Drying			4480
Irrigation			29620
Total input	0.37	6840	64460
Output	2.90	281,100	84120
Output/input ratio	7.8	41.1	1.3
Output/human input ratio	7.8	49.7	4206.0

Note: Units for inputs and outputs are Mj per hectare per year.
Source: Leach (1975).

Comparing industrial agriculture with pre-industrial agriculture, the total energy input increases by a factor of almost 10. Very little labour is used, and no animal power is used. The other inputs shown are supplied to agriculture by the industrial sector of the economy. In the case of machinery, the figure of 18,590 refers to the energy supplied – in the form of oil and electricity – to power the machinery used on the farm, and to the energy used in making the machinery. Similarly, the figure for drying refers to the energy used to run the equipment and to make it. The figures for pesticides and fertiliser are estimates of the energy used in making the amounts of these used on the farm, and that for irrigation is an estimate of the energy used in delivering the water used to the farm. The use of machinery, fertiliser and pesticide is characteristic for all industrial farming. The manufacture of fertiliser uses large amounts of energy. The use of energy for drying and irrigation is not a feature of all forms of industrial agriculture. Virtually all of the non-labour energy input used in industrial agriculture is based on fossil fuel combustion.

While this example of industrial agriculture uses 10 times as much energy input as the example of pre-industrial agriculture, it produces about 30 per cent as much output in energy terms, per hectare per year. The ratio of output to input drops from 41.1 for pre-industrial to 1.3 for industrial. In terms of the return to labour, however, industrial agriculture is very productive – its output to human energy input is about 80 times as high as that for pre-industrial agriculture, and more than 500 times as high as that for hunting and gathering. Modern industrial agriculture achieves very high labour productivity mainly by virtue of its use of extrasomatic energy based on fossil fuel combustion.

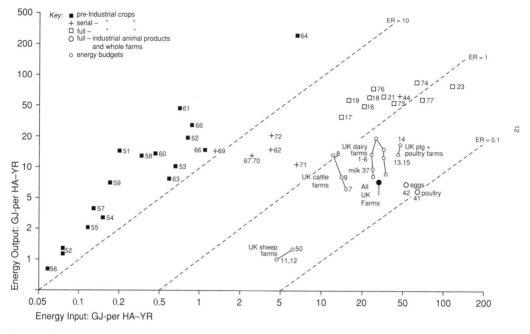

Source: Leach (1975).

Figure 3.2 The energetics of food production systems.

The data used in Table 3.1 refer to just one example of each of pre-industrial and industrial agriculture. Many studies of energy inputs to and outputs from agriculture have been done. Figure 3.2 shows the results from about 70 such studies, in terms of energy output in Gj per hectare per year, total energy input in Gj per hectare per year, and ER (energy ratios) the ratio of output to input. Figure 3.2 distinguishes between crop-production systems, and systems which produce animal products or combinations of crops and animal products. Food production systems are called 'Semi-industrial' where there is some use of fossil fuel-based extrasomatic energy, but where food production is not so heavily dependent on that as in the 'full-industrial' systems, of which the 'industrial agriculture' case in Table 3.1 is an example. The general picture in Figure 3.2 confirms the story told in Table 3.1. The dashed sloping lines indicate constant energy ratios. All of the pre-industrial crop systems shown have an energy ratio of greater than 10. They span a wide range of land productivity – from less than 1 Gj per hectare per year to more than 200 Gj per hectare per year. Industrial crop production achieves generally high outputs per unit land area, at the cost of high energy inputs per unit land area, so that energy ratios are less than 10, and in two cases less than 1. Not shown in Figure 3.2, but clear in the studies which it summarises, is the fact, noted above for Table 3.1, that industrial crop production achieves very high labour productivities. For mixed and industrial animal production systems, the energy ratios are generally less than one.

We have noted two great transitions in human history, that from hunting and gathering to agriculture which began about 12,000 years ago, and that from agriculture to industry which began about 200 years ago. Both transitions involved major shifts in the human position in terms of energy use.

As hunter-gatherers, humans operated within the limits set by photosynthetic capture and conversion in essentially the same way as did other animal species. Humans, largely due to their aptitude for culture, were a very successful hunter-gatherer animal species.

With the advent of agriculture, the human food-acquisition strategy changed fundamentally. Instead of operating within the given structure of a trophic pyramid as hunter-gatherers do, agriculturalists alter the structure of their local foodchains and trophic pyramids so as to serve their interests. However, for pre-industrial agriculturalists, the extent of operations in this respect is still essentially limited by the current inflow of solar radiation.

With industrialisation, humans begin the systematic use of fossil fuels, and their activities are no longer confined by the limits set by receipts of solar radiation and their conversion to plant and animal tissue. In the previous chapter we considered the origin of deposits of fossil fuels, and saw that they were organic, and that the deposits were accumulations over millions of years of some of the receipts of solar energy converted to plant and animal tissue. If we think of the annual inflow of solar radiation as an annual flow of income, then the fossil fuel deposits are like a savings account built up a long time ago. For the human species, discovering how to use the fossil fuels effectively as a source of energy was like an individual with income but no wealth inheriting a savings account built up out of somebody else's income. Whereas previously what could be done was limited by the annual income flow, the inheritance of wealth expanded the realms of the possible.

This transformation of the energy situation facing humanity affected all of its activities, including, as documented in this section, the most basic activity of all – the provision of food. One striking example of the way in which fossil fuel exploitation transformed the nature of agriculture and liberated humans from the bounds set by the current inflow of solar radiation is in regard to the substitution in the nineteenth and twentieth centuries of fossil fuel energy for animal muscle power. Prior to the extensive use of fossil fuels, in many economies horses were widely used as a source of power in agriculture, and were the dominant, non-human, source of power for land transport. The growing of food for these animals required the use of a lot of land – in the case of Great Britain, for example, it is estimated that in the late nineteenth century about 30 per cent of cropland was actually being used to produce fodder for horses. By the second half of the twentieth century, the use of horses in agriculture and transport in England was effectively non-existent, and in every former use they had been replaced by machines burning fossil fuels. The utilisation of fossil fuels had the effect of increasing the amount of land available in England for growing crops for human consumption by about 40 per cent. This effect has by now been replicated in all of the modern industrial economies, and in many of the currently developing economies.

Actually, the data on which Table 3.1 and Figure 3.1 are based understate the extent to which the provision of food to human individuals depends, in modern industrial economies, on the use of extrasomatic fossil fuel energy. These data cover only the inputs of energy that take place on the farms. In modern industrial economies most of the consumers of food live in urban areas, and getting the food to them in the forms that they use it requires further, large, amounts of energy for transport and processing.

As noted in the two previous chapters, given their origins, the total amount of the fossil fuels in existence is necessarily finite. The use of fossil fuels as extrasomatic energy in agricultural production cannot go on indefinitely.

3.7 THE EXTENT OF THE HUMAN IMPACT ON THE BIOSPHERE

The cultural evolution of the species *Homo sapiens sapiens* has resulted in a situation where the economic activities of that species have major impacts on the functioning of the biosphere. Particulars of this general situation will be dealt with at various places in the book. We have, for example, already noted the enhanced greenhouse effect and the climate change problem, and Chapter 13 will be entirely devoted to it. Here, we want to briefly convey a sense of the overall extent of the current human impact on the biosphere.

Chapter 2 showed that the basis for life on earth is the capture by plants of radiant solar energy, and its conversion to organic material by the process of photosynthesis. The rate at which plants produce plant tissue is primary productivity, measured in terms of energy per unit area per unit time – calories per square metre per year say. Gross primary productivity is the total amount of solar energy that is fixed by photosynthesis, whereas net primary productivity is that less the amount of energy lost to the environment as respiration, and so the amount that is actually stored in the plant tissue. Net primary productivity is the measure of the energy that is potentially available to the animals that eat the plants in question.

Table 3.2 shows estimates of the proportion of net primary productivity that is appropriated by humanity. About 70 per cent of the earth's surface is covered by water. The aquatic zone, the oceans, produces about 40 per cent of total global net primary productivity. The terrestrial zone, although accounting for only 30 per cent of the surface area, accounts for about 60 per cent of total primary productivity.

For each zone, and for both zones together, Table 3.2 shows estimates of human appropriation on three different bases:
(1)   Low – for this estimate what is counted is what humans and their domesticated animals directly use as food, fuel and fibre.
(2)   Intermediate – this counts the current net primary productivity of land modified by humans. Thus, for example, whereas the low estimate relates to food eaten, the intermediate estimate is of the net primary productivity of the agricultural land on which the food is produced.
(3)   High – this also counts potential net primary productivity that is lost as a result of human activity. Thus, with regard to agriculture, this estimate includes what is lost as a result, for example, of transforming forested land into grassland pasture for domesticated animals. It also includes losses due to desertification and urbanisation.

Table 3.2 Human appropriation of net primary productivity

	Percentages		
	Low	*Intermediate*	*High*
Terrestrial	4	31	39
Aquatic	2	2	2
Total	3	19	25

Source: Vitousek *et al.* (1986).

For the aquatic zone, it makes no difference which basis for estimation is used. This reflects the fact that human exploitation of the oceans is much less than it is of land-based ecosystems, and that the former is still essentially in the nature of hunter-gatherer activity rather than agricultural activity. It also reflects that what are reported are rounded numbers, to reflect the fact that we are looking at – for both zones – approximations rather than precise estimates.

For the terrestrial zone, the basis on which the human appropriation of net primary productivity is based makes a lot of difference. If we look at what humans and their domesticates actually consume – the low basis – it is 4 per cent. If we look at the net primary productivity of land managed in human interests – the intermediate basis – it is 31 per cent. Commenting on the high terrestrial figure, the scientists responsible for these estimates remark:

> An equivalent concentration of resources into one species and its satellites has probably not occurred since land plants first diversified.   (Vitousek *et al.*, 1986: p. 372)

Estimates (reported in Vitousek *et al.*, 1997) of the proportion of the global land area now used by humans for growing crops and as urban-industrial land range from 10 per cent to 15 per cent. For the proportion converted to animal pasture, the range is 6 per cent to 8 per cent. Estimates of the proportion of land transformed or degraded by human activity range from 39 per cent to 50 per cent. These estimates, like those reported in Table 3.2, are subject to large uncertainties. However, notwithstanding that, the extent to which humanity impacts on the biosphere is clearly great. Many scientists from a variety of disciplinary backgrounds take the view that the extent of the human impact on the natural environment is now such that it threatens its capacity to continue to support human activity in the ways, and at the levels, that it now does – threatens sustainability.

SUMMARY

For most of human history, economic activity took the form of hunting and gathering, and the size of the human population was small. About 12,000 years ago some societies began to practise agriculture, which could generally support higher population densities. Over time agriculture generally displaced hunting and gathering, and the human population grew slowly. The industrial revolution took place about 200 years ago, since when the size of the human population has grown very rapidly and the species now dominates the global ecosystem. The industrial mode of economic activity is characterised by the extensive use of extrasomatic energy, especially in the form of fossil fuels, in food production as well as manufacturing.

KEYWORDS

Agricultural revolution (p. 72): a misnomer for the domestic transition.

Culture (p. 67): social interaction between individuals and its consequences in terms of technologies, institutions, customs and the like.

Domestic transition (p. 72): the movement from hunting and gathering to farming.

Extrasomatic energy (p. 70): energy utilised by humans that comes from sources other than their muscles.

Human Energy Equivalent (p. 72): the amount of somatic energy per day required by a human individual.

Industrial revolution (p. 74): the emergence of factory manufacturing and the systemic use of fossil fuels as the dominant mode of economic activity.

Somatic energy (p. 70): the energy that an animal acquires from its food.

FURTHER READING

Tudge* (1996) is mainly about the 'five million years of human history' but also sets that history in the context of the history of planet earth. Ponting* (2001) is a comprehensive book, looking at the whole of human history in terms of man's interaction with environments. Ponting provides useful references to the literatures that are relevant to such a wide subject matter. The use of Human Energy Equivalents here follows Boyden *et al.* (1990), which covers much of the chapter's subject matter from a similarly energetic perspective, and which applies it in some detail to an analysis of modern Australia's situation. Diamond (1992) and Diamond (1998) are two books dealing with the biological evolution of humans and their early history. McNeill (2000) is 'the story of environmental change around the world in the twentieth century, its human causes and consequences' (page xix).

Current demographic data can be readily found in UNDP (2002). The world population projections mentioned in the chapter, and to be discussed further in Chapter 6, are from UN (2002).

Sahlins (1974) is a classic anthropological work on the economics of hunter-gatherer societies, which was influential in the reappraisal of their economic performance. Blainey (1975) is a highly readable general history of the Australian aboriginals, while Dingle (1988) focuses more specifically on their economic arrangements. Lee (1969) reports the results of a detailed study of the hunter-gatherer economy of the !Kung Bushmen of the Kalahari Desert. The energetics of agriculture is considered in Bayliss-Smith (1982).

Rojstaczer *et al.* (2001) report the results of a similar study to that of Vitousek *et al.* (1986) using a wider range of more recent data, confining their attention to terrestrial net primary production and looking at only the intermediate basis for estimation. Their mean estimate of the proportion of terrestrial net primary production appropriated by humans is 32 per cent. Vitousek *et al.* (1997) review a range of indicators for the extent to which the human species now dominates most ecosystems: see also Field (2001).

DISCUSSION TOPICS

1. Some regard the story of the fall and expulsion from the Garden of Eden at the beginning of the Judeo-Christian bible as being a mythical account of the transition to agriculture. Is this plausible?
2. The Australian aboriginals never invented the wheel. Some modern Australians of European origin consider that this shows that the Aboriginals were unintelligent and uncivilised. Others say that, on the contrary, it shows that they were intelligent enough not to get into situations where they had to move so much stuff about that they needed the wheel. Which is the correct view?
3. Do ecological economists need to study history?
4. How would human history have differed if there had been no accessible fossil fuel deposits?

4

The economy in the environment – a conceptual framework

In this chapter you will:

- Learn about the ways in which the economy and the environment are interdependent;
- Find out how natural resources can be classified;
- Look at waste flows and pollution;
- Learn how the use of natural resources and waste generation are related;
- Consider the amenities and life support services that the environment provides;
- See how the functions that the environment performs for the economy interact with one another, and may be competitive;
- Look at threats to sustainability that originate in economy–environment interdependence.

The purpose of this chapter is to look at the economic system in relation to the environment system that supports it. It concentrates on the big picture and on setting out the conceptual framework that will be used throughout the book. The perspective from which the framework is developed is that of a modern industrial economy. A supplement to this chapter, which fleshes out the conceptual framework with information and data, will be found on the website that goes with the book. You will also find on that website lots of links to other sites that give similar and related information and data.

The first section of the chapter briefly sets out the whole big picture of economy--environment interdependence, and subsequent sections are mainly about looking at parts of the picture. The final section considers threats to sustainability that have their origins in the relations between economic activity and the natural environment.

4.1 THE BIG PICTURE

Figure 4.1 is a representation of the relationships between human economic activity and the natural environment. The most basic and important point that it is

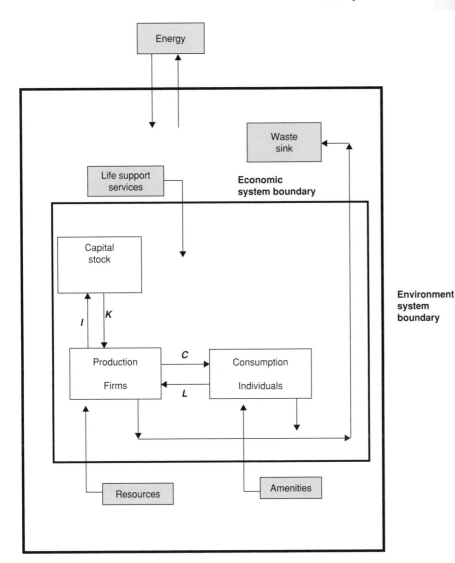

Figure 4.1
Economy–
environment
interdepen-
dence.

intended to bring out is that the human economic system is a subsystem of the system which is the environment. The economy depends upon the environment, what happens in the economy affects the environment, and changes in the environment affect the economy. Regarded as two systems, the economy and the environment are interdependent.

In Figure 4.1 the outer heavy-lined box represents the boundary of the environment system. This thermodynamically closed system exchanges energy, but not matter, with its environment, which is the rest of the universe. The exchange is shown by the arrows crossing the outer boundary at the top of Figure 4.1. The energy source is the Sun, and the incoming flow is solar radiation, which is the basis for all life on earth. The outgoing energy flow is thermal radiation emitted by the earth. The balance between these flows is affected by, among other things, the composition of the earth's atmosphere, and determines how warm the earth is. This will be discussed further in sub-section 4.10.3 below, and in Chapter 13.

The inner heavy-lined box represents the boundary of the economic subsystem. There are four lines crossing this boundary representing four classes of service that the environment provides to the economy.

Starting at bottom left, resources are extracted from the environment, and used in production. Resources are often referred to as 'natural resources'. Section 4.4 below looks at the differences between various types of natural resources.

At top right, there is shown a flow of wastes across the economy–environment boundary. These wastes arise in both production and consumption in the economy, but their real origin is in the flow of resources into the economy. It follows from the law of conservation of matter, considered in Chapter 2, that the mass of wastes inserted into the environment must be the same as the mass of resources extracted from it. This is discussed in sections 4.6 and 4.7 below. In relation to economic activity, the environment provides the service of waste sink. The connection between waste emissions and pollution is discussed in section 4.5.

The third flow crossing the economy–environment boundary in Figure 4.1, bottom right, is of amenity services. The environment provides humans with satisfactions in such forms of pleasure and stimulation as, for example, sunbathing, swimming in the ocean and wilderness recreation. This class of environmental service will be discussed in section 4.8 below.

Fourth, the environment provides basic life support services, shown top left in Figure 4.1. While the range of environmental conditions that humans can tolerate is greater than for many other species, there are limits to what can be tolerated, or adapted to, by humans. The maintenance by the environment of the conditions necessary for human life is a precondition for human economic activity of any kind. This fourth class of service is discussed in section 4.9 below.

Before looking at these services in more detail, we need to look more closely at the nature of economic activity. We do this in section 4.3. First, in the next section, 4.2, we will introduce some ideas that are relevant to thinking about both economic and natural systems, and about the interdependence of such systems.

4.2 STOCKS AND FLOWS

Stocks and flows, and the relationships between them, are fundamental to the operation of both economic and natural systems. A stock is a quantity existing at a point in time, and a flow is a quantity per period of time. A stock and the corresponding flow are related as shown in Figure 4.2. The size of the stock at the end of some period of time is given by the size at the beginning of the period and the relative sizes of the inflow and outflow over the period. That is

$$\text{Closing Stock} = \text{Opening Stock} + \text{Inflow} - \text{Outflow}$$

where stocks are quantities and flows are quantities per period. An example is water in a tank with a tap (faucet) which regulates the inflow, and an outlet drain which regulates the outflow. To increase the stock of water in the tank, you open the tap

Figure 4.2
Stock and flow.

more and/or close the drain more. To decrease it, you close the tap and/or open up the drain. If initially the tank is empty, and the inflow is 200 litres per hour and the outflow drain is completely closed, after 1 hour the stock of water in the tank will be 200 litres.

Let S_0 represent the initial stock size and S_1 represent the stock size at the end of the first period. Then

$$S_1 = S_0 + A_1 - O_1$$

where O_1 and A_1 are outflow and inflow during the first period. We do not use the obvious I for inflow because we want to use I in another way. A can stand for additions. At the end of the second period

$$S_2 = S_1 + A_2 - O_2$$

and so on and so on. Generally

$$S_t = S_{t-1} + A_t - O_t$$

where:

  S_t stands for the size of the stock at the end of some period t
  S_{t-1} stands for the size of the stock at the beginning of the period t (which
    is the end of period $t-1$)
  A_t stands for additions, the inflow, in period t
  O_t stands for the outflow during period t
Over any period, the change in the stock size is

$$S_t - S_{t-1} = A_t - O_t$$

During a period, the stock will increase, accumulate, if $A_t > O_t$ ($>$ means is greater than), while it will decrease, de-cumulate, if $A_t < O_t$ ($<$ means is less than).

As we shall see, many of the processes in both economic and natural systems can be analysed in terms of this simple basic framework of flows into and out from corresponding stocks. However, not all processes fit this framework.

First, there are what we can call non-consumptive processes. In the standard stock–flow relationship the flows are the same stuff as the stock, and outflow greater than inflow consumes the stock, as, for example, with the flows of water to and from a tank. Some stocks participate in processes involving flows of different stuff and are not consumed, or added to, as a result. Catalysts in chemical reactions are examples in natural systems. An example in the economic system is a statue, which is a stock of, say, marble that has been worked on. It gives pleasure to those who look at it, but the process by which it does so does not involve any consumption of the stock of marble that is the statue. It is true that the statue is involved in various processes on account of which it deteriorates, usually very slowly, over time. But the rates of those processes are not related to the rate at which the statue provides pleasure – they would go on just the same if nobody ever looked at the statue, or if it was an awful statue that did not give anybody any pleasure.

Second, there are what we can call multi-stock processes. These are processes where many stocks are involved, in ways that may in some cases be consumptive and others not. We saw in Chapter 2 that a living plant, as an example in natural systems, draws on stocks in its environment of various nutrients. We shall see, as another example in natural systems, that the balance of the energy flows across the boundary of our environment, shown at the top of Figure 4.1, depends, among other things, on the sizes of the stocks of several 'greenhouse gases' in the atmosphere. In the economic system, to continue the previous example, groups of statues are often put together to provide an aesthetic experience which is not simply the sum of the experiences that would separately occur from looking at each of the statues in isolation.

In the following sections of this chapter, we will be using these ideas to look at the economy and its relations to the environment. One final preliminary point needs to be made here. We need to be clear that processes that are consumptive of a stock do not violate the first law of thermodynamics as it applies to matter. If one stock of something is going up/down, then another stock of that something, or of some transformation of it, is going down/up somewhere – if the water in our tank is going up/down, then a stock of water somewhere else is changing in size.

4.3 THE ECONOMY

The basic activities that go on in the economy are consumption, production and investment. The discussion of these activities here will be brief – we look at economic activity in more detail in Part II of the book.

4.3.1 Consumption

Consumption is the use by human individuals of goods and services to satisfy some of their needs and wants. 'Goods and services' are often referred to as 'commodities', a practice that will be followed in this book. Figure 4.1 shows a flow C, for commodities, entering the Consumption/Individuals box. Consumption is the end to which economic activity is directed – the satisfaction of human needs and desires. Consumption, as shown in Figure 4.1, generates flows of wastes. Note that not all consumption is 'consumptive' in the material sense for which we used the term in the previous section. The consumption of food is materially consumptive, but the consumption of the services of art galleries, where statues are exhibited, is not.

4.3.2 Production

Firms are the organisations that undertake the **production** of the commodities that individuals consume. The flow C in Figure 4.1 originates in the Production/Firms box. Firms produce commodities using several kinds of inputs. They use labour services supplied by individuals, shown in Figure 4.1 by the flow L. They also use inputs, called 'raw materials' or 'natural resources', that are extracted from the environment, as indicated by the flow Resources in Figure 4.1. Also entering the Production/Firms box is a flow K, originating in the box Capital stock. The nature of this flow will be explained shortly, in connection with the activity of investment. Leaving the Production/Firms box is a flow, which like the Resources flow, crosses the boundary of the economic system, and goes into the Waste sink box.

The range of commodity types produced for consumption in a modern economy is very wide – from personal services to automobiles. Some firms may not directly use raw materials, as perhaps in the case of the provision of a personal service such as beauty care. However, as this example indicates, even where a firm's own input list does not include natural resources as such, its input list will include things that have been produced by other firms using inputs of natural resources – the beauty parlour uses various preparations based on chemicals produced using natural resources of several kinds. Figure 4.1 is drawn so as to avoid this complication of indirect use of inputs extracted from the environment, and shows the overall situation in regard to production and the environment. The indirect use by firms of inputs from the environment will be considered in Chapter 5, section 5.1.3.

4.3.3 Investment

Not all of what firms collectively produce is consumed by households. Figure 4.1 shows a flow I, for **investment**, from Production/Firms to the box Capital stock, which is the origin of the flow of capital services, labelled K, to Production/Firms. K stands for 'Capital', C having already been used for consumption of commodities. The use of K to refer to capital, or the services that it provides, and of I for investment is very widespread in economics. Using K to refer to the stock, the basic stock/flow equation in this context can be written as

$$K_t = K_{t-1} + I_t - D_t$$

where D stands for depreciation, the amount by which the stock would diminish if there were no investment, I. I is a flow into K, D is a flow which diminishes K.

The economy's **capital stock** has four component parts:

(1)   The collection of durable equipment for use in production – tools, machinery, buildings, vehicles, roads and the like. This component of the total capital stock is generally referred to as **durable capital**. Investment in it involves using labour, capital, and natural resources to produce such equipment rather than to produce commodities for consumption. In use, equipment wears out, and the amount by which it does so is the depreciation of durable capital.

(2)   The second component is known as **human capital** and consists of the stocks of learned skills, embodied in particular individuals, which enhances their productivity as suppliers of labour services. As with durable capital, so investment in human capital involves using inputs to acquire and disseminate skills, education and training, rather than to produce commodities for consumption. The individuals in whom human capital is embodied wear out, die, but culture means that they can pass on their acquired skills to other individuals.

(3)   The third component is **intellectual capital** which is the accumulated knowl-
      edge and skills available to the economy that is not embodied in particular
      individuals, but resides in books and other cultural artefacts such as com-
      puter memories. As with durable capital, so investment in intellectual capital
      involves using inputs to produce knowledge and disseminate it, rather than to
      produce commodities for consumption. While equipment necessarily wears
      out with use, this does not have to be true of knowledge. The books and
      the like in which intellectual capital is encoded may wear out, but can be
      replaced. In fact, any depreciation of intellectual capital as such is on account
      of non-use rather than use. Non-use leads to forgetting, which in this context
      is what depreciation is.

(4)   The fourth component is **social capital** which is the set of institutions and
      customs which organise economic activity. Investment in this kind of capital
      is using inputs which could otherwise be used to produce commodities for
      consumption to organise and run institutions – activities such as politics,
      legislation, law enforcement. Institutions and customs do not 'wear out', but
      may become obsolete as circumstances change.

Collectively these four are sometimes referred to as **reproducible** or **human-made
capital**. Both adjectives are used to distinguish capital resulting from the diversion
of productive activity away from consumption commodities to investment from
natural capital, which is a term used to refer to those stocks in the environment that
deliver services to the economy. We will be considering the components of natural
capital in the following sections of this chapter. When 'capital', or 'capital stock', is
used without a qualifying adjective it usually means reproducible or human-made
capital – we will follow this practice in this book.

The processes in which capital is used in production are non-consumptive of
capital. A machine which, for example, participates in the production of ice creams
does not end up embodied in millions of ice creams. The machine wears out, due
to friction and the like, as a result of its participation in ice cream production, and
the rate at which it wears out, depreciates, will be related to the rate at which ice
creams are produced. But, machines are different stuff to ice cream.

4.3.4 The productivity of capital accumulation

The four forms of human-made capital share the characteristic that investment
in them may be productive. Investment means forgoing some consumption now in
order to increase the future flow of capital services. To say that an act of investment
is productive means that the future increase in output due to the increased flow
of capital services arising is larger than the current reduction in consumption that
is involved.

The basic ideas here can be brought out by abstracting from the division between
production by firms and consumption by individuals, and looking at the economy
of Robinson Crusoe, who famously found himself alone on an island after a ship-
wreck. Suppose that Robinson was the only thing that reached the island from the
wrecked ship, so he initially lacked not only human companionship, but also any
tools or other productive equipment. At first, he was able to provide himself with
an adequate but uninteresting diet by spending all of his waking-time gathering

plants. Then Robinson decided to spend some of his time making a fishing line and hooks. This meant less time available for plant gathering, and, hence, reduced consumption – Robinson was investing. With the fishing tackle as his durable capital stock, Robinson can use it to improve his diet. The fishing tackle provides a flow of capital services into his production each day. Of course, the fishing tackle depreciates with use and needs maintenance, and eventually replacement. If Robinson is to continue to enjoy an improved diet he must keep on investing – spending some of his time working on the fishing line – so as to maintain his capital and the flow of services that it provides.

Now, we can imagine that as well as spending some time servicing his fishing tackle, Robinson further reduces the time spent actually fishing and gathering plants for consumption and uses the time made available to experiment and practise different fishing techniques, and fishing at new locations. Robinson is investing in his human capital. Going further, he could devote time to the study of the various fish species in the waters around his island, in terms of their movements and concentrations in different locations, their propensities to take different kinds of bait, and their abilities to get off from different kinds of hooks. He invests, that is, in his intellectual capital, and is thereby able to improve his fishing tackle, and to deploy it more effectively.

Given that Robinson is alone on the island, there is no scope for investment in social capital. Nor can he pass on his stock of human and intellectual capital to anybody else. However, we can imagine that another unfortunate fetches up on the island. In that case there is scope for teaching, passing on his human capital, and for social organisation and institution building. Robinson and the new arrival can spend time, which would otherwise be spent getting food, negotiating the terms on which they will share the island and according to which they will exploit its resources. We can imagine, for example, that it turns out that Robinson is better at fishing, while the new arrival is better at gathering plants. To the extent that they can devise and run institutional arrangements for each to specialise in production, their joint consumption opportunities will be improved. How this could work is discussed in Chapter 8 – the point here is that where there is more than one individual, institutions have a role in production.

4.3.5 Open and closed economies

In Chapter 2 we noted that in thermodynamics systems are defined as open, closed or isolated. An open system exchanges energy and matter with its environment. A closed system exchanges energy with only its environment. An isolated system exchanges neither with its environment.

An economy is a system, and economists classify economies as open or closed. However, the way that they use these terms is different from the way that they are used in thermodynamics. In the terminology of economics, an **open economy** is one that trades with other economies, exchanging goods and services and raw materials with those other economies, while a **closed economy** is one that does not trade with other economies. In the terminology of economics, there is no definition of an isolated economy. In fact, since in economics trade includes both energy and matter, closed in economics terminology corresponds to isolated in thermodynamic terminology. Note, however, that the economics definitions refer to exchanges with other economies, not to exchanges with the natural environment.

Figure 4.1 relates to an economy which is closed in the economic sense, and open in the thermodynamic sense. It shows only one economy. There are no other economies for the economy of interest to trade with. Figure 4.1 is drawn, in fact, for the global economy. If we wanted to use something like Figure 4.1 to represent the situation of a national economy – such as that of the UK or the USA – we would need to have within the outer heavily lined box lots of less heavily lined boxes representing that economy and all of the other economies. Each of these less heavily lined boxes would have within it the same boxes and lines as inside the less heavily lined box in Figure 4.1, and crossing its boundary would have the same four flows to and from the natural environment. In addition, each such box would have lines from it to all the other economy boxes representing flows of produced goods and services and of raw materials.

Clearly, this would be a messy and complicated diagram. This is one reason why we show only one economy in Figure 4.1 – it makes the representation of the interdependence of economic activity and the natural environment clearer. There is another important reason for showing just one economy in Figure 4.1. As noted, drawn this way, what it actually represents is an economy closed in the economic sense and open in the thermodynamic sense, which is what the global economy is. The second reason why Figure 4.1 is thus simplified is because the problems of sustainability and sustainable development are fundamentally problems for the global economy, rather than for national economies. We will come back to this at the end of this chapter, after we have looked at the flows across the economy boundary in Figure 4.1.

4.4 RESOURCE EXTRACTION

We look first at the flow of natural resources to productive activity, shown at bottom left in Figure 4.1. Natural resources used as inputs to production can be classified in various ways. The classification used here follows mainly from an interest in sustainability. The first distinction is between resources that exist in the environment as a flow and those that exist in the environment as a stock. The second distinction is as between two classes of stock type resources: renewable and non-renewable.

Both of these distinctions are important for sustainability. With **flow resources**, the amount used today has no implications for the amount that could be used in the future. With **stock resources**, the amount used today does have implications for future availability. In the case of a non-renewable resource, there is no rate of use that can be sustained for ever. In the case of a renewable resource, there are rates of use that can be indefinitely maintained.

4.4.1 Flow resources

Flow resources have no corresponding stocks of the same stuff. They neither accumulate nor de-cumulate. The amount used today has no implications for the amount available in the future.

The most important example of a flow resource is solar radiation. The flow of solar radiation at a given location is, approximately, constant over a suitably defined period such as a year, irrespective of the rate of use by the economy. An example of a particular use of the flow of solar radiation by the economy is the use of a solar voltaic panel to provide electricity. The amount of electricity generated today has no implications for the amount that can be generated tomorrow, or at any time in the future. While the daily amount of solar radiation falling on the panel varies with season and weather, it is not affected by the amount converted to electricity at any time – covering part of the panel today is not going to increase the amount that could be generated tomorrow with the cover off.

There is, of course, an upper limit to the amount of electricity that can be generated in a day, which is set by the size of the panel, the amount of solar radiation at its location, and the efficiency with which the panel operates. It is also the case that incident solar radiation at a given location can be used for only one resource input purpose. It is not possible to grow plants on land covered by a solar panel. Land used to grow food crops cannot simultaneously produce timber.

Other flow resources are wave power, wind power, hydro power and tidal power. These are all sources of energy inputs to production. They, and the extent of their use, are looked at in the supplement to this chapter on the book's companion website.

4.4.2 Stock resources

Stock resources exemplify the standard stock–flow relationship

$$S_t = S_{t-1} + A_t - O_t$$

where stocks and flows are of the same stuff. Where this relationship is used for stock resources it is convenient to use 'growth' for the inflow and 'extraction' for the outflow and to write it as

$$S_t = S_{t-1} + G_t - E_t$$

with G for growth and E for extraction. Renewable and non-renewable resources are distinguished from one another by the fact that for the latter, G is necessarily and always zero.

4.4.2.1 Renewable resources

Renewable resources are biotic populations which can reproduce. As explained in Chapter 2, all life is ultimately based on solar radiation – plants fix it by photosynthesis and animals eat plants. It is conventional to refer to the flow extracted by humans in a period as the harvest, and to the amount added, by reproduction, as natural growth. Flows and stocks can be measured as numbers of individuals or as biomass.

If E_t and G_t are equal, they cancel out and then S_t and S_{t-1} are equal. Where a renewable resource stock is exploited so that the harvest is always equal to the addition from natural growth, the stock size is constant over time. This is known as sustainable harvesting. If E_t is greater than G_t, then that is an unsustainable

Figure 4.3
Density-
dependent
growth.

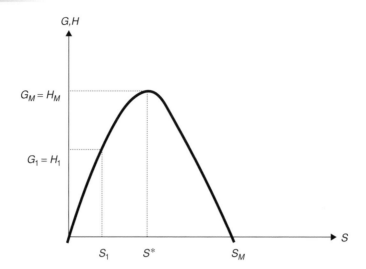

harvest level as it will mean that S_t is less than S_{t-1}. If E_t is less than G_t, then S_t will be greater than S_{t-1} (provided that the environment can support a larger population). Provided that the environment for the harvested resource stock does not change, keeping E_t equal to G_t at some constant level H means that the harvest H is sustainable indefinitely. If E_t is persistently greater than G_t then the resource stock will be harvested to extinction.

It is not true that if E_t is persistently less than G_t then S_t will grow indefinitely. The environments which support renewable resource stocks have an upper limit to the stock size that they can support, the carrying capacity for the stock. In Chapter 2 we looked at density-dependent growth, and particularly logistic growth, as describing how a biotic population size behaves in the absence of extraction. In the analysis of the exploitation of renewable resources it is often assumed that the natural growth of the population that is the resource is density-dependent.

The graph in Figure 4.3 is one representation of logistic growth – Figure 2.9 is an alternative representation. Figure 4.3 plots the amount of growth, G, against the stock size, S. The basic idea is that when the population is small it is not fully exploiting the potential of its environment, and the amount of growth increases with population size as there are more individuals around to have offspring, for which, given under-exploitation of the environment, the survival rate will be high. However, the rate at which the amount of growth increases with stock size declines as the stock increases. The amount of growth reaches a maximum at G_M corresponding to S^*, and thereafter declines with stock size at an increasing rate, as crowding of the environment increases and food/solar radiation per individual decreases. Eventually the population size reaches a level, S_M, at which the population is exploiting its environment to the maximum and, hence, natural growth is zero. Now, if the stock were to be exploited sustainably with $G=H$ always, the graph for G in Figure 4.3 would also be the graph for H, sustainable harvests. It would be the graph showing how sustainable harvests, or sustainable yields as they are often referred to, varied with the size of the exploited stock. Taking, for example, a constant harvest of size of H_1 equal to G_1 with the stock size initially at S_1 would keep the stock at that size. The largest sustainable harvest is when the stock size is kept at S^*, taking the harvest of size H_M. This is known as the **maximum sustainable harvest**, or maximum sustainable yield.

The exploitation by humans of biotic populations is hunting when it is an animal population that is involved, and gathering when it is a plant population. As discussed in the previous chapter, hunting and gathering are not activities that are characteristic of modern human societies, though it was once the case that all human economic activity was hunting and gathering. In modern societies, hunting activity is, recreation and pest control aside, targeted at just one class of animal – fish. Fishing is discussed in the supplementary material on the website. It also looks at forestry, which is the only significant form of gathering in a modern economy, and at agriculture, the method for human exploitation of biota based on solar radiation that has displaced hunting and gathering.

4.4.2.2 *Non-renewable resources*

For **non-renewable resources**, natural growth is zero, so that

$$S_t = S_{t-1} - E_t$$

always. Strictly, the statement G is always zero is true only for timescales of human interest. In geological time, new stocks of non-renewable resources do come into being. We will stick to human timescales and treat non-renewable resources as being defined by $G_t = 0$ for all t. If E_t is greater than zero, S_t must be less than S_{t-1}. This is the distinguishing characteristic of non-renewable resources. Given that the initial stock, prior to human exploitation, of any non-renewable resource must be finite, there is no constant extraction rate that can be maintained for ever for any non-renewable resource. For non-renewables, unlike renewables, there is no sustainable harvest, other than zero. For this reason, non-renewable resources are sometimes called 'exhaustible', or 'depletable', resources. However, this terminology is not really very useful as it is not the fact that they can be exhausted, or depleted, that distinguishes non-renewables from renewables. As noted above, renewables can be harvested to exhaustion by persistently extracting more than natural growth.

It is useful to distinguish between two classes of non-renewable resources – minerals and fossil fuels.

Stocks of minerals exist as the result of geological processes operating on the abiotic materials present at the creation of the planet. There are two broad classes of minerals – 'metallic' and all the others. The former are the ores that can be transformed into metals, such as bauxite (aluminium), iron ore (iron and steel), and copper, for example. The others include minerals used in construction (sand, gravel, clay), as inputs to chemicals production (various salts), as fertiliser (phosphate), and as the raw materials for glass production (silica, feldspar), as a few examples. Generally, the metallic minerals are more valuable per unit mass than the others. Again generally but not universally, other minerals are extracted close to their point of use as input to production, whereas metallic minerals are often extracted at mines which are far distant from the location where they enter production as inputs. Data on stocks and use rates, and the implied lifetimes for the stocks, for some important metallic minerals are given in the supplement on the website.

Stocks of fossil fuels are the result of geological processes operating on what was once the living tissue of biological organisms, as described in Chapter 2. They are, then, based on past incoming solar radiation, which was captured by photosynthesis. The fossil fuels – oil, gas and coal – are predominantly, but not exclusively, used, as the name suggests, as a source of energy inputs to production and as fuels for consumption by individuals. In most modern industrial economies fossil fuel combustion is the source of more than 80 per cent of the energy consumed – it is a defining characteristic of such an economy. Fossil fuels are also used as inputs, feedstocks, in the production of a wide range of commodities produced by the chemicals industries. Where the fossil fuels are burned to provide energy, they cannot be recycled. Where they are used as feedstocks, recycling is possible. Data on fossil fuels use and stocks are given in the website supplement. It also looks at uranium, which is a mineral used to produce energy via the process of nuclear fission – it is the basic input to nuclear power.

4.5 WASTE INSERTION

Given that economic activity involves the extraction from the natural environment of resource inputs to production, it follows, from the law of conservation of matter, that it also involves the insertion into the natural environment of wastes arising in production, and consumption, as shown in Figure 4.1. Before getting into our consideration of some of the issues arising, it will be useful to define some terms that we will be using.

By a **waste** we mean something that is an unwanted by-product of economic activity. The flow of a waste into the receiving environment will be called emissions, or discharges. Thus, for example, the smoke from a factory chimney is a waste, involving a flow of emissions, or discharges, into the atmosphere of x tonnes per hour, say. Sometimes people use the term 'pollution' as synonymous with, meaning the same as, emissions – any waste flow into the environment, that is, is called pollution. We do not use the term in that way. We define **pollution** as: any chemical or physical change in the environment due to waste emission that is harmful to any living organism. Given that not all emissions of waste damage the environment, it makes sense to reserve the term pollution for those that do.

4.5.1 Stocks and flows

Once in the environment, wastes may accumulate there as stocks. As when discussing natural resources, use S to represent the size of a stock, so that

$$S_t = S_{t-1} + W_t - D_t$$

is a standard stock–flow relationship, with stocks and flows measured in the same units, where W_t stands for the size of the waste flow during period t, and D_t stands for the amount by which the size of the stock declined during period t on account of environmental processes.

It is often assumed that the amount by which environmental processes reduce stock size is proportional to the size of the stock, i.e. that

$$D_t = d \times S_{t-1}$$

where d is a parameter with a value in the range 0 to 1, so that D_t lies in the range 0, when $d=0$, to S_{t-1} when $d=1$. With this assumption

$$S_t = S_{t-1} + W_t - (d \times S_{t-1})$$

and for $d=0$

$$S_t = S_{t-1} + W_t$$

To see the implications of this, start with zero stock at the start of year one, so that at the end of that year

$$S_1 = W_1$$

At the end of the second year

$$S_2 = S_1 + W_2$$

which for $S_1 = W_1$ is

$$S_2 = S_1 + W_2 = W_1 + W_2$$

At the end of the third year

$$S_3 = S_2 + W_3 = W_1 + W_2 + W_3$$

and so on and so on. Generally, for $d=0$

$$S_t = W_1 + W_2 + W_3 + \cdots + W_t$$

and the stock of waste is the sum of all of the previous yearly waste flows.

This is a perfectly persistent waste. At the other extreme, $d=1$ and

$$S_t = S_{t-1} + W_t - S_{t-1} = W_t$$

so that waste never accumulates from one period to the next. This is a non-accumulating waste. Most waste-accumulation situations are characterised by inter-mediate value for the parameter d, i.e. it is greater than 0 and less than 1.

The value taken by d would depend both on the nature of the waste itself and on the nature of the receiving environment. In regard to the latter, think of a lake. There are basically two ways that wastes dumped into the lake disappear from it – there is physical transport out of the lake, and there is biochemical transformation within the lake. For some wastes, such as heavy metals for example, the second of these does not operate at all, and the value for d depends solely on the physical nature of the lake system. If the lake sediment is little disturbed and remains in the lake for a long time, then for such wastes d will be close to 1 in value. For organic wastes, physical transport and biochemical transformation are both relevant, and for some such wastes in some lakes d could approach a value of 0.

In many cases it is the concentration of a waste that is of interest. The concentration is the amount of the waste per unit of the relevant receiving environment. Concentrations are expressed as parts per million, ppm, or parts per billion, ppb, so that 1 ppm is equal to 1,000 ppb. An important example of a waste where it is the concentration that matters is that of carbon dioxide in the global atmosphere.

4.5.2 Damage relationships

Thus far we have discussed wastes rather than pollution, having defined pollution as: any chemical or physical change in the environment due to waste emission that is harmful to any living organism. Much of the waste that is discharged into the environment does not give rise to pollution so defined either because the material concerned lacks the capacity for harm, or because potentially harmful wastes are rendered harmless by processes operating in the environment. There are also processes that work in the opposite direction.

The process of **biomagnification** involves the increasing concentration of toxic materials in animals higher up in a foodweb. Some of the toxic wastes released into the environment by human economic activity do not pass through the bodies of the animals that ingest them, but get incorporated in some parts of the body tissue. Predators on such animals then ingest those toxic materials. Typically, a predator over its lifetime consumes many prey individuals. All of the toxic material in all of the consumed prey gets incorporated into the predator's tissue. Predators get eaten by other predators. Moving up the food chain, the concentration of the toxic material in the tissue of an individual increases up to the level of the top carnivore. In some of the relevant contexts, the top carnivore is man.

One example of such a toxic material is DDT, which was first manufactured in the 1940s as a pesticide to control insects involved in the spread of human disease, and which was later widely used against insects that attacked crops. By the 1970s it was discovered that many species of carnivorous birds had high concentrations of DDT in their bodies. It interferes with calcium production and leads to the production of thin-shelled eggs and impaired reproduction. DDT has also been found in concentrations in excess of those regarded as safe in human breast milk. In many developed economies the use of DDT is now banned, though, because it is cheap to produce and easy to use, it is still used in many developing economies. Another example of biomagnification is the mercury poisoning of humans who eat fish that have ingested mercury.

Some of the processes by which wastes cause damage are synergistic, in that they involve two, or more, waste materials interacting in the environment to produce a pollutant which is more damaging than the simple sum of the damage that would be caused by each individually. An example of **synergy** in pollution damage is the 'smog' which is a combination of fog and smoke due to burning coal in the presence of prolonged temperature inversion. The most famous historical example occurred in London in the early 1950s, and it was the first time that an effect from smog to higher human mortality was definitely established. The sulphur dioxide released in coal burning and trapped in the smog reduces the efficiency with which contaminants are cleared from the lungs. This allows more smoke particles, also produced by the coal burning, to get into the lungs and do more damage.

The relationship between the amount of waste in the environment and the damage that it does to an organism is known as the dose–response relationship. Figure 4.4 shows two types of dose–response relationship that have been found to exist.

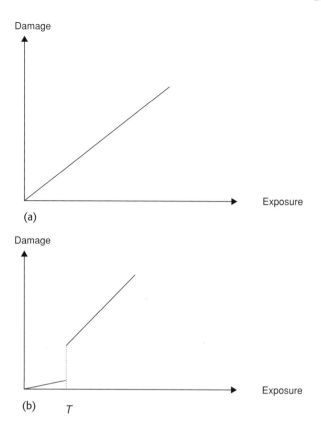

Figure 4.4
Dose–response
relationships.

That in Figure 4.4(a) is where the level of damage increases proportionately to the level of exposure to some waste, the dose, over the whole range of exposure. In the case shown in Figure 4.4(b) there is a **threshold effect** at T. Up to the level of the threshold increases in exposure have little or no effect on the level of damage. At the threshold there is a large increase in damage for a small increase in exposure, and thereafter damage increases in line with exposure. Crossing the threshold in case b has some similarities with what is involved in the loss of resilience discussed in Chapter 2, in that there is a sudden discontinuity. Clearly, in thinking about the problems that a particular kind of waste poses to the environment it is important to know before it is reached if there is a threshold as in b. As with the matter of resilience, it is generally not possible to know whether thresholds exist before they are crossed.

Further information on various kinds of wastes and pollution can be found in the supplementary material for this chapter on the companion website. Fossil fuel combustion is responsible for several kinds of atmospheric pollution, and is the major anthropogenic source of the most important greenhouse gas, carbon dioxide. One attraction of nuclear power is that it does not give rise to the atmospheric pollution that fossil fuel combustion does. However, as discussed in the supplementary material, it does give rise to major problems in terms of the wastes of other kinds that it generates.

4.6 IMPLICATIONS OF THE LAWS OF THERMODYNAMICS

The laws of thermodynamics, which we looked at in Chapter 2, have important implications for economic activity.

4.6.1 Conservation of mass

According to the first law of thermodynamics, energy and matter are conserved – neither can be created or destroyed. Economic activity does not really 'produce' or 'consume' anything – the labelling of these two boxes in Figure 4.1 merely follows the standard usage in economics, which from a physiochemical viewpoint is wrong. What economic activity does is to transform things. Production transforms inputs of resources, capital services and labour services into commodities, and wastes: consumption transforms commodities into satisfactions of needs and desires, and wastes.

In terms of Figure 4.1, it follows from the conservation of matter that the mass of the flow of resources from the environment into the economy is equal to the mass of the flow of wastes from the economy into the environment. The composition of the two flows is, of course, different as the result of the transformations that take place in the economy. But the mass, weight, of the two flows is the same.

This is the simplest way of stating a very important fact about the interdependence of the economy and the environment – using a larger mass of resources necessarily means generating a larger mass of wastes, or conversely that reducing the mass of the waste flow requires reducing the mass of the resource-extraction flow. The statement does, however, require some qualification. It does not necessarily hold exactly, as resources extracted from the environment may spend time in the economy locked up in durable structures.

Consider the extraction of iron ore, processed into steel used in the manufacture of motor cars. Of the mass of iron ore extracted only a small proportion is metal which ends up in the steel – the rest is waste, which gets returned to the environment almost instantaneously. That part of the extracted mass that gets embodied in the structure that is the motor car remains in the economy for many years. The car has a useful lifetime of say 10 years, after which it is left to rot away, we will assume for the moment (see section 4.7 below on recycling). The process of the disintegration of the steel – rusting – and the return to the environment of the iron molecules will take many years to complete – say 50. If the steel had been used in the construction of a building it could have been fixed in the economy for longer – perhaps hundreds of years.

Eventually, the entire mass of all of the iron ore, or whatever, extracted from the environment in any given year will return to the environment. Looking at the extraction flow and the insertion flow in any one year, the masses will not be equal to the extent that part of the extraction flow gets locked up in durable structures in the economy. Recall

$$S_t - S_{t-1} = A_t - O_t$$

as a statement of the standard stock–flow relationship. Now let S refer to the amount of material locked up in durable structures in the economy, A to additions to that stock due to extractions from the environment, and O to subtractions from it in the form of insertions into the environment. If S_t is greater than S_{t-1}, then A_t is greater than O_t and vice versa. If, that is, the stock of durable equipment and commodities in the economy is increasing, insertions will be less than extractions. Insertions equal extractions for an economy where S is constant.

4.6.2 Entropy

As seen in Chapter 2, entropy is a measure of disorder, and the reduction of entropy requires energy. The second law of thermodynamics says that the entropy of a system will increase unless it imports energy from its environment.

The commodities that economic activity 'produces' have lower entropy than the natural resources that are their material origin: the wastes that economic activity inserts into the environment have higher entropy than the natural resources that are their material origin. Think again about iron ore, motor cars and rusting. Motor cars are clearly less disordered than iron ore. Using energy, work is done on iron ore, and other materials, to make steel, on which more work is done to make a motor car. A motor car is a very highly ordered system. Once manufactured, a motor car starts to deteriorate, to become less ordered – the rate at which it deteriorates varies with the amount and nature of use, the conditions of storage, etc. But, in the absence of the replacement of parts of the original motor car system with new parts, deterioration – increasing entropy – is inevitable. At some point, the car is no longer usable as such. Beyond that point it falls apart, disintegrates and the steel rusts away. Given complete disintegration, all of the matter that was once the new motor car remains in existence, but it has been returned to the environment in a highly disordered state. The iron molecules that were embodied for a while in the structure of the car were in a less disordered state as iron ore than they are after the disintegration of the car.

As compared with most of the matter in the natural environment, the materials that humans recognise as natural resources are so recognised precisely because of relatively low entropy. Iron molecules, for example, exist everywhere in the earth's crust, but in very low concentrations. An iron ore deposit is where the concentration has been increased by geological processes. Low entropy is necessary for a lump of matter to qualify as a natural resource for humans, but it is not sufficient. All natural resources are characterised by low entropy, but not all low-entropy matter is a natural resource. Consider poisonous mushrooms – as thermodynamically open systems they exhibit low entropy, but they are certainly not resources.

Looked at in this way, the big-picture view of human economic activity over the long term involves three stages. First, low-entropy matter – natural resources – is extracted from the environment. Second, that matter is transformed so that it satisfies human needs and wants. This transformation requires work and heat, and results in commodities that generally have lower entropy than the resources. Third, high entropy matter – wastes – is put into the environment.

Box 4.1 reports an attempt to put some of the implications of all of this in terms of images of widely different modes of economic behaviour.

Box 4.1 Economics of 'Spaceship Earth'

In a classic paper written in 1966, 'The economics of the coming Spaceship Earth', Kenneth Boulding, one of the early ecological economists, argued that a change in perception is required if mankind is to achieve a sustainable economy. The general perception was, Boulding claimed, that the economy exists in an environment which is an open system. In fact, as he pointed out, the economy exists in an environment which is a closed system.

Boulding called the erroneous perception that of a 'cowboy economy'. The prevailing image which man has of himself and his environment is a state of affairs in which the natural environment is that of a limitless plain, on which a frontier exists that can be pushed back indefinitely. According to the cowboy economy perception, no limits exist on the capacity of the environment to supply or receive energy and material flows – the economy can grow indefinitely. Given this perception, Boulding argued that it would be reasonable to see economic performance in terms of the flows of energy and matter into the economy, and to regard it as desirable that these flows should be as large as possible.

In fact the environment's capacity to supply the economy with energy and matter is limited, as is its capacity to receive wastes from the economy. Boulding's argument was that the general perception needed to change so as to correspond to the reality – rather than perception of the cowboy we need the perception of a spaceman. The environment, earth, should be visualised as a spaceship, without unlimited reserves of anything. Spaceship earth is a thermodynamically closed system, which is the economy and its environment as in Figure 1.1, with a fixed supply of energy inputs from the outside in the form of solar radiation.

On the basis of this perception, it is not, Boulding argued, reasonable to simply identify improved economic performance with increased flows between the environment and the economy. Given the finite availability of material resources and waste disposal facilities, a higher level of movement across the economy–environment boundary means a shorter period over which the environment can support the economy. For the cowboy, there was always somewhere else to go if the local environment currently in use got into trouble. For the spaceman, there is nowhere else to go if the environment gets into trouble, and it makes sense to put off for as long as possible the time when trouble arrives. Boulding argued that, far from looking to emulate the cowboy, the prudent spaceman would seek to minimise, so far as is consistent with survival needs, the flows across the economy–environment boundary.

Writing in 1966, Boulding was arguing that while the cowboy perception had not been a major problem to date, it was now, because of the increased scale of human economic activity. He was arguing that the frontier had vanished, that the world had become full-up, so that there was nowhere else to go for new sources of materials or sinks for wastes. He hoped that the then recent pictures of planet earth taken from spacecraft, and associated developments in space exploration, would promote the replacement of the cowboy by the spaceman as the dominant image of economic man. Almost four decades on, many would argue that his hope is far from being realised.

Source: Boulding (1966).

4.6.3 Energy flow as an approximate measure of environmental impact

Transforming low-entropy natural resources into lower-entropy commodities involves heat and work, and hence energy conversion. The greater the quantity of natural resources extracted from the environment by the economy, the more energy is 'used' in the economy. Also, subject to the qualifications noted above – and another to be noted in the following section of this chapter – the greater the quantity of natural resources extracted from the environment, the greater the quantity of material inserted into it by the economy. It follows that the size of the flow of energy reflects the size of the environmental impact. If more energy is being 'used' in the economy, then more matter is being moved and transformed by the economy, and vice versa.

If one wants to compare the environmental impacts of economies at different points in time, or in different locations, then a simple measure is energy use. Note that what this measures is impact as the aggregate movement and transformation of matter. It does not measure environmental damage. Some movements and transformations do more damage than others, for the same amount of energy used. Dumping mercury in a lake will kill more fish than dumping an energetically equivalent amount of lime, for example. Despite such qualifications, when looking at modern industrial economies, energy use can be regarded as a good first approximation measure of environmental damage. This is because, as well as energy use being necessary for the movement and transformation of materials, in such economies the major source of energy is fossil fuel combustion, which, as discussed in the supplementary material, is itself a major direct source of waste emissions of several kinds.

4.7 RECYCLING

Figure 4.1 actually omitted one form of economic activity that is relevant to waste insertion into the environment by the economy – recycling. Figure 4.5 corrects that, while leaving out some aspects of economy–environment interdependence shown in Figure 4.1. As shown in Figure 4.5, **recycling** involves the diversion of some activity away from production for consumption or investment to the interception of some of the waste stream before it crosses the economy–environment boundary. The intercepted wastes are processed and then reused as inputs to production. Recycling has two consequences. First, the amount of waste inserted into the environment is reduced. Second, to the extent that recycled material is used, the amount of the corresponding resource extracted from the environment is reduced for a given level of input to production. Where the resource is non-renewable, this has the effect of stretching the lifetime of the resource stock.

For non-renewables we wrote

$$S_t = S_{t-1} - E_t$$

where E is the amount extracted and used in production. With U for the amount used in production and R for the amount made available by recycling, this becomes

$$S_t = S_{t-1} - (U_t - R_t)$$

which is

$$S_t = S_{t-1} - U_t + R_t$$

With E now referring to the amount extracted

$$E_t = U_t - R_t$$

and for U given, higher R means lower E.

The extent to which recycling is possible varies across resources, products and waste streams. At one extreme is the use of fossil fuels as an energy source, where recycling after combustion is simply impossible – the energy content can be used only once. At the other extreme is the use of ferrous metals in durable structures where a high proportion of the iron content of, for example, a motor car can be recovered. Intermediate cases are where the materials into which extracted resources are transformed are dispersed and dissipated in use – examples would be lubricants made from oil, paints made from oil and/or minerals, etc. In some of these cases, for example lubricants, recycling is possible in principle but is not

Figure 4.5
Recycling.

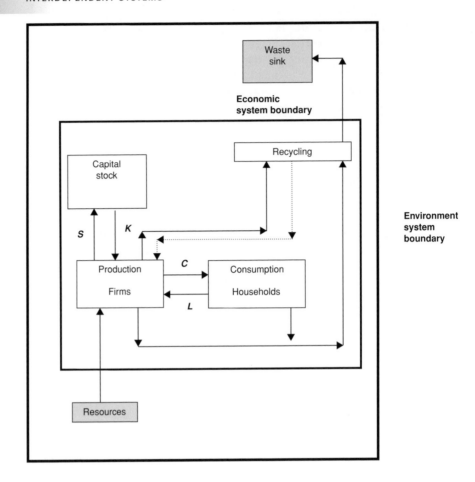

undertaken in practice. The extent to which recycling actually takes place depends on the extent to which it is possible, and on the amount of cost and effort that it involves as compared with the amount involved in extracting and using the corresponding virgin resource. The 'cost and effort' of recycling relative to that involved in the use of virgin resources is affected by legislation, as will be discussed later in the book (see Chapter 11).

Recycling involves diverting waste flows from the environment to economic production. Some waste flows are intercepted before reaching the environment, but are modified and then inserted into the environment, rather than being redirected to become an input to production. This is generally referred to as **waste treatment**, and the objective is to reduce the environmental impact of the waste. A widespread example, in developed industrial economies, is the treatment of human sewage before it is released into water bodies so as to reduce the risks to human health. The basic step in the treatment process is to allow the liquid sewage effluent to stand as still water in tanks so that the sludge can settle out. After removing the relatively clean water from the tank – possibly for further treatment before discharge into the water body – the sludge is dried out and compressed. The usual practice is then either to burn this material, or to dispose of it in landfill. Sometimes, after further treatment, the sludge is used to condition agricultural soils, which is partial recycling.

4.8 AMENITY SERVICES

Figure 4.1 shows amenity services as the third class of service that the natural environment provides to economic activity. There is an arrow from the Amenities box in the natural environment direct to consumption by individuals in the economy. The flow is shown as direct from the environment to individuals to make the point that for the provision of this kind of service, it is not necessary to combine an environmental input with an economic input. Amenity services from the environment can, that is, be consumed direct without being first transformed by productive activity – think of the pleasure derived from walking on a hillside on a fine evening to watch the sun go down. While it is true that transformation by productive activity prior to consumption is not an essential feature of the provision of environmental amenity services, it is also true that in modern industrial societies much of the consumption of such services does involve the joint consumption of commodities produced in the economy. For example, our walker admiring the sunset probably lives in an urban area and has travelled to the hillside in a motor vehicle. As another example, consider snorkelling so as to observe the flora and fauna associated with a coral reef – the consumer of the coral reef's amenity services is using manufactured equipment, and was probably transported many thousands of miles by air transport to a reef resort where he stays in a hotel and consumes imported food, drink and electricity.

The other important point about the consumption of amenity services provided by features of the natural environment is that it may be, and often is, a non-consumptive process. Observing geological features, water bodies, flora and fauna delivers satisfactions but does not entail any reduction in stocks existing in the environment. Environmental amenity service-consumption is different from the use of the resource-input and waste-sink services in that it does not necessarily involve any direct physiochemical impact. Admiring a beautiful landscape, or observing an animal, does not in and of itself give rise to any environmental impact, though it has to be noted that activities that may be associated with such acts in modern societies – travel, the construction of viewing facilities, etc. – do have impacts. Some amenity-consumption activities do directly entail impact – hunting wildlife as a form of recreation, for example.

The range of amenity services provided by the natural environment is wide, and of varied character. A clear and comprehensive definition is difficult, though the basic point is clear enough. For modern industrial-society humans we are looking at what might be called nature-based recreational activity, that is the use of leisure time in pursuit of pleasure and stimulation based mainly on features of the natural environment (where the consumption of produced commodities might be involved). Reflection on this, rough, definition will indicate that the provision of amenity services is a very important feature of economy–environment interdependence. It is, however, in the nature of the case that it is relatively difficult to fully quantify what is involved – sunset observations are not recorded in the way that, for example, oil extraction is. However, we do know, for example, that nature-based tourism accounts for about 20 per cent of all tourism, and is the fastest growing part of the industry. Some relevant data are noted in the supplementary material on the website.

The biologist E. O. Wilson developed the biophilia hypothesis, according to which, on account of our evolutionary background, human well-being is promoted by contact with nature. Wilson holds that humans have an innate sensitivity to and need for contact with other living things. There are numerous studies that show that contact with the natural world can benefit mental and physical health. For example, a comparison of post-operative patients whose rooms looked at either trees or a brick wall found that the former stayed in hospital for significantly less time, needed less strong medication, and had fewer negative comments in their nurses' notes. Studies of pet owners have found evidence of lower blood pressure than in non-pet owners, and of fewer visits to the doctor.

4.8.1 Sustainable amenity service consumption

Figure 4.6 shows some aspects of the recreational exploitation of the natural environment. Q_t stands for the quality of the recreational experiences during period t, assumed to be the same for all recreationalists using the particular environmental site – a national park say – being considered. V_t stands for the number of visitors during period t. Figure 4.6(a) shows the relationship between Q_t and V_t. Up to V^*, increases in the number of visitors have no effect on the quality of the recreational experience, whereas for V_t greater than V^* quality falls as numbers increase. There are two ways in which such a threshold effect can arise – crowding and damage. The first is where the quality of the recreational experience for any one person falls as the number of visitors increases once the number of visitors reaches a certain level, V^* in Figure 4.6(a). This crowding effect is independent of any damage that recreationalists might do to the attractive features of the environment, and relates simply to the presence of other visitors. Visitors, and the facilities provided for them, do cause damage to the environment. It is frequently assumed that the relationship is as shown in Figure 4.6(a), in that damage is insignificant up to a threshold then increases with visitor numbers. Examples of damage are vegetation trampling and effects on animals' breeding behaviour. There is, of course, no reason why the threshold number of visitors should be the same for crowding effects and for damage effects, or why the quality–numbers relationship should be the same for crowding and damage once the threshold is passed. Figure 4.6(a) is drawn for a common relationship for both crowding and damage so as to keep the presentation simple. For some sites V^* could be zero – this would be the case if either the crowding or the damage threshold were zero.

Figure 4.6(b) shows how visitor numbers respond to changes in the quality of the recreational experience. The vertical axis measures the deterrent effect of declining quality in the current period, and the horizontal axis measures quality in the previous period. The idea is that visits in this period are influenced by the reported experience of quality of those who have just visited. On the vertical axis, V_t^{**} is what visits would have been if quality were at Q^*, so $(V_t^{**} - V_t)$ is the number of visitors who do not come because of reported quality. On the horizontal axis, actual

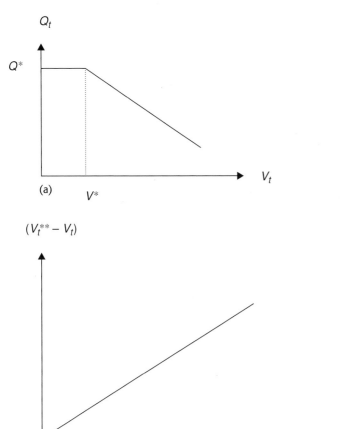

Figure 4.6
Recreational
use
relationships.

quality in period $t - 1$ declines moving to the right – the difference between Q_{t-1} and Q^* gets bigger. The visitor shortfall, compared with what it would have been for undiminished quality, increases as the reduction in quality increases.

If V_t is always at or below V^*, Q_t remains at Q^*, and future visitor numbers are unaffected. However, once visitor numbers exceed V^*, quality is affected, Q_{t-1} falls below Q^*, and visitor numbers are reduced below what they would otherwise have been. V^* identifies the maximum sustainable visitor rate for a site used for nature-based recreation, analogous to the maximum sustainable yield for a renewable resource, and visitor rates at or below V^* are sustainable, whereas those above it are not. The features of the environment that are the basis for amenity services can be over-used, but given that they are not, they can go on providing a constant level of service indefinitely. They are, in this respect, like stocks of renewable resources.

4.8.2 *Ex situ* consumption of amenity services

Nature-based recreation as discussed above involves the recreationalist visiting some site in the natural environment. The consumption is *in situ*. For completeness we need to note that in modern industrial societies environmental amenity services can also be, and in fact are, consumed *ex situ*. The most obvious manifestations of such consumption are TV shows about nature and wildlife, which are watched by millions of people. Zoos and exotic gardens are popular visitor attractions, and many people grow plants as a leisure activity. Books and magazines about nature and wildlife are also widely read.

4.9 LIFE SUPPORT SERVICES

As discussed thus far, the environment provides inputs to production by firms, serves as sink for the wastes arising in production by firms and consumption on the part of individuals, and is the source of amenity services for individuals. Figure 4.1 also shows a fourth box in the environment, and a flow from it across the boundary between the environment and the economy. The fourth class of environmental service distinguished in Figure 4.1 is 'Life support services' – the services that make human life, and hence economic activity, possible. These services include: the purification of our air and water; the stabilisation, and moderation, of the climate; nutrient cycling; the pollination of plants. All of the other plants and animals that we use as natural resources, which participate in waste assimilation, and which contribute to the provision of amenity services, also depend on these life support services.

Human beings are an animal species. As discussed in Chapter 2, all living animals are open systems requiring inputs of fresh water, oxygen, energy and nutrients. As well as providing such inputs, any animal's environment must provide the ambient conditions for which it is adapted by evolution, in terms of temperature, atmospheric pressure and the like. As compared with many other animal species, the range of environmental conditions that human physiology can tolerate is relatively wide. Also, cultural evolution has provided our species with many technological innovations – clothing, fire, shelters of various kinds – which extend still further the range of conditions within which members of the species can exist.

Currently, the biosphere functions in such a way that conditions suitable for human life obtain over a large proportion of the land surface of the planet, even without our cultural adaptations. Given those cultural adaptations, there is little of the planet's land surface (the polar regions, some desert areas) that cannot support human life. The human life-supporting conditions are maintained by the solar radiation balance, the functioning of the nutrient and hydrological cycles, and by the functioning of ecosystems. In its current overall operation, the biosphere provides the services necessary for the existence of human life. It did not always operate to maintain the conditions necessary for human life, and it will not continue to do so for ever into the future, though it might do so for a very long time – a few billion years.

Technological innovation means that life support services can now be provided independently of the functioning of the biosphere, as demonstrated most sharply in manned space flight. However, this has only been done, thus far, on a very small scale, whereas the scale of the provision by the biosphere is huge – the global population is now about six billion people, almost everyone of whom depends on the biosphere to maintain the conditions for her/his life.

Clearly, the life support services provided to economic activity by the natural environment are very important. Without them there would be no economic activity. Changes in any element of the solar radiation balance, the functioning of the nutrient and hydrological cycles, or the functioning of ecosystems could lead to changes in the provision of life support services with serious adverse implications for human interests. We will be looking at two particular instances of this – climate change and biodiversity loss – in the last two chapters of the book.

4.10 INTERACTIONS

In the preceding sections of this chapter we have seen that the ways in which economic activity depends upon, and affects, the natural environment are many and complex. The complexity of economy–environment interdependence is increased by the fact that the four classes of environmental service that we have distinguished – resource base, waste sink, amenity base and life support system – interact with one another. This is shown in Figure 4.7 by having the four boxes representing the origins in the environment of the four classes of service intersecting with one another. Also, the arrows representing the flows of energy between the environment and its own environment are shown as passing through these four boxes. This is to show that the services that the environment provides to the economy are affected by, and affect, the balance of these energy flows.

A comprehensive account of all of the interactions between services provided to the economy by the environment would itself be a long book. Here we will use three examples to illustrate what is involved. Another illustration is provided in the supplementary material on the website in the section on the economic services derived from an old-growth forest.

4.10.1 A river estuary

Consider a hypothetical but realistic river estuary. It serves as resource base for the local economy in that a commercial fishery operates in it. It serves as waste sink in that urban sewage is discharged into it. It serves as amenity base in that it is used for recreational purposes such as swimming and boating. It contributes to life support functions in so far as it is a breeding ground for marine species which are not commercially exploited, but which play a role in the operation of the regional marine ecosystem. At low rates of sewage discharge all four functions can coexist. If, however, the rate of sewage discharge exceeds the rate at which the estuary can decompose the sewage, then not only does a pollution problem emerge, but the other estuarine functions are impaired. Pollution will interfere with the reproductive capacity of the commercially exploited fish stocks, and may lead to the extinction of the fishery. This does not necessarily mean its biological extinction. The fishery may be closed on the grounds of the danger to public health. Pollution will reduce the capacity of the estuary to support recreational activity, and in some respects, such as swimming, may drive it to zero. Pollution will also impact on the non-commercial marine species, and may lead to their extinction with implications for regional marine ecosystem function.

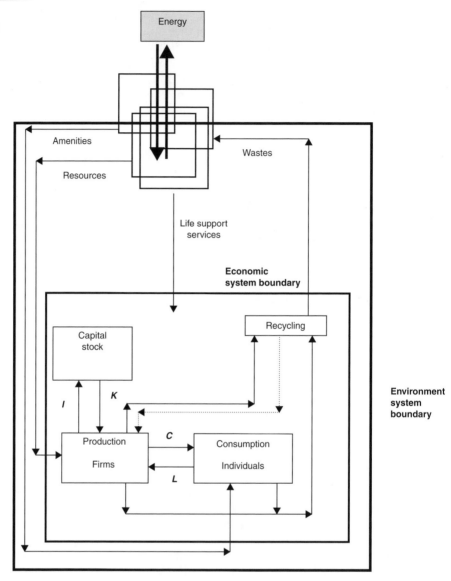

Figure 4.7
Environmental
service
interactions.

4.10.2 Resource quality, energy use and waste generation

The particular deposits of a mineral resource vary in quality as far as their use by the economy is concerned. Economic quality is measured by the cost of turning stuff in the ground into an input to production – the cost, for example, of turning bauxite *in situ* into aluminium. This cost depends on the location of the deposit, the ease with which it can be worked, and the grade of the ore. Usually, lower-cost deposits are worked before higher-cost. Moving from a lower- to a higher-cost deposit means one or more of: more transport, more digging, more processing. Each of these requires more energy and the last two mean more waste per unit of usable input to production. As the depletion of the mineral in question proceeds, that is, the general tendency will be for there to be more energy use and more waste generation per unit of usable input to production. The problem of mineral depletion necessarily, because of the laws of thermodynamics, entails a problem of increasing waste generation. It also entails increasing energy use per unit of usable input to production.

This does not apply to only mineral deposits. It also applies to the major form of renewable resource harvesting – ocean fishing. Worldwide, fishing boats are going further to find fish. It also applies to the major source of the energy used in mineral extraction and processing, and in fishing, the fossil fuels, especially oil and gas. Over time, the energy cost – in terms of finding, bringing to the surface and transporting to the point of use – of delivering usable energy based on fossil fuels shows a tendency to increase.

4.10.3 The enhanced greenhouse effect

As noted in Chapter 2, and to be discussed more fully in Chapter 13, the concentration of greenhouse gases in the atmosphere determines the balance between the incoming and outgoing energy flows shown in Figure 4.7, and hence affects how warm the earth is. In the last 200 years the concentrations of these gases have been increasing due to anthropogenic (due to human activity) emissions. If present trends continue, anthropogenic emissions will continue to increase, and most competent scientists consequently anticipate the warming of the earth – this is known as 'the enhanced greenhouse effect'. As noted above, carbon dioxide is the most important of the greenhouse gases, and the major contributor to anthropogenic carbon dioxide emissions is fossil fuel combustion.

Here is the first interaction between environmental services. Resource extraction and use, fossil fuel combustion, necessarily leads to waste insertion, emissions of greenhouse gases. The rate of use and insertion is such that the global climate system is affected. While the details are uncertain, particularly in regard to the magnitudes involved, it is clear that global warming would affect all of the classes of environmental services. This is the second, multi-faceted, interaction between environmental services, some aspects of which we now briefly outline. More detail is provided in Chapter 13.

In terms of the availability of resources, there would, first, be losses of agricultural and urban land in low-lying coastal areas due to sea-level rise. Changes in regional climates would mean changes in the crops that could be grown there. Some crops and wild species in some areas would grow faster with higher temperatures and carbon dioxide concentrations. Others would grow more slowly. The geographical patterns of availability of renewable resources and agricultural crops would change.

Changes would also occur in regard to the waste sink function. To take just one example, the assimilative capacity of a river for organic sewage decreases as water temperature increases. On the other hand, it is expected that higher temperatures would generally be accompanied by increased rainfall, which would suggest greater rates of stream flow and hence increased assimilative capacity in river systems. But again, it is expected that while average rainfall would increase this would in many areas be accompanied by greater variability over time. Increased average rainfall is not inconsistent with increased incidence of periods without rain. To the extent that this occurred there would be an increased temporal variability in the assimilative capacity of a river.

In regard to amenity services, in Scotland the viability of two skiing resorts is already highly questionable, and skiing opportunities are expected to be greatly reduced in many areas of the world where they are currently economically important. Coral dieback is already a major problem in some parts of the world, and is expected to increase with global warming, with serious affects on tourist business in the affected areas.

For some commentators, it is in the area of what are here called life support services that the possible implications of global warming are seen as most worrying. This worry arises via the prospects for biodiversity, and hence the functioning of ecosystems, in relation to the anticipated rate of climate change over the next century. The anticipated rate is greater than is thought to have occurred in the last 10,000 years, and high by the standards of much longer periods of history. Most species of flora have quite narrow ranges of climatic tolerance. Adaptation to climate change would involve genetic evolution and/or migration. The rates at which either of these processes can occur is slow relative to that anticipated for climate change, and the prospect envisaged is of the extinction of many species of flora. This would, in turn, have implications for species of fauna which have evolved to be dependent on particular species of flora. Reductions in biodiversity resulting from climate change would, in turn, have implications for amenity services – the natural recreational facilities available in particular areas would change.

4.11 THREATS TO SUSTAINABILITY

In Chapter 1 we said that sustainability is:

maintaining the capacity of the joint economy–environment system to continue to satisfy the needs and desires of humans for a long time into the future.

In the final section of this chapter we use the conceptual framework that it has developed to consider the ways in which economy–environment interdependence could threaten that capacity. This introduces many of the issues that we will be returning to in the rest of the book, so we can be fairly brief here.

4.11.1 Resource depletion

The most obvious kind of threat to the economic prospects facing future humans is the current use of non-renewable natural resources as inputs to production. Recall

$$S_t = S_{t-1} - E_t$$

for a non-renewable resource and it is clear that the larger is E_t, the smaller is S_t for given S_{t-1}. There is a trade-off between use now and in the future – using more of a non-renewable resource now means that there is less available for future use.

This kind of trade-off does not exist for flow resources.

The case of renewable resources is intermediate. It is possible to exploit them in such a way that S_t is equal to S_{t-1}, by taking a sustainable harvest which is equal in size to natural growth. But, if the amount extracted is greater than natural growth, S_t will be less than S_{t-1}.

In discussing Figure 4.6 we noted that the environmental features that support amenity services can be effectively similar to renewable natural resources – there are sustainable levels of visitation, and higher levels of use now decrease the future ability to deliver the service.

4.11.2 Waste accumulation

One of the implications of the laws of thermodynamics is that the flipside of resource extraction is waste insertion into the environment. In section 4.5 we looked at the accumulation in the environment of waste emissions and we defined pollution as any change in the environment due to waste emission that is harmful to any living organism. Some forms of pollution are directly harmful to human health, so persistent pollution reduces the capacity of the joint economy–environment system to satisfy the needs and desires of humans in the future, and is a direct threat to sustainability. Some other organisms are renewable resources, or are necessary for the existence of renewable resources, and pollution that harms such organisms threatens sustainability via the impact on renewable resource availability. Many species of plants and animals are involved in the delivery of amenity and life support services, and pollution which affects these organisms affects the delivery of those services.

4.11.3 Loss of resilience

In Chapter 2 we introduced the concept of ecosystem resilience. A resilient system is one that, when subjected to some shock, continues to exist and to function in the same essential ways. The functioning of ecosystems is what delivers many of the services that the environment provides to the economy. That functioning is involved in all of the flows in Figure 4.1 except flow resources and non-renewable stock resources. Things that promote ecosystem resilience promote sustainability, things that threaten ecosystem resilience threaten sustainability. As was noted when discussing resilience in Chapter 2, the determinants of resilience are not fully understood – apart from anything else, an ecosystem may be resilient with respect to one kind of shock, but not with respect to another kind. However, we did note that there appears to be agreement that reductions in biodiversity – loss of populations – in an ecosystem should be considered as threats to resilience.

It follows that biodiversity loss should be considered a threat to sustainability. We will be discussing biodiversity loss and its causes at length in Chapter 14. Here we can note that both resource extraction and waste accumulation are involved. Both, that is, threaten sustainability in terms of their implications for ecosystems resilience as well as in the particular ways noted in the previous two sub-sections here.

4.11.4 Responses

We have enumerated the ways in which economy–environment interdependence is the origin of threats to sustainability. We have *not* said that economy–environment interdependence means that sustainability is unattainable. We have *not* said, for example, that the depletion of stocks of non-renewable resources necessarily means that future generations will be worse-off because they are able to produce less. What *is* true is that economy–environment interdependence gives rise to problems to which human culture must adapt if sustainability is to be achieved – realising sustainability requires that the threats are responded to appropriately. It *may be* that human culture is incapable of evolving so as to make the necessary adaptations.

There are some ways in which Figure 4.1, in the interests of simplicity and getting the basic idea across, obscures some matters relating to the existence of possible responses to the threats that have been identified. One was rectified in Figure 4.5 – recycling. The most obvious threat to sustainability is non-renewable resource depletion. One possible response in regard to any particular resource is to recycle the wastes arising from its use. This also responds to the waste accumulation and pollution threat. The possibilities for recycling vary across resources – for the fossil fuels used as energy sources they are zero.

In Figure 4.1, and the following figures based on it, there is just one line for each service flow. In fact, and as the discussions in preceding sections have noted or implied, each service flow has many components – there are many kinds of natural resources, of wastes, of amenity services, of life support services. This raises the possibility of adaptation by switching between components of any given flow type – by making substitutions. In terms of resources, for example, it may be possible to switch from one mineral to another in many uses as the former is depleted – bauxite for copper is an historical example. Or it may be possible to substitute a renewable for a non-renewable – wood for fossil fuels, say. Or it may be possible to substitute a flow resource for a non-renewable – solar power for fossil fuels, for example.

Similarly in regard to wastes, in many cases processing can be done so as to transform a more to a less harmful waste before return to the environment. Substitutions as between natural resources will entail different waste streams.

The fact that a substitution that addresses a threat to sustainability is possible does not necessarily mean that it will happen so as to offset the threat in any given case. Whether or not a substitution that is feasible in the light of the laws of nature actually takes place or not is determined in the economy by cultural evolution. Basically it is necessary that it is known about and that the incentives for its adoption are in place. One of the questions that we will be concerned with in Part II, especially in Chapter 9, is whether market institutions can drive the responses that would promote sustainability in the light of threats originating in economy–environment interdependence. Part III looks at the role of government – it turns out that markets alone are not sufficient.

The substitutions just mentioned are of one environmental service flow for another. There is another kind of substitution that is relevant to responding to threats to sustainability that is not shown in Figure 4.1. That is the substitution of the services of reproducible capital for environmental service flows, sometimes referred to as substitution of man-made for natural capital. Examples would be:

- resource inputs – installing better control systems in a building so as to reduce energy consumption;
- waste flows – building treatment plants.

The role of this kind of substitution is examined in Chapter 7.

4.11.5 The global perspective

In section 4.3.5 we noted that Figure 4.1 is drawn for a closed economy, one that does not trade with other economies. One reason given there for doing this was that it made for a clearer picture. The other was that the global economy is a closed economy, and that it is the global economy that is relevant when considering sustainability, and sustainable development. We now briefly elaborate on this second point.

As noted, the most obvious threat to sustainability is the depletion of non-renewable natural resources necessary for production. For the economy of Figure 4.1, the resources box in the environment is the only place to get such inputs from. For one economy trading with other economies, running down resource stocks located within its national territory is a different order of problem – it can import needed inputs, or what the inputs are used to produce, from other economies. The world as a whole cannot, at present and for the foreseeable future anyway, import natural resources from another planet.

Second, as noted in Chapter 1, sustainable development is about dealing with poverty without undermining sustainability. Poverty is also a global issue. There is poverty within national economies where average income is high, such as those of Europe and North America. But, most of the world's really poor people live in countries in Africa and Asia. Thinking about poverty alleviation solely in terms of what goes on in one national economy fails to address the big problem.

Third, the major threats to sustainability, and hence to sustainable development, are global in nature. The climate in every part of the world, for example, depends on the concentrations of various gases in the global atmosphere. One such gas is carbon dioxide. A given amount of carbon dioxide released into the atmosphere has the same effect on the global concentration, irrespective of where in the world the release takes place. The climate of India is affected by carbon dioxide emissions in the USA, and vice versa. The enhanced greenhouse effect cannot be dealt with by one nation, or even a group of nations such as the EU, acting alone. Environmental and poverty problems are linked at the global level – poor countries are less able and less willing to act for the global environment. We will be looking at this linkage in Chapter 13 on climate change, and Chapter 14 on biodiversity loss.

For these reasons, the perspective of ecological economics is global rather than national, and hence Figure 4.1 is drawn for the global economy, which is, in terms of the economics terminology, a closed economy. Generally in what follows we will have in mind a closed, global, economy. We will make it clear when the discussion concerns an open, national, economy.

SUMMARY

This chapter has set out a framework for thinking about the interdependence of the economy and the natural environment, and the implications arising for sustainability. We have looked at the four classes of services that the environment provides to the economy – resource inputs, waste sinks, amenities and life supports – and at the way that they interact with one another. If the economy extracts more resources from the environment, it necessarily inserts more wastes into it. Waste insertions at high rates have the potential to, and often actually do, reduce the environment's ability to provide renewable resource inputs, to provide amenity services and to provide life support services.

KEYWORDS

Biomagnification (p. 100): the process by which the concentration of a toxin in animal tissue increases at higher levels of the food chain.

Capital stock (p. 91): the result of past investment in the form of durable equipment, knowledge and institutions which contribute to current production.

Closed economy (p. 93): one that does not trade with other economies.

Consumption (p. 90): the use by individuals of goods and services to satisfy their needs and desires.

Durable capital (p. 91): the collection of durable tools, machinery, buildings, vehicles, roads and the like used in production.

Flow resources (p. 94): where the amount used today has no implications for the amount that could be used in the future.

Human capital (p. 91): the stock of accumulated knowledge and skills available to the economy.

Human-made capital (p. 92): the totality of durable, human, intellectual and social capital, also known as reproducible capital.

Intellectual capital (p. 92): the accumulated knowledge and skills available to the economy that reside in books and other cultural artefacts such as computer memories.

Investment (p. 91): that part of production added to the capital stock rather than consumed.

Maximum sustainable harvest (p. 97): the largest harvest of a resource that can be taken without reducing the size of the stock.

Natural capital (p. 92): the totality of the stocks existing in the environment that deliver services to the economy.

Non-renewable resources (p. 97): stock resources for which growth is always zero.

Open economy (p. 93): one that trades with other economies.

Pollution (p. 98): a chemical or physical change in the environment due to waste emission that is harmful to any living organism.

Production (p. 90): the use of labour, capital and resources to provide means to the satisfaction of needs and wants.

Recycling (p. 105): the interception of some of the waste stream before it crosses the economy–environment boundary and its reuse in production.

Renewable resources (p. 95): biotic populations.

Reproducible capital (p. 92): see human-made capital.

Social capital (p. 92): the set of institutions and customs which organise economic activity.

Stock resources (p. 94): where the amount used today does have implications for future availability.

Synergy (p. 100): the process whereby the joint effect of two pollutants is greater than the sum of their separate effects.

Threshold effect (p. 101): a discontinuous step change in a dose–response relationship.

Waste (p. 98): an unwanted by-product of economic activity.

Waste treatment (p. 106): the modification of waste before its discharge into the environment so as to reduce the damage arising.

FURTHER READING

There is no uniquely correct way to classify the services that the environment provides to the economy. Barbier *et al.* (1994), in Table 3.1, provide a four-way classification of what they call the 'life support functions of ecosystems' into regulation, production, carrier and information functions. Costanza *et al.* (1997) distinguish 17 classes of 'ecosystem service'. Nicholas Georgescu-Roegen is mainly responsible for developing the implications of thermodynamics for economic activity. His main work, Georgescu-Roegen (1971), is a long and difficult read: Georgescu-Roegen (1976) is shorter and easier. Dragan and Demetrescu (1991) covers the life and work, in other areas of economics as well as the thermodynamics of economic activity, of Georgescu-Roegen. Faber *et al.* (1996) develops conceptual foundations for ecological economics, building, in part, on Georgescu-Roegen's work. Hall *et al.* (1986) looks at economic activity using an energetic perspective for the conceptual framework. References to some more models of economy–environment interdependence will be provided in Chapter 7.

If you consult a standard introductory, neoclassical, economics text – such as Mankiw* (2001) or Begg *et al.** (2000), for example – you will find that the basic conceptual framework presented for economic analysis makes no reference at all to the natural environment. The basic picture presented is just what is inside the Economic System box of Figure 4.1. To the extent that such books deal with economy–environment interdependence it is as something of an afterthought, a matter of detail.

The supplement to this chapter on the book's companion website gives more information about and data on the various dimensions of economy–environment interdependence, and further references, and website links, will be found there.

Lomborg* (2001) is a useful point of entry to the vast array of statistical materials on, and analysis of, economic extractions from and insertions to the environment, and the state of the environment. The appearance of Lomborg's book generated a great deal of interest and controversy, as he argues that what the statistics show is that those 'environmentalists' who claim that the ability of the environment to support economic activity and human welfare is decreasing are, overall, quite wrong. Many of those environmentalists have, in turn, claimed that Lomborg is both wrong and irresponsible. Basically, the problem with his work is that it lacks any conceptual framework, so that each environmental problem is treated in isolation and interactions are ignored. Lomborg has a website, address given below, that provides links to various contributions to the controversy.

On the biophilia hypothesis see Wilson (1993). Pretty *et al.* (2003) is the source for the examples cited in the chapter on the beneficial effects of contact with plants and animals. The characteristics and extent of nature-based tourism, also known as 'ecotourism', are discussed in Buckley (2000), Hawkins and Lamoureux (2001), Hunter and Green (1995) and Valentine (1992).

DISCUSSION QUESTIONS

1. Many neoclassical economists would accept that Figure 4.1 is an ultimately correct representation of the nature of economic activity, but would justify the fact that they do not teach their students about it on the grounds that it is not necessary for an economist in a modern society to know about it. Is this correct?

2. In the terminology of Box 4.1, does your lifestyle correspond to that of a cowboy or a spaceman?

EXERCISES

1. Simulate the growth of the accumulated waste stock according to

$$S_t = S_{t-1} + W_t - (d \times S_{t-1})$$

for d taking the values 0, 0.25, 0.5, 0.75 and 1, where W_t is always 1. Take the intitial stock size to be 0. If the stock size is constant over time, what is the relationship between its constant size and the constant rate of flow of W?

2. The same basic model as in Exercise 4.1 can be used to look at the matter of the relative sizes of environmental extractions and insertions in a growing economy (sub-section 4.6.1). Now let S refer to the amount of material contained in durable structures in the economy, so that

$$S_t = S_{t-1} + E_t - I_t$$

where E is extractions from and I is insertions into the environment. If insertions are proportional to the existing stock of stuff in the economy, with a constant rate of decay d, and extractions grow at the rate g, simulate $(E_t - I_t)$ for $g = 0.025$ and $d = 0.05$. What happens if E is constant?

3. Simulate the recycling model from section 4.7 with R_t, the amount recycled, equal to 0.3 and 0.7 times the amount used in the previous period. Use an initial stock size of 100 and amount used of 1, with use growing at 2.5 per cent. After how many periods is the stock exhausted in each case? Would 100 per cent recycling prevent the eventual exhaustion of the stock?

4. The model of amenity service consumption depicted in Figure 4.6, and dis-
    cussed in sub-section 4.8.1, consists of the relationships

$$Q_t = Q^* \text{ for } V_t \leq V^*, \text{ otherwise } Q_t = Q^* - \alpha V_t$$

and

$$V_t = V_t^{**} - \beta(Q^* - Q_{t-1})$$

Simulate this model for $V^* = 200$, $Q^* = 1000$, V^{**} growing at 2.5 per cent,
$\alpha = 0.5$ and $\beta = 0.2$. Use initial values of 100 for V and V^{**}, and of 1,000 for
the environmental quality index Q. What happens if V^{**} stops growing after
it has grown past V^*?

PART II
ECONOMIC ACTIVITY

Economic activity is directed toward the satisfaction of human needs and desires. Some of the ways that have been developed for recording and analysing that activity are introduced in Chapter 5. One measure is national income, the limitations of which are discussed in Chapter 5. Increasing national income per head is what is known as economic growth, which is generally seen as a very good thing. Chapter 6 looks at what causes economic growth, and how it relates to the satisfaction of human needs and desires. Chapter 7 looks at economic growth in the light of economy–environment interdependence. The market is the dominant mode of organisation in modern economies, and Chapter 8 explains how market exchange can assist in satisfying human needs and desires, and provides some tools for studying the workings of markets. Finally, Chapter 9 is about markets in relation to the environment and sustainability. It establishes that markets themselves cannot be relied on to deliver sustainability.

5

Economic accounting

In this chapter you will:

- Learn about input–output accounting and national income accounting, and how they are related;
- See how production uses natural resources indirectly as well as directly;
- Explore the extent to which Gross Domestic Product differences truly reflect differences in economic performance;
- Be introduced to proposals for modifying national income accounting to reflect environmental costs.

In this chapter we will first look at a system of economic accounting – input–output accounting – that records the ways in which industries trade with one another, as well as produce for consumption and investment. Then we will consider national income accounting, in which, inter-industry trade is netted out. National income accounting is where numbers for GDP, Gross Domestic Product, and related concepts such as GNP, Gross National Product, come from. As we shall see, while many commentators treat GDP as the principal indicator of an economy's performance, it is, at best, rather a crude indicator.

5.1 INPUT–OUTPUT ACCOUNTING

Input–output accounts describe the structure of an economy in terms of the inputs to its various industry sectors and the disposition of the outputs from those sectors. They are the most comprehensive economic accounts at the level of the whole economy. They are particularly useful in looking at the economy's extractions from and insertions into the natural environment. In order to keep things simple, we will explain the essentials of input–output accounting for an economy that does not trade with any other economy, and in which there is no government economic activity.

5.1.1 The basic accounts

The basic unit of accounting is the industry – input–output accounting is sometimes referred to as 'inter-industry' accounting. An **industry**, sometimes known as a sector,

Table 5.1 Input–output transactions table, $ million

Purchases from	Sales to			
	Agriculture	Manufacturing	Final demand	Total output
Agriculture	0	200	800	1000
Manufacturing	600	0	1400	2000
Primary inputs Wages and salaries	300	1200		
Other factor payments	100	600		
Total input	1000	2000		

is a collection of firms all producing a single commodity. Firms use two sorts of input. **Intermediate inputs** are goods and services bought from other firms and used up in current production. **Primary inputs** are services bought from individuals: these services are sometimes known as factors of production, and the payments for them by firms to individuals are known then as **factor payments**. Firms are owned by individuals.

There are four classes of factor payment. Wages and salaries are payments for labour services. Interest is paid on borrowings. Rent is paid for the use of equipment, buildings and land. Profits are the residual that accrues to the owners of a firm after its sales receipts have been used to pay for intermediate inputs, wages and salaries, interest and rent. Profits are regarded as a payment for the factor of production known as entrepreneurship, which is the function of organising and risk-taking.

The first step in input–output accounting is the compilation of data about the receipts and expenditures of every industry in the economy into a **transactions table**. Table 5.1 is such a table for an imaginary economy, constructed so as to explain the essentials of input–output accounting as simply as possible. The economy to which Table 5.1 relates for some particular year, let us say 2000, has just two industry sectors, Agriculture and Manufacturing. Reading across the rows gives the breakdown of a sector's total sales. It is conventional in input–output accounting to subtract any use by an industry of its own output from its gross output and to report its output net, showing the industry as not using any of its own output. Agriculture, for example, does actually use some of its output itself – cereals are fed to animals, for example. But, as in Table 5.1, the transactions table does not explicitly show such intra-industry trade – the value of cereals produced but used in Agriculture as animal feed is subtracted from Agriculture's total sales before that total is recorded in the table. Given this convention, all intra-industry sales are shown as zero. We will use a capital when referring to an industry and the lower case when referring to a commodity – Agriculture produces agriculture.

In Table 5.1, the total, net, output of Agriculture is $1,000 \times 10^6$, of which, as shown in the Agriculture row, 200×10^6 is sold in inter-industry transactions to the manufacturing industry. From now on, in order to keep the discussion simple, we shall conduct it in terms of units that are millions of dollars. Then the remaining 800 units of Agriculture's output is sold to the sector called **Final demand**.

This terminology simply indicates that purchases by this sector are not for the purpose of use in production. The purchase of agricultural output by Manufacturing is for use as inputs in producing manufacturing output – such purchases are part of what is known as **Intermediate demand**, which term refers to inter-industry transactions. Purchases by the

Table 5.2 Input–output coefficient table

	Agriculture	Manufacturing
Agriculture	0	0.1
Manufacturing	0.6	0
W and S	0.3	0.6
OFP	0.1	0.3

Final demand sector comprise those by individuals for consumption, by firms for investment, by government, and by foreigners. In the economy to which Table 5.1 relates, there is no government and no foreign trade, and it will also help to keep things clear if we also assume no investment. In that case, all final demand purchases are for consumption and we will often refer to them as such. Reading across the Manufacturing row, we see that it has inter-industry sales of 600 and sales to Final demand, consumption, of 1,400.

The columns in a transactions table refer to purchases of inputs to production by industries. These comprise purchases of intermediate commodities from other industries, and purchases of primary inputs. In Table 5.1 these are denoted as Wages and salaries and Other factor payments, for the sum of interest, rent and profits. Agriculture purchases 400 units of primary inputs. Note that the sum of Agriculture's purchases of intermediate commodities and primary inputs is exactly the same as the sum of its sales of intermediate commodities and its sales to individuals (Final demand) – its expenditures are equal to its receipts. The same is true for Manufacturing.

This must always be true for every sector in a transactions table for input–output accounting. Expenditures equal to receipts is an accounting identity which must always hold. As explained above, firms do not retain any money – all the money that comes into a firm and is not used to buy inputs from other firms or to pay for services rendered by individuals is paid out to the individuals who are its owners as profits. The conventions followed in compiling transactions tables reflect this at the industry-sector level – all receipts are paid out.

In many economies, and in all advanced industrial economies, the national statistical agency compiles and publishes a transactions table every few years. Usually, along with it they publish an input–output coefficient table derived from it. Table 5.2 is the coefficient table that goes with Table 5.1. The coefficients are derived by dividing the transactions table entry for an input purchase by an industry by that industry's output, which is the same as its total expenditure on inputs. Thus, for example, in Table 5.1 for a total output of 2,000, Manufacturing spends 200 on inputs purchased from Agriculture, so in the Agriculture row of Table 5.2 $200/2,000 = 0.1$ appears in the Manufacturing column.

The **input–output coefficient table** shows the structure of an economy, in terms of inputs used in production and inter-industry flows, in a way that is independent of the sizes of the industrial sectors. Thus, for example, in Table 5.2 we see that whereas in Manufacturing 90 per cent of input expenditure is for primary inputs, in Agriculture it is just 40 per cent.

5.1.2 Input–output analysis

The input–output coefficient table has another use, the explanation of which requires the use of some symbols. Use Q_A to represent the total or gross output level for Agriculture and Q_M for Manufacturing, and use F_A and F_M to represent the final demand consumption of agricultural and manufacturing output. Then, using the coefficients from Table 5.2, we can write equations describing the dispositions of those outputs as

$$Q_A = (0.1 \times Q_M) + F_A$$
$$Q_M = (0.6 \times Q_A) + F_M$$

These are known as output balance equations. The first equation here says that Agriculture's output is equal to what it delivers to consumption plus the amount $(0.1 \times Q_M)$ required as intermediate input to Manufacturing, and the second says that Manufacturing's output is equal to what it delivers to consumption plus the amount $(0.6 \times Q_A)$ required as intermediate input to Agriculture. Treating consumption requirements as givens, we have here a pair of simultaneous equations that can be solved for Q_A and Q_M.

Set $F_A = 800$ and $F_M = 1,400$ as in Table 5.1. Then, substituting for Q_A in the second of these equations using the first gives

$$Q_M = (0.6 \times 0.1 \times Q_M) + (0.6 \times 800) + 1,400 = 0.06 \times Q_M + 1,880$$

which, on subtracting $0.06 \times Q_M$ from both sides is

$$0.94 \times Q_M = 1,880$$

and dividing both sides by 0.94 gives

$$Q_M = 1,880/0.94 = 2,000$$

and substituting this into the first equation, for Q_A, above, gives

$$Q_A = (0.1 \times 2,000) + 800 = 1,000.$$

We have found that the gross output levels for the two industries are what we knew they were to begin with from the transactions table, Table 5.1, which is not terribly useful. However, we do not have to use the Final demand numbers from the transactions table when we solve the output balance equations for gross output levels. Instead of solving

$$Q_A = 0 + (0.1 \times Q_M) + 800$$
$$Q_M = (0.6 \times Q_A) + 0 + 1,400$$

for Q_A and Q_M, we could, for example, solve

$$Q_A = 0 + (0.1 \times Q_M) + 600$$
$$Q_M = (0.6 \times Q_A) + 0 + 1,600$$

to get Q_A equal to 808.5106 and Q_M equal to 2,085.1064. Note that the solution for Q_A depends on both of F_A and F_M, as does that for Q_M. Note also reducing the consumption of agriculture by 200 does not reduce the total requirement for agriculture – the gross output of Agriculture – by 200, because the consumption of manufacturing goes up and Manufacturing uses agriculture as an input.

We can use the top part of the coefficient table to find the gross output levels for each industry that go with any set of consumption requirements. Given the gross output levels, we can use the lower part of the coefficient table to find the corresponding requirements for primary inputs. Thus, for example, $F_A = 600$ and $F_M = 1,600$ gives $Q_A = 808.5106$ which, from Table 5.2, means, for Agriculture, that Wages and salaries $= 0.3 \times 808.5106 = 242.5532$ and Other factor payments $= 0.1 \times 808.5106 = 80.8511$.

So, the input–output coefficient table derived from a transactions table describing flows in the economy in a particular year for a particular set of consumption levels can be used to calculate what industry output levels would have to be for different consumption requirements, and what that would imply for requirements for primary inputs. This is clearly very useful. In doing this kind of conditional – on a given set of consumption requirements – forecasting, it is important to keep in mind two things. First, that we are working with units which are worth millions of dollars. Second, that it is implicitly assumed that the coefficients are fixed, and do not change with the changes in consumption levels.

Input–output data can be used to answer 'what if' questions about technological change. Suppose, for example, that we wanted to know about the implications of a technological innovation in Agriculture for which it was claimed that it would reduce the use of manufacturing as an input by 50 per cent. This would reduce the Manufacturing into Agriculture coefficient from 0.6 to 0.3. Solving

$$Q_A = 0 + (0.1 \times Q_M) + 800$$
$$Q_M = (0.3 \times Q_A) + 0 + 1,400$$

we get Q_A as 969.072 and Q_M as 1690.72 for the total output levels to be compared with those in Table 5.1. There is a reduced requirement for agriculture, as well as manufacturing, because the former is an input to the production of the latter.

5.1.3 Accounting for direct and indirect requirements

The national statistical agency publications that contain the transactions table and the input–output coefficient table often also include a table derived from the latter which gives the gross output levels for each industry that go with unit deliveries of each commodity to Final demand. Table 5.3 is such a table for our hypothetical economy. It is derived as follows.

Using the coefficients from Table 5.2, we have

$$Q_A = (0.1 \times Q_M) + F_A$$
$$Q_M = (0.6 \times Q_A) + F_M$$

Table 5.3 Total output requirements per unit delivery to final demand

Industry	Final demand commodity	
	Agriculture	Manufacturing
Agriculture	1.0638	0.1064
Manufacturing	0.6383	1.0638

Substituting for Q_A in the second equation from the first gives

$$Q_M = 0.6 \times \{(0.1 \times Q_M) + F_A\} + F_M = (0.06 \times Q_M) + (0.6 \times F_A) + F_M$$

and subtracting $0.06 \times Q_M$ from both sides

$$0.94 \times Q_M = 0.6 \times F_A + F_M$$

and dividing both sides by 0.94

$$Q_M = 0.6383 \times F_A + 1.0638 \times F_M$$

and using this to substitute for Q_M in the first of the original equations leads, after rearranging, to

$$Q_A = 1.0638 \times F_A + 0.1064 \times F_M$$

We now have two equations which calculate the total output levels for each industry from the amounts of each commodity delivered to consumption. To find what each industry needs to produce to meet any levels of consumption of the commodities, you simply substitute for F_A and F_M in these equations and do the arithmetic – you can check that for 800 and 1,400 this gives 1,000 and 2,000 as in Table 5.1, and that for 600 and 1,600 it gives 808.5106 and 2,085.1064 as in the previous sub-section. The coefficients in these equations are set out in Table 5.3.

Table 5.3 says, for example, that to deliver one unit of the commodity agriculture to consumption requires the total production of 1.0638 units of agriculture – it requires more than one unit because Agriculture uses inputs from Manufacturing which itself uses inputs from Agriculture. A table such as Table 5.3 is often known as a **Leontief matrix** – a matrix is an array of coefficients – named after Wassily Leontief because he is the economist who first developed input–output accounting as the means to calculate the coefficients giving the direct and indirect output requirements for total industry outputs to meet final demand requirements. The Appendix 'Input–output algebra' provides a more general derivation of the total requirements coefficients.

5.1.4 Input–output accounting and the environment

If there are data available on the inputs of some natural resource to the industrial sectors distinguished in a set of input–output tables, they can be used with the coefficients for direct and indirect requirements to allocate the economy's total use of the resource across the consumption of the commodities that it produces. Similarly, given data on emissions of some kind by industrial sectors, the total for that kind of emissions can be allocated across commodities.

First, consider the case of some resource input, oil say. Suppose that for the economy and the year looked at in the previous sub-section we knew that Manufacturing used 1,000,000 tonnes of oil, while Agriculture used no oil. While Agriculture does not use any oil directly, it is not true that producing the commodity agriculture does not use oil. Agriculture uses oil indirectly when it uses output from Manufacturing as an input, oil being used directly in Manufacturing. This can be put another way. Of the total use of oil in Manufacturing, some part is actually attributable to the use of that industry's output in the production of the commodity agriculture. These statements can be made precise using the coefficients for direct and indirect requirements from Table 5.3.

For the Final demand levels of Table 5.1, for the total output for Manufacturing we get

$$Q_M = 0.6383 \times 800 + 1.0638 \times 1,400 = 510.64 + 1,489.32$$

which says that of the total manufacturing output of 2,000, 510.64 was attributable to final demand deliveries of agriculture and 1,489.64 to final demand deliveries of manufacturing. Of total manufacturing output, $510.64/2,000 = 25.53$ per cent is attributable to agriculture consumption, and $1,489.32/2,000 = 74.47$ per cent is attributable to manufacturing consumption. We can apply these percentages to Manufacturing's total use of oil, and say that 25.53 per cent was on account of the final demand for agriculture of 800, and 74.47 per cent was on account of the final demand for manufacturing of 1,400. Given that Manufacturing's oil use was 1,000,000 tonnes, and Agriculture's was zero, of the economy's total oil use, 255,300 (25.53 per cent of 1,000,000) tonnes is attributable to agriculture consumption of 800, and 744,700 (74.47 per cent of 1,000,000) tonnes is attributable to manufacturing consumption of 1,400. Using the methods from previous sub-sections, we can also allocate total oil use as between agriculture and manufacturing consumption for any levels of those consumptions, and investigate the effects of technological change. We will illustrate the latter by going back to the example from section 5.1.2 where the input coefficient for Agriculture into Manufacturing was cut from 0.6 to 0.3. What would happen to total use of oil in this case?

With $Q_M = 2,000$ we had oil use in Manufacturing at 1,000,000 tonnes so that Manufacturing uses 500 tonnes of oil per unit (which is one million dollars' worth) of output. For the technological change being considered, we have already found that it reduces Q_M to 1,690.72, so that it reduces total oil use in the economy to $500 \times 1,690.72 = 845,360$ tonnes. Note that a technological change which has no direct bearing on energy use has nonetheless reduced it by virtue of reducing the amount of manufacturing used as input to Agriculture. The important point here generalises. Energy is necessary for moving and transforming matter. It follows that energy can be 'conserved' by reducing the amount of matter that is moved and/or transformed. Materials conservation is an indirect means of energy conservation.

We have looked at the analysis of resource use. A similar analysis works for emissions. Suppose that we knew that for the Table 5.1 economy, the Agriculture sector released into watercourses 100 tonnes of some pollutant, while Manufacturing released 1,000 tonnes. From Table 5.3 we can write for this economy

$$Q_A = 1.0638 \times F_A + 0.1064 \times F_M$$
$$Q_M = 0.6383 \times F_A + 1.0638 \times F_A$$

which for $F_A = 800$ and $F_M = 1,400$ as in Table 5.1 is

$$Q_A = (1.0638 \times 800) + (0.1064 \times 1,400) = 851.04 + 148.96 = 1,000$$
$$Q_M = (0.6383 \times 800) + (1.0638 \times 1,400) = 510.64 + 1,489.32 = 2,000$$

so that of Agriculture's total output, $851.04/1,000 = 0.8510$ is attributable to consumption of agriculture with $148.96/1,000 = 0.1490$ attributable to manufacturing consumption, while of Manufacturing's total output, $510.64/2,000 = 0.2553$ is attributable to consumption of agriculture with $1489.32/2,000 = 0.7447$ attributable to manufacturing consumption.

We know that Agriculture produces 100 tonnes of emissions while Manufacturing produces 1,000 tonnes. Of Agriculture's 100 tonnes 85.10 per cent, i.e. 85.10 tonnes, is associated with agriculture and of Manufacturing's 1,000 tonnes 25.53 per cent, i.e. 255.30 tonnes, is associated with agriculture. Hence, 85.10 plus $255.30 = 340.40$ tonnes of emissions are attributable to the production of agriculture for delivery to Final Demand for consumption. Of Agriculture's 100 tonnes 14.90 per cent, i.e. 14.90 tonnes, is associated with manufacturing and of Manufacturing's 1,000 tonnes 74.47 per cent, i.e. 744.70 tonnes, is associated with manufacturing. Hence, 14.90 plus $744.70 = 759.60$ tonnes of emissions are attributable to the production of manufacturing for delivery to Final Demand for consumption. Note that 340.40 plus 759.60 is 1,100, so that we have exactly allocated total emissions between agriculture and manufacturing consumption, taking account of indirect as well as direct requirements in production.

If we look at the emissions arising in each industry, Agriculture accounts for $100/1,100 = 9.09$ per cent of the economy's total, while Manufacturing accounts for $1,000/1,100 = 90.91$ per cent. This does *not* mean that cutting the consumption of manufacturing would cut emissions by ten times as much per million dollars as would cutting the consumption of agriculture. Such a calculation ignores the fact that Agriculture uses a lot of manufacturing as input. The proper way to figure the emissions reductions that would follow from reducing the consumption of agriculture or manufacturing is as set out above. The results arising can be expressed in terms of the emissions intensities of commodity consumption. Taking account of the ways in which they are produced using each other as inputs, the emissions intensities of agriculture consumption and manufacturing consumption are $340.40/800 = 0.4255$ and $759.60/1,400 = 0.5426$ tonnes per million dollars' worth respectively. The industry Manufacturing has an emissions intensity – $1,000/2,000 = 0.5$ tonnes per unit – which is five times that of the Agriculture industry – $100/1,000 = 0.1$ tonnes per unit. The consumption commodity manufacturing has an emissions intensity which is $0.5426/0.4255 = 1.28$ times that for the consumption commodity agriculture.

In many of the industrial economies the national statistical agencies publish data on sectoral uses of some natural resources and on sectoral emissions of various kinds, as well as input–output data and coefficients, so that it is possible to conduct analysis of the kind set out above. Box 5.1 reports the results from one such exercise.

5.1.5 Input–output structures in history

Chapter 3 looked at human economic history in terms of cultural adaptation driving a transition from a hunter-gatherer system to an agricultural system and then to an industrial system. The stages in this process can be represented in terms of input–output accounts. The accounts to be presented here are not actual historical

Box 5.1　Accounting for carbon dioxide emissions

Table 5.5 gives the results for Australia obtained using input–output coefficients and data on industry sector CO_2 emissions. The latter were derived from published data on fossil fuel energy inputs to the industry sectors distinguished, using knowledge of the carbon contents of the fossil fuels. The amounts of CO_2 released into the atmosphere per unit of fossil fuel burned are given in Table 5.4.

Table 5.4　CO_2 releases from fossil fuel combustion

	Tonnes CO_2 per PJ
Natural gas	54,900
Oil	73,200
Black coal	104,100
Brown coal	112,700

In order to get the results shown in Table 5.5, the procedure described in the text was followed for each of the fossil fuels to get CO_2 emissions by sector from each fossil fuel, and then summing across the fossil fuels for each sector to get its total emissions arising in fossil fuel combustion. In the first column of Table 5.5 the results arising are expressed in terms of CO_2 intensities, they are tonnes of CO_2 per million dollars' worth of delivery to final demand of the output of the indicated sector, *taking account of indirect as well as direct requirements*. The second column expresses the results in the first as proportions of the total of Australian CO_2 emissions. In both of these columns the figures in brackets are the sectoral rankings according to the criterion at the head of the column. Among the interesting features of these results are the following:

1. In terms of CO_2 intensity, the secondary fuels Electricity, Petroleum and Coal Products (mostly petroleum products such as vehicle fuels in fact) and Gas rank 1st, 2nd and 3rd. This is mainly because of their direct use of primary fossil fuels – coal for Electricity, oil for Petroleum and Coal Products, and gas for Gas. In terms of total CO_2, and hence per cent share, the rankings are 1st, 2nd and 18th. The difference for Gas arises from the fact that, whereas Electricity and Petroleum and Coal Products are industries with large outputs, Gas is a relatively small industry.

2. While the Electricity industry is the largest single sector in terms of both intensity and total emissions, it accounts for only 15 per cent of total emissions. The term 'only' is used here because one often reads that the Electricity industry accounts for around 40 per cent of CO_2 emissions. It is true for Australia, and many other industrial economies, that if one looks at the emissions coming out of smokestacks, around 40 per cent comes out of smokestacks belonging to the Electricity industry. However, much of the electricity generated is used as input to the production of other commodities – to light factories and offices in all sectors, to run machines and computers, etc., etc. The accounting of Table 5.5 allocates the CO_2 arising in such intermediate uses of electricity to the deliveries to final demand by the purchasing sector – only the CO_2 associated with deliveries of electricity to final demand gets attributed to Electricity. For many purposes this is the most useful way of allocating emissions. Using the direct and indirect requirements coefficients for the various fossil fuels and the data from Table 5.4, one can figure out the implications for CO_2 emissions of changes in final demands, as shown for 'oil' in the chapter text.

Table 5.5　CO_2 intensities and levels for deliveries to final demand, Australia 1986/7

Sector	CO_2 intensity tonnes per $A \times 10^6$	Proportion of Australian CO_2 emissions %
Agriculture, forestry and fishing	1,800.7(6)	4.74(8)
Mining	985.4(11)	3.41(12)
Meat and milk products	1,036.8(10)	2.92(13)
Food products	1,532.5(8)	4.00(10)
Beverages and tobacco	921.3(12)	1.17(20)
Textiles, clothing and footwear	556.1(24)	1.05(21)
Wood, wood products, furniture	877.1(14)	0.70(23)
Paper, products, printing, publishing	870.7(15)	0.48(24)
Chemicals	1,238.5(9)	0.88(22)
Petroleum and coal products	10,727.2(2)	12.95(2)
Non-metallic mineral products	2,198.0(5)	0.12(26)
Basic metals products	4,497.7(4)	6.94(4)
Fabricated metal products	1,705.5(7)	1.19(19)
Transport equipment	740.6(20)	1.61(17)

(*cont.*)

Table 5.5 (cont.)

Sector	CO_2 intensity tonnes per $A \times 10^6$	Proportion of Australian CO_2 emissions %
Machinery and equipment	883.4(13)	1.82(16)
Miscellaneous manufacturing	772.7(18)	0.35(25)
Electricity	15,244.9(1)	14.99(1)
Gas	9,966.3(3)	1.60(18)
Water	668.0(22)	0.07(27)
Construction	756.7(19)	9.64(3)
Wholesale and retail	497.8(25)	6.25(5)
Transport and communication	815.7(17)	4.58(9)
Finance and business services	624.2(23)	1.96(14)
Residential property	199.2(27)	1.89(15)
Public administration and defence	840.9(16)	4.92(7)
Community services	443.7(26)	6.10(6)
Recreational and personal services	720.5(21)	3.71(11)

Source: adapted from Common and Salma (1992).

3. Agriculture, Forestry and Fishing, which sector is dominated by agricultural production in Australia, is the sixth most CO_2-intensive industry in Australia. Its ranking by intensity would be similar in any industrial economy. In Table 5.5, Agriculture, Forestry and Fishing is shown as more CO_2-intensive, because it is more energy-intensive, than, for example, Textiles, Clothing and Footwear, Mining, and Fabricated Metal Products. Many people are surprised by this. It comes about because, as discussed in Chapter 3, modern agriculture uses (non-solar extrasomatic) energy directly – to drive farm machinery, for example – and indirectly – fertiliser production is energy-intensive. Modern agriculture has, when account is taken of its indirect as well as its direct use, an energy intensity similar to, or greater than, that of many manufacturing industries. Given that most of the energy that it uses is based on fossil fuel combustion, this makes it also a relatively high CO_2-intensity activity. In Australia, the Agriculture, Forestry and Fishing sector is large, so that the high-intensity ranking produces a similar ranking by total emissions. In many industrial economies, this sector is small so that, despite a high intensity ranking, its total emissions ranking is fairly low.

4. The service sectors typically have low ranks by CO_2 intensity, and considerably higher ranks by total emissions – look at Wholesale and Retail, and Community Services, for example. This is because they are relatively large sectors.

Table 5.6 The input–output structure for a hunter-gatherer economy

	Input coefficients	Final demand proportion
	Hunting and gathering	
Hunting and gathering	0	100%
Labour	1	
Other factors	0	

accounts. The compilation of input–output data only began in the middle of the twentieth century in industrial economies, and since then has spread slowly so that input–output accounts of at least a rudimentary kind are now available for most economies. The accounts to be presented here are entirely fictional, are made up in order to illustrate broad trends in economic history. The numbers are not intended to represent any actual economy: they are intended to give a sense of the major differences between representative economies at each phase of the evolutionary process. In order to have tables of manageable size, only the economic inputs distinguished in standard input–output accounts will be explicitly represented in the tables: the use of the natural environment will be noted separately.

The input–output structure of the hunter-gatherer economy, shown in Table 5.6, is very simple. The only input to hunting and gathering is labour. A wide range

of renewable natural resources are exploited using labour and simple weapons and
tools. Since there is no specialisation
by individuals as between hunting and
gathering and the making of artefacts,
there is no separate sector for the latter
activity. Capital accumulation is trivial
and so no use of capital services is shown
against 'Other Factors'. Similarly, there is
no individual landownership and hence
no rent payment to show here. The output
from Hunting and Gathering accounts
for, as shown in the rightmost column,

Table 5.7 The input–output structure for an agricultural phase economy

	Input coefficients			Final demand proportion
	Agriculture	Manufacturing	Services	%
Agriculture	0	0.30	0.1	50
Manufacturing	0.10	0	0.1	20
Services	0.20	0.30	0	30
Labour	0.40	0.25	0.50	
Other factors	0.30	0.15	0.30	
Relative size	1	0.4	0.8	

all of final demand. The structure of the hunter-gatherer economy is so simple that
an input–output representation is really redundant – it is provided for comparison
with agricultural and industrial representations.

Table 5.7 shows the input–output structure for an agricultural phase economy.
Agriculture uses intermediate inputs from Manufacturing – tools – and from Services – wholesale and retail distribution. In terms of primary inputs, it uses labour,
land and capital services. The output from Agriculture is intermediate input to the
other sectors and delivered to final demand, where it accounts for half of total final
demand. Manufacturing uses intermediate inputs from Agriculture – raw materials
such as wood – and from Services – distribution, labour, capital services and land.
It is less labour-intensive and less land-intensive than Agriculture. It supplies both
of the other sectors, and its deliveries to final demand account for 20 per cent
of the total there – individuals use cooking and eating utensils, furniture, etc.
Services uses relatively small proportional intermediate inputs from Agriculture
and Manufacturing, but is very labour-intensive. The final row of Table 5.7 shows
the sizes of the sectors relative to Agriculture in terms of total output. Agriculture is the largest sector, and Manufacturing the smallest. In terms of the natural
environment, both Agriculture and Manufacturing use flow (e.g. solar radiation in
Agriculture, water power in Manufacturing) and renewable resources (e.g. timber in
Manufacturing). There is some use of non-renewable resources in Manufacturing.
Agricultural production and consumption are the source of organic waste products,
and there are small amounts of emissions from Manufacturing, originating in the
use of non-renewable resource inputs.

In order to represent an industrial economy, it is necessary, in Table 5.8, to
introduce two new industry sectors. The Primary sector extracts natural resources –
iron ore, trees, for example – from the environment and turns them into inputs to
Manufacturing – steel, sawn wood and woodpulp, for example. The Primary sector
is necessarily the origin of many kinds of waste emissions. The Energy sector also
extracts – fossil fuels, uranium, hydropower, for example – from the environment
and supplies secondary energy forms – electricity, petroleum, for example – to *all*
of the other industry sectors, and to final demand. The proportion of total final
demand accounted for by agricultural output is just 10 per cent, whereas services
account for more than 50 per cent. Services is a relatively labour-intensive industry.
It is also, by a large margin, the largest sector of the economy. The Agriculture sector
is small, as is the Primary sector. The main point here is that the means by which

Table 5.8 The input–output structure for an industrial economy

	Input coefficients					Final demand proportion %
	Agriculture	Primary	Energy	Manufacturing	Services	
Agriculture	0	0	0	0.10	0	10
Primary	0	0	0	0.25	0	0
Energy	0.10	0.10	0	0.15	0.05	10
Manufacturing	0.15	0.20	0.35	0	0.15	20
Services	0.40	0.30	0.15	0.15	0	60
Labour	0.10	0.10	0.10	0.20	0.45	
Other factors	0.25	0.30	0.40	0.15	0.35	
Relative size	1	1	2	5	10	

human needs and desires are met have become more complex, in the sense that the economy has more sectors and more inter-industry connectivity. This has been an important feature of human cultural evolution.

5.2 NATIONAL INCOME ACCOUNTING CONVENTIONS

In relation to input–output accounting, the main point about national income accounting is that it ignores inter-industry transactions and focuses exclusively on deliveries to final demand on the one hand, and on primary inputs on the other.

5.2.1 The basic ideas

National income is the sum of all of the incomes earned by all of the factors of production employed in an economy in a given period of time, usually one year. National product is the total value of deliveries to final demand. National expenditure is the total of expenditure on deliveries to final demand. According to the definitions used in national income accounting, often referred to as the national income accounting conventions, for a given economy over a given period, national income, product and expenditure must all be equal to one another. With NI for national income, NP for national product, and NE for national expenditure

$$NI \equiv NP \equiv NE$$

where the three-bar equality sign is an identity sign, which is used to indicate that, given that the conventions are followed, these three things *must be* equal. The things on either side of an identity sign are always equal because they are defined that way. We will use an identity sign when we want to make it clear that the relationship in question is a matter of definition.

Look again at Table 5.1, the transactions table for a simple imaginary economy where two industries produce output that is used by the other industry – intermediate demand – and by individuals – final demand. Each industry uses as inputs purchases from the other industry and the services of factors of production.

In Table 5.1 payments for primary inputs are classified as Wages and salaries, for labour services, or Other factor payments, which is the totality of payments for the services of capital, for the services of land, for entrepreneurship, and of interest on borrowed funds. For this economy, for national income we have

$$NI \equiv \text{Factor payments by Agriculture} + \text{Factor payments by manufacturing}$$

so that

$$NI = (300 + 100) + (1{,}200 + 600)$$
$$= 2{,}200$$

$ million.
National product for this economy is

$$NP \equiv \text{Agriculture's final demand delivery}$$
$$+ \text{Manufacturing's final demand delivery}$$

so that

$$NP = 800 + 1{,}400$$
$$= 2{,}200$$

National expenditure is

$$NE \equiv \text{Individuals' spending on consumption of agricultural output}$$
$$+ \text{individuals' spending on consumption of manufacturing output}$$

so that

$$NE = 800 + 1{,}400$$
$$= 2{,}200$$

This shows that in this economy it is true that national income, product and expenditure are equal. It is easy to see why, given the definitions, it must always be true that national product and expenditure are equal – the former is just total producers' receipts from sales of final demand deliveries to individuals, the latter is just total expenditure by individuals in purchasing the same deliveries. National product and expenditure are the same thing looked at from the two different sides of the transactions, that of the sellers and that of the buyers. National expenditure must be equal to national income because the latter is the sum of all payments to factors of production, which all gets spent, as the former, on buying deliveries to final demand. The necessary equality of *NI*, *NE* and *NP* is demonstrated formally in the Appendix at the end of the chapter.

In the simple economy for which Table 5.1 gives the basic accounts, an industry's production is for either use as an intermediate input in another industry or consumption by individuals. Put another way, in that economy, the only component of final demand is consumption. In fact, as noted in regard to input–output accounting, final demand as output that is not used as intermediate inputs to production has several components. Before looking at the other components of final demand in the national income accounting context, it will be useful to introduce the concept of value added and use it to put the basic ideas about national income accounting in a slightly different way.

5.2.1.1 *Value added measurement of output*

For a firm, or an industry, **value added** is the difference between sales receipts and payments for purchases of goods and services. Look again at Table 5.1. For Agriculture, value added is $1,000 million less $600 million spent on purchases from Manufacturing, so that value added in Agriculture is $400 million. For Manufacturing, value added is $1,800 million, the difference between sales receipts of $2,000 and purchases from Agriculture of $200. The total value added in this economy is $400 plus $1,800 equals $2,200 million. We have already seen that for this economy $NI = NE = NP = \$2,200$ million.

This is not a coincidence. An alternative way to define national product is as the total output of an economy measured in terms of value added, or, the same thing, as total value added in the economy. The necessary equality of national product and national income as the sum of factor payments then follows in a direct and obvious way. If value added is the difference between sales receipts and payments for purchased goods and services, it must be equal to total payments to all factors of production. Firms, and hence industries, do not themselves retain any of the money received for sales – it is all paid out either to suppliers of goods and services or to suppliers of the services of factors of production.

5.2.2 Gross and net national product

NP is the output delivered to final demand, rather than being used as inputs to production, i.e. as intermediate products. Thus far final demand has consisted only of consumption by individuals. Investment is another component of final demand. It is output bought by firms to add to the capital stock, the services of which are used in production. When a bakery buys flour, it is buying an intermediate input. When a bakery buys an oven, it is investing and adding to its capital stock. The flour is entirely used up in the current production of bread: the oven yields a flow of services to bread production over many years. Distinguishing between production for consumption and production for investment gives

$$NP \equiv C + I$$

where C represents total consumption and I represents total investment, where both are measured in value added terms.

While it is not used up in current production, capital equipment is not ever-lasting. In use, it wears out, or depreciates, over time. Of the production that is investment, some is used to replace equipment that has come to the end of its useful life, that is it is used to make good the **depreciation** of the existing capital stock. The total amount of production for investment is known as gross investment. The excess of gross investment over the amount required to make good depreciation is known as net investment. Net investment is the amount by which the size of the economy's capital stock increases over the accounting period.

The distinction between gross and net investment carries over to definitions of national product, expenditure and income. Gross national product (GNP), for example, is total deliveries to final demand, while net national product (NNP), is total deliveries to final demand less depreciation. With D for depreciation

$$GNP \equiv C + I$$

while

$$NNP \equiv C + I - D$$

National income and national expenditure are also defined gross and net. For national income

$$NNI \equiv GNI - D$$

defines net national income as total factor payments less depreciation, and for national expenditure

$$NNE \equiv GNE - D$$

defines net national expenditure as total expenditure on final demand less depreciation.

NNP is the output available for allocation as between consumption and investment after provision for depreciation has been made. This means that *NNP* is the maximum that an economy could consume without reducing the size of its capital stock. From the definition of *NNP*

$$NNP - C = I - D$$

so that C equal to *NNP* would imply $I = D$ – gross investment would only be large enough to just make good the depreciation of the existing capital stock.

5.2.3 Investment is necessarily equal to saving

In the period to which the accounts refer, individuals receive incomes for the supply of the services of factors of production, which they allocate between current spending on goods and services, consumption and saving. Across all individuals

$$GNI \equiv C + S$$

where S represents the total amount saved. Looking at production we have

$$GNP \equiv C + I$$

so that given $GNP \equiv GNI$, the righthand sides here are identically equal and

$$C + S \equiv C + I$$

where subtracting C from both sides gives

$$S \equiv I$$

As recorded in the national income accounts, saving and investment are always, by definition, equal. They are just the same thing looked at from different sides of the accounts. Investment is output added to the capital stock rather than consumed. Saving is income not spent on current consumption.

What we have shown here is that gross investment is necessarily equal to gross saving. Just as net investment is defined as total investment less depreciation, so net saving is defined as total saving less depreciation. Then, net investment and net saving are identically equal. From

$$NNP \equiv C + I - D$$

and

$$NNI \equiv GNI - D \equiv C + S - D$$

for $NNP \equiv NNI$

$$C + S - D \equiv C + I - D$$

and so, subtracting C from both sides

$$S - D \equiv I - D$$

5.2.4 Accounting for government

Governments play a large role in modern economies, and the national income accounting conventions discussed thus far have to be extended so as to accommodate that activity. We need to look at what government spends and how it raises the money to pay for its spending.

Government expenditures divide into two categories. First, there is expenditure on goods and services. The symbol G will be used for this expenditure, which is a component of final demand. Second, there is expenditure arising as payments to individuals, known as **transfer payments**, for which the symbol H will be used. G includes such diverse things as the purchase of military equipment and the payment of the salaries of teachers in state-financed educational establishments. H comprises pensions paid by government (to its ex-employees and to the generality of individuals where a national retirement pension system exists), welfare payments, unemployment benefits, etc. The definition of transfer payments is that they are payments for which there is no corresponding return flow of services or commodities.

Government tax receipts are broadly classified as direct or indirect taxation. **Direct taxes** are those levied on individuals' incomes, while **indirect taxes** are those levied on individuals' and firms' purchases, such as excise duties and sales taxes of various kinds. Direct taxation necessitates some modification to the foregoing discussion on the income side of the accounts: indirect on the expenditure side. T_D will represent direct taxation receipts, T_E indirect taxation receipts.

National income was defined above as the sum of payments by industries for the services of the factors of production employed. The sources of such payments must now be extended to include government, which is an employer of factors of production. The amount of money that individuals in total have to spend on consumption, or save, is known as personal disposable income (PDI), and is total factor payments by industry and government plus transfer payments less direct taxation

$$PDI \equiv \text{Total factor payments} + H - T_D \equiv GNI + H - T_D$$

Government spending on goods and services, G, has to be included in the definition of national expenditure, so that

$$GNE^m \equiv C + I + G$$

The superscript m here indicates that this definition holds when expenditure is recorded and totalled using the market prices that purchasers pay. Given the existence of indirect taxation, these market prices are not the prices received by sellers. It follows that GNE^m cannot be the same as GNI, which is total receipts by sellers paid out to factors of production. The GNE total which is the same as GNI is national expenditure measured at basic prices, GNE^b, that is net of taxes on expenditure

$$GNE^b \equiv C + I + G - T_E \equiv GNI$$

Note that consumption, C, as measured in national income accounts does not include the goods and services provided by government to households, as part of G, for which no price per unit is charged at the point of use. Thus, C does not include: defence and security services, state-provided education, state-provided medical services, publicly provided refuse collection and disposal, public parks, public broadcasting, publicly provided water and sewage services. These do show up in national output as components of G where they are entered at prices which are the costs of provision rather than what households would be willing to pay if these services were provided through markets. To note this, in the national income accounting literature, C is often referred to as private consumption.

In the previous sub-section we saw that in an economy without a government, saving and investment as recorded in the national income accounts are necessarily equal. This remains true when government is accounted for, so long as saving by government is accounted for. From the relationships immediately above, we get

$$S \equiv PDI - C \equiv GNI + H - T_D - C$$

and

$$GNI \equiv C + I + G - T_E$$

and substituting for GNI in the first of these using the second gives

$$S \equiv C + I + G - T_E + H - T_D - C$$

where cancelling the Cs and rearranging the other terms on the righthand side gives

$$S \equiv I + (G + H) - T_E - T_D \equiv I + (G + H) - (T_E + T_D)$$

Here $G + H$ is total government spending and $T_E + T_D$ is total government tax receipts, so that it can be written

$$S_I \equiv I + G_T - T_T \equiv I - T_T + G_T \equiv I - (T_T - G_T) \equiv I - S_G$$

where S_I stands for saving by individuals, G_T for total government spending, T_T for total tax receipts, and S_G for government saving as the excess of tax receipts over government spending. Rearranging this gives

$$S_I + S_G \equiv I$$

so that total saving is again seen as necessarily equal to investment.

5.2.5 Foreign trade: national and domestic national income

Thus far we have been looking at the national income accounting conventions as they would apply to a closed economy, by which is meant in the economics terminology introduced in Chapter 4 an economy that does not trade with any other economies. When dealing with an open economy, one that does trade with the rest of the world, it is necessary to make a distinction between domestic income and national income. In what follows here, the economy for which the accounting is being done is the 'domestic economy': all other economies are treated as the single entity, the rest of the world. It simplifies matters to discuss the national income accounting for an open economy as if the economy had no government economic activity to account for.

Exports, conventionally given the symbol X, are treated as a component of final demand: output shipped overseas is not available for C, I or G, and cannot be used as intermediate input in domestic production. Production for export generates incomes payable to factors of production in the domestic economy. Imports, conventionally M, are available for domestic use – as C, I, G or as intermediate inputs – but do not generate incomes for domestic factors of production. The factors of production used in the production of M are located in the rest of the world. Thus far, assuming no trade, we have used definitions which mean that national income as the sum of payments to domestic factors of production is equal to expenditure on consumption and investment. With trade, we define gross domestic income (*GDI*) as

$$GDI \equiv C + I + X - M$$

where C, I, X and M are measured in terms of value added. In that case, the addition of X picks up the extra factor incomes generated in production for export. The subtraction of M means that to the extent that the final demands C and I are met by imports, the domestic factor incomes thereby 'lost' are netted out.

GDI thus defined is the total of the factor incomes generated in the domestic economy. It is not the total of the factor income accruing to residents of the domestic economy. Some such residents own income yielding property overseas, and some earn incomes from overseas employment. Equally, some rest-of-the world residents own property in the domestic economy which yields income to them overseas, and some earn employment incomes arising in the domestic economy but paid overseas. Net income received from abroad is the balance of these two flows. It may be positive or negative. Using O for net income received from abroad, gross national income, *GNI*, is defined as

$$GNI \equiv GDI + O$$

For most economies, the difference between *GDI* and *GNI* is not very great, with factor payments to and from foreigners being either small or roughly in balance.

For some economies the difference is 5 per cent or more. Given that O can be positive or negative, *GDI* may exceed or be smaller than *GNI*. Countries which have many of their nationals working overseas and remitting much of their incomes home will have *GNI* greater than *GDI*. Many developing countries fit this pattern. A country which owns more property overseas than foreigners own in it will, ignoring migrant workers, have positive net income from abroad, and *GNI* greater than *GDI*. This pattern fits a number of industrial economies, such as the US and the UK, for example. On the other hand, a country which is host to extensive foreign-owned industry will thereby tend to have *GDI* greater than *GNI*. This will be more the case, the greater the extent to which the foreign-owned industry is operated by expatriates.

We have discussed the domestic/national distinction in terms of the incomes side of the national income accounting conventions, as it is in that context that it makes most intuitive sense. The distinction carries through in terms of expenditure and production. In the case of production

$$GNP \equiv C + I + X - M + O \equiv GDP + O$$

GDP measures the value of the output for final demand produced by factors of production located in the domestic economy, irrespective of the national origin of the factors or their ownership. **GNP** measures the value of the final demand output produced by domestically owned factors of production, irrespective of the physical location of the production activity. If the interest is in the level of economic activity in the domestic economy, GDP is the more appropriate measure. If the interest is in the incomes earned by domestic factors of production, *GNP* is the more appropriate measure.

With foreign trade, keeping track of the relationship between saving and investment gets complicated because it is necessary to distinguish between investment in the domestic economy and investment overseas, and between investment in the domestic economy by residents and by foreigners, for example. We will not go into these complexities here.

Table 5.9 Summary national income accounting for the United Kingdom 2001

	£ million	% of GDP
Consumption	655 265	66.32
Investment	+ 164 048	16.60
Government	+ 190 663	19.30
Exports	+ 268 451	27.17
Imports	− 290 912	29.44
GDE at market prices	= 987 515	
Statistical discrepancy	+ 499	0.05
GDP at market prices	= 988 014	
Net overseas income	+ 5 756	0.58
GNI at market prices	= 993 770	

Source: Office of National Statistics (2002): Table 1.2.

5.2.6 National income accounting in practice

Table 5.9 uses data taken from the annual national income accounting publication from the United Kingdom government that came out in 2002, where the most recent data refers to 2001. This publication contains an enormous amount of information – over 300 pages of data tables. The governments of most industrial nations, and some developing nations, produce similar volumes, following internationally agreed conventions.

In published national income accounts the main focus is on GDP, which is of interest as a measure of the overall level of activity in the domestic economy. This is important information for the management of the economy so as to avoid recession or inflation, and to promote economic growth. The table from which the data in Table 5.9 here are taken – Table 1.2 in the 'Blue Book', as it is often referred to – reports three numbers for GDP: one derived from production data; one from expenditure data; and one from data on the incomes of factors of production. As explained above, given the conventions followed, each of these approaches should produce the same number. In practice, they do not. As the source for Table 5.9 puts it:

> The resulting estimates however, like all statistical estimates, contain errors and omissions; we obtain the best estimate of GDP (i.e. the published figure) by reconciling the estimates obtained from all three approaches. (Office of National Statistics, 2002: p. 31)

In other words, the different approaches actually give different answers. This is not a criticism of the UK's Office of National Statistics – the same thing is true for the accounts prepared in every country, and is necessarily the case given the different sources of information used for each approach.

In some years complete reconciliation is impossible, and then a 'statistical discrepancy' is reported. For the UK the year 2001 was such a year, as shown in Table 5.9 here. The numbers for consumption, investment, government, exports and imports in Table 5.9 come from looking at expenditures, and in Table 5.9 their sum is shown as *GDE* for gross domestic expenditure. For the expenditure-based estimate of *GDP*, the statistical discrepancy reported is the difference between this *GDE* and the Office of National Statistics' reported 'definitive estimate' of *GDP*, shown against *GDP* at market prices in Table 5.9. This 'definitive estimate' is based on such reconciliation of the three independent estimates – from the output, expenditure and income approaches – as is possible given the available data. The fact that the statistical discrepancy is a very small percentage of the best estimate does not actually tell us much about how far apart the original independent estimates were. As the Office of National Statistics puts it, it is 'very difficult to comment on the accuracy of GDP' (Office of National Statistics, 2002: p. 40). GDP measurement is not an exact science.

In terms of the relative sizes of consumption, investment, government, exports and imports as proportions of GDP, the UK situation shown in Table 5.9 is broadly representative of a modern industrial economy, save that by such standards UK exports and imports are relatively high proportions of GDP. Net overseas income is small relative to GDP, but the actual levels of inward and outward income flows are large. UK receipts of wages and salaries and property and entrepreneurial income from the rest of the world in 2001 were £139,880 million, which is 14 per cent of GDP.

5.3 NATIONAL INCOME AS THE MEASURE OF ECONOMIC PERFORMANCE

The proper and primary interpretation of national income is as a measure of the level of economic activity, in terms of the production of goods and services.

However, national income data are widely used as indicators of economic performance, and an increase in an economy's GDP is often treated as equivalent to an improvement in the average well-being of its citizens. Of particular relevance for ecological economics is the argument that GDP should not be so treated because it neglects to account for the interdependence between the economy and the natural environment. However, there are a number of problems about GDP as a performance indicator that are independent of environmental considerations. We shall look briefly at these in this section. In the next we look at the question of accounting for the environment.

5.3.1 Income or consumption?

The purpose of economic activity is consumption, the satisfaction of wants and needs, not production. Consumption would seem to be the obvious economic indicator of well-being. In fact, comparisons of well-being in a single economy over time or across economies at a point in time are usually made in terms of national income, rather than consumption deliveries to final demand. The first point here is that, as noted above, consumption as recorded in the national income accounts does not include the goods and services provided to individuals by the government for which no charge is made at the point of use. The second point is that national income includes output invested, and that investment is directed at future consumption. Looking at income rather than consumption means looking at current well-being and enhancement of the capacity to deliver well-being in the future. Consider two economies with the same consumption levels, where economy A is investing while B is not – looking at income will show A as doing better than B, whereas looking at consumption will not.

5.3.2 Gross or net income?

It follows from the argument that income is a better indicator than consumption, because it looks at the future as well as the present, that income should be measured net rather than gross. That is, the proper income measure is net national income, which is the output available for allocation between current consumption and adding to the stock of capital, after provision for depreciation has been made. It would be possible for an economy's gross national income to increase, while its capital stock was being reduced.

Sustainable national income is the maximum that could be consumed in a period while not running down the economy's capital stock. Clearly, given the role of capital in production, a level of consumption that entails reducing the capital stock is not sustainable. Let K stand for the capital stock and use ΔK to indicate the change in its size over the period. Then

$$\Delta K = I - D$$

and for

$$GDP = C + I$$

which means that

$$I = GDP - C$$

then

$$\Delta K = GDP - C - D$$

To find the highest level of consumption consistent with a non-declining capital stock, set the lefthand side here equal to zero and solve for C. Use Y_{sus} to denote the solution. Thus

$$0 = GDP - C - D$$

gives

$$Y_{sus} = GDP - D = NDP$$

and sustainable national income is net domestic product. Consumption greater than sustainable national income leads to a diminishing capital stock.

Government and foreign trade have been ignored here in the interests of making the important point as clearly as possible. Introducing them does not affect the basic idea that the proper measure of income is net income after making good depreciation.

The point that it is the net figure that should be used if national income is to be used as a well-being indicator is generally accepted. However, in practice, and as noted above for the UK, national income accounts are built around the gross figure, GDP. This is largely because it is very difficult to measure accurately the depreciation of the economy's stock of durable capital equipment. Those responsible for preparing national income accounts take the view that it is better to work around a reasonably accurate estimate of GDP than around a less reliable estimate of NDP. This view also derives from the fact that national income statisticians regard the main point of their activities as being measuring the level of economic activity, rather than measuring well-being. From that point of view, GDP is more appropriate than NDP, as producing to make good depreciation creates jobs, for example, in just the same way as does producing for consumption or to increase the size of the capital stock. Typically, the published national income accounts do include estimated depreciation, so that users who want to can derive NDP from the available data. However, most analysis of and commentary on the accounts is in terms of GDP.

It needs to be emphasised that when we talk of measuring depreciation here, and deriving numbers for net national income, we are talking about expressing the wearing out of durable capital equipment in monetary terms. The national income accounts make no attempt to measure any depreciation of human and social capital. National income statisticians take the view that this cannot be done with any accuracy, and prefer to ignore these areas rather than include unreliable estimates in the published accounts. As we shall see, similar considerations arise in relation to the treatment of the natural environment in the national income accounts.

5.3.3 Adjustment for population size and growth

If comparisons of GDP across countries are to tell us anything about the comparative well-being of the average citizens of those countries, then clearly GDP needs to be divided by population size and expressed as GDP per capita. Similarly, comparisons over time for a single country need to be adjusted for changes in the size of the population, and we need to look at movements in GDP per capita.

While the first of these requirements is rarely overlooked, the second often is, and its neglect can seriously mislead. Taking representative figures, an annual growth rate of 3.0 per cent in GDP is halved to 1.5 per cent for GDP per capita for population growth of 1.5 per cent per year, for example.

5.3.4 What national income does not include

Essentially, GDP measures the market value of the output that passes through markets in a way that is detectable by national income statisticians, together with government services valued at the cost of providing them. This means that there are lots of things that many would regard as contributing to well-being that do not register in GDP, or do not register in full.

First, there are the goods and, mainly, services provided by the 'black economy', i.e. provided by activity that escapes the attention of the statisticians in various ways, such as avoiding paying tax by the exclusive use of cash in transactions for services such as gardening, plumbing, decorating, etc. For the UK the size of the black economy has been estimated as 10 per cent of GNP. In some countries it is thought to be proportionately larger, e.g. for Spain it has been estimated at 20 per cent of GNP, and for Poland at 34 per cent.

In addition to goods and services paid for but not recorded, there are the goods and, mainly, services produced by unpaid individuals in the domestic sector. The cooking of meals in the home does not register in GDP, but the cooking of meals in restaurants does, for example. For the same amount of food consumed, a switch away from eating at home to eating out would increase GDP on account of larger payments of wages and salaries, and profits, in the catering sector of the economy. To the extent that those eating out enjoy it more than eating in, the increase in GDP reflects an increase in the satisfactions and pleasures derived from the totality of economic activity. However, it needs to be recognised that there is a lot of economic activity going on in the domestic sector that does not show up at all in GDP. It has been estimated that in a modern industrial economy, valuing household production at the appropriate market wage rates and including the result in GDP would increase GDP by 25–30 per cent of the value of private consumption as recorded in the national income accounts.

Third, changes in the amount of work affect GDP only to the extent that they are reflected in the value of the production that it covers. If GDP goes up by 10 per cent because the amount of paid work increases by 10 per cent, it is not obvious that well-being has increased by 10 per cent, as the price of the increased output is less leisure (assuming a constant population). If total working hours are lower for the same output, and total remuneration, one might want to say that average well-being is higher – but GDP would not reflect this. It is, of course, possible in principle to adjust the published GDP figures by data on time spent working, but the latter kind of data is less readily available than GDP data, and one rarely sees this done.

Fourth, GDP tells us nothing about the distribution of well-being in the economy, nothing about equity. Two economies could have the same GDP per capita, when in one all citizens have equal consumption levels while in the other 10 per cent of the population consume 50 per cent of total output.

Finally, it needs to be noted that GDP treats all dollar expenditure equally. One million dollars of additional private consumption expenditure on cigarettes has exactly the same impact on GDP as one million dollars of extra government expenditure on healthcare, for example.

5.3.5 Defensive expenditure

Defensive expenditure is the purchase, or provision, of goods and services which are intended to offset harm rather than positively enhance well-being. A widely cited example is the public provision of police services. Suppose that criminal activity suddenly increases, and that the government responds by increasing its expenditure on the police, and that as a result criminal activity goes back to its original level. In the new situation nobody is better-off than they were in the original situation. However, GDP will have increased by the amount of the increase in government expenditure, less the amount by which private consumption expenditure falls as the result of the increased taxation necessary to finance the additional public expenditure. Other frequently cited examples of defensive expenditures are hospital treatment for the victims of traffic accidents, and cleaning up after pollution incidents such as spills from oil tankers.

5.3.6 The problem of differing relative prices

One reason for measuring economic performance is to be able to make comparisons, to be able to say that an economy's performance is better or worse now than it was previously, or to be able to say that economy *A*'s performance is better or worse than that of Economy *B*. The first is a comparison over time, the second an international comparison. It turns out that in both of these cases, the major problem about comparative performance assessment is differing relative prices.

5.3.6.1 Comparisons over time

To consider the problems that arise when prices change, let us go back to a closed economy with no foreign trade. Particularly, look at the data of Table 5.1 again. There all final demand deliveries were for consumption by individuals. Looking at such an economy makes it simple to show what the problems, and their solutions, are. The lessons that emerge are quite generally applicable.

Take it that Table 5.1 refers to the economy in some year, given the label 0. In that year, expenditure on the consumption of agricultural output was 800 million dollars and expenditure on the consumption of manufactured output was 1,400 million dollars, so that GDP was 2,200 million dollars. To make things simple, suppose that all agricultural output was apples which sold at $1 each, and that all manufacturing output was widgets which sold at $2 each. Then, the corresponding quantities, as shown in Table 5.10, were 800×10^6 apples and 700×10^6 widgets.

We are interested in comparing GDP in year 0 with GDP in some later year given the label 1. As between 0 and 1, as shown in Table 5.10, the quantities of both apples and widgets increase by 10 per cent, so that total consumption increases by 10 per cent.

Table 5.10 A numerical example for measuring the change in GDP				
	Year 0		Year 1	
	Apples	*Widgets*	*Apples*	*Widgets*
Quantity, millions	800	700	880	770
Price, dollars	1	2	1	2
Price × Quantity, $ × 10⁶	800	1400	880	1540
$ GDP, × 10⁶		2200		2420

If the prices of apples and widgets are the same in both years, we find that GDP increases by 10 per cent. In fact, prices rarely remain constant over time. With inflation, all prices increase in the same proportion and relative prices remain constant. In Table 5.11, quantities change as in Table 5.10 but the prices of apples and widgets both double as between year 0 and year 1, so that in both years widgets are twice the price of apples. In that case calculating year 0 GDP using year 0 prices and year 1 GDP using year 1 prices gives the result shown for **current price GDP**, sometimes also known as **nominal GDP**. Current price GDP increases by a factor of 2.2, whereas we know that consumption has increased by a factor of just 1.1. The problem is the doubling of the prices used. To measure GDP properly we need to use the same prices for apples and widgets in both years. We can either use year 0 prices for year 0 and year 1, or year 1 prices for year 0 and year 1. As shown in Table 5.11, the $ figure for each year's GDP depends on which way we do things, but both ways show GDP increasing by 10 per cent. When GDP for a year is calculated using the prices that obtained in some other year, rather than current prices, the result is referred to as **real GDP**, or **constant price GDP**. The year from which the prices are taken to calculate real GDP is known as the base year. Usually in published national income accounts, real GDP is calculated using a base year that is in the past – in this example year 0 would be such a base year. The date for the base year, for example 1995, is usually indicated stating that the GDP numbers shown are in, for example, 1995 dollars. Table 5.11 shows calculations in year 0 dollars and year 1 dollars.

Pure inflation, as illustrated in Table 5.11 with all prices increasing in equal proportions, is not what is actually experienced in real economies. In reality what is called inflation involves most prices increasing in similar, but not equal, proportions. That means that relative prices change. Changing relative prices give rise to problems for measuring real national income. Table 5.12 shows the price of apples doubling while the price of widgets triples, as between years 0 and 1. Current price GDP increases by a factor of 2.9. Proceeding as before for the measurement of real GDP, we see that as before while $ values differ according to whether year 0 or year 1 dollars are used, either way real GDP is found, correctly, to increase by 10 per cent.

From Table 5.12 it does not seem that changing relative prices present any real problems for GDP as a measure of well-being, where we equate well-being with total consumption. This is because the example being dealt with is still unrealistic. It has been constructed so that the quantities consumed of both commodities increase in the same proportion, in which case total consumption increases in the same proportion, and GDP measurement reflects this so long as we use base period prices

Table 5.11 Nominal and real GDP: constant relative prices

	Year 0		Year 1	
	Apples	*Widgets*	*Apples*	*Widgets*
Quantity, millions	800	700	880	770
Price, dollars	1	2	2	4
Price × Quantity, $ × 10⁶	800	1400	1760	3080
Current Price $ GDP, × 10⁶		2200		4840
Year 0 price, dollars	1	2	1	2
Year 0 price × Quantity, $ × 10⁶	800	1400	880	1540
Real GDP, year 0 $ × 10⁶		2200		2420
Year 1 real GDP ÷ year 0 Real GDP			1.1	
Year 1 price, dollars	2	4	2	4
Year 1 price × quantity, $ × 10⁶	1600	2800	1760	3080
Real GDP, Year 1 $ × 10⁶		4400		4840
Year 1 real GDP ÷ year 0 Real GDP			1.1	

Table 5.12 Nominal and real GDP: changing relative prices

	Year 0		Year 1	
	Apples	*Widgets*	*Apples*	*Widgets*
Quantity, millions	800	700	880	770
Price, dollars	1	2	2	6
Price × quantity, $ × 10⁶	800	1400	1760	4620
Current Price GDP, $ × 10⁶		2200		6380
Year 0 price, dollars	1	2	1	2
Year 0 price × quantity, $ × 10⁶	800	1400	880	1540
Real GDP, year 0 $ × 10⁶		2200		2420
Year 1 real GDP ÷ Year 0 real GDP			1.1	
Year 1 Price, Dollars	2	6	2	6
Year 1 Price × Quantity, $ × 10⁶	1600	4200	1760	4620
Real GDP, year 1 $ × 10⁶		5800		6380
Year 1 real GDP ÷ year 0 real GDP			1.1	

for both years. And, it does not matter which year is used as base year. In practice quantities consumed do not change in equal proportions, in which case there is a problem as illustrated in Table 5.13. Typically for real economies, rates of increase in quantity consumption vary across commodities, and for some commodities are negative. In such cases, the figure obtained for real GDP in a given year, as a percentage change in relation to any other year as well as in $ terms, will vary according to the base year the prices for which are used to calculate real GDP. Table 5.13 illustrates the problem for a case where prices change as in Table 5.12 – relative prices change – and where the consumption of apples falls while that of widgets increases.

Table 5.13 Measuring real GDP when quantities go down as well as up

	Year 0		Year 1	
	Apples	*Widgets*	*Apples*	*Widgets*
Quantity, millions	800	700	700	735
Price, dollars	1	2	2	6
Price × quantity, $ × 10⁶	800	1400	1400	4410
Current price GDP, $ × 10⁶		**2200**		**5810**
Year 0 price, dollars	1	2	1	2
Year 0 price × quantity, $ × 10⁶	800	1400	700	1470
Real GDP, year 0 $ × 10⁶		**2200**		**2170**
Year 1 real GDP ÷ year 0 real GDP			**0.9864**	
Year 1 price, dollars	2	6	2	6
Year 1 price × quantity, $ × 10⁶	1600	4200	1400	4410
Real GDP, year 1 $ × 10⁶		**5800**		**5810**
Year 1 real GDP ÷ year 0 real GDP			**1.0017**	

If year 0 is taken as base year, then real GDP is calculated as going down. If year 1 is used as base year, it goes up. Which is right? Does real GDP really increase or decrease? The answer to these questions is that it depends how you want to look at it. The relative prices that obtain in a market economy ideally reflect the relative values placed upon commodities by individuals, and changing relative prices reflect changing relative valuations. The prices in Table 5.13 are saying that whereas in year 0 consumers valued a widget twice as much as an apple, in year 1 they valued a widget three times as much. Using year 0 as base year is weighting quantities in both years by the relative values obtaining in year 0 – one widget is worth twice as much as one apple. Using year 1 prices to calculate real GDP in both years is using year 1 relative values to weight quantities in both years. One cannot say that one set of weights is right and the other is wrong. Essentially, working in year 0 dollars amounts to looking at things in terms of the preferences of individuals as they are in year 0, while using year 1 dollars means using year 1 preferences.

The numbers used in Table 5.13 were chosen so as to make the point in an extreme way, with the direction of change of real GDP depending on the year chosen as base year. In reality, the choice of base year will affect the assessment of the size of the proportional change in real national income, rather than the direction of change. Also, the magnitude of the effect is likely to depend upon how far apart the years being compared are. Large changes in relative prices do not generally happen very quickly. For a comparison of two years that are just a few years apart, 1995 and 2000 for example, it is unlikely to make a large difference to the estimated change in real national income which of the years is selected as base year. For two years that are far apart, 1950 and 2000 for example, it is going to make a big difference. For a comparison across two or more decades, real GDP changes will be very different according to whether relative prices from the start of the comparison period or its end are used, and do not really have much meaning. The problem of changing relative prices is, over such lengths of time, compounded by the appearance of new commodities and the disappearance of old ones. In 1980 PCs were virtually non-existent as something that individuals bought for their own use; in 1980 many people listened to music at home by putting vinyl discs on turntables; by 2000 hardly anybody did that. In practice, national income statisticians respond to these kinds of problems by using as base year for the measurement of this year's real GDP a year up to a decade or so ago, and changing the base year every decade or so.

5.3.6.2 International comparisons

International comparisons of well-being are often made in terms of national income per capita. While this should be done in terms of net national income, it is, for the reason discussed above, in practice always done in terms of gross national income, and usually in terms of GDP. The problem that immediately arises is that a country's GDP is measured in its currency units – £ in the UK, $ in the USA, Yen in Japan, etc. The simplest solution to this problem is to use the exchange rate against some selected currency to convert GDP for each country from local currency measurement to measurement in the selected currency. Where many countries are being considered it is universal practice to express all GDPs in terms of US$. Thus, Table 5.9 gave the UK's GDP in 2001 as approximately £1,000 billion, which for an exchange rate of $1.5 to the £ could be expressed as $1,500 billion.

The exchange rate for one nation's currency against another is determined by the forces of demand and supply as they operate on the two currencies in the foreign exchange markets. In principle, according to the **purchasing power parity theory**, this should mean that exchange rates reflect the purchasing powers of currencies. An exchange rate of US$1.5 to the £ should mean, for example, that $150 in the USA can buy the same basket of goods and services as £100 in the UK. In fact, market exchange rates do not accurately reflect purchasing power in this way, for two reasons. First, actual foreign exchange markets do not work as they should in principle, and exchange rates are affected by factors other than purchasing power. Second, relative prices differ as between countries, which gives rise to the same sort of problems for international comparisons as discussed above for comparisons over time in a single country. For both of these reasons, using exchange rates to convert local currency GDPs to US$ GDPs does not produce a set of GDP figures which accurately reflect consumption levels across countries. Box 5.2 reports on an investigation of the validity of the theory of purchasing power parity that uses a very simple 'basket of goods and services'.

The solution to the problem with exchange rates that is adopted is very similar to that adopted in the case of comparisons over time. All GDPs are expressed in US dollars, but by pricing goods and services at their USA prices rather than by simply multiplying local currency GDP by the exchange rate. The GDP figures so obtained are referred to as GDP measured in PPP US$, where PPP stands for Purchasing Power Parity. Table 5.15 provides a simple illustration. We are interested in comparing Country X and the USA. The currency in country X is crowns, denoted Cr. For both commodities, consumption in Country X is 10 per cent of what it is in the USA. In their own currencies, Country X GDP is Cr.300×10^6, and USA GDP is $7,000 \times 10^6$. The exchange rate is Cr./$ = 1.5 so that one crown buys 1.5 dollars. Then, using the exchange rate to express Country X GDP in US$ gives it as 450×10^6. The ratio of GDP for the USA to GDP for Country X measured this way is 7,000/450 = 15.56,

Box 5.2 The Big Mac Index

Each year *The Economist* looks at the, local currency, price of a McDonald's Big Mac in a number of countries. It looks at the Big Mac because it is a commodity which is very much the same wherever it is produced and consumed. According to the theory of purchasing power parity, a Big Mac should cost the same in US$ wherever it is consumed, when the US$ price is computed from the local price using the exchange rate for the local currency against the $. Table 5.14 shows some of the results for 2001. *The Economist* has been doing this since 1986, and similar marked departures from the predictions of the theory of purchasing power parity are found each year, though the pattern across countries varies over time.

Table 5.14 Departures from purchasing power parity according to Big Mac prices

	Big Mac price local currency	Exchange rate local/US$	Big Mac price US$s	Big Mac exchange rate local/US$	Over-valuation of local currency against the US$ %
USA	US$2.54		2.54		
Australia	A$3.00	1.98	1.52	1.18	−40
Canada	C$3.33	1.56	2.14	1.31	−16
China	Yuan9.90	8.28	1.20	3.90	−53
Denmark	DKr24.75	8.46	2.93	9.74	15
Indonesia	R14700	10855	1.35	5787	−47
New Zealand	NZ$3.60	2.47	1.46	1.42	−43
Philippines	Peso59.00	50.3	1.17	23.2	−54
Russia	R35.00	28.9	1.21	13.8	−52
Switzerland	SFr6.30	1.73	1.73	2.48	44
United Kingdom	£1.99	0.70	2.84	0.78	11

Source: The Economist, 21–27 April (2001), p. 98.

In Table 5.14 the second column shows the price of a Big Mac in the country indicated in the first column in the local currency. The third column shows the exchange rate as the local currency over dollars, so that for Australia, for example, an exchange rate of 1.98 means that the US$ was worth 1.98 times as much as an Australian $ in the exchange market – to buy US$1.00 would cost A$1.98. The fourth column shows the local price of a Big Mac converted to US$ using the corresponding exchange rate. For Australia, 3.00 divided by 1.98 gives 1.52 – if you were in Sydney and had US$, changing US$1.52 into Australian $ at the rate 1.98 would get you the price of a Big Mac. The Big Mac Exchange Rate, shown in the fifth column, is the rate implied by the price of a Big Mac in local currencies. It costs US$2.54 in the USA and A$3.00 in Australia, and 3.00/2.54 = 1.18. In terms of Big Macs, the US$ is worth A$1.18, whereas in terms of the exchange market it is worth A$1.98. Dividing the Big Mac exchange rate by the actual exchange rate, 1.18/1.98 = 0.60, so that the Australian $ is 40 per cent undervalued against the US$ according to the local prices of Big Macs. Somebody from the USA visiting Australia and buying a Big Mac with A$ bought using US$ at the exchange rate would be paying 40 per cent less for it in US$ than she would have done when buying a Big Mac back in the USA.

To the extent that the Australia/USA Big Mac picture holds for other goods and services in the two economies, this apparently shows that the prediction of the theory of purchasing power parity is falsified. The same holds for the other currencies considered in Table 5.14. However, the theory is only supposed to explain what happens in the long run, and it could be that it appears not to hold because the underlying forces that are supposed to make it work have not had time to work themselves out. Actually, *The Economist* claims that, despite some obvious limitations, the Big Mac Index – the discrepancy between the current actual exchange rate and the Big Mac exchange rate – is a good predictor of future movements in the actual exchange rate. It cites the case of the launch of the € in 1999, when the general view was that the € would rise against the US$ from its launch rate. However, at that time the Big Mac index showed the € as overvalued against the US$. In fact, after its launch the € fell against the US$.

whereas we know that consumption in the USA is ten times what it is in Country X. We can make such a statement without reference to prices because we made consumption of both commodities ten times greater in the USA. At the bottom of Table 5.15 the USA prices for apples and widgets are used with Country X quantities to compute Country X GDP in PPP US$ as 700×10^6, which is 10 per cent of USA

Table 5.15 Calculating GDP in PPP $US				
	Country X		USA	
	Apples	Widgets	Apples	Widgets
Quantity, millions	100	100	1000	1000
Local price	Cr.1	Cr.2	$5	$2
Local price × Quantity	Cr.100 × 10^6	Cr.200 × 10^6	$5000 × 10^6	$2000 × 10^6
Local price GDP	**Cr.300 × 10^6**		**$7000 × 10^6**	
US$ GDP using exchange rate	**450 × 10^6**		**7000 × 10^6**	
USA price × quantity	$500 × 10^6	$200 × 10^6	$5000 × 10^6	$2000 × 10^6
PPP $US GDP	**700 × 10^6**		**7,000 × 10^6**	

GDP calculated using the same prices. Doing things this way does give the correct ratio for aggregate consumption in the two countries. As you can readily check, in this example you get the same answer for this ratio if you measure GDP in both countries using County X prices in crowns. That is the case here only because USA consumption is ten times County X consumption for both commodities. Where this special assumption does not hold, comparisons between countries face the same problem as do comparisons over time for a single country – the answer depends on which country's prices are used.

In the next chapter we will look at some international GDP comparisons which use PPP US$. The practice of producing such GDP data is actually a good deal more complex, and subject to more ambiguity, than the example in Table 5.15 might suggest, and involves a large international research programme. Basically this involves drawing up a list of goods and services, estimating the quantity of each item on the list that is delivered to final demand in each country, and then aggregating over all quantities in each country using USA prices for all of the items in the list. In Table 5.15 making the GDP comparison using the exchange rate makes the poorer country appear worse-off relative to the USA than when PPP US$ are used. This is the case in the actual data as well – it is always the case that disparities between the rich countries and the developing world are greater using actual exchange rates to do the calculations.

5.4 NATIONAL INCOME ACCOUNTING AND THE ENVIRONMENT

While the limitations of GDP as an economic performance indicator have been well understood by economists for a long time, it is still much used as such an indicator. Why is this? There are several reasons. One is that many commentators do not properly appreciate the limitations of either GDP or the difficulties involved in measuring it accurately. Economists have not done as much as they should to spread awareness of the problems about GDP. A second reason is that among those who have a proper appreciation of the limitations of GDP, there are many who take the view that it is, nonetheless, the best single number indicator available. In the next chapter we will look at some evidence about the relationship between

GDP and other measures of economic performance as the satisfaction of needs and desires.

In the last two decades of the twentieth century there emerged environmentally driven criticism of national income per capita as a measure of economic performance. This criticism raises considerations additional to those already looked at here, and has three main components. These are that, as measured by the existing accounting conventions, national income per capita:

(1)   takes no account of the depletion of natural resources;
(2)   takes no account of environmental degradation affecting life support and amenity services; and
(3)   includes defensive expenditures to rectify or prevent environmental degradation.

The first two deficiencies mean that the measure of current well-being takes no account of the extent to which it is being achieved at the expense of future well-being. It overstates, that is, sustainable well–being. The third points in the same direction, in that per capita national income includes spending by individuals and government that is necessary only because of environmental degradation.

The United Nations Statistical Division, UNSTAT, has, in consultation with other national and international organisations, considered these problems and made proposals as to how the agencies responsible for preparing national income accounts should modify the conventions that they follow, and the data that they publish, so as to respond to them. We now look at these proposals.

5.4.1 Natural resource balance sheets

An account showing the value of a stock of assets at a point in time is known as a **balance sheet**, and UNSTAT proposes that the standard national income accounts publication for a given year should include for the beginning and end of the year a natural resource balance sheet. Table 5.16 provides some hypothetical numbers for an economy that exploits two natural resources: oil and fish. It shows that at the start of the year the economy's stock of resources was worth £20,000 million. During the course of the year both stocks were run down, but for each the unit value increased. The net effect was that at the end of the year, the balance sheet showed a smaller total value for the economy's stock of resources – £18,845 million. The amount by which the balance sheet value at the end of the year is less than that at the beginning of the year is the depreciation of the natural resource stock.

In reality, the practical problems of compiling natural resource balance sheets are considerable. The principal problems relate to determining unit values, though there are also problems about determining stock sizes. The unit values required are the prices of the unextracted resources – the price of oil in the ground and fish in the sea in our hypothetical economy. As will be discussed in Chapter 9, while *in situ* non-renewable resources such as oil in the ground often do have prices attached to them, *in situ* renewable resources such as fish in the sea generally do not. Rights to exploit minerals and fossil fuels are traded in markets, but rights to catch fish generally are not. What this means is that including a renewable resource such as an ocean fish stock in a natural resource balance sheet would require estimating an *in situ* unit value. There are techniques for doing this using market data on the

Table 5.16 Opening and closing natural resource balance sheets

	Oil stock		Fish stock		
	Quantity tonnes × 10⁶	Unit value £	Quantity tonnes × 10⁶	Unit value £s	Total value of resource stocks £ × 10⁶
Start of year	1000	10.00	10000	1.00	10000 + 10000 = 20000
End of year	950	10.50	9400	1.05	9975 + 9870 = 18845

price of caught fish and estimates of the unit cost of catching fish – basically the *in situ* unit value is treated as the difference between the landed price and the estimated unit cost of harvesting. The results that the techniques produce are estimates, not data, and subject to errors of unknown size.

It has been suggested that the environmental assets that provide waste assimilation, amenity and life support services should also be included in balance sheets for the natural environment. Currently UNSTAT does not endorse such proposals. This is mainly because of the difficulty of coming up with useful unit values. For these assets there are no market values. Economists have developed techniques for attaching monetary values to these kinds of environmental assets, but UNSTAT does not regard these techniques as robust enough to provide data that could be included in official statistical publications.

5.4.2 Satellite accounting

As noted above, neglect of depletion and degradation is taken to mean that, as currently measured, per capita national income overstates sustainable well-being. Some have argued that the conventions for national income accounting should be changed so that what gets measured is sustainable national income when allowance is made for the environmental impact of economic activity in the year in question. The idea here is that over a year the reduction in the balance sheet value of the economy's total stock of natural resources and other environmental assets should be subtracted from net national income measured in the usual way to give sustainable national income. This change can be called **environmental cost** (EC), in which case sustainable national income (SDP for sustainable domestic product) would be defined as

$$SDP \equiv NDP - EC \equiv GDP - D - EC$$

where D is the depreciation of the man-made capital stock during the year. Environmental cost can be regarded as the depreciation of the economy's stock of natural resources during the year, and the definition is sometimes presented as

$$SDP \equiv GDP - D_M - D_N$$

where D_M stands for the depreciation of man-made capital and D_N for the depreciation of natural resources and other environmental assets, which are often jointly referred to as natural capital.

In Table 5.16 the opening balance sheet value is £20,000 million and the closing balance sheet value is £18,845 million so that

$$EC = -[18{,}845 - 20{,}000] = £1{,}155 \times 10^6$$

Suppose that for the year in question *NDP* had been measured as £100,000 million. Then *SDP* would be $100{,}000 - 1{,}155 = £98845 \times 10^6$.

The UNSTAT guidelines do *not* include the recommendation that the national income accounting conventions get changed like this so that sustainable national income is reported. They *do* recommend that there is published along with the standard national income accounts the opening and closing natural resource balance sheets for the year in question. These balance sheets are referred to as satellite accounts. The idea is that it would be open to anybody to use the satellite accounts to calculate an SDP figure from the standard figure for NDP. The reason that UNSTAT takes this position is that, even when just resource depletion is considered, the estimate of EC is not a robust number. At the most basic level, to do what it is supposed to do it would have to cover the opening and closing stocks of *every* natural resource used in the economy. Most national statistical agencies are not currently able to do this. Even for a non-renewable natural resource where reasonable quantity data is available and estimates of the *in situ* price can be made in a reasonably straightforward way, it is not easy to come up with a unique and generally agreed EC-type number for its depreciation. Often there will be different estimates of the unit value of a resource. For this reason, the view taken by UNSTAT is that it is better to stick with a measure of national income which is robust, even though it is not a proper measure of sustainable income, than to switch a measure which, though proper in principle, is not robust.

The problem here can be illustrated using Table 5.16. The unit values shown for the fish stock are estimates. Suppose that there also exists another set of estimates, where the opening value is £1.20 and that at the end of the year is £1.26. Using these estimates gives EC as £181 million, and applying that to the above figure for NDP gives SDP as £99,819 million. The UNSTAT view is that such possibilities for disagreement are best left in the satellite accounts, rather than imported into the main income accounts.

UNSTAT does not recommend that the satellite accounts cover environmental assets other than natural resources. This is mainly because of the difficulties of putting meaningful and reliable monetary values on them, given that they are not traded in markets. The position with respect to defensive environmental expenditures is similar. UNSTAT does not recommend that defensive expenditures be deducted from NDP. It does recommend that such expenditures be identified in the accounts.

It should be emphasised that we have been discussing recommendations made by UNSTAT, which are not binding on any national statistical agency. Most national statistical agencies do not prepare satellite accounts covering all natural resources. Some countries – the UK for example – do now regularly publish, along with the standard national income accounts, balance sheets for some natural resources. In the UK the annual publication for the standard national income accounts – the 'Blue Book' discussed earlier – now has a section on 'Environmental Accounts'. It includes natural resource balance sheets, where the only resources covered are oil

---

Box 5.3 Estimating the depreciation of Australia's non-renewable resources

Much of Australian economic activity is based on the exploitation of the country's natural resources, so the question of the depreciation of those resources is a matter of some importance for Australian policy makers. In 1995 the Australian Bureau of Statistics (ABS) published a first set of balance sheets for a range of Australia's natural resources. In Australia the financial year runs from 1 July to 30 June. For each of 33 non-renewable resources, i.e. minerals and fossil fuels, the publication provided:
- estimates of the size of the stock at the end of the financial years 1988/89, 1989/90, 1990/91 and 1991/92;
- the prices that the extracted resource sold for at the end of the financial years 1988/89, 1989/90, 1990/91 and 1991/92;
- estimates of the unit (average) cost of extraction at the end of the financial years 1988/89, 1989/90, 1990/91 and 1991/92;
- production in each of the financial years 1988/89, 1989/90, 1990/91 and 1991/92.

From these, the ABS calculated estimates of the depreciation – the change over the year in the balance sheet value – of each of the 33 resources for each of the years covered. The price of the unextracted resource was calculated as the difference between the price of the extracted resource and the estimated unit cost of extraction. Adding across the 33 resources produced the figures shown in the second column of Table 5.17, under ABS, for the depreciation of all of Australia's non-renewable resources. The figures are negative mainly because of new discoveries of some of the resources, but in some cases the price of the extracted resource went up over a year. Using these figures to go from NDP to SDP would make the latter bigger than the former!

Table 5.17 Alternative estimates of the depreciation of Australia's non-renewable resources

Year	ABS AUS$ $\times 10^6$	El Serafy AUS$ $\times 10^6$
1989/90	−6500	1228
1990/91	−19900	1922
1991/92	−9700	2328

Source: Common and Sanyal (1998).

The ABS actually calculated opening and closing balance sheet values, and took the differences as depreciation as discussed in the chapter here. Other methods of calculating the depreciation of non-renewable resources have been proposed in the economics literature, which work with the amount extracted during a year. One of these is the El Serafy rule, named after the economist who worked it out. Applying that rule to the ABS data gives, after adding across the 33 non-renewable resources, the results for the depreciation of all of Australia's non-renewable resources shown in the third column of Table 5.17. These figures are very different from those in the second column and are all positive, so that they would make SDP less than NDP. There is no consensus among economists and national income statisticians as to which is the 'right' way to calculate the depreciation of non-renewable resources. Both of the methods featuring in Table 5.17 have been widely used in the academic literature. UNSTAT does not make an unequivocal statement about the matter, but a careful reading of its publications suggest a preference for the method used by the ABS. That method requires more data than the El Serafy method, which often is not available. The point that Table 5.17 exemplifies is that different analysts can come up with different answers for the size of the adjustment to go from NDP to SDP; even when taking account of only non-renewable resources, which are the easiest environmental assets to deal with.

---

and gas, and tables giving data on expenditure on environmental protection. There are also data, in physical units, on energy consumption, atmospheric emissions, and water use. Box 5.3 reports on some work with data published by the official statistical agency of Australia, which illustrates the problems of coming up with a unique and definitive number for EC, even when attention is confined to non-renewable resources.

SUMMARY

Input–output accounts contain a lot of detailed information about the industrial structure of an economy, and can be used with data on industries' uses of natural resources and emissions of wastes to relate environmental extractions and insertions to the consumption of different commodities. Analysis based on input–output accounts can be useful for investigating the economic and environmental implications of technological change. The economic accounts that attract most attention are the national income accounts which abstract from the industrial detail of the input–output accounts and focus on 'bottom line' magnitudes like GDP. National income as GDP is a measure of the level of activity in an economy, but is frequently treated as a measure of economic performance and as such has many defects. Not the least of these is that it completely neglects the impact of current economic activity on the environment. Proposals have been made as to how this type of defect could be addressed. In practice, at the level of official statistical sources, not much has been done about these proposals. Implementing them raises lots of problems – SDP cannot be measured accurately.

KEYWORDS

Balance sheet (p. 155): an account showing the value of a stock of assets at a point in time.

Constant price GDP (p. 149): GDP for a period using the prices that obtained in some other, usually some earlier, period, known as the base period.

Current price GDP (p. 149): GDP for a period measured using the prices that obtained during that period.

Depreciation (p. 138): the extent to which the existing capital stock is reduced by the use of its services in production, and hence the amount of investment that is needed to maintain the size of the capital stock. It is the difference between gross and net investment.

Direct taxes (p. 140): taxes levied on incomes and wealth.

Environmental cost (p. 156): the change in the balance sheet value of the stock of environmental assets over the period.

Factor payments (p. 126): payments to individuals for the services that they provide as inputs to production.

Final demand (p. 126): sales for consumption by individuals, investment by firms, consumption and investment by government, and use overseas.

GDP (p. 143): Gross Domestic Product is the value of the output for final demand produced by factors of production that are located in the domestic economy. It is necessarily equal, in principle, to the sum of all of the factor incomes arising in the domestic economy.

GNP (p. 143): Gross National Product is the value of the final demand output produced by domestically owned factors of production, irrespective of where the production takes place.

Indirect taxes (p. 140): taxes levied on purchases of goods and services.

Industry (p. 125): sector of an economy; consists of firms which produce a single commodity.

Input–output coefficient table (p. 127): the array of coefficients for intermediate and primary inputs used per unit output.

Intermediate demand (p. 127): sales by one industry to another industry of commodities that are used up in current production.

Intermediate inputs (p. 126): good and services bought from other firms and used up in the production of one of the final goods and services.

Leontief matrix (p. 130): an array of coefficients which give the direct and indirect input requirements for every industry to meet unit levels of final demand requirements.

Nominal GDP (p. 149): GDP for a period measured using the prices that obtained during that period.

Primary Inputs (p. 126): inputs other than intermediate commodities, the services of factors of production, and imports.

Purchasing power parity theory (p. 152): holds that exchange rates reflect the purchasing powers of the currencies concerned.

Real GDP (p. 149): GDP for a period using the prices that obtained in some other, usually some earlier, period, known as the base period.

Sustainable national income (p. 145): the maximum that could be consumed in a period while not running down the economy's capital stock. It is equal to net national income.

Transactions table (p. 126): the table showing for each industry all of its expenditures on intermediate commodities and factor services, and all of its sales to other industries and to final demand.

Transfer payments (p. 140): payments by government to individuals for which there is no corresponding return flow of services or commodities.

Value added (p. 138): for a firm or an industry, the difference between sales receipts and payments for purchases of goods and services, which is equal to the sum of payments to factors of production.

APPENDIX: INPUT–OUTPUT ALGEBRA

Calculating industry gross outputs

Bringing together symbols introduced in the body of the chapter, we can state the upper part of the transactions table as

		Sales to		
Purchases From	Agriculture	Manufacturing	Final Demand	**Total Output**
Agriculture	0	Q_{AM}	F_A	Q_A
Manufacturing	Q_{MA}	0	F_M	Q_M

with the corresponding set of inter-industry coefficients

	Agriculture	Manufacturing
Agriculture	0	a_{AM}
Manufacturing	a_{MA}	0

where these are defined as

$$a_{AM} \equiv \frac{Q_{AM}}{Q_M}$$

$$a_{MA} \equiv \frac{Q_{MA}}{Q_A}$$

With these definitions, the output balance equations are

$$Q_A = (a_{AM} \times Q_M) + F_A \tag{1}$$

$$Q_M = (a_{MA} \times Q_A) + F_M \tag{2}$$

Using the second to substitute for Q_M in the first gives

$$Q_A = a_{AM} \times ([a_{MA} \times Q_A] + F_M) + F_A$$

which is

$$Q_A(1 - [a_{AM} \times a_{MA}]) = (a_{AM} \times F_M) + F_A$$

which can be re-arranged to give the solution for Q_A as

$$Q_A = \left(\frac{1}{1 - [a_{AM} \times a_{MA}]}\right) \times F_A + \left(\frac{a_{AM}}{1 - [a_{AM} \times a_{MA}]}\right) \times F_M \tag{3}$$

Using this to substitute for Q_A in the second of the output balance equations gives

$$Q_M = \left(\frac{a_{MA}}{1 - [a_{AM} \times a_{MA}]}\right) \times F_A + \left(\frac{a_{MA} \times a_{AM}}{1 - [a_{AM} \times a_{MA}]}\right) \times F_M + F_M$$

$$= \left(\frac{a_{MA}}{1 - [a_{AM} \times a_{MA}]}\right) \times F_A + \left(\frac{[a_{MA} \times a_{AM}] + 1 - [a_{AM} \times a_{MA}]}{1 - [a_{AM} \times a_{MA}]}\right) \times F_M$$

which is

$$Q_M = \left(\frac{a_{MA}}{1 - [a_{AM} \times a_{MA}]}\right) \times F_A + \left(\frac{1}{1 - [a_{AM} \times a_{MA}]}\right) \times F_M \tag{4}$$

Equations 3 and 4 show explicitly and generally the way in which the gross output levels for each industry are related to the final demands for both agricultural and manufacturing output, according to the inter-industry input coefficients. The inter-industry coefficients are the a coefficients defined above. Using the values for the a coefficients given in Table 5.2, Equations 3 and 4 are

$$Q_A = \left(\frac{1}{1 - 0.06}\right) \times F_A + \left(\frac{0.1}{1 - 0.06}\right) \times F_M$$

$$= 1.0638 \times F_A + 0.1064 \times F_M$$

$$Q_M = \left(\frac{0.6}{1 - 0.06}\right) \times F_A + \left(\frac{1}{1 - 0.06}\right) \times F_M$$

$$= 0.6383 \times F_A + 1.0638 \times F_M$$

You can readily check that, subject to rounding errors, the above equations produce, for the same final demands, the same answers for gross outputs as in the chapter. Note also that the coefficients in these two equations are the entries for the direct and indirect requirements per unit delivery to final demand given in Table 5.3.

In published input–output accounts more than two industries are distinguished, usually there are twenty or more and some publications for industrial economies go to more than one hundred sectors. With large numbers of industries and commodities, the principles involved are exactly as set out above – one is solving a set of simultaneous equations. But, where there are n industries there are n equations, and for n greater than 2 the methods of ordinary algebra cannot be used. Because the equations are linear, they can for n large be solved by the methods of matrix algebra, the arithmetic of which can be done with a spreadsheet such as Excel^{TM}. The interested reader will find references giving more information about this in the Further Reading section.

Allocating resource use and emissions

With R_A and R_M for the resource input to Agriculture and Manufacturing respectively, define

$$r_A \equiv \frac{R_A}{Q_A} \quad \text{and} \quad r_M \equiv \frac{R_M}{Q_M}$$

as resource input coefficients. With R for the economy's total resource use

$$R = R_A + R_M = (r_A \times Q_A) + (r_M \times Q_M)$$

Substituting here for Q_A and Q_M from equations 3 and 4 gives

$$R = \left(\frac{r_A}{1 - [a_{AM} \times a_{MA}]}\right) \times F_A + \left(\frac{r_A \times a_{AM}}{1 - [a_{AM} \times a_{MA}]}\right) \times F_M$$
$$+ \left(\frac{r_M \times a_{MA}}{1 - [a_{AM} \times a_{MA}]}\right) \times F_A + \left(\frac{r_M}{1 - [a_{AM} \times a_{MA}]}\right) \times F_M$$

which on collecting terms is

$$R = \left(\frac{r_A + [r_M \times a_{MA}]}{1 - [a_{AM} \times a_{MA}]}\right) \times F_A + \left(\frac{[r_A \times a_{AM}] + r_M}{1 - [a_{AM} \times a_{MA}]}\right) \times F_M \tag{5}$$

Equation 5 allocates total use of the resource, R, across deliveries to Final Demand, F_A and F_M. If you make the appropriate substitutions for F_A and F_M and the a and r coefficient values in equation 5 and do the arithmetic you will get the results given in the body of the chapter.

With E_A and E_M for emissions from Agriculture and Manufacturing respectively, define

$$e_A \equiv \frac{E_A}{Q_A} \quad \text{and} \quad e_M \equiv \frac{E_M}{Q_M}$$

as emissions coefficients. With E for total emissions

$$E = E_A + E_M = (e_A \times Q_A) + (e_M \times Q_M)$$

Proceeding as above for the resource case leads to

$$E = \left(\frac{e_A + [e_M \times a_{MA}]}{1 - [a_{AM} \times a_{MA}]}\right) \times F_A + \left(\frac{[e_A \times a_{AM}] + e_M}{1 - [a_{AM} \times a_{MA}]}\right) \times F_M \tag{6}$$

which allocates emissions across final demand deliveries. Again, you can check that Equation 6 gives the results from the body of the chapter.

Establishing the identity of *NI*, *NP* and *NE*

Use WS_A and OFP_A for Agriculture's Wages and salaries and Other factor payments respectively, and WS_M and OFP_M similarly for Manufacturing. For each industry expenditure on inputs of all kinds must equal receipts from sales of all kinds, so that

$$Q_{MA} + WS_A + OFP_A \equiv Q_{AM} + F_A \qquad (7)$$

is expenditure identically equal to receipts for Agriculture, and

$$Q_{AM} + WS_M + OFP_M \equiv Q_{MA} + F_M \qquad (8)$$

similarly for Manufacturing. Now add the lefthand sides of Equations 7 and 8 to get

$$Q_{MA} + Q_{AM} + WS_A + WS_M + OFP_A + OFP_M$$

and add the righthand sides to get

$$Q_{AM} + Q_{MA} + F_A + F_M$$

The results of these two additions must be equal, so

$$Q_{MA} + Q_{AM} + WS_A + WS_M + OFP_A + OFP_M \equiv Q_{AM} + Q_{MA} + F_A + F_M$$

and subtracting Q_{MA} and Q_{AM} from both sides here gives

$$WS_A + OFP_A + WS_M + WS_M \equiv F_A + F_M$$

which says that total factor payments in the economy are equal to total expenditure on final demand, i.e.

$$NI \equiv NE$$

and since *NE* and *NP* are the same thing, this establishes that

$$NI \equiv NE \equiv NP.$$

FURTHER READING

Introductory economics texts always cover national income accounting, but rarely deal with input–output accounting. In fact, we cannot come up with a reference to a book that deals with input–output at an introductory level. A comprehensive input–output text is Miller and Blair (1985), which includes energy and environmental extensions to the basic accounting and analysis. Perman *et al.* (2003), ch. 9, covers it briefly, focusing mainly on the resource and environmental aspects. Perman *et al.* (2003), appendix to ch. 6, also provides a brief introduction to the matrix algebra necessary for doing input–output analysis where there are more than two industries. A fuller treatment of matrix algebra will be found in most mathematics for economists texts – Chiang (1984) is a good example.

A brief introduction to the use of the input–output analysis for analysing extractions from and insertions into the environment is Perman *et al*. (2003), ch. 9. Proops *et al*. (1993) uses input–output methods to analyse CO_2 emissions and options for their abatement. Vaze (1998) presents environmental input–output accounts for the UK and reports the results of analysis using them. Duchin and Lange (1994) uses input–output analysis of the impacts on emissions of technological change to investigate the feasibility of sustainable development as proposed in *Our common future* (WCED, 1987) – Box 7.1 in Chapter 7 of this book summarises some of the results from this study. Duchin and Steenge (1999) is a review of input–output methods for the analysis of economy–environment interdependence: see also Rose (1999).

All introductory economics principles texts deal with national income accounting, which is the starting point for what is called macroeconomics – the study of the behaviour of and interrelations between economic aggregates such as GDP, total consumption, investment, etc. Examples of such texts are Begg *et al*.* (2000) and Mankiw* (2001). The former is the source of the estimates of the size of the black economy cited in this chapter, which are attributed to Lacko (1996). Frey and Stutzer (2002a) also, in ch. 2, provide estimates of the size of the black economy, and of the size of the voluntary sector. Snooks (1994) looks at the importance of the household sector in economic activity, and estimates that in Australia at the end of the twentieth century it was responsible for about 30 per cent of total production. Estimates for other advanced economies come up with similar numbers. Most national statistical agencies produce an account of the details of the conventions used in the national income accounts that they produce, and a listing of their publications can usually be found on their website. Usher (1980) is a thorough examination of the interpretation of GDP as a measure of economic performance.

The basic UNSTAT proposals for satellite accounting are set out in UN (1992) and UN (1993). Up-to-date information on how these proposals are being developed and refined over time is available at the UNSTAT website, address given below. The difficulties involved in measuring sustainable income are explored in Neumayer (1999), ch. 5, and in Perman *et al*. (2003), ch. 19. Both of these provide lots of further references to the literature on what is sometimes known as 'green accounting'. The World Bank has become interested in accounting for the environmental impact of economic activity, and has taken up the idea of 'genuine saving', which is net investment after allowing for the depreciation of natural resources. Hamilton (2000) is a survey of work in this area – this paper can be accessed at the World Bank's website, address below. Common and Sanyal (1998), the source for Box 5.3 here, reviews the different methods that have been proposed for measuring the depreciation of non-renewable resources and uses Australian data to show that they can lead to markedly different results.

WEBSITES

The United Nations Statistics Division (UNSTAT) site, http://unstats.un.org, has lots of information about environmental accounting and national income measurement. The World Bank's work on adjusting national income measurement and measuring genuine saving can be accessed at http://www.worldbank.org/environmentaleconomics/. In the UK the national statistical agency is the Office for National Statistics – http://www.statistics.gov.uk.

DISCUSSION TOPICS

1. Given the problems associated with it, why does GDP figure so largely in discussions about economic policy?
2. If some of the results in Table 5.17, Box 5.3, were used in $SDP = NDP - EC$, then SDP would be higher than NDP. Does this make sense?
3. Discuss the arguments that could be made for and against the exclusion (or treatment as negative items) of expenditure on environment-defensive activities – such as pollution clean-up – in the measurement of national income. To what other things currently contributing positively to GDP would similar arguments apply?

EXERCISES

1. From the Transactions Table

		Sales to				
Purchases from	*Ag*	*Man*	*C*	*I*	*G*	*X*
Ag	0	500	1000	0	0	500
Man	1000	0	2000	1000	800	200
Primary Inputs						
$W + S$	500	3000				
OFP	300	1000				
M	200	500				
Total Input	2000	5000				

where *Ag* and *Man* are the two industrial sectors and $W + S$ is wages and salaries, *OFP* is other factor payments, *M* is imports, *C* is (private) consumption, *I* is investment, *G* is government expenditure and *X* is exports, do the following.
(a) Work out the input–output coefficient table and the total output requirements per unit delivery to final demand.
(b) Work out the proportionate increases in the gross output levels of each industry for a 25 per cent increase in the consumption of *Man* together with a 10 per cent increase in exports of *Ag*.
(c) For the changes at *b*, work out by how much the labour input increases in each industry.
(d) Work out *GNI* and GDP.

    (e)   If emissions are 1,000 tonnes in *Ag* and 5,000 tonnes in *Man*, work out the allocation of emissions to deliveries of *Ag* and *Man* to final demand.

    (f)   By how much would total emissions be reduced if 50 per cent of the input of *Man* used in *Ag* was replaced by imports?

2.   (a)   For the local price and quantity data given in Table 5.15, work out each country's PPP GDP using Country X prices, and confirm that the ratio of these PPP GDPs is the same as when using USA prices.

    (b)   Modify the data of Table 5.15 so that the quantity of Apples in X is 500 and of Widgets is 2,000, then work out PPP GDPs first using USA prices then using Country X prices. What is the ratio of USA GDP to Country X GDP in each case?

6

Economic growth and human well-being

In this chapter you will:

- Examine how GDP per capita differs across countries;
- Discover the extent of poverty in the world;
- Learn about why some countries are rich and others are poor;
- Be introduced to standard theories of economic growth;
- Learn why economic growth is a major objective of economic policy;
- Look at the relationship between economic growth and the satisfaction of needs and desires.

In the previous chapter you learned about economic accounting, and especially about the measurement of national income. This chapter is concerned with affluence and poverty in the world economy. Economic accounting, and other data, is used to consider differences in the extent to which human needs and desires are satisfied in various countries. The explanation of these differences is sought, and found to lie in different experiences in regard to economic growth. The determinants of economic growth are investigated using simple models. Economic growth is the means by which poverty can be alleviated, and there is no doubt that achieving it is very important in poor countries. It is widely believed that it is also an important objective in rich countries because it makes people happier. It turns out that beyond a certain level, increasing affluence does not do much to make people happier.

6.1 THE RICH AND THE POOR

We begin this chapter by looking at current variations in the level of national income per capita, GDP per capita, around the world, and at the extent of poverty. This sets the scene for an enquiry, in the next section, into why some countries are rich and others poor.

6.1.1 International comparisons of per capita national income

Table 6.1 gives data on average per capita GDP for five groups of countries, and on per capita GDP for selected countries from two of those groupings. Later in the chapter we will be looking at other data for these groupings and countries.

Table 6.1 International comparisons of per capita GDP		
	GDP per capita 2000 PPP US$	Ratio to high income OECD
High income OECD	27848	1.00
FSB	6930	0.25
Developing	3783	0.14
Least developed	1216	0.04
Sub-Saharan Africa	1690	0.06
USA	34142	1.23
UK	23509	0.84
Mexico	9023	0.32
Brazil	7625	0.27
China	3976	0.14
India	2358	0.09
Bangladesh	1602	0.06
Kenya	1022	0.04
Nigeria	896	0.03
Sierra Leone	490	0.02

Source: UNDP (2002): Table 12.

OECD stands for Organisation for Economic Cooperation and Development. The Organisation for European Economic Cooperation was set up in 1948 to promote recovery from the Second World War by coordinating a USA programme of aid for the countries of western Europe. This evolved into the OECD in 1961. There are now 30 members of the OECD, including several former members of the Soviet bloc, Korea, Mexico and Turkey. The High Income OECD group considered in Table 6.1 comprises the countries of western and northern Europe plus Australia, Canada, Iceland, Japan, New Zealand and the USA – 23 countries in all. These are the world's rich industrial economies. FSB stands for Former Soviet Bloc, a group of 25 countries in Asia, and central and eastern Europe. The data for Table 6.1 are taken from the *Human development report 2002* (UNDP, 2002). All of the other countries for which that publication provides comprehensive data are members of the group called 'Developing' – there are 125 countries in this group. There are 18 countries for which the *Human development report 2002* does not provide comprehensive data, so that they are not covered in Table 6.1 nor in subsequent tables here based on its data. In 2000 these countries had a combined population of about 110 million out of a world population of 6 billion – the data for High Income OECD, FSB and Developing cover about 98 per cent of the world's population.

As well as these three main groupings, Table 6.1 gives data for two sub-groups of the Developing countries. The United Nations distinguishes 44 countries as belonging to the category Least Developed. Inclusion in this category is on the basis of suffering from one or more of: very low per capita GDP; being land-locked; remoteness; subject to desertification; high exposure to natural hazards. Most of the Least Developed countries are in Africa. Among the non-African countries in this group are: Bangladesh, Cambodia, Haiti, Myanmar and Nepal. Sub-Saharan Africa comprises 44 countries, many of which are also in the Least Developed group.

The USA and UK are from the High Income OECD group. All of the other individual countries shown in Table 6.1 are members of the Developing group. As noted above, Bangladesh is a member of the Least Developed group. Kenya, Nigeria and Sierra Leone are part of Sub-Saharan Africa and Sierra Leone also belongs to the Least Developed group. In Table 6.1 per capita national income is measured as GDP per capita in PPP US$, and shown in the second column of the table, while the third gives the second-column figures as ratios to the second-column figure for High Income OECD. If per capita national income had been measured as GDP per capita using actual, rather than purchasing power parity, exchange rates to convert to US$, the inequalities in the third column would have been much larger than

Table 6.2 Current and projected population sizes

	Population 2000 million	Population 2000 % of total	Annual % growth rate 2000–2015	Population 2050 million	Population 2050 % of total
High income OECD	852	14.33	0.3	990	9.39
FSB	397	6.68	−0.2	145	1.38
Developing	4695	78.99	1.4	9409	89.24
Least developed	634	10.67	2.4	2075	19.68
Sub-Saharan Africa	606	10.20	2.4	1984	18.82
World	5944			10544	

Source: UNDP (2002): Table 5.

those shown. The inequalities shown are, anyway, very large. For Developing average per capita income is less than 15 per cent of the average for the High Income OECD countries, and for Least Developed average per capita income is less than 5 per cent of the average for High Income OECD. Per capita national income in the USA is 20 per cent higher than the average for High Income OECD. In Sierra Leone it is just 2 per cent of the average for High Income OECD.

6.1.2 Many poor, few rich

Table 6.2 shows data from the *Human development report 2002* on the populations in the year 2000 of the five groups of countries, and on population growth rate projections for 2000 to 2015. The world population figures in Table 6.2 are the sums of those for High Income OECD, FSB and Developing.

Of a global population of approximately 6 billion in 2000, the Developing countries accounted for almost 80 per cent. The fifth column of Table 6.2 gives the projected population sizes for 2050 that result from assuming the growth rates shown in the fourth column operate over 50 years from 2000. According to these projections, by 2050 almost 90 per cent of the world's population, which will have increased by more than 70 per cent, will live in Developing countries. The currently rich countries are projected to account for less than 10 per cent of the total population by 2050. In the former FSB as a whole the population growth rate is currently negative, and projecting this out to 2050 gives a population less than half of the current level. In Table 6.2, the total increase in human numbers to 2050 is 4,600 million, while the increase in the Developing countries is 4,714 million. The Least Developed and Sub-Saharan Africa countries have much higher population growth rates than the Developing group as a whole, and on these projections their populations increase more than three-fold by 2050, so that they each account for about 20 per cent of the world's population. The prospects for most of the human population are the prospects that face Developing countries.

6.1.3 Poverty in the world economy

Figures for per capita national income are derived by dividing the national income statisticians' estimate of GDP by the size of the population. The result is an average

Table 6.3 People living in poverty

	Survey date	Percentage below $1 PPP 1985 US$	Number below $1 PPP 1985 US$ million	Percentage below $2 PPP 1985 US$	Number below $2 PPP 1985 US$ million
Brazil	1998	11.6	19	26.5	43
Mexico	1998	15.9	15	37.7	36
Bangladesh	1996	29.1	36	77.8	97
China	1999	18.8	238	52.6	665
India	1997	44.2	415	86.2	809
Indonesia	1999	7.7	16	55.3	115
Pakistan	1996	31.0	39	84.6	107
Egypt	1995	3.1	2	52.7	32
Ethiopia	1995	31.2	17	76.4	43
Ghana	1999	44.8	9	78.5	15
Nigeria	1997	70.2	77	90.8	99
Zambia	1998	63.7	6	87.4	9
Total			889		2070

Source: World Bank, latest version, accessible at http://www.worldbank.org/data/databytopic/poverty.html#pdf

which tells us nothing about the distribution of people's actual incomes around that average. Take a hypothetical economy where per capita GDP is $10,000 and the population size is 1,000,000 so that GDP is $10,000 \times 10^6$. These figures are consistent both with a situation where everybody has an income of $10,000, and with a situation where 100,000 people get $50,000 each while 900,000 people get $555.56 each. If the income below which an individual can be said to be poor is $8,000, then in the first case nobody is poor, while in the second case most people are very poor. Without information on the distribution of incomes, national income data gives an incomplete picture of the extent of poverty.

Rather than looking at per capita national income, one can look at what households and individuals actually consume. Many Developing countries periodically conduct surveys to produce this kind of data, and the World Bank uses such survey data to calculate the percentage of the population living in poverty. Table 6.3 gives the results for a selection of the countries covered in the World Bank data. The national surveys give the proportions of the population with consumption levels in bands denominated in local currency, and the World Bank uses the purchasing power parity exchange rates discussed in Chapter 5 to convert local currencies to common PPP US$. It then computes the proportions of the populations living on less than one and less than two 1985 US dollars' worth of consumption per day, which are widely accepted poverty standards.

In Table 6.3, for each country the percentage of the population living below the stated poverty line has been multiplied by the country's population for the year in which the survey was conducted to give the number of people below the poverty line. The figures shown for Total are the totals across the countries shown in Table 6.3, so that they understate the actual total across all of the countries for which World Bank data is available. The countries shown in Table 6.3 were selected on the basis that they were, in population terms, among the largest in South America, Asia and Africa respectively. What Table 6.3 shows then is that there are around 900 million people consuming less than one 1985 PPP US$ per day, and over two billion consuming less than two 1985 PPP US$ per day. One 1985 US$ would, on account of inflation in the USA, have had the same purchasing power as about $1.35 there in 2000. So, the poverty lines in Table 6.3 can, in round terms, be expressed as $500 (1.35 × 365 = 493) and $1,000 per year, $10 and $20 per week, in current US dollars. At the £/$ exchange rate operative at the time of writing, this is, again in round terms, £350 and £700 per year, £7 and £14 per week. Despite the difficulties and approximations necessarily involved in these kinds of comparisons and calculations, it can safely be said that over two billion people live in poverty and about one billion live in extreme poverty.

6.2 WHY ARE SOME COUNTRIES RICH AND SOME POOR?

Table 6.1 shows that there now exist very large differences in per capita national incomes – in 2000, GDP per capita in the USA was 70 times as great as in Sierra Leone when both are measured in PPP $. Such large differences are a relatively recent phenomenon. It is clear that during the hunter-gatherer phase of human history and for most of the agricultural phase, the differences between per capita output and income levels across societies were much smaller than they now are. Many economic historians take the view that until around 1500 the differences were so small that all of the world's economies should be regarded as having had the same level of per capita income. What has happened since then is that different economies have grown at different rates. The reason why some countries are now rich and some are now poor is that the former have, on average, grown faster than the latter in the last few hundred years.

   Given the nature of exponential, or compound, growth, which was introduced in Chapter 2, growth rates do not need to differ greatly to produce large differences in levels over periods of the order of a century. If g is the annual growth rate expressed as a decimal rather than a percentage, then over 100 years we have

$$Y_{100} = (1 + g)^{100} \times Y_0$$

where Y_0 is national income in the base year and Y_{100} is national income 100 years later. This is to be read as Y_{100} is equal to Y_0 multiplied by $(1+g)$ raised to the power 100. Table 6.4 gives some results so obtained for the 100-year multiplier for a range of annual growth rates. Growth at 0.75 per cent per year will double national income in 100 years, growth at 1.25 per cent will more than triple it. One economic historian has estimated that in 1500 the world average for per capita national income was $550 measured in 1990 PPP dollars, a little above the lower of the poverty lines looked at in the previous section of this chapter, some way below the upper one. Most economic historians agree that throughout the world during the agricultural phase of human history most of the population

Table 6.4 Implications of 100 years' growth at different rates	
Annual growth rate %	Multiplier for 100 years
0.25	1.2836
0.5	1.6467
0.75	2.1111
1.00	2.7048
1.25	3.4634
1.50	4.4321
1.75	5.6682
2.00	7.2447
3.00	19.2186
4.00	50.5049
5.00	131.5010

lived in what we would now regard as poverty. If we assume that the 1500 average for per capita national income applied in all economies, we can work out the annual growth rate that got any economy's per capita national income to where it is now.

Using y_{2000} and y_{1500} to denote national income per capita 'now' and 500 years ago respectively

$$y_{2000} = (1 + g)^{500} \times y_{1500}$$

and we want to solve for g for given values of y_{2000} and y_{1500} equal to $550. Take the case of the USA, where from Table 6.1 y_{2000} is $34,142 – given the broad brush nature of this exercise we can ignore the fact that y_{1500} is expressed in 1990 PPP $ while y_{2000} is expressed in 2000 PPP $. From

$$34,142 = (1 + g)^{500} \times 550$$

dividing both sides by 550 gives

$$62.0764 = (1 + g)^{500}$$

Taking logarithms on both sides, this becomes

$$\log 62.0764 = 500 \times \log (1 + g)$$

or

$$\log (1 + g) = \log 62.0764/500 = 1.7929/500 = 0.003586$$

so that $1 + g$ is the antilog of 0.003586. Given the availability of a calculator, the easiest way to find out what this is is to use the button marked 10^x. Enter 0.003586 and press the 10^x button and you get antilog 0.003586 as 1.008291, so that g here is 0.008291. This answer can be checked by calculating per capita national income in 2000 for the USA from

$$y_{2000} = (1.008291)^{500} \times 550$$

where the multiplier over 500 years is 62, in round numbers.

Table 6.5 gives, for the national economies shown, the average annual growth rates that are implied by the per capita national income figures of Table 6.1 and the assumption that all these economies had per capita national income at $550 in 1500. These figures illustrate two main points: first, that, as already noted, quite low rates of growth sustained over long periods of time have massive impacts on the corresponding levels – for growth at 0.83 per cent per year, the level of per capita national income in the USA increased by a factor of 62; second, that given long periods of time, quite small growth rate differences translate into large differences in the resulting levels. Compared, for example, to the UK, the USA has an average growth rate that is 0.12 per cent higher, and a 2000 per capita income level that is 45 per cent higher.

The numbers produced here should not be taken too seriously at the level of detail. From the discussion of national income accounting in the previous chapter, you will be aware that the statement that one country's, never mind all countries', per capita national income was $550 in terms of 1990 PPP $ should be regarded sceptically. It is not even clear that the conventions for measuring GDP make much sense for an economy such as that of, say, the UK as it existed in 1500. Many of the nation states that now exist did not exist as such in 1500. The USA is an example. Nevertheless, it does seem clear that sustained economic growth is, in terms of the full span of human history, a very recent phenomenon. And, the arithmetic of compound growth is remarkable, independently of the precise historical accuracy of the numbers just considered – quite modest growth rates, and differences therein, maintained over long periods transform situations.

Table 6.5 Implied growth rates over 500 years	
	Growth rate %pa
USA	0.83
UK	0.75
Mexico	0.56
Brazil	0.53
China	0.40
India	0.29
Bangladesh	0.21
Kenya	0.12
Nigeria	0.10
Sierra Leone	−0.02

In order to keep things simple, we have been looking at the last few hundred years in terms of national growth rates that are constant over the whole such period. In fact, many economic historians consider that for the world as a whole this period should be treated as two sub-periods, with higher growth rates for the second. There are differences about the dating of the break between the two sub-periods, but most agree that it is associated with the industrial revolution discussed in Chapter 3. As we shall see later in this chapter, in the latter part of the twentieth century many national economies maintained for decades growth rates well in excess of that shown for the USA in Table 6.5. For the world as a whole, the average growth rate for per capita GDP for the period 1950 to 2000 was approximately 2 per cent per year.

6.3 WHAT DRIVES ECONOMIC GROWTH?

We have said that the reason why we now observe rich and poor countries is that over recent history the former have grown faster than the latter. This 'explanation' leads to another question – why have some economies grown faster than others? That is, what explains economic growth?

We shall not be paying much explicit attention here to the relationships between economic growth and the environment. The whole of the next chapter is devoted to considering those relationships. What we want to do here is establish some basic ideas and methods, which we will build on in the next chapter.

6.3.1 The basic growth model

Economists study economic growth by looking at the historical data and constructing models intended to replicate, and thus explain, the major patterns in that data.

The models generate hypotheses that can be tested against the data. A model is a set of relationships between the things of interest. It is intended in that regard to be a simplified version of reality, in which the important relationships appear but the ones that are not important do not. Of course, any given model may not capture the important features of the reality that it is intended to promote understanding of. Models are tested by their performance against the data – a model 'works' to the extent that the behaviours that it displays correspond to the behaviours of interest in reality.

Models can be expressed and used in various ways. The most common and most powerful way is to use mathematics. That is what we will be doing. However, we will be doing it in a way that minimises the pain for the non-mathematical. The pain will, in fact, be almost non-existent. We are going to use numerical simulations executed by a spreadsheet. We will explain what is done in the spreadsheet and look at the results. You can replicate these simulations for yourself, and look at variations on them – some of the exercises at the end of the chapter ask you to do that.

The basic model for the study of economic growth consists of three relationships – a production function, a savings function, and that between savings and the size of the capital stock.

6.3.1.1 The production function

The **production function** is the relationship between the size of national income and the amounts of factors of production used to produce national income. Using Y for the size of national income for any year, K for the size of the capital stock, L for the amount of labour used, and R for the amount of natural resources used, a general statement of the production function used in the basic growth model is

$$Y = f(K, L, R)$$

This is to be read as saying that Y is 'a function of' K, L and R, by which is meant that the level taken by Y depends in some particular, but unspecified, way on the levels of K, L and R, which are known as the 'arguments' of the function. Another terminology is to refer to K, L and R as the independent or explanatory variables, with Y as the dependent variable.

In the study of economic growth it is very widely assumed that the production function takes the particular form

$$Y = K^{\alpha} \times L^{\beta} \times R^{\delta}$$

where α, β and δ are the parameters of the function. **Parameters** are constants for a particular version of the model, but can vary across versions. This is known as a Cobb–Douglas production function, Cobb and Douglas being economists who first proposed the use of this particular form. In growth economics it is almost universally assumed that the parameters of a Cobb–Douglas production function can only take values that satisfy the condition

$$\alpha + \beta + \delta = 1$$

Given that condition, one particular version of this production function is

$$Y = K^{0.2} \times L^{0.7} \times R^{0.1}$$

where $\alpha = 0.2$, $\beta = 0.7$ and $\delta = 0.1$, and which is to be read as Y is equal to K raised to the power 0.2 multiplied by L raised to the power 0.7 multiplied by R raised to the power 0.1. Taking logs on both sides, this can also be written as

$$\log Y = (0.2 \times \log K) + (0.7 \times \log L) + (0.1 \times \log R)$$

When a Cobb–Douglas production function satisfies the condition $\alpha + \beta + \delta = 1$ it is said to exhibit **constant returns to scale**. This is because if all input levels are increased by the same proportion, the level of national income increases in that proportion. Suppose $K = 10$, $L = 5$ and $R = 2$, then

$$Y = 10^{0.2} \times 5^{0.7} \times 2^{0.1} = 1.5849 \times 3.0852 \times 1.0718 = 5.2408$$

whereas for $K = 20$, $L = 10$ and $R = 4$

$$Y = 20^{0.2} \times 10^{0.7} \times 4^{0.1} = 1.8206 \times 5.0119 \times 1.1487 = 10.4815$$

which is 1.9999815 times 5.2408 – 1.9999815 rather than 2 simply because working to four decimal places introduces a slight rounding error.

The following function is another particular constant returns to scale Cobb–Douglas production

$$Y = K^{0.3} \times L^{0.6} \times R^{0.1}$$

You can confirm the constant returns to scale for this function in the same way.

The use of a Cobb–Douglas production function with constant returns to scale in most growth economics models is largely a matter of convenience. We shall follow the standard usage here because it is the standard usage, and it is convenient. We need to note, however, one implication that will turn out to be particularly important when, in the next chapter, we focus on matters environmental. This is that the standard usage implies that factors of production can be substituted for one another in producing national income. Using a calculator, or a spreadsheet, you can readily check that if

$$Y = K^{0.2} \times L^{0.7} \times R^{0.1}$$

then a level of national income of 10 can be produced using, for example, the following combinations of input levels

K	L	R
6	16.0779	1
5	16.9385	1
4	18.0533	1
3	19.6004	1
2	22.0071	1

as well as, for further example

K	L	R
6	20	0.2170
5	20	0.3125
4	20	0.4883
3	20	0.8683
2	20	1.9531

and

K	L	R
31.6229	10	1
16.7058	12	1
9.7398	14	1
6.1035	16	1
4.0415	18	1

Generally, the nature of the substitution possibilities for

$$Y = K^\alpha \times L^\beta \times R^\delta$$

with $\alpha + \beta + \delta = 1$ are as shown in Figure 6.1. In each panel the level of input of the factor not shown on either axis is being held constant. In each panel a line such as Y_1Y_1 shows all the combinations of the inputs to which each axis refers that could be used, given the fixed input of the third factor, to produce the level of national income Y_1. Thus, in Figure 6.1(a) for example, Y_1 could be produced using K^*L^* or $K^{**}L^{**}$ or any other combination of K and L lying along Y_1Y_1. Y_2 is a higher level of national income than Y_1 so that for given K one reads off a higher L from Y_2Y_2 than from Y_1Y_1, and for given L one reads off a higher K from Y_2Y_2 than from Y_1Y_1. The other panels are to be similarly interpreted. Lines such as Y_1Y_1 and Y_2Y_2 are known as **isoquants**, as they are lines joining points representing equal quantities of output of national income. Isoquants are like contour lines on a map – everywhere along one has the same output level – where moving northeast is going uphill.

6.3.1.2 Saving and capital accumulation

The **savings function** used in the basic model of economic growth has the amount saved as proportional to the size of national income according to

$$S = s \times Y$$

where s is a parameter which can take values in the range 0 to 1, and S is the amount saved. For $s = 0$ savings would be zero for any level of income, while for $s = 1$ all of income would be saved.

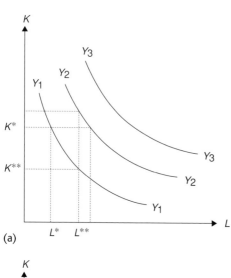

(a)

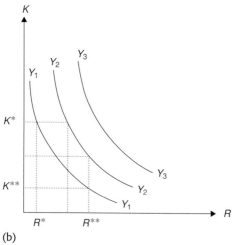

(b)

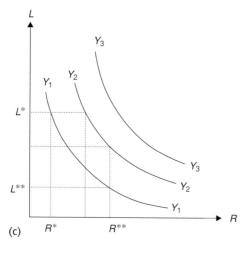

(c)

Figure 6.1
Substitution
possibilities
with a
Cobb–Douglas
production
function.

To complete the basic model of economic growth we need the relationship between saving and the size of the capital stock. This follows from the discussion of national income accounting in the previous chapter. Here we will assume, in the interests of simplicity, that capital does not depreciate. In that case we do not need to worry about the distinction between gross and net investment and we have

$$K_t = K_{t-1} + I_t$$

where K_{t-1} is the size of the capital stock at the beginning of year t, K_t is its size at the end of that year, and I_t is investment during the year t. Given that investment and saving are equal

$$K_t = K_{t-1} + I_t = K_{t-1} + S_t$$

6.3.1.3 Model simulation

The parameter values that we are going to use are: $\alpha = 0.2$, $\beta = 0.7$, $\delta = 0.1$ and $s = 0.15$. These values for the production function parameters are representative of the sorts of values that economists routinely assume, and 15 per cent is a reasonable approximation for the savings ratio. With these values the production function is

$$Y = K^{0.2} \times L^{0.7} \times R^{0.1}$$

and the savings function is

$$S = 0.15 \times Y$$

It simplifies the presentation of the simulation results a lot if we choose units of measurement for each variable such that initially the levels of K, L and R are all 1. It then follows from the fact that 1 raised to any power is equal to 1 (as you can easily check with your calculator) that Y is initially equal to 1.

Given an interest in economic growth in relation to human well-being, we are interested in per capita national income, which we denote by y. With P for the size of the population

$$y \equiv Y/P$$

We will be interested in proportional rates of growth, which will, as is conventional in economics, be denoted by putting a dot over the letter for the corresponding variable. Thus, for example, the proportional rate of growth for per capita national income for the year t is defined as

$$\dot{y}_t \equiv \frac{y_t - y_{t-1}}{y_{t-1}},$$

Again in the interests of simplicity, we will assume that the labour force is always fully employed and that it is always the same proportion of the population. We assume, that is, that

$$L = n \times P$$

where n is a parameter, which is the proportion of the population that is in the labour force. Looking at growth rates for the population and the labour force we have

$$\dot{P}_t \equiv \frac{P_t - P_{t-1}}{P_{t-1}}$$

and

$$\dot{L}_t \equiv \frac{L_t - L_{t-1}}{L_{t-1}} = \frac{(n \times P_t) - (n \times P_{t-1})}{n \times P_{t-1}}$$

where the ns on the top and bottom of the righthand side cancel out so that $\dot{L}_t = \dot{P}_t$ – for any constant n, the labour force grows at the same rate as the population. Given that, we may just as well set n equal to 1 and work with $L_t = P_t$. Doing this simplifies the calculations without affecting the results for proportionate growth rates. With $P = L = 1$ initially, $Y = 1$ means that $y = 1$ initially.

We assume that the population and the labour force grow at a constant rate, which is determined exogenously, that is outside the model. The growth rate of per capita national income is determined by the model – it is said to be an **endogenous variable**, whereas the population growth rate is an **exogenous variable**. We will assume that L and P grow at 2.5 per cent per year. We will also assume that the model economy's use of natural resources, R, grows at 2.5 per cent per year. Having resource input grow at the same rate as labour input and population means that the use of natural resources in producing national income does not affect the rate of growth of per capita national income. We make this assumption here so that we can focus on other – than natural resource use – things that affect the growth of per capita national income. In the next chapter, where we focus on growth and the environment, we will make different assumptions about the behaviour of resource inputs to production.

Here are the first few rows from the Excel™ spreadsheet for the simulation of this model. Rows 1 through to 6 identify the simulation by the parameter values that it uses, and identify the variables to which the columns relate:

	A	B	C	D	E	F	G	H	I	J
1										
2		0.7	0.1	0.2			WKSHEET1			
3										
4				s = 0.15						
5										
6	time	labour	rsces	captl	income	saving	inc pc	K/L ratio	incpc %	K/L %
7										
8	1	1	1	1	1	0.15	1	1		
9	2	1.025	1.025	1.15	1.048863	0.157329	1.023281	1.121951	0.023281	0.121951
10	3	1.050625	1.050625	1.307329	1.097577	0.164637	1.04469	1.244335	0.020922	0.109081
11	4	1.076891	1.076891	1.471966	1.146349	0.171952	1.064499	1.366867	0.018962	0.098472

Table 6.6 Income and capital per capita in the basic model				
Year	y	$\dot{y}$ %	k	$\dot{k}$ %
10	1.1593	1.18	2.0941	6.05
20	1.2641	0.68	3.2277	3.45
30	1.3342	0.45	4.2270	2.26
40	1.3847	0.32	5.0864	1.60
50	1.4221	0.23	5.8154	1.17
60	1.4508	0.18	6.4284	0.89
70	1.4733	0.14	6.9410	0.68
80	1.4910	0.11	7.3678	0.54
90	1.5050	0.08	7.7221	0.42
100	1.5163	0.07	8.0155	0.34

The simulation goes as follows. The initial values for time and the inputs are entered in columns A, B, C and D of Row 8. The entry in cell E8 is given by the formula

$$B8^{0.7} \times C8^{0.1} \times D8^{0.2}$$

which in Excel^{TM} notation is

$$(B8^{\wedge}0.7)^{*}(C8^{\wedge}0.1)^{*}(D8^{\wedge}0.2)$$

which gives the result for E8 as 1. For saving, F8 is given by $0.15 \times$ E8. 'inc pc' stands for income per capita, y, and so G8 is given by E8 $\div$ B8 which is E8/B8 in Excel^{TM} notation. 'K/L ratio' stands for the capital to labour ratio, so H8 is given by D8 $\div$ B8 (D8/B8 in spreadsheets such as Excel^{TM}).

Now move to row 9. The entry for cell A9 is determined by the formula A8 + 1, which can be copied down column A to date the rows as shown. The entry for B9 is given by the formula B8 $\times$ 1.025 (B8*1.025) and that for C9 by C8 $\times$ 1.025 (C8*1.025), and these can be copied down columns B and C. Column D records capital accumulation, so the D9 entry is given by the formula D8 + F7, as F gives savings and investment. This can be copied down the D column. To get the entries down the E column, for income, copy the formula from E8 given above down the column. The same applies to columns F, G and H. The last two columns determine the rates of change for income per capita and the capital to labour ratio, so they have no entries in row 8 for initial values. For income per capita percent change, the entry in I9 is given by the formula (G9 − G8) $\div$ G8, which is (G9 − G8)/G8 in spreadsheet notation, and J9 = (H9 − H8) $\div$ H8. These can also be copied down the columns to produce the results for the later years.

Table 6.6 shows, at ten-year intervals, the results of this simulation out to year 100. Here k stands for K/L, the capital–labour ratio, and $\dot{k}$ for its rate of change. The second and third columns of Table 6.6 show per capita national income growing at a decreasing rate. For the simulation that produced the data for Table 6.6, Figure 6.2 shows the plot of y against time. Because this pattern of per capita income growth

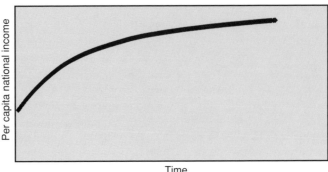

Figure 6.2
Growth in the
basic model.

at a declining rate is characteristic of the basic model that we are now considering we have dropped the numbers from the axes in Figure 6.2. The outcome shown there does not depend, except in one particular way, on the particular numerical values used for the parameters of the basic model. So long as it has a savings rate greater than the population growth rate, any model that consists of a Cobb–Douglas production function with constant returns to scale, a savings function that has saving and investment as a constant proportion of national income will produce this kind of outcome – growth at a declining rate – for per capita national income. If the population growth rate is larger than the savings rate, then per capita national income will decline at a decreasing rate. If the savings rate exceeds the population growth rate, then, as illustrated in Table 6.6, the amount of capital per worker grows. It is this that drives the growth of income per capita in the basic growth model. Given that capital services can be substituted for labour, more capital per head means more national income output per head – each worker is using more capital along with his labour and so producing more output. However, the amount by which a unit of additional capital increases output per worker decreases as the amount of capital per worker increases. Hence, the rate of income growth slows as capital accumulation proceeds, which in turn slows the rate at which capital per worker grows.

Table 6.7 Income per capita after 100 years			
		s	
L %	0.05	0.15	0.3
1	1.3351	1.7132	2.0235
2.5	1.1675	1.5163	1.7970
4	1.0550	1.3798	1.6382
7	0.9203	1.2091	1.4375

In the basic growth model, in which growth is driven by capital accumulation, growth eventually comes to an end, and per capita income remains constant. Achieving constant per capita income takes a very long time, but that this is what is eventually going to happen is clear in Table 6.6 and in Figure 6.2. In fact, for the particular model for which they show results, per capita national income eventually stabilises at 1.565.

6.3.1.4 *Varying the parameter values*

The rate at which per capita income grows, and the level at which it eventually stabilises, vary with the numerical values taken by the parameters of the model. It depends, first, on the relative sizes of s, the savings ratio and the rate at which the population grows. This is illustrated in Table 6.7 by looking at the level of per capita income after 100 years. The results there are obtained as described in the preceding sub-section, but using different numbers to 1.025 in column B and to 0.15 in column F. In order to continue to have resource use growing at the same rate as population, we also use in column C whatever the number is in column B.

In Table 6.7, reading across rows, for a given rate of growth for population, per capita income grows faster, and eventually attains a higher level, the higher the savings ratio. Reading down columns, for a given savings ratio, per capita income grows more slowly, and eventually attains a lower level, the faster the rate of population growth. Note that for a savings ratio less than the rate of population growth, the per capita income growth rate is negative. This is illustrated in the bottom left cell of Table 6.7, where for $s = 0.05$ and $\dot{L} = 0.07$, y after 100 years is less than it was initially. The growth rate also depends on the numerical values taken by the parameters of the production function. You are invited to investigate this in Exercise 2 at the end of the chapter.

6.3.2 The basic model and the data

In considering the adequacy of this basic model as an explanation of the phenomenon of economic growth as observed in the last few hundred years, economists focus on three of its properties – a higher savings ratio goes with faster growth, faster population growth goes with slower growth, the rate of growth slows down over time. This basic model generates, that is, three hypotheses about actual economic growth:

(1)   The rate of growth of per capita national income is higher in economies where the rate of savings is higher.

(2)   The rate of growth of per capita national income is lower in economies with higher rates of population growth.

(3)   In a given economy the rate of growth of per capita national income falls over time.

In general, economists consider that the evidence supports the first of these, but not the other two. Figures 6.3, 6.4 and 6.5 plot relevant data taken from the *Human development report 2000* and the *Human development report 2002*. In Figure 6.3, the horizontal axis measures saving and investment as a percentage of national income, and the vertical axis measures the annual percentage growth of per capita national income. The data covers 149 economies across the full High Income OECD to Least Developed range, and refers to the 1990s. There is a clear tendency for growth to increase as saving/investment increases.

In Figure 6.4 the horizontal axis measures the annual per cent growth rate for population while the vertical axis again measures economic growth as the annual per cent growth of per capita national income. The data, for the 1990s, covers 157 economies across the full High Income OECD to Least Developed range. In this figure there is no obvious relationship, positive or negative, as between economic growth and population growth. If we look at the High Income OECD group as a whole and the Developing group as a whole, over 1975 to 2000 the former has average annual population growth at 0.6 per cent and economic growth over 1990 to 2000 at 1.7 per cent per annum, while for the latter the corresponding numbers are 1.9 per cent and 3.1 per cent, so that higher population and higher economic growth go together, contrary to the hypothesis derived from the basic model.

As regards the third hypothesis, that an economy's growth rate falls over time, we have already noted that most economic historians consider that for the world as a whole, the growth rate was higher in the last couple of hundred years than in the previous couple of hundred years. Individual country studies frequently come up with the growth rate being higher in recent years than in the more distant past. However, as noted in this and the previous chapter, measuring national

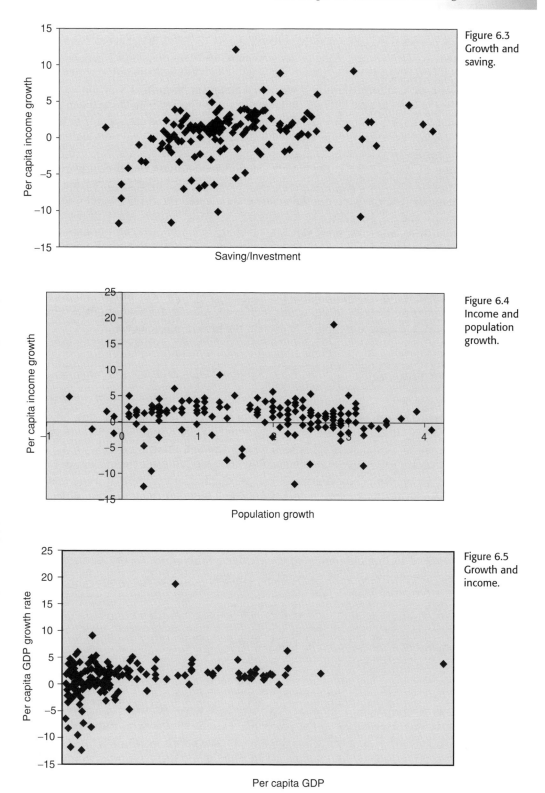

Figure 6.3
Growth and
saving.

Figure 6.4
Income and
population
growth.

Figure 6.5
Growth and
income.

income for years far in the past is problematic. Another way of looking at the third hypothesis is that it implies that growth should be slower in richer economies, given that economies are getting richer over time. The data plotted in Figure 6.5, which refers to the 1990s and covers 157 economies, does not support this hypothesis. Per capita national income is measured along the horizontal axis and its growth on the vertical axis. Overall, there appears to be no relationship between income and its growth, though at very low levels of income there does appear to be some tendency for growth to increase with income.

For the High Income OECD group of economies as a whole in 2000 per capita GDP in PPP\$ was 27,848 and the growth rate in the 1990s was 1.7 per cent per annum, whereas for Developing as a whole the corresponding figures are 3,783 and 3.1. On these figures, the poorer do grow faster. But, if we look at Least Developed we get \$1,216 and 1.3 per cent, and for Sub-Saharan Africa \$1,690 and −0.3 per cent, so that the poorer grew more slowly.

All in all, the general consensus on the basic model of economic growth considered here is that, while it is useful in drawing attention to the role of capital accumulation, it is not a satisfactory model of economic growth. Mainly this is because it generates a declining rate of growth. We now look briefly at some modifications to the basic model which seek to address the deficiencies of the standard model in regard to its ability to explain the growth phenomenon.

6.3.3 Efficiency

It is widely noted that output per worker is higher in some economies than it is in others. This can be explained in terms of the Cobb–Douglas production function, according to which, other things equal, output per worker is higher the greater the use of capital services, as seen above. However, there is evidence that output per worker varies across economies even after correcting for the amount of capital per worker. Some economies are, that is, simply more efficient at using available labour to produce national income. It turns out that there are also differences in the efficiency with which economies use capital and resource inputs. Do these differences have any implications for growth rates?

To investigate this question, the basic model considered in Table 6.6 can be modified so that differences in the efficiency with which inputs are used can be considered. Instead of the production function

$$Y = K^{0.2} \times L^{0.7} \times R^{0.1}$$

let us now look at the production function

$$Y = (a \times K)^{0.2} \times (b \times L)^{0.7} \times (c \times R)^{0.1}$$

This new production function has three additional parameters – a, b and c. In it, before being raised to the power 0.2, capital, for example is multiplied by a. The parameters a, b and c describe the efficiency with which each input is used.

Consider b, for example. Comparing an economy where $b=1$ with an economy where $b=1.5$, every unit of labour used is used 50 per cent more efficiently in the second economy, so that it is as if it had 50 per cent more labour for the same population size.

Table 6.8 Economic growth and efficiency in input use

year	y_{LE}	y_{ME}	$\dot{y}_{LE}$ %	$\dot{y}_{ME}$ %
10	1.1593	1.4268	1.18	1.33
20	1.2641	1.5693	0.68	0.74
30	1.3342	1.6629	0.45	0.48
40	1.3847	1.7295	0.32	0.34
50	1.4221	1.7790	0.23	0.25
60	1.4508	1.8167	0.18	0.19
70	1.4733	1.8461	0.14	0.14
80	1.4910	1.8692	0.11	0.11
90	1.5050	1.8876	0.08	0.09
100	1.5163	1.9022	0.07	0.07

Differences across economies could involve a, b and c differing in different proportions, but it makes things simpler to have each of these parameters differing in the same proportion. Consider one model economy where $a = b = c = 1$, and one where $a = b = c = 1.2$. In both model economies everything apart from the production function is as it was for Table 6.6. Table 6.8 reports the results from simulations with these two production functions, where the subscript LE is for 'less efficient' with $a = b = c = 1$ and ME is for 'more efficient' with $a = b = c = 1.2$. The results for LE are, of course, the same as those in Table 6.6. Comparing ME with LE, we see that y_{ME} is always greater than y_{LE}, but that while $\dot{y}_{ME}$ starts out higher than $\dot{y}_{LE}$ it eventually becomes the same. Over the long term, per capita income growth rates are the same in the two model economies.

The important general points that this particular numerical example illustrates are that introducing into the basic model differences in the efficiency with which inputs are used does generate differences in the level of per capita income, but does not generate difference in the growth rate (except in a transitory way), and does not eliminate the decline in the growth rate and the eventual stabilisation of per capita national income. We still do not have a model that can produce growth at a constant rate in the long run.

6.3.4 Technological change

We now introduce continuing technological change into the basic model, such that the efficiency with which inputs are used is changing over time. In that case, instead of a, b and c being constant over time, they change over time. Again, to keep things simple we make $a = b = c$ at each point in time. We will consider a simulation where the efficiency factor applied to each input grows at 5 per cent per year.

To see how the model now works consider how the simulation gets done in a spreadsheet. Start with the description for the basic model which produced the results for Table 6.6. Introduce a new column immediately after that for time. This has the common efficiency factor in it, so head it 'effcncy'. In row 8 the cell entry is 1. In row 9 the entry is given by the formula as the row 8 entry multiplied by 1.05. Then, in the columns for 'labour', 'rsces' and 'captl' the formulas are changed so that before being raised to the appropriate power the amount of whichever it is multiplied by the corresponding row value for the efficiency factor. Thus, for

Table 6.9   Income and capital per capita with technological progress

Year	y	$\dot{y}$ %	k	$\dot{k}$ %
10	1.8518	6.82	2.4235	8.97
20	3.5200	6.52	5.2448	7.47
30	6.5753	6.40	10.4025	6.85
40	12.1883	6.34	19.8515	6.56
50	22.5100	6.32	37.1959	6.43
60	41.4980	6.30	69.0702	6.36
70	76.4345	6.30	127.6845	6.32
80	140.7200	6.29	235.5081	6.31
90	259.0141	6.29	433.8894	6.30
100	476.6955	6.29	798.9177	6.29

example, in the case of labour, which would now be in column C with the efficiency factor in column B, the C9 entry would be given by the formula (C8 × 1.025) × B9 which is (C8*1.025)*B9 in spreadsheet notation, and this would be copied down the column. With the 'rsces' and 'captl' columns modified in the same way, the other columns stay the same and the results that come out are a simulation of a growth model in which technical change increases the efficiency with which each input is used over time at the common rate of 5 per cent per year.

The results that you get when you do this are in Table 6.9. The point about Table 6.9 as compared with Table 6.6 is that in the former the growth rate first declines, as in Table 6.6, but then stabilises and remains the same over time. Figure 6.6 plots the growth rate for this model against time. Comparing it with Figure 6.2, note carefully that whereas Figure 6.2 shows the level of per capita income against time, Figure 6.6 shows the growth rate of per capita income against time. With technical progress in the model, we do get growth at a constant rate in the long run. We now have, in the technology model, a model which produces ongoing per capita income growth, growth which does not die away in the long run. In all respects other than the introduction of technological progress, the inputs to the simulations for Tables 6.6 and 6.9 are the same.

6.3.5 Endogenous technological progress

In the Table 6.9 simulation, the growing efficiency with which the inputs are used is exogenous – comes from outside the model, is not explained within the relationships of the model. This is not really very satisfactory. As an explanation of continuing economic growth, this technology model merely says that if input use efficiency improves continually, and if things are otherwise as in the basic model, then you get growth that does not die away. It leaves unanswered, indeed unasked, the question as to why there is this kind of technological progress. In the literature exogenous technological progress has aptly been referred to as 'manna from heaven'.

Economists have considered this question. Technological progress has been brought into the relationships of the model, made endogenous, in a number of ways. The models arising can get quite complicated. We shall consider just one simple model, which captures one of the basic ideas. In it, what determines the efficiency with which factor inputs are used is the stock of knowledge which is the basis for the technological innovations that improve technology. The stock of knowledge is built up by investment in human and intellectual capital, that is by

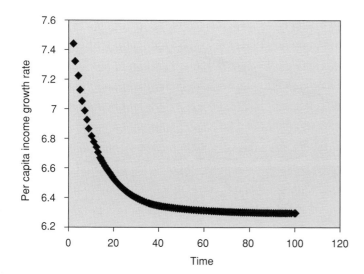

Figure 6.6
Growth with
technological
progress.

using some inputs to produce education and research rather than consumption goods. We provided a simple example of investment in Chapter 4 when we looked at Robinson Crusoe's economic activity.

The simplest way to model endogenous technical progress is to modify the model simulated for the results in Table 6.9 so that at each point in time the size of the efficiency factors applied to the inputs to production depends on the size of the capital stock. In the simulations that give the results in Table 6.10 the efficiency factors are given by

Table 6.10 Endogenous technological progress		
Year	y	$\dot{y}$ %
10	2.5404	10.60
20	6.7389	9.97
30	16.9963	9.49
40	41.2872	9.13
50	97.4269	8.84
60	224.7375	8.62
70	509.1718	8.45
80	1137.1630	8.31
90	2510.5910	8.19
100	5491.4520	8.10

$$a_t = b_t = c_t = K_{t-1}^{0.6}$$

The relationship that this describes between each efficiency factor and the size of the capital stock is shown, for a, in Figure 6.7. As K increases so the efficiency factors increase with it at a declining rate. To do the simulation here, start with the one described in the previous sub-section. All that needs modifying is the column headed 'effcncy'. As before the row 8 entry is 1. In row 9 the entry is given by the formula $E8^{0.6}$, E8^0.6 in Excel^{TM} notation, where E is the column for capital. This is copied down the column headed 'effcncy'. The common efficiency factor now increases at a rate that depends on the rate at which capital is accumulated as shown in Figure 6.7. The results in Table 6.10 show the rate of growth for per capita national income slowing with time, and converging on a positive growth rate. This is the same pattern as in Table 6.9 and Figure 6.6 for exogenous technological progress.

Figure 6.7
Endogenous
technical
progress:
efficiency and
capital

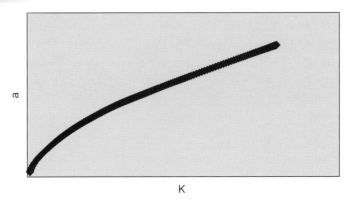

a

K

6.3.6 Explaining economic growth

On the basis of analysis of the behaviour of growth models, we see that an adequate (in the light of population growth) rate of saving and capital accumulation is
necessary for economic growth. However, saving and capital accumulation are not
sufficient, do not guarantee continuing growth. Without technical progress, growth
peters out eventually. What is needed to keep it going is ongoing enhancement of
the efficiency with which factors of production are used. Technical progress is itself
linked to saving and investment, in that the education and research that drive it
require that inputs be diverted from producing for consumption to providing education and research. Also, what education and research produce is knowledge, and
having knowledge deliver technical progress generally requires new types of capital
equipment.

If variations in economic growth rates are to be explained in terms of variations
in savings behaviour and technical progress, then questions arise, which growth
models do not answer, as to why savings behaviour and technical progress differ. The
models identify the proximate sources of economic growth, but not the underlying
causes. Why is the savings rate higher in one economy than another? Given two
economies with the same savings rate, why does one have more technical progress
than another, why is it more innovative?

At one level, the answers to these questions are fairly simple. People will save
more and innovate more when the incentives to do so are greater. Again, this
answer leads to more questions – what are the incentives to save and innovate, and
why do they differ across economies? A great deal has been written about these
questions in the last couple of hundred years. Much of it boils down to two basic
ideas:

- Individuals are motivated to save and innovate by the prospects of personal
  material gain from so doing, and the motivation increases with the amount
  of prospective gain.
- For individuals to see the prospect of gain from saving and/or innovating, they must have secure ownership of the results of their saving and/or
  innovating.

Saving and innovation flourish, that is, where laws exist, and are enforced, that
protect private property rights.

Box 6.1 Physioeconomics and the 'Equatorial Paradox'

The 'Equatorial Paradox' is the remarkable fact that there are no (with minor exceptions such as Singapore and Brunei) rich economies lying in the region from one thousand miles north of the equator to one thousand miles south of it. Why is this? Philip Parker, in *Physioeconomics: the basis for long-run economic growth* published in 2000, offers an explanation in terms of human physiology. The survival of an individual human animal requires that body temperature is maintained close to 37°C, which for a naked individual corresponds to an environment at 28–30°C. This reflects the evolution of humans as tropical animals. As latitude increases and environmental temperature decreases, so survival requires behavioural adjustments in terms of increased food intake, wearing clothing and using shelter and fire. The provision of more food, clothing and shelter amounts to defensive, in the sense introduced in the discussion of national income accounting in the previous chapter, economic activity. Parker's basic argument is that the amount of defensive economic activity increases with latitude, which is why we find GDP per capita increasing with latitude – historically, those who lived in colder climates had to do more work to produce more goods and services to satisfy their needs and desires. The systems of governance that they developed to accommodate to this need fostered economic growth. According to Parker, economies nearer to the equator may come to be as well-off in terms of average individual well-being as high-latitude economies, but will not then have such high GDP per capita because the same level of well-being is possible with less economic activity.

These ideas dominate modern neoclassical economic thinking about what drives economic growth through capital accumulation and technical progress – the emergence of the phenomenon of economic growth in the last few hundred years is to be understood primarily in terms of the emergence of a system of governance that respected and protected private property rights. This first took place in the economies of northern and western Europe, and their offshoots in North America and Oceania. Of course, one may then wonder why such a system of governance emerged in those societies at that point in human history. Various explanations have been offered, ranging from innate racial/ethnic characteristics to accidents of geography. Some suggestions as to how to find out more about these explanations are given in Further Reading at the end of the chapter. Box 6.1 summarises a recent contribution to this literature.

In our models of economic growth here we have had natural resources as an input to production, but we have had the amount used grow at the same rate as the population. In regard to constructing a model intended to mimic the history of the last few hundred years this is not unreasonable – the use of natural resources, and especially of the fossil fuels in the last 250 years, has grown. In fact, many models of economic growth constructed by neoclassical economists entirely overlook economy–environment interdependence and have only labour and various kinds of reproducible capital as inputs to production. Such models produce the same kind of results for per capita income as those reported in Tables 6.6 through to 6.10 here, but are a serious misrepresentation of history. And, they are also likely to be a poor guide to future prospects. These are matters we turn to in the next chapter, building on what we have learned about simulating growth models here.

The point is not that ecological economists think that the two basic ideas about the historical phenomenon of economic growth are wrong. It is that they think that they are a lot less than the whole story, and, therefore, that they mislead about future prospects.

6.4 THE DESIRABILITY OF ECONOMIC GROWTH

Economists study economic growth because it is the major economic phenomenon of the last few hundred years – it has totally transformed the conditions of human life in those economies that have experienced it. Neoclassical economists see growth as a very good thing, and to the extent that they understand it they hope to be able to advise on how to have more of it. Many neoclassical economists believe that, even in economies that are already rich, the pursuit of economic growth should be the most important objective of economic policy. In this section we will mainly be concerned to explain why neoclassical economists see economic growth as desirable. In the final sub-section, we will set out the ecological economics position on the desirability of economic growth – the remaining sections of the chapter look at the basis for that position.

6.4.1 Economists and dentists

John Maynard Keynes (1883–1946) was perhaps the most famous economist of the twentieth century. In 1930 he wrote of economics that:

> It should be a matter for specialists – like dentistry. If economists could manage to get themselves thought of as humble, competent people, on a level with dentists, that would be splendid. (Keynes, 1963)

In fact Keynes thought that within 100 years economists actually would have the status of dentists, due to economic growth.

Keynes was not saying that dentists are unimportant. On the contrary, they clearly do a very necessary and useful job. However, the views of dentists on social and political issues are not considered especially important. One does not see prominent dentists being interviewed on TV about the big questions of the day. The latest book on dentistry does not get discussed in the Sunday papers. There is no Nobel prize for dentistry. In contrast, the views of economists are sought on all manner of social and political issues, they are frequently interviewed on TV, and their books are reviewed in the Sunday papers and other journals addressed to a non-specialist audience. Each year, the identity of the winner of the Nobel prize for economics is widely reported and commented on.

According to one definition, economics is the study of how people cope with scarcity. The point that Keynes was making – in an essay entitled 'Economic possibilities for our grandchildren' – was that economic growth could abolish the problem that economics studied, could do away with scarcity. In order to make the case for addressing the then current problem of massive unemployment and negative economic growth, Keynes pointed out that, with full employment, growth at 2 per cent per year maintained for 100 years would mean that national income would increase by a factor of 7. Such affluence might not make economists entirely redundant, but it would greatly reduce their perceived importance. Their status would become the same as that of dentists.

While few economists would agree with Keynes about the desirability of a major reduction in the status of economists, most neoclassical economists share his belief in the ability of economic growth to go on transforming the human condition for the better, and, therefore, his belief in the desirability of economic growth. For most neoclassical economists, economic growth should be the principal objective of government policy – achieve it, they argue, and all other desirable objectives will either follow automatically or become more easily attainable.

6.4.2 Poverty alleviation

In particular, neoclassical economists see economic growth as the only feasible way to alleviate poverty. Their argument is that in the absence of economic growth, the only way to improve the lot of the poor is to redistribute in their favour by taking away from the better-off and giving to the poor. They cite three problems about this way of trying to alleviate poverty. First, the better-off tend not to like it, and to resist it. Attempted redistribution is a source of conflict, sometimes violent, as history demonstrates. And, if the better-off resist successfully, nothing is done for the poor. Second, typically the amount by which the better-off collectively are better-off than the poor collectively is not sufficiently large for it to be possible to solve the poor's problems this way even if it were possible to redistribute. Third, to the extent that redistribution is effected it may act as a disincentive to behaviour, such as saving and investing, which promotes the economic growth that is the best hope of the poor.

Box 6.2 illustrates, at the global level, the second problem with the redistributive approach and the appeal of the economic growth approach – many poor, few rich. It also notes that at the global level the redistributive approach faces the problem that there is no world government that might run the tax system to effect it peacefully.

Now look back at Table 6.1, which gives levels of GDP per capita for various groupings of countries and for selected countries in 2000. Call the High Income OECD grouping the 'rich' and the Developing grouping the 'poor'. In round numbers, for the rich GDP per capita is $28,000, and for the poor it is $4,000. Again in round numbers, there are 1 billion rich and 5 billion poor – see Table 6.2. So, total GDP for the rich is $28,000 \times 1 \times 10^9 = $28,000 \times 10^9$ and total GDP for the poor is $4,000 \times 5 \times 10^9 = $20,000 \times 10^9$, so that total world GDP is $48,000 \times 10^9$. If this total were divided equally among all of the 6 billion people, GDP per capita would be $8,000. Each of the rich would lose $20,000, or about 70 per cent of actual 2000 GDP per capita for the rich, and each of the poor would gain $4,000, 100 per cent of actual GDP per capita for the poor. The poor would get to a per capita income level which is a little less than one third of that actually enjoyed by the rich in 2000.

Now consider economic growth. Table 6.11 shows the average annual growth rates for the economies of Table 6.1 over the decade 1990–2000, and uses these to project what GDP per capita would be in 2050 if they were maintained over 50 years. The growth rates used in Table 6.11 do not refer to GDP per capita measured in PPP US$, as those data are not available. The growth rates refer to GDP per capita converted to US dollars using exchange rates. It is reasonable to assume that the broad trends and relativities in growth rates shown in Table 6.11 do apply to PPP US$ growth rates. The fourth column of Table 6.11 shows the ratio of GDP per capita in 2050 to GDP per capita in 2000.

The first point to note, again, is the power of compound growth even at modest rates when it is maintained over a few decades – in the case of Mexico, for example, growth at 1.4 per cent for 50 years doubles per capita national income. For the poor, Developing, growth at 3.1 per cent would increase per capita income to 4.6 times its 2000 level, $17,409, which is more than twice what we have just seen that sharing out 2000 world GDP equally would give them. China's growth in the

Box 6.2 Redistribution or economic growth to help the poor?

In the *Human development report 1998*, it is noted (in Box 1.3, 'The ultra-rich') that while:

> the world's 225 richest people have a combined wealth of over $1 trillion, equal to the annual income of the poorest 47 per cent of the world's people (2.5 billion). (UNDP, 1998, p. 30)

it is estimated that:

> the additional cost of achieving and maintaining universal access to basic education for all, reproductive health care for all women, adequate food for all and safe water and sanitation for all is roughly $40 billion per year. This is less than 4 per cent of the combined wealth of the 225 richest people. (*ibid.*)

Here, 1 trillion is 1,000 billion, i.e. 10^{12}. The combined wealth of the richest 225 people is reported as US$1.015 trillion. In what follows, to keep the calculations simple and transparent, this will be treated as US$1 trillion.

This might be, and seems to be intended to be, taken to imply that one way to help the poor would be to take some money away from the world's richest people and use it to benefit the poor, if that were possible. And, that the amount that it would be necessary to take away from the ultra-rich would, in relation to what they have, be quite small.

The first thing to note here is that the statement about the ultra-rich refers to their *stock* of wealth, whereas the statements about the poor refer to annual *flows*, of income and of cost. Comparing the wealth of the rich with the income of the poor, as in the first statement above, can give rise to confusion. Think of these ultra-rich as having their wealth in a savings account paying 5 per cent per year. Note that not many savings accounts pay that well in normal circumstances. Then, the income that their wealth yields is $0.05 \times 1 \times 10^{12} = 50 \times 10^9$, or $50 billion per year. The annual cost of the package to help the poor is 80 per cent of the annual income of the ultra-rich.

Look at this another way. Suppose that the entire wealth of the ultra-rich could be taken from them and used to help the poor, of whom there are 2.5 billion with an average income of $2,000 in round numbers. Consider the following ways of then helping the poor:

- The annual cost of the education and health package is $40 billion per year, so one trillion dollars would pay for it for 25 years.
- One trillion divided equally between 2.5 billion people is $400 each. If a recipient spent all the money in one year, her consumption would go up by 20 per cent (400/2000) in that year, and then drop back to its previous level.
- Again divide one trillion equally between 2.5 billion people, but now suppose that everybody puts their $400 in a savings account at 5 per cent, instead of spending it on consumption. In that case the income of each recipient would increase, on a permanent basis, by 1 per cent – at 5 per cent $400 delivers $20 per year, and 20/2,000 = 0.01.
- Suppose that the one trillion dollars was given to an agency for the poor, which put it in a bank account at 5 per cent interest. The agency would have an annual income of $50 billion, which would each year pay for the cost of the package and have $10 billion left over to finance other useful programmes for the poor.

Now forget about the ultra-rich and consider economic growth. Suppose that national income per capita in the economies where the 2.5 billion live could be made to grow at 2.5 per cent per year. With per capita income at $2,000 for 2.5 billion people, the relevant national income is initially 5,000 billion dollars. After one year at 2.5 per cent growth, this has become £5,125 billion – 5,000 × 1.025. The increment, 5,125 – 5,000 = 125, will pay the cost of the package and leave 125 – 40 = 85 billion dollars over. In the next year, total national income will be 5,125 × 1.025 = 5,253 billion dollars, so that after paying for the education and health package there is still more than $200 billion of national income than there was initially. And so on and so on.

In order to make the basic point – that economic growth is a much more effective way of dealing with poverty than redistribution – as clearly as possible, these calculations ignore some finer points. But, taking those on board would not alter the basic message.

Two other points need to be made. First, none of this should be taken to mean that there is no reason to redistribute from the rich to the poor. If we think that inequality matters, as well as absolute poverty, then redistribution is needed to reduce inequality. However, and second, at the international level there is no means of redistributing from rich individuals to poor individuals because there is no world government to do the taxing and spending that would be involved. There is some movement of money from rich governments to poor countries, but the extent of this redistribution is very small.

1990s, according to these data, was phenomenal. If maintained for the next 50 years it would increase per capita GDP in China more than eighty-fold, to a level several times that of the USA as currently projected for 2050. India's performance was less spectacular, but if continued would increase GDP per capita more than seven-fold out to 2050. The entries for FSB, Sub-Saharan Africa and three African countries show that the power of compound growth also works in reverse – the projected per capita income for Sierra Leone is just $17 per year, which would not support life.

Table 6.11 Recent growth rates and per capita GDP projections

	Annual growth rate 1990–2000 %	Projected GDP per capita 2050	Ratio to GDP per capita 2000
High income OECD	1.7	64690	2.32
FSB	−2.4	2057	0.30
Developing	3.1	17409	4.60
Least developed	1.3	2320	1.91
Sub-Saharan Africa	−0.3	1454	0.86
USA	2.2	101352	2.97
UK	2.2	69788	2.97
Mexico	1.4	18082	2.00
Brazil	1.5	16052	2.11
China	9.2	324025	81.50
India	4.1	17583	7.46
Bangladesh	3.0	7023	4.38
Kenya	−0.5	795	0.78
Nigeria	−0.4	733	0.82
Sierra Leone	−6.5	17	0.03

Source: UNDP (2002): Table 12.

6.4.3 Growth and inequality

As well as the effect of growth on absolute per capita income levels, there is the question of global inequalities. What happens to these in the future depends on the relative growth rates of the various groupings and countries. Table 6.12 shows the implications of the growth rates from Table 6.11 for per capita GDP inequalities as between the groupings in 2050. The gap between Developing and High Income OECD is projected to narrow, between Least Developed and High Income OECD to stay the same, and between Sub-Saharan Africa and High Income OECD to widen. If the contraction of the FSB continues for 50 years, its position relative to High Income OECD will be similar in 2050 to that of the poorest developing countries in 2000. These projections are suggestive, but should not be taken too seriously and should not be regarded as forecasts. They are simply intended to show what would happen *if* the growth rates of Table 6.11 operated for 50 years. It is, for example, very unlikely that the FSB economies will continue for 50 years to experience per capita GDP shrinking at 2.4 per cent per year, or that China will keep up growth at 9.2 per cent per year.

There are, however, basic general points about income growth and inequality. If the rich and the poor experience growth at the same rate, the difference between them in absolute terms increases, while in proportionate terms it remains the same. Reducing inequality in proportionate terms requires faster growth for the poor. Reducing it in absolute terms requires much faster growth for the poor.

To see what is involved, take the same round numbers from Table 6.1 as before – the rich on $28,000 in 2000 and the poor on $4,000. The rich to poor ratio is 7. Suppose both experience growth at 2.5 per cent per year for 50 years. Per capita

Table 6.12 The implications of recent growth rates for global income inequalities

	Annual growth rate 1990–2000 %	Ratio to high income OECD 2000	Ratio to high income OECD 2050
High income OECD	1.7	1.00	1.00
FSB	−2.4	0.25	0.03
Developing	3.1	0.14	0.27
Least developed	1.3	0.04	0.04
Sub-Saharan Africa	−0.3	0.06	0.02

income is $96,239 for the rich and $13,748 for the poor. The ratio stays at 7, but the dollar gap has grown from $24,000 to $82,491.

Now suppose that it is known that the rich are going to experience growth at 2.5 per cent. How fast would per capita income for the poor have to grow for the initial $ gap of $24,000 to be cut by 50 per cent – to $12,000 – after 50 years? After 50 years at 2.5 per cent the rich get to $96,239 so the target for the poor is $84,239. Using your calculator, or a spreadsheet, you can check that growth at 6.3 per cent will slightly over-achieve that target. To halve the absolute $ difference over 50 years requires that the poor's income per capita grows two-and-a-half times as fast each year as that of the rich.

6.4.4 Ecological economics on the desirability of economic growth

No ecological economist can dispute any of the foregoing arithmetic – as arithmetic it contains no mistakes. Ecological economists do not, however, share neoclassical economists' unqualified enthusiasm for economic growth as a dominant policy objective everywhere. There are two broad reasons for this. The first is that they consider that for the world as a whole, economic growth is not, on account of economy–environment interdependence, a feasible long-run objective. They think, that is, that it is very likely that continuing growth in average world income per capita will threaten the sustainability of the joint economy–environment system. The basis for this view will be set out in the next chapter.

The second reason has to do with the desirability of economic growth. Ecological economists do not think that it is desirable in the rich economies. They do think that it is very desirable in the economies where there are many poor people. The basis for this view is set out in the rest of this chapter.

6.5 NON-ECONOMIC INDICATORS OF WELL-BEING

There are many indicators of well-being, other than per capita GDP, that we could look at. We will look at four basic indicators. Data on others can be found in references cited in the Further Reading section at the end of the chapter – the annual Human Development Reports put together by the United Nations Human Development Programme are particularly useful, and are what we draw on here.

Table 6.13 Some basic indicators of well-being				
	Life expectancy at birth 2000 years	Infant mortality 2000 per 1,000 live births	Calories per day 1997	Adult literacy 2000 % at age 15
High income OECD	78.2	6	3380	*
FSB	68.6	20	2907	99.3
Developing	64.7	61	2663	73.7
Least developed	51.9	98	2099	52.8
Sub-Saharan Africa	48.7	135	2237	61.5

Sources: UNDP (2002): Tables 1 and 8 and UNDP (2000): Table 23.
Note: * data not available.

6.5.1 International comparisons

Table 6.13 gives data on our four basic well-being indicators for the groupings of national economies looked at previously in this chapter. Life expectancy at birth is obviously a very basic indicator of the extent to which needs and desires are being satisfied. Infant mortality rates reflect healthcare standards. An adequate diet is a fundamental need – recall that the intake requirement for a healthy adult leading a moderately active life is considered to be around 2,500 calories per day. The figure for calories per day shown for the High Income OECD group in Table 6.13 actually refers to the whole of the OECD. Adult literacy reflects educational performance, which may be seen as the source of intellectual nourishment. Table 6.13 shows that, by the standards of the rich world, conditions in the developing world, and especially in some parts of it, are very bad. In Sierra Leone in 2000, life expectancy at birth was just 39 years, about half of that in High Income OECD, and infant mortality was 180 per 1,000 live births, 30 times that in High Income OECD. While for the Developing countries as a whole the average availability of food energy exceeds the 2,500 standard, for Least Developed and Sub-Saharan Africa it falls short – in the case of Least Developed by 15 per cent. For the other indicators also these two groups do much less well than Developing.

6.5.2 Are things getting better?

An obvious question is whether conditions for the world's poor have, in terms of these indicators, been improving in the recent past. Table 6.14 looks at this question. In the first column we see that over the last quarter of the twentieth century life expectancy at birth increased everywhere except in the FSB. For infant mortality, a lower number is better, and for this indicator 1970 to 2000 saw improvements everywhere except in Sub-Saharan Africa. The availability of food energy increased in Developing, but in Least Developed it remained constant – below the average requirement for health – and in Sub-Saharan Africa it declined by a small amount. Over 1985 to 2000, adult literacy increased everywhere where data are available. The very small increase for FSB simply reflects the fact that in 1985 it was already the case that 99.3 per cent of those over 15 years of age were literate. For all of these indicators, Table 6.14 shows improvement for Developing as a whole. For

Table 6.14   Recent trends in well-being indicators

	Life expectancy 2000 ÷ 1970–1975	Infant mortality 2000 ÷ 1970	Calories per day 1997 ÷ 1970	Adult literacy 2000 ÷ 1985
High income OECD	1.09	0.30	1.11	*
FSB	0.99	0.59	*	1.01
Developing	1.16	0.57	1.17	1.18
Least developed	1.17	0.66	1.00	1.34
Sub-Saharan Africa	1.08	1.00	0.99	1.39

Sources: UNDP (2002): Tables 1 and 8 and UNDP (2000): Table 23.
Note: * data not available.

Least Developed, three indicators show improvement and one – calories per day – is constant. For Sub-Saharan Africa, three indicators show improvement and one – calories per day – shows a small deterioration. In the main then, things have improved, on average, for the world's poor in the last few decades. However, given that things have also improved in High Income OECD, it could still be true that the relative position of the poor has worsened – that inequality in life expectancy and the like has increased. It turns out that this is true for some indicators and groupings, but not for others. Exercise 5 invites you to look at this using the data from Tables 6.13 and 6.14.

6.5.3 Relationships between GDP per capita and well-being indicators

Table 6.15 brings together per capita GDP data with data on three of the indicators considered in the previous sub-section for the same groupings as already considered in this chapter. For the three main groupings, the rankings are the same for all three indicators, and that ranking is the same as that by GDP per capita. Least Developed has lower GDP per capita than Sub-Saharan Africa, but does a little better on life expectancy and infant mortality.

The data in Table 6.15 are for averages across groups of countries. Figures 6.8, 6.9 and 6.10 show the plots of each of these indicators against GDP per capita for data on the individual countries that make up the groupings of Table 6.15. These data show, in each case, an interesting and important pattern – indicator performance improves rapidly with GDP per capita at low levels of GDP per capita, but at higher levels the rate at which the indicator improves as GDP per capita increases falls.

Table 6.15   GDP compared with other indicators

	GDP per capita 2000 PPP $US	Life expectancy at birth 2000 years	Infant mortality 2000 per 1000 live births	Adult literacy 2000 % at age 15
High income OECD	27848	78.2	6	*
FSB	6930	68.6	20	99.3
Developing	3783	64.7	61	73.7
Least developed	1216	51.9	98	52.8
Sub-Saharan Africa	1690	48.7	135	61.5

Note: * data not available.

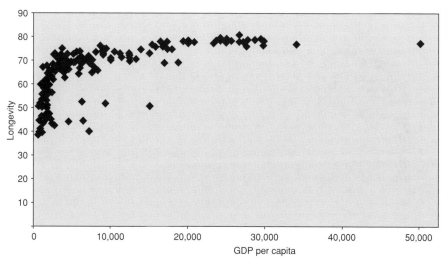

Figure 6.8
Longevity and
GDP per capita.

Note: data points from 166 countries.

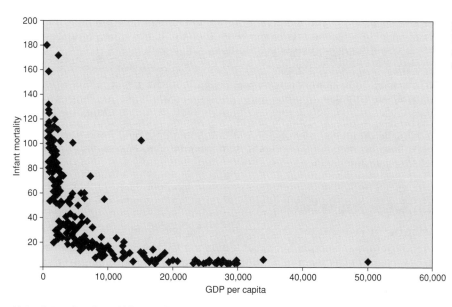

Figure 6.9
Infant mortality
and GDP per
capita.

Note: data points from 165 countries.

The data for these Figures is taken from Tables 1 and 8 of the *Human development report 2002*.

In Figure 6.8, data on 166 countries, life expectancy mainly increases very rapidly with increasing GDP per capita up to about $5,000, and beyond $10,000 there is virtually no effect of the level of GDP per capita on longevity. The picture in Figure 6.9, data on 165 countries, is similar. Note that in this case, infant mortality

Figure 6.10
Literacy and
GDP per
capita.

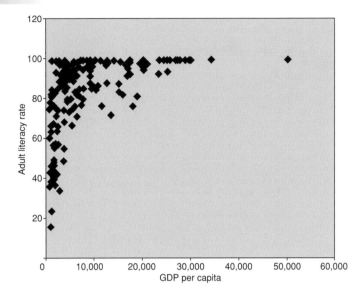

Note: data points from 166 countries.

cannot possibly go below 0. Over the range $500 to $10,000 infant mortality drops from over 100 deaths per 1,000 live births to below 20, whereas the drop over the range $10,000 to $50,000 is barely perceptible in Figure 6.9. For Figure 6.10, data on 166 countries, adult literacy cannot possibly go above 100 per cent. Some countries with very low GDP per capita get near this upper limit, but below $5,000 there is clearly a strong positive association between GDP per capita and the literacy rate. Beyond $10,000, increasing GDP per capita is only very weakly associated with the literacy rate because for countries in that position the latter is very close to its upper limit of 100 per cent.

6.5.4 GDP per capita and happiness

One of the attractions for many people of GDP per capita as a measure of economic performance appears to be that it purports to capture everything in a single number – it is seen as a sort of 'bottom line' indicator. It avoids the need to look at several measures of performance and to cope with the fact that different indicators tell different stories. If nation *A* does a lot better than *B* for literacy, but a little worse for life expectancy, how does one say which economy is performing better? Looking at per capita GDP solves this problem it seems. Indeed, given the fixation with GDP per capita it seems plausible that there is a general belief that there are no other 'bottom line' indicators available. This is not true.

To the extent that peoples' needs and desires are more or less satisfied, we could expect them to feel more or less happy. Then, a proper and comprehensive indicator of economic performance is human happiness. To use this indicator it has to be possible to measure human happiness. We will discuss this in the next

Happiness (index)

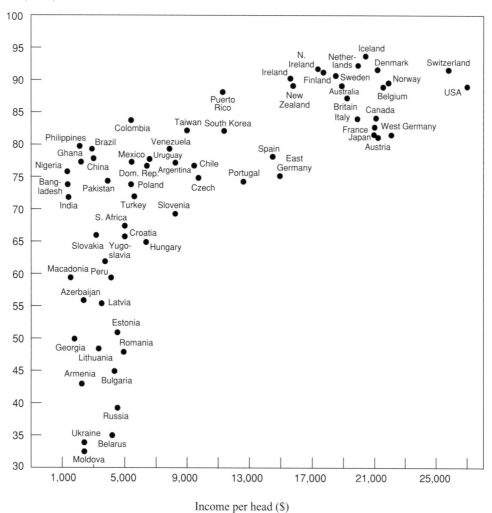

Income per head ($)

Source: Inglehart and Klingemann (2000).

section. For the moment, take it that it is possible to measure human happiness reasonably accurately. Certainly, while it is true that national statistical agencies do not regularly publish happiness data, it is also true that surveys asking people about their happiness, or satisfaction with their lives, are routinely conducted in most countries of the world by research institutes and polling organisations.

Figure 6.11 plots data on an index of happiness against GDP per capita (PPP$) for countries with a wide range of per capita income levels. The relationship is very similar to those in Figures 6.8, 6.9 and 6.10 – at low levels of income the happiness index increases rapidly as per capita income increases, but beyond about $10,000

Figure 6.11
Happiness and
GDP per capita.

the relationship becomes much weaker. The finding in Figure 6.11 is replicated in other studies – references are in the Further Reading section at the end of the chapter.

Taking Figures 6.8, 6.9. 6.10 and 6.11 together, the reasonable conclusion is that economic growth is very important for improving human well-being at income levels typical of the developing world today, but not very important in that respect at income levels typical of the developed world today.

6.6 HUMAN NEEDS AND DESIRES – WHAT MAKES PEOPLE HAPPY?

Finally in this chapter we look briefly at what is known, mainly as the result of the work of psychologists, about how satisfying various human needs and desires contributes to happiness. We will, in particular, explore further the relationship between income and happiness.

6.6.1 Measuring and explaining happiness

In the nineteenth century economists believed that happiness, which they called utility, could in principle be measured. By the 1950s this view had been almost entirely abandoned by neoclassical economists. They still use the term utility, meaning happiness or satisfaction in ordinary language, but do not try to measure it. They do not believe that utility, happiness, levels are measurable in a way that permits comparisons across individuals or groups of individuals. To most neoclassical economists today it makes no sense to say, 'A is happier, has more utility, than B' or 'The citizens of X are on average happier, have more utility, than those of Y'. However, for the last few decades psychologists – and a few economists – have been studying peoples' feelings and investigating what makes them happy. The emerging insights are very important in relation to the proper study of the satisfaction of human needs and desires, but are largely ignored in neoclassical economics.

6.6.1.1 Measuring happiness

The first question that needs to be looked at is whether happiness can actually be measured. Happiness is a state of mind, of feeling, and psychologists ask people how they feel. A typical question in a survey intended to study happiness and its determinants would be something like: 'Taking everything into account, how would you say things are for you these days – would you say that you are very happy, happy, unhappy or very unhappy?' An alternative form of question that gets used is to ask the interviewee, 'How satisfied are you with your life as a whole these days?' and to get them to respond on a scale of 1, for 'completely dissatisfied', to 10, for 'completely satisfied'.

The fact that people answer these kinds of questions does not necessarily mean that their happiness is being accurately measured. However, there are good reasons for believing that when these kinds of surveys are done carefully the answers that they elicit do mean something, that people who get higher scores are happier. One way in which such surveys have been evaluated is by asking the same people the same questions at different points in time. If an individual's circumstances do not change, then her happiness score should not change significantly – this is what has been found to be the case. Another test of these subjective, self-assessed, measures of an individual's happiness is to see if they correlate with other indicators of happiness. It has been found that, compared with the average person, individuals with higher than average self-assessed happiness scores are, for example, more likely to:

- be rated as happy individuals by family and friends
- be more optimistic about the future
- be less likely to attempt suicide
- recall more positive than negative life events
- smile more during social interaction
- be more healthy.

These surveys have been done in many countries, as Figure 6.11 indicates. An obvious concern here would be that 'happy' might mean different things in different languages. This appears not to be a major problem. Countries have, for example, been rated on three different approaches – asking people how happy they are, asking people how satisfied they are, and asking them to give their lives a score on a scale running from 'worst possible life' to 'best'. It was found that the rankings of countries were almost identical across the three approaches.

Finally, in recent years it has been found that the feelings that people report correspond to objectively measurable activity in the brain. Positive feelings correspond (for right-handed people) to activity in the left side of the brain, negative feelings to activity in the right side of the brain.

6.6.1.2 What determines happiness?

Psychologists consider that an individual's level of happiness can be assessed relative to that of other individuals, by asking appropriate questions, to a reasonable degree of accuracy. It is then possible to investigate the determinants of individual happiness by comparing variations in happiness across individuals with variations in genetic endowment and life circumstances. A number of studies of this kind have been done now, and in broad terms they all tell the same story.

The first point to note is that individuals do differ in their genetic predispositions in relation to feeling happy or otherwise. This is a matter of everyday observation, which is confirmed in experiments and surveys. Some people are basically cheerful by nature, others are not. Research into the determinants of happiness is based on the answers given to questions about happiness and life circumstances by a random sample of the population. The idea is to look for correlations between happiness scores and other attributes. By use of proper statistical methods, the correlation between the happiness score and attribute x score is after allowing for, or controlling for, the influence of other attributes. Only those attributes that are

Table 6.16 Effects of changes on happiness

	Fall in happiness index
Income	
Family income down 33 % relative to average	1
Work	
Unemployed (rather then employed)	3
Job insecure (rather than secure)	1.5
Unemployment rate up 10%	1.5
Inflation rate up 10%	0.5
Family	
Divorced (rather than married)	2.5
Separated (rather than married)	4.5
Widowed (rather than married)	2
Health	
Own health assessment down 1 point (5-point scale)	3

Source: Layard (2003).

recorded in the survey can be controlled for. Genetic make-up is not recorded in the survey, and is not controlled for. This is not considered to be a problem for using such surveys to study how life circumstances affect happiness, as genetic make-up is thought to affect the overall disposition to happiness, rather than the responses to particular life circumstances. It is thought, for example, to mean that A will be happier than B for exactly the same life circumstances, rather than to mean that more of x makes A happier but B less happy.

Surveys to generate data on the determinants of happiness have included questions about the respondent's self-assessed happiness (or satisfaction with life), age, physical health, family situation, employment status, educational attainment, and income. Table 6.16 reports results from three studies put together in such a way as to make the interpretation of the results as straightforward as possible. The happiness index is scaled so that the effect on it of having a family income 33 per cent lower than the average family income is, all other influences held constant, 1. It is the relative sizes of the other effects that we are interested in.

The effect on happiness of being unemployed, even when family income is not affected, is three times as big as the effect of a 33 per cent fall in family income. Just feeling that one's job is insecure affects happiness more than such a fall in family income, as does an increase in the general unemployment rate for the whole economy, even though one is not oneself unemployed. The effect on happiness of inflation at 10 per cent, i.e. the general level of prices increasing at 10 per cent per year, is less than the income effect, and hence less than the effect of an increase of 10 per cent in the unemployment rate.

The family situation has a big impact on self-assessed happiness. As compared to being married, for all other influences such as income and work status held constant, being separated lowers the score on the happiness index by 4.5 times as much as the income effect, being divorced by 2.5 times as much, and being widowed by twice as much.

Health is very important. A respondent whose self-assessed health score on a 5-point scale is one point lower has, all other influences held constant, a happiness index score which is lower by three times the amount that the index falls for a family income 33 per cent below average.

The general nature of these results is the same across all studies of the determinants of individual happiness. Income, and hence consumption, differences do affect happiness, but, except for big differences, by less than being in or out of work, being married or not, and feeling more or less healthy. We will now look more closely at the nature of the relationship between income and happiness.

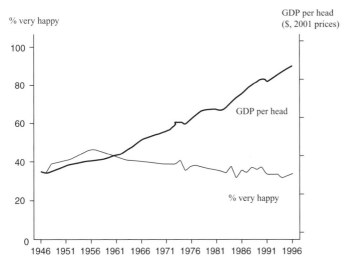

% very happy

GDP per head
($, 2001 prices)

Figure 6.12
Post-Second
World War
trends in
happiness and
GDP per capita
in the USA.

Source: Layard (2003).

6.6.2 Relationships between income and happiness

Actually, as indicated by the heading to this sub-section, the last statement should have referred to 'relationships' rather than 'the relationship'. We can look at the happiness–income relationship across individuals in a given country, across country averages, or over time in a given country.

6.6.2.1 *Across individuals*

Considering advanced economies, if we look at data on individuals in a given country at a given point in time, we find that, as in Table 6.16, individual happiness increases with individual income. However, most such studies find that as income increases so the happiness index increase associated with a given increase in income decreases. The relationship is essentially the same form as that shown in Figure 6.11 – the curve becomes less and less steep as income increases. In terms of happiness, there are decreasing returns to income increases. A $500 increase in income delivers a greater increase in happiness for an individual on $5,000 per year than it does for an individual on $20,000 per year.

6.6.2.2 *Across countries*

This is the case to which Figure 6.11 relates, looking at the average happiness index score in different economies at different levels of GDP per capita at a point in time. Again, happiness increases with income at a decreasing rate.

6.6.2.3 *Over time*

Figure 6.12 shows the trends in GDP per capita and the percentage of people reporting themselves as 'very happy' in the USA for the period 1946 to 1996. GDP per capita

Table 6.17 Percentages reporting various states of happiness by income group, USA

State reported	Proportion of people with incomes in the top quarter of the range %		Proportion of people with incomes in the bottom quarter of the range %	
	1975	1998	1975	1998
Very happy	39	37	19	16
Pretty happy	53	57	51	53
Not too happy	8	6	30	31

Source: Layard (2003).

has increased steadily, while the very happy proportion has actually fallen slightly. Essentially there is no relationship between average income as measured by GDP and this measure of national happiness. This is what turns out to be the case for virtually all of the rich economies for which data is available over a few decades or more – GDP per capita grows steadily while happiness remains unchanged.

6.6.2.4 Why does growth not increase happiness in rich countries?

There seems to be a paradox here. If we look across individuals, or across countries, at a point in time, then increasing income goes with increasing happiness, albeit at a declining rate as income increases. On the other hand, when we look at a whole rich economy over time, rising per capita GDP does not go with increasing happiness. Surely, if having more income makes an individual happier, individuals on average becoming richer over time should mean individuals on average becoming happier over time.

Table 6.17 restates this paradox. It refers to the USA, but what it reports is what is found in the recent history of many rich economies. A higher percentage of rich people than of poor people report themselves as 'Very happy', and a higher percentage of poor people than of rich people report themselves as 'Not too happy', in both 1975 and 1998. At a point in time, those with higher incomes are happier. However, despite the incomes of both rich and poor growing at something like 2 per cent per year for over 20 years, the proportions for 'Very happy', 'Pretty happy' and 'Not too happy' were much the same, for both groups, in 1998 as they were in 1975. Average income grew a lot, but average happiness clearly did not. Why? The explanation is that an individual's happiness depends on the match between what he aspires to and what he experiences, and that his aspirations depend on his own experience and what he observes about others' experience. Aspirations are formed by adaptation, or habituation, and rivalry.

In regard to adaptation, a rise in an individual's income permits a new higher level of consumption – more, or more stylish, clothes say. Initially this gives a higher level of satisfaction/happiness, but she soon gets used to the new clothes, and satisfaction/happiness returns to its former level, that is, in a widely used phrase, 'the novelty wears off'. To the extent that income and consumption rise steadily over time, that gets built into experience and steadily rising income and consumption become the aspirational norm – they do not deliver much more happiness.

Rivalry involves comparing oneself to others. The source for Table 6.17 reports a recent study in which students were asked, assuming that prices were the same in both cases, whether they would prefer a situation in which they earned $50,000 per year while others got half that, or one in which they earned $100,000 per year while others got twice that. The majority said they would prefer the first situation. Again, a widely used phrase puts it briefly – 'keeping up with the Jones'. If an individuals' peers are experiencing the same income and consumption growth as he is, his own income and consumption growth do not do much to increase his happiness/satisfaction.

Together, adaptation and rivalry explain why at a point in time individuals with higher incomes are usually happier than those with lower incomes, although over time generally rising incomes do not produce generally increasing happiness. Once all this is pointed out, it is fairly obvious, and, on reflection, consistent with our everyday experience, as indicated by the widely used phrases cited. It is, however, generally ignored in neoclassical economics. It is why, in rich economies, ecological economists do not accord the pursuit of per capita GDP growth the priority that neoclassical economists generally do.

6.6.3 Does inequality matter?

We saw in section 6.4.3 that economic growth as such does not reduce proportionate inequality, and increases absolute inequality – if the incomes of the poor and the rich grow at the same rates, their ratio stays the same and the absolute difference in $ increases. Reducing inequality requires differential growth, with the income of the poor growing faster than that of the rich.

There is a view that given economic growth, continuing inequality is not something to be concerned about. The argument is that so long as economic growth lifts the poor out of poverty, the fact that the rich are getting even richer, and the absolute gap between poor and rich is increasing, is fine. On this view, policy should seek to encourage growth but does not need as well to seek to reduce inequality – it is said that 'the rising tide lifts all the boats'.

The discussion of the relationship between income and happiness suggests that there are two problems with this view. First, if an extra $ of income increases the happiness of the poor by more than it increases the happiness of the rich, then it makes sense to seek policies that favour the poor. Second, the phenomenon of rivalry means that inequality is itself a source of unhappiness. If it is accepted that the point of economic activity is human happiness via the satisfaction of wants and needs, and that poverty is a problem to be addressed, then inequality does matter, and growth alone is not enough. Policies to reduce inequality within and between national economies are needed. This is the position of most ecological economists.

SUMMARY

A significant proportion of the world's population, at least 2 billion people, live in what is, by the standards of North America and Europe, serious, and for many abject, poverty. Economic growth is the major policy objective in every country in the world. In poor countries it is clear that economic growth improves the extent to which human needs and desires are satisfied, and makes people healthier and happier. In rich countries, economic growth does not make people generally happier. While it is obvious that poor countries need economic growth, it is not obvious that having it as a major policy objective in rich countries makes a lot of sense. This is very important for the problem of sustainable development, which we consider in the next chapter.

KEYWORDS

Constant returns to scale (p. 175): where increasing all input levels by x per cent leads to an x per cent increase in output.

Economic growth (p. 167): continuing increases in per capita national income.

Endogenous variable (p. 179): a variable whose value is determined by the model, for given values for the exogenous variables.

Exogenous variable (p. 179): a variable whose value is determined outside the model.

Isoquants (p. 176): lines joining points representing equal quantities of output.

Parameters (p. 174): constants for a particular version of the model, but can vary across versions.

Production function (p. 174): the relationship between the output level and the levels of inputs to production.

Savings function (p. 176): the relationship between the amount saved, and invested, and the level of national income.

FURTHER READING

The calculations in section 6.2 are based on data from Kuznets (1966) and Madison (1995) as reported in Parker (2000). According to Parker, Kuznets has economic growth starting 'sometime after 1500' and Madison identifies 1500 as the start of the period during which western Europe pulled ahead of the rest of the world in terms of economic development. Madison estimates that the world average for per capita national income in 1500 was $565 in 1990 PPP dollars.

The phenomenon of economic growth is dealt with in standard general introductory economics texts such as Mankiw *(2001) and Begg *et al.* (2000), for example, where it is explained in terms of the kind of growth models considered in the chapter here, save that they do not have natural resources as an input to production. These models are the basis for what is known as 'neoclassical growth theory'. For an excellent, and comprehensive, introductory treatment of this see Jones (2002), where the use of natural resources in production is considered. These models take the savings rate as an exogenously given parameter. In 'optimal growth theory' the savings rate is a variable to be determined by preferences as between current and future consumption and the terms on which sacrifices of current consumption generate gains to future consumption. We will come back to this in Chapter 9, and then provide some references.

The underlying sources of economic growth are considered in Jones (2002), which provides many references to the literature: see also Parker (2000). These books are written from the perspective of neoclassical growth theory. Mokyr (1990) is an economic historian's account of technological innovation and its impact on economic growth. Diamond (1998) relates technological innovation to environmental conditions.

Arndt (1978) gives a good account of how economic growth became the dominant policy objective in the years following the Second World War. Arndt also looks at the questioning of that objective from an environmental position that took place in the early 1970s – we will be considering this in the next chapter. Beckerman (1974) is a response to that assault and a very good statement of the neoclassical economist's position on the desirability of economic growth.

Each year the *Human development report* (UNDP, 2002, for example) reports for each of some 170 countries its score on the UNDP's Human Development Index, which combines measures of GDP per capita with a measure of health performance (longevity) and a measure of educational performance (adult literacy and enrolment). Dissatisfaction with per capita GDP as a measure of economic performance has led to a number of proposals for alternative single-number measures, such the Genuine Progress Indicator (GPI) and the Index of Sustainable Economic Welfare (ISEW). These are rather similar. They start with Consumption as measured in the national income accounts and make a series of adjustments to it to take out defensive expenditures, to put in non-marketed production of consumption goods and services, and to account for resource depletion and environmental damage. The ISEW was originally proposed in Daly and Cobb*(1989). The organisation Redefining Progress does work on the GPI, which can be accessed via its website, address given below. The journal *Ecological Economics* frequently publishes papers on ISEW and GPI.

Until quite recently few economists took much interest in studying the sources of human happiness, it being taken that it depended on only, and increased with, the consumption of goods and services. An exception is the work of Scitovsky (1976, 1986). This is changing and more economists are taking more notice of the work of psychologists, the nature of which can be seen in, for example, Argyle* (1987), which is a non-technical account. The treatment in the chapter here draws on Frey and Stutzer (2002a) and Layard (2003), which both provide extensive references to the economic and psychological literature. See also Lane (2000) and Frey and Stutzer (2002b). One approach to an understanding of what makes for physical and mental health in humans is to look at the conditions for which their genetic make-up was selected by biological evolution: see, for example, Boyden (1987) or Boyden *et al.* (1990). Boyden distinguishes between physical and psychological needs and their satisfiers – whereas the former were fixed by biological evolution, the latter change with cultural evolution. Max-Neef (1992) makes a similar distinction. Reisch (2003) is a survey of work on consumption in relation to ecological economics that covers some of these issues.

The nature of needs also relates to what is understood by poverty, and the relationship between poverty and inequality. In a classic study, Townsend (1979) took poverty to be unmet needs and noted that needs are culturally, as well as physiologically, determined. See also Sen (1985). Townsend noted that this was not a new idea, and quoted the founding father of economics, Adam Smith, as writing in the eighteenth century that: 'By necessities I understand, not only the commodities which are indispensably necessary for the support of life, but whatever the custom of the country renders it indecent for creditable people, even of the lowest order, to be without.' In the essay on the virtues of economic growth cited in section 6.4.1, Keynes distinguished between 'absolute' and 'relative' needs. The latter 'satisfy the desire for superiority, and may be insatiable'. Keynes did not spell out the arising implications for the ability of economic growth to deliver increasing happiness for all once absolute needs are met – this is done in Hirsch (1977) and in the works on the income–happiness relationship cited above.

DISCUSSION TOPICS

1. Should people in High Income OECD countries care about poverty in Developing countries?
2. Does inequality matter?
3. Given that in rich countries economic growth does not do much to increase happiness, and given that these countries are democracies, how can its importance as an objective of government policy be explained?

EXERCISES

1. Assuming that each had per capita income of $550 in 1500, work out the growth rates through to 2000 for High Income OECD, FSB and Developing that go with the GDP per capita figures in Table 6.1.
2. Simulate the basic growth model of section 6.3.1 for

$$Y = K^{0.3} \times L^{0.6} \times R^{0.1}$$

and for

$$Y = K^{0.1} \times L^{0.8} \times R^{0.1}$$

and compare your results with those in Tables 6.6 and 6.7. Explain the comparison.
3. Simulate the endogenous technical progress model for

$$a_t = b_t = c_t = K_{t-1}^{0.3}$$

and for

$$a_t = b_t = c_t = K_{t-1}^{0.8}$$

and discuss what the three sets of results for this model show.
4. Table 6.1 gives GDP per capita for 2000 and Table 6.11 gives growth rates for 1990–2000. Use these data to work out GDP per capita in 1990 for the three main groupings, and for Least Developed and Sub-Saharan Africa. Then

find out what happened over the decade to income inequalities relatively and absolutely.

5. From the ratios given in Table 6.14, or by going to the cited sources, produce a table like Table 6.13 for the base years that Table 6.14 refers to. Use this to consider how relative and absolute inequalities in these indicators changed over the periods that the data cover.

7

Economic growth and the environment

In this chapter you will:

- Learn about the construction of scenarios for the environmental impact of economic and population growth;
- Look at the effect of the composition of GDP on the environmental impact of economic growth;
- Study models of economic growth and resource availability;
- Consider the importance of substitution possibilities in production and technological change for growth prospects when there are natural resource constraints;
- Be introduced to *The Limits to Growth* controversy;
- Learn about the ways in which economic growth can be good for the environment;
- Look at what sustainable development would involve.

In the previous chapter we saw why economic growth is so widely regarded as a very good thing. In that chapter we largely ignored the natural environment. However, we know from Chapter 4 that studying what goes on in the economy without considering the implications for the environment is a serious mistake. In this chapter we are going to begin to correct that mistake, by looking at economic growth and the environment. There are two, related, big issues here. First, there is the widely held view that economic growth damages the environment. Second, there is the idea that environmental constraints mean that economic growth must come to an end. Before getting into these two areas, we begin by considering a simple way of looking at the roles of population growth, economic growth and technological change in how the economy impacts on the environment.

7.1 THE IPAT IDENTITY

In general terms, it is fairly obvious that the impact that an economy has on the environment will depend on the number of people, what each person consumes, and the technologies by means of which goods and services are produced. Other things being equal, the impact will increase with population size. Other things being equal, it will increase with the average quantity of goods and services consumed by an individual. Other things being equal, impact will increase as the technologies become more resource-intensive. The IPAT identity is a precise way of saying this for a particular environmental impact.

The identity is

$$I \equiv P \times A \times T$$

where:

      I stands for impact
      P stands for population
      A stands for affluence
      T stands for technology

The three-barred equality sign signifies that this is an identity – something that must always be true given the way that the things involved are defined.

The way things are defined is as follows. I is an extraction from the environment – oil, coal, or timber, for example – or an insertion into the environment – CO_2 into the atmosphere, sewage into a river, for example. I can be measured in various units – tonnes, litres, cubic feet, etc. – so for the moment we will say simply that it is measured in 'units', leaving the actual units to be defined later in particular applications. P is measured as number of people. Affluence is measured as the economy's total output of goods and services divided by population, where total output is measured in currency units as Gross Domestic Product (GDP). If the currency unit is \$, GDP is an amount of \$. Technology is measured as units of whatever it is that we are looking at, a particular extraction from or insertion into the environment, per \$ of GDP.

Given these definitions, the righthand side of the IPAT identity is

$$\text{number} \times (\text{GDP per capita}) \times (\text{units per \$ of GDP})$$

which is

$$\text{number} \times \frac{\$}{\text{number}} \times \frac{\text{units}}{\$}$$

where number cancels with number, and \$ cancels with \$, to leave units, as on the lefthand side.

Consider a particular example, global emissions of CO_2. In round numbers for the year 2000:

      P, the global population, was 6 billion, 6×10^9
      A, average GDP per capita for the world as a whole, was \$7,000
      T, the average amount of CO_2 released into the atmosphere for each \$ of
         global GDP produced in 2000, was 0.00055 tonnes

Using IPAT we find total global CO_2 emissions in 2000 as

$$I = (6 \times 10^9) \times 7,000 \times 0.00055 = 23.1 \times 10^9 = 23,100 \times 10^6$$

      or 23,100 million tonnes

In order to set this example up, the figure used for T was calculated by dividing total global CO_2 emissions, $23,100 \times 10^6$, by total global GDP given by $P \times A$ as

$(6 \times 10^9) \times 7{,}000$. Figures for global CO_2 emissions, global population and average global GDP per capita are available in standard published sources – those used here were taken from the *Human development report 2001*. The point here is to emphasise that IPAT is an accounting identity – given the definitions, I equals PAT must always be true.

IPAT is a tautology – it states what must be true. It is, nonetheless, very useful. It points us to the proximate determinants of the environmental impacts of economic activity. It does not tell us about the fundamental, or underlying, determinants. If we have two economies with very different levels of CO_2 emissions, for example, IPAT tells us that they must differ in population size, and/or in affluence, and/or in the technologies in use.

It does not tell us why the economies have different populations, and/or different levels of affluence, and/or different technologies. It does direct our attention to those questions as the relevant questions. Again, IPAT cannot tell us what will happen to environmental impacts in the future, but it is a useful way to begin thinking about such things and does call attention to important issues. We will now look at the use of IPAT in thinking about the future, in constructing scenarios.

7.1.1 Scenarios for the near future

A **scenario** is an internally consistent story about one way in which the future could unfold. It is not a prediction or a forecast. Rather, the point about studying scenarios is to consider a range of possible futures with the intention of identifying some of the implications of some possible, or desired, futures. We are going to use the IPAT identity to generate some scenarios which are focused on the environmental impact of population growth and increasing affluence. To fix ideas we will continue with the impact example introduced above – global CO_2 emissions.

7.1.1.1 Population

In Chapter 3 (section 3.5.2) we noted the difference between the demographic experiences of the developed world and the developing countries in the period following the Second World War. For the world as a whole, population grew at an average of 2 per cent per annum over 1950 to 1975. Over 1975 to 1999 the annual growth rate dropped to 1.6 per cent, and in 2000 it was 1.3 per cent. By the end of the twentieth century, the population growth rate for the developed countries as a whole was less than 0.5 per cent, and in some of them (Sweden and Denmark, for example) the population was falling. For the developing world as a whole, by the end of the century the growth rate was a little over 2 per cent per annum.

It is important to note that the absolute sizes of the increases in world population each year were larger at the end of the twentieth century than they were in 1950, despite the lower growth rate. In 1950 the world population was 2.2 billion, 2 per cent of which is 44 million. For 1975, 1.6 per cent of 4 billion is 64 million, and for 2000, 1.3 per cent of 6 billion is 78 million. This phenomenon – larger absolute increases despite falling rates of increase – is known as **demographic momentum**.

Despite the falling growth rate, by 2000 the annual increase in the number of people in the world was greater than the population of the UK.

Demographers, those who study population behaviour, generate projections of future population size on the basis of assumptions about future mortality and

Table 7.1 United Nations population projections for 2050, millions	
Low fertility	7866
Medium fertility	9322
High fertility	10934

Source: UN (2001).

fertility rates. The **fertility rate** is the average number of children produced by a female during her lifetime. Table 7.1 gives a set of projections, for different fertility rate assumptions, for world population in 2050, recently prepared by demographers at the UN. The mortality rate assumptions are the same for all of the projections. Recall that in the previous chapter we applied population growth rates for groupings of economies to their population in 2000 to project a world population of 10,544 billion for 2050, which is close to, but lower than, the High Fertility projection in Table 7.1. The UN demographers take the view that fertility rates in the developing world in the next 50 years will behave in a similar way to those in the developed world in the last 50 years, so that the global average fertility rate will fall. While they are confident about the direction of change in the fertility rate, the size of the change is uncertain. We can be reasonably confident that the world's population will increase, from 6,000 million in 2000, by at least 1,500 million to 2050. The increase may be almost 5,000 million. We are sure that the global population will increase, but unsure by how much.

By constructing scenarios we can examine the environmental implications of the range of population projections. We will use the UN population projections as input to IPAT to generate scenarios for global emissions of CO_2 in 2050. Recall that for the 2000 data

$$P = 6 \times 10^9$$
$$A = \$7,000$$
$$T = 0.00055 \text{ tonnes}$$

we got

$$I = (6,000 \times 10^6) \times 7,000 \times 0.00055 = 23,100 \times 10^6 \text{ or } 23,100 \text{ million tonnes}$$

Table 7.2 shows the projected levels of global CO_2 for 2050 for each of the three UN population projections of Table 7.1, assuming that A and T in 2050 take the same values as in 2000. The third column shows the percentage increase over emissions in 2000.

7.1.1.2 Affluence

We now use IPAT to consider the effects on global CO_2 emissions of increasing average GDP per capita. We will consider economic growth rates of 1 per cent, 2.5 per cent and 4 per cent per annum. The reasons for considering these rates are as follows. In terms of historical experience, an economy that grew at 2.5 per cent per annum over several decades would be growing reasonably fast. Some economies

Table 7.2 The effect of population growth on global CO_2 emissions

	2050 emissions tonnes	Percentage increase on 2000
Low fertility	$I = (7866 \times 10^6) \times 7000 \times 0.00055 = 30284 \times 10^6$	31%
Medium fertility	$I = (9322 \times 10^6) \times 7000 \times 0.00055 = 35890 \times 10^6$	55%
High fertility	$I = (10934 \times 10^6) \times 7000 \times 0.00055 = 42096 \times 10^6$	82%

Table 7.3 Economic growth and CO_2 emissions

Economic growth % per annum	2050 GDP pc $	2050 CO_2 emissions tonnes $\times 10^6$	Ratio of 2050 emissions to 2000 emissions
1	11512	37990	1.65
2.5	24060	79398	3.44
4	49747	164165	7.11

Table 7.4 CO_2 emissions for population growth and economic growth

Economic growth rate	CO_2 million tonnes		
	Low fertility	Medium fertility	High fertility
1% pa	49804 (2.16)	59023 (2.56)	69230 (3.00)
2.5% pa	104091 (4.51)	123358 (5.34)	144690 (6.26)
4% pa	215220 (9.32)	255058 (11.04)	299164 (12.95)

have grown faster, some slower in recent years – see the previous chapter. We use 1 per cent to represent a global economy doing poorly in terms of average growth. The argument has been advanced, as will be discussed later in this chapter, that in order to deal with the problem of poverty, the global economy needs to, and could, grow at a rate higher than it has done in the recent past – 4 per cent per annum is used to represent this view.

Table 7.3 shows, in the second column, the level that A as GDP per capita would reach in 2050 if it grew at the indicated annual rate from 2000 until 2050, starting from the base of $7,000 in 2000. Note that for a growth rate of 2.5 per cent, 50 years is long enough for something to increase more than three-fold. The third column of Table 7.3 shows the level of CO_2 emissions calculated using IPAT with the 2050 level of GDP per capita shown in the second column for A and the actual 2000 levels for P and T, i.e. $6,000 \times 10^6$ and 0.00055. The final column in Table 7.3 shows the proportionate increase in CO_2 emissions due to the increase in A – 50 years of economic growth at 4 per cent would, all else constant, increase emissions by a factor of 7. Even at 2.5 per cent growth, emissions would increase more than three-fold. However, all else constant is not a tenable assumption. In the previous subsection here we considered UN projections for global population growth out to 2050, and their implications for CO_2 emissions. We can now use IPAT to figure what would happen to emissions as the result of population growth together with increasing GDP per capita, assuming T remains constant. Results are given in Table 7.4. They use P figures from Table 7.1, A figures from Table 7.3, and T is 0.00055. The figures in parentheses in Table 7.4 are the ratios of the 2050 emissions to emissions in 2000, $21,300 \times 10^6$ tonnes. Note that the combined effect of population growth and economic growth is *not* the sum of their separate effects. On its own, low fertility assumption population growth leads (see Table 7.2) to a 31 per cent increase in emissions. On its own (see Table 7.3) 1 per cent economic growth leads to a 65 per cent increase in emissions. The sum of these effects is 96 per cent. The effect on emissions of low fertility population growth together with 1 per cent economic growth is actually (Table 7.4) an increase of 116 per cent. It follows from $I \equiv PAT$ that the joint effect of changes in P and A on I is multiplicative rather than additive. The effect is striking for the combination of high fertility and 4 per cent economic growth. The sum of the separate effects is 693 per cent, whereas the joint effect is actually an increase of 1,195 per cent.

7.1.1.3 Technology

As already noted at various points, CO_2 is the most important of the greenhouse gases which are generally considered to be responsible for observed global warming in the twentieth century. The majority of expert scientists take the view that the amount of CO_2 in the atmosphere is already greater than is desirable, and that we should be working to stabilise emissions of CO_2, and ideally to reduce them. The scenarios considered above show that on conservative assumptions about population and per capita GDP growth, CO_2 emissions would double in the next 50 years, and that on central assumptions about these things they would increase by a factor of about 5.

These results assume that technology does not change, that the average amount of CO_2 released into the atmosphere per \$ of world GDP produced remains the same for the next 50 years. This is extremely unlikely. Apart from anything else, the enhanced greenhouse effect, to which CO_2 emissions contribute, is widely recognised as a very serious problem and many of the developed nations have committed themselves to reducing their emissions, as will be discussed in Chapter 13. If emissions are to be reduced, and if there is to be no reduction in either population or GDP per capita, then clearly T, tonnes of emissions per \$ of GDP, must fall. If emissions are to be reduced while population and GDP per capita are growing, as expected in the former case and hoped for in the latter, then T must fall even more.

IPAT can produce scenarios which include population growth assumptions, GDP per capita growth assumptions and technology change assumptions. One would simply postulate the change in T, and calculate I for the new T, A and P as shown above. Rather than go through such a calculation here, it is instructive to note another way in which IPAT can be used to address questions about technology change.

We can ask: given postulated changes in P and A, how would it be necessary for T to change in order that I be at some specified level? To illustrate, we can continue with the CO_2 emissions case, and consider a specified level for I which is the 2000 level. The question then is: given postulated changes in world population and average per capita GDP to 2050, by how much would T have to change in order that CO_2 emissions in 2050 be no higher than in 2000?

To answer this question, we need to solve

$$23{,}100 \times 10^6 = (P_{2050} \times 10^6) \times A_{2050} \times T_{2050}$$

for T_{2050} given values for P_{2050} and A_{2050}, where P_{2050} is the population for 2050 in millions, and so on. Rearranging and cancelling 10^6 here gives

$$T^*_{2050} = \frac{23100}{P_{2050} \times A_{2050}}$$

where T^*_{2050} is the required value for T. Substituting 7,866 for P_{2050} from Table 7.1 and 11,512 for A_{2050} from Table 7.3, for example, we find that for low fertility assumption population growth and economic growth at 1 per cent, the value of T^*_{2050} that gives emissions at the 2000 level is 0.0002551. Recall that T for 2000 was 0.00055, so that in this case

$$\frac{T^*_{2050}}{T_{2000}} = 0.4638$$

which means that in order for the postulated population and income growth to be consistent with constant emissions, the amount of emissions per \$ of GDP has to fall by more than 50 per cent. Proceeding in the same way for high fertility assumption population growth – to $10{,}934 \times 10^6$ from Table 7.1 – and economic growth at 4 per cent – to GDP per capita of \$49,747 from Table 7.3 – gives T^*_{2050} equal to 0.000043, so that

$$\frac{T^*_{2050}}{T_{2000}} = 0.0772$$

and total global emissions at the 2000 level would require that per \$ of GDP emissions were less than 10 per cent of their 2000 level.

IPAT-generated scenarios can show what needs to be done in terms of T to meet given targets in terms of I, for given assumptions about population and income change. They cannot, of course, tell us whether what is needed can be done, nor how to do it if it can be done.

7.1.2 The commodity composition of GDP – 'consumption technology'

As normally understood, 'technology' refers, as in the previous chapter, to methods of production. However, the commodity composition of GDP can be regarded as the 'technology' by means of which needs and desires are satisfied in a particular economy. Given the observed variation of the commodity composition of GDP across economies, it is clear that this 'technology' is not rigidly fixed. Consumption technology, as much as and along with production technology determines the value taken by I. In considering economic growth and the environment in terms of IPAT, it is important to think about changes in consumption technology as well as changes in production technology. The question of, for example, whether CO_2 emissions can be held constant while population and affluence increase is about what is consumed as well as about how it is produced.

To see what is involved here it is useful to start by revisiting the IPAT identity. Let us restate it as

$$I_i \equiv P \times A \times T_i \quad \text{for } i = 1, 2, 3, \ldots n$$

where the subscript i indexes particular forms of environmental impact, of which there are n in total. Thus, for example, I_1 could refer to coal extraction, I_2 to CO_2

emissions, I_3 to oil extraction, I_4 to SO_2 emissions, and so on. Writing IPAT in this way makes the point that population and GDP per capita affect all environmental impacts, whereas technology is impact-specific – the effect that P and A have on any particular I_i depends on T_i. Reducing P and/or A would reduce all I_i. I_i for an economy can also be affected by the pattern of commodity production that goes to make up GDP, for given A and P. The simplest way to see what is involved is to look at a simple constructed numerical example.

Take an economy where two commodities are produced. The production of X uses 1 tonne of coal per unit X, whereas Y production uses 10 tonnes of coal per unit Y. Suppose that for the purposes of measuring GDP X and Y both have unit value \$1, and that 50,000 million units of X and Y are the only things that the economy produces. Then

$$GDP = \text{value of X production} + \text{value of Y production}$$
$$= \$(1 \times 50,000 \times 10^6) + \$(1 \times 50,000 \times 10^6)$$
$$= \$100,000 \times 10^6$$

i.e. one hundred billion dollars. Suppose that the population is 10 million, so that GDP per capita is \$10,000.

The total amount of coal used is

$$C = \text{coal used in X production} + \text{coal used in Y production}$$
$$= (50,000 \times 10^6 \times 1) + (50,000 \times 10^6 \times 10)$$
$$= 550,000 \times 10^6 \text{ tonnes}$$

so that for the use of coal in this economy

$$T_i = \frac{C}{GDP} = \frac{550,000 \times 10^6}{100,000 \times 10^6} = 5.5$$

where i indexes the extraction of coal.

Now consider an economy the same in all respects save that 25,000 million units of X and 75,000 million units of Y are produced. Then

$$GDP = \text{value of X production} + \text{value of Y production}$$
$$= \$(1 \times 25,000 \times 10^6) + \$(1 \times 75,000 \times 10^6)$$
$$= \$100,000 \times 10^6$$

i.e. one hundred billion dollars, as before. The total amount of coal used is

$$C = \text{coal used in X production} + \text{coal used in Y production}$$
$$= (25,000 \times 10^6 \times 1) + (75,000 \times 10^6 \times 10)$$
$$= 775,000 \times 10^6 \text{ tonnes}$$

so that for this economy

$$T_i = \frac{C}{GDP} = \frac{775,000 \times 10^6}{100,000 \times 10^6} = 7.75$$

GDP production in the second economy is more coal-intensive, although both economies use the same production technologies in commodity production.

Looking at whole economies, the value of T_i, and of I_i, depends on the commodity composition of GDP, as well as on P, A, and the production technologies in use. Of course, any reduction of coal use achieved by changing consumption technology (or production technology) may involve more use of some other resource or resources.

We have explained the way in which the commodity composition of GDP affects environmental impact by looking at an example concerning resource extraction. Clearly, the same sort of story applies to threats originating in waste insertions into the environment.

7.2 MODELLING GROWTH AND THE ENVIRONMENT

The IPAT identity is a very useful truism. Given numbers for population, affluence and technology it tells us what the corresponding impact must be. Or, given numbers for population and affluence, we can use it to work out what the number for technology must be if impact is to be of given size. It does not, however, give us any insights into what determines, for example, affluence. For such insights we need to look at models rather than accounting identities.

In the previous chapter we looked at models of economic growth based on a production function

$$Y = f(K, L, R)$$

a savings function

$$S = s \times Y$$

and the relationship between saving and the size of the capital stock

$$K_t \equiv K_{t-1} + S_t$$

We considered some of the properties of this model, and some variants, by conducting simulations in which the resource input grew at the same rate as the labour input. In this way we were able to ignore the role of resources in production.

We now want to look at the relationship between economic growth and the environment. We will do this using the same basic model, but without the special assumption about resource input levels. In this section we use simple abstract models to bring out some of the fundamentals of the growth and the environment relationship. We will assume, for example, that just one kind of natural resource is used in production. We will look at renewable resources, and then at non-renewable resources.

In Chapter 6 we found that savings behaviour and technological change were key drivers of economic growth. They are also important to the relationship between economic growth and the environment. Also important are the possibilities for input substitution between capital services, labour services and environmental services. In order to bring this out we need to consider some alternative forms for the production function, and it is with this that we begin.

7.2.1 On substitution possibilities

In the models in Chapter 6, the production function took the form

$$Y = K^{\alpha} \times L^{\beta} \times R^{\delta}$$

where Y represents national income, K represents capital, L labour and R is the input of the natural resource. We used the constant returns to scale version of this Cobb–Douglas production function, where the parameters satisfy the condition $\alpha + \beta + \delta = 1$. In Figure 6.1 we showed isoquants for such a production function, which illustrate how inputs can be substituted for one another while holding the output level constant. Figure 7.1(b) here shows the isoquants for this production function in terms of substitution between K and R – it is the same as Figure 6.1(b).

A different particular form that the production function could be given in this kind of model is

$$Y = \alpha K + \beta L + \delta R$$

and the K/R isoquants that go with this are shown in Figure 7.1(a). According to this production function, K, or L, can be substituted for R with Y constant at a constant rate. The substitutability of K, or L, for R is such that any given level of Y could be produced using no R at all if there is enough K, or L. Setting $R = 0$ in

$$Y = \alpha K + \beta L + \delta R$$

gives

$$Y = \alpha K + \beta L$$

so that Y can be produced with no resource input. Given the laws of nature, this cannot be a description of the production of national income – it involves material commodities and so must involve some material extraction from the environment.

Any algebraic statement of a production function that is to be acceptable as a simplified description of reality must have the property that if R is equal to zero, then Y is equal to zero. The Cobb–Douglas form does have this property. Setting $R = 0$ in

$$Y = K^{\alpha} \times L^{\beta} \times R^{\delta}$$

obviously gives $Y = 0$. What Figures 6.1(b) and 7.1(b) show is that K can be substituted for R at a decreasing rate as more K is used. In Chapter 6 we saw that, with $\alpha = 0.2$, $\beta = 0.7$ and $\delta = 0.1$, Y equal to 10 could be produced using the following combinations of inputs:

K	L	R
6	20	0.2170
5	20	0.3125
4	20	0.4883
3	20	0.8683
2	20	1.9531

Figure 7.1
Isoquants for
three types of
substitution
situation.

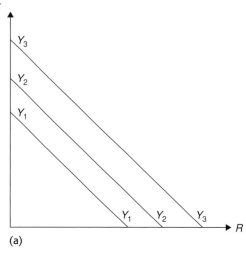

(a)

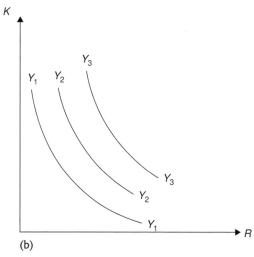

(b)

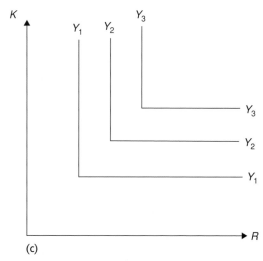

(c)

Holding Y at 10 and L constant at 20, increasing K from 2 to 3 reduces R by 1.9531 − 0.8683 = 1.0848, whereas increasing K from 3 to 4 reduces R by 0.38, and increasing K from 5 to 6 reduces R by just 0.0955.

Figure 7.1(c) shows K/R isoquants for

$$Y = \min(\{\alpha \times K\}, \{\beta \times L\}, \{\delta \times R\})$$

which is known as a **Leontief production function**, which is a production function that does not allow for any substitution between input factors. This is to be read as follows. Y takes the value that is the smallest of $\{\alpha \times K\}$, $\{\beta \times L\}$, and $\{\delta \times R\}$. Suppose, for example, that $\alpha = 0.01$ and $K = 100$, $\beta = 2$ and $L = 10$, and $\delta = 5$ and $R = 10$. Then $\alpha \times K = 1$, $\beta \times L = 20$ and $\delta \times R = 50$, so that Y is equal to 1. This form for the production function satisfies the condition that R equal to zero gives Y equal to zero − the minimum of $\alpha \times K$, $\beta \times L$, and 0 is 0 whatever the values taken by α, K, β and L. With this kind of production function, no input can be substituted for by another. Suppose, for example, that $\alpha = 1$ and $K = 100$, $\beta = 2$ and $L = 100$, and $\delta = 5$ and $R = 10$. Then $\alpha \times K = 100$, $\beta \times L = 200$ and $\delta \times R = 50$, so that Y is equal to 50. Reducing R to 9 reduces Y to 45, and there are no increases in K and/or L that can maintain Y at 50 given this, or indeed any, reduction in R.

Figure 7.1(a) and (c) correspond to polar extremes in regard to substitution possibilities. In Figure 7.1(a) they are so great that any Y can be produced without any of any one input, provided that there is enough of the other two. In Figure 7.1(c) they are zero, in that if any one input is zero then Y is zero however much of each of the other two inputs could be used. The Cobb–Douglas case is intermediate, in that while it is true that if any input level is zero then Y is zero, it is also true that more of either or both of any two inputs can be used to hold Y constant as the level of the third input is reduced. The amount of one input required to substitute for a given reduction in another increases as the level of its use increases.

Given that the Figure 7.1(a) situation cannot be a simple description of reality, we will not consider it further. We shall look further at the production functions that go with Figure 7.1(b) and (c). Not surprisingly, it turns out that relationships between economic growth and the environment differ according to which of these is used in the model.

7.2.2 Renewable resources

We look first at renewable (stock) resources. In Chapter 6, in order to avoid having to consider matters environmental, it was assumed that the resource input to production simply grew in line with the labour input. Obviously, given our discussion of renewable stock resources and their population dynamics in Chapters 2 and 4, this cannot be a generally realistic assumption − populations of flora and fauna do not grow indefinitely. So, we begin by looking at the population dynamics of the harvested renewable resource.

7.2.2.1 Stock size and harvesting

In Chapters 2 and 4 we introduced density-dependent growth as a standard assumption about how biotic populations grow. In Chapter 2 we considered the logistic model of population growth, which is a widely used particular model of density-dependent growth. With N for the size of the renewable resource population, the logistic growth model is

$$N_t = N_{t-1} + \left[r \times \left(\frac{K - N_{t-1}}{K} \right) \times N_{t-1} \right]$$

where r is the intrinsic growth rate and K is the carrying capacity of the environment for this population.[1] This says that over a period, the population size increases by an amount which is r times the proportionate distance that the population size is from carrying capacity times the population size at the start of the period. As discussed in Chapter 2, we can study the logistic growth model by doing simulations with a spreadsheet – Figure 2.9 in sub-section 2.3.2.2 is a plot of N against time produced that way. Figure 2.9 tracks N in the absence of exploitation by humans, which we refer to as harvesting. With harvesting

$$N_t = N_{t-1} + \left[r \times \left(\frac{K - N_{t-1}}{K} \right) \times N_{t-1} \right] - H_t$$

where H_t stands for the size of the harvest in year t.

In Chapter 6 we looked at simulations where the amount of the resource used increased over time at the same rate as the human population. With an upper limit, K, to the size of the exploited stock here, it is clear that this could not go on indefinitely, since taking an increasing harvest would reduce the stock to zero. You can confirm this by simulations (see Exercise 2 at the end of the chapter). As in the previous chapter, have the human population grow from an initial level of 1 (million, say) at 2.5 per cent, and have the harvest also start at 1 and grow at 2.5 per cent. For $r = 0.4$ and $K = 10$, and with the stock size initially at 10, the stock is harvested to extinction in 22 years, for example.

In Chapter 4 we introduced the idea of a sustainable harvest, a harvest that could be maintained indefinitely, being equal to the growth of the resource stock. If, as with logistic growth, the growth of the resource stock varies with the stock size, so does the sustainable harvest. As shown in Figure 4.3 there is a largest sustainable harvest known as the maximum sustainable yield. The size of this harvest, and of the stock size that goes with it, depends on the values of the parameters r and K. For $r = 0.4$ and $K = 10$, the maximum sustainable yield is 1 and the corresponding stock size is 5. Exercise 2 asks you to verify this by simulating

$$N_t = N_{t-1} + \left[0.4 \times \left(\frac{100 - N_{t-1}}{100} \right) \times N_{t-1} \right] - H_t$$

---

1 We apologise for the use of the symbol K for carrying capacity here, and for capital in stating the production function. These are standard usages, in ecology and economics respectively, which we prefer to conform to. It should not give rise to any confusion. A similar problem arises with r, used here, as is standard in ecology, for the intrinsic growth rate, and later, as is standard in economics, for the interest rate.

for H_t always equal to 1, and for N initially at 5. You will find that N stays at 5 indefinitely, as at that stock size natural growth is 1, which is always equal to the harvest size.

7.2.2.2 Growth and sustainable yield harvesting

If a renewable resource stock is not to be harvested to extinction, then the harvest must be held at, or below, a sustainable level. The largest constant harvest that can be taken indefinitely is the maximum sustainable yield. We now want to look at the implications of sustainable yield harvesting for economic growth. We will do this for logistic growth with $r=0.4$ and $K=10$, as just considered, where the human population grows at 2.5 per cent per year.

First, consider the growth model with a Leontief production function

$$Y = \min(\{\alpha \times K\}, \{\beta \times L\}, \{\delta \times R\})$$

$$S = s \times Y$$

$$K_t \equiv K_{t-1} + S_t$$

where R is always the maximum sustainable yield harvest of 1. Given our earlier discussion of substitution possibilities with this kind of production function, we know that Y can never be greater than $\delta \times R = \delta \times 1$. There is an upper limit to Y, which is determined by the value of δ, which limit is the same however much capital is accumulated and however large the population grows. Once Y reaches its upper limit, if population continues to grow, then y, income per capita, falls at the rate at which population grows.

To see how the possibility of substituting capital and labour for the resource input affects this, we can consider the growth model with a Cobb–Douglas production function

$$Y = K^\alpha \times L^\beta \times R^\delta$$

$$S = s \times Y$$

$$K_t \equiv K_{t-1} + S_t$$

where R is always the maximum sustainable yield harvest of 1, where $\alpha = 0.2$, $\beta = 0.7$ and $\delta = 0.1$, and where $s = 0.15$. These are the basic values for the parameters of the production function and the savings rate that were used in Chapter 6, and the simulation outcomes here are to be compared with those there.

Here are the first few rows from an Excel™ spreadsheet for this simulation. Rows 1 through to 6 say what the columns are, and give the parameter values used in the simulation. Reading down B from row 9 onwards, each entry is 1.025 times the one above – B9 is given by B8*1.025, for example. All column C entries are 1. In column D, D9 is given by D8 + F7, D10 by D9 + F8, and so on. The entries in column E for national income come from the production function so that (B8^0.7)*(C8^0.1)*(D8^0.2) gives the E8 entry, and is copied down the column. Column F works out saving as the savings ratio 0.15 times national income. Column G divides national income by population – which is the same as the size of the labour force in column B – to get per capita national income y. Column H works out the

	A	B	C	D	E	F	G	H	I	J
1	time	lab	rsce	cap	ntnl	saving	inc pc	grwth	cap pc	grwth
2		input	input	stock	inc		y	rate	k	rate
3								for y		for k
4						save		$\dot{y}$		$\dot{k}$
5		beta	gamma	alpha		ratio				
6		0.7	0.1	0.2		0.15				
7										
8	1	1	1	1	1	0.15	1		1	
9	2	1.025	1	1.15	1.046276	0.156941	1.020757	0.020757	1.121951	0.121951
10	3	1.050625	1	1.306941	1.092106	0.163816	1.039482	0.018344	1.243966	0.108752
11	4	1.076891	1	1.470757	1.137701	0.170655	1.056469	0.016342	1.365744	0.097896

Table 7.5   Sustainable yield input to a Cobb–Douglas production function

Year	y	$\dot{y}$ %	k	$\dot{k}$ %
10	1.1323	0.91	2.0800	5.92
20	1.2010	0.40	3.1594	3.28
30	1.2324	0.17	4.0671	2.08
40	1.2430	0.03	4.8034	1.40
50	1.2407	−0.05	5.3840	0.97
60	1.2298	−0.11	5.8289	0.67
70	1.2131	−0.15	6.1582	0.46
80	1.1923	−0.19	6.3909	0.31
90	1.1687	−0.21	6.5436	0.19
100	1.1433	−0.23	6.6306	0.09

Table 7.6   Varying the importance of the resource input

Year	$\delta = 0.05$ y	$\dot{y}$ %	$\delta = 0.01$ y	$\dot{y}$ %
10	1.1925	1.39	1.2447	1.80
20	1.3157	0.75	1.4224	1.06
30	1.3941	0.45	1.5480	0.71
40	1.4438	0.28	1.6412	0.50
50	1.4752	0.17	1.7120	0.37
60	1.4937	0.09	1.7667	0.28
70	1.5028	0.04	1.8093	0.21
80	1.5049	0.00	1.8424	0.16
90	1.5017	−0.04	1.8682	0.12
100	1.4945	−0.06	1.8880	0.09

growth rate for y, $\dot{y}$– the entry for H9 is (G9-G8)/G8, which is copied down the column. Columns I and J work out the per capita capital stock, k, and its rate of growth, $\dot{k}$.

The results for this basic version of the growth model with sustainable yield harvesting of a renewable resource are shown in Table 7.5, to be compared with Table 6.7.

Somewhere between 40 and 50 years out, per capita national income reaches a peak, and thereafter it declines at an increasing rate. Out to 100 years, capital per capita is still increasing, but at a declining rate. Despite capital accumulation and substitution, not only is economic growth in this model a transitory phenomenon, but it eventually goes into reverse. Can a higher savings rate offset this effect of the fixed level of the resource input? No. Simulations for this model with various levels for s up to 0.99 simply delay the date at which per capita income peaks. Even for s = 0.99, the peak is delayed only until year 51.

In Chapter 6 we saw that increasing the importance of capital in production, increasing the value for α in the production function, increased the growth of per capita income for given s and population growth rate. Does the effect of the fixed level of the resource input depend on the importance of the resource input in production, on the size of the parameter δ? Yes. Table 7.6 shows results for two cases where the resource is less important in production than in Table 7.5. In order to maintain the constant returns to scale feature of the production function, as δ is reduced to make the resource less important in production, so α is increased so that $\alpha + \beta + \delta$ is kept equal to 1. For δ equal to 0.05 the peaking of per capita income is delayed until somewhere between years 80 and 90. For δ equal to 0.01 per capita income is still growing at year 100, though the rate of growth is declining. In this case, extending the length of the simulation out to 200 years reveals that per capita income peaks in year 170, declining thereafter at an increasing rate.

7.2.2.3 Technical progress

So, even with capital accumulation and substitution, fixing the input of the renewable resource at a sustainable harvest level, so that the resource is not exhausted, means that for a growing human population the growth of per capita income eventually goes into reverse and per capita income falls.

We now consider endogenous technical progress, which we model as in Chapter 6. Let us look first at this for the case where the production function is a Cobb–Douglas with constant returns to scale. Table 7.7 gives the simulation results which we get for a model which is that just considered – results in Table 7.5 – modified to feature endogenous technical progress. See the first few rows from an Excel^{TM} spreadsheet for this simulation in the table below.

	A	B	C	D	E	F	G	H	I
1	time	a	lab	rsce	cap	ntnl	saving	inc pc	grwth
2			input	input	stock	inc		y	rate
3									for y
4							save		ẏ
5			beta	gamma	alpha		ratio		
6			0.7	0.1	0.2		0.15		
7									
8	1	1	1	1	1	1	0.15	1	
9	2	1	1.025	1	1.15	1.046276	0.156941	1.020757	0.020757
10	3	1.087474	1.050625	1	1.306941	1.187636	0.178145	1.130409	0.107422
11	4	1.174231	1.076891	1	1.485087	1.338518	0.200778	1.242947	0.099555

We have introduced a new column at B for the efficiency factor applied to all inputs, *a*. Its size depends on the size of the capital stock, so that B9 is given by E8^0.6 and so on down the column. The input levels from columns C, D and E are multiplied by this factor before being used in the production function. The entry for national income in F9 is given by ((E8*B8)^0.2)*((C8*B8)^0.7)*((D8*B8)^0.1) which is Excel^{TM} notation for $(E8 \times B8)^{0.2} \times (C8 \times B8)^{0.7} \times (D8 \times B8)^{0.1}$. This is copied down column F. The entries in columns G, H and I are determined as previously.

Table 7.7 is to be compared with Table 7.5, which is for the same model with no technical progress. In both cases the population and labour force grow at 2.5 per cent, and the resource input is always the maximum sustainable yield, 1. The

Table 7.7 Technical progress with a Cobb–Douglas production function

Year	y	$\dot{y}$ %
10	2.1695	9.54
20	5.2260	8.93
30	11.9860	8.45
40	26.4559	8.08
50	56.6438	7.78
60	118.3469	7.54
70	242.4033	7.35
80	488.4987	7.19
90	971.3480	7.06
100	1910.1630	6.95

Table 7.8 Technical progress with a Leontief production function

Year	$\dot{y}$ % $a_t = K_{t-1}^{0.6}$	$a_t = K_{t-1}^{0.9}$
10	3.45	9.32
20	1.79	8.00
30	0.85	6.94
40	0.26	6.07
50	−0.16	5.34
60	−0.46	4.73
70	−0.70	4.21
80	−0.88	3.75
90	−1.03	3.36
100	−1.15	3.01

growth rate in Table 7.7 is declining, but at a decreasing rate and eventually it will become constant. Given sufficient technological progress, ongoing economic growth is possible with a growing human population using a sustainable yield from a renewable resource. This result arises in a model where there are possibilities for substitution between inputs. What is the situation if the production function is of the Leontief kind, where there are no substitution possibilities? It turns out that, even in this case, sufficiently fast technical progress can keep the growth of per capita income going for a very long time. Table 7.8 gives the per capita income growth rate outcomes for simulations which is the same as that just considered except that now the production function is

$$Y = \min(\{a \times K\}, \{a \times L\}, \{a \times R\})$$

with a determined as shown at the top of Table 7.8. For $a_t = K_{t-1}^{0.6}$, the rate of growth of per capita income becomes negative – so that per capita income starts to fall – in less than 50 years. But for $a_t = K_{t-1}^{0.9}$, after 100 years per capita income is still growing at 3.01 per cent per year.

7.2.2.4 Constant population

Given a growing human population, if the harvest of the renewable resource input increases with that population, the resource is harvested to extinction. If the resource is harvested on a sustainable yield basis, then economic growth soon comes to an end unless there are possibilities for substituting for the resource in production, and/or technological progress. What if the size of the human population is constant? Does capital accumulation without technical progress then mean continuing economic growth? Given the need to harvest the renewable resource on a sustainable yield basis, if it is not to be harvested to extinction and income to go to zero, could population stabilisation be a means to per capita income growth?

Suppose first that the production function is of the Leontief form, so that there are no substitution possibilities. The levels of resource input and labour input are constant, while the capital stock is growing in size as a result of saving. In that case, in the absence of any technical progress, Y cannot get bigger than whichever is the smaller of $\{\beta \times L\}$ and $\{\delta \times R\}$, where L and R are the constant labour input/population size and the constant resource input. Maximum Y is the smaller of these, and maximum *y* is maximum *Y* divided by the constant *L*. With these production possibilities, capital accumulation alone does not produce economic growth with constant resource use, even if the population is not growing.

Now suppose that the production function is of Cobb–Douglas form, so that there are possibilities for substitution in production. Table 7.9 shows in the right two columns results from a simulation model which is the same as the basic Cobb–Douglas case reported in Table 7.5 except that the human population is constant at its initial level of 1. The corresponding results from Table 7.5 are reproduced

Table 7.9 The effects of population stabilisation

Year	Population growth 2.5% pa		Population growth 0% pa	
	y	*ẏ %*	*y*	*ẏ %*
10	1.1323	0.91	1.1993	1.49
20	1.2010	0.40	1.3439	0.94
30	1.2324	0.17	1.4530	0.68
40	1.2430	0.03	1.5420	0.54
50	1.2407	−0.05	1.6107	0.45
60	1.2298	−0.11	1.6843	0.38
70	1.2131	−0.15	1.7438	0.33
80	1.1923	−0.19	1.7977	0.29
90	1.1687	−0.21	1.8472	0.26
100	1.1433	−0.23	1.8930	0.23

at the left of Table 7.9, under Population growth 2.5 per cent pa, for ease of comparison. With no technical progress, the outcome with sustainable yield harvesting of a renewable resource and zero population growth is essentially the same as it was for the basic model in the previous chapter – economic growth is a transitory phenomenon with the growth rate declining to zero eventually. But, 'transitory' can mean many years, and in those years the level of per capita income can increase a lot. From the point of view of per capita income and its growth, Table 7.9 shows that zero population growth is better than positive population growth – positive growth rates persist out to beyond 100 years, rather than 40 odd years. In fact, with zero population growth, per capita income is still growing, albeit at just 0.07 per cent pa, after 350 years.

7.2.2.5 *Renewable resources in classical economics*

The discipline of economics is generally taken to have come into being in the late eighteenth century. The economists who worked from then until the middle of the nineteenth century are now known as 'classical economists'. Although living and working during the early stages of the industrial revolution, these economists thought in terms of an agricultural economy. Accordingly, they considered the inputs to the production of national income to be labour, capital and the land on which crops were grown and animals grazed. In their models of economic growth, they took land to be an input which was constant in size over time. Those models were, then, effectively the same as the models we have just been looking at where a renewable resource is harvested on a sustainable yield basis.

In its classical phase, economics was known as the 'dismal science'. This was because it argued that economic growth was, at best, a transitory phenomenon and that the long-run prospects for the material human condition, for per capita national income as we would now refer to it, were poor. The classical economists considered that the possibilities for substituting capital for land were limited, and ignored technological progress. Their models included one feature missing from those that we have been looking at.

In the foregoing models, the rate of growth of the human population is exogenous – it is a constant given outside the model, not affected by what happens in it. In the classical economists' growth models, the population growth rate was endogenous – determined in the model. They took it that there was a subsistence level of per capita income, below which the birth rate declined and the death rate increased, so that the population size decreased. In their models, per capita income growth was episodic. With it, once it took per capita income above subsistence, the population started to grow. With the availability of land fixed, this eventually led to the cessation of growth and declining per capita income. When it fell below subsistence, population growth ceased and went into reverse, so increasing land per capita and permitting the growth of per capita income. In the long run, per capita income varied around the subsistence level.

It is widely asserted that the classical economists got things spectacularly wrong, in that during the nineteenth and twentieth centuries population grew continuously and per capita national income increased fairly steadily. It is also asserted that they got things so wrong because they ignored substitution possibilities and, especially, technical progress. While our models show that the possibility of substitution of capital for land and of endogenous technical progress should not be overlooked, both of these assertions are over-simplifications in regard to the historical record.

First, until the second half of the twentieth century, population and economic growth were confined to the European economies and their offshoots in North America, Australia and New Zealand. As we have seen, it was only in the second half of the twentieth century that population and economic growth became global phenomena, and even then experience with the latter was patchy.

Second, for those economies which experienced economic growth in the nineteenth century, one of the key assumptions of the classical economists' model was not operative. The European economies and their offshoots did not, during that period, operate with a fixed amount of land. The European economies used land outside their boundaries through colonisation and trade, and in North America, Australia and New Zealand the boundaries were extended. This is not to say that technical progress was not important for these economies. It was very important. We discussed one particular manifestation, the increasing use of extrasomatic energy, in Chapter 3.

7.2.3 Non-renewable resources

As discussed in Chapter 3, the defining characteristic of non-renewable resources is that the stock does not grow. Whereas the history of an exploited renewable resource is given by

$$N_t = N_{t-1} + \left[r \times \left(\frac{K - N_{t-1}}{K} \right) \times N_{t-1} \right] - H_t$$

that of a non-renewable resource is given by

$$N_t = N_{t-1} - H_t$$

since r is zero for a non-renewable resource. Further, since the initial size of the stock is finite, there is no positive constant value for H that can be maintained indefinitely – for a non-renewable resource there is no sustainable yield (other than 0). If, for example, the initial stock is 100 units and each year 0.001 units are extracted – harvested – then the stock will be exhausted after 100,000 years. We will ignore recycling possibilities so as to look at the non-renewable resource problem in its starkest form. Recall that fossil fuels that are burned, as is mostly the case, cannot be recycled.

In this section we are going to use the growth models of the previous section to examine the situation of an economy that uses a non-renewable resource, along with capital and labour, to produce its national income. To do this we simply change the assumptions about the behaviour of the level of resource input, so that they reflect the non-renewable nature of the resource input.

7.2.3.1 Depletion profile

Given non-renewability, we know that any constant, or increasing, level of resource use will exhaust the resource. Given that we are working with production functions such that zero resource input means zero national income, this means that any constant, or increasing, level of resource use implies that national income will eventually go to zero. There is no need for simulations to consider the implications for economic growth where a non-renewable resource is used at a constant, or increasing, rate.

There is one kind of time profile for resource use that it is worth running simulations for. If the amount of the resource extracted and used is always a constant proportion of the remaining stock of the resource, then the amount used and the amount remaining get smaller and smaller over time, but never actually become zero. In technical terms, use and stock size 'approach zero asymptotically'. For this kind of depletion profile

$$R_t = H_t = k \times N_{t-1}$$

where R_t and H_t are the amount extracted and used during period t, N_{t-1} is the stock remaining at the start of period t, and k is some constant less than 1. Suppose N is initially 100 and k is 0.01. Then stock and use behave as shown, for a few early years, in Table 7.10. Figures 7.2 and 7.3 show the same information out to year 500. These graphs show use and stock size 'approaching zero asymptotically' – around about year 400 they get to be so small that the graph is indistinguishable from the horizontal axis, but if you do the Excel^{TM} simulations you will find that out to year 500 they produce very small numbers different from zero. For this kind of depletion profile, stock size and use fall over time at the same proportionate rates. You can confirm this by calculating the

Table 7.10 Extraction as a constant proportion of the remaining stock

Year	Opening stock N_{t-1}	Extraction and use $R_t = H_t$
1	100	1
2	99	0.99
3	98.01	0.09801
4	97.0299	0.9703
5	96.0596	0.9606
6	95.0990	0.9510

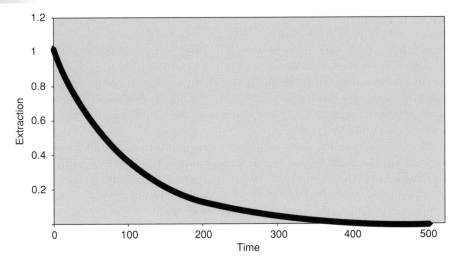

Figure 7.2
Extraction as a
constant
proportion of
remaining
stock.

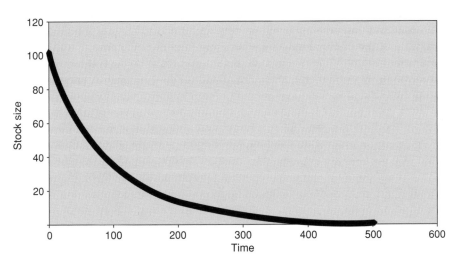

Figure 7.3
Resource stock
for declining
extraction.

proportionate rates of change in the simulation. You will find that the common rate is equal to, but of opposite sign to, the proportion of the remaining stock that is always used.

Before looking at the implications of this kind of resource depletion profile, there is the question of whether it is the sort of thing that we might actually observe. Could we ever expect to see non-renewable resource use declining over time? As we shall see in Chapter 9, we might expect to see this kind of pattern if the level of use were determined solely by the resource price, and if the resource price rose as the resource was depleted.

Given what we saw when looking at a constant level of input for a renewable resource, we can anticipate the implications of a declining level of input in the absence of substitution possibilities and/or technical progress – economic growth will be a transitory phenomenon. We could guess that if the substitution

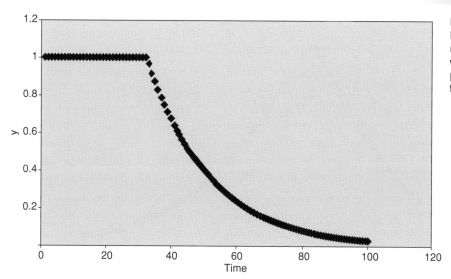

Figure 7.4
Non-renewable
resource use
with a Leontief
production
function.

possibilities are great enough, if the resource is sufficiently unimportant in production, and/or there is enough technical progress, growth can go on for a very
long time. We will now look at simulations that confirm these anticipations.

7.2.3.2 *The Leontief production function case*

We do this first using a growth model where national income is produced according
to a Leontief production function, so that there are no substitution possibilities.
The model is

$$Y = \min(\{\alpha \times K\}, \{\beta \times L\}, \{\delta \times R\})$$
$$S = s \times Y$$
$$K_t \equiv K_{t-1} + S_t$$
$$R_t = k \times N_{t-1}$$

In the simulations, we use the numerical parameter values $\alpha = 1$, $\beta = 1$, $\delta = 1$,
$s = 0.15$ and $k = 0.05$. The initial size of the non-renewable resource stock is 100.
For K and L, the initial values are, as in all previous simulations, 1. For R, the initial
value is $0.05 \times 100 = 5$. Setting the production parameters all equal to 1 makes it
easier to see what is going on. Having 5 per cent of the remaining stock used each
year makes the things that we are interested in happen relatively quickly. Given
the results for renewable resource use, we will look at simulations where human
population, and hence labour input, is constant over time – L equals 1 always.

Figure 7.4 shows the results for this simulation when there is no technical
progress. Out to year 32, per capita income y is constant at 1. This is because out
to that year the smallest of K, L and R is L, which is constant at 1. Over these years
the capital stock increases more than five-fold in size, but cannot be substituted
for labour or resource input. Over these years the resource input declines from 5
to 1.0195 in year 32. In year 33 the resource input goes to 0.9686, which is smaller

Figure 7.5
Non-
renewable
resource use
with a Leontief
production
function and
technical-
progress.

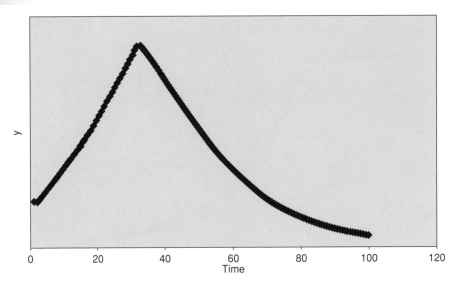

than the values for L (1) and K in that year, so income and per capita income drop to 0.9686. Thereafter, given that there are no substitution possibilities, despite continuing capital accumulation, y falls at the constant rate of 5 per cent per year because that is the rate at which the resource input is falling.

For the model economy simulated for Figure 7.4 there are no substitution possibilities, and there is no technical progress. What difference would technical progress make? Figure 7.5 shows the results for the Figure 7.4 model modified to include technical progress in the same way as previously – an efficiency factor a is applied to each input at each point in time where

$$a_t = K_{t-1}^{0.6}$$

and K represents the size of the capital stock. Because of technical progress, per capita income grows initially. The effective labour input is $a \times L$, but L is always 1. Out to year 32, R is greater than 1 so $a \times R$ is greater than $a \times L$, so that Y, and hence y, is equal to $a \times L = a$. In year 33 R drops below 1, so that $a \times R$ is less than $a \times L$ and hence $Y = a \times R$ in year 33 and subsequently. From year 33 onwards, Y and y move as $a \times R$, which is downwards because technical progress is not fast enough to outpace the decline in R. For the simulations of Figures 7.4 and 7.5, technical progress raises the maximum level that y attains but does not stop it declining. Can more rapid technical progress prevent per capita income declining? The rate of technical progress in this model depends on the value of π in $a_t = K_{t-1}^{\pi}$ and on the value of s in $S = s \times Y$. Leaving s fixed at 0.15, increasing π does not have much effect on the results – for $\pi = 0.7$ y peaks in year 34, for $\pi = 0.8$ y peaks in year 37, and for $\pi = 0.9$ y peaks in year 44. For $\pi = 0.9$, increasing s does not greatly affect the results – for $s = 0.3$ y peaks at year 50, for $s = 0.5$ y peaks at year 54, for $s = 0.7$ y peaks at year 56. If the production function is of the Leontief, no substitution, form, then the use of a non-renewable resource in production means,

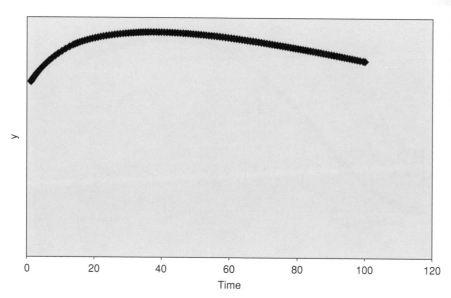

Figure 7.6
Non-renewable
resource use
with a
Cobb–Douglas
production
function.

even for a constant population, that per capita national income growth is at best a transitory phenomenon.

7.2.3.3 The Cobb–Douglas production function case

With no possibilities for substitution, capital accumulation and technical progress cannot overcome the fundamental problem presented by the use of a non-renewable resource in production. If the resource is used at a constant, or increasing, rate, it runs out and national income goes to zero. If the resource is used at a declining rate, so that it never completely runs out, economic growth can only go on for a limited time – eventually per capita income goes into decline. This is true even for a constant population size.

Does this fundamental problem exist if there are substitution possibilities in production? To examine this question we go to simulations of the model with a Cobb–Douglas production function. This model, without technical progress, is

$$Y = K^{0.2} \times L^{0.7} \times R^{0.1}$$
$$S = 0.15 \times Y$$
$$K_t \equiv K_{t-1} + S_t$$
$$R_t = 0.05 \times N_{t-1}$$

The initial values for K, L and R are as above for the model with the Leontief production function, and again the human population size is constant.

The results for this simulation are shown in Figure 7.6. Initially per capita income grows as capital accumulation proceeds and capital services substitute for the declining resource input. However, by year 39 the declining resource input effect is stronger than the capital substitution effect and y starts to decline continuously. The rate at which y declines is increasing, and eventually it will go to

Figure 7.7
Non-
renewable
resource use
with a
Cobb–Douglas
production
function and
technical-
progress.

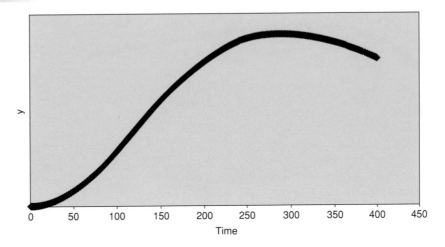

zero. Can a higher saving rate overcome this? No. Increasing s to 0.9 postpones the date at which y peaks to year 45. When looking at renewable resource use, we saw that the implications of sustainable yield resource input depended on the relative importance of capital and resource inputs in production. This is also true for non-renewable resource input. Holding $s = 0.15$, we get the dates (see following table) for the peak in y as the coefficients on capital, α, and resource input, δ, are varied, holding the coefficient on labour input, β, constant at 0.7.

α	δ	date for peak y
0.25	0.05	year 112
0.275	0.025	year 244
0.29	0.01	y growing at 0.02% at year 500

If the non-renewable resource is sufficiently unimportant in production, then despite its input declining to very low levels, per capita income can, by virtue of the substitution of capital services, grow for a very long time.

The effects of introducing endogenous technical progress are shown in Figure 7.7. For this simulation, L is constant at 1 and R declines as for Figure 7.6, s is 0.15, and the production function is the same as for Figure 7.6 save that each input is multiplied by the efficiency factor $a_t = K_{t-1}^{0.6}$. In Figure 7.7 y is still growing at year 100 though the rate at which it is growing is declining slowly. Here y peaks in year 291 and then declines. If π in $a_t = K_{t-1}^{\pi}$ is increased to 0.7, all else the same, y will keep growing for 404 years, and if it is increased to 0.8 at year 500 y is still growing slowly.

7.2.4 Summary and overview

The simulation modelling exercises that we have considered here were intended to bring out as clearly as possible the importance of substitution possibilities and technical progress in relation to the possibility of long-term economic growth given the use of natural resources in production. What we found was as follows.

For an economy that uses a renewable resource on a sustainable yield basis, in the absence of technical progress, economic growth is a transitory phenomenon even if capital can be substituted for the resource. Where substitution is possible, sufficiently rapid technical progress can keep growth going. The necessity of technical progress for continuing growth applies even if the human population is constant. If resource use is persistently in excess of sustainable yield, then eventually the resource is exhausted and production goes to zero. All this is for an economy that is closed in the economic sense, an economy that cannot import the resource from some other economy. The world economy is a closed economy in this sense.

Where the resource is non-renewable, there is no constant rate of use that can be maintained indefinitely, no sustainable yield. If use is a constant proportion of the remaining stock, then it gets smaller and smaller over time and gets very close to, but never actually becomes, zero. In this case we considered only simulations with constant population. With no possibility of substituting capital for the resource, growth is a transitory phenomenon even with technical progress. Where substitution is possible, we found that if the resource is sufficiently unimportant in production, per capita income is still growing after 500 years. Introducing technical progress has a similar effect to making the resource unimportant. Together, technical progress, unimportance of the resource in production, and sufficient saving mean that falling income, and hence falling per capita income with constant population, can be postponed indefinitely. Again, all this is for a closed economy. For an open economy, domestic sourcing of resource input to production can be supplemented, or replaced by, imports.

The models that we have looked at have ignored some important features of economy–environment interdependence in the interests of bringing out the foregoing important lessons as clearly as possible. The lessons – the importance of capital accumulation, substitution possibilities, and technical progress – carry over into models which include more of the relationships that follow from economy–environment interdependence. Among the important features of reality not included in the models that we have considered in this section are the following;

- Multiple resource inputs – the economy uses renewable and non-renewable resource inputs, and different kinds of each of these. There are possibilities for substitution as between the class of renewable and the class of non-renewable resources, and as between different kinds within each class.
- Insertions – we modelled only extractions from the environment, and ignored the insertions into it – the waste flows – that, by the first law of thermodynamics, necessarily go with the extractions.
- Recycling – we ignored the possibility of reducing extractions (and insertions) by recycling.
- Amenity and life support services – do not feature in our models.
- Interactions – given that they look only at extractions, our models cannot include interactions between, for example, waste flows and life support services.

Clearly, a comprehensive model of economy–environment interdependence would be complicated. In the next section we look at a simulation modelling exercise that did try to be comprehensive.

7.3 LIMITS TO GROWTH?

The models and simulations that we looked at in the previous section were not intended either to reproduce historical patterns of natural resource use as actually observed in any real economy or to identify the prospects for future economic growth in any actual economy.

The main purpose of this section is to look briefly at a simulation modelling exercise that did seek to reproduce the main features of the historical experience of the world economy, and which did claim, in that way, to be able to identify future growth possibilities for the actual world economy. Before looking at that exercise, we briefly review actual historical experience in relation to resource use in the world economy.

7.3.1 Growth and the environment in history

In Chapter 3 human history was divided into three phases. The hunter-gatherer phase lasted, for *Homo sapiens sapiens*, about 90,000 years. At its end, the human population was about 4 million. For hunter-gatherers economic activity involved little more than the provision of food and basic clothing. In terms of the IPAT identity, the hunter-gatherer economy had both low P and low A. The technologies employed were simple, and involved the per capita use of about 1 HEE (Human Energy Equivalent, defined in Chapter 3) of extrasomatic energy. This economic system generally had low environmental impact, and persisted for a long time. It did give way to agriculture eventually – it did not last for ever. Two sorts of explanation for this transition, not mutually exclusive, were noted in Chapter 3 – the growth of P beyond the level that the environment could sustain given the hunter-gatherer technology, and climate change which reduced the productivity of that technology. Some hunter-gatherer societies adapted and evolved into agricultural societies, others ceased to exist.

The agricultural phase has lasted some 12,000 years, and is now effectively over. Its end began 200 years ago, by which time P for the world had grown to about 900 million. For most members of farming society, consumption comprised little more than basic food, clothing and shelter. As compared with hunter-gatherer societies, agricultural societies involved greater inequality, and in them minorities enjoyed luxuries beyond physiological subsistence needs. As compared with the hunter-gatherer system, agriculture involved much higher P and, on average, somewhat higher A. The technologies employed were more complex and involved higher T – by the end of the agricultural phase, the per capita use of extrasomatic energy was about 2 or 3 HEE. Given the increase in population, by 200 years ago the total human use of extrasomatic energy was several hundred times what it had been in the hunter-gatherer phase.

The general environmental impact of agriculture was much greater than that of hunting and gathering. Agriculture did not persist as the dominant mode of economic activity for anything like as long as hunting and gathering. As noted in Chapter 3, many explanations, which are not mutually exclusive, have been offered for the emergence of the industrial economic system. According to one, the start of the systematic exploitation of coal, in England, was triggered by the depletion of a renewable resource, timber, driven by increasing P and A there.

The industrial phase began a little over 200 years ago. Globally, P and A have increased enormously in the last 200 years, as documented in Chapters 3 and 6. Technologies have also changed greatly. In regard to technology, the global average for per capita extrasomatic energy use is now about twenty times what it was 200 years ago. Total human use of extrasomatic energy has increased more than a hundred-fold.

We know that energy use reflects the amount of transformation and transportation of matter, so that this tells us that the extraction of resources generally has increased hugely since the end of the eighteenth century. While there are exceptions, in the historical record of the last couple of centuries, renewable resources have *not* generally been harvested on a sustainable yield basis, as we assumed in the previous section's modelling exercises. In the historical record of the last couple of centuries, non-renewable resources have *not* generally been used at declining rates, as we assumed in the previous sub-section's modelling exercises. With growing human numbers and rising levels of per capita income, the rates of use for most, renewable and non-renewable, resources have been increasing.

The models of the previous section produced results about the possibility, or otherwise, of continuing economic growth on the basis of sustainable yield use of renewables and declining use of non-renewables. It follows that while useful in identifying the roles of substitution and technical progress, they are no basis for taking a view about future growth prospects for the world economy if it continues to function as it has in recent history.

7.3.2 *The limits to growth*

A book published in 1972, *The limits to growth* (Meadows *et al.*, 1972), reported the results from an exercise in simulation modelling which sought to assess the prospects for continuing economic growth in the actual, as opposed to some imaginary, world economy. The model that was simulated was claimed to have represented in it all of the essentially important relationships in the actual world economy. The 'world model', as it was referred to, comprised many more relationships and many more endogenous variables than any of the growth models considered in this and the previous chapter.

To see how such a model relates to our simple models, and introduce a way of stating a model graphically, consider human population growth. In the growth models that we have been looking at, the population growth rate is given exogenously, determined outside the model, as, for example, 2.5 per cent per annum. With P for population, we have been modelling its growth as

$$P_t = P_{t-1} + (g \times P_{t-1})$$

Figure 7.8
Exogenous
fertility and
mortality.

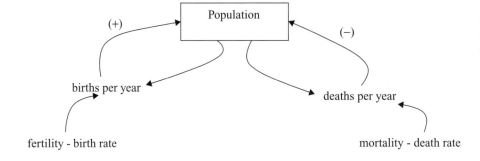

where g is the exogenous growth rate. We could state this model in terms of birth and death rates, rather than a single growth rate. Let b represent the birth rate, and d represent the death rate. Then total births are

$$B_t = b \times P_{t-1}$$

and total deaths are

$$D_t = d \times P_{t-1}$$

and

$$P_t = P_{t-1} + B_t - D_t = P_{t-1} + (b \times P_{t-1}) - (d \times P_{t-1}) = P_{t-1} + (b-d)P_{t-1}$$

The exogenous growth rate g is the difference between the exogenous birth and death rates. If there are 40 births per 1,000 population and 15 deaths per 1,000 population, then b is 0.04 and d is 0.015, so that g is 0.025 or 2.5 per cent.

Figure 7.8 represents that way of modelling population growth graphically. Births are determined by the birth rate and population size, as shown by two arrows from 'population' and 'fertility – birth rate' to 'births per year'. Births per year add to population size, as shown by the arrow from 'births per year' to 'Population', and similarly for deaths, save that they reduce population size. The loop from Population through births per year back to Population has a plus sign next to it as it is a positive feedback loop – for a given birth rate, an increase in population increases the number of births which increases the population. The loop through deaths per year has a minus sign as it is a negative feedback loop – more people means more deaths. Population growth is the net outcome of the positive and negative feedbacks.

Figure 7.9 shows how the world model from *The limits to growth* makes the birth and death rates into endogenous variables. It is assumed that mortality depends on the level of provision of health services, which in turn depends on the availability per capita of all kinds of services. That availability also affects the amount of education and family planning services which affects fertility, which is also affected by industrial output per capita. Industrial output and services per capita are themselves affected by the size of the population – for given total levels of industrial and services output, the per capita levels go down as population goes up.

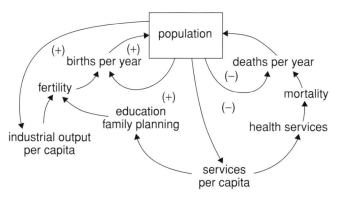

Figure 7.9
Endogenous
fertility and
mortality.

In the world model, the levels of industrial output and services output are themselves endogenous variables. At the bottom of an extended version of Figure 7.9 there would be arrows into industrial output per capita and services per capita from industrial output and services output respectively. There would also be arrows into those things representing what determines them in the model, and so on and so on. The world model has many relationships in it, and many endogenous variables. Figure 7.10 shows the whole model in terms of its feedback loops. We present Figure 7.10 only to give some sense of the nature of the world model – it has lots of interconnected endogenous variables. If you want to learn more about this and similar models, guidance is provided in Further Reading at the end of the chapter.

The authors of *The limits to growth* gave the parameters of the various relationships in the world model numerical values that they regarded as accurately reflecting conditions in the actual world economy. Figure 7.11 shows the behaviour of some of the variables in the world model for those numerical values. It shows some of the results from the standard simulation run of the model. The horizontal axis goes from 1900 to 2100. Out to almost halfway along this axis the paths followed by the variables could be compared with historical data. To the extent that the paths generated in the model here correspond to those in history the model could be regarded as having credibility as a means of considering the likely future behaviour of the world economy. The creators of the world model considered that in its standard run version it did have such credibility. In Figure 7.11 you can see that during the twentieth century population, food per capita and industrial output per capita all grow steadily, as they did in fact. According to *The limits to growth* the other variables in the world model but not plotted in Figure 7.11 also followed the historical record.

Also plotted in Figure 7.11 are the fraction of 1900 resource reserves remaining, labelled 'resources', and the level of waste discharge into the environment scaled so that its 1970 value is 1, labelled 'pollution'. In this run of the model, food per capita and industrial output per capita peak early in the twenty-first century. Economic growth comes to an end because natural resources have become very scarce by that time. As a result of declining food and industrial output per capita, fertility declines and mortality increases, and around the middle of the twenty-first century the world population peaks and then goes into decline. Pollution peaks a little earlier due to the declining rate of use of resources.

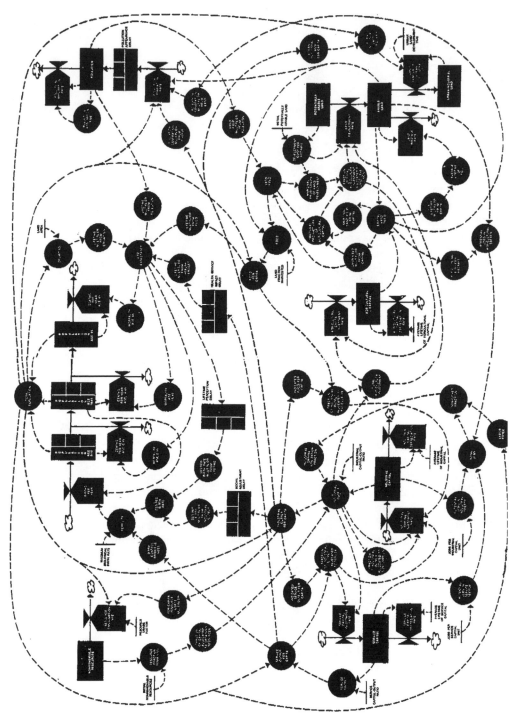

Figure 7.10 The World Model.

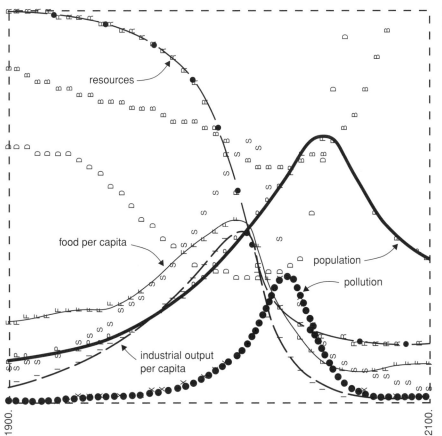

Figure 7.11
Standard run.

The authors of *The limits to growth* interpreted this standard run as demonstrating that given unchanged human behaviour and technology, economic growth in the world economy would come to an end sometime during the twenty-first century, and human numbers would go into decline. They did not assert that such outcomes were inevitable. The forecast of disaster was conditional on the perpetuation of the historical relationships between the variables in the model, which relationships reflect behaviour modes and technology. In fact, a major motivation for the construction of the world model was to be able to use it to investigate what changes to the historical relationships would be needed to avert the collapse in the world economy. The idea is to use runs of the model with different numerical values for the parameters as 'what if?' experiments, just as we did with the much simpler models earlier in this chapter.

The first such experiment directly addressed the problem revealed in the standard run – running out of natural resources. This experiment involved only one change to the numerical values used for the standard run. That was to double the initial, 1900, stock of natural resources available to the model world economy. The simulation output for some of the model variables for this run of the world model is shown in Figure 7.12. The plot for 'resources' does not look that

Figure 7.12
Increased
resources run.

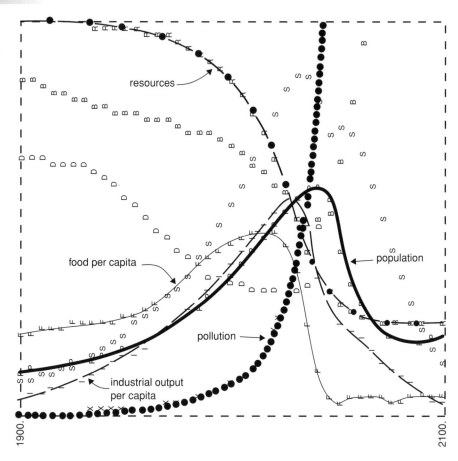

different because what is being plotted is the fraction remaining – the rate of resource use in Figure 7.12 is much higher than in Figure 7.11. That is what produces the most obvious difference between the two figures – the behaviour of the pollution variable. In the simulation run for Figure 7.12, by virtue of the law of conservation of matter (see Chapter 2 here), insertions into the natural environment grow to a much higher level than in Figure 7.11 precisely because there is no scarcity of resources for extraction from the natural environment. The relationships in the model are such that waste generation affects food production, which peaks early in the twenty-first century, leading via effects on fertility and mortality to a crash in human numbers in the middle of that century.

According to this experiment, if economic growth is not brought to an end by resource scarcity, it will be brought to a halt by the problems of waste generation and pollution. In another experiment, it was assumed that natural resources were available in unlimited quantities, and that there is technological change late in the twentieth century so that thereafter the waste generated per unit of industrial and agricultural production is one quarter of its former level. A series of such experiments were conducted with the world model, until a set of changes to its

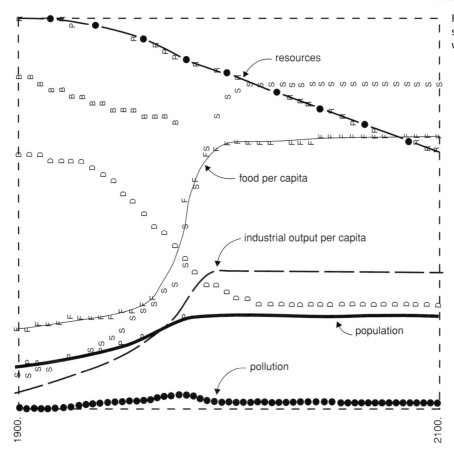

Figure 7.13 The sustainable world run.

standard run settings were found such that the model world economy did not collapse before 2100. Figure 7.13 shows the plots for the same variables as in the two previous figures, for a run of the world model where the main changes to the standard run settings are that:

- with effect in 1975 the size of the human population is stabilised
- with effect in 1975 there is technical progress such that thereafter resource use per unit of industrial production is one quarter of what it was in 1970
- with effect in 1975 there is technical progress such that thereafter waste generation per unit of industrial and agricultural output is one quarter of what it was in 1970
- with effect in 1975 peoples' tastes shift away from industrial output in favour of services
- with effect from 1975 the average lifetime of units of the capital stock used in industrial production is increased, and with effect from 1990 the size of this capital stock is held constant, with more of investment going into agricultural production
- with effect from 1975 the rate of soil erosion in agriculture is reduced.

With all of these changes, collapse is avoided and around the beginning of the twenty-first century the model world economy gets into a state which is sustainable, at least, throughout the twenty-first century.

The stable twenty-first century level of world food per capita is more than twice its 1970 level, industrial output per capita is up by about 50 per cent, and service output per capita (not shown in Figure 7.13) is up by a factor of three. Adding these three forms of production and consumption together gives a stable twenty-first-century level of per capita GDP roughly 50 per cent of what USA per capita GDP was in 1970, which is three times what the world average for GDP per capita was in 1970. According to the authors of *The limits to growth*, what this model experiment shows is that while economic growth cannot, because of environmental constraints, continue indefinitely, it is technologically feasible to provide all of the human population with a decent standard of living within those constraints.

However, it is important to note that this conclusion depends upon the results of an experiment conducted in 1970 where all of the model changes noted above take effect in 1975, i.e. very quickly. A further experiment showed that if the date at which those changes took effect were put back to 2000, then the model world economy did not get into a sustainable configuration during the twenty-first century. The central message of *The limits to growth* was that, while global economic growth could not continue indefinitely, the needs and desires of all of the human population could be satisfied if effective policies directed to that purpose were implemented quickly.

7.3.3 Reactions to *The limits to growth*

The publication of *The limits to growth* in 1972 attracted enormous interest worldwide, and generated much controversy. It came in for a great deal of criticism, especially from neoclassical economists. Much of this criticism simply misrepresented the content of the book. It was, and still is, often stated that the central message was that the world economy would soon collapse on account of running out of non-renewable natural resources. In the 1970s neoclassical economists pointed to falling prices for most non-renewable natural resources as showing that they were becoming less rather than more scarce. Today those who misrepresent *The limits to growth* in this way point out that for many non-renewables reserves are as big as, or bigger, than they were in 1970. This mistake was made, economists argue, because the world model did not contain relationships which captured the way that markets work to conserve resources and to promote the discovery of previously unknown deposits (see Chapter 9, this book).

As the summary given above makes clear, this line of criticism largely misses the point of *The limits to growth* exercise, and one is tempted to believe that many of those who advanced it had not really read the whole book. The authors of *The limits to growth* claimed that putting such relationships into the model made no essential difference to the conclusions that could be drawn on the basis of the many different runs that they performed. Generally, the world model was criticised for leaving out important relationships, and/or getting the numbers for the parameter values wrong. Clearly, some of such criticism was valid. Clearly, as complicated as the model is (see Figure 7.10) it is an enormous simplification of the reality – the interdependence of the world economy and the natural environment – that it seeks to provide insights into. Its authors claim that it is not a gross over-simplification, and that the behaviour pattern of the model system is a guide to what we should expect of the real system, either under a continuation of historical trends – Figure 7.11, the standard run – or under some major policy-driven changes to those trends – Figure 7.13, the sustainable world run.

This is not the place to go into a detailed account and evaluation of the criticisms of *The limits to growth* – some pointers to the literature will be found in Further Reading at the end of the chapter. What can be said is that the statement by one neoclassical economist that *The limits to growth* was 'a brazen, impudent piece of nonsense that nobody could possibly take seriously' was quite unjustified. Though more strongly worded than most of the evaluations offered by neoclassical economists, this statement does convey the sense of outrage that many of them obviously felt. Why was there so much hostility toward *The limits to growth* on the part of neoclassical economists? One reason was probably a sense of defending territory – the study of economic growth should be left to the economists whose business it is. The authors of *The limits to growth* were systems analysts. Another, given the first reason, was the attention that the book received.

There is a deeper and more important reason. As explained in the previous chapter, neoclassical economists have a strong attachment to economic growth, particularly in relation to the alleviation of poverty. It is an important implication of limits to economic growth that there are limits to the extent that it can be relied upon to solve the problem of poverty in the world. To the extent that economic growth is abandoned, dealing with poverty will involve redistribution. This implication is mentioned but not given a lot of emphasis in *The limits to growth*, but all economist readers would have picked it up and realised its significance.

Some simple arithmetic makes the point. As noted above when discussing Figure 7.13, the level of per capita income that is sustainable according to the world model is about half of the 1970 level of per capita GDP in the USA. That is what the 1970 level of per capita GDP in Europe was, and is about 12,500 current (2000) US$. The Figure 7.13 outcome in the world model has the world population stabilising at its 1975 level, which in round numbers was 4 billion, 4×10^9. In 1975, 3 billion lived in the developing world and 1 billion in the developed world, again in round numbers to make the arithmetic easy. We will assume the continuation of these relative sizes. With 4 billion people and an average per capita GDP of \$12,500, total world GDP is $4 \times 10^9 \times 12.5 \times 10^3 = 50 \times 10^{12}$ US\$2000. Basically, what the world model is saying is that this is the level of world economic activity that meets environmental constraints – above this level the world economy runs into environmental problems that feed back into economic problems.

Now, if this total world GDP were shared out equally among all of the 4 billion people each would get the average of \$12,500. That is about half of what European GDP per capita is at time of writing – economic growth in Europe since 1975 has more or less doubled per capita national income in constant price terms, i.e. after allowing for inflation. Even if the world population had stayed at its 1975 level, respecting environmental constraints with equal shares would mean everybody being half as well-off, as measured by GDP per capita, as Europeans actually are now. If, a big if, the programme for sustainability from *The limits to growth* had been implemented in 1975 along with equal shares, Europeans would have forgone all of the increase in per capita GDP that they have actually experienced since then. North Americans would have seen their per capita GDP decrease.

Equality is not the historical norm, and it is inconceivable that Europeans and North Americans would have agreed to the above scenario had it been presented to them. Suppose that they could have been persuaded to accept stabilisation of their average per capita GDP at $25,000 in terms of current US dollars – this is roughly what European per capita GDP actually is now, considerably less than current North American per capita GDP. Then given population stabilisation, the one billion people in the developed world would get $25 \times 10^3 \times 10^9 = 25 \times 10^{12}$ in current US$, leaving the same amount to be shared among the three billion people in the developing world. Average per capita GDP there would then be 25×10^{12} divided by 3×10^9 which is $8,333, which is about three-quarters of what European per capita GDP was in 1975.

7.3.4 *Beyond the limits*

Beyond the limits is the title of the sequel (Meadows *et al.*, 1992), published in 1992, to *The limits to growth*. Three of the four authors of the original are the authors of the sequel. It uses essentially the same world model as the original. In response to the criticisms of the original world model, some modifications to the form of some of the relationships were made, and some of the numerical values for parameters were changed. The basic nature and structure of the world model is unchanged as between the original and the sequel. The conclusions stated in *Beyond the limits* are:

> As far as we can tell from the global data, from the World 3 model, and from all we have learned in the past twenty years, the three conclusions we drew in *The limits to growth* are still valid, but they need to be strengthened. Now we would write them this way;
>
> 1. Human use of many essential resources and generation of many kinds of pollutants have already surpassed the rates that are physically sustainable. Without significant reductions in material and energy flows, there will be in the coming decades an uncontrolled decline in per capita food output, energy use, and industrial production.
> 2. The decline is not inevitable. To avoid it two changes are necessary. The first is a comprehensive revision of policies and practices that perpetuate growth in material consumption and population. The second is a rapid, drastic increase in the efficiency with which materials and energy are used.
> 3. A sustainable society is still technically and economically possible. It could be much more desirable than a society that tries to solve its problems by constant expansion. The transition to a sustainable society requires a careful balance between long-term and short-term goals and an emphasis on sufficiency, equity and quality of life rather than on quantity of output. It requires more than productivity and more than technology; it also requires maturity, compassion, and wisdom.   (Meadows *et al.*, 1992, p. xvi)

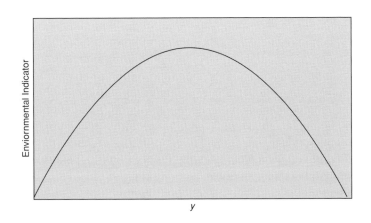

Figure 7.14
Hypothesised
EKC
relationship.

7.4 GROWTH AS THE SOLUTION TO ENVIRONMENTAL PROBLEMS?

Whereas the authors of *The limits to growth* and *Beyond the limits* argue for the need to respect environmental constraints in order to avoid future economic problems, in the last decade some neoclassical economists have advanced the argument that economic growth is, if there is enough of it, actually good for the environment. As usually made, the argument relates to insertions into the environment, and the damage that they cause. It is known as the Environmental Kuznets Curve, or EKC, hypothesis.

7.4.1 The EKC hypothesis

In its most general form, the **EKC hypothesis** is that as economic growth proceeds so environmental damage first increases, then levels off, then declines. Figure 7.14 illustrates the inverted *U* form of this hypothesised relationship. The level taken by some indicator of environmental damage is measured on the vertical axis, and per capita income, *y*, on the horizontal axis. The reason why a relationship such as that shown in Figure 7.14 is known as an 'Environmental Kuznets Curve' is as follows. In the 1960s an economist named Kuznets hypothesised that the relationship between income inequality and average per capita income in a growing economy took the form of an inverted *U*. At low levels of per capita income, inequality increased with per capita income, but after a certain level of per capita income further economic growth was accompanied by decreasing inequality. When, in the early 1990s, some economists came up with the idea of a similar inverted *U* relationship for environmental damage and per capita income, they identified it as the environmental version of the Kuznets idea.

    The basis for hypothesising this kind of relationship involves several elements. First, there is the matter of the structure of the economy at different stages of economic growth. The argument is that at low levels of per capita income economic growth involves industrialisation, so that more energy and other raw materials are extracted from the environment, leading to increasing insertions into it. On the other hand, it is the recent historical experience of the High Income OECD countries that the structure of the economy has changed with growth so that the manufacturing sector has got relatively smaller and the service sector relatively bigger. Modern high-income economies are sometimes referred to as 'post-industrial' in recognition of this. Since the service sector is less resource-intensive, it is argued, its expansion at the expense of the manufacturing sector would imply the economy extracting less from the environment, and hence inserting less into it.

The second idea is that as people become better-off, so they are willing and able to spend more of their income on improving environmental quality. At low levels of per capita income, the satisfaction of basic needs such as food and shelter takes priority. As per capita income increases so these basic needs are increasingly satisfied, and people have money to spend on 'luxuries', such as waste treatment facilities for the improvement of environmental conditions. Given that basic needs are satisfied, people are more likely to be concerned about the quality of the environment. Once economic growth goes beyond a certain point, the argument goes, so people increasingly have both the desire and the means to reduce the impact of further growth on the quality of their environment.

There is a third consideration that is relevant to the recent historical experience of many of the High Income OECD countries. As well as the relative shift into services and away from manufacturing noted above, there has been a shift within manufacturing away from basic raw materials processing towards activities requiring more highly trained labour and more technologically sophisticated capital equipment. For example, iron and steel production has actually declined in volume terms in the most advanced economies, which increasingly import the steel to be used in, say, motor vehicle manufacturing, from developing countries. This process has been largely driven by the fact that the developing countries can do basic raw materials processing more cheaply than the developed countries can. Basic raw materials processing is more environmentally damaging than high technology engineering – moving iron and steel works from, say, Germany to, say, India and having Germany import Indian-made steel to make cars is good for the quality of the environment experienced by people in Germany.

It is important to note that while this can work to improve environmental quality for an open national economy, it cannot work for the world economy as a whole, which is closed – there is no 'overseas' in which to relocate dirty basic raw materials processing activities. It also needs to be noted that there are some environmental problems for which this kind of relocation is irrelevant. In regard to the climate change problem, for example, what affects the climate everywhere is the global concentration of CO_2. It does not matter where the CO_2 was emitted. Simply moving a steel works and its CO_2 emissions from Germany to India has no implications for the future climate in India or Germany.

7.4.2 The empirical status of the hypothesis

The curve shown in Figure 7.14 is the graph of the quadratic equation

$$I = (\alpha \times y) - (\beta \times y^2)$$

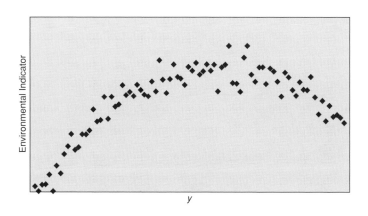

Figure 7.15
Data consistent
with the EKC
hypothesis.

over the range of y for which I, the environmental damage indicator, is equal to or greater than zero – a negative value for I makes no sense. As usual, y represents per capita national income. Even if this was the underlying form of the relationship between some damage index and per capita income, using data on I and y for different countries you would not expect to plot I against y and get all the points lying exactly along a curve like that in Figure 7.14. There are other influences on I. But if these other influences on I are less strong and less systematic than y, then you would expect the relationship between I and y to dominate and to produce a plot such as that shown in Figure 7.15.

In the last decade a lot of work has gone into looking at data on a whole variety of indices of environmental damage in order to ascertain for which, if any, the EKC hypothesis is true. It turns out, as documented in the references provided in Further Reading at the end of the chapter, that the EKC appears to be true for some forms of damage but not others. Broadly, most studies find that where the damage is generated and suffered within a nation state (or within adjacent and cooperating nation states) the data plot looks like Figure 7.15. Examples of this are plots for particulates, nitrous oxide and sulphur dioxide. On the other hand, where the problem crosses national boundaries, most studies conclude that the EKC hypothesis does not hold. The outstanding example of an environmental problem that crosses national boundaries is that of carbon dioxide emissions, noted above and to be discussed more fully in Chapter 13.

Figure 7.16 is the plot of the data on CO_2 emissions and per capita GDP for 158 countries. The data are taken from the *Human development report 2002* and the *Human development report 2003*. The vertical axis measures tonnes of CO_2 per capita (1999), the horizontal axis measures PPP \$ of per capita GDP (2000). Comparing Figure 7.16 with Figure 7.15, you can see that the former is not consistent with the EKC hypothesis. There is in Figure 7.16 no tendency, at any level of per capita income, for per capita emissions to fall with increasing per capita income. The line that best fits the data of Figure 7.16 is a straight line with slope 0.0004, so that if country A has per capita GDP \$1,000 higher than country B, it will have per capita CO_2 emissions 0.4 tonnes higher. Several studies have come to the conclusion that the EKC hypothesis does not hold for CO_2.

Figure 7.16 An
EKC for carbon
dioxide?

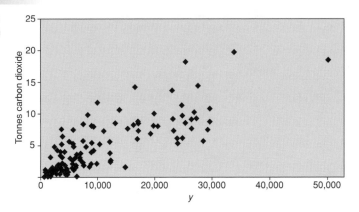

Recall that one part of the argument suggesting the EKC hypothesis is that the structure of the economy, in terms of the relative sizes of manufacturing and services, changes with growth at high income levels. This argument would also suggest an EKC-type relationship for resource inputs and per capita national income. As with emissions and environmental damage, the evidence on this is mixed – for some natural resources the EKC hypothesis appears to work, for others it does not.

It needs to be emphasised that this is a brief summary of a lot of technical research done by a large number of economists. One can find disagreements in the literature regarding any particular kind of environmental damage or type of resource. These disagreements reflect differing definitions, data sets and statistical methods. For example, while most studies find that the EKC holds for sulphur dioxide, at least one finds that it does not. Similarly, there is one study for CO_2 that finds that it fits the EKC hypothesis.

The next question to be considered is whether the proposition that economic growth is good for the environment, eventually, necessarily follows from the EKC. If the EKC were true, could we rely on it to accommodate the economy to the environment?

7.4.3 EKC implications

There are several reasons why even if it were true that all environmental impacts behaved according to the EKC hypothesis, it would not be generally true that economic growth is good for the environment. We look first at the matter of environmental thresholds, and then at lower limits to environmental impacts.

7.4.3.1 Thresholds and population growth

To illustrate this, consider first a situation where per capita emissions and per capita income are related in the way shown in Figure 7.14, so that

$$e = (\alpha \times y) - (\beta \times y^2)$$

where e represents per capita emissions and y per capita income. We will look at simulations where the parameters α and β take the values 1 and 0.1 respectively,

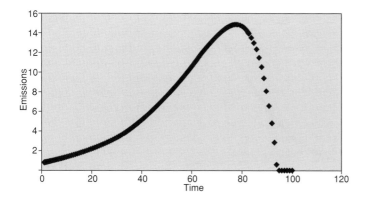

Figure 7.17
Emissions for
population
growth at
2.5 per cent.

so that

$$e = y - (0.1 \times y^2)$$

Suppose that per capita income grows at 2.5 per cent per year so that

$$y_t = 1.025 \times y_{t-1}$$

and the initial level of y is 1. Now, what matters for the state of the environment is total emissions rather than per capita emissions, so that we need to consider also what is happening to population size. With E for total emissions and P for population

$$E_t = P_t \times e_t$$

We will consider first a simulation where population grows at 2.5 per cent per year, i.e.

$$P_t = 1.025 \times P_{t-1}$$

starting at an initial level of 1. To do this we generate the numbers for P_t and y_t in each year using the growth rates, calculating

$$e_t = y_t - (0.1 \times y_t^2)$$

and then

$$E_t = P_t \times e_t$$

The results are shown in Figure 7.17. Emissions peak at approximately 15 in year 78, then rapidly decline to zero.

Now, we do exactly the same simulation except that population grows at 5 per cent per year, i.e.

$$P_t = 1.05 \times P_{t-1}$$

In this case, as shown in Figure 7.18, total emissions peak at approximately 100 in year 83, then rapidly decline to zero. For the same EKC relationship, the peak level of emissions increases by a factor of more than six for a doubling of the population growth rate. Suppose that the emissions in question are such that up to

Figure 7.18
Emissions for
population
growth at
5 per cent.

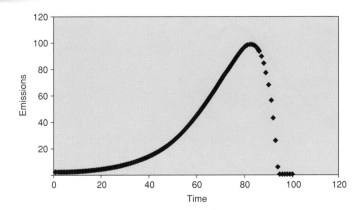

a threshold level of 50 they cause no damage, whereas beyond that threshold they mean the loss of resilience for an exploited ecosystem. Then clearly the fact that an EKC relationship exists for this type of emission does not necessarily mean that economic growth is good for the environment – crossing the threshold is consistent with the existence of an EKC relationship. Of course, in any particular case the threshold for the loss of resilience could be higher than the level at which total emissions peak. In the Figure 7.18 case, for example, the threshold could be 200. Equally, in the Figure 7.17 case the threshold for the loss of resilience could be 10. The point is that the numbers matter. Whether the fact that

$$e = \alpha y - \beta y^2$$

means that economic growth is good for the environment depends on the numerical values taken by the parameters α and β, on the rate of population growth, and on the level at which any threshold effects cut in.

7.4.3.2 A lower limit to per capita emissions

In Figures 7.17 and 7.18, total emissions eventually go to zero and stay there notwithstanding the continuation of population and economic growth. For

$$e = (\alpha \times y) - (\beta \times y^2)$$

there are two levels of per capita income that give zero per capita emissions. One is zero, obviously. To find the other write the equation with e equal to zero so that

$$0 = (\alpha \times y) - (\beta \times y^2)$$

where dividing both sides by y gives

$$0 = \alpha - (\beta \times y)$$

so that

$$y = \alpha \div \beta$$

is the second level of y for which per capita emissions are zero. For the numerical example that we have been using in the simulations, $\alpha = 1$ and $\beta = 0.1$ so that e is 0 for $y = 0$ and for

$$y = 1 \div 0.1 = 10.$$

Does an EKC relationship according to which a high enough level of per capita income results in zero emissions per capita, and therefore in total, make sense? It could be true for a particular environmental impact for a particular open economy, but it follows from the necessary dependence of economic activity on environmental extractions and insertions that it cannot be true of all environmental impacts for the world economy. Some advocates of economic growth as the means to protect the environment overlook the fact, considered in Chapter 5, that sectors of the economy use environmental inputs indirectly as well as directly – while the services sector may not buy iron ore, say, it very likely does buy inputs the provision of which requires the use of iron ore. And, it certainly buys inputs the provision of which requires the use of energy. However rich and service sector-dominated it becomes, a modern economy cannot function without environmental extractions and, hence, insertions.

One could imagine an open national economy which produced only services, say banking and software writing, which it sold to other economies from which it bought all of its manufactured requirements and all its food. One could further imagine that its energy supply came entirely from solar panels, manufactured overseas, and that all waste products arising in consumption in the economy were themselves shipped overseas. An effectively zero environmental impact open national economy is conceivable, if implausible. But, an effectively zero environmental impact world economy is, apart from a return to the hunter-gatherer mode of existence, inconceivable.

A more appropriate form for an EKC relationship of general applicability would be

$$e = \max(\{e = (\alpha \times y) - (\beta \times y^2)\}, e^*)$$

where e^* is a lower limit to per capita emissions. Here per capita emissions are whichever is the largest of $e = (\alpha \times y) - (\beta \times y^2)$ and e^* – they cannot fall below e^*. For some economies and some impacts, e^* might, in fact, be zero. Figure 7.19 plots the results of a simulation that shows the implications of e^* being greater than zero. It uses $\alpha = 1$ and $\beta = 0.1$ as in previous simulations here, and e^* equal to 0.1 – however large per capita income gets, per capita emissions cannot fall below 0.1. It also uses a population growth rate of 2.5 per cent per year, and is to be compared with Figure 7.17. In both of Figures 7.17 and 7.19 emissions peak at about 15 in year 78, and in both they then fall rapidly. However, where there is a lower limit to per capita emissions, the growth of total emissions resumes once that limit is reached, given a growing population. In the absence of population growth, total emissions would remain constant at a level of e^* times the size of the constant population. While it is true that in some particular cases economic growth is good for the environment, it is not true that economic growth is the solution to all environmental problems. Note, however, that if economic growth is taken

Figure 7.19
Emissions
when there is
a lower limit
to per capita
emissions.

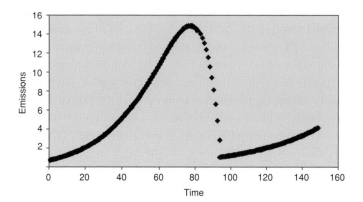

as a given, we see, here as previously, that, other things equal, its environmental consequences will be less if there is a constant population size.

7.5 SUSTAINABLE DEVELOPMENT?

In Chapter 1 we introduced the idea of sustainable development as:

a form of economic growth that would meet the needs and desires of the present without compromising the economy-environment system's capacity to meet them in the future

and we attributed the idea to the 'Brundtland Report', as *Our common future*, produced by the World Commission on Environment and Development in 1987, is often known. The definition given in the Brundtland Report is slightly different in the form of words used but the same in meaning:

> Sustainable development seeks to meet the needs and aspirations of the present without compromising the ability to meet those of the future. Far from requiring the cessation of economic growth, it recognizes that the problems of poverty and underdevelopment cannot be solved unless we have a new era of growth . . . policy makers guided by the concept of sustainable development will necessarily work to assure that growing economies remain firmly attached to their ecological roots and that these roots are protected and nurtured so that they may support growth over the long term. Environmental protection is thus inherent in the concept of sustainable development.   (WCED, 1987: 40)

Basically, the Brundtland Report has two points of departure – the existence of mass poverty in the world, and the fact of economy–environment interdependence. It accepts that growth in the world economy is the only feasible way of dealing with the poverty problem. It accepts that the continuation of the past pattern of economic growth would run into environmental problems that would affect future economic prospects. But, it argues, growth in the future does not have to be like growth in the past. There could, and should, be, it argues, a new pattern of growth which respects the fact of economy–environment interdependence and does not undermine future economic prospects – sustainable development.

In order to address the poverty problem, the Brundtland Report considered that GDP per capita needed to grow at around 3 per cent per annum in the developing world. It also saw the need for continuing growth in the developed economies, at around 1.5 per cent per annum, so that the markets for developing country exports would grow. To get some broadbrush appreciation of what sustainable development would involve, let us take it that it requires these economic growth rates, which correspond to an average of 2.5 per cent for the world as a whole, together with no increase in the environmental impact of economic activity. There are many environmental impacts of concern. Let us look at again one of the major concerns, carbon dioxide emissions. We did some IPAT calculations for CO_2 emissions in section 7.1, which we now revisit. We take it that sustainable development requires that CO_2 emissions are no higher in 2050 than they are now.

We want to know what the Brundtland Report conception of sustainable development implies about technology. As before, let us use 2000 as base and look ahead as far as to 2050. If we write

$$I_{2050} \equiv P_{2050} \times A_{2050} \times T_{2050}$$

and

$$I_{2000} \equiv P_{2000} \times A_{2000} \times T_{2000}$$

then no increase in impact means I_{2050} equal to I_{2000}, which implies

$$\frac{P_{2050} \times A_{2050} \times T_{2050}}{P_{2000} \times A_{2000} \times T_{2000}} = 1$$

which is

$$\left(\frac{P_{2050}}{P_{2000}}\right) \times \left(\frac{A_{2050}}{A_{2000}}\right) \times \left(\frac{T_{2050}}{T_{2000}}\right) = 1$$

For economic growth at 2.5 per cent, A_{2050} is $A_{2000} \times 1.025^{50}$, so A_{2050} divided by A_{2000} is 1.025^{50} which is 3.4371. Back in Table 7.1 we gave UN population projections for three assumptions about fertility. Using these with a 2000 population of 6 billion, gives P_{2050} divided by P_{2000} as 1.3110 for low fertility, 1.5537 for medium fertility, and 1.8223 for high fertility. So we get

$$\left(\frac{T_{2050}}{T_{2000}}\right) = 0.22 \text{ for low fertility}$$

$$\left(\frac{T_{2050}}{T_{2000}}\right) = 0.19 \text{ for medium fertility}$$

$$\left(\frac{T_{2050}}{T_{2000}}\right) = 0.16 \text{ for high fertility}$$

Depending on population growth, technology has to change such that emissions per dollar GDP in 2050 are 22 per cent, 19 per cent or 16 per cent of what they were in 2000.

Box 7.1 Input–output analysis of *Our common future* scenario – is it feasible?

According to the Brundtland Report, sustainable development is feasible – given the political will and the necessary institutional changes, it is economically and technologically feasible for the world economy to grow fast enough to reduce poverty without increasing environmental damage. In the Brundtland Report, this is asserted rather than demonstrated. The discussions of economic and technological possibilities in the various areas considered are never put together and examined for consistency. Duchin and Lange (1994 – DL) is a report on the use of input–output analysis, the nature of which was explained in Chapter 5, to do just that.

DL use an input–output model of the world economy based on a transactions table for 16 regional economies with 50 commodities and sectors. This is used to generate two scenarios for the period 1990 to 2020. The reference scenario assumes that over this period world GDP grows at 2.8 per cent per year, while the global population increases by 53 per cent. The economic growth assumption is taken to be what is implicit in the Brundtland Report's account of what is necessary for sustainable development. In the reference scenario there is no technological progress after 1990. The other scenario is the OCF scenario, where OCF stands for 'Our Common Future'. This uses the same global economic and demographic assumptions as the Reference scenario, but incorporates a lot of technological improvements which are quantifications of what DL take to be what the Brundtland Report considers to be feasible. These include energy conservation, materials conservation, changes in the fuel mix for electricity generation, and measures to reduce SO_2 and NO_2 emissions per unit energy use. They require increases in investment to be realised, especially in the developing countries. They are incorporated into the analysis as described in Chapter 5 – by alterations to the input coefficients in the sector columns. The OCF scenario also includes big increases in the flows of aid from the developed to the developing countries.

As indicators of environmental impact, the analysis tracks fossil fuel use and emissions of CO_2, SO_2 and NO_2. Under the Reference Scenario, all of these indicators increase by about 150 per cent over 1990 to 2020. The OCF scenario represents a big improvement on this, but the indicators still go up – fossil fuel use by 61 per cent, CO_2 by 60 per cent, SO_2 by 16 per cent, and NO_2 by 63 per cent. The changes that DL incorporate into the OCF scenario do not hold these environmental damage indicators constant, given economic and population growth. On this analysis, sustainable development as envisaged in the Brundtland Report is not feasible. As DL puts it, 'the position taken in the Brundtland Report is not realistic' (p. 5) in as much as their analysis shows that 'the economic and environmental objectives of the Brundtland Report cannot be achieved simultaneously' (p. 8). It is, of course, possible that the DL assessments of what is economically and technologically feasible are too pessimistic.

It is generally agreed that sustainable development would require improvements in technology of this order of magnitude – major reductions in materials and energy use, and therefore in waste emissions, per unit output. It seems to be widely agreed that such improvements are in a technological sense feasible – some references which discuss technological possibilities are given in Further Reading at the end of the chapter. In the energy sector, the technology now exists by means of which the use of fossil fuels could be greatly reduced by the use of nuclear fission and renewable energy sources such as biomass, solar power, wave and wind power. This would greatly reduce CO_2 emissions.

Unfortunately, the fact that the technologies which would make sustainable development feasible are known about, and in that sense exist, does not itself mean that sustainable development is feasible. What is required is not just that the technologies exist, but that they are widely used, or at least brought into use in the coming decades. In this respect, there are two, related, problems. First, at current market prices, they are generally more expensive than the technologies now in use – electricity from nuclear fission costs more than electricity from fossil fuels, even before the waste-handling problems of the former are fully taken into account. Second, putting them into use would involve creating lots of new capital equipment in which the new technologies would be embodied – new nuclear power stations, for example. It would require, that is, lots of saving and investment.

The WCED in the Brundtland Report took the view that these problems could be dealt with, that sustainable development is feasible, but that this would require major political and institutional changes. The publication of the Brundtland Report did set in train a series of political and institutional developments, which we will briefly outline in Part III. However, not all are convinced that these are enough, or will be enough, to realise sustainable development. As we will see in Parts III and IV, the problems that those who are pessimistic about future prospects see are economic and political rather than technological. Box 7.1 reports some results from a study that used the input–output methods introduced in Chapter 5 to consider the prospects for sustainable development.

SUMMARY

The relationship between economic growth and the natural environment is complex and multi-faceted. It is not true that economic growth always increases environmental degradation, nor is it true that it always decreases it eventually. Outcomes depend on what is happening to the size of the human population, the pattern of consumption, and the technologies used in production. What is clear is that achieving sustainable development requires major changes to the technologies in use, which in turn requires investment and capital accumulation.

KEYWORDS

Demographic momentum (p. 212): larger absolute increases in population size despite a falling rate of increase.
EKC hypothesis (p. 247): the idea that as economic growth proceeds so environmental damage first increases, then levels off, then declines.
Fertility rate (p. 213): the average number of children produced by a female during her lifetime.
Leontief production function (p. 221): a production function such that there is no possibility of substituting one input for another.
Scenario (p. 212): an internally consistent story about one way in which the future could unfold.

FURTHER READING

The IPAT identity was introduced in Ehrlich and Holdren (1971): see also Ehrlich and Ehrlich (1990). It was originally set out as $I \equiv PCT$ where C stands for consumption, but IPAT is a better-sounding acronym than IPCT. The feasible prospects for technological change are discussed in von Weizsäcker *et al.** (1997) – it is claimed that T could be reduced by a factor of 4, so that affluence could double and impact be cut by 50 per cent, for constant population. Lovins *et al.* (2000) is even more optimistic about technological possibilities.

The publication of *The limits to growth* in 1972 was a factor in the reawakening of economists' interest in natural resources in relation to long-run economic growth, and some of the early contributions to the modern economic literature were responses to it. For example, the Economics Nobel prize-winner Robert Solow (Solow, 1974a) rigorously examined the question of whether a non-renewable resource stock could last for ever under various assumptions about substitutability in production, population growth and technical progress. His results parallel the discussion here. See also Solow (1974b) and Dasgupta and Heal (1979). Jones (2002) is a good textbook on modelling economic growth, which has a chapter on natural resources.

The source of the brazen impudent nonsense quotation regarding *The limits to growth* is Beckerman (1972). The quotation is from Beckerman's inaugural lecture as Professor of Economics at University College London. Some sense of the stir created by *The limits to growth* can be gained from the fact that an abridged version of this lecture appeared as a major feature article in *The Times* newspaper within a few days of the lecture being given. The same Professor of Economics later published a more measured, but still highly critical, appraisal of *The limits to growth* – Beckerman (1974) – which also sets out very clearly why economists are so committed to economic growth. This book provides the references to much of the contemporary criticism of *The limits to growth*. A particularly robust, and quite influential, economist's attack on the idea that the environment might set limits to economic growth is Simon (1981). It is interesting that the sequel, *Beyond the limits* (Meadows *et al.*, 1992), came in for a lot less criticism, and notably a lot less criticism from neoclassical economists, despite the fact that the analysis and conclusions had changed very little. Common (1995) discusses this, and considers the nature of Simon's arguments about limits. Van den Bergh and de Mooij (1999) survey and categorise a number of different positions on the 'growth versus the environment' question.

As noted in the chapter, many neoclassical economists treated *The limits to growth* as if it simply involved the proposition that further economic growth was threatened by the increasing scarcity of natural resources. There have been a number of attempts to use various kinds of data to determine whether resources are, in fact, becoming more scarce. The possibility that they might not be becoming more scarce is attributed to new discoveries and technical progress. The results depend upon what kind of scarcity indicator is used. Interpretation of the empirical evidence often overlooks the fact that proponents of the increasing scarcity hypothesis have in mind the world economy, whereas much of the cited evidence relates to the economy of the USA. Good points of entry to this literature are Smith (1979), Hall *et al.* (1986), and Cleveland and Stern (1999); see also Common (1995).

Given modern computing power and software, constructing and analysing even complicated simulation models is relatively straightforward and does not require great competence in computer programming. Gilbert and Troitzsch (1999) cover several types of simulation modelling, and provide guidance to the software available for each type. The world model of *The limits to growth* was simulated using DYNAMO, which was the first software specifically designed, in the late 1960s, for dynamic models. The simulations for *Beyond the limits* were done using STELLA^{RM}, a development of DYNAMO which is more user-friendly and has a graphical user interface. Hannon and Ruth (1994) is a book about dynamic modelling using STELLA, which covers applications in economics, ecology, chemistry, biology and engineering.

The EKC hypothesis quickly generated a substantial literature concerning both the reasoning behind it and the evidence for it. Rather less attention has been paid to the implications that would follow if the hypothesis were true. The literature is mainly in the form of papers published in journals such as *Environmental and Resource Economics, Ecological Economics, Environment and Development Economics*, and the *Journal of Environmental Economics and Management. Ecological Economics* devoted a whole special issue to the EKC in May 1998, Number 2 of Volume 25. Good overviews are Stern (1998) and de Bruyn and Heintz (1999).

The literature on sustainable development is now huge. Ekins (2003a) is a useful introduction to some of it. The seminal 'Brundtland Report' (WCED, 1987) is still well worth reading. Reid* (1995) is a short introductory treatment. Van den Bergh and Hofkes (1999) surveys relevant economic modelling: see also Faucheux *et al.* (1996).

WEBSITES

A good point of entry to the EKC literature is the entry 'The EKC' in the ISEE encyclopedia at http://www.ecoeco.org. Chapters from Lovins *et al.* (2000) can be downloaded from http://www.natcap.org/. Lovins is associated with the Rocky Mountain Institute – see http://www.rmi.org/. Useful sites in relation to sustainable development are those of the International Institute for Sustainable Development, http://www.iisd.org, the Sustainable Development Communications Network, http://www.sdgateway.net, the Division for Sustainable Development at the UN, http://www.un.org/esa/sustdev/index.html, and the UK's Sustainable Development Commission, http://www.sd-commission.gov.uk/. The UN's population projections, and other demographic information, can be accessed at the site for the UN's Population Division http://www.un.org/esa/population. Population Connection is an organisation advocating action 'to stabilize world population at a level that can be sustained by the earth's resources' – see http://www.populationconnection.org/.

DISCUSSION QUESTIONS

1. Some critics of *The limits to growth* argued that it was really just a restatement of the classical economists' position, and was wrong for the same reasons as they were. Is this a valid criticism?
2. Do you think it is reasonable to use a Cobb–Douglas production function in a model of economic growth?
3. If sustainable development is not feasible, then what does the future hold?

EXERCISES

1. Some scientists consider that climate change prospects require that global CO_2 emissions are cut by 50 per cent. Using IPAT and data given in the chapter, work out by how much T would have to change for this to happen given current population and global average GDP per capita. By how much would it have to change if population and per capita income were to double?

2. (a) Simulate the history of a renewable resource stock with logistic growth, where the carrying capacity is 10 and the intrinsic growth rate is 0.4, where the initial stock size is 10 and the harvest is initially 1 growing thereafter at 2.5 per cent. By how much is the date of extinction delayed if the rate of growth of the harvest is reduced to 1 per cent?

    (b) Consider the history for the same resource stock with an initial size of 5 when a constant harvest of 1 is taken. What happens if the constant harvest is 2? If it is 0.5?

3. Simulate per capita income growth for an economy with the production function

$$Y = R^{0.1} \times L^{0.7} \times K^{0.2}$$

where R is input of a non-renewable resource, set at 0.05 times the remaining stock of the resource. The initial stock is 100. Initially L and K are 1. L grows at 2.5 per cent and the savings rate is 0.15. Assume that there is endogenous technical progress with

$$a = K^{0.6}$$

which applies: (a) to all inputs as in the chapter; (b) to resource and capital inputs; and (c) just to capital inputs.

4. Consider a world economy comprising two economies, in both of which

$$e = \max(\{e = y - 0.1y^2\}, e^*)$$

where in economy 1 y grows at 2.5 per cent and population grows at 2.5 per cent from year 1, whereas in economy two neither grows until year 40 when y starts to grow at 2.5 per cent and population at 4 per cent. All initial values are 1. Use simulations out to year 150 to consider predicting the path of future total world emissions based on experience out to year 94: (a) for $e^* = 0$; and (b) for $e^* = 0.1$.

8

Exchange and markets

In this chapter you will:

- Learn about the benefits of exchange based on the specialisation of production;
- Learn how the use of money facilitates exchange and specialisation;
- See how markets work in terms of demand and supply functions;
- Be introduced to elasticities of demand and supply;
- Consider the distinction between short- and long-run market adjustments;
- See what determines who – buyers or sellers – pays most of the tax on a commodity;
- Learn about financial markets and how the rate of interest is determined.

M arkets are the dominant form of economic organisation in modern societies. The main purpose of this chapter is to use demand and supply analysis to explain how markets work. It will also use that analysis to explain how the interest rate is determined, and how it influences the level of saving and investment. Before getting to those matters, we begin by discussing the benefits that can flow from exchange and specialisation, which are what markets are really all about.

8.1 EXCHANGE AND SPECIALISATION

Markets are social institutions which facilitate the process by which potential gains from exchange and specialisation are realised. In this section we consider the nature of the gains that markets can realise. First, we look at the gains that can exist on the basis of the fact that where people have different tastes exchanging things may make people feel better off. Second, we shall show that in a world where productive capabilities differ specialisation can make everybody better off.

8.1.1 Exchange

Consider a world of just two individuals, Jane and Tom, where there are two consumption goods, loaves and fishes. For the moment, we do not enquire into the production of loaves and fishes. We just assume that they have given amounts of each, known as their endowments, and preferences concerning quantities of each. Suppose that Jane's endowment is 40 loaves and 20 fishes, while Tom's is 20 loaves and 40 fishes. Suppose that both would prefer more of both commodities to what they have in their endowment, which can be stated as (41,21)P(40,20) for Jane and (21,41)P(20,40) for Tom, where (x,y) refers to the commodity bundle x loaves and y fishes and P means 'is preferred to', so that (41,21)P(40,20) means that 41 loaves and 21 fishes are preferred to 40 loaves and 20 fishes. Given just Jane and Tom and their endowments of loaves and fishes, Jane cannot consume (41,21) while Tom consumes (21,41) – this would be total loaves consumption of 62 and total fish consumption of 62, whereas there are just 60 of each in existence.

Suppose also that (39,21)P(40,20) for Jane and (21,39)P(20,40) for Tom – both would prefer a slightly more balanced diet. A move from the initial endowments position of (40,20) for Jane and (20,40) for Tom to (39,21) for Jane and (21,39) for Tom is feasible – for such an allocation total consumption of loaves is 60 and total consumption of fish is 60. Jane can move to a preferred position by giving Tom 1 loaf in exchange for 1 fish, which exchange also moves Tom to a preferred position. The voluntary exchange of 1 loaf for 1 fish makes both Jane and Tom feel that they are better off – there is a gain from exchange.

This simple example illustrates an important point – voluntary exchange makes both parties feel better off. If an exchange is not going to make both feel better off it will not take place voluntarily. It follows from this that if, given fixed endowments of commodities, all possible voluntary exchanges have taken place, then it will not be possible to make either of Jane or Tom, in our simple world, feel better off. Except, that is, by making the other feel worse off. Suppose that both Jane and Tom always prefer a more to a less balanced diet. Then clearly, voluntary exchanges will take them to (30,30) for Jane and (30,30) for Tom, and then stop, with both feeling better-off than they did with their original endowments. From this position, Jane/Tom could be made better off if some of both commodities were taken from Tom/Jane and given to Jane/Tom, but this would involve coercion – Tom/Jane would not voluntarily participate in such a reallocation. The point is that voluntary exchange means both parties feeling better off, otherwise both would not participate.

It is important to be clear that the endpoint to a process of voluntary exchange does not have to involve equal shares of the totals available, and generally will not. It did in the above Jane and Tom example because of the initial endowments and the preferences. Altering either, or both, would produce a different outcome. Suppose, for example, that the initial endowments were (40,30) for Jane and (70,80) for Tom, and that as above each preferred a more to a less balanced diet. Then voluntary exchanges would eventually lead to (35,35) for Jane and (75,75) for Tom – Tom starts and ends with more of both commodities.

8.1.2 Specialisation in production

Now consider the production of loaves and fish by Jane and Tom. It is reasonably obvious that if both can produce both commodities, and Jane, say, is better at producing loaves while Tom is better at producing fish, then there would be more of both fish and loaves produced if Tom specialised in producing fish and Jane in producing loaves. If more of both commodities is produced, then both Jane and Tom could be better off with specialisation than if both produced both commodities. What is less obvious is that there can be specialisation gains for both even where one of the parties is better at producing

Table 8.1 Production and opportunity costs without specialisation

	Jane	Tom
Loaves per hour	1.5	0.625
Fish per hour	0.3	0.25
Opportunity cost 1 fish	5 loaves	2.5 loaves
Opportunity cost 1 loaf	0.2 fish	0.4 fish

both commodities, provided that the degree of superiority differs across commodities. This is the **principle of comparative advantage**, which we now explain.

Suppose that Jane and Tom both work a 40-hour week. The first two rows of Table 8.1 show output per hour for Jane and Tom in each line of production. In one hour Jane produces more loaves *and* more fish than Tom, but the extent of her superiority is greatest in the production of loaves – she produces $1.5/0.625 = 2.4$ times as many loaves per hour as Tom and $0.3/0.25 = 1.2$ times as many fish. Jane's comparative advantage lies in the production of loaves, which means that Tom has a comparative advantage in the production of fish. The production possibilities for Jane and Tom are shown as the solid lines in Figure 8.1. If Jane devotes all her time to producing loaves she produces 60 of them; if she devotes all her time to fish she produces 12 of them. By varying the amounts of working time devoted to each kind of production, she could produce any combination of loaves and fish lying along the line joining 60 loaves (and no fish) and 12 fish (and no loaves), the slope of which is $60/12 = 5$. In Figure 8.1(b) for Tom, the line joining 25 loaves (and no fish) and 10 fish (and no loaves) has the slope $25/10 = 2.5$. We will assume that Jane and Tom's preferences are such that in the absence of specialisation, Jane produces and consumes 6 fish and 30 loaves, while Tom produces and consumes 4 fish and 15 loaves. The state of affairs in which Jane and Tom are self-sufficient, each consuming what they themselves produce, is known as **autarky**.

In a state of autarky the lines in Figure 8.1 showing the production possibilities for Jane and Tom also show the consumption possibilities that are open to each of them. Consumption opportunities can be expressed in terms of opportunity costs. The **opportunity cost** of something is what has to be given up for it. For Jane, switching one hour from the production of loaves to the production of fish would increase fish output and consumption by 0.3 at the cost of reducing loaf output and consumption by 1.5 – the opportunity cost of 1 fish is 5 loaves. Note that this is the slope of the solid line in Figure 8.1(a): reading off from it, going from 2 to 4 fish would reduce loaves from 50 to 40. Tom's opportunity cost for 1 fish is worked out in the same way. The opportunity costs for 1 loaf are worked out by considering the switching of one hour of labour in the opposite direction, and are the reciprocals of (i.e. one divided by) the opportunity costs for 1 fish. Note that Jane has the lower opportunity cost for a loaf, while Tom has the lower opportunity cost for a fish. This is just another way of saying that Jane has a comparative advantage in loaf production, while Tom has a comparative advantage in fish production. Jane has to give up less fish to have an extra loaf, while Tom has to give up less bread to have more fish.

According to the principle of comparative advantage, both Jane and Tom can do better if each specialises in the line of production where she/he has comparative

Figure 8.1
Gains from
production
specialisation.

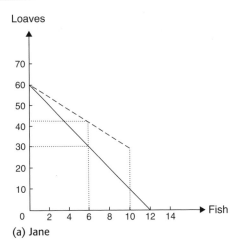

(a) Jane

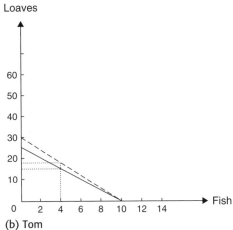

(b) Tom

Table 8.2 Consumption opportunities with specialisation in production and exchange at three loaves for one fish

Jane		Tom	
Loaves	Fish	Loaves	Fish
60	0	0	10
57	1	3	9
54	2	6	8
51	3	9	7
48	4	12	6
45	5	15	5
42	**6**	**18**	**4**
39	7	21	3
36	8	24	2
33	9	27	1
30	10	30	0

advantage, even though Jane is actually superior in both lines of production in an absolute sense. Suppose then that Jane produces 60 loaves and no fish, and Tom produces 10 fish and no loaves, and that they agree to exchange their output with each other on the basis of one fish for three loaves. Table 8.2 shows the consumption opportunities then open to Jane and Tom. The first row shows the consumption situation when there is specialisation in production, but no exchange. The next row shows that Jane could, by exchanging with Tom, consume one fish at the cost of a reduction in her bread consumption of three loaves, in which case Tom would get to consume three loaves at the cost of consuming one less fish. Following rows show the results of more exchange at the ratio of one fish for three loaves. In the highlighted row we see that given production specialisation with exchange, Jane could consume the same amount of fish (6) and more loaves (42) than she did in the absence of specialisation (30), as could Tom (4 and 18 compared with 4 and 15). Consumption opportunities based on specialisation and trade at the exchange ratio of three loaves for one fish are also shown as the dashed lines in Figure 8.1. Note that these two dashed lines have the same slope, reflecting the fact that given production specialisation and exchange Jane and Tom both face the same opportunity costs – Jane has to give up as many loaves for a given amount of extra fish, and vice versa, as Tom

Table 8.3 Consumption opportunities at different exchange rates

| Exchange ratio is 5 | | | | Exchange ratio is 2.5 | | | |
| Jane | | Tom | | Jane | | Tom | |
Loaves	Fish	Loaves	Fish	Loaves	Fish	Loaves	Fish
60	0	0	10	60	0	0	10
55	1	5	9	57.5	1	2.5	9
50	2	10	8	55	2	5	8
45	3	15	7	52.5	3	7.5	7
40	4	20	6	50	4	10	6
35	5	25	5	47.5	5	12.5	5
30	**6**	**30**	**4**	**45**	**6**	**15**	**4**
25	7	35	3	42.5	7	17.5	3
20	8	40	2	40	8	20	2
15	9	45	1	37.5	9	22.5	1
40	10	50	0	35	10	25	0

does. For both, the opportunity cost of one fish is three loaves, while the opportunity cost of one loaf is one third of a fish. The slope of the dashed line is three. Note that for Jane the dashed line ends where fish equals 10 and loaves equals 30. After specialisation Jane cannot consume more than 10 fish because that is the most that Tom can produce.

So long as the exchange ratio that Jane and Tom use is between the opportunity costs that each faced in the state of autarky, both can benefit from specialisation and exchange. The closer the exchange rate to Jane's opportunity costs in autarky, the more of the gains to trade go to Tom: the closer the exchange ratio to Tom's opportunity costs in autarky, the more of the gains to trade go to Jane. Table 8.3 is constructed in the same way as Table 8.2 and shows the consumption opportunities with specialisation and trade when the exchange ratio is five loaves for one fish – the opportunity cost that Jane faced under autarky – and when it is 2.5 loaves for one fish – the opportunity cost that Tom faced under autarky. Looking at the bread consumption levels that go with the fish consumption levels that applied under autarky, in the row with bold figures, we see that for an exchange ratio of 5 Tom's situation improves with trade while Jane's does not, while for an exchange ratio of 2.5 Jane's situation improves but Tom's does not. Between these limits, increasing the exchange ratio from 2.5 towards 5 increases Tom's gain and reduces Jane's. Exercise 1 asks you to confirm this, using Tables 8.2 and 8.3, and some further simple calculations of your own. We see, then, that given differences in opportunity costs in a state of autarky, specialisation in production according to comparative advantage plus trade can improve the lot of both Jane and Tom. We also see that Jane and Tom do not necessarily gain equally, and that the way that the gains from trade are shared depends on the exchange ratio at which trade takes place. Given the production possibilities, what the agreed rate will actually be depends on Jane and Tom's preferences as between fish and bread.

The principle of comparative advantage is important in understanding why productive specialisation and exchange, rather than autarky, characterises much of economic activity. It is used, for example, to explain patterns of trade between national economies, as we shall see in Chapter 12. In regard to specialisation as between individuals, as in the story about Jane and Tom, it needs to be kept in mind that in telling that story we have implicitly assumed that Jane and Tom have no preferences as between different kinds of work. If, for example, Jane actually preferred spending time catching fish to spending it growing wheat and making bread, then complete production specialisation might not be the outcome despite the consumption advantages that it offers. There are other reasons why comparative advantage does not always lead to complete specialisation. One is that exchange involves costs – the institution of money is one way of reducing those costs, as discussed below.

8.1.3 Money and prices

In discussing specialisation and exchange for Jane and Tom, we had them agree the ratio at which they would trade fish for bread and vice versa. For the case of Table 8.2, for example, Jane gave Tom three loaves for each fish that he gave her. An alternative way of realising the gains from specialisation and trade would be to use money as a **medium of exchange**. Under such a system, instead of directly exchanging bread and fish, each would be exchanged for money. Suppose that the currency is £. Instead of agreeing on an exchange ratio of three loaves per fish, Jane and Tom could agree that a loaf would exchange for £1 and a fish for £3. The **price** of a loaf would be, that is, £1 and the price of a fish would be £3. To move from the first to the second row in Table 8.2, Jane would sell three loaves to Tom to get £3, which she would use to buy three fish from Tom.

In considering money as a medium of exchange and the role of prices, it is important to be clear about the difference between relative price and absolute price. The **absolute price** of a commodity is the quantity of currency units that it exchanges for. It is what is meant by 'price' in common usage. The **relative price** of a commodity is its absolute price divided by the absolute price of some other commodity. If all absolute, or nominal, prices change in equal proportion, all relative prices remain the same. Given that the, absolute, prices of loaves and fish are £1 and £3, the relative price of fish in terms of bread is 3 and the relative price of bread in terms of fish is $\frac{1}{3}$. Relative prices give the terms on which the commodities concerned exchange for one another. Multiplying the price of fish and the price of bread by the same factor leaves the relative prices unchanged – if the price of a loaf goes to £10 and the price of a fish to £30, the rate at which they exchange one for another stays the same, as do the relative prices of 3 and $\frac{1}{3}$.

Different relative prices do mean different rates for commodity exchange. If the, absolute, prices of loaves and fish are £1 and £5, five loaves exchange for one fish as in the left part of Table 8.3 – this is also the case for any absolute prices which are £$(1 \times k)$ for loaves and £$(5 \times k)$ for fish, where k is some positive number. If the, absolute, prices for loaves and fish are £1 and £2.5, 2.5 loaves exchange for one fish as in the right part of Table 8.3 – this is also the case for any absolute prices which are £$(1 \times k)$ for loaves and £$(2.5 \times k)$ for fish. Clearly, in thinking about money as a medium of exchange, it is relative prices, not absolute prices, that matter. It is the relative prices of bread and fish that Jane and Tom agree on that determines how the gains from trade are shared between them, not the absolute prices in which those relative prices are expressed. The commodity exchange ratio is the same for loaf price £1 and fish price £3 as it is for loaf price £2 and fish price £6, which commodity exchange ratio is different from that at loaf price £1 and fish price £5 or any common multiples of 1 and 5.

Where there are just two parties trading just two commodities the benefits of using money as a medium of exchange, rather than simply exchanging the commodities directly, are not obvious. The exchange of commodities for commodities is known as **barter**. Effecting their trades by means of money and prices rather than bartering would not obviously benefit Jane and Tom. But their situation is a special one constructed so as to bring out the basic ideas about the potential benefits of production specialisation and exchange over autarky as simply and clearly as possible. Economies actually involve large numbers of individuals – millions – and large numbers of commodities – thousands. Where there are many traders and many things to be traded the advantages of the use of money as medium of exchange, as compared with barter, are easy to see, and explain its widespread use.

The problem with barter is that it requires the double coincidence of wants, which means that it requires that two parties be in contact each of whom has something that the other wants some of. In the example that we used to explain specialisation based on comparative advantage this requirement was satisfied because there were just two parties and two commodities, both of which each party wanted to consume. Now suppose that as well as Jane and Tom there is someone called Sally, and that:

Jane has comparative advantage in bread production, and wants to eat bread and meat;
Tom has comparative advantage in fish production, and wants to eat fish and bread;
Sally has comparative advantage in meat production, and wants to eat meat and fish.

In this case there is no double coincidence of wants, and if production were specialised barter could not take place. There would be no basis for direct exchange between any two of the specialised producers.

Now, suppose that there exists money in the form of £1 coins and that Jane, Tom and Sally are all willing to accept money in exchange for bread, fish and meat respectively, at rates to be agreed. Then Jane can sell bread to Tom and use the money she gets to buy meat from Sally, Tom can sell fish to Sally and use the money he gets to buy bread from Jane, and Sally can sell meat to Jane and use the money she gets to buy fish from Tom. The use of money as medium of exchange means that trade does not require the double coincidence of wants, and facilitates specialisation.

Money came into existence as a means of exchange but now has two other functions. It serves as a store of value and as unit of account.

At one level the store of value function is just a necessary feature of its use as a medium of exchange. It is the fact that the commodity for money exchange can take place at one date and the exchange of the money for another commodity at a later date that really cracks the coincidence of wants problem. Jane, for example, can sell her bread for money today, and use the money to buy meat at some time in the future. If money did not act as a store of value in this way, it would not be much use as medium of exchange. Note that in order for money to act as a store of value, the form that it takes must be durable not perishable – gold and silver have served as money, fish have not.

Given that many goods and services have prices, money has come to be used as a common denominator, a unit of account. It is sometimes said that you cannot add apples and pears. That is true. But you can add the money value of a quantity of apples – apple price times quantity of apples – to the money value of a quantity of pears – pear price times quantity of pears – to get the money value of the apples together with the pears. And, you can compare the money value of the apples and pears with the money value of, say, some bananas. Given the prices of apples and pears, the money value of a number of apples together with a number of pears could be expressed in terms of apple equivalents or pear equivalents. But neither of those is directly comparable with bananas, whereas the money value of the apples and pears is directly comparable with the money value of bananas.

We looked at the use of money as unit of account in Chapter 5. As the term 'accounts' is normally used it refers to money values, prices times quantities. It is because of the comparability of money values that accounts as usually understood can have a 'bottom line' where the overall situation is expressed in a single number – the profit or loss in a firm's accounts, GDP in a nation's accounts. Things that do not have prices attached to them cannot be included in accounts of money values. This is one of the reasons that some people object to looking at a nation's economic performance in terms of GDP – that measure does not account for damage to the environment, which for reasons to be discussed in the next chapter, does not have a price attached to it.

8.2 HOW MARKETS WORK

A **market** is a system in which buyers and sellers of something interact. At one time, the interaction necessarily involved buyers and sellers physically coming together, and a market was a place where they did that. The word 'market' is still sometimes used to mean a place where buying and selling occur, but we will, along with all economists, use it with the more general meaning given above. Some markets today, for example, involve transactions effected via the Internet. A market is a system in which buyers exchange money for something, and sellers exchange that something for money. Rather than a place, it can be thought of as a set of arrangements that makes such exchanges possible. The range of things bought and sold in markets is very wide, from titles to property through iron ore to haircuts. Market participants, as both buyers and sellers, can be individuals, firms and governments. We will look at the market for a commodity produced by firms and bought by individuals, and we shall call the commodity a widget. The analysis to be explained in terms of the market for widgets here applies, in general terms, to any kind of market.

8.2.1 Demand and supply functions

The basic elements of market analysis are the demand function and the supply function. The **demand function** is the relationship between the quantity that buyers wish to buy and price, given that other influences on the quantity that buyers wish to buy are held constant. A demand function can be represented as a set of pairs of numbers for price and quantity, as an algebraic relationship, or graphically. Thus, for example, for quantity demanded varying with price as shown in Table 8.4, the corresponding algebraic statement, using P to represent price and Q to represent quantity is

$$Q = 10 - (0.5 \times P)$$

and the corresponding graphical statement is shown in Figure 8.2(a). You should check that this equation and the graph in Figure 8.2(a) do summarise the relationship set out in Table 8.4.

Table 8.4 A demand function	
Price	Quantity demanded
20	0
18	1
16	2
14	3
12	4
10	5
8	6
6	7
4	8
2	9
0	10

In this book we shall always work with demand functions such that quantity demanded increases/falls as price falls/increases, and that have graphs which are straight lines, as in Figure 8.2. The inverse relationship between price and quantity demanded is a general property of demand functions – very few cases have been found where, other things being equal, quantity demanded moves in the same direction as price. While demand functions almost always have downward slopes, it is not generally true that this relationship takes a form that has a graph which is a straight line. However, using straight-line relationships makes the analysis using demand functions much easier, and does not mislead, so that is what we do.

It is not difficult to understand why quantity demanded generally moves in the opposite direction to price, when nothing else changes. If the price of widgets increases, while other prices remain the same and widget consumers have constant incomes, then they must give up more of the consumption of commodities other than widgets per widget consumed. An individual's preferences would be strange if in such circumstances she chose to increase her consumption of widgets. Holding widget consumption constant would imply a very strong preference for widgets as against all other commodities. Conversely, a fall in the price of widgets, other prices and incomes unchanged, would mean that an individual could consume more widgets without consuming less of anything else, and widgets would be a strange commodity if consumers did not increase their consumption of them at all in such circumstances.

In Figure 8.2(a) we have put quantity on the vertical axis and price on the horizontal. Given the interpretation that the demand function is telling us about how the amount that buyers want to buy changes as price varies, so that price is the independent and quantity the dependent variable, this would seem the natural way to do things. However, in economics it is conventional to put price on the vertical and quantity on the horizontal axis, and we shall follow that convention in the diagrams in the rest of this book. Figure 8.2(b) corresponds to Table 8.4 for this way

Figure 8.2
Graphical
representation
of a demand
function.

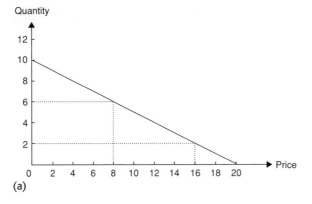

(a)

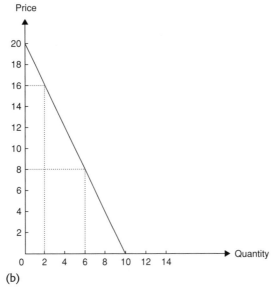

(b)

of drawing the demand function. From

$$Q = 10 - (0.5 \times P)$$

for quantity dependent on price, adding $0.5 \times P$ and subtracting Q gives

$$0.5 \times P = 10 - Q$$

and multiplying both sides by 2 gives

$$P = 20 - (2 \times Q)$$

for price dependent on quantity. This is the equation that goes with the graph in Figure 8.2(b).

The **supply function** is the relationship between the quantity that sellers wish to sell and price, given that other influences on the quantity that sellers wish to sell are held constant. Generally, the supply function slopes upwards, so that the quantity offered for sale increases/decreases with increases/decreases in price. This

is because the higher the price of, say, widgets, the greater the incentive in the form
of profits for firms to produce widgets. As
with a demand function, a supply function can be represented as a set of pairs
of numbers for price and quantity, as an
algebraic relationship, or graphically, with
either quantity or price as dependent variable. In this book we shall show supply
functions as graphs which, with price on
the vertical and quantity on the horizontal axis, are upward-sloping straight lines.
Similar remarks apply here as were made
above in regard to the way that demand
functions will be represented graphically

Table 8.5 A supply function	
Price	Quantity supplied
0	0
2	3
4	6
6	9
8	12
10	15
12	18
14	21
16	24
18	27
20	30

in what follows. First, while it might seem more natural to put quantity on the
vertical axis as dependent variable, the convention in economics, which we shall
follow, is to put price on the vertical axis. Second, whereas supply functions do
generally slope upwards, showing them as straight lines is a matter of convenience
not a statement of fact. Table 8.5 shows some of the price–quantity combinations
that go with the algebraic statement

$$P = (2/3) \times Q$$

which is equivalent to

$$Q = 1.5 \times P$$

Figure 8.3 brings together the demand and supply functions, as the straight lines
DD and *SS*, for widgets. The **market equilibrium** is where supply equals demand
giving an equilibrium price P^e and an equilibrium quantity Q^e. At price P^e the
quantity that buyers wish to buy is equal to the quantity that sellers wish to sell,

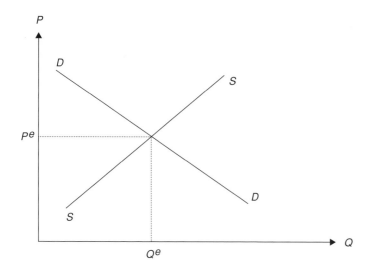

Figure 8.3
Equilibrium
price and
quantity.

Figure 8.4
Excess supply
and demand.

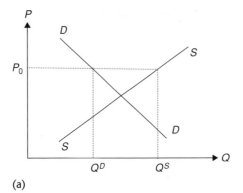

(a)

(b)

and it is in that sense that it is the equilibrium price. If you carefully draw the graphs for the demand and supply functions represented in Tables 8.4 and 8.5, you will find that they intersect where price is 5 and quantity is 7.5. An alternative way of establishing the equilibrium price and quantity in this particular case is to do some simple algebra, solving the pair of simultaneous equations

$$P = 20 - (2 \times Q) \tag{i}$$

and

$$P = (2/3) \times Q. \tag{ii}$$

Substituting for P in (ii) from (i)

$$20 - (2 \times Q) = (2/3) \times Q$$

so

$$20 = (8/3) \times Q$$

which is

$$Q^e = (60/8) = 7.5$$

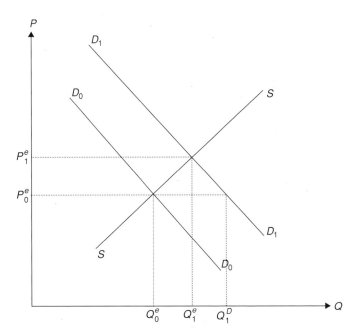

Substituting this into (ii)

$$P^e = (2/3) \times 7.5 = 15/3 = 5$$

If an equilibrium price is established, then in the absence of external shocks
to the market that price will persist. Figure 8.4 shows non-equilibrium prices. In
Figure 8.4(a), at the price P_0 the amount that widget producers want to sell, Q^S,
is greater than the amount that widget users want to buy, Q^D, and there is a
condition of **excess supply**. In such circumstances, the market price of widgets
will be driven down as sellers compete for sales. In Figure 8.4(b), at the price $P_0 Q^D$
is greater than Q^S and there is a situation of **excess demand** which will drive the
market price up as would-be buyers compete to get their hands on widgets.

Demand and supply functions show how the plans of buyers and sellers vary
with price, given that all other influences on buying and selling plans are constant.
If one of those other influences changes, then an existing market equilibrium will
be disturbed and there will be initiated a process of adjustment to a new market
equilibrium. The 'other influences' on demand and supply will be discussed shortly.
For now let us look at demand, where the average level of individuals' incomes will
influence their demand for widgets – at any given price for widgets, more will be
demanded the higher the average level of income for actual and potential widget
users. An increase in income will shift the demand function as shown in Figure 8.5,
from $D_0 D_0$ to $D_1 D_1$. The initial effect of such a shift is to create a situation of excess
demand. At the original equilibrium price P_0^e with the higher level of income the
amount demanded is Q_1^D and the amount supplied is Q_0^e, so that there is excess
demand equal to $Q_1^D - Q_0^e$. The excess demand will push up the price of widgets,
which will both reduce demand and increase supply. As price increases, buyers will

move along D_1D_1 to northwest and sellers along SS to the northeast. In the absence of any further external shocks to the system that is the market for widgets, a new market equilibrium will be established where supply again equals demand, with price P_1^e and quantity Q_1^e.

8.2.2 Non-price influences on demand and supply

When we draw, or tabulate or state algebraically, demand and supply varying with price, we are not asserting that price is the only thing that influences the quantity demanded and supplied. The relationships between demand and price and supply and price that are demand and supply functions are the relationships that hold when other influences on demand and supply are held constant. We now look briefly at those other influences.

8.2.2.1 Demand

Other than its price, the main things that affect the demand for some commodity are: incomes; preferences; and the prices of other goods and services.

The first of the 'things held equal' when looking at a demand function is the incomes of the, actual and potential, consumers of the commodity. For most commodities, the demand function will shift upwards and outwards with an increase in consumers' incomes, so that more is demanded at every price. The shift of the demand function from D_0D_0 to D_1D_1 in Figure 8.5 was taken to be the result of an increase in consumers' incomes.

Preferences are sometimes referred to as tastes. The position and slope of the demand function reflects consumer preferences for the commodity as against the other commodities that compete with it for a share of consumers' incomes. A change in tastes in favour of the commodity would act like an increase in consumers' incomes, shifting the demand function outwards so that more is demanded at a given price.

In relation to any commodity, other commodities are classified as **substitutes** or **complements**. If the price of a substitute falls/increases, the demand for the commodity falls/increases, other things equal. If the price of a complement falls/increases, the demand for the commodity increases/falls, other things equal. An example of substitutes would be apricot jam and plum jam – an increase in the price of one would, other things being equal, increase demand for the other. An example of complements would be motor cars and urban parking space – an increase in the price of one would, other things equal, decrease the demand for the other. Most commodities are, because they compete for consumers' spending, substitutes for one another. Where commodities are complements it is usually because of some specific technological relationship, as in the case of CD players and CDs for example.

8.2.2.2 Supply

Other than its price, the main things that affect the supply of some commodity are: technology, and the costs of the inputs used in producing it. Together, these determine the costs of producing the commodity, which for given price determine profit per unit produced.

The supply function for a commodity is constructed for a given technology used in its production. In this context, we mean by 'technology' the terms on which inputs are used to produce the commodity. A production function, as introduced in Chapter 6, describes a technology. An improvement in technology is anything that allows more of the commodity to be produced using the same levels of the same inputs, or allows the same amount of the commodity to be produced using a collection of inputs that, for unchanged input prices, has lower total cost. An improvement in the technology used in the production of the commodity will shift the supply function downwards and to the right, so that more is supplied at any given price.

In the absence of any change in the technology of production, production costs will change with changes in the prices of the inputs that the technology uses, such as labour, capital equipment and raw materials. An increase in the unit cost of any input will increase the cost of any level of output and shift the supply function upwards and to the left, so that less is supplied at any given price.

8.2.3 Elasticities

Elasticities are measures that are used to convey information about the responsiveness of demand and supply to the various things that influence them, and to classify commodities accordingly. The basic idea of an elasticity is that it is the ratio of the proportional change in demand/supply to the proportional change in whatever, price or income, it is caused by.

8.2.3.1 Own-price elasticity of demand

The own-price elasticity of demand is the ratio of the proportionate increase/decrease in the demand for a commodity to the associated proportionate decrease/increase in the price of that commodity, other things held equal. It is often referred to as just the price elasticity of demand, or just the **elasticity of demand**. It is given by the formula

$$E_P \equiv \left(\frac{\Delta Q}{Q} \div \frac{\Delta P}{P} \right) \times -1$$

where:

E_P is the own price elasticity of demand
ΔQ is the change in quantity demanded
Q is initial level of demand
ΔP is the change in price
P is the initial price level

Given that price and quantity move in opposite directions, with ΔQ^D being negative/positive for ΔP being positive/negative, the ratio of proportionate changes is multiplied by minus 1 in this definition so that the elasticity is a positive number.

Consider the demand function represented in Figure 8.2 and Table 8.4, which algebraically is

$$Q = 10 - (0.5 \times P)$$

Figure 8.6
Elasticity of
demand.

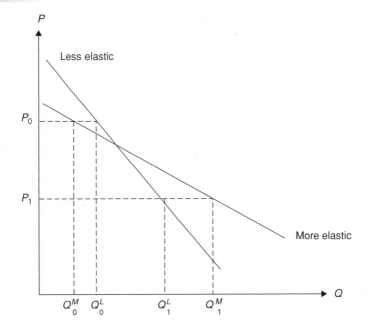

with quantity on the vertical axis, or

$$P = 20 - (2 \times Q)$$

with price on the vertical axis. Suppose that P increases by 10 per cent from $P_0 = 8$, so that it goes to $P_1 = 8.8$. The corresponding levels of quantity demanded are $Q_0 = 6$ and $Q_1 = 5.6$. Using the definition

$$E_P = \left(\frac{-0.4}{6} \div \frac{0.8}{8} \right) \times -1 = \left(\frac{-0.06666}{0.1} \right) \times -1 = -0.6666 \times -1 = 0.6666$$

Now suppose that P increases by 10 per cent from $P_0 = 2$, so that $P_1 = 2.2$. Then $Q_0 = 9$ and $Q_1 = 8.9$ so that E_P is found to be 0.1111. The elasticity of demand varies along a given demand function. This is generally true for all linear demand functions, with the elasticity getting smaller as price falls.

When the demand function is graphed with price on the vertical axis, less steeply sloped demand functions have larger elasticities, and we say that they are 'more elastic'. Figure 8.6 illustrates. For both demand functions the price change is the same, and for the more elastic case demand increases from Q_0^M to Q_1^M whereas for the less elastic case it increases from Q_0^L to Q_1^L. It is conventional to refer to commodities for which the elasticity of demand is equal to or greater than one as having an 'elastic' demand, while those for which E_P is less than one are said to have an 'inelastic' demand.

What determines the elasticity of a commodity's demand function? Basically it is a matter of the tastes of consumers and the extent to which it is possible to substitute for the commodity. Commodities, such as cigarettes, which are essentially addictive and have no substitutes have very inelastic demand functions. Note, however, that this statement refers to cigarettes rather than to brands of cigarettes. Brand X is a reasonably close substitute for Brand Y, and the demand for Brand X is more elastic than the demand for cigarettes in general. Whereas a general increase of, say, 10 per cent in the price of all brands of cigarettes will have a small impact on total cigarette consumption, an increase in the price of Brand X alone will have a much larger proportional impact on its sales. Energy and fuels have relatively inelastic demand functions – we shall discuss this below when looking at short- and long-run adjustments.

8.2.3.2 Cross-price elasticity of demand

The **cross-price elasticity of demand** for a commodity is defined with respect to a change in the price of some other commodity. If we use the subscript i to identify the commodity concerned, and j to identify the other commodity, the cross-price elasticity of i with respect to the price of j is the proportionate change in the quantity of i demanded divided by the proportionate change in the price of j. The definition is

$$E_i^{CP} \equiv \frac{\frac{\Delta Q_i}{Q_i}}{\frac{\Delta P_j}{P_j}}$$

Note that in this definition, unlike that for own-price elasticity, we do not multiply by minus one as we want to get both negative and positive numbers as values for E^{CP}.

If an increase in the price of j of 10 per cent leads, other things being equal, to an increase in the demand for i of 5 per cent, the cross-price elasticity of demand for i with respect to the price of j is 5 ÷ 10 equals 0.5, a positive number. If an increase in the price of j of 10 per cent leads, other things being equal, to a decrease in demand for i of 5 per cent, the cross-price elasticity is −0.5, a negative number. Pairs of commodities where the cross-price elasticity is positive are substitutes, where it is negative they are complements. In terms of the examples previously used for substitutes and complements, an increase in the price of plum jam leads to an increase in the demand for substitute apricot jam and E^{CP} is positive, while an increase in the price of CD players leads to a decrease in the demand for complementary CDs and E^{CP} is negative.

8.2.3.3 Income elasticity of demand

The **income elasticity of demand** for a commodity is the ratio of the proportionate increase in demand for the commodity to the associated proportionate increase in the incomes of consumers of the commodity, other things held equal. The definition is

$$E_Y \equiv \frac{\frac{\Delta Q}{Q}}{\frac{\Delta Y}{Y}}$$

where Y represents income. If consumers' incomes on average rose by 10 per cent, and everything else remained unchanged except that the demand for apples rose by 5 per cent, then the income elasticity of demand for apples would be measured as 0.5.

For most commodities E_Y is found to be positive, but there are some for which it is negative so that demand falls as, other things being equal, incomes increase. Examples of commodities with negative income elasticities are, in the richer economies, foods such as potatoes and bread – meat, on the other hand, has a positive income elasticity of demand. As incomes increase, beyond a certain level, so people typically eat less grain and more meat. Commodities with positive income elasticities are known as 'normal' commodities, whereas those with negative elasticities get called 'inferior'. Normal commodities are sometimes further classified as 'necessities' if their income elasticity of demand is equal to or less than one, and 'luxuries' if it is greater than one. Luxuries are commodities the demand for which increases at a proportionate rate greater than that at which income is growing, given that their (relative) prices are constant.

8.2.3.4 Elasticity of supply

When economists refer to the **elasticity of supply** they mean the own-price elasticity of supply, a measure that describes a property of the supply function in the same way as does the, own-price, elasticity of demand for the demand function. The definition for the elasticity of supply is

$$E_S \equiv \frac{\frac{\Delta Q}{Q}}{\frac{\Delta P}{P}}$$

where Q is the quantity supplied, and the definition refers to situations where only price and quantity supplied change. Note that there is no multiplication by minus one here, as with ΔP and ΔQ both being either positive or negative, E_S will come out as a positive number without such multiplication – the supply function slopes upwards.

When we graph the supply function with price on the vertical axis, the flatter it is the higher is the value of the elasticity of supply – flatter supply curves are 'more elastic'. This is illustrated in Figure 8.7. For the same price increase from P_0 to P_1, supply in the less elastic case increases from Q_0^l to Q_1^l whereas in the more elastic case it increases from Q_0^M to Q_1^M.

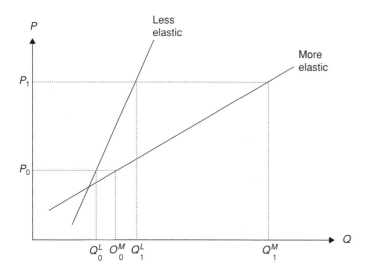

Figure 8.7
Elasticity of
supply.

8.2.3.5 Short- and long-run elasticities

Price elasticities are measures of the responsiveness of demand and supply quantities to price changes. In both cases, responsiveness varies with the length of time considered. It is conventional to distinguish between short- and long-run elasticities, with the latter always being at least as large as the former. For most commodities, long-run elasticities are larger. Short and long run are not defined in terms of particular numbers of weeks, say. Rather, the **short run** is defined as a length of time during which buyers and sellers, actual and potential, can make only limited adjustments to the new price situation, while the **long run** is a length of time during which all possible adjustments are made. Given this, the calendar length of the long run varies across commodities.

The short- versus long-run distinction on both the demand side and the supply side can be illustrated in the energy sector. Take the demand side first, and consider an upward shift in the supply function for motor vehicle fuel, as in Figure 8.8(a). In the short run motor vehicle users can reduce their consumption only by travelling less, and the operative demand function has a low elasticity as in the case of $D_S D_S$. Given more time, they can switch to smaller and/or more fuel efficient vehicles, and/or switch transport modes (from car travel to bus travel, for example), and/or relocate so that less travelling needs to be done. Given the greater scope for behavioural adjustment in the longer run, there is a greater capability to reduce motor fuel consumption, and the demand elasticity is greater, as for $D_L D_L$ in Figure 8.8(a). Because the demand elasticity is larger in the long run, in the long run the market for motor fuel attains a new equilibrium where the price change is smaller, and the quantity change larger, than in the short run. In Figure 8.8(a) Q_S^e and P_S^e are the temporary short-run equilibrium quantity and price following the supply shock, and Q_L^e and P_L^e are the long-run equilibrium quantity and price.

Figure 8.8
Short- and
long-run
market
adjustments.

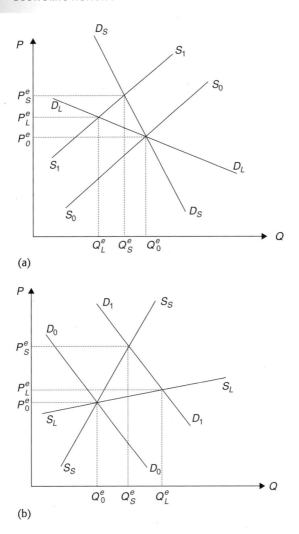

(a)

(b)

Another illustrative example from the energy sector is the case of home heating. If the price of oil rises relative to the price of coal, householders with oil-fired heating systems cannot switch to using coal without changing the equipment installed in their homes. Some whose equipment is old and nearing the end of its useful life may do this straightaway, but for many immediate switching to coal-burning equipment would entail junking valuable oil-burning equipment and hence substantial costs – their fuel-switching response will be delayed, and in the short run their reduction in oil use will be limited to that made possible by turning down the thermostat, wearing more clothes around the house, etc. Similar considerations apply to oil versus coal use in production – switching from oil to coal means changing equipment which takes time, and money.

Figure 8.8(b) shows long- and short-run supply functions, and again it is the long-run function which has the larger elasticity. Again, the energy sector illustrates what is involved. Suppose that Figure 8.8(b) refers to a shift in the demand function for electricity due to an increase in household incomes. The suppliers of electricity can in the short run respond only by working existing generating plants closer to capacity. Unless the situation was initially one of considerable excess capacity, the scope for this is quite limited, and there will be, in the short run, just a small increase in electricity supplied and its price will rise so as to reduce demand – in the figure $S_S S_S$ is the short-run supply function, and Q_S^e and P_S^e are the temporary short-run equilibrium quantity and price following the demand shock. Given time, and the expenditure of money on new generating equipment, the amount of electricity generated can be increased more, and with the supply function $S_L S_L$ the long-run response produces a long-run equilibrium with Q_L^e and P_L^e.

In the energy sector, on both the demand side and the supply side, the long run in the sense used by economists can, as these examples suggest, be a long time. Motor vehicles have normal lifetimes of the order of 10 years, and domestic heating equipment is similar. It takes a similar length of time to plan and build a new electricity-generating station, which once brought on line would normally be expected to supply electricity for more than 25 years. In the short run, energy sector shocks generally entail large price and small quantity changes. It takes a long time to effect large changes in energy supply and energy-using systems. And, it requires lots of investment in new equipment of various kinds.

For energy commodities, the long term is typically several years or more, and the difference between long- and short-term elasticities is large. Considering the demand for all forms of energy in an industrial economy, the short-term elasticity is typically around 0.25 – a 10 per cent price increase leads to a 2.5 per cent reduction in demand – whereas the long-term elasticity is typically around 0.75 – a 10 per cent price increase leads eventually to 7.5 per cent reduction in demand.

For some commodities, short- and long-term elasticities are much closer together in size, and the long term is not very long in terms of calendar time. On the demand side, consider, for example, a particular kind of breakfast cereal – oatmeal say. Switching from oatmeal to, say, muesli does not involve changing the equipment used for eating breakfast, and there will be very little difference between the short and long run, or between the corresponding elasticities. On the supply side, consider, for example, an outward shift in the demand function for domestic services as a result of rising household incomes and more females going out to work. House cleaning involves little capital equipment, and anyway most of what is needed is already in place – outsourcing the cleaning just means changing who uses the equipment. In this case, supply can adjust very quickly to demand shifts.

The point here is that demand and supply analysis, considering elasticities and what determines them, facilitates understanding of how a market economy will respond to shocks of different kinds. Shocks to the energy sector, such as the 1973/4 crisis when oil prices to the industrial economies more than doubled in a matter of months due to concerted action to reduce output by the major oil-producing countries, cause large price and small quantity effects in the short run, as the scope for immediate adjustment by producers and consumers is limited. In the longer run, a decade or so, quantity adjustments – smaller cars, more electricity from nuclear fission, etc. – greatly mitigate the price effects.

8.3 APPLICATIONS OF MARKET ANALYSIS

The apparatus of demand and supply functions introduced above can be used to analyse many issues in the functioning of a market economy. Here we use the apparatus to look at three issues involving government intervention in markets. Most economists want to see the extent of government intervention in markets kept as small as possible, but recognise that some intervention is desirable. In the next chapter we will look systematically at the basic issues that arise in considering how much intervention is desirable, and where it is desirable. For the moment we leave such general questions to one side to provide examples of the usefulness of the demand and supply function concepts. The relevance of each example to issues in sustainable development – poverty alleviation and environmental protection – will be noted.

8.3.1 Price ceilings

Price ceilings are a form of intervention sometimes used by government with the intention of protecting the poor from the effect of a high market price for some commodity considered to be necessary for a decent standard of well-being. Historically, price ceilings have been imposed, in various countries, in respect, for example, of staple foods, fuels and rental accommodation, when it has been considered that the price in an uncontrolled market would be too high for the poor to consume adequately.

In Figure 8.9 P^e is the equilibrium market price and Q^e the corresponding quantity. In the interests of the poor, the government passes a law which says that the price charged by a seller cannot exceed P^c, the price ceiling. Given that P^e is greater than P^c, P^c will be the ruling price. At that price, the amount that buyers want to buy is Q^D, while the amount that sellers want to sell is Q^S, and there is excess demand in amount $Q^D - Q^S$. Note that for a given difference between P^e and P^c, the amount of excess demand created by the price ceiling depends on the elasticities of supply and demand. Given the price ceiling, price cannot, legally, rise to eliminate the excess demand by increasing the amount supplied and reducing the amount demanded. Given that demand exceeds supply on a permanent basis, some way must be found to allocate what is produced as between those who want to consume it. Usually this takes the form of a rationing system, such that in order to, legally, acquire units of the commodity it is necessary to hand over to a supplier not just money but also government-issued ration coupons. Usually, the coupons are issued so that each person gets an equal amount. The main problem with this is that, given that some people are willing and able to pay more than the ceiling price, there is an incentive for sellers to cheat and sell to such people amounts in excess of their ration entitlements. Also, some people will sell some of their ration coupons. In these ways, a 'black market' develops, which works against the objective of the price ceiling – ensuring that the poor get enough of the commodity – and increases criminal behaviour.

Economists are strongly opposed to price ceilings except as short-term solutions to exceptional short-term problems. The imposition of a price ceiling with rationing does nothing to encourage producers and sellers to look for, legal, ways, in the long

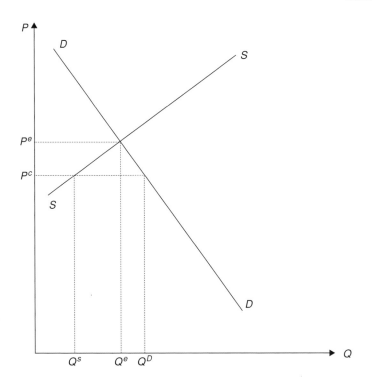

Figure 8.9 Price ceiling.

run, of shifting the supply function outwards. There are, economists argue, other ways of addressing the problem. One possibility would be to subsidise the production of the commodity in question, though this too entails some problems, notably the need for the government to raise, by taxation, the money to pay the subsidies. More fundamentally, economists argue, the solution is to address the problem of poverty rather than to intervene in the markets for particular commodities, raising the incomes of the poor so that they can afford to buy enough at the equilibrium market price.

8.3.2 Price floors

A price floor is where the government sets the price below which the commodity cannot, legally, be sold. Figure 8.10 shows what is involved. As before, P^e is the equilibrium price at which the amount that buyers want to buy is equal to the amount that sellers want to sell, Q^e. If the government sets the price floor at P^F, Q^D is demand, Q^S is supply, and there is excess supply $Q^S - Q^D$. In many industrial economies, average incomes in agriculture tend to be lower than those in the manufacturing and service sectors and governments have used price floors for agricultural products to raise farm incomes. This has given rise to major problems. As Figure 8.10 shows, at P^F more is produced than buyers will take off the market. In order to prevent the excess supply driving down the price below the floor, it has somehow to be absorbed. This is done by having the government buy and store the quantity $Q^S - Q^D$. Storing agricultural products can be expensive, and in

Figure 8.10
Price floor.

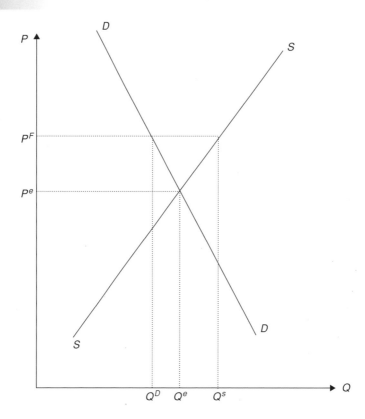

some cases the excess supply is simply collected and destroyed, as a less expensive alternative. Another problem is that the benefit to individual farmers is directly related to the amount that they produce – for every potato sold every farmer gets P^F instead of P^e. So in addition to causing over-production, the price-floor system for helping farmers rewards owners of larger farms more than owners of small farms, though the former are generally better off than the latter, and are frequently very well-off. The system also creates incentives to increasing farm sizes, which implies fewer farmers and what many consider less attractive countryside.

There are alternative ways of addressing the problem of low agricultural incomes. One is simply to make grants to those farmers whose incomes are judged too low, sufficient to bring them up to an acceptable level. The important point is not to link the amount of grant to the amount produced, irrespective of the income of the recipient, which is what the price-floor system does. Box 8.1 considers some aspects of the recent history of policy to address the problem of low farm incomes in what is now the European Union.

Another example of a price floor is minimum wage legislation intended to raise the incomes of those in low-paid jobs. For many purposes, economists look at human labour in paid employment as a commodity traded in labour markets. In such markets the demand function relates to how much employers want to buy, the supply function to how much workers want to sell. Remember that these functions relate to what happens to demand and supply as price, in this case the wage–salary

Box 8.1   Agricultural support policy in the EU

The European Union (the EU), started life as the European Economic Community, the EEC, which was brought into being in 1957 by the Treaty of Rome. The EEC's Common Agricultural Policy, the CAP, was introduced in 1962. The stated objectives of the CAP were to:
(1)   increase agricultural productivity;
(2)   ensure a fair standard of living for agricultural producers;
(3)   stabilise agricultural markets;
(4)   ensure secure supplies of foodstuffs;
(5)   make food available to consumers at reasonable prices.
From the outset, the principal means by which these objectives were pursued was a system of price support for agricultural commodities. The support price for a commodity, P^F in Figure 8.10, was generally set well above the world price, P^e in Figure 8.10. The same support price applied in all member states. Intervention agencies in each member country bought surplus domestic production at the support price, and levied taxation on imports so that their price in the domestic market was at least as great as the support price. These agencies also paid refunds – subsidies – to exporters so that they could sell in overseas markets at the world price.

During the 1960s and 1970s agricultural production and average farm incomes increased in all the member states, which collectively became self-sufficient or net exporters for almost all temperate zone agricultural commodities. For most such commodities, member state demand grew much less rapidly than domestic output. The CAP delivered on its first four objectives. In regard to the fifth, it depends what 'reasonable' means. European consumers were paying well above world prices, but for most, the share of their income spent on food was falling.

Higher food prices were not the only cost of the CAP. Consumers in member states also had to pay the taxation to finance the buying and storing of excess production, the payment of export subsidies, and the non-price support assistance given to agriculture under the CAP. By the early 1980s these costs amounted to over 60 per cent of the total EEC budget. By guaranteeing farmers a good price for whatever they produced, the CAP encouraged more intensive farm practices and larger farms – damage to the natural environment in Europe was another cost of the CAP. Finally, subsidised EEC food exports reduced the amount that other countries could export, even if they were lower-cost producers than EEC countries. Many of the countries thus hurt were, and are, developing countries so that the world's poor bear some of the costs of the CAP. It should be noted that some other developed economies – notably the USA – subsidise agricultural exports.

Beginning in 1984, attempts have been made to reform the CAP. The first steps involved trying to reduce over-production by introducing output quotas for some commodities and paying farmers compensation for not producing. Some support price levels were also reduced towards market-clearing levels, and the affected farmers given direct income support payments unrelated to their production levels. In the cause of environmental protection, and output reduction, set-aside payments have been introduced, whereby farmers are given grants to take environmentally important land out of production. Measures have been introduced to encourage environmentally friendly agricultural practices.

As a result of a series of such reforms in the 1980s and 1990s, the importance of the price support part of the CAP was reduced. In 2000, of a total CAP budget of about €40 billion, about €11 billion went on price support, €26 billion on direct payments to farmers, and the rest on schemes to promote non-agricultural development in rural areas and protect the environment. In June 2003 the Agriculture Ministers of the member states of the EU agreed a package of reform measures intended, over the next few years, to (largely) decouple the level of payments to farmers from their current levels of production. This abandonment of price floors as the means of agricultural support in the EU is intended to reduce over-production in the EU, thus doing environmental good there and reducing competition with producers in developing countries. Farmers will continue to receive income support via the CAP. On exactly what basis they will be paid is to be left to individual member states to decide. It is intended that payment will be conditional on good practice in regard to environmental protection and animal welfare.

rate, varies when all else relevant to demand and supply is constant. Given that vital caveat, it is plausible that employers will want more hours worked as they get cheaper. Neoclassical economists arrive at the conclusion that workers will want to work more as the pay per unit time or effort goes up by assuming that people work only to get the money to consume, that people get no satisfaction from paid work other than indirectly via the pay. This is an assumption that is consistent neither with thinking about one's own motivations, nor with the evidence that has been assembled about where and how people derive satisfaction and well-being, which was discussed in Chapter 6. It needs to be noted, however, that the satisfactions that people get from working are likely to be less in low-paid jobs than in well-paid jobs – status and working conditions tend to be correlated with pay.

Given the assumption that work is all pain, Figure 8.10 is drawn for the market for low-skill, low-pay employment, and on this basis many economists argue that the effect of minimum wage legislation would be to create unemployment at the bottom end of the labour market. In this case the vertical axis refers to the hourly wage rate and the horizontal to hours of work. As compared with the market equilibrium, the legislation increases the number looking for work so that they would want to work Q^S hours, but reduces the amount of work that employers want done to Q^D hours. In fact there is little evidence that minimum wage legislation has this effect, provided that the difference between P^e and P^F is not too large. One factor involved is that SS is likely to be steep, to have a low elasticity of supply on account of non-wage influences, so that the minimum wage does not induce a large increase in the supply of labour. Also, given that all employers of low-paid workers are affected, employers will be able to increase their selling prices to cover the extra costs without any loss of sales. In effect this makes DD steep, inelastic, so that the reduction in labour demand is small.

8.3.3 Commodity taxation

Governments need revenue to finance their activities. A popular way of raising revenue is the taxation of some of the goods and services traded in markets. Supply and demand analysis can explain why some commodities are more often the subject of such taxation than others, and what determines who suffers most, buyers or sellers, from such taxation.

Figures 8.11(a) and (b) show the demand and supply functions for two commodities. In order to bring out demand side considerations clearly the supply functions in the Figures 8.11(a) and (b) are exactly the same. The elasticity of demand is greater in Figure 8.11(a). In both markets we are looking at the imposition of the same rate of tax, indicated by T. The government requires sellers of these commodities to pay it an amount of money T for every unit that they sell. SS is the supply function prior to the imposition of the tax, which makes it shift upwards, with the same slope, by the distance T to become $S_T S_T$. To understand why the tax has this effect, recall that the supply function shows how the quantity offered for sale varies with price. SS shows this relationship in terms of the price that sellers receive after passing the tax to the government. $S_T S_T$ shows it in terms of the price that sellers charge buyers, the price that buyers actually pay. The government gets T on every unit sold, so that its total tax revenue is T times the quantity sold with the tax in place.

Consider Figure 8.11(a). Without the tax an amount Q_0^e is sold at price P^e, which is the price that buyers pay and sellers receive. As the result of the introduction of the tax, the quantity sold drops to Q_T^e. Buyers pay a price of P_T^B. Sellers take P_T^B per unit from buyers but pass T per unit to the government, so the price they actually receive is P_T^S. The price paid by buyers has gone up, the price received by sellers has gone down. Of the tax rate T, an amount $P_T^B - P^e$ shows up as a higher price paid by buyers, and an amount $P^e - P_T^S$ shows up as a lower price received by sellers. In this case the effect of the tax on sellers' price is greater than the effect on the price that buyers pay, and the tax is borne mainly by sellers. The incidence of the tax is, that is, mainly on sellers.

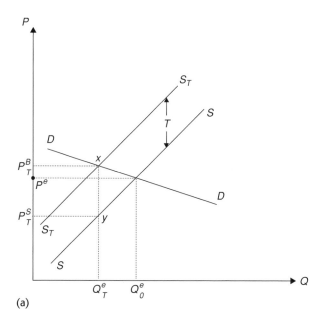

Figure 8.11
Commodity
taxation.

(a)

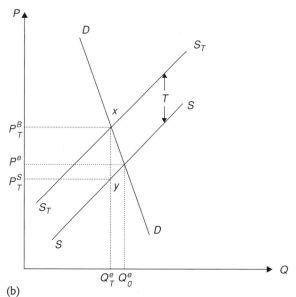

(b)

Now consider Figure 8.11(b) where supply conditions are the same and the tax rate is the same, but demand is less elastic and the demand function has a steeper slope. As compared with the situation in Figure 8.11(a), in Figure 8.11(b) we have:

- a bigger change in the market price due to the tax – $P_T^B - P^e$ is bigger;
- a smaller change in the quantity bought and sold – $Q_0^e - Q_T^e$ is smaller;
- more of the tax is borne by the buyers – for the same T, $P_T^B - P^e$ is bigger and $P^e - P_T^S$ is smaller.

These results hold generally, so that the more elastic is demand:

- the smaller the increase in the market price;
- the larger the reduction in the quantity traded;
- the less of the tax is borne by buyers.

You can see that as demand gets more and more elastic and DD gets near to being a horizontal line, so the price change would tend to zero and the tax would tend to fall entirely on sellers. At the other extreme, if demand had zero elasticity – a vertical DD – there would be no change in quantity and the tax would fall entirely on buyers.

The elasticity of demand also affects the total revenue that the tax raises. This is the tax rate, T, multiplied by the quantity sold after the imposition of the tax, Q_T^e. Given that the tax rate is the same in both Figure 8.11(a) and Figure 8.11(b), while Q_T^e is bigger in Figure 8.11(b), the total revenue from the tax is also larger. The rectangle with corner P_T^B, x, y and P_T^S is bigger in Figure 8.11(b) than in Figure 8.11(a). Again, this illustrates a general result – the more elastic is demand, the smaller the total revenue raised by a given rate of tax.

It is this last result that explains why across many jurisdictions one finds the same commodities taxed. Cigarettes, alcohol and private motor vehicle fuels are major examples of such commodities. They are frequently taxed because they have relatively low price elasticities, and so the total revenues arising are large, while the level of consumption is little affected. In the case of cigarettes and alcohol, governments often argue that these things are taxed to discourage consumption, because they are bad for health. Governments actually have conflicting interests in such cases. To the extent that the taxes serve this stated purpose, reducing consumption, they are less effective in raising revenue. Historically, the taxation of private motor vehicle fuels was not justified on the grounds that it was good for people. However, given that private motor vehicle use is now recognised as a major source of urban air pollution and of carbon dioxide emissions, which contribute to global climate change (see Chapter 13), such taxation is increasingly defended on health and environmental grounds by governments.

The use of taxes for environmental protection will be discussed is some detail in Chapter 11. Here we note two important points. First, by taxing environmentally damaging commodities, government can both reduce environmental damage and raise revenue. That revenue can be used to reduce other taxes or to finance additional government expenditure. Second, when government does this, there is a trade-off. The more effective the tax is in reducing environmental damage, the less revenue it raises.

We have considered commodity taxation in terms of variations in the elasticity of demand. From Figure 8.11 it should be clear that the effects of imposing a tax will also vary with the elasticity of supply – you can imagine the rotation of SS and $S_T S_T$ in Figure 8.11(a) or (b), or actually draw two market diagrams where the demand function is the same but the supply functions have different slopes. If you do, you will find that as supply gets more elastic, so, for given demand conditions and tax rate, the quantity change gets bigger and the market supply change smaller, while the incidence of the tax falls more on sellers. For given demand conditions and a given tax rate, commodities where supply elasticity is greater raise less total revenue.

8.4 LENDING AND BORROWING, SAVING AND INVESTING

In this section we want to explain how financial markets work, and why their operation is important to the way the economy as a whole works. Basically, their operation is important because it is where the economy's levels of saving and invest-ment are determined. As we saw in Chapter 7, investment, capital accumulation, is important in relation to economic growth and the question of whether it can continue in a closed environment. In subsequent chapters we will be considering further the importance of saving and investment in relation to sustainability and sustainable development. Here we are going to explain how the levels of saving and investment for a market economy are determined in its financial markets.

In a modern economy there are very many, interconnected, financial markets, and many different kinds of firms, financial institutions, operating in them. In what follows, we abstract greatly from the complexity of reality and explain the basic issues in simple terms. We will consider an economy where there are just indi-viduals and firms in the business of producing goods and services, and where there is just one kind of financial market, the bond market. We shall assume that the firms borrow to invest, and that individuals lend to save. The investment behaviour of firms and the savings behaviour of individuals are brought together in the bond market. Before looking at it, we need to explain compounding and discounting, what bonds are, and how profit-maximising firms should decide on how much investment to undertake.

8.4.1 Compounding and discounting

The processes of compounding and discounting are fundamental to lending and borrowing and to the operation of all financial markets.

Compounding is one manifestation of exponential growth, which was intro-duced back in Chapter 2, and was shown graphically in Figure 2.8. When the interest is re-lent, money lent at interest compounds, i.e. grows exponentially. A sum of money N_0 left to compound at an annual interest rate of r for t years will accumulate to

$$N_t = (1 + r)^t \times N_0$$

It is standard in economics to use r for the interest rate. For reasons which will become clear shortly, let us also use V_t instead of N_t, and PV instead of N_0, and write this as

$$V_t = PV \times (1 + r)^t$$

V_t stands for value after t years, and PV is the initial sum, or the principal. Thus, if the interest rate is 0.05 (5 per cent) after 1 year a principal of $1 will have grown to $1.05 = 1 \times 1.05$. If principal and interest are re-lent, i.e. left to compound, after two years the amount to be paid back would be $1.1025 = (1 \times 1.05) \times 1.05 = 1 \times 1.05^2$. After three years the amount to be paid back would be $1.157625 = 1.05^2 \times 1.05 = 1.05^3$. And so on and so on. As noted in Chapter 2, doing the arithmetic here is very easy on a decent calculator, or using a spreadsheet such as Excel.

What would a, completely reliable, promise to pay $(1 + r)$ a year hence be worth now? Call such a promise a **bond** – a document that says that on presentation at the appropriate place, the legal owner can exchange it for a certain sum of money on a certain date. Then, the question above is: what is the value today of a bond with value $\$(1 + r)$ a year from now? Given that $\$1$ lent today at r will be worth $\$(1 + r)$ a year from now, the answer to this question is clearly $\$1$. If the bond could be bought for less than $\$1$, everybody would want to buy it. If more than $\$1$ was asked for it, nobody would want to buy it. At a price of $\$1$, people would be indifferent between buying this bond and lending out $\$1$ at the ruling rate of interest r.

Discounting is compounding in reverse. At interest rate r, the value today of a certain receipt of $\$(1 + r)$ a year from today is just $\$1$. The discount rate is the rate that converts the future value to its current value, known as its **present value**. As the bond example above shows, with an interest rate of r, the discount rate is $1/(1 + r)$. Just as compounding can be extended over many years, so can this idea of discounting. What would be the value of a bond that promised to pay $\$V$ t years from now? The amount of money that would have to be invested now at the ruling interest rate to realise $\$V$ t years from now. From

$$V_t = PV \times (1 + r)^t$$

rearranging tells us that that is

$$PV = V_t/(1 + r)^t$$

We initially used PV, which stands for 'present value', to represent the principal in a lending operation to make it clear that discounting is compounding in reverse.

Suppose that the interest rate is 0.05. What is the present value of $\$100$ five years from now? From the equation for PV it is

$$100/1.05^5 = 100/1.2763 = 78.35$$

If $\$78.35$ were lent out now and left to compound for 5 years at 0.05 per annum, what would it then be worth? According to the equation for V_t the answer is

$$78.35 \times 1.05^5 = 78.35 \times 1.2763 = \$100.$$

The present value of a sum of money in the future is its current equivalent, where equivalence is in the sense that, given the existence of facilities for lending and borrowing, an individual would currently be indifferent between the certain promise of the future sum and the offer of the present value now.

An obvious next question is: what determines the interest rate? Before answering that question, we need to look at saving and lending by individuals, and at investing and borrowing by firms.

8.4.2 Saving and lending

Saving means spending less than one's income on current consumption. One reason for doing this is so as to be able to spend more than one's income in the future, by running down a stock of accumulated savings, one's wealth, in the future. Individuals save during their working life, so as to able to consume when their earnings go to zero on retirement. For some individuals, such saving is involuntary and in the form of contributions to some kind of compulsory, state- or employer-run, pension scheme. Some individuals save more than they intend to consume in retirement so as to leave some wealth to their heirs. Some individuals dis-save, spending more on consumption than their current income, thus running down their wealth, or, once wealth has gone to zero, running up debts. Saving is effected by lending, dis-saving by borrowing. In saying that saving is lending, we are assuming that people do not keep cash under the mattress, and that there are no banks. We return to the matter of money as a possible vehicle for saving in section 8.4.4.2. To keep things simple we are now assuming that the only financial assets are bonds. Lending means buying bonds, borrowing means selling bonds.

It helps to keep things simple to also assume that the only kind of bonds in existence are one-year bonds, such as were considered above when explaining discounting. As noted above, a bond is a promise to pay a certain sum of money at a future date. The sum of money is written on the document that is the bond, and is called the 'coupon'. We will assume that all bond trading is done on the first day of the current year, with the coupons payable on the first day of next year. We will also assume that all bonds have the same coupon, $€x$. On the first day of this year, those wishing to borrow offer their bonds for sale in the bond market, where the buyers are lenders. From the latter's point of view, it works as follows. I pay a price for each bond that I buy now, and at the start of next year I present my bonds to the person whose name appears under the promise, who then gives me $€x$ for each bond returned.

The demand for bonds originates with would-be lenders. Figure 8.12(a) shows the demand function, $D_B D_B$, for these bonds. It slopes downwards in the usual way, and in the usual way it assumes that the only thing that is varying is P_B. For a given coupon, $€x$, fewer people will want to buy bonds the higher their price, P_B. The rate of interest is given by the relationship between the coupon and P_B with

$$r = \frac{x - P_B}{P_B} = \frac{x}{P_B} - 1$$

Suppose, for example, that $€x$ is $€1.10$. Then, for P_B at $€1$ the interest rate earned by buying a bond is

$$r = \frac{1.10 - 1}{1} = 0.10$$

whereas for P_B at $€1.05$ it is

$$r = \frac{1.10 - 1.05}{1.05} = 0.048$$

Given the fixed coupon, as the price of the bonds goes up, so the interest rate goes down. In Figure 8.12(b) LL (L for lending) is the relationship between the demand for bonds, that is the amount of lending, and the interest rate. The amount of lending, and hence saving, that individuals want to do increases with the interest rate. This makes sense. Lenders are reducing their consumption now below their current income in return for the possibility of consumption in excess of their income one year from now. They give up P_B now to get $€x$ one year from now. The interest rate is the proportional difference between $€x$ and P_B, the reward for deferring consumption by one year. What Figure 8.12(b) shows is that as this reward increases

Figure 8.12
Lending and
saving.

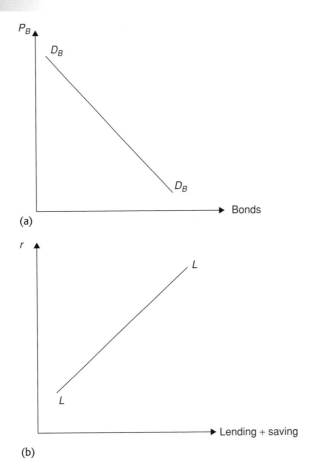

(a)

(b)

so does the amount of deferred consumption that individuals will want to go in
for, the amount that they will wish to lend and save.

As noted, some individuals are borrowers. They become issuers of bonds. The
logic works in reverse for such individuals. For them, r is the penalty that they
pay for consuming now rather than one year from now. It makes sense that they
will borrow less/more as the interest rate rises/falls, other things remaining the
same. When we use $D_B D_B$ later in the analysis of the market for bonds, we will
interpret it as referring to the overall net position of individuals, showing, that is,
the demand for bonds less the supply of bonds by individuals varying with the price
of bonds. Similarly, $L L$ will refer to net lending by individuals taken all together –
their total lending minus their total borrowing.

8.4.3 Investing and borrowing

Firms invest when they spend now to secure a future stream of receipts. Since
firms pay out all of their receipts to their owners, they have to borrow to invest.
At any point in time there will be a number of investment opportunities open to
any given firm, each involving adding to its stock of capital in different ways. The

standard examples concern buying new machines and equipment. The firm has to decide which investment projects to undertake, and which not to undertake. The decision-making process here is often referred to as **project appraisal**.

The basic problem that project appraisal has to deal with is that different projects involve different time profiles for the delayed receipts to be achieved by spending now. Given different time profiles, the simple addition of expenditures and receipts over project lifetimes, to see which gives the largest surplus, will not do. Consider the two projects, A and B, for which the time profiles of expenditures, receipts and net cashflow are shown in Tables 8.6 and 8.7. Both, we can suppose, involve buying, installing and operating some machine. Both projects involve the expenditure of £100 now, the first day of the first year

Table 8.6　Project A			
Year	Expenditure	Receipts	Net cashflow
0	100	0	−100
1	10	50	40
2	10	50	40
3	10	45.005	35.005
4	0	0	0

Table 8.7　Project B			
Year	Expenditure	Receipts	Net cashflow
0	100	0	−100
1	0	0	0
2	0	0	0
...	...	...	...
...	...	...	...
48	0	0	0
49	0	115.005	115.005
50	0	0	0

of the project lifetime, to acquire the machine. This capital cost is shown as Year 0 expenditure in Tables 8.6 and 8.7, which also show expenditure on running costs (labour, energy and raw materials) and receipts from sales in the following years. It is assumed that all payments are made on the first day of each year. Against Year 1, for example, are shown outgoings and incomings one year from now, against Year 2 two years from now, and so on. In each year the Net cashflow is just Receipts minus Expenditure. The numbers in these tables were made up so as to be convenient, as will become clear shortly. Each project has a lifetime given by the date at which Expenditures, and hence Receipts, go to zero.

If we sum the Net cashflow over time for these two projects, we find that both have a cumulative Net cashflow of £15.005. However, whereas for *A* it takes four years to realise this surplus, for *B* it takes 50 years and for most of its lifetime Net cashflow is zero. Clearly, no firm's management would regard these two projects as equally good ways of spending £100 now. A proper comparison of the two projects requires some method that takes account of the time profile of the Net cashflow, as well as its cumulative total. For firms where the management objective is the maximisation of the firm's net worth, such a method is the Net present value, or NPV, test. We first show how that test is done, and then explain how it serves the objective of maximising net worth.

8.4.3.1 *The Net Present Value test*

The Net present value, **NPV**, of an investment is the discounted present value of the Net cashflow associated with it. If an investment has a positive NPV, then it should be undertaken. If it has a negative NPV, then it should not be. If the NPV is 0, then it is a matter of indifference whether the project is undertaken or not.

Table 8.8 The general project

Year	Expenditure	Receipts	Net cashflow
0	E_0	R_0	N_0
1	E_1	R_1	N_1
2	E_2	R_2	N_2
...	...	...	...
	E_t	R_t	N_t
...	...	...	...
T−2	E_{T-2}	R_{T-2}	N_{T-2}
T−1	E_{T-1}	R_{T-1}	N_{T-1}
T	E_T	R_T	N_T

The decision rule is, that is, go ahead with the project if NPV > 0, do not if NPV < 0. Following this rule will lead to going ahead only with projects that increase net worth, NPV > 0, or leave it unchanged, NPV = 0.

To see how the NPV test is done, denote expenditure in year t as E_t, and receipts as R_t so that any project can, with T for the project's lifetime and $N_t = R_t - E_t$ for the net cashflow, be represented as in Table 8.8. Then, the present value of Expenditures is

$$PV_E = E_0 + \frac{E_1}{(1+r)} + \frac{E_2}{(1+r)^2} + \cdots + \frac{E_T}{(1+r)^T} = \sum_0^T \frac{E_t}{(1+r)^t}$$

and the present value of Receipts is

$$PV_R = R_0 + \frac{R_1}{(1+r)} + \frac{R_2}{(1+r)^2} + \cdots + \frac{R_T}{(1+r)^T} = \sum_0^T \frac{R_t}{(1+r)^t}$$

and the project's Net present value is given by

$$NPV = PV_R - PV_E = \sum_0^T \frac{R_t}{(1+r)^t} - \sum_0^T \frac{E_t}{(1+r)^t}$$

which is equivalent to

$$NPV = N_0 + \frac{N_1}{(1+r)} + \frac{N_2}{(1+r)^2} + \cdots + \frac{N_T}{(1+r)^T} = \sum_0^T \frac{N_t}{(1+r)^t}$$

Here, $\sum$ (from the Greek alphabet, said as sigma) is standard notation which indicates the addition of the things which immediately follow, and the 0 below $\sum$ and the T above it show that N_t divided by $(1+r)^t$ are to be added for t from 0 to T inclusive.

Applying either version of this formula to the data for Project A from Table 8.6, for $r = 0.05$ (an interest rate of 5 per cent) gives its NPV as £4.61, to two decimal places. According to the NPV test, Project A should be undertaken. The calculations, using the figures for Net Cashflow, are shown in Table 8.9. You can easily check that you get the same answer by finding the present values for the flow of Expenditure and of Receipts, and subtracting the former from the latter. Table 8.7 related to Project B which involved £100 expenditure now for a one-off net receipt of £115.005 in year 49. For this project, with $r = 0.05$:

$$NPV = \left(\frac{115.005}{1.05^{49}}\right) - 100 = \left(\frac{115.005}{10.9213}\right) - 100$$
$$= 10.5303 - 100 = -89.4697 = -£89.47$$

Whereas Project A passes the NPV test for $r = 0.05$, Project B has a negative NPV and fails it.

Table 8.9 Calculating Project A's NPV

Year	Expenditure	Receipts	Net cashflow	Discount factor $\dfrac{1}{(1+r)^t}$	Present value of net cashflow
0	100	0	−100	1	−100 × 1 = −100
1	10	50	40	$1/1.05 = 0.9524$	40 × 0.9524 = 38.0960
2	10	50	40	$1/1.05^2 = 0.9070$	40 × 0.9070 = 36.2800
3	10	45.005	35.005	$1/1.05^3 = 0.8638$	35.005 × 0.8638 = 30.2373
4	0	0	0	$1/1.05^4 = 0.8227$	0 × 0.8227 = 0
					Sum = 4.6133

If you repeat the calculations of Table 8.9 for $r = 0.075$ and 0.10, you will find that the NPVs are £0 and −£4.28 respectively. At 5 per cent A passes, at 7.5 per cent it is on the margin, and at 10 per cent it fails. It is obvious from the formulae for NPV given above that for a given set of Net cashflow data, the NPV will be lower the higher the interest rate. These calculations confirm that. Put another way, what they confirm is that for any particular project whether or not it passes the NPV test depends on the interest rate, and that a project that passes at one rate may fail at a higher rate, and vice versa. The numbers for Project A were made up so that for the middle interest rate here, the NPV for Project A came out as zero. The reason for doing this will become clear in the next section.

For projects with Net cashflows that go on for more than a few years, calculating the NPV by, as in Table 8.9, working out and applying the discount factor for each year is time-consuming and prone to error. Time can be saved and errors reduced by using a spreadsheet such as Excel^{TM}, which includes the worksheet function NPV, as well as many closely related financial worksheet functions involving compounding and discounting. In using Excel^{TM}'s financial worksheet functions it is necessary to be clear about the timings of payments and receipts, as explained in the Excel^{TM} Help notes.

8.4.3.2 Net worth maximisation

Now we want to use Project A to show how the NPV test selects projects that increase the firm's net worth. To do this, we will assume that the firm finances the project by issuing one-year bonds. The same logic applies if longer-dated bonds are used, but looking at one-year bonds makes things clearer. A firm's **net worth** is the present value of its future profit stream, the sum of present values of profits in future years.

Take the 5 per cent case first. In order to acquire the machine, the firm must on day one of year 0 sell its bonds to the value of £100. Given $r = 0.05$, it thus incurs the liability to redeem the bonds for £105 on day one of year 1. At that time, it will have a Net cashflow from using the machine of £40, a shortfall of £65. It covers this shortfall by issuing new bonds in the amount of £65, which generates a liability of £68.25 (65 × 1.05) for day one of year 2. At that time its receipts in respect of using the machine are £40, so there is a shortfall of £28.25 as between the Net cashflow and expenditure on bond redemption. This can be covered by issuing further one-year bonds to the value of £28.25, incurring a liability of £29.6625 (28.25 × 1.05) for day one of year 3. On that day, Net cashflow will be £35.005, so that there will be a current surplus of 35.005 − 29.6625 = £5.3425 at the end of the project lifetime.

What is the present value of this surplus when considered at the time, day one of year 0, that a decision has to be made on the project? It is 5.3425 × $1/(1 + r)^3$ = 5.3425/1.1576 = £4.61, which is the answer that we got from NPV formula for this project with an interest rate of 5 per cent, see Table 8.9. The NPV is just the present value, at the time of making a decision about it, of the surplus that the project yields at the end of its lifetime, taking into account the costs of financing it. If this kind of surplus exists, it represents an increase in the net worth of the firm at the time that the decision is taken. It is the maximum extra amount that somebody would be willing to pay to buy the firm with the project as compared to without the project. This is because they could do as well by buying the firm without the project and lending £4.61 at 5 per cent for the project lifetime.   .

Working through the 7.5 per cent case in the same way:

t

0   sell £100 of bonds
1   redeem bonds for £107.5, sell £67.5 of new bonds (107.5−40)
2   redeem bonds for £72.5625, sell £32.5625 of new bonds (72.5625−40)
3   redeem bonds for £35.005, surplus of £0

In this case, we previously found NPV = 0 according to the formula. At this rate of interest, going ahead with the project leaves the net worth of the firm unchanged − the maximum that anybody would pay for the opportunity to undertake the project is zero.

Working through the 7.5 per cent case in the same way:

t

0   sell £100 of bonds
1   redeem bonds for £110, sell £70 of new bonds (110 − 40)
2   redeem bonds for £77, sell £37 of new bonds (77 − 40)
3   redeem bonds for £40.7, surplus of −£5.695 (35.005 − 40.7)

In this case, we previously got the answer NPV = −£4.28. This is the present value at 10 per cent of −£5.695 three years hence; £4.28 is what would have to be invested at 10 per cent to meet the £5.695 liability that would arise if the firm went ahead with this project when the interest rate was 10 per cent. It is the reduction in the firm's net worth − the minimum that it would necessary to pay somebody to buy the firm with the project rather than without it.

So, undertaking those projects for which the NPV is positive will increase the firm's net worth, while undertaking those for which it is negative will reduce it. It follows that, in order to maximise its net worth, a firm should undertake all those projects that have non-negative NPVs. A firm that wants to maximise its net worth should list all the projects that it could undertake and their NPVs. It should then arrange the list by descending order of NPV, and draw a line under the project for which NPV = 0. It should go ahead with all the projects above the line. The project for which NPV = 0 is the marginal project at the current rate of interest. It follows from the above discussion that as the interest rate varies so the list of projects

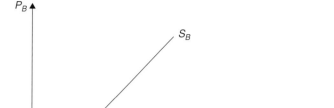

Figure 8.13
Borrowing and
investing.

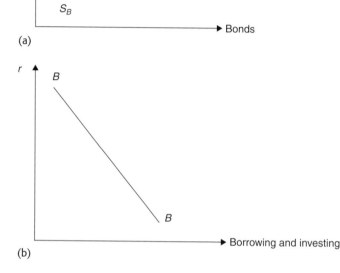

above the line will get shorter or longer – shorter if r goes up, longer if it goes down.

Finally here we can note that the NPV test would be equally appropriate if the firm was thinking in terms of financing any project from its own cash reserves. The firm could, instead of using its cash to finance the project, lend it at interest. You should be able to modify the discussion above to see that for a project with a positive NPV the firm would do better for its net worth by putting cash into the project rather than lending it at interest for the life of the project, whereas if the NPV is negative it would do better to lend at interest.

8.4.3.3 *The supply function for bonds*

Figure 8.13(a) shows the supply function for bonds that arises when firms seek to maximise net worth by using the NPV test to appraise investment projects. Figure 8.13(b) shows the relationship between the amount of borrowing and investing that firms do and the interest rate. Look at Figure 8.13(b) first. We noted above that for any firm using the NPV test, the total amount that it wants to invest will increase as the interest rate falls. This is true for all such firms. Rather than thinking about listing one firm's projects by descending NPV, we can think of listing all the projects for all of the firms in order of descending NPV. As r falls so the line for NPV equals zero will move down the list, and the amount that firms want to borrow will increase. As they borrow by issuing bonds, this means that the amount of bonds that they want to sell increases with reductions in r.

Figure 8.13(a) shows the supply of bonds against P_B. We have seen that the price of bonds and the interest rate move in opposite directions. It follows that if supply of bonds increases as r falls, it decreases as P_B falls, as shown in Figure 8.13(a). This looks like a standard supply function, and it is. Think of all bonds as one-year bonds all with the same coupon value. For a given amount to pay back in a year, firms will want to sell more bonds the higher the price that they can get for them now, the higher is P_B. For a given coupon, higher P_B means lower r.

8.4.3.4 The Internal Rate of Return to investment

An alternative test for project appraisal is the Internal Rate of Return, **IRR**, test, according to which a project should be undertaken if its internal rate of return is equal to or greater than the rate of interest. The internal rate of return for a project is the rate at which the Net cashflow must be discounted to produce an NPV equal to 0.

Recall that NPV is given by the formula

$$\text{NPV} = N_0 + \frac{N_1}{(1+r)} + \frac{N_2}{(1+r)^2} + \cdots + \frac{N_T}{(1+r)^T} = \sum_{0}^{T} \frac{N_t}{(1+r)^t}$$

Let us use the symbol i for a project's IRR. Then, we find i as the solution to

$$0 = N_0 + \frac{N_1}{(1+i)} + \frac{N_2}{(1+i)^2} + \cdots + \frac{N_T}{(1+i)^T} = \sum_{0}^{T} \frac{N_t}{(1+i)^t}$$

In other words, the IRR for a project is the rate of interest which if used to compute its NPV would give the result 0. For the project of Table 8.6, we know that the IRR is 0.075 because we found NPV equal to 0 when we calculated it for an interest rate of 7.5 per cent. At that interest rate it made no difference to net worth whether the firm undertook the project or not. In this case, the IRR test also says that it is a matter of indifference whether the project goes ahead or not.

For an interest rate of 5 per cent, we found that the NPV test said that the project should go ahead. The IRR test gives the same answer, as in this case $i > r$. For an interest rate of 10 per cent, we found that the NPV test said that the project should not go ahead. The IRR test again gives the same answer, as in this case $i < r$. In fact, the IRR test always gives the same answer as the NPV test. The reason for this is not hard to see. The IRR test works out what the rate of interest would have to be for the project to be marginal, to have no effect on the firm's net worth. If that rate is higher than the actual interest rate, then the firm can increase its net worth by borrowing and going ahead with the project. If that rate is lower than the actual interest rate, then by going ahead with the project the firm would reduce its net worth.

Just as all projects can be ranked by their NPV, so can they be ranked by their IRR. And in the same way as the NPV listing gives rise to borrowing and investing increasing as the interest rate falls, so does the IRR listing – as the interest rate falls, so more IRRs are larger than r.

The IRR for a project is actually harder to calculate than its NPV. Given that spreadsheet software will do the calculations for you – there is in Excel a worksheet function IRR – this is not a major concern. However, it is also true that for some time profiles for the Net cashflow, calculating a unique result for the IRR is impossible. There is never a problem about calculating the correct NPV, whatever the Net cashflow time profile. Hence, as a practical matter it makes sense to stick to the NPV test. Why then bother introducing the IRR test? Because, as we will see in the next chapter, it is the easiest way to understand the claim that markets can bring about desirable patterns of investment, the claim that financial markets will ensure that an economy's total investment is made up of the most productive projects available.

8.4.4 Savings, investment and the interest rate

We have seen in Figure 8.12 that the amount that savers want to lend increases with the interest rate and that they save by buying bonds, and we have seen in Figure 8.13 that the amount that firms want to borrow to invest decreases with the interest rate and that they borrow by selling bonds. This suggests that the interest rate and the equilibrium levels of lending and borrowing, and thus saving and investment, are determined in the bond market.

8.4.4.1 The bond market

Figure 8.14(a) shows equilibrium in the bond market. The story is just like that for any market. The price of bonds will settle at P_B^e, at which price supply and demand are equal and B^e of bonds are traded. Figure 8.14(b) shows the same equilibrium in terms of savings, investment and the interest rate. Remember that P_B and r move in opposite directions – a lower price for bonds means a higher interest rate, and vice versa. The II function reflects the $S_B S_B$ function in Figure 8.14(a), and the SS function reflects the $D_B D_B$ function there. At the equilibrium interest rate r^e that goes with P_B^e, savings and investment are equal to each other, $S^e = I^e$, and to the equilibrium quantity of bonds traded, B^e in Figure 8.14(a). According to Figure 8.14, the amount of saving and investing done in an economy is determined, along with the interest rate, by the positions of the II and SS functions, which reflect the positions of the $D_B D_B$ and $S_B S_B$ functions. Saving, investment and interest rate are determined, that is, by savings behaviour of individuals and the investment opportunities open to firms. You should confirm for yourself that it follows from Figure 8.14 that:

- an economy where individuals save more at any given rate of interest will, other things being equal, have more investment and a lower interest rate than one where they save less at every rate of interest
- an economy where firms have more opportunities for profitable investment, so that investment is higher at any given interest rate, will, other things being equal, have more saving and a higher interest rate than one where there are fewer opportunities for profitable investment

Figure 8.14
Bond market
equilibrium.

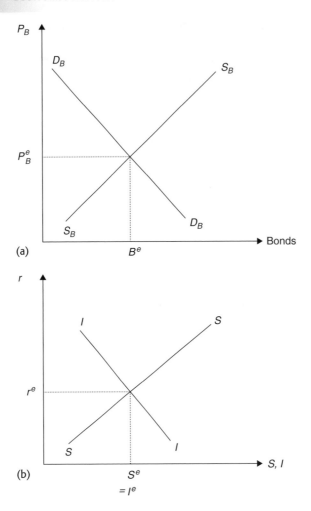

(a)

(b)

●   comparing an economy with a high propensity to save and lots of profitable
     investment opportunities with one with a lower propensity to save and less
     profitable investment opportunities, the former will do more saving and
     investing for the same interest rate.

As we noted at the beginning of this section, we saw in the previous chapter the crucial role of saving and investment in relation to economic growth, and in relation to
how growth is affected by resource availability. Broadly, investment is necessary for
growth and for reducing the drag on it caused by the depletion of non-renewable
resources. We can say that an economy with thrifty individuals where firms see
lots of opportunities for profitable investment will do relatively well in terms of
economic growth and meeting resource availability problems.

    We said at the beginning of this section that we were going to abstract greatly
from the complexities of the financial markets. Most of the complexity that we
have ignored has no impact on the story that we have told here. Considering, for
example, bonds with maturities greater than one year would have no major effect

on the conclusion that the interest rate is determined by savings and investment. Given that bonds with different maturities would have different prices there would be a spectrum of interest rates rather than just one, and the conclusion would be that the average level of interest rates is determined by savings and investment.

There is, however, one simplification in the story here that does matter, and we now need to consider it and its implications.

8.4.4.2 *Money and bonds*

We have assumed so far that bonds are the only financial asset. Ignoring most other financial assets – various kinds of shares, for example – does not make any real difference to the story about interest rate determination. Ignoring money as a financial asset does make a difference, and we now need to correct our account of interest rate determination. In so doing we answer a question that has likely been troubling you – how does the story about saving and investing fixing the interest rate square with the fact that I often read in the newspaper that the Bank of England – or the Federal Reserve Bank in the US, or the European Central Bank for the European Monetary Union – raised/lowered the interest rate yesterday? All of these are what are known as central banks, institutions which control the amount of money in existence. Exactly how they do this varies from country to country, and will not concern us here. We do need to note that central banks usually exercise their control so as to stabilise the economy, and do so according to pursuing objectives set for them by the government. In the United Kingdom, for example, the Bank of England is required by the government to act so as to keep inflation below a specified level.

Money is a financial asset. Earlier in this chapter we noted three roles for money – medium of exchange, store of value, and unit of account. It is the first two roles that are relevant here. Money is useful because it facilitates exchange and can be used to defer exchange. We introduced bonds as a means of saving and shifting consumption over time. Clearly, money can serve the same purpose. If we assume away banks and the like to keep the story as simple as possible, money is cash and I can save cash rather than buy bonds in order to be able to spend more than my income at some future date – figuratively, I can save by keeping cash under the mattress.

A given amount of saving can be divided between money and bonds. Each has advantages and disadvantages as a savings vehicle. Bonds earn interest, but they mean that the spending power that they represent is unavailable until the bond matures. Money as cash, on the other hand, earns no interest but its spending power is instantly available at any time. The opportunity cost of holding money is the forgone interest. Other things equal, the amount of money that people will want to hold will vary inversely with the rate of interest. If the rate of interest goes up, the opportunity cost of holding money rather than bonds goes up, and people will want less money and more bonds. And vice versa.

With just two financial assets, people who want to transfer consumption over time must hold some of one or both of them. Total saving in the economy will be the sum of money and bonds. It is conventional to talk about the 'money market', though there is not an actual market in which money is traded. Leaving aside foreign currency, people do not exchange cash for cash. There is, however, a sense

Figure 8.15
Joint
equilibrium in
two financial
asset markets.

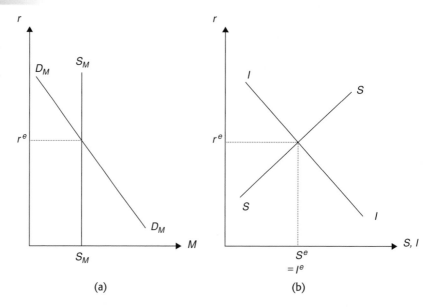

(a)   (b)

in which there is a demand for money, in that in order for people to want to hold more or less of it the interest rate must go down or up. The interest rate is the opportunity cost of holding money, and it can be thought of as the price of money. Figure 8.15(a) shows as $D_M D_M$ the relationship between the amount of money that people will want to hold and the rate of interest. $D_M D_M$ stands for 'demand for money', and this demand function has the usual property of sloping downwards – as r goes down, the amount of money that people want to hold goes up.

Now we get to the matter of the central bank. It controls the amount of money that exists. Figure 8.15(a) has a vertical line $S_M S_M$. This is the supply of money, the amount in existence. $S_M S_M$ is a supply function with zero elasticity – the supply of money does not vary at all with the price of money, r. In order for people to want to hold the amount of money that exists, the interest rate must move to r^e. Figure 8.15(a) does not describe a market as normally understood – there is no trade taking place in money. But, what goes on has a market-like outcome in that there is an equilibrium price at which supply is equal to the amount of money that people will willingly hold. Hence, Figure 8.15(a) is often referred to as depicting the money market. The caption to Figure 8.15 refers to 'two financial asset markets'.

The other market is the bond market, shown in Figure 8.15(b). It shows the bond market in equilibrium at the same interest rate as in Figure 8.15(a). The two equilibria must have the same price, interest rate, since they are linked by the fact that each reflects the same decision – to hold either money or bonds to transfer spending over time. The details of the linkage are the subject matter of the study of short-run fluctuations in the overall level of economic activity – recessions and booms, inflationary pressures and the like. Such short-run fluctuations are not very important in relation to sustainability and sustainable development and we will not go into details. Basically, the point is that savings and investment are not solely determined by the rate of interest. Particularly, they also depend on the level of economic activity, on GDP. If the money and bond markets are out of equilibrium,

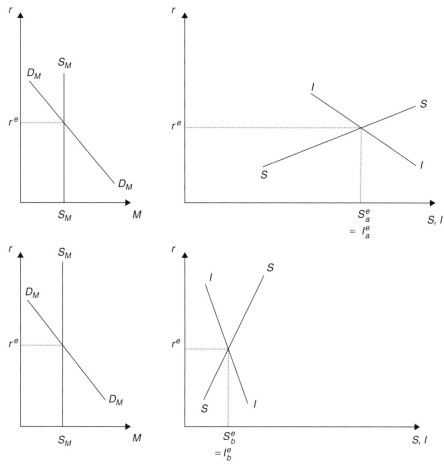

Figure 8.16
Joint equilibria
in two
economies.

then equilibrium in the bond market will be restored by movements of *SS* and/or *II* driven by changes in the level of GDP. And, from the perspective of central bank control, this is exactly the point. The central bank alters the money supply, so as to alter the interest rate – which effect is what it announces – so as to affect the level of economic activity. It cuts interest rates so as to stimulate the economy to avoid recession, and raises them so as restrict the economy and thus avoid inflation.

The important point for our purposes is that the interest rate is not determined by savings behaviour and investment opportunities. It is determined by the central bank, operating, usually, on behalf of the government in pursuit of short-run stabilisation objectives. Those objectives may point in a different direction to sustainable development objectives. We have seen, and will see again, that sustainable development requires, to put it loosely, lots of investment. Stabilisation objectives may work against that.

While the existence of money means that savings behaviour and investment opportunities do not determine the interest rate, it does not mean that they are irrelevant to the sustainability-promoting objective of having a high level of investment. Figure 8.16 shows what is involved. Figures 8.16(a) and (b) refer to two economies which have the same money demand functions and the same money supply. It follows that both have the same interest rate. In economy (a) people have a higher savings propensity than in (b) – save more at any rate of interest – and there are better investment opportunities than in (b) – more investment at any interest rate because of more high NPVs. As a result there is, for the same interest rate, more saving and more investment in economy (a). Given the importance of this to sustainable development, it would be nice if we could look at economies like (a) and (b) and come to firm conclusions about a simple list of the things that make an economy like (a) rather than like (b). It would then be possible to consider how an economy like (b) might become more like (a). This is very like the sort of questions that we ended up with when looking at the causes of economic growth – why do some countries save more and innovate more? As in that case, beyond broad generalisations about social and political conditions, there is no shortlist of obviously correct ways to promote high savings propensities and investment opportunities.

SUMMARY

In this chapter we have looked at the workings of a product of cultural evolution – the market – which greatly increases the possibilities for the realisation of the gains that can be had from exchange and specialisation in production. The market is a remarkable institution which has come to dominate the organisation of modern economies, and modern economies dominate the human world. Recent years have seen the virtual disappearance of the main modern alternative to the market mode of organisation, which was the command-and-control system practised, mainly, in the former Soviet Union and its satellites. In the next chapter we will look at the extent to which it can be claimed that market outcomes are socially desirable. From an ecological economics perspective there are two aspects of this that are particularly important – whether market systems look after the environment, and whether they look after the least well-off.

KEYWORDS

Absolute price (p. 266): the amount of money that exchanges for a unit of some good or service.

Autarky (p. 263): a state of self-sufficiency, in which there is no exchange or trade.

Barter (p. 267): the exchange of commodities for commodities.

Bond (p. 289): a document that, says that, on presentation at the appropriate place, the legal owner can exchange it for a certain sum of money (the coupon) on a certain date.

Complements (p. 274): commodities for which the cross-price elasticity of demand is negative.

Compounding (p. 289): when interest payable is added to the amount outstanding to earn more interest (is equivalent to exponential growth of the amount outstanding).

Cross-price elasticity of demand (p. 277): the ratio of the proportionate change in quantity demanded to the proportionate change in the price of some other commodity.

Demand function (p. 268): the relationship between the quantity that buyers wish to buy and price, given that other influences are held constant.

Discounting (p. 290): the opposite of compounding, the process by which a sum due at a future date is given a present value.

Elasticity of demand (p. 275): the ratio of the proportionate change in the quantity demanded to the proportionate change in the price of the commodity (own-price elasticity of demand).

Elasticity of supply (p. 278): the ratio of the proportionate change in the quantity offered for sale to the proportionate change in the commodity's price.

Excess demand (p. 273): where at the ruling price more is demanded than is offered for sale.

Excess supply (p. 273): where at the ruling price more is offered for sale than is demanded.

Income elasticity of demand (p. 277): the ratio of the proportionate change in the quantity demanded to the proportionate change in income.

IRR (p. 298): the internal rate of return is the interest rate that would make the NPV of a project equal to zero.

Long run (p. 279): the length of time required for complete adjustment to changed circumstances.

Market equilibrium (p. 271): the state where supply equals demand.

Market (p. 268): system in which buyers and sellers exchange commodities and money. Markets are shaped by and consist of social institutions.

Medium of exchange (p. 266): something (money) that is universally acceptable in exchange for goods and services.

Net worth (p. 295): sum of present values of profits in future years.

NPV (p. 293): the net present value is the amount by which a project would, if undertaken, increase the firm's net worth.

Opportunity cost (p. 263): that which has to be forgone in order to have what is chosen.

Present value (p. 290): the most that anybody would pay now for a promise to pay in the future.

Price (p. 266): the amount of money needed to purchase something.

Principle of comparative advantage (p. 263): specialisation according to comparative, as opposed to absolute, advantage can make all of those involved better off.

Project appraisal (p. 293): making investment decisions.

Relative price (p. 266): a commodity's absolute price divided by the absolute price of some other commodity.

Short run (p. 279): a length of time such that adjustment to changed circumstances is incomplete.

Substitutes (p. 274): commodities for which the cross-price elasticity of demand is positive.

Supply function (p. 270): the relationship between the quantity that sellers wish to sell and price, given that other influences are held constant.

FURTHER READING

The subject matter of this chapter is covered at greater length in all introductory, first-year undergraduate, economics textbooks. Examples are Begg *et al.** (2000) and Mankiw* (2001). Beyond the first year, the core of economics is usually treated in two separate courses each with standard intermediate and advanced textbooks. Microeconomics is, mainly, about the behaviour of individuals and firms in markets and the determination of the relative prices of commodities and inputs to production.

Macroeconomics is about economic behaviour in the aggregate, about short-run fluctuations in the overall level of economic activity and long-term economic growth. Sections 8.1 through to 8.3 above are essentially about topics in microeconomics. Readers wishing to pursue neoclassical microeconomics beyond the introductory level should find, for example, Katz and Rosen (1998), Pindyck and Rubinfeld (2001), or Varian (1987) useful. Kreps (1990) is an advanced text. Himmelweit *et al.* (2001) covers institutionalist as well neoclassical microeconomics.

The material in section 8.4 on the determination of interest rates and levels of savings and investment is usually treated as part of macroeconomics, building on the analysis of the savings behaviour of individuals and of the investment behaviour of firms in microeconomics. Examples of intermediate macroeconomics texts are Blanchard (2003) and Mankiw (2000). The investment behaviour of firms is dealt with in business economics type texts as well as micro texts. Perman and Scoullar (1999) is a good introduction to business economics.

DISCUSSION QUESTIONS

1. What are the arguments for, and against, treating cannabis like tobacco or alcohol?
2. Some people argue that lending money at interest is immoral, as the interest is unearned income, and should be banned. Do you agree?
3. Why is water, a necessity, cheap while diamonds, a luxury, are expensive?

EXERCISES

1. Using the information given in section 8.1.2, set out, in a manner similar to Table 8.3, the consumption opportunities facing Jane and Tom if the exchange ratio is 4. From this table, along with Tables 8.2 and 8.3, derive a table showing, for fish consumptions at their levels under autarky, the bread consumption gains to Jane and Tom for exchange ratios of 5, 4, 3 and 2.5.
2. For the demand function $Q^D = 12 - P$ and the supply function $Q^S = 5 \times P$, find the equilibrium price and quantity. You can do this either by tabulating the functions, or by drawing an accurate diagram, or by solving the simultaneous equations for $Q^D = Q^S$. What is the effect on P^e and Q^e of a shift in the demand function, due to increased incomes, such that it becomes $Q^D = 15 - P$?

3. Find the demand and supply elasticities at the market equilibrium – consider a 10 per cent price reduction – for $Q^D = 12 - P$ and $Q^S = 5 \times P$.

4. For each of the following cases, find the effects on equilibrium price and quantity of the imposition of a tax of $1 per unit of the commodity, and how much of the tax is paid by buyers:

   (a) $Q^D = 12 - P$ and $Q^S = 5 \times P$

   (b) $Q^D = 12 - (2 \times P)$ and $Q^S = 5 \times P$

   (c) $Q^D = 12 - P$ and $Q^S = 6 \times P$

   What do the results show about the incidence of the tax in relation to the elasticities of demand and supply?

5. A project has the following Net cashflow profile

Year	0	1	2	3	4	5
Net cashflow, $	−220	60	60	60	88.9524	0

   Work out the project's NPV for interest rates of 0.05, 0.08 and 0.1. What is its IRR?

6. A firm is considering buying some equipment that will, if energy prices remain constant, reduce its energy expenditure by £3,000 for each of the next 10 years. The machine costs £30,000 and at the end of its useful life will have a scrap value of £10,000. The interest rate is 5 per cent. Should the firm buy the machine? What if the interest rate were 3 per cent? Or if it were 5 per cent and the firm expected energy prices to rise at 5 per cent per year?

7. If v is a constant annual flow of £ for ever and the interest rate is r, show that the corresponding present value is

$$PV = \frac{(1+r) \times v}{r}$$

   if the money arrives on the first day of each year, and

$$PV = \frac{v}{r}$$

   if it arrives on the last day. If n is the number of years, how good an approximation would this be for $n = 30$, $n = 50$ and $n = 100$?

9

Limits to markets

In this chapter you will:

- Learn what the 'invisible hand' of market forces would do in an 'ideal' world;
- Find out how and why the 'invisible hand' does not work in fact;
- Study the distinction between efficiency and equity;
- Explore the role of property rights in the functioning of markets;
- Consider how well markets look after the environment;
- Learn that efficiency is not the same as sustainability.

In the previous chapter we studied how markets work. In this chapter we are concerned with the nature of the outcomes that markets produce. We are concerned, that is, not just with whether the economic problems facing society can be left to markets, but also with the question of whether they should be left to markets. Whereas the previous chapter was mainly about positive analysis, this one is concerned with normative questions as well. We shall see that while market outcomes can have desirable features, they cannot be relied upon to protect the environment, and there is no guarantee that they produce outcomes that are fair, or consistent with sustainability.

9.1 MARKETS AND EFFICIENCY

The economic problem facing a human society is often stated as three questions:
(1)   Which commodities to produce and in what quantities?
(2)   How, in terms of quantities of inputs, to produce the commodities?
(3)   How to share the produced commodities as between the individual members of the society?

Various ways of answering these questions and implementing the answers can be imagined, and have been employed at some stages of human history. For a small and technologically simple society, a hunter-gatherer band say, a leader could decide the answers and tell people what to do so as to implement her solution to the economic problem. An economy where some authority determines the solution to the economic problem is known as a **command economy**. At the opposite extreme to a command economy is a **pure market economy** where economic decision making and activity are completely decentralised. In such an economy there is no leader to draw up a plan and tell individuals what to do in pursuit of it. On the contrary, each individual pursues her own self-interest and there is no coordinating authority.

It is a remarkable fact that markets do permit some decentralisation of the solution to the economic problem. No modern economy is a pure market economy, but in most such economies the role for central planning and control is limited to such matters as defence, law and order, public health services and the like. In such economies, the provision of most goods and services is left to firms owned by individuals. These firms decide what to produce, in what quantities, and on the methods and inputs to be used in production, and are free, subject to health and safety regulation and the like, to implement their plans. The goods and services so produced are shared between individuals on the basis that individuals deal with the firms producing the goods and services. Firms sell to individuals who pay the going price. In the same way, individuals sell their services to firms for use in production.

As inhabitants of a modern economy we live on a daily basis with the evidence that markets work. The food supply system, for example, is not run by some central agency but consists of many firms in the businesses of farming, food processing, and wholesale and retail distribution. There is no central coordination of these diverse activities, but we get fed. The market system, or the price system as it is sometimes called, is a remarkable social institution which coordinates the plans and activities of millions of firms and individuals such that society's economic problem is solved.

Now, for any given society, there will be lots of solutions to its economic problem. Go back to a society consisting of Jane and Tom. Consistent with the survival of each of them, there could be lots of different combinations of fish and bread outputs, each of which could be shared between Jane and Tom in different ways. There is a branch of modern neoclassical economics, **welfare economics**, which is about the relative merits of the available alternative solutions to a society's economic problem, and how to achieve the best solution. According to welfare economics, the pure market system would be, if it operated in some very special circumstances, doubly remarkable. It can be shown that, in such circumstances, not only would a pure market system produce a solution to the economic problem, but that the solution produced would be, in a particular sense, the best solution available. The argument for market solutions to economic problems is not just that markets work in the sense of producing a solution, but also that the solution produced is a good one.

9.1.1 The invisible hand -- allocative efficiency

Adam Smith (1723–1790) is generally taken to be the first economist. He was certainly the first writer to make the argument that self-interested behaviour in a system of markets produces a desirable solution to the economic problem. His major work, *An Inquiry into the Nature and Causes of the Wealth of Nations* (1776), contains the famous statement of the role of the 'invisible hand':

> But it is only for the sake of profit that any man employs a capital in the support of industry; and he will always, therefore, endeavour to employ it in the support of that industry of which the produce is likely to be of the greatest value, or to exchange for the greatest quantity, either of money or of other goods.
>
> As every individual, therefore, endeavours as much as he can both to employ his capital in the support of domestic industry, and so to direct that industry that its produce may be of the greatest value; every individual necessarily labours to render the annual revenue of the society as great as he can. He generally, indeed, neither intends to promote the public interest, nor knows how much he is promoting it . . . he is, in this as in many other cases, led by an invisible hand to promote an end which was no part of his intention . . .
>
> . . . By pursuing his own interest he frequently promotes that of society more effectively than when he really intends to promote it.
>
> (Smith, 1776, Book IV, ch. 2, p. 477)

The core of modern welfare economics is a rigorous examination of this claim that the pursuit of self-interest promotes the interest of society.

The outcomes of that examination can be stated as follows. Imagine a society consisting of many individuals and many firms owned by those individuals. Firms produce various commodities by using input services which they buy from individuals. Individuals use the income that they derive from the ownership of firms and the sale to firms of services to buy the commodities that the firms produce. Firms and individuals separately pursue their own self-interests as they see them. Given certain conditions, to be discussed in the next section of this chapter, it can then be proved that:

(1)   There will exist a **general competitive equilibrium**, that is a state of affairs where the markets for all commodities and all inputs to production are in equilibrium (as described in the previous chapter).

(2)   If such a general competitive equilibrium exists, it will be an **efficient allocation**.

An efficient allocation is sometimes referred to as a Pareto-efficient allocation or a Pareto-optimal allocation – Pareto is the name of the economist who developed the concept. Another way, sometimes used, of stating the second proposition here is to say that, given certain conditions, a general competitive equilibrium would be allocatively efficient.

9.1.2 What is allocative efficiency?

We need first to explain what an allocation is. To do this, we can go back to the imaginary economy consisting of just Jane and Tom from the previous chapter. Their labour is used with land to produce two commodities: bread and fish. As their labour inputs are shifted between the production of bread and fish, so the outputs of bread and fish will vary. For any given outputs of bread and fish, each can be shared between Jane and Tom in a number of ways. An allocation is a particular share-out of available inputs to each line of production, and a particular share-out of the outputs of bread and fish arising as between Jane and Tom. Clearly, even for a very simple, imaginary, economy like this there are a very large number of possible allocations – each possible share-out of available inputs as between bread and fish production gives rise to a particular pair of levels of bread and fish output, and for each possible pair of bread and fish output levels there are lots of different divisions of the total available amounts of bread and fish as between Jane and Tom.

For this simple economy, an allocation is efficient if it is such that it is not possible to make Jane/Tom feel better off except by making Tom/Jane feel worse off. An allocation is not efficient if, for example, it is such that shifting some labour from bread to fish production could yield enough extra fish output so that both Jane and Tom could have their fish consumption increased by enough so that both felt better off despite some reduction in bread consumption. Generally, an allocation is efficient if there is no possible rearrangement of inputs to production, levels of production or share-outs of what is produced that could make somebody feel better off without making anybody else feel worse off. An allocation is not efficient if it could be changed so as to make some individual, or individuals, feel better off without making anybody feel worse off.

Closely related to the concept of allocative efficiency is the idea of the **compensation test**. Suppose that we want to compare two allocations, call them A and B. We want to be able to say whether one of these allocations is better than the other. Think of A as an existing allocation and B as some alternative, and the question is whether the move from A to B is desirable or not. Generally, a move from one allocation to another will mean that some individuals get to feel better off, gain, and some get to feel worse off, lose. According to the compensation test, a move from A to B is an improvement if the gainers could compensate the losers and still feel better off. Clearly, if A is an efficient allocation there cannot be any alteration to it that satisfies this compensation test, as by definition there is no alteration to A that can make anybody feel better off except by making at least one other person feel worse off. This can be put the other way round. An efficient allocation is the state of affairs that would exist if all reallocations that pass the compensation test are undertaken.

The test that we have described is sometimes called the potential compensation test, to emphasise that it relates to potential rather than actual compensation. This is important because this test is fundamental to the way that neoclassical economists advise on policy questions. A policy in this context means some change to the existing allocation. Asked to advise on such a policy, a neoclassical economist would recommend the change if her calculations indicated that those who gained would do so by more than the losers lost, and so could compensate the losers and still be better off. It is not required that compensation is actually to take place. Nor is it required that the gains go to the worst-off.

9.1.3 How markets could achieve allocative efficiency

The essential basic intuition for the result that, in certain circumstances, the pursuit of self-interest in a market system will produce an outcome that is allocatively efficient is really very simple. In the previous chapter we looked at Jane and Tom exchanging with one another, on the basis that they had given endowments of bread and fish. We saw that for some initial endowments and preferences voluntary exchanges of bread and fish could make both Jane and Tom feel better off. Exchanges proceeded until the opportunities for mutually beneficial exchanges were exhausted. A situation of no exchange would be one where the existing allocation was such that it would be impossible for *both* Jane and Tom to feel better off as the result of any possible proposed exchange – there would be, that is, no possible alternative allocation that could make Jane/Tom feel better off without making Tom/Jane feel worse off. Considering voluntary direct exchange, an equilibrium – the cessation of exchange – must be an efficient allocation.

This Jane-and-Tom story ignores the use of money to facilitate exchange and the production of the commodities to be exchanged. The basic intuition as to why a pure exchange–barter equilibrium entails allocative efficiency extends without difficulty to money-mediated exchange and to production.

As regards the role of money, all that is necessary is that the money prices of bread and fish are known to Jane and Tom. An exchange of bread or fish for money is then an exchange of bread or fish for the ability to get fish or bread, rather than directly for fish or bread as such. Clearly, trading using money, rather than direct barter exchange, does not make any real difference – trades will cease when mutually beneficial opportunities are exhausted, so that a situation with no trades, equilibrium in the bread market and the fish market, means no possibility of making Jane/Tom better-off without making Tom/Jane worse-off.

Taking production into account extends the range of contexts where trade, using money, takes place, but does not affect the basic idea. Imagine an economy with lots of Janes and Toms, in which bread and fish are produced by firms using inputs of labour supplied by the Janes and Toms. There is a labour market in which hours of labour are voluntarily exchanged for money, are sold by individuals to firms. The money received by the individuals is exchanged for bread and fish in the markets for those commodities, where the discussion of the previous paragraph applies. In the labour market firms, knowing the money prices of what they produce and sell and of labour, exchange money for labour up to the point where it ceases to serve their interest to do so, while individuals, knowing the prices of commodities and of labour, exchange labour for money up to the point where it ceases to serve their interests so to do. Just as with a commodity market, in the labour market the market equilibrium will obtain when there are no further opportunities for mutually beneficial voluntary exchange.

Given the right conditions, to be discussed in the next section, the story is that when there is equilibrium in all markets, then the allocation is efficient in that nobody could be made better-off except at the cost of making somebody worse-off. Let us look at this idea again, using supply and demand analysis of the market for some commodity, widgets, produced by firms and sold to individuals. *We will assume in the rest of this section that 'the right conditions' are satisfied.*

The demand function slopes downwards reflecting the fact that as price increases, so, with a fixed level of income, people will want to buy less. There is another way of looking at the demand function and its downward slope. This is to interpret it as the relationship between **marginal willingness to pay** and quantity consumed. Look back to Figure 8.2(b) now. On this interpretation, what that demand function says is that for widget consumption at the level two, people would be willing to pay £16 for a small increase in widget consumption, whereas for widget consumption at the level six they would be willing to pay £8 for a small increase in widget consumption. In economics, a small (strictly speaking a very, very small) change is known as a marginal change, so Figure 8.2(b) shows marginal willingness to pay for widgets falling as widget consumption increases. Now, what people are willing to pay for a marginal increase in widget consumption is a measure of what, in terms of the consumption of other commodities, they are willing to give up to get it, and, hence, a measure of what it is worth to them.

On this interpretation, what a demand function shows is how marginal worth declines as consumption increases. The term 'marginal worth' is not used in economics. Instead, what people are willing to pay for a marginal increase in consumption is known as **marginal benefit**, and the demand function shows how the benefit that people get from a small increase in consumption declines as the level of consumption increases, and increases as the level of consumption decreases. Benefit is, in neoclassical economics, measured in terms of willingness to pay, willingness to give up other forms of consumption. It is important to be clear that in neoclassical economics, what something is worth, what its value is, is what people are willing to pay for it. In Figure 9.1 we have drawn the demand function for widgets, and labelled it *MB* for marginal benefit, as well as *DD*.

Now think about the supply function for widgets. It shows how the quantity that producers wish to sell increases as the price increases. It can also be interpreted, under the conditions being assumed, as showing how the **marginal cost** of production increases as the level of production increases. Marginal cost is the increase/decrease in the total cost of production for a small increase/decrease in production. As the output of widgets increases, so the production of widgets must use more inputs, such as labour, for example. More inputs used in the production of widgets means less available for the production of other commodities. The cost of increased widget production is in terms of the reduced availability of commodities other than widgets. As more inputs are transferred into widget production, so this cost of a small increase in widget production increases. In Figure 9.1 we have drawn the supply function for widgets, and labelled it *MC* for marginal cost, as well as *SS*.

At the market equilibrium marginal benefit is equal to marginal cost, and this is why the equilibrium is efficient. The first way to look at this is to consider situations where marginal cost, *MC*, and marginal benefit, *MB*, are not equal. In Figure 9.1(a), at Q_1, MC_1 is greater than MB_1. This means that a marginal reduction in the quantity of widgets produced and consumed would reduce costs by more than benefits. It would release inputs from widget production which are, in terms of what they could produce elsewhere in the economy, worth more than the widgets they are currently being used to produce. Those gaining from such a reallocation – reducing widget output below Q_1 and using the inputs thus released in production elsewhere in the economy – would gain more than the losers would lose. The gainers could, that is, compensate the losers and still feel better-off. It follows that Q_1 could not have corresponded to an efficient allocation. Now consider Q_2 in Figure 9.1(b), for which level of widget production and consumption MB_2 is greater than MC_2. This, $MB_2 > MC_2$, means that a marginal increase in the production and consumption of widgets would increase benefits by more than costs. The additional widgets would be worth more than the output lost elsewhere as a result of the increase in widget

Figure 9.1 The efficiency of market equilibrium.

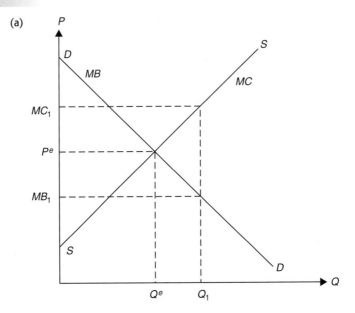

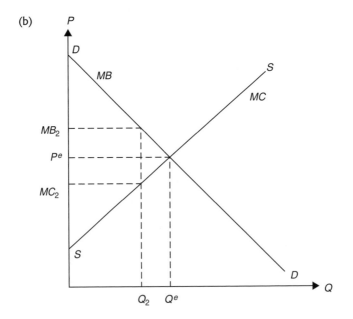

production. Again, those gaining from increasing Q from Q_2 could compensate those losing and still feel better off, so that such an increase in widget production would pass the compensation test.

These arguments about an increase in Q from Q_2 and a reduction in Q from Q_1 hold for Q_2 anywhere to the left of Q^e and Q_1 anywhere to the right of Q^e. However close to Q^e the level of Q is, so long as it is not at Q^e, a move in the direction of Q^e passes the compensation test. On the other hand, for the production of widgets at the market equilibrium level Q^e there is no move in either direction that generates gains greater than the losses, that passes the compensation test. It follows that Q^e corresponds to an efficient allocation.

9.1.3.1 Net benefit maximisation

A second way to look at this introduces a result that is very widely used in economics. Corresponding to MB for marginal benefit let B represent benefit, and corresponding to MC for marginal cost let C represent cost. Define net benefit as the excess of benefit over cost, i.e.

$$NB \equiv B - C$$

Now go back to Figure 9.1(a), and look at Q_1 for which MC_1 is greater than MB_1. Recall that MB is the amount by which benefit increases/decreases for a marginal change in consumption and that MC is the amount by which cost increases/decreases for a marginal change in production. $MC_1 > MB_1$ means that a marginal movement along the horizontal axis from Q_1 towards Q^e will reduce cost by more than it reduces benefit – it will therefore increase NB. This is true for $Q_1 > Q^e$ by any amount. Now look at Figure 9.1(b). For Q_2 less than Q_e MB_2 is greater than MC_2, which means that marginally increasing Q towards Q_e will increase benefit by more than it increases cost, and will, therefore, increase NB. This is true for $Q_2 < Q^e$ by any amount.

What this means is that the excess of benefit over cost, NB, is at its greatest, is maximised, at the market equilibrium level of widget production and consumption Q^e. This is another way of looking at the efficiency property of market outcomes – they maximise net benefits. Note that this is an example of the use of money as unit of account. Costs and benefits are measured in money terms, and efficiency is where the excess of the money value of the benefits over the money value of the costs is at its maximum.

Now, in establishing this we have also found that net benefit is maximised where marginal cost equals marginal benefit – NB attains its largest value where

$$MB = MC$$

This is a general result that is widely used, in various slightly different particular forms, in economics. Where the marginal benefits of an activity decrease with the level of the activity and the marginal costs increase, the level of the activity that maximises the net benefits is that at which marginal benefit equals marginal cost. Many standard results in economics are just particular forms of this general result, according to the particular interpretation of net benefit, benefit and cost. For example, in looking at a firm rather than an economy, benefit would be sales revenue and net benefit would be profit equal to revenue minus cost. The standard result is that in order to maximise profit, the firm should produce at the output level for which marginal revenue is equal to marginal cost. The argument to this famous result is just that above based on Figure 9.1, save that revenue replaces benefit and profit replaces net benefit so that the standard result is that to maximise

$$\text{Profit} \equiv R - C$$

the firm should operate where

$$MR = MC$$

with R for revenue and MR for marginal revenue.

9.1.4 Intertemporal efficiency

'Inter' means between and 'intra' means within. Thus far in this section we have been discussing intratemporal efficiency, or static efficiency as it is sometimes referred to. We have been looking at allocative efficiency within a period of time. Intertemporal efficiency is allocative efficiency between periods of time, sometimes referred to as dynamic efficiency. An allocation is intertemporally efficient if it is not possible to make individuals in one period of time better-off except by making those in some other period of time worse-off.

9.1.4.1 The rate of return

In order to explain what intertemporal allocative efficiency requires and how markets can achieve it, we will simplify by considering just two adjacent years which we will label 0, this year, and 1, next year. In the previous chapter we looked at project appraisal, and introduced the related concepts of Net present value, NPV, and Internal rate of return, IRR. You may find it helpful to look back there before continuing here. We will use i to represent IRR, and from now on we will refer to it as just the rate of return. For a project with a two-year lifetime, the rate of return is i in

$$0 = N_0 + \frac{N_1}{1+i}$$

where N_0 and N_1 are the Net cashflow in years 0 and 1. Subtracting N_0 from both sides gives

$$-N_0 = \frac{N_1}{1+i}$$

so that

$$N_1 = -N_0 \times (1+i)$$

and the Net cashflow next year is opposite in sign to this year's, and $(1+i)$ times as large.

The initial Net cashflow is the investment, and so is a negative number. To illustrate, suppose the investment required by some project is $100, so that N_0 is -100. Then

$$i = -0.05 \text{ means } N_1 = (-1 \times -100) \times (1 - 0.05) = 100 \times 0.95 = \$95$$
$$i = 0 \text{ means } N_1 = (-1 \times -100) \times (1) = 100 \times 1 = \$100$$
$$i = 0.05 \text{ means } N_1 = (-1 \times -100) \times (1 + 0.05) = 100 \times 1.05 = \$105$$

Recall that Net cashflow is the excess of the value of output, sales receipts, over the value of inputs, expenditure associated with the project. A positive rate of return means that the surplus next year is bigger than the deficit this year.

For a two-year project i is the percentage by which N_1 is bigger than N_0. From

$$N_1 = -N_0 \times (1 + i)$$

dividing by $-N_0$ gives

$$\frac{N_1}{-N_0} = 1 + i$$

so that

$$i = \frac{N_1}{-N_0} - 1 = \frac{N_1 + N_0}{-N_0}$$

For an initial investment of $100 and a Net cashflow next year of $105, for example, N_0 is -100 and N_1 is 105 so that

$$i = \frac{105}{(-1) \times (-100)} - 1 = \frac{105}{100} - 1 = 1.05 - 1 = 0.05$$

Suppose that the total amount available for investment this year is fixed at $100 and that there are two possible projects each requiring $100 investment. Project A has $i_A = 0.05$ and project B has $i_B = 0.1$. How should these projects be ranked? If A, then $N_1 = \$105$, whereas for B N_1 would equal $110. Provided that the prices used for calculating N_0 and N_1 accurately reflect the relative values that society places on inputs and output, it makes sense to say that for a given investment cost, N_0, society should rank projects by N_1. Given that i puts things in proportionate terms, projects with differing investment costs can be ranked, with projects with higher rates of return preferred to projects with lower rates of return.

9.1.4.2 The allocation of investment

Intertemporal efficiency requires that the total amount of investment is allocated across the alternative particular forms that it could take so that the marginal rates of return are equal across the alternatives. To show what this means and how it works, suppose that there are two sorts of investment, for each of which there are lots of projects with varying rates of return. Investment projects of type A are for the production of widgets, say, while projects of type B involve, say, smidget production. Imagine that for each type of investment, the projects are listed by rate of return in descending order. As the total amount of investment of a given type increases, so the rate of return on the marginal project decreases. Figure 9.2 shows the graphical representations of such lists for widget and smidget production. As more widget production projects are undertaken so the level of investment in widget production, I_W, increases, and the rate of return, i_W, on the marginal project falls as shown by the line $i_W i_W$; similarly for I_S and i_S. There is no reason why the rates of decline of i should be the same in different sorts of investment. Generally, we would expect them to be different as in Figure 9.2, where the slope of $i_W i_W$ is steeper than $i_S i_S$ – the marginal rate of return to investment in widgets falls more rapidly than that for smidgets.

Figure 9.2
Rates of return
and levels of
investment.

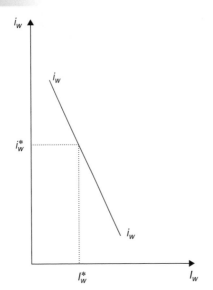 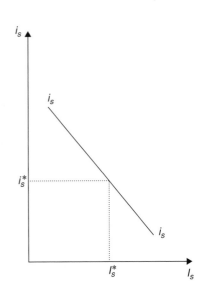

The total amount of investment is

$$I = I_W + I_S$$

which we take, for the moment, to be fixed so that more I_W means less I_S and vice versa. I fixed means that saving and total consumption are also fixed. As shown in Figure 9.2, the levels of I_W and I_S are such that the marginal rate of return to investment is higher in widget production than in smidget production. That means that switching a small amount of total investment out of smidgets and into widgets, keeping total investment constant, would increase the total return to all investment next year. Suppose i_S is 0.09 and i_W is 0.1, for example, and consider cutting I_S by \$100 and increasing I_W by \$100. In regard to smidgets N_0 is a positive number as investment is being cut, so that

$$N_{1S} = -N_{0S} \times (1 + i_S) = (-1 \times 100) \times 1.09 = -109$$

while in regard to widgets there is an increase investment, so that

$$N_{1W} = -N_{0W} \times (1 + i_W) = (-1 \times -100) \times 1.10 = 110$$

The total return to this reallocation of investment as between smidgets and widgets is

$$N_1 = N_{1W} + N_{1S} = 110 - 109 = \$1.$$

Suppose that matters had been the other way round from that shown in Figure 9.2, with i_S larger than i_W. Then by replicating the calculation above for a switch out of widget investment where i_W is 0.09 and into smidget investment where i_S is 0.1, you can see that for the same total level of investment now, next year's total return to investment gets increased. Clearly, any switch of investment from where the marginal rate of return is lower to where it is higher will, for a constant level

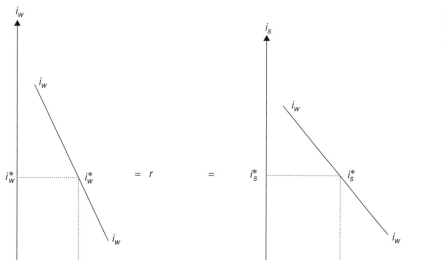

Figure 9.3
Equalisation of
rates of return.

of total investment, increase the total return to investment next year. And, the only circumstance in which it would not be possible to increase the total return for a given total level of investment would be where the two rates of return were equal.

It follows from the definition of intertemporal allocative efficiency as a situation where it is not possible to make individuals in one period of time better-off except by making those in some other period of time worse-off, that it requires that the rates of return to investment in widgets and in smidgets are equal. If they are not, at no cost now – total investment and hence consumption now staying the same – next year's total return to investment in widgets and smidgets together can be increased by reallocating investment in favour of the line where the rate of return is higher. It should be fairly obvious that although made here for just widgets and smidgets, this argument holds where there are many different sorts of investment opportunity. And, it holds however many periods are considered, so long as the rates of return are multi-period rates of return worked out as described in the previous chapter. The general proposition is that intertemporal efficiency requires that marginal rates of return to investment are everywhere equal.

9.1.4.3 *Financial markets and intertemporal efficiency*

Given certain conditions, it can be shown that financial markets will bring about an efficient intertemporal allocation of total investment. The basic reasoning here is very simple, and is illustrated in Figure 9.3 for investment in widgets and smidgets.

In the previous chapter we saw that firms driven by the objective of maximis-ing net worth would undertake investment projects by working down the list of available projects arranged in descending order of IRR and going ahead with all projects for which the IRR is greater than the interest rate. Consequently, given that all firms face the same interest rate, all such firms will be operating where the rate of return on their marginal project is equal to the interest rate, which means that all such firms will be operating with the same marginal rate of return. This is, as we have just seen, exactly what intertemporal allocative efficiency requires – given the right conditions, financial markets allocate total investment efficiently across the alternative lines of investment.

9.2 MARKET FAILURE AND ITS CORRECTION

We have explained what allocative efficiency is, and how a system of markets would produce it if certain ideal conditions are satisfied. In this section we will spell out what the conditions that must hold for markets to deliver allocative efficiency are. We shall see that no actual or conceivable economy could satisfy these conditions. No economist believes that markets alone can deliver allocative efficiency. What many neoclassical economists do believe is that markets subject to a modest amount of government intervention can deliver it, and that government intervention in the economy should be mainly directed toward achieving allocative efficiency. The point about markets under ideal conditions is then that they serve as a benchmark against which to appraise actual markets and from which to derive policy recommendations about desirable interventions in the workings of actual markets.

Having spelt out the ideal conditions, we can then look at **market failure** – where allocative efficiency is not achieved – and what neoclassical economists have to say about how to put it right. We shall also briefly discuss the ethical basis for using allocative efficiency as the basis for policy recommendation, and note some of the difficulties involved in attempting to correct market failure.

In what follows we will sometimes use the term **agent** to refer to any, non-government, actor in the market system – an agent may be a firm or an individual. To cover the case of firms, we will use 'it' rather she/he for an agent.

9.2.1 The conditions needed for markets to produce allocative efficiency

In order for it to be true that society's economic problem can be solved solely by a system of markets, and that the resulting pure market economy solution be an efficient allocation, it is necessary that the following set of conditions are all satisfied.

9.2.1.1 Well-behaved technologies and preferences

Production technologies are the relationships that determine the terms on which firms can use different combinations of inputs to produce various levels of output. Preferences are what determine the demands of individuals for the various commodities that are produced. Both technologies and preferences need to be such that they permit the existence of a general competitive equilibrium. A proper explanation of what this involves is well beyond the technical level of this text. Roughly, what is necessary is that the market supply-and-demand functions that the production technologies and preferences give rise to are smooth and continuous – do not have kinks or gaps in them. In the case of production technologies it is also necessary that there are no increasing returns to scale. Increasing returns to scale exist when increasing all input levels by x per cent leads to an increase in output in excess of x per cent.

9.2.1.2 The complete markets condition

If a pure market system is to produce an efficient allocation, then clearly all of the things that affect how well-off individuals feel and all of the things used as inputs to production have to be traded in markets. In order for this complete markets condition to be satisfied, it is necessary that all of the things that affect how well-off individuals feel and all of the things used as inputs to production are owned by individuals or firms. Market trading requires that the things to be traded are owned by the traders. There cannot be a market for something in which there are no private property rights giving some particular individual or firm the right to dispose of it. Things which have no owners cannot be bought and sold.

9.2.1.3 The price taker condition

Every agent must be a price taker. Agents are **price takers** when they act on the belief that the terms on which they can transact cannot be affected by their own behaviour. Particularly, they take the prices that they face as given and as incapable of being altered by anything that they might do, so that they can buy/sell any quantity at the ruling price. In order for a pure market system to have a general equilibrium which is an efficient allocation, *all* agents must be price takers in *every* market.

An agent will lack the power to influence the terms on which trade takes place when it is one of many competing agents. **Perfect competition** is a market situation where there are so many buyers and sellers that no individual or firm can influence the market price. At the other end of the spectrum of market classification by the degree of competitiveness are monopoly and monopsony. With **monopoly** there is just one seller, who can influence the market price by varying the amount put onto the market – reducing/increasing the quantity it offers for sale will drive up/down the price. **Monopsony** is where there is just one buyer. When there is a very large number of sellers, variations in the amount offered for sale by any one seller are such a small proportion of the total supply that they have no effect on the market price, and the sellers are all price takers. When there is a very large number of buyers, variations in the amount bought by any one buyer are such a small proportion of the total demand that they have no effect on the market price, and the buyers are all price takers. When both sellers and buyers are price takers there is perfect competition.

Between the extremes of perfect competition and monopoly/monopsony, economists distinguish two additional market forms. **Imperfect competition** is where there are many price-taking buyers, and lots of sellers who are not price takers. **Oligopoly** is where there are many price-taking buyers, and a few sellers who are not price takers. The difference between imperfect competition and oligopoly is that in the latter case the number of sellers is so small that action by one seller has a noticeable effect on the firm's competitors, whereas in the former case it does not. What this means is that whereas an imperfectly competitive firm can make decisions without worrying about provoking reactions from its competitors, an oligopolistic firm needs to take account of its rivals' reactions in its decision making.

It is in only the case of perfect competition, where there are enough buyers and sellers so that both sorts of agent are price takers, that the market equilibrium corresponds to efficiency in allocation.

9.2.1.4 *The rationality condition*

Agents are rational when they do the best that they can for themselves, as they understand that, in the circumstances that they face. The rationality condition that is necessary for markets to have equilibria that are allocatively efficient is actually a special version of rationality. In the case of firms the necessary condition is profit maximisation, and in the case of individuals it is utility maximisation. As used by neoclassical economists, see Chapter 1, 'utility' is an index of *self-assessed* individual well-being. For individuals, what is required is that they choose between available alternatives so as make themselves feel as good as is possible. For firms, what is required is that managers care about nothing but profit, which they seek to maximise.

9.2.1.5 *The complete information condition*

Every agent must have complete information about the consequences for itself of making any market transaction that is open to it. The complete information condition requires that all agents know the prices ruling in all markets, and know what effect making any prospective market trade would have on their profits, in the case of firms, or on their utility, for individuals. Without this condition, rationality itself would not make much sense and would not lead to efficiency in allocation, as, for example, an individual aiming to maximise utility might fail to do so by virtue of spending £x on widgets when £x spent on, say, whisky would have delivered a larger improvement in her own assessment of her well-being.

9.2.2 Market failure is the norm

It should be clear that the conditions under which a pure market system would lead to an efficient allocation are very stringent. In fact no actual economy could satisfy them. The invisible hand story is fiction. Self-interest – as utility and profit maximisation – operating through a system of markets could, of itself, never bring about efficiency in allocation. As Box 9.1 reports this is also the assessment of some recent recipients of the Nobel prize for economics, based on consideration of the rationality and information conditions. It is obvious to the most casual observer of any actual economy that very few markets are anything like the perfect competition ideal on the sellers' side whereas allocative efficiency requires that all markets satisfy the perfect competition ideal. Many of the things that individuals care about, and that affect firm's profits, are not traded in markets. As we shall

Box 9.1 There is no invisible hand

'There is no invisible hand' is the title of an article by the economist Joseph Stiglitz which appeared in *The Guardian* on 20 December 2002. Stiglitz was Chair of the Council of Economic Advisers to President Clinton, worked for a while as Chief Economist at the World Bank, and was one of three joint winners of the Nobel prize in economics in 2001. His article was about the work of the winners of the prize in 2002: Daniel Kahneman and Vernon Smith.

Kahneman is a psychologist who has 'demonstrated how individuals systematically behave in ways less rational than orthodox economists believe they do'. Smith is a leading practitioner of experimental economics, in which hypotheses about economic behaviour are tested in laboratory conditions. As Stiglitz puts it, in such experiments 'the irrationality of market participants, which was the focus of Kahneman's work, has been repeatedly verified'.

Stiglitz notes that in honouring work that exposes the limitations of 'simplistic market economics', the 2002 prizes followed the pattern of 2001, when the laureates 'emphasised that different market participants have different (and imperfect) information', which fact means that markets cannot be taken to be, generally, efficient. According to Stiglitz, what the work that won the Nobel prizes in 2001 and 2002 means is that:

> Adam Smith's invisible hand – the idea that free markets lead to efficiency as if guided by unseen forces – is invisible, at least in part, because it is not there. (2002)

'Rational expectations' models assume that all market participants have the same information and act perfectly rationally. Stiglitz comments that the fact that such models were for many years the received wisdom in neoclassical economics, and 'especially in America's graduate schools', 'bears testimony to a triumph of ideology over science'.

Stiglitz draws attention to some results that have emerged from experimental work in economics, which he describes as 'amusing', about selfishness and altruism. In laboratory contexts, human subjects are not as selfish as economists hypothesise, except for one group – economists. Is this because the study of economics attracts more selfish individuals, or because being taught economics makes individuals more selfish? Stiglitz suspects that the answer is a little bit of both, and entertains the hope that further work in experimental economics will throw more light on this.

see shortly, missing markets are very common in regard to the services that the environment provides to economic activity. All economists recognise that market failure – violations of the conditions under which markets deliver allocative efficiency – is pervasive in actual economies. Given that the story about the invisible hand is known to be a fairy story, why do so many neoclassical economists spend so much time on it? Why, indeed, have we spent so much time on it in a book about ecological economics?

The first point is that the neoclassical economics approach to the proper role of government is dominated by the pursuit of allocative efficiency. Then, studying the ideal world of the fairy story is the way to come up with policy prescriptions for the real world. The idea is to go around correcting market failure so that the real world approaches more closely the ideal world, so that allocative efficiency is more closely approximated to in the real world.

The second point is that neoclassical economics is currently the dominant school of thought in economics, and economic advice on policy in relation to the environment and sustainable development carries a lot of weight with elected politicians and their advisors. If you want to understand a lot of what goes on in the world of government decision making you have to have some appreciation of the way that neoclassical economists think.

The third point is that, as we shall see, that way of thinking generates some useful insights into the origins of problems with the environment, equity and sustainability in market economies. Ecological economics does not deny the validity of the fairy story given its assumptions. To do so would be foolish, as the logic is without fault – if the assumptions hold, the stated consequences follow. Ecological economics does not claim that efficiency considerations should always be ignored. It does claim that they are not the only thing that matters, and that sometimes they may have to be overridden. It does point out that correcting market failure does not ensure sustainability.

9.2.3 Consumer sovereignty

Allocative efficiency in neoclassical economics is a state where nobody could be made to *feel* better off except at the cost of making somebody else *feel* worse off. This is not, necessarily, the same as a state where nobody could be made better-off except by making somebody worse-off. The point is that the idea of allocative efficiency uses individuals' self-assessments of their state of well-being. This is the doctrine of **consumer sovereignty** – the idea that individuals should, as far as possible, get what they want, that the proper measure of economic performance is the preferences of individuals as expressed in willingness to pay.

Self-assessed well-being is not the only way that we could, at the level of principle, use the idea of allocative efficiency. We could, for example, assess an allocation in terms of the physical and mental health of members of the population, and say that it was efficient if it was the case that nobody could be made healthier without making somebody else less healthy. What individuals feel makes them better or worse off is not necessarily the same as what makes them more or less healthy. As discussed in Chapter 1, the ethical basis for neoclassical economics is the view that what people want should be the basis for judging whether one allocation is better or worse than another. Many philosophers would argue that what people want should not be the basis for judging whether one situation is better than another.

In health terms, some of the things that many individuals obviously want are not actually good for them, and some of the things that many individuals have an aversion for are actually good for them. Tobacco is an example of the first kind, broccoli is an example of the second kind. In practice most neoclassical economists would accept that there are commodities such that the principle of consumer sovereignty has to be overridden. Such commodities are known as **merit goods** – broccoli – or 'bads' – tobacco. The point about such commodities is not that consumers do not know how they will affect how they feel. It is that with such commodities, how the consumer feels is a poor guide to her true interests. The problem is how to decide exactly which goods to put in this category, and most neoclassical economists recognise the existence of the category only with reluctance – it seems to undermine consumer sovereignty.

Ecological economists do not accept that individuals' preferences should be the *only* criterion for assessing the relative merits of alternative allocations. There is some debate among ecological economists about what its ethical basis should be. There is wide agreement that equity is important, and we return to this later. Most ecological economists would agree that individuals' preferences should have some role in determining what gets produced, and how it gets produced. Most would argue that it would be right to override individuals' preferences if they represent a threat to sustainability. In practical terms, many ecological economists are in much the same sort of position on consumer sovereignty as many neoclassical economists, in that they recognise limits to the applicability of consumers' sovereignty. The difference here is that ecological economists want to treat sustainability as a generalised merit good. Most are happy for preferences to determine what goes in the economy, so long as that does not threaten sustainability. Given that there are many aspects of the behaviour of individuals and firms that affect the environment and have implications for sustainability, this means that there are many particulars where ecological economists might be prepared to compromise on consumer sovereignty.

A related point of difference between neoclassical and ecological economics concerns the matter of the determination of individuals' preferences. In the former, individuals' preferences are taken as given, and their determination is outside the field of enquiry that is seen as relevant. In effect it is assumed that individuals are born with preferences which remain unchanged throughout their lifetimes. This assumption is obviously wrong. Preferences are not part of an individual's genetic endowment, but are acquired characteristics determined by both genetic endowment and the environment in which the individual develops. In the terminology introduced in Chapter 2 when considering evolution, an individual's preferences are phenotypes, not genotypes. Since the environment in which any individual develops includes the behaviour of other living individuals, as well as the ideas and information bequeathed by individuals now dead, the way the preferences present in a society change over time involves cultural coevolution.

In ecological economics it is recognised that individuals' preferences are phenotypes, and that the distribution of different types of preferences in society is subject to cultural coevolution. Many of the particular implications of this general statement have yet to be worked out, and are at the frontiers of research in ecological economics, drawing on work, for example, in social and evolutionary psychology, as well as recent advances in simulation methods. What can be said is that the general level of recognition means that ecological economists see individuals' preferences not as eternal givens of the economic problem, as neoclassical economists effectively do, but as one of the manifestations of the constantly changing and complex pattern of responses to the problem. Ecological economists would, for example, have much less of a problem about using the education system to promote preferences consistent with sustainability than neoclassical economists would.

9.2.4 Correcting market failure

In advising on public policy, neoclassical economists are mainly interested in correcting market failure. They want, that is, to see the economy operating in a way that corresponds to an efficient allocation. Given that it will not do that under the direction of markets as they exist, there is a role for government to improve the way markets work by addressing and correcting the sources of market failure, or, if this cannot be done, by government itself doing what allocative efficiency requires. Rather than work exhaustively through the whole gallery of market failure categories and the corresponding sets of possible correction policies, we will look briefly at just three problems and some policy responses to them.

9.2.4.1 Public goods

A commodity which is a public good has two characteristics. It is non-rivalrous and non-excludable in consumption. A commodity is **non-rivalrous** if an increase in one agent's consumption does not reduce the consumption of other agents.

A commodity is **non-excludable** if an agent cannot be prevented from consuming or using it. Private goods are rivalrous and excludable. Ice cream is an example of a private good. There is rivalry in that an ice cream eaten by me is not available for somebody else to eat. There is exclusion in that individuals can be prevented from consuming. Private goods are 'ordinary' goods and services. An example of a public good is national defence by the armed forces. The provision of defence to me does not reduce the amount available to anybody else – non-rivalry. Nobody resident in the country can be prevented from consuming service provided by its armed forces – non-excludability.

The fact that agents cannot be excluded from non-rivalrous consumption of a public good means that it cannot be supplied through a market by a firm. Markets operate on the basis that buyers hand over money in return for particular units of the commodity. Buyers who do not hand over money are excluded from consumption. Where such exclusion is impossible, private firms and markets have no role. Individuals cannot be sold particular units of defence services for their exclusive enjoyment – everybody consumes whatever level is provided.

Public goods have to be provided by government, which, unlike a firm, has the power to tax, so that consumption and payment can be separated. The government does not need to *sell* units to particular individuals. It can *give*, provide free of charge, the commodity to agents and raise the money to pay for the inputs used in its production by taxing agents. Given that the government, unlike a firm, has the power to tax, it does not need to cover production costs by sales receipts.

Neoclassical and ecological economists recognise the inability of firms working in markets to supply public goods as one limit to the scope of markets, and as necessitating economic activity by government. The question that then arises is: how much of the public good to supply? In neoclassical economics the existence of public goods is one form of market failure, and the question is to be answered by correcting that so that the amounts supplied should be those which go with allocative efficiency. A public good should be supplied, that is, at the level where the marginal cost of provision is equal to the marginal benefit, as in Figure 9.1, where benefit is to be assessed in terms of willingness to pay. To do this, the government needs to know how marginal benefit varies with the level of provision. The problem with this advice for the government is that it cannot observe the marginal benefit function in the form of a demand function in a market for the public good, and it is very difficult to ascertain it in any other way.

Precisely because of non-excludability and non-rivalry, rational self-interested people are held to lack the incentives to truthfully reveal their preferences in regard to a public good. This is called the **free rider problem**. Because they know that if it is supplied they cannot be prevented from consuming it, purely self-interested people will try to 'free ride', concealing their own willingness to pay and letting others say they want, and therefore pay for, the public good. Neoclassical economists have devoted a lot of effort to trying to devise systems for the supply of public goods whereby people are induced to truthfully reveal their willingness to pay. Such efforts have not yet produced results used by governments, and decisions about the levels of supply of public goods are made by political processes.

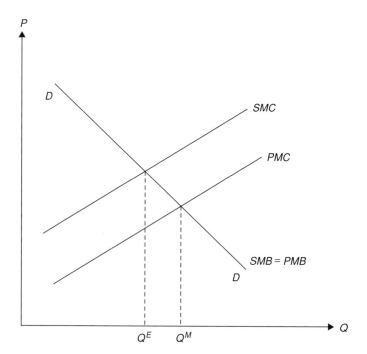

Figure 9.4 The externality problem.

9.2.4.2 *Externalities*

An **externality**, or an external effect, is said to exist when the actions of one agent have an unintended effect on some other agent or agents. The unintended effect may be beneficial or harmful. An externality is a market failure in that a system of markets will produce an allocation with more of it, in a harmful case, or less of it, in a beneficial case, than allocative efficiency requires. Why is this? Because of the lack of intentionality, which is in turn due to the fact that there is no bargaining about the effect, which is in turn due to the fact that there are no property rights in it. The terminology arises because the effects involved are 'external' to the operation of systems of markets.

To explain what is involved, we will look first at a harmful externality where waste emissions by one agent cause harm to another agent. Suppose that a widget-producing firm discharges wastes into a lake which is the source of the water supply for a firm producing smidgets using a process that requires clean water. The smidget firm has to treat water drawn from the lake before using it. This entails costs. Figure 9.4 shows what is involved, and introduces some widely used terminology. *DD* is the demand function for widgets. *SMB* stands for social marginal benefit and *PMB* stands for private marginal benefit. We will explain why *SMB* = *PMB* shortly. *PMC* stands for private marginal cost and *SMC* stands for social marginal cost. *PMC* refers to the costs that the widget firm faces and uses in its decision making. *SMC* refers to the costs that the firm's activities generate, the costs that are relevant to the whole society in which the widget firm operates. *SMC* exceeds *PMC* by the marginal cost of treating the water from the lake, which is a cost that is not borne by the widget firm – is external to it – but is a real cost borne by the smidget firm and hence by those who buy smidgets. The difference between SMC and PMC is known as **marginal external cost**, MEC, so that

$$MEC = SMC - PMC$$

The widget firm bases its decisions on the costs and benefits that accrue to it: PMC and PMB. It will maximise profit by producing at the output level Q^M (M for market) where $PMC = PMB$. However, what allocative efficiency requires is that it produce at the level Q^E (E for efficient) where $SMC = SMB$. Because the costs of water treatment are not borne by the firm responsible for the need for that treatment, that firm will ignore those costs and produce too many widgets, putting into the lake an amount of waste that is too great from the perspective of efficiency in allocation. If the widget firm had to pay for the water treatment, its PMC would then be the same as SMC and equating the marginal costs and benefits that it faced would lead it to produce Q^E widgets, as required for efficiency in allocation. SMB and PMB are the same here because we are assuming that the externality problem attending the widget firm's use of the lake is the only sort of market failure associated with the production and consumption of widgets. As we shall see, this is a highly unrealistic assumption. The reason for making it is only to bring out as clearly as possible the essential nature of the externality problem. If there are no other departures from the ideal conditions, then marginal willingness to pay by individuals – PMB for private marginal benefit – is the same as the marginal benefit looked at from the point of view of society – SMB for social marginal benefit.

The widget firm over-produces and over-pollutes because it does not bear the cost of its use of the lake. Why does it not bear the cost? It must be because the smidget firm can neither charge the widget firm for its use of the lake, nor extract from the widget firm compensation for the harm it has done. It could do the former if it owned the lake, or it could do the latter if it had a legal right to use the lake's water in an unpolluted state. The origin of the externality is in the lack of a property right in either the lake itself or in access to clean water from the lake. The point here generalises – externality problems arise because of incomplete private property rights, on account of which absence there can be no market trading or other bargaining.

The solution to this market failure problem would seem to be obvious – legislate to create the missing private property rights. In the case illustrated in Figure 9.4, for example, the obvious solution is to legislate so that the smidget firm has a right to the use of clean water from the lake. Given that right, it could threaten to take legal action against the widget firm for cost recovery. Against such a legal background, the widget and smidget firms would bargain over the amount of waste that the former should put into the lake. Such bargaining would lead to the widget firm producing the quantity of widgets, Q^E, and the associated level of waste discharge, that go with efficiency in allocation because SMC would be the marginal cost function used in the widget firm's decision making. Actually, it can be shown that Q^E would also be the outcome if the widget firm owned the lake or had a legal entitlement to pollute it, so that the smidget firm would pay it to pollute less than it would otherwise do.

This insight about private property rights as a solution to an environmental problem was first written about in 1960 by Ronald Coase, who was subsequently awarded the Nobel prize for economics. It is frequently referred to as the 'Coase Theorem'. We are not going to work though a detailed demonstration of this 'theorem' here. It is not difficult and is left as an exercise for you to do. In order to demonstrate that the Coase Theorem works, it is necessary to make assumptions. Unfortunately, for all except special cases, the obvious and simple solution to the harmful externality problem cannot actually be used because the assumptions do not hold in reality. Our widget/smidget example was special in that there was one source of the externality and one sufferer from it. In all important actual harmful externality problems, there are many sources and/or many sufferers. All non-trivial environmental pollution problems involve many sources and/or many affected agents. As the numbers involved increase, so the costs of bargaining increase, and for large numbers it is impossible – imagine trying to deal with urban air pollution in a city of 5 million residents and 1 million motor vehicles by giving the residents individually the right to clean air so that they can bargain with the vehicle operators, the factory owners, the power plants and all of the other pollution sources.

There is another problem that arises once there are many agents affected by the externality. In many cases the unintended effect that they experience is in the nature of a public bad, in that it is non-rivalrous and non-excludable. This is true of virtually all pollution problems. Think again about urban air pollution as an example. If one citizen increases her consumption (by breathing more deeply?) this does not meaningfully reduce the amount available for consumption by others – non-rivalry. No citizen can avoid consumption – non-excludability. We saw above that public goods cannot be supplied through the market by a firm. The efficient level of pollution cannot be delivered by bargaining based on private property rights for the same reasons – bargaining requires rivalry and excludability. As with public goods such as defence, so with public bads such as pollution there is an essential role for government.

There are several ways in which government can intervene in the functioning of a market system so as to reduce this kind of pollution, which will be discussed in Chapter 11. One would be to put a tax on widget sales, or on the emissions that widget production gives rise to. Neoclassical and ecological economists would both see some kind of tax as a possible response to this kind of externality problem. They would differ over how to decide the tax rate. Neoclassical economists would insist that the tax be at a rate equal to the marginal external cost. In that case the marginal costs facing the widget firm would be the same as the social marginal costs of widget production – with the tax in place, *PMC* in Figure 9.4 would shift to merge with *SMC* – and the firm would produce Q^E as required for efficiency in allocation. Ecological economists would not necessarily want the tax rate fixed this way. The difference in the ways that neoclassical and ecological economics approach the setting of the standards at which environmental protection measures, such as taxes, should aim are discussed in the next chapter.

9.2.4.3 Monopoly

Profit is the difference between revenue from sales and the cost of production, and, as noted in section 9.1.3.1, for profit to be maximised it is necessary that

$$MR = MC$$

where MR is marginal revenue and MC is marginal cost. Let a marginal change be a change of one unit, one widget say. MR is the increase in sales revenue when one more unit is sold. If the firm is a price taker, so that selling more does not affect price, the increase in revenue when an additional widget is sold is just the unit price, and the condition for profit maximisation becomes

$$P = MC$$

where P stands for price. Where firms fix their output levels so that price equals marginal cost, they are behaving as allocative efficiency requires, with marginal willingness to pay equal to marginal cost.

Whereas in perfect competition there are so many sellers that variations in the quantity sold by any one seller have no effect on the market price, with a monopoly there is just one seller and variations in the amount it sells do affect the market price. If there is just one firm producing and selling widgets, then the demand function that it faces is the market demand function for widgets, which slopes downwards so that selling more means a lower price. If, on the other hand, widgets are produced by perfectly competitive firms, then each of them faces a horizontal demand function so that more can be sold at the ruling price. For the perfectly competitive firm, price and marginal revenue are the same. For the monopolist, they are different.

In fact, for a downward-sloping demand function, marginal revenue is always less than price, $MR < P$. Table 9.1 shows what is involved for the demand function

$$P = 1,000 - (50 \times Q)$$

where R stands for revenue, $R = Q \times P$, and MR is found by looking at the change in R for a unit increase in the quantity sold, Q. For example, for $Q = 2$ $R = \$1,800$ whereas for $Q = 3$ $R = \$2,550$ so that for $Q = 2$ MR is $750 – increasing sales from 2 to 3 would increase revenue by $750. Clearly, for a downward-sloping demand function, marginal revenue must always be less than price, because price must fall to sell more. Price equal to marginal revenue is the special case where the demand function is horizontal.

Figure 9.5 shows why and how monopoly gives rise to market failure. Profit maximisation means that the monopolist's output level is Q_M where $MC = MR$. The MR function is also labelled PMB because for the monopolist the MR function shows how the firm's private marginal benefit, its

Table 9.1 Marginal revenue for a downward-sloping demand function

Q	P	R	MR
1	950	950	
2	900	1800	850
3	850	2550	750
4	800	3200	650
5	750	3750	550
6	700	4200	450
7	650	4550	350
8	600	4800	250
9	550	4950	150

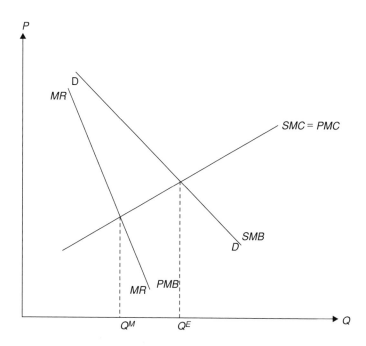

Figure 9.5 The
monopoly
problem.

revenue, varies with its output and sales. The demand function, *DD*, is also labelled
SMB because it shows how marginal willingness to pay for the commodity, and
hence the social marginal benefit, varies with output and sales. Since we are
assuming that the only departure from the ideal conditions is that we have a
monopoly – the production of widgets does not now give rise to any polluting
emissions into a lake, for example – the monopolist's marginal cost function shows
both social and private marginal costs, $SMC = PMC$. Allocative efficiency requires
that $SMC = SMB$ and so an output level of Q^E. Because a profit-maximising monopolist produces where $MR = PMC = SMC$ its output level is lower than allocative
efficiency requires – monopoly is a form of market failure. As with excessive production by the generator of a harmful externality, so with under-production by a
monopolist, there are several ways in which government could seek to correct
the market failure. One way would be to legislate so that the monopoly was
required to produce and sell Q^E. In many cases, it turns out that the monopolist's cost structure is such that this would mean its making a loss rather than a
profit. For this reason, monopolies have often been taken into public ownership
with the government making good the losses from tax revenue. An alternative
is to leave a monopoly in private ownership and to pay subsidies to cover the
losses.

9.2.5 Multiple sources of market failure

Thus far we have looked at situations where there is only one violation of the ideal
conditions under which a set of market equilibria would produce an efficient allocation. Suppose instead that there are two violations of the ideal conditions, two

sources of market failure. It then turns out that correcting just one of them is not guaranteed to improve things, to move in the direction of efficiency in allocation – it could make things worse. Take as an example a situation where the production of widgets is entirely by a monopoly firm which discharges waste emissions into a lake, in which there are no private property rights and where nobody has a legal entitlement to the use of clean water. By virtue of being a monopoly the firm will, as noted above, be producing and selling less widgets than efficiency in allocation requires. Because it is not paying for its use of the lake as a sink for some of its wastes, it will be over-using the lake, producing more widgets and more pollution of the lake than efficiency in allocation requires. Government intervention to deal with the monopoly market failure will worsen the waste discharge problem. Government intervention to deal with the waste discharge problem will worsen the under-production problem.

If both sources of market failure can be dealt with, things definitely get better in that the result is an efficient allocation. If only one can be dealt with things may get better or worse. In principle, in any particular case it could be determined whether dealing with just one source of market failure would improve or worsen things from the efficiency point of view. But, there is no general rule, and every particular case needs to be individually assessed. This is often referred to as the **second best problem**. If one violation of the conditions for markets to produce allocative efficiency cannot be dealt with, then the first best outcome, allocative efficiency, is not attainable. A second best solution is attainable, but it will not be attained by following the standard prescription for dealing with the violation that can be dealt with. Some other prescription, that takes account of the existence of the non-fixable problem, has to be worked out.

The second best problem makes policy recommendation based on allocative efficiency analysis very difficult. Given that not all sources can be dealt with, simple prescriptions derived from looking at just one source of market failure in isolation may do more harm than good. In practice, in using ideas about allocative efficiency and market failure to make policy recommendations, neoclassical economists mainly ignore the second best problem.

Although we have presented the problem in terms of a monopolist, a type of firm that in the strict sense is rare, it actually applies for any producers which are not price takers. Most commodities are produced by firms that are not price takers, and the production of many commodities involves waste emissions. The second best problem, like market failure, is pervasive.

9.3 MARKETS AND EQUITY

If all of the necessary conditions were satisfied everywhere in the economy, a system of markets would bring about an efficient allocation. There is, however, no reason to suppose that such an allocation would be in any sense fair or equitable. Efficiency, that is, is not the same thing as equity. If equity is considered important, securing it is another recognised role – in addition to the market failure correction role – for government in an economy mainly organised around markets. Just as efficiency has an intratemporal, or static, dimension and an intertemporal, or dynamic, dimension so does the question of equity.

9.3.1 Intratemporal equity

The simplest way to see the efficiency equity distinction here is to go back to the pure exchange economy, consisting of Jane and Tom with endowments of bread and fish, that we looked at in the first section of the previous chapter. We have already noted that in such an economy the idea that the pursuit of self-interest leads to an equilibrium which is efficient is very straightforward. An equilibrium will exist when Jane and Tom have made all mutually beneficial voluntary exchanges – given that there remain no mutually beneficial trades, any such equilibrium must be efficient in the sense that Jane/Tom cannot be made to feel better off except by making Tom/Jane feel worse off. At the start of the previous chapter, we considered two sets of initial endowments. One led to both Jane and Tom ending up with 30 loaves and 30 fish, the other to Jane ending up with 35 loaves and 35 fish while Tom ended up with 75 loaves and 75 fish. Both of these final equilibria are allocatively efficient, but they differ markedly in regard to equity.

In this barter illustration, Tom ended up with more when he had a much larger initial endowment than Jane. This carries through to market trading – those who start with more will end up with more. We can show what is involved by looking again at Jane and Tom and the widget market. *We assume that there is no market failure.* For both Jane and Tom, weekly widget demand depends on income and price such that

$$D = Y - (5 \times P)$$

where Y stands for weekly income and P for the price of a widget. Jane has an income of €140 and Tom has an income of €60 per week, so that their demand functions are

$$D_J = 140 - (5 \times P)$$

for Jane and

$$D_T = 60 - (5 \times P)$$

for Tom. These two demand functions are shown in the upper part of Figure 9.6(a). To get the market demand function from individual demand functions we add the quantities demanded by each relevant individual at each possible price. Thus, for example, when the price is €10 Jane's demand is $140 - (5 \times 10) = 140 - 50 = 90$ and Tom's demand is $60 - (5 \times 10) = 60 - 50 = 10$, so that the market demand for widgets at price €10 is $90 + 10 = 100$. Working through prices from €28 – the price at which Jane's demand is zero – down to €0 gives the market demand function shown in the lower part of Figure 9.6(a). Note that this market demand function has a kink at price €12, which is the price at which Tom's demand is zero. Above €12 only Jane would buy any widgets, so to the left of $Q = 80$ the market demand function is just Jane's demand whereas to the right of $Q = 80$ both individuals are buyers. (Where there are many individuals, the scale of the diagram will usually be such that kinks like this do not show up in the market demand function as it gets drawn.)

The supply function is shown as SS in the lower diagram, along with the market equilibrium price, €10, and quantity, 100 widgets. Going to the upper parts of Figure 9.6(a), for $P = €10$ Jane consumes 90 widgets per week while Tom consumes

Figure 9.6
Two widget
market
equilibria.

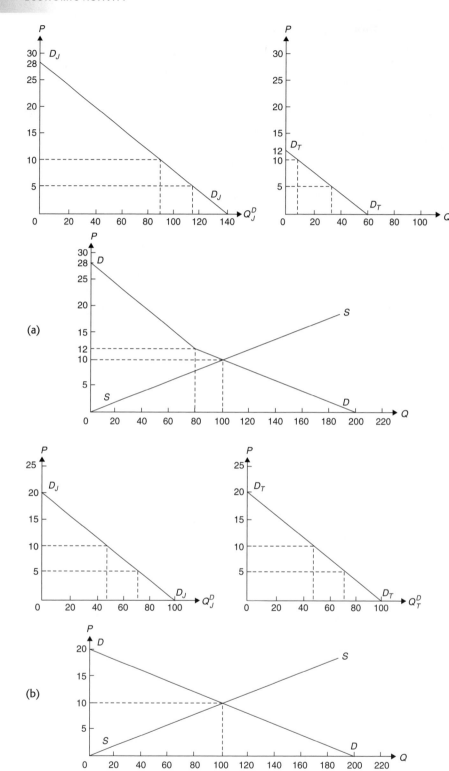

just 10. The market equilibrium is efficient, but the widget consumption levels that go with it are very unequal, reflecting the fact that Jane has a much larger income than Tom.

Suppose that Jane and Tom had the same incomes of €100 per week. Then

$$D_J = 100 - (5 \times P)$$

and

$$D_T = 100 - (5 \times P)$$

as shown in the upper part of Figure 9.6(b). Proceeding as before, adding the demands of Jane and Tom at each possible price, gives the market demand function shown as *DD* in the lower part. The market equilibrium price is €10, the equilibrium quantity is 100, and Jane and Tom both consume 50 widgets. Given that Jane and Tom have equal incomes, and the same preferences for widgets as against other things that they might spend their money on, the efficient market allocation has both consuming equal amounts of widgets. If Jane and Tom had different preferences for widgets, if their demand functions had different slopes, then even with equal incomes they would consume different amounts of widgets.

Jane and Tom were given the same preferences here to make the story simple, and to bring out clearly the point about efficiency's not being the same as equity. The important points that this simple story illustrates, which do not depend on individuals all having the same preferences, are first that an efficient allocation is not unique, and second that a particular efficient allocation may or may not be equitable. Given the ideal conditions that we are assuming to operate, any market allocation is efficient – both of the allocations in Figure 9.6 are efficient. As the distribution of incomes is varied, so the particular efficient allocation that the market brings about varies. The more equitable is the distribution of incomes, the more equitable will be the efficient allocation that the market produces be.

Suppose that widgets were a commodity generally agreed to be essential to a minimally decent life, such as a staple foodstuff. In that case, the situation in Figure 9.6(a) would generally be agreed to be seriously inequitable, and increasing Tom's consumption of widgets would be seen as an important policy objective. This does not require intervention in the widget market to reallocate widgets from Jane to Tom, or to cap the price of widgets so that Tom could afford to buy more. Those kinds of intervention would involve departing from an efficient allocation. The desired result can, instead, be achieved by redistributing income, in which case efficiency in allocation is retained.

Most people would agree that there is a redistributional role for government in a market system, that it should use taxes and grants to make the distribution of income more equal than that which emerges from markets. There is much less agreement about how much redistribution there should be. The better-off tend to want less and the worse-off more. But, even when these kinds of vested interests are ignored, it turns out to be very difficult to come to firm conclusions about what would represent a fair allocation as between individuals alive at a point in time. Many books have been written about what comprises economic justice, by philosophers as well as economists. The question involves, in the terminology introduced in Chapter 1, normative as well as positive issues. It is not, to put it another way, a purely scientific question. It also involves ethics.

Defining absolutely and precisely what comprises economic intratemporal economic justice is difficult. Rather than try to do that, we could ask whether, starting from where we now are, there should be more, or less, redistribution from the better-off to the worst-off. This is still a difficult question about which there is disagreement. The ethics of the authors of this book lead them to believe, given the sort of evidence referred to in Chapter 6, that in most modern industrial economies there is a case for more redistribution than currently occurs. We believe even more strongly, again based on the evidence reviewed in Chapter 6, that if we look at the world as a whole there is a case for more redistribution from the better-off in the rich industrial economies to the poor in the developing economies. Global redistribution is difficult to achieve because there is no world government to run the tax and grants system required.

9.3.2 Intertemporal efficiency and distribution

The intertemporal efficiency–equity relationship is the same as the intratemporal efficiency–equity relationship – there are many intertemporal allocations that are efficient, and there is no guarantee that the particular efficient allocation that an ideal system of markets produces will be desirable on equity grounds.

In Figure 9.3 we saw that efficiency requires that rates of return in different lines of investment are equalised at the margin. In an ideal system of markets, where all firms expand their investment to the point where the IRR on their marginal project is equal to the interest rate, rates of return will be equalised at the margin. Hence, an ideal system of markets delivers intertemporal efficiency. Note, however, that nothing has been said here about what the rate of interest is, or about what the corresponding level of total investment is. In Figure 9.7, a development of Figure 9.3, we show two interest rates, r^* and r^{**}, and the corresponding levels of investment in widget and smidget production arising in ideal markets. I_W^{**} with I_S^{**} is an efficient allocation as is I_W^* with I_S^*. Clearly, we could consider lots of levels for r, instead of just two, and for every level for the interest rate there is a corresponding intertemporally efficient allocation that an ideal system of markets will bring about.

In Figure 9.7 the total level of investment that goes with r^* is higher than that which goes with r^{**} – $I^* = I_W^* + I_S^*$ and is greater than $I^{**} = I_W^{**} + I_S^{**}$. This fits with the discussion of the determination of levels of savings and investment in section 8.4.4 of the previous chapter. Since total investment and savings are equal, and since what is produced is either consumed or saved, $I^{**} < I^*$ means $S^{**} < S^*$, which means $C^{**} > C^*$, where C stands for total consumption. While both of the situations shown in Figure 9.7 correspond to efficient intertemporal allocations, the one that goes with r^* has lower consumption than the one that goes with r^{**}. At r^* more consumption is being forgone now than at r^{**}, which means that at r^* a larger stock of capital is being passed on to the future than at r^{**} – an interest rate of r^* favours the future in relation to the present more than r^{**} does.

Exactly what variations in the current level of saving and investment mean for future income and consumption is complicated. As we saw in Chapters 6 and 7, capital accumulation is necessary for economic growth and variations in the savings

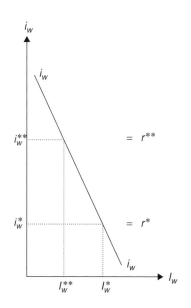
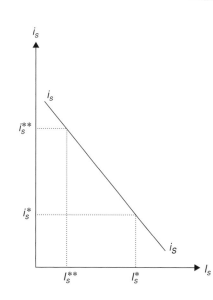

Figure 9.7 Two efficient intertemporal allocations.

rate give rise to variations in the growth rate. Outcomes depend on the importance of natural resources in production, on the possibilities for substitution, and on technological progress. We shall return to intertemporal equity in the final section of the chapter when we look at the question of whether leaving things to market forces guarantees sustainability.

9.4 MARKETS AND THE ENVIRONMENT

In Chapter 4 we distinguished four routes through which the interdependence of economy and environment operates. The environment is:
- the source of inputs of natural resources to production;
- the receptacle for the wastes arising in production and consumption;
- a source of amenity services to consumption;
- the source of life support services to humans.

We are now going to consider the extent to which each of these functions is controlled by markets, and to what extent such markets as exist approximate to the conditions required for market attainment of efficiency in allocation. From earlier sections of this chapter it is clear that one fundamental aspect of this is the question of the existence of property rights, so before working through the list above, we will look at a simple classification of property rights.

9.4.1 Property rights

Property rights actually come in many forms, but for our purposes we can distinguish private and common property rights, and situations where there are no property rights at all.

Private property rights are held by individuals and firms, and are transferred between them. In most such transfers a property right is exchanged for money, and one agent buys it from another agent. Individuals sell their services to firms, from which they buy goods and services. Gifts, where there is no reciprocal movement of money corresponding to the movement of a property right, usually involve individuals rather than firms. Private property rights are the basis for markets. Without them, markets cannot exist.

Common property rights are held by collectives of individuals. In a modern economy, common property rights are mainly held by the government of the nation state, as, for example, in the cases of the coastal sea out to territorial limits (currently 12 miles) or of the airspace of the nation state. Government can allow use of its property by individuals and firms, as with coastal fishing and overflying. Whereas the use of private property is mainly regulated by market transactions involving the payment of a price, the use of common property owned by government is regulated in a variety of ways, or may not be regulated at all. Until recently, government rarely used prices to regulate the use of its common property, but, as we will discuss in Chapter 11 mainly, this is becoming more common now.

The government of a nation state is not the only kind of collective that can hold common property. The nation state is an institution that did not exist throughout most of human history, for most of which – the hunter-gatherer phase – private property was rare. In that phase of history, some land, and the plants and animals on it, was common rather than private property and its use was regulated in a variety of ways by a variety of institutions. The term 'common property' actually comes from Europe in the agricultural phase of history. Under the feudal system of government there was private agricultural property, from which the owners could exclude others, which coexisted with the 'commons', which was land to which all had access for the grazing of livestock. The feudal system included rules and conventions regulating the use of the common land. There are still examples of common land, not owned by government, in modern nation states. In the UK, for example, parts of the New Forest remain as common land, use of which is regulated by a collective of individuals whose historical rights to control are still recognised in law.

In the early part of the hunter-gatherer phase of human history much of the planet was not used at all by humans, and was subject to neither private property rights nor common property rights. With the growth of the human population the unexploited proportion of the planet has declined, and consequently the proportion subject to property rights of one kind or the other has increased. Since the transition to agriculture the extent of private property rights has increased, and common property rights have increasingly become government property rights. However, it is still the case that not everything is subject to property rights of some kind. The oceans that lie outside territorial waters remain outside the ambit of property rights, being owned neither by individuals, firms and governments, nor non-government collectives. To the very limited extent that there is regulation of the use made of the open oceans, it is as the result of agreements between the governments of nation states. As far as fishing is concerned, with some minor exceptions (regarding whales for example), any firm can legally exploit waters outside territorial limits in any feasible manner that serves its interests.

Such a situation of no property rights is known as **free access**, alternatively **open access**. The terminology is a little misleading. The point is not that access for use is not charged for, though that is true. The point is that access and use is totally unregulated by virtue of the complete absence of any kind of property right. It should also be noted that the term free access is also used sometimes in a different way to this. In some cases a property right exits but is so expensive to enforce that it is not exercised, and such a situation is also often referred to as a free-access situation. An example would be a large privately owned area of forest on remote and mountainous terrain. The owner has the legal right to fence the area and exclude would-be recreationalists, but they are few and fencing and excluding is very expensive, so that the would-be recreationalists effectively have free access.

9.4.1.1 The tragedy of the commons

The 'tragedy of the commons' is a phrase that is now widely used in relation to economy's use of the natural environment. It stems from a famous article in the journal *Science* in 1968, with the title 'The tragedy of the commons', by Garrett Hardin. Hardin was referring to the commons of the European feudal system of agriculture noted above. According to Hardin, because everybody could graze as much livestock as they wanted to on the common land it was over-used so that the number and quality of animals that it could support – the amount of food it could produce – was reduced. The tragedy was over-grazing, caused by free access.

The phrase 'tragedy of the commons' is now widely used to refer to the over-use of renewable natural resources and environmental services. This is unfortunate. The problem that it refers to is actually one of free or open access, not common property. The title of the article should have been 'The open access tragedy'. Hardin's idea was that too many livestock would graze the common land because any owner could put as many animals on it as he liked, while not taking account of the consequences of over-use because of not owning the land. This story could apply to land subject to free or open access, but did not apply to the feudal commons. As noted above, they were common property, and it was not true that access was uncontrolled. There were problems with the feudal system and its commons, but they were not due to free access. Common property need not suffer over-use, and is not a 'tragedy'. Historically, there have been many common property systems for regulating use of the natural environment that have worked well over long periods of time.

We will now work through the ways in which the environment and the economy are interdependent, looking at the typical property rights regime and its implications for the ability of a market to regulate use of the environment.

9.4.2 Natural resources

As explained in Chapter 4, natural resources can be classified as stock resources and flow resources, and within the first of these classifications there is a distinction between renewable and non-renewable resources. We will work though that list in reverse order.

9.4.2.1 Non-renewable resources

Non-renewable resources are deposits of minerals and fossil fuels. Such deposits are either private or government property. Where they are government property, exploitation rights are often sold, or leased, to firms. Either way, prices and markets regulate the depletion of these resources.

Where a deposit is owned by a firm, it can be shown that, if the ideal conditions hold, it will be depleted in a way that is consistent with intertemporal efficiency. In order to understand what is involved, it helps to suppose that a firm that owns a deposit sells extraction rights to other firms which actually do the extracting. The unit price for extraction rights is called the **rent**, or the royalty. The rent is the price of a barrel of oil, say, in the well. This is to be distinguished from the price of a barrel of extracted oil, and the difference between the two is the unit cost of extraction.

Now, at the beginning of the year the owner of an oil well has to decide how many units of extraction rights for the coming year to sell. Selling a unit right brings in revenue in the amount of the unit rent, and entails no cost. That revenue could be lent at interest, so that if we denote it as R_0, at the end of the year for every unit right sold the oil well owner will have $(1 + r) \times R_0$, where r is the interest rate. Extraction rights not sold at the beginning of this year are available for sale at the beginning of next year, at the price R_1. What would the relationship between R_0 and R_1 have to be for an oil well owner to be indifferent between selling now and selling one year from now? The answer to this question is reasonably obvious, and is

$$R_1 = (1 + r) \times R_0$$

If this is true, it makes no difference to net worth whether an owner sells now or one year from now – either way, one year from now, the proceeds will be one plus the interest rate times the price now.

Now suppose that there is a perfectly competitive market in rights to extract units of oil, barrels say, with a 'large' number of firms selling them and a 'large' number of buyers. In that case, the relationship between the market equilibrium price one year from now and now will be

$$R_1 = (1 + r) \times R_0$$

If R_1 were less than this, owners would want to sell more extraction rights as they could do better by doing that and lending the proceeds. If R_1 were more than this, owners would want to sell less extraction rights as they could do better by keeping the oil in the ground for a year and then selling the extraction rights.

The basic point here is that for an owner, keeping oil, or any non-renewable resource, in the ground, rather than selling the right to extract it, is a form of investment. The question of how many unit rights to sell is also the question of how much oil to hold, how much to invest in oil? In the previous chapter we saw that a firm motivated by net worth maximisation would invest in all projects with rates of return greater than the interest rate. The above relationship is just a particular of that general principle. The rate of return to investment in oil by an oil well owner is just the future increase in the value of oil in the ground divided by the current value of oil in the ground, that is

$$\frac{R_1 - R_0}{R_0}$$

Setting this equal to the rate of interest r gives

$$\frac{R_1 - R_0}{R_0} = r$$

where multiplying both sides by R_0 gives

$$R_1 - R_0 = r \times R_0$$

and thus

$$R_1 = R_0 + (r \times R_0) = (1 + r) \times R_0$$

as above.

In section 9.1.4 we saw that intertemporal efficiency requires that rates of return are equal across all lines of investment, and that, given ideal conditions, markets would bring this about. We have just worked through a special case of this argument for investment in oil, or any non-renewable resource, in the ground. Leaving some of a non-renewable resource *in situ*, rather than extracting it, is a form of investment. Intertemporal efficiency requires that renewable resources are depleted, dis-invested in, so that their unit rent increases at a proportional rate equal to the rate of interest.

There are two very important things to be noted about this argument. First, it establishes that in a system of markets that satisfy the ideal conditions, non-renewable resources would be depleted in ways that go with allocative efficiency. We saw, in section 9.3.2, that intertemporal efficiency is *not* the same as intertemporal fairness. If non-renewable resources were being depleted consistently with efficiency that would not necessarily mean that they were being depleted in a way that was fair to future generations. It could be that they were being depleted so as to leave future generations to be worse-off than the current generation, possibly much worse-off. As we saw in Chapter 7, if capital can be substituted for resources in production, whether or not this is the case depends not only on the rate of resource depletion but also on the savings rate.

The second thing to be noted is that, in fact, markets do *not* satisfy the ideal conditions necessary for them to produce an efficient allocation. In regard to the markets that are directly involved in non-renewable resource extraction, they are not, for example, perfectly competitive – owners of deposits are generally not price takers, nor are firms in the extraction business. It is not found that the unit rent increases over time at a proportionate rate equal to the interest. The extraction, and use, of most non-renewable resources also involves external effects in the form of waste emissions of many kinds.

This is not to say that markets have no influence on the way that non-renewable resources are exploited. They do. Because non-renewable resource deposits are subject to property rights and can be traded in markets, their depletion is subject to the forces of supply and demand. As depletion proceeds, so increasing scarcity tends to increase unit rent. With P for the price of the extracted resource and C for

Figure 9.8 The market for a non-renewable resource.

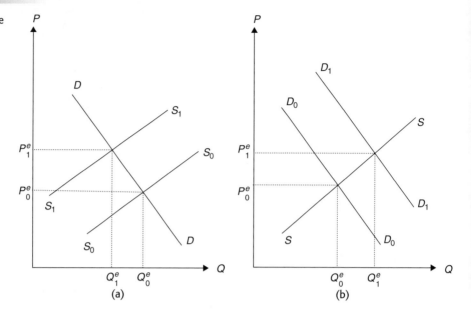

the unit cost of extraction

$$P = C + R$$

so that higher R will mean higher P, and hence reduced demand for the extracted resource and extraction rights, unless C falls. Typically C rises, rather than falls, as depletion proceeds. This is because the resource stock generally consists of deposits that differ in quality, cost of extraction, and proximity to where the extracted resource is to be used. Deposits of lower quality, higher extraction cost or greater remoteness will not be used until those of higher quality, lower extraction cost or lesser remoteness have been exhausted. As extraction shifts from the latter to the former, so the supply function shifts upwards as shown in Figure 9.8(a), where the subscript 0 refers to now and 1 to the future. Over time P rises and the quantity of the extracted resource used falls. This effect may be offset temporarily by the discovery of new high-quality and/or low-cost deposits. As P rises, so the incentive to explore for new deposits is increased. This is the explanation for the phenomenon of known reserves staying more or less constant in size over time. New discoveries left aside, and other things being equal, market forces will tend to slow down the rate of use of a non-renewable resource. The extent of this conservation effect will depend on the size of the shifts in the supply function, the elasticity of supply, and the elasticity of demand.

However, other things are not generally equal in fact. As discussed in Chapter 6, a dominant feature of recent economic history has been the growth of the level of global economic activity, due to population growth and increasing average per capita income. As discussed in the previous chapter, demand depends on income as well as price. As individuals' incomes increase, other things being equal they demand more of most commodities, so that the demand for most non-renewable resources, used as inputs to the production of those commodities, increases. With economic growth, for most non-renewable resources, the demand function will shift outwards, as in Figure 9.8(b), where, in order to focus on the demand-side of things, the supply function does not shift. Other things being equal, for most non-renewable resources, economic growth will lead to a higher price for the extracted resource and a higher amount used. The extents to which price and quantity each increase will depend on the income elasticity of demand for the extracted resource, the elasticity of supply, and the (price) elasticity of demand.

In history, the effects considered separately in each of the two elements (a) and (b) of Figure 9.8 are operating simultaneously – rising costs and/or rents are working to reduce the level of use, increasing income is working to increase the level of use. Both effects tend to drive up the price of the extracted resource. Whether this goes with increasing, static, or declining levels of use depends on the circumstances of the particular resource in question. One of the important circumstances is the extent to which it is possible to substitute for the use of the resource in production. The easier it is to substitute for the resource, the more elastic will the demand for it be. In terms of Figure 9.8(a), the slope of *DD* is less the easier it is to substitute for the resource, so that a given shift in the supply function will result in a smaller price increase and a larger reduction in demand. The slope of *DD* will reflect both the technological opportunities for substitution and the costs involved. The substitution may be of another resource for the resource in question, as, for example, with the use of aluminium instead of copper in many products. Or, it may involve substituting capital or labour for resource use.

9.4.2.2 *Renewable resources*

As seen in Chapter 3, renewable resources are biotic populations exploited by hunting and gathering rather than by agriculture. In modern economies the main renewable resources are trees and fish.

Forests are either private or common, and in that case almost invariably government, property. Often they provide a range of services to the economy, as discussed in the companion website's supplement to Chapter 4, including the supply of timber as an input to production. Private owners regulate timber harvesting by selling permits to cut timber. In the forestry context the price of such a permit is often referred to as a stumpage fee rather than a rent or royalty. Government owners can and often do use stumpage fees, but also use other means of regulation of the extraction of trees from their forests. Forestry economics is a specialised area which we are not going to go into here – you will find references in the Further Reading section at the end of the chapter.

In considering fish we will look at fish in the sea. Marine fish stocks are either common property or open access. Those stocks inside the limits of territorial waters are government property, those outside such limits are open access resources.

9.4.2.2.1 PRIVATE PROPERTY RIGHTS OUTCOMES

Despite the fact that no marine fish stocks are privately owned, much of the fisheries literature in neoclassical economics is about what would be the case if the populations of some particular species of fish were privately owned. It is shown in that literature that *if* the populations were privately owned and *if* the ideal conditions for market operations were satisfied throughout the economy, then fish would be harvested as required for efficiency in allocation. In general terms, the argument to this conclusion is the same as that developed above for non-renewable resources. We imagine that there are a 'large' number of firms each of which owns a population of some species of fish, and that there are a 'large' number of fishing firms who have to buy the rights to catch this kind of fish from such owners. Owners invest in their stocks by not selling the rights to take all of the fish that they own. They maximise net worth by doing the amount of such investment that equates the rate of return to it with the interest rate. This is how they decide how many extraction permits to sell at any given time. Given a single interest rate, this means that all such owners operate with the same rate of return to fish investment, which is the same rate of return as in all other lines of investment in the economy, which is what intertemporal allocative efficiency requires.

If, as is standard in the fisheries economics literature, we assume that the population dynamics of the species is density-dependent growth as discussed in Chapter 2 (and see also Chapters 4 and 7) and that owners ensure sustainable yield harvesting, it turns out that the perfect market/intertemporally efficient outcome has two interesting properties. First, it will involve a harvest smaller than the maximum sustainable harvest. Second, it may involve maintaining the stock size so low as to risk the exploited species going extinct. This is more likely the slower growing the species and the higher the interest rate.

A rigorous demonstration of these results is fairly difficult (see references in Further Reading) but the basic point involved is simple. It is that the rate of return to investment in fish in the water depends on reproductive behaviour of the fish stock. Think of a fish stock owner contemplating a reduction in the quantity of extraction permits she sells now, i.e. increasing her investment in fish in the water. What is the future pay-off to such an investment? In the future she would have available for sale permits for the fish that got left in the water now, *and* the offspring of those fish. If F less fish are taken now, there will be $F + (g \times F)$ or $(1 + g) \times F$ more fish to be taken in the future, where g is the ratio of the additional growth to the increase in stock size, which ratio depends on stock size. The rate of return to this increase in investment is the excess of the future pay-off over the current sacrifice as a proportion of the current sacrifice, so that

$$i_F = \frac{\{(1 + g) \times F\} - F}{F}$$

where i_F is the rate of return. Cancelling F's on the righthand side this is

$$i_F = \frac{(1 + g) - 1}{1}$$

so that

$$i_F = g$$

The fish stock owner operating under the ideal conditions for markets will invest in fish in the water up to the point where the rate of return to so doing is equal to the interest rate, up to the point where

$$i_F = r$$

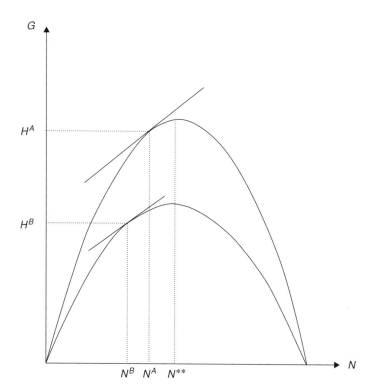

Figure 9.9
Efficient fish
harvesting.

which is

$$g = r$$

where r is the interest rate.

Figure 9.9 shows density-dependent growth for two species: A and B, with the vertical axis measuring the amount of growth in tonnes or whatever, and the horizontal axis measuring stock size in the same units. The curves plot sustainable harvest size, as well as natural growth, against stock size. N^{**} is the maximum sustainable harvest for both species. Species A grows more than B at all stock sizes other than 0 and carrying capacity. The slope of the curve is g, which differs between the species. For both species g starts out high and declines to 0 at N^{**}, after which it becomes negative. If g is to be equal to r, the interest rate, it must be positive. Harvests that have $g = r$ as intertemporal efficiency requires will involve keeping N below N^{**}, and will be less than the maximum sustainable harvest. This is the first property of intertemporal efficiency.

To show the second property we have drawn two parallel straight lines tangential to each curve in Figure 9.9. You can see that N is smaller for B than for A where the slopes of the two curves are equal, at the points of tangency, and that this will be true for all positive slopes for the lines. As the lines get steeper so both points of tangency move towards the origin, but that for B will always be nearer to it. The slope of the straight lines is representing the interest rate r, and the points of tangency where $g = r$ identify the intertemporally efficient sustainable harvests,

Figure 9.10
Open access
means
overfishing.

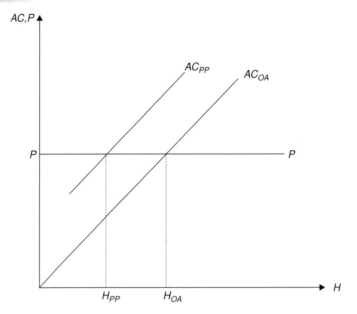

H^A and H^B, and the corresponding stock sizes, for each species. If r were 0, the points of tangency would both be directly above N^{**} where for both populations g is zero. As r gets bigger the slope increases, and the stock sizes under the points of tangency, N^A and N^B, move toward zero with N^A always bigger than N^B. For a slow-growing species such as B and a high interest rate, the constant stock size could be very small with the species vulnerable to extinction if its environment deteriorates. Intertemporal efficiency does *not* guarantee the survival of slow-growing species.

9.4.2.2.2 OPEN ACCESS OUTCOMES

Now we consider open, or free, access fishing. This is what happens in the seas outside the territorial limits of nation states. It is also what happens if the exploitation of common property fisheries is left to market forces, as is the case within territorial limits where the state does not regulate the fisheries in any way.

Open access fishing will, for the same species, involve larger harvests than would occur if the fish populations being exploited were subject to private property rights. The reason for this is shown in Figure 9.10. Fishing is carried out by firms in the fish extraction industry. This industry is more like perfect competition than it is like monopoly. There are typically many firms in the industry. New firms set up and enter the industry when there are profits to be earned in it. In Figure 9.10 AC stands for average cost, the total divided by the harvest size. As new firms enter the industry harvest size increases and average costs rise, because, for example, it is necessary to harvest more remote populations of the target species. Also, more fishing boats exploiting a given population usually means lower catches, and hence higher average cost, per boat. Profits are positive so long as average cost is less than the price for which caught fish sell, P. New firms stop entering the industry when $AC = P$.

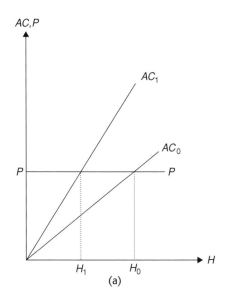

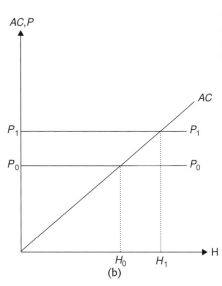

Figure 9.11
Effects of
depletion on
open-access
harvesting.

The basic point is that where the fish populations are privately owned average costs, AC_{PP}, for the fishing industry are higher than they are where there is open access, AC_{OA}, for any level of industry harvest, because of the need to buy extraction rights, which is a cost to the fishing industry. Consequently, the industry harvest level at which new firms cease to enter the fishing industry will be higher, for the same extraction costs, with open access. Note that where government owns the rights to take fish, it could sell them to fishermen. Fisheries economists have long argued that this would be a good way for governments to regulate use of the fisheries within their territorial limits. Generally, the higher the charge per unit right to extract, the more will the harvest be reduced below the open access level.

It is sometimes claimed that open access necessarily entails the targeted fish species being harvested to extinction. This is not true in general, though it may be in particular cases. Even with open access there are market forces that work to protect harvested species, and may save them from extinction. The average cost functions in Figure 9.10 are drawn for a given total stock size. As the total stock, and the size of the individual populations, is reduced by harvesting, so it would be expected that average cost as a function of harvest size would shift upwards, as shown in Figure 9.11(a), on account of fish being harder to find. For any given price for caught fish, this would reduce the size of the open access industry harvest, thus reducing the rate of depletion. The relationship between stock size and average cost would vary across fish species – for some this effect may be a strong influence on the rate of depletion, in other cases it may be weak. Another, related, factor that historically has operated against the possibility of open access leading to extinction is the fact that fishing boats and equipment are not generally species-specific. When the costs of extracting one species rise substantially, some of the fishing firms in that industry may be able to switch into an industry based on a different, more abundant and/or less costly species. Given that almost all of the world's fish species are now being heavily exploited, the potential for this is much less than was the case a few decades ago.

There is, however, a demand side-effect that works in the opposite direction, possibly increasing the propensity for open access fishing to lead to extinction of the target species. This is illustrated in Figure 9.11(b), where a higher price for caught fish increases the harvest size. The demand function for a given fish species will shift out with economic growth at a rate depending on the income elasticity of demand for that species, which will, other things being equal, lead to an increase in the price and a larger harvest. The demand function can also shift outwards as the result of other fish species moving from open access to government-owned and -regulated.

When we looked at fishing outcomes under a private property regime we ignored the costs of catching fish, in order to keep things simple. If the private property case is examined with stock and catch sizes affecting costs, the story gets more complicated but the outcome is not essentially different – intertemporally efficient harvesting will generally involve harvests below maximum sustainable yield, stock sizes will be lower the higher the interest rate, and stock sizes will be lower for slower-growing species.

9.4.2.3 Flow resources

As discussed in Chapter 4, flow resources are energy resources frequently referred to as 'renewables' – solar, wind, wave, tidal, hydro. These are all open-access resources in themselves, but using them requires access to land or water which is subject to private or government property rights. This is not strictly true of the wave power that could be generated in seas outside territorial limits, or of the wind power that could be generated over such seas. At present the open oceans are not potential sites for the location of equipment to generate electricity from water or air movements.

Where sites for flow energy sources are privately owned, the owners will require payment for this use. This applies mainly to land-based developments in solar, wind and hydro. The amount of this kind of rent that landowners can charge will depend on the alternative uses of the land and on the willingness to pay of the firms generating the electricity – supply and demand again. While there is no market in, for example, solar radiation, there is a market in the land needed to exploit solar radiation, which has competing uses. There are external effects associated with the use of land for electricity generation. While the solar, wind and hydro ways of generating electricity do not give rise to waste emissions, as the use of fossil fuels does, they do impact on the amenity services provided by the land that they are situated on. While some people claim to enjoy looking at, for example, wind turbines, the impact of energy developments on amenity services is generally regarded as adverse.

Where sites for flow energy sources are government-owned, the government could act like a private owner and charge for use, it could allow open access, or it could regulate access in some non-market way such as the granting of free licences.

9.4.3 Waste flows and sinks

The waste flows generated in production and consumption are owned by their generators. Generally they are desired neither by their owners nor by others, which is just another way of saying that they are wastes. In some cases the by-products of production and consumption are desired by their owners or others, as inputs to recycling. In that case they do not become waste flows.

When economists consider property rights in relation to wastes, what they are normally interested in is not the flows as such but the environmental sinks into which they are inserted. When we looked at an emissions problem as an example of a detrimental externality situation, in 9.2.4.2 above (see also Figure 9.4), the excessive level of emissions was explained in terms of the lack of property rights in the lake into which the emissions went. As we noted there, another sort of property right question relevant to waste problems is whether people have the legal right to an undamaged sink even though they do not own it.

The legal status of the various kinds of environmental sink and of peoples' interests in them varies widely. Land is usually private or common property, and in the latter case it is usually in the hands of the government. The situation is similar with rivers and lakes. The air over a nation is government property, otherwise it is open access. As we shall see in Chapter 13 when we look at climate change, in regard to some emissions the air over the whole of the earth is the single relevant sink, which gives rise to problems in regard to the incentives for governments to exercise control over those emissions. Inside territorial waters the seas are common, government, property, but outside those limits the seas are open access. Historically, governments have often not done much to control the use made of their property as waste sink, but, particularly since the industrial revolution, the trend has been for them to do so to an increasing extent. This has been driven by the increasing volumes of wastes of all kinds, by increasing knowledge of the damage done by many wastes, and by increasing voter awareness and concern.

Given all this, markets as such have a limited role in regulating the amount of wastes dumped into environmental sinks, a job that must be done largely by government. It should be noted, however, that it follows from the first law of thermodynamics, conservation of mass, that to the extent that markets regulate the use of non-renewable resources they do affect waste flows. If a rising price for some resource reduces its use, then that will reduce the waste flows that originate with its extraction and use.

9.4.4 Amenity and life support services

Amenity service flows are based on features of the natural environment which may be private property, common property or open access. Only in the first case can control of use be left solely to market forces. Even where the environmental bases for amenity services are privately owned, market failure often exists because the services are non-rivalrous and/or non-excludable.

The environmental features and processes that support the provision of life support services typically do not align with the boundaries of nation states, and are often global in scope. Given the absence of a world government, this means that they are generally open access unless international agreements between nation states exist to control use. A prime example of what is involved is the case of climate change due to the enhanced greenhouse effect, which we will look at in detail in Chapter 13. Broadly, emissions of the gases which affect global temperature mix uniformly throughout the earth's atmosphere – it is the global concentration that matters. Without international cooperation, the sink for these wastes is open access, and is over-used.

9.5 MARKETS AND SUSTAINABILITY

We have seen that the invisible hand does not in fact work. Market failures of various kinds mean that actual market outcomes are not allocatively efficient. Further, achieving efficiency does not guarantee equity, between either those alive at a point in time, or different points in time. Even under 'ideal' conditions, market outcomes may be very unfair.

We have defined sustainability as:

maintaining the capacity of the joint economy–environment system to continue to satisfy the needs and desires of humans for a long time into the future

Sustainability is about equity as between those alive at different points in time, about intergenerational equity. Adopting sustainability as an objective means acting now so as to leave the joint economy–environment system as well able to satisfy the needs and desires of future generations as it is able to satisfy ours. Sustainable development means increasing the capability of the joint system to do that. If sustainability is not achieved, sustainable development will not be.

Correcting market failure does not guarantee sustainability, and, hence, does not guarantee sustainable development. This follows from the fact that intertemporal efficiency is not the same as intertemporal equity. It is also the case that achieving allocative efficiency at a point in time does not guarantee that there will not occur environmental damage that hurts the interests of future generations. Both of these points are implicit in the analysis looked at thus far in this chapter. They are so important that we will spend a little time finishing up the chapter by looking at particular examples that make the points explicitly.

9.5.1 Non-renewable resource depletion and sustainability

Imagine a closed economy such as that considered in Chapter 7, where national income is produced using inputs of labour, capital services and a non-renewable natural resource. The production function is Cobb–Douglas with constant returns to scale. The population size is constant. There is no technological progress. It can be shown that for such an economy, provided that the natural resource is sufficiently unimportant in production, it is possible, despite the finite size of the resource stock, to maintain per capita consumption constant indefinitely. Sustainability, as equal per capita consumption across successive generations for ever, is possible. This requires that the resource is depleted efficiently.

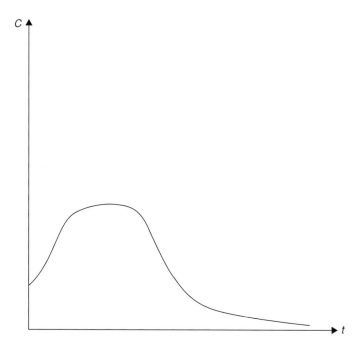

Figure 9.12 An
intertemporally
efficient
consumption
path.

Now imagine that this economy is run by a benevolent dictator who is all-knowing and all-powerful. He makes sure that the resource is depleted in an intertemporally efficient way. He can and does ensure that for all future time the savings rate reflects the current generation's preferences as between current and future consumption. If they prefer current to future consumption, so that they regard £1 of consumption now more highly than £1 worth in the future, as most people do, then for this economy consumption over time will behave as shown in Figure 9.12. Given a constant population this refers to total and per capita consumption, on the vertical axis. The horizontal axis measures time. Consumption first increases, reaches a peak and then goes into decline. In this model economy, consumption 'approaches zero asymptotically' – once it has turned down it gets closer and closer to zero over time, but it never actually gets there.

The outcome shown in Figure 9.12 is not sustainability. Early generations experience increasing consumption, later ones experience declining consumption, and in the distant future consumption is very low for a very long time. The problem is not that constant consumption is not possible. It is. There exists a savings policy which if adopted at the outset would ensure that consumption remained constant for ever. As explained in Chapter 7, in this sort of model capital can be substituted for the resource. Given enough savings, capital accumulation would offset resource depletion so as to hold consumption constant. The reason that this does not happen for the situation that Figure 9.12 represents is that the dictator does not enforce the necessary savings behaviour, but accepts the savings behaviour that individuals prefer. The problem is *not* market failure. The resource *is* being depleted as required for intertemporal efficiency.

If the dictator ensured that the amount saved and invested was always equal to the total amount of rent – the unit rent or royalty multiplied by the amount extracted – arising in the depletion of the resource, then consumption would be constant for ever. Such a savings rule is called the **Hartwick rule**, named after the economist John Hartwick who first showed that such a rule would give constant consumption in this kind of model economy, provided that the resource was depleted efficiently. Left to their own devices, individuals will not save as required for sustainability in this model economy. The Hartwick rule is a constraint on individual behaviour that would have to be adopted in such an economy if it was to achieve sustainability. The point of the story here is that intertemporal efficiency is not sufficient for sustainability. The point carries over into more complex models. Adding endogenous technological progress to the model here, for example, does not of itself produce constant consumption – it can do if there is enough saving and accumulation, but 'enough' may not be forthcoming if individuals get what they want.

9.5.2 The efficient level of waste emissions

Back in section 9.2.4.2 we looked at waste emissions as an example of an adverse externality. We saw in Figure 9.4 that because of the externality involved, emissions and widget production would be larger than allocative efficiency requires – in terms of the latter Q^M rather than Q^E. Correcting the market failure would involve bringing about Q^E and the corresponding level of emissions. The corresponding level of emissions is not, it is important to note, zero. Allocative efficiency does *not* require zero emissions. It *does* require the level of emissions at which Social marginal costs are equal to Social marginal benefits. This level may involve a lot of pollution in the sense that we defined it in Chapter 4 – harm to any organism – and may threaten sustainability.

The social costs and benefits of an activity reflect only those effects that it gives rise to that agents in the economy are aware of and care about. In constructing Figure 9.4 we envisaged a lake into which wastes were discharged where they imposed costs on a firm using the lake as water supply. Suppose instead that the wastes impose no such costs on any productive activity, but do harm plant and animal life in the lake, i.e. pollute it. Is Q^M greater than allocative efficiency requires in this case? Not necessarily. If no human agent cares about pollution in this lake, there are no external costs and Q^M goes with allocative efficiency. From the perspective of neoclassical economics there would be no basis for policy to reduce the level of emissions and pollution in this case, as there is no market failure to correct.

In many such cases, of course, human agents will care about the pollution of the lake. It could, for example, impact on the amenity services that the lake delivers. In such a case, external costs would arise as the monetary valuation of the damage done to those services. Neoclassical economists would estimate the external costs in such a case by figuring out what those affected would be willing to pay to avoid the damage. The point is *not* that neoclassical economics and efficiency ignore pollution that does not impact on production costs. It *is* that they take account of it only to the extent that somebody is willing to pay to avoid it. Pollution that does not affect production costs or give rise to any effects that anybody cares about may well, nevertheless, have implications for the future ability of the joint economy–environment system to satisfy human needs and desires. The harmed organisms may be, for example, members of a keystone species, the loss of which would lead to a loss of ecosystem resilience.

What is involved here can be looked at on the basis of a reinterpretation of Figure 9.4. Suppose that it has been established by research scientists that emissions continuing at the level that goes with Q^M would mean the disappearance of the lake's population of some species of fauna. It has also been established that reducing widget production to Q^E would reduce emissions such that there would be no threat to the population. Should the government induce the widget firm to cut back its output to Q^E? On neoclassical allocative efficiency criteria the answer to this question depends on whether it can be established that there are external costs great enough to draw *SMC* where it is in Figure 9.4, or higher. If it can, the biologically based proposal for a reduction in widget production is justified on efficiency criteria, otherwise it is not, and a neoclassical economist government advisor would recommend against bringing about the reduction to Q^E.

Assuming as we are now that the emissions do not affect production costs anywhere, any external costs must originate with individuals, and the question is whether they care about the fate of this organism, and if so how much? Do they care enough to put *SMC* high enough to cut at, or to the left of Q^E? Neoclassical economists would answer this question by asking people about their willingness to pay to protect the population in the lake. Whether meaningful answers to such questions can be obtained is somewhat controversial in neoclassical economics, but we will assume that they can.

We have not suggested yet what kind of organism is at risk. Consider two possibilities. In case *A*, the threatened fauna is a population of large fish that recreational fisherman go after, and for which the lake is famous. In case *B*, it is a population of detritivores (decomposers) – bugs – that nobody except a biologist has ever heard of. It is obvious that the prospects of finding enough willingness to pay to save the population, to justify Q^E, are much greater in case *A* than in case *B*. Willingness to pay to save a population of bugs may well be very small. It is entirely plausible to assume that the bugs are a keystone species the disappearance of which would threaten the resilience of the lake ecosystem, whereas the fish are not. The efficiency criteria could well justify the extinction of a keystone species.

It could be objected here that if this is so, it must be because of imperfect information. If they knew, this argument would go, that the bugs were a keystone species, people would be willing to pay enough to save them because they would realise that without them the lake ecosystem might collapse, possibly taking with it some of the populations that they do like, such as the case *A* fish. While this kind of information is clearly important, and neoclassical economists asking about willingness to pay take great care to provide it, complete information does not ensure that a threatened population will pass the efficiency/willingness to pay test. Even with complete information, people's preferences may not be consistent with what environmental protection for sustainability requires. The situation here is like that which we saw for a slow-growing fish species subject to private property rights held by agents facing a high rate of interest – although the efficiency criterion is met, it does not guarantee non-extinction.

All of this is made much more difficult by virtue of the fact that in reality things are rarely as clear-cut as in the story here. Scientists would not, for example, know that Q^M means extinction while Q^E means safety. Rather, they would know that the probability of extinction was much higher at Q^M than at Q^E. In the next chapter, we will look at how ecological economists think that environmental standards should be set in circumstances where knowledge is uncertain.

SUMMARY

Sustainability is about intertemporal equity – not leaving our successors worse-off than we are. Sustainable development recognises that many are now insufficiently well-off and seeks to remedy that by leaving our successors better-off, on average, than we are. Both are about equity. Both require environmental protection, capital accumulation and technological progress. Market forces alone cannot be relied on to do what sustainable development requires in these respects – government intervention in market systems is required. This intervention needs to go beyond the correction of market failure, as efficiency, which is what an ideal market system delivers, is not the same as equity and may not protect the environment as sustainability requires. As we shall see, the fact that what the market delivers is not sustainability, does not mean that we cannot use market mechanisms in the pursuit of sustainable development. While ecological economics does not accept efficiency as the pre-eminent objective of policy, it does not reject markets and price incentives as instruments of policy.

KEYWORDS

Agent (p. 320): a firm or an individual.
Command economy (p. 309): where some central authority determines what will be produced, how it will be produced, and by whom it will be used.
Common property (p. 338): rights are held by collectives of individuals.
Compensation test (p. 311): the normative judgement that if the gainers could compensate the losers from some change then it should happen.
Consumer sovereignty (p. 324): the idea that the measure of economic performance is the preferences of individuals.
Efficient allocation (p. 310): there is no possible rearrangement of inputs to production, levels of production or share-outs of what is produced that could make somebody feel better-off without making anybody else feel worse-off.
Externality (p. 327): when the actions of one agent have an unintended effect on some other agent or agents.
Free access (p. 339): where property rights do not exist or are not enforced (see also **open access**).
Free rider problem (p. 326): where selfish individuals conceal their willingness to pay for public good provision hoping that others will not and will pay for provision which all can enjoy for nothing.

General competitive equilibrium (p. 310): where the markets for all commodities and all inputs are in equilibrium.

Hartwick rule (p. 352): constant consumption in a model economy can be achieved if the total value of the economy's stock of reproducible capital together with its stock of non-renewable resources is held constant over time by investing the rent.

Imperfect competition (p. 321): a market where there are many price-taking buyers and lots of sellers who are not price takers.

Marginal benefit (p. 313): the benefit associated with a small increase in consumption.

Marginal cost (p. 313): the cost associated with a small increase in production.

Marginal external cost (p. 328): the difference between social marginal cost, or just marginal cost and private marginal cost, the marginal cost borne by the externality generator.

Marginal willingness to pay (p. 312): what people would be willing to pay for a small increase in consumption; the demand function shows the variation of the marginal willingness to pay with the amount they already have.

Market failure (p. 320): where market equilibria do not correspond to allocative efficiency.

Merit goods (p. 324): commodities for which the principle of consumer sovereignty does not hold.

Monopoly (p. 321): where there is just one seller.

Monopsony (p. 321): where there is just one buyer.

Non-excludable (p. 326): where an agent cannot be prevented from consuming the commodity in question.

Non-rivalrous (p. 325): where an increase in one agent's consumption does not reduce the consumption of other agents.

Oligopoly (p. 321): where there are many price-taking buyers and a few sellers who are not price takers.

Open access (p. 339): where property rights do not exist or are not enforced.

Perfect competition (p. 321): where there are so many buyers and sellers that no agent can influence the market price.

Price takers (p. 321): agents who act in the belief that the market terms they face cannot be affected by their own behaviour.

Private property (p. 338): rights are held by individuals and firms.

Public goods (p. xx): things which an individual or firm cannot be denied use of because of non-payment for use, such as the atmosphere.

Pure market economy (p. 309): where all economic decision making and activity are completely decentralised to individuals and firms with coordination by markets.

Rent (p. 340): the unit price for extraction rights.

Second best problem (p. 332): as the government tries to address one market failure (e.g. by introducing a green tax) it could contribute to other existing or generate new market failures. If so, correcting just one of the market failures to achieve marginal cost pricing, will not necessarily improve overal efficiency in the economy.

Welfare economics (p. 309): a branch of neoclassical economics concerned with the relative merits of alternative solutions to the economic problem, and how to achieve the best solution.

FURTHER READING

Introductory economics principles texts always extol the virtues of markets and usually explain the conditions necessary for them to deliver allocative efficiency, though they often fail to make sufficiently clear how restrictive those conditions are, and to properly differentiate between efficiency and equity. Examples are Begg *et al.** (2000) and Mankiw* (2001). Intertemporal allocative efficiency is not usually dealt with adequately in introductory texts. More advanced microeconomics texts are often less than comprehensive on intertemporal issues: an exception is Varian (1987). Boadway and Bruce (1984) is a good, intermediate level, welfare economics text. Perman *et al.* (2003) is a resource and environmental economics text which provides summaries of static (ch. 5) and dynamic (ch. 12) welfare economics. Cornes and Sandler (1996) is a comprehensive treatment of the neoclassical theory of externalities and public goods. On the latter, see also Ledyard (1995). On property rights see Ostrom (1990) and Ostrom *et al.* (2002).

Most of neoclassical resource and environmental economics is about market failure and its correction in relation to resource extraction and waste insertion. Most textbooks in these areas assume prior knowledge of economics, as in economics programmes these subjects are options in the later undergraduate years. An exception is Common (1996). Tietenberg (2000) does not require much prior knowledge of economics. Standard texts at the advanced undergraduate or postgraduate level are: Dasgupta and Heal (1979); Baumol and Oates (1988); Hartwick and Olewiler (1998); Kolstad (2000); Grafton *et al.* (2003); and Perman *et al.* (2003). Van den Bergh (1999) is a very comprehensive collection of survey articles in resource and environmental economics: see also Bromley (1995).

Fisheries economics, which is most of the neoclassical economics of renewable resources, is dealt with in all of the texts just cited: Clark (1990) is solely about renewable resources. Most resource economics texts deal with forestry. Johansson and Löfgren (1985) is a good account of the basic theory of forestry economics, while Bowes and Krutilla (1989) focuses particularly on the management of government-owned forests for multiple uses – amenity services (recreation) and resource supply (timber), for example. The amenity service provision role of the environment is looked at, from the market failure perspective, in most of the texts cited above – see, for example, chs. 11–13 in Perman *et al.* (2003). We will look at major issues in regard to life support services in Chapter 13 (on climate change) and Chapter 14 (on biodiversity loss) later in this book.

Journals such as *Environmental and Resource Economics* and the *Journal of Environmental Economics and Management* are basically all about neoclassical environmental and resource economics. The May 2000 issue of the latter marked the journal's 25th anniversary and contains articles reviewing the major developments in the field over the journal's history. That history is pretty much the modern history of the field. In 1974 the May issue of the *Review of Economic Studies* was a symposium on non-renewable resources, which contained some seminal papers in relation to the issues discussed in section 9.5.1 – sustainability when non-renewable resources are used in production. Solow (1974a) showed that constant consumption for ever may be possible, while Dasgupta and Heal (1974) established the result shown in Figure 9.12. The original demonstration that saving all of the rent would produce constant consumption is found in Hartwick (1977).

DISCUSSION TOPICS

1. While neoclassical economists see creating private property rights as a good way of looking after the environment, many environmentalists consider doing so to be immoral. What do you think? Suppose, for example, that an endangered species could be protected by the government declaring that company X now owned it. Would that be acceptable?
2. Should people be made to save more to look after the interests of future generations?
3. Do you think that giving the vote to children would mean that the future would be better cared for in democratic societies? Or would taking it away from people over 70?

WEBSITES

The International Association for the Study of Common Property seeks to improve understanding of institutions for managing collectively used environmental resources – http://www.indiana.edu/~iascp/. The International Institute of Fisheries, Economics and Trade is an organisation for the exchange of information about fisheries – http://oregonstate.edu/Dept/IIFET.

EXERCISES

1. In Figure 9.4, suppose that

$$PMC = 10 + (0.5 \times Q)$$
$$SMB = PMB = MR = 30 - (0.5 \times Q)$$
$$MEC = 10$$

   What is the firm's profit maximising output (Q^M)? What is the allocatively efficient output for the firm (Q^E)? How large would MEC have to be for Q^E to be zero?
2. This exercise shows how the Coase Theorem works. There is a lake into which a widget firm discharges effluent, imposing clean-up costs on a smidget firm that extracts water from the lake. For the widget firm total costs are Q^2 and widgets sell at $12 each. By working out costs and receipts for $Q = 1, 2, \ldots 10$ confirm that the profit maximising output is 6. Now suppose that costs for the smidget firm vary with widget output as $C = 20 + (0.5 \times Q^2)$, and that the widget firm has to compensate the smidget firm for its extra costs due to widget production. By working out the amount of compensation for $Q = 0, 1, 2 \ldots 10$ show that for the widget firm profits less compensation is maximised at $Q = 4$ and that the smidget firm's costs after compensation are the same for any level of Q. Now suppose that the widget firm has the right to discharge into the lake, and the smidget firm can pay it to reduce its output and effluent discharge. For $Q = 10, 9, \ldots 1, 0$ work out the levels of payment that would compensate the widget firm for producing at that

level rather than at $Q = 6$, and what the smidget firm's costs inclusive of compensation would be. Confirm that these net costs are minimised when $Q = 4$. Explain how all this shows that bargaining leads to an efficient outcome irrespective of the assignment of property rights.

3. In the market for a non-renewable resource input, the demand function is

$$Q^D = (a \times Y) - (b \times P)$$

where Q^D is the quantity demanded, Y is national income and P is price, and the supply function is

$$Q^S = (c \times P) - (d \times \Sigma Q)$$

where Q^S is quantity supplied and ΣQ is cumulated past extraction. The parameters take the values $a = 0.1$, $b = 0.5$ and $c = 2$, and the initial level for Y is 100. Simulate the histories of Q and P out to year 100 for:

(a) Y constant and $d = 0$
(b) Y growing at 2.5 per cent per year and $d = 0$
(c) Y growing at 2.5 per cent per year and $d = 0.01$
(d) Y growing at 2.5 per cent per year and $d = 0.05$

4. (a)   Consider an open access fishery where the cost per unit of catching fish is

$$AC = \frac{W \times H}{N^2}$$

where AC is average cost, W is the cost of a unit of fishing input effort, H is the catch size, and N is the size of the fish stock. Sketch the relationship between AC and H for different levels of N. Firms will cease entering the fishery when profits are zero, which is where

$$P = AC$$

with P for the price of a caught fish.

For logistic growth of the stock, sustainable harvests, from Chapter 7, are given by

$$H = 0.4 \times \left(\frac{100 - N}{100} \right) \times N$$

(b)   Find the stock size for this fishery for 'bioeconomic equilibrium' – where the size of the fishing fleet is constant and a sustainable harvest is being taken – for $P = 6$ and $W = 500$. By repeating the calculation for $P = 7$ and $W = 550$ show that the bioeconomic equilibrium stock size goes down for higher P and up for higher W. Explain this.

(c)   Repeat these calculations for

$$H = 0.5 \times \left(\frac{100 - N}{100} \right) \times N$$

and discuss the results.

PART III
GOVERNANCE

For sustainability, markets alone do not suffice – governance is also needed. Governance is a broader notion than government. Both words can be traced back to the Greek word 'kyberbes', which means a 'helmsman', whose skill involves knowing where to go, making decisions about a course to get there, and taking the actions needed to stay on that course. Government refers to the state, which has the authority to take decisions on behalf of the entire community. Governance refers also to the myriad other organisations and institutions involved in steering society. In Part III we are going to look, in Chapter 10, at sustainable development as destination, the policy objectives intended to get society and economy there, and, in Chapter 11, at policy instruments for pursuing these objectives.

10

Determining policy objectives

In this chapter you will:

- Find out how the principle of sustainable development was put on the policy agenda;
- Learn how researchers from different academic fields have suggested operationalising the principle of sustainable development;
- Find out why imperfect knowledge makes scientific analysis and decision making much more difficult;
- Learn about the precautionary principle;
- Consider how policy objectives are set in democratic societies.

I n this book so far we have seen that the human economy is located within the environment and that our economic activities are jeopardising the sustainability of the environment and hence of the economy itself. Policy makers worldwide therefore face the massive task of finding ways to organise economic activities such that they address the needs of the current generation better (alleviate poverty) and maintain the capacity of the joint economy–environment system to continue to satisfy the needs and desires of humans for a long time into the future – of finding ways for achieving sustainable development. In the last chapter we saw that, for two reasons, this task cannot be left to markets alone. First, market failures of various kinds mean that the actual market outcomes are not allocatively efficient. Second, achieving efficiency does not guarantee either inter- or intragenerational equity, both of which are essential features of sustainable development. Hence, aiming for sustainable development requires more than correcting market failure.

We now need to look at the roles of government and civil society in the pursuit of sustainable development. How do, and can, the public sector (government), the private sector (firms and individuals as consumers) and civil society (e.g. non-governmental organisations, NGOs) work together towards this goal? This is the question of '**governance**', which is the title of this part of the book. In it we will review how governments and other organisations have tried in recent decades to organise economies in such a way that they generate more sustainable outcomes. Solving the global economic, social and environmental problems is in the first place a political challenge – to be tackled by transnational institutions, national governments and the active participation of civil society. Let us start by exploring what national and international organisations have done to get the principle of sustainable development on the respective policy agendas and what economists have contributed to finding ways for making more sustainable production and lifestyle choices.

10.1 THE HISTORY OF THE SUSTAINABLE DEVELOPMENT PRINCIPLE

As we saw in Chapter 3, the human population has increased significantly over the last few hundred years. Material demands have risen at even higher rates. In a situation where large-scale redistribution of wealth is unacceptable, economic growth is generally considered as the solution to the problem of poverty. However, the world's resource base is limited and contains a complex interrelated set of ecosystems, which already shows clear signs of fragility. In recent years the ability of the global economic system to continue to grow without undermining the natural systems which are its ultimate foundation has increasingly been questioned.

10.1.1 The early days of sustainable development

As discussed back in Chapter 7, in 1972 a team of researchers from MIT published the results of their simulation modelling, which indicated that economic growth as it had been experienced until then could not continue in the long term. The book *The limits to growth: a report for the Club of Rome's project on the predicament of mankind* (Meadows *et al.*, 1972) was widely understood to claim that environmental limits would cause the collapse of the world economic system by the middle of the twenty-first century. The book was severely criticised by economists. However, it played an important role in bringing concerns about the over-use of natural resources into the political debate, and stimulating the interest of some economists in such matters.

In the same year, the United Nations Stockholm Conference on the Human Environment marked the first occasion on which the state of the environment was recognized as a global problem to be addressed by all nations. Some 6,000 people from 114 countries attended the conference. The Declaration of the United Nations Conference on the Human Environment was adopted at the conference, and the United Nations Environmental Programme (UNEP) was formed to provide an essential coordinating function, informing and assisting with the work of existing UN specialised agencies. UNEP has since played a major role in focusing attention on environmental issues in the international arena, and in encouraging many countries to improve environmental governance.

10.1.2 The 'Brundtland Report' – our common future

As noted in Chapter 1, in 1983 the UN General Assembly set up the World Commission on Environment and Development (WCED) chaired by Ms Gro Harlem

Brundtland, then Prime Minister of Norway. The WCED's mandate comprised three objectives:

(1)   To re-examine the critical environment and development issues and to formulate realistic proposals for dealing with them;

(2)   To propose new forms of international cooperation on these issues that will influence policies and events in the direction of needed changes;

(3)   To raise the levels of understanding and commitment to action of individuals, voluntary organisations, businesses, institutes and governments.

The WCED focused its re-examination (1) and awareness-raising (3) on the issues of: population growth, food security, biodiversity loss, energy, resource depletion, and pollution and urbanisation.

The WCED's report, entitled *Our Common Future*, contains the most widely cited definition of sustainable development: 'Sustainable development is development that meets the needs of the present without compromising the ability of future generations to meet their own needs' (p. 43). The report also says, 'The next few decades are crucial. The time has come to break out of past patterns. Attempts to maintain social and ecological stability through old approaches to development and environmental protection will increase instability' (p. 22). It clearly indicated a need for sustainable development instead of continuing 'past patterns'.

However, the WCED found itself in a dilemma. On the one hand, it was clear by the mid-1980s that technological change had failed to reverse some of the most worrying environmental trends, which meant that easy solutions were not available. On the other hand, all parties involved had to agree to the report. The WCED consisted of 23 commissioners from 21 different countries, including countries as diverse as the US and Sudan. It was considered politically impossible to revert to 'limits to growth' arguments. In many countries of the South there was, and is, mass poverty. Besides leading to low human well-being, poverty was perceived as causing a sizable share of the global environmental damage. In the North periods of zero economic growth had led to economic crises, unemployment, fiscal instability and difficulties in funding public services. A recommendation of no economic growth was therefore considered likely to be unacceptable to countries in both the South and the North. A redistribution of wealth for the benefit of the South (i.e. a new social contract with the South) was considered unacceptable to the electorates in the rich countries of the North. Hence, a global no-growth strategy was deemed impossible.

The WCED concluded that there needed to be 'a new era of economic growth – growth that is forceful and at the same time socially and environmentally sustainable' (WCED, 1987, p. xii). This is how this definition of the sustainable development principle came into being, which envisaged a continued pursuit of economic growth and social progress, but without the environmental damage which had historically accompanied this pursuit.

Unfortunately the report was not very clear on specific details about how to move from 'past patterns' to sustainable development. The report urges, e.g. 'merging environment and economics in decision-making' by nations, but gives few specific recommendations. However, there was one: that the UN General Assembly convene an international conference in order to 'review progress made and promote follow-up arrangements that will be needed over time to set benchmarks and to maintain human progress within the guidelines of human needs and natural laws' (WCED, 1987, p. 343). This recommendation was acted on, and the result was a conference in Rio de Janeiro in 1992.

10.1.3 The United Nations Conference on Environment and Development (UNCED)

UNCED took place in Rio de Janeiro in June 1992. It was preceded by two years of preparatory international negotiations. The title indicated the intention to consider development issues alongside environmental concerns, because of their strong links. The Stockholm conference had been criticised for ignoring the specific problems of the large group of poor countries. To effectively deal with environmental problems, it was argued, it is necessary to adopt a new approach which tackles social and environmental problems jointly.

UNCED was the largest international conference to that date, with 178 nations sending delegations, and 107 heads of government/state attending. The involvement of NGO representatives was a relatively novel feature. It is estimated that over 30,000 people attended in total. The major UNCED outcomes were:

- The Rio Declaration on Environment and Development was adopted. It is *non-binding* and comprises 27 statements of principle for global sustainable development (see Box 10.1);
- Agenda 21, which covers over 100 'programme areas' for action to promote global sustainable development. Many of these involve transfer of money from rich to poor countries. It is *non-binding* and was adopted.
- The establishment of a Commission for Sustainable Development as part of the UN, with the aim to ensure effective follow-up of UNCED, was proposed and subsequently implemented. The Commission started operating in 1993.
- The *binding* Framework Convention on Climate Change was adopted and signed by 153 nations. As discussed in Chapter 13, it called for action by the rich but not the poor nations. It did not place specific emissions reduction commitments on any of the signatories. Future negotiations, COPs, were to establish specific commitments and rules. This process started in 1995, and the progress since made is reported in Chapter 13.
- The *binding* Convention on Biological Diversity was adopted and signed by 156 nations (US not until 1993). As discussed in Chapter 14, it deals with two issues: the economic exploitation of genetic material and biodiversity conservation. On the latter, all signatories agreed to create systems of protected areas and to draw up national plans for conservation, but no specific commitments were made as regards, for example, the extent of protected areas.
- A Convention on Forest Management was *not* adopted. A short, *non-binding*, statement of principles for a global consensus on forest management was adopted.
- The rich countries reaffirmed their existing commitment each to provide 0.7 per cent of their GNI, Gross National Income, as Official Development

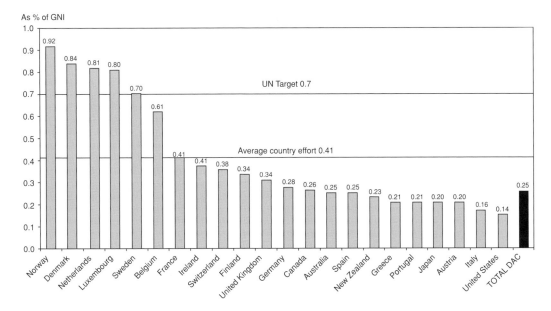

As % of GNI

Source: OECD (2004, p. 6).

Assistance[1] (ODA) to the poor countries. This has not happened. For example, in 2003 the UK gave ODA of 0.34 per cent of GNI, Norway 0.92 per cent of GNI, US 0.14 per cent of GNI, and Australia 0.25 per cent of GNI; see Figure 10.1 for the contributions of further countries.

Figure 10.1 Net Official Development Assistance as percentage of GNI (2003).

Many of the points highlighted in the 'Rio Declaration on Environment and Development' have already been discussed in this book. In Chapter 1 we defined an anthropocentric approach as one which is centred on human beings. With such an approach the effects of an action on non-human beings are taken into account only in so far as they produce pain or pleasure for human beings. As we can see from proclamation (1) in Box 10.1, the 'Rio Declaration on Environment and Development' is explicitly anthropocentric.

In Chapter 4 we saw in conceptual terms, and in Chapter 7 in empirical terms, that the relationship between economic activities and environmental quality is problematic and therefore needs to be addressed with new concepts and policies. Proclamation (2) highlights some aspects of protection of the environment.

In Chapter 9 we showed that an efficient allocation may or may not be equitable. Proclamation (3) of the Rio Declaration addresses the need to find solutions with high intra- and intertemporal equity. This means that the benefits and the costs of development need to be distributed fairly between current and future generations as well as between rich and poor countries and within countries.

---

1 Official development assistance, or foreign aid, consists of loans, grants, technical assistance and other forms of cooperation extended by governments to developing countries. A significant proportion of official development assistance is aimed at promoting sustainable development in poorer countries, particularly through natural resource conservation, environmental protection and population programmes.

Box 10.1 The Rio Declaration on Environment and Development

- The United Nations Conference on Environment and Development,
- Having met at Rio de Janeiro from 3 to 14 June 1992,
- Reaffirming the Declaration of the United Nations Conference on the Human Environment, adopted at Stockholm on 16 June 1972, and seeking to build upon it,
- With the goal of establishing a new and equitable global partnership through the creation of new levels of cooperation among States, key sectors of societies and people,
- Working towards international agreements, which respect the interests of all and protect the integrity of the global environmental and developmental system,
- Recognizing the integral and interdependent nature of the Earth, our home, Proclaims that:

(1) Human beings are at the centre of concerns for sustainable development. They are entitled to a healthy and productive life in harmony with nature.

(2) States have, in accordance with the Charter of the United Nations and the principles of international law, the sovereign right to exploit their own resources pursuant to their own environmental and developmental policies, and the responsibility to ensure that activities within their jurisdiction or control do not cause damage to the environment of other States or of areas beyond the limits of national jurisdiction.

(3) The right to development must be fulfilled so as to equitably meet developmental and environmental needs of present and future generations.

(4) In order to achieve sustainable development, environmental protection shall constitute an integral part of the development process and cannot be considered in isolation from it.

(5) All States and all people shall cooperate in the essential task of eradicating poverty as an indispensable requirement for sustainable development, in order to decrease the disparities in standards of living and better meet the needs of the majority of the people of the world.

(6) The special situation and needs of developing countries, particularly the least developed and those most environmentally vulnerable, shall be given special priority. International actions in the field of environment and development should also address the interests and needs of all countries.

(7) States shall cooperate in a spirit of global partnership to conserve, protect and restore the health and integrity of the Earth's ecosystem. In view of the different contributions to global environmental degradation, States have common but differentiated responsibilities. The developed countries acknowledge the responsibility that they bear in the international pursuit to sustainable development in view of the pressures their societies place on the global environment and of the technologies and financial resources they command.

(8) To achieve sustainable development and a higher quality of life for all people, States should reduce and eliminate unsustainable patterns of production and consumption and promote appropriate demographic policies.

(9) States should cooperate to strengthen endogenous capacity-building for sustainable development by improving scientific understanding through exchanges of scientific and technological knowledge, and by enhancing the development, adaptation, diffusion and transfer of technologies, including new and innovative technologies.

(10) Environmental issues are best handled with participation of all concerned citizens, at the relevant level. At the national level, each individual shall have appropriate access to information concerning the environment that is held by public authorities, including information on hazardous materials and activities in their communities, and the opportunity to participate in decision-making processes. States shall facilitate and encourage public awareness and participation by making information widely available. Effective access to judicial and administrative proceedings, including redress and remedy, shall be provided.

(11) States shall enact effective environmental legislation. Environmental standards, management objectives and priorities should reflect the environmental and development context to which they apply. Standards applied by some countries may be inappropriate and of unwarranted economic and social cost to other countries, in particular developing countries.

(12) States should cooperate to promote a supportive and open international economic system that would lead to economic growth and sustainable development in all countries, to better address the problems of environmental degradation. Trade policy measures for environmental purposes should not constitute a means of arbitrary or unjustifiable discrimination or a disguised restriction on international trade. Unilateral actions to deal with environmental challenges outside the jurisdiction of the importing country should be avoided. Environmental measures addressing transboundary or global environmental problems should, as far as possible, be based on an international consensus.

(13) States shall develop national law regarding liability and compensation for the victims of pollution and other environmental damage. States shall also cooperate in an expeditious and more determined manner to develop further international law regarding liability and compensation for adverse effects of environmental damage caused by activities within their jurisdiction or control to areas beyond their jurisdiction.

(14) States should effectively cooperate to discourage or prevent the relocation and transfer to other States of any activities and substances that cause severe environmental degradation or are found to be harmful to human health.

(15)   In order to protect the environment, the precautionary approach shall be widely applied by States according to their capabilities. Where there are threats of serious or irreversible damage, lack of full scientific certainty shall not be used as a reason for postponing cost-effective measures to prevent environmental degradation.

(16)   National authorities should endeavour to promote the internalisation of environmental costs and the use of economic instruments, taking into account the approach that the polluter should, in principle, bear the cost of pollution, with due regard to the public interest and without distorting international trade and investment.

(17)   Environmental impact assessment, as a national instrument, shall be undertaken for proposed activities that are likely to have a significant adverse impact on the environment and are subject to a decision of a competent national authority.

(18)   States shall immediately notify other States of any natural disasters or other emergencies that are likely to produce sudden harmful effects on the environment of those States. Every effort shall be made by the international community to help States so afflicted.

(19)   States shall provide prior and timely notification and relevant information to potentially affected States on activities that may have a significant adverse transboundary environmental effect and shall consult with those States at an early stage and in good faith.

(20)   Women have a vital role in environmental management and development. Their full participation is therefore essential to achieve sustainable development.

(21)   The creativity, ideals and courage of the youth of the world should be mobilized to forge a global partnership in order to achieve sustainable development and ensure a better future for all.

(22)   Indigenous people and their communities and other local communities have a vital role in environmental management and development because of their knowledge and traditional practices. States should recognize and duly support their identity, culture and interests and enable their effective participation in the achievement of sustainable development.

(23)   The environment and natural resources of people under oppression, domination and occupation shall be protected.

(24)   Warfare is inherently destructive of sustainable development. States shall therefore respect international law providing protection for the environment in times of armed conflict and cooperate in its further development, as necessary.

(25)   Peace, development and environmental protection are interdependent and indivisible.

(26)   States shall resolve all their environmental disputes peacefully and by appropriate means in accordance with the Charter of the United Nations.

(27)   States and people shall cooperate in good faith and in a spirit of partnership in the fulfilment of the principles embodied in this Declaration and in the further development of international law in the field of sustainable development.

In Chapter 6 we explored the relationships between poverty, well-being and economic growth. The large number of people living in poverty worldwide and the severe impacts on health and happiness make poverty one of the most pressing political problems. For people living in poverty increasing income is a key to satisfying their human needs and desires better. Proclamation (5) highlights the pivotal role of poverty alleviation for sustainable development.

Proclamation (10) focuses on citizen participation and Proclamation (15) talks about the Precautionary Principle. We will come back to both of them later in this chapter.

The adopted conventions are legally binding and have led to further developments of commitments in the areas that they cover. However, the most publicised element of UNCED, namely Agenda 21, remains merely a declaration of intent and its implementation rests solely on the goodwill of each country. This becomes evident with regard to the UN Commission for Sustainable Development (CSD), established just after Rio 1992. The main objective of the CSD is to assure the follow-up procedure to the Rio 1992 conference as well as to oversee the implementation of the national and international agreements. The CSD is one of the nine functional Commissions of the Economic and Social Council (ECOSOC) of the United Nations and is subject to the General Assembly. The CSD has almost no decision-making powers; it cannot adopt any legally binding agreements or conventions. The task of supervising the implementation of the Rio 1992 resolutions was difficult, because

Box 10.2 The changing relationship of the UN and NGOs

The influence of NGOs on the UN has a long tradition. The formal basis of NGO participation in the UN is Article 71 of the Charter, which says: 'The Economic and Social Council may make suitable arrangements for consultation with non-governmental organizations which are concerned with matters within its competence. Such arrangements may be made with international organizations and, where appropriate, with national organizations after consultation with the Member of the United Nations concerned'. NGOs can give their opinions on social and economic matters, but in the powerful political organs – the General Assembly and the Security Council – they do not have a direct role.

Until the late 1980s it was mostly International NGOs (INGOs) of different varieties, including professional and business associations that were granted formal consultative relations with the UN, which had influence. However, there was little actual engagement of INGOs in the work of the UN. NGO forums were organised around UN Conferences but they remained more or less autonomous, commenting on UN deliberations at arm's length. Nonetheless, they brought many new ideas to the UN and established the right of non-governmental actors to participate in UN deliberations.

During the 1990s large numbers of non-governmental actors, in particular national NGOs from developing countries and from the Western hemisphere and, to a lesser extent, from Central and Eastern European post-communist societies, appeared around the major UN Conferences. The newly emerged national and regional NGOs sought to engage directly in intergovernmental deliberations and, through advocacy and mobilisation work, influence their outcomes. At the same time many of the traditional INGOs began adapting to these new realities and reinventing themselves. In 1996, ECOSOC reviewed and expanded its arrangements for consultation with NGOs and recommended that the General Assembly examine the question of the 'participation of NGOs in all areas of work of the UN'. The UN system now knows three levels of NGO participation: At the top is consultation with the Economic and Social Council (ECOSOC). This status allows some direct participation in the intergovernmental process. Below ECOSOC status, there is 'association' with the Department of Public Information (DPI), which does not allow participation, but does permit access to the UN. And finally, there is accreditation to conferences and other one-time events, which can permit considerable participation and lobbying in informal sessions, but of course does not allow a continuing relationship with the UN. The number of participating NGOs is large. In August 2003 there were 2379 NGOs in consultative status with ECOSOC and many others which were accredited only for specific events. Over time the UN has shifted from an organisation in which only governments spoke to only governments, to one that now brings together the political power of governments, the economic power of the corporate sector, and the 'public opinion' power of civil society as participants in the global policy dialogue.

Source: Hill (2004). *Three Generations of UN–Civil Society Relations, Global Policy Forum*, http://www.globalpolicy.org/ngos/ngo-un/gen/2004/0404generation.htm (accessed 19 June 2004)

the CSD depended upon information obtained from the different governments by way of their national reports. Still, the CSD has a pivotal role to play in terms of the entire UN system since the participation of the NGO community is pervasive. The dialogue and cooperation between governments and NGOs have improved to the point where it has become possible for NGOs and other civil groups to take part in some of the informal discussions as well as in the actual negotiations. More about NGOs in the UN system can be found in Box 10.2.

All things considered, was UNCED a success? Many incline to the answer 'No', because no binding commitments to specific programmes to promote sustainable development, with reference to either poverty alleviation or environmental protection, were agreed.

But, given the difficulty of securing international agreements across the 'North/South divide' that was too much to expect. It could be regarded as somewhat successful because it did:

- raise awareness and issues, and put them on political agendas
- get national governments to agree to some principles
- put in place processes (e.g. Conference of the Parties, COPs for The Framework Convention on Climate Change, FCCC) for continuing negotiations and thus create the potential for the emergence of future binding commitments.

10.1.4 The World Summit on Sustainable Development (WSSD)

WSSD, also called Rio+10, took place in Johannesburg from 26 August to 4 September 2002. It was attended by 9,000 governmental delegates, including 104 heads of state or government, 8,000 representatives from NGOs, 4,000 members of the press and many business representatives. The large number of attendees from the business sectors was new compared to the previous conferences on sustainable development.

The summit was intended to assess progress on implementation of the results of the Rio Summit, in particular Agenda 21, and whether countries had adopted National Sustainable Development Strategies as it had been agreed that they would by 2002. And it was to identify new challenges that had come up in the decade since 1992.

No new conventions were on the table at Johannesburg. Many considered it important that some of the conventions from Rio still awaiting implementation were fully ratified by member states so they could enter into force. The Kyoto Protocol, for example, which took the 1992 UNFCCC forward with specific commitments, had not been ratified by enough signatories for it to come into force. Apart from that, fighting poverty was to be another crucial focus of WSSD as the mutually enhancing nature of poverty and environmental degradation has been one of the main obstacles for achieving global sustainability. The summit was intended to develop programmes to eradicate poverty by addressing the underlying causes that relate to the principle of equity and an equitable access to resources, to opportunities and to decision-making structures on the one hand and debt relief programmes for the poorest nations on the other hand.

WSSD was widely seen as putting more emphasis on the economic dimension of sustainable development than had been the case in Rio. Economic growth featured prominently in the list of goals. Many governments, international agencies (e.g. the World Bank) and businesses took the opportunity to announce their own actions for sustainable development. For example:

- the UK announced that it was increasing its ODA by 50 per cent and
- Canada and Russia announced that they were going to ratify the Kyoto Protocol – see Chapter 13 for the current situation on ratification and the coming into force of the Kyoto Protocol.

All nations signed up to the Johannesburg Plan of Implementation, which consisted largely of statements of intent, often without clear targets, time frames or funding for implementation. Firmer results had been expected with regard to renewable energy, but targets for its expansion were not generally agreed. A smaller group of countries, including the EU, acted independently to commit themselves to increase the share of renewable energies. In their joint declaration, 'The Way Forward on Renewable Energy', the small group of signatory states commit themselves to 'work together to substantially increase the global share of renewable energy sources, with regular review of progress, on the basis of clear and ambitious time bound targets set at the national, regional and hopefully at the global level'. In the Johannesburg Plan of Implementation itself, limited targets were agreed on issues such as biodiversity loss, restoration of fish stocks and the use of toxic chemicals. (The full text of the plan and the declaration can be found at the conference web page – see

Box 10.3 Views on WSSD

We invited the leaders of the world to come here and commit themselves to sustainable development, to protecting our planet, to maintaining the essential balance and to go back home and take action. It is on the ground that we will have to test how really successful we are. But we have started off well. Johannesburg is a beginning.
(Kofi Annan, United Nations Secretary-General, The Johannesburg Summit Test: What Will Change? Feature Story United Nations; 25 September)

Compared to the 1992 Earth Summit in Rio, this summer's World Summit on Sustainable Development (WSSD) in Johannesburg was bound to be somewhat disappointing. The negotiations leading up to Johannesburg had not provided any reason to expect dramatic break-throughs, and there were none. After the meeting, many non-governmental organizations denounced the WSSD as a failure. Even seasoned U.N. officials, while relieved that the Summit had not broken down completely, were rather muted in their responses.
(Hilary French, Worldwatch Institute, From Rio to Johannesburg and Beyond: Assessing the Summit)

The Plan of Action is not much of a plan, and it contains almost no action. We've spent the last year and half doing damage control. We now have to move forward with a 'coalition of the willing,' those countries, communities, organisations, and people who want to deliver a sustainable energy future.
(Steve Sawyer, Greenpeace Climate Policy Director, 'Exxon buys summit, planet', Greenpeace press release, 3 September 2003)

With the world's most powerful governments fully behind the corporate globalisation agenda, it was agreed even before the Summit that there would be no new mandatory agreements. Rather the focus was to be on implementation of old agreements, mainly through partnerships with the private sector. In other words, those aspects of sustainability that are convenient for private sector would be implemented.
(Kenny Bruno, CorpWatch, 'The Earth Summit's Deathblow to Sustainable Development', CorpWatch article; 4 September 2003)

The Earth Summit should have been about protecting the environment and fighting poverty and social destruction. Instead it has been hijacked by free market ideology, by a backward-looking US administration and by global corporations that help keep reactionary politicians in business. This is the worst political sell-out in decades.
(Charles Secrett, Friends of the Earth, UK)

Source: http://www.worldsummit2002.org/

web page section at the end of this chapter.) On economic development signatories agreed, for example, to:

- halve, by 2015, proportion of global population living on $1 or less per day
- halve, by 2015, proportion of global population without access to safe drinking water
- halve, by 2015, the proportion of people living in hunger
- improve access to (environmentally sound) energy services for the poor
- ensure that, by 2015, all children completed primary education.

On environmental protection the signatories agreed, for example, to:

- 'substantially increase the global share of renewable energy sources'
- develop, by 2005, integrated water resource-management plans
- eliminate subsidies that 'contribute to illegal, unreported and unregulated fishing and to overcapacity'
- achieve, by 2010, 'a significant reduction in the current rate of loss of biological diversity'.

Note that some economic targets are quantified, but none of the environmental targets are.

Together with a Political Declaration, which expresses commitments and the direction for implementing sustainable development, the Plan of Implementation is known as Type-I-Outcome. Additionally Partnership Initiatives, often referred to as Type-II-Outcomes, were agreed. These Partnership Initiatives, which are voluntary and non-binding, include action-oriented programmes between governments, business and civil society. Analysts often saw the Partnership Initiatives as a possibility of delivering some results as they could not be blocked by reluctant countries.

However, there were no clear criteria of what would qualify for a Type-II-Outcome, and NGOs feared that the partnerships option would take pressure off governments to negotiate firm agreements (Type-I-Outcomes).

What did WSSD achieve? It acknowledged the links between poverty alleviation and environmental protection more explicitly than UNCED had done. It reaffirmed two key principles agreed at UNCED: first, the Precautionary Principle, which is stated in proclamation (15) of the Rio Declaration (see Box 10.1; we will discuss the Precautionary Principle in section 10.4 below); second, the paradigm of Common but Differentiated Responsibility, which is stated most explicitly in proclamation (7) of the Rio Declaration (we will return to this in Chapters 13 and 14). According to some commentators, WSSD promoted a greater sense of urgency to comply with the commitments made in Rio. About two-thirds of the final Plan of Implementation consists of reiterations of earlier commitments. Many commentators were disappointed with the Johannesburg outcomes. Box 10.3 contains snapshots of what representatives from international and national organisations thought about WSSD.

In this section we have discussed the most significant international events concerning sustainable development. Besides these there were many activities at the local, national and international level aiming for governance for sustainable development. We end the section with a selection of some of the main events (including those just explored) in Box 10.4.

Box 10.4 The Sustainable Development Timeline

Selection of key events relating to sustainable development.

Source: IISD 2002, updated by the authors; for fuller version see http://www.iisd.org/pdf/2002/sd_timeline2002.pdf

1972 – Club of Rome publishes *Limits to Growth*. The report is extremely controversial because it predicts dire consequences if growth is not slowed. Northern countries criticize the report for not including technological solutions while Southern countries are incensed because it advocates abandonment of economic development. http://www.clubofrome.org/

1972 – UN Conference on Human Environment /UNEP held in Stockholm under the leadership of Maurice Strong. The conference is rooted in the regional pollution and acid rain problems of northern Europe. The conference leads to establishing many national environmental protection agencies and the United Nations Environment Programme (UNEP). http://www.unep.org/

1980 – World Conservation Strategy released by the International Union for the Conservation of Nature, IUCN. The section 'Towards Sustainable Development' identifies the main agents of habitat destruction as poverty, population pressure, social inequity and the terms of trade. It calls for a new international development strategy with the aims of redressing inequities, achieving a more dynamic and stable world economy, stimulating economic growth and countering the worst impacts of poverty. http://www.iucn.org/

1980 – US President Jimmy Carter authorises study leading to the Global 2000 report. This report is the first that recognises biodiversity as a critical characteristic in the proper functioning of the planetary ecosystem. It asserts that the robust nature of ecosystems is weakened by species extinction.

1987 – *Our Common Future* also known as the Brundtland Report. Report of the World Commission on Environment and Development weaves together social, economic, cultural and environmental issues and global solutions. Chaired by Norwegian Prime Minister Gro Harlem Brundtland. Popularises term 'sustainable development'.

1992 – The Business Council for Sustainable Development publishes *Changing Course*. Establishes business interests in promoting SD practices. http://www.wbcsd.ch/

1992 – UN Conference on Environment and Development (UNCED) also known as the Earth Summit held in Rio de Janeiro, under the leadership of Maurice Strong. Agreements reached on Agenda 21, the Convention on Biological Diversity, the Framework Convention on Climate Change, the Rio Declaration, and non-binding Forest Principles. Concurrent NGO Global Forum publishes alternative treaties. http://www.unep.org/unep/partners/un/unced/home.htm

1992 – The Earth Council is established in Costa Rica as a focal point for facilitating follow-up and implementation of the agreements reached at the Earth Summit, and linking national SD councils. http://www.ecouncil.ac.cr/

1993 – President's Council for Sustainable Development in US announced by President Bill Clinton. They publish Sustainable America: A New Consensus for Prosperity, Opportunity, and a Healthy Environment for the Future in 1996. http://clinton2.nara.gov/PCSD/

1993 – First meeting of the UN Commission on Sustainable Development established to ensure effective follow-up to UNCED, enhance international cooperation and rationalise intergovernmental decision-making capacity. http://www.un.org/esa/sustdev/

1995 – World Summit for Social Development held in Copenhagen, Denmark. First time that the international community has expressed a clear commitment to eradicate absolute poverty. http://www.un.org/esa/socdev/wssd/index.html

1996 – The Summit of the Americas on Sustainable Development held in Santa Cruz, Bolivia. This Summit identified the joint efforts needed to reach SD in the hemisphere. http://www.summit-americas.org/boliviaplan.htm

1997 – UN General Assembly review of Earth Summit progress, a special session which acts as a sober reminder that little progress has been made in implementing the Earth Summit's Agenda 21 and ends without significant new commitments. http://www.iisd.ca/linkages/csd/ungass.html

2000 – United Nations Millennium Summit, this largest-ever gathering of world leaders adopted the United Nations World Summit Declaration, which spells out values and principles, as well as goals in key priority areas. World leaders agreed that the UN's first priority was the eradication of extreme poverty and highlighted the importance of a fairer world economy in an era of globalisation. http://www.un.org/millennium/summit.htm

2001 – EU Sustainable Development Strategy (EU SDS) agreed in Gothenburg. It has four key priorities: climate change, sustainable transport, public health and natural resources. http://europa.eu.int/comm/environment/eussd/

2002 – World Summit on Sustainable Development held in Johannesburg, South Africa. World governments, concerned citizens, UN agencies, multilateral financial institutions, and other major groups participate and assess global change since the United Nations Conference on Environment and Development (UNCED) in 1992. http://www.johannesburgsummit.org/

2003 – UK Sustainable Development Task Force set up to help ensure effective delivery of sustainable development, including WSSD commitments. Composed of ministers from across government and the devolved administrations and some key opinion-formers from outside government. Led to publication of the second edition of the UK Sustainable Development Strategy in 2004. http://www.sustainable-development.

10.2 OPERATIONALISING THE PRINCIPLE

After looking at declarations of principle and objectives from politicians and diplomats, we turn to the specific policy objectives which follow from a commitment to sustainable development and to the role of researchers from various disciplines who try to inform the deliberations of policy makers.

10.2.1 What is the principle meant to deliver?

For the organisers of WSSD sustainable development meant the following:

Sustainable development calls for improving the quality of life for all of the world's people without increasing the use of our natural resources beyond the earth's carrying capacity. While sustainable development may require different actions in every region of the world, the efforts to build a truly sustainable way of life require the integration of action in three key areas.

(1) Economic Growth and Equity – Today's interlinked, global economic systems demand an integrated approach in order to foster responsible long-term growth while ensuring that no nation or community is left behind.

(2) Conserving Natural Resources and the Environment – To conserve our environmental heritage and natural resources for future generations, economically

viable solutions must be developed to reduce resource consumption, stop pollution and conserve natural habitats.

(3) Social Development – Throughout the world, people require jobs, food, education, energy, health care, water and sanitation. While addressing these needs, the world community must also ensure that the rich fabric of cultural and social diversity, and the rights of workers, are respected, and that all members of society are empowered to play a role in determining their futures (WSSD Brochure, page 2, http://www.johannesburgsummit.org/html/brochure/brochure12.pdf).

This statement reflects the economic, environmental and social aspects, which have been widely recognised as the essential components of sustainable development. While it can be useful for purposes of analysis and understanding to treat each separately, we need to keep in mind that the economy, society and the environment are not independent – they are interdependent systems.

In comparison to pursuing the relatively simple goal of short-term economic success, the three interconnected component dimensions of sustainable development make their pursuit much more complicated. For every policy decision to take the multiple dimensions into account raises the questions of how to balance objectives and how to judge success or failure. For example, what if generating electricity from renewable energy sources instead of non-renewable sources is more expensive and therefore increases the burden on the poor, who spend a larger share of their income on fuels like electricity? What if tourism generates value added for a remote community, but threatens the ecosystem health of the local environment? Which goal should carry more weight? The need for deciding the weights to assign to the different dimensions of sustainability highlights the strong normative content of the concept of sustainable development. As discussed in Chapter 1, all policy recommendation involves normative elements. Policy decisions cannot be derived purely from scientific analysis, but also require information about societal preferences. In democracies such preferences are supposed to derive from the preferences, or ethical positions, of citizens. In practice this also involves elected representatives, lobby groups (such as NGOs as well as those representing business interests), stakeholders and opinion formers in the media. Since different groups in societies attach different weights to the dimensions of sustainable development, there are a large number of views about what particular policies it entails.

Once agreed, the general principles of sustainable development need to be adapted to the specific circumstances of place and people to become operational policies. The statements of the sustainable development principle in the Brundtland Report (UNCED, 1992) and in WSSD 2002 (UN, 2002b) have in common that they intend to deliver economic growth and social progress, while ensuring effective protection of the environment and prudent use of natural resources. The specific guidelines for sustainable development may require different actions for different groups of the human population. For example, economic growth in some form is required for those who lack fulfilment of essential needs, the world's poor, but the environmental impact from economic production must be subject to global limits if sustainable development is to be realised. Therefore, while it is obvious that sustainable development requires economic growth in the developing countries, it is not at all clear that it should be the prime objective for countries which are already at high levels of consumption. In such countries, the principle of sustainable development implies that the growth objective should have less weight attached to it than social and environmental objectives. In developing countries, on the other hand, sustainable development implies that a lot of weight be attached to the growth objective, though, of course, the environment cannot be given zero weight.

In Chapter 1, we defined sustainability as:

maintaining the capacity of the joint economy–environment system to continue to satisfy the needs and desires of humans for a long time into the future.

Sustainability is a necessary condition for sustainable development, which, at the global level, wants to not just maintain the joint system's capacity, but increase it. Sustainable development as currently understood involves growth in what the global economy delivers – that is the development part. It requires that this does not damage the environment – that is the sustainability part. We now want to look at the way that economists and ecologists approach the question of what sorts of policy sustainability requires.

10.2.2 Sustainability in neoclassical economics

We looked at this in Chapter 9, when we considered whether markets alone would produce sustainable outcomes. For neoclassical economists, sustainability is primarily about what happens to human welfare over time. Most simplify further by identifying welfare with consumption. While this may be criticised as an over-simplification, it certainly includes many important elements of human welfare (food, shelter, clothing, transport, health and education services). The sustainability questions that most interest neoclassical economists are about the time profile of consumption. They first started thinking about these questions in connection with the depletion of non-renewable resources.

As we saw in section 9.5.1 of Chapter 9, the obvious question there is whether consumption can be held constant indefinitely, if the population is constant in size, given that non-renewable resources are a necessary input to production. If this is not possible, more ambitious goals, such as increasing per capita consumption, will clearly be infeasible. Studying this question in models, neoclassical economists have found that constant consumption may be possible notwithstanding the use of non-renewable resources in production, and even without technical progress. Sustainability, as constant consumption, is possible in such circumstances:

- if human-made, or reproducible, capital can be substituted for the resource in production as per the Cobb–Douglas production function (see Chapter 7, p. 233);
- if the resource is sufficiently unimportant in production; and
- if the resource stock is depleted in an intertemporally efficient way (see Chapter 9, p. 350).

Sustainability as constant consumption will be the outcome in such circumstances if, as well, the economy follows the Hartwick rule, always saving and investing all of the rent arising in the extraction of the resource. This is not what is guaranteed to happen if the determination of savings and investment is left entirely to markets. The Hartwick rule is a policy rule – government needs to see that it is satisfied.

This study of a model economy is one of the foundations of the neoclassical approach to sustainability. The other, also discussed in Chapter 9, is correcting market failure so that allocative efficiency is attained. To the extent that people care about protecting the environment from damage, internalising externalities will protect the environment.

Back in Chapter 4 we called the capital that is the result of investment and saving human-made or reproducible capital. To recapitulate, it comprises:

- Durable capital: plant, equipment, buildings and other infrastructure, accumulated by devoting part of current production to capital investment.
- Human capital: stocks of learned skills, embodied in particular individuals, which enhances the productive potential of those people.
- Intellectual capital: disembodied skills and knowledge. This comprises the stock of useful knowledge, which we might otherwise call the state of technology. These skills are disembodied in that they do not reside in particular individuals, but are part of the culture of society. They reside in books and other cultural constructs, and are transmitted and developed through time by social learning processes.
- Social capital: the set of institutions and customs, which organise economic activity, and features of social behaviour that facilitate coordinated actions, such as trust and norms. Examples of the latter are solidarity, civic engagement and reciprocity.

We also noted in Chapter 4 the use of the term natural capital to refer to those stocks in the environment that deliver services to the economy – such as aquifers and water systems, fertile land, crude oil and gas, forests, fisheries and other stocks of biomass, genetic material and the earth's atmosphere. The total stock of capital available to the economy can be seen as consisting of two parts: natural and human-made capital.

From the neoclassical perspective there is no particular reason to conserve natural capital. The Hartwick rule does not require the maintenance of any particular stock of natural capital. In the model for which it was discussed above, natural capital is the non-renewable resource. Consumption is held constant indefinitely by running down the stock of natural capital and building up the stock of human-made capital, with the latter substituting for the former in production. Following on from the work of Hartwick, various economists have shown that his rule generalises to hold where many different resources of both the non-renewable and renewable kind are used as inputs to production. If human-made capital can be substituted for the resources sufficiently, and they are sufficiently unimportant in production, and if all of the rents arising in exploiting the resources in an intertemporally efficient way are invested in human-made capital, then constant consumption is the outcome. This extended Hartwick rule is a major and pervasive influence on the thinking of neoclassical economists about sustainability, and, therefore, on their thinking about sustainable development.

They would argue, for example, if we cut the trees of a forest and use the wood for building tools and houses, we are better off provided the economic value of the new tools and houses exceeds the economic value of the lost forest. In that case, they would argue, the value of the total stock of capital, human-made together with natural, has increased. For neoclassical economists what matters is the value of the total stock of capital, which is taken to reflect the value of the total amount of satisfaction of human needs and desires that is taking place. How that total is split between human-made and natural capital does not matter, *so long as it is assumed that market failures due to externalities have been corrected.* If this were not so, then it would be impossible to claim that the prices used to measure human-made and natural capital stocks properly reflected peoples' preferences. If market failures are not corrected when measuring the sizes of the capital stocks, having the total size increase does not necessarily mean that more satisfaction of needs and desires is being delivered.

10.2.3 Sustainability in ecology

Ecologists look at sustainability from the point of view of an ecological system of which humans are just one part. They think about sustainability in terms of the extent to which the prevailing structure and properties of the ecosystem can be maintained. This perspective focuses on the resilience of ecosystems. We looked at what resilience means in Chapter 2 (see section 2.3.3 especially). To re-cap, an ecosystem is resilient if it maintains its functional integrity in the face of a disturbance. This does not require that the disturbance does not change the system at all. It does require that the system continues to function in the same way, so that, for example, productivity is maintained.

Natural scientists and ecologists are accustomed to the idea of limits. The laws of thermodynamics and observations of biological systems and of population behaviours inform us of and demonstrate such limits, as we saw in Chapter 2. Organisms with high rates of population growth will inevitably encounter limits set by their environment. From an ecological perspective sustainability must involve some limits to the increase of human population and consumption levels, since such limits apply to all biological systems and humans are part of a biological system. While humans may appear to evade them for some time period, they must ultimately accept the boundaries of a finite planet.

As discussed in Chapter 2, the generation of genetic diversity and the resultant processes of evolution and change in species and ecosystems are fundamental concepts in ecological analysis. Ecologists consider that genetic diversity is likely to promote resilience in ecosystems. In many ecosystems, it is the existence of a wide variety of species, interacting with each other and providing a reservoir of genetic forms, that provide the potential to adapt to changing conditions and is the key to resilience. As we will discuss in Chapter 14, the current level of human economic activity is reducing biodiversity, and, therefore, ecologists argue threatening the resilience of ecosystems worldwide.

Often ecologists face the problem that the factors which are relevant to sustainability are not known for certain, or are not known at all. The imperfect knowledge may be about the basic form of the relationships between variables, the parameters that quantify the relationships, or exogenous factors (events outside the ecological system of concern). How ecologists can deal with such situations depends a lot on what aspects of the necessary information are unknown. We will see in section 10.3

what techniques have been developed in order to support decision making despite imperfect knowledge.

Another problem which ecologists are struggling with is that biophysical systems are not simple, but rather complex and that they change all the time. At any time a large number of factors may influence the outcome of a particular event, each one to a greater or lesser extent. At another time the strength of those same causative factors on the same event may be very different. The relative intensity of causal relations in the system changes from time to time. This makes prediction of outcomes very difficult. Extreme examples are the regime shifts such as those which have occurred in response to environmental changes in many places around the world. Under these conditions similar species may be present but in such radically altered proportions that predictions based on extrapolations of past relationships would be far off the mark. Less extreme changes are the normal course of events in **complex systems**, in which components are continually adapting and evolving in response to developments in the system itself. Examples are changes in the species distribution as a result of industrial agriculture, or as farmers respond to a change in regulations about organic farming. Even with all these changes there is order in these systems, which we can observe in the form of patterns. Recognition of the patterns of change in a particular complex system can lead to an understanding of that system. Imperfect knowledge and the difficulties of dealing with complex systems require from us a more prudent approach to development, which allows time for the acquisition of understanding, than if all current and future impacts were fully understood and known.

In fact economic systems are also complex, evolving, systems. However, neo-classical economic models typically do not reflect this reality. There is a school of economics which seeks to do that. You will find references to introductions to evolutionary economics in Further Reading.

10.2.4 Sustainability in ecological economics

For ecological economists the question obviously is: how do these two perspectives on sustainability fit together? In particular, there are two questions. Do we need to worry about sustainability as resilience? If so, would following the economists' prescriptions – the Hartwick rule and correcting market failure – take care of it? For ecological economists the answers to these questions are 'yes' and 'no'.

With regard to the first question, ecological economists argue that we need to worry about sustainability as resilience if we have any concern for the interest of future generations. This concern normally entails our hope that the social, economic and environmental systems are in a position to fulfil the same functions for future generations that they fulfil for us. For example, that the economy can provide the economic means for high levels of well-being, the natural system provides services such as the assimilative capacity of the atmosphere and the social system provides fair conditions for men and women. Aiming to maintain the ability to fulfil the same functions of these systems even after disturbances is based on the resilience concept. It follows from the interdependence of economic systems and environmental systems, discussed in Chapter 4, that if we want to maintain the resilience of one system, we need to take the other system into account.

As regards the second question, the answer is no because, as we discussed in Chapter 9 (see especially 9.5.2) the principle of allocative efficiency only refers to individuals' preferences and there is no reason to assume that those preferences will always reflect the requirements of resilience. Individuals may be willing to pay nothing to preserve a keystone species, in which case correcting market failure will not guarantee its survival, and hence does not guarantee the resilience of the relevant ecosystem.

In sum, ecological economists accept that resilience is important for sustainability, and they argue that following the Hartwick rule and correcting market failure will not suffice to achieve sustainability.

Based on this perspective, how can the principles of sustainability be operationalised and paths of sustainable development be determined? Unfortunately there is no agreed blueprint. That is largely because we do not know, for example, in detail how to promote resilience. Since we are not sure which are and which are not keystone species, developing and measuring indicators is not enough and decisions need to be made with imperfect knowledge. The question of how to make decisions with imperfect knowledge will be discussed in the next section. In the light of that discussion some ecological economists have come up with some ideas about broad strategies. For example, Costanza and Daly (1992) suggest minimum conditions for sustainability, which lead to two decision rules which aim to ensure that natural capital is maintained:

(1)   for renewable resources, the rule is to limit resource consumption to sustainable yield levels;

(2)   for non-renewable resources the rule is to reinvest the proceeds from non-renewable resource exploitation into renewable natural capital.

These rules build on a perspective which assumes that natural and human-made capital are complements rather than substitutes. For example, a sawmill is of no use without trees. This perspective is known as **strong sustainability**. Many ecological economists adopt this perspective because they find the perspective generally used in neoclassical economics, **weak sustainability**, insufficient. Weak sustainability requires, as per the Hartwick rule, that the total of natural and human-made capital together remains constant over time. This rule makes sense, and delivers sustainability as constant consumption, only if the two types of capital are substitutable. By introducing **critical natural capital**, which acknowledges substitutability close to zero for some parts of capital and assumes higher substitutability for others, the weak sustainability approach comes closer to the strong sustainability perspective. For example, proponents of the critical natural capital approach argue that keystone species need to be maintained under all circumstances, but other elements of ecosystem can see significant change.

The debate over the different, especially the former two, approaches has caused a lot of disagreement. Clearly, the weak and strong sustainability question is multifaceted, and it is not possible to give precise answers except in particular contexts and with full information. There is no answer to the general question: how far is human-made capital substitutable for natural capital? (The different ways of conceptualising substitution between factors of production were discussed in Chapter 7.) Following the weak sustainability approach requires a full accounting of natural capital depletion. However, the natural capital stock is not a homogenous thing, but consists of many qualitatively different components. It is extremely difficult to aggregate the heterogeneous elements of the natural capital stock and to measure its depreciation.

Finally, note that the fact that ecological economists consider the Hartwick rule and the efficiency goal insufficient to deliver sustainability does not mean that they think that saving and investment are unimportant or that externalities do not matter. First, an adequate level of saving and investment is necessary to look after the interests of the future. However, it does not guarantee a sustainable outcome, because the outcome depends, for example, on substitution possibilities; they are very difficult to measure, especially in the long term. Second, probably all economists accept the idea that in a market system the natural resources and ecosystem services are over-used because users do not bear all the costs. Hence, ecological economists are normally in favour of making people bear the costs of their actions. However, they question whether assessing the costs according to allocative efficiency criteria will ensure sustainability in the sense of ecosystem resilience. What needs to be done instead is to assess the level of protection that is required for sustainability as resilience.

In order to protect critical natural capital under the condition of imperfect knowledge, specific decision rules need to be defined. For this purpose we first review the different types of imperfect knowledge and their influence on decision making. Then, in section 10.4 we will discuss the Precautionary Principle and safe minimum standards, two frequently cited principles for protecting critical natural capital under conditions of severely restricted knowledge.

10.3 DECISION MAKING UNDER IMPERFECT KNOWLEDGE

So far we have discussed the difficulties which result for policy makers from having to balance different dimensions of sustainability and the interests of different groups of a population. Even with full knowledge this would be a challenging task. However, often we have only imperfect knowledge, but we still need to make decisions because doing nothing might make the situation worse.

Clearly, the degree to which knowledge is imperfect and the extent of the possible (positive or negative) impact of a decision vary between situations. Some types of imperfect knowledge are much easier to deal with than others. For example, we may not have gathered all available information yet, but we could do so. In another situation it may be that information on key aspects of the question has not been produced yet or that the information which we get is contradictory. Or we may be able to find out certain aspects of what we want to know, but not others. For example, when rolling a dice, we know that six outcomes are possible and how likely they are to happen, but we do not know what the outcome of one particular throw will be. In other situations we may not even know the probability of the individual outcomes or what the possible outcomes are. It is normal for us to make decisions every day about minor issues with or without knowing about the probabilities of the different outcomes (e.g. order food for lunch in the university's cafeteria in the former case; ordering food for lunch in a new restaurant in the latter). But we find it much harder to make decisions about major issues without having complete information (e.g. accepting one or the other job after your graduation).

Imperfect knowledge can take four basic forms:

(1) **Risk**: the different possible outcomes are known exactly and a probability can be assigned to each possibility;

(2) **Ambiguity**: the probabilities are known but the outcomes to which they attach are not known exactly;

(3) **Uncertainty**: the different possible outcomes are known but probabilities cannot be assigned to them;

(4) **Ignorance**: the definition of a complete set of possible outcomes is problematic and probabilities cannot be assigned.

In order to explain this classification and introduce the approaches to decision making that can be adopted in each case, we will begin by looking at project appraisal, leaving environmental problems aside for the moment.

10.3.1 Project appraisal with imperfect information

Consider a project being appraised by a profit-maximising firm. It involves expenditure now of £100. It would run for three years. When we looked at project appraisal in Chapter 8 we assumed that the firm knew what the Net cashflow would be one, two and three years from the time of taking the decision on the project. This is, of course, unrealistic. Nobody knows what the future will bring. We will now look at each of the above four imperfect knowledge situations in terms of this project.

10.3.1.1 Risk

In situations where the imperfect knowledge situation can be categorised as one of risk, the firm can precisely identify the alternative cashflows that could arise if it goes ahead with the project, and it can assign probabilities to each alternative. To keep things simple, let us assume that there are just two possible, mutually exclusive, futures. If market conditions turn out to be favourable, the firm knows that the cashflow will be as shown under 'State F' in the table below – F stands for 'Favourable'. If they turn out to be unfavourable, it knows that what is shown under 'State U' will eventuate – U for 'Unfavourable'. The interest rate is 5 per cent, which means that the NPVs under each possible future state of the world are as shown, positive for State F and negative for State U – under F the project should go ahead, under U it should not.

	State F	State U
0	−£100	−£100
1	£40	£30
2	£40	£30
3	£40	£30
NPV at 5%	£8.93	−£18.30
Probability	0.7	0.3

Supposing that the firm can assign the probabilities 0.7 and 0.3 to F and U respectively, how should it decide whether or not to go ahead with the project? In this case, instead of the simple NPV test it should use the Expected NPV test, and go ahead with the project if the expected NPV is positive. The expected value, or expectation, for a decision to be taken in the face of risk is the probability-weighted sum of the mutually exclusive possible outcomes. The following table shows how

	Expected net cashflow	Present values for expected net cashflow
0	$(0.7 \times [-100]) + (0.3 \times [-100]) = -100$	-100
1	$(0.7 \times 40) + (0.3 \times 30) = 28 + 9 = 37$	$37 \div 1.05 = 35.2381$
2	$(0.7 \times 40) + (0.3 \times 30) = 28 + 9 = 37$	$37 \div 1.05^2 = 33.5601$
3	$(0.7 \times 40) + (0.3 \times 30) = 28 + 9 = 37$	$37 \div 1.05^3 = 31.9621$
Expected NPV		£ 0.76

the expected NPV is calculated in the example we are considering. The Expected net cashflow in any year is 0.7 times the State F cashflow plus 0.3 times the State U Cashflow. For each year the Present Value of the Expected net cashflow is calculated using the appropriate discount factor for the interest rate of 0.05. These present values are then summed in the usual way to give the Expected net present value. In this example, the Expected NPV is, just, positive and the project should go ahead. Although the loss under state U is much larger than the gain under state F, it is also much more unlikely. Two points need to be made about the Expected NPV decision rule and this illustration.

First, the decision rule works where the decision maker, the management of the firm in the illustration, is 'risk neutral'. A decision maker is risk neutral if she regards an expected value of $X as equivalent to the certainty of $X. A risk-neutral person would be indifferent between the offer of $4 if a tossed coin comes up heads and nothing if it comes up tails, and the offer of $2 cash in hand now. The expected value of the former is, assuming a fair coin $(0.5 \times 4) + (0.5 \times 0)$, equal to $2. Decision makers are not necessarily risk-neutral. Risk aversion is where $2 cash in hand now is considered more attractive than the statistically equivalent offer of $4 for heads and nothing for tails. If the decision maker is risk-averse, then she should not use the Expected NPV rule as set out above when appraising projects. The modifications to the Expected NPV rule required for appraising projects for a risk-averse decision maker are explained in books cited in Further Reading at the end of the chapter.

Second, as you may well have noticed, there is a quicker way to get to the result of £0.76 for the Expected NPV. You get this if you just weight the NPVs in each state of nature by the respective probabilities and add them. This works in this illustration because of the special time profiles for the Cashflows – in both cases they are constant over time after the initial outlay. Where the time profiles are not both constant, the shortcut will not work, which is why we did the calculation the long way in this case – it is the correct way in general.

10.3.1.2 Ambiguity

We now modify the illustrative project appraisal so that it conforms to the situation defined as ambiguity. In that case, the firm would know that F and U were the possible future states, and would be able to assign probabilities to each state, but it would not know the cashflows arising in each state. To keep things simple, we will suppose that it knows what the cashflow would be under F but not, apart from the initial outlay, under U, as in the following table.

	State F	State U
0	−£100	−£100
1	£40	?
2	£40	?
3	£40	?
NPV at 5%	£8.93	?
Probability	0.7	0.3

Ambiguity is where the firm does not know for sure what would happen under U, but has some idea. Suppose that it considers that under U for each of the years 1, 2 and 3 the Net cashflow will be in the range £25 to £35. It can then approach its decision making by way of **sensitivity analysis**, as in the table below. It defines three variants of the U state – A is the middle of its range, B is the lower end and C is the upper end.

	State F	State U_A	State U_B	State U_C
0	−£100	−£100	−£100	−£100
1	£40	£30	£25	£35
2	£40	£30	£25	£35
3	£40	£30	£25	£35
Probability	0.7	0.3	0.3	0.3

It can then work out the Expected NPVs for each variant of state U. You can check that the results are: A £0.76, B −£3.33, C £4.85. This kind of analysis does not produce a decision in the way that the Expected NPV rule does. Rather, it provides input to the decision maker's thinking about her problem. The decision that she takes is essentially a subjective matter. It involves some kind of judgement. In all of the relevant circumstances, as illuminated by the Expected NPV calculations, which decision does she consider best for the firm?

10.3.1.3 Uncertainty

It is also the case with uncertainty that there are no rules that a decision maker can follow in all circumstances, no rules that can be shown to produce 'best' decisions. For our simple project appraisal illustration, the uncertainty situation is as in the table below. The firm knows that there are two possible states of the world, and knows what the cashflows would be in each of them, but it does not know what the probabilities for each state are.

	State F	State U
0	–£100	–£100
1	£40	£30
2	£40	£30
3	£40	£30
NPV at 5%	£8.93	–£18.30
Probability	?	?

When dealing with uncertainty, decision makers can find it useful to organise the available information into a pay-off matrix. This states the possible decisions and the outcomes that go with them given the possible states. The pay-off matrix for our project appraisal illustration is:

	State F	State U
Yes	£8.93	–£18.30
No	0	0

The decision on the project can be either Yes for go ahead with it or No for reject it. If the decision is Yes, the pay-off to that decision is that the firm's net worth increases by £8.93 if F, but decreases by £18.30 if U comes about. If the decision is No, then there is no change in the firm's net worth whatever the state of nature turns out to be.

Given the information assembled in a pay-off matrix, various decision-making rules have been proposed. One is the 'maximax' rule. This says make the decision that gives the largest best outcome. To follow maximax the decision maker forms the maximax table by adding to the pay-off matrix a new column which shows the best outcome for each possible decision. In our case this is:

	State F	State U	rowmax
Yes	£8.93	–£18.30	£8.93
No	0	0	0

She then looks for the biggest entry in the 'rowmax' column, and makes the decision that goes with that. In this case, that is to go ahead with the project.

For the 'minimax' rule, which says make the decision that leads to the least worst outcome, the decision maker forms the minimax table in which the additional column shows the lowest figures in the corresponding rows. In our example this is:

	State F	State U	rowmin
Yes	£8.93	–£18.30	–£18.30
No	0	0	0

She then looks for the least bad outcome shown in the new column and makes the decision that goes with that. In this case, that is No.

Which of these rules, maximax or minimax, is the right one? Neither is 'right'. The former would suit an adventurous decision maker looking for big gains; the latter would suit a cautious decision maker concerned not to make big losses.

There is a third rule that has been proposed – the minimax regret rule. To follow it, the first step is to derive the regret matrix from the pay-off matrix. The entries in the regret matrix are the difference between the pay-off and what the pay-off would have been if the right decision had been taken. For our illustration the regret matrix is:

	State F	State U
Yes	0	£18.30
No	£8.93	0

The entry in the top-left cell is 0 because under state F the right decision would be Yes with a pay-off of £8.93, which is what the pay-off is in the pay-off matrix. For the bottom-left cell, the correct decision would be Yes with pay-off of £8.93 so that deciding No with pay-off of £0 means a regret of £8.93. The entry in the top-right cell is the difference between the loss of £18.30 that would occur with Yes given state U and the £0 outcome if the right decision – No – had been taken for state U. Because the right decision for U is No, the bottom-right entry is 0.

We now do minimax on the regret matrix. The minimax regret table is:

	State F	State U	rowmax
Yes	0	£18.30	£18.30
No	£8.93	0	£8.93

and we go for the decision with the smallest entry in the new column – we take the decision which minimises the maximum regret – which is No.

Minimax regret is another cautious rule. In this case, the two cautious rules say decide against the project, the adventurous rule says go ahead with it. Things will not always work out this way. It depends on the numbers. The important point is that these rules are ways of organising the information that is available. No one of them is 'the right way' in all circumstances. All of them should really be applied to any given decision-making problem. Then, it is down to the decision maker's judgement.

10.3.1.4 Ignorance

In a state of ignorance the decision maker cannot say what all the possible outcomes are, let alone assign probabilities to them. Ignorance combines features of ambiguity with features of uncertainty. We can illustrate ignorance as in the following table:

	State F	State U
0	−£100	−£100
1	£40	?
2	£40	?
3	£40	?
NPV at 5%	£8.93	?
Probability	?	?

The decision maker knows that if things turn out favourably, the project will have a cashflow that will produce a positive NPV. She also knows that things may not turn out favourably, but she has no idea what that might mean in cashflow terms. And, she has no idea how likely it is that things will turn out favourably. How can she proceed?

The available information can be assembled in a pay-off matrix as follows:

	State F	State U
Yes	£8.93	−£X
No	0	0

where £X is an unknown amount. She could then ask 'how big would X have to be to lead to a No decision if I went for minimax?', and then ask 'is that credible?'. If the answer is 'yes' here, it could be seen as reasonable to decide not to go ahead with the project; if it is 'no', it could be seen as reasonable to decide to go ahead with it.

This way of dealing with ignorance is, as we shall see, one way of understanding the nature of the Precautionary Principle, and the related idea of setting safe minimum standards.

10.3.2 Imperfect information and the environment

We have been looking at a two-fold distinction, in terms of knowledge about (1) probabilities and (2) outcomes or magnitudes. This yields four logical categories, as displayed in Table 10.1. This scheme provides us with a heuristic for thinking about concepts of risk, ambiguity, uncertainty and ignorance. Why is this distinction important for us as ecological economists? An example of economic analysis of impacts of the enhanced greenhouse effect illustrates the relevance of these concepts. As we shall see in Chapter 13, this problem is very complex with every aspect characterised by imperfect knowledge. The generally accepted estimates of the costs of climate change lie in a range of 1.5–10 per cent of national GDP, with the higher percentages mostly relating to developing countries. These estimates are based on the assumption that all costs can be determined and that the temperature rise is limited to not more than 4°C. More drastic outcomes cannot be ruled out. Outcomes such as damage from climate change in excess of a loss of 10 per cent of GDP in 2050, and a steady decline of per capita income after 2100,

Table 10.1 The formal definitions of risk, uncertainty, ambiguity and ignorance

Knowledge of probabilities	Knowledge of outcomes	
	Well defined	Poorly defined
Yes	Risk Use expected values	Ambiguity Use sensitivity analysis Precaution
No	Uncertainty Use scenario analysis Sensitivity analysis Precaution	Ignorance Use diversity Flexibility precaution

Source: based on Stirling and Mayer (2005).

are not impossible. However, in all major economic studies of climate change the problem of imperfect knowledge has been predominantly addressed through non-extreme scenarios and sensitivity analysis. In addition, existing economic research has mainly emphasised uncertainty in relation to over-investment in the reduction of greenhouse gas emissions. Extreme environmental events have received almost no attention.

For problems such as this, characterised not only by risk but also by uncertainty, ambiguity and/or ignorance, it is crucial to acknowledge them in the research design. Not taking extreme events into account in economic studies does not mean that they won't happen. If policy makers base their decisions on studies which systematically exclude some possibilities, we cannot be sure that the good decisions are made. Let us now look at environmental decision making in the face of imperfect knowledge of the future.

10.3.2.1 Environmental decision making under conditions of risk

For situations characterised by risk we said that probabilities can be assigned to outcomes. For example, in roulette the probabilities are assigned on the basis of the known properties of the gamble – unless cheating is involved. In insurance, probabilities are assigned on the basis of lots of past experience – as with the incidence of accidents for motor vehicle drivers of different age or gender. In some gambling situations, such as horse racing, probabilities are also assigned on the basis of past 'form', albeit differently by different observers. Where probabilities are assigned on the basis of experience, they are sometimes referred to as 'objective' probabilities.

In many environmental decision contexts probabilities are derived from models, which help us to develop in a structured way an understanding of a situation about which we have no relevant experience. In the case of urban air pollution, for example, for given levels of emissions from a given set of sources, ambient pollution levels at locations will vary with meteorological conditions. Physical models of the airshed can be used to simulate probabilities of different ambient levels at locations of interest. While we may have experienced all possible combinations of emissions and metereological conditions, they may not have been recorded (fully). Or we may want to investigate potential future situations in terms of emissions and weather which we have not experienced yet. What interests us in environmental analysis is often outside the range of experience. For more discussion in the context of climate change, see Chapter 13.

The probabilistic risk-based approaches are useful conceptual tools in dealing with well-understood self-contained systems and for addressing highly repetitive events. However, in the case of investments, policies or technological systems, in the real world conditions are far less circumscribed and tractable. The economic and environmental systems impinging on the development of energy technologies, chemicals and genetically modified organisms, for example, are imperfectly understood, open-ended, complex and dynamic. In such circumstances, decision makers are dealing with novelty – there is no previous experience to guide them. Serious doubts emerge over the crucial assumption of comparability between past and future circumstances and outcomes. Together, these features undermine the concept of a hypothetical series of trials, which is so central to classical notions of probability.

Some economists deal with situations like this, where the assignment of objective probabilities is seen as impossible, by treating the decision-making problem as being dealt with by the assignment of 'subjective' probabilities. This approach, which is known as the 'Bayesian' approach, conceives probabilities as an expression of the 'relative likelihoods' of different eventualities, given the best available information and the prevailing opinions of specialists. The idea is that the decision maker proceeds by assigning, on the basis of judgement, to each of the possible outcomes which he has identified a set of weights that satisfy the requirements for probabilities. The weights must be positive numbers which sum to unity. However, this assumes that the decision maker feels able to do this, and more fundamentally, feels able to enumerate all possible outcomes. The amount of information required and analysis necessary for the identification of all possible outcomes will be difficult to attain for decision makers concerning issues such as global warming, novel chemicals or genetically modified organisms. Where there is no past 'form' and/or the underlying properties of the situation to be affected by the decision are not well understood, probabilities cannot be assigned by these means.

10.3.2.2 Environmental decision making under conditions of uncertainty

Where these difficulties are recognised, we confront the condition of uncertainty in the strict sense introduced originally nearly eighty years ago by the economist Frank Knight (1921). In Table 10.1 we are now in the lower lefthand quadrant. This is a situation where it is possible to define a finite set of discrete outcomes (or a single continuous scale), but where it is acknowledged that there simply exists no credible basis for the assignment of probabilities. Where environmental decision making involves the condition of uncertainty, the decision-making aids discussed previously in connection with project appraisal in the face of uncertainty can be used. However, techniques involving definitive assignments of probability can no longer be used.

10.3.2.3 Environmental decision making under conditions of ambiguity

Serious as they are, these difficulties of assigning probabilities are unfortunately only a part of the problem usually faced in environmental decision making. We may also find that the outcomes are poorly defined. These states are represented in the righthand column of Table 10.1. 'Ambiguity', which is sometimes also called 'indeterminacy', describes a situation where a variety of divergent – but equally reasonable – framing assumptions precludes imposing any single definitive scheme of outcomes. In such a situation we find that there are a number of different perspectives concerning the scope, characterisation and prioritisation of the various magnitudes involved.

One way to deal with ambiguity may be to capture all pertinent features of the outcomes in question in a series of dichotomous categories: such as 'high' or 'low' values on some predetermined decision parameter like 'emissions' or 'growth'. Here techniques such as 'fuzzy logic', where numbers are interpreted as sets instead of precise numbers, offer ways to capture certain ambiguities in terms of dualistic category schemes. Similarly, sensitivity and scenario analysis can be applied to address aspects of ambiguity as well as uncertainty, as illustrated in the previous section.

10.3.2.4 Environmental decision making under conditions of ignorance

The condition of ignorance is the most difficult to address. Ignorance is a state of knowledge under which we are neither able to fully quantify probabilities nor to characterise all the possible outcomes. Ignorance arises from many sources, including incomplete knowledge, contradictory information, conceptual imprecision, divergent frames of reference and the intrinsic complexity and systemic indeterminacy of many natural and social processes. Put simply, ignorance is a reflection of the degree to which 'we don't know what we don't know'. It represents our uncertainty about our uncertainty. It is an acknowledgement of the importance of the element of 'surprise'. Ignorance emerges especially in complex and dynamic environments where actors and their cognitive and institutional commitments may themselves influence supposedly exogenous 'events'.

While this all may sound quite abstract, the condition of ignorance has important practical implications in relation to environmental decision making and sustainability. The most important environmental problems are characterised by ignorance. Many of the imponderables associated with global climate change, biodiversity loss, the number and functional unpredictability of chemical reactions and the unprecedented nature of genetic modification technology all present elements of 'ignorance' alongside 'risk', 'uncertainty' and 'ambiguity'. Crucially, ignorance does not necessarily imply the complete absence of knowledge, but simply the possibility that certain relevant parameters may be unknown or unknowable. This raises important questions over the precise operational locus of ignorance.

Key elements of knowledge may quite simply be unavailable to society more broadly. This was the case, for instance, with endocrine-disrupting chemicals such as dioxin and DDT prior to identification of the associated hazardous properties. Alternatively, the operational locus of ignorance may sometimes best be understood at a more specific institutional level. Key elements of pertinent knowledge may be available somewhere in society – among affected workers or consumers, for instance – but nevertheless remain effectively excluded from the governance process itself. Historically, this has arguably been the case in the early stages of recognition of many occupational and public health hazards such as asbestos, benzene and various organochlorine chemicals. The stratosphere is the region of the atmosphere above the troposphere and below the mesosphere, and is characterized by its concentration of ozone molecules which form the ozone layer. With stratospheric ozone depletion, relevant knowledge was available at an early stage in some areas of science, but the policy arena was slow to translate this knowledge into mitigation and prevention policies.

All the above examples are real cases where problems lay not so much in determining probabilities, as in anticipating the very possibilities themselves. In different ways, all were surprises born of a state of ignorance. The ancient Chinese philosopher Lao-Tzu is reputed to have said that 'knowing one's ignorance is the best part of knowledge'.

In the next section we examine responses to the problems of uncertainty, ambiguity and/or ignorance as they affect environmental decision making and the pursuit of sustainability.

10.4 THE PRECAUTIONARY PRINCIPLE AND SAFE MINIMUM STANDARDS

The **Precautionary Principle** states that where the environmental consequences of regulatory inaction are (1) in some way uncertain/ambiguous but (2) non-negligible, regulatory inaction is unjustified. Safe minimum standards are a closely related constraint approach to environmental policy, whereby in conditions of uncertainty cautious minimum levels are set.

10.4.1 The Precautionary Principle

If all resource-use decisions were reversible, then much of the force behind sustainability arguments would be lost. If we were to discover that present behaviour was unsustainable, we could change our behaviour in whatever way and at whatever time was deemed appropriate. Reversibility would imply that nothing was irretrievably lost. However, many decisions about the use of environmental services cannot be reversed, particularly those that involve the extraction of resources, the development of undisturbed ecosystems, or species extinction. When irreversibility is combined with imperfect knowledge of the future then decision rules need to change significantly. In such a situation there are good reasons for keeping options open and behaving in a relatively cautious manner. For problems in which the environmental cost of economic activity is highly uncertain/ambiguous, potentially catastrophic, widespread and possibly irreversible, it can be argued that, if we are seriously concerned for future generations, precaution is the only sensible strategy.

Although there is no consensus definition of what is termed the Precautionary Principle, one often-cited statement from the so-called Wingspread conference in Racine, Wisconsin in 1998 sums it up: 'When an activity raises threats of harm to human health or the environment, precautionary measures should be taken even if some cause and effect relationships are not fully established scientifically.'

The Precautionary Principle can be thought of as a hierarchical approach to setting targets. The sustainability criterion is considered to have overriding significance and requires that any target do as well as possible in terms of this measure. If this leaves us with more than one option, then other desirable criteria can be employed to choose among this restricted set of options. A prime example of this sort is the climate change problem, where a strong sustainability approach results in not accepting a wait-and-see policy in the face of uncertainty. An often-heard argument against the Precautionary Principle in this context is that the costs of a proactive climate policy would mean that alternative public goals have to be sacrificed. However, whereas, for instance, less healthcare and education can indeed reduce growth and welfare, they are not connected to extreme and possibly irreversible changes at a global scale. For this reason, climate policy deserves to be treated as fundamentally different from other areas of public policy.

The roots of the Precautionary Principle lie in the German 'Vorsorgeprinzip' (Boehmer-Christiansen, 1994). The first legal use of the concept was the 1969 Swedish Environmental Protection Act, which introduced the reversed burden of proof with regard to environmentally hazardous activities – they have to be proved innocent rather than guilty. Since then, largely through the campaigning and lobbying efforts of international environmental NGOs, precaution has moved from the field of hazardous waste into diverse areas such as marine pollution, climate change, biodiversity, genetic modification, chemicals regulation, food safety, public health and trade policy. As a result, the Precautionary Principle has become a potent and pervasive element in contemporary risk and environment policy.

The classic and most globally influential exposition is found in Principle 15 of the 1992 Rio Declaration on Environment and Development, as reported in Box 10.1. 'Where there are threats of serious or irreversible damage, lack of full scientific certainty shall not be used as a reason for postponing cost-effective measures to prevent environmental degradation' (UNCED, 1992). The precautionary principle differs from the principle of prevention, as for the former the uncertain nature of the threats at hand is central. However, the precautionary principle does not specify what should trigger action, nor does it specify what action should be taken. It is not a decision rule. It has mainly served to justify action rather than to ascertain what exactly should be done. A core element of the suggested principle is the 'shift of the burden of proof'.

Some authors suggest that the Precautionary Principle goes further than this and includes:

(1)   Research and monitoring for the early detection of hazards,
(2)   A general reduction of environmental burdens,
(3)   The promotion of 'clean production' and innovation,
(4)   A cooperative approach between **stakeholders** to solving common problems via integrated policy measures that aim to improve the environment, competitiveness and employment.

Funtowicz and Ravetz (1990) give another reason for stakeholder involvement in cases of uncertainty, ambiguity and ignorance. These conditions cause severe problems for the role of science in decision making. Funtowicz and Ravetz argue that if facts are uncertain, values are in dispute, stakes are high and decisions are urgent, decision making needs to be supported by '**postnormal science**'. This methodology includes the introduction of the **extended peer community**, i.e. the involvement of laypeople in quality assurance through participatory processes. Postnormal science has been widely used as the conceptual foundation of various forms of participatory integrated assessment.

As discussed above in relation to postnormal science, the difficulties arising from uncertainty, ambiguity and ignorance as well as the diverse interests within pluralist societies, which are characterised by different value systems and world-views, have in recent times increasingly persuaded policy makers to include public participation in the public policy decision-making process.

Most formulations of the Precautionary Principle contain some threshold regarding the scope or magnitude of threat involved which must be crossed to require a response. In the Rio formulation, this is 'threats of serious or irreversible damage'. The threshold cannot be universally prescribed, but rather is socially and politically determined. In the specific context triggering conditions and a required response to the triggering conditions need to be defined. This reasoning extends the need for stakeholder involvement beyond the more common argument that the diverse interests within pluralist societies, which are characterised by different value systems and worldviews, call for more public and stakeholder participation in public decision-making.

The historical practice of policy making regarding polluting substances has often used scientific uncertainty as a reason for inaction or continuing the status quo – they have to be 'proved guilty'. The lack of defined causal relationships has frequently been used in support of the option to defer a regulatory decision until further research becomes available. For example, in the case of the North Sea evidence was building up during the 1980s that pollution was causing large-scale damage, but action was repeatedly delayed because scientists were unable to establish the proof of causality. A 1990 declaration on protection of the North Sea called for action to be taken even if there is 'no scientific evidence to prove a causal link between emissions and effects'. More generally, in its least demanding formulation, the Precautionary Principle simply requires that scientific uncertainty not be used as a reason for inaction. The potential threat becomes a necessary but not a sufficient condition for precautionary action. The most widely accepted formulation of the principle acknowledges that one cannot always wait for proof of harm before acting. In the more demanding formulations, such as in the case of the North Sea, a potential threat is both a necessary and sufficient condition for precautionary action.

The greatest problem of the Precautionary Principle as a policy tool is the extreme variability possible in its interpretation. Agreements (like the Treaty on European Union) merely refer to the principle without defining it. In its strongest formulations, the principle can be interpreted as calling for absolute proof of safety before allowing new technologies to be adopted. For example, the World Charter for Nature (1982) states, 'where potential adverse effects are not fully understood, the activities should not proceed'. If interpreted literally, no new technology could meet this requirement. Other formulations open the door to consideration of costs and discretionary judgement. For example, as noted above, the Rio Declaration (1992) says that lack of 'full scientific certainty shall not be used as a reason for postponing cost-effective measures to prevent environmental degradation'.

Despite seemingly widespread political support, the Precautionary Principle has engendered much controversy, in part because some critics have interpreted 'precautionary' decisions as veiled forms of trade protectionism (see Chapter 12). Critics have also asserted that the principle's definition and goals are vague, leaving its application dependent on the regulators in charge at the moment. Others are concerned that the application of the principle will limit innovation.

An illustrative example should help to make clear the nature of the Precautionary Principle, and some of the problems associated with it. Suppose that a power
supply company wants to construct a hydro-electric facility, which would entail
the flooding of a remote river valley, which is currently used by people only as a
wilderness recreation site. Suppose that it is also known that the valley hosts a
population of some plant, and that as far as is known this is the only population
of this plant existing anywhere in the world. Flooding the valley would destroy the
plant population. Given that this would, as far as is known, entail the irreversible
extinction of the plant species, the developers have modified their proposal so that
it includes attempting to re-establish the plant population elsewhere.

Now we want to consider the position of the government's Environmental Protection Agency, the EPA, which has to decide whether this project can go ahead or
not. If it rules against the hydro plant, a wind-driven electricity generating plant
will be built instead. Suppose that all of the costs and benefits associated with the
hydro plant and the alternative can be calculated by the EPA and are as summarised
in NPV terms, in millions of $, in the following pay-off matrix:

	State of Nature	
Decision	F	U
Hydro	70	−20
Wind	20	20

If the state of nature is favourable, the relocation of the plant population is successful, and building the hydro plant has a higher NPV than the wind farm because
of lower construction costs and more reliable availability of power. If the state of
nature is unfavourable, the NPV of the wind farm is unaffected, but the NPV for
the hydro plant goes negative when it is charged with the cost of the irreversible
species loss.

The EPA is unable to attach probabilities to F and U, so it cannot use the Expected
NPV rule. It has to use one of the rules for responding to uncertainty that we discussed above. If you apply maximax, minimax and minimax regret to the hypothetical numbers above – as you are invited to do in Exercise 2 – you will find that the
arising decisions are hydro, wind and hydro respectively. If the EPA followed the
Precautionary Principle strictly it would go for the wind option. The hydro option
carries with it the threat of serious and irreversible damage: species extinction.
The burden of proof is on the proponents of the hydro plant to satisfy the
EPA that this threat will not eventuate as the relocation programme will be successful. They cannot do this so the EPA has to find against hydro and for wind. Following
the Precautionary Principle strictly means ignoring all the information about the
two projects except that one may entail serious and irreversible damage to the
environment.

10.4.2 Safe minimum standards

The basic idea of Safe minimum standards (SMS) relates to situations of ignorance,
and was originally developed in the 1950s, in the context of thinking about species

extinction. We can illustrate the basic ideas by continuing with the story about the EPA having to decide for Hydro or Wind.

In order to illustrate the nature of the Precautionary Principle, it was convenient to assume that the EPA could put a price on species extinction so as to come up with a figure for the NPV of the hydro plant if the state of nature were unfavourable. It would be more reasonable, SMS advocates would argue, to assume that it cannot do this and that the NPV for hydro given U is a negative number of unknown size. The pay-off matrix is then:

	State of Nature	
Decision	F	U
Hydro	70	−X
Wind	20	20

and the corresponding regret matrix is:

	State of Nature	
Decision	F	U
Hydro	0	X + 20
Wind	50	0

so that the maximum regrets are $X + 20$ for hydro and 50 for wind.

According to SMS we should presume that X is large enough to make Wind the preferred decision on the minimax regret criterion. The argument for this goes as follows. Any species extinction involves an irreversible reduction in the stock of potentially useful things in the environment. There is no way of knowing now how large the value to future humans of any of the existing species will turn out to be. In terms of the degree of imperfect knowledge, we are now dealing with the case of ignorance. Our ignorance takes two forms. First, we do not know what the future conditions for humans will be. We cannot know what their specific needs and desires will be, nor what the resources and technologies for meeting those needs and desires will be. Second, we are ignorant about the characteristics of most existing species in regard to their usefulness for given needs and desires and technologies. As we shall see in Chapter 14, we do not even know, approximately, how many species there are now in existence.

We should, therefore, presume that the extinction of any species carries very large costs, costs large enough to make it wrong to go ahead with anything that might entail the extinction of any species. From the point of view of economic development, SMS is very conservative. Strictly applied, it would mean not going ahead with anything that might entail the extinction of any species. More generally, where serious and irreversible environmental damage is involved, critics argue that it means forgoing current gains, however large, in order to avoid future losses of unknown size. Accordingly, just as the Precautionary Principle has often come to be qualified with cost-effectiveness caveats, so a modified SMS has been proposed, whereby possible species loss, or possible serious and irreversible environmental damage, is to be avoided unless that involves unacceptable social costs. The question remains as to how to decide in any particular case what 'unacceptable' means, which is a matter of, essentially political, judgement. Decision making in the face of ambiguity, uncertainty and/or ignorance cannot be reduced to simple rules that apply in all circumstances. Standards based on SMS-type decision making have been put in place in regard to habitat designation for endangered species, and for minimum flow and purity requirements for water quality.

10.4.3 The Precautionary Principle in the EU

The Precautionary Principle was introduced into EU environmental policy making by the EU Treaty that constitutes the European Union, which expressly provides that EU environmental policy shall be 'based on the Precautionary Principle' (EU Treaty 1993, article 174). In the absence of a definition of the principle in this document, its meaning remained unclear. On 2 February 2000, the European Commission adopted a communication on the Precautionary Principle, in which it defined this concept and explained how it intended to apply it. In this document, the European Commission sets out the specific cases where this principle is applicable:

- where the scientific data are insufficient, inconclusive or uncertain;
- where a preliminary scientific evaluation shows that potentially dangerous effects for the environment and human, animal or plant health can reasonably be feared.

In both cases, the risks are considered incompatible with the high level of protection sought by the European Union. The Communication also sets out the three rules which must be followed for the Precautionary Principle to be respected:

- a complete scientific evaluation carried out by an independent authority in order to determine the degree of scientific uncertainty;
- an assessment of the potential risks and the consequences of inaction;
- the participation, under conditions of maximum transparency, of all the interested parties in the study of possible measures.

Finally, the European Commission points out that the measures resulting from recourse to the Precautionary Principle may take the form of a decision to act or not to act, depending on the level of risk considered 'acceptable'. The Union applied the Precautionary Principle in the area of GMOs, for instance, with the entry into force of a moratorium in 1999.

10.4.4 The Precautionary Principle in the US

The US has taken a precautionary approach in some policy areas for many years, e.g. the 1958 Delaney Clause overseeing pesticide residues in food and requirements for environmental impact statements. However, while the US used to be more precautionary than Europe in the 1970s, since the 1980s the obverse has often been the case.

The US has not officially adopted the Precautionary Principle as a general basis for all risk regulation, although it has ratified the Rio Declaration on Environment and Development, which obliges nations to exercise the Precautionary Principle. After endorsements of precautionary regulation in cases like *Ethyl Corp.* v. *EPA* (1976) and *TVA* v. *Hill* (1978), the US Supreme Court held in the *Benzene case* (Industrial Union Dept., *AFL-CIO* v. *API* (1980)) that the Occupational Safety and Health Administration cannot regulate on the basis of mere conjecture about uncertain risks; the court ruled that the agency must demonstrate 'significant risk' before regulating. This decision, and a 1983 guidebook from the National Academy of Sciences, spurred widespread adoption of scientific risk assessment as the basis for American risk regulation over the past two decades, while European regulation has remained more qualitative and informal. The US insisted on qualifying the statement of the Precautionary Principle contained in the 1992 Climate Change treaty (see Chapter 13), and the US Department of State responded to the European Commission's endorsement of the Precautionary Principle with a long list of sceptical questions.

10.5 SCIENCE AND PRECAUTION

In many countries public trust in politicians and scientists has been jeopardised in recent years by issues such as BSE in the UK and elsewhere, dioxins in Belgium, and HIV-contaminated blood transfusions in France. These are stark reminders of the challenges that arise from uncertainty and ambiguity for science and policymakers. Box 10.5 provides historical examples where decisions were made on the basis that the activities were harmless and that known levels of exposure would prevail and could be controlled. Later, evidence about the harmful effects emerged. Early warning signs were generally ignored because the scientific basis was still weak. If decisions had been made based on the Precautionary Principle the impacts would have been reduced, if not avoided.

Box 10.5 Late lessons from early warnings

- Fisheries
  Fisheries worldwide had to deal with uncertainties for centuries. Scottish fisheries from the Middle Ages through to the nineteenth century, the mid-twentieth-century Californian sardine fishery crash and the collapse of Canadian northern cod stocks in the 1990s provide examples of wrong or ineffective fishery policies. The Scottish fisheries have suffered dwindling total catch of major fish species by UK vessels by about half between mid-1960s and 1999 and left the industry with low profit prospects. The major fish stocks were concerned, cod, haddock, whiting, saithe and plaice. Overexploitation of marine fisheries remains a serious problem worldwide, even for many fisheries that have been intensively managed by coastal nations. Many factors have contributed to these system failures. Irreducible scientific uncertainty about marine ecosystems in combination with the typical levels of uncontrollability of catches and incidental mortality imply that traditional approaches to fisheries management are persistently unsuccessful.

- Asbestos
  In 1879 asbestos mining began in Canada and soon thereafter mines in Australia, South Africa and the former USSR followed. Within 20 years of the start-up of the asbestos mining over 100 products made from the 'magic mineral' had been developed, but reports of serious disease had

also begun to appear. In 1998 the annual production of all types of asbestos was 2 million tonnes. Imports to the EU dropped significantly after the mid-1970s due to negative health impacts. For decades asbestos regulations were only partially enforced and/or lung cancer was not covered by work-related hygiene standards. It is estimated that 250,000 deaths will result from asbestos use in the EU over the next 35 years. Asbestos use is continuing, now largely in developing countries.

- Polychlorinated biphenyls (PCBs)
  Mass production for commercial use of PCBs started in 1929. They were well received in the marketplace as they replaced products that were more flammable, less stable and bulkier. This new group of chemicals facilitated the production of smaller, lighter and what was thought to be safer electrical equipment. By the late 1930s Monsanto, the US producer of PCBs, was certainly aware of adverse health effects on workers exposed to PCBs. It took 37 years for PCBs to become generally recognised as environmental pollutants and a danger to animals and humans. Large-scale production worldwide and in particular in some eastern European countries continued until the mid-1980s.
  From the analysis of 14 case studies Harremoes *et al.* (2002) derive the following lessons:
- Acknowledge and respond to ignorance, as well as uncertainty and risk, in technology appraisal and public policy making;
- Provide adequate long-term environmental and health monitoring and research into early warnings;
- Identify and work to reduce 'blind spots' and gaps in scientific knowledge;
- Identify and reduce interdisciplinary obstacles to learning;
- Ensure that real-world conditions are adequately accounted for in regulatory appraisal;
- Systematically scrutinise the claimed justifications and benefits alongside the potential risks;
- Evaluate a range of alternative options for meeting needs alongside the option under appraisal, and promote more robust, diverse and adaptable technologies so as to minimise the costs of surprises and maximise the benefits of innovation;
- Ensure use of 'lay' and local knowledge, as well as relevant specialist expertise in the appraisal;
- Take full account of the assumptions and values of different social groups;
- Maintain regulatory independence from interested parties while retaining an inclusive approach to information and opinion gathering;
- Identify and reduce institutional obstacles to learning and action;
- Avoid 'paralysis by analysis' by acting to reduce potential harm when there are reasonable grounds for concern.

Source: Harremoes *et al.* (2002).

10.6 FROM POLICY PRINCIPLES TO POLICY OBJECTIVES

In this chapter we have so far explored how policy principles relating to sustainable development have been negotiated over the last few decades and what economists' and ecologists' perspectives on sustainability are. We have seen by reference to the sustainable development principle that policy objectives are determined by government in consultation with the private sector (firms and consumers) and civil society (NGOs, etc.).

Recent examples of stakeholder engagement in UK policy decision-making can be found in Box 10.6. When facing continuous change, uncertainty and multiple legitimate perspectives of systems, decision making can be perceived only as an adaptive process, where the individuals taking part in one form or another in the decision-making are continuously learning. If decision making is not simply a strategic action to satisfy individual actors alone, but rather a social learning process, this requires the stimulation of trust, identity and solidarity within the respective society. These are social phenomena, which are products of communication and mutual understanding. Public participation, which includes deliberation and inclusion, can initiate social learning processes which translate uncoordinated

Box 10.6 Recent examples of public consultation in the UK

Energy White Paper
In 2001 the Department of Trade and Industry set out to write a new strategy paper about the future of the UK energy system. In addition to drawing on scientific and administrative expertise, a public consultation took place from May to August 2002. In total, over 6,500 individuals and groups took part in the consultation, which was organised in two streams:
(1)   Consultation of stakeholders – web-based and regional and thematic seminars;
(2)   Consultation of the general public – focus groups and deliberative workshops. More information can be found at – http://www.dti.gov.uk/energy/developep/index.shtml

The GM Nation? Debate
GM Nation? was part of a broader process of discussion and research that will influence the government's decision on GM crop commercialisation in the UK. Over 600 meetings across the UK took place over six weeks in 2003. GM Nation? was a novel approach to public participation in the decision-making process and, despite sometimes being critical of the process, many organisations and members of the public were willing to get involved. More information can be found at – http://www.gmnation.org.uk/index.html

Ministers 'Taking On' sustainability challenge
Ministers from six government departments joined forces to launch, on 21 April 2004, the consultation to develop new UK sustainable development strategy. The three-month consultation, run by the UK government, together with the Scottish Executive, the Welsh Assembly government and Northern Ireland, included local and regional events and an online consultation. More information can be found at – http://www.sustainable-development.gov.uk/taking-it-on/index.htm

individual actions into collective actions supporting and reflecting collective needs and understanding.

SUMMARY

Sustainable development entails doing better now in terms of satisfying the needs and desires of all the world's people while not impairing, via resource depletion and environmental damage, the ability to do that in the future. Doing this will require investment and technical change, as well as measures to protect the natural environment. Many of the policy decisions that have to be taken in pursuit of the sustainable development objective involve dealing with situations of uncertainty and ignorance, and are often irreversible. In such circumstances, decisions cannot follow simple general rules, and necessarily involve judgement as well as conventional scientific input. Increasingly, governments are looking to wider participation in decision making for sustainable development.

KEYWORDS

Ambiguity (p. 380): state of knowledge where the probabilities are known but the outcomes to which they attach are not known exactly.

Complex system (p. 377): composed of several interacting elements. The complexity of a system depends on the number of elements, the number of interactions among the elements, and the characteristics of the elements and the interactions.

Critical natural capital (p. 378): the set of environmental resources which performs important environmental functions and for which no substitute in terms of human, manufactured, or other natural capital exist.

Governance (p. 361): Governance encompasses collective decisions made in the public sector, the private sector and civil society.

Extended peer communities (p. 390): Participants in the quality-assurance processes of knowledge production and assessment in postnormal science, including all stakeholders engaged in the management of the problem at hand.

Ignorance (p. 380): state of knowledge where the definition of a complete set of possible outcomes is problematic and probabilities cannot be assigned.

Postnormal Science (p. 390): Methodology that is appropriate for decision making when 'facts are uncertain, values in dispute, stakes high and decisions urgent'.

Precautionary Principle (p. 389): view that when an activity raises threats of harm to human health or the environment, precautionary measures should be taken even if some cause-and-effect relationships are not fully established scientifically.

Risk (p. 380): state of knowledge where the different possible outcomes are known exactly and a probability can be assigned to each possibility.

Sensitivity analysis (p. 382): Sensitivity analysis is the study of how the uncertainty in the output of a model (numerical or otherwise) can be apportioned to different sources of uncertainty in the model input.

Stakeholders (p. 390): Stakeholders are those actors who are directly or indirectly affected by an issue and who could affect the outcome of a decision-making process regarding that issue or are affected by it.

Strong sustainability (p. 378): the view that natural and human-made capital are generally complementary and therefore natural capital levels should be maintained.

Uncertainty (p. 380): state of knowledge where the different possible outcomes are known but probabilities cannot be assigned to them.

Weak sustainability (p. 378): the view that natural capital depletion is justified as long as it is compensated for with increases in human-made capital; assumes that human-made capital can substitute for most types of natural capital.

FURTHER READING

Redclift (1992) examines a number of the dimensions within which the idea of sustainable development can be explored, as do Pezzey (1992, 1997), Barbier and Markandya (1990), Common (1995) and Lele (1991). Good general surveys are presented in Barbier (1989), Klaassen and Opschoor (1991), Markandya and Richardson (1992), Toman *et al.* (1995), and Neumayer (1999) which has a very comprehensive bibliography. The argument that policy should be directed towards maintaining a non-declining natural capital stock appears to have first been developed in Pearce and Turner (1990).

The ecological economics approach to sustainability is explored in various contributions to Köhn *et al.* (1999); see also Pearce (1999), Costanza (1991), Common and Perrings (1992), Söderbaum (2000) and Bossel (1998). Page (1997) compares two approaches to the problem of achieving the goals of sustainability and intergenerational efficiency. Spash (1999) gives a very good overview of the different strands of thinking which have contributed to the evolution of ecological economics.

Business economics books such as Perman and Scouller* (1999) explain project appraisal in the face of risk. Chapter 13 of Perman *et al.* (2003) deals with cost–benefit analysis in the face of uncertainty and irreversibility, and provides references. The original contribution arguing for a cautious approach to environmental conservation is Ciriacy-Wantrup (1968), which suggested establishing a Safe Minimum Standard (SMS). The concept of the SMS has since been refined by Bishop (1978) and others and put into practice in the form of critical habitat designation for endangered species, minimum flow and purity requirements for water quality, and others. Norton and Toman (1997) suggested an SMS could play a role in a 'two-tiered' decision-making system, in which utilitarian calculus would give way to a more conservationist approach as irreversibility and justice issues increase in importance. Farmer and Randall (1998) show that SMS is a common feature of agreements negotiated among citizens with varying moral positions.

A major contribution of social science to the instrumental understanding of imperfect knowledge lies in acknowledging and addressing the condition of ignorance. Knight (1921) was the first economist to distinguish clearly between risk and uncertainty. Loasby (1976) emphasised contractual incompleteness which we face in most situations. Collingridge (1980, 1982) argued that the more a system (of thought) is entrenched, and the longer the time it has been operating, the more difficult and expensive it becomes to change that system. Ravetz (1986) and Funtowicz and Ravetz (1990) emphasised that the presence of uncertainty causes severe problems for science as we know it and that different rules for public decision making are necessary in situations with high uncertainty. Public decision making thus perceived becomes a social learning task (Wynne, 1992). Faber and Proops (1994) draw on evolutionary theory and highlight irreversibility and uncertainty as omnipresent principles in economic analysis. For introductions to evolutionary economics see Dosi and Nelson (1994), Gowdy (1994), Norgaard (1994), Foster and Metcalfe (2001), Nelson and Winter (2002), or Hodgson (2004). Stirling and Mayer (2005) clarify the difference between and consequences of risk, uncertainty, ambiguity and ignorance. Young (2001) is an interesting investigation into the applicability of Shackle's ideas about decision making in the face of uncertainty in the environmental context.

WEBSITES

http://www.unep.org/ – UNEP key documents on environment and development; includes the texts of the official declarations from Stockholm to Johannesburg.
http://www.un.org/esa/sustdev/csd/ – Commission for Sustainable Development
http://www.europa.eu.int/comm/sustainable/index_en.htm – European Commission on Sustainable Development
http://www.johannesburgsummit.org – World Summit 2002 web page by UNEP.

http://www.worldsummit2002.org/ – World Summit 2002 web page by the Heinrich Böll Foundation, which gives a thorough insight into the event from an NGO perspective.

http://www.sd-research.org.uk/ – UK-based Sustainable Development Research Network

http://www.nusap.net – Uncertainty in integrated assessment.

http://www.un.org/esa/sustdev/index.html – United Nations Commission on Sustainable Development (UN/CSD) have developed a set of indicators and are producing guidance for a menu of indicators countries might use in their reporting on sustainable development. In addition

http://www.oecd.org/env/indicators/ – Organisation for Economic Co-operation and Development (OECD) published a preliminary core set of environmental indicators in 1991. These have been revised and are used in country performance reviews.

http://www.europa.eu.int/comm/sustainable/index_en.htm – European Commission (EC) developed a set of 'headline' environmental indicators and also indicators which reflect the success of integrating environmental concerns into European Union sectoral policies, particularly for transport, energy and agriculture.

http://reports.eea.eu.int/signals-2004/en – European Environment Agency (EEA) publishes annually a report on environmental indicators, 'Environmental Signals'.

http://www.sdgateway.net/ – operated by the International Institute for Sustainable Development (http://www.iisd.org/) for the Sustainable Development Communications Network, which is a group of NGOs seeking to 'accelerate the implementation of sustainable development' by improving communications and disseminating information.

http://www.ase.tufts.edu/gdae/ – the Global Development and Environment Institute at Tufts University is concerned to promote understanding of how societies 'can pursue their economic goals in an environmentally and socially sustainable manner'.

DISCUSSION QUESTIONS

1. Why did the idea of sustainable development appear in the last quarter of the twentieth century?
2. Would the Precautionary Principle be a sensible basis for personal decision making?

EXERCISES

1. The governance structure which is relevant to the place where you live consists of various organisations in the public, private and voluntary sectors. Find out how one national or local governmental organisation, one firm and one NGO in your area define sustainable development. How do the definitions compare? Are they consistent? If not, can you imagine why one organisation would favour one aspect over another?

2. Refer to the example of renewable energy technologies (hydro and wind) in section 10.4 and apply maximax, minimax and minimax regret rules. How would you decide? Give a reasoning for your decision and use the terminology introduced in this chapter (risk, uncertainty, ambiguity, ignorance) in your answer.

3. Find issues which have been recently discussed in the national media of your country and for which you think that the Precautionary Principle should be applied; discuss also how pursuing the Precautionary Principle could be exploited by some groups (e.g. justification for trade barriers such as the case of beef fed with hormones, dealt with by the World Trade Organization).

11 Environmental policy instruments

In this chapter you will:

- Find out what needs to be considered for implementing environmental policy;
- Learn about the instruments available to attain environmental goals;
- See by which mechanisms these instruments operate;
- Consider their respective merits and limitations;
- Learn why uncertainty complicates the implementation of environmental policy immensely.

The previous chapter dealt with the evolution of environmental policy over the last few decades and how environmental targets are set. In this chapter we study the instruments that have been used to pursue the agreed environmental targets. Over time economists and political scientists have developed many different instruments for implementing environmental policy goals.

Before going into details of the different policy instruments and how to choose between them, let us take a step back and think about why we need policy instruments. Well obviously, we want to avoid or reduce environmental damage. But why is it that we cannot leave this task to markets? As we saw in Chapter 9, in neo-classical economics excessive anthropogenic environmental damage stems from the failure of the institutions of which markets consist, and in which they are embedded, to incorporate the full cost and benefits of economic activities. When do markets fail? They fail if the institutions are missing which require producers and consumers to take responsibility for the consequences of their actions. This leads to a divergence of private and social costs and as a consequence private profit-maximising decisions are not socially, that is allocatively, efficient. The divergence between private and social costs causes problems for society, the environment and in the long run for the economy.

The institutions, which might persuade the economic actors to take responsibility, could be:

(a) a social norm which makes it unacceptable to behave in a way which jeopardises the stability of local or global ecosystems,

(b)   an eco-label which informs consumers that choosing the labelled product is probably better for the environment,

(c)   an individual's conviction to do the right thing for the environment (as a result of information received from governmental or other sources or because of their altruistic behavioural trait),

(d)   a law which forbids certain activities,

(e)   the assignment to individuals and firms of quantified entitlements to resource use or emissions generation

(f)   an economic incentive which is set to reduce the consumption of environmentally harmful goods; it becomes more expensive to buy the good.

For example, driving a car causes emissions and resource use for the production of the car. In that case the types of institutions listed above would be:

(a)   A is part of a social network within which it is for environmental reasons unacceptable to own a car; buying and driving one would reduce A's social status significantly;

(b)   while B needs/wants a car, she makes sure to buy the brand and make with the lowest fuel consumption and excellent emission test results;

(c)   while C's friends have cars and in his current situation it would be difficult for C to get around without a car, he decides to move closer to the places where he needs to go, relies mostly on his bicycle and joins a car-sharing club for occasional long-distance trips;

(d)   D would love to drive a big and very powerful car, which consumes 15 litres of petrol per 100 km, but a new national law forbids selling new cars that consume more than 10 litres per 100 km;

(e)   E would like to drive her car 20,000 km per year, which would mean using 3,000 litres, but the government restricts individual petrol consumption to 2,000 litres per year;

(f)   the government implements a new tax which increases the price of petrol by 10 per cent.

The problem of external effects can be overcome by altruistic behaviour (c) or by some kind of social coordination (a–b) and (d–f). We will discuss the institutions described in (a–c) as 'moral suasion' in section 11.2, direct regulation or 'command-and-control' as in (d) in section 11.3, creation of (quasi) property rights as in (e) in section 11.4, and economic incentives or 'market-based instruments' as in (f) will be discussed in sections 11.5 and 11.6. First, however, let us consider what policy makers might want from environmental policy instruments and which criteria they need to fulfil.

11.1 CHOICE OF ENVIRONMENTAL POLICY INSTRUMENTS

Choosing from the array of possible policy instruments is a challenging task. This is particularly so, because governments typically have multiple goals. In daily political life, these goals develop from a network of influences and pressures within the political and administrative systems. The goals can be read as criteria for comparing policy instruments against each other. The preferred policy instrument will then be the one which scores highest against these criteria.

All environmental policy instruments have in common that they aim to:
(1)   achieve environmental improvements (e.g. a certain reduction in CO_2 emissions),
(2)   cause the lowest possible cost for economic actors (businesses, households and governments) and
(3)   avoid negative, and create positive, impacts in other areas of society (e.g. employment, income distribution).

However, different policy instruments put different emphasis on these aims. For example, environmental standards focus on (1), while market-based instruments, like taxes, highlight (2). Every policy has some impacts on other areas of society, which is where (3) comes in. To what extent this happens and whether they are positive or negative depends not only on the instrument applied, but also on the specific design of the institutions which implement the policy. For example, an energy tax makes energy more expensive, which normally leads to a reduction in the quantity of energy demanded and therefore lower CO_2 emissions. Energy taxes have been criticised because they can lead to lower employment. However, using the revenues from the energy tax for reducing payroll taxes may lead to positive employment effects. Policy makers are concerned about their country losing competitiveness after introducing an energy tax. Depending on whether firms or households are mostly taxed and depending on whether other countries (competitors) are introducing a similar tax at the same time, the tax will lead to a negative or near-neutral effect on competitiveness. Taxing household energy demand may hit poor households harder than rich ones because they spend a larger share of their household income on energy (especially for heating and transport). This is in many countries considered unfair. It can be counterbalanced by increases in benefits for poor households.

In addition to these three main goals, there are a number of more technical requirements for good policy instruments. For achieving the stated goals, the instruments should:
(4)   create continuing incentives to improve products or production processes in environmentally less harmful directions (often referred to as 'dynamic efficiency'),
(5)   be dependable so that the stakeholders can rely upon the target being achieved,
(6)   be able to adapt to changing conditions,
(7)   avoid excessive information requirements.

There is no one policy instrument which scores highest against all of these criteria under all circumstances. The use of any instrument is likely to involve conflicts or trade-offs between alternative criteria. The choice of instrument depends on how important the individual criteria are in the specific situation and to the particular policy maker.

We can arrange environmental policy instruments into three groups: (1) decentralised, such as moral suasion, property rights and liability laws; (2) command-and-control (direct regulation), such as ambient, effluent or technology standards combined with enforcement; and (3) market-based, such as emissions taxes, subsidies and tradable permits. We will discuss these types of instruments in detail in the other sections of this chapter.

Economists, especially neoclassical economists, tend to favour market-based instruments, which means control via a price mechanism. This is a relatively new type of environmental policy instrument, whose appeal stems from the promise to reduce the total cost for achieving the environmental policy goal (or to achieve more for the same cost). The logic behind this argument is that those polluters for whom it is easiest (cheapest) shall be encouraged (paid) to reduce their emissions by more than their equal share. As a result the environmental policy goal can be achieved at a lower cost to society. In other words, economic incentives not only allow firms to take different actions, but they also allow them to end up with varying levels of emissions reduction. Because manufacturing plants, even those within the same industry, differ widely in their levels of technology and production processes, some will find it less expensive to undertake a given amount of emissions reductions than others. An economic instrument can achieve a given level of environmental protection for lowest overall cost by creating a framework that enables companies to respond according to their ability to make reductions. Ultimately, firms are either rewarded or penalised for their efforts. One company may continue to emit more pollution, but pays a price for doing so. Another may undertake further control measures and achieve a lower tax bill, or revenues from sold permits. The overall impact on the environment will be the same, but the aggregate cost of the **regulation** will be reduced.

Market-based instruments, such as emission charges, product charges, tax differentiation, subsidies, deposit-refund systems and tradable permits, change the economic incentive structure for firms and/or consumers. These more indirect interventions leave room for a flexible response to the environmental demands of society, mobilising the (search for) knowledge of technological feasibilities and considering local physical constraints of individual actors.

While market-based instruments are becoming more widely used, they have not come anywhere close to replacing the conventional, command-and-control, approach to environmental protection. These regulatory techniques, such as uniform reduction percentages across pollution sources, input restrictions, product requirements and technology-specific prescriptions, require specified economic actors to change their behaviour for the sake of achieving specified environmental goals, such as emission standards. The widespread application of command-and-control instruments can be explained by the fact that they seem to serve most interest groups (polluting firms, environmentalists, regulators) best, despite difficulties which these groups may have in agreeing on a specific pollution target. From the viewpoint of the polluting firm, a tax increase costs more than an equivalent emission standard because as well as the cost of reducing emissions there is the tax liability. Environmentalists often oppose market-based instruments on the grounds that they may fail to secure the desired environmental improvement. There is also the fear that these instruments may give legitimacy to the act of polluting, or that pricing it may erode the level of environmental quality society desires to attain. Compared to market-based instruments, command-and-control instruments are seen by politicians to offer better opportunities for demonstrating care for the environment.

Another reason for the slow change lies in some weaknesses of market-based instruments. Even when and where market-based approaches have been used in their purest form and with some success, such as in the case of tradable permit systems in the United States noted below, they have not always performed as anticipated. A number of disadvantages of market-based instruments have become apparent with their actual use, such as negative distributional effects, less certain environmental effects than direct regulations, and difficulties in determining the required tax levels.

In practice, the key issue is to design mechanisms for economic incentives to complement and integrate with a well-established regulatory system. For example, in the case of the UK's landfill tax, operators of landfill sites must: comply with planning consents and waste management licensing conditions which set requirements for site design, operation and restoration; demonstrate that they are fit and proper persons to hold a waste management licence; make financial provision for site restoration; pay landfill tax on waste they accept for landfilling. The regulatory instruments ensure that the environmental impacts of the landfill are within acceptable limits in the short and long term, whilst the economic instrument is designed to promote switching between landfill and other forms of waste management that are less harmful to the environment and to provide a long-term incentive for waste reduction.

Now let us scrutinise each of the main environmental policy instruments.

11.2 MORAL SUASION

Moral suasion is persuasion exerted or acting through and upon the moral nature or sense. An authority (e.g. the US EPA, EC, ministry of the environment) applies pressure without applying force in an attempt to get firms and/or individuals to behave in ways that serve a policy. Moral suasion aims to manipulate the cultural environment. It involves attempts to change the preferences of economic agents, without adopting command-and-control measures and without directly changing price incentive structures. An important vehicle of moral suasion is providing information about the (environmental) consequences of behaviour. As discussed in Chapter 1, what is thought to be morally correct depends on an appreciation of the relevant facts as well as on ethics and/or preferences.

Examples of moral suasion as an environmental policy instrument are:
- finance of campaigns to raise public awareness;
- product-labelling requirements;
- voluntary agreements by emissions sources on emissions targets;
- subsidisation of research and development for alternative technologies;
- finance of basic research.

These approaches have been widely used in practice. Politicians seem to like moral suasion because they are seen to be encouraging people to do the (morally) right thing, but they do not risk criticism on account of forcing people to change their behaviour, or of increasing taxation. Firms prefer voluntary approaches because they can use them as part of their public relations campaigns – and they leave more room for the firm to decide whether or not to fulfil them in case the competitive pressure becomes too fierce.

Neoclassical economists are generally dismissive of moral suasion approaches, which is probably a reflection of the assumptions of given preferences and consumer sovereignty, which we discussed back in Chapter 9. Certainly changing prices that firms and individuals face so as to reflect better environmental costs conveys information and aims to change behaviour. However, the ability of prices to communicate relevant information about the environment–economy relationship is limited and prices influence rich and poor people in very different ways. Ecological economists have adopted a different approach, which aims to make fuller use of moral suasion approaches. Their models explicitly allow for preferences to change over time. The crucial question is, however, what the (democratic and non-exploitative) mechanisms for changing preferences are. To date there has been relatively little systematic research on the cost-effectiveness of moral suasion in relation to other instruments. In particular when aimed at long-run sustainability issues it appears that there could be much greater room for approaches of moral suasion than currently practised. Once the cultural environment has been changed, moral suasion approaches require much less attention and reinforcement than other policy instruments.

Next we take a closer look at different types of preferences and changing preferences.

11.2.1 Changing preferences

People form their preferences in interaction with other people. In Chapter 6 we saw, for example, that people's sense of happiness depends largely on relations with other people. People adapt their basic beliefs and norms to others, and imitate peers with regard to spending patterns, but show a great diversity in both respects. Preferences are also influenced by education, advertising and public policies.

Understanding how preferences change is important for environmental policy because achieving a shift in preferences (e.g. about social responsibility of firms or lifestyles of households) means that economic agents will act in more environmentally friendly ways and feel good about it, instead of being forced to do so.

11.2.2 Varieties of preferences

The variegated repertoire of needs and values, opportunities and abilities, which people bring into a decision process, translates into an array of preferences. These include the categories of self-regarding, other-regarding and process-regarding preferences. Whereas self-regarding preferences concern the individual's own outcomes, other-regarding preferences concern the outcomes for others, and process-regarding preferences concern the manner in which the individual in question and others behave, including the ways in which they attain outcomes of interest. The latter, the process-regarding preferences, include values, codes of behaviour and mores. In this extended framework, other- and process-regarding preferences are embraced rather than just acknowledged as unexplained oddities. Experiments by social psychologists and economists, as well as ethnographic and historical studies of collective sacrifice towards common objectives, point to the importance of a wider framework. These empirical studies also show which role particular institutional settings play to prompt individuals in drawing one or another response from their varied behavioural repertoire. For example, face-to-face communication, an existing common personal history, or continued interaction will enhance an individual's disposition to take the interest of others into consideration.

Preferences appear to be defined over processes as well as outcomes *per se*. Individuals make different choices depending on how a given opportunity set was determined. Also the large literature in the social sciences, especially in psychology, political science and sociology, which attributes a positive value to participatory processes, points to the importance of processes. They enhance people's perception of self-determination. Citizens may gain satisfaction from such participation rights over and above the outcome generated in the political process, because they provide a feeling of being involved and having political influence, as well as a notion of inclusion, identity and self-determination.

A recent Swiss study investigating the benefits of political participation rights found that an increase by one point in a residents' participation scale raised the proportion of those who said they were 'very happy' by 2.7 per cent. This represents half of what moving from the lowest to the highest income band (a sevenfold increase of income) created. The authors also examined whether perceived benefits from higher public participation were due to the outcome, better government, or to the process. Foreigners, who are not allowed to vote, enjoy the outcomes but cannot take part in the process. In fact, foreigners' happiness resulting from better government rose by only one third as much as the increase for nationals. The findings thus suggest that two-thirds of the benefits lie in the process, meaning in the ability to participate in a decision-making process. This indicates that not only the outcome but also the process matters considerably in people's perceptions. The reference for this study can be found in the further reading section.

Understanding the different types of preferences and under what conditions people base their behaviour on which type is crucial for designing effective policy instruments. Policies which address people via their other-regarding and process-regarding preferences, and which provide sufficient reasoning and adequate institutions to assure individuals that they are contributing to the larger good, will open opportunities which are beyond the reach of other policy instruments. Also, policy makers who understand that the process of coming to a decision will influence its acceptance will normally be more successful in achieving (environmental) policy targets than others. However, attempting to change behaviour simply by the provision of information may often be ineffective. Among the reasons for this are:

- people are often confronted with too many decisions, too much information, and too little time to process it all;
- a great number of decisions are made every day by routine/out of habit – the situation occurs often and/or the decision is perceived as not important enough to collect all information and deliberate about it;
- once somebody has acquired new information and wants to behave differently, if under time pressure they may well revert to old behavioural patterns.

Box 11.1   Eco-Labelling

Eco-labelling is a practice of providing information to consumers about a product which is characterised by improved environmental performance compared with similar products. Germany's 'Blue Angel', which pioneered eco-labelling, was launched in 1978 to denote 'environmentally friendly' products. Since then, products with labels promoting attributes like 'recyclable', 'degradable' or 'ozone-friendly' were introduced into the marketplace. More recently, eco-labels promoting environmentally friendly production methods, such as 'dolphin-safe tuna', 'organic' food, furniture made from wood from sustainably managed forests or fish from sustainable fisheries, were introduced.

The trend towards eco-labelling is based on the increased concern of consumers for the environment and food safety. Eco-labels are institutions which inform consumers in a concise way about minimum standards of product characteristics and/or the environmental impacts of producing, processing, transporting and using a product. Besides pooling (environmental) information, their aim is to generate trust in the product. (Similar arguments motivate fair trade labels which focus on working conditions and the price which producers receive.)

To some degree their popularity is defeating the purpose as more labels arise which focus on different aspects of the production process or product characteristics. As economies become more integrated national labels also need to be replaced by internationally recognisable ones. While national eco-labels are well known in some countries (above 50 per cent in Japan, Singapore, Canada and Norway), international labels are much less known (e.g. the European label, the flower, ranges between 0 and 2 per cent in different European countries).

The attractiveness of eco-labels stems largely from their compatibility with existing market structures – potential buyers are provided with information and left to make their choice.

However, this popularity is not without controversy. Developing countries are afraid of losing market access if they cannot prove that their production techniques or product characteristics meet the standards of the eco-label. This is why many developing countries view eco-labels as non-tariff trade barriers (see Chapter 12).

11.2.3 Innovations in measuring and reporting economic and environmental performance

Back in Chapter 5 we noted some proposals for modifying the national income accounting conventions so that what would get measured would be sustainable national income. The proponents have the idea that politicians and the public would be more likely to support policies to promote sustainability if they were more informed about the extent of natural resource depletion and environmental damage. National income statisticians share the view that such information should be made available, but are sceptical about the possibility of using it to produce an accurate and meaningful measure of sustainable national income. Hence, as reported in Chapter 5, while official national income publications are moving in the direction of including data on resource depletion and environmental damage, the intention is to put it in 'satellite accounts' rather than to use it in the main national income accounts.

Some economists argue that in order to provide proper information on economic performance, and the environmental impact of economic activity, one should not start with per capita national income. Rather, they argue, one should start with personal consumption per capita, as measured in the national income accounts, and make adjustments to it so as to measure 'sustainable welfare'. The proposed adjustments include resource depletion and environmental damage estimates. The result is known as an 'index of sustainable economic welfare', ISEW, or sometimes as a 'genuine progress indicator', GPI. Historical series for these have been constructed for a number of developed countries – most show that since around 1970, per capita sustainable welfare has remained more or less static while per capita national income has grown. You will find references to some of these studies in Further Reading: see also the websites listed at the end of the chapter.

There has also been a lot of interest in providing biophysical information on the state of the environment, and how it is affected by economic activity. Again, part of the motivation is the idea that if people were better informed there would be more chance of their behaving consistently with the requirements of sustainability, and voting for policies to protect the environment. There are two, related, problems about expecting such biophysical information to have much impact on public opinion. First, it is difficult for many people to take on board what scientific data mean. Second, there are lots of different biophysical indicators expressed in different units of measurement. One of the attractions of the economic indicators – GDP or ISEW – as sources of public information is that they come as single numbers, not as a whole series of different measurements.

One interesting attempt to get round these problems and to come up with a single easily understood indicator is the 'ecological footprint'. This is:

> The aggregate area of land and water in various categories that is claimed by participants in the economy to produce all the resources they consume, and to absorb all the wastes they generate on a continuing basis, using prevailing technology.
>
> (Wackernagel and Rees, 1996)

There are problems about actually measuring all of the land requirements, so footprint results should not be regarded as precise. However, they are striking and easily understandable, and are indicative of the basic situation. Wackernagel *et al.* (2002) estimated the footprint for the global economy for each year from 1961 to 1999. They found that the ratio of the footprint size to the land actually available increased from approximately 0.7 in 1961 to approximately 1.2 in 1999. In the latter year, as they put it, it would require 1.2 earths to regenerate what humanity used. There are wide differences in the size of the per capita footprint across different national economies. Whereas the global average is about 2 hectares per capita, for the USA the footprint is 9.7 hectares. The implication is that if all of the world's people were to consume at the US level, using current technology, it would require a few earths to support them.

11.3 COMMAND-AND-CONTROL INSTRUMENTS

Command-and-control instruments (or 'direct regulation' as they are also known) have been the dominant method of environmental regulation in the majority of countries. They are mostly used for pollution control and the management of common property resources (such as ocean fisheries within territorial waters). The benefits are measured in physical units, which avoids the problems of monetary valuation.

The command-and-control instruments which are currently in use operate at various stages of the production and pollution-generation process: inputs used, production technique, quantity of goods produced, emissions output, location of emissions and ambient pollution levels. Directing the controls at points closest to what is the target, namely ambient pollution levels, gives polluters most flexibility in how a pollution reduction is achieved. Examples of direct regulation in the US include ambient air quality standards (Clean Air Act), effluent emissions

(Clean Water Act), standards for hazardous waste disposal (Resource Conservation and Recovery Act) and restrictions on the use of dangerous substances (Federal Insecticide, Fungicide and Rodenticide Act; Toxic Substance Control Act).

Direct regulation may ban substances or production techniques if they are deemed too dangerous for humans or the environment. Otherwise the quantity of a pollutant that can be produced or the share of a resource stock that can be used will be limited or the technology or location restricted. In the following we explore the three most commonly used types of command-and-control instruments.

11.3.1 Non-transferable emissions licences

Setting emission targets (or **environmental standards**) is normally a political process, which is based on scientific findings about safe emission levels and which take into account what policy makers and stakeholders consider as technically and economically feasible. Remember, as we saw in the previous chapter, that under conditions of uncertainty it is often difficult (or impossible) to establish what 'safe' emission levels are. However, the alternative of doing nothing is even less attractive. Therefore, targets are set and producers are asked to comply with them. Being aware of the problems which scientists and policy makers face when setting targets under conditions of uncertainty, we should not be surprised that we often observe targets which were considered safe in one year, but later have to be significantly revised as better or novel information arises and as we acquire a better understanding of the environmental impact of a production process.

In order to achieve a given overall emissions target for a particular kind of pollutant, the environmental regulatory authority creates licences (depending on the context, also called permits or quota), which limit the amount of emissions permissible for each production unit. As the name indicates, the licences cannot be transferred or traded – we look at licences that can be traded, which are a market instrument, later. The authority needs to have sufficient information for allocating the licences adequately. Examples of emissions licences are the 'eco-points' (Ökopunkte), which hauliers have to buy from the Austrian government when passing through Austria. Per EU Member State up to 8,000 trips through Austria are granted per year. Lorries with modern engines which produce less emissions require fewer points (they can make more trips) than lorries with older engines. How effective the system is environmentally depends on the total number of licences issued per year.

For the licence scheme to function well, levels of emissions need to be monitored regularly and penalties for non-compliance need to be in place (and enforced). If these conditions are fulfilled, emission licences will normally deliver the expected environmental improvement. If the cost structures for abatement are different for various emissions sources, the scheme will, however, cost society more than is strictly necessary. The reason for this is that each source has to fulfil its target independently, irrespective of how difficult (expensive) it is for it and it cannot ask (pay) somebody else to reduce emissions by a larger quantity on its behalf. The way in which this makes total abatement costs higher than they need be will be explained in detail when we look at how tradable licences, and uniform emissions taxes, work.

Box 11.2 Best Available Technology Regulation in Europe

While pollution from industrial installations in many European countries has been controlled to some extent for over 150 years, the definition of best available technology was only recently harmonised. In October 1999 a European Directive on Integrated Pollution Prevention and Control (EC/96/61) was passed, and by 2004 most Member States have integrated it into their respective national environmental laws. The Directive defines 'best available techniques' as: 'the most effective and advanced stage in the development of activities and their methods of operation which indicate the practical suitability of particular techniques for providing in principle the basis for emission limit values designed to prevent and, where that is not practicable, generally to reduce emissions and impact on the environment as a whole'. The Directive outlines a framework requiring Member States to issue operating permits for certain installations carrying on certain industrial activities. The Directive applies to new or substantially changed installations with effect from October 1999 and no later than October 2007 for existing installations. These permits must contain conditions based on BAT. The European Integrated Pollution Prevention and Control Bureau organises an exchange of technical information on best available techniques and creates reference documents (BREFs) which must be taken into account when the respective national authorities of Member States determine conditions for integrated pollution prevention and control permits. The BREFs inform the relevant decision makers about what may be technically and economically available to industry in order to improve their environmental performance.

11.3.2 Minimum technology requirements

Another command-and-control instrument regulates the technology which firms (and/or households) can use. The aim of required technology standards is to control pollution by banning or phasing out technologies which are known for causing severe or unnecessary environmental damage. In other words, it is a technology-forcing process which is intended to reduce future emissions to prevent unnecessary pollution. Required technology standards have been implemented as 'best practicable means' (BPM), 'best available technology' (BAT) and 'best available control technology' (BACT). More recently, policy makers have become more sensitive to causing high costs to firms in their country and therefore the 'best available technology not entailing excessive cost' (BATNEEC) was introduced.

For examples, such regulations have required polluters to use flue-gas desulphurisation equipment in power generation, designated minimum stack heights, required the installation of catalytic converters in vehicle exhaust systems and maximum permitted lead content in engine fuels. BACT regulations play an important role in the US clean air laws.

11.3.3 Regulation of location of polluting activities

For pollutants for which physical processes operate so that the pollutant quickly becomes dispersed to the point where the spatial distribution is uniform, the location of the pollution source is not important. Many pollutants are, however, not easily dispersed. For example, ozone accumulation in the lower atmosphere, oxides of nitrogen and sulphur in urban airsheds, particulate pollutants from diesel engines and trace metal emissions are cases where emissions source location matters. In such cases, in order to reduce human exposure it is common to regulate by zoning or planning procedures which control where sources or residences can be built. For example, incinerators are usually located on the outskirts of cities or industrial zones are separated from residential ones. Only on rare occasions are people relocated from existing residences in response to high pollution levels. For example,

Box 11.3　Environmental racism and classism

There is evidence that poor people and residents in ethnic communities have experienced disproportionate exposure to hazardous waste and pollution, although there are conflicting views as to the cause. In the literature the proposition that environmental hazards disproportionately affect minorities and the poor is called the environmental racism–classism hypothesis. Quantitative research supports both propositions by reporting race/class correlates for a variety of environmental hazards. Studies, which were mostly conducted during the early to mid-1990s, documented particular exposure for air pollution and lead among urban African Americans, pesticide contamination for Chicano farmworkers, radiation exposure among the Navajo and waste management facilities in African American and Hispanic communities. Allen (2001) tests the environmental racism–classism hypothesis and focuses on environmental racism in relation to toxic releases in American counties. Allen uses data on 2,083 counties in 1995. The major findings in this study support the environmental racism and classism hypothesis. Minorities and the poor are disproportionately affected by environmental hazards. However, the results also demonstrate that the race–class–risk nexus, as regards toxic releases, is more complex than anticipated. As the percentage of the Black population in American counties in 1995 increased, so did the level of toxic releases; however, this relationship was stronger in the Sunbelt, indicating that larger proportions of Black Americans are exposed to higher levels of toxic releases in Sunbelt counties than is the case elsewhere in the nation. Class and race relationships are conditional: while high social class reduces the level of toxic releases, it does so by moderating the relationship between fiscal capacity, pollution potential and thus environmental harm.

Such outcomes do not need to be explained in terms of overt racism or classism. They could be the result of decision making based solely on efficiency or cost-effectiveness criteria. Locating waste facilities where they pose the least risk to the general population, have the lowest operation expenses and entail the smallest opportunity cost for alternate land uses, in combination with a low propensity for protest, seems to make a lot of sense in such terms. However, this is a clear reminder that public policy decisions should not be solely based on the efficiency goal. Efficiency and fairness need to be considered at the same time. In order to produce good recommendations for environmental policy, our economic framework needs to take into account equity as well as efficiency and cost effectiveness. This is what ecological economics aims to do.

In response to such academic studies and the strengthening environmental justice movement, on 11 February 1994 US President Clinton signed the Executive Order 12898 on Environmental Justice. In the spring of 1998 the US EPA issued Interim Guidance for investigating Title VI of the Civil Rights Act of 1964 to ensure that the issuance of pollution control permits does not negatively impact low-income and minority communities. The Office of Environmental Justice in the US EPA was founded to 'provide a central point for the Agency to address environmental and human health concerns in minority communities and/or low-income communities – a segment of the population which has been disproportionately exposed to environmental harms and risks'.

the radioactive pollution in Chernobyl was far too high for people to live there after the nuclear accident in 1986. Planning controls and other forms of command and control directed at location have a large role to play in the control of pollution with localised impacts and for immobile source pollution. They are used to prevent harmful spatial clustering of emission sources.

However, separating people from pollution sources does not reduce the impact on the non-human biophysical systems. In addition, people are not homogenous. Some groups are more able to avoid exposure to negative environmental impacts than others. As reported in Box 11.3, during the 1980s and 1990s evidence from many cases in the US showed that the poor and ethnic communities were more likely to be exposed to hazardous waste and pollution.

11.4 CREATION OF PROPERTY RIGHTS

The twentieth century has witnessed many efforts to improve the management of economy–environment interdependencies through reforms of **property rights**, the rights of an owner of property; these typically include the right to use the property as one sees fit (subject to certain restrictions, such as zoning) and the right to sell it. The reasoning behind this is that the absence of private property rights in natural resources or ecosystem services is responsible for many environmental problems. With the creation of private property rights in these assets, markets would change the relative prices of all assets. The prices of environmental assets being depleted would rise, so that their use would decline. This trend would also encourage the development and use of substitutes, where possible. As a result of the changed relative prices, production and consumption patterns would become less environmentally damaging, and the prices of goods and services would better reflect their environmental impacts.

This approach is problematic for three reasons. First, the range of applicability is limited since many environmental assets are inherently non-rival and/or non-exclusive in use. Second, where private property rights can be created, and other problems for the operation of markets are absent, the outcomes will be those that protect the environment as required by efficiency criteria. These outcomes are not necessarily consistent with sustainability requirements. Third, it overlooks the role of common property rights.

As discussed in Chapter 9 – see 9.2.4.2 on externalities – Ronald Coase showed that government intervention is not necessary if the people affected by the externality and the people creating it get together and bargain. However, the likelihood that bargaining will actually take place is low unless private property rights exist which can be enforced at low cost. The 'Coase Theorem' is of very limited applicability to important environmental problems, because they usually involve public goods/bads. This is the first point above. The second is that while bargaining would, in the circumstances assumed by Coase (rivalry and exclusion), lead to an efficient outcome, there is no reason to suppose that it would be equitable, or meet the requirements of sustainability.

The third problem with the focus on creating private property rights in environmental assets is that common property regimes may be an equally effective basis for managing environmental assets. The focus goes back to Hardin's 'tragedy of the commons', which was, as we discussed in Chapter 9, based on a confusion of open access and common property resources. Since then Elinor Ostrom and her co-workers have pointed out that common property resources are closer to a drama which may have a favourable or an unfavourable ending. A long list of historical and current examples show that common property regimes may be as effective a basis for managing environmental assets as private property rights. They also emphasise that it is not only formal institutions (laws), but also informal institutions (traditions, norms, etc.) that constitute an effective basis of property rights in many societies. References to this work were provided in Further Reading for Chapter 9.

This is not to deny a role for the creation of private property rights for using environmental assets more sustainably. There are, no doubt, situations where it is useful to create them where they do not currently exist and where the resulting outcomes would provide better protection for environmental assets than current arrangements. The point is that the usefulness of this type of policy instrument is to be judged on a case-by-case basis, in light of a full consideration of all particular circumstances. For some there is an ethical presumption that critical environmental assets should be collectively, rather than privately, owned. Collective or common ownership does not preclude leasing usage rights to individuals.

11.5 TAXATION

The idea of taxing environmentally damaging activities, such as pollution generation, in order to reduce their scale has a long history in economics. It was Arthur Cecil Pigou in his book *Economics of Welfare* (1920) who first introduced the idea that waste emissions were an externality and proposed imposing a tax equal to the marginal external cost so as to bring about the level of emissions that goes with allocative efficiency. Recall from Chapter 9 that externalities are the unintended effects of one agent's behaviour on some other agent or agents which the current institutional arrangement does not require the former to take responsibility for. While externalities can also be positive,[1] in environmental policy we are mostly concerned with negative externalities, such as, for example, air pollution from car exhausts causing respiratory problems for the human population living near a motorway.

Pigou argued that taxing emissions would reduce them to the level corresponding to allocative efficiency in the most efficient manner possible. An emissions tax is levied on each unit discharged. By raising the price for polluting to reflect social cost, environmental taxes ensure that polluters take responsibility for the full cost of their actions. In the absence of taxes or other control mechanisms, environmentally damaging activities are carried to excess by the operation of market forces. The reliance of emissions taxes on a price mechanism is a way to reduce overall compliance costs. This is so because taxes encourage the greatest pollution abatement by the firms able to adjust at the lowest cost, as we will demonstrate below when we look at the least cost theorem in section 11.7, and because they encourage deployment of new technologies.

We now want to consider at what level the regulatory authority should set the emissions tax in order to achieve: (1) the economically, *that is allocatively*, efficient level of emissions abatement; and/or (2) a sustainable level of production.

11.5.1 Taxation for allocative efficiency

Let us start with aiming for an economically efficient level of emissions abatement. First we need to identify the efficient level of pollution, which is the one that minimises the sum of total abatement cost plus total damage cost. Abatement cost is the cost to society of pollution reduction. Abatement may involve a reduction in the activity that produces the emissions, or the application of some emission-reducing measures, or some combination of the two. For example, emissions from driving a car could be reduced by driving less, by smoother driving, or a combination of the two. Damage cost is how affected individual firms value the damage. The sum of the total costs is minimised where the marginal damage and the marginal abatement cost are equal.

Back in Chapter 9, see section 9.1, we discussed the principle of equalising marginal costs and marginal benefits to maximise net benefits for allocative

---

1 For example, the effect child-rearing can have on society. Societies benefit greatly from an upbringing which makes young people responsible, well-educated and competent citizens. This is the reason why it makes sense for a society to support families, child-care centres, schools, training facilities, universities, etc. with public funds.

Figure 11.1
The
economically
efficient level
of pollution
minimises the
sum of
abatement
and damage
cost.

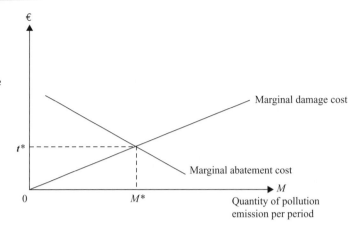

Figure 11.2
Economically
efficient level
of emissions
abatement.

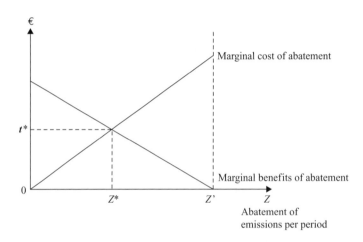

efficiency. Here we apply the same principle. By equalising the marginal damage cost and marginal abatement cost we find the economically efficient level of pollution emission per period. Figure 11.1 shows the intersection of the two curves. The marginal damage cost curve is upward sloping because the damage per additionally produced unit of pollution goes up because an additional ton, of say CO_2, at a high pollution level causes more environmental damage than the same quantity emitted in a situation with low pollution level. The marginal abatement cost curve is downward sloping because when pollution is high, incremental abatement, i.e. a small reduction, is relatively inexpensive, but the cleaner the environment, the more expensive it is to achieve further gains. If you think that the abatement cost curve slope should be the other way around, note that emissions are an economic 'bad', i.e. the less the better. In Figure 11.2 we will replace the label 'quantity of pollution emission per period' by 'abatement of emission per period', and then we are back to thinking in economic 'goods'.

At the intersection of the marginal abatement cost and the marginal damage cost, we find the economically efficient level of emissions M^*, which neoclassical economists call the 'optimal level of pollution', and the economically efficient tax rate t^*. If it was the rate charged it would bring about the required amount of emissions. This is easier to explain if we look at things in a slightly different way as in Figure 11.2. Looking at the same situation from another angle, namely abatement of emissions instead of emissions level, we can, in Figure 11.2, identify the economically efficient level of emissions abatement Z^*. Note that on the horizontal axis Z' is zero emissions, and 0 is no abatement. The marginal benefit curve is the marginal damage from Figure 11.1, but from the abatement perspective instead of the pollution emission perspective. Z^* corresponds to the same level of emissions as M^*. This is the level at which the marginal costs and benefits of emissions abatement are equal. Z^* equals the pre-tax level of emissions minus the economically efficient quantity of emissions, i.e. the amount which needs to be abated in order to get from the original emissions level to the economically efficient emission level. Z^* is efficient, given that all social costs and benefits are included, because of the by now familiar argument about the equality of marginals. To the left of Z^* abatement cost is less than damage cost at the margin, so more abatement will reduce the sum of abatement and damage costs. To the right of Z^* abatement cost is greater than damage cost, so less abatement will reduce the sum of abatement and damage costs. You should see that the same argument gives M^* as the efficient level of emissions in Figure 11.1.

Taking Figure 11.2 as applying to a representative firm, we can see why profit maximising firms do what is needed in the same way – t^* is the (constant) marginal cost of emitting and the firm will maximise post tax profits when that is equal to marginal abatement cost (MAC). If MAC $> t$ it pays to abate less, if MAC $< t$ it pays to abate more.

11.5.2 Taxation for an arbitrary standard

In order to identify the allocatively efficient level of pollution as its target for emissions control the environmental regulatory authority would need to know the marginal costs and benefits of abatement. The intersection of the marginal cost and benefit functions determines the proper rate for (**Pigouvian** or externalities) taxation (t^*) and the desired emissions level. Generally the information that is needed to do this is not available to the authority. While neoclassical economists have devoted a lot of time and effort to devising means for estimating the marginal costs and, especially, benefits of pollution abatement, most recognise, with regret, that control to allocatively efficient levels is not feasible.

The policy-relevant questions are about methods of control to achieve what neoclassical economists call 'arbitrary standards'. This terminology merely means that the policy target does not derive from a precise balancing of the marginal costs and benefits of abatement. It does not, necessarily, mean that it is arbitrary in the sense of having been adopted impulsively or capriciously. Arbitrary pollution standards, in this sense, may be, and generally are, the result of a great deal of scientific research and political deliberation. For example, the standard could be a level which scientists and stakeholders consider to the best of their knowledge to be a sustainable level. For any target so determined we can identify the corresponding abatement level. Even though this level is not an allocatively efficient target, the argument used about the cost-efficiency of taxation as an instrument remains true. An arbitrary standard can be attained at least cost by the taxation of emissions, as we will show later. The regulatory authority does not need to know the aggregate marginal abatement benefit function, nor does it need to know the abatement cost function for each firm.

We need to note that choosing approach (1), aiming for allocative efficiency, or approach (2), aiming for an 'arbitrary standard', can have major implications for the biophysical environment. The economic efficiency approach is focused on economic costs and human perceptions of benefits, and knowledge that the result of emissions taxation is the economically efficient pollution level does not inform us that the outcome is sustainable. It may not be. In contrast, in approach (2) a standard is set that to the best of current knowledge and understanding is considered as a sustainable level of emissions, i.e. a level that can be absorbed by the sinks of the environment for an indefinite, or at least very long, time period without damaging it or humans. After this biophysical analysis in combination with democratic deliberation, the tax and the market mechanism are used to deliver what it is thought is the sustainable level at least cost. Approach (2) shows how ecological economists want to use the market mechanism. They have no problem with using it to attain standards set by sustainability criteria. They do not want standards set by consumer sovereignty criteria.

However, even with this more limited use of market mechanisms, we should not forget the problems resulting from uncertainty and irreversibility in the environment and society. We cannot be sure that the arbitrary standard adopted guarantees sustainability, and we cannot be sure that the tax actually imposed will deliver the standard aimed at. Joan Martinez-Alier, one of the founding fathers of ecological economics, reminds us that nobody knows for sure what the correct prices to bring about sustainability are. As he puts it: 'There are no 'ecologically correct' prices, although there might be 'ecologically corrected' prices' (Martinez-Alier, 2000:4018). He argues that when externalities are uncertain and irreversible, then it is impossible to set 'ecologically correct' prices. By 'ecologically corrected' he means prices modified by taxes and the like that move things in the direction of sustainability.

In some pollution problems, such as those arising with emissions from fossil fuel combustion for example, monitoring and enforcement costs will be lower if some input is used as the point of control, rather than emissions as such. It has been shown that if the relationships between the levels of some input and the level of emissions are known to the regulatory authority, then the least cost property of uniform emissions taxation carries over to input taxation – the authority can tax the input rather than the emissions and achieve an arbitrary standard at least cost. In the case of carbon dioxide releases in fossil fuel combustion when people talk of 'carbon taxation' in connection with mitigation of the enhanced greenhouse effect, discussed in Chapter 13, what they actually mean is taxation of the fossil fuels at rates which reflect their carbon contents. We come back to carbon taxation in the next subsection.

11.5.3 Taxation and the goods market

Taxing emissions, or the input which is the origin of the emissions, raises the costs of production. As we saw in Chapter 8, increasing the costs of production shifts the supply function upwards. This impact of emissions or input taxation is shown

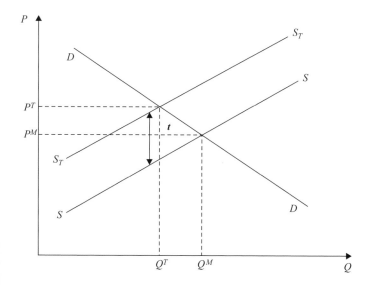

Figure 11.3
Impact of
environmental
tax on goods
market.

in Figure 11.3, where SS is the supply function for some commodity before the imposition of the tax and $S_T S_T$ is the supply function with the tax in place. DD is the demand function for the commodity. As a result of the tax, the equilibrium quantity falls from Q^M to Q^T and the equilibrium price increases from P^M to P^T. As we saw in Chapter 8, the size of these changes due to the imposition of the tax will depend upon the elasticities of demand and supply, as will the incidence of the tax as between producers of the commodity and its buyers.

Let us now look briefly at carbon taxation. A carbon tax is aimed at reducing the carbon dioxide emissions that come from fossil fuels and which threaten to change the climate. More than 80 per cent of the world's CO_2 emissions come from fossil fuel combustion. In practice the tax would be applied not to emissions as such, but to fossil fuels. You can think of a carbon tax as a product charge placed on fossil fuels in proportion to their carbon content. Coal, which has a higher carbon content than oil and natural gas, is thus taxed relatively more. Once implemented, the rising prices of fossil fuels would induce people to use oil and gas in favour of coal; to use more renewable energy sources instead of fossil fuels; and to be more efficient in their use of energy generally. Applying such a tax enables an economy as a whole to reduce its level of carbon dioxide emissions for the lowest overall cost. Because of the scale of fossil fuel use in the economy, a carbon tax is attractive to governments as it can raise significant amounts of revenue, which could be used to finance environmental projects or to reduce other taxes, such as taxes on labour. In the latter case the relative prices of input factors would be changed. Labour would become cheaper and energy would become more expensive. This would increase the demand for labour, and reduce the use of energy, and hence carbon dioxide emissions. Increasing the demand for labour would work in the direction of reducing unemployment.

The amount of CO_2 released into the atmosphere when a barrel of oil is burned, for example, is known. Let us say it is z tonnes. Suppose that we want to tax CO_2

emissions at $w per tonne. Then taxing the extraction of oil at $w \times z$ per barrel is equivalent to taxing CO_2 emissions from oil combustion at $w per tonne of CO_2. The extractor of oil would raise the price for which it sells oil to reflect the tax. Users of oil to produce other goods and services would have to pay a higher price for oil, and would raise the price for their outputs. The extent to which other commodity prices would rise would vary according to the amounts of oil used in their production. Final consumers would end up facing increases in the prices of all goods and services, with the sizes of the increases varying with the extent to which they used oil and, hence, were responsible for carbon dioxide emissions.

The effects on commodity prices can be figured out using input–output analysis, which we looked at in Chapter 5. The point about input–output analysis is that it picks up the ways in which commodity production uses inputs indirectly as well as directly. In section 5.1.3 we looked at input–output accounting and the environment and considered a numerical example economy in which manufacturing used 1,000,000 tonnes of oil, while agriculture used no oil directly. We saw that although agriculture does not directly use oil, the delivery of agriculture to final demand is responsible for some of the oil use in the economy. The production of the commodity agriculture uses the commodity manufacturing, and the production of the latter does directly use oil. We found that of this economy's total oil use, 25 per cent was indirectly attributable in this way to the production of agriculture for delivery to final demand.

Now suppose that each tonne of oil used in manufacturing releases 0.1 tonnes of CO_2 into the atmosphere, and that the government wants to tax CO_2 emissions at $1,000 per tonne – this is equivalent to a tax of $100 per tonne of oil. Clearly, the price of manufacturing will go up with the imposition of the tax. But so will the price of agriculture, because while agriculture does not directly use any oil in this example, it does buy manufacturing, and the selling price of agriculture will have to cover the increased costs on that account. In general, the carbon tax will affect the prices of all commodities in this way – their prices will increase by amounts reflecting their indirect as well as their direct responsibility for CO_2 emissions.

Using input–output analysis we can figure out from input–output accounts and information on the direct responsibility for CO_2 emissions in each industry what the price rises for all commodities would be for any given rate of carbon tax. In the numerical example here, for a $1,000 per tonne carbon tax, the price of agriculture would rise by 3.19 per cent and the price of manufacturing by 5.32 per cent – although agriculture does not use oil directly, as the transactions table shows, it does use a lot of manufacturing, and hence oil is an important indirect input to its production. The Appendix to this chapter shows how these results are obtained, and working through it will enhance your understanding of how carbon taxation would work.

In real economies all industries directly use energy inputs based on fossil fuels, and use inputs produced in several other industries using such energy inputs – all industries are directly and indirectly responsible for CO_2 emissions. Box 11.4 shows the estimates for the price rises that introducing carbon taxation would produce in a real economy. Table 11.2 lists the taxes levied on electricity consumption and production in various OECD countries. Electricity generation accounts for about 40 per cent of carbon dioxide emissions in modern industrial economies. Note, however, that much of the electricity produced is used in the production of other

Box 11.4   Input–output analysis of carbon taxation and commodity prices in Australia

Table 11.1 gives the results for carbon taxation-induced price increases, obtained from calculations of the same nature as those set out in the Appendix, using actual input–output data for Australia – the same data as was used to produce the results for CO_2 intensities given in Table 5.5. The main difference in the calculations is that those for Table 11.1 have to take account of the fact that Australia, like all industrial economies, uses not just oil, but also coal and gas. The three fossil fuels have different carbon contents per unit energy – the ranking from most to least carbon per PJ is coal, oil and gas.

Table 11.1   Price increases for a carbon tax of $20 per tonne in Australia

Sector	Percentage price increase	Ranking
Agriculture, forestry and fishing	1.77	9
Mining	1.69	12
Meat and milk products	1.77	9
Food products	1.46	16
Beverages and tobacco	0.84	24
Textiles clothing and footwear	0.95	21
Wood, wood products, furniture	1.31	15
Paper, products, printing, publishing	1.12	20
Chemicals	1.56	16
Petroleum and coal products	9.97	4
Non-metallic mineral products	1.89	8
Basic metals products	9.00	5
Fabricated metal products	2.76	6
Transport equipment	0.82	23
Machinery and equipment	0.71	26
Miscellaneous manufacturing	0.89	23
Electricity	31.33	1
Gas	21.41	2
Water	1.34	18
Construction	1.60	13
Wholesale and retail	10.14	3
Transport and communication	2.28	7
Finance and business services	1.21	19
Residential property	0.42	27
Public administration and defence	1.73	11
Community services	0.93	21
Recreational and personal services	1.62	13

Source: adapted from Common and Salma (1992).

The figures in the rightmost column of Table 11.1 are the rankings by proportionate price increase – electricity goes up by the largest percentage, residential property by the smallest. If you look back at Table 5.5 you will see that the rankings there and in Table 11.1 are very similar. The commodities whose production involves more CO_2 emissions – when indirect as well as direct pathways are taken into account – are those with larger price increases following the imposition of the carbon tax. All commodity prices go up because all production involves energy, and hence fossil fuel, use when indirect use is accounted for. The reason that the rankings in the two tables are not exactly the same is because of the impact of existing commodity taxes in the data, and because of the way these input–output tables handle payments for distribution services.

While these kinds of calculations bring out the implications of the indirect use of fossil fuels in commodity production and show how the effects of carbon taxation would hence cascade throughout the whole economy, they would not accurately predict the long-run pattern of commodity price changes. This is because the input–output analysis assumes that the imposition of the carbon taxation has no effect on production technologies – the input–output coefficients that it uses are constant. This is a reasonable assumption in the short run, but not in the long run – on the difference between the long and short runs see Chapter 8. In the long run, there would be some substitution of other inputs for fossil fuel inputs, and the input–output coefficients would change. Also, as you can see in the Appendix, these calculations assume that the producers are able to pass all of the tax increase price effects forward to the buyers of their outputs. As we saw in Chapter 8 when looking at tax incidence, they are not generally able to do this to an extent that depends on the elasticities of supply and demand.

goods and services, rather than delivered to final users of electricity. Hence, the proportion of CO_2 emissions accounted for by deliveries to final demand of the commodity electricity is typically well below 40 per cent. If you look back at Table 5.5, you will see that for Australia that proportion is just 15 per cent – this is a representative figure for a modern industrial economy. Table 11.2 shows that electricity is widely taxed, and that the rates of taxation differ greatly between countries.

Carbon taxation as we have described it is not currently in use in any economy. For the United Kingdom, Table 11.2 shows, as a tax on electricity consumption, something called the Climate Change Levy. This was originally intended to be a tax on carbon emissions that would reduce them so as to enable the United Kingdom to meet its international obligations and domestic policy objectives. In the event what emerged from the political process was a tax on some forms of energy consumption, which will not be very effective in terms of reducing CO_2 emissions. The story of how the original intention became the actual Climate Change Levy throws lots of light on the actual process by which policy is determined. Unfortunately, there is no space to tell it properly here – you will find out about it on the book's companion website. Basically, it looks as if the UK government retreated from a proper carbon tax because it feared the electoral consequences of the price rises that would have been attributed to such a tax.

11.5.4 Environmental taxes raise revenue

For policy makers emissions taxes, or energy taxes, are welcome for another reason. They generate income for the government. As discussed in Chapter 8, the revenue from the tax depends on the elasticity of demand, which is the percentage change of quantity demanded of the taxed good in response to a one per cent increase in the price. In our context of energy taxes the elasticity of demand measures how firms and households react to the increase in the prices of energy. From empirical estimates we know that the price elasticity of demand for energy is low, at least in the short run. This is due to energy demand arising from earlier decisions, which are difficult to revise in the sort run. For example, energy used for home heating is the result of a housing decision, which can only be corrected in the longer term (e.g. by installing better insulation or moving to a different house). Other decisions relating to energy depend on collective decisions. For example, one may prefer to use a train or bus instead of a car as sole occupant, but if there is no, or an inadequate, public transport system in place, the possibility for substitution does not exist in the short run. In the longer run, policies may change or the individual can move to a place which offers public transport.

Table 11.2 Taxes in OECD member countries levied on electricity

Country	Tax	Specific tax-base	Tax rate national currency	Units	Tax rate – euro	Units
Austria	Energy tax	Electricity consumption	0.0150	€ per kWh	0.015	€ per kWh
Belgium	Cotisation sur l'energie	Électricité basse tension	55.0000	BEF per MWh	1.3641	€ per MWh
Denmark	Duty on CO₂	Electricity	0.1000	DKK per kWh	0.0134	€ per kWh
Denmark	Duty on electricity	Electricity consumption for heating of dwellings and other purposes	0.5010	DKK per kWh	0.0673	€ per kWh
Denmark	Duty on electricity	Electricity consumption for other purposes	0.5660	DKK per kWh	0.076	€ per kWh
Finland	Excise on fuels	Electricity used in the manufacturing sector, etc.	25.0000	FIM per MWh	4.2073	€ per MWh
Finland	Excise on fuels	Electricity used in the rest of the economy	41.0000	FIM per MWh	6.9	€ per MWh
Finland	Strategic stockpile fee	Electricity consumption	0.7500	FIM per MWh	0.1262	€ per MWh
Germany	Duty on electricity	Electricity consumption	0.0250	DEM per kWh	0.0128	€ per kWh
Italy	Additional tax on electricity – towns / provinces	Electricity consumption for private dwellings				
Italy	Additional tax on electricity – towns / provinces	Electricity consumption for industrial purposes				
Italy	Tax on electrical energy – State	Electricity consumption for industrial purposes	6.0000	LIT per kWh	0.003	€ per kWh
Italy	Tax on electrical energy – State	Electricity consumption for private dwellings	4.1000	LIT per kWh	0.0021	€ per kWh
Japan	Promotion of power resources development tax	Electricity consumption	0.4450	JPY per kWh	0.0041	€ per kWh
Netherlands	Regulatory Energy Tax	Electricity consumption – up to 10,000 kWh per year.	0.0601	€ per kWh	0.0601	€ per kWh
Netherlands	Regulatory Energy Tax	Electricity consumption – between 10,000 kWh and 50,000 kWh per year.	0.0200	€ per kWh	0.02	€ per kWh

(cont.)

Table 11.2 (cont.)

Country	Tax	Specific tax-base	Tax rate national currency	Units	Tax rate – euro	Units
Netherlands	Regulatory Energy Tax	Electricity consumption – between 50,000 kWh and 10 million kWh per year.	0.0061	€ per kWh	0.0061	€ per kWh
Norway	Tax on consumption of electricity	Electricity consumption	0.1030	NOK per kWh	0.0128	€ per kWh
Spain	Tax on electricity	The production or importation of electricity	4.864%	4.864%	4.864%	4.864%
Sweden	Energy tax on electricity	Electricity consumption – households	0.1980	SEK per kWh	0.0214	€ per kWh
Sweden	Energy tax on electricity	Electricity consumption – manufacturing and commercial greenhouses	0.0000		0	
Sweden	Energy tax on electricity	Electricity consumption – other sectors	0.1740	SEK per kWh	0.0151	€ per kWh
Sweden	Energy tax on electricity	Material permitted for abstraction > 200 000 tons	0.1400	SEK per kWh	0.0015	€ per kWh
United Kingdom	Climate change levy	Electricity consumption – ordinary rate	0.0043	GBP per kWh	0.0069	€ per kWh
United Kingdom	Climate change levy	Electricity consumption – reduced rate	0.0008	GBP per kWh	0.0014	€ per kWh
United States	Delaware – public utilities tax	Electricity consumption	4.25% of gross receipts	4.25% of gross receipts		4.25% of gross receipts

Taxes on Electricity production

Country	Tax	Specific tax-base	Units	Units
Lithuania	Excise tax on energy products	Electricity	1% of the value of kWh	1% of the value of kWh
United Kingdom	Non-fossil fuel obligation levy	Electricity production	0.7% of the price.	0.7% of the price.
United States	Connecticut – electricity company tax	Income from electricity distribution to residential service	6.8% of income.	6.8% of income.
United States	Connecticut – electricity company tax	Income from electricity distribution to other than residential service	8.5% of income.	8.5% of income.

Source: OECD/EEA Environmentally Related Taxes Database, http://www1.oecd.org/scripts/env/ecoInst/index.htm

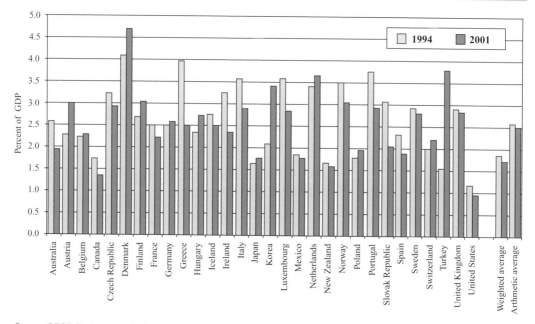

Percent of GDP

1994 · 2001

Australia · Austria · Belgium · Canada · Czech Republic · Denmark · Finland · France · Germany · Greece · Hungary · Iceland · Ireland · Italy · Japan · Korea · Luxembourg · Mexico · Netherlands · New Zealand · Norway · Poland · Portugal · Slovak Republic · Spain · Sweden · Switzerland · Turkey · United Kingdom · United States · Weighted average · Arthmetic average

Source: OECD Environmentally Related Taxes database
http://www.oecd.org/document/29/0,2340,en_2649-34295 1894685_1_1_1_1,00.html

Revenues from environmental taxes may or may not be earmarked for funding environmental projects. Environmental taxes face the fundamental problem that the tax base shrinks if the tax is effective. An example here is the recently introduced congestion charge in London, which reduced traffic by 18 per cent within the first year, and consequently did not produce enough revenue to increase capacity of public transport as had been planned. For more information see http://www.londontransport.co.uk/tfl/downloads/pdf/congestion-charging/cc-12monthson.pdf.

Figure 11.4 shows that the degree to which environmental taxes are charged and raise revenue in various countries differs widely. This is an issue, which we will revisit in the next chapter, where we will discuss the international dimension of environmental problems and environmental policy instruments. An often-used argument against the introduction of environmental taxes in a country has been the fear that doing so would make it less competitive in international trade.

Figure 11.4
Revenue from environment-related taxes as percentage of GDP.

11.6 TRADABLE PERMITS

Tradable permits are another type of market-based policy instrument, under which rights to discharge pollution or exploit resources can be exchanged through either a free or controlled permit-market. Like taxes they generate economic incentives to economic agents to move towards less environmentally harmful behaviour. As used to date, they have mainly impacted directly on firms.

Tradable permits differ from taxes in a fundamental way. Consider the control of pollution. With taxes the monetary incentive facing the agent is the fixed price to be paid for each unit of emissions. With permits the agent faces a quantitative emissions target which is fixed by the amount of permits held, and the agent can vary her holding by buying or selling permits at a variable price. From the point of view of the regulatory authority, taxes fix the price at which agents can emit but not the amount that they emit individually or collectively, whereas permits fix the amount that agents can collectively emit but not the price at which they do it or the amount they emit individually.

So, how do tradable permits work? A tradable permit is an environmental policy instrument which organises the exchange of rights to discharge a particular kind of waste into some environment, or to use a particular natural resource. In the former case, instead of being charged for releases, one needs to hold a permit to discharge the amount that one actually does discharge. The regulatory authority sets a limit (expressed in biophysical units) on the total amount of emissions permits in existence. By controlling the total number of permits, the regulating authority can control the aggregate pollution quantity. While the regulating authority sets the total amount permissible, they do not attempt to determine how that total allowed quantity is allocated among individual sources of emissions. Tradable permits are based on the principle that any increase in emissions from one source must be offset by an equivalent decrease elsewhere. Sources can vary the amount of permits that they hold, and hence their emissions levels, by buying and selling from and to other sources. The main advantage of the scheme is that it is cost-effective and generates dynamic incentives for cost reduction. The regulatory authority could issue a total amount of permits equivalent to the allocative efficiency target, if it knew what it was, or an amount equivalent to an 'arbitrary standard'.

The basic principles are the same in the case of permits to use a natural resource – a regulatory authority determines what the level of use is to be and issues a corresponding total amount of permits, denominated in terms of tonnes or number of individuals for a fish stock, for example. Once issued by the authority, permits can be bought and sold among the resource-harvesting firms and individuals.

Examples include individual transferable quotas in fisheries, tradable depletion rights to mineral concessions and marketable discharge permits for water-borne effluents. The United States began emissions trading after passage of the 1990 Clean Air Act, which authorised the US EPA to put a cap on how much sulphur dioxide (which causes acid rain) the operator of a fossil-fuelled plant was allowed to emit. The tradable permit scheme as applied under the US Clean Air Act led to reductions of smog and acid rain emissions at lower economic cost than would have been the case with a command-and-control instrument. Other initiatives for more sector-specific use of the tradable permit concept have been developed, e.g. for municipal waste management (in the UK) and the use of renewable energy sources (e.g. in Denmark and Italy). Currently researchers are working on options for more systematic use of tradable permits in the transport sector. For an overview of past and current tradable permit schemes see Table 11.3. More details can be found in Further Reading.

Box 11.5 Emissions trading in the European Union

On 1 January 2005 the European Union launched its Europe-wide Emissions Trading Scheme. This aims to reduce the impacts of climate change through lowering carbon emissions by providing clear incentives for investment in energy efficiency and cleaner technologies. Under the terms of the Scheme, industrial emitters of carbon dioxide (CO_2) will be allocated tradable allowances, on an installation-specific basis, specifying the amount of CO_2 they can emit each year. The key principle of the scheme is the ability of companies to trade their allowances in order that emissions reductions are achieved at least cost to Europe as a whole.

The EU Emissions Trading Scheme (EU ETS) will establish the world's largest-ever market in emissions. Participation in the scheme will be mandatory for companies in sectors covered by the first phase of the scheme. These are electricity generators, oil refineries, iron and steel production, cement clinker and lime production, glass manufacturing, brick and tile manufacturing and pulp and paper. In addition, installations in any sectors that have combustion plants of a thermal input of over 20MW, including aggregated plants on a single site, are also covered (hospitals, universities and large retailers may find themselves included under this provision). For further details see http://www.europa.eu.int/comm/environment/climat/emission.htm.

There are two broad types of tradable permit system – the 'cap-and-trade' scheme and the 'emission reduction credit' scheme. For the latter, a baseline is agreed for every participant source before the start of the operation of the system. A participant is credited with any over-achievement, and is allowed to sell the credits arising. The 'cap-and-trade' scheme involves a decision by the regulatory authority about the total quantity of emissions (or natural-resource use) that is to be allowed – the 'cap' – and shares the total among the participating agents. This scheme establishes a quantified ceiling assigned to each participant for a given period. No one is allowed to emit (or use) more than the amount for which it possesses emission (or natural-resource use) permits. As with the emissions reduction scheme, the participants can buy and sell permits from and to one another.

As with all environmental policy instruments monitoring emissions (or natural-resource use) and implementing a system of penalties for non-permitted emissions (use) is crucial. The control authority devises the total quantity of permits issued and the initial allocation. The initial allocation to firms and/or individuals can be either by auction, which generates revenue for the government, or it can be without charge. Adequate safeguards need to be put in place to ensure that permits can be freely traded between participating firms and/or individuals at whichever price they have agreed for that trade. In Table 11.3 you will notice a 'Greenhouse gas trading scheme' for Sweden and UK. We will be looking at greenhouse gas emissions and the problems that they cause in Chapter 13, where we will come back to the use of tradable permits for their control.

11.7 THE LEAST COST THEOREM

What economists (and in fact many others) find attractive about market instruments is the prospect of their delivering the desired outcome at least cost. The **least cost theorem** says that total abatement costs are minimised where the regulatory authority taxes emissions from all firms at a uniform rate per unit. However, the theorem does not, as is widely believed, establish a presumption in favour of emissions taxation over command-and-control instruments of the form that specify

Table 11.3 Past and current tradable permit schemes in OECD countries

Country	Name of permit system	Type of permit system
Australia	Individual transferable fishing quotas	Quota
	New South Wales – Hunter River Salinity Trading Scheme	Quota
	Pilot Interstate Water Trading Project	Transferable usage rights
Canada	Alberta – Tradable hunting rights	Transferable usage rights
	Allowance system for HCFCs	Quota
	Allowance system for methyl bromide	Quota
	Maple grove permits	
	NO$_x$ and VOC emissions	Quota
	Transferable fishing quota	Quota
Denmark	Emissions trading in the electricity sector	Quota
France	Tradable development rights for land preservation	
Iceland	Individual transferable fish quota	Quota
Mexico	Tradable hunting permit	Transferable usage rights
Netherlands	Tradable fishery quota	Quota
New Zealand	Revised district scheme (tradable development rights)	
	Transferable fishing quota	Quota
Norway	Quota system for greenhouse gases	Quota
Poland	Chorzow – VOC control (demonstration project 1991–92)	Quota
Sweden	Greenhouse gas emissions trading scheme	Quota
Switzerland	Basel Canton – Control of VOC and NO$_x$ emissions	Quota
UK	Greenhouse gas emissions trading scheme	Quota
US	Acid rain allowance trading	Quota
	Colorado – Tradable phosphorous discharge rights – Dillion Reservoir	Quota
	Mobile sources averaging, banking and trading	Averaging
	Montgomery County – Land management	
	Northeast USA – Ozone transport commission NO$_x$ Programme	
	Ozone-depleting substances (ODS)	Quota
	RECLAIM (Regional Clean Air Incentives Market)	Quota
	Tradable development rights for Lake Tahoe watershed management	
	Tradable development rights for pinelands management	
	Tradable permits for lead in gasoline (1983–1987)	Quota
	Transferable fishing quota	Quota
	Transferable rights for wetlands conservation	
	Wisconsin – Lower Rox River Trading Scheme	Quota

Notes: VOC control: control of Volatile Organic Compounds, which comprise any carbon compound that evaporates under standard test conditions. All paint and caulk solvents except water are classified as VOCs. Government regulations limiting the amount of volatile organic compounds permitted in paint are in place in several countries.

NO$_x$ emissions: Nitrogen Oxide emissions. Nitrogen Oxides is a term used to refer to nitric oxide (NO) and nitrogen dioxide (NO$_2$). The major sources of man-made NOx emissions are high-temperature combustion processes, such as those occurring in automobiles and power plants.
Source: OECD/EEA database on economic instruments and voluntary approaches used in environmental policy and natural resources management.

allowable emissions levels. The regulatory authority could achieve the same target at the same minimum cost in other ways:

- by setting the emissions level for each firm;
- by creating permits tradable as between firms with the total amount of emissions permitted equal to the arbitrary standard for total emissions.

We will look first at uniform emissions taxation, and then at these alternatives.

The least-cost property of uniform emissions taxation derives from the fact that it loads total abatement across firms such that those for which it costs less do more. Each firm would abate up to the level where its marginal abatement cost

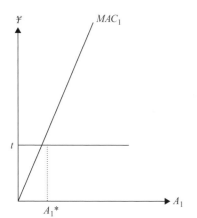
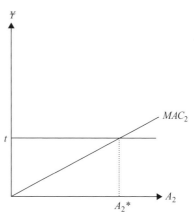

Figure 11.5
Least cost
theorem.

was equal to the tax rate, so as to minimise its costs inclusive of tax. As a result, all firms would be operating with the same marginal abatement cost. Given this, there would be no reallocation of the total abatement cost as between firms that could reduce the total cost of abatement. The regulatory authority does not need to know each firm's abatement cost function to identify the differential abatement targets for each firm that minimise total cost. The reaction of the firms to the uniform tax identifies the least-cost solution.

Figure 11.5 shows how the least-cost property works for the case of two firms. The regulatory authority levies a tax at the rate t per unit of emission. Both firms will move toward the point $t = $ MAC, because if $t > $ MAC it would pay to abate more and if $t < $ MAC it would pay to abate less. They will abate to levels A_1^* and A_2^*, which adds up to A^* total abatement. To see that this is least-cost combination of abatement by firm 1 and firm 2 that gives total abatement A^*, suppose that firm 1 abated less than A_1^* and firm 2 an equal amount more in order to stay at total abatement level A^*. The increase in cost for firm 2 is more than the decrease for firm 1. Try to think through for yourself the same idea, but with firm 2 abating less than A_2^* and firm 1 making up for it. What is the outcome in terms of total abatement costs? If the regulating authority knew MAC_1 and MAC_2, desiring total abatement A^*, it could work out what the cost minimising A_1^* and A_2^* were, and use command-and-control to require firms to abate these specified amounts of emissions. But the regulator does not know the necessary details of abatement costs for individual firms. Hence, it cannot work out these abatement levels and will normally go for an overall target of A^* via equal proportional cutbacks in each firm. This procedure is generally considered as 'fair'.

If command-and-control is to involve the same abatement cost total as uniform taxation, then the levels of abatement enforced by the environment regulatory authority will have to differ across firms such that more is done by those firms where abatement costs are lower. For the environment regulatory authority to be able to issue the individually tailored regulations, it would have to know the marginal abatement-cost function for each firm. This is generally infeasible, and the operational version of command-and-control is seen as involving each firm cutting back emissions by the same x per cent so as to achieve an overall x per cent reduction. Because firms' abatement-cost functions differ, uniform percentage cut-backs would not be efficient.

Not requiring complete information on the costs of abatement in each firm is what gives uniform taxation the cost advantage over command-and-control. However, a problem for the argument for uniform taxation as we have just presented it is that without complete information, the authority cannot calculate the tax rate that goes with its target level of abatement. In the absence of complete information in the authority about the firms' marginal abatement-cost functions, uniform taxation is not guaranteed to achieve the target level of total abatement. Hence, uniform taxation is not dependable.

In the absence of such information, the authority can set a tax rate, which will achieve some overall abatement level at the lowest cost that is possible. You can see that whatever is done is done at the least cost from Figure 11.5 – the least-cost property follows from the fact that both firms face the same tax rate. But, the achieved overall abatement level will not, except by chance, be the reduction in total emissions desired. The regulatory authority could proceed by trial and error, setting a tax rate, observing the outcome, and adjusting the rate up or down as necessary. This would involve additional adjustment costs, and would be very unpopular with the affected firms.

Tradable permits are both least cost and dependable without requiring that the regulatory authority has complete information about the costs of abatement in each firm. They are dependable because the total quantity of permits created by the environment regulatory authority is equal to the emissions total that corresponds to the desired overall cutback. They are least cost because the market in permits allocates them to firms where it is cheaper to buy a permit than to abate. Given that the permits are tradable, a single price for a unit permit will be established. The argument as to why they are least cost is exactly as for the uniform tax. All firms face the same price. The price will depend on the amount of permits issued, and given ideal conditions will turn out to be what the tax rate would have needed to be to reach the target desired. Firms where abatement is relatively cheap will abate rather than buy permits. The loading of total abatement across firms so as to minimise total cost is automatically generated by the cost-minimising behaviour of the firms.

This outcome, however, is crucially dependent on two other assumptions, namely that all of the firms are price-takers and that the environment regulatory authority can both monitor emissions and enforce compliance without cost. Where there are few firms, one may be able to exercise power in the permit market and distort its operation. Monitoring firms' compliance, ensuring that their actual emissions correspond to their permit holding, may involve the environmental regulatory authority in substantial costs. Note that such potential problems aside, the dependability and least-cost properties of permits hold irrespective of how the environmental regulatory authority initially allocates the permits. It could give polluters permits in proportion to past pollution (**grandfathering**) or it could sell them (e.g. by auction).

To conclude, how do tradable permits compare to environmental taxes? If we were ready to make strong simplifying assumptions, cost-minimising solutions could be calculated by the regulatory authority and either type of market-based policy instrument could be used with the same result. In reality, uncertainty about abatement costs (present and future), interdependencies of impacts, and responses of economic actors make the design of such policy instruments a less straightforward task. We know now that uncertainty about abatement costs may make quantity-based regulation (e.g. standards or tradable permits) more attractive. Because of the risk of missing the target when using taxes, in cases where it is considered important not to miss the target the regulatory authority will be attracted to tradable permits by virtue of their dependability.

11.8 ENVIRONMENTAL PERFORMANCE BONDS

Most environmental problems involve uncertainty and hence it has always been a difficulty in formulating and implementing environmental policy. Recall from the previous chapter that uncertainty differs from risk. While policy makers may know about the possible states following a decision, if they cannot attach probabilities to those states they are facing uncertainty rather than dealing with risk. In the previous chapter we focused on the severe problems which uncertainty causes for setting policy goals. In regard to implementation and policy instruments, we have just seen the difficulties arising from uncertainty.

A good example of the problems which uncertainty arising from major novel technologies creates for policy makers is provided by Genetically Modified Organisms (GMOs). They are particularly difficult to assess for policy makers, as there is no past experience according to which probabilities can be assigned to some of the possible adverse environmental outcomes. Some of these, according to some scientists, could have potentially huge irreversible impacts. How can governments deal with such situations? On what basis can they decide whether to embrace such innovations and reap the benefits for society or whether to stop them because they are too dangerous? What if it is impossible to make a well-informed decision at the beginning of a technological development? Are there any policy instruments that can help to address irreversibility and uncertainty in a satisfactory way?

Until a few decades ago, it was common practice in policy circles to ignore or deny the existence of uncertainty, or to apply arbitrary numerical fudge factors, and then to proceed as if everything was known with certainty, or at least that probabilities were known. More recently uncertainty has become more widely recognised and the need for the adoption of safe minimum standards and the precautionary principle, discussed in the previous chapter, is gaining widespread acceptance in policy-making and advice circles.

As we saw in the previous chapter, a major problem for the implementation of the precautionary principle remains that its definition and goals are vague, leaving its application dependent on interpretation by the regulators in regard to any particular problem. Another problem is a lack of experience with policy instruments aiming to operationalise and implement the principle. A rather recent idea for a policy instrument is that of environmental performance bonds. In general terms, a performance bond is a promise to pay compensation in the event of non-fulfilment of a particular contract. Performance bonds are common in the construction industry. Before a job begins, a construction company puts up a bond, i.e. an amount of money that is held by a third party. If the construction is completed satisfactorily and on time, the bond monies are returned to the construction company. However, if the work is unsatisfactory or late, part of, or the entire bond will be forfeited. An environmental performance bond is a deposit that possible polluters and violators of environmental standards must pay into an environmental fund to be held there until a specified period of time has elapsed.

It is aimed at providing a financial incentive to a firm undertaking a project or running some process to adhere to environmental requirements and to deal with uncertainty. Environmental performance bonds have a different aim to the command-and-control, taxation or tradable permit schemes, which we looked at earlier in this chapter. They do not directly focus on the reduction of emissions, but are designed to make companies responsible for the unknown environmental impact of their future activities. In keeping with the precautionary principle, they require a commitment of resources up front to offset potentially catastrophic future effects.

The basic idea is that before a firm introduces, for example, a new (chemical) substance or a new technology, a bond is fixed, which is equal in size to the current best estimate of the money value of the largest potential future environmental damage. The bond plus part of the interest is returned if the polluter proves that the suspected damage has not occurred or certainly will not occur. If damage does occur, the bond will be forfeited to a corresponding amount to the value placed on the damage. While the bond is being held it earns interest, and the part of the interest that is not returned to the polluter is used to finance the administration necessary for the environmental bonding system and research into environmental pollution-control technology and management.

Environmental performance bonds also create an incentive for the proponent of a project to conduct research to reduce the uncertainties about its environmental impacts. The incentive effect could be enhanced by having the size of the bond posted periodically adjustable. If the firm could show that the worst case was very unlikely to happen, part of their bond would be refunded to them. This would give proponents an incentive to fund independent research or, alternatively, to change to less damaging technologies. The implementation of the scheme requires an environmental regulatory agency with assistance from a scientific advisory board consisting of independent environmental experts.

In general, the applicability of environmental performance bonds is impeded by several factors. One difficulty is to measure the value of environmental damage in monetary terms. If it is impossible to express the damage in monetary terms, the part of the bond which is forfeited and the damage cannot be equivalent. The application of bonds might also be restricted by the necessity to prove causation. An additional problem arises if the actual damage is higher than the originally estimated maximum possible loss, as then the size of the bond is not sufficient to pay for the damage. Hence, the scheme only works successfully if the regulatory body takes a cautious view of the available evidence, implying a high amount for the performance bond, so that society would not find itself under-compensated. In

Box 11.6 Suggestion for an application of environmental performance bonds to wetland restoration

Wetlands are increasingly recognized as valuable natural systems providing useful services to society such as flood abatement, water purification, groundwater recharge, erosion control and biological diversity. International recognition of the value of wetlands is apparent through collective action in the Convention on Wetlands of International Importance (Ramsar Convention). Historical degradation of wetlands in the United States has led to a federal 'no net loss policy' for wetlands authorised by the Clean Water Act. The Clean Water Act mandates the restoration and maintenance of the chemical, physical and biological integrity of the nation's surface waters including certain wetlands. Gutrich and Hitzhusen (2004) review the situation in the state of Ohio and find that 90 per cent of the original wetlands in the United States has led to a federal 'no net loss policy' for wetlands over the last two centuries. Under the rules guiding the protection of water quality in Ohio, wetland losses are prohibited without compensatory 'mitigation': restoring or creating a wetland to make up for the one destroyed in the process of development.

Wetland mitigation is viewed as a means to balance the need for economic development with environmental protection. The extent and rate to which mitigation wetlands can replace the functions of natural ones remains uncertain and the value of the temporary loss of social wetland benefits have yet to be adequately addressed.

In an attempt to identify the ecological substitutability of mitigation inland freshwater marshes for natural ones, to estimate economic restoration lag costs to society and to address least-cost approaches to successful mitigation, Gutrich and Hitzhusen (2004) assessed sixteen mitigation wetlands, comprising of eight low-elevation inland freshwater emergent marshes in Ohio and eight high-elevation ($>2,285$ m) freshwater emergent marshes in a wetland complex in Colorado, USA. Years required for achieving full functional equivalency for both flora and soils for the Ohio sites under logistic growth ranged from 8 to 50 years with a median of 33 years. Years required for achieving floristic functional equivalency for the Colorado sites ranged from 10 to 16 years with a median of 13 years. Restoration lag costs are a function of ecological rates of wetland substitution and decrease with the increased ability of a mitigation wetland to restore all the functions of a natural site quickly. Per acre (0.4 ha) in Ohio restoration lag costs ranged from $3,460 to $49,811 per acre with an average of $16,640 per acre (US$ in 2000). This suggests that society is currently incurring significant wetland restoration costs due to time lags of mitigation sites. Therefore, Gutrich and Hitzhusen (2004) suggest the posting of an interest-accruing performance bond, which can serve to internalise the time lag costs to the permittee and provide an incentive for more cost-effective wetland restoration efforts.

order to avoid favouring big corporations over small and medium-sized enterprises (SMEs), organisational arrangements for cooperation of SMEs need to be devised.

The problems relating to SMEs are not unique to environmental performance bonds. While in most countries the share of firms classified as SMEs is about 98 per cent, it is by no means certain that environmental policy instruments that are effective with large companies are equally effective when applied to small and medium-sized ones. It is likely that they will need to be adapted to the particular circumstances of SMEs. In Europe there are few specific allowances made for SMEs in terms of environmental legislation; most Member States apply the same requirements to all companies. The UK and the Netherlands have given most consideration to sectoral and even company-specific economic issues. Other Member States worry that lighter administrative and legislative burdens for SMEs could lead to a lowering of environmental standards in such companies.

Given the problems encountered with uncertainty and irreversibility, environmental performance bonds are clearly an interesting idea for a potential addition to the existing menu of environmental policy instruments. To our knowledge they are not in use yet anywhere in the form set out above. Box 11.6 describes a proposed application of the idea. As with all environmental policy instruments, the success of an environmental bond scheme would depend heavily on the specific institutions created for its implementation. Especially, the procedure for setting the amount of the performance bond and the approach to addressing the problems related to SMEs will be crucial.

11.9 INTERDEPENDENCE OF POLICY GOALS

While the main aim of environmental policy is clearly to achieve environmental targets, it cannot be pursued independently of other policy goals. In fundamental terms, we find that in complex evolving systems, such as the social–ecological systems which we are dealing with here, the effects of different policies interact and therefore policies in different areas cannot be pursued independently of one another.

For example, as we will see in Chapter 13, consideration of climate policy really needs to take into account the link between the extremely skewed international distribution of income, and human history over the last few centuries. The relevance of history has two dimensions. First, the risks of climate change are the result of an accumulation and long residence time of green house gases (GHGs) in the atmosphere. Second, economic history is characterised by unfair trade, colonialism and other historical contingencies. Western countries have a historical responsibility because they have enjoyed high economic growth since the Industrial Revolution associated with the intensive use of fossil fuels, the fundamental cause of the human contribution to GHGs in the atmosphere. The neglect of historical responsibility, and of equity issues, in some of the current analyses may serve to reinforce the pursuit of opportunistic strategies in international climate negotiations.

Interdependencies among policy goals will also influence whether a proposed environmental policy gets the necessary political support to become a reality. The differing distributional consequences of the various possible pollution control policy instruments will be very important in determining which instrument is selected in practice. For example, as we have seen, an emissions tax imposed upon fossil fuels will affect final consumers who purchase goods that have energy inputs, directly or indirectly, to their production as well as affecting purchases of the fuels for heating and the like. That means that all final consumers are affected to an extent that depends on the energy intensity of their consumption behaviour. Individuals, for example, for whom heating comprises a large proportion of their budget – as is typically the case with the poor in northern countries – may well experience quite large falls in real income following the imposition of fossil fuel taxation. Indeed, many kinds of 'green taxes' (environmental taxes) are likely to have regressive effects upon income distribution, that is to reduce the real incomes of the poor more than the better-off. Many European governments initially rejected energy taxes because they feared the negative distributional effects.

On the other hand, environmental policies may generate so-called double dividends. The first benefit, or dividend, is an improvement in the environment. The second dividend is a reduction in the overall economic costs associated with the tax system by using the revenue generated to displace other more distortionary taxes that slow economic growth at the same time. For more details on the second dividend see Further Reading.

SUMMARY

In this chapter we have studied the main characteristics of the available environmental policy instruments, and looked at examples in various countries. The main lesson is that there is no single instrument type that is best in all situations. Tradable permits can be depended on to meet the target, whereas taxation cannot. On the other hand, taxation raises revenue. Both taxation and tradable permits have abatement cost advantages over command-and-control-type instruments. Changing the information and/or preferences that people have can affect their behaviour and its environmental impact. The question of instrument choice, like the question of policy targets, is made much more difficult to deal with by the fact that there is usually a lot of uncertainty involved, and by the fact that an instrument adopted in pursuit of one target is likely to affect other sustainable development policy objectives.

KEYWORDS

Command-and-control instruments (p. 410): policy instruments, used for pollution control and the management of common property resources, which require polluters to meet specific emission-reduction targets and often require the installation and use of specific types of equipment to reduce emissions.

Environmental standard (p. 411): a quantifiable characteristic of the environment against which environmental quality can be assessed. It is a surrogate for the environmental values that are to be protected.

Grandfathering (p. 430): An initial allocation of emission permits which rejects the relative amounts emitted by the various sources prior to the introduction of the permit system.

Green taxes (p. 434): taxes with a potentially positive environmental impact, hence comprising energy taxes, transport taxes and taxes on pollution and resources; also called environmental taxes.

Least cost theorem (p. 427): total abatement costs are minimised where the regulatory authority taxes emissions from all firms at a uniform rate per unit.

Market-based instruments (p. 405): policy instruments which seek to address environmental problems via a price mechanism.

Moral suasion (p. 406): A type of approach used by an authority to get members to adhere to a policy, goal or initiative. It involves applying pressure on members, rather than using legislation or force, to achieve a desired result.

Pigouvian tax (p. 417): A tax on an externality, such as pollution, designed to use market forces to achieve an efficient allocation of resources. Named after A. C. Pigou, one of the first economists to study market failure due to externalities.

Property rights (p. 413): social institution carrying the right of ownership.

Regulation (p. 405): control by means of rules and principle; includes formal rules introduced by national and international governing bodies as well as traditions and group norms.

Tradable permit (transferable pollution permits) (p. 425): An environmental policy instrument under which rights to discharge pollution or exploit resources can be exchanged through either a free or a controlled permit-market. Examples include individual transferable quotas in fisheries, tradable depletion rights to mineral concessions and marketable discharge permits for water-borne effluents.

FURTHER READING

Common* (1996), Tietenberg* (2003), Harris* (2002) and Hanley *et al.** (2001) are introductory environmental economics textbooks which discuss in greater detail how policy instruments work, especially market-based instruments. Perman *et al.* (2003) is a good intermediate/advanced text which offers a thorough discussion of the least cost theorem. Common* (1995) explores policy options for sustainable development, not only environmental policy but also population and welfare policy. Articles in van den Bergh (1999) give an overview of different environmental policy instruments. A classic article which explores the advantages and disadvantages of price incentives compared to setting quantitative standards is Weitzman (1974). The role of the decision process for the outcome is explored in Frey and Stutzer (2002c). For further details about the double dividend of environmental taxation see Goulder (1994).

For the reader who wishes to explore tradable permits in greater depth, Tietenberg (2001) is a collection of leading articles important in the development of the use of emissions trading to control air pollution, from its earliest implementation in the USA in 1976, to its application to global warming in the Kyoto Protocol. A recent innovative suggestion for using tradable permit schemes for households is presented in Anderson and Starkey (2004). The Domestic Tradable Quotas (DTQ) scheme is premised on the assumption that stabilising greenhouse gas concentrations in the atmosphere at a level that will prevent dangerous anthropogenic interference with the climate system will require very large reductions in global greenhouse gas emissions. Furthermore it is assumed that these reductions will be achieved through some form of international agreement establishing binding national emissions reduction targets. The DTQ scheme is a new instrument designed to enable nations to meet the component of their emissions reduction targets that is related to energy use. A nation implementing a DTQ scheme establishes the maximum quantity of greenhouse gases that it can emit from energy use during any given year. This carbon budget is reduced year on year up to and including the year by which a nation must have achieved its emission reduction target. Each carbon budget is divided into carbon units, with, for example, 1 carbon unit representing 1 kg of carbon dioxide. A proportion of these units is allocated by government, free and on an equal per capita basis, to all adult citizens. This free allocation is known as the Entitlement. The remaining carbon units are allocated to firms and other organizations through a government-regulated auction. A computer database holds the carbon unit account for all citizens and organizations, The database records all carbon unit transactions – issuing, surrendering, buying or selling. See also OECD (2002).

In section 11.2.3 we discussed novel ways for measuring and reporting economic and environmental performance. The ISEW proposal first appeared in Daly and Cobb (1989), where it is calculated for the USA. Another example, showing a similar path over time, is in Stockhammer *et al.* (1997). Further references, and discussion, can be found in of Perman *et al.* (2003) ch. 19. A good straightforward account of the motivation for, and methods used in, ecological footprinting is Wackernagel and Rees (1996). The March 2000 issue (vol. 32, no. 3) of *Ecological Economics* has twelve articles on ecological footprinting, including several setting out its limitations.

Further discussions on environmental racism/classism can be found in Faber (1998), Cole and Foster (2001), Gottlieb (2001), Lester *et al.* (2001), Roberts and Toffolon-Weiss (2001) and Fletcher (2003).

WEBSITES

http://www.epa.gov/ – Environment Protection Agency (EPA), which develops and implements national environmental policy in the US.

http://www.eea.eu.int/ – European Environmental Agency (EEA), which delivers background information for environmental policy in Europe; their webpage has a helpful glossary: http://glossary.eea.eu.int/EEAGlossary

http://europa.eu.int/comm/environment/index_en.htm – European Commission (EC) – General Directorate Environment, which implements environmental policy in Europe.

http://www.oecd.org/department/0,2688,en_2649_33713_1_1_1_1_1,00.html – OECD – Environment Directorate, which advises OECD countries on environmental policy.

http://www.oecd.org/document/29/0,2340,en_2649_34295_1894685_1_1_1_1,00.html – OECD Environmentally Related Taxes database.

http://www2.oecd.org/ecoinst/queries/index/htm/ – OECD and EEA have also prepared a complementary database with information concerning other economic instruments (such as tradable permits schemes, deposit-refund systems and environmentally motivated subsidies) and voluntary approaches used in environmental policy.

http://www.colby.edu/personal/t/thtieten/trade.html – Bibliography on tradable permits compiled by Tom Tietenberg.

http://www.ieta.org/ – international tradable permit schemes.

http://www.europa.eu.int/comm/environment/climat/emission.htm – EU tradable permit scheme

http://www.defra.gov.uk/environment/climatechange/trading/uk/index.htm – UK tradable permit scheme

http://www.futureforests.com/acabalog/index_shop_calculators.asp/ – Carbon calculator for air travel

http://www.fairtrade.net/ – Fairtrade labelling organisation.

http://www.rprogress.org/ – the website for the organisation Redefining Progress, which has lots of material on ecological footprinting and the Genuine Progress Indicator.

DISCUSSION TOPICS

1.   Proponents of eco-labels consider them as an alternative to traditional governmental regulation. Is this a viable option? What are the drawbacks of eco-labels?

2.   Some environmental activists argue that tradable pollution permits are immoral because they confer the right to damage the natural environment. Do you agree?

EXERCISES

1   (a)   Energy prices rose sharply in the early 1970s, stimulating interest in energy conservation. Companies installed more energy-efficient equipment, individuals insulated their homes, and the average fuel efficiency of the vehicle fleet was improved. Despite all this, UK energy demand was 210.1 million tons of oil equivalent in 1970 while by 2000 it was 231.9 million tons of oil equivalent. How can you explain this result?

(b)   Part of the explanation may be the 'rebound effect', which describes the increase in demand for a resource, although more efficient technology is used. How does this relate to the claim of ecological economists that the focus on efficiency is insufficient, and that the total level of energy and material throughput needs to be targeted as well?

(c)   Many ecological economists regard the current level, and pattern in terms of the fuels and resources used, of energy consumption as unsustainable. What scenarios and policy measures for this can you think of that would address their concerns?

APPENDIX INPUT – OUTPUT ANALYSIS OF CARBON TAXATION

This appendix builds on the Appendix in Chapter 5, and you may find it useful to go back and look again at it before working through this one.

We first extend the symbolic transactions table to include primary inputs:

			Sales to	
Purchases from	Agriculture	Manufacturing	Final demand	Total Output
Agriculture	0	Q_{AM}	F_A	Q_A
Manufacturing	Q_{MA}	0	F_M	Q_M
Primary input	V_A	V_M		

Note that we have now consolidated W and S and OFP into one primary input so as to simplify the algebra, and recall that OFP includes the payments for oil.

The corresponding coefficient table is:

	Agriculture	Manufacturing
Agriculture	0	a_{AM}
Manufacturing	a_{MA}	0
Primary inputs	v_A	v_M

where

$$a_{AM} \equiv \frac{Q_{AM}}{Q_M}$$

$$a_{MA} \equiv \frac{Q_{MA}}{Q_A}$$

$$v_A \equiv \frac{V_A}{Q_A}$$

$$v_M \equiv \frac{V_M}{Q_M}$$

With P for price and Q for quantity, we have

$$\text{Agriculture sales receipts} = P_A \times Q_A$$
$$\text{Agriculture expenditures} = (P_M \times Q_{MA}) + V_A$$

and

$$\text{Manufacturing sales receipts} = P_M \times Q_M$$
$$\text{Manufacturing expenditures} = (P_A \times Q_{AM}) + V_M$$

Since receipts are always equal to expenditures in input–output accounting, this is

$$P_A \times Q_A = (P_M \times Q_{MA}) + V_A$$

and

$$P_M \times Q_M = (P_A \times Q_{AM}) + V_M$$

The definitions of the coefficients mean that

$$Q_{AM} = a_{AM} \times Q_M$$
$$Q_{MA} = a_{MA} \times Q_A$$
$$V_A = v_A \times Q_A$$
$$V_M = v_M \times Q_M$$

and making these substitutions in the two sales equals receipts statements gives

$$P_A \times Q_A = (P_M \times a_{MA} \times Q_A) + (v_A \times Q_A)$$

and

$$P_M \times Q_M = (P_A \times a_{AM} \times Q_M) + (v_M \times Q_M)$$

where dividing both sides of the first by Q_A and of the second by Q_M gives

$$P_A = (a_{MA} \times P_M) + v_A \tag{1}$$

and

$$P_M = (a_{AM} \times P_A) + v_M \tag{2}$$

as a pair of simultaneous equations which can be solved for P_A and P_M in terms of the coefficients a_{MA}, v_A, a_{AM} and v_M.

Substituting from (2) into (1) and rearranging gives

$$P_A = \left(\frac{1}{1 - a_{AM} \times a_{MA}} \right) \times v_A + \left(\frac{a_{MA}}{1 - a_{AM} \times a_{MA}} \right) \times v_M \tag{3}$$

and using this to substitute in (2) leads to

$$P_M = \left(\frac{a_{AM}}{1 - a_{AM} \times a_{MA}} \right) \times v_A + \left(\frac{1}{1 - a_{AM} \times a_{MA}} \right) \times v_M \tag{4}$$

The prices of both commodities depend on all of the coefficients describing the structure of the economy – the input–output coefficients and the primary input coefficients.

For the numerical illustration from the chapter, repeated from Chapter 5, we have

	Agriculture	Manufacturing
Agriculture	0	$a_{AM} = 0.1$
Manufacturing	$a_{MA} = 0.6$	0
Primary inputs	$v_A = 0.4$	$v_M = 0.9$

and substituting these values in (3) and (4) leads to $P_A = 1$ and $P_M = 1$. This seemingly strange result arises from the fact that the entries in the transactions table are expenditures, that is they are price times quantity. When we treat them as quantities, as we have done here, we are measuring quantities in units that are (millions of) dollars' worth. This is standard practice in input–output accounting; as the industry sectors distinguished each produce many different actual commodities, this is the only way to proceed. The price of such a unit is just 1.

So, solving the equations (3) and (4) for the numerical coefficient values derived from the transactions table data gives the prices implicit in that data, which is as it should be. We can now use these equations to derive the result stated in the body of the chapter for the effect on prices of a carbon tax. With oil as base, the tax is $100 per tonne, so that given the use of 1,000,000 tonnes of oil it costs Manufacturing $100,000,000 or 100×10^6. The tax is treated as an expenditure on primary inputs, which increase from $1,800 million to $1,900 million for Manufacturing. Hence, with the tax in place

$$v_M = 1900 \div 2000 = 0.95$$

and substituting in (3) and (4) for the original a_{AM}, a_{MA} and v_A and this value for v_M gives $P_A = 1.0319$ and $P_M = 1.0532$.

Using these prices with the original quantities for commodities

		Sales to		
Purchases from	Agriculture	Manufacturing	Final demand	Total output
Agriculture	0	200	800	1000
Manufacturing	600	0	1400	2000

gives expenditure flows, in $ million as:

		Sales to		
Purchases from	Agriculture	Manufacturing	Final demand	Total output
Agriculture	0	206.38	825.52	1031.9
Manufacturing	632.92	0	1474.48	2106.4

where subtracting intermediate purchases from total sales revenue gives 399.98 for Agriculture and 1,900.02 for Manufacturing. Allowing for rounding errors, these are the payments for primary inputs in each sector with the carbon tax in place.

With many sectors, the algebraic method used here will not work to solve many simultaneous equations. However, multiple simultaneous equations can readily be solved using matrix algebra, where the arithmetic can be done quickly using a spreadsheet such as Excel^{TM}. The interested reader can find out more about matrix algebra from references in the Further Reading section of Chapter 5.

PART IV
THE INTERNATIONAL DIMENSION

In previous chapters we referred to sustainable development as a principle of global concern. However, we have not yet explored how problems of unsustainable development which have an international dimension can be addressed. So far we have treated environmental problems and policies as if the generators and victims of unsustainable economic activities resided within a single country. This allowed us to focus on the governance mechanisms which induce or enforce more sustainable production and consumption choices. These mechanisms can operate because the primacy given to the nation state in political affairs provides the legitimacy and authority needed to support them. However, many important environmental problems concern effects on individuals who live (or are yet to live) in different nation states. Humankind faces an unprecedented array of truly global and regional environmental problems, the reach of which is greater than any single national community (or generation). Chapter 12 sets out some basic ideas and information about trade between states in relation to sustainable development. Then, in Chapters 13 and 14, we look at two global threats to sustainability: climate change and biodiversity loss.

12

A world of nation states

In this chapter you will:

- Find out why international trade is generally considered beneficial to the parties involved;
- Learn how national environmental and trade policies interact;
- Find out in what sense globalisation reaches further than international trade;
- Look at the means by which environmental policy can be implemented in the context of international trade;
- Consider the advantages and disadvantages of living in a world where nations move closer together.

The nations of the world are increasingly interlinked. They are exchanging more goods and services than ever before, but they now also share transboundary and global environmental problems. In this chapter we will consider the linkages between trade and the environment, and their implications for sustainable development.

12.1 THE CASE FOR INTERNATIONAL TRADE

In this section we are going to look at the standard argument as to why trade between nations is a 'good thing', and to note some qualifications to that argument. We will also take a first look at the connections between trade issues and environmental issues.

12.1.1 The principle of comparative advantage

For thousands of years peoples have exchanged regional specialities in order to get a taste of different cultures. Trade has permitted access to goods and services unavailable otherwise. For example, Austria has produced white wine for centuries and in particular its eastern and southern regions are well suited for growing it. Iceland in turn has a clear geographic advantage for harvesting cod. Austria is a land-locked country and therefore does not have any seafish of its own. The short growing period and low average temperature in Iceland does not allow for producing wine. Wine is well liked in Austria and cod is prominent in Icelandic cuisine. However, by trading wine for cod, Austrians can enjoy seafish as a complement to their usual diet and Icelanders can enjoy wine with their fish.

While the benefits of this type of trade are clear and require little explanation, we saw in Chapter 8 that even if both parties can produce both commodities and one party is in a better position to produce both commodities, specialisation in production according to comparative advantage, plus trade, can improve the economic situation of the trading partners. In Chapter 8 we looked at the example of Jane who was better than Tom at both making loaves and catching fish, but was even better – had a comparative advantage – at the production of loaves. In total Jane and Tom can produce more by specialising in making the commodity for which each of them has the lower opportunity cost, i.e. for which they have a comparative advantage.

The same principle of comparative advantage can be applied to countries. Then the theory of comparative advantage explains why it can be beneficial for two countries to trade, even though one of them may be able to produce every kind of commodity more cheaply than the other country. It is not the absolute costs of production that matter, but rather the ratio of the costs at which the two countries can produce different commodities. The principle was first described by Robert Torrens in 1815 in an essay on the trade of corn. Two years later David Ricardo explained the principle of comparative advantage clearly in his book *The principles of political economy and taxation*. Ricardo used the example of Portugal, where it is possible to produce both wine and cloth with less work than it takes in England. However, the relative costs of producing these two goods are different in the two countries. In England it is very hard to produce wine, and only moderately difficult to produce cloth. In Portugal both are easy to produce. Therefore, while it is cheaper to produce cloth in Portugal than in England, it is cheaper still for Portugal to specialise in wine production, and trade that for English cloth. Conversely, England benefits from this trade because its costs for producing cloth have not changed but it can now get wine at a cost closer to that of cloth. If all countries specialised where they had a comparative advantage, then all countries could consume more of every commodity.

David Ricardo's story about England and Portugal and wine and cloth works in the same way as our Chapter 8 story about Jane and Tom and loaves and fish. In fact, if you go back to Chapter 8 and call Jane Portugal, call Tom England, call loaves wine, and call fish cloth, then you have a numerical illustration of the Ricardo exposition of the principle of comparative advantage as it works between nations with the countries and commodities that he used.

We do need to note one point about terminology. In Chapter 8 we called the terms on which Jane and Tom traded, the number of loaves exchanged for a fish, the 'exchange ratio', or the 'exchange rate'. In the international trade context this rate is known as the **terms of trade**, and the **exchange rate** is the rate at which the currencies of the two countries exchange for one another. In Chapter 8, Jane and Tom lived in the same country and used the same curency, £, so they could trade fish for loaves by selling fish for £ and buying loaves with £, and vice versa.

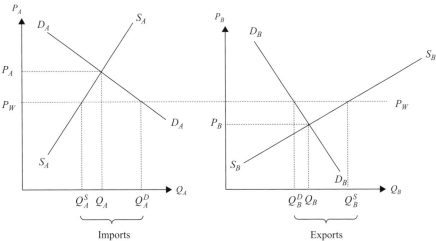

Figure 12.1 The effects of trade.

With international trade another step is introduced into the trade process. English buyers need € to pay Portuguese wine producers and Portuguese buyers need £ to pay English cloth producers. The exchange rate here is the rate at which € and £ exchange for one another, which is determined in the foreign exchange, or currency, market.

What matters for the share-out of the benefits from trade between nations is the underlying rate at which the traded commodities exchange for one another, that is the terms of trade. We saw this when we considered Jane and Tom in Chapter 8, and the story there applies to Portugal and England and loaves and fish, save that in this case 'terms of trade' would be used instead of 'exchange ratio'. Where the terms of trade end up within the range that permits both countries to get some gain from trade depends on the sizes of the two countries and on the demand functions for the commodities in the two countries. The terms of trade change with changes in demands for the various commodities traded. If a country's terms of trade deteriorate, it has to export more per unit imported, just as Jane/Tom would have to give up more loaves/fish per unit fish/loaves obtained from Tom/Jane as the terms of trade moved against Jane/Tom.

12.1.2 Domestic winners and losers

To explore the principle of comparative advantage further in the international trade context, we can look at Figure 12.1. The important point to be made is that while the principle applies as much to countries as to individuals, a country comprises groups with different interests who are affected differently by specialisation and trade. This fairly obvious point, and its implications, are sometimes overlooked.

Figure 12.1 refers to the production and consumption of some commodity, widgets say, in two countries, and shows what happens when they move from a situation of autarky to one where they trade with one another. In the state of autarky, the domestic widget markets clear with demand equal to supply at prices P_A and P_B. With free trade there is a single world price, P_W. In country A this is below the

Figure 12.2 An
import tariff.

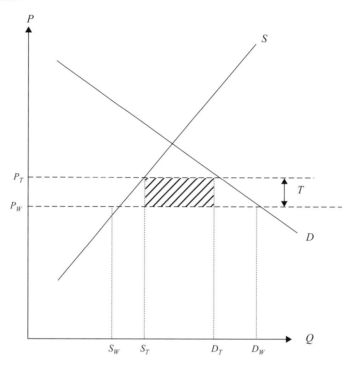

autarky price and A becomes an importer of widgets. In country B, it is above the
autarky price so B exports widgets. In A domestic production is Q_A^S, consumption is
Q_A^D, and imports are $Q_A^D - Q_A^S$. In B domestic production is Q_B^S and consumption
is Q_B^D so that exports are $Q_B^S - Q_B^D$. As compared with the autarky situation, in A
consumers of widgets get to consume more at a lower price, while producers in A
sell less at a lower price – consumers gain and producers lose. In B, consumers get
to consume less at a higher price with trade, and producers sell more at a higher
price. If the winners in each country were to be required to compensate their country's losers, then the losers would be no worse off, and the winners would still
be better off. In both countries, the winners gain more than the losers lose. You
can find a proof of this in most intermediate microeconomics texts: see Further
Reading. The important point is that there are winners and losers, and that compensation is not in fact usually paid. While the principle of comparative advantage
says that all countries can gain from trade, it does not say that everybody in every
country does actually gain from trade.

All this helps to explain why free trade is not the universal rule, why national
governments often restrict the free movement of goods and services between countries, and why it is imports, rather than exports, that are usually subject to restriction. If country A opens its borders to imports, its widget manufacturers lose. Naturally, they will seek to persuade the government not to do this. Widget consumers in
the same country would gain, but are likely to be less easily organised to influence
the government than are the widget producers. Often there are many consumers

and few producers, and the latter's potential losses, of jobs for example, are often more obviously important than the former's potential gains: cheaper widgets.

Where a government wishes to reduce imports the main options are restrictions on the quantity imported, often known as **import quotas**, or a tax per unit imported. Taxes on imports are known as **tariffs** and all forms of import restriction other than taxes are often referred to as **non-tariff restrictions**. Tariffs have the advantage that as well as restricting imports they raise government revenue and are an alternative to, for example, income taxation. Figure 12.2 shows how a tariff works. P_W is the world price, at which domestic demand is D_W, domestic output is S_W, and imports are $D_W - S_W$. The tariff T raises the price in the domestic market to P_T, at which domestic consumption is D_T and domestic output is S_T. As the result of the tariff domestic output increases, domestic consumption falls and consumers pay more, and imports are reduced to $D_T - S_T$. The revenue raised is given by the amount imported multiplied by the tariff, which is the area of the hatched rectangle between P_T and P_W over S_T to D_T.

12.1.3 Some qualifications to the principle of comparative adavantage

Before looking at how environmental damage might affect the case for trade, we need to take a look at some non-environmental potential problems with the comparative advantage argument for free trade. We will go through them rather briefly; more analysis and information can be found via Further Reading. The problems to note are:

1. The principle of comparative advantage states that the total of goods and services produced will be higher, so that all nations could consume more if they were to specialise according to the principle. It says nothing about the distribution of the extra commodities produced which depends on the terms of trade. When we looked at specialisation and exchange based on comparative advantage for individuals in Chapter 8, we saw that while it led to allocative efficiency, it did not necessarily produce equitable outcomes. The situation is the same with international trade – the distribution of gains is not necessarily fair.

2. We have neglected the costs of transport. Zero transport cost is not such a strong assumption when accounting for only the monetary cost of transport under current institutional arrangements. However, if we took the full costs, including environmental damage, into account, they would be more significant and correcting for such external costs might in some cases undermine the case for trade based on comparative advantage. We will come back to this in section 12.5.

3. We have assumed that specialisation in one commodity following an opening to trade comes at no cost. In reality, there will be costs of adjustment – capital equipment will not be readily transferable and people from the shrinking sectors will need retraining before being able to produce a commodity which they have not made before.

4. Specialisation is a risky strategy. What if after a few years of production nobody wanted to buy the product which the country has specialised in?

Specialisation helps to reduce production costs, but this gain comes at a price. Diversity is expensive, but provides economic resilience in that a severe decline in one sector need not bring down the whole economy. Countries and regions need to consider this trade-off when deciding on their strategies of national and regional development.

The last two points are related to what is known in the literature as the '**Dutch disease**'. The phenomenon is named after the effects of natural gas discoveries in the Netherlands from 1959 onwards, which had an adverse effect on the country's other industries. The phenomenon occurs when one industry substantially expands its exports, causing a real appreciation of the country's currency. In the given scenario, the value of the country's currency rises (making its manufactured goods less competitive because at a higher exchange rate non-nationals have to give up more of their own currency to get a unit of the country's currency), imports increase, exports decrease and productivity falls. Most commonly this scenario is applied to explain the impact of exports by natural-resource-extractive industries on manufacturing.

Comparative advantages are determined at a single point in time, but the long-term consequences of specialisation depend on their dynamic effects on the economy. For example, two countries may at present have comparative advantages in bananas and information technology, respectively. Specialisation in bananas does little for technological innovation, the development of labour skills, or diversification into high value-added products whereas specialisation in information technology usually performs well in all these areas. Where trade takes place on the basis of such technologically unequal comparative advantages, the countries that specialise in the least dynamic comparative advantages may find themselves locked into economic stagnation and at the bottom end of growing inequality. For example, Costa Rica focused on the production of agricultural crops for exports – coffee, bananas, sugar – which led to a sluggish economic development as well as substantial soil loss. Finland on the other hand has been able to transform itself over the last 150 years from a tar- and wood-exporting peripheral economy into a technologically highly advanced country.

Economists have developed formal models of such situations by associating positive externalities with the industrial sector and showing that trade with developed nations prevents industrialisation in less developed countries, which specialised in less dynamic sectors. From this followed widespread concern that the contraction of a country's manufacturing sector that follows natural resource discoveries is a bad thing. The worry is when the natural resources run out, the lost manufacturing sector will not come back because the equipment was sold and the skills forgotten. The home country's market share and relative wage will turn out to have been permanently reduced by the country's temporary good fortune.

These issues clearly need to be taken into account when assessing the expected economic and social consequences of international trade. In addition there has been a long debate about the impacts of international trade on the environment, with some environmentalists arguing that trade is bad for the environment, and some economists arguing that it is not. Our next step is to take our first look at these issues. We will come back to them in section 12.3.

12.1.4 Trade and the environment -- a first look

We can make a start using Figure 12.1. Although we did not say so explicitly, our discussion of winners and losers from opening to trade, in section 12.1.2, assumed that the production of widgets did not give rise to any external costs. Suppose now that the production of widgets in both countries results in emissions into the atmosphere of some particulate matter which is injurious to the health of the citizens of the country where production takes place. And suppose, initially, that these emissions are not regulated in any way.

In this case, trade is good for the environment in country *A*, but bad for it in country *B*. In the country that becomes an importer, domestic production, and hence emissions, go down. In the country that becomes an exporter, domestic production, and hence emissions, go up. In the country that becomes an exporter, trade is, in the case of widgets and particulates anyway, bad for the environment. In considering whether or not trade is a 'good thing' for country *B*, the gains to producers in excess of the loss to consumers on account of lower widget consumption at a higher price have to be compared with the increase in environmental damage. If they are larger, the producers could compensate those affected by the particulate matter and still be better off. Whether or not this is the situation will vary from case to case – there can be no general presumption one way or another. In the case where the emissions are unregulated, domestic environmental damage may undermine the case for trade.

Suppose that emissions are regulated in country *B*. Does it then follow that the increased environmental damage that goes with the increased production once trade takes place will not be great enough to undermine the case for trade? Obviously the answer to this question depends on the amount of regulation, which as well as reducing the increase in environmental damage, also reduces the gains to producers. Only in one case is it possible to be sure that opening up to trade still involves net benefits in the sense that the gainers could compensate the losers and still be better off. That is when the level of regulation is just what is required to correct market failure, that is the level that goes with allocative efficiency. As we saw in Chapter 11, regulatory authorities rarely have the information that is needed to regulate at this level. That being the case, when neoclassical economists say that pollution generation does not undermine the case for free trade provided the proper pollution controls are in place, they are right on their own terms (compensation could be paid, rather than is paid). But, the 'provided' means that the assurance is, for practical purposes, invalid. In the real world, with environmental regulation as it actually is, trade-induced production expansion may entail environmental damage costs in excess of the producers' gains.

The argument is often made that environmental protection is bad for competitiveness, will reduce a country's exports. Suppose that countries *A* and *B* in Figure 12.1 regulate the emissions arising in widget production by taxing it. Then the supply functions will move up and to the left. At the given world price this will mean lower production in both countries. In the exporting country *B*, exports go down, and in *A* imports go up. If all countries in the world tax widget production, then global widget production falls. If all countries tax at the same rate, there is no loss of competitiveness for any country. Production falls everywhere as the worldwide correction of market failure requires. No country suffers a 'loss of competitiveness'.

When the argument that protecting the domestic environment will hurt the economy is made, it is not usually envisaged that all countries will tax at the same rate, or regulate to the same level. Rather, proponents have in mind a situation where one country, B say, acts to protect its environment, but others do not, or do so to a lesser extent. Suppose B acts but other widget exporters do not act at all. Then its supply function shifts, but its competitors' do not. Its output is cut, but that of its competitors is not.

As we will note later, there are reasons to believe that this kind of effect on a country acting unilaterally to protect its environment will generally be small. The available evidence appears to support this view. Note also that other domestic industries may benefit if a country acts in this way. Other things being equal, the reduction in widget exports will reduce the exchange rate, which will make it easier for all domestic industries to export.

12.2 PATTERNS OF INTERNATIONAL TRADE

In 2002 some $6.4 trillion of goods were sent from one country to another. While the global economy has been expanding at about 3 per cent a year since 1950, the volume of trade has been rising at a compound annual rate of about twice that. Merchandise[1] trade is now sixteen times what it was in 1950, while world GDP is only six times as big as it was. Figure 12.3 compares the postwar evolution of world trade volumes in goods compared to world real GDP. Merchandise trade growth was particularly strong during the 1990s. Note that the vertical axis in the figure is indexed so that 1990 = 100 for both trade volumes and GDP. The ratio of world exports to GDP climbed since 1950 from 7 per cent to 15 per cent in 2000. Particularly since the mid-1980s, increasing growth rates of international trade of merchandise were observed. On average the value of traded merchandise increased between 1990 and 1997 by 7 per cent per year. Particularly high growth rates were observed in 1994 (13 per cent) and 1995 (almost 20 per cent). In 2001 we saw a decline in world trade (−4 per cent). The annual rate of merchandise trade expansion in 2002 was limited to 3 per cent in real terms, only half the rate observed in the 1990s. The trade recovery in 2002 benefited from strong import demand in developing Asia and the transition economies of Central and Eastern Europe. Sluggish import demand in Western Europe and a sharp contraction of Latin America's imports slowed international trade down. China's recent trade expansion (both exports and imports) is outstanding. In the 1990s, China's trade growth was three times faster than global trade growth and between 2000 and 2002 its exports and imports rose by 30 per cent, while world trade stagnated. China has become the fourth largest merchandise trader (if the EU in counted as a single trader) in 2002. The evolution of the distribution of exports of merchandise and services by country group can be

---

1 Following the UN recommendations, the international merchandise trade statistics record all goods which add to or subtract from the stock of material resources of a country by entering (imports) or leaving (exports) its economic territory. Goods simply being transported through a country (goods in transit) or temporarily admitted or withdrawn (except for goods for inward or outward processing) do not add to or subtract from the stock of material resources of a country and are not included in the international merchandise trade statistics.

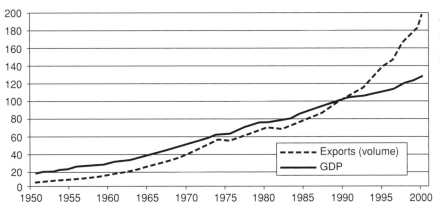

Figure 12.3
Trends in world
trade in goods
(volume)
vs. real GDP
(1990 = 100).

Source: Data from WTO (2001).

seen in Table 12.1. Developing countries are playing an increasingly significant role in merchandise trade. As shown in Table 12.1 the share of merchandise accounted for by developing country exports rose from 24.7 per cent in 1960 to 31.7 per cent in 2002. Increasing amounts of trade now flow between developing countries, but the poorest countries continue to play only a marginal role in international trade. Some countries, in particular those of Sub-Saharan Africa, have seen their share in world trade drop during the last two decades and have experienced a deterioration of their terms of trade.

Trade agreements, which allow countries to trade goods and services on preferential conditions, were important for increasing trade worldwide and for the developing countries in particular as they had found, and to some degree still do find, themselves barred from trade opportunities. To date trade agreements remain biased. Recently the World Bank investigated 91 trade agreements negotiated since 1980 and tested for reciprocity in free trade agreements (Freund, 2003). Reciprocity here means a 'balance of concessions' between the trading partners who are parties to an agreement. The results of the World Bank study offer strong evidence of reciprocity in North–North and South–South free trade agreements, but there is little empirical support for reciprocity in North–South trade agreements.

As well as reductions in trade barriers, which will be discussed further in section 12.4, and the opening to trade of countries like China and Mexico, the increase in the relative importance of international trade has been based on the falling costs of getting goods to market. Not only the volume, also the kinds of goods traded have changed significantly over recent decades. In 1900 'crude materials' and 'crude food' made up 41 per cent of America's exports, by value, and 45 per cent of its imports. These products are heavy and bulky. The cost of transporting them is relatively high, compared with the value of the goods themselves. Today, finished manufactured products, not raw commodities, dominate the flow of trade. As the costs of shipping matter less and less, distance becomes less relevant.

Another trend has been towards global production sharing and hence trade in semi-finished products which now involves more than $800 billion in manufactures

Table 12.1 Share of merchandise and services exports – world exports in million US$ and shares as % by country group

Regions	1960	1970	1980	1990	2000	2002
Merchandise						
World	130 135	316 428	2 031 219	3 500 278	6 426 893	6 414 058
Developing countries	24.7	19.2	29.4	24.1	32.0	31.7
Countries in Central and Eastern Europe	10.6	10.1	8.0	5.0	4.2	4.9
Developed countries	64.7	70.7	62.6	70.8	63.8	63.5
Services						
World	..	..	385 352	824 724	1 511 935	1 610 608
Developing countries	..	..	17.9	18.1	23.1	22.6
Countries in Central and Eastern Europe	..	..	..	..	3.6	4.2
Developed countries	..	..	79.1	79.9	73.2	73.2

Note: figures in this table are in current $US
Source: UNCTAD (2004).

trade annually, or at least 30 per cent of trade in manufactured products. The trade in components and parts has been growing at a considerably faster pace than that of other (finished) products. This reflects the growing interdependence of countries in international trade and production operations. This is reflected in increased **foreign direct investment** flows, with firms creating and expanding overseas branches and subsidiaries. In the past two decades, the world stock of capital owned by non-nationals has grown more than ten-fold to reach $7.1 trillion in 2002.

International trade in services – such as banking, insurance, accountancy and consulting, for example – expanded rapidly in the late twentieth century, growing on average much faster than both world GDP and world merchandise trade. In current US dollars, total exports of services more than quadrupled between 1980 and 2002, from approximately $400 billion to about $1,600 billion. Some 60 per cent of foreign-owned capital is now in the services industries, compared to less than 50 per cent a decade ago. The share of manufacturing in foreign-owned capital has fallen from more than 40 per cent in 1990 to 35 per cent today, while the share of the primary sector has declined from 10 per cent to 6 per cent.

With decreasing transportation costs and the increasing importance of product differentiation the share of similar products traded rose. Product differentiation means that similar products (like brands of breakfast cereals or soft drinks) are perceived to differ from one another and thus are imperfect substitutes. For example, German cars are exported to France and vice versa, and British butter exported to New Zealand and vice versa.

12.3 INTERNATIONAL TRADE AND SUSTAINABLE DEVELOPMENT

Is international trade good for sustainable development? That question raises two further questions. How does trade affect the environment? What does it do for poverty and inequality? In this section we will first look at the ways in which it is argued that trade is good for sustainable development. Then we will consider arguments that trade is bad for the environment and bad for poverty and inequality. It turns out that there is no simple bottom line – in some ways trade promotes sustainable development, in others it does not.

12.3.1 Positive consequences of international trade

International trade has benefited people in two important ways: first, by promoting economic growth; second, by enabling households to consume goods not produced domestically and to pay less for some other goods. For example, in China incomes have increased six-fold in the last twenty years and the Chinese population has much more choice of products.

12.3.1.1 Increase of income

International trade and investment have been the engines of world growth over the past fifty years. As we saw earlier, the quantity of goods traded around the world has grown more than sixteen-fold since 1950, reflecting the lowering of tariff barriers and growth in the world economy. The growth of trade in services is even greater. The benefits of economic growth have been shared unequally among nations. The countries that are getting poorer are those that are not open to world trade, notably many nations in Africa. Some evidence indicates that inequalities in global income and poverty are decreasing and that globalisation has contributed to this turnaround. For example, the World Bank notes that China's opening to world trade has brought it growth in income from $1,460 a head in 1980 to $4,120 by 1999. Over the same period the ratio of US per capita income to Chinese per capita income declined from 12.5 to 7.4. Other data have been used to argue that the gap between the rich and poor nations of the world is increasing. The figures used most frequently for this purpose are those from the UNDP 1999 Human Development Report which finds that over the previous ten years the number of people earning $1 a day or less had remained static at 1.2 billion, while the number earning less than $2 a day had increased from 2.55 billion to 2.8 billion people. The ratio of the incomes of the top 20 per cent of people in the richest countries to those of the bottom 20 per cent in the poorest countries grew from 30 to 1 in 1960 to 74 to 1 in 1995. For a fuller discussion of poverty and inequality in the world economy see Chapter 6 and its Further Reading suggestions.

Besides the comparative advantage argument which we discussed above, it is also argued that **economies of scale** based on international trade are an argument for free trade. Economies of scale are the lower per-unit production costs for the firm that usually go with increased production levels (also called '**internal economies of scale**'), where long-run average costs are falling as output increases. The case is less clear for trade based on '**external economies of scale**'. These are economies of scale which apply at the level of the industry rather than at the level of the firm. They can arise as an industry builds up a sizeable pool of trained labour that each individual firm can make use of. Another way for external economies of scale to arise is as an industry grows and other businesses start up in support of that industry, increasing competition among themselves and experiencing their own internal economies of scale. This means they can sell components and services at a lower unit cost to the industry. Cooperation of firms in an industry is another pathway to external economies of scale. For example, small hotels frequently combine to publish shared advertising material. In the presence of external economies of scale it is possible that trade is not beneficial to all countries. While there may be gains to the world economy from concentrating production in particular industries to realise external economies (e.g. Silicon Valley or Swiss watch production), there is on the other hand no guarantee that the right country will produce a good subject to external economies, and it is possible that trade based on external economies may actually leave a country worse off than it would have been in the absence of trade. External economies potentially give a strong role to historical accident in determining who produces what, and may allow established patterns of specialisation to persist even when they run counter to comparative advantage.

12.3.1.2 Economic growth and the environment

Based on the above arguments, and assuming also that free trade gives the consumers the greatest opportunity to choose 'green' products and establishes the best climate for multilateral cooperation to solve environmental problems, many argue that trade restrictions motivated by environmental concerns would be harmful. From the neoclassical economics point of view, what sustainability requires is the internalisation of environmental externalities (see Chapters 9 and 11). Neoclassical economists argue that a failure to place the 'right' value on environmental damage and resource depletion would undermine sustainable development even in complete autarky. Trade is seen not as a source of environmental problems, but rather as a 'magnifier' of the adverse effects of not having the proper environmental policies in place. If the policies necessary for the proper levels of environmental protection are in place, trade promotes development that is sustainable.

Some economists go further, and argue that economic growth, enhanced by free trade, is itself good for the environment. This is the Environmental Kuznets Curve hypothesis (EKC), which we discussed in Chapter 7. One idea behind this hypothesis is that the poor have little demand for environmental quality, and are constrained by their present consumption needs to degrade their environment. Thus, for example:

> As a society becomes richer its members may intensify their demands for a more healthy and sustainable environment in which case the government may be called upon to impose more stringent environmental controls. (Grossman and Krueger, 1991)

Not only are consumers with higher incomes more willing (and able) to spend more for green products, as citizens they are also expected to exert increased pressure through the political system for environmental regulation.

In most cases where emissions have declined with rising income, the reductions have been due to local and national institutional reforms, such as environmental legislation and market-based incentives to reduce environmental impacts. A review of the available evidence on instances of pollution abatement suggests that the strongest link between income and pollution in fact is via induced policy response. Thus, the inverted U-relation is evidence that in some cases institutional reforms led private users of environmental resources to take account of the social costs of their actions (Arrow *et al.*, 1995).

As incomes increase, individuals are willing and able to spend more (in absolute terms) for all normal goods, which most economists take to include environmental services such as cleaner air and water. Some authors have argued that individuals would increase their demand for environmental quality by a greater percentage than the rise in income – that environmental quality has an income elasticity greater than unity and is a superior good. However, there is a lack of evidence to support this hypothesis. In a recent analysis of evidence from European countries, environmental quality was found to be a normal economic good for which demand rises less than proportionately with income, i.e. with an income elasticity of about 0.4 (Kristöm and Riera, 1996). Separate studies of environmental pollution cases corroborate this general finding (Carson *et al.*, 1997; Flores and Carson, 1997; Sipes and Mendelsohn, 2001). Since demand for pollution abatement policies appear to be quite income-inelastic (at least beyond a certain threshold), it will increase with income, but to a lower extent than often assumed.

Poor people, especially rural poor people, are often the most directly dependent on their environment and its resources, and the most vulnerable to its degradation. Such people do not need to become richer to become concerned about the environment. Of course, it is not our intention to argue for keeping poor people poor. Decent income is certainly a determining factor of quality of life. However, the argument that higher income is a precondition for higher environmental awareness and concern does not hold. The fact that the poor do not show much willingness to pay often simply reflects a lack of ability to pay for, rather than a lack of interest in, environmental protection. In fact, especially where their survival may be at stake, many low-income societies have evolved both conserving and sustainable patterns of use of the resource on which they depend. Such patterns depend on these societies preserving their control over the resources in question, yet they may have little capability to defend them against outside expropriation. In some cases where external agents degraded poor people's environments, such people became environmental activists. You will find references to discussions of such cases in the Further Reading section.

Income does not always appear to be the main determinant for environmental legislation. Education and possibilities for organising are probably good alternative candidates. The mechanism of getting richer as stimulation for people to look for environmental improvement works for some situations, but not for others. In general, it is neither necessary nor sufficient. As we noted in Chapter 7, the EKC hypothesis appears to hold where localised problems are concerned, but not for global problems.

12.3.1.3 *International trade and the transfer of cleaner technology*

International trade leads to the diffusion of new technologies in several ways. Technologies are embodied in traded products and services, and can also be transferred

**Figure 12.4
Diving through
the EKC.**

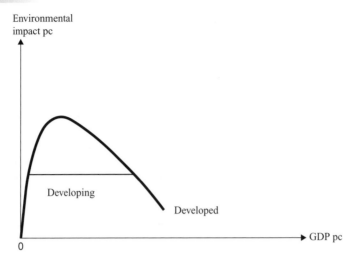

via foreign investment and trade in education. The diffusion of technology means that economic latecomers can have lower levels of materials and energy inputs per unit of GDP than older industrialised countries did at the same stage of development in terms of GDP per capita. Some authors have suggested that this might allow developing countries to 'dive through' the EKC. The basic idea is shown in Figure 12.4. The heavy curve shows an EKC relationship as experienced historically by what is now a developed country. For a developing country, technology transfer from the developed world could cut off the upper part of the EKC relationship, as shown by the lighter horizontal line. With regard to this technique effect there are different classes of the transfer and diffusion of technologies for more efficient resource use, substitutions between resources, and containment of wastes. Examples can be found in car manufacturing. Germany developed efficient Volkswagen cars, which were then produced in Brazil (more efficient resource use). Daimler Benz has replaced synthetic fibres for making seats and mats by coconut fibres and latex (substitution between resources). The legal requirement for manufacturers in Europe to take back a car after its use has led to production techniques which contribute to the containment of wastes and this will ultimately be also beneficial for reducing wastes in the South. However, it needs to be noted that many alternatives have secondary environmental effects. When appraising benefits from advances in technology one must always incorporate these secondary effects into an environmental assessment.

12.3.1.4 Environmental policy learning and benchmarking

National governments learn about how to solve environmental problems from their own experience. At the same time they are looking for best practice, observing other governments. Successful environmental policy innovations by one government – institutions, instruments, strategies – are thus often adopted by other governments. This improvement by imitation is an important mechanism of global environmental

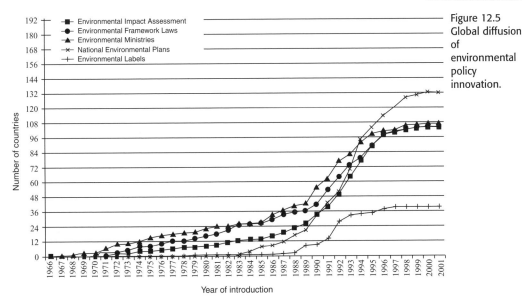

Figure 12.5
Global diffusion of environmental policy innovation.

Source: Busch and Jörgens 2002, after Jänicke 2002, p. 4.

policy development and policy convergence. International institutions such as the OECD or UNEP play an important role as policy arenas for pioneers and as agents of diffusion for environmental policy innovations. This role seems to be more important than the creation of policy innovations by the international institutions themselves. Figure 12.5 shows some examples of the diffusion of environmental policy innovations – such as environmental ministries or green plans – from pioneer countries to the rest of the world. The speed of diffusion increased in the 1990s, which may imply capacity building at the national level. An example is the so-called 'California Effect' in the US. After the passage of the US 1970 Clean Air Act Amendments, California repeatedly adopted stricter emissions standards than other US states. Instead of a flight of investment and jobs from California, however, other states began adopting similar, tougher emissions standards. A self-reinforcing 'race to the top' was thus put in place in which California helped lift standards throughout the US. Vogel (1995) attributes this largely to the 'lure of green markets' – car manufacturers were willing to meet California's higher standards to avoid losing such a large market and once they had met the standard in one state, they could easily meet it in every state.

The globalisation of environmental policy has changed the conditions of the world market. Regulatory imitation in regard to the environment often creates first-mover advantages for national economies. This is an advantage which one economy has by virtue of having been one of the first to introduce a policy, which then stimulates domestic firms to develop new technologies which can be the basis for exports when other countries adopt similar policies (e.g. wind turbines, to substitute for fossil fuel combustion, in Denmark and Germany). First movers risk making some domestic industry uncompetitive, but in practice this risk is often not great because the cost of meeting standards is low.

12.3.2 Negative consequences of international trade

Having looked at ways in which it can be argued that international trade can have positive implications for poverty and environmental protection, we now move on to look at arguments in the opposite direction. We look first at arguments concerning the environment, then at arguments to the effect that trade perpetuates poverty in some developing countries.

12.3.2.1 Environmental spillovers

The economics literature distinguishes three different types of situation in regard to trade and the environment. While in all three types the production of goods and services crosses national frontiers, in terms of the crossing of national frontiers by environmental impacts they differ. These environmental impacts may arise from either production or consumption activity. The different types give rise to different kinds of policy issues. In Type I situations environmental impacts do not cross national frontiers – there are no spillovers. In Type II situations, unidirectional spillovers, the impact flow is one way – an activity taking place in *A* gives rise to damage in *B* but not in *A*, or vice versa. In Type III situations, reciprocal spillovers, the impacts flow two ways – activity in *A* causes damage in *A* and *B*, and activity in *B* causes damage in *A* and *B*. In Type II and III situations, the damage inflicted on the other party is incidental to domestic production and/or consumption and is unintended. Following the terminology introduced in Chapter 9, these situations are also known as unidirectional and reciprocal external effects, or externalities, respectively. Clearly, more than one other country could suffer the cross-border environmental damage – having just one keeps the discussion of the basic ideas simple.

Type I situations are what we looked at back in section 12.1.5. In such situations the basic question is whether domestic environmental policy should be adopted to deal with the domestic environmental problem. The question has a trade dimension in so far as unilateral action to protect the environment is held to imply adverse effects on the country's trade situation. As we saw, acting unilaterally to protect the domestic environment does have trade implications, but whether or not they are sufficient to mean that the action is not justified on allocative efficiency criteria depends on the circumstances of the case.

In Type II situations the basic questions are about the appropriate way for the nation suffering the damage to seek to protect its environment, given that it cannot use domestic environmental policy. Where some activity in *A* is causing damage in *B*, but not in *A*, the situation between the nations is analogous to that of the two firms considered in standard expositions of the Coase Theorem (see Chapter 9). If a supranational environmental protection agency existed, it could assign a property right to either *A* or *B*, who could then bargain an improvement over the situation of no property rights. On one assignment *A* would offer *B* compensation, on the other *B* would offer *A* inducements to curtail the level of its damaging activity. In the former case the 'polluter pays' principle would be operative. In the latter case, the 'victim pays' principle applies. This is the operative principle in the absence of any supranational agency with property rights granting powers. Given no damage arising in A, A otherwise has no incentive to introduce policies to curtail the damage occurring in B. The prospect of conditional payment from B would create such an incentive.

Suppose A exports to B the commodity X, the production of which gives rise to the damage experienced in B. Then prohibition by B of imports of X from A is sometimes argued as the way to deal with the unidirectional spillover arising. For example, environmentalists in a number of industrial countries have called for bans on the import of tropical timber in order to reduce the rate of forest clearance in tropical countries, with a view to halting biodiversity losses there. The effectiveness of such an approach is generally questionable. First, import bans would be a second-best policy in that they would involve forgoing some of the gains from trade. Bribery, on the other hand, could in principle be tailored so as to retain the gains from trade while limiting the damage. Thus, in the logging case, B's payment to A could be conditional on the observance of logging practices that minimise environmental damage. Second, it will not generally be the case that B is the only destination to which A exports X. If there are many nations importing X from A, an import ban by B alone will be ineffective, and securing general agreement to ban imports may be difficult.

Where, as in the case of acid rain for example, the damage arising in B is not due to a single identifiable production activity in A, the possibility of this kind of import ban does not exist. A problem which arises with bribery is that of monitoring compliance. In the case of payment for following less damaging logging practices, for example, B would need to prescribe the nature of those practices and to be assured that the prescriptions were being followed. It could be argued in favour of import bans that, where feasible and effective, they avoid monitoring problems in that, for example, there is a direct reduction in the quantity of timber felled.

The prime example of a Type III situation is the role of carbon dioxide emissions in the enhanced greenhouse effect. All countries burn fossil fuels, releasing carbon dioxide into the atmosphere, where all emissions mix globally. The climate-relevant parameter is the global atmospheric concentration of carbon dioxide in the upper atmosphere. The origin of any particular molecule of carbon dioxide is irrelevant to its role in the world climate system. Driven by increasing rates of fossil fuel combustion, global carbon dioxide concentrations are increasing, which causes changes in temperatures around the world and more extreme weather events. All nations are involved in driving up atmospheric carbon dioxide concentrations: all nations would experience climate change and its consequences.

In Type III situations the essential issue is seen as the incentive structure facing nations in regard to action to reduce environmental damage. Basically the problem with reciprocal externality situations is that in the absence of an effective and credible international agreement that all will act, each nation's self-interest would lead it to try to free ride on the efforts of other nations to reduce the environmental damage. We will leave explaining this until section 13.2.1 in the next chapter.

12.3.2.2 *Internationalisation of market failure*

Trade can export market failure as well as goods and services. Suppose country A produces corn more cheaply than country B, but in doing so generates more pollution. In the absence of countervailing policies, trade liberalisation will cause production to shift from country *B* to country *A*, with a corresponding increase in pollution and its external costs. Similarly, if producers in country *B* generate higher positive externalities than those in country *A* – for example, via the conservation of crop genetic diversity – trade liberalisation will erode the supply of these benefits. Whether the social gains from trade liberalisation will exceed the social losses from the attendant market failures is an empirical question, one which cannot be answered by theoretical inquiry – as is often the case. What it can do is set out the possibilities and highlight the key issues.

Boyce (2002) explores two actual cases which illustrate what is involved here:

(1)   the displacement of natural fibres by synthetic substitutes, resulting from competition in which the higher pollution costs associated with the latter are not internalised in world prices; illustrated by the competition between jute and polypropylene;

(2)   erosion of crop genetic diversity, arising from the fact that markets do not reward farmers for their provision of this public good.

Another concern relates to environmental regulation. It has been argued that international competition for investment could cause countries to lower environmental regulations (or to retain poor ones), leading to a 'race to the bottom' in environmental standards as countries fight to attract foreign capital and keep domestic investment at home. In fact, lower environmental standards do not appear to encourage industrial mobility between countries. The empirical evidence seems to show that it has not happened in the past and many economists consider that it is unlikely to happen in the future. Basically, the reason is that the costs of compliance with environmental standards are not high – in the developed countries of the North it has been estimated that typically they are less than 3 per cent of total costs. Factors such as labour and raw material costs, transparent regulation and protection of property rights are likely to be much more important, even for polluting industries. On the other hand, using differences in standards to attract international capital may not be a good strategy because, if it works, it may generate strong local resistance due to deterioration in the quality of life.

Overseas investors may prefer to adopt standards from the headquarter-country to homogenise procedures, and also to avoid local and international legal suits and the possible cost of complying with subsequent changes in the local environmental legislation. Most multinational companies adopt near-uniform standards globally, often well above the local government-set standards. Indeed, foreign-owned plants in developing countries, precisely the ones that according to the theory would be most attracted by low standards, tend to be less polluting than indigenous plants in the same industry. This suggests that they relocate plants to developing countries for reasons other than low environmental standards. While it is widely accepted that 'the race to the bottom' is largely fictional, Zarsky (2002) argues that the primary impact of globalisation is to keep environmental policy initiatives 'stuck in the mud' by which she means that it will be very difficult for governments to introduce new environmental policies. Reforms of environmental regulations are held back by the potential for relocation, which makes policy makers hesitant to implement major shifts to environmental policy.

12.3.2.3 Unequal exchange

In the discussion of trade and the environment at multilateral forums such as the United Nations Conference on Trade and Development (UNCTAD) and the World Trade Organization (on which see below) it is often assumed that negative externalities are more prevalent in the developing countries of the South, while in the North, tougher regulations have led to a greater internalisation of environmental costs. The threat of 'ecological dumping' – exports at prices below the full cost of production, including the social costs of pollution – is therefore viewed primarily as a route by which Southern producers may win markets at the expense of their Northern competitors. The two cases discussed in Boyce (2002) cited above illustrate the opposite possibility: international trade can result in the displacement of relatively clean and sustainable Southern production by environmentally more costly and less sustainable Northern production. Indeed, if one reflects on the history of international commerce since the Industrial Revolution, it is arguable that the main direction of environmental dumping has been from the North to the South. Southern governments have been slow to call for policies that would help them to translate the comparative environmental advantage of their farmers into comparative economic advantages.

Recent trends in volumes and prices for some raw materials may also indicate transference of environmental costs from North to South. In a study of the percentage change between 1971 and 1976 and 1991 and 1996 in the imports (total weight and averaged price) of the US, Japan, France, Italy, Germany, Netherlands, Spain, Sweden, Denmark, UK and Ireland of non-renewable materials coming from developing countries, Muradian and Martinez-Alier (2001) find that physical de-linking between economic growth in the North and non-renewable resources imported from the South is not taking place. They also find that prices for most of these products have gone down considerably in those twenty years. Table 12.2 shows some of their results. One hundred per cent of change means an increase by a factor of 2. These data suggest that the North's economic growth goes together with: (a) increasing consumption of non-renewable resources coming from developing countries; and (b) worsening terms of trade for exporting countries specialised in non-renewable resources. Oversupply, rather than decreasing demand, is likely the principal cause of price deterioration and probably it is the result of the 'specialisation

Table 12.2 Change in South–North non-renewable resources flows and prices between 1971–1976 and 1991–1996

Item	% change	
	Weight	*Price (US$ 1987)*
Aluminium	660	−12
Pig iron	306	−26
Iron and steel shapes	238	−31
Petroleum products	230	−21
Nickel (alloys)	196	−22
Gas, natural and manufactured	128	10
Zinc	87	−35
Copper ores	70	−52
Copper (alloys)	32	−35
Bauxite	30	71
Tin (alloys)	12	−63
Lead	9	−46
Zinc ores	8	−45
Nickel ores	−3	−46
Iron ores	−10	−32
Lead ores	−10	−34
Crude petroleum	−12	10
Fertilisers	−51	−17
Tin ores	−97	22

Source: Muradian and Martinez-Alier (2001), p. 289.

trap'. As discussed in relation to the 'Dutch disease', when specialisation means 'de-industralisation' and the expansion of natural resources exports, the exploitation of comparative advantages may in the long term exacerbate the already large gap between rich and poor regions of the world.

Environmental problems associated with trade in or export of natural resources include habitat destruction (especially deforestation), species loss, land, water and air pollution, and promotion of human diseases. Worsening terms of trade prevent internalisation of these environmental externalities due to the costs involved. If international conditions determining prices make the South less able to internalise externalities, then there is a transfer of wealth from poor countries to rich countries. This mechanism has been called unequal (ecological) exchange (Martinez-Alier, 1993; Hornborg, 1998). By this is meant that the North is transferring environmental costs, in the form of reductions of natural capital, to the South, at the same time as the terms of trade are moving against the South. For an empirical perspective by use of input–output analysis see Further Reading.

12.4 INSTITUTIONS REGULATING INTERNATIONAL TRADE

Over the last few decades international institutions have been built up to regulate and promote international trade and to deal with environmental problems that cross national frontiers. With the increasing integration of world markets comes a corresponding need for international policy responses to market failures. Unilateral measures by individual governments can have only limited impacts on trade-related and trade-driven market failures.

12.4.1 Trade measures – WTO rules

The **World Trade Organization** (WTO) is a global international organisation that specifies and enforces rules for the conduct of international trade policies and serves as a forum for negotiations to reduce barriers to trade. It was founded in 1995 to replace the **General Agreement on Tariffs and Trade** (GATT), which had existed since 1948. The key difference between the WTO and the GATT is that the WTO is a permanent organisation with judicial powers to rule on international trade disputes. The WTO also covers trade in services, whereas GATT only covered trade in goods. The WTO aims to lower tariffs and non-tariff barriers so as to increase international trade. The 146 member states meet in ministerial sessions at least once every two years. Non-governmental organisations (NGOs) and poor countries fear that further liberalisation of trade will only benefit rich countries. Critics claim that WTO negotiations tend to favour the interests of investors and neglect agricultural protectionism by rich countries. Critics also often make the charge that the WTO functions undemocratically and that it has opaque negotiation procedures that harm the interests of the poor.

At its centre, the GATT–WTO regime is a multilateral institution that exists to promote the liberalisation of global trade. The GATT–WTO regime seeks to promote a common set of international trade rules, a reduction in tariffs and other barriers to trade, and the elimination of discriminatory treatment in international trade relations. The GATT–WTO regime also attempts to provide an effective dispute resolution system to facilitate the settlement of trade disputes among its member nations.

In general, the GATT–WTO regime does not impose an affirmative requirement that members (and their domestic regulatory regimes) meet a minimum baseline standard of compliance with its goals. The GATT–WTO regime accomplishes many of these goals primarily through the use of 'negative' obligations. This means that instead of requiring actions, it regulates what member countries cannot do in relation to international trade. Additionally, the liberalised trade regime does not establish minimum benchmark levels for individual member protection of the environment and public health. Instead, the GATT–WTO regime seeks to distinguish national standards adopted for legitimate health and environment purposes from those regulatory standards enacted to promote protectionism.

If a regulatory standard is deemed inconsistent with the GATT–WTO regime, a 'negative' obligation to remove or correct the offending measure is imposed on the member. The core principles of the GATT–WTO regime are reflected in the original GATT 1947 text. Article I of GATT 1947 establishes the Most-Favoured-Nation principle (MFN), and aims to ensure that each member grant any privilege or advantage it provides to a product from one member immediately and unconditionally to like products from, or destined for, all GATT–WTO members. MFN effectively requires all members to treat products from all other members in the same manner. Article III establishes the national treatment principle and requires members to treat any imported 'like product' in the same manner as they would treat domestic 'like products'. National treatment is designed to prevent the discrimination against imported products in order to secure market advantages for domestic products. Article XI establishes a prohibition on quantitative restrictions and seeks to prohibit such trade actions as quotas, embargoes and licensing schemes on imported or exported products.

If a GATT–WTO member is challenged with violating any of the above obligations, the member has recourse to the GATT 1947 Article XX on General Exceptions. Article XX only permits exceptions when it can be shown that the 'measures are not applied in a manner which would constitute a means of arbitrary or unjustifiable discrimination between countries where the same conditions prevail, or a disguised restriction on international trade'. Clauses (b) and (g) of Article XX are the exceptions most frequently cited in trade disputes that involve the environment and natural resources. Articles XX(b) and XX(g) do not apply to all measures taken to protect the environment. Rather, Article XX exceptions are only applicable when a violation of a general obligation of the GATT–WTO regime is alleged to have occurred. Article XX(b) allows members to take measures 'necessary to protect human, animal or plant life or health.' Article XX(g) allows measures 'relating to the conservation of exhaustible natural resources if such measures are made effective in conjunction with restrictions on domestic production or consumption'. Article XX also allows exceptions from the GATT–WTO general obligations to, among other things, protect public morals, distinguish products manufactured with prison labour, exclude commodity agreements that meet certain criteria, and meet emergency shortages of supplies.

The WTO Agreement on Technical Barriers to Trade (TBT Agreement) seeks to ensure that the non-discrimination and national treatment provisions of the GATT–WTO regime as a whole are specifically applied to the adoption of technical regulations by members. The TBT Agreement emphasises deference to international standards in the creation of regulations governing, among others, product characteristics, process and production methods, labelling and packaging.

When a trade dispute does arise between members, the WTO Understanding on Rules and Procedures Governing the Settlement of Disputes (DSU) encourages members to enter into informal negotiations in an effort to reach a mutually agreed solution. If a resolution of the matter is not forthcoming, a challenging member invoking the dispute settlement procedures is entitled to a *prima facie* assumption that the measure being challenged is inconsistent with the GATT–WTO regime. The burden of proof to rebut the charge is on the defendant member. A complaining party may request the appointment of a panel to settle the disagreement. The panel hearings are between governments and are generally closed to the public and non-governmental organisations (NGOs). Panel reports are adopted within sixty days of their issuance unless a member initiates an appeal or it is the consensus of the other members not to adopt the report. If a member chooses to ignore the recommendations of a panel, the complaining member may seek compensation in the area of trade directly related to the dispute or, if necessary, may cross-retaliate in another trade sector.

Work on trade and environment at the WTO takes place in the Committee on Trade and Environment (CTE), which was established in January 1995. The Committee is charged with two primary duties: to identify the relationship between trade measures and environmental measures, and to make appropriate recommendations on whether any modifications of the provisions of the multilateral trading system are required for environmental reasons.

During negotiations at the Fourth WTO Ministerial Meeting in Doha, Qatar, in 2001 members agreed upon a negotiating agenda that includes several issues relevant to the environment. Members have started to address the relationship between the WTO and Multilateral Environmental Agreements (MEA), which are discussed below; clarify procedures for regular interaction between the WTO and MEA secretariats; and trade liberalisation for environmental goods and services. Members also decided to begin discussing the environmental aspects of fisheries subsidies, product labelling and intellectual property rights. The CTE has commenced a process which involves sector-by-sector Secretariat briefings on the environmental aspects of the negotiations. A negotiation covering so many issues and involving so many members will always be difficult, and it is to be expected that progress in the early stages will be slow, as members define their interests and reach an understanding of the issues at stake and the positions of other members. A concerted effort must now be made to identify positive linkages and trade-offs between and within sectors and move all areas of the negotiations forward together to reach a balanced overall outcome by 1 January 2005.

The WTO's Fifth Ministerial Conference was held in Cancún, Mexico from 10 to 14 September 2003. Disagreements about agricultural subsidies in the North and suggested new liberalisation regulations in the areas of investment, competition and public purchasing were unacceptable for countries in the South. No agreement was reached.

WTO rules expressly permit countries to take actions to protect human, animal or plant life or health, and to conserve exhaustible natural resources. However, such restrictions must pursue legitimate environmental objectives, and not be a disguised form of trade protectionism. A good example is the US prohibition of imports of tuna and tuna products from Canada. In 1981 Canada had seized 19 US tuna fishing vessels and arrested their fishermen in waters that it considered to be within its sole jurisdiction. The US disputed Canada's jurisdiction claims and imposed a ban on imports of tuna and tuna products from Canada in retaliation. The US argued before the GATT panel that the prohibition was undertaken 'in order to avoid and deter threats to the international management approach which the United States considered essential to conservation of the world's tuna stocks' and therefore justified under Article XX(g). The panel decided that the US import ban fell within the preamble of Article XX. But it noted that the US import prohibition was not 'made effective in conjunction with restrictions on domestic production or consumption' as required by Article XX(g). Also the import restriction was evidently imposed in retaliation for the arrest of US fishing vessels and therefore could not 'in itself constitute a measure of a type listed in Article XX'. As a result the panel ruled that the US import prohibition was inconsistent with GATT. References for more examples are listed in the Further Reading section.

12.4.2 Multilateral Environmental Agreements

It is widely recognised that environmental regulation is better accomplished multilaterally rather than through numerous bilateral agreements. To this end, at the WCED in 1992, conference participants endorsed what are now commonly known as **Multilateral Environmental Agreements** (MEA). They are voluntary commitments among several or many sovereign nations that seek to address the effects and consequences of global and regional environmental degradation. MEA address environmental problems with transboundary effects, traditionally domestic environmental issues that raise extra-jurisdictional concerns, and environmental risks to the global commons. International agreements to protect human health and the environment have used trade measures in varying forms since the 1870s.

According to the WTO, out of over 200 MEA in existence only twenty-two concern trade. Of these trade-relevant MEA, thirteen are global agreements and nine are regional. It needs to be noted that some MEAs have more parties than does the WTO. For example, the **Convention on International Trade in Endangered Species of Wild Fauna and Flora** (CITES) has 152 parties, the **Montreal Protocol** 175, the **Basle Convention** 147, the **Convention on Biological Diversity** (CBD) 168, and the UN Framework Convention on Climate Change (UNFCCC) has 176, compared to the 141 nations that are party to the WTO. In addition, a number of other MEA have been negotiated that will have trade implications when they go into effect. Major pending agreements include the **Cartagena Protocol on Biosafety**, the Kyoto Protocol, the Rotterdam Convention on the Prior Informed Consent Procedure for Certain Hazardous Chemicals and Pesticides in International Trade, and the Persistent Organic Pollutants Convention.

Because MEA and WTO trade agreements address many of the same issues and concerns from different perspectives, occasional conflict between the two must be mitigated in some way to ease controversy for future environmental regulations. The resolution of the interface problem between MEA and the WTO was cited as a key negotiating issue and mandated as a topic of discussion in paragraph 31(i) of the **Doha Declaration** document agreed upon by the trade ministers of the member countries of the WTO at the Doha Ministerial meeting, initiating negotioations on a wide range of subjects, particularly the interests of developing countries. Just how to reconcile the two remains to be decided.

No WTO member has ever challenged any trade measure that another WTO member has undertaken in compliance with an MEA – no case law and binding interpretations exist – but clearly potential for conflict exists. Most MEAs with explicitly mandated or permitted trade provisions restrict trade between parties and non-parties or even trade between parties. These restrictions might violate the general most-favoured-nation treatment obligation in the GATT Article 1. If these restrictions take the form of import or export bans, export certificates or access restrictions rather than duties, taxes or other charges, they might violate the general elimination of quantitative restrictions obligations in GATT Article XI.

This means that in some ways trade measures in MEA and WTO need to be reconciled. There are several options to do this: temporary waiver, interpretative statement or amendment of GATT. The latter is the most far-reaching and needs a two-thirds majority of the WTO membership. An example would be the introduction of a sustainability clause which would set out agreed principles of environmental policy, such as the 'polluter pays' principle and the precautionary principle, against which trade measures can be judged. The sustainability clause would mitigate but not solve the conflict. The Agreement establishing the WTO already contains a commitment to sustainable development in the preamble.

Hudec (1996) proposed a new exception to Article XX, which would introduce a two-tier approach modelled on the existing Article XX(h), which excepts international commodity agreements. According to this proposal, in its first part such a new exception would lay down pre-specified criteria as to the substance, structure and negotiating procedure that an MEA would need to fulfil to qualify for the exception. In its second part, the new exception would allow the submission of any MEA to WTO members for approval and the granting of the exceptional status, which would be possible whether or not the criteria in the exception's first part were met or not.

This could take the form of either an environmental side agreement or a simple MEA exception clause in a renegotiated GATT. Against such a proposal, Caldwell (1994) raises the fear that an MEA exception clause might reinforce the perception, particularly on the part of the environmental community, that the GATT and the goals of liberalised trade it represents have priority over all other concerns.

12.5 TOWARDS TRADE RULES FOR SUSTAINABILITY

The WTO claims that:

> Elimination of barriers to merchandise trade in both industrialized and developing countries, in which the Doha Development Agenda will be vital, could result in welfare gains ranging from US$250 billion to US$620 billion annually, of which about one third to one half would accrue to developing countries. Removal of agricultural

supports would raise global economic welfare by a further US$128 billion annually, with some US$30 billion to developing countries. The more rapid growth associated with a global reduction in protection could reduce the number of people living in poverty by as much as 13 per cent by 2015. Trade liberalization and poverty reduction go hand in hand. (WTO Annual Report, 2003)

For ecological economists international trade is potentially better than autarky, but whether this is actually so in any particular case depends on the conditions prevalent. As one of them puts it:

> Trade is not necessarily regarded as something inherently good, something that should be defended in all cases. Therefore, it is not appropriate to pose the problem as a conflict between interests in preserving the trading system on the one hand and environmental concerns on the other. Instead, it is a more open question as to what are the relations between trade and the environment. (Røpke, 1994:14)

Neoclassical and ecological economists agree on the existence of externalities, but whereas neoclassical economists tend to regard them as somewhat exceptional, ecological economists consider them to be pervasive. It is useful to distinguish between competitive advantage and comparative advantage. The former refers to advantage at existing market prices, which, generally, are not corrected for external costs. The latter refers to what would be the case if prices properly reflected all costs including external costs. Unfortunately, in much of the economics literature these two terms are used interchangeably. They should not be. In practice external costs are not generally internalised and the pattern of trade based on competitive advantage is not what it would be if based on comparative advantage, and the former must be presumed to involve more environmental damage than would the latter.

Ecological economists maintain that trade has beneficial effects for sustainability only if it occurs within an institutional framework that explicitly accounts for the natural capital on which social and economic development depend. Without this framework, it is more likely that the increased pressures for resource exploitation that arise from free trade will exacerbate environmental problems. Trade increases the need for taking account of resource depletion and environmental damage in production and consumption decisions. This requires that environmental policy operates at the level where the problem occurs – global, regional, national and/or local.

To this end several suggestions for amendments of GATT–WTO rules have been made. They include:

1. implementation of countervailing duties on countries with more lenient environmental regulations (the lax standard could be seen as an unfair subsidy); a 'countervailing' duty is an extra duty on subsidised imports that are found to be hurting domestic producers;
2. implementation of domestic subsidies for environmental control cost; allowing governments to subsidise pollution-abatement equipment to avoid competitive disadvantage of the industry (under current rules this may lead to charges of unfair export subsidies);
3. distinguishing not only by product characteristics, but also by production processes according to their impact on essential ecological functions.

To realise these measures in a transparent, open and non-protectionist manner, the following means have been suggested:

- Product life cycle analysis: quantification of the cumulative impacts generated by a product from the point where materials are extracted from the earth to the final disposal of the remaining wastes back into the earth. For imported products (product regulation) the 'border to grave' portion of the life cycle information is considered, and for products produced nationally (process regulation) the relevant part is the portion concerning 'cradle to border'. Using such a physical inventory system, countries could agree upon the actual size of countervailing measures to be introduced for various products. For the cases where countries could not agree on actual measures, the physical inventory could alternatively form the basis of a more consumer-oriented regulatory system, such as eco-labelling as discussed in the previous chapter. However, considerable problems exist as the administrative demand would be high and there are in general no truly unambiguous criteria for comparing physical emissions in different countries. Process regulations are not allowed under current WTO rules.

- Balancing disparities in environmental expenditures on a cost basis: in order to allow a national government to determine its environmental quality levels independently of trade considerations, it should be allowed to shelter domestic production from foreign 'environmental competition' by charging import levies according to the size of the control cost differences. A country could also be allowed to subsidise exports in the same way. Setting domestic environmental quality targets would still involve decisions about how much of the nation's inputs to devote to such objectives, but there would be no trade effects to worry about when making such decisions, as there is under the current regulatory framework. This could be achieved by changes of Articles III and XVI of GATT. The attribution of environmental costs remains a problem. It might be practical to distinguish for this measure between global, regional and local environmental externalities. It would be mostly the latter which could be dealt with by the product life cycle analysis measure suggested above. For regional and global externalities international cooperation is indispensable.

- Ecologically accelerated trade liberalisation agreements: a separate 'Code on process standards and environmental agreements' could be prepared. It would express the nature of trade-related environment provisions consistent with GATT, and would establish a mechanism for agreement between international trade policy and international environmental policy. Thereby, the trade-influencing dimensions of international agreements on the environment would become more transparent. The abuse of trade measures to achieve environmental objectives and vice versa would become harder. To make it an innovation-friendly and acceptable framework, the 'ecologically accelerated trade liberalisation agreements' would need to:

  (a)   give tariff-free and quota-free access to all products produced in a manner consistent with the agreement, which, for example, might require full application of the 'polluter pays' principle;

(b)   be restricted to production processes that involve the use of CFCs, the production of CO_2 and other similar substances that have (or might have) a significant adverse impact on global environments,

(c)   have open membership and be signed by at least three countries,

(d)   be valid only if it can be shown that, consistent with the agreement, at least one firm is obtaining tariff-free and quota-free access to the markets of a participating country, and

(e)   entitle any country or firm whose resource and environmental practices are consistent with the agreement to obtain tariff-free and quota-free access for all agreement-consistent products including related value-added products. (Steininger, 1994)

In addition to such proposals, there are changes to WTO procedures which would help to harmonise its workings with the requirements of sustainable development, such as increased openness to outside, non-governmental, views during the dispute-settlement process, and consultation with environmental scientists if environmental problems are involved. To conclude here, since the economy is embedded in both the social and biophysical systems, instead of the uniform liberalisation of trade on the basis of competitive advantage, what is needed is a trading framework which, while multilateral, non-discriminatory, rule-based and global, promotes open markets for trade on the basis of true comparative advantage.

12.6 GLOBALISATION

So far we have talked about internationalisation, which refers to the increasing interrelationship of nations in terms of international trade. This is only one aspect of the more fundamental process of globalisation, which also includes the growth and extended reach of multinational corporations and greatly increased international interaction between civil society organisations. Globalisation is a process (or a set of processes) which embodies a transformation in the spatial organisation of social relations and transactions, generating transcontinental or interregional flows and networks of activity, interaction and power (Giddens, 1990).

Globalisation is characterised by four types of change:

- First, it involves a *stretching* of social, political and economic activities across political frontiers, regions and continents.
- Second, it suggests the *intensification*, or the growing magnitude, of interconnectedness and flows of trade, investment, finance, migration, culture, etc.
- Third, the growing extent and intensity of global interconnectedness can be linked to a *speeding up* of global interactions and processes, as the evolution of worldwide systems of transport and communication increases the velocity of the diffusion of ideas, goods, information, capital and people.
- Fourth, the growing extent, intensity and velocity of global interactions can be associated with their *deepening* impact such that the effects of distant events can be highly significant elsewhere, and even the most local developments may come to have enormous global consequences. In this sense, the boundaries between domestic matters and global affairs can become increasingly blurred. (Held *et al.*, 1999)

In response to these developments, in 1998 the UN Committee on Economic Social and Cultural Rights issued a 'Statement on Globalization'. It stated that 'if not complemented by appropriate additional policies, globalization risks downgrading the central place accorded to human rights by the Charter of the United Nations in general and the International Bill of Human Rights in particular'. As market activities become more international, so must be their regulation. In section 12.4 we discussed some of the institutions that have been implemented over the last few decades for this purpose.

More specifically the Statement on Globalisation asks for the following changes:

> The Committee calls upon the International Monetary Fund and the World Bank to pay enhanced attention in their activities to respect for economic, social and cultural rights, including through encouraging explicit recognition of these rights, assisting in the identification of country-specific benchmarks to facilitate their promotion, and facilitating the development of appropriate remedies for responding to violations. Social safety nets should be established by reference to these rights and enhanced attention should be accorded to such methods of protecting the poor and vulnerable in the context of structural adjustment programs. Effective social monitoring should be an integral part of the enhanced financial surveillance and monitoring policies accompanying loans and credits for adjustment purposes. Similarly the World Trade Organization should devise appropriate methods to facilitate more systematic consideration of the impact upon human rights of particular trade and investment policies. (Committee on Economic, Social and Cultural Rights, 1998)

In sum, this statement highlights the urgent need for regulation of global economic activities in order to reduce their negative consequences. The UN Committee does not call for stopping globalisation, but it suggests the need for a different type of globalisation, one which is carefully shaped by the democratic institutions of the countries involved and by international organisations. This plea is necessary because the intensified and deepened economic relationships risk coinciding with insufficient feedback on the environmental and social consequences caused. Globalisation prolongs the apparent illusion of unlimited environmental sources and sinks on the part of many decision makers, and postpones the shift from an 'empty-world' (or cowboy in the terminology of Box 2.2) view of economics to a 'full-world' (or spaceman) perspective that all must eventually make if sustainable development is to be realised.

12.6.1 Role of transnational and multinational corporations

Transnational corporations (TNCs) are large companies that conduct their business operations in several states. The primary defining factor for TNCs is that they keep their financial headquarters offshore to protect themselves from taxes. Thereby, they lack financial accountability to the states in which they conduct their primary operations. Although multinational corporations (MNCs) are often considered synonymous with TNCs, they are in fact a particular class of TNC. A pure MNC would truly be global in nature: operating across borders with no predominant relationship to a particular country. However, this is rarely the case. Generally, TNCs are controlled by a parent company, typically located in the developed world, through which they conduct the bulk of their research and to which they repatriate profits.

After years of expansion, the foreign operations of the top 50 non-financial TNCs worldwide (as measured by foreign assets, sales and employment) stagnated in 2001 as shown in Table 12.3 below. Despite the bursting of the information and communication technology bubble, the industrial composition of the top 50 did not change significantly compared to earlier years. Petroleum and automobile companies remain high on the list. In general, the top 50 span a wide range of industries covering all major sectors. Owing to privatisation programmes in many developed and developing countries, the list has in recent years included an increasing number of TNCs involved in telecommunications and utilities. Most TNCs are headquartered in the United States, the European Union or Japan: the so-called Triad, which also accounts for the largest share of foreign direct investment worldwide. The United States is home to the largest number of TNCs (11), followed by France (8), Germany (8), the United Kingdom (7) and Japan (4). The list also includes numerous TNCs from smaller countries such as Switzerland, Finland and the Netherlands, demonstrating that a large home market is not an indispensable precondition for the emergence of large TNCs. In recent years, the number of developing-country TNCs on the top-50 list has increased. In 2001, the list included four companies from developing countries – Hutchinson Whampoa, Singtel, Cemex and LG Electronics. This trend is expected to continue as companies from developing countries (especially in Asia) increasingly internationalise their operations, not just within the region but also worldwide.

A key concern with regard to TNCs is their mobile nature. In pursuit of low costs and high profits, they tend to establish subsidiaries in countries where conditions are most favourable to their business operations. However, circumstances change and TNCs can move their operations from one country to another. In their negotiations with the governments of potential host countries, their mobility provides them with a great deal of leverage over states looking to get the jobs they can provide. A TNC may be able to induce governments to compete with one another over the terms on offer to it, in regard to taxation and regulation.

Host governments do have some bargaining power, but, particularly in developing nations, where economies are often weak, the concerns of the host government over how the TNC operates in their country must often take a back seat and investment concerns are dominant. Therein lies the risk of exploitation. Some of these large corporations are more important economic actors than the states with which they negotiate.

TNCs are important vehicles for the movement of foreign direct investment (FDI). With FDI, a firm in one country creates or expands a subsidiary in another through the use of international capital flows. The distinctive feature of direct foreign investment is that it involves not only a transfer of resources but also the acquisition of control. That is, the subsidiary does not simply have a financial obligation to the parent company; it is part of the same organisation. Table 12.4 illustrates the increase of worldwide FDI until 2000 and its rapid decline in 2001 and 2002. In 2003 FDI recovered somewhat, but showed only moderate growth. FDI tends to be much more volatile than trade in merchandise or services. Cross-border mergers and acquisitions became significant during only the late 1980s. Sales of foreign affiliates increased more than six-fold within the two decades from 1982 to 2002.

Table 12.3 World's top 50 non-financial TNCs in 2001 (million US $ and number of employees)

	Corporation (home economy)	Industry	Foreign assets	assets	Total sales	employees
1	Vodafone (UK)	Telecommunications	187 792	207 458	32 744	67 178
2	General Electric (US)	Electrical and electronic equipment	180 031	495 210	125 913	310 000
3	BP (UK)	Petroleum expl./ref./distr.	111 207	141 158	175 389	110 150
4	Vivendi Universal (FR)	Diversified	91 120	123 156	51 423	381 504
5	Deutsche Telekom AG (GE)	Telecommunications	90 657	145 802	43 309	257 058
6	Exxonmobil Corporation (US)	Petroleum expl./ref./distr.	89 426	143 174	209 417	97 900
7	Ford Motor Company (US)	Motor vehicles	81 169	276 543	162 412	354 431
8	General Motors (US)	Motor vehicles	75 379	323 969	177 260	365 000
9	Royal Dutch/Shell Group (UK/NL)	Petroleum expl./ref./distr.	73 492	111 543	135 211	89 939
10	Total Fina Elf (FR)	Petroleum expl./ref./distr.	70 030	78 500	94 418	122 025
11	Suez (FR)	Electricity, gas and water	69 345	79 280	37 975	188 050
12	Toyota Motor Corporation (JP)	Motor vehicles	68 400	144 793	108 808	246 702
13	Fiat Spa (ITA)	Motor vehicles	48 749	89 264	52 002	198 764
14	Telefonica SA (SP)	Telecommunications	48 122	77 011	27 775	161 527
15	Volkswagen Group (GE)	Motor vehicles	47 480	92 520	79 376	324 413
16	ChevronTexaco Corp. (US)	Petroleum expl./ref./distr.	44 943	77 572	104 409	67 569
17	Hutchison Whampoa Ltd (HK)	Diversified	40 989	55 281	11 415	77 253
18	News Corporation (AUS)	Media	35 650	40 007	15 087	33 800
19	Honda Motor Co., Ltd (JP)	Motor vehicles	35 257	52 056	55 955	120 600
20	E.On (GE)	Electricity, gas and water	33 990	87 755	71 419	151 953
21	Nestlé SA (CH)	Food and beverages	33 065	55 821	50 717	229 765
22	RWE Group (GE)	Electricity, gas and water	32 809	81 024	58 039	155 634
23	IBM (US)	Electrical and electronic equipment	32 800	88 313	85 866	319 876
24	ABB (CH)	Machinery and equipment	30 586	32 305	19 382	156 865
25	Unilever (UK/NL)	Diversified	30 529	46 922	46 803	279 000
26	ENI Group (ITA)	Petroleum expl./ref./distr.	29 935	55 584	43 861	80 178
27	BMW AG (GE)	Motor vehicles	29 901	45 415	34 482	97 275
28	Philips Electronics (NL)	Electrical and electronic equipment	29 416	34 070	28 992	188 643
29	Carrefour SA (FR)	Retail	29 342	41 172	62 294	358 501
30	Electricité de France (FR)	Electricity, gas and water	28 141	120 124	36 502	162 491
31	Repsol YPF SA (SP)	Petroleum expl./ref./distr.	27 028	45 575	39 135	35 452
32	Sony Corporation (JP)	Electrical and electronic equipment	26 930	61 393	57 595	168 000
33	Aventis SA (FR)	Pharmaceuticals	26 368	34 761	20 567	91 729
34	Wal-Mart Stores (US)	Retail	26 324	83 451	217 799	1 383 000

(cont.)

Table 12.3 (cont.)

Corporation (home economy)	Industry	Foreign assets	assets	Total sales	employees
35 DaimlerChrysler AG (GE/US)	Motor vehicles	25 795	183 765	137 051	372 470
36 Lafarge SA (FR)	Construction materials	24 906	26 493	12 280	82 892
37 Nissan Motor Co., Ltd (JP)	Motor vehicles	24 382	54 113	47 091	125 099
38 AES Corporation (US)	Electricity, gas and water	23 902	36 736	9 327	38 000
39 Roche Group (CH)	Pharmaceuticals	22 794	25 289	17 463	63 717
40 BASF AG (GE)	Chemicals	20 872	32 671	29 136	92 545
41 Deutsche Post AG (GE)	Transport and storage	20 840	138 837	29 924	276 235
42 Bayer AG (GE)	Pharmaceuticals/chemicals	20 297	32 817	27 142	116 900
43 GlaxoSmithKline Plc (UK)	Pharmaceuticals	20 295	31 758	29 689	107 470
44 Royal Ahold NV (NL)	Retail	19 967	28 562	59 701	270 739
45 Compagnie de Saint-Gobain SA (FR)	Construction materials	19 961	28 478	27 245	173 329
46 BHP Billiton Group (AUS)	Mining and quarrying	19 898	29 552	17 778	51 037
47 Diageo Plc (UK)	Food and beverages	19 731	26 260	16 020	62 124
48 Conoco Inc. (US)	Petroleum expl./ref./distr.	19 383	27 904	38 737	20 033
49 Philip Morris Companies Inc. (US)	Diversified	19 339	84 968	89 924	175 000
50 National Grid Transco (UK)	Electricity, gas and water	19 080	24 839	6 308	13 236

Source: UNCTAD (2004).

Table 12.4 Selected indicators of FDI and international production, 1982–2002 ($ billion and %)

Item	Value at current prices ($ billion)			Annual growth rate (%)						
	1982	1990	2002	1986–1990	1991–1995	1996–2000	1999	2000	2001	2002
FDI inflows	59	209	651	23.1	21.1	40.2	57.3	29.1	−40.9	−21.0
FDI outflows	28	242	647	25.7	16.5	35.7	60.5	9.5	−40.8	−9.0
FDI inward stock	802	1 954	7 123	14.7	9.3	71.2	19.4	18.9	4.5	7.8
FDI outward stock	595	1 763	6 866	18.0	10.6	16.8	18.2	19.8	5.5	8.7
Cross-border M&As	..	151	370	25.9	24.0	51.5	44.1	49.3	−48.1	−37.7
Sales of foreign affiliates	2 737	5 675	17 685	16.0	10.1	10.9	13.3	19.6	9.2	7.4
Gross product of foreign affiliates	640	1 458	3 437	17.3	6.7	7.9	12.8	16.2	14.7	6.7
Total assets of foreign affiliates	2 091	5 899	26 543	18.8	13.9	19.2	20.7	27.4	4.5	8.3
Export of foreign affiliates	722	1 197	2 613	13.5	7.6	9.6	3.3	11.4	−3.3	4.2
Employment of foreign affiliates (thousands)	19 375	24 282	53 094	5.5	2.9	14.2	15.4	16.5	−1.5	5.7

Source: UNCTAD, based on its FDI/TNC database and UNCTAD estimates.

In the past two decades, the world stock of FDI has grown more than ten-fold to reach $7.1 trillion in 2002. In 2002, FDI inflows declined by 21 per cent to $651 billion, or just half the peak amount in 2000. The decline was distributed across all major regions and countries except Central and Eastern Europe, where inflows were up by 15 per cent. The decrease resulted mainly from weak economic growth, tumbling stock markets that contributed to a steep decline in cross-border mergers and acquisitions, and institutional factors such as the winding down of privatisation in several countries. The recent downturn has not changed the importance of FDI in the integration of global production activities. The global stock of FDI continues to grow, albeit more slowly. The increase in FDI also reflects the increase of components made partly overseas.

SUMMARY

There is no doubt that international trade can play an important role in the satisfying of human needs and desires. But the gains from trade are not necessarily shared equitably either within or between countries. Trade may increase the impact of economic activity on environmental systems. In order to be consistent with the pursuit of sustainable development there need to be the right kinds of agreed rules governing international trade.

KEYWORDS

Basel (or Basle) Convention (p. 467): A convention restricting trade in hazardous waste, some non-hazardous wastes, solid wastes and incinerator ash, adopted at a United Nations conference in 1989.

Cartagena Protocol on Biosafety (p. 467): A protocol of the Convention on Biological Diversity (CBD), Article 19.3 of which provides for parties to consider the need for and modalities of a protocol on the safe transfer, handling and use of living modified organisms that may have an adverse effect on biodiversity. The protocol was adopted as a supplementary agreement to the CBD in 2000.

Convention on Biological Diversity (CBD) (p. 467): drawn up by UNEP and adopted at the Rio Conference in June 1992.

Convention on International Trade in Endangered Species of Wild Fauna and Flora (CITES) (p. 467): an agreement among originally 80 governments effective in 1975 to prevent trade in wild animals and plants from threatening their survival. It works by requiring licensing of trade in covered species.

Doha Declaration (p. 468): The document agreed upon by the trade ministers of the member countries of the WTO at the Doha Ministerial meeting. It initiates negotiations on a range of subjects. A distinctive feature is the emphasis placed on the interests of developing countries.

Dutch disease (p. 450): The adverse effect on a country's other industries that occurs when one industry substantially expands its exports, causing appreciation of the country's currency.

Economies of scale (p. 455): Economies of scale occur when long-run average costs are falling as output is increasing.

Economies of scale, external (p. 455): External economies of scale occur as the output of the industry increases.

Economies of scale, internal (p. 455): See economies of scale.

Exchange rate (p. 446): price of one currency stated in terms of another currency.

Foreign direct investment (p. 454): Foreign direct investment (FDI) is investment involving a long-term relationship and lasting interest in and control by a resident entity in one economy in an enterprise resident in another economy. FDI inflows are capital received, either directly or through other related enterprises, in a foreign affiliate from a direct investor. FDI outflows are capital provided by a direct investor to its affiliate abroad.

General Agreement on Tariffs and Trade (GATT) (p. 464): A multilateral treaty entered into in 1948 by the intended members of the International Trade Organization (ITO), the purpose of which was to implement many of the rules and negotiated tariff reductions that would be overseen by the ITO. With the failure of the ITO to be approved, the GATT became the principal institution regulating trade policy until it was subsumed within the WTO in 1995.

Import quota (p. 449): A limit on the maximum quantity of a good that may be imported into a particular country.

Montreal Protocol (p. 467). Montreal Protocol on Substances that Deplete the Ozone Layer, signed in 1987; stipulates that the production and consumption of compounds that deplete ozone in the stratosphere–chlorofluorocarbons (CFCs), halons, carbon tetrachloride and methyl chloroform–are to be phased out by 2000 (2005 for methyl chloroform).

Multilateral Environmental Agreements (MEA) (p. 467): Commitments among several or many sovereign nations that seek to address the effects and consequences of global and regional environmental degradation. The main MEAs are: Convention on International Trade in Endangered Species of Wild Fauna and Flora (CITES), 1975; Montreal Protocol on Substances that Deplete the Stratospheric Ozone Layer, 1987; Basle Convention on the Control of Transboundary Movement of Hazardous Wastes and their Disposal, 1992; Convention on Biological Diversity, 1993; Framework Convention on Climate Change (FCCC), 1994; Rotterdam Convention on the Prior Informed Consent Procedure for Certain Hazardous Chemicals and Pesticides in International Trade (PIC), 1998; Cartagena Protocol on Biosafety, 2000.

Multinational corporation (MNC) (p. xx): See transnational corporation.

Non-tariff restrictions (p. 449): measures other than tariffs which effectively prohibit or restrict import or export of products.

Tariffs (p. 449): Customs duties on goods imported into a country.

Terms of trade (p. 446): The relative price of a country's exports compared to its imports.

Transnational corporation (p. 472): business organisation that operates extraction, production and distribution facilities in multiple countries.

United Nation Framework Convention on Climate Change (UNFCCC) (p. xx): over a decade ago, most countries joined the international treaty to facilitate management of greenhouse bases. In 1997 governments agreed to an addition to the treaty, called the Kyoto Protocol, which has more powerful (and legally binding) measure. The Protocol took effect in February 2005.

World Trade Organization (WTO) (p. 464): A global international organisation that specifies and enforces rules for the conduct of international trade policies and serves as a forum for negotiations to reduce barriers to trade. Formed in 1995 as the successor to the GATT, it had 147 member countries as of April 2004.

FURTHER READING

The subject matter of this chapter is also discussed in Ekins* (2003b), Krutilla (1997) and Stagl (2002). For proofs of gains and losses with and without pollution as discussed in section 12.1 see Common (1996, ch. 10). Krugman and Obstfeld (2002) is a good intermediate textbook on international economics and Krutilla (1999) or Ulph (1997) are concise intermediate overview articles.

Daly and Cobb (1989) discuss whether free trade and sustainability are mutually reinforcing and conclude that they are not. One of their arguments is that Ricardo based his principle of comparative advantage on the assumption of capital and labour immobility. In fact capital is very mobile between countries. Under conditions of international capital mobility investors would seek the greatest absolute profit opportunities and consequently they would invest in the country with the lowest production cost. It is only if capital cannot follow absolute advantage that investors will go for the next-best solution, which is to follow comparative advantage specialisation at home. In reality capital is becoming more mobile every year. However, there are a number of reasons why it is not completely mobile: language and/or cultural barriers for investors, lack of skills, unsatisfactory infrastructure and insufficient political stability in some countries. Ekins highlights the need for compensation in order to maintain benefits from trade for the involved parties: 'While the potential for everyone to be made better off with freer trade undoubtedly exists, the achievement of this all-win outcome requires compensation for the losers under such liberalization' (Ekins, 1997: p. 65). For more detailed discussions of specific aspects of trade and environment from an ecological economics perspective see also the special issue of the journal *Ecological Economics*, vol. 9, no. 1, in 1994.

UNEP and IISD* (2000) and Neumayer* (2001) give more details on the various institutions that regulate trade and environment. The last includes a detailed discussion of the use of environmental protection as argument for trade restrictions as well as suggestions for reform of current trade institutions.

On the distributional effects of trade see Broad (1994), Martinez-Alier (1993) and Martinez-Alier and O'Connor (1999). Proops *et al.* (1999) use input–output analysis to explore the idea of unequal ecological exchange.

Empirical studies which examine the relationship between the openness of an economy and environmental quality distinguish between the technique effect (result of the introduction of cleaner technologies) and the composition effect (changes sectoral composition as a result of trade). Some of these studies suggest that openness reduces pollution (Wheeler, 2001), while others claim evidence to the contrary (Rock, 1995). The 'ecological dumping' discussions can be explored further in Rauscher (2001) and Muradian and Martinez-Alier (2001).

Stiglitz (2002) explains the functions and powers of the main institutions involved in globalisation (the WTO which we have discussed, and also the international financial institutions IMF and World Bank which we did not cover in this chapter) along with the ramifications, both good and bad, of their policies. He strongly believes that globalisation can be a positive force around the world, particularly for the poor, but only if the IMF, World Bank and WTO dramatically alter the way they operate, beginning with increased transparency and a greater willingness to examine their own actions closely. The next two authors take a broader perspective on globalisation. They consider the impact of globalisation on various aspects of society. Castells (1996, 1997, 1998) investigates the relationship of information technology and globalisation. Giddens (1999) explores the impact of globalisation on various aspects of people's lives. It assesses this change as broadly positive, liberating women, spreading democracy and creating new wealth.

WEBSITES

http://www.wto.org/english/tratop_e/envir_e/envir_e.htm – WTO Environment and Trade – presents the perspective of the most powerful institution in international trade on the relationship of environment and trade and related international negotiations.

http://www.unep.ch/etu/ – United Nations Environment Programme (UNEP) – Environment and Trade Branch.

http://globstat.unctad.org/html/index.html – Development and Globalization: Facts and Figures.

http://www.unctad.org/Templates/Page.asp?intItemID=1584&lang=1 – UNCTAD data site includes several databases: UNCTAD Handbook of Statistics, Commodity Price Bulletin, UNCTAD-TRAINS on the Internet (Trade Analysis and Information System) and Foreign Direct Investment database.

http://globstat.unctad.org/html/index.html – Development and Globalization: Facts and Figures, new webpage by UNCTAD with concise information and statistics.

http://www.wto.org/english/res_e/statis_e/its2003_e/its03_bysubject_e.htm #trends – International Trade Statistics 2003.

http://www.cid.harvard.edu/cidtrade/ – Center for International Development at Harvard University – the Global Trade Negotiations webpage gathers and disseminates information and research on the multilateral trade system.

http://www.citizen.org/trade/index.cfm – Global Trade Watch (GTW) – a division of Public Citizen, promotes government and corporate accountability in the globalisation and trade arena.

http://www.iatp.org/ – Institute for Agriculture and Trade Policy (IATP) – promotes resilient family farms, rural communities and ecosystems around the world through research and education, science and technology, and advocacy.

http://www.maketradefair.com/en/index.htm – Make Trade Fair is a campaign by Oxfam International and twelve affiliates, calling on governments, institutions and multinational companies to change the rules so that trade can become part of the solution to poverty, not part of the problem.

http://www.globalisationguide.org/index.htm – Useful globalisation resources organised around 'key questions'. Provides both the 'pro-' and 'anti-' globalisation perspectives.

http://www.tradeknowledgenetwork.net/publication.aspx?id=631 – The Trade Knowledge Network (TKN) is composed of research and policy institutions in Africa, Asia, Europe, and North and South America that are exploring the connection between trade and sustainable development.

DISCUSSION QUESTIONS

1. In your own words – is international trade beneficial for the environment? How does the EKC help you in answering this question?
2. In your own words – is international trade beneficial for eradicating poverty?

EXERCISES

1. Let's consider the production of bicycles and clothes worldwide. Comparing two countries, one country (Vietnam) has an absolute advantage in the production of both goods. For simplicity we focus on labour input; the same logic holds with more input factors. The amount of labour needed to produce one unit of bicycles and one unit of clothes is given in the following table:

	Labour input required for producing one unit of		
	bicyle	clothes	Total labour available
Vietnam	5	10	120
Laos	30	15	120

(a) Please calculate the labour productivity for producing bicycles and clothes for each country.

(b) What are the opportunity cost of each country for producing one bicycle and one unit of clothes? What does this mean with regard to comparative advantage?

(c) Use the results from (a) and (b) to show how Vietnam and Laos can benefit from trade.

2. What are the main reasons why the coordination of environmental policy is preferable over national policies? What are the downsides of policy coordination?

3. Suppose that under the terms of an international agreement, US CO_2 emissions are to be reduced by 200 million tons, and those in Brazil by 50 million tons.

Here are the policy options that the US and Brazil have to reduce their emissions:

US Policy options	Total emissions reduction (million tons carbon)	Cost ($ billion)
A: Efficient machinery	60	12
B: Reforestation	40	20
C: Replace coal-fuelled power plants	120	30

Brazil Policy options	Total emissions reduction (million tons carbon)	Cost ($ billion)
A: Efficient machinery	50	20
B: Protection Amazonas	30	3
C: Replace coal-fuelled power plants	40	8

(a)   What are the most efficient policies for the US and Brazil to use in meeting their targets? What will be the costs to each nation if they must operate independently?

(b)   Suppose a market of transferable permits allows the US and Brazil to trade permits to emit CO_2. Who has an interest in buying permits? Who has an interest in selling permits? What agreement can be reached between the US and Brazil so that they can meet the overall emissions reduction target of 250 at the least cost? Can you estimate a range for the price of a permit to emit one ton of carbon? (Hint: calculate the average cost per unit for each reduction policy.)

13

Climate change

In this chapter you will:

- Learn how the greenhouse effect works;
- Find out what future climate change is expected by the vast majority of competent scientists due to the enhanced greenhouse effect;
- See what effects future climate change is expected to have;
- Learn why the enhanced greenhouse effect is so difficult to deal with;
- Find out about the ways in which it could be responded to;
- Learn about what is actually being done in response to the problem, and what effect it is expected to have.

We have referred to various aspects of the climate change problem at a number of points in earlier chapters, usually in order to illustrate some point. Now we are going to look at the problem itself in its entirety. It is one of the most serious threats to sustainability. This is because of the impacts that it could entail, and because of the difficulties that responding to the problem involves. We first set out what is known about climate change due to the enhanced greenhouse effect. Then we shall explain exactly why it is such a difficult problem to deal with. Next we consider issues to do with the setting of targets and the choice of instrument. Finally, we will describe and assess what is actually being done about climate change in terms of targets and instruments.

13.1 THE NATURE AND EXTENT OF THE PROBLEM

Basically the 'climate change problem' relates to the fact that virtually all competent climate scientists consider that the global climate is changing as the result of human economic activity, and will continue to do so in the future. What is changing the climate is the 'enhanced greenhouse effect'. Most of the scientists who have considered the impacts that future climate change is likely to have are of the view that most will be harmful to human interests. In this section we are going to explain the basis for these positions. Before looking at the enhanced greenhouse effect we need to begin with the greenhouse effect itself.

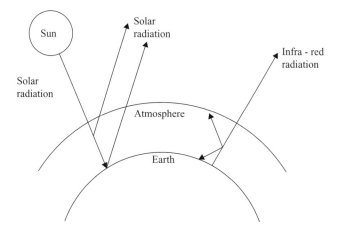

Figure 13.1
Physics of the
greenhouse
effect.

13.1.1 The greenhouse effect

The existence of a greenhouse effect is universally accepted. Without it, life, at least as we know it, would not exist on planet earth, as it would have an average surface temperature of about−6°C, rather than the actual 15°C. Figure 13.1 shows the main features of the basic physics of the greenhouse effect. Some 60 per cent of the solar radiation arriving at the earth's atmosphere reaches the surface of the earth, of which about 18 per cent is reflected back into space, with the remainder warming the earth's surface. With warming, the earth's surface emits infra-red radiation. The so-called 'greenhouse gases' in the atmosphere absorb some of this radiation, and re-emit it in all directions, including back towards the surface of the earth. The effect of this reflected infra-red radiation is to warm the lower atmosphere and the surface of the earth. The greenhouse gases act like a blanket around the earth's surface. The effect is also like that of the glass in a gardener's greenhouse – hence the terminology.

This basic physics has been known about for almost two centuries. It was first pointed out by Fourier in 1827, who noted the similarity with the way a greenhouse works. In the middle of the nineteenth century it was suggested that the ice ages might have been caused by reductions in carbon dioxide, CO_2, recognised as a greenhouse gas. In 1896 the Swedish chemist Arrhenius noted the CO_2 released into the atmosphere by coal combustion since the Industrial Revolution and estimated the effect of a doubling of the amount of CO_2 in the atmosphere as an increase in the average global surface temperature of about 5°C. In the late twentieth century understanding of the role of the composition of the atmosphere in determining global temperature, and other features of climate, was enhanced by the collection of data on conditions on other planets in the solar system.

The amounts of greenhouse gases in the atmosphere are not the only determinants of global average surface temperature. The amount of solar radiation arriving at the earth's atmosphere varies with solar activity, and with the earth's movement around the sun. The proportion that reaches the surface of the earth is affected by the amounts of aerosols – particulates in the atmosphere.

Figure 13.2
The enhanced
greenhouse
effect.

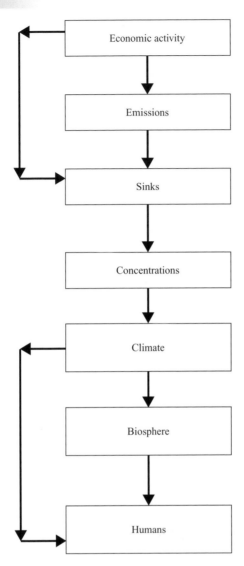

Figure 13.2
The enhanced greenhouse effect.

13.1.2 The enhanced greenhouse effect

Since the industrial revolution, concentrations of greenhouse gases in the atmosphere have been increasing as the result of human economic activity. In the last century it appears that the world's climate has been changing, and particularly that the global average surface temperature has been increasing. The term 'the enhanced greenhouse effect' refers to the proposition that the global climate is changing mainly due to increasing greenhouse gas concentrations caused by human activity.

Figure 13.2 shows the outlines of the operation of the enhanced greenhouse effect. Economic activity gives rise to emissions into the atmosphere of greenhouse gases. What matters for climate is not the emissions *per se* but the atmospheric concentrations of the gases. The concentrations depend on emissions and on the operation of processes which remove the gases from the atmosphere, known as **sinks**. The functioning of the sinks is affected by economic activity. The enhanced greenhouse effect has been the subject of controversy. It has been claimed that the climate has not changed beyond limits that would be expected from its normal variability, and/or that such change as there has been cannot be definitively put down to the effects of human activity. There is now much less controversy than was the case ten years ago. In sub-section 13.1.5 we report assessments of the climatic results of the enhanced greenhouse effect that the great majority of the scientists working in the area would endorse.

Most of those who accept the enhanced greenhouse effect as real also take it that the effects on humans are mainly adverse. Figure 13.2 shows two pathways linking climate to humans. There are direct effects on human health and well-being, due to heat stress, increased storms, flooding, for example, and there are indirect effects transmitted through the impact on other plants and animals of agricultural productivity reductions, biodiversity losses, for example. There is some continuing controversy over how bad the effects for humans of continuing climate change will be. We shall report on an authoritative mainstream assessment in sub-section 13.1.6.

The area where there is most disagreement over the enhanced greenhouse effect is what, if anything, to do about it – how to respond to it. Whereas questions about the existence and impact of an enhanced greenhouse effect can be treated as positive questions, the question of what to do about it is a normative one (see Chapter 1 on the distinction between positive and normative questions). We shall begin to look at this question in sub-section 13.1.7, and, in one way or another, the following sections also mainly deal with it.

13.1.3 The Intergovernmental Panel on Climate Change

Work like that of Arrhenius did not attract much attention when it was published. The enhanced greenhouse effect did not become the subject of much scientific enquiry until the 1960s. The first World Climate Conference took place in 1979, and a number of conferences and workshops took place during the 1980s. The Intergovernmental Panel on Climate Change, the IPCC, was established in 1988 under the auspices of the United Nations Environment Programme, UNEP, and the World Meteorological Organisation, WMO. The purpose of the IPCC is to provide authoritative assessments of the state of knowledge on climate change.

In order to appreciate the status of the reports that the IPCC has produced, it is necessary to understand how it works. It does not itself undertake research. The IPCC is organised as three Working Groups. Each of these produces reports which bring together the results of many scientists working in the fields that it covers. The process of producing an IPCC Working Group report starts with member governments – almost all members of the UN are members of the IPCC – nominating experts to participate in the preparation of the report. From those nominated, writing teams are selected by an intergovernmental committee for each of the Working Groups. The overall report for a Working Group begins with a Summary for Policymakers. This is drafted by a writing team, but the final text is the outcome of detailed negotiation by governmental delegates. Following this summary, each report contains a Technical Summary, which is not the result of line-by-line negotiation but is 'accepted' by the Working Group – this means that the IPCC endorses it as 'a comprehensive, objective and balanced view of the subject matter'. The main text of each Working Group report is a series of chapters, each of which is the responsibility of its writing team. The chapter that a writing team produces is peer-reviewed by many other scientists working in the field, and will have gone through a number of drafts before being finalised.

The IPCC reports do not make policy recommendations. The intention is for them to provide those who do make recommendations, and take decisions, with the best available information. It is generally accepted by the scientific community, and by governments, that this is exactly what they do. There is very little dissent from the state of knowledge as portrayed in the IPCC reports.

As noted above, the IPCC is organised into three Working Groups. Working Group I is concerned with the science of climate change – it deals with the boxes from Economic activity down to Climate in Figure 13.2. Working Group II is concerned with the effects of climate change – the bottom two boxes in Figure 13.2. Working Group III is concerned with possible responses to climate change.

To date, the IPCC has produced three sets of reports from its three Working Groups. Its First Assessment Report in 1990 was a major input to the deliberations on the United Nations Framework Convention on Climate Change adopted in 1992, to be discussed in section 13.4 below. Its Second Assessment Report in 1995 (sometimes referred to as the SAR) provided the scientific basis for the next major step in the evolution of the international response to the problem: the Kyoto Protocol of 1997, also to be discussed in 13.4. Its Third Assessment Report (sometimes referred to as the TAR) came out in 2001. The rest of this section of the chapter is based mainly on the three volumes of the TAR: Houghton *et al.* (2001) for Working Group I; McCarthy *et al.* (2001) for Working Group II; and Metz *et al.* (2001) for Working Group III. Each of these is several hundred pages long, and we mainly use, and quote from, the Summary for Policymakers and the Technical Summary in each of the reports. As noted above, these summaries reflect the collective IPCC assessment, and in the former case are accepted in detail by the member governments. In the rest of this section, unless stated otherwise, all quotations are from these summaries.

13.1.4 The greenhouse gases

The gases which are responsible for the greenhouse effect exist in very small quantities in the atmosphere, which consists mainly of nitrogen, 78 per cent, and oxygen, 21 per cent. Of the remaining 1 per cent, argon accounts for 90 per cent, leaving just 0.1 per cent of the atmosphere to be accounted for by all other gases in it. Table 13.1 shows the atmospheric concentrations of three of the main greenhouse gases as estimated for before the Industrial Revolution and as measured for 1998. As is standard, the concentrations are stated as ppm, which stands for 'parts per million' – the pre-industrial figure of 280 ppm for CO_2 corresponds to 0.028 per cent of the atmosphere. These gases differ in the effectiveness with which they absorb and re-emit infra-red radiation. Per molecule, CO_2 is much the least effective, and

Table 13.1 Greenhouse gas atmospheric concentrations

	Carbon dioxide CO_2	Methane CH_4	Nitrous oxide N_2O
Pre-industrial concentration, ppm	280	0.70	0.27
Concentration in 1998, ppm	365	1.75	0.31
Increase, %	30	150	15

N_2O is the most effective. However, as shown in Table 13.1, there is much more CO_2 in the atmosphere, so that CO_2 actually plays a bigger role in the greenhouse effect than either CH_4 or N_2O.

The gases shown in Table 13.1 all have long **atmospheric lifetimes**: the time between the emission of a molecule into the atmosphere and its removal from the atmosphere. For CO_2 the lifetime varies from five to several hundred years according to the sink involved in the removal. For methane it is about 10 years, and for nitrous oxide it is about 100 years.

We looked at the ways in which carbon cycles between the atmosphere and other stores in Chapter 2 – see section 2.4.1 and Figure 2.14. The relevant cycle in regard to the greenhouse effect is the fast cycle, in which the other stores are the oceans and terrestrial biota. The increase in the atmospheric concentration of CO_2 shown in Table 13.1 has been due to anthropogenic influences. In terms of Figure 13.2, these have been mainly the burning of fossil fuels and biomass causing emissions into the atmosphere, and deforestation and other land-use changes reducing the sink effect of terrestrial biota. Currently, CO_2 is estimated to account for about 60 per cent of the estimated total additional warming, compared to the pre-industrial, effect of all of the long-lived greenhouse gases.

The main anthropogenic sources of methane emissions into the atmosphere, which have driven the increase shown in Table 13.1, are the paddy cultivation of rice, ruminant animals, fossil fuel production, and the disposal of wastes in landfills. The main non-anthropogenic source of CH_4 emissions is wetlands. Methane is removed from the atmosphere by chemical reactions taking place in it. Methane is estimated to account now for about 20 per cent of the estimated total additional warming, compared to pre-industrial, effect of all of the long-lived greenhouse gases.

The main anthropogenic sources of nitrous oxide are fossil fuel combustion and the use of nitrogen fertilisers in agriculture. Non-anthropogenic sources include bacteria in soils, the oceans, and biomass combustion. The main sink for atmospheric nitrous oxide (N_2O) is its breakdown by sunlight, producing nitrogen oxide and nitrogen dioxide. Nitrous oxide is estimated to account now for about 6 per cent of the estimated total additional warming, compared to pre-industrial, effect of all of the long-lived greenhouse gases.

The gases shown in Table 13.1 are not the only ones with long lifetimes that have a role in the enhanced greenhouse effect. Chlorofluorocarbons (CFCs) are man-made, synthetic chemicals, the production of which started in the twentieth century for use as refrigerants, solvents and aerosol propellants. When released into the atmosphere they give rise to two environmental problems. First, they destroy stratospheric ozone. Second, they are greenhouse gases. On a molecular basis, the

CFCs are much more effective at absorbing and re-emitting infra-red radiation than CO_2 is. The processes by which they are removed from the atmosphere operate very slowly. CFC atmospheric lifetimes vary from tens to hundreds of years. It is estimated that the CFCs account now for about 14 per cent of the estimated total additional warming, compared to pre-industrial, effect of all of the long-lived greenhouse gases.

The use of CFCs is now regulated by an international treaty, and is being greatly reduced. This has come about not because of their greenhouse-gas role, but because of the ozone-depletion problem. However, CFCs are being replaced by other synthetic chemicals, hydrofluorocarbons or HFCs, which, while not ozone-destroying, are greenhouse gases. You will find references to accounts of the stratospheric ozone-depletion problem and discussion of the treaty which responds to it in Further Reading at the end of the chapter.

Ozone, O_3, is a greenhouse gas which differs from those considered thus far in several respects. First, ozone as such is not emitted into the atmosphere. It is formed there by processes operating on other emissions. Second, the gases considered thus far all mix well throughout the atmosphere so that it is their global concentrations that matter for the global climate system, whereas ozone does not mix well and concentrations vary spatially. Third, ozone's atmospheric residence time is short – weeks or months rather than years. Fourth, changes in ozone concentrations have varied with altitude. As noted above, stratospheric ozone has been depleted in recent times, giving rise to a cooling effect. Also as noted above, the depletion of stratospheric ozone is set to decrease. Tropospheric ozone has been increasing in recent years, due to anthropogenic emissions of its precursor gases. It is estimated that tropospheric ozone is currently of similar warming importance to the CFCs.

In this sub-section we are going to look at what the IPCC Working Group I TAR has to say about the existence of an enhanced greenhouse effect and the climatic change that might result from it in the future. We do this in three steps. First we outline how climate scientists approach the enhanced greenhouse effect question: by modelling. Then we look at what they have to say about climate change and its causes in the recent past. Finally we look at what they have to say about future climate change.

13.1.4.1 Modelling

The main tools that climate scientists use are models of the global climate system. Essentially what these models do is to use the relationships thought to determine how that system works to translate inputs of greenhouse gas concentrations into outputs that are features of climate such as temperature and precipitation. Greenhouse gas concentrations are not the only inputs. The models also use input data on solar radiation, and on atmospheric levels of sulphur particulate matter, which, by preventing solar radiation reaching the earth's surface, have the opposite effect to the greenhouse gases – other things being equal, more atmospheric sulphur means lower temperature.

While the basic physics of the greenhouse effect as described above is reasonably simple, the climate models are large and complicated. The complications arise mainly from trying to incorporate into the models four feedback mechanisms at work in the climate system. The first and most important is the water vapour feedback. Warmer air can hold more water vapour, which is itself a greenhouse gas. This is a positive feedback effect – warming means more water vapour means more warming. The second is the effect of the oceans, which warm more slowly than the atmosphere and tend to reduce the rate at which the latter warms. Ocean circulation also plays an important role in the spatial patterns of climate around the globe, and these circulations are themselves affected by global warming. The third is the effect of cloud cover. Increased cloud cover reflects more solar radiation back into space, but also acts like an increasing greenhouse gas concentration, absorbing thermal radiation from the earth's surface and reflecting some of it back towards that surface. Which of these effects is the stronger depends on a number of factors, and varies with circumstances. It is conceivable that relatively small changes in the extent of cloud cover could have a warming effect of similar magnitude to that of CO_2. The fourth feedback effect is via changes in the extent of ice and snow cover of the earth's surface. As warming occurs so this cover is reduced, so that more solar radiation is absorbed by the earth's surface rather than being reflected back into space. There is thus more infra-red radiation emitted by the earth's surface to be trapped by the greenhouse gases.

These feedbacks are well understood in general terms, but the strengths of the effects involved are not definitively known. There are several climate models in existence, each of which represents these feedbacks somewhat differently. This is the main reason why the various models give different climatic outputs for the same inputs in terms of greenhouse gas concentrations and solar radiation. The IPCC Working Group I TAR reports results obtained using several different climate models. It notes the lack of definitive quantitative understanding of the feedback effects, particularly in regard to water vapour and clouds. The direction – positive or negative – of the net effect from cloud cover is not known for sure, and 'clouds represent a significant source of potential error in climate simulations' using the models.

13.1.4.2 Has there been an enhanced greenhouse effect at work?

The first way that these models are used is to investigate whether the apparent recent changes in global climate can be attributed to an enhanced greenhouse effect. Basically the question is: given what we think we know about climate change in the recent past, can the increasing concentrations of greenhouse gases explain it? The answer to this question is sought by inputting the historical record on concentrations, the solar flux and atmospheric sulphur levels into climate models to see whether their climatic outputs match the historical record. Broadly, the IPCC's assessment is that there has been an enhanced greenhouse effect at work in the last 100 years.

In regard to what has happened to the climate, the main point is that over the course of the twentieth century the global average surface temperature increased by $0.6 \pm 0.2°C$. The band $\pm 0.2°C$ represents a 95 per cent confidence interval – the IPCC is saying that it is 95 per cent confident, not absolutely certain, that temperature increased by between $0.4°C$ and $0.8°C$. It is 'very likely' that snow cover has decreased by 'about 10 per cent' since the late 1960s – by 'very likely' the IPCC means that it is 90 per cent to 99 per cent confident that the statement referred to is true. It is certain that non-polar mountain glaciers have retreated during the twentieth century. In the northern hemisphere there is evidence of a reduction in the extent of ice, especially during the summer. With a warmer world, the water in the oceans would expand and the sea level would be expected to rise because of this and the ice melt. In fact, 'Tide gauge data show that global average sea level rose between 0.1 and 0.2 metres during the 20th century'.

In regard to what has caused the observed changes in the climate:

> The best agreement between model simulations and observations over the last 140 years has been found when all the above anthropogenic and natural forcing factors are combined . . . These results show that the forcings included are sufficient to explain the observed changes, but do not exclude the possibility that other forcings may also have contributed.   (J. T. Houghton *et al.*, 2001: 10)

The **anthropogenic forcing factors** input to the climate models are changes in greenhouse gas concentrations and sulphur emissions. The natural forcing factors are the solar flux and the effects of major volcanic events, which release particulate matter into the atmosphere. The SAR had said that 'The balance of evidence suggests a discernible human influence on global climate.' The TAR says that 'There is new and stronger evidence that most of the warming observed in the last 50 years is attributable to human activities.' It also says that it is 'very likely' that the twentieth-century warming 'has contributed significantly to the observed sea level rise, through thermal expansion of sea water and widespread loss of land ice'.

13.1.4.3 Future prospects

In terms of Figure 13.2, the modelling work that seeks to explain the origins of climatic change in the recent past deals with the link between 'Concentrations' and 'Climate'. It can do this because there are data on greenhouse gas concentrations to input to the climate models. For considering future prospects, such data are not available, and the scope of the necessary modelling has to move back up the chain in Figure 13.2.

Most of the work on future prospects looks out to 2100. A range of economic scenarios for this period are modelled for their implications regarding greenhouse gas emissions. The IPCC considered a lot of different scenarios derived from four families of 'storylines'. All the scenarios in a family share the same broad features but each differs in detail. The A1 family has global population peaking mid-century, with rapid economic growth and technological change. The A2 family has continuing population growth, but slower economic growth and technological change than in the A1 family. The B1 storyline family involves the same population assumptions as A1, but has more rapid economic and technological change reducing resource use. The B2 family has continuously growing world population, at a rate lower than for A2, and slower economic and technological change than for A1 and B1. In none of the scenarios is there any action modelled which is primarily intended to affect climate change – the effects of the UNFCC and the subsequent Kyoto Protocol, to be discussed below, are not taken into account. In that sense, when looking at climate change, these are all Business as Usual (BAU) scenarios. Of course, many of the things that differ across the scenarios – such as demographics – do affect greenhouse gas emissions levels.

As indicated in Figure 13.2, in order to derive a time path for concentrations out to 2100, as well as having projections of what happens to emissions, it is also necessary to have projections for what happens to sinks. And, again as shown in Figure 13.2, what happens to sinks is affected by economic activity. Looking at future climatic prospects requires using, in addition to climate models, models that translate assumptions about the demographic and economic future into emissions futures and into sinks futures. Actually, in the work reported by the IPCC, the only greenhouse gas for which sink behaviour is explicitly modelled is CO_2. For the others, concentrations as such are projected. CO_2 is the most important greenhouse gas, and the interconnections between the operation of its sinks – notably growing plants – and economic activity are thought to be important and reasonably well understood.

Future climatic prospects out to 2100 are investigated by using the emissions and sink modelling with the climate models. The result is a range of projections – the modelling described in this sub-section produces a range of projections for concentrations, and the several climate models used each produce different climatic outputs for a given concentrations projection. The final range of climatic projections reflect, that is, both different assumptions about the demographic and economic futures and their implications for emissions and sinks, and different understandings, as reflected in the climate models, of how the global climate system works. It is the assessment of the IPCC that these two sources of difference for the final climatic projection contribute about equally to producing the range of climatic outcomes that they report: 'differences in emissions in the SRES scenarios and different climate model responses contribute similar uncertainty to the range of global temperature change'.

That range is large: 'The globally averaged surface temperature is projected to increase by 1.4 to 5.8°C over the period 1990 to 2100'. It is of interest that the IPCC's range of projections is moving upwards over time: 'Temperature increases are projected (in TAR) to be greater than those in the SAR, which were about 1 to 3.5°C.' The projected rate of warming is 'much larger than the observed changes during the 20th century' and is 'very likely' (90 per cent to 99 per cent confidence) 'to be without precedent during at least the last 10,000 years'. The projected warming is not uniform around the world: 'it is very likely that nearly all land areas will warm more rapidly than the global average, particularly those at northern high latitudes in the cold season'.

Other climatic changes are projected along with warming. Beyond 2050, 'it is likely that precipitation will have increased over northern mid to high latitudes and Antarctica in winter': this likely means that the IPCC attaches a probability in the range of 66 per cent to 90 per cent. In other parts of the world increases and decreases in precipitation are projected. Where increases are projected, larger year-to-year variations are 'very likely'. Among the changes in relation to extreme events assessed as 'very likely' during the twenty-first century are 'more intense precipitation events', as well as higher maximum temperatures and more hot days over nearly all land areas. Rated 'likely' are increased risk of drought over 'most mid-latitude continental interiors', increased peak wind intensities and peak pre-cipitation intensities in tropical cyclones in some areas.

Across all the emissions scenarios, global mean sea level is projected to rise from 0.09 m to 0.88 m out to 2100. This is due to the water already there expanding with warming, and to loss of mass from glaciers and land ice caps. These projections for sea-level rise are a slightly lower range than the 0.13 m to 0.94 m range given in SAR.

While most attention is focused on projections out to 2100, it is in the nature of the case that enhanced greenhouse effects need to be looked at for longer time horizons. This would be true even if greenhouse gas concentrations stopped rising by 2100, or sooner: 'Global mean surface temperature increases and rising sea level from thermal expansion are projected to continue for hundreds of years after sta-bilisation of greenhouse gas concentrations (even at present levels).' In fact, for CO_2, which is expected to account for 70 per cent of the warming due to all greenhouse gases out to 2100, all the scenarios considered by the IPCC have concentrations higher in 2100 than in 1990. The effects of the enhanced greenhouse effect would not stop when temperature stabilised:

> Ice sheets will continue to react to climate warming and contribute to sea level rise for thousands of years after climate has been stabilised . . . Ice sheet models project that a local warming of larger than 3°C, if sustained for millennia, would lead to virtually a complete melting of the Greenland ice sheet with a resulting sea level rise of about 7 metres.   (J. T. Houghton et al., 2001: 17)

Most of the IPCC Working Group I TAR is concerned with prospects out to 2100 under the assumption that the climate system continues to work in the way that it does now, in which case change due to increasing greenhouse gas concentrations happens rather slowly. It is, however, recognised that the climate system is non-linear, involves positive feedbacks which are not now properly understood, and may exhibit rapid, and unanticipated, change if thresholds are crossed. Such events can be seen in the historic climate record. Chapter 1 says that 'Because the probability of their occurrence may be small and their predictability limited, they are colloquially referred to as "unexpected events" or "surprises"', and that the climate system 'may experience as yet unevisionable, unexpected, rapid change'. Catastrophic climate change cannot, that is, be ruled out.

Among the longer-term possibilities, discussed in Chapter 7 of the report, are:

- reorganisation of the **thermohaline circulation** in the North Atlantic, result-ing in a more southerly course for the Gulf Stream, with major implications for the climate of northwest Europe;
- a possible rapid disintegration of part of the Antarctic ice sheet, with dra-matic consequences for the global sea level;
- large-scale and possibly irreversible changes in the terrestrial biosphere and vegetation cover, which would affect the operation of that carbon sink.

There may be other, 'as yet unenvisionable', effects – the IPCC recognises that we are dealing here with a state of imperfect knowledge of the future classified as ignorance in Chapter 10. According to chapter 7 of Working Group I's TAR:

model simulations indicate that such transitions lie within the range of changes that are projected for the next few centuries if greenhouse gas concentrations continue to increase. A particular concern is the fact that some of these changes may even be irreversible. (p. 456)

They are saying that it is possible that humanity will permanently and substantially alter the way the global climate system works.

13.1.5 The enhanced greenhouse effect -- impacts of climate change

In this sub-section we are looking mainly at what the TAR by Working Group II has to say about the impacts of the climate change, actual and prospective, out to 2100, described in the previous sub-section based on the TAR by Working Group I.

The first point to note is that climate change impacts on natural systems are already observable:

> Available evidence indicates that regional changes in climate, particularly increases in temperature, have already affected a diverse set of physical and biological systems in many parts of the world. Examples of observed changes include shrinkage of glaciers, thawing of permafrost, later freezing and earlier break-up of ice on rivers and lakes, lengthening of mid- to high-latitude growing seasons, poleward and altitudinal shifts of plants and animal ranges, declines of some plant and animal populations, and earlier flowering of trees, emergence of insects, and egg-laying in birds . . . Associations between changes in regional temperatures and observed changes in physical and biological systems have been documented in many aquatic, terrestrial, and marine environments. (J. J. McCarthy *et al.*, 2001: 3)

Given this evidence, 'there is high confidence that recent regional changes in temperature have had discernible impacts on many physical and biological systems' – high confidence means that the authors are 67–95 per cent confident.

It is more difficult to separate out climatic from other effects on human systems, but there is 'emerging evidence that some social and economic systems have been affected by the recent increasing frequency of floods and droughts in some areas'.

The natural systems at risk from prospective climate change include glaciers, coral reefs and atolls, mangroves, boreal and tropical forests, polar and alpine ecosystems, prairie wetlands and remnant native grasslands. Biodiversity will be affected: 'While some species may increase in abundance, climate change will increase existing risks of extinction of some vulnerable species and loss of biodiversity.' It is 'well established' that the extent of these risks increases with the 'magnitude and rate of climate change'.

The human systems at risk 'include mainly water resources; agriculture (especially food security) and forestry; coastal zones and marine systems (fisheries); human settlements, energy and industry; insurance and other financial services; and human health'.

Among the adverse effects of the prospective climate change on human systems are:
- reduced crop yields in most tropical and sub-tropical regions;
- reduction in crop yields in mid-latitudes for changes of more than a few degrees C;
- decreased water availability in water-scarce regions;

- increase in human exposure to vector-borne (malaria) and water-borne (cholera) diseases;
- increase in heat stress mortality;
- increased risk of flooding – more heavy precipitation events and sea-level rise;
- increased energy demand for summer cooling.

Among the beneficial effects are:

- increased crop yields in some mid-latitude regions for changes of less than a few degrees C;
- increased timber supply 'from appropriately managed forests';
- increased water availability in some water-scarce regions (parts of SE Asia);
- reduced winter mortality in mid- and high latitudes;
- reduced winter demand for energy.

In looking at climatic prospects we noted more intense precipitation events as very likely. These would have the following impacts:

- increased flood, landslide, avalanche and mudslide damage;
- increased soil erosion;
- increased flood run-off could increase recharge of some floodplain aquifers;
- increased pressure on government and private flood insurance systems and disaster relief.

Also noted as very likely were higher maximum temperatures and more hot days over nearly all land areas, which would have the following impacts:

- increased incidence of death and serious illness in older age groups and urban poor;
- increased heat stress in livestock and wildlife;
- shifts in tourist destinations;
- increased risk of damage to a number of crops;
- increased electric cooling demand and reduced energy supply reliability.

The sea-level rise associated with global warming out to 2100 would have serious consequences. Large numbers of people live in low-lying coastal areas, where many of the world's major cities are located. In addition to increased frequency and levels of flooding, coastal areas will experience 'accelerated erosion, loss of wetlands and mangroves, and seawater intrusion into freshwater sources'. Also, the 'extent and severity of storm impacts, including storm-surge floods and shore erosion, will increase as a result of climate change including sea-level rise'.

Given this wide range of impacts, including some beneficial ones, it is difficult to get some sense of how bad the overall impact is expected to be. It is tempting to look for some kind of 'bottom line' summary of the overall impact. In its TAR, Working Group II resisted this temptation. In the SAR, Working Group III did not, and attempted to put a monetary value on the damage that the enhanced greenhouse effect would do – this working group was composed mainly of neoclassical economists. This proved to be a highly controversial exercise. Among other things, it involved valuing lost human lives, and the value used for a human life lost in the developed world was much higher than that used for a human life lost in the developing world. Given that many more lives were expected to be lost in the developing than in the developed world, this had the effect of making the overall money value of climate change lower than it would have been if all lives had been valued at the developed world level. Many, mainly non-economist, commentators objected to the differential valuation because it produced this effect, and argued that the differential valuation was, anyway, immoral. The dispute was largely unresolved. The contentious monetary estimates remained in the relevant chapter of Working Group III's SAR, which did not require approval by governmental delegates, but the Summary for Policymakers, which did require such approval, largely ignored the estimates of the cost of climate change.

In its TAR, Working Group II states that:

> Estimates of aggregate impacts are controversial because they treat gains for some as cancelling out losses for others and because the weights that are used to aggregate across individuals are necessarily subjective. (p. 958)

Accordingly, it makes no attempt to come up with a global bottom line for the economic impact of prospective climate change. It does note that a number of studies find that many developing countries would suffer net losses, while developed countries would show a mix of gainers and losers for an increase in global mean temperature of up to a few degrees C. Its assessment is that the anticipated distribution of economic impacts would increase the economic disparities between developed and developing economies. There are two reasons given for this. First, 'most less-developed regions are especially vulnerable because a larger share of their economies are in climate sensitive sectors' (p. 16) such as agriculture. Second, the capacity of less-developed economies to adapt to the impacts of climate change is low 'due to low levels of human, financial and natural resources, as well as limited institutional and technological capability' (*ibid.*).

13.1.6 Responding to the enhanced greenhouse effect

What can and should be done about all of this? Most of the next two sections are about various aspects of these questions. Here we want to make some preliminary observations, and to say a little more about the work of the IPCC. The IPCC does not itself make recommendations about what should be done. It does try to spell out what the results of, and costs of, alternative courses of action could be.

First, we can distinguish three types of human response to the enhanced greenhouse effect:

(1) *Adaptation* would involve simply letting it happen, and making adjustments to the changing climate. Examples of adaptive responses would be breeding new strains of crops to cope with higher temperatures, limiting future development in coastal and other flood-prone areas, building coastal defences against flooding.

(2) *Offsetting* would involve doing things intended to have the opposite climatic effects to the build-up of greenhouse gases in the atmosphere. It has been suggested, for example, that it would be possible to release particulate matter into the atmosphere, or to put into orbit devices to reflect solar radiation back into space.

(3) *Mitigation* involves trying to reduce the climatic impacts by reducing the rate of increase in greenhouse gas concentrations, either by reducing the rate at which emissions increase or by enhancing the operation of the sinks for the gases.

Note that the last two of these options are open to only the human species. Other species of plants and animals will have to adapt, or not, to the climate change that results from the choices that humans make about these responses.

While it is useful to distinguish these response classes, it is important to be clear that they do not have to be mutually exclusive – all three types of response could be adopted simultaneously. It follows from the IPCC assessments set out above that there is going to be some enhanced greenhouse effect-driven climate change to adapt to whatever humanity now decides to do about offsetting and/or mitigation. As noted, it is the IPCC assessment that we are already experiencing enhanced greenhouse effect-driven climate change. To the extent that something is done about offsetting and/or mitigation there will be less climatic change to adapt to.

The second class of responses does not get much serious attention. Most attention focuses on the third class of response – measures to slow down the rate of increase in greenhouse gas concentrations. And, most of that attention is focused on reducing the rate of growth of emissions and enhancing sinks for CO_2. This is because, as we have seen, it is the gas that is expected to contribute the most to warming out to 2100: about 70 per cent of the total greenhouse gas-warming effect. It is also the case that it is the gas for which most is known about sources and sinks: and where there are reasonably straightforward ways, in a technical sense, for enhancing sinks: by growing and harvesting more trees. While enhancing terrestrial carbon sinks in this way is reasonably straightforward in the technical sense, it is attended by lots of economic and political problems. As we shall see in the remaining sections of this chapter, this is general in regard to mitigation responses to the enhanced greenhouse effect.

Some sense of the extent of the mitigation response that would be required to make a significant impact on prospective global warming via acting solely on CO_2 emissions was given by the simple IPAT calculations that we did in Chapter 7. We found there that given conservative assumptions about the growth of the human population out to 2050, and modest aspirations in terms of economic growth to that date, holding CO_2 emissions at their current global level would require that emissions per $ of GDP would have to fall by more than 50 per cent. Reducing CO_2 emissions per $ of GDP is known as **de-carbonisation** of the economy. Most experts consider this amount of de-carbonisation to be technically achievable, but unlikely – in the absence of strong policy measures in pursuit of it globally. The political problems of putting in place the necessary policy measures are considerable. More population growth and/or more economic growth would mean more de-carbonisation was necessary. Holding CO_2 emissions constant at the current level would not stabilise the concentration at the current level.

The TAR of IPCC Working Group III has the title *Climate change 2001: mitigation*. It looks at the amounts of mitigation needed for the stabilisation of the CO_2 concentration at different levels under different scenarios, at the technological options for and feasibility of various levels of mitigation, and at the costs of mitigation. It does not, unlike the SAR Working Group III report, address the question of the monetary value of the benefits of mitigation, i.e. the monetary value of the costs of climate change that mitigation would avoid.

The report notes that progress in developing greenhouse gas emissions-reduction technologies has 'been faster than anticipated' since 1995 and reviews a vast range of mitigation options now known to be technologically feasible. It also reviews the literature on the costs of such options. Looking out to 2020 it comes up with a range of 3,600–5,050 Mt of CO_2 equivalent for total 'Potential emissions reductions' in that year. This is to be compared with a range of 12,000–16,000 Mt of CO_2 equivalent for what emissions would otherwise be across a range of scenarios. Very roughly, and this is all that is appropriate, in their TAR, Working Group III is saying that there is the technological potential to mitigate so that 2020 emissions are cut by about 30 per cent of what projection on the basis of the current emissions intensity of GDP production would give. In terms of costs, the assessment is that about half of this potential could be realised at zero or negative cost. The assessment of the total potential excludes options for which the estimated cost exceeds US$100 per tonne of CO_2 equivalent emission avoided.

Note that it is implicit in this assessment that there are things that could be done now that have negative costs, but which are not being done. It is widely recognised that this is the case. Mitigation options that carry negative costs are often referred to as **no-regrets options**: they are things that it would make sense to do independently of the climate-change problem. It is well documented, for example, that there are many feasible energy-saving measures the adoption of which would save many firms money – would increase their profits – but which are not being adopted by those firms. Contrary to the standard assumptions of neoclassical economics – see Chapter 9 – many firms are not in possession of complete information about the opportunities open to them, and/or are not profit maximisers. Similarly, it is well documented that many households do not do energy-conserving things – insulating their roofs for example – that would save them money without any loss of comfort or well-being. In modern industrial societies, given that fossil fuels are the dominant energy source, energy conservation is equivalent to mitigation of the enhanced greenhouse effect.

Over and above this, government policy can contribute to the existence of situations such that mitigation measures with negative or zero real costs are not adopted. As discussed in Chapter 9, the costs that firms and individuals face in the market may not fully reflect the real social costs that their activities give rise to – where they do not, external costs exist. In many cases, correcting for (non-greenhouse) external costs, so that firms and individuals face the real costs of their actions, would lead to mitigation measures that are not currently cost-reducing at market prices becoming cost-reducing at, corrected, market prices. There are other cases where government policy actively encourages the non-adoption of mitigation measures that would reduce real social costs, as, for example, when the prices paid by fossil fuel consumers are subsidised and held below what even uncorrected market prices would be. Once in place, it can be very difficult politically to remove such subsidies.

Working Group III's TAR looks at these kinds of barriers to the adoption of feasible mitigation possibilities. We know look at some of the essential features of the enhanced greenhouse effect-problem that make it difficult for humanity to respond to by way of mitigation.

13.2 WHY THE PROBLEM IS DIFFICULT

Basically the enhanced greenhouse effect is a pollution problem, and what the IPCC calls mitigation is what is often called – see Chapter 11 – abatement. It is a very difficult pollution problem, for reasons which we now explain.

13.2.1 A global public bad

Back in Chapter 9 we saw that markets could not supply public goods because there is no way of tying payment for them to use of them. We also saw that for the same reason – the free-rider problem – it is difficult for government to use willingness to pay to figure out how much of a public good to supply. The pollution due to increasing greenhouse gas concentrations in the atmosphere is a global public bad – the associated damage is non-rival and non-excludable – and dealing with it involves the free-rider problem. The agents involved are nation states rather than individuals. Anthropogenic climate change is the prime example of the reciprocal spillover, or externality, problem introduced in section 12.4.2.1 in Chapter 12.

The free-rider problem can be analysed using **game theory**. This is a way of analysing situations where the outcome of a decision by one agent, or player, depends on the decisions made by the other agents. At the time that decisions have to be made, no decision maker knows what the decisions of the others will be. Game theory is a powerful tool with lots of applications in economics. Here we only use the basic elements – references to expositions of game theory and its application appear in Further Reading.

The major greenhouse gases mix uniformly in the atmosphere, and it is the global concentration that affects the earth's heat balance, and hence the global climate. The climatic effect of a given molecule of a greenhouse gas in no way depends on where it originated. To bring out the nature of the free rider problem here as clearly as possible, we will assume that there are just two nations, called North and South. We will also assume that the two nations have the same population sizes, the same GDP per capita, the same technologies, and are affected in the same way by climate change. In respect to the climate-change problem, each nation has two possible courses of action: it can do nothing (BAU for Business As Usual); or it can reduce its greenhouse gas emissions by a fixed amount, Mitigate. Table 13.2 sets out the pay-offs to each nation for each course of action. This is a constructed example, so the numbers in Table 13.2 are made up to make a point. In the four cells showing pay-off numbers, the one to the left of / refers to South, the one to the right to North. To make things simple, we fix the numbers for the status quo where neither country abates at 1 for each country, shown in the top-left cell in Table 13.2. Now suppose that if a country mitigates the cost to it is 0.3, and that the amount of mitigation involved is such that climate-change damage avoided can be valued at 0.2, which benefit applies to both countries. Suppose that South mitigates but North does not. South incurs 0.3 cost and gets 0.2 benefit, while North incurs 0 cost and gets 0.2 benefit, so that the pay-offs are 0.9/1.2 as shown in the bottom-left cell in Table 13.2. If North mitigates but South does not, then these outcomes are reversed as shown in the top-right cell. If both countries mitigate both incur 0.3 cost but now there is twice as much mitigation and the benefit to both countries is 0.4, so that both gain by 0.1 compared to BAU/BAU, as shown in the bottom-right cell in Table 13.2

If each country is going to pursue its own interest in isolation, then neither will mitigate. Acting alone would make a country worse off. The best thing would be to free ride on the mitigation of the other country. Look at the possibilities from North's point of view. If South mitigates,
North gains most by not mitigating. If South does not mitigate, North would lose by mitigating whereas it neither gains nor loses by BAU. For North, the **dominant strategy** – the choice that offers the best outcome irrespective of the choice made by the other agent – is not to mitigate. BAU is clearly the dominant strategy for South as well. Neither country will mitigate.

Now suppose that North and South acted cooperatively, rather than in isolation. Suppose that a credible and binding agreement could be negotiated according to which North would mitigate if South did, and vice versa. With such an agreement in place, things look very different. Now Mitigate is the preferred strategy for both countries. Only the top-left and bottom-right cells in Table 13.2 are relevant now – it is BAU for both, or Mitigate for both. For both countries the latter is better than the former.

Note that this requires that the negotiated agreement is credible and binding. What Table 13.2 also shows is that it would be in either country's interest to negotiate such an agreement and subsequently defect while the other complied. This implies that, in order to be credible and lasting, the agreement would have to involve penalties for non-compliance.

While Table 13.2 does bring out the essential nature of the free-rider problem in relation to climate change, there are a number of ways in which it departs from the actual conditions, some of which mean that negotiating an agreement to act cooperatively will be difficult. In particular:

(1)   There are almost 200, rather than 2, countries;
(2)   The countries are not equal in population size, are not equally rich, and do not have the same technologies;
(3)   The countries would not suffer equally from climate change, and so would not benefit equally from mitigation;
(4)   The costs and, especially, the benefits of mitigation are very imperfectly known – we are dealing with ignorance in the terminology introduced in Chapter 10.

We will now consider these matters further.

Table 13.2 A simplified free-rider problem

		North	
		BAU	Mitigate
South	BAU	1/1	1.2/0.9
	Mitigate	0.9/1.2	1.1/1.1

13.2.2 Equity issues

In this sub-section, in order to be reasonably brief, we just look at CO_2. It is by far the most important greenhouse gas in terms of contributions to warming.

Table 13.3 Current P and A for developing and developed

	Population P million	Population share %	GDP per capita A PPP$s
Developing	4695	78.99	3783
Developed	1249	21.01	21199
Total	5944		

We will look first at the question of equity between countries as it affects both the problems about getting an agreement and about what form it should take if it is to be effective. In doing this we will, mostly, continue to treat the world as comprising two economies, so as to be brief. Then we will look at the question of intergenerational equity.

13.2.2.1 Past and future differences between countries

We divide the countries of the world into two groups, Developed and Developing. In Chapter 6 we divided the world into three groups of countries: High-Income OECD; FSB; and Developing. Developing here is defined as in Chapter 6, and Developed here is High-Income OECD and FSB combined. We will use the IPAT identity, introduced in Chapter 7, to look at the differences between these two groups of countries. In Chapter 7 we used IPAT to look at CO_2 scenarios for the world treated as one economy. Here we are going to use it to generate scenarios for Developed and Developing, which will then be added to look at the global situation. The sources for the data used here are the same as in Chapters 6 and 7.

Table 13.3 shows the current situation in terms of population sizes, P, and GDP per capita, A. It also shows the current shares of total world population. Table 13.4 shows the total emissions for each group, I, and the emissions per $ of GDP, T. It also shows CO_2 per capita, derived by dividing I by P. Developing accounts for almost 80 per cent of total population, but less than 40 per cent of emissions. Per capita emissions are five times as high in Developed as in Developing. The CO_2 intensities, T, for the two groups are similar. There are substantial differences in per capita and per $ of GDP emissions between countries within these groups as shown in Table 13.5.

We now want to look at future prospects for CO_2 emissions in Developing and Developed, which depend on the futures for P, A and T. As regards P, we will use growth rates for 2000–2015 taken from the source for the P data in Table 13.3, which we also used in Chapter 6 (see Table 6.2) – 1.4 per cent per year for Developing and 0.15 per cent for Developed. As regards A we will use 2.5 per cent per year GDP per capita growth for Developing and 1 per cent for Developed – these are the sorts of figures that go with sustainable development as envisaged in the Brundtland Report. We will assume initially that T, carbon intensity, is constant. We will look out 100 years. The results arising are shown in Table 13.6. These results are obtained

Table 13.4 Current I and T for developing and developed

	CO_2 emissions tonnes $\times 10^6$ I	CO_2 share %	CO_2 intensity T	CO_2 emissions per capita tonnes
Developing	8921	39.48	0.0005023	1.9
Developed	13673	60.52	0.0005164	10.95
Total	22594			

by using $I \equiv P \times A \times T$ for Developing and Developed separately, given the above assumptions about P, A and T, and then summing for the global Total. To 2025 global CO_2 emissions almost double. To 2100 they increase twenty-fold. By 2025 Developing accounts for more than half of the total, and by 2100 it accounts for more than 90 per cent. Another way of looking at this is as follows:

- for 2000 to 2025, emissions increase by 19,028 tonnes, of which 76 per cent comes from Developing;
- for 2000 to 2050, emissions increase by 63,095 tonnes of which 83 per cent comes from Developing;
- for 2000 to 2100, emissions increase by 443,632 tonnes of which 93 per cent comes from Developing.

Most analysts consider that assuming constant T is unrealistic even in the absence of active mitigation policies. In thinking about future emissions under BAU, the usual assumption is that there will be some de-carbonisation – that T will fall over time. All of the IPCC emissions scenarios, for example, assume some de-carbonisation. Table 13.7 shows the results arising when the calculations just described are repeated save that T is assumed to decline by 2 per cent per year in Developing and Developed. This cuts the increase in global emissions to 2100 to less than three-fold, but the proportions of the total are the same as before because both groups de-carbonise at the same rate. Most of the increase in global CO_2 concentrations in the last 200 years is due to emissions from Developed. Part of the reason that these countries are now rich is that they have burned lots of

Table 13.5 Current data for some selected countries

	Per capita CO_2 tonnes	CO_2 intensity	Population million
USA	19.9	0.0005829	283.2
Russian Federation	9.8	0.0011698	145.5
UK	9.2	0.0003913	59.4
Japan	9.0	0.0003364	127.1
France	6.3	0.0002601	59.2
China	2.5	0.0006288	1275.1
Brazil	1.8	0.0002361	170.4
India	1.1	0.0004665	1008.9
Indonesia	1.1	0.0003615	212.1
Sierra Leone	0.1	0.0002041	4.4

Table 13.6 CO_2 emissions projections – no de-carbonisation

	Current		2025		2050		2100	
	Millions of tonnes	Share %	Millions of tonnes	Share %	Millions of tonnes	Share %	Millions of tonnes	Share %
Developing	8920	39.49	23410	56.25	61451	71.72	423258	90.78
Developed	13670	60.51	18208	43.75	24234	28.28	42964	9.22
Total	22590		41618		85685		466222	

Table 13.7 CO_2 emissions projections – de-carbonisation at 2% per year

	Current		2025		2050		2100	
	Millions of tonnes	Share %	Millions of tonnes	Share %	Millions of tonnes	Share %	Millions of tonnes	Share %
Developing	8920	39.49	14129	56.25	22376	71.72	56120	90.78
Developed	13670	60.51	10987	43.75	8823	28.28	5691	9.22
Total	22590		25116		31199		61811	

fossil fuels since the Industrial Revolution. Because they are rich they are more able to afford the costs of mitigation. Developing countries are poor, and need to grow economically, and mitigating their emissions could damage their growth prospects. Equity requires, it could be argued, that Developed do the mitigating. This is what countries in Developing do argue. On the other hand, while the future is unknown, we can be reasonably sure that most of future emissions increases will come from Developing.

13.2.2.2 A long-term problem

The time spans relevant to decisions about CO_2 mitigation are much longer than those that decision makers are used to dealing with. Costly action to reduce emissions now would be to secure benefits, that is avoided harm from climate change, far into the future. The current generation would be bearing costs to reduce the harm to future generations. If the decision were for no mitigation now, the current generation would be avoiding costs at the expense of future generations.

We can show the time dimension of the CO_2 problem by using data on the carbon cycle provided in Chapter 2 with the model of pollution accumulation introduced in Chapter 4, see section 4.5. That model is

$$S_t = S_{t-1} + E_t - (d \times S_{t-1})$$

where S refers to the stock size, E to emissions and where d is the parameter that gives the rate at which the existing stock decays. As a model for the dynamics of the atmospheric carbon stock this is a huge over-simplification, in that it treats decay as a constant proportion of the stock, but it will suffice to indicate the orders of magnitude involved. The IPCC Working Group I TAR reports results based on more satisfactory models, which tell the same broad story as this one, though they look out only 100 years.

In section 2.4.1 of Chapter 2 we saw that the atmospheric stock of carbon is about 750 Gt – note that now we are working in terms of carbon rather than CO_2. We saw also that each year the land sink takes up about 1.4 Gt and the ocean sink about 1.7 Gt. Adding 1.4 to 1.7 and dividing by 750 gives 0.00413, which we will approximate with the round number 0.005 for the parameter d in our model. Each year, the operation of the (fast) carbon cycle removes about 0.5 per cent of the stock of carbon in the atmosphere as CO_2. So, our numerical model is

$$S_t = S_{t-1} + E_t - (0.005 \times S_{t-1})$$

with which we can do simulations for different assumptions about the time path for E, with an initial level of S equal to 750.

Figures 13.3 to 13.5 show some Excel^{TM} simulation results, with S the atmospheric carbon stock in Gt, on the vertical axis and time on the horizontal. In each case the initial value of S is 750 Gt. In Figure 13.3 emissions start at the actual current level of 6.3 Gt per year (see section 2.4.1) and grow at 1.4 per cent per year out to fifty years from now, and then remain constant at the level they have then got to, which is 12.85 Gt, near enough double what they are now. The atmospheric stock is still growing 500 years out. It eventually stabilises at 2,570 Gt. Suppose

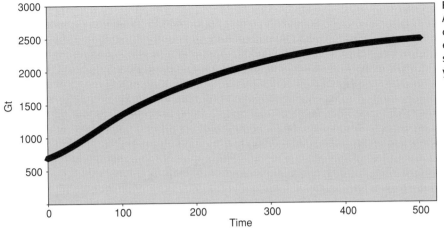

Figure 13.3
Atmospheric
carbon stock for
emissions
stabilisation 50
years out.

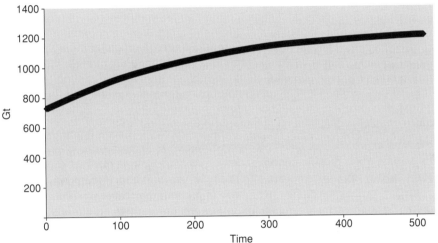

Figure 13.4
Atmospheric
carbon stock for
emissions
stabilisation
now.

that emissions were stabilised now at their current level of 6.3 Gt. Then the model
gives the result shown in Figure 13.4 – the atmospheric stock is still growing 500
years out and will eventually stabilise at 1,260 Gt. Figure 13.5 shows the results
when emissions are stabilised now at 3.125 Gt, just under half the current level.
The atmospheric stock declines slowly, and is still going down 500 years out. It
will stabilise at 625 Gt. It is interesting to note that the carbon stock prior to the
Industrial Revolution was about 600 Gt. Cutting emissions to 50 per cent of the
current level would, according to this model, slowly return the atmospheric stock
to its pre-industrial level. This is, in general terms the story that models considered
to be better descriptions of the carbon cycle tell – emissions cuts take a long time
to show up in concentrations, and major cuts on current levels would be necessary
to get back to pre-industrial levels.

Figure 13.5
Atmospheric
carbon stock
for a 50 per
cent emissions
cut now.

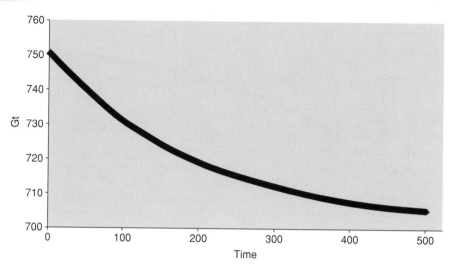

13.2.3 Complexity and ignorance

In Figure 13.2 we showed some of the linkages in the operation of the enhanced greenhouse effect. It actually left out some important feedbacks, which are now included in Figure 13.6, where they are shown as the lighter lines. Climate change-induced changes in the biosphere have two sorts of feedback effect. First, there are effects on the ways in which sinks work, which will affect the relationships between emissions and concentrations. For example, plant growth rates, and hence the rates at which they take up CO_2, are affected by temperature, available moisture and carbon dioxide concentrations. The relationships involved differ across plant species. Second, there are effects on the way that climate responds to greenhouse gas concentrations. The proportion of incident radiation absorbed, and hence the amount of warming, is affected by the vegetation cover, which is affected by climate.

Climatic change itself, and its effects on the biosphere and on humans, both directly and via effects on the biosphere, will affect economic activity in many ways, which will, in turn, affect anthropogenic emissions back at the top of the Figure. Examples are:

- Higher temperatures and increased humidity could lead to increased use of air conditioning, leading to an increased demand for electricity and increased fossil-fuel combustion with increased CO_2 emissions;
- In regard to biosphere impacts, climate change would lead to changes in the spatial patterns of agricultural activities, which would affect trade flows and generate needs for investment in new infrastructure, increasing economic activity levels with effects on anthropogenic emissions;
- One form of economic activity directly affected by climate change itself, as well as indirectly, would be tourism. Higher summer temperatures in northern Europe, for example, would reduce the push effect for temporary summer migration to southern Europe, where higher temperatures could well reduce the pull effect.

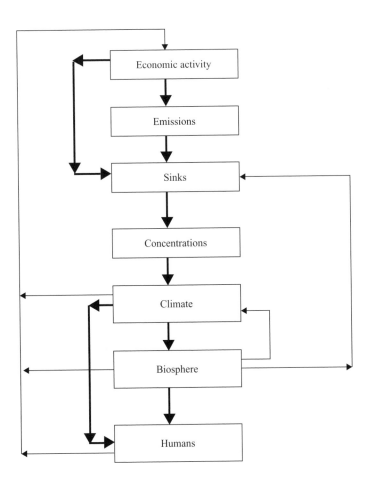

Figure 13.6
Some
feedbacks in
the enhanced
greenhouse
effect.

The important general point is that the enhanced greenhouse effect involves human and natural systems, with complicated feedback effects. The systems and their inter-actions are not all well understood. Some are very poorly understood. In terms of being able to say what will happen in the future, we are, in the terminology of Chapter 10, in a state of ignorance. The future could evolve in many different ways. Not only can nobody assign probabilities to the possibilities, nobody can set out all of the possibilities.

As we noted in section 13.1.5 when discussing IPCC Working Group I's TAR, we are dealing with a non-linear system with positive feedbacks. Such systems are not just complicated. They are also **complex systems**, in the sense that the behaviour of the system cannot be inferred from the behaviour of its components considered separately. Non-linearity means that the whole is not just the sum of its parts. Such systems are inherently unpredictable: they may experience changes that are currently not envisaged, that have not been thought of as possibilities.

As discussed in Chapter 10, decision making in the case of ignorance cannot be reduced to following a simple, or even a complicated, set of rules that produce some kind of 'best' decision. This would be true even if the decision did not involve the need for international cooperation and sensitive equity issues, as the climate-change problem does.

13.2.4 Energy use and supply

The last characteristic of the climate-change problem to be noted here is the fact that it is closely bound up with energy use and supply. We have noted the dependence of the industrial economic way of life on the use of lots of extrasomatic energy – see Chapter 3 especially. We have also noted that in an industrial economy all economic activities use extrasomatic energy, indirectly if not directly – see Chapter 5. High and pervasive dependence on extrasomatic energy is a defining characteristic of a modern industrial economy. Most of that energy is derived from fossil-fuel combustion which releases CO_2 into the atmosphere, and CO_2 is by far the most important gas involved in the enhanced greenhouse effect. In broad terms, CO_2 accounts for about 70 per cent of the warming anticipated out to 2100, and, for the world as a whole, fossil-fuel combustion accounts for about 80 per cent of CO_2 emissions. It is also an important source for NO_2 emissions, and fossil-fuel production gives rise to CH_4 emissions.

Any substantial mitigation of greenhouse gas emissions must involve substantial reductions in fossil-fuel combustion. This would have major impacts on most areas of the industrial way of life. We saw, in Chapter 11, how a carbon tax levied on the extraction of fossil fuels would feed through into increases in the prices paid for all commodities. This, or some other way of reducing fossil fuel-based CO_2 emissions, is something that elected politicians do not want to have to try to persuade the electorate to accept.

13.3 MITIGATION TARGETS AND INSTRUMENTS

We now want to look at the questions of mitigation targets and instrument regimes. In order to clarify the issues, we will assume that the nations of the world have all agreed to set up a global Climate Change Authority (CCA) and given it the power to set a global mitigation target and to do whatever it deems necessary, anywhere in the world, in pursuit of that target. This is a useful but patently unrealistic assumption, as we will discuss in the final sub-section.

13.3.1 Setting a global target

The first point to note here is that what affects the climate is greenhouse gas concentrations, rather than emissions. However, any system of targets and instruments adopted by the CCA would have to work in terms of emissions. Broadly, there are two ways that the CCA could go about global emissions-targeting.

If it followed the advice of ecological economists, it would follow the Precautionary Principle. It would figure out the maximum amount of greenhouse gases in terms of warming potential that should be allowed to be in the atmosphere in order to avoid significant climate change, and the date by which stabilisation at that level should be achieved. From these targets it would, using models of the sort we discussed in sub-section 13.2.2.2, work out the required time paths for emissions. The CCA would have to use judgement to translate 'significant' into an amount of warming potential. Given a number for that, the CCA could translate it into different sets of concentrations targets for the various greenhouse gases, and hence different sets of time paths. Most statements of the Precautionary Principle require its implementation in a cost-effective way, so one criterion that the CCA could use to pick from among the possible time paths for the various gases would be least cost. Much of the information that it would need is not actually available.

If the CCA followed the advice of neoclassical economists, it would look for the emissions time paths that would maximise the excess of benefits over costs. Benefits here are the monetary value of the avoided damages due to climate change, and costs are the mitigation costs. Basically, this approach requires the same information as following the Precautionary Principle plus information on benefits. One problem with this approach that quickly becomes apparent when trying to implement it follows from the long timescales involved. Costs are to be incurred now and in the near future to secure benefits, avoid damages, in the more distant future. It is difficult to translate the biophysical impacts of climate change into $ values. Basically, as noted in Chapter 9, neoclassical economists try to do this by assessing what people would be willing to pay. But the people who would suffer the damage in the future are not around now to answer questions about what they would be willing to pay. So, it is assumed that willingness to pay to avoid impact X in the future will be the same as it is now thought to be.

There is a deeper problem even than this. Suppose that we could actually figure out a money value for the damage that some emissions mitigation programme would avoid in each future year out to some agreed date at which the analysis stops. What weights should be used to add $ at different dates? This is the intertemporal distribution question encountered in Chapter 9. We saw there that achieving intertemporal allocative efficiency does not ensure intertemporal fairness – what it means is that people alive at one point in time cannot be made better off except by making people alive at some other point in time worse off. But when we are asking what mitigation programme to follow, exactly what we are asking about is how much people at one time should give up to make people at some other time better off. In particular, we are asking how much people now alive should give up to make those alive 50, 100, 200 and more years into the future better off. Note the use of 'should' here. This is an ethical question involving normative as well as positive dimensions. There is no 'scientific' answer to the question of how to weight $ of cost now and $ of benefit in the future so as to compare them in a cost–benefit analysis of climate change.

Not surprisingly, it turns out that the answer to this question has a big influence on what cost–benefit analysis has to say about the optimal time path for emissions abatement. Other things being equal, the lower the weight given to $ of future benefit, the less mitigation now and in the near future. Note that following the Precautionary Principle does not really avoid this ethical element in targeting. Just as views about the weights to attach to $ at different dates can differ, so can views about what constitutes 'significant' climate change. The determination of what constitutes 'significant' here is not a purely scientific matter, is not a purely positive question. It involves ethics and judgement.

Supposing that the CCA has, somehow or other, decided what is to be done about mitigation, how can it pursue its targets?

13.3.2 Instrument regimes

To keep the discussion clear, we will just look at CO_2, and we will assume that the target is a once-and-for-all reduction of X tonnes in emissions below their current level. We discussed instruments for pollution control in Chapter 11, in the context of the operations of a regulatory body within a nation state. Given what we are assuming about the CCA, its position is no different from that of such a regulatory authority, and the discussion of the merits of the various instruments largely applies here, so we can be fairly brief.

13.3.2.1 Taxation

The CCA could tax CO_2 emissions everywhere in the world at a uniform rate. Actually, it would, as discussed in Chapter 11, make more sense to tax the extraction of fossil fuels at rates reflecting their relative carbon contents. This would achieve some cut in global emissions at the lowest global cost that it could be achieved at. But, it would not necessarily be the cut that the CCA wanted – uniform taxation is not dependable, given the knowledge available to the CCA. Further, there is no reason to suppose that the incidence of the tax would fair as between nations – the tax rate would be the same in India as in the USA. The CCA would be in receipt of enormous amounts of money. It could use these in pursuit of equity, by, say, dividing its revenues between countries according to a formula such that per capita payments were inversely related to per capita GDP.

13.3.2.2 Command and Control

The CCA could set allowable emissions limits for each country, and impose penalties on countries not in compliance. Assuming compliance, this would achieve the target, but it would not do so at least cost. The main question for the CCA would be how to divide up its global amount of allowed emissions as between countries. One option would be equal percentage reductions: if reducing the global total by X tonnes is a global Z per cent cut, then every country has to cut by Z per cent. Given global disparities in GDP and CO_2 per capita, this would widely be seen as inequitable, with India cutting by the same percentage as the USA, for example. What many would regard as a more equitable approach would be to take the global level of emissions implied by a cut of X tonnes, and to divide it by the world's population to give a global per capita allowance of y tonnes. Each country's emissions limit would then be the product of y and its population size. Countries like India would get allowances greatly in excess of their current emissions, while countries like the USA would get allowances much smaller than their current emissions.

13.3.2.3 *Tradable permits*

The CCA could give an amount of emissions permits to each country, and the permits would be tradable as between countries, with a country allowed the level of emissions covered by its permit holding after trade. The theory that we looked at in Chapter 11 showed that tradable permits are least-cost and dependable – given compliance, the global target would be hit at the lowest global cost. The equity properties of such a regulatory system would depend on the initial allocation of permits as between countries. Issuing them in line with what would be equal percentage reductions in each country would perpetuate existing disparities – the USA would get a lot more than India, for example. If they were allocated on the equal per capita shares of total global emissions basis described above, countries like India would have permits to sell to countries like the USA, and there could be major transfers of wealth as between large-population poor countries and small-population rich countries.

13.3.2.4 *Sinks*

These descriptions of the alternative instrument regimes that the CCA could adopt ignore many practical details of implementation. For example, what matters in regard to the enhanced greenhouse effect is concentrations rather than emissions as such, and concentrations depend on sinks as well as emissions. A country would be contributing to mitigation if it enhanced sinks, and each of these regimes would need to allow for this. Under taxation, for example, a country could be paid at the tax rate for each tonne's worth of sink enhancement. If at the margin, sink enhancement was cheaper than emissions abatement the country would enhance rather than abate. The least cost property would be retained.

13.3.3 National sovereignty and mitigation

The CCA was a useful invention in order to make some important points about climate change-mitigation targets and instruments, but is not a realistic prospect, for the foreseeable future, in regard to how the climate-change problem might actually be addressed. Setting up such a body would involve unacceptable diminutions of the sovereignty of the nation states that govern the world. If the climate-change problem is to be addressed, it will be by treaty arrangements covering targets and instruments, negotiated by national governments.

If such a treaty is to be negotiated, its terms will have to create the incentives for nation states to join it. In this context, the relevant questions about targets and instruments are as much questions about incentives for participation as they are questions about dependability and cost minimisation.

When nation states enter international negotiations they are mainly concerned to look after national interests. They are interested in what a proposal would cost them, rather than what it would cost the world. The global least cost property of taxes and tradable permits will not be of great interest to negotiators – least cost for the world could be high cost for many individual countries. This would be the perception of the developing countries in regard to a global CO_2 tax, for example. In fact, such countries see their main problem as poverty now, and are not much interested in incurring costs now for uncertain future benefits. A globally administered CO_2 tax with the revenues going mainly to developing countries might attract the developing countries, but would be unacceptable to developed countries. Similarly, if tradable permits were issued on an equal per capita entitlement basis, large-population poor countries would have incentives to sign in terms of short-run gains from surplus permit sales, but the developed nations would see disincentives.

In fact, perhaps surprisingly, most nations have signed an international treaty to address the climate-change problem, which we look at in the next section.

13.4 WHAT IS BEING DONE ABOUT THE PROBLEM?

We now look at what is actually being done about the climate-change problem. Of necessity, we can not go into a lot of detail but must look at the general features of what is being done – whole books have been written about what we are going to cover in a few pages. You can learn more about particulars by following up suggestions from Further Reading, and/or by visiting the websites noted at the end of the chapter.

13.4.1 The United Nations Framework Convention on Climate Change

The IPCC was established in 1988 and produced its first report in 1990, which was a major input to the negotiations towards the United Nations Framework Convention on Climate Change (UNFCCC) which began early in 1991. The UNFCCC was tabled and signed by more than 150 nations at the Earth Summit in Rio de Janeiro in June 1992. As noted in Chapter 10, that conference was part of the process set in motion by the Brundtland Report, and was intended to promote sustainable development – it brought together concerns for the global environment and concerns about poverty in developing countries. The UNFCCC reflected the larger process of which it was part, and is to be understood as one, important, particular manifestation of the pursuit of sustainable development.

As stated in Article 2, the objective is:

> stabilization of greenhouse gas concentrations in the atmosphere at a level that would prevent dangerous anthropogenic interference with the climate system. Such a level should be achieved within a time frame sufficient to allow ecosystems to adapt naturally to climate change, to ensure that food production is not threatened and to enable economic development to proceed in a sustainable manner.

Article 3 states the principles which should guide the parties to the convention in pursuit of this objective. These state that equity requires that 'the developed country Parties should take the lead', and that 'the specific needs and circumstances of developing country Parties' should be given full consideration. Article 3 also endorses the Precautionary Principle (see Chapter 10), stating that:

Where there are threats of serious or irreversible damage, lack of full scientific certainty should not be used as a reason for postponing such measures, taking into account that policies and measures to deal with climate change should be cost-effective.

In pursuit of the objective, all Parties to the UNFCCC were committed to preparing national greenhouse inventories, to reporting on mitigation activities, to preparing to adapt to climate change, and to cooperating on research into climate change. Following the principles, Parties were divided into three categories: Annex I; Annex II; and the others. The Annex II Parties were basically the members of the OECD. The Annex I Parties were the Annex II Parties plus the countries that formerly comprised the Soviet Union and its satellites. The Annex I Parties were basically the industrial economies and the rest were basically the developing economies – the two groups corresponded closely to the 'North' and the 'South' as those terms had been used in the international relations context, and to Developed and Developing as used in sub-section 13.2.2.1 here.

Article 4 of the UNFCCC set out the commitments of the Parties. Those applying to all are stated above. Annex II Parties undertook to provide unspecified amounts of financial assistance to developing countries to help them meet their UNFCCC commitments, to help vulnerable developing countries to adapt to climate change, and to help with the transfer of environmentally sound technologies to developing countries. The Annex I Parties also undertook to adopt mitigation policies, operating on emissions sources and sinks. It was widely reported at the time that this commitment involved a target of returning emissions to their 1990 level by 2000, but on a careful reading of the relevant paragraphs it is not clear that this was the case.

What is clear is that the industrialised countries were intended to take the lead and bear the burdens, at least in the first instance. All Parties were, however, committed to what was really the most important, and somewhat novel, feature of the UNFCCC. This was the provision for subsequent annual Conferences of the Parties, or COPs as they became known. These were charged with sorting out issues not resolved in the course of the UNFCCC negotiations, and with reviewing progress towards the stated objective of the UNFCCC in the light of changing knowledge and circumstances. The UNFCCC itself thus became but the first step in an ongoing international process aimed at addressing the climate-change problem.

Signing an international treaty does not bring it into force. This requires that it is ratified by a specified number of the signatories by being approved by the domestic legislative apparatus. The UNFCCC required ratification by 50 countries, which was achieved by December 1993. By normal standards, this was quick. The lack of specific binding commitments no doubt helped here. As of 2004 the UNFCCC has been ratified by more than 170 countries.

13.4.2 The Kyoto Protocol

The next major development in the process initiated at Rio de Janeiro was the third COP which took place in Kyoto, Japan in 1997. After a lot of difficult negotiations prior to and at this COP, it adopted a Protocol to the UNFCCC, the Kyoto Protocol (hereafter the KP). The text of the KP, and of the UNFCCC, is available on the UNFCCC website (address given at the end of this chapter).

As compared with the UNFCCC, the KP did not involve any new commitments for the developing countries. A number of industrialised countries, listed in Annex B to the KP and known as the Annex B Parties, did take on a new commitment. The membership list for Annex B is effectively the same as that for Annex I to the UNFCCC. These countries undertook to ensure that their greenhouse gas emissions did not exceed their 'assigned amounts' by the 'commitment period 2008 to 2012' (Article 3). The 'assigned amount' for each country is stated, in Annex B, in terms of a reduction on the country's 1990 level of emissions. The reductions vary from 8 per cent (several countries) to −10 per cent, i.e. an increase of 10 per cent (Iceland). The USA reduction listed is 7 per cent: Australia is listed for an increase of 8 per cent. It was calculated that the overall effect of the reductions listed in Annex B would be a reduction of 5.2 per cent on 1990 for all the Annex B countries taken together.

If you look at Annex B you will see that it lists all the 1997 members of the European Community and the European Community itself, and that all the individual members have the same percentage reduction commitment as the European Community itself – all are shown as cutting by 8 per cent. The KP allows countries to come together as a group which is the entity which has an emissions reduction commitment – it is then for the group to decide individual commitments for its members so as to meet the group commitment. To date, the European Community is the only such group. It agreed Member State emissions-reduction targets in 1998. Mainly, the richer countries are to reduce emissions, while the poorer can increase them. The range is from a 28 per cent reduction for Luxembourg to a 27 per cent increase for Portugal.

The adoption of quantified emissions-reduction targets by the Annex B countries, but not by any others, is the key feature of the KP. It also included so-called 'flexibility' provisions relating to how these commitments could be met. These can be classified as internal and external.

Internal flexibility had two dimensions. First, the targets referred to the total of several greenhouse gases to be added together in terms of their CO_2 equivalences. Thus, for example, if methane were twice as effective as carbon dioxide in its warming effect, a unit of CH_4 is equivalent to two units of CO_2 for the purposes of the KP emissions reductions. The KP did not say by how much emissions of each greenhouse gas should be cut – this was left to each Annex I Party to decide for itself. The point here is that the costs of cutting differ across the gases in different ways in different countries, so that this flexibility left it open to each Party to choose a mix that minimised its costs. Second, the effects of land-use changes could be taken into account. This relates to CO_2 and vegetation, where sink enhancement through, for example, reafforestation could be counted against the emissions-reduction target. Again, this was about the costs of meeting the target – for some countries reafforestation could be cheaper than reductions in, say, CO_2 emissions from fossil-fuel burning.

External flexibility took three forms: emissions trading; joint implementation; and the clean development mechanism. In each case, the basic point is again about cost reduction.

Emissions trading relates to only the Annex B Parties. We have previously discussed, in Chapter 11, emissions trading within a country: how and why it works, and how it reduces total costs. In the context of the KP, where it is covered by Article 17, the idea is that rather than reduce emissions within its borders, Party X may claim against its reduction target a reduction in emissions taking place in Party Y. Party X would pay Party Y for the right to do this. Party Y would lose the right to claim the reduction for itself in meeting its commitment.

Joint implementation, Article 6 of the KP, relates only to Annex 1 countries. Where a firm or government entity from country X finances an investment project in country Y that has the effect of reducing emissions or enhancing sinks in Y, country X may claim this result for itself. Country Y cannot then claim it against its commitment. In some circumstances this may be cheaper for country X than doing the equivalent amount of emissions reduction at home.

The Clean Development Mechanism, Article 12 of the KP, relates to Annex I and non-Annex I countries. Apart from that, it is very like joint implementation. Annex I countries can fund development projects in non-Annex I countries and claim any emissions reductions entailed for themselves. Again, the point here is about costs to Annex I countries – financing a project that would benefit a developing country could be a cheaper way of meeting some of the KP commitment than action at home.

In regard to these flexibility mechanisms, the KP was about establishing principles rather than specifying the exact rules according to which they were to operate. This was intentionally left for future COPs, and especially for the sixth COP to be held in The Hague in November 2000. To somewhat over-simplify a complex situation, this COP was dominated by disagreement between the USA and the EU over the extent to which Annex I countries could meet their commitments by way of credits obtained through the external flexibility mechanisms. The EU's position was that the intention at Kyoto was that these mechanisms were to be 'supplemental': that the main burden of meeting the commitment should fall on domestic action to reduce emissions and enhance sinks. The USA did not want to see any restrictions placed on the extent to which these mechanisms could be used, so that it would be possible for an Annex I Party to meet its commitment entirely on the basis of things that actually took place outside its boundaries. There was also disagreement over the allowable extent of reliance on domestic sink enhancement, and over whether the Clean Development Mechanism provisions should be interpreted to include sink enhancement or to be restricted to emissions reduction. The USA wanted no restrictions on the former and a wide interpretation in relation to the Clean Development Mechanism. The EU disagreed on both issues.

The sixth COP ended without agreement on these issues. In March 2001 the USA announced its withdrawal from the UNFCCC. As well as concerns over what meeting its KP commitment would cost it in the absence of the ability to make maximum use of the flexibility mechanisms – over the cost, that is, of reducing emissions, especially of CO_2, domestically – the USA has always been concerned that the developing nations – where most of the future growth in emissions will occur – have no commitment to do anything to reduce their greenhouse gas emissions.

The situation in regard to the KP at the time that this chapter was written will now be outlined – you can check the situation at the time that you are reading it by visiting the UNFCCC website. Since Kyoto there have been three further COPs. These have made quite a lot of progress in spelling out precise rules for the flexibility mechanisms. At COP7, which the USA attended as only an observer, it was agreed that Annex I Parties, in their annual reports, would have to demonstrate that their use of flexibility mechanisms is 'supplemental to domestic action'. No quantified limit was set on the use of the flexibility mechanisms. This remains the situation.

Article 24 of the KP states that it will:

> enter into force on the ninetieth day after the date on which not less than 55 Parties to the Convention, incorporating Parties included in Annex I which accounted in total for at least 55 per cent of the total carbon dioxide emissions for 1990 of the Parties included in Annex I, have deposited their instruments of ratification, acceptance, approval or accession.

As of April 2004 the KP had not come into force. The first requirement had been met, but not the second. The KP had then been ratified by 122 of the Parties to the Convention. Those Parties accounted for 44.2 per cent of 1990 Annex I CO_2 emissions. Clearly, from the data on CO_2 emissions given earlier, had the USA ratified the second requirement would have been met, and the KP would now be in force. It is also the case that Russia has yet to ratify – ratification by Russia would mean that the second requirement was met. The only other significant non-ratifier is Australia – Australian ratification alone would not satisfy the 55 per cent of 1990 Annex I emissions condition.

Notwithstanding that the KP is not yet actually in force, there is already some emissions trading, and some joint implementation projects have gone ahead, as have projects falling under the Clean Development Mechanism umbrella. Some countries have stated that they will meet their commitments even if the KP does not come into force. You can find out more about these things from the Further Reading suggestions and keep abreast of the unfolding situation by visiting the appropriate websites – the companion website to this book will flag major developments. Now we want to look at what effects the KP would have if it was implemented.

13.4.3 What would Kyoto's impact be?

While they differ in detail, all assessments of what the KP cuts in global greenhouse gas emissions would do to the climate change that would occur without those cuts agree that the effect would be small. This follows from the fact that the cuts are a small proportion of emissions from a group of countries that will not be the main source of greenhouse gas emissions in the future. The KP calls for a 5.2 per cent cut on 1990 levels for the Annex B Parties – which are effectively the developed countries as defined for Tables 13.3 through to 13.7. It calls for no cuts at all by the developing countries.

While it is concentrations of all greenhouse gases that affect the climate, we can get a sense of the orders of magnitude involved by looking at the CO_2 emissions figures from Table 13.6. If the developed countries cut now by 5 per cent, and stay at the level that results, their emissions out to 2100 are constant at, in round numbers of millions, $13,000 \times 10^6$ tonnes. Adding this to the 2100 figure of 423,258 for developing we get 436,528 rather than the 466,222 million tonnes shown in Table 13.6 – a reduction of about 6 per cent in the 2100 level of emissions. If we assume de-carbonisation in the no-Kyoto situation an in Table 13.7, then the effect of Kyoto is even smaller. Repeating the calculations there save that Developed starts at 13,000 now leads to total world emissions of 61,497 million tonnes in 2100, which is less than 1 per cent down on the figure shown in Table 13.7.

Assessing the impact of the KP on climate change depends on an assessment of what would happen without it. As we saw earlier, the IPCC reports a wide range of 'business as usual' climate-change scenarios, due to different assumptions about population growth, economic growth, technical change, and the responsiveness of the climate system to changing concentrations of the greenhouse gases. Assumptions about all of these things affect an assessment of the climatic impact of Kyoto, so in detail there are a wide range of assessments of that. In terms of global average surface temperature, estimates of how much lower it would be in 2100 range from $0.03°C$ to $0.3°C$ – recall that the IPCC range for the increase to 2100 on business as usual is $1.4°C$ to $5.8°C$. Higher figures for the Kyoto impact go with higher figures for business as usual. The best that can be said for the KP emissions-reduction commitments is that they would delay climate change by a few years – what would have happened in 2100 on a business-as-usual basis would happen instead around 2110. The magnitude of the effect on sea-level rise would be similar.

As noted above, the UNFCCC adopts the precautionary principle as the basis for its approach to mitigation, and its objective is to 'prevent dangerous anthropogenic interference with the climate system'. Given the IPCC assessment of what is likely to happen with business as usual, and the small difference that the KP emissions-reduction commitments will make, it is very unlikely that achievement of those commitments would realise the UNFCCC objective. Certainly, it would not avoid the need for adaptation to climate change. It should also be noted that some commentators doubt that ratification of the KP would actually deliver the commitments – it contains no enforcement mechanisms, and there are no provisions for sanctions against countries that do not meet their commitments. On the other hand, most countries that enter into international agreements do strive to honour them most of the time.

Article 3 of the UNFCCC also refers to the need for 'policies and measures to deal with climate change' to be 'cost-effective'. As with assessments of what will happen if the KP commitments are realised, so there are a range of estimates of what those commitments would cost. What is generally agreed is that the flexibility mechanisms would lower the cost of achieving a cut in global emissions equivalent to 5.2 per cent of those of the Annex B countries in 1990. The point of putting it this way is that under the provisions of the Clean Development Mechanism some of this cut would actually take place in non-Annex B countries.

One set of estimates of costs is given in Nordhaus and Boyer (2000). According to their modelling results, out to 2105 the global costs of the KP commitments would be $59 billion with the flexibility mechanisms working and $884 billion without them working at all (these are in 1990 US$). If, that is, each Annex B country had to realise its commitment entirely by domestic action, the global cost would be fifteen times what it would be if there were emissions trading, joint implementation and the Clean Development Mechanism were operating. Nordhaus and Boyer also looked at how these costs would be distributed across nations. They found that without the flexibility mechanisms working, the USA would bear $852 billion of cost, out of the global total of $884 billion, whereas with flexibility the cost to the USA would be $91 billion. The Nordhaus and Boyer results are illustrative of those from a number of studies which show the importance of the flexibility mechanisms in reducing the costs of its commitment, since abandoned, to the USA. These sorts of calculations were an important input to the processes by which the US government reached its decision to withdraw from the UNFCCC following the failure to agree on the extent to which flexibility mechanisms would be used at COP6.

What do these sorts of numbers really mean? If they are reasonable estimates of the costs involved, should we think the costs are high, or low? Certainly, $884 billion sounds like a lot of money. To give some perspective let us look at the cost to the USA in the no-flexibility case: $852 billion. This is the present value of the annual costs over the period 1995 to 2105 – we looked at the calculation of the present value of a stream of money values in Chapter 8. Using the approximation:

$$PV = v \div r$$

where v is a constant annual sum of money (see Exercise 7 in Chapter 8) this present value goes with a constant annual cost of $42.6 billion per year for an interest rate of 5 per cent. Taking the population of the USA to be 270 million, that is $160 per person per year, or about $3 per week. In 1995 US per capita GDP was about $23,000 in 1990 $ – $160 is about 0.7 per cent of that. Of course, the standard assumption is that per capita US GDP would grow over 1995 to 2105, and if that happened the cost each year would be a smaller proportion of per capita GDP.

13.4.4 Assessment

Given our discussion of the nature of the climate-change problem, and of the incentives facing potential signatories to an international agreement to address it, the main features of the existing international agreement are not surprising.

The UNFCCC endorses the Precautionary Principle as the means by which the objectives of mitigation policy should be set, but it is questionable whether the KP global emissions-reduction commitments would be enough to 'prevent dangerous anthropogenic interference with the climate system'. We say 'would be enough' because there are no penalties for non-compliance, and because at the moment the KP is not in force. The total global cost involved does not appear to be very great.

In terms of the mitigation instrument regime, it is command-and-control-modified, by the flexibility mechanisms, in the direction of tradable permits. The scope of the regime is restricted, with only the Annex B, essentially the developed, countries contributing to the global mitigation target. The costs of meeting the global target are borne entirely by the Annex B countries.

Many commentators consider that not enough is being done to satisfy the Precautionary Principle. Others, mindful of the difficulties involved in negotiating an international treaty to address a problem as difficult as climate change, take the view that considerable progress, more than might have been expected, has been made.

In considering whether the KP represents success or failure, we need to keep in mind that the UNFCCC set in motion, in terms of the COPs, a process in which Kyoto was an early stage. According to one commentator:

> Achieving the commitments in the industrialised countries would presumably be accompanied by the development of new infrastructure, technologies and industries that would set their energy economies on a different course over subsequent years and decades. These changes would also tend to spread globally.   (Grubb *et al.*, 1999)

SUMMARY

While the basic physics of the enhanced greenhouse effect is straightforward, the environmental systems involved in the climate change problem are complicated and complex, and are not well understood. In terms of assessing the climatic consequences of alternative future emissions paths we are in a state of ignorance. What we do know is that choices made now will have consequences stretching far into the future. The human systems that will determine future emissions paths are also complicated and complex. The climate-change problem is global in nature, but there is no world government to respond. Any international response must be negotiated by sovereign nation states pursuing what they see as their national interests. An international response has been negotiated, and it reflects, especially in its open-ended character, the nature of the problem.

KEYWORDS

Anthropogenic forcing factors (p. 490): factors with origins in human behaviour that are able to disturb the balance of a system and thus potentially alter system characteristics; here: changes in greenhouse gas concentrations and sulphur emissions.

Atmospheric lifetimes (p. 487): the time between the emission of a greenhouse gas molecule into the atmosphere and its removal from the atmosphere.

Complex systems (p. 505): where the behaviour of the system cannot be inferred from the behaviour of its components considered separately.

De-carbonisation (p. 496): reducing CO_2 emissions per $ of GDP.

Dominant strategy (p. 499): the choice in a game that offers the best outcome irrespective of the choice made by the other players.

Game theory (p. 498): the analysis of situations where the outcome of a decision by one player depends on the decisions made by the other players, which are not known at the time.

No-regrets options (p. 497): mitigation activities involving negative costs.

Sinks (p. 485): processes which remove greenhouse gases from the atmosphere.

Thermohaline circulation (p. 492): global ocean circulation which is driven by differences in the density of the sea water which is controlled by temperature (thermal) and salinity (haline).

FURTHER READING

The literature on climate change and the enhanced greenhouse effect is enormous. What follows is but a small selection from that literature. Many of the websites cited below provide access to papers and reports on all aspects of the problem.

The IPCC TAR reports: Houghton *et al.* (2001) for Working Group I; McCarthy *et al.* (2001) for II; and Metz *et al.* (2001) for III, are authoritative, but apart from the summaries they are hardgoing for those without a reasonable background in the academic disciplines on which the chapters draw. Houghton (1997) is an excellent short introduction to climate science and climate modelling. Part V of Lomborg (2001) looks at all aspects of the problem – and is somewhat sceptical about its severity and of the case for incurring costs to mitigate.

Chapter 10 in Perman *et al.* (2003) takes the game-theoretic analysis of the free-rider problem in dealing with international environmental problems further than we did in section 13.2.1, and provides references to the literature on this. Ramussen (2001) is a general text on game theory: see also Varian (1987) for an economics-based treatment. Sandler (1997) is a book-length treatment of the application of game theory to international environmental problems. Chapter 10 of Perman *et al.* (2003) looks at acid rain and stratospheric ozone depletion as well as climate change. The stratospheric ozone problem shares several characteristics with the climate-change problem, but the CFCs are subject to more effective control, under the Montreal Protocol, than are the greenhouse gases under the Kyoto Protocol. Why this is so is an interesting and important question which is considered in Barrett (1999). The book in which Barrett's analysis appears, Kaul *et al.* (1999), is all about global public goods and bads, and methods for their analysis.

Grubb (1999) is an excellent account of the Kyoto Protocol, of the negotiations that lead to the signing of it, and of its implications. Toman (2001) is a collection of papers from Resources for the Future, a US 'think tank', which give the neoclassical economics take on most aspects of the climate-change problem. Spash (2002) is an ecological economics look at some of the issues, especially to do with valuation, associated with policy making in respect to the problem. Nordhaus and Boyer (2000) is a well-documented report on results obtained from a model which has both a climate component and an economic component – it models all of the stages in Figure 13.2, albeit in a much simplified way as regards climate. The link between the enhanced greenhouse effect and fossil fuel use is explored in many books, reports and papers. The websites cited below are a useful point of entry to this literature. Read (1993) sets out the basic situation and argues for a policy of replacing fossil-fuel combustion with biomass combustion, with the biomass being harvested on a sustainable basis so that the CO_2 released is taken up by the biomass growth. Read argues, in broad terms, that a programme of this nature on a scale sufficient to significantly slow global warming is both technically feasible and cost-effective. Royal Commission on Environmental Pollution (2000) is a report looking at what could be done in the UK energy sector, and the costs involved, in order to reduce UK fossil-fuel combustion by 60 per cent of its 1998 level by 2050. It did this on the basis that this is the sort of target that would be consistent with a truly precautionary approach to the climate-change problem.

WEBSITES

For the texts of the 1992 UNFCCC and the Kyoto Protocol and up-to-date information on the situation in regard to ratification, COPs, etc., visit the UNFCCC website at http://unfccc.int. The latest information on the work of the IPCC is at http://www.ipcc.ch/. In the UK the government department mainly responsible for climate change matters is the Department for Environment Food and Rural Affairs, DEFRA, at http://www.defra.gov.uk/. Two useful USA sites are http://www.epa.gov/ for the Environmental Protection Agency, EPA, and http://www.rff.org/ for Resources for the Future (RFF), a 'think tank' primarily concerned with environmental issues. At http://www.epa.gov/ozone/ the former provides information about the stratospheric ozone-depletion problem, and the Montreal Protocol which addresses it. The ISEE encyclopedia, at http://www.ecoeco.org, has a very good entry 'The Kyoto Protocol and its flexibility mechanisms' which gives addresses to websites where can you can get up-to-date information on how the use of them is evolving. The Global Commons Institute aims to promote the protection of global common property, and focuses mainly on the enhanced greenhouse effect, where it advocates 'contraction and convergence' whereby global emissions are progressively reduced and everybody in the world has an equal share of the global total: http://www.gci.org.uk/. See also the World Resources Institute at http://www.wri.org/climate/.

DISCUSSION QUESTIONS

1. Groucho Marx (a twentieth-century American comedian) asked: 'Why should I do anything for posterity – what did it do for me?' Would you want to persuade him that as far as climate change goes this is the wrong way to look at things? How would you persuade him?
2. According to a neoclassical economist, on the best estimates out to 2100 adaptation to climate change would involve lower net costs than mitigation, and therefore we should adapt rather than mitigate. Do you think that the recommendation follows from the analysis?
3. In relation to the assessment of the Kyoto Protocol in the quotation which ends section 13.4.4, discuss the view that the EU was right to want to limit flexibility to a supplementary role since it reduces the technology-forcing effect of the emissions-reduction commitments.

EXERCISES

1. Rework the calculations for Tables 13.6 and 13.7 on the assumptions of: (a) zero population growth in both groupings after 2025; and (b) zero population growth in both groupings with effect now.
2. Suppose that there was an agreement that global CO_2 emissions should be cut by 10 per cent on their current level and held there. Using the data from Tables 13.3 and 13.4, work out what allowable emissions from Developing and Developed would be if these were determined on the basis of equal per

capita entitlements. Suppose that population growth was as in Tables 13.6 and 13.7, and that new allowances were worked out in 2025, 2050 and 2100. What would those allowances be?

3. Do an Excel simulation for 500 years using the model from section 13.2.2.2 for CO_2 concentrations under the emissions scenario of question 2. At what level would concentrations stabilise? Convert CO_2 to carbon by dividing by 3.7 – 1 Gt of carbon is equivalent to 3.7 Gt of CO_2.

4. Take the answers from question 2 for what current allowances for Developed and Developing would be. Suppose that Developed bought permits from Developing so that they could continue to emit $13,670 \times 10^6$ million tonnes as in Table 13.6. What would the financial transfer from Developed to Developing be if a permit to emit 1 tonne of CO_2 had a price of $10?

14

Biodiversity loss

In this chapter you will:

- Learn that due to human activities biodiversity is being lost at a much higher rate than is normal;
- Consider why this matters to humans;
- find out why reducing the rate of biodiversity loss is difficult;
- Learn about the main features of the international treaty intended to address the problem.

The problem of biodiversity loss has a lot in common with the climate-change problem, and the main international treaty intended to deal with it shares a number of features with the UNFCCC discussed in the previous chapter. We will look at the treaty in section 14.4. In the first section we explain what biodiversity loss is, what is driving it, and why it matters to humans. Section 14.2 is about the characteristics it shares with the climate-change problem, and section 14.3 identifies some of the main issues arising in policy formulation.

14.1 THE BIODIVERSITY-LOSS PROBLEM

In this section we are going to set out the essential features of the biodiversity-loss problem. We begin by explaining what biodiversity is, and what is known about how much of it there is.

14.1.1 What is biodiversity?

Most generally, **biodiversity** is the diversity of living organisms, the genes that they contain and the ecosystems in which they exist. The most fundamental level at which to consider biodiversity is the genetic. As discussed in Chapter 2, genes determine the potentialities of individual organisms. A population is a group of individuals which are involved in reproduction, and a species is a collection of individuals that could be involved in reproduction. Populations are reproductively isolated sub-groups of a species. There is genetic diversity within a population

Table 14.1 Species numbers described and estimated 1995

Taxa	Species described	High estimate	Low estimate	Working figure	Accuracy
Viruses	4,000 (1%)	1,000,000	50,000	400,000	V. poor
Bacteria	4,000 (0.4%)	3,000,000	50,000	1,000,000	V. poor
Fungi	72,000 (5%)	2,700,000	200,000	1,500,000	Moderate
Protoza	40,000 (20%)	200,000	60,000	200,000	V. poor
Algae	40,000 (10%)	1,000,000	150,000	400,000	V. poor
Plants	270,000 (84%)	500,000	300,000	320,000	Good
Nematodes	25,000 (6%)	1,000,000	100,000	400,000	Poor
Crustaceans	40,000 (27%)	200,000	75,000	150,000	Moderate
Arachnids	75,000 (10%)	1,000,000	300,000	750,000	Moderate
Insects	950,000 (12%)	100,000,000	2,000,000	8,000,000	Moderate
Molluscs	70,000 (35%)	200,000	100,000	200,000	Moderate
Chordates	45,000 (90%)	55,000	50,000	50,000	Good
Others	115,000 (46%)	800,000	200,000	250,000	Moderate
Totals	**1,750,000 (13%)**	**111,655,000**	**3,635,000**	**13,620,000**	**V. poor**

Note: ( ) gives Described as % of Working
Source: Table 3.1.2 in Heywood (1995).

Table 14.2 Species numbers described and estimated 2002

Kingdom	Described	Estimated number
Bacteria	4,000 (0.4%)	1,000,000
Protoctists (Algae, Protozoa, etc.)	80,000 (13%)	600,000
Fungi	70,000 (5%)	1,500,000
Plants	270,000 (90%)	300,000
Animals	1,320,000 (12%)	10,600,000
Total	**1,744,000 (13%)**	**14,000,000**

Note: ( ) gives Described as % of Estimated
Source: Table 1.1 Global biodiversity outlook at http://www.biodiv.org

and within a species. Individuals from different species differ genetically from one another more than do individuals from different populations of the same species.

Most work on genetic diversity takes the species as the unit of account – biodiversity is said to be lost when a species goes extinct. We shall follow this practice. The extent of biodiversity can then be expressed as the number of species in existence. Tables 14.1 and 14.2 give information about what is known about this. The important points are that we do not know how many species exist, but we do know that there are a lot of them. The two tables refer to data and estimates put together seven years apart, but tell essentially the same stories, albeit for slightly different classifications of species. In total some 1,750,000 different species have actually been identified and described by taxonomists. This represents less than 15 per cent of the widely accepted estimate, or 'Working Figure', for the number of species. The total number could be over 100 million, or as low as 3.7 million. The percentage of the estimated number of species that have been described varies greatly across Kingdoms and Phyla. In terms of the former, the Plant and Animal Kingdoms are much better described than the others. Chordates – mammals, birds, amphibians, reptiles, fish and a small number of invertebrates (without backbones) – are what most people think of as 'animals' and (see Table 14.1) are 90 per cent described. Anthropods comprise by far the largest animal phylum, and include insects and crustaceans – for insects 950,000 species have been described, but this is only 12 per cent of the working figure.

Described species are not evenly distributed around the world. The most obvious spatial pattern is that **species richness**, the number of species per unit area, increases moving towards the equator. This correlates with the pattern for primary production, which was noted in Chapter 2: solar radiation increases with decreasing latitude. Also of interest in regard to the spatial pattern of biodiversity is **endemism**: a species is endemic to an area when it occurs only in that area. Places, such as Australia, that were isolated for long periods have high levels of endemism.

14.1.2 How fast is biodiversity being lost?

Species have been going extinct since life began – extinction is a 'natural' event. The fossil record indicates that, on average, species have come into existence at a higher rate than they have gone extinct, so that biodiversity has been increasing over time. There have been five, relatively brief, periods in the history of the earth during which the extinction rate was very high. The most recent was about 65 million years ago, when 10 per cent of terrestrial species, including the dinosaurs, and 15 per cent of marine species went extinct. This is generally thought to have been caused by climate change, possibly associated with an asteroid impact. About 250 million years ago up to 90 per cent of the marine animals present in the fossil record appear to have gone extinct, and again extreme climate change is thought to have been involved.

Table 14.3 gives the number of recorded species extinctions in the plant and animal kingdoms in the last 400 years. Other species in these kingdoms may have gone extinct without ever having been described. The number shown in Table 14.3 for plants is thought to be a serious underestimate. For the other kingdoms the data on recent extinctions is very limited and patchy. It would be reasonable to assume that rates there are similar to those for plants and animals. For animals, in the last 400 years, the rate of extinction in Table 14.3 is 180 per century, and for birds and mammals, where the data is most reliable, it is 32 and 22 per century respectively. How do these rates compare with those in the fossil record, the 'normal' rates of extinction? The fossil record suggests that the normal rate is something like 250 species per century for a total number of species in existence of 10 million. If 250 is divided by 10,000,000 this gives a rate of 0.000025, which, when applied to the existing numbers of bird and mammal species of

Table 14.3 Species extinctions since 1600	
Kingdom	*Extinct Species*
Vertebrates	**337**
Mammals	87
Birds	131
Reptiles	22
Amphibians	5
Fishes	92
Invertebrates	**389**
Insects	73
Molluscs	303
Crustaceans	9
Others	4
Plants	**90**
Mosses	3
Conifers, cycads, etc.	1
Flowering Plants	86

Source: Global biodiversity outlook, Table 1.4 at http://www.biodiv.org

Table 14.4 Threatened species

Kingdom	Described species	Species evaluated 2003	Species threatened 2003	Percentage of described threatened	Percentage of evaluated threatened
Vertebrates	**56,586**	**17,127**	**3,524**	**6%**	**21%**
Mammals	4,842	4,789	1,130	23%	24%
Birds	9,932	9,932	1194	12%	12%
Reptiles	8,134	473	293	4%	62%
Amphibians	5,578	401	157	3%	39%
Fishes	28,100	1,532	750	3%	49%
Invertebrates	**1,190,200**	**3,382**	**1,959**	**0.2%**	**58%**
Insects	950,000	768	553	0.06%	72%
Molluscs	70,000	2,098	967	1%	46%
Crustaceans	40,000	461	409	1%	89%
Others	130,200	55	30	0.02%	55%
Plants	**297,655**	**9,708**	**6,776**	**2%**	**70%**
Mosses	15,000	93	80	0.5%	86%
Ferns	13,025	180	111	1%	62%
Gymnosperms	980	907	304	31%	34%
Dicotyledons	199,350	7,734	5,768	3%	75%
Monocotyledons	59,300	792	511	1%	65%
Lichens	10,000	2	2	0.02%	100%

Source: Summary Statistics, from the IUCN Red List of Threatened Species, Table 1, accessed at http://www.redlist.org on 03/04/2004.

10,000 and 5,000 (in round numbers – see Table 14.4), gives 0.25 and 0.125 extinctions per century respectively as the **background rate**. So for birds the rate in the last 400 years is $32 \div 0.25 = 128$ times the normal background rate, and for mammals it is $22 \div 0.125 = 176$ times the background rate.

These results are based on very rough-and-ready calculations, and the precise numbers should not be taken too seriously. They do, however, make the incontrovertible point that for birds and mammals the extinction rate in the last 400 years is very high by long-term historical standards. The same is almost certainly true for all other forms of life.

The IUCN-World Conservation Union's Species Survival Commission is a worldwide network of experts which regularly produces estimates of the number of threatened species among some animal and plant categories: the so-called IUCN Red List. Table 14.4 gives the latest **Red List** data. Threatened species are those considered to be at risk of extinction. The second column of Table 14.4 shows the numbers of species for which status as threatened or non-threatened has been considered. For mammals virtually all, and for birds all, known species have been evaluated, and 23 per cent and 12 per cent respectively are considered to be threatened. For most other categories the proportion of known species whose status has been considered is much lower and for these the threatened proportion of those evaluated is much higher than the threatened proportion of the numbers of species described. Evaluation effort is concentrated on species thought likely to be threatened. From Tables 14.1 and 14.2 it is clear that there may be many species not yet described, and therefore not evaluated, that are threatened. Many species may go extinct before they are known about.

14.1.3 Why is it being lost so fast?

There is no doubt that species are going extinct now at a rate much greater than normal. In an article that appeared in *The Guardian* on 29 November 2001, Lord May, a physicist and ecologist who had been the UK government's Chief Scientist and was then President of the Royal Society, said that:

> There is little doubt that we are standing on the breaking tip of the sixth great wave of extinction in the history of life on earth.

As to the cause, he said that the current extinction wave:

> is different from the others in that it is caused not by external events, but by us – by the fact that we consumed somewhere between a quarter and a half of all the plants grown last year.

By 'us' here Lord May means our species, humans.

Back in Chapter 3 we looked at the current level of human appropriation of net primary productivity (see Table 3.2). On the most conservative basis for calculation, humans take 4 per cent of global net primary productivity. The fundamental reason for the current wave of extinctions is the enormous impact on the biosphere of humanity's economic activity.

In looking a little further into this we can distinguish proximate from underlying causes. The proximate causes of biodiversity loss are:

- Habitat loss due to agriculture, forestry and urban development.
- The overharvesting of targeted renewable resource species, and by-catches (secondary catches) of non-targeted species.
- Pollution, of which a major future form is, as seen in the previous chapter, likely to be climate change.
- Exotic species – humans have been responsible, both deliberately and inadvertently, for spreading many species into new environments around the world where they become involved in competition or predation relationships with the native species, the suite of which is not adapted to the exotic's presence with the result that some go extinct.

The most important underlying causes are human population growth and the growth in per capita energy and materials consumption, the extent of which in the last few hundred years we documented in Chapters 3 and 7. The arising problems can be exacerbated by institutional failures. In Chapter 9 we considered the role of property rights in regard to the exploitation of renewable resources, and saw that free access leads to over-use. In some cases ignorance has been a contributory factor – when an alien species is introduced, it will never be known for sure what its impact on the local flora and fauna will be. In many cases of deliberate introduction, it is clear that had the future consequences been known, it would not have taken place.

14.1.4 Why does biodiversity loss matter?

When we speak of 'the biodiversity-loss problem' we mean the accelerated rate of loss due to human impacts on the biosphere. In what sense is this a problem? Does the extinction of a few hundred, or possibly a few thousand, species of all kinds each century matter? There are several sorts of reasons why the rapid rate of loss of genetic diversity matters. At the outset we need to note that the extinction of a species is irreversible – once gone, a species is lost for ever.

The first class of reason concerns production. Some non-domesticated species are the renewable resources that we hunt and gather for food and fibre. As noted in Chapter 4, these are now mainly fish and tree species. Domesticated species of plants and animals are the basic inputs to agriculture. Wild species provide genetic material for cross-breeding with domesticated species aimed at producing better varieties to suit changing conditions – this is likely to become more important with climate change. Wild species are also important as sources of inputs to the manufacture of drugs and medicines. Presumably many of the species known but not currently much researched, and many of the currently unknown species, could prove to be useful in these ways. Their loss would mean the loss of opportunities for research and of possible future inputs to production.

The second class of reason concerns consumption. Biodiversity is part of the basis for the provision of amenity services by the natural environment. Humans would generally find an environment with less biodiversity less enjoyable. There is considerable evidence that, as well as being willing to pay for their own consumption of the environment's amenity services, many people in modern economies would also be willing to pay to preserve species that they themselves will never see – except possibly on TV. When asked, many people say that they would be willing to pay to conserve species for future generations. Many people clearly get satisfaction from simply knowing that species of animals and plants, and the ecosystems in which they operate, exist, and would get satisfaction from knowing that they will continue to exist.

The third class of reason concerns the functioning of ecosystems, and hence the services, such as waste assimilation and life support services, that they deliver. Functioning ecosystems also deliver amenity services – people like to look at woodlands in their entirety, for example, as well as at particular species, such as bears, that inhabit them. The exact role that most species play in the functioning of the ecosystems in which they exist is largely unknown. It follows from the state of knowledge regarding the species that exist, reviewed above, that the existence of many species that are keystone species is simply unknown. In Chapter 2 we noted that the resilience of an ecosystem will be threatened by the removal of a keystone species. This might be taken to imply that so long as it is not keystone species that are lost, extinction does not threaten resilience. This is not what ecologists understand to be the case – they consider that biodiversity loss should be presumed to threaten resilience. While the functions that keystone species perform are fixed, the identity of the species that carry them out need not be. What are currently 'redundant' species may be reservoirs of replacement keystone species should the ability of the current keystone species to perform the functions be affected. And, while currently redundant species may not themselves be able to perform keystone functions, they may be the reservoirs of the genetic material from which new species that can do so may evolve.

An aircraft rivet analogy is sometimes used to make the point in the previous paragraph. Aircraft are held together by very large numbers of rivets, many more than the designers consider strictly necessary. On boarding your aircraft for a long flight, you notice that an engineer is removing every fifth rivet. He explains when asked that they are needed elsewhere, and that there is nothing to worry about as he has done this several times before without any problems ensuing. Would you still want to board the aircraft?

One reason for the existence of this analogy is that it is an answer to those who argue that species extinction is not really anything to worry about, as it has happened lots of times before, and nothing much seems to have gone wrong. The other point that needs to be made about this kind of response to the current extinction problem is that it ignores the fact that ecosystems are now being subjected to other unusual changes and stresses, notably climate change and a very high level of primary productivity appropriation by humanity.

14.2 WHY IT IS A DIFFICULT PROBLEM

In the previous chapter we noted and discussed several characteristics of the climate-change problem that make it a very difficult problem to deal with. The biodiversity-loss problem shares a number of these characteristics, and it too is a very difficult problem to solve.

14.2.1 Publicness

First, in many respects biodiversity is a global public good, its loss a global public bad. Recall from Chapter 9 that a public good is something where use is non-excludable and non-rival. As noted in the previous section, use of a species by economic activity involves direct and indirect channels. Directly, it may be an input to production or to consumption. In the former case, use is generally consumptive in the material sense, and is rivalrous – fish caught by firm *A* cannot be caught by firm *B*. In the latter case use may be rival – as with recreational fishing – but in many cases is not. The pleasure that, for example, I get from seeing bears, or from knowing that they exist, is not at the expense of your bear-based pleasure, and I cannot prevent you from getting pleasure from knowing that bears exist.

There are two aspects of the indirect use of species. First, populations are what interact to make ecosystems function. Functioning ecosystems provide amenity, waste assimilation and life support services, the use of which is thus indirect use of the species represented in the ecosystem concerned. The use of these services is not generally consumptive in the material sense, and so is not generally rivalrous. Generally it is not excludable either.

Second, as exemplified by research directed at the production of medicines, the genes that are embodied in living organisms are a form of knowledge which can be exploited in production. Making use of such knowledge is non-rivalrous. The loss

Table 14.5 National Biodiversity Index values	
	NBI
Indonesia	1
Colombia	0.935
Mexico	0.928
Brazil	0.877
Ecuador	0.873
Australia	0.853
Venezuela	0.850
Peru	0.843
China	0.839
Costa Rica	0.820
Madagascar	0.813
Malaysia	0.809
United Kingdom	0.320
Sweden	0.304
Canada	0.299
Ireland	0.279
Kuwait	0.224
Iceland	0.113
Greenland	0

Source: *Global biodiversity outlook*, Annex 1, at http://www.biodiv.org

of species means a reduction in the size of this stock of knowledge. The knowledge may be excludable. A country could, for example, restrict access to a population within its borders. If this were the only population in existence, it would be denying access to the species. As populations differ genetically, even if there were other populations elsewhere, such denial of access would restrict the generally available knowledge.

Clearly, these public good dimensions of biodiversity will often cross national borders. A species extinction in country X affects the citizens of country Y. The most obvious manifestation of this is the willingness to pay on the part of citizens of developed countries to preserve populations in the developing world. Many such contributors to wildlife preservation will never actually see the animals that they are paying to keep alive. The beneficiaries of a medicine developed on the basis of the study of organisms found in only country X will be from many countries.

14.2.2 Equity

Action to reduce the current rate of biodiversity loss involves both intertemporal and intratemporal equity issues.

In so far as avoiding species extinction now incurs costs, as it will generally be perceived to do, the benefits arising accrue to many future generations, as well as to the current generation. Conversely, not incurring the costs now means an irreversible loss to future generations.

As regards the distribution of costs, and benefits, now, there is a North–South dimension to the biodiversity-loss problem which is very similar to the climate-change case. As already noted in this chapter, species richness is inversely correlated with latitude on account of solar radiation levels. As noted in Chapter 6 (see Box 6.1), GDP per capita is also inversely correlated with latitude. The rich developed countries are biodiversity poor, while many of the poor developing countries are biodiversity rich.

Table 14.5 shows the values taken by the National Biodiversity Index for the 12 'mega-diversity' countries, Indonesia through to Malaysia. This index combines a measure of species richness with a measure of endemism – having lots of species many of which are not found in other countries makes for a high score. The index is scaled so that the highest score, for Indonesia, is 1, and the lowest score, for Greenland, is 0. Table 14.5 also shows the scores for a selection of countries with scores at the low end of the range. Of the 12 mega-diversity countries, only one, Australia, is not a developing country. As already noted, Australia has lots of endemic species. In terms of species richness, the presence of tropical rainforests is a major factor – it has been estimated that while these forests account for some 7 per cent of the earth's surface area, they contain about 50 per cent of all species.

These data clearly indicate that biodiversity conservation to prevent species extinction is especially important in low-latitude countries. On the other hand, those are generally the countries least able to afford the costs that would be involved. These considerations have been important in determining the nature of the Convention on Biological Diversity which was negotiated in 1992, to be discussed in section 14.4 below. It has several features in common with the UNFCCC, discussed in the previous chapter, negotiated at the same time.

14.2.3 Uncertainty

The biodiversity-loss problem is like the climate-change problem in that, while its broad features are reasonably well understood, there is much ignorance about particulars. We know that biodiversity is now being lost at a rate much faster than normal, and that this is driven by the activities of the human species. We know that this species appropriates an enormous amount of net primary productivity, and that it, in various ways, reduces or damages the sustenance available to other species. We do not, however, know how many other species there are, and are very likely endangering species that we do not know the existence of.

When we consider those species that we think we are endangering, we do not know what the consequences of their extinction for us would be. If we wanted to decide, in any particular such case, whether or not we should do what was considered necessary to avoid the extinction, we would be dealing with a situation of decision making in conditions of ignorance. We discussed this, in general terms, in Chapter 10. The next section now looks at some issues in relation to action to preserve biodiversity.

14.3 CONSERVATION POLICY

In this section we introduce some of the main issues and ideas in regard to policy measures intended to slow down the rate of biodiversity loss.

14.3.1 *Ex situ* versus *in situ* conservation

In situ **conservation** is the preservation of species in their natural habitats, in the wild. It is what we generally think of when we talk about biodiversity, or nature, conservation, and what we are mainly concerned with in this chapter. However, given the pressure on habitats, and other threats to survival in the wild, there is now considerable interest in the conservation of biodiversity in facilities constructed by humans. This is *ex situ* **conservation**.

Zoos and botanical gardens have existed for many centuries, but it is only relatively recently that they have been seen as an *ex situ* means of biodiversity conservation. For most of their history they have been intended to provide pleasure to those who visit them to look at exotic plants and animals. They have also been used to provide facilities for the work of botanists and zoologists. Seedbanks, where plant seeds as opposed to growing plants are stored, have also been in existence for a long time. Again, it is only relatively recently that their role in biodiversity conservation has been emphasised. Historically they have mainly been seen as facilities for the breeding of new and improved varieties of domesticated plants.

Particularly for animals, *ex situ* conservation can be expensive. A major problem is that it is necessary to keep a large number of individual animals in order to avoid declining genetic diversity in the captive population. It is estimated that a breeding population of 250 individuals is necessary to maintain 95 per cent of a species' genetic diversity over 50 generations. To some extent this problem can be overcome by cooperation between zoos so that populations from different zoos can inter-breed. There is now considerable interest in using such zoo-based programmes to breed animals for reintroduction into their natural habitats. To date these have met with mixed success. Some argue that such programmes ignore the basic problem of biodiversity loss, habitat destruction, and that zoos would better promote biodiversity conservation by using the money spent on them to buy land for the creation of protected areas. On the other hand, the money is only available because of the opportunity to see the animals that is created by the captive breeding programmes.

Recent technological developments may offer the prospect of reducing the costs of *ex situ* conservation. Whole plants and animals can be stored by means of cry-opreservation – freezing to very low temperatures. DNA itself can now be isolated and stored. In this case the volume of material that needs storage can be very small. The regeneration of whole organisms from such material has yet to demonstrated, but its introduction into other organisms is now the source of Genetically Modified Organisms (GMOs). To date this activity has been directed at agricultural production, rather than biodiversity conservation, and is controversial. Basically, the problem is ignorance about all of the consequences of cultivating GMO crops outside laboratory conditions.

Ex situ conservation, if it does not eventually lead to reintroduction, preserves the genetic material of the species, but does not maintain its role in the ecosystem which is the natural habitat. It does not, that is, necessarily preserve ecosystem structure and function. This is one reason why many conservationists argue that ecosystems and habitats, rather than species and genes, are the proper proximate target for biodiversity conservation. The other reason for preferring *in situ* conservation is the preservation of within species genetic diversity mentioned earlier.

14.3.2 Which species to preserve?

Many argue that however it might be done, it simply is not feasible that all known endangered species can be preserved. Preservation has costs, the argument goes, either in the use of inputs to construct *ex situ* conservation facilities, or in the non-use of inputs from areas set aside for *in situ* conservation – protected areas. Costs of the latter kind are likely to be particularly high in low-latitude developing countries with high human population growth rates where there is pressure to convert forested land to agriculture, and to exploit natural resources so as to generate export earnings and economic growth. As we have seen, such countries are also likely to be the very place where biodiversity conservation is important. The institutional problem is that while the costs of establishing protected areas are clear and tangible, it is difficult for individuals or government to derive substantial reward from such action. Because of the global public good nature of biodiversity, those who could preserve it often cannot capture all of the benefit that preservation generates and so do not do enough preservation. One of the features of the Convention on Biological Diversity to be discussed below is an attempt to address this problem.

If all endangered species cannot be preserved the question which arises is: which ones to preserve? For neoclassical economists the obvious answer is: the ones for which the excess of the benefits of preservation over the costs is greatest. Given a limited budget for biodiversity conservation, this means ranking the endangered species by Net Benefit and working down the list until the budget is all spent. Species ranked below the point at which funds are exhausted are left to go extinct. Net Benefit here is the money value of the difference between the value of preserving the species in question and the cost of so doing.

Clearly the difficult crucial question here is the size of the preservation benefits. The costs of preservation will be comparatively easy to assess, as, say, the development benefits forgone by creating the necessary protected area in which development is prohibited. It would be, for example, the value of the forgone agricultural output. The benefit from preserving a species cannot be derived solely from market data in this kind of way. There are no markets in the commodity 'preservation of species X'. Basically what neoclassical economists want to know here is what firms and individuals collectively would be willing to pay for this commodity if there was a market in it. They have devised a whole variety of methods and techniques intended to generate an answer to this question. As we have noted elsewhere, there is controversy among neoclassical economists as to the extent to which these methods and techniques can answer this question, but among neoclassical economists it is widely agreed that it is the right question.

Some neoclassical economists argue that it is only part of the right question. They argue that what we are willing to pay for preservation is not the whole story. They argue that the value that we should put on the preservation of a particular species should reflect not just how much we like the species or find it useful, but should also reflect how different it is, in terms of its genetic make-up, from other species. For two species for which willingness to pay is the same, the one that differs genetically more than the other from all the other species should be given the higher preservation value. This argument is based on the idea, noted above, that genes are carriers of information. This being the case, more information is lost when a species with a more distinct set of genes is lost.

Ecological economists do not think that willingness to pay is irrelevant to biodiversity conservation decision making, and they would agree that it ought to take into account the degree of distinctiveness of species. However, they do not think that these are the only things to be considered, and they see the problem mainly in terms of decision making in the face of ignorance. We discussed this in Chapter 10, where we introduced the Precautionary Principle and the associated idea of the Safe Minimum Standard. These lead to a presumption in favour of the preservation of every known endangered species. Each case would be considered from this perspective, and each threatened species would be preserved unless the costs of so doing were socially unacceptable. Adopting this approach does not mean that costs are irrelevant. They cannot be. It does mean framing the questions about costs differently.

14.3.3 Habitat preservation and protected areas

The discussion in the preceding sub-section is concerned mainly with the principles that might be followed in making decisions about *in situ* species preservation. In practice, biodiversity conservation decision making focuses on habitat preservation rather than species preservation. This only partly reflects the arguments of principle, noted above, for a focus on ecosystems and habitats rather than species. Mainly it reflects the fact that the main element of any plan to preserve a species *in situ* must be the preservation of, at least, some of its habitat. As a practical matter, *in situ* preservation decisions are decisions about protected areas. By a **protected area** we mean an area where human activities are to some degree constrained in the interests of biodiversity conservation.

Then the basic questions about protected areas are where, and how big? Answering these questions involves the same sorts of issues as we just looked at in relation to species. The same sort of difference in approach, at the level of principle, as between neoclassical and ecological economists applies. The former would want to select area locations and sizes on the basis of maximising the excess of benefit over cost, the latter would follow a safe minimum standard approach. Whereas the former would be mainly interested in willingness to pay as it would be expressed in markets if they existed, the latter would be mainly interested in the social acceptability of the costs of setting aside the protected area.

One of the interesting things about asking people about their willingness to pay for species preservation is that they, understandably, report much greater amounts for charismatic large mammals, such as bears or tigers, than for worms or beetles, say. In terms of ecosystem function, it will generally be the case that large charismatic mammals are not keystone species, while 'creepy crawlies' often are. There generally appears to be a low correlation, that is, between the rankings that people would give to species for preservation and the rankings that ecologists would give. However, given that *in situ* species conservation actually works in terms of habitat conservation, many conservation ecologists are, as a practical matter, happy to see decision making based on willingness to pay criteria. This is because the minimum viable area for the preservation of a large charismatic mammal is generally a large area, certainly larger than the minimum viable area for a beetle species, for example. Setting up protected areas for animals like bears or tigers will mean large areas, within which many other populations from a range of species get protected. Endangered species of charismatic mammals are sometimes known as **flagship species**, because protecting them protects other species, and because it is relatively easy to generate public support for their preservation. They are usully large.

Protected area establishment has not always been motivated primarily by biodiversity conservation. In some cases the motivation has been more to do with the provision of wilderness recreation facilities. To some degree, wilderness recreation and biodiversity conservation can be joint uses of a protected area. We discussed

Box 14.1 The Galápagos Islands

The Galápagos Islands are a group of 170 volcanic islands on the equator, situated at about 600 nautical miles west of Ecuador, of which they are politically part. Most of the islands are very small and have no resident human population. The total area of the islands is 7,800 km², and the total resident population is around 20,000, occupying just 3 per cent of the total area. Fresh water is scarce, the soils are generally poor and building materials are scarce. Until the sixteenth century the islands were uninhabited. From the seventeenth to the nineteenth century they were used by whaling ships for collecting fresh water and food (native animals, especially turtles), and there was a small resident population. Whaling declined at the end of the nineteenth century. By the early 1960s the resident population was a few hundred.

In 1835 Charles Darwin visited the Galápagos on HMS *Beagle*. He was there for just six weeks, but the experience was a major factor in the evolution of his thinking and is credited with greatly influencing his book *On the origin of species by means of natural selection* published in 1859. In particular, Darwin was struck by the fact that different species of finches existed on different islands. A species is said to be endemic to a locality if it is found nowhere else. For the Galápagos, 95 per cent of reptile species found there are endemic, as are 50 per cent of birds, 40 per cent of plants, 70 per cent of insects and 17 per cent of fish.

In 1959, to coincide with the centenary of the publication of Darwin's major work, the government of Ecuador declared 97 per cent of the land area of the Galápagos a national park, from which humans were excluded as permanent residents. In 1986 it declared the waters around the islands up to 15 nautical miles offshore as a marine reserve, an area of about 50,000 km². In 1998 this was extended to include waters out to 40 nautical miles, an area over 130,000 km².

Ever since the visit of HMS *Beagle* small numbers of people have visited these islands to view the flora and fauna. Mostly, until the late twentieth century, they were scientists following in Darwin's footsteps. In the early 1970s an airlink between the islands and mainland Ecuador was opened, and tourism began. Tourist numbers grew from about 6,000 in 1972 to 62,000 in 1996. Ecuador is a poor country, and the incomes that could be earned catering for the tourists in the Galápagos attracted Ecuadorians to migrate to the islands, so that, as noted above, the resident population grew from a few hundred in the 1960s to 20,000 by the end of the century.

Given the remoteness of the islands they are relatively expensive destinations for European and North American tourists. Also, the beaches are not attractive. All of the tourists from these origins are attracted by the flora and fauna, and perhaps the scientific associations. Mainland Ecuadorians now account for about one quarter of total visitors to the islands.

It is generally considered that to date tourism has had little impact on the terrestrial flora and fauna that mainly attract the overseas visitors. There is some evidence of erosion and vegetation loss at the most visited sites, and of changes in the behaviour of some animals, but the problems are not regarded as serious. The national park administration is generally thought to have done a reasonably good job of managing visitors – its finances and powers were enhanced by the enactment of the Special Law for the Conservation of the Galápagos in 1998. This law does not put any cap on future visitor numbers, but it does set some limits to future developments to provide tourist facilities.

The deliberate and unintended importation by the rapidly growing human population of species of plants and animals not native to the islands has had major impacts on native flora and fauna. On some islands some species of turtles have gone extinct due to competition for food from goats and predation on eggs by rats. Cats are also a problem. Until recently systems intended to control the introduction of alien species were ineffective, mainly on account of inadequate funding. The Special Law includes provisions intended to address this problem.

Another problem is commercial fishing. The marine reserve allows small-scale fishing activity by locals for local consumption, but there has been a history of illegal 'industrial' fishing for export markets. The Special Law tightened the limits on fishing and put their enforcement in the hands of the national park administration. This led to serious social and political unrest in the Galápagos, with many of the recent immigrants to the islands protesting against controls on fishing activity.

Sources: Chapter 4 of Honey (1999) and C. MacFarland (1998) 'An analysis of nature tourism in the Galápagos Islands', accessed at the website of the Charles Darwin Foundation, http://www.darwinfoundation.org/articles/br15049801.html. See also the Galapagos Conservation Trust at http://www.gct.org/.

some aspects of this briefly in Chapter 4 in connection with the amenity services that the natural environment provides. In recent years wildlife viewing has become a highly desired leisure activity on the part of people from developed countries. As noted above, low-latitude developing countries are where much of the world's biodiversity is to be found, including charismatic mammal species. International tourism based on such attractions, often called **ecotourism**, is now a large and rapidly growing phenomenon. It can be a means by which developing countries can derive income from biodiversity conservation. Box 14.1 provides some information on an interesting case, which illustrates the problems that can be associated with ecotourism. You can find out more about ecotourism and developing countries from references provided in Further Reading.

14.4 THE CONVENTION ON BIOLOGICAL DIVERSITY

The Convention on Biological Diversity (CBD), was opened for signing at UNCED in Rio de Janeiro in June 1992. It was signed by 156 countries, and came into force in December 1993, 90 days after the 30th signatory had ratified it. There are now over 180 parties to the CBD – most of the world's nations. The USA signed in 1993, but has not yet (April 2004) ratified the CBD.

14.4.1 Objectives and principles

The CBD addresses two distinct but related issues – the conservation of biodiversity and its use by biotechnology. Both of these have a North–South dimension. We have already noted that developing countries are where most of the biodiversity is, while those are the countries least able to bear the costs of conservation. In regard to the use of genetic material, while most of it is located in developing countries, most of the use of it is by firms from developed countries which have the necessary technological expertise. Developing countries argued that they were not compensated for the use of their biodiversity resources as inputs to medicinal and other research, that they had to pay high prices for the products based on that research, and that they did not participate in the technological development involved. The two issues and their developed–developing dimensions are clear in the stated objectives and principles of the CBD.

The objectives, stated in Article 1, are:

> the conservation of biological diversity, the sustainable use of its components and the fair and equitable sharing of the benefits arising out of the utilization of genetic resources, including by appropriate access to genetic resources and by appropriate transfer of relevant technologies, taking into account all rights over those resources and to technologies, and by appropriate funding.

The Preamble to the CBD states the principles. While it is affirmed that biodiversity conservation is 'a common concern of humankind', it is also affirmed that states 'have sovereign rights over their own biological resources' and are responsible for their use. The Precautionary Principle is endorsed:

> where there is a threat of significant reduction or loss of biological diversity, lack of full scientific certainty should not be used as a reason for postponing measures to avoid or minimize such a threat.

It is accepted that the main approach to conservation has to be the 'in situ conservation of ecosystems and natural habitats'.

The need for 'the provision of new and additional financial resources and appropriate access to relevant technologies' is noted along with the need for 'special provision' to 'meet the needs of developing countries' in respect of finance and access to technology. It is recognised that 'economic and social development and poverty eradication are the first and overriding priorities of developing countries'.

The CBD is unusual in recognising the importance of the traditional knowledge of indigenous peoples and local communities, and calls for such knowledge to be more widely used, with the approval of its holders, with the benefits arising being shared with them.

14.4.2 Instruments

We now look at what the CBD involved in terms of the means by which its objectives were to be pursued. In this respect it had much in common with the UNFCCC, as might be expected given the shared features of the problems that each addressed, including the North–South dimension.

Like the UNFCCC, the CBD establishes a process for its future development in the form of the Conference of the Parties (COP). The remit of the CBD COP is very similar to that of the UNFCCC COP – to review progress towards objectives and to take such further steps in pursuit of the objectives as may be agreed to be necessary in the light of experience. The COP is empowered to establish new subsidiary bodies and to adopt protocols.

Like the UNFCCC, the CBD imposes different obligations on developed and developing country parties – all parties accept some common obligations, but developed country parties accept additional ones.

The common obligations do not involve quantified targets, nor do they involve any specific prescriptions as to how countries should go about meeting their obligations. While the CBD accepts the primary role of *in situ* conservation, it does not, for example, specify minimum standards for, or the extent of, protected areas for any party. The CBD itself places few precise binding obligations on parties, and subsequent COPs have not gone far in that direction either.

All parties are required (Article 6) to prepare national biodiversity conservation plans consistent with the aims and principles of the CBD, and to integrate biodiversity conservation into national decision making in other areas. All parties are required (Article 7) to identify 'components of biodiversity important for its conservation and sustainable use' and to monitor such. All parties are required (Article 8) to establish 'a system of protected areas' and otherwise conserve biodiversity *in situ*. They are, for example, required to control or eradicate alien species which threaten ecosystems, habitats or species. While this applies to all parties, the final clause of the relevant article does introduce some differentiation – it calls on parties to provide financial and other support for *in situ* conservation measures, 'particularly to developing countries'.

All parties are called on 'as far as possible and as appropriate' to complement *in situ* with *ex situ* measures. They are required to structure economic and social incentives to encourage conservation, to promote relevant research and training, and to introduce 'appropriate procedures' for environmental impact assessment. Every party is required, at intervals to be set by the COP, to submit a report on 'measures which it has taken for the implementation of the provisions of this Convention and their effectiveness in meeting the objectives of this Convention'.

We now look at where the CBD treats developed and developing countries differently. These provisions are dealt with in Articles 15 to 21 of the CBD. Essentially these articles specify the potential benefits to developing countries from participation. Without these benefits as incentive, it is very unlikely that more than a few developing countries would have signed or ratified the CBD.

Article 15 does not actually refer to developed or developing countries, but given the spatial distribution of biodiversity and its correlation with the spatial pattern of development, noted above, its differential implications are clear. Article 15 has the title 'Access to Genetic Resources', which the CBD defines as material of plant, animal, microbial or other origin containing functional units of heredity which is of actual or potential value. Prior to the CBD such material was generally treated as a free access resource, and was often removed from developing countries by developed country biotech firms without payment. Article 15 recognises that a nation has the right to determine access to genetic resources located within its borders. Given that recognition, and the elimination of the free access situation, the CBD contains other provisions for the relationships between host countries and the users of genetic resources. These are intended to enable host countries to capture more of the benefits that flow from conservation, which should provide them with incentives to do more of it.

Articles 16, 17 and 18 cover access to and transfer of technologies, exchange of information, and technical and scientific cooperation. Developing countries are to have access to technology 'under fair and most favourable terms'. The exchange of information is to take account of 'the special needs of developing countries'. All parties are to promote technical and scientific cooperation with other parties and 'in particular developing countries', and special attention is to be given to the strengthening and development of national capabilities. Article 19 calls on all parties to provide for the effective participation in biotechnical research of the countries that provide the genetic resources for it, and especially developing countries. It makes a similar statement in regard to the results and benefits of such research. Article 19 also requires all parties to work towards a protocol on the safe handling of any living modified organism that may adversely affect biodiversity – this is what the Cartagena Protocol on Biosafety of 2000 covered.

Articles 20 and 21 relate to money. By 20, all contracting parties undertake to finance their national programmes adopted under the CBD, in accordance with their capabilities. What is in accordance with capabilities is left for individual parties to decide for themselves. The developed countries agreed to:

> provide new and additional financial resources to enable developing country Parties to meet the agreed full incremental costs to them of implimenting measures which fulfil the obligations of this Convention.

The mechanism by means of which these international transfers were to take place was left to the first COP meeting. We will come back to this shortly. First, we need to make clear what is intended by this provision in Article 20. What was intended was that this financial assistance would be additional to existing bilateral and multilateral development aid flows. These financial resources were to meet the additional costs, the 'full incremental costs', to a developing country of undertaking projects relevant to the objectives of the CBD.

The institutional mechanism for raising and disbursing these financial resources that was chosen at the first COP meeting was the Global Environmental Facility (GEF). This had been set up in 1991 by an agreement between the World Bank, UNDP and UNEP. The GEF gets its funds from developed donor countries. It uses the funds to support projects relating to six global environmental issues:

- Biodiversity
- Climate change
- International waters
- Land degradation
- The ozone layer
- Persistent organic pollutants.

Since 1991 the GEF has provided grants for more than 1,300 projects in 140 developing countries. It has itself provided $4.5 billion in grants, and generated an additional $14.5 billion in co-financing of projects. The GEF is also the financing mechanism for the UNFCCC. You can find out more about the work of the GEF, and the projects that it has financed, at its website address given below.

14.4.3 Assessment

The range of views on the CBD and its achievements is very similar to that on the UNFCCC and its achievements. Many consider that given the nature and importance of the problem, not enough is being done about global biodiversity loss. On one hand, the CBD does not involve enough specific and binding commitments – to the creation of protected areas for example – to be considered a proper realisation of the Precautionary Principle. On the other hand, given the difficulty of securing any kind of international agreement, many take the CBD to be a major achievement. And, it must be remembered that, like the UNFCCC, it is, through the COP, a work in progress rather than a final product.

SUMMARY

It is natural, and part of the process of the evolution of life on earth, for species to become extinct. However, the rate at which species are currently becoming extinct is very much faster than the natural rate, and the cause of this is human economic activity. This biodiversity-loss problem is difficult to deal with because it transcends the boundaries of nation states. Most biodiversity exists in developing countries which can least afford the costs of conservation. The Convention on Biological Diversity made a start on a global approach to the problems of conservation and equitable exploitation. Whether it will lead to a slowing of the rate of extinction remains to be seen.

KEYWORDS

Background rate (p. 524): the average rate of extinctions in the fossil record.
Biodiversity (p. 521): the diversity of living organisms, the genes that they contain and the ecosystems in which they exist.
Ecotourism (p. 533): tourism based on viewing wildlife in its natural habitat.
Endemism (p. 523): a species is endemic to an area when it occurs only in that area.

***Ex situ* conservation** (p. 529): the conservation of biodiversity in facilities con-
structed by humans.

Flagship species (p. 532): a species, usually a charismatic mammal, the preservation
of which *in situ* commends public support, and requires a large protected area.

***In situ* conservation** (p. 529): the preservation of species in their natural habitats.

Protected area (p. 532): where human activities are constrained in the interests of
biodiversity conservation.

Red List (p. 524): a list of plant and animal species prepared by IUCN (International
Union for Conservation of Nature) classifying various threatened species and
evaluating their risk of extinction.

Species richness (p. 523): the number of species per unit area.

Taxa (p. 522): named groups or organisms of any rank, such as a particular species,
family or class.

FURTHER READING

Heywood (1995) is a comprehensive, 1,100 page, report on all aspects of biodiversity, its loss and its conservation, prepared for the United Nations Environment
Programme. Data used in this chapter was also taken from the *Global biodiversity
outlook* put together by the Secretariat to the Convention on Biological Diversity and
accessible at http://www.biodiv.org, and from the website of the IUCN-The World
Conservation Union at http://www.redlist.org. Gaston (1996) is a useful collection of
chapters, written by natural scientists, on all aspects of biodiversity, generally written so as to be understandable by those without a strong background in biology.
Swanson (1995) is a collection of papers from economists and ecologists about why
biodiversity is currently being lost quickly. The estimate that the tropical forests
contain 50 per cent of all species is from Wilson (1988). Tudge (1996) is a highly
readable account of the processes and events associated with the appearance of our
species, and of its history.

The text of the CBD can be accessed at http://www.biodiv.org, and it is discussed
in Chapter 2 of the *Global biodiversity outlook*, also accessible there.

Lomborg (2001) notes, and argues against, much higher estimates of the current
rates of species extinction than those given here. Lomborg also argues that species
loss *per se* is not really a major problem, except in those cases where people care
about them, or find them useful. Simon and Wildavsky (1993) is an example of the
position that biodiversity loss does not matter much. The rivet analogy, intended
to rebut this kind of argument, is from Ehrlich and Ehrlich (1992): see also the
chapter by Kunin and Lawton in Gaston (1996).

The prioritisation of species for conservation has been called 'the Noah's Ark
Problem' – see Metrick and Weitzman (1998) where the idea that the ranking
should take account of distinctiveness as well as conventional measure of worth
to humans is developed. The measurement of diversity is dealt with in papers
reprinted in Polasky (2002) and chapters in Gaston (1996): see also Heywood (1995).
The economics literature on what people are willing to pay to preserve species is
now enormous: see chapter 12 of Perman *et al.* (2003) for an introduction to the
techniques and some of the issues, and Loomis and White (1996) for a survey of

results. Journals such as the *Journal of Environmental Economics and Management, Land Economics*, and *Environmental and Resource Economics* regularly carry articles on methods and results. A seminal exposition of the Safe Minimum Standard approach is Bishop (1978).

The characteristics and extent of nature-based tourism/ecotourism are discussed in Buckley (2000), Hawkins and Lamoureux (2001), Hunter and Green (1995) and Valentine (1992). Weaver (1998) looks at nature-based tourism in developing countries and provides case studies including Nepal, Costa Rica and Kenya. The environmental impacts of nature-based tourism are surveyed in Buckley (2001) and Newsome *et al.* (2001), and both provide further references to the specialised literature; see also Hunter and Green (1995).

WEBSITES

For up to date information on where the CBD process is now at, and related matters, visit http://www.biodiv.org, where national reports can be accessed. For information on the GEF go to http://www.gefweb.org. Details on the IUCN Red List can be found at http://www.redlist.org from where you can get to the main IUCN–World Conservation Union site. There is an international agreement intended to control international trade in endangered species and the convention's web address is http://www.cites.org/index.html. UNEP runs a World Conservation Monitoring Centre and lots of information can be accessed at http://www.unep-wcmc.org. The address for the World Wildlife Fund (WWF) is http://www.wwf.org.

DISCUSSION QUESTIONS

1. Some people argue that all other species have a right to exist, and that arguing for biodiversity conservation in terms of human interests, as we have done, is wrong because species that do not serve human interests may then be allowed to become extinct. Do you agree?
2. Do animal lovers in the rich world have the right to expect poor countries to establish protected areas where no logging and farming are allowed?

References

Allen, D. W. 2001. 'Social class, race, and toxic releases in American counties, 1995', *The Social Science Journal* 38: 13–25.

Anderson, K. and Starkey, R. 2004. Domestic tradable quotas: a policy instrument for the reduction of greenhouse gas emissions, *An interim report to the Tyndall Centre for Climate Change Research*, 7 January 2004 http://www.tyndall.ac.uk/whatsnew/DTQs.pdf

Argyle, M. 1987. *The psychology of happiness*. London, Methuen.

Arndt, H. W. 1978. *The rise and fall of economic growth: a study in contemporary thought*. Sydney, Longman Cheshire.

Arrow, K., Bert, B., Costanza, R., Dasgupta, P., Folke, C., Holling, C. S., Jansson, B., Levin, S., Maler, K., Perrings, C. and Pimentel, D. 1995. 'Economic growth, carrying capacity, and the environment', *Science* 268: 520–521.

Australian Bureau of Statistics (ABS), 1995. *National Balance Sheet for Australia, issues and experimental estimates 1989 to 1992*, Occasional paper, 5241, Canberra.

Ayres, R. U. 1978. 'Application of physical principles to economics', in Ayres, R. U. (ed.). *Resources, environment and economics: applications of the materials/energy balance principle*. New York, John Wiley and Sons (reprinted in Costanza, R., Perrings, C. and Cleveland, C. J. (eds.) 1997 *The development of ecological economics*. Cheltenham, Edward Elgar), pp. 260–294.

Ayres, R. U. 1999 'Industrial metabolism and the grand nutrient cycles', in van den Bergh, J. C. J. M. (ed.) *Handbook of environmental and resource economics*. Cheltenham, Edward Elgar, pp. 912–945.

Barber, W. J. 1967. *A history of economic thought*. London, Penguin.

Barbier, E. B. 1989. *Economics, natural resource scarcity and development: conventional and alternative views*. London, Earthscan Publications.

Barbier, E. B. and Markandya, A. 1990. 'The conditions for achieving environmentally sustainable growth', *European Economic Review* 34: 659–669.

Barbier, E. B., Burgess, J. C. and Folke, C. 1994. *Paradise lost? The ecological economics of biodiversity*. Earthscan, London.

Barrett, S. 1999. 'Montreal versus Kyoto: international cooperation and the global environment', in Kaul, I., Grunberg, I. and Stern, M. A. (eds.) *Global public goods: international cooperation in the 21st century*. Published for the United Nations Development Programme. Oxford, Oxford University Press, pp. 192–219.

Baumol, W. J. and Oates, W. E. 1988. *The theory of environmental policy, externalities, public outlays and the quality of life*. 2nd edn. Englewood Cliffs, NJ, Prentice-Hall.

Bayliss-Smith, T. P. 1982. *The ecology of agricultural systems*. Cambridge, Cambridge University Press.

Beckerman, W. 1972. 'Economists, scientists and environmental catastrophe', *Oxford Economic Papers* 24: 237–244.

Beckerman, W. 1974. *In defence of economic growth*. London, Jonathan Cape.

Begg, D., Fischer, S. and Dornbusch, R. 2000. *Economics*. 6th edn. London, McGraw-Hill.

Bishop, R. 1978. 'Endangered species and uncertainty: the economics of a safe minimum standard', *American Journal of Agricultural Economics* 60: 10–18.

Blainey, G. 1982. *Triumph of the nomads: a history of ancient Australia*. Melbourne, Sun Books.

Blanchard, O. J. 2003. *Macroeconomics*. 3rd edn. London, Prentice-Hall.

Blaug, M. 1985. *Economic theory in retrospect*. 4th edn. Cambridge, Cambridge University Press.

Boehmer-Christiansen, S. 1994. 'The precautionary principle in Germany – enabling government', in O'Riordan, T. and Cameron, J. I. (eds.) *Interpreting the precautionary principle*. London, Earthscan, pp. 31–60.

Bossel, H. 1998. *Earth at a crossroads: paths to a sustainable future*. Cambridge, UK and New York, Cambridge University Press.

Boulding, K. E. 1966. 'The economics of the coming spaceship earth', in Jarrett, H. (ed.) *Environmental quality in a growing economy*. Baltimore, Resources for the Future/Johns Hopkins University Press, pp. 3–14. (Reprinted in Costanza, R., Perrings, C. and Cleveland, C. J. (eds.) 1997. *The development of ecological economics*. Cheltenham, Edward Elgar).

Bowes, M. D. and Krutilla, J. V. 1989. *Multiple-use management: the economics of public forestlands*. Washington DC, Resources for the Future.

Bowler, P. J. 1992. *The Fontana history of the environmental sciences*. London, Fontana.

Boyce, James K. 2002. *The political economy of the environment*. Cheltenham, Edward Elgar.

Boyden, S. 1987. *Western civilization in biological perspective: patterns in biohistory*. Oxford, Oxford University Press.

Boyden, S., Dovers, S. and Shirlow, M. 1990. *Our biosphere under threat: ecological realities and Australia's opportunities*. Melbourne, Oxford University Press.

Brennan, A. 2003. 'Philosophy', in Page, E. A. and Proops, J. (eds.) *Environmental thought*. Cheltenham, Elgar, pp. 15–33.

Broad, R. 1994. 'The poor and the environment: friends or foes?', *World Development* 22: 811–822.

Boadway, R. W. and Bruce, N. 1984. *Welfare economics: theory and applications*. Oxford, Blackwell.

Bromley, D. W. (ed.) 1995. *The handbook of environmental economics*. Oxford, Blackwell.

Buckley, R. 2000. 'Neat trends: current issues in nature, eco- and adventure tourism', *International Journal of Tourism Research* 2: 437–444.

Buckley, R. 2001. 'Environmental impacts', in Weaver, D. B. (ed.) *The encyclopaedia of ecotourism*. Wallingford, CABI Publishing, pp. 379–394.

Caldwell, D. J. 1994. 'International environmental agreements and the GATT: an analysis of the potential conflict and the role of a GATT "waiver" resolution', *Maryland Journal International Law and Trade* 18: 173–198.

Carson, R. T., Jeon, Y. and McCubbin, D. R. 1997. 'The relationship between air pollution emissions and income: US data', *Environment and Development Economics* 2: 433–450.

Castells, M. 1996, 1997, 1998. *The information age: economy, society, and culture*, three vol. Oxford and Malden, MA, Blackwell Publishers.

Chapman, P. 1975. *Fuel's paradise: energy options for Britain*. Harmondsworth, Penguin.

Chapman, P. and Roberts, F. 1983. *Metal resources and energy*. London, Butterworth.

Chiang, A. C. 1984. *Fundamental methods of mathematical economics*. 3rd edn. New York, McGraw-Hill.

Ciriacy-Wantrup, S. V. 1968. *Resource conservation: economics and policy*. Berkley, University of California Press.

Clark, C. W. 1990. *Mathematical bioeconomics: the optimal management of renewable resources*. 2nd edn. New York, John Wiley.

Cleveland, C. J. and Stern, D. I. 1999. 'Indicators of natural resource scarcity: a review and synthesis', in van den Bergh, J. C. J. M. (ed.) *Handbook of environmental and resource economics*. Cheltenham, Edward Elgar, pp. 89–108.

Cole, L. W. and Foster, S. R. 2001. *From the ground up: environmental racism and the rise of the environmental justice movement*. New York, New York University Press.

Cole, S. 1996. 'Which came first, the fossil or the fuel?', *Social Studies of Science* 26: 733–766.

Collingridge, D. 1980. *The social control of technology*. New York, St. Martin's Press.

Collingridge, D. 1982. *Critical decision making*. New York, St. Martin's Press.

Committee on Economic, Social and Cultural Rights 1998. Statement on globalization and economic, social and cultural rights, Geneva, Office of the United Nations High Commissioner for Human Rights. http://www.unhchr.ch/tbs/doc.nsf/0/ adc44375895aa10d8025668f003cc06e?Opendocument

Common, M. S. 1995. *Sustainability and policy: limits to economics*. Melbourne, Cambridge University Press.

Common, M. 1996. *Environmental and resource economics: an introduction*. 2nd edn. Longman, Harlow.

Common, M. and Perrings, C. 1992. 'Towards an ecological economics of sustainability', *Ecological Economics* 6: 7–34.

Common, M. and Salma, U. 1992. 'Accounting for Australian carbon dioxide emissions', *Economic Record* 68: 31–42.

Common, M. and Sanyal, K. 1998. 'Measuring the depreciation of Australia's non-renewable resources: a cautionary tale', *Ecological Economics* 26: 23–30.

Copeland, Brian R. 2001. 'International trade in waste products in the presence of illegal disposal', in Batabyal, A. A. and Beladi, H. (eds.) *The economics of international trade and the environment*. Boca Raton, Lewis Publishers, pp. 33–50.

Cornes, R. and Sandler, T. 1996. *The theory of externalities, public goods and club goods*. 2nd edn. Cambridge, Cambridge University Press.

Costanza, R., Perrings, C. and Cleveland, C. J. (eds.) 1997. *The development of ecological economics*. Cheltenham, Edward Elgar.

Costanza, R. 1991. *Ecological economics: the science and management of sustainability*, New York, Columbia University Press.

Costanza, R. and Daly, H. E. 1992. 'Natural capital and sustainable development', *Conservation Biology* 6: 454–464.

Costanza, R., d'Arge, R., de Groot, R., Farber, S., Grasso, M., Hannon, B., Limburg, K., Naeem, S., O'Neill, R. V., Paruelo, J., Raskin, R. G., Sutton, P. and van den Belt, M. 1997. 'The value of the world's ecosystem services and natural capital', *Nature* 387: 253–260.

Crocker, T. D. 1999. 'A short history of environmental and resource economics', in van den Bergh, J. C. J. M. (ed.) *Handbook of environmental and resource economics*. Cheltenham, Edward Elgar, pp. 32–45.

Daly, H. E., and Cobb, J. B. 1989. *For the common good: redirecting the economy toward community, the environment, and a sustainable future*. Boston, Beacon Press.

Daly, H. and Goodland, R. 1994. 'An ecological-economic assessment of deregulation of international commerce under GATT', *Ecological Economics* 9: 73–92.

Dasgupta, P. and Heal, G. M. 1974. 'The optimal depletion of exhaustible resources', *Review of Economic Studies* 41 (May): 3–28.

Dasgupta, P. and Heal, G. M. 1979. *Economic theory and exhaustible resources*. Cambridge, Cambridge University Press.

de Bruyn, S. M. and Heintz, R. J. 1999. 'The environmental Kuznets curve hypothesis', in van den Bergh, J. C. J. M. (ed.) *Handbook of environmental and resource economics*. Cheltenham, Edward Elgar, pp. 656–677.

Diamond, J. 1992. *The rise and fall of the third chimpanzee*. London, Vintage Press.

Diamond, J. 1998. *Guns germs and steel: a short history of everybody for the last 13000 years*. London, Vintage Press.

Dingle, T. 1988. *Aboriginal economy*. Fitzroy, McPhee Gribble.

Dosi, G. and Nelson, R. R. 1994. 'An introduction to evolutionary theories in economics', *Journal of Evolutionary Economics* 4: 153–172.

Dragan, J. C. and Demetrescu, M. C. 1991. *Entropy and bioeconomics: the new paradigm of Nicholas Georgescu-Roegen*. 2nd edn. Rome, Nagard.

Duchin, F. and Lange, G.-M. 1994. *The future of the environment: ecological economics and technological change*. New York, Oxford University Press.

Duchin, F. and Steenge, A. E. 1999. 'Input–output analysis, technology and the environment', in van den Bergh, J. C. J. M. (ed.) *Handbook of environmental and resource economics*. Cheltenham, Edward Elgar, pp. 1037–1059.

Ehrlich, P. R. and Ehrlich, A. E. 1990. *The population explosion*. London, Hutchinson.

Ehrlich, P. R. and Ehrlich, A. E. 1992. 'The value of biodiversity', *Ambio* 21: 219–226.

Ehrlich, P. R. and Holdren, J. P. 1971. 'Impact of population growth', *Science* 171: 1212–1217.

Ekins, P. 1997. 'The future of the World Trade Organization: proposals for fair and environmentally sustainable trade', *Democracy & Nature* 3: 57–89.

Ekins, P. 2003a. 'Sustainable development', in Page, E. A. and Proops, J. (eds.) *Environmental thought*. Cheltenham, Edward Elgar, pp. 144–172.

Ekins, P. 2003b. 'Trade and Environment', in International Society for Ecological Economics (ed.) *Internet Encyclopaedia of Ecological Economics*. http://www.ecoeco.org/publica/encyc_entries/TradeEnv.pdf

Ekins, P., Folke, C. and Costanza, R. 1994. 'Trade, environment and development: the issues in perspective', *Ecological Economics* 9: 1–12.

Faber, D. (ed.) 1998. *The struggle for ecological democracy: environmental justice movements in the United States*. New York, Guilford Press.

Faber, M. and Proops, J. L. R. 1994. *Evolution, time, production and the environment*. Heidelberg, Springer-Verlag.

Faber, M., Manstetten, R. and Proops, J. 1996. *Ecological economics: concepts and methods*. Cheltenham: Edward Elgar.

Farmer, M. C. and Randall, A. 1998. 'The rationality of a safe minimum standard of conservation', *Land Economics* 74: 287–302.

Faucheux, S., Pearce, D. and Proops, J. (eds.) 1996. *Models of sustainable development*. Cheltenham, Edward Elgar.

Field, C. B. 2001. 'Sharing the garden', *Science* 294: (21 December): 2490–2491.

Fletcher, Thomas, H. 2003. *From love canal to environmental justice: the politics of hazardous waste on the Canada–U.S. Border*. Ontario, Canada, Broadview Press Ltd.

Flores, N. E. and Carson, R. T. 1997. 'The relationship between income elasticities of demand and willingness to pay', *Journal of Environmental Economics and Management* 33: 287–295.

Folke, C. 1999. 'Ecological principles and environmental economic analysis', in van den Bergh, J. C. J. M. (ed.) *Handbook of environmental and resource economics*. Cheltenham, Edward Elgar, pp. 895–911.

Foster, J. and Metcalfe, J. S. 2001. *Frontiers of evolutionary economics – competition, self-organization and innovation policy*. Cheltenham, Edward Elgar.

Freund, C. 2003. *Reciprocity in free trade agreements*. Washington, DC, The World Bank.

Frey, B. S. and Stutzer, A. 2002a. *Happiness and economics*. Princeton, Princeton University Press.

Frey, B. S. and Stutzer, A. 2002b. 'What can economists learn from happiness research?', *Journal of Economic Literature* 40: 402–435.

Frey, B. S. and Stutzer, A. 2002c. *Beyond outcomes: measuring procedural utility*, Zurich, University of Zurich Economics Working Paper No. 76. http://ssrn.com/abstract=569347.

Funtowicz, S. O. and Ravetz, J. 1990. *Uncertainty and quality in science for policy*. Dordrecht, Kluwer.

Gaston, K. J. (ed.) 1996. *Biodiversity: a biology of numbers and difference*. Oxford, Blackwell Science.

Georgescu-Roegen, N. 1971. *The entropy law and the economic process*. Cambridge, MA: Harvard University Press.

Georgescu-Roegen, N. 1976. 'Energy and economic myths', in *Energy and economic myths: institutional and analytical essays*. New York, Pergamon.

Giddens, A. 1990. *The consequences of modernity*. Cambridge, UK; Oxford, UK, Polity Press in association with Basil Blackwell.

Giddens, A. 1999. *Runaway world – how globalisation is reshaping our lives*. London, Profile Books Ltd.

Gilbert, N. and Troitzsch, K. G. 1999. *Simulation for the social scientist*. Buckingham, Open University Press.

Glasser, H. 1999. 'Ethical perspectives and environmental policy analysis', in van den Bergh, J. C. J. M. (ed.) *Handbook of environmental and resource economics*. Cheltenham, Edward Elgar, pp. 981–1,000.

Gleick, J. 1988. *Chaos: making a new science*. Harmondsworth, Sphere.

Gold, T. 1999. *The deep hot biosphere*. New York, Springer-Verlag.

Gottlieb, R. 2001. *Environmentalism unbound: exploring new pathways for change*. Cambridge, MA, MIT Press.

Goulder, L. H. 1994. *Environmental taxation and the 'double dividend:' a reader's guide*. Cambridge, NBER Working Paper No. W4896. http://ssrn.com/abstract=227957.

Gowdy, J. M. 1994. *Coevolutionary economics: the economy, society, and the environment*. Boston, Kluwer Academic Publishers.

Grafton, R. Q., Adamowicz, W. A., Dupont, D., Nelson, H., Hill, R. and Renzeth, S. 2003. *The economics of the environment and natural resources*. Oxford, Blackwell.

Grossman, G. M. and Krueger, A. B. 1991. *Environmental impacts of the North American Free Trade Agreement*. Cambridge, MA, NBER.

Grubb, M. with Vrolijk, C. and Brack, D. 1999. *The Kyoto Protocol: a guide and assessment*. London, Royal Institute of International Affairs and Earthscan.

Gutrich, J. J. and Hitzhusen, F. J. 2004. 'Assessing the substitutability of mitigation wetlands for natural sites: estimating restoration lag costs of wetland mitigation', *Ecological Economics* 48: 409–424.

Hall, C. A. S., Cleveland, C. J. and Kaufmannn, R. 1986. *The ecology of the economic process: energy and resource quality*. New York, Wiley-Interscience.

Hamilton, K. 2000. *Genuine saving as a sustainability indicator*. Environmental Economics Series Paper No 77, World Bank, Washington DC.

Hanley, Nick, Shogren, J. F. and White, B. 2001. *An introduction to environmental economics*. Oxford, Oxford University Press.

Hannon, B. and Ruth, M. 1994. *Dynamic modelling*. New York, Springer-Verlag.

Hardin, Garrett, 1968 'The tragedy of the commons', *Science* 162 (December): 1243–1248.

Harremoes, P., Gee, D., Macgarvin, M., Stirling, A., Keys, J., Wynne, B. and Guedes Vaz, S. (eds.) 2002. *The precautionary principle in the 20th century – late lessons from early warnings*. London and Sterling, VA, Earthscan.

Harris, J. M. 2002. *Environmental and natural resource economics – a contemporary approach*. Boston, Houghton Mifflin Company.

Hartwick, J. M. 1977. 'Intergenerational equity and the investing of rents from exhaustible resources', *American Economic Review* 67: 972–974.

Hartwick, J. M. and Olewiler, N. D. 1998. *The economics of natural resource use*. 2nd edn. New York, Harper and Row.

Hawkins, D. E. and Lamoureux, K. 2001. 'Global growth and magnitude of ecotourism', in Weaver, D. B. (ed.) *The encyclopaedia of ecotourism*. Wallingford, CABI Publishing, pp. 63–72.

Heilbronner, R. L. 1991. *The worldly philosophers: the lives, times and ideas of the great economic thinkers*. London, Penguin.

Held, D., Mcgrew, A., Goldblatt, D. and Perraton, J. 1999. *Global transformations: politics, economics and culture*. Cambridge, Polity Press.

Heywood, V. H. 1995. *Global biodiversity assessment*. Cambridge, Cambridge University Press, for United Nations Environment Programme.

Himmelweit, S., Simonetti, R. and Trigg, A. 2001. *Microeconomics: neoclassical and institutionalist perspectives on economic behaviour*. London, Thomson Learning.

Hirsch, F. 1977. *Social limits to growth*. London, Routledge and Kegan Paul.

Hodgson, Geoffrey 2004. *The evolution of institutional economics: agency, structure and Darwinism in American institutionalism*. London, Routledge.

Holling, C. S. 1973. 'Resilience and stability of ecological systems', *Annual Review of Ecological Systems* 4, 1–24.

Holling, C. S. 1986. 'The resilience of terrestrial ecosystems: local surprise and global change', in Clark, W. C. and Munn, R. E. (eds.) *Sustainable development of the biosphere*. Cambridge, Cambridge University Press, pp. 292–317.

Honey, M. 1999. *Ecotourism and sustainable development: who owns paradise?* Washington, WC, Island Press.

Hornborg, A. 1998. 'Towards an ecological theory of unequal exchange: articulating a world system theory', *Ecological Economics* 25: 127–136.

Houghton, J. 1997. *Global warming: the complete briefing.* 2nd edn. Cambridge, Cambridge University Press.

Houghton, J. T., Ding, Y., Griggs, D. J., Noguer, M., van der Linden, P. J., Dai, X., Maskell, K. and Johnson, C. A. (eds.) 2001. *Climate change 2001: the scientific basis.* Cambridge: Cambridge University Press, for the Intergovernmental Panel on Climate Change.

Houghton, J. T., Jenkins, G. J. and Ephraums, J. J. (eds.) 1990. *Climate change: the IPCC scientific assessment.* Cambridge, Cambridge University Press for the Intergovernmental Panel on Climate Change.

Hudec, R. E. 1996. 'GATT legal restraints on the use of trade measures against foreign environmental practices', in Bhagwati, J. and Hudec, R. E. (eds.) *Fair trade and harmonization*, vol. II: *Legal analysis.* 2 vols, Cambridge, MA, MIT Press, pp. 95–174.

Hunter, C. and Green, H. 1995. *Tourism and the environment: a sustainable relationship?* London, Routledge.

Inglehart, R. and Klingemann, H.-D. 2000. 'Genes, culture, democracy and happiness', in Diener, E. and Suh, E. M. (eds.) (2000) *Culture and subjective well-being*, Cambridge MA, MIT Press.

Jackson, A. R. W. and Jackson, J. M. 2000. *Environmental science*, 2nd edn, Harlow, Pearson.

Johansson, P. and Löfgren, K. 1985. *The economics of forestry and natural resources.* Oxford, Blackwell.

Jones, C. I. 2002. *Introduction to economic growth.* 2nd edn. New York, Norton.

Katz, M. L. and Rosen, H. S. 1998. *Microeconomics.* 3rd edn. Boston, McGraw-Hill.

Kauffman, S. 1995. *At home in the universe: the search for the laws of complexity.* Harmondsworth, Penguin.

Kaul, I., Grunberg, I. and Stern, M. A. (eds.) 1999. *Global public goods: international cooperation in the 21st century.* Oxford, Oxford University Press, for the United Nations Development Programme.

Keynes, J. M. 1931. 'Economic possibilities for our grandchildren', in Keynes, J. M. *Essays in persuasion.* London, Macmillan, pp. 358–373.

Klaassen, G. A. J. and Opschoor, J. B. 1991. 'Economics of sustainability or the sustainability of economics: different paradigms', *Ecological Economics* 4: 93–115.

Knight, F. 1921. *Risk, uncertainty, and profit.* Boston, Houghton Mifflin.

Köhn, J., Gowdy, J., Hinterberger, F. and Straaten, J. Van Der (eds.) 1999. *Sustainability in question: the search for a conceptual framework.* Cheltenham, Edward Elgar.

Kolstad, C. D. 2000. *Environmental economics.* Oxford, Oxford University Press.

Krebs, C. J. 2001. *Ecology: the experimental analysis of distribution and abundance.* 5th edn. New York, Harper and Row.

Kreps, D. M. 1990. *A course in microeconomic theory.* New York, Harvester Wheatsheaf.

Kristöm, B. and Riera, P. 1996. 'Is the income elasticity of environmental improvements less than one? Evidence from Europe and other countries', *Environmental and Resource Economics* 7: 45–55.

Krugman, P. M. and Obstfeld, M. 2002. *International economics: theory and policy*, Reading, MA, Addison Wesley.

Krutilla, K. 1997. 'World trade, the WTO, and the environment', in Caldwell, L. K. and Bartlett, R. V. (eds.) *Environmental policy: transitional issues and environmental trends.* Greenwood, CT, Greenwood Publishing, pp. 127–142.

Krutilla, K. 1999. 'Partial equilibrium models of trade and the environment', in van den Bergh, J. C. J. M. (ed.) *Handbook of environmental and resource economics.* Cheltenham, Edward Elgar.

Kunin, W. E. and Lawton, J. H. 1996. 'Does biodiversity matter? Evaluating the case for conserving species', in Gaston, K. J. (ed.), *Biodiversity*, pp. 283–308.

Kuznets, S. 1966. *Modern economic growth: rate, structure and spread*. New Haven, Yale University Press.

Lacko, M. 1996. *Hungarian hidden economy in international comparisons*. Budapest, Institute of Economics.

Lane, R. E. 2000. *The loss of happiness in market economies*. New Haven, Yale University Press.

Lawton, J. H. 1973. 'The energy cost of food gathering', in Benjamin, B., Cox, P. R. and Peel, J. (eds.) *Resources and population*. New York, Academic Press.

Layard, R. 2003. *Happiness: has social science a clue?* The Lionel Robbins Memorial Lectures 2002/3, delivered at the London School of Economics 3rd, 4th and 5th March 2003 – downloaded from http://www.cep.lse.ac.uk/events/lectures.

Leach, G. 1975. *Energy and food production*. Guildford, IPC Press.

Ledyard, J. O. 1995. 'Public goods: a survey of experimental research', in Kagel, J. H. and Roth, A. E. (eds.) *The handbook of experimental economics*. Princeton, NJ, Princeton University Press, pp. 111–181.

Lee, R. D. 1969. '!Kung Bushmen subsistence: an input–output analysis', in Vayda, A. P. (ed.) *Environment and cultural behaviour: ecological studies in cultural anthropology*. New York, The Natural History Press, pp. 47–79.

Lele, S. M. 1991. 'Sustainable development: a critical review', *World Development* 19: 607–621.

Lester, J. P., Allen, D. W. and Hill, K. M. 2001. *Environmental injustice in the United States: myths and realities*. Boulder, CO, Westview Press.

Loasby, B. J. 1976. *Choice, complexity and ignorance*. Cambridge, Cambridge University Press.

Lomborg, B. 2001. *The skeptical environmentalist: measuring the real state of the world*. Cambridge, Cambridge University Press.

Loomis, J. B. and White, D. S. 1996. 'Economic benefits of rare and endangered species: summary and meta-analysis', *Ecological Economics* 18: pp. 197–202 (reprinted in Polasky, S. 2002. *The economics of biodiversity conservation*. Aldershot, Ashgate).

Lovelock. J. E. 1979. *Gaia: a new look at life on earth*. Oxford, Oxford University Press.

Lovelock, J. E. 1988. *The ages of Gaia*. New York, Norton.

Lovins, L. H., Hawken, P. and Lovins, A. B. 2000. *Natural capital: the next industrial revolution*. London, Earthscan.

Ludwig, D., Walker, B. and Holling, C. S. 1997 'Sustainability, stability and resilience', *Conservation Ecology* [online] 1(1): 7. URL http://www.consecol.org/vol1/iss1/art7.

McCarthy, J. J. *et al.* (eds.) 2001. *Climate change 2001: impacts, adaptation and vulnerability. Contribution of Working Group II to the Third Assessment Report of the Intergovernmental Panel on Climate Change*. Cambridge, Cambridge University Press, for the Intergovernmental Panel on Climate Change.

MacFarland, C. 1998. *An analysis of nature tourism in the Galápagos Islands*. http://www.darwinfoundation.org/articles/br15049801.html, accessed 13 June 2004.

McNeill, J. R. 2000. *Something new under the sun: an environmental history of the twentieth century*. London, Penguin.

Madison, A. 1995. *Monitoring the world economy 1820–1992*. Paris, Organisation for Economic Cooperation and Development.

Mankiw, G. N. 2000. *Macroeconomics*. 3rd edn. New York, Worth Publishers.

Mankiw, G. N. 2001. *Principles of economics*. 2nd edn. Fort Worth, Harcourt.

Markandya, A. and Richardson, J. 1992. *Environmental economics: a reader*. New York, Palgrave Macmillan.

Martinez-Alier, J. 1993. 'Distributional obstacles to international environmental policy', *Environmental Values* 2.

Martinez-Alier, J. and O'Connor, M. 1999. 'Distributional issues: an overview', in van Den Bergh, J. (ed.) *Handbook of environmental and resource economics*. Cheltenham and Northampton, Edward Elgar, pp. 380–392.

Martinez-Alier, J. 2000. 'Ecological economics'. *International Encyclopedia of the Social and Behavioral Sciences* Article 4.9: 4016–4023.

Max-Neef, M. 1992. 'Development and human needs', in Ekins, P. and Max-Neef, M. (eds.) *Real-life economics: understanding wealth creation*. London, Routledge, pp. 197–214.

Meadows, D. H., Meadows, D. L., Randers, J. and Behrens, W. W. 1972. *The limits to growth: a report for the Club of Rome's project on the predicament of mankind*. New York, Universe Books.

Meadows, D. H., Meadows, D. L. and Randers, J. 1992. *Beyond the limits: global collapse or a sustainable future?* London, Earthscan.

Metrick, A. and Weitzman, M. L. 1998. 'Conflicts and choices in biodiversity preservation', *Journal of Economic Perspectives* 12 (3): 21–34 (reprinted in Stavins, R. N. (ed.) *Economics of the environment: selected readings*. 4th edn. New York, Norton).

Metz, B. et al. (eds.) 2001. *Climate change 2001: mitigation. Contribution of Working Group III to the Third Assessment Report of the Intergovernmental Panel on Climate Change*. Cambridge, Cambridge University Press, for the Intergovernmental Panel on Climate Change.

Miller, R. E. and Blair, P. D. 1985. *Input–output analysis: foundations and extensions*. Englewood Cliffs, N.J., Prentice-Hall.

Mokyr, J. 1990. *The lever of riches: technological creativity and economic progress*. New York, Oxford University Press.

Muradian, R. and Martinez-Alier, J. 2001. 'Trade and the environment: from a 'Southern' perspective', *Ecological Economics* 36: 281–297.

Nelson, R. R. and Winter, S. G. 2002. 'Evolutionary theorising in economics', *Journal of Economic Perspectives* 16: 23–46.

Neumayer, E. 1999. *Weak versus strong sustainability: exploring the limits of two opposing paradigms*. Cheltenham, Edward Elgar.

Neumayer, E. 2001. *Greening trade and investment: environmental protection without protectionism*. London, Earthscan Publications.

Newsome, D., Moore, S. A. and Dowling, R. K. 2002. *Natural area tourism: ecology impacts and management*. Clevedon, Channel View Publications.

Nordhaus, W. D. and Boyer, J. 2000. *Warming the world: economic models of global warming*. Cambridge, MA, MIT Press.

Norgaard, R. B. 1994. *Development betrayed: the end of progress and a coevolutionary revisioning of the future*. London; New York, Routledge.

Norton, B. G. and Toman, M. A. 1997. 'Sustainability: ecological and economic perspectives', *Land Economics* 73: 553–568.

OECD 2002. *Implementing domestic tradeable permits – Recent developments and future challenges*, Paris, OECD. http://www.oecdbookshop.org/oecd/display.asp?lang= EN&sf1=identifiers&st1=972002121p1

OECD 2004. *ODA Statistics for 2003 and ODA Outlook*, Paris, OECD. http://www.oecd.org/dataoecd/40/63/31508396.pdf

Office of National Statistics 2002. *United Kingdom National Accounts: The Blue Book 2002*. London, The Stationery Office.

Ostrom, E. 1990. *Governing the commons: the evolution of institutions for collective action*. Cambridge; New York, Cambridge University Press.

Ostrom, E., Dietz, T., Dolsak, N., Stern, P., Stonich, S. and Weber, E. U. (eds.) 2002. *The drama of the commons*. Washington, DC, National Academy Press.

Page, Talbot 1997. 'On the problem of achieving efficiency and equity, intergenerationally', *Land Economics* 73: 580–596.

Park, Chris 2001. *The environment: principles and applications*. 2nd edn, London: Routledge.

Parker, P. 2000. *Physioeconomics: the basis for long-run economic growth*. Cambridge Mass., MIT Press.

Pearce, D. 1999. *Economics and environment: essays on ecological economics and sustainable development*. Cheltenham, Edward Elgar.

Pearce, D. and Turner, K. R. 1990. *Economics of natural resources and the environment*. New York, Harvester Wheatsheaf.

Perman, R., Ma, Y., McGilvray, J. and Common, M. 2003. *Natural resource and environmental economics*. 3rd edn. Harlow, Pearson.

Perman, R. and Scouller, J. 1999. *Business economics*. Oxford, Oxford University Press.

Pezzey, John 1992. 'Sustainability: an interdisciplinary guide', *Environmental Values* 1: 321–362.

Pezzey, J. C. V. 1997. 'Sustainability constraints versus "optimality" versus intertemporal concern, and axioms versus data', *Land Economics* 73: 448–466.

Pigou, A. C. 1920. *The economics of welfare*. London, Macmillan.

Pindyck, R. S. and Rubinfeld, D. L. 2001. *Microeconomics*. 5th edn. New Jersey, Prentice-Hall.

Polasky, S. (ed.) 2002. *The economics of biodiversity conservation*. Aldershot, Ashgate.

Ponting, C. 2001. *World history: a new perspective*. London, Vintage.

Pretty, J., Griffin, M., Sellens, M. and Pretty, C. 2003. *Green exercise: complementary roles of nature, exercise and diet in physical and emotional well-being and implications for public health policy*. CES Occasional Paper 2003–1, Centre for Environment and Society, University of Essex. (available at http://www2.essex.ac.uk/ces/).

Proops, J. L. R., Faber, M. and Wagenhals, G. 1993. *Reducing CO2 emissions: a comparative input–output study for Germany and the UK*. Berlin, Springer-Verlag.

Proops, J. L. R., Atkinson, G., Von Schlothein, B. F. and Simon, S. 1999. 'International trade and the sustainability footprint: a practical criterion for its assessment', *Ecological Economics* 28: 75–97.

Ramage, J. 1983. *Energy: a guidebook*. Oxford, Oxford University Press.

Rasmussen, E. 2001. *Games and information: an introduction to game theory*. 3rd edn. Oxford, Blackwell.

Rauscher, Michael 2001. 'On ecological dumping', in Batabyal, A. A. and Beladi, H. (eds.) *The economics of international trade and the environment*. Baco Raton, Lewis Publishers, pp. 67–82.

Ravetz, J. R. 1986. 'Usable knowledge, usable ignorance: incomplete science with policy implications', in Clark, W., Collin and Munn, T. E. (eds.) *Sustainable development of the biosphere*. Cambridge, Cambridge University Press, pp. 415–434.

Read, P. 1993. *Responding to global warming: the technology economics and politics of sustainable energy*. London, Zed Books.

Redclift, M. 1992. 'The meaning of sustainable development', *Geoforum* 25: 395–403.

Reid, D. 1995. *Sustainable development: an introductory guide*. London, Earthscan.

Reisch, L. A. 2003. 'The place of consumption in ecological economics', in Page, E. A. and Proops, J. (eds.) *Environmental thought*. Cheltenham, Edward Elgar.

Roberts, T. J. and Töffolon-Weiss, M. M. 2001. *Chronicles from the environmental justice frontline*. Cambridge, Cambridge University Press.

Rock, M. T. 1995. 'Pollution intensity of GDP and trade policy: can the World Bank be wrong?' *World Development* 24: 471–479.

Rogers, J. J. W. and Feiss, P. G. 1998. *People and the earth: basic issues in the sustainability of resources and environment*. Cambridge, Cambridge University Press.

Rojstaczer, S., Sterling, S. M. and Moore, N. J. 2001. 'Human appropriation of photosynthesis products', *Science*, 294: (21 December): 2549–2552.

Røpke, I. 1994. 'Trade, development and sustainability – a critical assessment of the "free trade dogma"', *Ecological Economics* 9: 13–22.

Rose, A. 1999. 'Input–output structural decomposition analysis of energy and the environment', in van den Bergh, J. C. J. M. (ed.) *Handbook of environmental and resource economics*. Cheltenham, Edward Elgar.

Royal Commission on Environmental Pollution 2000. *Twenty-second report: energy – the changing climate*. London, HMSO.

Ruth, M. 1999. 'Physical principles and environmental economic analysis', in van den Bergh, J. C. J. M. (ed.) *Handbook of environmental and resource economics*. Cheltenham, Edward Elgar.

Sahlins, M. 1974. *Stone age economics*. London, Routledge and Kegan Paul.

Sandler, T. 1997. *Global challenges: an approach to environmental, political and economic challenges.* Cambridge, Cambridge University Press.

Scitovsky, T. 1976. *The joyless economy.* New York, Oxford University Press.

Scitovsky, T. 1986. *Human desire and economic satisfaction: essays in the frontiers of economics.* Brighton, Wheatsheaf.

Secretariat to Biodiversity Convention 2001. *Global biodiversity outlook.* access pdf version at http://www.biodiv.org/gbo/gbo-pdf.asp#.

Sen, A. 1985. *Commodities and capabilities.* Amsterdam, Elsevier.

Sen, A. K. 1987. *On ethics and economics.* Oxford, Blackwell.

Simon, J. L. 1981. *The ultimate resource.* Princeton, Princeton University Press.

Simon, J. L. and Wildavsky, A. 1993. *Assessing the empirical basis of the 'biodiversity crisis'.* Washington, DC, Competitive Enterprise Foundation.

Singer, P. 1993. *Practical ethics.* 2nd edn. Cambridge, Cambridge University Press.

Sipes, K. N. and Mendelsohn, R. 2001. 'The effectiveness of gasoline taxation to manage air pollution', *Ecological Economics* 36: 299–309.

Slesser, M. 1978. *Energy in the economy,* London: Macmillan.

Smith, A. 1776. An inquiry into the nature and causes of the wealth of nations. Dublin: Whitestone.

Smith, V. K. (ed.) 1979. *Scarcity and growth reconsidered.* Baltimore, Johns Hopkins University Press.

Snooks, G. D. 1994. *Portrait of the family within the total economy: a study in long-run dynamics, Australia 1788–1990.* Cambridge, Cambridge University Press.

Söderbaum, P. 2000. *Ecological economics – a political economics approach to environment and development.* London, Earthscan.

Solow, R. M. 1974a. 'Intergenerational equity and exhaustible resources', *Review of Economic Studies* 41 (May): 29–46.

Solow, R. M. 1974b. 'The economics of resources and the resources of economics', *American Economic Review* 64: 1–14.

Spash, C. L. 1999. 'The development of environmental thinking in economics', *Environmental Values* 8: 413–435.

Spash, C. L. 2002. *Greenhouse economics: value and ethics.* London, Routledge.

Stagl, S. 2002. 'Free trade and its effects: some critical comments', in Wohlmeyer, H. and Quendler, T. (eds.) *The WTO, agriculture and sustainable development.* Sheffield, Greenleaf Publishing, pp. 165–188.

Steininger, K. 1994. 'Reconciling trade and environment: towards a comparative advantage for long-term policy goals', *Ecological Economics* 9: 23–42.

Stern, D. I. 1998. Progress on the environmental Kuznets curve? *Environment and Development Economics* 3(2): 173–196.

Stiglitz, J. E. 2002. *Globalization and its discontents.* New York, Allen Lane.

Stirling, A. and Mayer, S. 2005. 'Confronting risk with precaution: a multi-criteria mapping of a GM crop', in Getzner, M., Spash, C. L. and Stagl, S. (eds.) *Alternatives for environmental valuation.* London, Routledge, pp. 159–184.

Stockhammer, E., Harald, H., Obermayr, B. and Steiner, K. 1997. 'The Index of Sustainable Economic Welfare (ISEW) as an alternative to GDP in measuring economic welfare: the results of the Austrian (revised) ISEW calculation 1955–1992', *Ecological Economics* 21: 19–34.

Swanson, T. M. (ed.) 1995. *The economics and ecology of biodiversity decline: the forces driving global change.* Cambridge, Cambridge University Press.

Tietenberg, T. H. 2000. *Environmental and natural resource economics.* Fifth Edition. New York, Harper Collins.

Tietenberg, T. 2001. *Emissions trading programs,* Aldershot, Ashgate Publishing Limited.

Tietenberg, T. H. 2003. *Environmental and natural resource economics.* Reading, MA, Addison Wesley.

Toman, M. A. (ed.) 2001. *Climate change, economics and policy: an RFF anthology.* Washington, DC, Resources for the Future.

Toman, M. A., Pezzey, J. and Krautkraemer, J. 1995. 'Neoclassical economic growth theory and "sustainability"', in Bromley, D. W. (ed.) *The handbook of environmental economics*. Oxford and Cambridge, Blackwell, pp. 139–165.

Townsend, P. 1979. *Poverty in the United Kingdom: a survey of household resources and standards of living*. Harmondsworth, Penguin.

Tudge, C.1996. *The day before yesterday: five million years of human history*. London, Pimlico.

Ulph, A. 1997. 'International trade and the environment: a survey of recent economic analysis', in Folmer, H. and Tietenberg, T. (eds.) *The international yearbook of environmental and resource economics 1997/1998*. Cheltenham, Edward Elgar, pp. 204–242.

UNCED 1992. *Agenda 21 and the UNCED Proceedings*, New York, Oceana Publications.

United Nations 1972. *Report of the United Nations Conference on the Human Environment*, Stockholm, 5–16 June 1972 (United Nations publication, Sales No. E.73.II.A.14 and corrigendum), chap. I.

United Nations 1992. *Integrated environmental and economic accounting*. New York, United Nations.

United Nations 1993. *Handbook of national accounting: integrated environmental and economic accounting*. Studies in Method (Series F, No 61), New York, Department for Economic and Social Information and Policy Analysis, Statistical Division, United Nations.

United Nations 2002a. *World population prospects: the 2000 revision. Volume III Analytical report*. New York, Population Division of Department of Economic and Social Affairs, United Nations. (accessible at http://www.un.org and search for 'population'.)

United Nations 2002b. The World Summit on Sustainable Development, 26 August–4 September 2002, Johannesburg, http://www.johannesburgsummit.org/html/brochure/brochure12.pdf

United Nations Development Programme 1998. *Human development report 1998*. New York, Oxford University Press.

United Nations Development Programme (UNDP) 1999. *Human Development Report 1999 – globalization with a human face*. Oxford and New York, Oxford University Press.

United Nations Development Programme (UNDP) 2000. *Human rights and Human development – for freedom and solidarity*, Oxford and New York, Oxford University Press.

United Nations Development Programme (UNDP) 2001. *Human Development Report 2001 – making new technologies work for human development*, Oxford and New York, Oxford University Press.

United Nations Development Programme (UNDP) 2003. *Human Development Report 2003 – millennium development goals: a compact among nations to end human poverty*. Oxford and New York, Oxford University Press.

UNEP and IISD 2000. Environment and trade – a handbook, Geneva, http://www.iisd.org/pdf/envirotrade_handbook.pdf.

Usher, D. 1980. *The measurement of economic growth*. Oxford, Blackwell.

Valentine, P. S. 1992. 'Review: nature based tourism', in Weiler, B. and Hall, C. M. (eds.) *Special interest tourism*. London, Bellhaven, pp. 105–127.

van den Bergh, J. C. J. M., and de Mooij, R. A. 1999. 'An assessment of the growth debate', in van den Bergh, J. C. J. M. (ed.) *Handbook of environmental and resource economics*. Cheltenham, Edward Elgar, pp. 643–655.

van den Bergh, J. C. J. M., and Hofkes, M. W. 1999. 'Economic models of sustainable development', in van den Bergh, J. C. J. M. (ed.) *Handbook of environmental and resource economics*. Cheltenham, Edward Elgar, pp. 1108–1122.

van den Bergh, J. C. J. M. (ed.) 1999. *Handbook of environmental and resource economics*, Cheltenham, Edward Elgar.

Varian, H. R. 1987. *Intermediate microeconomics*. 2nd edn. New York, W. W. Norton.

Vaze, P. 1998. 'Environmental input–output tables for the United Kingdom', in Vaze, P. (ed.) *UK environmental accounts 1998*. London, The Stationery Office.

Vitousek, P. M., Ehrlich, P. R., Ehrlich, A. H. and Matson, P. A. 1986. 'Human appropriation of the products of photosynthesis', *Bioscience* 36: 368–373.

Vitousek, P. M., Mooney, H. A., Lubchenco, J. and Mlillo, J. M. 1997. 'Human domination of earth's ecosystems', *Science* 277: 494–499.

Vogel, D. 1995. *Trading up. Consumer and environmental regulation in the global economy.* Cambridge, MA, Harvard University.

von Weizsäcker, E. U., Lovins, A. B. and Lovins, L. H. 1997. *Factor four: doubling wealth, halving resource use.* London, Earthscan.

Wackernagel, M. and Rees, W. 1996. *Our ecological footprint: reducing human impact on the earth.* Gabriola Island, British Columbia, New Society Publishers.

Wackernagel, M., Shulz, N. B. *et al.* 2002. 'Tracking the ecological overshoot of the human economy'. *Proceedings of the National Academy of Sciences* 99(14): 9266–9271.

Waldrop, M. M. 1994. *Complexity: the emerging science at the edge of order and chaos.* Harmondsworth, Penguin.

WCED. 1987. *Our common future.* New York, Oxford University Press.

Weaver, D. B. 1998. *Ecotourism in the less developed world.* Wallingford, CABI Publishing.

Weitzman, M. L. 1974. 'Prices vs. quantities', *Review of Economic Studies* 41: 477–491.

Wheeler, D. 2001. 'Racing to the bottom? Foreign investment and air pollution in developing countries', *Journal of Environment and Development* 10: 225–245.

Whittaker, R. H. and Likens, G. E. 1975. 'The biosphere and man', in Leith, H. and Whittaker, R. H. (eds.) *Primary productivity of the biosphere.* New York, Springer-Verlag, pp. 305–328.

Wilson, E. O. 1988. 'The current state of biodiversity', in Wilson, E. O. (ed.) *Biodiversity.* Washington, DC, National Academy Press, pp. 31–41.

Wilson, E. O. 1993. 'Biophilia and the conservation ethic', in Kellert, S. R. and Wilson, E. O. (eds.) *The biophilia hypothesis.* Washington DC, Island Press.

World Trade Organization (WTO) 2003. *WTO Annual Report 2003.* Geneva, WTO Publications.

Wynne, B. 1992. 'Uncertainty and environmental learning – reconceiving science and policy in the preventive paradigm', *Global Environmental Change* Vol. 2, no. 2: 111–127.

Young, M. D. 1994. 'Ecologically-accelerated trade liberalisation: a set of disciplines for environment and trade agreements', *Ecological Economics* 9: 43–51.

Young, R. A. 2001. *Uncertainty and the environment: implications for decision making and environmental policy.* Cheltenham, Edward Elgar.

Zarsky, L. 2002. 'Stuck in the mud? Nation states, globalisation and the environment', in Gallagher, K. P. and Werksman, J. (eds.) *International Trade & Sustainable Development.* London, Earthscan Publications, pp. 19–44.

Index

This item is to be returned or renewed before the latest date above. It may be borrowed for a further period if not in demand. **To renew your books:**

- **Phone the 24/7 Renewal Line 01926 499273 or**
- **Visit www.warwickshire.gov.uk/libraries**

Discover • Imagine • Learn • with libraries

Warwickshire
County Council

...ing for ...wickshire

KT-449-058

MIDSUMMER MAGIC

Engaged Josie is visiting Cornwall with best friend Diane, fiancé Harry and his pal Ant. Josie can't wait to start wedding planning, if only Harry was more interested, and Diane and Ant weren't at war with each other. As the four make amends, they meet Freddie Puck, a well known TV hypnotist and find themselves agreeing to a dare – to stay all night on the hills by the standing stones. Local mythology says a young married couple will find true happiness if they can last a whole night there on Midsummer's Eve. But as night time falls, not everyone seems to have remembered the boundaries of love...

MIDSUMMER MAGIC

MIDSUMMER MAGIC

by

Julia Williams

Magna Large Print Books
Long Preston, North Yorkshire,
BD23 4ND, England.

British Library Cataloguing in Publication Data.

Williams, Julia
    Midsummer magic.

        A catalogue record of this book is
        available from the British Library

        ISBN   978-0-7505-3894-7

First published in Great Britain by Avon
A division of HarperCollins*Publishers* 2013

Cover illustration by arrangement with HarperCollins Publishers

Julia Williams asserts the moral right to be identified as the author of this work

Published in Large Print 2014 by arrangement with
HarperCollins Publishers

Magna Large Print is an imprint of Library Magna Books Ltd.

Printed and bound in Great Britain by
T.J. (International) Ltd., Cornwall, PL28 8RW

For Dot with love and gratitude

Prologue

'Thou speakest aright:
I am that merry wanderer of the night.
I jest to Oberon and make him smile'
                    A Midsummer Night's Dream:
                                    Act II, Scene 1

'"Lord what fools these mortals be..." *You could*
say that's my mantra. It's easy to hypnotise the
gullible, but I've managed to hypnotise sceptics too. I
like to think Shakespeare knew a thing or two about
hypnotism.'
                    Freddie Puck interviewed in *The Sun,*
                                    June 1982

1982: Tatiana

'You're late,' Freddie Puck was standing languidly by the stage door, as Tatiana came flying down the street straight from dinner with her agent, Susan Peasebottom, where she'd both eaten and drunk more then she should have. He was smoking a cigarette, and as usual, looked calm and in control. She hated the way he always did that; she always felt ill at ease around Freddie, as if he knew a secret about her that she did not. But then that was part of what he did, play mind games on people to screw them up.

'You're lucky I'm here at all,' she muttered. After the offer Susan had put to her this evening, she had been very tempted not to turn up.

Freddie looked her up and down quizzically – honestly, sometimes she felt like she was just a lump of meat to him.

'You done something to your hair?'

Tatiana blushed. She wasn't sure about her new haircut, a drastic departure from the Farrah look she'd been sporting for the last couple of years. Her hairdresser, Julie, had produced an article from an American mag which pronounced that long flickbacks were out, short was in, and hair for some reason should be red. So Tatiana had been persuaded to have it dyed, trimmed and hacked, so now she had a longish piece at the back, but the hair at the top was cut short and swept back in waves – or it had done when she'd come out of the salon this afternoon. After a couple of hours in a smoky dive with Susan Peasebottom, followed by an undignified race up the road, Tatiana felt sure her hair wasn't quite the crowning glory the article had promised.

'Yes,' she mumbled, almost wishing he hadn't noticed.

'Nice,' said Freddie, nonchalantly flicking out his ash as she walked past him into the theatre, and as usual she had no way of knowing whether he really meant it, or whether he was just kidding her.

'Tati, darling, love the hair!' Damn. Bron came out of his dressing room (it still irked her that he had his own dressing room, while she had to share) and gave her a hug. 'How was dinner?'

'Great,' said Tati, hoping he hadn't noticed the slight flinch as he touched her. It was still the same between them. It was. She kept telling herself that. She had to believe it.

'Any news?' he said lightly. She'd let slip there might be something, now she wished she hadn't. She wanted time to work out what she was going to do.

'There might be a part in a soap coming up,' she said.

'A soap?' Bron's face was almost comic in his dismay. 'You can't do a soap, darling, Tati, you can't. It's selling out.'

The frustration spilled out of her.

'And this? This isn't selling out?' she said. 'Freddie bloody Puck's promises won't pay the rent.'

'He's in talks with a TV production company,'

14

said Bron, 'it's only a matter of time…'

Tati put her hands up, 'I don't want to hear it,' she said. 'Freddie's always in sodding talks with a TV company. This is *real*, Bron. I want you to be happy for me.'

Bron slumped, and gave her the sad look she'd seen too much of late. 'But what about us?' he said. 'What about our plans?'

'I know, we'll have our own theatre company,' she said. She'd heard it too many times before. 'Perhaps I had plans too, but we all know what happened to *them*.'

She couldn't disguise the bitterness in her voice.

'Tati,' said Bron, there were tears in his eyes, 'You know I'm sorry–'

'Don't.' Tati looked at him sadly. 'It's too late for all that. I have to think about the future now.'

'We both do,' said Bron, reaching out and holding her hands. 'Come on, Tati, we're still young, I still want to do Shakespeare with you. One day…'

'Maybe I can't wait for one day anymore.'

She'd said it. Words that she'd never wanted to say, and when she saw how Bron slumped even more, she wished them back. 'Look,' she said, letting go of his hands gently, 'I'm late, we've got a show to do. We'll talk about this later.'

Giving him a swift kiss and a hug, she left him in the corridor and went to get ready, her thoughts churning. Susan's offer was tempting, but was it the right thing to do?

As usual, it was squashed in the girls' dressing

room. Bron didn't have this problem in his single dressing room, thought Tatiana bitterly as she found her dressing table in the corner. Naturally the *male* star of the show couldn't slum it like she did. She was so mixed up. She loved Bron, she really did, but she hated this, and it wasn't fair. Someone had laughingly written 'Star' in lipstick on her mirror. Ha, bloody ha. The joke was certainly on her, she thought sourly as she sat herself down, and with the practice of an old hand started to apply her stage make-up.

The room was hot and crowded, and full of the noise of women's chatter. Like so many cheeping hens, Tatiana thought bitchily. She was more of a man's woman. Women and their idle talk bored her. Which didn't make for popularity among her peer group, but Tatiana didn't really care. This batch of hens was even duller than most, so she didn't feel she was missing out. They were the backstage chorus dancing to Freddie Puck's tune, as all of them were on this *Illusions* tour. As she was. As Bron was.

She sighed and looked at herself in the mirror. Pushing twenty-five and was this all there was to offer? She thought again about the deal on the table, and felt her stomach churn. It was all very well for Bron to tell her to be patient, that Freddie's incessant talks with production companies about a TV series of *Illusions* would eventually come to fruition, but she couldn't see it herself.

Tatiana scrutinised her face. Still pretty, she judged – pretty enough to do what she had to do in Bron's show, at any rate. But for how long? This was a cruel business for a woman. Twenty-five wasn't far from thirty. Then what would happen to her? When she and Bron had started out, he'd promised her an equal part in the act; equal shares in the profits, and then, when they could afford it, their own theatre company, Shakespeare, *proper* acting. So how come it was still her looking decorative and pretty, Bron taking all the credit, the gasps and plaudits from the crowd, as he performed yet another incredible trick? If she hadn't been so damned in thrall to Bron...

They'd met as extras in rep, doing Shakespeare in dreary towns to uninterested punters. It had been a far cry from her drama school ambition to play Juliet at Stratford, and the only bright spot had been Bron, with his lean handsome look and sardonic manner. They had laughed their way through most of the misery of the tour, and he'd taught her card tricks and outlined his twin obsessions of magic and owning his own theatre company. When, after the tour was over, he rang her to say he and his friend Freddie had got a gig doing a magic show in Brighton, it had seemed like a lifeline. Regular money, regular work. After months of scrabbling to pay the rent, it was an easy option. It had always been meant to be temporary – Bron was never going to give up on his theatre plans, but as time went on, they seemed to recede into the distance. And now Tati often found herself wondering if he still wanted it as much as he said he did.

Tatiana formed a cupid's bow, and painted her lips bright red in a fury. With her green and blue sparkly eye shadow, over-blushed cheeks, and the new haircut (which despite her best efforts didn't

17

look anything like the photo Julie had shown her), she looked like a painted doll. Which is all she was. Being pretty and decorative was all she was good for. Unless…

Unless she took the offer. She hadn't been quite straight with Bron. It wasn't just any old soap: she'd been offered the leading role in a new soap opera the Beeb had just commissioned. Susan thought she should; couldn't understand her hesitation. 'You don't want to be doing this forever do you?' she'd said with uncharacteristic honesty. Tatiana knew she was right. So why was she still hesitating? Misguided loyalty to Bron was what Susan had called it. But, Bron and her … a future without him was unthinkable, even after what had happened. She pulled on her spandex bodysuit, wincing as she realised how tight it was getting. She still hadn't managed to shed all her excess weight. Even Bron had noticed and Freddie had made sarky comments too. All the time she was getting older and fatter and there were any amount of silly hens in this hen coop desperate to take her place.

So why don't you let them?

As Tatiana stood waiting in the wings for the fanfare which heralded her arrival on stage, the thought came to her more strongly than ever. As she let Bron tie her up, throw knives at her, try to cut her in two, and pull hankies out of her ear, while she span and danced like a pretty doll around him, with the same fixed grin on her face, she felt her strongest urge yet to leave. What was there for her here now? She and Bron were growing apart, she could feel it. She knew Bron was

18

hurting too, but what had happened was forming an insurmountable barrier between them. And Freddie was too much of an influence not to suggest she was replaced when she got too fat, too wrinkly, too old.

At the climax of Bron's act, he produced doves out of a hat, which flew onto Tatiana. As she paraded round the stage (hating what she did with a passion) the bird that had landed on her head shat on her.

In that instant her decision was made. Susan was right. She could do much better than this.

'Sorry babes, about Henrietta,' Bron said as they came off the stage. Bron had the absurd habit of naming all his birds. 'Hope your new hairdo can stand it.' He laughed, and Freddie, who was standing with him, laughed too. Tati was enraged, it was as if their earlier conversation had never taken place.

'My hair, yes,' said Tatiana. 'Me, no.'

'Sorry?' Bron looked confused.

'That's it,' she said. 'It's the last straw. Tomorrow I sign up for *Sail for the Sun*. I'm going to be on the TV.'

'What about the act?' said Bron, aghast.

'What about it?' said Tatiana. 'You don't need me. You just need a pretty face. Well Auberon Fanshawe, I'm tired of being your Debbie McGee. I'm better than that.'

With that, she turned and left the theatre, without even taking her make-up off.

She'd done it. She was free. And a shining future beckoned.

Halloween

'Combining your moving-in party with a Halloween one was a brilliant idea,' declared Diana. She looked gorgeous as ever, in a little black dress which accentuated her curves, her auburn hair piled high on her head, with some fetching curls escaping, as she bustled round Josie's kitchen. From the lounge – which they'd spent the afternoon decorating with wispy bits of cobweb, spiders dangling from the ceiling, flashing skull-shaped lights and pumpkin-shaped candles – came a loud set of expletives, as Harry tried to plug in various bits of electrical equipment to make a sound system any nightclub would have been proud of, but which Josie was somewhat doubtful was needed in a small London flat on a Saturday night.

'I seem to remember it was more your idea,' laughed Josie, as she got out plastic cups and put them on the kitchen drainer with the copious amounts of wine and beer that Harry had cheerily brought back from Sainsburys. 'Josie, it's so fab that you and Harry are moving in together, why don't you have a party?' she mimicked. 'Josie, Halloween's coming up, you can combine them, wouldn't that be *amazing!*'

'Well if I left it up to you, you'd have just snuck in here like a pair of sneak thieves, as if you were embarrassed about the whole thing, rather than celebrating the wonderfulness of you two becoming a proper partnership,' declared Diana. 'Honestly, I don't know what you'd do without me.'

'Er, get on with my life without being bossed about?' said Josie, and ducked as Diana chucked some peanuts in her direction.

'I can only hope Harry's more domesticated than you are,' said Diana. 'I don't know how you'll manage to keep this place clean without my help.'

Until recently Diana had been renting Josie's spare room, but when it became clear that Harry was becoming a permanent fixture, she'd tactfully moved out to live with friends down the road. 'Three is definitely a crowd,' she'd said, 'and I don't fancy being a gooseberry to you two lovebirds'

'I miss this,' said Josie, 'are you sure you're okay about leaving?'

Di had been incredibly positive and supportive since Josie had first broached the awkward subject of Harry moving in, but Josie knew how good she was at covering up her emotions. Di didn't have a huge social network, didn't get on immensely well with her family, and for all her playing the 'I love being single' card, Josie had the sneaking suspicion that she was secretly yearning to settle down herself.

'Of course I am,' said Diana, 'I mean, it is bloody annoying being best friends with someone as pretty, rich and successful as you are, who's managed to nab a gorgeous man to boot, but I'll survive.'

'Oh, Diana, now I feel terrible,' said Josie,

giving her friend a hug.

'It was a *joke*, Josie,' said Diana affectionately. 'You are so gullible.'

'Still,' said Josie wistfully, 'it's not going to be the same now, is it?'

Josie had met Di five years earlier, through a mutual friend, Carrie, who worked with Josie and had been to school with Di. They both quickly decided they didn't like Carrie as much as they did each other. They'd started meeting once a week for drinks, and soon it had turned into regular weekends on the pull – Diana's confidence taking Josie places she would never have been alone. Without Diana pushing her, Josie doubted she would have followed up Harry's tentative calls when they'd first met up again. It was no good, happy as she was, Josie was going to miss sparky, lively Diana, who called a spade a spade and always let you know when you were in the wrong, but was also an incredibly loyal, fun friend.

'No, it won't,' said Diana, 'but it will be different. And that's good too.'

She was being so positive about it, Josie hoped she wasn't protesting too much.

'And you really don't mind?'

'Don't be daft, of course I don't,' said Diana, 'I'm happy for you. You and Harry are made for each other. Now what else do we need to do? How's the punch?'

Josie looked at the punch into which Harry had cheerfully flung a bottle of vodka, copious amounts of red wine, and not nearly enough orange juice, in Josie's opinion. It seemed to be a bit lacking in the fruit department, and they'd run out of oranges. 'What do you think about this punch? Does it need more fruit?'

'Haven't you got any more apples?' said Diana. 'It's Halloween, you have to have apples. It's the law.'

'I think I might still have some left in the cupboard,' said Josie.

She rummaged around, and then produced a couple of rather wrinkled-looking apples.

'Great,' said Diana, 'here, let me peel them.'

'Why?' said Josie.

'Because...' said Diana. 'It's Halloween and you need to see the name of the man you're going to marry ... which will begin with H, obviously.'

Despite her straight talking and often cynical nature, Diana was extremely superstitious, always walking round a ladder, and freaking out if a black cat strolled across her path.

She grabbed one of the apples from Josie and peeled it with a flourish.

'Now,' she instructed, 'you have to fling it over your shoulder, and it should fall in the shape of the letter that begins the name of your future husband.'

'What are you talking about?' said Josie.

'Famous Halloween tradition, young maids did it all the time in olden days, don't you know *anything?*' Diana was a force to be reckoned with so, feeling incredibly foolish, Josie threw the apple peel over her shoulder. It landed with a plop on the floor, and despite herself Josie turned round to see what the result was.

'Knew it was stupid,' she said, 'look, it's formed

the letter A. I don't know anyone whose name begins with A, apart from Harry's mate Ant, and I'm hardly going to marry him.'

'Oh,' said Diana, looking a bit despondent. 'I can't believe it hasn't worked.'

'Come on, Di, you can't believe all that mumbo jumbo,' said Josie, laughing. She could never get over how gullible Di could be.

'Well, you never know, Halloween is a strange time of year,' said Diana. 'I just think there are things out there we know nothing about.'

'Go on then, you have a go,' said Josie indulgently.

Diana peeled the other apple and with a great sense of drama, slowly threw it behind her shoulder. This time the apple peel landed with a more definite thud, and split into three pieces which, if you were being very imaginative, may just have formed the letter H.

'Well that's not right, either,' said Diana, 'the only H I know is Harry.'

'There you go,' said Josie, 'I knew it was daft. Besides, I'm not marrying Harry just yet. Without your help I'd never have persuaded him to move in here. I might just get him convinced about marrying me in the next decade.'

'Get me convinced of what?' Harry came into the kitchen holding a pair of leads and looking a bit bemused. Josie's heart did the little leap it always did when she saw him. Lovely dependable Harry, with his brilliant blue eyes, curly black hair and cute smile. It made her feel warm all over thinking they were now a proper item again. They had first met at university, although Josie might never have paid much attention to the quiet studious boy on her course if he hadn't tagged along on a group weekend away at her parents' home in Cornwall. When he was the only person who was prepared to go and watch Shakespeare with her on a rainy summer's night at the local open air theatre she knew he was special. And for a while there it looked like they might go the distance, then time and space and work intervened and somehow they lost touch. It still seemed such luck not only to have met Harry again at Amy's wedding, but for him to have still remembered, and (apparently) thought about her, just as she'd thought about him over the years. In one way their relationship had been a whirlwind, they'd only been 'together' properly for a few months, but in other ways it felt like she was coming home. Harry in her mind had always been the one who got away.

'I think I'm going to have to head out to B&Q to find another lead,' he said – 'there's a connection I'm missing.'

'Nothing,' said Josie, digging Diana in the ribs and glaring at her to stop her spilling the beans. But as usual it did no good.

'Josie's been doing an old Halloween trick of seeing the name of the man she'll marry,' said Diana. 'She threw a piece of apple peel over her shoulder, and look, it fell down in the shape of the letter H. I wonder what that could mean?'

Josie felt herself blush deeply. Marriage was something she wanted with Harry, of course it was, but given how fast they'd moved so far, she thought marriage might be rushing things a bit.

25

She wanted him to ask her in his own way, at the right time.

Harry peered at the floor, 'Are you sure that's an H?' he said. 'What about that one?'

'Oh, that was my turn,' lied Diana glibly. 'I got an A.'

'Ah, shame Ant's still in Oz, otherwise I'd introduce you,' said Harry with a grin.

'Ant? You want to inflict Ant on my best friend?' said Josie as she swept the peel away. 'It's all foolish nonsense anyway. As if an apple peel can tell you who you're going to marry.'

'As if indeed,' said Harry, but he looked thoughtful as he picked up the car keys and left the room.

'There, he's going to ask you now,' Diana teased her, 'sure as eggs is eggs. Did you see the look on his face?'

'Don't you ever stop interfering?' said Josie, blushing. 'He'll ask me if and when he's good and ready.'

'Well, there's no harm in pushing him along a bit,' said Diana. 'You know you two are made for each other. You just need a little help from Cupid's arrow, that's all.'

'What was all that about?' Harry muttered to himself as he got in the car and drove the short distance to B&Q. One of the most restful things about being with Josie was that she had never ever mentioned the 'M' word. Not that Harry was against the idea, but things had already moved faster then he'd anticipated, and he wasn't in a hurry to get married. Indeed, his best friend,

Ant, had laughed like a drain when he found out that Harry was even contemplating moving in with Josie.

'You are joking?' he'd said over the phone, when Harry had tracked him down to a bar in Australia to tell him the good news. 'Before you know it, you'll have his 'n' hers slippers and she'll be walking you down the aisle. And then it will be only a matter of time before she starts mentioning babies, and your life will effectively be over. Don't do it, mate. You'll really live to regret it.'

Knowing that he really wouldn't regret it, or at least regret taking the first step of sharing a home with Josie, allowed Harry to pass off Ant's teasing in a good-humoured fashion. 'You're only saying that because you're a jealous saddo who doesn't have a clue how to attract, let alone keep a beautiful woman,' he joshed back. 'Women, beware, Ant's here.'

Ant had always had plenty of women, but no one serious, apart from one mysterious relationship after uni, which he rarely mentioned, but had clearly left a scar.

'Your funeral, mate,' said Ant. 'Don't say I didn't warn you.'

Ant, who was currently taking the gap year he'd been threatening ever since before he and Harry had been students, had sent him a very rude Facebook message when he found out that Harry actually had gone the whole hog and was going 'all domesticated', as he put it.

Harry didn't happen to think Ant was right. Sure, when they were young guns straight out of college there had been a certain cachet in seeing who got the most women – getting any women at all had been Harry's main aim when he'd arrived at university, in the autumn of the millennium – but once Harry met Josie again at a mutual friend's wedding, nights on the pull had definitely lost their charm. It hadn't taken long for Harry to realise he'd fallen swiftly, deeply, irrevocably in love. He and Josie had got together at the end of university, and he'd always regretted letting her get away. He'd never been quite sure how it had happened, but he and Josie had been together such a briefly short time, and once they went to work – him to a small local newspaper in Newcastle, her to be a marketing assistant in a factory in Swindon – things had fizzled out. He had always thought he should have fought harder to keep her. So now they had found each other again, nothing was going to keep them apart. However much Ant might bitch about it, no amount of teasing would change his mind.

But ... marriage? Harry thought about it as he scanned the electrical shelves in B&Q for the right scart lead, wishing, not for the first time, that manufacturers would just make a universal lead which adapted to fit every bit of electronic equipment it seemed necessary for a modern man to have in his possession. Were he and Josie ready for that? He had to admit to a certain amount of relief and pleasure when they'd made the decision to move in together. No longer the need to be out there in the savage forest of dating; time to hang up his spurs, sit by the fire, and sip wine with his one true love. Simples, as the meerkats would say, but true.

Eventually buying two leads, certain that one of them would fit, Harry made his way back home, where he found Josie and Diana already giggly, having tried out his punch to 'see that it was strong enough', according to Diana, although Josie was worried it had too much vodka. 'Nonsense!' said Diana, 'you can never have too much vodka!' and promptly poured the remaining half of the bottle Harry had resisted pouring in before. Diana was a whirlwind. One he quite liked, he thought, but so different from Josie, Harry sometimes wondered how they could be friends. She was vivacious, lively, pretty and incredibly flirty: like a female version of Ant, a good-time girl out on the pull. She often gave off a tough vibe, but underneath it all Harry suspected she hid a vulnerability she wasn't prepared to let most people see. And she liked him and seemed genuinely happy for them both. Harry had a huge soft spot for her.

Josie poured some more orange juice into the punch, while Diana answered the door to their first guests. Once Harry had sorted out the music, the next few hours went by in a blur of congratulations, drinking and laughter. By midnight, Harry was feeling distinctly the worse for wear, and sitting happily ensconced on the sofa, watching Josie dance to the dulcet tones of Lady Gaga. He could sit and watch her dance for hours, she moved so gracefully, it was mesmerising. He was so lucky to have her. Josie was so beautiful, and kind, and wonderful. And she was his ... sometimes he couldn't quite believe it.

Maybe it *was* time to make things more permanent between them.

Someone had put something slower on, and a few of their friends were cosying up together – Diana, he noticed with amusement, was smooching with Josie's boss – 'Come on, lover boy,' Josie came swaying towards him, as drunk, he realised, as he was, 'time to dance.'

'Always time to dance with you,' he smiled, and pulled her close. She leant against his shoulder, and he felt her softness, and smelt her perfume. He was suddenly overcome with a dizzying sense of what could only be described as joy. He wanted to hold her and keep her and never let her go. 'You are so perfect,' he said, kissing her softly on the lips, 'how did I get this lucky?'

Josie blushed, and said, 'I'm the lucky one,' as she kissed him back, and he was overcome with a happiness he could never remember feeling before. With her small trim figure, her gorgeous fair pre-Raphaelite curls, and her stunning blue eyes, Josie was perfect in every way. She was kind, sweet, funny, loyal and he already knew he wanted to spend the rest of his life with her. So why not make it formal? What was wrong with marriage, after all? A perfectly sensible institution which had been round for centuries.

'Josie,' he said, feeling his heart hammering with happiness, 'will you marry me?'

'Oh my God, Oh my God!' An overexcited and slightly pissed Josie dragged Diana away from a rather interesting situation with Josie's to-die-for good-looking boss, Philip (trust Josie to nab a lovely guy *and* have a good-looking boss) into the kitchen. 'It worked, I can't believe it, but it worked.'

'What worked?' Josie wasn't the only one who'd drunk too much, Diana realised, as the walls came crashing in on her suddenly. 'What are you talking about?'

'Your Halloween thing,' said Josie, 'you know, the apple peel.'

Diana dragged herself away from the delicious prospect of a night in a penthouse with Philip, to focus on a faint memory of the early evening. 'But you got an A!'

'No I didn't,' said Josie, 'I got an H, remember? Ta-da!'

She waved her ring finger in front of Diana's bleary eyes. There was a platinum-looking ring on it.

'What? He didn't?'

'Yup, Harry just proposed!' said Josie triumphantly. 'Of course we need to get a proper ring, but this will do for now.'

On closer inspection, Diana realised Josie was wearing the ring pull from a Coke can on her finger.

'That's, that's – words fail me,' Diana suddenly felt the urgent need to sit down, and slumped against the wall and slid down it. She wanted to say something more effusive, but somehow the words wouldn't come.

'I know,' said Josie, sliding down to join her, 'and it's all down to you. You *are* going to be my bridesmaid, aren't you?'

Diana screamed in delight.

'You're getting married!' she whooped, 'and

31

I'm going to be bridesmaid. That is fabulous!'
Fabulous. That was the word she'd been searching for.

'I know!' said Josie, 'isn't it great?'

Diana suddenly felt a sudden, sober chill. It was great, of course it was great, but drunken misery set in, 'What about u-u-uss?' she wailed. 'You're going off to get married and you'll be shacked up and happy and I'll be on my own and single for ever!'

Great sloppy tears were running down her cheeks. Damn, that punch had been a serious mistake.

'Oh, Di, don't say that,' said Josie, clutching her in panic, 'you're my best friend, I couldn't live without you.'

She was crying too.

'You couldn't?' Diana paused and blew her nose, not very attractively. She hoped Philip didn't choose that particular moment to look for her.

'Of course not,' said Josie, sobbing nearly as loudly as Di was, 'you're always going to be my best friend. What would I do without you?'

'But it's not going to be the sa-aa-me,' hiccoughed Diana.

'It will, it will,' said Josie, 'pinkie promise.'

She linked her little finger in Diana's, setting off a fresh round of wailing, 'Oh, that's so lovely,' she wept, 'I love you so much.'

'And I love you too,' howled Josie, hugging her tightly.

'But you love Harry more,' said Diana.

'I do,' said Josie, her eyes shining through her

32

tears, 'I really do.'

Diana looked around her, suddenly surprised that they were sitting on the floor.

'Then what are we doing sitting here?' she said. '*You're* getting married. That is *so* fantastic. C'me on, let's dance!'

She staggered up, dragging Josie after her, and went to find Harry who was sitting looking slightly dazed in the corner, 'Woohoo, you two getting married, that is so brilliant! Listen up, everyone, Harry and Josie have just got engaged!'

'This calls for champagne!' someone shouted.

'We don't have any,' laughed Josie, 'we'll have to make do with vodka.'

'Vodka it is!' said Diana. She busied herself filling people's glasses, and then declared a toast, 'To Harry and Josie!' she said. 'Harry and Josie!' everyone said, raising their glasses and cheering, and the next half hour disappeared in a flurry of congratulations and back slapping. It was only as the party began to die down that Diana remembered Philip. She looked round for him and couldn't see him anywhere. Sneaky bastard. A bleep from her phone confirmed it. *Sorry, had to dash. Catch you soon?* This year, next year, sometime, never. She looked over at Josie caught in a romantic clinch with her future husband, and tried not to feel that she was getting left behind.

In a bar in Australia, Anthony Lambert, known to his friends as Ant, opened his laptop and checked his emails. He'd sent a rude message to his best friend, Harry, the previous day in response to the dire (in Ant's mind at least) news that he was settling down and moving in with his girlfriend, Josie, after a ridiculously whirlwind romance lasting a few short months. Ant had been horrified, not least because at twenty-eight the notion of settling down seemed as far removed as it had when he'd first met Harry at uni ten years ago, but also because Harry had already dated Josie back then, and they'd lost touch. If she was so great, why hadn't they stuck together before? Hmm? Ant's motto was always look forward, never look back. He felt sure that Harry was making a big mistake, and had told him so in so many words. Well. Very few words actually. It had been more along the lines of What are you doing you stupid bastard? I thought Josie was all in the past?

It seemed Harry had been remarkably swift in his reply. Their correspondence while Ant had been away had been in the main, short and sweet, and they'd often been known to go weeks without hearing from one another. It was only the imperative need to tell his best friend not make a complete dickhead of himself which had impelled Ant to write yesterday.

From: Harry@gmail.com
To: Antonhistravels@gmail.com

Hi mate,
1 I hope you're sitting down...

2 And I hope you are in a bar...

3 And I also hope you have a drink in your hand.

What the...? Ant had a sip of his beer, and scrolled down to the bottom of the email where he read words which caused him to nearly spill his drink. He had to reread in case he'd got it wrong, but no, there it was in black and white.

I know you're not going to like this, mate, but it's my life.

So ... the big news is Josie and I are getting married. Next year, September, we think.

I know, I know. It's sudden. And I'm going to have to put off travelling for a bit. But ... I let her get away once. I'm not going to make that mistake again. Try to be happy for us.

Harry.

P.S. We'd like you to be best man.

Best man. Harry wanted him to be best man? Could it get any worse?

'Fuck me sideways,' said Ant out loud. 'I think it's time I went home.'

Part One

There May I Marry Thee

'Four days will quickly steep themselves in night
Four nights will quickly dream away the time...'
A Midsummer Night's Dream:
Act I, Scene 1

'Magic tricks are all about dissembling. Distract the
punter with your voice, or a bit of stage business, and
they miss the actual trick itself. It's easy when you
know how.'
Freddie Puck: *The Art of Illusion*

Chapter One

'Is that the lot?' said Harry as he paused to take a breather. Though early in the morning, the June sun was already hot and he was already working up a sweat. He looked on in horror as Josie, still somehow looking cool and collected in a strappy summer dress and sandals, came down the flat steps, with the second large holdall she had apparently packed for a simple weekend away. 'How long are we planning to be away again?'

'This one isn't mine, it's Di's,' said Josie. Di had come to stay the night before, terrified of oversleeping on her own. 'And before you start bitching about how Diana always takes advantage of me, she's bringing her bigger one.'

'She's got a bigger bag than *this?*' Harry said as he took the bag from Josie, and tried to squeeze a space for it in the not-too-huge boot of his Honda Civic. A car that, not unnaturally, Ant had sneered at very loudly, as being 'a girl's car.' Sometimes Harry wished Ant would keep his opinions to himself. But there was no chance of that. Ant, back from his travels, was louder and more opinionated than ever since his time away. It hadn't taken him long to be employed by a flash advertising company ('Recession, what recession?' he'd queried) with more cash than sense and was driving down alone in his brand new top of the range Merc. He was planning to meet them at a motorway service station en route, as, hilariously for Ant who was always overconfident, he appeared to have had an attack of nerves at the thought of arriving before them and meeting Josie's parents on his own.

'I don't think I'm going to be able to fit this all in,' said Harry, looking despairing as Diana, her ginger curls escaping from a straggly bun, tottered down the steps in high wedges, skinny jeans which accentuated every curve and a skimpy top which left nothing to the imagination, dragging an even bigger and more cumbersome bag behind her.

'Di, you're going to have to have your bag in the back with you,' said Josie when she realised that there really was no more room in the boot. 'Either that, or we'll ring Ant up to see if he can take you in his car.'

'No, it's okay,' said Diana as she squashed herself into the back, complete with the offending bag. 'Ant's an unusual name.'

'It's short for Anthony,' said Harry, 'though sometimes he goes by the name of Tony.'

'I knew a Tony once, he was a total wanker. What's yours like?'

'A total wanker,' said Josie, and Harry dug her in the ribs. 'Well, he is,' she protested, 'as far as women are concerned. He's charming and witty and funny of course, but I wouldn't trust him as far as I can throw him.'

'He's not that bad,' protested Harry half-heartedly as he started up the car.

'He so is,' said Josie. 'Don't you remember Suzie at uni? Poor cow was so in love with Ant,

40

and I lost count of the number of girls he cheated on her with. And still she came back for more.'

'I'd forgotten about her,' said Harry.

'Then there was the time we were out for my birthday and he started the evening with one girl and went home with another.'

'Oh, God, and the time we met him at the cinema and he pretended not to see us because he was with the wife of the local landlord,' said Harry. 'I'd forgotten all that. But you never know. Maybe he's changed since he's been away.'

'I doubt it,' said Josie. 'He hasn't stopped sulking since you asked him to be best man. Anyone would think you were committing suicide the way he goes on about the fact that you're getting married.'

'Well, to Ant, marriage *is* a form of suicide,' said Harry, as he turned left out of their road and headed for the main road which led to the motorway. 'I can't see him ever getting hitched. He'll be trying to pull birds when he's old and grey.'

'Birds,' groaned Diana. 'Does he really use the word birds?'

'Afraid so,' said Josie, 'but it's all right, he doesn't bite, honest.'

'To be fair to him,' said Harry, 'I think there was someone after uni he was quite serious about, and she ditched him. He's always been really cagey about it, but I think she really hurt him.'

'Well then, maybe it's time he got over it,' said Diana.

'Perhaps you can help,' said Josie slyly.

'Don't look at me,' said Di firmly, 'he really doesn't sound like my type.'

41

Within half an hour they were on the motorway and heading down to Cornwall, to Josie's parents, where Josie's mum was indulging in a spot of pre-wedding hysteria. After much dithering, Harry and Josie had only recently fixed the date for next June. They'd talked vaguely about September when they first got engaged, but it turned out getting married was like planning a military operation and no one in their right minds would attempt to organise a wedding in such a short space of time. Harry, who'd been hoping for something small and quiet, was beginning to realise his wishes were unlikely to be met. Josie's mum, Nicola, had firmly taken charge since Christmas, and now most of their spare time seemed to be taken up with wedding plans. Harry was beginning to find it a little wearing.

Nicola had insisted on having a long weekend with Josie, Harry, the best man (Ant, naturally) and bridesmaid (Diana, of course), to plan things. Quite why he and Ant were needed was a mystery to Harry. So far his input into preparations was to have been told things, like what he had to wear (morning suit, top hat, and pink ties – Josie was very insistent on the pink) – who he was inviting ('we get twenty-five friends each and twenty-five family, or in my case, forty family and twenty friends, as I have more family'), and where the event was going to take place ('St Cuthbert's of course,' Josie's mum opined, 'it's where we got married, and Josie was christened, and Reverend Paul has known her since she was little, so it's perfect').

Just recently, the tone of the long phone

conversations Josie was having with her mum seemed to have ratcheted up a notch. Having read in a magazine that it was all the rage to have live entertainment in the evening, Josie had got a bee in her bonnet about having not only fireworks, but possibly hiring jugglers and magicians for the night. Harry's protests about the money had been ignored – he was beginning to appreciate his fiancée had a steely side of which he'd been hitherto unaware – 'Dad won't mind,' Josie had assured him, which was true. Josie's dad Peter doted on his daughter and would spend any amount of money to keep her happy.

But Harry minded. Peter was always polite to him, but he had the distinct impression that his future father-in-law was disappointed that his daughter had come home not with a City magnate, but a lowly paid journalist without much ambition. Harry would much rather have had a smaller affair, to which he and Josie could contribute financially, without him feeling so indebted to Josie's parents. Harry still felt his career had time to get going. He'd always wanted to get into travel journalism, and had been planning to join Ant out in Australia when he met up with Josie again. Since then, everything had happened so fast that Harry had laid aside his ambitions to see something of the world. And when he'd tried to talk about it to Josie, she'd laughed and said, 'There'll be plenty of time for that later.' But the further the wedding preparations went on, the more he could feel that particular ambition receding, particularly as he had the sneaking suspicion that Nicola was already laying plans for them to

43

move down to the neighbouring village as soon as they were able. She was a very forceful woman, and sometimes, he worried what Josie might be like in middle age – whether behind that mild-mannered image was a female tiger, just waiting to pounce on him. Harry sighed; he was beginning to wonder if he'd rushed into this marriage thing. He felt he was on a roller coaster and couldn't get off.

'Why the heavy sigh?' said Josie. 'Is anything wrong?'

The lightness of her touch on his arm, and her quick and ready sympathy were enough to bring him to his senses. He was marrying Josie, who was gorgeous, and everything he wanted in a woman. Of course it would be all right.

'Nothing,' he said. 'Nothing at all. In fact, nothing could be more right.'

Diana was regretting the amount of packing she'd done for a weekend away. But she was nervous. She'd only met Josie's parents once or twice when they'd come up to London to see Josie and they were so posh, they'd turned her into a gibbering wreck. She wasn't often ashamed of her council house upbringing, but a few days with Josie's mum and dad had managed to make her feel inadequate. Josie hid her privileged upbringing well, and because she was so kind, went out of her way to put people at ease, so most people who met her in London would have had no idea of the luxury awaiting her at home. Of course, she took that for granted too, and was often puzzled when Diana mentioned that she couldn't afford something, giving a delicate little frown and a perplexed smile. With anyone else, Diana might have felt envious, particularly since she'd bagged such a great prize in Harry, but Josie was such a joy to be around, envy just seemed like the wrong emotion.

Harry was the kind of man any girl would be happy to have. Lovely, solid dependable Harry – a bit dull maybe for her tastes, but Diana had a soft spot for him. He was always kind and welcoming to her; she could do worse than have a Harry of her own. But men like Harry never came Diana's way, which was partly her own fault of course. Diana had had to fight to get where she was – opposing her parents' plans for her to go into law, to take advantage of the opportunities they never had, and choosing travel as a career instead (and the way that was going at the moment, she was going to have to admit to her dad soon it might have been a big mistake) – and learning the hard way that people let you down, especially in love. Josie had never had those kinds of experiences. Things had a habit of going her way, and sometimes that was an annoying trait in a best friend. But Josie was the kind of person it was impossible not to love, so Diana put such thoughts behind her as unworthy. She was the unkind one, Josie was not, and didn't deserve anyone to be bitter and nasty about her.

'So where are we meeting this friend of yours?' Diana said, from her uncomfortable position in the back of the car, squashed up as she was against her big suitcase. She knew taking it had been a mistake, but she'd wanted to make sure she had something to wear for any occasion.

'There's a service station not far from Honiton,' said Josie, 'we thought we'd catch up with him there.'

'And how soon will we be there?' said Diana, looking at her watch. They seemed to have been in the car for hours, and she felt hot, cramped and awkward. Diana didn't drive herself. Although she'd miraculously passed her test, after having a car in the first few months she'd lived in London she'd decided the stress of driving the mean city streets was far too much to be going along with. Besides, after three prangs in as many weeks, she couldn't afford the insurance any more. As a result, most of her travelling was done by train, and she really hadn't a clue how long this journey would take.

'Not for another half an hour at least,' said Josie. 'Honestly, it's like having a small child in the back. That's the fourth time you've asked since we set off.'

'Well, you two are like my surrogate mum and dad,' grinned Diana. 'Okay, I'm going to have a kip. Wake me when we get there.'

Josie was a bundle of nerves. It was only the second time she and Harry had visited her parents since their engagement, and this time she was bringing Diana and Ant. Her mother could be a terrible snob, and Josie knew that while she was too polite to say so, she thoroughly disapproved of Diana, whom she thought rather common. What she was going to make of Ant, the Lord only knew. Josie just hoped he could manage to keep his mouth shut and behave himself. Knowing Ant, that was highly unlikely.

She was also nervous about how Harry was going to get on with her parents. They seemed to like him, but she suspected they were slightly disappointed in her choice. They'd wanted her to marry someone in the City, not an impoverished journalist – her dad's clumsy jokes about them starving in garrets making it clear what he really thought. It didn't matter either that Josie had a good career in marketing and was earning enough for both of them, and that more importantly she loved Harry to pieces and had never been happier than the last few months when they'd been living together; her parents were desperately old-fashioned about life. As soon as Josie was married, she would be expected to stay at home and raise a family, which was why marrying someone rich was so important.

They couldn't see that that was what appealed to Josie about Harry. That he wasn't rich, didn't set much store by all of that. He was kind and compassionate, and the loveliest person Josie knew. They'd originally met and had a brief fling on their English course at university years before, but the physical distance between them afterwards had meant they'd drifted away from one another. Meeting Harry again at Amy's wedding, after years of dating unsuitable and complicated men and seeing how straightforward and uncomplicated he was, had made him instantly attractive. The fact that he didn't earn much money didn't matter. She earned enough for the pair of them.

It was a pity Mum and Dad didn't see it like that. No doubt Dad at least, would be more impressed with Ant. He had the flash job and car, and was annoyingly good at charming the birds off the trees. Josie hoped Dad wouldn't compare Harry unfavourably to his friend.

'You all right, hon?' she said to Harry, squeezing his knee hard. He was very quiet, and she had a feeling he was even more nervous than she was. It was going to be a long weekend.

'Yeah, fine,' he said. 'Just hope I can get through the weekend without making too much of an idiot of myself.'

'You'll be fine,' Josie assured him, 'Mum and Dad love you.' She crossed her fingers behind her back while she said this. Perhaps if she wanted it to be true enough, it would be...

She looked at her watch, they'd been on the road for nearly three hours and they weren't too far from Honiton now. Josie turned back to Diana who was snoring in the back.'

'Wakey, wakey, sleepyhead. We're nearly there. Time to meet up with the man of your dreams.'

'Wha-a?' Diana jerked herself awake.

'Just saying, we're nearly at Honiton. And finally you get to meet Ant. It could be a match made in heaven.'

'From everything you've said, I doubt it,' snorted Diana.

'You never know,' said Josie, 'he might surprise you.'

'Hmm, we'll see,' said Diana, but Josie was amused to see she'd got out her compact and was anxiously checking to see her make-up hadn't smudged.

'The best man and bridesmaid have to get together,' declared Josie. 'It's the law.'

'In your dreams, pal,' said Diana, chucking an empty crisp packet at her friend. 'I'm happily single, and however good-looking the best man is, that's how I plan to stay.'

Ant sat leaning on his convertible, sipping a coffee, and smoking a cigarette. The sun was very bright and the sky a clear blue, so the sunglasses he had put on, part affectation, part a means of deflecting the hangover from the night before, had turned out useful. His head was pounding and he could have done with a couple of hours more kip. God, he wished he hadn't been persuaded to go to Cornwall for the weekend to meet Harry's new in-laws. He wasn't quite sure how he'd even agreed to do it, but Harry was his best mate. And despite being certain that he was making a huge mistake, Ant felt duty bound to support him, and even he had to concede, certain as he was that it would all go pear-shaped, Josie was pretty gorgeous and a lovely person to boot. If Harry hadn't got in there first... In fact, thinking about it, how had Harry got in there first? From memory it was Ant who had introduced them at some party or other. And then she'd invited them all down to her place one summer. Ant felt sure he'd gone down with the express intention of nabbing Josie, but it hadn't happened. Unbelievable that Josie could have possibly chosen dull old Harry over him.

49

He looked at his watch. Harry had thought they'd be arriving around midday, but there was no sign of them, yet. Ant had been at a sales conference in Salisbury (hence the hangover) and come straight on from there. He checked his BlackBerry and dealt with a few outstanding work issues, before ringing up Harry to see where he'd got to.

'Harry, where are you, mate? I'm feeling like a right idiot standing here in this car park on my own.'

'It's Josie,' said a crisp clear voice on the other end. Josie's voice sparkled like a babbling brook, he'd forgotten what a lovely sound it was. 'And we'll be with you in about five minutes. Don't be so impatient.'

Delicious. Josie even sounded lovely when she was telling him off. Harry was a lucky man. No doubt about that.

Five minutes later, true to Josie's word, Harry's poxy little Honda Civic drove into the car park. It really was a girl's car.

Putting out his cigarette, Ant unrolled himself from his position and strode over to say hello.

'Harry, great to see you, mate!' he said giving him a thump on the back and feeling absurdly affectionate towards his oldest friend.

'You, too!' said Harry punching him in the ribs.

'Josie, you look lovely as ever,' he said, giving her a hug and a huge kiss on the lips.

'Flatterer,' said Josie, neatly escaping from his grasp.

'And who have we here?' Ant noted with pleasure a very fetching pair of legs encased in a pair of skinny jeans, emerging from the back of the Civic.

'Ant, meet my friend, Diana,' said Josie with a smile. 'Diana, this is Ant.'

Ant nearly dropped his coffee in shock, as he followed the legs up (via the jeans and busty top) to a ginger (she said auburn) head of hair and pretty face, with those emerald-green eyes he remembered with clarity even though they'd last met eight years ago.

'You!' they said simultaneously.

Chapter Two

Diana was shaking as she got back into the car. She'd have recognised him anywhere, the arrogant tilt of his chin, the fair hair swept back off his face, revealing deep brown eyes that had once been tender, but then cruel. *Teflon Tone?* Harry's mysterious best friend Ant and best-man-to-be. Teflon Tone? How could they be the same person? How was that even possible? Since Josie and Harry had been together, Ant had been mentioned frequently, but he had only recently returned from his travels. Of late, she'd seen less of Josie then she would have liked, so she'd been aware that Ant was back on the scene, but had never met him. She couldn't believe this was happening to her. Teflon Tone. The guy who'd ruined her life. And she had to spend a whole weekend with him.

'So what's the deal with you and Ant, then?' Josie turned round in the car to face her friend. 'How do you know each other?'

'We don't,' mumbled Diana. 'Not anymore.'

'Come on,' teased Josie, 'I saw that reaction. There must be a story there.'

'Well, there isn't,' said Diana shortly. 'Can we just drop it now, please.'

'Oh,' said Josie, in surprise. 'Okay.'

She settled back into the front and started making small talk with Harry, while Diana stared out of the window and remembered...

She'd been twenty-two when she met Tony eight years earlier, and happily whiling away a winter working as a chalet rep in Switzerland. At a loose end after university, Ant had taken a temporary job working for her firm, while he worked out what to do with his life. She'd noticed him the first time he'd walked into the bar, it was impossible not to: good-looking, tall, fair, charming as he was. Her instant reaction had been that he wasn't for her, particularly as he seemed such a flirt, but there'd been something about him from the start. And then she'd fallen in so deep, she couldn't get out easily, and it was too late to escape the broken heart that had ensued. Eight years she'd spent trying to forget him. Eight years, and now she had to spend the whole weekend with him.

Diana sighed. That was the past, this was the present. She was here for Josie and Harry, she'd just have to try and ignore Tony/Ant/whatever his name was. Because this was Josie and Harry's weekend and she didn't want to ruin it for them.

Diana had envied their relationship from the start. A couple truly suited to one another, truly at ease, truly in love. She could never imagine that happening to her. She was far too difficult and spiky, as all the boyfriends she'd ever had had told her. There were reasons for that of course. Having once given her heart irrevocably, and been hurt so badly she thought she might never recover, Diana had sworn never to let herself be so vulnerable again. So she cultivated her tough exterior, sought out short-term relationships she knew would go nowhere, and resolved to stay single and in control for the rest of her life.

Which was all very well, but the downside was she was sometimes lonely. A fact she barely ever admitted to herself, let alone anyone else. Particularly since Josie and Harry had been living together. Diana had little in common with her new flatmates, who were friends of friends, and when not working late, spent most evenings alone watching crap TV. Recently the offers from men seemed to be less forthcoming than in the past. Josie had once told her that she scared them off. The trouble with cultivating an image of invulnerability of course, meaning that people thought it was true. If only they knew...

Diana wished in a way she could be more like Josie, who was most definitely not spiky. Everyone loved Josie. It was impossible not to. Josie was kind and open and friendly, all the things Diana found it hard to be. It wasn't that she didn't have friends, but people didn't love her the way they loved Josie. Not at work, where her ambitious nature had given her a reputation for ruthlessness, nor in her social life, where she'd ended up dropping most of her girlfriends once they were shacked up. Apart from Josie. But that was because Josie was exceptionally kind. As was Harry. Diana felt sure he didn't quite get his fiancée's sarcastic, difficult friend, and put up with her for Josie's sake.

While Josie, Josie was kind and tolerant of their differences. And one of her special gifts was bringing people together in difficult social situations. When she realised the extent to which her best friend and Harry's actually did know each other, she'd talked of other things, and Tone had followed Di's line of *we've met but we barely know each other* with barely concealed relief.

Another memory resurfaced, searing Diana with a pain she'd forgotten she was capable of. Tone promising her the earth then abandoning her in her hour of need. No one had ever let her down that badly, and she'd sworn never would again.

Oh, God. Teflon Tone. Best Man. And she was Chief Bridesmaid. This was going to end up being the wedding from hell.

Ant sped along the motorway in a state of – what? Fury? That wasn't quite the word. But agitation, certainly. Bloody hell. Fancy quiet little Josie having made friends with Dynamite Di. How the hell had that happened? How the hell had he not known? He'd only been out of the country for two years, and it seemed like everything had turned upside down in his absence. Bad enough that Harry had had to go sentimental on him, and decided to get married. But to have Dynamite Di as a bridesmaid? That was adding insult to injury. *And* he had to spend a weekend with her, being polite? Bloody Hell. Bloody Bloody Hell.

Mind you, there had been a time when he couldn't get enough of her. Diana still remained one of the sexiest women he'd ever encountered, and he'd fallen for her in a way he'd never fallen for anyone before or since. But then it had disintegrated into a mess of bitterness and accusation. And the last time they'd met, she'd unceremoniously tipped a pint of beer over his head and called him a bastard of the finest order, in front of everyone they knew. He found out why much too late, and by then she wouldn't see him, wouldn't hear his side of the story. Ant couldn't bear to admit to anyone how heartbroken he'd been about everything that had happened – only briefly telling Harry the details – so he'd buried those feelings deep, and sworn never to let a woman get that close again. He'd certainly never imagined meeting Diana again. And now here she was, larger than life, looking just as gorgeous as ever. And they had a whole weekend to get through.

He'd been thinking about it so much, Ant nearly missed the turning to Tresgothen, the village where Josie's parents lived. He vaguely remembered the pretty little lane, with high hedges and scary bends, as he drove down it. Some time ago – a lifetime it seemed now – when they were still students, Josie had invited them all down here for a long weekend, and they'd had a fine boozy time of it, as he recalled. Josie's parents had been away so they had the place to themselves, which at the time had been amazing. Josie's parents were hugely wealthy and their house had been the height of luxury, even then. He'd brought a girl – he couldn't remember who now – Kim? Kelly? He could barely recall her, but had vague and rather erotic memories of skinny dipping with her at midnight.

The place was bigger than he remembered: a beautiful oak-beamed house on three floors with pitched roofs and ivy growing up the side. To be this rich, Ant thought, as the car crunched across the enormous gravel drive, *that* really would be something. Josie, Harry and Diana were already getting out of Harry's car, to be greeted by Josie's mum, a tiny, older version of Josie, dressed in a cream linen dress and flat sandals.

'Welcome, welcome,' she said. 'I see you've brought the lovely weather with you. I've put you in the annexe, as I thought you'd be more comfortable there.'

The annexe? Ant followed them in awe, for once silenced. The house had six bedrooms as he recalled it, and now they'd built an annexe? Maybe Harry had a point about this getting married lark. As an only child, Josie presumably stood to inherit the lot.

'The annexe is for our guests,' Josie's mum was saying cheerfully, as she took them into the enormous hall, which had expensive looking rugs on the parquet flooring and a wide-panelled oak staircase. It was light and airy, a welcoming, rather than an intimidating space, the kind of hall Ant would like to have some day. 'It's so much nicer for people to have their privacy.'

Of course, thought Ant. The way she said it, was like this was normal. Ant immediately decided whatever else he did with his life, he wanted to end up with a property portfolio like Josie's parents.

'More like for Dad to have his,' laughed Josie.

'Did someone take my name in vain?'

Josie's dad, an ambling six-foot academic-looking type, wandered in from an enormous room on the side, which looked like a lounge.

'Dad!' Josie shrieked and threw her arms around him.

'Lovely to see you too, darling. Harry, good to see you again.'

He shook hands with Harry, who looked unaccountably nervous. Ant dimly recalled Harry saying how terrifying he found his future father-in-law.

'Diana, always a pleasure,' he continued, 'and you must be the elusive Ant. Peter Hampton at your service.' He looked him up and down appraisingly, with sharp blue eyes, which reminded him suddenly of Josie. For an instant, Ant felt sorry for Harry; great to be marrying into the money certainly, but despite the scatty professor persona Ant had a feeling Peter was a hard man to impress.

'At your service,' said Ant, then felt ridiculous. What a stupid thing to have said.

'Are we eating outside, darling?' said Peter, 'as it's such a beautiful day?'

'I thought we would,' said Nicola. 'We don't often get the opportunity, and it's so lovely that you could all be here.'

She beamed cheerfully at them, and Ant tried to smile back, but suddenly he felt quite claustrophobic. He wasn't good at families, this felt all too domestic and cosy for him. Surely it was time for the pub soon? Otherwise it was going to be a very long weekend...

'You know there's a local plan to revive the theatre, don't you?' Nicola said, ushering Harry and Josie straight into the dining room as soon as they'd deposited their bags, while she left Peter sorting out drinks for Ant and Diana on the patio. Harry looked after them longingly, even more so when he saw to his horror a huge array of wedding catalogues lying open on the magnificent mahogany dining table.

'I hadn't, no,' said Josie.

'Well, they might be hiring it out for weddings,' said Nicola.

Hang on a minute. Harry was confused. The last conversation they'd had, Nicola had been insisting on a church wedding.

'That would be awesome!' said Josie, 'could we get a marquee up there?'

'Well, I've been looking into it,' Nicola said. 'It's worth a thought.'

'Don't you think it would be nicer to have a marquee at home?' asked Harry, but he knew the answer straight away.

'No!' Josie and Nicola said simultaneously.

'I think it would be amazing to have our wed-

58

ding on the cliff edge looking out to sea,' said Josie. 'It would be different, stand out; be a wedding like no other. No one would ever forget it.'

Why did their wedding have to stand out? Harry wondered. He didn't care if anyone else forgot it, he knew he never would.

'And what about getting married in St Cuthbert's?' he continued, though he knew it was futile. The idea of that had been filling him with dread, but now he clung onto it longingly, 'I thought that's what you wanted.'

'I did,' said Josie, 'but the open-air theatre would make such a great setting for the wedding. So romantic. You can't have forgotten our first date there?'

Of course he hadn't. The first time he'd ever been to this house, years ago, with a group of their university friends, he'd found himself suddenly alone with Josie, the only one wanting to go out to the theatre for the night. It had rained, and they'd huddled together in their plastic macs under an umbrella, watching a magical version of *A Midsummer Night's Dream*. It had been a wonderful, incredible evening and he'd fallen head over heels in love. Though they'd drifted apart after uni, Harry had never forgotten either that night, or Josie. He still couldn't believe his luck in finding her again.

'Of course not,' he said taking her hand. 'It was one of the most amazing nights of my life.'

'Aah,' said Nicola fondly, 'what a romantic.'

'Of course he is,' said Josie, 'that's why I'm marrying him.'

Harry blushed. He never quite knew what to do

59

when Josie was so public about her feelings for him.

'Stop it,' scolded Nicola, 'you're shaming the poor boy. Now, what do you think about these bouquets?'

'Oh, Mum, they're gorgeous.' Josie was peering at pictures of pale pink roses entwined with white carnations and wound in unknown greenery. There were pages and pages of pictures of bouquets that all looked the same to Harry. He endured five minutes of Josie rhapsodising about flowers and then, deciding his presence wasn't necessary, beat a retreat into the garden, hoping he wasn't going to face a grilling from Peter about his latest prospects.

Diana had disappeared to take a nap, claiming a headache in a very pointed manner, evidently her desire not to spend time with Ant over-coming her normal politeness in front of Josie's parents. What was going on there? They clearly knew one another, but were being icily polite to the point of freezing. And Ant was pretending to barely know Diana, which was clearly not true. Harry wondered which of Ant's many conquests Di must have been. It was always hard to keep track with Ant, but for the life of him he couldn't recall Ant mentioning her before. He wondered if she was the one who'd broken Ant's heart. It would explain an awful lot. Resolving to ask him at the first opportunity, Harry went into the garden where he found Ant animatedly talking business with Peter.

'So what do you think about us losing our triple A rating then?' Ant was saying as he approached.

'The country's being run by idiots.'

'You're not wrong there,' said Peter. 'This bunch is no better than the last lot. I worry about the future for you kids, I really do.'

'It could be worse, at least we're not Italy,' said Ant, provoking a hearty laugh from Peter which made Harry feel like punching a wall. He'd never made Peter laugh like that once, not in all the months he'd been coming here.

In truth, while Harry had grown very fond of Nicola, Peter terrified him. A self-made millionaire who'd used Nicola's money to make one fortune in the dot com bubble, which had enabled him not only to buy this house, but a pied-a-terre in London, a villa in Spain, and another fortune in the technological boom of more recent times. And he appeared to be recessionproof, living evidence that money made more money.

Harry, who came from a more modest background and was quite happy to be earning what he regarded as a reasonable income in a job he enjoyed, was totally baffled when Peter started on about stocks and shares, and even more so when Ant joined in. How the hell did Ant even know all this stuff? It wasn't even as if he was any good at maths.

Gloomily, Harry sat between them as Ant quizzed Peter ever more heavily about the future of the economy, then Josie and Nicola joined them and went into frenzies about menus, venues, and other things which he felt were insignificant. When he'd impulsively asked Josie to marry him last October, he hadn't foreseen this. There seemed to be no end to the minutiae that had to be planned for a wedding. All he wanted to do was go into a wood somewhere and plight his troth with his lady love, like in some kind of mediaeval knight's tale. He loved Josie, she loved him. All the rest was frippery. But she clearly didn't see it like that...

Chapter Three

'You'll never guess who's staying in the village?' Nicola said gleefully as they sat down to a huge lunch on the vast patio by the pool. Josie had tried to stop her, told her they'd be just as happy to head to the pub for lunch (she could see Harry and Ant were already getting twitchy), but her mother was unstoppable. Nicola was the perfect matriarch. She'd been made to mother a huge family, and it had been a source of unending disappointment to her that she had only been able to have one child. She made up for it by feeding anyone who came within a mile of the house. Josie felt sure Nicola kidnapped people from the highways and byways when she wasn't there.

'It makes me feel useful,' her mother had once confided in her daughter. Josie tried not to feel irritated that her mother could only see one way of being useful, and bit her lip so as not to retort, well go and do something properly useful if you feel at a loose end. It exasperated her that her mother seemed to be so happy with so little, having given up on any career aspirations long before Josie was born. Her own father had been wealthy in his own right and Nicola had never been expected to work. When she met Peter who even then was on the up, she devoted herself to being a full-time wife and mother. She wouldn't even work with Dad, saying the figures were beyond her. It was exasperating. But it wasn't in Josie's nature to quarrel, and she didn't want to hurt her mum's feelings, so she said nothing.

'No, who?' said Josie, laughing as her dad rolled his eyes.

'Only Tatiana Okeby,' said Nicola triumphantly.

She was met with a stunning silence and blank looks.

'Er. Tatiana who?' said Diana.

'Tatiana Okeby. You must know her. *Sail for the Sun?*'

'Nope, not ringing any bells,' said Harry.

'Sandy Kane, tart with a heart. Who went through abortion, rape, several husbands, and sailed off into the sunset, never to be seen again? How can you not remember *Sail for the Sun?*'

'Might be a bit before our time, Mum,' said Josie.

'What, none of you ever saw *Sail for the Sun?*' Nicola looked baffled. 'I could have sworn we watched it together, Josie.'

'Did we? I don't remember. When?'

'Let me see... It must have been around 1983, I suppose,' said Nicola. 'Tatiana Okeby was tipped to appear as Auberon Fanshawe's assistant on Freddie Puck's *Illusions* show, but she quit to play Cassandra instead. She and Auberon used to have a bit of a thing.'

'Now, *Illusions* I do remember,' said Harry 'It was awesome.'

'Do you remember the trick they did with the lighted candle?' said Ant. 'You know the one where Auberon's assistant lit the candle and he made it disappear. I still can't work out how they did that.'

'Oh, I remember that! It was brilliant!' Di burst in, then reddened when she realised she'd agreed with something Ant had said.

'Well, that aside,' said Nicola, 'I'm very excited. Tatiana Okeby's staying in that new place with the yurts near the open-air theatre, and the rumour is she's going to be playing Titania in this summer's production of *A Midsummer Night's Dream*. I was telling Josie earlier, the theatre has been a bit down in the doldrums in the last few years, and they're thinking of hiring it out for weddings.'

'What, you two getting married in a theatre?' said Diana, 'what about a church wedding?'

'That's so passé,' said Josie, nonchalantly. 'I want our wedding to be different. To be the one everyone will be talking about for years to come. I think the theatre's the perfect venue. And in the evening it will be brilliant for entertainment: jugglers, acrobats, magicians, that kind of thing. Won't it, Harry?'

Harry didn't appear to be paying any attention, and she had to kick him under the table before he mumbled, 'Oh, yes, great,' rather unconvincingly.

'Wow,' Diana seemed slightly stunned. 'Sounds amazing.'

Josie checked to make sure Di wasn't being

sarcastic, but she seemed genuine.

'Anyway,' Nicola continued, 'if we could get someone of Tatiana Okeby's calibre playing at the theatre, it could help put us back on the map.'

'Now, that I would like to see,' said Josie. 'The open-air theatre is so special. Isn't it, Harry?'

'Oh, er, yes,' said Harry, looking a little guilty. He'd been deep in conversation with Ant about the many and varied delights of *Illusions,* and Josie wasn't entirely sure he'd heard her. She wondered whether it had been a good idea to bring Ant along this weekend. Especially as there was clearly something weird going on with him and Di. She'd been dying to find out what was going on there, but hadn't had a moment alone with Diana since they'd arrived. She hoped whatever it was wouldn't spoil the atmosphere of the weekend, especially as she didn't trust Ant not to make trouble. He'd never been a good influence on Harry in her eyes, and so far this weekend seemed intent on dragging him away from anything to do with the wedding. She'd already caught them muttering about going for a pint. The only reason she'd let Harry bring him along was because he'd been so worried about spending the weekend with her parents, and she'd wanted Harry to have some moral support. There was a point to Di coming. They were going searching for hers and Di's dresses tomorrow, and although the boys were getting fitted for their suits, Ant didn't really need to be here. She hoped he wasn't going to ruin everything...

'Does anyone fancy a walk?' Diana said after

lunch. She was getting fed up with Ant, who kept sending her significant looks across the table. The last thing she wanted to do was to have deep meaningful chats with him. What was done was done. She'd long ago consigned him to her past, and wasn't at all interested in having him in her future. She was hoping that he'd be more interested in going to the pub, then she and Josie could at least have a girlie chat. It felt like ages since they'd had any time on their own together, and Diana missed her friend more than she'd thought she would.

'I'd rather have a pint,' said Ant. Good. True to form.

'A walk would be great,' said Josie. 'We can get up to the Faerie Ring from the footpath at the end of the lane, walk along the cliff edge and then make our way down to the village, and have a pint in the Lover's Rest. It'll only take us an hour or so. And it's a glorious day.'

Diana frantically tried to signal to Josie that this wasn't her intention, but Josie was looking fixedly at Harry, as if to say, *Don't you dare think about going straight to the pub.* Harry clearly understood the look, because he responded with, 'A walk sounds like a brilliant idea.'

Great. Now Ant would feel obliged to come.

'I suppose we could stretch our legs,' said Ant. 'So what's this Faerie Ring place then?'

'They're a bunch of Standing Stones on the cliff,' explained Josie. 'Local legend says magic happens there on Midsummer's Eve.'

'Don't tell me, young lovers plight their troth while fairies dance around them,' snorted Ant.

'Something like that,' admitted Josie. 'All nonsense of course.'

'How about it, Di,' Ant said slyly. 'Fancy finding yourself a red-hot lover on the cliffs at midnight?'

'I think the key word that is wrong in that sentence is lover,' said Diana sarcastically. 'And until you can find me a red-hot lover worthy of me, I can safely say the answer is no.'

'As if I'd be interested in you,' said Ant. 'You clearly still have no sense of humour.'

'Not for puerile infants, no,' said Diana. She was furious. A couple of hours in Ant's company was all it had taken her to remind him what a prick he was.

'Woah! Children!' said Josie. 'What is it with you two?'

'Nothing!' said Diana and Ant, simultaneously glaring at one another.

'Okay point taken,' said Josie throwing her hands up, and tactfully changing the subject, to Diana's relief. She sighed deeply. She couldn't wait for the weekend to be over.

But, as they set off down the lane that led past Josie's house to the footpath that took them up to the cliffs, Diana felt a bit better. The hedgerows were alive with birdsong, and the air heavy with scent from the riot of wildflowers that lined the path: the pinks and whites of scarlet pimpernels and red campions jostled with blue mallow and purple speedwell and other flowers Di couldn't identify. There was barely a cloud in the azure sky, and the sun was so warm, they soon discarded cardigans and jumpers. She breathed a deep sigh of contentment. It was great to be away from London for once and the tension that she'd left behind at work.

'This way,' said Josie, confidently leading them over a stile which led onto a sandy cliff path, where the foliage gave way to yellow gorse, green bracken and pink heathers, and tall cow parsley bowed down in the breeze. It was a steepish climb, but with the wind on her face and the sun on her skin, Diana was beginning to enjoy herself – until she caught sight of Ant whispering to Harry, and glancing in her direction. She felt sure it was about her, and her stomach plummeted. How utterly miserable. To think she not only had to spend a whole weekend with him but also a whole wedding, when she'd be forced to be nice to him. Diana couldn't think of anything worse.

'So what's the deal with you and Di, then?' Harry said as he and Ant forged their way up the cliff path. After the little display of histrionics between them, he and Josie had decided it would be better for now if they kept their warring friends apart.

'Dynamite Di?' said Ant, looking back down the path at her, affecting nonchalance. 'Oh, nothing.'

'Didn't look like nothing to me,' said Harry. 'You reacted like a scalded cat when you saw her.'

Ant stopped to take a breather and stared back at the lane, Josie's house reflecting the sunshine in the distance.

'We knew each other a long time ago. Had a bit of a thing. Didn't work out.'

'Which is why you're so down on her,' snorted

Harry, not believing a word of it, and feeling more convinced than ever, she was the one. He paused too and took a sip of the water he had thought to bring in his small backpack. It was hot work climbing the path. Last time he'd done this walk it had been in the winter and much easier.

'I'm not down on her,' protested Ant. 'You've seen the way she is with me. She's a cow of the highest order. Can't think why someone as nice as Josie could be mates with someone as chippy as Di.'

'Oh, Di's okay,' said Harry, 'and she's been a good friend to Josie; really helped her through some tough times. So do me a favour, mate, and be nice to her. Just for the weekend. If not for me, do it for Josie.'

'All right,' said Ant. 'Anything you say.'

The sun was out and the walk was invigorating. Soon they'd reached the top of the cliffs, and could look out to sea. To their left, the green of the cliffs fell away to the sea, and the path led down towards the dip where the Standing Stones stood, hidden from sight from this angle. To their right, a path led to down to a little cove in the distance. Boats on their way back to Tresgothen bobbed on the turquoise-green sea below, and seagulls keened in the sea breeze. The sparkling blue-green waves, dancing in the sunshine, looked really inviting. Harry had the mad impulse to throw himself off the edge. Here, out in the fresh air on such a glorious sunny day, Harry had a sudden urge to get away from everything, to be free. He'd had the feeling for a while now:

that life was becoming more constricted, constrained, even. Particularly since Ant had been back, and Harry had listened to his travelling tales with increasing envy. The lure of going abroad was rearing its head again. And today, the thought of diving out, getting away, suddenly seemed irresistible. Particularly when they reached the famed Faerie Ring, which stood in a dip, a slight way from the cliff.

Approaching them, Harry, who wasn't often given to fanciful notions, felt a shiver go down his spine. The stones were so old, and weathered; had stood here for generations, through wind and shine. It wasn't hard to think somehow there was something deeply magical here.

'Well, go on then,' said Di, pushing Josie at Harry. 'Time to plight your troth. It will bring you luck at your wedding.'

'Don't be daft,' said Josie, 'it's only a silly superstition. And you have to do it at midnight on Midsummer's Eve. Plus, you need love-in-idleness.'

'What's that?' asked Ant.

'A flower; a sort of wild pansy,' said Josie. 'The legend goes that if your true love picks love-in-idleness at midsummer, your love will be eternal.'

'Oh, that is so romantic,' Di clapped her hands together with glee. 'I do love all these old tales.'

Harry could see they were both angling for him to say something, but he laughed it off and said, 'I wouldn't know a wild pansy from a geranium,' till Di said lightly, 'See, there are some growing here, by this stone.'

At that moment, he could have cheerfully

70

strangled her. It had been the same, the day he'd proposed. That had been Di's doing too. Would he even have thought about marriage without Di's interference? Sometimes he wondered. To Josie's evident dismay, he laughed it off, saying, 'We've got two days to Midsummer's Eve, I'd hate to get it wrong, and anyway, as Josie says, it's all nonsense.' He tried to ignore her hurt look as he strode through the Standing Stones and made his way to the path that led back to the town. It was just a silly local legend. She must see that. So why did he feel so guilty?

Ant's bad mood had dissipated as the afternoon wore on. True, he still had to spend the weekend with Di, but despite moaning about it, he did enjoy a blow in the country, something he didn't get to do very often now he was working back in the big smoke. The sun was shining, it was a beautiful summer's day, and it was hard to stay cross for long. Besides, Peter had given him a great tip for an investment. He'd checked it out and it seemed sound. He was still reeling from the thrill of having had a chat with *the* Peter Hampton. It was the stuff that dreams were made of.

As they left the Standing Stones, Ant sidled up to Di. He was beginning to enjoy this weekend and he didn't want her sour looks ruining things.

'Look, Di, I know this isn't ideal, us both being here—'

'I should say so,' snorted Di.

'But let's just get on with it, for Harry and Josie's sake. We don't want to ruin things for

71

them, do we?'

'No, that would be too dreadful,' Diana sounded as sarcastic as ever. Ant felt doubtful his approach was working.

He tried again, 'I know you think I'm a dick.'

'Because you are,' said Diana.

He'd said it partly in jest, and was surprised by the power she still had to hurt him. For a moment, he really wanted her not to think badly of him, wanted her to think of him the way she used to, but he tamped the thought down. No point going there; that door was long since bolted.

'And I think you're a cow,' continued Ant, putting more venom into his words than he'd intended, wanting to hurt her the way she'd hurt him. She looked cross at that, but couldn't really say anything, given that she'd just insulted him, 'but we can at least be polite to one another, can't we?'

'I suppose,' Diana said grudgingly. 'But don't think you're going to use that famous charm to worm your way back into my affections. I never make the same mistake twice.'

'Understood,' said Ant, raising his hand. 'Wouldn't dream of it.' He resisted the impulse to say *you should be so lucky*.

'Good,' said Di.

'Good,' agreed Ant, wondering if he could risk shaking on it, but decided it was best not to. There being very little else to say, they sped up to catch up with the other two, and Ant naturally fell back into conversation with Harry, while Diane and Josie resumed their chat about whatever girls chat about. Even after all these years of bedding and chasing them, Ant wasn't entirely sure what that was.

1983: Tatiana

Tatiana heard the phone go as she knelt on the floor, checking and rechecking the contents of her suitcase: passport, plane tickets, clothes, bikinis, sunglasses, suntan lotion – not that she'd get much time to sunbathe probably. By all accounts the workload on *Sail for the Sun* was phenomenal, but you never knew.

The phone was still ringing as she finally zipped up her suitcase, and placed her tickets and passport in her handbag, but she decided to ignore it. It would only be Bron, begging her to come back. God knows why he'd suddenly turned so needy after all these years. Who'd have thought?

Walking out on a five-year relationship hadn't been quite as easy as she'd imagined. Bron had half his stuff at her flat for a start, and she wasn't quite angry enough to dump it all out in the corridor for him to collect. So instead she'd endured several excruciating visits, when he'd begged her to change her mind.

'I know the last few months haven't been easy,' he'd said.

'Who for, you? Don't make me laugh.' Fear that she might crumble made her cruel. She knew he'd been hurting too, but she pushed the

73

thought to one side. She needed this. She needed to get away, if she had any hope of surviving.

'No, you,' he mumbled, his face creased with guilt and pain. He stood underneath the hall light looking forlorn, a little boy lost – a familiar tug pulled at her heart but she ignored it. 'Of course, for you, they've been tough. And I haven't helped, I know.'

'No, you haven't,' said Tati, then, briskly changing the subject, 'We seem to have two copies of *Rumours,* do you want one?'

She went into overdrive, tidying, cleaning, sorting, organising. Anything to stop herself from actually talking to him. All those months, and all she'd wanted was for Bron to listen, to hold her, to share it with her. And now he was ready to, and it was too late. If she let him pull her back now, she'd be lost again, and this opportunity would be gone.

'Can't I at least hope?' Bron had pleaded on his last visit, the one where she'd eventually banned him from seeing her again.

'You can hope,' she said, hardening her heart, 'but it probably won't do you any good.'

Hearing the catch in his voice as he left made her stronger once more, particularly when she could see tears in his eyes. It meant she was able to resist the heart-melting hug he gave her as he left. She'd cried a river over him, time for him to cry one over her.

Tatiana had spent so long in thrall to Bron it was quite satisfying to discover that while she could manage perfectly well without him (she ignored the painful little twist of her heart that still persisted whenever she thought of him), Bron was finding it difficult to do without her. Well, he'd have to manage, wouldn't he? Her contract on *Sail for the Sun* was only three months, to be extended if her character proved popular. When she came back, Bron might be suitably sorry. *Then* she could think perhaps about having him back.

The beeping of a horn outside signalled the arrival of her taxi, while the beep from the answerphone told her that Bron had left his latest message. Well, he could wait. She'd wasted enough time on Bron. Time to seize her future. Time for Tatiana Okeby to have her day in the sun. Taking one last look at the small flat where she and Bron had shared so many happy times (she felt that familiar twist again, and reminded herself they'd had their fair share of bitter times too), she picked up her suitcase, strode through the door, and locked it for the last time. She was on her way. The future was bright and shining and golden.

As she got into the taxi and sped off, the phone in her flat rang again.

'Tati – I know you're there. Pick up, please. I've got some great news. *Illusions* is going to be on TV. And we can have equal shares this time. I promise. Tati? Are you there? Tati?'

Chapter Four

The pub was heaving, when they got to it. It was a lovely whitewashed old building with a thatched roof, wisteria growing up the sides, and hanging baskets tumbling down with bright red geraniums, blue and purple lobelia and yellow petunias. There was a pretty beer garden overlooking the harbour, and Diana was hugely relieved when the boys elbowed their way to the bar, and Josie suggested going outside. They managed to squeeze into a wobbly wooden table in the farthest corner of the beer garden, by a low granite wall, with a great view of the harbour. The sea was a turquoise green, and the sun was bright and warm. There was the constant humming of sails as the summer breeze danced its way through the myriad of boats bobbing in the harbour. On any other day it would have been perfect. But Ant's presence had unsettled Diana more than she would have liked to admit. Dammit. How bloody typical of her pathetic little life, that Harry's best mate should turn out to be Tony. The only man she'd ever let close enough to break her heart...

Christmas 2005 had found a twenty-two-year-old Diana working a season in the Alps as a chalet girl. She'd loved it. She was out of England, and therefore away from the ever-present sense of her father's disappointment that she

76

hadn't made more of herself, and her mother's rueful comments about 'If only I'd had the opportunities you've had'; Diana's decision to not go to uni and saddle herself with a load of debt having gone down badly with her parents.

But she was good at what she did. She enjoyed the challenge of organising skiing parties, plus she loved the outdoor life, and the partying hard aspect of the job. Life was for living, and the young Diana had wanted to seize it with both hands. She was earning good money, and unlike her peers, independent of her parents. She couldn't see what their problem was.

She'd been having a ball, and then Anthony sodding Lambert had walked into her life and ruined it all. He'd knocked her sideways from the minute they met. For a while there, she – cynical, hard-bitten Di, who was never going to let a man near enough to break her heart – had even considered he might be the one person to make her change her mind about settling down. Which just goes to show how wrong you can be...

'So go on then,' Josie cut bluntly into Diana's reverie. 'What's the story with you and Ant?'

'There is no story with me and Ant,' said Diana. 'We worked together once. It was years ago.'

'Yeah, right,' Josie said. 'Which is why you both looked as though you'd seen a ghost when you met.'

Diana had been dreading Josie's interrogation since the morning. Josie had clearly given her some leeway about Ant, and not asked too many questions so far. Besides, she was happy to chat for England about what kind of flowers she was having, and Diana had kept her talking for as long as she was able. But it was clear Josie wasn't prepared to be fobbed off anymore.

'It was just a shock to see him,' mumbled Diana. 'It was years ago.'

'Spill,' said Josie, looking accusatory.

'There is nothing *to* spill,' protested Diana. 'I worked with him one Christmas when I was doing the ski chalet thing. I barely know him. There is nothing to tell.'

'Oh my God!' Recognition suddenly dawned on Josie's face. 'Ant's Teflon Tone, isn't he?'

Diana felt the bottom fall out of her world. She really didn't want to have this conversation.

'No,' she said unconvincingly.

'You don't fool me,' continued Josie mercilessly. 'Ant, Teflon Tone. No way.'

'Yes, way,' said Diana, realising there was no point denying it any longer. 'Now can you see why I'm so freaked?'

'He's the one who–?'

'Yes,' said Diana. 'That's him. The bastard of all bastards.'

'Oh bloody hell,' said Josie. 'If I'd had any idea, I'd have told Harry not to have him as best man, and I *certainly* wouldn't have invited him for the weekend. God, Di, I'm so sorry. I'll tell Harry he has to get another best man. It's not as if Ant's even that interested in the job.'

'Not your fault. You weren't to know,' said Diana. 'Just my godawful luck, as usual. Besides, whatever's happened between Tony and me, it's nothing to do with you two. Harry has to choose his own best man. I'll cope.'

Josie sat looking thoughtful.

'I still can't get over Ant being Teflon Tone. What on earth possessed you? Or was he different when he was out there? At uni he always had a terrible reputation with women.'

'Youth, stupidity, vodka?' said Di. There'd been more to it than that of course. But she couldn't bear to let her friend know quite how foolish she'd been. She'd heard Josie rant often enough about the idiocy of women who'd fallen for Ant's charms and didn't want to admit quite how easily she had done the same. It had all seemed so different back then.

'Anyway, it was ages ago. All forgotten now.' Diana looked round, desperate to change the subject; when talking to Josie about Tony in the past, she'd always played up the bad stuff, never mentioned any of the good, but there had been a reason why she was in love. 'Where are the boys with those drinks? The bar isn't that packed.'

'Oh,' said Josie. 'Look. Seems like we've got more than one local celebrity.'

Di looked to where Josie was pointing, to see Harry and Ant standing on the patio, deep in conversation with none other than Freddie Puck, the famous TV illusionist.

'So go on,' Ant was saying, clearly puppishly in awe of his childhood hero. 'Spill the beans. How does the candle trick work? Is it sleight of hand, a false candle, what?'

'You should know by now that I never speak of how the show works,' said Freddie with a mischievous smile. 'Shh, it will spoil the magic.'

'He said it!' Ant roared in delight.

'Shh, it will spoil the magic,' had been Freddie Puck's catchphrase back in the day, solemnly chanted in playgrounds up and down the country every Monday morning after the show was aired the previous Saturday.

'Yes, brilliant,' said Harry, feeling somewhat embarrassed by his friend. He was beginning to wonder if he'd made a big mistake bringing Ant with him this weekend. He'd forgotten in the two years that Ant had been away, just how loud, how forward, how full of hot air, how *thrusting*, his best friend could be. They'd been mates a long, long time, and Harry had always felt slightly overshadowed by his funnier, more confident, better-looking friend. And today, as Ant grew more expansive, Harry felt himself shrivel a bit, partly from embarrassment (Ant *would* insist on talking to Freddie Puck), partly from an old and familiar feeling that in Ant's presence no one was interested in what he had to say. Luckily Freddie seemed to have an ego to match Ant's and was revelling in the attention.

'I'll just get the drinks to the girls, shall I?' Harry muttered as Ant went into an interminable discussion about how he'd watched *Illusions* week after week, and tried to work out how they did the tricks. Freddie just smiled enigmatically as Ant came up with ever more outlandish theories about how they were done.

Sensing they didn't really need him, Harry took the tray of drinks over to the girls.

'Sorry about that,' he said, sliding gratefully into his seat. 'Ant would insist on holding court with Freddie Puck. Honestly, he's incorrigible.'

'That's one word for him,' Diana said pointedly.

'Look, Di,' Harry felt even more embarrassed, 'I'm sorry. I had no idea that you and Ant knew each other. I'd never have brought him if I'd known.'

'It's okay,' said Diana, with a grateful smile. It almost made her look vulnerable, and he noticed with slight surprise how pretty she was. 'Past history. Done and dealt with a long time ago. Now let's get onto something far more interesting. Like you two getting hitched.'

Harry tried to smile with enthusiasm. He wasn't sure he wanted to talk about the wedding either. For reasons he felt uncomfortable dwelling on, the thought of the wedding was making him feel more and more uneasy. But he'd do anything to avoid a row, so he smiled again and said, 'Yes, it's going to be great, isn't it?'

'I know,' said Josie grabbing his hand. 'We're so excited, aren't we, Harry?'

'Yes,' said Harry, with more enthusiasm than he felt. 'We can't wait.'

He felt mean then. He squeezed Josie's hand and kissed her on the lips. Of course she was excited. They were getting married; they were going to spend the rest of their lives together. The thought of spending the rest of his life with Josie made him tingle all over. She was so gorgeous and she was his; he was very, very fortunate.

Diana was looking at her texts, and frowning.

'Shit, first signal I've managed to get all day, and apparently I need to ring work. Will you excuse me for a moment? You two can keep wedding planning in peace.'

'Wonderful,' said Harry, trying very hard to feel it *was* wonderful.

The afternoon was turning out better than expected. Ant still hadn't come to join them, as soon after Harry had sat down with Josie and Di, Freddie had been joined by none other than Auberon Fanshawe, the star turn in the *Illusions* show. While Freddie's act had been all about the art of illusion and the power of the mind, Auberon Fanshawe had been everyone's favourite TV magician. They'd made a formidable duo, and a formidable fortune in the process. Ant looked like all his Christmases had come at once, sitting between them; a small puppy trying to please two masters.

'Look at that,' Diana smirked, having sat back down after being unable to get a signal. 'It makes a change to see Tony, I mean Ant, looking overawed. That is something positive to take from this weekend, at any rate.'

Josie laughed. 'I know what you mean,' she said, 'Ant is always so much in control. Hilarious. Anyway, back to the wedding; let's talk table plans...'

Josie was feeling a little out of sorts, and she couldn't work out why. The sun was still really warm, and the beer she was drinking was making her feel ever so light-headed. She didn't often drink in the day. It was pleasant sitting basking in the sun, and watching the seagulls whirl above the cliffs, and dive down to catch fish. Part of her wished she could stay here always. She missed

Cornwall when she was up in London. It should have been a perfect afternoon, but somehow she felt that Diana and even Harry just weren't as interested in talking about wedding plans as she was. Diana kept drifting off, looking across at the bay, and acting as if she hadn't heard what Josie was talking about, while Harry... Well. Sometimes she wondered why he'd asked her to marry him. He couldn't have appeared less interested if he'd tried.

Josie wasn't the sort of person to get irate, or worked up about things; she normally hated taking charge, and being confrontational, but this was her's and Harry's wedding and she just wanted it to be special. So she decided that she would have to take charge for once, and be more forthright.

'Look, Harry,' she said, as she caught him drifting off again, 'this is important. We can't just sit your Auntie Vi with Dad's sister. It won't work. Lulu is a huge snob and an alcoholic to boot. She'll be vile to Vi, I just know it.'

'I can't believe we're even talking about the tables,' said Harry. 'The wedding's next *year*. Auntie Vi might not come.'

'Fail to prepare, prepare to fail,' said Josie. 'I do not want my wedding to turn into an episode of *My Big Fat Gypsy Wedding*, with brawls at the top table.'

'Come on, it can't be as bad as all that,' laughed Diana, 'weddings aren't normally that exciting, except in films.'

'And we'll have to keep Ant away from pretty much everyone. He's bound to upset somebody.'

'Now that, I can agree on,' said Di.

'Oh come on, Josie,' said Harry. 'I think you're being unfair now. And you're worrying about nothing. Why would anyone want to fight at our wedding?'

'I just want things to be perfect,' said Josie, wishing he'd understand.

'I know,' said Harry, 'and they will, I promise. But the most important thing is we're getting married, and nothing else matters.'

He grabbed her hand, and squeezed it tight, then gave her that little grin she found endearing, and she was instantly mollified. Harry was right; she was getting hung up on detail. Everything would be fine.

'Excuse me while I barf,' said Diana, with characteristic sarcasm. 'I think I'll just leave you two lovebirds to it.'

'Di,' said Josie, stricken. She hadn't meant to make her friend feel left out, but she knew sometimes she felt she and Harry were in their own little bubble and the rest of the world was excluded.

'It's all right,' said Diana, 'I really need to get hold of work. I might get a signal on top of the cliffs. And I fancy watching the sunset anyway. I'll wander back up to the Stones, and see you back at home. At least it means I get to avoid Tony for a bit longer. Result.'

'If you're sure,' said Josie.

'Absolutely,' said Di firmly. 'So lose the stricken face. You and Harry can have some time to yourselves. I'm sure you need it.'

And with that, she was gone.

'Okay,' said Josie, 'time to talk about flowers…'

'Josie,' said Harry with a groan, 'do we have to?'

'Yes,' she said firmly, 'we absolutely do. Now shut up and listen.'

'I love it when you come over all dominant,' said Harry, giving her a grin that made her go shivery all over.

'Oh, do shut up,' said Josie, throwing a beer mat at him, but she felt better. Organising weddings was hard work, it was bound to make them tense with each other sometimes. So long as Harry always looked at her like that, they'd never have anything to worry about. 'And concentrate, we have a lot to organise.'

Ant was having a whale of a time. Freddie Puck was fascinating company and Auberon Fanshawe a master of the discreet, or not-so-discreet, celeb story. Ant couldn't believe his luck. Fancy meeting his boyhood heroes. No one, but no one would ever know how much time the young Ant had spent alone in his parents' shed with a box of matches and a firelighter, trying out Auberon's 'How Do You Light The Burnt Match?' trick. It was his little secret, but for the first time in his life he felt able to share it. They would understand. Freddie and Auberon were both good sports too, happy to have their photos taken with him, joking that their pictures would no doubt be all over Twitter and Facebook in an instant. Discreetly, when he thought they weren't looking, Ant had done exactly that. He felt a little foolish when they caught him out, but it wasn't every day you met your heroes…

85

'So what's your next project going to be?' Ant asked.

'Hush, hush, my boy,' Auberon tapped his nose. 'Early doors and all that. Let's say my agent is in some ... interesting discussions. And I have a few irons in the fire production-wise. I'm more in the production side of things now, with Freddie here.'

Freddie gave Auberon a sly look.

'You could always sign up for *A Dream*. I hear an old friend of ours is playing Titania soon.'

Auberon blushed, and looked flustered. 'I don't think so,' he said.

'What about you, Freddie? Any chance we'll be seeing *Illusions* back on our screens?' asked Ant.

'Possibly,' said Freddie, 'but actually, I'm down here researching a new project.'

'Which is?'

'Going to different locations in the UK, and trying to work out if the local myths have any grain of truth in them.'

'Such as?'

'Well, here it's the Standing Stones,' said Freddie. 'Locally people claim to plight their troth at midnight, and fall in love for ever. I'm going to see whether by suggestion and hypnosis, we can actually make two people fall in love with one another.'

'Right,' said Ant. 'Now *that's* something I'd like to see. Because I don't believe it can be done. Take me for instance. I'm not in the slightest bit suggestible.'

'Really?' said Freddie. 'In my experience most people are a bit suggestible.'

'Well, if you could say, make me fall in love with – *that* woman,' said Ant, 'then maybe I'd believe you.' He pointed in the direction of Diana, then realised Diana had disappeared and he was pointing at Josie.

'What, that pretty little girl?' said Freddie. 'Easy peasy.'

'No, not her,' Ant looked round wildly for Diana. 'She's marrying my best friend. The other one – she was here a minute ago, tall, large, redheaded, loud, thoroughly obnoxious. She must be round here somewhere. I can honestly tell you she is the last person on earth I would want to be with, and vice versa. If you could make *her* fall in love with me, then maybe I'd believe you.'

'Are you a betting man?' said Freddie with a smirk.

'Okay,' said Ant. 'Tenner says it can't be done.'

'Twenty, that it can,' said Freddie.

He extended his hand to Ant.

'You have a deal, my friend.'

Chapter Five

'Well, that was exciting,' said Ant, finally making his way over to where Harry and Josie were sitting. Auberon and Freddie, no doubt glad to be free of their most enthusiastic fan, had settled down with their drinks in the far corner. Harry felt guiltily relieved. Maybe Josie would calm down on the wedding chat for a bit. He had tried to be as fascinated about flowers as she was, but he found he just couldn't do it. All he really wanted was to spend time alone with Josie and not have to mention weddings for a week.

'You've come to join us at last,' said Harry, 'and save me from this endless talk of weddings.'

He'd intended it as a joke, but a trace of irritation had entered his voice, and he could see from Josie's slight wince it wasn't lost on her. He immediately felt guilty again. He didn't want to upset Josie.

'What happened to Dynamite?' said Ant as he sat down.

'Gone for a walk to the Standing Stones,' said Harry.

'And don't call her that,' said Josie.

'Talking about the Standing Stones,' said Ant – before he was interrupted by a dramatic figure striding into the beer garden, followed by a retinue of apologetic-looking people clearly trying to calm her down.

'Who does he think he is?' she was saying angrily, 'coming here, spoiling my moment.'

'Don't worry about him, darling,' said a rather androgynous creature dressed in the tightest chinos that Harry had ever seen, and a long flowing top. Harry would have hazarded a guess at the figure being male, if it weren't for the long painted nails, and the high heels. He/she appeared to be following the woman, a blowsy-looking blonde dressed in tight leather clothes thirty years too young for her and dripping in gold, touching up her make-up at every opportunity. 'Don't frown, darling. You've only just had the Botox done.'

'Which means I can't frown, Gray,' snapped the woman.

'Is that?' asked Harry.

'Tatiana Okeby, yes,' said Josie, 'I remember her now. She and Auberon Fanshawe were all over the papers at one time. But, God, she's gone to seed.'

'Put your claws away,' said Ant. 'I think she's rather magnificent.'

Harry couldn't see it himself, she was a bit bold and brassy for his tastes, but she certainly had ... something. The whole beer garden had stopped to listen to her, enthralled by the situation unfolding before them.

'Tatiana, my darling, what a lovely surprise,' Auberon Fanshawe drawled. He and Freddie had been sitting quietly in the far corner. Harry could see that Freddie was sniggering into his pint glass, clearly enjoying the drama.

'Surprise, my arse,' said Tatiana. 'You planned this, didn't you? You and Freddie. Just couldn't wait to spike my guns, could you?'

'What do you mean?' said Auberon, wide-eyed and innocent. 'Freddie and I are here quite by chance. Freddie's researching a new TV programme. We're staying at Tresgothen Manor.'

'How very convenient,' said Tatiana. 'That you just happen to turn up in the same village, where I've been staying already, negotiating to play Titania in *A Dream*. I've been in talks with Mike Slowbotham about it for days. You'd better not screw this up for me.'

'As if I would, Tati, as if I would. I'm sure the world is waiting with bated breath for your Titania.'

'Don't you dare,' she glared at him angrily. 'And don't call me Tati.' But she seemed mollified enough to calm down. Suddenly aware of her audience, she smiled graciously around her at the holidaymakers packing out the pub.

Before long someone had plucked up courage to ask for her autograph, and she smilingly obliged, as if the previous scene had never occurred. Soon she was surrounded by an adoring crowd and the chatter had returned to normal.

'Well, that was entertaining,' said Ant. 'What a woman. Never a dull moment.'

Josie laughed and took Harry's hand. 'At least we're not like that,' she said.

'I should hope not!' said Harry, squeezing her hand tight.

She smiled and squeezed his hand back.

'I do love you, Harry,' she said, leaning in to kiss him.

'Give me a break,' groaned Ant, and Harry threw a beermat at him.

'Sorry, mate, I am not going to pretend not to be in love, just to please you,' said Harry, kissing Josie full on the lips.

'Oh, Harry,' sighed Josie, blushing in a manner which was both sexy and endearing, and Harry felt a burst of happiness.

Josie was no diva, thank God. She was lovely and down to earth and straightforward. It was true at the moment she was going overboard on the wedding thing but it was a big deal for her, even if he'd rather have kept things simpler. But the bottom line was they loved each other very much. And that was the most important thing.

Josie walked back from the pub alone. After their all too brief moment of solidarity following Tatiana Okeby's outburst, when she and Harry had started to actually relax and enjoy some banter about the wedding instead of rub each other up the wrong way, Ant had come along and spoiled it all. Within minutes Harry had become absorbed in a deep conversation about rugby. As Josie had no interest whatsoever in the subject, this was tedious to say the least. She resented the way Ant seemed to expect to have Harry's attention by virtue of being his best friend. *But I'm his fiancée, I get preference,* she wanted to scream, even knowing it was childish. In the end, feeling like a spare part as Ant was extolling the virtues of some rugby prop she'd never heard of, she kissed Harry on the cheek, got up and left, telling him not to be too long.

'I promise I won't,' he said, squeezing her hand and mouthing *sorry* at her, which made her feel a little better. Ant could be overwhelming. It wasn't easy for Harry, she could see that.

The sun was low in the sky, and a warm breeze played through her long fair curls as she left the pub and walked through the rambling network of streets that made up Tresgothen. The shops were busy, tourists spilling out onto the streets, mingling among locals eating ice creams, and bearing gifts from the Piskie Shop, which prided itself on selling the widest variety of piskies this side of the Tamar. As Josie made her way up the steep winding hill home, past the little grey and white houses nestling in the hillside, she felt a wonderful sense of peace. Josie loved it down here; the colour of the sky, the sound of the sea, the call of the gulls, the briny tang in the air. While she enjoyed her life in London, Cornwall was in her blood, and she missed Tresgothen. The pace of life was slower, calmer, and *it's 200 miles away from Ant,* she caught herself thinking. She felt uneasy that he was here. Josie remembered that long-ago summer, when she'd invited a crowd from uni to stay. She'd actually been interested in Ant, she recalled, blushing. She remembered the way he'd looked at her, remembered the way he'd been back then: exciting, alluring ... dangerous. But as soon as they'd arrived he'd been all over some girl, Kerry, was it? Josie had forgotten now. And then, Harry had been there, quiet, sweet Harry, the only person who'd been prepared to come out to see Shakespeare at the theatre with her. Harry. Her lovely Harry. How glad she was she'd found him again. She couldn't wait for them to be married.

Although ... Harry didn't seem quite as enthusiastic as he had done. Josie blamed Ant, who kept making snide remarks about wearing a ball and chain. Di had told her not to be so stupid when she'd voiced her fears earlier in the day, but Josie was worried. Harry just didn't seem the same since they'd got here. She wasn't sure if it was just nerves. There was a strange feeling in the air. It was unsettling and Josie couldn't put her finger on it...

'How was the pub?' Josie's mum came to greet her. So warm, so reassuring. Some things never changed, and knowing Mum was always there was one of them.

'Great fun, the boys are staying a bit longer,' said Josie. 'We saw Tatiana Okeby–'

'–Who had a fight with Auberon Fanshawe,' continued Nicola. 'I know.'

'Who told you?' said Josie, laughing. She'd forgotten how swiftly news travelled in Tresgothen.

'Well, Mrs Allison was just coming out of the butchers, when she met Jenny Osgood, who'd been walking past the beer garden and heard the whole thing.'

'More like snooping past the beer garden,' said Josie. Jenny Osgood was a well-known local gossip.

'So what happened, then?' Mum was all agog. 'Those two have history, you know.'

'We gathered,' said Josie. 'She accused him of following her down here. It wasn't pretty.'

'I bet,' said Josie's mum. 'The most exciting thing to happen in Tresgothen for years, and I missed it.'

'Oh, and she's apparently talking to Mike Slowbotham about being in *A Midsummer Night's Dream*,' said Josie. 'I didn't think he was anything to do with the theatre.'

'Oh, it's his new thing,' snorted Josie's mum. 'Somehow he's got on the board of directors who are behind the renovation project. He's got a bee in his bonnet about being an influential producer, and he's planning a production of *A Midsummer*

Night's Dream. He claims that he's always wanted to see it put on at the theatre, but I'm not convinced. He's just interested in women, that one. He'd do anything to add someone like Tatiana Okeby to his bedpost. He's a total ass. Poor woman. Someone should tell her.'

'I'm not sure I'd like to be on the receiving end of that conversation,' said Josie. 'Now, come on, let's look at those wedding dresses again. I think I'm getting an idea of what I want...'

Ant and Harry had moved into the bar, and Ant was beginning to feel slightly drunk. It was a while since he'd had a session this early in the day, and he wasn't as used to it as he once was.

The bar had cleared out somewhat, and most of the tourists seemed to have moved on. Tatiana Okeby hadn't stayed long either. Auberon Fanshawe had also disappeared. Maybe he'd gone to try and appease her. But Freddie Puck was still propping up the bar when they came inside.

'Have you persuaded your friend to take part in my experiment?' Freddie gave an ingratiating smile.

'What experiment?' Harry looked puzzled.

'You know, the hypnotic thing,' said Ant. 'Freddie here thinks he can hypnotise us all. It's for a TV show.'

'Ha,' said Harry. 'Hypnotise us. I don't think so.'

'Oh, well, it was worth a punt,' said Freddie. 'There's a bit of money in it.'

Harry thought about that.

'Enough to go travelling?' he said.

94

'Not quite,' said Freddie, 'but maybe enough to have a great weekend away somewhere.'

'That would be nice,' said Harry. 'I'd at least like to pay for our honeymoon suite. Or maybe take Josie away for a long weekend – soften her up to go travelling with me.'

'I thought Josie's folks were paying for everything to do with the wedding,' said Ant, surprised.

'Yeah, well, it would be nice to pay for something,' said Harry, 'and I would like us to splash out on our wedding night.'

'So you'll think about it?' said Freddie.

Harry looked sheepish.

'Better run it by Josie first,' he said. 'Talking of which...' He looked at his watch. 'I think it's time we were heading back.'

'God, she really has got you under the thumb, hasn't she?' said Ant. 'One more can't hurt.'

Harry looked mortified. 'I'm not under the thumb,' he muttered. 'Josie's mum; it would be rude to her.'

'I suppose you're right,' said Ant, unconvinced. He had a feeling Harry and Josie might be having words when they got back. Prime reason if ever he needed one to remind him never to get married. 'See you around, Freddie.'

'So what about my show?'

'We'll think about it,' said Harry.

'I shall just have to bring all my powers of persuasion to bear on Josie, won't I?' laughed Ant.

'Don't,' said Harry, 'please don't.'

Diana found herself wandering the coastal path and getting a bit lost, before she eventually reached the Standing Stones.

It was so peaceful up here. The wind tangled her hair, and she sat down and looked over the bay. The sun was dropping low on the horizon, casting out golden rays on a sparkling sea. Seagulls whirled high in the sky above her. It was just perfect. Diana felt free and happy for once. It wasn't a feeling she was very familiar with. Much of the time, she felt grouchy and miserable. Life hadn't quite panned out the way she'd thought. From such promising beginnings, when she'd got promotion after promotion in the travel company she worked for, her career had stalled of late. The global recession had meant big cutbacks in her industry. And now she was beginning to think the unthinkable; maybe her job wasn't safe. The text she'd received before losing the signal had been ominous. Perhaps her dad had been right all those years ago. She should have done that law degree. The world always needed lawyers.

She heard her phone give a familiar beep. Brilliant, there must be a signal up here. Two seconds later she wished she hadn't checked. *Sorry to have to tell you but your services are no longer required*, followed by dozens of texts from work colleagues similarly affected. Overnight the company had gone into liquidation and everyone had been given the sack. Shit, shit, shit. Now what was she to do? She could just imagine Dad's reaction when she told him.

Stop, stop, stop. Old familiar feelings of self-hatred surged through her. Dad couldn't be right. Otherwise the life she'd carved for herself over the last few years was meaningless.

That was why Ant had seemed so special, of course. He'd been the first person to see through her spiky defences and find the real Diana, the vulnerable Di she kept hidden from the world. And for a time they'd been happy. She'd been properly happy, for perhaps the only time in her life. And then ... he'd let her down. As everyone did. Ant had reminded her why she didn't let anyone get close to her, why she didn't trust anyone. She'd vowed never to make that mistake again, and up till now, she'd been true to her word.

But Ant, here; this weekend, when it was all about Josie and Harry and their marriage (despite having eschewed it for herself, she loved her friends and was genuinely happy for them). It was unsettling looking at him, and remembering a time when life had been very different.

This was no good at all. She and Ant were history. Diana took one last look at the view, and got up. Time to get back before they sent out a search party. No point letting Ant get to her. After the weekend she wouldn't have to see him till the wedding, and then he could disappear out of her life again. This time she hoped, for ever.

Chapter Six

'Do you really think that Freddie can hypnotise people?' Josie was laughing at Ant, who was pontificating once more about the conversation he'd had with the wonderful Freddie. He'd talked about nothing else since they came back from the pub, when Harry had whispered a hurried apology for staying out so long. Josie had never seen Ant so in awe of anyone. It was quite funny, as was the idea that he thought it was so real. Josie was a complete sceptic about that kind of thing. 'I thought all of that was just nonsense for the TV.'

Laughing at Ant was at least making her not so cross with Harry, who'd been behaving like a naughty little schoolboy since he came back. Why could he not just stand up to Ant and have come back at a sensible time?

'No, straight up. I went to see him when I was still at school. He could do it, definitely. He had people dancing with complete strangers on the stage, doing handstands. All sorts. You couldn't have faked it!'

'They might have been plants,' suggested Di, who had found her way back from the Standing Stones a few minutes earlier. She seemed flushed and thoughtful, but was making an effort to talk to Ant.

Ant bridled, 'I don't see how everyone could

98

have been a plant,' he said. 'At one point he had the whole audience doing the *Birdy Song*. Well, I don't quite remember doing it myself – I just remember him talking and standing up in the aisles with everyone else – it's weird, I've watched that episode and *everyone* took part.'

'Mass hallucination,' said Josie swiftly. 'Don't believe a word of it.'

They were sitting round the pool sipping cocktails, while Peter made his usual song and dance about the barbie, which was the sole interest he had in family cooking. In fact doing the barbie was about the only time Peter got involved with anything domestic. Josie loved her dad, but she was glad Harry, who was a keen cook, wasn't like that; if truth be told, Harry was better at cooking than Josie.

'What are we doing tomorrow?' said Harry, yawning.

'Di, Mum and I are dress shopping,' said Josie, 'and you, Dad and Ant have an appointment at Garratt's.' Garratt's was the local gentleman's outfitters.

'No, no, no,' said Ant looking horrified. 'You didn't tell me you'd dress me up like a penguin!'

'Sorry,' said Harry. 'You don't get a say in it, and neither do I.'

'Yeah, I can see that, mate,' drawled Ant. 'You've really got him jumping to your beat, haven't you, Jose? I can see I didn't come home a minute too soon.'

Josie felt like throttling him, but she smiled sweetly and said nothing. She hated conflict, and didn't want to start a row. She waited for Harry to say something, put Ant straight about their relationship, but Harry was silent. What was it about being round Ant that turned him into a Neanderthal? Why couldn't he stick up for her? Saying nothing was much worse than anything Ant had said.

'Right, I'd better see if Mum needs some help,' she said, more brightly then she felt. She got up to go inside, and looked back at Harry hunched over his chair looking miserable, while Ant goaded him about the loss of his freedom. At least Harry didn't look happy about his lack of support, but she wanted to tell him to get some backbone. It had been a huge mistake having Ant here. He was going to ruin everything.

'You could at least try to tone it down, for Josie's sake,' hissed Diana at Ant, as Harry got up abruptly and went to help Peter on the barbecue.

'What? What did I say?' Ant thought he'd been rather jovial and friendly. He couldn't think why Diana was being so aggressive.

'All those jokes about Harry giving everything up for love. Do you think that's fair?'

'I'm only having a laugh,' said Ant. 'Though I don't expect you'd know anything about that.'

'Mainly because it's not funny,' said Diana.

Had she always been such a sullen cow? he thought. They'd had fun once.

'Oh, lighten up will you?' he said crossly. 'I'm just teasing them. Anyway, Harry *has* gone all dappy since he's got loved up with Josie. It's my duty as a friend to point it out.'

'Just because you wouldn't know what love is if

it hit you between the eyes,' said Diana with feeling.

'And I know who I have to thank for that,' Ant shot back.

'That aside,' said Diana, 'other people do fall in love. And you should leave them be.'

'Why shouldn't I point out to my best mate that he's making a big mistake?' said Ant.

'Because he's not,' said Diana. 'You're just jealous.'

'I'm not jealous,' said Ant.

'Of course you are,' said Diana. 'You know that you're incapable of loving a woman the way Harry loves Josie, and you can't stand it.'

'That's because the only woman I ever loved turned her back on me.'

There was a pregnant pause, and then Diana turned accusing eyes on him. He felt deeply uncomfortable under her gaze.

'And why not, after what you did?'

'Who said I was talking about you?'

'Weren't you?' said Di.

They sat glaring at each other.

'This is ridiculous,' said Ant, finally, breaking the silence. 'I don't have to put up with this crap.'

He got up and wandered over to the men, where he felt safer. There was a reason he was single, and Diana had just reminded him of it. He felt hot under the collar just thinking about their time together. Being tied down to a woman screwed up your life. He didn't envy Harry one little bit. Diana had got that completely wrong. He was young, free and single and quite content to stay that way. Harry could settle into boring domesticity if he wanted to. There was a whole world out there and Ant wasn't done exploring it yet...

Diana felt like a spare part. The boys were happily ensconced with Peter at the barbie, trying to outdo each other in their efforts to impress him. Annoyingly, she had the feeling that Ant was winning. She knew if she joined Josie and Nicola indoors she'd be driven mad within minutes by the incessant wedding chat. She was happy for her friend, really she was, but the wedding seemed to be Josie's only topic of conversation. She knew that was the point of the weekend, but still... True, Josie had been suitably sympathetic when Di had told her about her redundancy, immediately offering to help out financially if she could, but Di had waved her away, with a 'don't worry, I'll be fine' response, which Josie seemed to be taking literally.

'Come on, let's take your mind off things,' she'd said. 'Here look at some of these dresses, see what you think.'

So Di had been forced to endure half an hour of flicking through bridal magazines, looking at dresses she wouldn't be seen dead in.

'You'll find another job in no time,' she'd said, when she realised Di wasn't quite as focused on the dress issue as she was.

'Will I?' Di wanted to say, but she didn't have the heart. What was the point in ruining Josie's weekend, going on about how anxious she was? She'd have to face up to what had happened when she got home. Nothing she could do about it now.

Instead she smiled, and said 'That one's lovely' (it wasn't, but Josie seemed satisfied), and tried to throw herself into wedding chatter. It was why she'd come down, after all.

Diana took a sip of her cocktail and sat back, looking up at the evening sky. It was really warm and the bats were out in flight. As the night drew in, stars appeared, brighter then she'd ever seen before in England. There was so little background light here, she realised. In London you never saw the stars.

'Oh–' she looked in wonder as a shooting star flashed across the sky.

'Beautiful, isn't it?' Harry had reappeared. 'I could sit and watch the night sky for ever.'

'Could you?' said Diana.

'I wish I knew what they were all called though,' said Harry. 'I can just about tell what the evening star is. The rest of it is a complete mystery to me.'

'Aren't you needed at the barbie?' said Diana.

'Hardly,' said Harry. 'Particularly now Ant's started talking economics with Peter. I have no idea what they are talking about. I've never felt so unnecessary.'

'Me, you both,' laughed Diana. 'I couldn't face going inside to have another dull conversation about table decorations.'

'At least you can get away from it when you get home,' said Harry. 'Feel for me. I'm living with wedding mania 24/7.'

He looked sombre and a little sad.

'Are you okay?' said Diana. 'Only if you don't mind me saying, for the groom, you seem to be a bit down.'

'I'm fine,' said Harry. 'Just Ant being here has reminded me of how much fun I had when I was single. And that before I met Josie, I was planning to go travelling...'

'Harry, you're not having doubts, are you?' Diana looked horrified.

'No, of course not,' said Harry hastily, 'I adore Josie, you know that. It's just...'

'Just what?' said Diana, looking baffled. 'I thought you wanted to get married.'

'I do,' said Harry. 'I did. But, Christ, I had no idea how much planning would be involved.'

Diana burst out laughing.

'Oh, Harry, you poor fool. Girls love planning weddings. Surely you realised that.'

Harry felt completely stupid.

'I hadn't actually,' he said. 'I thought it would be simple. We decide to get married, we have a few friends to church, we have a party, and that would be that. But...'

'Josie is overcomplicating things?'

'A bit,' said Harry. 'At the moment, I think I'd rather just go off to a desert island and get married without anyone else. I feel we're drowning in all this wedding preparation; forgetting the reason why we're doing it.'

'Well, why don't you, then?' said Diana. 'You could do that, go on your travels, do your travel journalism. Why not? I'm sure Josie would love it.'

'But you see how happy she is,' said Harry. 'This is what she wants, this is how she wants to do it. I'm being selfish. Although I would really love to talk about something other than the wedding for a change.'

'I know how you feel,' said Diana. 'I can't talk to Josie like I used to. I told her I'd been made redundant earlier, and she barely acknowledged it.'

'Oh, no, Di, I'm so sorry,' said Harry.

'I don't suppose Josie meant to be unkind,' said Diana with a sigh.

'What are you going to do?'

'Don't know yet,' said Diana. 'I expect I'll think of something. Don't fret too much about Josie. She's just so wrapped up in the wedding she's not thinking about anyone else at the moment.'

Harry gave her a rueful hug.

'I expect she'll calm down about it eventually.'

'Sorry,' said Diana. 'I shouldn't be bitching about it. It's not fair.'

'Neither should I,' said Harry. 'I'm just feeling stressed, that's all. I hate coming down here at the best of times. Josie's dad always makes me nervous. I'm sure he'd rather she was marrying someone like Ant.'

Di glanced over at Ant, who was holding court with Peter in a suave and sophisticated way. She could see that cute, quiet, slightly bumbling Harry might feel he couldn't compete.

'But she chose you, didn't she?' said Diana encouragingly. 'And it's Josie you're marrying, not her dad...'

Harry was feeling more and more out of sorts. When they'd got back from the pub and seen that Josie and her mum were knee-deep in paper, sorting out menus and seating plans, he'd felt he should have been helping, but Josie had dismissed his apology with an airy, 'Oh, we don't need you for this bit,' and yet he still felt in the wrong. To his horror, their quiet little wedding had morphed into a larger and larger affair. As well as the 150 guests who were now coming to the reception ('How do we even know 150 people?' he'd asked, perplexed), a further 100 ('From the village,' Nicola had said glibly) were coming for a disco buffet in the evening. A marquee the size of Buckingham Palace had been ordered to accommodate them all, and if Nicola had her way, it would be erected on top of a cliff, which struck Harry as a mental idea. When he thought of how much this was all going to cost, Harry felt slightly weak at the knees. But Josie was blasé about it. He supposed that was what coming from a moneyed background did for you. But he couldn't help feeling it was all a bit wasteful. And he felt a gnawing worry about the honeymoon. After all this, Josie would be expecting something really special.

'I never knew that I could feel so emasculated by my own wedding,' he said to Diana.

'In what way?' Di laughed at him. She often did. Other people found Diana prickly and difficult, but Harry had always liked her. She was refreshingly honest, and never dressed things up to make them better. And – a guilty thought crept into his head – she was feistier and more vivacious then Josie.

'It's just that there doesn't appear to be much for the groom to do, other then turn up,' he said.

'Well, that is your main job,' said Diana. 'Weddings are really for mothers and daughters. If you're worried about it, why not talk to Josie about it.'

It was the obvious thing to do, Harry knew.

'She's so into it all,' he said, 'I don't want to upset her. I expect I'm making a fuss about nothing.'

'I expect you are,' said Di touching his arm sympathetically. 'It won't last for ever.'

'As long as Josie calms down after it's all over,' said Harry. 'It's enough to send me back on the fags.'

'If you're that desperate,' said Di, 'I've been sneaking down to the end of the garden for the odd puff. I've got through most of the packet this evening thinking about my lack of prospects. I can't face the thought of Peter quizzing me about my future, when he finds out I've been made redundant. That is, if Josie even remembers to tell him.'

Harry laughed. His in-laws' house was definitely not the place you could ask to smoke in. He was sorely tempted. He'd given up smoking shortly after he and Josie had got together – her dislike of them being enough to keep him on the straight and narrow. But one ... one couldn't hurt.

'Okay, you're on,' he said.

Feeling like a naughty schoolboy, he followed Di nonchalantly down the garden, where she lit a cigarette and passed it to him.

The first puff made him light-headed. He breathed it in deeply and enjoyed the moment. He'd forgotten how much he enjoyed the sensation. Before he knew it, he was halfway through his second fag.

'We'd better be getting back,' said Di, stubbing hers out and throwing the stub over the hedge into the field that backed onto Josie's parents' garden.

'Wouldn't do to get caught,' Harry agreed. 'Josie would be livid.'

He grinned conspiratorially at Diana. It was a relief to be doing something he actually wanted to do for once. It seemed like ages since he'd led a life of his own.

They made their way up the garden, giggling like two naughty school kids.

As they emerged from behind the bushes, Josie walked out onto the patio, carrying a salad bowl. She looked over at them and a sudden stab of pain shot across her face. She covered it up quickly, saying brightly, 'So, what have you two been up to?'

'Just had a stroll around the garden,' said Harry, trying not to feel guilty, but she looked so stricken he suddenly realised she'd drawn the wrong conclusion. 'Josie–' he began, but she slammed the salad down on the table and fled into the kitchen. Oh God, what had he done?

1986: Tatiana

'Tatiana, darling, give us your best smile.'

The cameras flashed as she spun and smiled and pouted and grimaced on the red carpet, on the way into the newly inaugurated UK TV Awards, held this year at the Royal Opera House, Covent Garden. And it was all for her. *Sail for the Sun* was a huge success, and this year, Sandy Kane's heartbreaking storyline, involving a miscarriage, a nervous breakdown, and an unfaithful husband, had ensured that *Sail for the Sun* had been topping the TV charts for week after glorious week. And she was its star. Finally, all the years of hard work had paid off and she was at the top of the tree.

'Come on, love, show us a bit more cleavage,' said Snifter Suggs, a particularly loathsome member of the paparazzi who'd gained his moniker from being able to sniff out where the good stories were to be found. Tatiana smiled sweetly but failed to oblige, and shoved back the unwelcome thought that despite her success, she was still the painted doll, preening to give men pleasure.

'Yes, Tati, do show us your tits,' a sneering voice behind her said.

Bron. That was all she needed. Annoyingly, he and Freddie were also up for several awards tonight. *Illusions* was the most-watched TV show on a Saturday night, 'great family viewing,' the *Mail* had called it, and it regularly got viewing figures of over twenty million, not quite as good as *Sail for the Sun,* which had maxed out at twenty-nine million for the episode in which Sandy Kane's discovery of her husband's infidelity had led to her miscarriage, but it grated on her that Bron and Freddie were having such success. Freddie had finally got what he'd always wanted, and he and Bron were reaping the rewards.

'Bron, Tati, give us a picture together, go on,' said Snifter.

Ever the professional, Tati duly obliged, but as she draped herself seductively on Bron's shoulder, she whispered in his ear, 'Got another child bride?' and nodded at the young girl hovering awkwardly on the red carpet. Tati felt sorry for her; she was only the latest of a string of young starlets whose name Bron was being linked to. No doubt to replace the current Debbie McGee (who'd earned her spot on the show by the same means) as soon as her contract was up.

'Over here, Tati!' shouted a voice from the other side of the barrier, and Tati duly smiled as she leaned over in the other direction.

'Really, Bron, you're getting to be a bit of a joke, chasing after young women, when everyone can see that bald patch every week on TV.'

That was a low blow. She knew how sensitive he was about his hair.

'At least I have a love life.' Tatiana's last boyfriend's parting gift had been to describe their sexploits to the *Sunday Sport.*

'At least my hair's all my own,' snapped Tatiana, before smiling sweetly once more for the cameras and sweeping off inside the theatre.

Please God let me win tonight, and not Bron, she thought. If there is any justice in this world, that's how things should be. She felt nervous as hell. By rights, she should win for her portrayal of Sandy Kane, but she was up against stiff competition from her rival Candida Cordwell, whose portrayal of brave Merry Edwards coping with cancer in *Meet Me in Manhattan* had also garnered huge praise.

It was the first time Tati had been to an event like this and she was still star-struck by the comedy compere, whose TV show she'd watched since childhood, and terrified at the thought of having to speak to the Hollywood film actor who was giving out the prize for best actress, should she win. Susan Peasebottom was doing her best to hold Tati's hand, throughout the course of a long evening, in which the prize for Best Light Entertainment Show, Best TV Duo, Best Production and Best Direction went to *Illusions*, but it wasn't helping. Tati had taken two Valium before she came out but her nerves were still jangling all over the place, and despite her best intentions, she drank rather a lot of champagne. More, certainly, than she'd intended. She was just vainly looking around for another refill when Antony Hayward, the gorgeous Hollywood star of yesteryear, got up to announce the winner of the Best Actress category. Tati was so tense, she didn't hear a word he'd said, and it was only when Susan prised the glass out of her hand and started steering her towards the stage that Tati realised what had happened.

Everyone in the room seemed to be on their feet; she'd never heard so much applause. And it was all for her. Tati staggered towards the bright lights of the stage, feeling more than a little tipsy, and sick to the core. What the hell was she supposed to do now? Damn, they'd rehearsed this in case she won, but nerves combined with champagne made her forget what she was supposed to be doing.

'Well, well, your little TV show made the grade,' a voice said in her ear, and she realised Freddie Puck was raising his glass to her. Without thinking, she grabbed the glass from his hand, marched up to the stage, practically wrestled the award from Antony Hayward's unsuspecting grasp, and said, 'I'd like to thank everyone on the cast of *Sail for the Sun,* without whom I wouldn't be here today, and my wonderful agent Susan Pease-bottom, thank you from the bottom of my heart, I couldn't have done it without you.' She paused and looked around the room, lighting eventually on Bron and Freddie's table. 'There are some people here who never thought I could do this, and I did. Which just goes to show you should follow your dreams. Cheers, everybody,' she raised her glass, before staggering unceremoniously offstage. As she walked past Bron and Freddie's table, she quietly poured the champagne on Freddie's head, and then went back to sit with the cast and crew of *Sail for the Sun* and bask in their adulation.

She had her crown. She had her victory. So why did it feel so hollow?

Chapter Seven

Diana was at the Standing Stones. She was standing, staring out to sea, the wind blowing through her hair. The sun was going down and the cliff was alive with burnished gold.

She heard someone call her name, and turning, she thought she saw Ant coming towards her, before the figure dissolved into Tatiana Okeby, saying, 'What angel wakes me from my flowery bed...'

'Rise and shine!' Josie came bounding into Diana's room ridiculously early for a Saturday, particularly one when they were away for the weekend.

'What time is it?' Diana came slowly to.

'Nine a.m., sleepyhead, I've been up for hours,' said Josie. Although she seemed bright and breezy, Diana thought she could detect a note of something else, as though Josie was determined to put on a show. An uncomfortable feeling of guilt shot through her. Josie hadn't said anything, but Diana saw how it could have looked, her and Harry coming up the garden like that. But he'd sworn her to secrecy about his smoking, and she felt it wasn't her secret to share with Josie.

'Come on, time to get out and at 'em. We're going to Penzance to do some serious dress shopping.'

'Ugh,' said Diana, pulling the duvet back. Maybe she was wrong. Maybe Josie hadn't been affected by last night.

'I'm a woman on a mission,' said Josie.

'I can see that,' grumbled Diana, but she got out of bed. Her throat was sore from smoking too much, her mouth tasted sour and her head was thumping. Drinking always seemed like a good idea at the time.

Half an hour later, she, Nicola and Josie were having breakfast. There was no sign of the boys.

'Sleeping off their hangovers, bless them,' smiled Nicola, as if she were talking about children. Diana noticed Josie give a little wince of annoyance. Diana didn't blame her. Nicola was so meek and mild it made Diana really impatient. She hoped that Josie wasn't cast in the same mould, and wouldn't turn into a carbon copy of her mum once she was settled down with Harry. Di thought her friend had more about her than that, but looking at Nicola, she did wonder sometimes.

'Where's Peter?' asked Diana.

'Working,' said Nicola. 'I never disturb him when he's working.'

No, I bet you don't, thought Diana, snaffling another piece of toast. Wouldn't want to disturb the great man, would we?

'Come on,' said Josie, before she'd finished, 'time we were off.'

'Oh, right,' said Diana, feeling a little miffed. She liked her breakfast to be relaxed at the weekends. She had realised they were going to be busy today, but not quite how regimented things were going to be. She got up with a sigh, and went to get ready.

'What are the boys going to do while we're out?' said Diana, as she climbed into the car behind Josie and Nicola.

'As little as possible,' said Josie firmly, exchanging looks with her mother. 'I've booked them in with Garratt's in the village to sort out their suits, but that's it. I don't trust Ant anywhere near the arrangements for my wedding, and as for Harry... Well, let's just say his efforts so far have been somewhat less than helpful.'

'Oh,' said Diana, preparing to settle down for a journey of endless bridal chatter.

After twenty minutes in the car with Josie discussing the minutiae of flowers for the button-holes, Diana felt like slitting her wrists. Did it matter that the bride's side had pink, and the groom's white? Or how big the mums' corsages were going to be? Had she known it was going to be like this, Di might never have put the idea of weddings into Josie's head. She was beginning to feel quite sorry for Harry. No wonder he'd wanted a fag last night. By the end of the weekend he'd probably be on forty a day. Josie's search for the perfect wedding was beginning to grate.

But it was hard to remain irritated when they arrived in Penzance and Josie took both Diana and Nicola by the arm, saying, 'This is so fabulous. I'm going to choose my wedding dress with my two favourite people. What could possibly be better?'

Her enthusiasm was so infectious, Diana felt a heel. Josie was so lovely and so thrilled about getting married, it was mean-spirited and churlish not to feel happy for her. Di squeezed her arm tight and said, 'Penzance here we come!' and happily followed Josie's lead through the streets on the search for the perfect wedding dress.

'Oh, Josie, that's beautiful.'

Josie emerged from the changing room, wearing a simple but elegant gown in ivory silk, with a lacy bodice, long lacy sleeves, and a skirt that swirled as she walked.

'I don't know,' said Nicola critically. 'I think you can do better.'

'Really?' Diana was flabbergasted. 'I think she looks amazing.'

'Nah, don't think I like this one,' said Josie.

Half an hour later they left the shop empty-handed, and then proceeded to make their way through every bridal shop in Penzance. Josie tried on dozens of dresses, but none of them was right.

'It pinches too much,' she said of one dress, which admittedly looked as if it was made for a size zero American model, or 'I look all boobs and bum,' she wailed of another which accentuated her body into a Marilyn Monroe-type shape. But not in a good way.

Whichever dress Josie tried on was wrong. It was either too short, or too long, didn't show enough cleavage, or showed too much. It didn't matter that Diana and Nicola pointed out that each offending dress could be altered to suit, Josie found something to criticise about every single one, though Diana and Nicola had agreed there were at least three which made Josie look stunning. Even Nicola, whom Diana had never heard raise her voice before, said rather tetchily at one point, 'Come on, Josie, surely something must be right?'

'You're going to kill me,' said Josie. 'But you know that very first dress we saw...'

Diana had known the elegant lace gown, which had shown Josie off to complete advantage, was the one, but Josie wouldn't be told.

'I'm sorry,' she said, 'I just want everything to be perfect.'

Perfect. Of course she did. And of course it would be. Perfect – because Josie's life was always perfect, from her looks, personality, to her boyfriend, job and home. She didn't have messy relationships or redundancy issues. Josie's life *was* perfect.

Hang on? Where had that come from? Diana was pleased for her friend, really she was. And yet suddenly she felt herself being ever so slightly jealous...

Harry woke up with a thumping head. He rolled over. Josie wasn't beside him. She'd gone to bed before him last night, without saying a word, and had been fast asleep when he came to bed. And now she appeared to have got up and left without saying anything either. She must be very angry with him. He glanced at his watch. Ten-thirty already. Damn. Where was she? The thought of braving the breakfast table so late, without Josie, filled him with horror. His future in-laws always breakfasted early, and it was usually cooked. It was the only home he'd ever been in where

117

breakfast felt formal. Josie must be furious with him to let him face the outlaws alone.

He got out of bed gingerly. Those vodka shots with Ant at two a.m. had been a mistake.

'Go on if you want, lightweight,' Ant had taunted when Harry had muttered something about going to bed, 'but since Peter has given us the full run of his drinks cabinet, it seems rude not to indulge.'

So indulge they had. Blearily, he even wondered if Peter had actually given them permission to raid his drinks cabinet. Ant certainly seemed to think so – he and Peter having bonded more in six hours than Harry had in six months. But even if Peter was fancying Ant as an alternative son-in-law (as no doubt he was), would he be happy to see quite how much they'd consumed?

Ugh. He tried to stand up and the room spun. The sun was shining in. It was very, very bright, and the sound of the seagulls outside was driving him crazy. And he thought living in London was noisy. Harry was tempted to go back to bed, but that was only putting off the inevitable. Reluctantly he showered, shaved, got dressed and tried to make himself look vaguely presentable, though the hollow gauntness round his eyes rather gave the game away.

When he finally made it to the main house, Ant and Peter were drinking coffee and eating toast, bonding some more over the *FT*. Ant, he was irritated to see, was looking distinctly bright-eyed and bushy-tailed.

'Ah there you are, old boy,' said Peter, with such forced joviality that Harry wondered if he was finding this weekend as excruciating as Harry was. 'We were about to send out search parties. The girls have gone swanning off to Penzance to buy dresses, and it's my job to take you two reprobates to try on our monkey suits.'

'Great,' said Harry faintly. 'Look forward to it.'

'You're looking quite green, mate,' said Ant. 'Hope your head isn't throbbing too much.'

'Yours is clearly fine,' snapped Harry, feeling uncharacteristically irritated with his friend.

'Some of us can take it,' grinned Ant in an infuriatingly superior manner, and Peter grinned with him, making Harry's sense of humiliation complete.

'I do find that weekends like this sort the men from the boys,' said Peter. Great. His future father-in-law clearly saw him as a total lightweight. Not for the first time, Harry wished he were somewhere else.

Josie was also feeling irritable. She'd been planning this day for weeks, and it had gone horribly wrong. She'd so wanted Mum and Diana with her to help choose her wedding dress and they'd been no help at all. Mum, who never raised her voice, had yelled at her at one point, and Di was clearly getting exasperated that Josie couldn't make up her mind. 'Surely there must be one you like,' she kept saying.

'But it's the most important dress I'll ever wear,' Josie had wailed, 'I just want it to be right.' Josie felt they were both fed up with her, particularly Di. This wasn't the way things were supposed to be. Plus, while she'd been immersing herself in

119

dress shopping, it had kept her from thinking too deeply about what she'd witnessed in the garden last night.

Josie had played the scene over in her head from the previous evening, again and again. She had been too upset to say anything to Harry last night and gone to bed early to avoid a confrontation, but he and Di had looked so guilty as they'd walked up the path, almost as if they were hiding something. Though surely, surely, they couldn't have? Josie hadn't trusted herself to ask Harry directly, in case she'd seen something in his eyes to confirm her suspicions, so she'd gone to bed early, feeling utterly miserable. She'd tried to hint to Harry to join her, but he'd avoided her eye and seemed intent on drinking the night away with Ant. It was as if he didn't want to spend time with her. He was dead to the world when she'd got up this morning, and so she'd left with a feeling of unresolved misery.

And now Diana was acting funny too. She seemed so grumpy and stressed. What if her suspicions *weren't* unfounded? What if Di and Harry were–?

'So, are you going to make me wear this meringue or not?' Diana was standing in front of her, looking fed up in a pale pink ridiculously frilly dress. With her flaming red hair and fair complexion, it made her look washed out and anaemic. Even Josie had to admit that it would be a mistake to make Di wear it.

Perhaps I should make her wear it anyway. The thought crept into her head, although she tried to shake it off. She was being unkind; a feeling Josie

120

was unfamiliar with and which wasn't making her feel good about herself.

'She certainly won't.' For the first time that day, Mum took charge. 'Really, Josie, what were you thinking,' she scolded. 'That colour makes poor Diana look pasty faced, and shows off her natural charms a little too amply.'

'Let's have a change of tack,' Josie said brightly. 'Why don't we go for lunch and leaf through some more of those bridal magazines, to get some fresh ideas.'

'Anything to get me out of wearing this monstrosity,' said Diana.

'Great,' said Josie more cheerfully than she felt. 'Lunch it is then.'

Ant stood in the men's changing room, feeling as if Paul Whitehouse was about to peer round the corner at any minute. Despite cockily trying to pretend he was used to these places, he'd never had a made-to-measure before. True, his suits were expensive, but they were always off the peg.

He felt uneasy and uncomfortable. He'd spent the best part of last night trying to persuade Harry he was making a mistake. 'Come on mate, admit it. You know you're going to regret this,' he said, but Harry wasn't having any of it, replying, 'Pisshoff and pass the vodka.' So Ant had to give up, and now his head was pounding from the vast quantities of vodka he'd drunk (not that he was going to admit that to Harry).

'You don't understand,' Harry had slurred earnestly. 'I love her, she's perfect.'

121

Ant could understand that. If Ant had Josie as a girlfriend, maybe he'd have changed his mind about marriage too. She was gorgeous, and sweet and funny. He'd known it when they'd first met all those years ago, and inexplicably, she'd chosen Harry over him. The knowledge that she was now utterly unattainable made her both more alluring to him, and viciously nastier about the wedding, despite the fact he could see it was annoying both Josie and Harry. Ant wasn't quite sure why he was behaving like such a bastard, but Diana's presence wasn't helping. Why people felt the need to get married, he had no idea. He felt the world would get on much better if the sexes kept themselves separate apart from for purely recreational reasons, or perhaps, occasionally to procreate.

'Right, sir, let me just take a tape measure to your inner thigh,' the shop assistant was unfailingly polite, but it didn't stop Ant from feeling incredibly awkward.

'Suits you, sir,' joked Ant. The guy was probably sick of that joke.

'Indeed, sir,' said the assistant, which instantly put him in his place. This was utter torture. Ant couldn't believe he was being made to go through it, or how long it seemed to take to get measured up.

'That was such an ordeal,' he said as he emerged from the dressing room, to find Peter and Harry waiting for him. 'I've never felt so uncomfortable in my life. Suits you indeed.'

Peter guffawed with laughter. 'I've always thought Mr Garratt bore a passing resemblance

122

to Mark Williams,' he said. 'Very good. I say, that was good, wasn't it, Harry?'

'Yes,' said Harry, 'hilarious.'

But he looked down and miserable as he said it. This would never do.

'Pint to celebrate getting through that?' said Ant.

'Why not?' said Peter. 'The girls will be gone for hours. I think we deserve a drink.'

'My thoughts exactly,' said Ant, rubbing his hands.

The day was looking up already.

Chapter Eight

Harry cradled his pint, feeling miserable.

'Hair of the dog's what you need, old boy!' Peter had clapped him on the back in bonhomie, and ordered a pint of Idle Brew, the strongest beer Tresgothen had to offer. Harry's constitution was still feeling pretty delicate, and he wasn't quite ready for beer yet. By teatime, maybe he'd be up for it, but it wasn't even one o'clock. Besides, he didn't think Josie was going to be too happy with him if he came back drunk.

Knowing how exacting Josie could be about sharing out domestic tasks, Harry also felt uneasy about the state they'd left the kitchen in after breakfast. But Peter had insisted that Nicola 'wouldn't mind' clearing up, so Harry had tried to pretend that Josie wouldn't mind either. After all, it wasn't her house. But the nagging feeling that she might be cross wouldn't quite go away. And he was certain she'd be angry with him for drinking again. That coupled with the guilt he was still feeling about last night, made him sip his beer slowly, and when Ant and Peter tried to persuade him to a second, he said no.

How's it going? He texted Josie carefully.

Rubbish. was the response. *You?*

Suits ordered. In pub. Back soon.

DON'T BE LATE.

The capitals didn't bode well, but at least she'd responded, he thought.

'I really think we ought to get going soon,' Harry said. He didn't want to be back after Josie.

'Nonsense,' boomed Peter. 'Nicola's just texted me to say they're having a spot of lunch. We'll be back long before them. I just want to have a chat with Lionel Roberts about some golf club business and then we'll have another pint.'

Golf club business. Of course he did. Harry really wondered sometimes about the world he was entering.

'Harry, come on, mate, there's no hurry,' said Ant. 'I bet they'll be ages.'

'Josie asked me not to be late back,' mumbled Harry.

'And we won't be,' said Ant, wafting away his concern. 'Come on, one more pint can't hurt.'

Harry, who had only just managed to finish his first pint, allowed himself to be persuaded. Just as they sat down with it outside, a familiar figure came over to them.

124

'Ant, great to see you again.' Freddie Puck was pumping Ant's hand enthusiastically. 'And, Henry, isn't it?'

'Harry,' he reminded him.

'How are you both today?' said Freddie. 'Enjoying this glorious Cornish sunshine?'

'I would if my head wasn't pounding so much,' said Ant, clearly delighted that Freddie had joined them.

'So, have you thought any more about my offer?'

'Your offer?' Harry was puzzled for a minute.

'Do you want to be hypnotised?' said Freddie.

'Oh, that,' said Harry.

'Only, Bron and I are staying at Tresgothen Manor and we wondered if you guys wanted to come over there tomorrow and give it a go? What do you think?'

'I think it's a great idea,' said Ant. 'Don't you, Harry?'

'Er,' Harry hadn't actually talked to Josie about it yet, but judging by how sceptical she'd been, he couldn't see her agreeing to it with any great pleasure.

'Don't forget about the money,' said Ant, teasingly.

'The money isn't that brilliant,' said Harry, 'but I'll think about it.'

'Excellent,' said Freddie. 'Here's my card, give me a ring and we'll see what we can do.'

He walked away with the confidence of one who knew just what he was doing, and Harry's heart sank further. Now what had he got himself into?

'I think that calls for another pint,' said Ant triumphantly, and Harry's heart sank further. It was going to be a very long afternoon.

Lunch proved a welcome distraction, and Josie even managed to talk about something other than wedding matters, mainly because Nicola had been talking non-stop about how Mrs Bertram in the post office was sure that Tatiana Okeby was going to be staying in her yurt for a long time.

'The rumours about her playing at the theatre must be true,' said Nicola, in delight. 'It's so exciting. I hope I can get her autograph.'

'You might not have to wait too long,' said Diana drily, and she and Josie had to practically gag Nicola's squeals when she pointed out Tatiana Okeby (in what she clearly thought was a heavy disguise of sunglasses and headscarf) sneaking into the café and discreetly finding a spot in the corner. This time she was completely alone, minus her entourage.

'Ooh, I wonder what she's doing in here,' said Nicola, who almost passed out with joy as Tatiana brushed past their table. Diana had never seen Josie's prim and proper mum so excited.

'I think I can guess,' said Josie. 'Look, it's Mike Slowbotham. Do you think he's trying to use his powers of persuasion on her?'

Mike Slowbotham swept in, in an attempt at grandeur. He clearly thought the whole café would stop to look at him.

'Tatiana, my darling,' he said loudly, greeting her like a long-lost friend.

126

'So much for anonymity,' said Josie. 'He clearly wants everyone to know who he's meeting.'

'Shh, shh,' said Tatiana, 'I'm trying to be incognito.'

'I've never seen anyone less incognito in my life,' snorted Diana.

They watched in fascination as Tatiana and Mike outdid one another in over-politeness.

Just then, the door of the café opened again. 'Surprise, surprise,' said Diana, as a photographer entered, along with a woman holding a dictaphone.

'Jenny Barrow, *Tresgothen Gazette*,' she thrust her dictaphone in Tatiana's face. 'Is it true you are in talks with Mr Slowbotham about bringing *A Midsummer Night's Dream* to our famous theatre?'

Tatiana drew herself up regally, as if about to hold court. She looked around in some disappointment and said, 'Only two of you?' but then, consummate performer that she was, overcame her dismay and gave a charming account of the interesting conversation she'd had with Mike Slowbotham. 'whom I'm sure can tell you more about it than I can.' Then she got up and went to leave the café.

As Tatiana walked past their table, Nicola pounced.

'Miss Okeby, I'm a huge fan of yours. Please, may I have your autograph?'

Tatiana was evidently in a hurry, but couldn't resist the lure of an actual fan who actually wanted her autograph.

'Delighted, I'm sure.' Diana noticed that it was

said with some reluctance, but she consented to have her picture taken with Nicola, who had descended into simpering schoolgirl levels of idiocy. Diana had never seen Nicola anything but unruffled and in control, and it was amusing to see her so overwhelmed.

'So are we going to see you tread the boards in Tresgothen?' gushed Nicola. 'It would be so wonderful for the village if you could.'

'We'll see,' said Tatiana. 'If I have to talk to that odious little man about it any more, I might lose the will to live.'

'Oh, please,' said Nicola. 'It's a while since we've had a star in the village. It would be such an honour. Only, I'm not sure Mike–'

'I'll be delighted then,' said Tatiana graciously. 'I can't let my fans down.' And with that, she swept out.

'I was going to warn her about Mike Slowbotham,' said Nicola.

'I think she's got his measure,' laughed Diana. 'Look at him.'

Mike was still deep in conversation with the journalist. Every other word seemed to be 'Tatiana, said this, or Tatiana has promised that.' Unbeknownst to him, the journalist was edging away, trying to wrap it up.

'That has been the perfect end to the morning,' sighed Nicola.

'And the day's not over yet,' said Josie. 'Time to look at some more dresses.'

'Oh, God,' groaned Diana.

'Just kidding,' said Josie, 'we're going back to the first shop, and I'm going to buy the first one

I tried on, and you are going to choose whichever dress you really want to wear.'

'Thank God for that,' said Diana.

Two hours later, Josie was feeling relieved that at least she'd got her wedding dress sorted, and Diana had chosen a sensational strapless turquoise gown, which showed her colouring off to perfection. God alone knew what kind of flowers would go with it – the pink and white theme was clearly going to have to go out – but Josie was past caring. At least they hadn't come away empty-handed.

They'd been so long, Josie was sure the boys would have been back by now. She hadn't heard from Harry since a text a couple of hours earlier saying they were in the pub, and when she tried to ring him, his phone was off.

'Tea, anyone?' said Nicola, going into the kitchen, and then saying, 'Oh.'

Josie followed her in. The kitchen, which they had left neat and tidy, now looked like a bomb had hit it. The boys had clearly had breakfast and left everything for someone else to clear up.

'I'll kill Harry,' said Josie. 'I asked him specifically before we came to help out in the kitchen.'

'It's all right, dear, I'll tidy up,' Josie's mum took on a martyred air which she knew too well, and was precisely why Dad never did anything round the house. And why Josie had sworn she wasn't going to spend her married life running round after Harry the way her mum had after her dad. Mum always said she didn't mind. 'It gives me something to do,' she'd say, but Josie was often frustrated by her lack of ambition. Surely there was more to life than keeping her house clean, especially when you had two cleaners who came in every week?

Josie wanted to protest that Mum should leave it for the men to do when they came back, but cross and all as she was, it wasn't her house, and they weren't her rules. She was furious that Harry hadn't at least tried to improve the situation, but resorted to slobby behaviour just because Ant and her dad did.

'I can't believe they're not back from the pub yet,' she said, starting to help Mum as she couldn't bear the thought of her doing everything. It was another thing that was making her cross. Harry would be fit for nothing for the afternoon at this rate.

'Boys will be boys,' said Nicola indulgently. 'And really, you don't need to help. I'll do it. You two sit by the pool, and enjoy the sunshine while it lasts. Heaven knows when we'll get another weekend like this.'

Reluctantly feeling like she was dumping on her mum, while simultaneously seething that the boys had got away with it, Josie joined Diana at the pool. It was shaping up to be a boiling hot afternoon, and Di was already slathering suntan lotion on and didn't seem to share Josie's irritation.

'If your mum wants to be a martyr, let her,' she said. 'I bet she gets her own way with other things. I wouldn't want to cross her too much if I were your dad. Come on. Your mum's right. You need to take a break from all this frantic wedding planning and relax for five minutes. It won't kill you.'

Josie slid into place next to Di. She felt churned up and miserable and now Diana seemed to be saying...

'You don't think I've turned into the bride from hell, do you?'

'No,' said Diana, 'but you could calm it down a bit. I think you're terrifying poor Harry.'

'Harry?' Josie felt jumpy and suspicious again.

'Yes, Harry, your fiancé, Harry,' said Diana.

'What's he been saying to you?' said Josie, really wanting to know and *when* had he been saying it?

'Nothing. Just last night, he hinted. Well, he mentioned – he's feeling a bit overwhelmed.'

'What, when you had your nice little tête-à-tête in the garden?' the words were out before Josie could stop herself.

'Look, Josie, that wasn't what you think–' Diana started to say before the boys marched in, loud and leery. Just what Josie didn't want.

'I think I will go and help Mum after all,' Josie said, and ignoring Diana's hurt look, went indoors. Not trusting herself to go into the kitchen in case Mum asked if anything was wrong, she hurried into the lounge instead.

'Oops,' she thought she heard Ant say, 'Think you're in big trouble, mate.'

Not as much as me, Josie thought, not as much as me.

When they finally made it back to the house, Harry was like a cat on hot bricks.

'Calm down, mate, you'll give yourself a heart attack.'

Peter seemed to have the right attitude, as far as Ant could tell. The girls would all have been chatting about the wedding and wouldn't have missed them. Ant couldn't see what the big deal was, and was dismayed that his best mate was so domesticated now he seemed to be unable to enjoy himself for five minutes without Josie's company.

But when they got in, and he saw the way Josie glared at Harry, even Ant felt a slight twinge of guilt. Bugger, he might have unwittingly caused a domestic, which meant this weekend could only get more unpleasant. Maybe he ought to help them out.

Peter, who seemed oblivious to any awkward atmosphere that had built up, tried to fix Harry a drink, despite Harry half-heartedly saying he only wanted an orange juice.

'You'll have to do better than that on your stag night,' Ant heard Peter say as he slipped into the house and went in search of Josie.

He found her in the lounge, flicking through wedding magazines in a desultory manner. She looked pale, and he thought she might have been crying. Ant was good at telling the signs. Women seemed to cry a lot around him, for some reason. Even when he laid it on the line and did the whole consenting adults thing, they always seemed to cry.

'Oh, it's you,' she said with barely concealed distaste.

'Er, is everything all right, Jose?' he said.

132

'Not really,' said Josie, 'No thanks to you.'

Ant sat down, 'I'm sorry, Josie. It's not Harry's fault we're late, he's been trying to come home for hours and it was your dad who was stopping him, mainly.'

'And I expect you had nothing to do with it,' said Josie, unbending a little.

'Maybe a bit,' he said. 'But your dad is pretty determined when he gets going.'

'That is true,' said Josie, managing a small smile. That was better.

'It's not just that, though,' said Josie. 'I'm probably being silly...'

'But...?'

Josie shook her head. 'I must be going mad. Why on earth am I talking to you, of all people?'

'Because despite it all, you know you're making a huge mistake and should marry me?'

'Definitely not that,' said Josie, giving him a shove.

'Then, what?'

'Then... It's ... last night,' she burst out miserably. 'I saw Harry and Di coming up the garden together. And I'm sure I caught him giving her a hug earlier. They looked so secretive. I'm sure it's nothing, but...'

'You thought?' Ant burst out laughing.

'It's not funny!' said Josie.

'You dozy cow,' laughed Ant. 'Harry didn't tell you, then?'

'Tell me what?' said Josie, looking puzzled.

'He was feeling so stressed about this weekend, he cadged a fag off Diana and the stupid twat didn't tell you.'

'Oh.' Josie looked simultaneously relieved and annoyed. 'Now I feel really stupid. God, I was thinking all sorts.'

'You are daft, Josie,' said Ant. 'Harry adores you. You're all he ever talks about.'

'That's as may be,' said Josie, 'but if he does it again, I am going to bloody kill him.'

Chapter Nine

'Surprise!' Harry, who'd made his excuses and gone back to the annexe for a lie down and a think about how best to tackle Josie, woke up bleary-eyed as Ant came bounding in, followed by Josie, a sheepish look on her face.

'What?' said Harry.

'I think it's time you two had a little chat,' said Ant.

'Sorry?' Harry still felt totally befuddled.

Josie was looking a little awkward, so Ant pushed her towards Harry and said, 'Go on, love-birds. Do what lovebirds are meant to do – kiss and make up.'

Feeling sick with misery, Harry tried to work out how to say sorry for making Josie suspicious, when all he was doing was having a fag, which sounded lamer than lame, and sorry for coming home drunk.

Josie helped him out.

'Why didn't you just say you'd been smoking?' she said.

It sounded pretty stupid when she put it like that.

'Because I'm an idiot?' said Harry. 'I knew you wouldn't like me smoking, so I didn't tell you. But that's all I was doing. Honestly. I'm sorry.'

'I know,' said Josie, sitting down on the bed. 'But since we've been here, you've been ... so distant, like you're not interested in the wedding ... and you came to bed so late last night, I thought you were avoiding me ... and then I thought... I thought...'

Her composure faltered, and to Harry's dismay, he saw she was about to cry. He couldn't bear that he'd made her cry. She was his gorgeous Josie, and he wanted to spend every day of her life making her happy, not making her cry.

'Oh, Jose,' he said. 'You mean everything to me. I could never ever let you down. Come here, you dope.'

He pulled her close and held her tight.

'My work here is done,' said Ant and left the room, but Harry barely noticed. He drank in the smell of her, felt her respond to his touch. His gorgeous, gorgeous Josie. He only ever wanted to be with her.

'Sorry about staying out so late,' he said. 'Your dad's a hard man to resist.'

'Tell me about it,' said Josie laughing as she snuggled back up to him. 'Years of Mum putting up with him, means he does more or less exactly as he pleases.'

'I shall have to take a leaf out of his book, then,' teased Harry.

'You most certainly will not,' said Josie. 'I'm not

135

going to spend the next twenty years playing the little wifey at home, or there'll be trouble.'

'Hmm, I like the sound of that,' said Harry, and started tickling her. They romped around on the bed for a bit and then Josie stopped and sat up. She looked at him really seriously and said, 'Harry, you are okay about all this, aren't you?'

'About this?' said Harry snaking his arm up her back.

'Not that,' said Josie, smacking his hand, 'though that of course is very nice. No, I mean about the wedding. Only you don't seem to be as enthusiastic as you once were. I know I've been a bit OTT about it...'

Harry smiled, 'A bit?' he said.

'That bad?' said Josie looking stricken.

'Worse,' said Harry.

'I'm sorry. I just want everything to be right.'

'And it will be,' said Harry.

'So you're okay?'

'Apart from being super intimidated by your dad,' said Harry, 'I'm fine. Don't worry, it's all going to be wonderful. Now, where were we?'

Josie sank back onto the bed with a blissful expression on her face. Harry gently bent over her and stroked her face. 'It's all going to be brilliant,' he said, 'you wait and see.' But as he took her in his arms, he wasn't sure if he was convincing Josie or himself...

Everyone seemed to have disappeared. Peter, ostensibly to his study to work, but Diana suspected he was having a little snooze. She'd spotted a recliner in there when Josie had shown them round. Nicola had disappeared into the kitchen again to prepare another huge meal, and Ant, Harry and Josie had all gone off to the annexe. Diana didn't know whether to join them or not.

She was just thinking about going in, when Ant came strolling back, dressed in the briefest of swimming briefs. His tanned torso was broad and rippled in all the right places. Clearly he still worked out. Diana watched him carefully from underneath her sunglasses, while pretending to read her magazine.

He certainly still had it, she thought, what a bod. If she didn't know him, it might have been fun to have a pre-wedding flirty fling with Ant. But she did know him, and despite her hormones betraying her horribly, she wouldn't go there again.

Being Ant, he was acting as if he had an audience anyway. His every move was slowly calculated. He walked up to the pool, dived in and swam several lengths of perfect crawl, scything his way through the water with impressive speed. Then he hauled himself lightly out of the pool. Diana had to smother a giggle. Any minute now he'd shake himself off like a springer spaniel.

'Move over Michael Phelps,' said Diana. 'Is there no end to your talents?'

Ant glared at her. He'd clearly been hoping she was impressed. She *was* impressed, but she certainly wasn't going to let him see that.

'You didn't honestly think I was going to fall for that little piece of peacock behaviour, did you?'

said Diana.

'No more than I'd fall for you baring yourself to the world, like some floozy,' sneered Ant.

'Floozy, am I?' said Diana. 'That's rich, coming from the biggest male stud I know.'

They glared at each other angrily, and then Ant burst out laughing.

'What's so funny?' said Diana crossly.

'Us,' said Ant. 'I told Freddie Puck it would never work.'

'What would never work?'

'He reckons he could hypnotise a couple and make them fall in love on Midsummer's Eve at the Standing Stones, like in the legend. He's invited us all over to Tresgotben Manor tomorrow to give it a go. He even thought he could make it happen for us.'

'Ha, ha, ha,' Diana nearly spilt her drink. 'I don't think so.'

'That's what I told him,' said Ant. 'In fact, I've got a bet on it.'

'A bet I think you'll win,' said Diana. 'Maybe we should get him to work on Josie and Harry, though. I'm a bit worried that Harry's getting cold feet.'

'It's all right,' said Ant. 'I sorted it. Put Josie right about your little rendezvous in the garden with Harry last night.'

'It wasn't a rendezvous,' snapped Diana, cross again. 'Poor guy was feeling stressed and I gave him a fag.'

'Which is what I told Josie,' said Ant. 'Anyway, they should be okay now.'

'Why do you care?' said Diana curiously. 'You've

hardly been the biggest fan of this wedding.'

'Harry's my best mate,' said Ant, looking a little embarrassed. 'I don't like seeing him down.'

Diana felt something unfamiliar squirm inside her. A small nasty part of her had been slightly enjoying Josie's misery today, and here was Ant thinking about their friends, trying to put things right for them. It shamed her to think it, but since being here, she'd felt jealous of her friend and unexpectedly drawn to Harry. Shut up, she said to herself, shut up. You're not to think that.

'So what do you think?' said Ant. 'Shall we do this stupid experiment? We even get paid a bit for it.'

'We get paid?' Diana's ears pricked up. She'd got some savings, but any little extra was a help till she found a new job.

'Didn't I say?'

'Nope,' said Diana. 'As it happens, I could do with the money. We know it will never work, but it might be a laugh.'

Ant was feeling quite pleased with himself. Josie and Harry had arrived together for dinner, looking pleasantly flushed and slightly coy. No prizes for guessing what they'd been up to. Maybe Josie would get off his case now. Despite Diana's admiration of his actions, he hadn't been entirely straight with her. If Josie thought he was on her side, maybe she wouldn't be quite so hostile. It had alarmed him this weekend how much Harry seemed to take store by what Josie said, and how little time he was prepared to give his friend. Once they were married Josie could stop Harry seeing Ant altogether, and that would be a disaster.

Personally, Ant thought Harry should take a leaf out of Peter's book. He seemed to have got things completely sussed. Nicola seemed happy pottering around at home and Peter seemed to do exactly what he liked. Ant suspected he would have happily stayed out all afternoon, had Harry not insisted they get back. Peter had been far more relaxed about things. 'Nicola won't mind,' he'd said. Ant was overcome with admiration. What a man. And Nicola really hadn't seemed to mind, rustling up sandwiches when they got back without a murmur, despite the fact the girls had eaten in town. And now producing another delicious meal. She must spend her whole life in the kitchen, but she seemed quite content. If you had to get married, the answer was clearly to marry someone like Nicola, Ant thought. Yup, Peter had it sorted; he got to do what he liked, when he liked, and had a pretty appreciative wife when he came home. If Ant did ever settle down, he was going to have that kind of marriage.

'Everything okay now?' he whispered, as Josie came to sit down.

'Yes, thanks, Ant,' she glanced fondly over at Harry, and squeezed Ant's shoulder in thanks as she sat down. Ant grinned. Project win over Josie was underway. Now if he could get this hypnotist thing to work and have Diana fall for him again as a laugh, his cup of happiness would be complete. It might even have been worthwhile, his coming for the weekend...

Josie was feeling much better as they sat down to dinner. Mum had produced yet another fantastic meal – braised lamb and onion stew, with new potatoes and asparagus from the garden, followed by raspberry cheesecake and steaming apple pie. She could tell Harry was in heaven. He loved her mum's apple pie. She wondered if that was what had won Nicola around.

'I thought you could have done better than a journalist,' had been her mum's plaintive complaint when she'd first been introduced to Harry, but she softened when Harry had used all his natural charm on her, including helping her with the washing up; something Dad never did.

'So what's the plan for the evening then?' said Diana as they passed the pudding around.

'I thought a stroll to the Lover's Rest might be in order,' said Ant. 'Unless Harry's still recovering from his hangover. Freddie Puck said he might be in again.'

'You're not still thinking about that stupid programme, are you?'

'Why not? At least let's find out more about it,' said Ant. 'It might be a laugh. We can earn some dosh and we'd be on the telly.'

'Sounds ridiculous,' sniffed Peter.

'Is it dangerous?' said Nicola. 'You do hear such funny things.'

'I don't think so,' said Ant. 'Otherwise they'd never get anyone to do it.'

'I still think it sounds silly,' said Josie.

'I don't know,' piped up Harry. 'It could be fun.'

'I bet it won't work.' Diana looked levelly at Ant

141

when she said this.

'What? Frightened you'll fall for me?' said Ant.

'Frightened I won't?' shot back Di.

'Children, children,' said Nicola. 'Go on, off to the pub with you. I'll clear up here.'

'No, Mum, you *won't*,' said Josie firmly. 'You've been running round after us all day.'

'Yes, let me help, Nicola,' said Diana, jumping up.

Harry sat where he was, until Josie nudged him.

'Of course,' he said. 'Here, let me. Sit down, Josie.'

He took the plates out of Josie's hands and followed Nicola and Diana into the kitchen.

Peter and Ant had no such qualms and much as she loved her dad, Josie felt like thumping him. That was never ever going to happen to her.

Harry smiled at her as he went out, a secret, shared smile that warmed her to her core. He was hers, not Ant's, and for the first time all weekend, Josie felt herself relax.

1988: Tatiana

Tatiana held the phone as she rifled through her Filofax, wondering if she should really go ahead with it. God, how many numbers did she have for him? Bron seemed to have moved around such a lot since she'd left him, never staying in one place or with one woman for very long.

Aha! Here was the latest number. She felt shaky, this might be a big mistake, but she didn't want to do this without hearing his voice; without, she could admit now, having his blessing.

She'd waited till she was completely alone in her hotel room, having dismissed everyone, even her mum, saying she wanted a lie down before dinner. When really she wanted this. One last chance to hear his voice.

'Darling, how are you?' Tatiana hadn't been sure of the reception she'd get. Hell, she wasn't even sure till the last minute she was going to dial his number. She'd had to down nearly a bottle of wine to have the confidence to ring him. And when he answered the phone, her knees sagged, and she thought she might faint. His voice resonated on the other end of the phone. So near, and yet so far. How could he still have this power over her? After all this time, it didn't seem possible.

Help, I think I'm drowning, is what she wanted to say. *Save me.* She was shouting inside.

This was stupid. Why was she ringing Bron of all people? As if he'd be interested in her now.

Instead, she said, 'I'm getting married tomorrow.'

There was a pause, and then, 'I know, I read it in the papers.'

Below the belt, but fair point. They hadn't spoken to each other in months.

'Sorry, I didn't know how to tell you.'

'Tati, my darling, it is of no consequence to me,' his voice was light, ironic, wounding. 'We're both grown-ups and we've moved on. I'm

143

thinking of settling down myself. Time we both did, don't you think?'

Tatiana felt a punch in the stomach. He didn't care any more. She'd been idiotic to phone. She was getting married in the morning. What on earth had she expected? Auberon to come riding along on his white charger and rescue her at the last minute? And rescue her from what? She and Simon were in love, and were going to live happily ever after. The tabloids told her so daily. It must be true.

'Oh,' she squeaked. 'Good for you.'

Inside, she felt herself die a little. That chapter of her life was finally over. Bron was closing the door. And it was all her own fault. She let out a half sob, but suppressed it, hoping he hadn't heard.

There was a pregnant pause.

'Tati, is everything all right?' It was the old Bron, the one she fell in love with, all touching concern.

He's only being nice, she reminded herself, it's what he does.

'Of course it is,' said Tatiana brightly. 'I'm marrying a wonderful man tomorrow. I suppose... I just wanted your blessing.'

No, no, she screamed inside, I want you to stop me. I want you to come over here and tell me you can't live without me.

'You have it, always,' Bron said. 'Good luck, darling. Be happy.'

'You too,' she whispered. 'You too.'

She put down the phone, blinked the tears back from her eyes. He was never coming back

144

to her. Finally, it was over. Time for her to move on.

Be happy. If only it were that simple.

Part Two

Ill Met by Moonlight

'Love looks not with the eyes, but with the mind;
And therefore is wing'd Cupid painted blind.'
A Midsummer Night's Dream:
Act I, Scene 1

'It's not a trick. You don't have to do anything you
don't want to. I make suggestions. Some people are
more susceptible than others, that's all.'
Freddie Puck: The Art of Illusion

Chapter Ten

It was another warm, balmy evening as they walked down to the pub. Everyone was feeling pleasantly mellow and relaxed. Diana, in a post-meal, alcoholic-infused warm glow, was feeling a little more positive about her future – she had a lot of experience, she was still young, something would turn up – and even more kindly towards Ant, keeping up a steady banter about how easy it was going to be for Freddie Puck to dupe him.

'You're already half in love with the guy,' she teased, 'if he hypnotises you, you'll do anything he says.'

'I am not, as you put it, in love with him,' said Ant, prickling a little, 'I just respect his abilities, that's all.'

'It was a joke,' said Di, touching him lightly on the shoulder. 'I'm a real sucker for this kind of thing, so he'll probably persuade me more.'

'Do we really want to do this?' said Josie, as they sat down with their drinks in the pub. She scanned the pub, looking to see if Freddie had turned up yet. 'I'm not sure it's a good idea.'

'Oh go on, Josie, it might be a laugh,' said Diana. 'Haven't you always wanted to be on TV?'

'Not especially,' said Josie. 'Besides, Harry and I are already in love, so what can a hypnotic experiment do?'

'Ah, but he hasn't plighted his troth to you at the Standing Stones, has he?' said Ant. 'Perhaps hypnosis will bring out his romantic side.'

'I thought Harry had been showing Josie his romantic side all afternoon,' said Diana.

Josie and Harry blushed, and even Ant laughed at the joke.

'You people all seem to be having fun.' Freddie Puck appeared as if by magic. 'May I buy you all a drink?'

'Ha, that's how hypnotism works is it?' snorted Diana. 'Get us all plastered and then we'll do what you suggest? Not really rocket science is it?'

'Oh ye of little faith,' said Freddie, with a hurt look on his face. 'Let me show you what I can do. If you come to Tresgothen Manor tomorrow, I can take you through it properly. But I could do a simple demonstration here, tonight, if you'd like.'

'Like what?' Josie still seemed suspicious.

'I could hypnotise someone else, so you can see how straightforward it is.'

'I'll think about it,' said Diana. She was sipping an elderflower wine, a local brew known as Love in the Mist. It was stronger than it looked and on top of the wine she'd had at dinner, was making her feel a bit giddy. 'Do I have to sign anything?'

'Disclaimers at the ready,' said Freddie with a wolfish smile.

'No, seriously,' said Diana, 'I do like to know what I'm getting into. Do you have a contract or anything?'

'Bron's sorting out the finer detail, and we can go through it properly tomorrow,' said Freddie,

150

'but here's a basic version. Honestly, I have been doing this for a long time, I am properly licensed. You really have nothing to worry about. And you can put an end to the experiment at any time. I won't make you do anything you don't want to do. You don't have to go through with it, if you change your mind.'

Reading through the disclaimers Freddie had given her, Diana felt a bit better. There didn't seem anything too horrendous there, and the few hundred quid on offer was enough to put aside her qualms. Beggars couldn't be choosers.

'Right, gather round folks.' Ever the showman, Freddie had worked the crowd in the pub, and they were all gathering round a chair in the middle of the room, where his victim was waiting.

Harry pushed forward and nearly burst out laughing when he realised that Freddie's first punter was Mike Slowbotham.

'Am I okay here?' Mike was saying. He looked simultaneously nervous and proud. See, he appeared to be saying, the great Freddie Puck has chosen me to be his first subject. It was all Harry could do not to giggle out loud. Little did Mike know how little the locals were impressed with him.

'You're fine,' said Freddie. 'Now I want you to take a deep breath, while I count you down.'

'Look into my eyes, look into my eyes, you're under,' said Mike, in a very poor attempt at a *Little Britain* impression.

'It's not quite like that,' said Freddie. 'Just try

and relax and think soothing thoughts. Imagine you're climbing down a spiral staircase, and at the bottom, something really pleasant and lovely is waiting for you.'

Harry watched in fascination as Freddie put Mike under. He didn't seem to be asleep, although he had shut his eyes. In actual fact, it seemed like no big deal. All Freddie suggested was that when he awoke Mike would think he was a donkey, until Freddie clicked his fingers. It didn't seem like a lot. Just a bit of light entertainment. Much like he'd used to do in his TV shows.

'Do you think it will work?' said Diana, equally fascinated.

'I guess the proof will be in the pudding,' said Harry. 'Shh, watch.'

Freddie was bringing Mike round. '...and three, two, one – you're awake.'

'Eee ore,' said Mike, promptly going down on all fours, much to the amusement of the pub at large.

He put his hands above his head to make ear shapes and said 'Eee ore,' again, more loudly this time, making the place erupt.

'Do you think he fancies a carrot?' shouted a wag.

Mike eee-ored enthusiastically, and one of the bar staff fetched one from the kitchen, which Freddie fed to him while patting him on the head, saying 'Good donkey.'

'I'm not sure I like this,' said Josie uneasily. 'Freddie could do anything to us when we're asleep.'

'It's only a bit of fun,' said Harry. 'Freddie, you wouldn't do anything like that to us, would you, right?'

'Of course not,' said Freddie, 'I'm just showing how easy it is to hypnotise someone. I promise I won't make you look silly.'

Josie still looked unconvinced, but Harry gave her a hug and said, 'You worry too much. I'm sure it will be fine.'

He sipped another sip of Idle Brew. God this stuff was good. His hangover had completely cleared and he felt up for an adventure. This hypnotism lark didn't look too onerous and – who knew? – it might even be fun.

Josie was still feeling uncomfortable about the whole hypnosis thing. She'd watched Freddie put Mike under, which she had to admit had been quite a mesmerising experience in itself. But while the atmosphere was joshing and light-hearted, Josie didn't like the fact that Mike didn't realise he was being made a figure of fun. Granted the guy was self-delusional – he'd promised more than one woman over a certain age in the village fame and fortune – but this seemed cruel. And maybe a little dangerous.

Josie wasn't the only one who was having doubts.

'What the hell's going on here?' Tatiana Okeby arrived and her retinue; camp M'stard, willowy little Ariadne, and fussy Gypsy, tumbled in after her.

'I'm conducting a little experiment, and I've hypnotised Mike here to think he's a donkey.'

153

'You're making a laughing stock of the poor man.'

'Eee ore,' said Mike and the pub erupted.

'What's wrong with that?'

'What's right with it?' Tatiana was furious. 'This is typical of you, Freddie. You always have to make people look foolish, don't you? And as for you, Bron, isn't it about time you stopped putting up with all this crap? I despair, I really do.'

'What would you have me do?' said Freddie, shrugging his shoulders to his audience as if to say, look what I have to contend with. 'Be reasonable. Mike here consented to be hypnotised–'

'The man is a well-respected member of this community, and you are making a mockery of him,' said Tatiana, oblivious to the sniggers in the audience. 'Go on, snap him out of it.'

'You are such a spoilsport, Tati,' sighed Freddie, 'but if you insist. Three, two, one and you're awake.'

Mike came round, looking a little confused.

'I was dreaming I was a donkey,' he said, 'and how come I'm holding a carrot?'

'This idiot played a rotten trick on you,' said Tatiana. 'I think he should apologise.'

'Oh, no need, no need, all in the spirit of the thing.' Mike took her hand earnestly and planted a kiss on it, 'but thank you dear lady, for thinking of me in my hour of need.'

'See, no problem,' said Freddie. 'All a bit of harmless fun. I was just demonstrating what I could do to these lovely people who are going to join in an experiment with me tomorrow. You could come along too if you want.'

Josie looked anxiously at the others; she was even less sure now than she'd been at the beginning.

'Over my dead body,' said Tatiana. 'I wouldn't trust you with a bargepole. Come on, everyone, party's over. Let's get back to the yurt.'

With that, she swept out, leaving Freddie smirking in the corner.

'So is that how it works?' said Josie. 'You make us look idiots? I can't speak for the others, but I'm really not up for that.'

'No, no, no,' said Freddie. 'That was my little joke. Mike understands, don't you? And if he's prepared to have another go, I'll show you that there really is nothing to worry about.'

'I'd be delighted old boy,' said Mike, preening himself. It didn't look as though he'd been harmed by his encounter. Maybe she was worrying over nothing.

'All right, Mike, now let's try and relax you once more...'

Ant came back from the bar with another round of drinks, as Mike slipped under again. This time he was snoring really loudly. Ant couldn't see what Tatiana was making a fuss about. The guy was a prize idiot. He could make himself look like an ass without Freddie's help.

'I think we could have a bit more fun with this,' he said to Auberon Fanshawe, who was sitting nearby looking sardonically amused by it all. 'Just to stir things up a bit for Tati.'

'Go for it,' said Auberon. 'She deserves everything she gets in my opinion.'

Ouch. Still no love lost there then. Their fiery relationship had clearly not been exaggerated in the press. Bron made Ant feel he was being positively charitable to Di.

Freddie turned to the still-snoring Mike and said very solemnly, 'When you awake you will be convinced that you are a famous London producer with lots of connections to the stage, and you can bring a certain famous actress back into the fold. Tatiana Okeby is going to be the key to your golden future. Three, two, one ... now you are awake.'

'That's so mean,' said Josie, who still looked uncomfortable. 'I really don't like this at all.'

'It's only a bit of fun,' said Di. 'I bet it won't work. And doesn't that guy have ideas above his station anyway?'

'Yes, but I feel sorry for Tatiana Okeby,' said Josie. 'She's clearly the butt of the joke.'

'So,' Freddie grinned. 'What do you think? Are you going to come by my place tomorrow and sign yourselves up?'

'I'm your man,' said Ant. 'What do the rest of you think?'

'I think it looks like a laugh,' said Diana, who had clearly slightly overindulged in Love in the Mist. 'I'm game if everyone else is.'

'Ditto,' said Harry.

That only left Josie.

'I'm really not sure,' she said.

'There's nothing to it,' said Freddie. 'I promise I won't do anything you don't want me to, and you can stop the experiment at any time.'

'Go on, Josie,' said Harry, putting an arm

round her. 'It doesn't look too bad, and I'll be there. What could possibly happen?'

'I suppose,' said Josie.

'Brilliant, it's agreed,' said Freddie. 'So you'll come by Tresgothen Manor in the afternoon, then? Say two-ish?'

'You have a deal,' said Ant, shaking Freddie by the hand.

The hypnosis session over, the rest of the pub returned to what they were doing. The four of them sat back down at a table and carried on chatting – Josie clearly making strenuous efforts to talk about something other than the wedding.

'I'm really tuckered out,' Harry yawned eventually. 'I think I'm ready for my bed.'

'Me too,' said Josie.

'Are you sure you'll be getting any sleep?' said Diana with a grin.

'Behave,' said Josie.

Bed. Yes, bed seemed like a good idea. Ant suddenly felt very sleepy. Too much beer on top of a heavy session the previous night.

'Yeah, let's go,' he said.

They got up to leave. It wasn't actually that late. And the cool evening air was refreshing, and suddenly Ant felt more wakeful. The evening sky was a darkening blue, and a blood-red moon sat huge and still over the sea.

'Wow, that's amazing,' said Josie.

'Wouldn't it look better from the cliffs?' said Diana. 'And we could check out what it's like up there in the dark, so we know whether we'll be safe if we do go along with the hypnotism.'

'That's a great idea,' agreed Harry. 'The fresh

air's woken me up a bit.'

'Sounds like a good plan,' said Josie. 'Besides, I feel there's magic in the air tonight.'

Ant followed them up the path with a growing sense of excitement. Like Josie, he felt as if something momentous was about to happen. He just didn't know what...

Chapter Eleven

Josie walked up the hill in a dream. The evening had taken a surreal turn. Several glasses of Love in the Mist had taken the edge off her slight anxiety over the whole hypnosis thing. She was probably making a fuss about nothing, and Mike seemed unharmed by the experience. She should probably relax a bit more.

It was another lovely warm evening as they made their way up the cliff path. Harry strode forward, lighting their way with the torches that Dad had fortunately made them bring as it got so dark walking home from the pub. The moon was so bright, it was scarcely necessary. Although it was shrinking slightly, it still looked amazing against the blue-black sky, and the calm shimmering sea. Josie felt like she was floating on air.

It was harder going in the dark. Although moonlight still lit the path, the trees and shadows meant you occasionally tripped on a hidden rabbit hole. Josie was regretting wearing her strappy sandals. She always forgot when she came home how unsuitable London footwear was for day to day living, and twice now she'd ricked her ankle. In the end she took her shoes off. The path was sandy rather than stony, and it hadn't rained in a while. The top of the cliff was full of soft heather and grass, and it was good to feel the sand between her toes, just as she had done when she was a child.

'Are we nearly there yet?' Diana plaintively called behind her. She was wearing flip-flops, which were equally unsuitable and she kept having to stop when they pinged off her feet. 'It seems so much further than in the day time.'

'Not much further now,' said Josie. 'I think Harry's made it to the top.'

'Come on you lazy sods,' shouted Harry, from high above them. 'We're nearly there.'

Josie scrambled up, needing to use her hands to pull her up the last bit, till she got near the summit, and Harry stretched out his hand before her.

Diana soon followed, and Ant came up last.

Josie walked towards the Standing Stones and looked at them in awe. She'd been coming here all her life, and yet it was as though she were seeing them for the first time. The moon was higher in the sky now, still with a hint of red, but bathing the stones in a shimmering silvery light. The stones themselves cast dark mysterious shadows across the grass, which waved softly in the gentle sea breeze. Josie felt that if she reached out and touched the air she would be transported somewhere, different; other. For the first time, the myths felt they could almost be real. You

159

really could imagine fairies here.

'Wow,' she said. 'Just wow. This is amazing.'

'Isn't it?' said Harry. He came over and squeezed her hand tight.

'Love you,' said Josie as he pulled her towards him, and kissed him. The air seemed full of promise and mystery. She was glad she'd come.

Ant climbed down into the Faerie Ring, his sense of anticipation growing. There was a strange atmosphere in the air. Harry and Josie had gone all moony on each other, and even Diana seemed chilled and less aggressive.

The sea rose and fell below them, and the moon shone as bright as day. A soft breeze ruffled his hair, and the silvery beams of the moon cast weird shadows on the grass. For all that Ant didn't believe in this nonsense, he had the shivery sensation that something – unusual? – was about to happen. It even made him feel more warmly to Diana for a moment. But only for a moment, because she opened her mouth and spoilt the atmosphere.

'So when do the hordes of fairies arrive?' she said. 'I can't believe we've walked all the way up here in the middle of the night. We must be off our trolleys.'

'But you have to admit it is rather beautiful,' said Josie. 'I'm so pleased we came up here.'

'Me too,' said Ant, surprising himself. He felt almost poetic as he looked out to sea; this feeling was unlike one he had ever experienced before. 'And I feel ... different. As if I could do anything. As if I were invincible.'

'In your dreams,' snorted Diana. 'You've had too much beer, and allowed yourself to get sucked into the whole stupid hypnotism thing. We should all just go home to bed!'

'Don't be so bad-tempered,' said Josie. 'Come on. Lie down on the grass, and look up at the stars. This is a perfect evening. Enjoy it.'

'Yes, Di,' said Ant, 'don't be so bad-tempered.'

Diana looked as if she was going to bite off a retort, but then changed her mind, and sat down instead.

'So, you two, isn't it time you plighted your troth in the light of the moon?' said Ant, also sitting down.

'Not while anyone's looking,' said Harry. 'What about you and Diana? Maybe being hypnotised tomorrow will change your feelings towards one another.'

'No!' shrieked Ant and Diana in unison.

'I'm as likely to plight my troth with Harry,' Diana added. 'Which is not at all likely.'

But Ant wasn't sure it was entirely true. There was something odd in the air tonight, and he felt suddenly quite nervous around Diana. Once upon a time, she'd meant everything to him. Could you ever put those feelings away for good?

Diana was feeling very strange. She'd been quite happy when they left the pub. But the nearer they got to the top of the cliff, the more anxious she felt. What were they doing up here, in the middle of the night? And what if Freddie Puck had secretly hypnotised them, without them realising it? She'd been quite clear in her own mind that

161

she wasn't going anywhere but home to bed after the pub, and yet, here she was.

And Josie and Harry had gone into sappy mode again. She felt shut out of their world and it made her feel lonely. When she and Josie had first flat-shared, they'd both been single and then Harry had moved in, and she'd moved out – and nothing had ever been the same again. Diana hadn't realised how difficult she was going to find it without Josie. She felt she was in mourning for the best friend she'd ever had, and it was all her own fault. She'd pushed them together. Thanks to Diana, Harry and Josie would be married next year, and she'd be on the sidelines for ever.

She looked over to where Josie and Harry were sitting up, talking quietly together. Ant was lying on his back, looking dreamily up at the stars. He'd been giving her some funny looks all evening. She did hope he wasn't going to try anything on. She wouldn't put it past him to pretend the past hadn't happened, and see what he could get away with this weekend. From what Josie had said about him, eventually Ant tried it on with every woman he met. She hoped given their past history she would be the exception.

She tried to relax, and remember the happy feelings drinking Love in the Mist had induced in her. She'd been having fun then, but now she felt edgy and irritable. Everyone seemed to be enjoying the moment but her.

This was no good, Diana admonished herself; she should try to cheer up. No one liked people who behaved like a wet weekend in November, as her mother was fond of saying. She was the only person responsible for her own happiness. Maybe she just needed to liven things up.

'I know,' she found herself saying, 'let's play a game of Truth or Dare.'

Harry was leaning his head on Josie's lap and looking up at the stars. He was feeling deeply content. This was turning out to be a quite magical evening. He smiled happily up at Josie, who smiled happily back.

'Penny for your thoughts?' she said.

'Thinking how lucky I am,' said Harry, 'that I nabbed you.'

'And me you too,' said Josie, leaning over and kissing him on the lips.

'Ugh, you two. Do you have to?'

'Sorry,' said Harry. 'Did you just say something?'

'I thought it might be fun to play Truth or Dare,' said Diana.

'Why?' said Josie.

'I don't know,' said Diana. 'I feel like it. Sorry, I don't know why I suggested it, it's a silly idea.'

'No it's not,' said Harry, suddenly feeling this could be the funniest thing ever.

'I'm game,' said Ant.

'Me too,' said Josie.

'Who's going first?' said Ant.

'I will,' said Harry.

'So what's it to be, Truth or Dare?' said Ant.

'Truth,' said Harry.

'Okay,' said Diana, 'what do you want most of all in the world?'

'To spend my life with Josie,' said Harry. 'Simple.'

'Okay, my go,' said Diana, 'I'll do a dare.'

'I dare you to kiss Ant,' said Josie sneakily.

Diana blushed, but went and kissed him on the cheek.

'Don't put yourself out too much,' said Ant. 'Okay. Josie, your turn.'

'Dare,' said Josie.

'Finish this bottle of Idle Brew I brought with me,' said Ant.

'Down in one, down in one,' they shouted, as Josie finished it triumphantly.

'Now you, Ant,' said Harry. 'Truth or Dare?'

'Truth,' said Ant.

'What's the question you want to know the answer to most in the world?' said Josie.

'That's easy,' said Ant. He turned to Diana. 'What did I do to make you hate me so much? I've never really known.'

Chapter Twelve

'So what's the score today?' Nicola said brightly over the breakfast table, as if sensing a bit of an atmosphere. After Ant's question, which Diana had refused to answer, they'd given up on Truth or Dare and come home. Diana had gone straight to bed, and this morning was barely speaking to Ant. Ant and Harry were both looking pale and wan, thanks to their overindulgence the previous day, so Josie had decided a more active day was in order.

'I think we've spent enough time in the pub this weekend,' she said. 'We need to get some fresh air. Let's go kayaking. I was thinking we could do it on my hen night, so I'd like to try out the new centre near St Ives.'

'Kayaking? You are joking,' said Diana, who had been very quiet since last night. 'Who goes kayaking on their hen night?'

'Me,' said Josie. 'I don't want a strippogram. I'd just like us to have some active fun in the day, before we get down to drinking later.'

'Are you sure you wouldn't prefer a spa?' said Diana. 'That was more what I had in mind.'

'Nope,' said Josie. 'It's my hen night. And if I want to go kayaking, that's what we're going to do.'

'I wouldn't bother arguing, dear,' said Nicola, 'Josie's just like her father, stubborn through and through.'

'I'm not getting in a boat,' said Diana. 'Even if you pay me.'

'Oh, go on,' said Harry. 'I've been before. It's fun. If I can do it, anyone can.'

'That's true,' laughed Josie, 'he was pretty hopeless at it.'

'What about going over to Tresgothen Manor?' said Ant.

'We agreed we'd go and see Freddie at some point today.'

'We can go after the kayaking,' said Josie.

'Okay then,' Ant said, 'I'm in.'

'I hope you haven't got any other mental ideas

planned for your hen night,' said Diana.

'I was thinking about a parachute jump,' said Josie. 'I've always wanted to do one.'

'You are joking–' Diana looked pale.

'Of course I am, you idiot. I don't want to hobble up the aisle.'

'Right, are we all set?' Twenty minutes later, Josie had marshalled everyone together. She was determined to have a good day today, and was doing her best to keep the W word out of the conversation. But it was so hard. She kept having to sneak off and look through the dozens of bridal mags Mum had saved for her. And despite having suggested the kayaking, a part of her just wanted to sit chatting to Mum about place settings and table decorations. Although the wedding was still a year away, Josie felt a crippling worry that she had to organise as much as possible, as soon as possible, in order to avoid mishaps. No one else felt like that clearly, but she did. She couldn't help it.

Harry drove faster down the country lanes than he'd intended. Every bump felt as if the car was lifting in the air, and he had to slam his brakes on a couple of times, eliciting a 'Harry!' from Josie, but he didn't care. He wasn't that keen on going kayaking, but Josie was so determined, he wasn't at all likely to get his own way. He'd noticed she'd started doing that to him; making little decisions (mainly about the wedding) without him, and then confirming them in public with that lovely smile of hers. Which meant he couldn't do anything but seethe quietly. He wished she'd be a bit

166

more inclusive sometimes.

'Woah,' said Ant as Harry slammed on the brakes so as not to hit a passing tractor.

'Sorry,' said Harry, 'thinking of other things.'

But he drove more soberly till they got to the outdoor centre where the kayaking was taking place. Harry's heart sank. It looked very outdoorsy and energetic. The sort of place he hated and Josie, he was beginning to realise, loved. He still hadn't quite got round to letting her know just how much he wanted to go travelling. He'd hinted at it several times, but she'd not picked up on the hint. Harry had the horrible feeling that his future plans would just slip away from him without him being able to stop them.

'So what's it going to be?' asked Harry, as he looked at the activities on offer. 'Are we going on the lake, or are we going to brave the sea?'

'I am not going in the sea,' said Diana firmly. 'I want to make it back in one piece, thank you very much.'

'God, you're dull,' said Ant. 'Bags I don't go with you.'

'I know,' said Harry peaceably, 'why don't you and Josie go together and I'll go with Diana, as she's not done it before.'

'Fine by me,' said Ant. 'You've done this before, right, Josie?'

'Once or twice,' said Josie. 'I've been kayaking since I was a little girl.'

'Ha,' thought Harry uncharitably. That would teach her. Ant was not in the slightest bit capable of listening to instructions. Particularly not from a girl.

'Right, Di,' he said with a smile. 'Are we all set?'

Diana was terrified. She'd hated boats ever since she was a kid and had gone adrift in one with her dad. They hadn't been far from the shore, but she'd never forgotten the feeling of panic when the motorboat's engine had shut down, or the look of fear on his face, and the way it felt to be drifting, helpless, further away from the shore. The whole incident had probably only taken ten minutes or so. But she'd never really got over it.

'You okay?' said Harry. 'Only you seem a bit nervous.'

That was Harry all over. Kind and thoughtful. She was glad he'd opted to have her in his boat. She could imagine all too well how unkind Ant would have been, and to a degree, Josie. Josie always failed to understand how other people found difficult the things she made look effortless. It was a really irritating characteristic, and today would be shown to its full, no doubt.

'Okay,' said Harry once they were sorted with lifejackets, helmets and sculls, 'it really is quite straightforward. You take your lead from me.'

Blanching at the reason why they were wearing headgear ('So if you fall out of the boat, you minimise any head damage,' said the cheerful instructor), Diana gingerly climbed into the boat, while Harry nobly stepped into the water. God, Josie was lucky to have him. What a gent. She noted with some amusement that Ant had leapt in first, leaving Josie to push their boat into the water. Not that Josie seemed to mind. She was in her element, teasing Ant when he complained about the cold.

The boat rocked alarmingly when Harry clambered in and Diana let out an involuntary scream, and then felt really stupid.

'Sorry,' she said, 'that was really pathetic of me.'

'Don't worry,' said Harry. 'If I can do this, anyone can. Honestly, it's easier than it looks.'

Harry turned out to be right. Soon, with his gentle instructions, she found they were skimming across the water, and gradually her nerves deserted her.

'This is actually quite a lot of fun,' she said, surprising herself. It was the first time she'd felt comfortable on the water for years.

'Isn't it?' said Harry. 'I think we should race the others to the island and back.'

'You're on,' said Diana. 'I don't think we're going to have too many problems.'

She pointed Harry in the direction of Josie and Ant's boat, which was going round in circles.

'When I say right, I mean you paddle to your left, you idiot,' Josie was saying, 'so we can turn right. I thought you'd done this before.'

'I have,' said Ant.

'Could have fooled me,' said Josie grumpily. 'Right.'

Ant pushed to his left.

'No, I meant left that time!' Josie's exasperation was obvious. 'Come on. Let's start again. I want us to go left, so we paddle to the right. Okay?'

Gradually they got the boat under control and Harry shouted across, 'Race you to the island and back. Loser buys the first round.'

'That's like a red rag to a bull,' said Diana.

'You're on,' said Ant, and with that, he and Josie flew away.

'Bugger, we'll never catch them.'

'Oh yes we will,' said Harry. 'Steady as she goes. Ant will cock it up by wanting to go too fast. You mark my words. It's in the bag.'

Ant was beginning to regret going out with Josie. She was much bossier than he'd thought she would be, constantly nagging him about which oar he was supposed to be using. The very unwelcome sight of Harry and Diana gliding effortlessly through the water while laughing their heads off at him was deeply irksome.

So it was with some satisfaction that when Harry (foolishly, in Ant's opinion) proposed a race, that Ant and Josie finally got it together and were soon flying across the waves.

'Go for it, Ant!' Josie shrieked in delight.

He glanced round to see her flushed face, sparkling eyes and fair hair flying back, and he was reminded of the vivacious girl whom he'd met all those years ago. He remembered spotting Josie in the uni bar, surrounded by male admirers, and at the time he'd been as smitten as the rest. Funny that he'd forgotten how attractive she was. But it was a long time since he'd spent so much time in her company.

'We'll show them, Josie,' he said, 'make up for them laughing at us.'

'I think they were laughing at you, actually,' said Josie. 'But let's not quibble.'

Then the race was on in earnest. The little

kayak scythed through the water, which sparkled and shone in the June sun. Ant felt like he was flying. He'd never felt so elated. This was so much fun. Before too long, they'd reached the island. They were miles ahead of Di and Harry, who were ploughing steadily through the water. Josie's expertise and his brute strength were going to win the day. Except...

'Right, Ant. You need go to right.'

Ant ploughed on to the right and the boat spun in the opposite direction.

'I mean left,' said Josie. 'You should be paddling left to go right.'

'What?' said Ant paddling frantically to his left.

'That's right,' said Josie.

'Did you say right?' said Ant paddling to his left again, and making the boat veer suddenly to his right.

'No, left,' said Josie, 'paddle on your right.'

Ant tried to do as he was told, but there were some big waves coming up, and one slurped alarmingly in the boat.

'Bugger,' said Josie, 'we're taking on too much water. We need to bail out.'

'Do I go left or right?' said Ant, before a wave crashed over his head, and the next thing he knew, he was in the water, without a paddle, and a very, very long way from his canoe.

1992: Bron

Bron was exhausted. They'd just finished filming series 4 of *Illusions,* and they still had all the brouhaha of interviews and other nonsense to get through. It seemed to get worse every time. Especially as the inevitable questions about his love life always seemed to come up. Couldn't journalists think of anything else to ask him about?

One more drink with the crew, and he was done. He still had the age-old problem that had beset him ever since Tati had left, of how to say goodbye to his latest assistant. He would only let Freddie employ them from now on.

'It would help if you didn't keep shagging them, Bron,' Freddie would drawl, and he knew in that at least, Freddie was right.

Ever since Tati had gone and got herself married – hell, ever since she'd left (could it really be ten years ago?) – Bron had been looking for a substitute. But no one had ever matched up. There could never be another Tati, not on stage, nor in his bed. And yet he still kept searching, kept kidding himself he could find her. Sometimes he toyed with ringing Tati up for old times' sake. But what would he say? She'd made her choice a long time ago, and she hadn't chosen him. Nothing was ever going to change that.

He sipped mournfully at his pint, unable to join in the high jinks of the rest of the crew, who were

172

persuading Freddie it was a really good idea to try out one of his mind games on them now. That was a waste of time, as Freddie rarely drank, and he'd clean them all out in minutes.

'Well, well, well. Look what the cat brought in.' A very familiar voice cut into his thoughts. 'Auberon Fanshawe, as I live and breathe.'

'Tati,' Bron couldn't help but be cut to the quick that she'd used his full name. His heart sank. It was one thing thinking about her, imagining what he'd say to her, but to have her there in front of him was too much to bear. He felt stifled, like he couldn't breathe, and his clothes suddenly felt uncomfortably tight. His palms were hot and sweaty and he was aware that he was breathing faster than normal. A small knot formed in the pit of his stomach. She was just the same. Beautiful; distant; unattainable. Why did she still have this effect on him, why?

'Mind if I join you?'

'Be my guest.' As he said it, Bron knew it was a really bad idea. They'd been apart now longer than they'd been together. All they ever did was hurt one another. He was tired of it, and didn't want to open himself up to any more pain.

Tati sat down next to him, and he was over-whelmed by her perfume. Word on the street was that her marriage was on the rocks, and so, the whispers went, was her career. Drunk on set, was what people were saying. But there were always rumours about Tati; it went with the persona she'd created for herself. She'd never made it her business to make friends, and had plenty of enemies, not least among his cast-offs, who'd

173

sought to emulate her career trajectory. If they were hoping for a friendly helping hand from one of the sisterhood, they were certainly mistaken.

'You look lovely,' he said. 'How's Simon?'

'Fine,' she said coolly. 'And – how's – is it Emily?'

'Amelie,' said Bron. 'And she's not – we're not together anymore.'

'A drink for old times' sake?'

'I'm not sure that's a good idea, Tati,' he said uneasily. 'Your marriage–'

'Is over, in all but name,' she said. 'Come on. One drink. What harm can it do?'

Chapter Thirteen

'You have to admit, it was funny,' Harry said for the hundredth time as they got in the car, ready to drive to Tresgothen Manor. They'd all agreed that it was worth giving Freddie the benefit of the doubt, even though Josie was still expressing her doubts.

'Ha bloody ha,' said Ant, whose mood didn't seem to have improved since he'd had to be fished out of the water by the people running the kayak hire. Josie had managed to get back into the kayak, but had ended up drifting round the wrong side of the island, and it had taken her nearly half an hour to get back.

'Lucky one of us knew what we were doing,' she said, looking over her shoulder as she buckled her seatbelt.

'Shame you don't know your left from your right,' said Ant grumpily.

'Me?' said Josie. 'I was giving you perfectly clear instructions. It's you who have the problem with left and right.'

'Oh do shut up, you two!' said Harry, looking in the rearview mirror as he did a nippy three-point turn out of a very crowded spot in the car park. 'Let's not squabble.'

He was feeling much happier than when they'd come out. He'd actually enjoyed rowing with Di. When he'd kayaked in the past with Josie, he was always aware of his inadequacy in the face of her eminent superiority in the rowing department. Not that she rubbed it in or anything, but he could feel her impatience. By contrast, it had been nice and restful being with Di, who knew less than he did and was willing to learn. And she'd impressed him with her courage. Scared as she'd been when she got in the boat, once she'd stopped shrieking, she'd settled down.

'I'd have hated going in the water,' said Di. 'You've actually gone up in my estimation, Ant. You dealt with it pretty well.'

'Wonders will never cease,' laughed Josie, 'that's the first nice thing you've said to Ant all weekend.'

'I suppose it *was* funny,' said Ant grudgingly.

'Funny,' said Harry, 'it was bloody hilarious.'

He felt quite triumphant. It wasn't often he got one over Ant, and he was enjoying the unusual feeling of having come out on top.

'Harry's right,' Josie started to giggle, breaking

the mood, 'the look on your face...'

Her laughter was infectious, and before long Diana had joined in, and in the end, even Ant started to smile. 'Okay, okay,' he said, 'I made an idiot of myself. But Josie, I never want to go kayaking with you ever again.'

'Deal,' said Josie.

She wound down the window, and the scent of freshly mown grass and roses drifted past them, as Harry sped down the country lanes.

'You sure you know the way?' he said.

'Of course I do,' said Josie, 'Tresgothen Manor is on the road past Mum and Dad's, about a mile from the open-air theatre. You can't miss it.'

Josie put one arm out of the window and sat back, enjoying the ride.

'Are we still sure about this?' she said. 'Freddie made Mike Slowbotham look pretty stupid in the pub last night. I don't want to look like an idiot.'

'He did deserve it though,' laughed Diana. 'The guy's a total ass.'

'...Hole,' joked Ant. 'I'm sure Freddie won't be making us look that stupid.'

'I hope not,' said Josie. 'I'm still not sure this is such a good idea.'

Harry looked at the others. 'What do you think?' he said.

'So long as I'm not made a fool of, I'm up for it,' said Diana, 'it sounds like fun.'

'And the cash will be handy,' added Ant.

'I don't know...' said Josie.

'Oh don't be such a stuffy bore,' said Diana, 'it'll be fun. What can possibly go wrong?'

Harry had a funny feeling that possibly a lot

could go wrong, but then he thought about the money. It wasn't a great deal, but enough for the two of them to go to a really nice hotel on their wedding night, and maybe have enough left over for a weekend in Europe. Maybe if he took Josie somewhere fun and interesting, she'd get the travel bug too. He could but hope.

Diana was enjoying herself. She'd beaten her demons and proved she could kayak with the best of them. A slightly ignoble part of her also felt quite triumphant. Josie was so damned good at *everything*, it felt quite nice to have done better for once. And as to having seen Ant ending up in the water, she hadn't enjoyed anything so much in ages. It had even made up for the shakiness she'd felt after Ant had asked her that question last night. Why he had to bring it up during the game and not when they were alone, she couldn't fathom. She hadn't bothered to answer him. A memory of sitting alone in a hospital bed, waiting for him, came searing back into her consciousness. How could he possibly not know why she hated him? If it wasn't obvious to him by now, it never would be.

Deciding to put thoughts of Ant out of her mind, which wasn't as easy as all that, with him sitting right next to her, Diana leaned against the window and stared out dreamily as they sped through the beautiful Cornish countryside. It really was a glorious day, and above the car engine, she could just make out the murmur of bees, and the summer breeze blowing through the fresh green grass. It was so lovely here. Part

177

of her wished she could stay for ever.

She lay back and shut her eyes, letting her mind drift.

She wasn't exactly daydreaming, but her thoughts wandered to a scenario where a tall dark stranger came striding up the beach and whisked her off her feet. He was lovely, soulful, caring and looked like – *Harry?* She jerked awake suddenly, feeling herself blush. She'd never looked at him that way before, and after what had happened on Friday night, didn't want any more misunderstanding. She flushed again, as Josie said, 'Are you okay? You look a bit flustered.'

'Yes, fine,' said Di, brushing away the guilty feeling that her daydream had left her with. It was only a dream. Nothing had happened.

'Daydreaming about anyone nice?' teased Josie.

'No one nice,' said Di, and glanced at Ant to throw Josie off the scent.

Josie giggled and whispered something to Harry.

Phew. That had worked. But how strange. To be dreaming about Harry. Strange and embarrassing. Best she forgot all about it.

Ant's temper had finally improved as they pulled up at Tresgothen Manor. If Ant had been impressed by Josie's parents' house, this was mindblowing. A long driveway, lined with poplars, gave way to a massive drive with a cultivated lawn, which looked as though someone had cut it with nail clippers, and led up to a massive Elizabethan-style house, with red brick chimneys and a huge oak door, which was thrown dramatically open as

Freddie came out to greet them.

'Welcome, welcome,' said Freddie, 'do come in. We're having drinks on the lawn, and we can sit down and go over the finer points of the contracts.'

He ushered them through the house, and Ant looked around him at the cool interior, with marble floors and a magnificent wooden staircase, paintings of long-dead aristocrats lining the walls, before they were led out into a glorious garden.

If the front garden had looked impressive, the back garden was magnificent. A large lawn, with neat flowerbeds at either side, led to a terraced garden at the bottom which was a riot of colour. A rose arch made way for a sunken garden, from where the tinkling sound of water suggested the pond at the bottom of the terrace had been carefully laid to create the illusion of a waterfall. Even Ant, who knew nothing about gardens, could see it was amazing.

'I'd heard they'd done up the gardens here,' said Josie, 'I hadn't realised they were quite so beautiful. When I was a child they were a wilderness.'

'Aren't they magnificent?' said Auberon Fanshawe coming towards them, his hand extended in greeting. 'I've stayed in lots of wonderful places over the years, but I can honestly say I would really love to make this my permanent home.'

'Drink, anyone?' Freddie clicked his finger, and as if by magic a waiter appeared bearing a tray of champagne and Bucks Fizz. Everyone took a glass except Harry, who opted for orange juice.

'To all of you,' said Freddie, raising his glass, 'and thank you for sharing in my experiment.'

'Are you sure it's safe?' said Josie, who still seemed down on the whole idea.

'Quite sure,' said Freddie. 'Look, Jack here, our lawyer, will go through it with you, but honestly, as I told you before, you don't have to do anything you don't want to, and we can stop the experiment at any time. Why don't I demonstrate how easy it is on one of you? And we'll take it from there.'

Ant put his hand up.

'I'm up for it,' he said.

'All right,' said Freddie, and led Ant to a chair in the middle of the lawn. A blank screen had been set up behind the chair, and a camera was also in place.

'This is Will, our cameraman,' said Freddie, 'and he'll be with us tonight, to record what happens.'

Ant sat down, slightly nervous now that it was about to happen, but Freddie put a light hand on his shoulder.

'Nothing at all to be worried about,' he said. 'I just want you to think about something that makes you relax.'

Ant immediately imagined himself on a beach in Australia.

'Take a few deep breaths, and imagine you are descending a spiral staircase,' began Freddie. 'I'm going to count down from two hundred, and when you get to one, you will be at the bottom...'

Ant was vaguely aware of Freddie counting,

and before he knew it, Freddie had reached one.

'Now you are completely relaxed,' he heard Freddie saying; his mind was drifting and Freddie's voice sounded as if it came from a long way away. 'I'd like you to go and let the person you're closest to here know how you feel about them.'

Overcome with a strong emotion and fuzzy warmth, Ant got up and walked over to Harry and gave him a huge bear hug.

'Aw, mate,' he said, 'Aw, mate.'

Harry squirmed a little under his embrace, but Ant didn't mind, he just felt a beatific sense of warmth that he was here on this lovely day with Harry, Josie and Diana.

'Now go back and sit down and go to sleep.'

Ant wandered back to his chair, and sat down, and within seconds was fast asleep. He was dreaming about Diana, about how she'd been when they were young; remembering the joy he'd felt in her presence, when he heard Freddie say, '…and one and you're awake.'

He shook his head, and said, 'Was that it?'

'That was it,' said Freddie. 'Now, that wasn't so bad, was it?'

'I still don't like it,' said Josie, even though the others were convinced by Freddie's display, and had eagerly agreed to meet Freddie at sunset at the Standing Stones so they could begin the experiment.

She couldn't put her finger on why, but Josie had a sudden bad feeling about this. There were strange undercurrents in the air. Diana and Ant were still on edge with each other, and she had

181

the distinct impression that Harry was not telling her something. Having seen Ant suddenly come over all affectionate to Harry made her wonder if under hypnotism, they might all reveal things they'd rather keep hidden. Josie wasn't sure she wanted to know his innermost thoughts at the moment. She had a horrible feeling they wouldn't chime with hers.

'I'm not sure,' she said. 'I think we should let things lie.'

'Oh, don't be a spoilsport, Josie,' said Harry, tickling her.

'Yes, go on, Josie,' urged Diana. 'Nothing happened to Ant, and I know it was a bit mean, but seeing what Freddie did to Mike was quite funny.'

Everyone but her seemed to think being hypnotised was a huge laugh. But Josie had the weirdest feeling that she'd regret it if she did.

'What if we cause things to happen that we don't intend?' said Josie.

'What things?' laughed Harry.

'I don't know. We might all turn into axe murderers, or kill ourselves.'

'I doubt that is going to happen,' said Harry, laughing. 'You have far too vivid an imagination.'

'Maybe that is a bit extreme,' said Josie. 'But I think we're playing with fire. All I'm saying is that I don't want to get burnt.'

Chapter Fourteen

The sun was dipping low in the sky as they clambered up to the Standing Stones, casting long shadows across the grass. It was a warm balmy evening, but Diana kept shivering. She was slightly apprehensive about what was going to happen, especially as Nicola had been quite frantic when she found out about it.

'But what if you all get attacked, or fall off the edge of the cliff,' she'd wailed.

'I really don't think that's going to happen, Mum,' said Josie, which was a bit rich considering she'd also been worrying about it.

Nicola had only consented when they'd promised to go well prepared, with proper trainers, warm clothes, torches for when it got dark, and even a food parcel, but she was still fretting about it when they set off.

Luckily Peter was more worried about being late for a golf dinner dance they were attending at a hotel fifty miles away where they were staying the night, and told them they were idiots, but it was on their heads. Diana didn't like to say, 'I'm only doing it for the money'; she didn't imagine for one moment they'd understand. But it was her only motivation.

'Okay,' said Freddie, as they gathered by the Standing Stones at eight thirty. 'You met Will earlier. With your permission, he's going to follow us round this evening and film anything interesting that happens.

'What I'd like to do, if you have no objections, is to take each of you individually, and make some suggestions that the others can't hear,' continued Freddie. 'Don't worry, Bron and Will are going to be sitting with me all the time. Nothing's going to happen.'

'So who's first?'

'Okay,' said Diana, 'I'll go for it.'

She followed Freddie to the middle of the Standing Stones, where Freddie had set up two chairs, and Will had his camera set up.

The sun's last rays cast golden shadows on the grass, the sound of seagulls keening floated from high in the sky, and there was the constant thrum of waves crashing against the rocks below.

It was quite breathtakingly beautiful, and Diana felt her misgivings fade away. Somehow, she knew this was going to be a night to remember.

'Where do you want me?' she asked.

'If you just sit there, we'll check out the sound and lighting,' said Freddie.

Another ten minutes of fiddling went on before Freddie appeared happy.

'No need to be worried,' he said eventually, 'just let your mind empty.'

'Do I have to look into your eyes?' said Diana.

'No, nothing like that,' said Freddie calmly. 'I just want you to relax, take some deep breaths and imagine somewhere that makes you feel safe and happy. If at any time you feel worried, go to your safe place, and everything will be fine. Shut your eyes if it helps.'

'Okay,' said Diana. She felt a little shiver of excitement. Now it came to it, it was quite thrilling being hypnotised. She shut her eyes, and tried to think of the last time she'd felt safe. A picture popped into her head of her being eight years old, and lying by the fire, staring into the flames. She saw sprites, and fairies and magic in those flames, and she knew somewhere in the house her mum would be cooking dinner for her. She felt secure in a way she hadn't done for years.

'Now I want you to imagine climbing down a spiral staircase, till we get to your safe place. I'm going to count down from ten. Ten; you are descending the first couple of stairs...' his voice rolled over her like warm melted hot chocolate. 'Think calming thoughts.'

Despite herself, Diana began to relax. Freddie's voice was like a summer's breeze blowing gently through every corner of her mind, making her feel safe, warm, content. She was vaguely aware that when they reached the bottom of the stairs, a picture came into her head of playing by the fire with a small furry black and white kitten. He'd been a present for her eighth birthday. A deep feeling of contentment stole over her and she felt utterly relaxed.

'I'm going to unlock your deepest desires,' Freddie purred. 'When the film crew have gone, you're going to have a little sleep, and when you hear an owl hoot, you will wake up, completely refreshed. The first person you see when you wake will be the person you plight your troth with at midnight, tonight.'

Diana felt detached from herself, but very happy. She let out a deep sigh. Slowly she became aware that she was resurfacing, 'Three, you are climbing back up the stairs...' Freddie's voice soothed her, and she could see the next step, feel the metal handrail, 'Two, nearly at the top now... One, wake up...'

Diana shook her head, blinking a little.

'Was that it?' she said, feeling a little disorientated.

'That's it,' said Freddie. 'Now go and join your friends, and we'll have the next person. Let's say, Ant.'

Ant came strolling into the centre of the circle. He was feeling more confident tonight. Whatever suggestions Freddie might think he'd planted earlier, nothing had happened, apart from him feeling mildly affectionate towards Harry which was undoubtedly the booze talking, proving the whole hypnotism thing was pure bunkum. Easy money.

'So, Ant, how do you feel tonight?' said Freddie, as he sat down.

'Fine,' said Ant. 'I still don't think you can do it.'

'Really?' said Freddie, with an amused smile. 'We'll see, shall we?'

Ant settled into his seat, vaguely aware that Freddie had started speaking again. Once more he was descending a spiral staircase, one step at a time, 'three, two, one, you're asleep...' said Freddie, and then Ant had the strangest sensation of floating. He was soaring high above the earth, feeling that the stars were almost within his grasp.

It was a dizzying, intoxicating sensation. Looking down, he could see his own body slumped over a chair, while Freddie was leaning in and whispering in his ear. Freddie was saying something like, '...as this was your idea, you are responsible for your companions. If anything goes wrong tonight, it is up to you to put it right...'

That didn't seem too bad, Ant thought lazily, wondering if he could float as high as the gulls. It was a pleasant sensation up here, with the soft sea breeze on his face, and the sensation of wheeling, arching up, up and away. He felt freer then he'd ever felt, and almost wished he could stay here for ever. '...Three, two, one, and you're awake.'

Ant sat up with a jolt. For a minute, he felt cheated, as if deprived of some great treat, and then a little foolish. Had he really imagined he'd been floating up in the sky? How daft was that?

'We done?' he said, to hide his embarrassment.

'We're done,' said Freddie.

'I think your wallet is going to be somewhat lighter by the end of the evening,' said Ant. 'I don't feel any different at all.'

'We'll see,' said Freddie. 'We'll see.'

Josie went next. Despite her forebodings, Diana and Ant had come back seeming very chilled and relaxed about the whole thing. Maybe she was making a fuss about nothing.

'Still nervous?' said Freddie, as she sat down.

'A bit,' said Josie. 'Are you sure you're not going to do anything bad to us?'

'On my life,' said Freddie. 'Hypnotism is really

harmless. I've done it on Bron dozens of times, haven't I?'

'Absolutely,' said Bron, 'there's nothing to it. And I promise you, I won't let any harm come to you.'

'Okay,' said Josie, slightly mollified. Bron was like your favourite uncle. She couldn't imagine him letting anything bad happen. 'Now what?'

'I'm just going to chat to you for a bit. Think of lovely things, and things that make you happy.'

Josie could hear Freddie's voice floating over her, tinkling like a running stream. 'I am going to take you to your safe place,' she heard him say and then she was walking through a beautiful forest that had a river running through it, filled with flowers, birds, sunshine and laughter. It was wonderful, she had the sensation of being truly alive and at one with nature. She had never felt so incredible in her life.

'You will find your heart's desire tonight,' Freddie's voice flowed overhead from a long way off. 'The first person you see when you wake up is your life's partner. You know you are meant to be together for ever...'

Josie smiled happily as Harry came running through the woods towards her, and she flung herself into his arms.

'...And, two, you are at the top of the stairs, and one, you're awake.'

Josie felt absurdly happy, as if someone had just given her the best present in her life, if only she could remember what it was.

'I feel fantastic,' she said in surprise.

'And you will continue to do so,' assured Freddie. 'You're in for a magical and surprising evening.'

By the time it was Harry's turn, he was feeling both a little bored and a little concerned about what they were doing. He couldn't help but feel that maybe Nicola was right and they were making themselves very vulnerable out on the cliffs after dark.

'Don't be daft,' joshed Ant, when he mentioned his fears. 'We're all going to be together anyway. And it probably won't work. What's the worst that can happen?'

'What indeed?' agreed Harry; put like that, his fears seemed foolish.

'Okay,' he said, as he sat down in the circle. 'How do you want me?'

'You're fine, just there,' said Freddie. 'Now sit still, and breathe deeply and cast your mind back to a happy positive point in your life.'

Josie. Harry's heart leapt as his thoughts automatically turned to Josie.

'You're getting married soon, I gather,' Freddie's smooth mellifluous tones continued. 'Think of that happy day.'

Harry felt a jerk of concentration. Josie made him happy, but the cheerful positive feelings fled away the minute he tried to picture her in a wedding dress.

'Sorry, lost concentration for a second.'

'That's okay...' Freddie's voice soothed. 'Think only good thoughts. You are very, very relaxed. Now, I want you to find your safe place...'

Harry resisted the urge to giggle. What was he

189

doing here? A grown man. This was ridiculous. But he couldn't seem to keep hold of Freddie's words, they seemed to flow over and past him, sounding meaningless, yet dragging him further down into himself. Until eventually he found himself at the bottom of a spiral staircase, rooted in the earth, his arms round Josie, the safest place he could possibly be.

'...And you will reveal the secrets of your heart,' he heard Freddie say as he pulled his arms tighter still round Josie.

Harry stifled a yawn and heard Freddie say, 'You are ascending, slowly climbing back up the stairs...' again the words flowed around him, and he could barely remember what Freddie was saying till he heard, 'Three, two, one. Now you are awake.'

Harry roused himself, feeling a bit confused about what had just happened.

'Now what?' he said.

'Now you go back to the others,' said Freddie, 'and when you hear me count to three, all four of you will fall asleep.'

Harry went back and sat down next to Ant, as Josie and Diana were preoccupied in a giggling girlie session.

'What are you doing?' said Harry to Josie.

'Look, I'm making daisy chains,' she grinned. 'Here's a crown for the king of my heart.'

Harry blushed, but accepted the gift and the kiss Josie gave him.

Then Freddie was standing before them.

'When I click my fingers, you will all go to sleep. But when you hear an owl hooting, you will wake up.'

Harry let out a yawn; he felt enormously tired, as if he just had to lie down. He saw the others were also struggling to keep awake too. And then Freddie clicked his fingers.

'Just might put my head down for a bit,' said Josie sleepily.

'Me too,' yawned Diana.

'This is ridiculous, I'm not going to sle–' Ant's words were muffled by the sound of his snoring.

Sleep washed over Harry. No point fighting it. He lay down, curled up and in seconds was fast asleep.

Chapter Fifteen

Ant was wandering through a forest, feeling kind of dreamy. He had never been out at night like this in the country. The silver beams of the moon danced through the trees, casting a light shimmer, which meant he wasn't afraid. He heard the snuffling sounds of woodland creatures in the undergrowth.

It was such a lovely evening, such a pretty copse. He felt that no one would mind if he lay down here and stayed for a while. Ant lay flat on his back and looked up at the stars, feeling pleasantly detached, and then suddenly the dream changed...

It wasn't summer any more, it was winter, and he and Diana were holding hands, laughing, at the top of a mountain. He could feel the crisp cold air against his cheeks, see the majestic mountains around him. He was with her and nothing mattered at all. He could hear the others falling out of the bar, screaming and laughing, but nothing else mattered but this moment, with Diana by his side. He had never felt such exquisite happiness.

'I will never ever let you go,' he whispered, kissing her softly on the lips.

Laughing, she tugged him by the hand, and then they were tobogganing down the mountain at a dizzying and thrilling rate. Time and time again they ended up in heaps of snow, only to remount and carry on. It was mad, furious and funny and he never wanted the moment to end. But end it did, with a bump, as they fell off the toboggan for one last time and ended up in a soggy giggling heap in the snow.

'I'm so lucky to have found you,' he said, 'don't ever change.'

'Tony–' she began, just as he heard the sound of an owl hooting. 'I need to tell you something…'

'What?' Ant asked, but the dream was already fading, and the snow and Diana disappeared as quickly as they'd come.

What? What was she going to tell him? He felt sure it was important, and simultaneously sad, as if he'd lost something very dear to him.

He felt his cheek and realized to his surprise that tears were coursing down them. He remembered more then. Diana had never answered his question, and two weeks later she'd dumped him in front of everyone, by pouring a pint of beer over his head. At the time he had no idea, why.

And by the time he'd found out why, it was too late.

Ant sat up and looked around him, and gasped. He was alone in a beautiful copse, the silvery moon casting its light in the gaps between the trees. How had he got here? He glanced at his watch, nearly ten o'clock already. He must have been sleepwalking. Suddenly it felt imperative he get back to them, especially to Diana. He'd done her a great wrong and it was time he put it right.

Diana was dreaming she was lying on pillows in the base of a boat, being rowed down a river. Kingfishers darted across the bows, and fish jumped up out of the river. She lay back drowsily, letting her hands drift in the river, feeling the warmth of the sun on her cheek, deeply content. She wondered idly who was rowing the boat; all she could see were strong arms rhythmically rowing back and forth. She had never felt so safe and secure.

She heard the sound of a bird – an owl at this time of the day? – and sat up to see what it was. Smiling, Diana took in the face of the rower, but the dream faded before she could tell who it was. The warmth of the sun was gone, and she was completely alone in the midst of the Standing Stones. She felt sure she'd woken up earlier and looked over and seen Harry next to her. Where had he and the others gone? What was happening? She should be feeling alarmed, she supposed, but somehow she wasn't. They would probably turn up in a minute. Perhaps she should go and look for them? Although there was no

193

sense of urgency.

'Hello?' a voice called out to her. 'It's Freddie, just wondering how you are?'

Freddie? Oh. Then Diana remembered. She'd been hypnotised, they all had. Not that she felt any different.

'Fine,' she said, looking up as Freddie came towards her, shadowed by the cameraman, Will. 'Where's everyone else?'

'They're scattered about,' said Freddie. 'Part of the experiment is waiting to see what happens now.'

'Okay,' said Diana. 'Should I go and find them?'

'If you wish,' said Freddie. 'Is there anyone in particular that you'll be looking for?'

Diana thought for a moment.

'I don't think so,' she began, and then realised it wasn't true.

Her mind flashed back to the dream, and the face she'd just glimpsed when she woke up. No, it couldn't have been.

'Well?' prompted Freddie gently.

'There's only one person I want to see,' said Diana, puzzled, 'and I have to find him now.'

'And who's that?' Freddie smiled at her, and she was vaguely aware the camera was still rolling.

The face from the dream swarmed in front of her again. 'Harry,' she said slowly. 'I need to find Harry.'

Harry was on a boat – no, not on one, *driving* one. He was powering a speedboat across the waves, blinking into the sun. The wind was blowing

194

through his hair, and he was exhilarated by the speed and the spray. He was wearing sunglasses, tee shirt and jeans, but felt like something in a James Bond movie. Even more so when he realised there was a beautiful girl by his side, shrieking her pleasure as he sped up, causing waves behind them.

'This is awesome!' she shrieked.

'Isn't it?' He turned and smiled. 'I'm so glad we're doing this together.'

'Me too,' said Josie. 'Me too.'

Harry woke with a start, a smile on his face. What a great dream. He wondered if he could perhaps persuade Josie to go travelling after the wedding. His dream had left him feeling restless, as if something were missing from his life.

He looked down, and realised he'd been sleeping curled up with Josie on a bench at the top of the cliff. He had vague memories of them waking up after Freddie had hypnotised them, and deciding they wanted to sit here together looking out to sea.

Josie was still asleep, and he didn't like to wake her. She was so beautiful, so precious. Their relationship was still new enough for him to be grateful that he'd found her. Not for him any more the thrill of the chase, the misery of the rejection. He'd found the woman of his dreams, and he wasn't ever going to let her go.

Josie stirred in her sleep and then blinked and looked up at him. She stretched and yawned.

'Where are we?' she said as she sat up. 'I was dreaming I was wandering through a vast forest, and I couldn't find you. I'm so glad you're here.'

'Me too,' said Harry. 'I was dreaming we were taking a round-the-world trip on a massive speedboat. It was amazing.'

'Ha.' Josie sat up properly now, 'I can't see you ever being able to drive a speedboat.'

'You never know,' said Harry, 'I've never had the chance.'

'And aren't likely to,' said Josie.

'Is it such a mad idea?' said Harry.

'Is what?' said Josie.

'Us going travelling together?'

'Woah,' said Josie, 'where's this come from? Have you been talking to Ant again?'

'Ant has nothing to do with it,' said Harry. 'You know before I met you I was planning to go travelling?'

'I didn't think you were serious,' said Josie. 'How can we go travelling? We can't afford it, not with the wedding and everything.'

The wedding. Harry suddenly felt as if he'd been hit between the ribs. He was beginning to hate the sodding wedding.

'We could go afterwards,' said Harry. 'Save up and...'

'No,' said Josie, 'I'm sorry Harry, I don't want to go travelling. I can't believe you've suddenly suggested it. We need to get ourselves straight first.'

'Oh,' said Harry, feeling deflated. He hadn't realised till now just how much it meant to him. 'I suppose you're right.'

'You know I am,' said Josie. 'You've got commitments now. You can't just up sticks when you feel like it anymore. That's Ant's department.'

'Then maybe,' said Harry slowly, 'we should

have a rethink.'

'About?' said Josie.

The words were out of his mouth before he could stop them.

'The wedding,' he said.

Josie stared at him in dismay. It was the last thing she'd expected. She'd woken up feeling un-accountably anxious, after uncertain dreams in which she was searching for Harry and unable to find him. And now Harry had started wittering on about doing some kind of grown-up gap year, which was the last thing she wanted to do at the moment, and now he seemed to be saying...

'What about the wedding?' said Josie.

'We could put it off,' said Harry. 'Wait a couple of years, have some fun. Then get settled. What's the rush?'

'I thought you wanted to marry me,' said Josie in a small voice. A feeling of cold dread washed over her. Had he changed his mind?

'I do,' said Harry.

'But?'

'But, I think we're rushing things,' he said. 'We've been together less than a year. We have still so much to learn about one another. You didn't know I wanted to travel that badly, for example...'

'More than you want to get married to me, it would seem.' Josie felt as if her world were crumbling. Harry couldn't be saying all this stuff.

'That's not what I meant,' said Harry.

'So, what did you mean?' said Josie. 'Do you still want us to get married or not?'

There was a pause, before Harry said, 'Yes, of

197

course I do.'

The pause hadn't been long, but it was long enough.

'But you'd rather go travelling first?' said Josie. 'Thanks for nothing, Harry.'

'It's not like that,' protested Harry.

'Then what *is* it like?' said Josie. 'It feels like my fiancé has cold feet, is what it's like from my perspective.'

'I love you,' said Harry.

'Really?' said Josie. 'You could have fooled me.'

Shaking with anger, she got up and walked away. Harry had taken her completely by surprise. She thought that everything was perfect, that he was happy, and wanted to get married. But now it appeared he wasn't. He said he loved her, but seemed to be unable to prove it in the one way she felt mattered. What did it mean? Could they still be together and not get married?

1995: Bron

'So it's over then?' Bron said sombrely.

'Sorry, mate, but I'm afraid it is,' said Freddie sighing. 'They've said the viewing figures are really down from last series. And to be honest, I want to look at doing something new. Time for a change for both of us, old boy.'

'I suppose,' he replied. He'd hated the last two seasons of *Illusions,* but even so Bron felt cast off. It was work, and it was regular. It stopped him

198

having to think too hard about what happened next.

'There's always producing and directing,' said Freddie. 'You have been banging on about doing both forever.'

That was true. Maybe he'd have time for that now...

He felt melancholy though. And he knew the reason why. Bloody stupid after all these years to be still hankering after her, but he'd always imagined that Tatiana Okeby would be the first leading lady he'd ever direct. But then, he'd always imagined that they would have been together with a horde of kids by now. What had stopped him? He could have had that future, and it was his own fault for not making it happen.

Tati had more or less intimated that to him on their last, and he hoped final, meeting. One drink had led to another, and another, and then, of course the inevitable. And he thought it was their chance to put things right. They'd talked about everything that night; about their hopes, their fears, their failures, the pain they'd caused one another, and he'd really thought it was a new beginning. But whereas he had been over the moon, thinking that finally, here was the second chance he'd been wanting all those years, Tati had made it very clear to him what it was all about for her.

'It's called a revenge shag, darling,' she'd said in the morning. 'Poor little Bron, did you really think I was coming back to you? After all this time? Give me strength.' But she'd been so drunk by the time they went to bed, he didn't even think it had been that calculated.

And then to make matters worse, the next thing he knew it was all over the Sunday papers. 'Bron and me: The True Story', 'Bron the Bastard'; 'How Auberon Fanshawe broke my heart'.

Poor lovely Tatiana. Such a waste. They said she was in rehab now, but he didn't enquire too often. He really thought they'd cut through the bullshit of the last few years on that evening. But he'd been so wrong. Bad enough that she had rejected him in the morning, but to sell their story to the papers: his heart had broken all over again.

However much of a mess Tati was in, Bron was staying well clear. He knew he was still vulnerable to her charms. Probably always would be. The problem was, she was bad for his mental health.

Chapter Sixteen

Diana's happiness from earlier on had completely dissipated. She'd been wandering around for over half an hour and was now grumpily lost. After her chat with Freddie, she had left the Standing Stones to find the others, feeling unsettled by the emotions she'd had when she woke up. She'd just been having a weird dream, with Harry rowing her in a boat. It didn't mean anything, surely? Diana felt sure that once she saw him again, she'd put it all in perspective, but couldn't rid herself of the stomach-churning excitement she felt at the thought – which was ridiculous, especially as he was getting married to Josie. Your best friend, Diana reminded herself. How could she harbour feelings for her best friend's fiancé? Especially since she'd never let herself fall for anyone properly since Ant.

Diana's mind fled back eight years, to when she and Ant had been an item. They had been so happy, or so she'd thought. But he'd let her down in her hour of need. And when she'd come look-ing for him – afterwards – she'd found him cosied up in the bar with Sian. Sian, who'd been her best friend. Ant claimed to have had no idea why she'd poured the glass of beer over his head. He'd denied anything was going on – yeah, right. Diana had seen first hand how flirtatious Ant could be, and Diana had never known anyone resist Sian's seduction technique. All Diana knew was that during the most traumatic experience of her life, her boyfriend had been betraying her with her so-called best friend. Josie was the first proper friend Diana had trusted since then, but now she seemed to be harbouring feelings for Harry. She couldn't do to Josie what had been done to her. She had to put these thoughts out of her mind.

The moon was really bright and shone on the path, which gave way to some woods. Where the hell was Harry? Or Josie? Or even Ant? Or *anyone*. Diana wasn't really a country girl, and the sound of hooting owls freaked her out. But the path shimmered in the moonlight, and something drew her on. Despite her anxiety and irritation, Diana felt a sense that something magical was about to happen, and if only she could find her way through to the right path, she could almost reach out and touch it.

Harry was not feeling the magic. His head was thumping, and he felt heartsick at what he'd said to Josie. She had looked so hurt when he'd talked about delaying the wedding and the last thing he'd ever wanted to do was cause her pain. Harry wished she'd given him time to explain properly, but she'd run off into the darkness and now he didn't know where she'd gone.

He wasn't even sure which direction he should be looking in. Perhaps he should think about heading home. Maybe Josie had gone straight back there. He'd find her, sit her down, have a proper chat, and sort it all out. They'd had a silly misunderstanding, that was all; it could be easily resolved. Descending the cliff path, he found himself walking through woods which swayed gently in the breeze. The soft calls of owls and the odd rustling in the bushes were the only sounds to disturb him. After he'd been walking about ten minutes, he found himself in a clearing. In the far distance he could hear the rhythmic roar of the waves. There was a real sense of something – magic? – in the air. Harry paused for a moment and then sat down. He didn't know why.

Then he heard voices. He got up gladly. Maybe it was Josie. But as the voices came nearer, he realised they were male voices.

'Oh,' he said, 'it's you.'

'Hello, Harry,' Freddie was all urbane charm, while Auberon Fanshawe huffing and puffing behind him nodded hello, and Will wandered

202

nonchalantly behind them with a camera.

'I thought you were going to show me where Tati is,' Auberon grumbled. 'Where in God's name are we?'

'I believe we're not too far away from the farm where she's camping,' said Freddie with a smile.

'Tati, camping? I'd like to see that,' snorted Auberon.

'I believe it's more of a glamping experience,' said Freddie, 'she's holed up in a yurt with all mod cons. But I'm hoping she might be up for a little midnight adventure.'

'What did you say to her?' said Auberon.

'I may have possibly suggested subliminally that if she wanted that part, a late-night assignation at the theatre might be the thing,' said Freddie. 'You're not getting cold feet, are you? It was your idea.'

'No,' said Auberon, but he didn't sound too convinced.

'Ah, Midsummer Eve,' said Freddie, breathing a deep sigh. 'Such a magical night, don't you think? You could almost believe fairies and elves and Cornish piskies exist, couldn't you?'

'Tommy rot,' said Auberon.

'Um, I think I gave up believing in fairies some time ago,' said Harry.

'Oh well,' said Freddie. 'How's the experiment going?'

'Not well at all,' said Harry. 'I can honestly say that if I get through this evening, I will never be hypnotised ever again. Thanks to you, Josie's run off and I don't know where she is.'

'So no one's plighted their troth yet.'

Harry rolled his eyes.

'The likelihood of Diana and Ant ever making it is somewhat less than zero, and thanks to me getting a dose of verbal diarrhoea as a direct consequence of your hypnotism, my fiancée isn't speaking to me.'

'Ah,' said Freddie. 'I'm sure it will all be all right in the end. Why don't you go and find her and have a chat?'

'That was the plan,' said Harry, 'but I'm not sure where she's gone.'

'Well, we're heading for the theatre,' said Freddie. 'If I see her, I'll tell her to meet you there.'

'Okay,' said Harry. 'It's a deal.'

Josie had planned to go back to the Standing Stones, to see if the others were there. She really wanted to talk to Diana and ask what she thought. A bit of her thought maybe she'd been unfair on Harry. Perhaps he was right, maybe they had rushed things – but it had been a bit of a shock, hearing that he still wanted to go travelling. He'd mentioned it when they first got together, but she hadn't realised he was serious about it. Josie felt a little stab of guilt. She knew Harry really wasn't happy in his job. Working on a local rag for London suburbia covering school fetes, lost pets and the occasional petty crime wasn't exactly what Harry had had in mind when he left the journalism course he'd taken after uni. Josie could remember all those years ago, when they first met, he'd had the burning ambition to be a prizewinning journalist. That wasn't going to happen at the *Hornsey Echo*, but she hadn't twigged that he was so determined to do travel writing. Harry had mentioned it once or twice, but in such a diffident manner, Josie had assumed he wasn't that serious.

She couldn't help feeling it was partly Ant's fault. No doubt he'd been stirring Harry up with thoughts of getting away and finding his freedom again. Despite Ant's intervention the previous day, Josie didn't quite trust him. He was so against marriage – or commitment even, Josie had read the excoriating email he'd sent Harry when Harry told him they were moving in together – he couldn't seem to bear it happening for other people.

Josie had reached a fork in the path; one way carried on round the coast, and another path went down to the open-air theatre. A third made its way down to a pretty little beach where she'd spent much of her teenage years having illicit barbies on the beach.

Josie struck off for the cliff path and, hearing voices, thought for a moment it must be Diana or Ant, but as she came further up the path, she realised the sounds were coming from a field where she could make out a brightly lit campsite – oh of course, this was the new place Mum had mentioned recently. A smart young couple from London had moved in and converted an old farm into a luxury caravan site, complete with yurts, and log burners, and 'massage parlours', according to Mum. Josie had checked, and it turned out there was a healing tent offering everything from Ayurvedic massage to hot stone therapy. And according to Mum, it was where Tatiana Okeby

205

and her entourage were staying.

'Please don't go, Tati,' she heard the high-pitched voice of Gray M'stard pleading, 'Darling, you might get lost out there.'

'Who knows what creatures are lurking in the woods,' said the flighty little assistant, whom Josie had heard Tati refer to as Gypsy.

Their voices were getting nearer, they were clearly heading across the fields for the path she was on.

'Will you all stop making such a fuss,' said Tatiana grandly. 'I am going for a little walk down to the woods, where I am going to meet Mr Slowbotham and discuss this part further.'

'But why so late?' said the final member of the entourage, Ariadne, Josie thought she was called. 'What if he's an axe murderer?'

'Hallo there,' called Josie, 'it's me, Josie, I met Tatiana yesterday. You really don't need to worry. I've known Mike all my life, I can promise you he isn't an axe murderer.'

'You see,' said Tatiana triumphantly. 'There really is no need to worry. Mike wants me to perform for him at midnight, so as to get the ambience right. I think it's a wonderful idea. Now please, children, leave me be. I'll be fine. This young lady seems to know her way round, so I'm sure she won't mind escorting me to the theatre.'

'Er,' Josie was going to mention that she was looking for her friends, but didn't get a chance as Tatiana bowled past her, grabbed her arm and said forcefully, 'Now, I believe it's this way, isn't it?'

Ant was lost in the woods. He'd walked round and round in circles, and was no nearer to finding anyone, least of all Diana. Which in a way was a relief. Although he still had the strongest feeling that he needed to find her, a part of him was hoping he didn't. From her reaction last night, when he tried to talk about what had happened between them, she didn't seem too keen to go over old ground. Maybe he should let sleeping dogs lie.

He was just about to throw the towel in and take any path down the hill, just so he could get out of this wretched wood, when he heard voices. Female voices. It must be Josie and Diana, he decided. Well, it was now or never.

He walked towards them and then realised Josie was with someone else entirely.

'Oh,' he said. 'Where's everyone else?'

'I haven't seen Di,' said Josie, 'and Harry's still on the cliff somewhere. Tatiana was a bit lost, so I said I'd show her the way to the theatre.'

'Thank you so much,' said Tatiana graciously, 'I couldn't have found my way on my own.'

She was wearing highly inappropriate clothing; a light gossamer dress, which was far too revealing for a woman her age, and high strappy sandals, which looked like they'd break your ankles if you fell over.

'I must say, the countryside is rather tiring,' she continued. 'I don't sleep a wink in that yurt. All I can hear is strange snuffling noises all night long. It is most concerning.'

Ant suppressed a laugh. What did the woman expect from camping?

207

'At least you've got the glamorous version,' said Josie tactfully. 'Now, if you just follow the path that way for five minutes, you should be able to find the theatre. You can't miss it.'

'Thank you, my dear,' said Tatiana, 'it was very kind of you.'

'Are you sure you don't want me to take you all the way?'

'No, thank you,' said Tatiana, 'I think I can manage.'

And with that she walked off dramatically in the wrong direction, till Josie pointed her the right way again.

'God, what a drama queen,' said Josie. 'I'm glad to see the back of her. What's been happening with you?'

'Not a lot,' said Ant. 'I'm glad I've met you, as I've been getting hopelessly lost.'

'Where were you trying to get to?'

'Back to the Standing Stones to find Di,' said Ant.

'Really?' Josie looked confused. 'So the hypnotism thing actually worked, then?'

'No!' said Ant, 'I just want to talk to her.'

'About what?' said Josie. 'Only after last night, I wouldn't have thought bringing up the past is a good idea, do you? Diana hasn't even told me what really happened, what makes you think she'll discuss it with you?'

Ant shrugged his shoulders.

'She probably won't, but it's worth a try,' he said. Ant looked around him. 'Where did you say Harry was again?'

Josie shrugged.

'I left him on the cliff,' she stubbed her toe in the ground. 'We had – we had a row.'

'About?'

Josie looked miserable. 'He wants to delay the wedding and go travelling. I said I didn't. And then we fought.'

'Come on,' said Ant, suddenly feeling he wanted to make her smile again. 'I'm sure you two can sort this out. Let's go back and find him.'

'Okay,' said Josie.

They turned back up the path together, Josie leading the way. She seemed so sad, which upset Ant for some reason. He felt an overwhelming urge to make sure she was happy again, and as he followed her up the path, he couldn't for the life of him think why.

Chapter Seventeen

Harry was struggling to find the right path to the theatre. The one and only time he'd been there, on his first date with Josie, they'd come from a different direction altogether. And now with the light of the moon fading, and the beginnings of a sea mist slowly curling its way across the cliffs, he was getting quite disorientated. All he knew was that he must find Josie. Surely she'd understand how he felt if he explained it to her better? He'd been clumsy and spoken without thinking. Maybe he could persuade her that instead of a honeymoon and buying a house, they should take a year off and travel instead. That would be a good compromise, he felt.

As he came out of the woods, he ran into Diana, who was looking pale and ghostly; ethereal almost.

'Harry,' she said, flushing slightly, and he thought with a jolt that she was very pretty. He hadn't really noticed it before.

'Di,' he said, 'have you seen Josie?'

'No,' she said, 'I assumed you were together.'

'We were,' said Harry with a sigh, 'but we had a row, and I've lost her.'

'Never mind,' said Diana. 'I expect she'll turn up.'

'I hope so,' said Harry, feeling morose and out of sorts. 'I can't bear the thought that I've made her upset.'

'I hope she realises how lucky she is,' said Diana. She sounded rather sad, and Harry looked at her in surprise.

'Is everything okay, Diana? Only you seem a little different.'

'Do I?' said Diana. She gave him a shy and tender smile, which was rather disconcerting, to say the least. If she hadn't been Josie's best friend, he might have thought...

Suddenly she grabbed hold of him, and said, 'Have you ever danced under the light of the moon?'

And then he did think, very rapidly and in an increasingly panicky manner. What on earth was happening? Di was Josie's mate; could she? – was it possible? – was she coming on to him?

'Er, no,' said Harry.

'Everyone should try it at least once,' said

210

Diana, starting to croon Frank Sinatra lyrics at him, which was a tad alarming. She'd just got to the bit about there being trouble ahead, when he managed to extricate himself from her embrace.

'I think we really ought to be looking for the others,' he said, but she pulled him back to her. 'Oh, Harry, you're so staid,' she said. 'Live a little.'

'Are you drunk?' said Harry. It was the only way he could account for her behaviour.

'Yes, I'm drunk on love, and high on you,' said Diana, grabbing him and spinning him around.

Harry was stunned.

'Diana–' he began, just at the moment Josie burst down the path.

'Harry,' she said. 'What's going on?'

Josie stopped dead in her tracks. Diana and Harry? Diana and *Harry?* She'd been prepared to be conciliatory when she was talking to Ant, but here was Harry, *her* Harry, dancing with Diana, looking for all the world as if he had forgotten all about their argument.

'So now we know the real reason you want to put off the wedding,' she said; 'you're more into the bridesmaid than the bride. Great. Absolutely great.'

Josie's legs felt like jelly and her heart was pounding so loudly she thought it might explode.

'I *thought* there was something going on on Friday, but I told myself I was being stupid. But now, this…'

She turned to run back down the path, and Harry ran after her.

'Josie, it's not like that.' Harry looked aghast,

urgently grabbing hold of her hands to try and remonstrate with her. 'Diana, well Diana's in a bit of a funny mood.'

'And was Diana in a funny mood when you were dawdling together down the garden the other night?' said Josie. 'I can't believe you two. I trusted you both.'

Her voice cracked, and she wiped furious tears from her eyes. Why was Harry doing this to her? This weekend was supposed to be perfect. And now it was all ruined.

'Josie,' Harry looked gobsmacked, as if the truth of what had happened had only just dawned on him. 'Josie, you're wrong. Nothing is going on. I love you.'

'I don't believe you,' said Josie, flinging his hands away.

Just then, Ant came panting up the path. 'What's wrong?' he said.

'Nothing,' said Josie, 'and everything.' And with that she was gone again, unable to stand it one moment longer. The world had gone mad and she wasn't sure what to do next.

'What? You did what?' Ant felt like smacking his head against a brick wall. What on earth did Harry think he was doing? Why was he mucking around with Diana, when he had Josie? He couldn't have made a bigger fool of himself if he'd tried.

'Nothing,' said Harry, 'I did nothing. Diana launched herself at me, and we were dancing when Josie came up. She got the wrong idea, that's all.'

He was standing as far away from Diana as he possibly could, so perhaps he was telling the truth, though it would be difficult to persuade Josie of that.

Diana was leaning against a tree, looking slightly defiant.

'What about me?' said Diana in a small voice.

'What about you?' said Harry. 'I'm sorry, Di, I'm not sure why you did that. But thanks to you, Josie thinks I'm cheating on her. I need to find her, now.'

'What do I do?' wailed Diana. 'I love you.'

She started to walk towards him, but Harry pushed her away, and took off in the direction that Josie had taken. She looked so undignified, Ant snorted to himself, and then felt bad. Poor Di was going to end the night disappointed, he felt sure of it. Poor Di? When had Diana become poor Di? Good God, he was losing the plot too. It was bad enough that he felt the need to become friends again with Diana, it was a bit much to have to feel sorry for her too, especially as he felt miffed that she'd chosen his friend above him. It was about time he found Freddie bloody Puck and got him to sort this mess out once and for all.

'Excellent, excellent,' he heard a voice in the bushes. 'Did you get all that?'

'Who's there?' Ant said suspiciously.

'It's only us,' said Freddie, emerging from the bushes with a debonair smile, followed swiftly by Bron and Will, whose camera seemed surgically attached to his body. 'We've been catching up with what's happening. Oh, dear. It's all gone a bit pear-shaped, hasn't it?'

'You're enjoying this, aren't you?' accused Ant. 'Did you do this on purpose?'

'No, of course I didn't,' said Freddie, 'but the course of true love never did run smooth. I'm sure it will all work out.'

'It better had,' said Ant. 'Otherwise you'll have me to answer to.'

Again, that feeling of responsibility. Where had that come from? It was becoming rather annoying.

Di was well and truly lost this time. The moon had vanished, hidden by swirling clouds which made the place resemble something from a Daphne du Maurier novel. Bushes rustled in the wind as she walked past, and she had never seen anywhere so dark. She lit her way with the torch, but its light didn't spread very far. Diane shivered; it was a bit creepy out here on the cliffs. Suddenly she felt foolish for having come.

Oh, dear God, what was she doing here? There was no point in chasing after Harry. Whatever moment of insanity had led her to dance with him had passed. She could see how pathetic she looked now. Harry was in love with Josie. Josie was in love with Harry – she had no right to interfere. But Diana felt very strange. She was in the grip of a really strong emotion which possessed her whole being. She loved Harry with all her heart, and the pain of knowing that he could never be hers was sharp and intense. As usual, Diana's timing was off, and she'd made the mistake of falling for the one person she couldn't have. How she could have been so dense as to not see it before, she didn't know.

'There's nowt so stupid as folk in love,' she muttered to herself.

'You can say that again,' a voice startled her in the darkness.

'Jesus!' Diana nearly leapt out of her skin. 'Who's there?'

'We met in the pub, I think,' a woman got up from where she was crouching on the ground, and Diana saw it was Tatiana Okeby. 'Your friend, Josie, was showing me the way to the theatre, but then the mist came down and I got a little lost. I sat down here and I think I might have dozed off. I feel sure I'm meant to be meeting someone, only I can't remember who.'

'Is it the guy we saw you with at the café? Mike, isn't it?' said Diana. 'Something about a play?'

'Ah, yes, that's it. He wanted to meet me at midnight in the open air theatre, so I can audition to play Titania. How immensely thrilling. I'd best be off,' Tati said and, surprising Diana with her sprightliness, walked very fast towards the theatre.

Diana couldn't think where else to go, so she got up and followed her.

Chapter Eighteen

'What on earth have you done?' said Ant. 'Harry and Josie have fallen out, Di thinks she's in love with Harry and I have this overwhelming urge to look after everyone.'

215

'Aah ... I think that might have been a small thing I did,' said Freddie.

'Which was?'

'When you were under, I might have made a few suggestions to liven things up. Josie is supposed to find her deepest desire, Harry was supposed to reveal his true thoughts, and Diana was to find her true love.'

'And me?'

'Ah, yes,' said Freddie, 'I did suggest that you might have to take responsibility for everyone, as this was all your idea.'

'When? When did you say that?' Ant couldn't remember Freddie saying anything like that. Mind you, the hypnosis itself felt blurry now anyway.

'Earlier on, when you were at the Standing Stones,' said Freddie.

'Oh,' said Ant, vague memories of the words, 'You will take responsibility,' seeping through his memory banks.

'I'm sorry, I was just trying make things more interesting,' said Freddie.

'You certainly did that,' said Ant.

'It was part of the experiment,' said Freddie. 'I had no idea that all this would happen.'

'But you can fix it, right?'

'I *should* be able to,' said Freddie, but he didn't sound too convinced. 'Where are they all now?'

'Harry followed Josie to the theatre, I think,' said Ant. 'God knows where Di's got to.'

'Well, best foot forward,' said Freddie.

'No,' said Ant firmly, 'I want you to rid me of this responsible behaviour thing. It's cramping my style.'

'First things first,' said Freddie, 'I think we need to find Josie and Harry, don't we?'

'All right,' said Ant, 'but I'm next. I don't want to be the one in charge.'

He turned to Will who was following behind with his camera clamped to his shoulder. 'And will you please stop filming my every move?' he said. 'It's making me paranoid.'

After it turned out that the open-air theatre was further away than they thought, Tatiana decided to take a breather. 'Need to rest my legs,' she gasped. 'You go on.'

Diana had never been to the open-air theatre before and, intrigued, she walked on till she found the entrance, which was covered in weeds. Apparently it wasn't in use as much as it had been. She wasn't even sure if the gate was locked. But then she pushed it and it swung open with a creak.

Diana stepped through the entrance and was immediately entranced. A stone gateway lead through to a grass stage, surrounded by seats in a half circle looking out to sea. The mist rolling from the sea, was swirling around the theatre, reflecting the silvery shimmer of a moon just trying to peep through the clouds. Shafts of moonlight caught the stone seats, and cast long shadows on the grass. It felt magical and mysterious. Diana felt herself shiver in anticipation. Of what, she wasn't quite sure.

'Josie? Harry?' she called. 'Are you there?'

But there was no answer, just the crashing of

the sea on the rocks below and the cries of the seagulls. She shivered. What was she doing here really? She had a sudden feeling that coming at all had been a mistake. Josie and Harry were meant to be together. She was Josie's friend. She should never have entangled herself in their love life, should have seen her feelings for what they were. Now, she risked losing the best friend she'd had since ... Sian. She'd never allowed anyone to get that close again. And now Diane had pretty much done to Josie what Sian had done to her. She'd never felt so bad about anything in her life before.

'Is that you, my love?'

Diana nearly jumped out of her skin.

'Um – no, I don't think so,' she said cautiously. Oh God. She was on a cliffside at midnight with a weirdo. To her relief, the weirdo turned out to be Mike Slowbotham.

'I thought you might be Miss Okeby. We have an assignation.'

'She's heading this way, but just stopped for a rest,' said Diana. 'Are you quite sure she's expecting the same thing you are?'

'I know it,' said Mike, dramatically. 'I saw it the first time we met. We're kindred spirits, you see. Fellow thespians. Mere mortals couldn't begin to understand. But through her, I'm going to revive the fortunes of this place. This theatre will live and breathe again. She will be a glorious Titania, and magic our way back on to the map. It is going to be wonderful.'

'If you say so,' said Diana, edging away nervously. The guy was barking. 'I think I really must

218

just go and find my friends.'

'And if you see Tatiana, tell her I'm waiting, won't you?'

'Of course,' said Diana escaping thankfully, and striking out on a path back to the forest. The mist had come down really heavily now, and it wasn't long before she was hopelessly lost...

Harry ran and ran, frantically calling Josie's name. But if she was there and listening, she certainly wasn't answering. And who could blame her, after what he'd done? She had every right to be angry with him. Every right.

Eventually he caught sight of her sitting by the edge of the forest. She looked beautiful, wistful and lost.

He longed to go and hug her, but held back in case she turned away from him.

'It's all right, Harry,' she said. 'I know you're there.'

'Oh.' Harry came forward feeling foolish.

'Look Josie, I'm so sorry. Nothing happened with Diana, honestly. It's been a strange evening and a pretty odd weekend. Can we just start again?'

'It's okay,' said Josie, 'I'm sorry too.'

She took his hand and held it.

'But I feel a bit strange. It's been such a weird night, and I think I need a bit of space. I've clearly been pressurising you about the wedding, and I feel stupid I didn't know how serious you were about your travel plans. Sorry, Harry, but I need some time to think this all over.'

Whatever Harry had been expecting, it wasn't

this. He opened his mouth and shut it again.

'What is there to think over?' he asked weakly.

'Everything,' said Josie, holding his hand, but it felt cold to the touch. 'I'm worried we may have rushed things. Perhaps we should slow it all down, delay the wedding–'

Delay the wedding? Harry felt seriously alarmed now. He'd not been sure about the wedding itself, and should have felt pleased. But a cold clutch of fear held him in its grip. What if *delay* the wedding, meant *cancel* the wedding? He'd always felt so lucky to have found Josie, and amazed that someone as gorgeous as her had chosen him. Maybe she was the one getting cold feet? Perhaps she didn't want him at all, and his worst fears were going to come to pass.

'Look, all this hypnosis stuff has clearly played around with all our minds,' he said. 'This is nothing. We'll get over it. I'm sure we can work it out. I never meant to hurt you.'

'You haven't,' said Josie. 'It's okay, really. I hope you and Di are very happy together. Now if you don't mind, I have some serious thinking to do. I'll see you later.' With that, she got up and walked away.

Harry slumped back with his head in his hands. Now what? Josie sounded like she had been really serious. What if she left him? He loved her now more than anything. He'd been a prize idiot, and it could cost him dear.

Josie walked away from Harry, feeling oddly numb. It was as if a veil had been lifted from her eyes. Once she'd got over the shock of seeing

Diana and Harry together, she'd known what she had to do. If Harry was having doubts about their relationship, now was the time to say it. Better now than later, and at least it would stop her worrying that her parents secretly felt she was making a mistake.

She had been so thrilled to see him again at Amy's wedding, remembering how well they'd got on when they dated at university, and had thrown herself headlong into the relationship. She'd wanted it to work, she'd wanted to get married. She'd got so caught up with the excitement of a wedding, she'd forgotten the important person, Harry. And maybe she'd pushed him away. If he ended up in Di's arms, she only had herself to blame.

The mist had come up even thicker now, so Josie was a little uncertain of the way. Which path had she come down? The trouble was, in the dark and in this mist, they all looked the same. She struck off to the left, feeling sure that was the direction she'd come in, but in only a few moments, she realised she'd lost her way.

Bushes loomed at her alarmingly and the path she was on grew smaller and smaller until it vanished altogether, and she found herself scrambling through undergrowth to get out into the open.

'Oh.' She'd arrived by chance at the open-air theatre. Should she go in, or should she just call it a night? There seemed no point pursuing this hypnotism thing, it had been such a disaster.

She was about to turn back, but then she noticed the gate was open, and a faint voice was declaiming, 'I know a bank where the wild thyme blows...'

Intrigued, Josie pushed open the gate and walked in.

1998: Bron

She was coming out of the hotel, just as he was entering it. Swathed in furs, her hair covered with a scarf, eyes hidden behind dark glasses, her lips, bright red in a cruel smile. He hadn't seen her for five years, but he'd have recognised her anywhere. Still the same, beautiful Tati. A bit sadder and wiser now, perhaps, but for all the talk in the tabloids of how Tati had lost 'it' – whatever 'it' was – she would always remain beautiful to him.

'Bron,' she said, 'what a delight.'

Her voice was dripping with sarcasm, and he felt a sharp blow in the pit of his stomach. Why did she always have to be so unkind to him?

'The pleasure's all mine,' he responded, cursing himself for still getting that weak-kneed feeling in her presence. It was that damned perfume. Got him every time.

'Still toiling away behind the cameras?' her smile said it all; you've lost it, career over, just like me.

'How's rehab?' It was a low blow, but the pain she perpetually caused him, and the memory of the way she'd treated him still rankled.

'I've been clean for three years!' she snapped.

222

'I've just been meeting my agent, if you must know. A possible part in Hollywood.'

'London's loss is Hollywood's gain,' said Bron, with only the slightest trace of irony.

'Hmm, well it's not a done deal,' she said, 'so not a word, understood?'

'My lips are sealed,' Bron bowed politely.

She softened slightly. 'You always were a gentleman, Bron,' she said.

There was a pause and then she said quickly, 'I hear you're married. I hope you're luckier than I was.'

And then she was gone in a blur of scarves and perfume, and Bron stood looking after her, not sure if he felt happy or sad.

Part Three

The Course of True Love

'I know a bank where the wild thyme blows,
Where oxlips and the nodding violet grows.
Quite over-canopied with luscious woodbine,
With sweet musk-roses and with eglantine.'
                    A Midsummer Night's Dream:
                                Act II, Scene 1

'People enjoy what I do. I enjoy what I do, otherwise I
wouldn't do it. Do I owe them anything? No, I don't
think so. It's their choice after all.'
        Freddie Puck: interview with *Loaded;* 2000

Chapter Nineteen

Diana was hacking her way through the bushes. Leaving the theatre, she'd decided the best thing she could do was to go home and get some sleep. This evening had turned into a total farce, and she just wanted it to be over, so she could forget all about it, before she made an even bigger fool of herself.

But with the mist now fully entrenched on the cliffs, she had become lost within minutes and ended up in some woods, where owls hooted, creatures rustled and there were all sorts of mysterious and intimidating noises. Before long the path petered out, and she found herself scrambling under branches and pushing her way through nettles and brambles, before tumbling into a hedge, from which she was now unceremoniously pulling herself. She was grateful for her fleece, which not only was keeping her warm as the temperature dropped but had stopped her arms from being completely scratched to bits, though she'd stung her hands after grabbing a nettle by mistake, and her hair, which had been in a very fetching up-do, was now straggling round her face. She was filthy dirty and very, very cross. So the last voice she wanted to hear was Ant's.

'Di, is that you?' he said.

Emerging from the mist like a phantom, Ant hove into view.

'Hang on, I'll help you out of there.'

Great, now her humiliation was complete.

'Don't you dare laugh,' Diana said, trying to summon what little dignity she had left as Ant pushed brambles and bracken out of his way to reach her.

'Watch out, there are some stingers there – oh.'

Ouch. Ant's warning had come too late; Diana simultaneously put her hand in among the nettles, and accidentally dragged her leg through them as she stumbled through the gap.

'Damn, that hurts.'

Diana wrung her hand, and checked Ant suspiciously for laughter, but he seemed surprisingly solicitous. Perhaps she'd underestimated his capacity for chivalry.

'Here, let me find you a dock leaf. Hang on.'

Ant half dragged, half yanked Diana the rest of the way out of the bushes and sat her down.

'Where's it stinging?'

'Everywhere,' said Diana crossly, then, aware that she might be appearing like a prima donna, said, 'I'm scratched everywhere, but the sting's on my leg.'

'Oh, I'm just going to rub this dock leaf on it.'

'What are you doing?' said Diana in alarm. The first time Ant had touched her leg, on around their second or third date, she'd got into all sorts of trouble. She could still remember the treacherous feelings of excitement, nerves and delicious anticipation as if it were yesterday. She had no intention of her body betraying her in that way now.

'It will make it feel better, honestly,' he said.

And to Diana's surprise, it did. Whatever was in the leaf soothed the stinging sensation, and soon it had gone altogether.

'That's amazing,' she said. 'How did you know how to do that?'

Ant shrugged his shoulders.

'Dunno, I just do. Seriously, did you never rub dock leaves on your leg as a kid? I thought everyone did.'

'City girl through and through, me. I don't think I ever saw a nettle till I left home,' Diana said. She looked at Ant suspiciously. 'What's with you? You're not normally this helpful.'

'Blame it on Freddie. He apparently threw in a little, *you're going to be responsible for everyone* thing into my hypnosis experience. It's a right pain in the arse. I've sent him to find Harry and Josie and get them talking again. Then I'm going get him to make me irresponsible again.'

'I think I prefer the responsible version,' said Diana.

'I don't,' said Ant with feeling.

'That's because the real you is an arse,' said Diana. 'Take it from one who knows, you're much better like this.'

'We'll have to disagree on that,' said Ant. 'I do not want to be responsible for everyone. Especially not you.'

'There's no need for you to,' Diana bristled. The real, obnoxious Ant was in there after all.

'Di, you can't have Harry. I saw the way you looked at him,' said Ant, more gently then he expected. 'It'll ruin everything.'

'I don't know what I feel about Harry,' said Di,

229

'I'd never thought of him like that till tonight. This hypnotism has muddled everything up.'

'Maybe Freddie can fix it so we go back to normal,' said Ant.

'So now what?'

'I said I'd wait here for Freddie and Bron,' said Ant.

'I suppose I could stay with you,' said Diana, though not entirely relishing the prospect. 'I doubt Harry and Josie want to see me, and I've nothing else to do.'

Harry wandered through the mist, also lost in more ways than one. He wished he'd kept his mouth shut, and not mentioned anything about his travel plans. Then he might be lost, but at least Josie would be at his side. Why had he opened his big mouth?

Because it's true, a voice said in his head, and he realised with sudden clarity it was. He loved Josie, truly, with all his heart, and would do anything for her, but he also wanted to travel, see the world, have a proper attempt at being a travel journalist, instead of marking time at the *Hornsey Echo*. If he hadn't met Josie again, he'd have probably been off by now. But he had, and fallen head over heels with her. In the first flush of new romance and the excitement of getting married, his plans had fallen by the wayside. No wonder she hadn't taken them seriously. He'd forgotten to take them seriously himself. If he found her, Harry thought, and explained it properly, maybe she'd understand. This was just a blip in their relationship, the first no doubt of many. He needed to find Josie as quickly as possible and put things right.

He'd been walking aimlessly for about an hour before he realised he must have gone round in a circle. The bush and rock he'd seen half an hour ago loomed up once more.

'Can this sodding evening get any worse?' he said, sitting down in exasperation. If ever he needed a fag it was now.

'Harry? Is that you?' A voice came out of the gloom, and Auberon Fanshawe lurched towards him. 'I keep getting lost in all this fog.'

'Me too,' said Harry. 'What are you doing?'

'The idea was that I'd find you and bring you back to Freddie for a little – erm – hypnotic re-adjustment, so we can start again.'

'So it *is* Freddie's fault,' said Harry. 'I should have known this hypnosis thing was a bad idea.'

'Steady on,' said Auberon. 'You were supposed to wake up next to Josie. But you didn't.'

'No, because when I got back, she was chatting to Diana and oh–'

'Diana fell in love with the first person she saw – you. So if I can get you back to Josie and Freddie and he puts you all under again, Josie can forget what she saw, and then Freddie can make Diana forget she's in love with you.'

'That easy?'

'That easy.'

'Okay, what are we waiting for?'

'Right, good,' said Auberon. 'Off we go, then.'

'Er, which way?' said Harry.

'This way,' said Auberon firmly. 'I know I haven't been down here before.'

231

Harry followed Auberon down a path that had cleared a little as the mist escaped. He was damned if he was going to get lost again. Not now there was a chance to put things right.

Josie came into the theatre to see Mike Slowbotham standing dramatically declaiming his lines.

'Miss Okeby,' he rushed forwards expectantly.

'Erm, sorry, no,' said Josie. Oh, God, please don't let Mike come on to her. That would be too much to bear after the trials of this evening.

'Oh, it's you. Darling little Josie, how are you?' he said exuberantly. Nicola had spent many years on the committee of the local theatre, and Josie had been darling little Josie nearly all her life, much to her disgust.

'I have the most exciting news to impart,' Mike said portentously. 'We will soon be graced with the presence of that angel of the small screen, that beauty, that wondrous being, the divine Tatiana Okeby, treading the very ground we walk on. And then I hope she will consent to be mine.'

'Right,' said Josie. 'And she knows this, does she?'

It sounded most unlikely, and she wondered if Freddie Puck could be somehow involved.

'Without a doubt,' said Mike. 'Tatiana and I are soulmates, two halves of a whole. You saw her last night, in the pub, how she stood up for me. I've finally met someone who can match me in every way. Tatiana is perfect.'

'Well, good luck with that,' said Josie. 'I think she's just intending for you to give her a part in your production.'

'Production? Of course she's going to have a leading role, as befits the leading lady in my life.'

'Oh, God, you really mean it, don't you?' Josie laughed out loud, forgetting her own troubles for a moment. Mike had always had delusions about his ability to attract women, but this took the biscuit. 'Sorry to disappoint you, but I think you might be punching a tad above your weight, there.'

The door creaked open behind them and Tatiana swept in.

'Where do you want me, darling,' she said. 'I can't wait to begin.'

Mike looked as if all his Christmases had come at once.

'Right, erm, okay,' he began, voice squeaking (perhaps he wasn't as confident as he appeared), 'I thought we could start with...'

Josie wondered what she should do. She still hadn't sorted out the mess in her head about Harry and the wedding yet, and wasn't quite ready to find him. She sat down instead. This could be fun, she thought. May as well stay and watch.

Ant felt very strange, sitting here with Di. Something about the intimacy of putting the dock leaf on her leg had sparked something. Regret? Maybe... Why had he let her go all those years ago? Till their split, he'd thought her the best thing that had ever happened to him. Yes, he knew the reasons she'd given him later, but why had he never told her how he'd felt about it? *Because she never gave you a chance.* The thought

233

came unbidden, and he realised it was true. Suddenly he wanted her to hear him out, as she hadn't all those years ago.

'So go on, now we're alone, answer the question I asked you last night,' he said.

'What question was that?' said Diana, looking uncomfortable.

'Why you hate me so much,' he said. 'You do realise you never actually told me.'

Diana rolled her eyes.

'You're bringing that up now?'

'Why not?' he said. 'It's the first time we've had a chance to properly talk all weekend. You never gave me the chance before.'

'Maybe I don't want to talk,' said Diana.

'And maybe I do,' said Ant.

'Why? What good will it do? It's a long time ago. We were in love. You were a bastard. End of story.'

'Because it was good, wasn't it?' he said softly. 'I'm not making that up. At one point I thought...'

A memory sprang unbidden into his head, of having brunch with Di and looking across the table at her and realising how very lucky he was. It hadn't just been good; it had been amazing.

'Well, you thought wrong,' said Diana, savagely ripping out his memory. 'Look, what is this? Do you want to make amends for what you did? You had your chance. It's too late.'

'That's the thing, though,' said Ant. 'I've never known what it was that I did wrong. As far as I knew everything was fine, and then you ditched me in front of everyone. It was humiliating.'

'Humiliating? Humiliating?' Diana practically screamed. 'I'll give you humiliating. Ant, I lost our baby all alone in a foreign hospital and you weren't there. It wasn't just humiliating, it damn near broke my heart.'

Ant felt like he'd been punched in the stomach. Despite what Diana may have thought of him, he still felt the pain of that loss, though over the years he'd buried it deep.

'But at the time I didn't even know you were pregnant,' he protested. 'And it was my baby too.'

'And when I came out looking for you, there you were, cosied up with Sian. All those messages I left. And you never came.'

He heard the catch in her throat, and instinctively leaned over to touch her. But she shook him off and got up.

'You broke my heart, Ant,' she said, getting up. 'And I don't think I can ever forgive you.'

'What messages?' said Ant, puzzled, to her departing back. 'I never got any.'

Chapter Twenty

'Okay,' said Harry, after they'd gone round in circles for the tenth time. 'Admit it, you're just as lost as I am. Have you any idea where Freddie is?'

'Can't get a signal on this damned phone,' admitted Bron sheepishly. 'The only thing it's good for at the moment is as a torch.'

'You won't get one up here,' said Harry. 'I think there are only about three places in Tresgothen that you can get a signal. I swear one of them is on my in-laws' roof.'

Possible ex-in-laws, Harry corrected himself. Auberon was putting a lot of faith in Freddie's skills, and what if he got it wrong again?

'I think we should try going downhill,' said Harry. 'We keep heading upwards, and I really don't fancy tumbling off a cliff in the fog.'

'Good idea,' said Auberon.

They found a path that Harry didn't think they'd taken before, and wandered down it before it gave way and opened up towards a clearing, at the edge of which a gate attached to a stone wall lurched out of the fog.

'Aha!' said Harry. 'I do believe that's the theatre. Isn't that where Freddie was headed? Josie seemed determined to go there.'

'With any luck,' said Auberon.

'With any luck, what?' said Freddie, who was leaning against the wall looking nonchalant. 'Shh, I've got Will in there, secretly recording Tati and that Slowbotham fellow. It's hilarious.'

'Sorry?' Harry was confused.

'Another little unexpected bonus of the project,' said Freddie with a mischievous grin. 'Bron has a long-running feud with Tati which goes back into the mists of time. We thought we'd have a little fun with her while she's here.'

Bron looked a tad uncomfortable when Freddie said this. 'You won't be too unkind, will you, Freddie?'

In the dim recesses of his mind Harry seemed to remember his mum going on about how Bron and Tati were like the Taylor and Burton of light entertainment. He could even vaguely remember how distraught she'd been when their relationship had ended for good. 'It's so tragic,' she'd said, 'those two are star-crossed lovers if ever I saw them.'

'Do you know if Josie is in there?' said Harry. 'I have to see her.'

'Hold your horses, mate,' said Freddie. 'This requires very careful handling. I think the best way to do this is if we go back to basics. I put you under again, and we'll start from scratch.'

'And Josie won't be angry with me anymore?' said Harry. He wondered if this actually was the best way to resolve their differences; there was the small matter of him wanting to go travelling to sort out.

'Can guarantee it,' said Freddie, 'don't you worry about a thing.' Harry just had to hope he wasn't crossing his fingers behind his back.

Diana strode away from Ant in a blind fury. She was shaken, rocked to the core. Why had Ant had to go and bring that all up again? She'd just about coped with seeing him this weekend by blanking out all the really bad stuff, but having him bring it up again had really shocked her. She'd worked so hard at forgetting, hardening herself up, never letting herself get too close to anyone, and now... With a few words he'd ripped away those barriers. She felt pathetic, but the gentle way Ant had touched her leg had awoken something in her, brought her back to the time when they had been into each other.

Back then, she remembered now, she'd woken

every day to a fuzzy world of blissful imaginings. A world where every day she'd known she would meet Ant, that Ant (or Tony as she'd known him then) was in her life and all was right with the world. It hadn't even been all about the sex either – though that had been fantastic, which was a new experience for Diana at the time. But there had been something more. Every time she saw him, she'd felt dizzy with delight that he was hers and that she was his. Every hour spent away from him had been an agony; every reunion sweeter than the last. And then, like the greenest girl in the world, she'd fallen pregnant and her world had collapsed.

She'd tried to tell Ant, the night they'd been tobogganing together, but the moment had passed and then she hadn't known how. A further two weeks had elapsed, when she and Ant had been so busy working separate shifts there'd barely seen each other. Thinking about it now, Sian had been in charge of the rotas. She wondered if? – no, surely Sian hadn't been that devious?

And then on the evening she'd planned to tell Ant, she'd started bleeding. No one else knew about the pregnancy, Diana had hugged her secret to herself, not wanting anyone to know till he did. Frantically she'd tried to get hold of Ant, but he wasn't at his chalet, and she remembered too late that he'd agreed to do a late shift. She told Sian, sure that she would pass the message on, and then gone alone in a taxi to the hospital, where they'd confirmed she was losing her baby. Sian had offered to come with her, but at the time, Di had been so desperate for her to find Ant, she'd begged her to stay and look for him.

She'd stayed overnight, waiting and waiting for Ant, certain he would have got away, and come to find her in her hour of need. But he hadn't come, and she'd sat in her wretched hospital bed, sobbing and alone. It was the greatest betrayal of her life, and part of her had never got over it.

And when she'd been discharged and got back, there was a text saying *You OK Babe? Missed you earlier. Bar later?* She'd left her phone at home in her hurry to get away.

So she'd gone to the bar, and he'd been with Sian. The full force of that betrayal and the sense of loss she'd had that evening hit her again. She'd marched straight up to him, tipped beer over his head and vowed to never let another man hurt her like that again.

Ant had tried to get in touch, but she refused to see him. She'd assumed that he'd got her messages, and couldn't be bothered to come. And that knowledge had kept her hatred of him burning long. But tonight for the first time she had doubts. 'What messages?' he'd said. Maybe he hadn't received them after all.

Ant was also lost in the past. He had been so shocked that night when Di had poured beer over his head. He'd had no idea what had happened. That poisonous cow Sian had been whispering sweet nothings in his ear – not that he'd been in the remotest bit interested in her. But Sian seemed to have been always there, drip-feeding him stuff for weeks about how Di was changing shifts to avoid him; feeding his insecurities about why a girl like Di would be with someone like him. And when Di had ditched him, Ant had assumed it was true, she'd never loved him. Like an idiot, rather than sorting it out with Di straight away, hurt pride meant he'd fallen straight into Sian's arms, as no doubt Sian had always intended. By the time he'd found about the miscarriage from a message Diana later left on his answerphone (Sian had never once mentioned it) it was too late. Diana wasn't answering his calls and refused to see him. She'd left soon afterwards to go back to the UK, and so had he, and he'd put her out of his thoughts ever since.

And the baby. He'd tried not to think about the baby. If it had lived it would have been seven or eight by now. Instead of the self-indulgent life he'd lived up until now, he'd have been a dad – been responsible. Normally the thought terrified him, but tonight it made him feel sad. It was a long time ago, but the thought of what might have been was heartbreaking. This evening, something inside him had changed. Despite insisting that Freddie de-programme him, Ant suddenly felt he was taking the easy way out. He'd ruined Di's life all those years ago, albeit unintentionally. Till tonight, he'd had no idea she'd tried to contact him before she went to hospital, believing instead she hadn't wanted to have anything to do with him. No wonder she hated him.

And thanks to his idiocy in pushing this hypnotism thing, his best friends had fallen out. He needed to go and make sure that Freddie was really making things better. And he needed to make his peace with Di. After all this time, he owed her.

'I pray thee, gentle mortal, sing again.'
Mine ear is much enamoured of thy note...'
Tatiana was really getting into character, and to her surprise, Josie was enjoying the performance. She was very good. A shame she'd never had the chance to prove it. Josie found herself hoping that this could actually be her comeback to the theatre world. She only prayed if Mike managed to put on the play he didn't elect to play Bottom himself. He was dreadful. As Tatiana lay languidly back, he pawed over her, and was blurting out 'Me thinks mistress you should have little reason for that. And yet to say the truth–' before Tatiana stopped him and said, 'Maybe we should run that through one more time, a little slower, perhaps, with pause for feeling.'
Mike's response to pausing for feeling was to take such long pauses between words that Josie was liable to nod off waiting for the next sentence. She was giggling to herself about this when there was a tap on her shoulder.
It was Freddie Puck.
'I feel responsible,' he said.
'What for?' said Josie.
'For everything that's happened tonight,' he said. 'It's my fault that you and Harry have had a row.'
'It's okay,' said Josie. 'I think I might just need some space away from him. Maybe we rushed this marriage thing.'

'Oh, bugger, much worse than I thought,' said Freddie, 'Time for you to find your safe place again. I'm going to snap my fingers and you'll fall asleep, and when you wake up the first person you meet will be the one you love.'

Josie stretched sleepily, and lay against the seat in the theatre, feeling cosy and warm. Over her head, she could hear Auberon saying anxiously, 'Isn't that a bit risky? Suppose she doesn't see Harry straight away?'

'Shh, I know what I'm doing,' said Freddie. 'Now let's leave her and go back to Harry, just to make sure he is the first person she sees when she wakes up...'

Josie stretched herself languorously on her seat. It was turning out to be a strangely entertaining evening. She dozed off, and was soon dreaming. She and Harry were in the woods dancing. It was lovely, she felt all happy and floaty. Then she turned, and there was Diana, coming towards her. Oh, good, she'd had a feeling they'd fallen out, but here she was smiling. 'Oh, Diana,' said Josie, giving her a hug. 'I'm so glad we're friends again...'

Slowly, she became aware of someone shaking her. 'Oh, Josie,' Diana was saying, tears pouring down her cheeks. 'I've been such an idiot. I'm so sorry. I've let you down so much. You're my best friend in the world.'

Josie sat up, feeling bewildered.

'Di, it's okay, sweetie. You've got nothing to be sorry about. You know I love you.'

'And I love you too, Josie,' said Diana. 'Are we still mates?'

'Of course,' said Josie. And leant forward and planted a smacker on Diana's lips. 'I'll love you for ever. You're my one and only.'

Chapter Twenty-One

'You what?' Diana was stunned. Had she heard what she thought she'd just heard? As Josie leant forward to grab her, she realised she had.

'Gerroff me, what are you doing?'

'Don't be like that, Di,' said Josie. 'Don't you see we're meant to be together?'

'No,' said Diana firmly, 'we really really aren't. I mean you're my best mate, and I love you dearly, but...'

'See, you said it,' said Josie, 'you said the L word.'

'I meant love as in a *sister*,' said Diana.

'Oh, you silly,' said Josie. 'Don't be shy. We're all grown-ups here. You know you feel the same way.'

Diana started to edge her way backwards.

'I don't, Josie, honestly I don't,' said Diana. 'Hot-blooded hetero me. I mean, I've got nothing against lesbians. Some of my best friends are lesbians, including apparently you, which is a surprise – and is fine – but seriously, girls don't do it for me.'

Josie had a scary gleam in her eye, as if she wasn't prepared to be thwarted.

Oh dear.

'Look, I understand,' she said grabbing Diana's hand and clutching it hard as if she'd never let it go. 'You're in denial. It's been sudden–'

'You can say that again,' said Diana.

'But you don't know what you're missing. Just think of it, how wonderful it would be if the two of us were living together.'

'Yeah, I remember that,' said Diana, 'we were flatmates, I used to nag you about tidying up. And then you fell in love with Harry.'

'Harry, Shmarry,' said Josie airily. 'I was blind then. But now I can see. Don't you get it? We're meant to be together?'

'I don't think so,' said Diana.

'Just think of the fun we'll have,' urged Josie. 'Two girls, chilling out in our onesies, being able to watch all the chick flicks we want to, whenever we want to–'

'I'm more of a horror film girl myself,' said Diana.

'The house will be spotless–'

'Yeah, right,' said Diana. Josie, having been waited on all her life, didn't 'do' housework.

'And best of all–'

'What?' said Diana, wondering at what revelation was about to pour from Josie's lips...

'The loo seat will never be left up!' said Josie triumphantly. 'Come on Di, embrace your inner lesbian. You know it makes sense.'

'Right, going now,' said Diana, extricating herself from Josie's hand with difficulty. She ran down the aisle to escape her friend. But Josie was too fast for her.

'Ooh, playing hard to get,' she said. 'I like it.'

'Nooo, this cannot be happening,' said Diana. 'This isn't real, Josie, Freddie's hypnotised us, remember?'

'It's real to me,' laughed Josie.

Di tried to run in the opposite direction, but Josie blocked her.

'You won't get far,' said Josie with a grin. 'You know I'm faster than you.'

Of course, another sodding thing that Josie was better at than her.

'Oh God,' moaned Diana, 'someone, please get me out of here!'

Ant had pounded all the way down the path and quickly reached the theatre, where he found Freddie standing over Harry saying, 'When you wake up, you will see Josie and it will be as if your argument never happened...'

'Did you tell Josie the same thing?' said Ant.

'More or less,' said Freddie.

'What was it, more or less?' said Ant.

'I told her when she woke up she'd fall in love with the first person she saw.'

'You idiot,' said Ant, 'what happens if the first person is one of us?'

'But it won't be,' said Freddie, 'because you're going to stay back while Harry goes in.'

'Did Di pass this way, by the way?' said Ant, trying to keep things casual.

'Not that I've seen,' said Freddie. He turned his attention back to Harry.

'Now, Harry, go get her.' Freddie gently propelled Harry through the creaking gate to the theatre and underneath the archway, where Ant suddenly heard a squeal of, 'Bloody hell, Josie, don't you dare do that again!'

As Harry walked into the theatre, arms wide open, saying, 'Josie, I am so sorry, I truly love you, please let's start again,' Diana leapt over the seats and came tearing towards them.

'You've got to help me, please!' she said. 'Josie's gone mad and thinks she's in love with me.'

'I don't think,' said Josie with a lascivious wink, 'I know. Diana, you're what's been missing all my life.'

'That should make bedtime more interesting,' said Ant. 'Honestly Harry, you lucky bugger.'

'Who said anything about him?' said Josie. 'I'm so done with *him*. All men are good for is providing sperm. I'm sure Diana and I can get along just fine without you two.'

'Freddie, what on earth's going on? Josie's gone mad,' said Harry in disbelief.

'You have to admit it is quite funny,' said Freddie. 'I've never had a reaction like that before. Fascinating.'

'Fascinating? You think it's *fascinating*? You wouldn't say that if it was happening to your fiancée,' said Harry. 'Do something!'

'Okay, point taken,' said Freddie looking a tiny bit remorseful. 'Josie, sweetheart, I think you need to have a little sleep again, while we think things through.'

'No chance,' said Josie. 'You're not going to get me that way again, not now I've found the love of my life.'

And with that she bounded down the stage and headed off round a path at the side of the cliff.

Harry raced after Josie and Ant followed him.

'Sorry.' he shouted as he barged past Tatiana Okeby and Mike Slowbotham who were standing open-mouthed, looking at them. 'Bit of a crisis.'

Good God, could this evening get any madder?

Josie felt ridiculously light-hearted. Falling in love with a girl was the most fabulous thing. They could paint each other's nails, sit down and chat about make-up for hours. It would be so much fun. Like having a sister as well as a lover. Josie had always wanted a sister. Josie felt all girlish and giddy. She'd never felt so light and happy before. It was the most wonderful feeling.

After a while, she grew weary, and finding a bench that looked out to sea, sat down. Never in her life had she felt more content. Josie yawned slightly. All this excitement had made her feel sleepy. Maybe she could just lie down and take a little nap...

Soon Josie was dreaming. She was in a wood, a dark, spooky wood, and she had lost her way. Somehow, she knew she had got things wrong and she needed badly to find her way back to someone, but who? Her path was blocked with brambles which scratched her arms, as she fought her way through. She had to find her way back; had to make things right.

Eventually, she saw a light flickering on and off in the distance, and she made her way towards it. She could just make out the shape of a large wall, and a tower behind it. Gradually she hacked her way through the branches, more determined than ever that she must find her way to whoever was on the other side of the wall.

Breaking through the last tangles of brambles, and could it be? Roses? Josie ran towards the wall, where she found a gate creaking slightly open. Without thinking, she pushed her way through, and saw the source of the light, a lantern hanging above a gate, by the entrance to the tower. She grabbed the lantern, and raced up the stairs two at a time, determined now to find the person she knew was waiting for her.

And finally at the top of the stairs, there he was curled up on a sofa, fast asleep, with a gentle smile playing on his lips.

'Oh, Harry,' said Josie, and kissed him.

Ant and Harry were both exhausted by the time they found Josie curled up asleep on the bench.

'She can't half run fast,' grumbled Ant. 'I'm knackered.'

'She's used to it,' said Harry, leaning over and breathing fast. He had a massive stitch in his side. 'She grew up doing cross country round here. Even at home she does mad long runs all the time. I can't keep up with her. Now what?'

'Wait for Freddie to sort this out, I guess,' said Ant, 'and hope she doesn't wake up before he gets here.'

Harry threw himself onto the grass and let out a snort. 'I suppose it is quite funny in a way,' he said.

'What is?'

'Josie, falling for Di. The look on her face ... priceless.'

'I still think you should go for a threesome,'

248

said Ant. 'I mean, you and Di...'

'...Was never meant to happen,' said Harry firmly. 'It's this bloody hypnotism. It's all gone horribly wrong.'

'I know,' said Ant. 'Sorry. It's my fault. I should never have suggested it.'

'You've found her then,' Freddie came puffing up the hill, Diana and Bron behind him. 'I'm sorry, I had no idea she'd do that. I think the best thing now is if we start again.'

'Don't you think you've done enough damage?' said Harry. 'Can't you just get us back to square one?'

'As you wish,' said Freddie. 'Let's have a little reboot. When I snap my fingers you will all go to sleep. And when you wake none of this will have happened. Everyone will be in love with the person they should be.'

Harry wasn't even aware of feeling sleepy this time. One minute he was awake and the next he was in a deep dreamless sleep, feeling utterly content.

2002: Tatiana

'You can't even get me on *Celebrity Big Brother?* What kind of agent are you?' Tatiana practically screamed down the phone. 'I cannot possibly be less well known than Melinda Messenger.'

'Sorry, Tats,' Sally Peasebottom said. 'They say you're not well remembered enough.'

'Me, not remembered? God, the public are fickle.' Tatiana took a drag on her cigarette. 'What about this new Jungle thingy. I hear Tony Blackburn is up for it. If an old has-been like him can get in, surely it must be a shoo-in for me?'

'I'll try,' said Sally with a sigh, 'but don't hold your breath. Word on the street is they've signed everyone up already.'

'So it's another season doing panto for me, then?' Tatiana drooped. Oh, God. How had it come to this?

'Looks like it,' said Sally, 'but I'll do my best.'

Tatiana put the phone down and stubbed out her fag. She looked at herself critically. A few crows' feet here and there. But not too bad. Maybe she should try this new Botox thing people were talking about. Or a face-lift. Her hair still had a natural sheen and bounce, thanks to the magical hands of her favourite stylist, Colin. He could do amazing things with a bottle, that man.

She was still looking good for her age. Despite the drinking, she'd managed to invest her soap star money wisely, which meant the odd nip and tuck had been available to her. In the good times she'd always remembered the bad, and now the bad were rolling round again, it was just as well she had...

But what would she do when the parts dried up? She was still occasionally in the papers with stories about her latest toyboys – usually an escort she'd paid to hang on her arm – but that wasn't enough to keep the wolf from the door. She was in danger of being a washed-up has-been.

And that wasn't even the worst of it. The thing

was, her life felt so empty. There had been no one significant for a number of years, and she'd screwed up the one fleeting moment she might have had to get back with Bron. How she could have done that kiss and tell demolition with the *News of the Screws,* she couldn't now tell. She still curled up in shame when she thought about it. No wonder he didn't want anything to do with her, even though she'd read recently he'd split from his wife. Tati couldn't blame him either. If Bron had done that to her, she'd never have wanted to see him again. But she'd been a different person then. Drink and drugs had a lot to answer for.

And now, here she was, middle-aged, fast losing her looks, with her career going down the pan. And so very, very alone.

Chapter Twenty-Two

Ant stretched and yawned. He was sitting on the ground, on top of a cliff, looking out at a calm and placid sea. It was very dark, the moon shining faintly through the mist, swirling clouds spreading their tendrils across the cliffs. What was he doing here? He had only vague memories of the evening so far. They'd come up to the Standing Stones and then ... it was all a bit patchy. Though he had a feeling he'd been doing an awful lot of running; he was aching all over.

He looked around. Josie was asleep on the

251

bench and suddenly it hit him square between the eyes, and he realised how blind he'd been. Holy crap. He felt like his heart was about to explode with happiness. *Josie*. Josie was what he'd been searching for his whole life. How could he not have seen that before? Beautiful, gorgeous Josie. It had always been her, from that very first moment in the uni bar. If she did but know it. But how could he have forgotten?

Next to him, he heard a groan, and a 'Where the hell are we?'

Oh. Diana. He had a feeling they had been at odds this evening and somehow it was important – that he was supposed to have sorted something out. But he couldn't remember.

'On top of a cliff. Last thing I remember, I was talking to Freddie, and–' he suppressed a yawn, 'then I woke up here.'

'Do you think this daft experience is over yet?' said Diana. 'I really want to go home.'

Harry stirred. Ant hadn't clocked him next to Josie, and suddenly feelings of utter jealousy flooded over him. It was so unfair. Why did Harry – quiet, dull Harry – get someone as gorgeous as Josie? It was all wrong.

'Hi, Josie,' Harry said, a little shyly. 'Are we okay now?'

Josie woke up and the smile on her face made Ant light up inside. But then she ruined it by flinging her arms around Harry and saying, 'Oh babe. I was dreaming I'd lost you, and then I found you.' Ant felt a knife twist in his heart.

Josie got up, a little flustered. First she'd flung

her arms around Harry, thinking they were alone, and then she'd spotted Ant and Diana were there; and Ant seemed to be radiating negativity on a major scale – but why? Surely he was happy about Harry and Josie, wasn't he? She vaguely remembered she and Harry had been arguing, and that Ant had been supportive, but now the evening's squabbles seemed to have diminished from a major storm to a minor squall. Josie couldn't work out what all the fuss had been about, why she'd got so angry. She and Harry could sort whatever it was out. They could do anything together. She was sure of that.

'I think I've had enough of this nonsense,' she said. 'Let's go home.'

'Good idea,' said Diana. She looked quite sad and lonely, and Josie felt for her friend. She hoped that Di didn't resent her own good fortune. 'I think I've had enough. Is this the way back?' She got up and walked off in the wrong direction, till Josie called her back.

'This has been an odd evening and no mistake,' said Harry, holding her hand and squeezing it tightly as they made their way up the track towards the theatre. 'But everything's fine now, isn't it?'

'Yes, of course it is,' said Josie, kissing him on the lips.

'Do you have to?' Ant sounded quite put out, which was unlike him. He was normally the one to make a bawdy comment.

'Sorry,' said Josie. 'I'm just so glad everything's back to normal.'

They had nearly reached the theatre when Freddie emerged. 'Everything all right now?' he said. 'Good, good. Then we can start filming again.'

'Actually, Freddie, we were all thinking of calling it a night,' said Josie. 'We're knackered.'

'But it's not yet midnight,' said Freddie persuasively. 'And in order to see if my experiment has worked, you should be up at the Standing Stones at midnight plighting your troth. At least hang around till then.'

'Do we have to?' groaned Diana. 'I want my bed.'

'It was in the contract you all signed,' said Freddie. 'And I'm afraid there won't be any money if you don't fulfil that part of the contract.'

Josie hesitated. She knew Harry had wanted the money to do something special for their wedding night. And although it wasn't much, now Diana had lost her job, she probably couldn't afford to turn it down.

'The money would be nice,' said Harry.

'I could do with some extra dosh,' said Diana grumpily. 'Okay, I'm in.'

'What about you, Ant?' Josie asked.

Ant shrugged his shoulders. 'I'm happy to go wherever you are,' he said enigmatically. 'Come on, let's get it over with.'

Harry felt he'd spent a whole night climbing up and down this wretched cliff. He'd know his way round perfectly by the end of the night. Freddie was keen for them to go back to the Standing Stones where they'd started from. It seemed like a daft idea to him. Ant and Diana were hardly likely to declare undying love and he and Josie –

well, if he were going to do anything like that, he'd rather do it in private, without a camera crew watching. But money was money, and he couldn't afford to be choosy.

They made good time back to the Stones. The mist was beginning to clear, and there was a clear view of the moon again, and the stars sparkled and shone. Harry looked up at the sky, getting a sense of how small he was in an infinitely huge universe. Whatever troubles he and Josie had had seemed petty now.

It was still quite warm, despite being so late, and a soft breeze played on his face. He looked at Josie as the wind ruffled her fair curls, marvelling at how someone as beautiful as her could have chosen him. He loved everything about her: the way when she smiled it lit up her whole face, the little dimple on her chin; her clear blue eyes; her heart-shaped face; her flawless complexion. If nothing else came of tonight, at least he'd learned how utterly, irrevocably in love he was with Josie. There was still a huge discussion to be had about what they did about his career, and whether or not to go travelling after the wedding, but he felt they could weather anything now. They were together, united, a complete pair. And nothing else really mattered.

When they arrived, everyone sat down looking more than a little self-conscious.

'Now what?' said Diana, who seemed very grumpy, and, he felt, somewhat sad.

'Now we wait,' said Freddie with a smile. 'We wait and see…'

Diana had never felt so discontented in her life. Unlike the others, who appeared to either have blanked out what had happened, or had genuinely forgotten, she remembered snatches of the evening so far. She was filled with mortification at the memories; her dancing with Harry and *Josie* kissing her were two moments that were making her go hot under the collar. How could Josie be acting as if neither had happened? And then there was that painful conversation with Ant. Diana was uncomfortably aware that she might have got it a bit wrong with Ant, who had been kinder to her then she'd expected. She didn't want to let him back in her life, ever – least of all by being sympathetic. She could bear his scorn, but not his pity.

Her watch showed that it was nearly midnight. Midnight on a Midsummer's Eve... She took a sharp intake of breath. Maybe anything was possible. Diana had a feeling of anticipation, of waiting, as if something momentous was about to occur...

'We should have dressed up as druids,' said Josie dreamily, leaning back on Harry, clearly feeling the same. 'I feel all tingly, as if something amazing is about to happen.'

'Yeah, right,' said Ant. 'I didn't know you were some New Age hippy.'

'I'm not,' said Josie looking a bit hurt. 'But the setting calls for it, don't you think? I really feel that there's magic in the air tonight...'

The moon was brighter than it had been all night, the sea breeze gently blowing the remnants of the mist away. Perhaps Josie was right; perhaps it was a night when magic could happen. Diana looked at Ant, and was overcome with a sudden impulse which, try as she might, she couldn't resist. All those long-repressed feelings came rushing back – images of them kissing, of them being in bed, of them laughing, of them being together, the pair of them against the world, just the way that Harry and Josie were – came flooding back.

'Ant,' she said, slowly, as if a great truth had just been revealed to her, 'Ant.'

'Why do you keep saying my name?' Ant looked confused.

As if in a dream, and despite knowing that once the words were said they couldn't be unsaid, Di walked over to Ant's side, knelt down and said, 'This midnight, on a Midsummer's Eve, I plight my troth to you.'

Chapter Twenty-Three

'What? You like Ant now?' Josie was as stunned as Ant, who was standing open-mouthed.

'What's it to you?' said Diana. 'You've got Harry. Why should you care who I'm in love with?'

Which was true – Josie wasn't remotely interested in Ant, but for some reason it niggled her that Di suddenly was. After everything she'd said. It was none of her business, but it felt like Di wasn't being true to herself.

'I'm your friend,' she said lamely. 'And I just do. Ant's hurt you before – remember he's Teflon Tone, the guy you've hated for years – I don't want you to be hurt again.'

'It's none of your business,' said Diana. 'Besides, you can hardly take the moral high ground, considering you were chasing me round the theatre not so long ago.'

'I – I...' Oh, God, the theatre; it all came flooding back Josie flushed deep red. She'd thought she'd dreamt the theatre, and now the memories of pursuing Diana were returning with dreadful clarity.

'That wasn't me,' she said. 'That was the stupid hypnosis. And so is this. You don't really love Ant. Freddie's just been messing with your mind, like he has with the rest of us.'

Of course. It all made sense. Di was jealous of her. Josie had money, looks, Harry. Diana had nothing. Not even a job anymore. Josie took a deep breath and said, 'Look, I know you've had it tough and you've screwed things up in the past. But what makes you think Ant would suddenly be interested in you?'

'Well, Ant?' said Diana. 'How about it? We've got unfinished business after all.'

Ant's mouth snapped shut, and he attempted to articulate a response, but all that came out was a strangled gasp.

'I told you,' said Josie, 'he's so useless he can't even say it, but this is Ant we're talking about, he hasn't changed. No offence, Ant.'

'None taken,' said Ant, who seemed to have temporarily recovered the power of speech.

'You spoilt, spoilt little princess.' Josie had never seen Diana so enraged. 'You think the world revolves around you. Why can't I be happy too?'

'That's not what I'm saying–' Josie protested, but Diana was on a roll now and oblivious to anything her friend was saying.

'Why poor Harry still wants to marry you after the fuss you've made about this sodding wedding is anyone's guess,' she continued. 'All he wants to do is keep things simple, but no, *perfect* little Josie has to have her *perfect* wedding, sod what everyone else wants. He's put everything on hold for you, even his travel plans, but you don't care, do you? It's all about you. Christ, I didn't just create a bridezilla, I've created a wedding monster.'

Josie was flabbergasted. In all the years she'd known Di, she'd never been subjected to the full force of Diana's bitterness, though she'd often witnessed Di demolishing others. It was like sharp shards of glass falling on her from a great height, each more painful than the last.

'Di, that's a bit strong,' said Harry. Her hero. Why wasn't he standing up for her more? 'I think you should apologise.'

'I have nothing to apologise for,' said Diana, looking truculent and moody.

'You were out of order and should say sorry immediately,' Ant butted in.

Diana looked as if she'd been punched in the stomach.

'I might have known you'd take Miss Goody Two-Shoes' side,' said Diana bitterly. 'Three against one. Nice. I'm done here. I'm going back to the house, and tomorrow I'm going to make my own way home.'

'What about the contract?'

'What about it?' said Diana. 'I stayed till midnight; it's been an utter disaster. I'm out of here.'

'Diana–' Josie started to protest. Underneath the bravado, she could see that Di was struggling to hold it together.

'Find yourself another bridesmaid, Josie. That is, if you ever make it down the aisle, which somehow I doubt.' Getting up, Diana stormed off down the path, leaving the three of them stunned.

'And then there were three,' said Harry, trying to sound light-hearted.

'Oh, shut up, Harry,' Josie said. She was devastated. It looked as though she'd just lost her best friend.

Harry was stunned, first by Diana's declaration, and then by the bile that had spewed from her lips. He'd always seen her as Josie's feisty friend. Sure, she could be a bit sharp sometimes, but essentially she meant well. He'd had no idea that she had been harbouring such bitter thoughts against Josie. Nor that she still had feelings for Ant. She'd spent so much of the weekend on his case, it was the last thing he'd been expecting. But then again, maybe she'd been protesting too much.

'She'll get over it, Josie,' he said, putting a tentative arm round her shoulder. 'I'm sure in the morning she'll have calmed down and everything will be okay.'

'But it won't, though, will it?' said Josie, 'I only

260

wanted Di as my bridesmaid. How can I have a bridesmaid who doesn't want to speak to me?'

'Fair point,' said Ant.

Josie flopped down on the grass, and started tearing clumps of grass out of the ground. She looked as if she was pondering something. Eventually she burst out with 'Do you think she's right about the wedding? Have I been a complete nightmare about it?'

Harry said nothing, staring into the darkness, chewing his lip and wondering what to tell her. The silence that followed was almost unbearable.

'I think she deserves an answer, mate,' Ant said quietly, and Harry felt like thumping him. Since when did Ant have the monopoly on relationship advice?

'Well?' Josie looked at him. 'You do still want to get married, don't you?'

Oh God. He wasn't ready for this.

'Look, Josie, I love you, you know I do,' said Harry. 'Earlier, when I thought you'd walked out on me, I felt as if my whole world had collapsed...'

'You haven't answered my question,' Josie fixed him with those piercing blue eyes. He felt like a rabbit caught in the headlights.

'Josie, I want to spend the rest of my life with you,' he began.

'I sense a *but* here,' Josie replied.

'But it's too soon,' Harry said miserably. 'I'm not ready for marriage, there are too many things I want to do...'

'I see,' said Josie, tight-lipped, but it was clear she didn't.

'And I want to do them with you,' said Harry helplessly.

'But not married to me,' said Josie. 'I can be forever dangling at your side, but you will never commit, will you? I'm sorry, Harry. I'm an all-or-nothing kind of girl. I just can't do that.'

They stared at one another in dismay, until Josie finally looked away.

'It's very late,' she said. 'Di's right. We should go home. But at the moment I can't be around you. Can you just go away, please?'

'Do you want me to stay with you?' Why was Ant being so solicitous to Josie? It was really annoying.

'Kind offer, Ant, but I really want to be on my own,' said Josie.

'Yes, of course,' said Ant. 'Maybe we should go and see if Di's okay.'

'I don't really care,' said Josie, 'so long as you don't involve me.'

'Josie,' said Harry. 'Please, you can't mean it?'

'Just go,' she said. 'If you really loved me, you'd let me be.'

Feeling dejected and miserable, and not knowing quite what to do, Harry got up to go. It had been a disastrous evening and he wasn't sure if there was a way back from it.

Diana was furious with herself. Why had she acted on impulse like that? It was completely unlike her. Those things she'd said to Josie. She hadn't even realised she felt like that until she'd said them. And she'd made a total tit of herself in front of Ant. He wasn't interested in her anymore, and who could blame him. She'd been on his case ever since she got here. He probably thought she was winding him up. Bugger, bugger, bugger. If only she had a car, she'd drive off to find a hotel; she doubted that any of the little B&Bs in the village would open their doors to her at this time of night.

'What a sodding nightmare,' she said. Her fury had propelled her so far, but now she was slumped down and leaned against a tree, feeling utterly bereft. Her whole life seemed to be leading up to this moment: the disappointment of her parents, all the failed relationships, the loneliness – it all went back to that day in the hospital, when Ant had let her down.

Tears rolled down her cheeks. The baby. She'd made a point of never letting herself think about it. But tonight, after that conversation with Ant and everything that had happened since, she couldn't box it away anymore. Huge sobs overwhelmed her. She was hugging her knees and feeling pathetically sorry for herself, and still the tears came.

'Oh, dear, are you all right?' Auberon Fanshawe was standing before her. 'I was just going back to the theatre to meet Freddie and Will,' he said, 'and I couldn't help noticing you were a bit upset.'

Mortified, Diana tried frantically to wipe away her tears.

'It's okay,' said Auberon, 'I'm an actor, I'm used to women crying. Hell, most of the time, it's my fault they're crying. May I?'

He pointed to a patch of ground next to her,

and when she nodded sat down beside her.

'Fancy telling me what a nice girl like you is doing all alone in the woods bawling your eyes out?'

'An old trouble,' said Diana. 'One I thought I'd put behind me. Stupid really.'

'The worst kind,' said Auberon, looking rather sad. 'They have a habit of biting you on the bum.'

'You and Tatiana?' guessed Diana.

'You and...?'

'Ant,' said Diana. 'I thought he was the love of my life once, a long time ago. But he let me down really badly. And tonight I thought maybe I should let him back into my life again. But he's not interested, he's let me down again.'

'We men can be good at that,' said Auberon with a rueful sigh. 'I made a big mistake once. I've regretted it forever. You never know, your Ant may have done the same.'

'Maybe,' said Diana. 'But I doubt it.'

Ant followed Harry down the hill, feeling a mixture of emotions. Despite himself, he still felt the need to sort everything out; still felt responsible, and he felt really guilty about Diana. That had come as a bolt from the blue. What was he going to do about that? And more importantly, what about Harry and Josie? At the moment, he felt like thumping Harry. The look on Josie's face when they'd left had nearly cut him in two. She'd looked so lost and lonely.

'Why did you ask Josie to marry you if you didn't want to get married?' said Ant. 'I told you it was a bad idea.'

'I thought I did,' said Harry. 'I think I still do. But not now. Not yet. And not like this. All this wedding business. It's been like living with a demented hen for the last few months. It's all she ever talks about, and it's driving me nuts. I hadn't realised quite how bad it was till we got here and her mum ratcheted it up even more. Do you know Josie was looking up fire-eaters on the internet yesterday to have as evening entertainment? I tell you, it's insane.'

'So have a small wedding,' said Ant.

'But Josie set her heart on it being like this,' said Harry. 'I didn't want to let her down.'

'Too late for that, mate,' said Ant. 'I think you already have.'

'Thanks for the vote of confidence,' said Harry.

'So lie, then,' said Ant. 'That's what I'd do.'

'Yeah, and we all know how that goes,' said Harry.

'Meaning?' Ant bristled.

'Meaning you've never had a meaningful relationship in your life, partly because you lie. I want my relationship with Josie to be honest.'

'Then more fool you,' said Ant angrily. 'And that's not quite true. Di and I had something special once.'

'The emphasis there being on "had",' said Harry. 'You can't tell me anything about relationships.'

'I can tell you you're a bloody idiot. You have a gorgeous girlfriend and you are in serious danger of losing her.'

'Butt out of this, Ant,' said Harry. 'You know nothing about love. You're incapable of it. You've even managed, God knows how, to get Diana falling at your feet again, and you can't deal with that. You have no right to talk.'

Harry walked off into the darkness, leaving Ant fuming.

The two conflicting emotions, his loyalty to Harry and the way he was feeling about Josie, struggled to overcome one another, intertwined with a sense of responsibility towards Diana. But he realised if he went and found her now, he'd just make things worse. Bugger it, he'd tried. Harry didn't deserve her. Ant turned round and went back to search for Josie.

Chapter Twenty-Four

Harry strode on down the path, furious with bloody Ant. How dare he give him advice about his love life? How bloody dare he? As if Ant had ever really been in love. Apart from possibly whatever had gone on between him and Di, and look how that turned out. Ant had been down on the idea of him and Josie being together right from the start. He just couldn't stand for his friend to be happy.

But how happy was he, really?

Harry paused, and finding a convenient rock, sat down on it. He shivered and zipped up his fleece, glad Josie had made him wear it now. The night was colder now, and the last of the mist was dissipating. He could see the stars twinkling in the distance. It should have been a magical evening, spent in the company of the woman he loved and his best friends. Now none of them were speaking to one another. How could it have gone so badly wrong? And what did he really feel about the wedding?

Thinking back, this was his fault, Harry realised miserably. He should never have proposed when he did. He'd been thrilled to move in with Josie, and it had been enough for him. If it hadn't been for all that Halloween nonsense that Di had started, the thought of marriage wouldn't have entered his head. And he might have spent the last six months persuading Josie to come travelling with him, instead of feeling all his options were being shut down in the inexorable march to the Wedding Day. Had he not rushed things, he might have been able to explain to Josie how much he wanted to change his life, how he wanted to shake off his rut, and how much a part of that she could be.

Instead, he felt he was condemning himself to a life of stability and sensible behaviour. There was no reason why getting married shouldn't stop them travelling, but to Josie, it seemed to signal that the adventurous part of their life was over; whereas for Harry, he felt it had only just begun.

This was ridiculous. Sitting here thinking to himself wasn't going to alter anything. He just needed to go back, find Josie and have a sensible chat with her about what he really wanted. Harry felt sure if she could just give him the opportunity to explain, everything would be all right. He'd be happy enough to go along with the wedding plans if it meant that they could go travelling afterwards. Hell, if the only good thing that came out of this ridiculous hypnosis experiment was him persuading Josie to see the world with him, then it had been worth doing. Josie would surely see that too, once she'd had a chance to think about it.

With that, Harry got up and returned the way he'd come. There was only one way of finding out what Josie thought; he simply had to ask her.

'So what's the story with you and Tatiana?' said Diana, mildly amazed that she was sitting down in a wood discussing the love life of someone she'd grown up watching on TV.

'Same as you, I guess,' sighed Auberon. 'We were in love. It was all going well. She'd been pushing for an equal share on the show – it was before we were on TV, and Tati wanted her cut. Which was fair enough, but Freddie ... well Freddie felt differently. He saw Tati as a nuisance. "There are plenty more fish in the sea," he used to say, "pretty assistants are replaceable." Except Tati, Tati wasn't.'

Bron sighed again.

'I never let her see how I felt, like an idiot, and she thought I agreed with Freddie. So when she fell pregnant, she booked herself into a clinic. She got rid of our baby and never said a word to me till afterwards. When I found out, she said it wasn't my decision, it was her body.'

'She was right, wasn't she?' said Diana. 'What would have happened to her career if she'd got pregnant then?'

'To my shame, I'd probably have let her go. I didn't really think of it from her point of view. Just that the show didn't need a pregnant assistant. I was wrong, of course.'

He looked into the distance, and sighed. 'I still think about that baby, you know. I always pictured it as a she, a little clone of my Tati. She'd have been thirty by now.'

Diana sat staring into the darkness. It felt like a warm cloak around her, and she found herself finding it remarkably easy to open up to Auberon, with whom she felt a natural affinity. Hearing his story emboldened her to tell him hers.

'I lost a baby too,' she said eventually. 'And until tonight, I've spent every day of the last eight years pretending it didn't exist.'

'Was it Ant's?'

'Yes, but he didn't know, till it was too late. I hadn't got round to telling him, and then it was gone. I was barely pregnant at all.'

'So what did Ant do?'

'That's it,' said Diana. 'Nothing. I called him from the hospital, and he never came. And when I came out, I found him in the arms of my best friend. It broke my heart.'

'You never know,' said Auberon, patting her hand, 'he might regret that now. Lord alone knows I do.'

'He says he never got my messages,' said Diana, 'but I don't know whether or not I believe him.'

'Give him a chance,' said Auberon: 'Before you ruin your life with bitter regrets, like I've done.'

Give Ant a chance? It was still a strange thought, after she'd spent so many years hating him, but Auberon was right, it was time she put her past behind her.

'I'd love to,' she said sadly, 'but he's made it abundantly clear he doesn't want me.'

Ant walked back to the place where they'd left Josie, but she was no longer there. Where on earth could she have gone? Why couldn't the wretched girl stay in one place? It was infuriating.

Perhaps she'd gone back to the theatre. Harry had mentioned it earlier as the place where they'd been on their first date. Maybe if she were still feeling upset about Harry, she'd want to go there and remember a happier time.

Bloody Harry. Stealing a march on him. He'd seen Josie first, in the bar at uni. He'd been the one who got to know her; inveigled himself into her crowd, turned up at her parties, and eventually wangled an invitation down here. They'd always got on well, and Ant had intended to ask Josie out, but then Kerry or Kelly got under his skin and he'd been distracted. By the time he realised his mistake, Harry had snuck Josie out from under his nose.

At the time it had been utterly baffling. Harry was a good mate, but so quiet and retiring compared to Ant. What had Josie seen in him, that she hadn't seen in Ant? After all, she had flirted with Ant quite a lot, and never paid any attention to Harry before that week. Ant wasn't surprised it hadn't lasted after they left university and all went their separate ways. It was clearly never meant to be. Like an idiot, he hadn't kept in touch with Josie, and he was stunned when Harry had emailed him out of the blue to say they were an item again.

Ant still didn't get why Josie had chosen Harry to share her life with. He was so modest and unambitious. Surely a girl like Josie deserved someone with more get up and go? Ant had more money and prospects, was better looking, drove a faster car. Hell, even her dad liked him better than he liked Harry. The more Ant thought about it, the more furious he became. He was going to go and show her what was what. How a real man behaved. Show her just how masterfully he could sweep her off her feet. Show her what she'd been missing.

What about Harry? The responsible pricking of his conscience kept butting in. Ant ruthlessly repressed it. He hadn't got as far as this in life paying too much attention to his conscience. What *about* Harry? He'd had his chance with Josie and blown it. Now it was Ant's turn.

Josie sat for a while staring out to sea, where a pale moon was just visible through the swirling clouds. So much for the exciting magical evening Freddie had promised. She was cross with everyone: Harry for being so frustrating, Di for the things she'd said, and Ant for, well, being Ant. God knows why he'd appointed himself relationship guru for the weekend, but he'd made a dreadful fist of it. She decided she'd preferred it when he was just playing the field.

After a little while she got up. It was no good; she couldn't stay here all night. Time to get home. Even if she ended up leaving them all in

271

the annexe, and sleeping in her own bed. Thank God Mum and Dad had gone away for the night, she wouldn't have any explaining to do. Time to sort everything out tomorrow.

She was halfway down the path which led to the back of the theatre, when she saw torches dancing among the bushes.

'Hello,' called a quavering voice, sounding as if it was about to jump out of its skin any moment. 'Is anyone there? Only we're terribly lost.'

'Where on earth are you trying to get to?' Josie could make out three huddled figures in the gloom. On closer inspection she realised it was Tatiana's retinue. What on earth were they doing out here at this time of night?

'We're looking for the theatre. Tati went out hours ago, and we don't know what's happened to her. We think that that Slowbotham fellow might have done something to her.'

'He hadn't last time I saw,' said Josie with a grin. 'She was auditioning for *A Midsummer Night's Dream*.'

'Oh, thank goodness,' cried M'stard with relief. 'I've been so worried. My auras just don't feel right. I couldn't imagine what I was going to say to her agent.'

'Come with me,' said Josie, 'you're not too far away. I'll show you the way.'

2007: Tatiana

'Look can you book me in on Wednesday or not?' Tatiana said in exasperation.

'We're pretty busy,' the girl on the other end sounded both bored and vague. 'I'll ring you if there's a cancellation.'

'You do that,' said Tatiana crisply, and tried to turn her phone off. It promptly came back to life. Damned thing. She swore her new mobile required more fingers than she had.

Time was when people would have bent over backwards to have her in their salon. But these days most people didn't even recognise her. Tatiana who? To her humiliation *The Sun* had recently run a *Where Are they Now?* feature and she hadn't even been in it. Bron had. There'd been a big piece on him and Freddie and the whole *Illusions* phenomenon. The article had even mentioned they might be making a comeback. It didn't seem fair that people still remembered Bron, whereas their eyes would glaze over politely when she introduced herself, shrugging their shoulders and muttering about people being past it when they thought she wasn't listening. It was galling to think that despite everything she'd achieved, she might have been better known as Bron's Debbie McGee after all. It was so hurtful. And unfair.

Bron was still in vogue, popping up on the

occasional chat show, his and Freddie's company
going from strength to strength, thanks to some
shrewd investment in several successful movies.
And Bron had started directing Shakespeare too.
She'd always wanted to do Shakespeare. But
these days, she was even lucky to get a panto.
Thank God for UK Gold and repeat fees.

'What am I to do?' she said. 'They can't fit me
in till God knows when. My roots are showing.
It's a disaster!'

'Darling, we'll just get you booked into
Anthony's,' said Gray M'stard, her new stylist.
'Everyone's going there.'

'I need more than a new hair style,' said
Tatiana, with a sigh. 'I need to get my profile
raised. Get back on to Susan as quickly as you
can. The sooner we start, the better.'

Chapter Twenty-Five

Josie led them through the theatre, to where
Tatiana was lying prone on the stage, with Mike
hovering awkwardly around her.

Tatiana sat up, stretching languorously.

'What angel wakes me from my flow'ry bed?'
she declaimed.

'The finch, the sparrow and the lark,' warbled
Mike, woefully out of tune. 'Who would set his
wit to what?' He paused, 'sorry, just lost my
place, ah yes, let me see...'

'And thy fair virtue's force perforce doth move...'

274

'Methinks mistress…'

'No, no, no! Darling,' Tatiana held up her hand. 'You need to wait for me to finish the line. Your cue is "To swear I love thee".'

'Which of course, dear lady, I do,' said Mike, bowing ingratiatingly.

Tatiana waved him away as if swatting a gnat, 'Now carry on…'

Josie was in pieces. Mike's attempts to prove his actor credentials hadn't improved as the night wore on; he was appalling. He was trying to make Bottom seem a romantic lead, but was channelling his inner buffoon. Plus he was so loud, he kept drowning out Tatiana's lines, and Josie could see Tatiana was getting very fed up with it.

When Mike got to the line 'if I had wit enough to get out of this wood', it was all Josie could do not to burst out laughing at the look on Tatiana's face. She was probably hoping he'd do just that. Josie found herself wishing Harry was sitting here with her watching it together, laughing at Mike, rather than with Tatiana's bunch of lunatics, who kept standing up, applauding every line she delivered. She was good, though maybe not deserving of a standing ovation after delivering three lines.

Could you break off an engagement and still stay together? Josie wondered. That's what Harry seemed to be suggesting, and she wasn't sure how she felt about it. She didn't want to lose him, but how could they carry on after that?

'…And when she weeps, weeps every little flower,

Lamenting some enforced chastity.

275

Tie up my lover's tongue, bring him silently.' Tatiana finished triumphantly.

'Oh, bravo, Tati, Bravo!' M'stard stood up clapping loudly. 'Isn't she good,' he said enthusiastically, 'I say, isn't she good?'

'Marvellous, darling. Marvellous,' said Gypsy.

'You were magnificent,' said Ariadne, 'simply magnificent.'

'Thank you, darlings,' said Tatiana gracefully. 'One does one's best.'

Josie had to suppress another snigger. Poor Tatiana. Everyone around her was so unctuous and self-serving, she probably never had a true word spoken to her in her life. Or certainly not for years. Josie felt sorry for her in a way. All that fame and fortune, to end up surrounded by arse lickers and having to butter up the likes of Mike Slowbotham, who she noticed with amusement was being very touchy-feely with Tatiana.

Tatiana seemed to be responding, but Josie couldn't be sure if she was just acting. Surely she couldn't find a creep like Mike attractive, could she? However desperate she was.

'Let's run through that again,' said Tatiana, lying back down on the ground. 'Now, from the top…'

'Oh well,' thought Josie, repressing a yawn. 'I may as well stay here.'

For all she knew, the others might have all gone back to the house by now, Harry had a spare set of keys. She didn't want to go home and face whatever was there. Much better to stay put. At least she'd have a laugh.

Ant was determined to find Josie before Harry got it into his head that he needed to sort things out. Maybe if Ant got there first, she'd be prepared to listen to him. For a moment he indulged in a fantasy that he and Josie were alone on a desert island and she had agreed that he was the only man for her...

But where had she gone? He made his way down the cliff path and was nearly back in the village when he ran into Freddie, who said, 'How's it going?'

'How do you think?' said Ant. 'Can't you get anything right? Josie is over Di, but has fallen out with Harry, Di is in love with me, and I apparently am in love with Josie. What have you done to us?'

'I'll sort it, I promise,' said Freddie.

'Why not sort it this time that Josie falls for me, eh?' said Ant. 'That's what I'd call a result.'

'Hmm,' said Freddie. 'Look, I haven't seen any of the others coming this way, but I think Josie might have been heading for the theatre.'

'Right, I'm off, then,' said Ant, and he went haring back up the path. He ran and ran as if his life was depending on it. He had to get to Josie before Harry did. Soon he was puffed out and exhausted. Maybe it was time to knock the fags on the head. He was sweating profusely by the time he got back to the theatre, but there was no sign of Harry, so that was something.

He found Josie sitting among Tatiana's retinue, trying not to giggle as they fell over each other in their bids to get her attention. Tatiana was looking as if she was finding Mike's attentions a bit too much. He appeared to have developed into a very amorous Bottom...

'You okay?' Ant sat down next to Josie. He wanted to play this carefully, didn't want to frighten her off.

'Not sure yet,' said Josie. 'I'm trying not to think about it.'

'Well, if you need me, I'm here,' said Ant. And for once it wasn't a corny come-on. He actually meant it.

'You're not so bad under all that bravado, are you?' said Josie, smiling. 'I've seen a different side to you tonight.'

'Shh, don't tell anyone,' said Ant, 'it would ruin my reputation.'

He could do it, make her fall for him, he knew he could. She was vulnerable and upset. He was the obvious shoulder to cry on. He'd done it dozens of times in the past, so what was making him hesitate? Why did he feel so different?

Because she's in love with your best mate, you cretin. He could almost feel Freddie's words splintering in his head. Damn. This responsibility shit was still sticking. Sod, sod, and double sod.

Diana was feeling much better after her chat with Auberon, who'd insisted she call him Bron. He seemed to completely understand what had happened to her. No one had done that before. Not even Josie, she realised. Josie was a good listener, and was always sweetly sympathetic, but she hadn't ever been through any of the things that Di had, and her charmed life hadn't prepared her for the kind of pain Di had experienced. It meant

278

there was a gap in empathy sometimes, and Di could see now that she hadn't really understood.

'You've been very sweet,' she said. 'I've never told anyone else the whole story.'

'Curse of old age, my dear,' he said. 'You finally learn empathy when it's far too late.'

'You're not that old,' said Diana. 'And anyway, maybe it's not too late. Have you tried talking to Tatiana since you've been here?'

'No,' admitted Bron, 'but I don't think she'll want to talk to me, particularly with Freddie around. She can't stand him. And anyway ... it's probably too late now.'

'Why?'

'Like an idiot I let Freddie persuade me it would be fun to take Tati down a peg or two. It was after the scene in the pub the other night. I was really cross with her, so I told Freddie I wanted revenge.'

'And?'

'Freddie's hypnotised Mike Slowbotham to think she's in love with him. She thinks he's genuinely offering her a part when he hasn't even got proper funding, and all he really wants to do is get inside her knickers.'

'I gathered that,' said Diana drily. 'Do you always go to Freddie for your relationship advice? Because quite frankly that's the worst idea I've ever heard...'

'Freddie can be very persuasive,' said Bron. 'It used to drive Tati nuts.'

'I'm not surprised,' said Diana. 'If I were you I'd get myself another mate. And stop Freddie before it's too late. What you're doing to Tatiana

279

is monstrous. The poor woman thinks she's in with a chance of a leading role.'

'Oh,' said Bron, looking mournful. 'It did seem funnier in the pub when I was in my cups. Freddie can be very cruel. Speak of the devil.'

Freddie came puffing up the hill.

'Why you lot can't stay in one place, I don't know,' he complained. 'Diana, can you possibly stay here, and I'll get you all together again, and see if we can finally get this to work. Have you seen Harry?'

'Someone mention my name?' said Harry.

'Where did you spring from?' said Diana in surprise.

'I just came through those bushes,' said Harry, 'and here you all were. I was looking for Josie. Have you seen her?'

'What do you think?' said Diana. 'I'm the last person she wants to see at the moment.'

She felt like kicking herself. She'd been a horrible cow to Josie tonight.

'I'm sorry about earlier,' she said to Harry.

'No worries,' he said. 'It's been a funny old night.'

'You can say that again,' said Diana with feeling.

Despite everything that had happened, Harry felt sorry for Diana, it was clear she'd been crying, and she obviously regretted what she'd said to Josie earlier. He'd have to make sure Josie was prepared to forgive her when they caught up with one another.

'As you're both here,' said Freddie, interrupting his thoughts, 'can we get some of your response to this evening on camera?'

'I don't think you'd like what I've got to say,' said Harry, spotting that Will was hovering behind Freddie, camera in hand. Bloody hell, they never stopped.

'Nor me,' said Diana. 'Disastrous doesn't cover it.'

'All you've done is bugger things up,' said Harry. 'So far I don't think your experiment has been a success.'

'The night is still young,' said Freddie, 'plenty of time to put things right before morning.'

'You're enjoying this, aren't you?' Diana accused Freddie.

'No, of course I'm not,' said Freddie, 'but hypnotism isn't an exact science; things sometimes take an unexpected turn. Everything will work out in the end, I'm sure. And the money will make it all worthwhile.'

The money. That was the main reason Harry was doing this, so he could show Josie how much he loved her when they got married – if they got married. But what was the point in that, if Josie wasn't going to come with him?

Suddenly feeling tired, defeated and very sorry for himself, Harry sat down with a thump.

'Three, two, one,' he heard Freddie say.

Bloody hell. Not again.

Harry was out like a light, dreaming of being rooted to the spot while Josie endlessly danced in among the moonbeams. When he went to reach her she ran away laughing...

Chapter Twenty-Six

Ant was trying to do the decent thing, and had been planning to tell Josie she should go and talk to Harry, when he was suddenly aware that she was weeping silently beside him. Suddenly his resolve to do the right thing was sorely tempted, it would be all too easy to take advantage of her vulnerability.

'Here Josie, don't cry,' he said awkwardly patting her arm. He desperately wanted to put his arm round her, but didn't want to appear too pushy.

'Here, have a tissue,' he felt in his pockets and pulled out his fags, 'no sorry, here, I do have one.'

Gently, he wiped her eyes.

'He's an idiot, you know,' said Ant. 'If you were mine, I'd never let you go.'

'But I'm not, am I?' said Josie. 'I just can't believe he'd do this to me. I thought he really wanted to marry me. But now...'

This could be his moment, and in the past would have been, but the damned sense of responsibility was hovering over him with a vengeance.

'Maybe you rushed things,' he found himself saying. 'Maybe he needs more time.'

'He's had six months,' said Josie.

'Well, if it were me, I'd need at least two years, probably five,' said Ant with a grin. 'And I certainly couldn't handle all that chat about dresses and flowers. You've talked about nothing else since we got here.'

'You think I've become a bit obsessed?' Josie looked appalled.

'Just a smidgeon,' said Ant. 'What do I know? I've never been engaged. But I think the circus acts may have been a tipping point.'

'Oh, God, I've turned into a bridezilla, haven't I?' Josie groaned. 'Why did no one tell me?'

'You can be quite hard to resist,' said Ant, 'and to be honest I don't think anyone wanted to upset you.'

'Really?' Josie looked stricken. 'Am I really that bad?'

'No,' said Ant, cursing himself for his clumsiness. 'I think it might have been a bit overwhelming for Harry, that's all.'

'Maybe 250 guests *is* too many,' said Josie slowly. 'Harry did mention it, but I ignored him.'

She looked as if something was dawning on her.

'Perhaps it's my fault,' she said, 'perhaps I've been ignoring Harry too much.'

'No, no, no,' said Ant, 'I think you've just got a bit more involved than him. It's natural, I'm sure.'

'All I wanted was for things to be perfect,' said Josie rather sadly. 'I didn't want to put Harry off.'

'And you probably haven't,' said Ant. 'Maybe you need to talk to him about it.'

'Maybe I do,' said Josie. 'Thinking about the sort of people my mum and dad want to invite, I can understand Harry being intimidated. I never meant to upset him, I got a bit carried away.'

'Maybe just a little bit,' said Ant. 'Come on, let's go and see where Harry's got to. Maybe we can try and work this out.'

Still not quite believing he could be so noble, Ant took Josie by the hand and led her out of the theatre.

Diana sat watching Harry sleeping, wishing it was Ant lying there. Freddie, Bron and Will had wandered off to see what was happening at the theatre and, nervous of the reaction she would get when she saw Ant again, she'd elected to stay put. What was she going to do? She was overcome with the strength of her feelings for Ant. They'd come like a bolt from the blue, a real *coup de foudre*. Only, maybe it hadn't been that sudden. Talking to Bron had made her remember how much she'd loved him. In her hurt and bitterness she'd forgotten that. But maybe it was time to let that hurt and bitterness go. At least he'd been prepared to talk to her tonight, and thinking again about the whole situation with Sian, perhaps she had misjudged him.

Maybe he was being so standoffish with her because he was still hurting too. Perhaps all she needed to do was come clean, say sorry, and say what was going on in her head. She can't have imagined what they'd had between them. It had been special. She knew he'd felt it too. If only she could remind him of how they used to be, everything would be all right again and they could put the past behind them...

It was a nice dream. But a foolish one. This story wasn't going to end the way she wanted. They never did. Diana should be used to it by now. She was coming to the conclusion that she was never going to find someone to live happily ever after with.

Still, a girl could fantasise... It was getting a little chilly and Harry looked cosy and warm. There could be no harm in snuggling up to him...

She lay down next to him, and Harry rolled over and put his arms round her. For a moment, she lay in blissful happiness, imagining that she was lying next to Ant, before he ruined it entirely, by saying 'Josie' really loudly.

She knew she was kidding herself, Ant was never going to fall for her again. But she was tired, and if she just shut her eyes, in her dreams he could be hers...

Harry was having a lovely dream about Josie, about when they'd first met. She was coming towards him in a pretty floral dress, her long fair curls flapping in the breeze, saying shyly, 'It's Harry isn't it?'

He could still remember the thrill when he closed his hand over hers, and said 'yes,' and they'd walked off together, as they went to the theatre as if it was the most natural thing in the world to do. Things like that never happened to Harry. They happened to Ant all the time, but not to Harry. It had been such a sweet moment, he recalled, as he woke up slowly and found himself cuddling her. How lovely. This whole mad night had been a bad dream. Here was Josie in bed beside him, and everything was going to be okay.

Except ... something wasn't quite right. He was lying on something hard and stony. A bush was poking in his back. And as the person lying beside him rolled round and stared at him, he groaned in dismay.

'Diana?' he said, incredulous. What was she doing here? At that moment, he heard voices coming down the path towards them, and the next thing he knew...

'Harry, you bastard, you bloody bastard!' Josie was standing over him, looking shattered.

'Josie, this isn't how it looks,' Harry got up to try and remonstrate.

'I trusted you!' said Josie, delivering a stinging slap around his cheeks, before running into the darkness.

'What's going on?' Diana was sitting up, looking really confused.

'I have no idea,' said Harry. 'But thanks for nothing!'

He shot off in the darkness to find Josie. He had to make her understand that nothing had happened, or they really were finished.

Chapter Twenty-Seven

Ant was flabbergasted. Of all the things he'd expected to see, it hadn't been that. Maybe despite his denials, Harry did have a thing going on with Diana, although it didn't seem likely. He'd looked so distraught when Josie had slapped him. Ant was at a loss as to what to do now. They seemed locked in a nightmarish situation, which looked like never getting resolved.

But maybe you've got more chance with Josie now, said a whispering voice in his head. Maybe. Or maybe she'll be blaming you for setting the whole thing up...

'Oh, God, oh, God, I'm such a fool.'

Ant had almost forgotten Di. What was going on there? Had she changed her mind about him, and transferred her attentions to Harry? She was rocking herself backwards and forwards, crying. Awkwardly, Ant sat down next to her. Another crying woman. What had he done to deserve this? He'd never spent so much time comforting crying women without some kind of reward. It was an odd feeling.

'Hey, it's not as bad as that,' he said. 'I can see you're a bit confused this evening, but how do you know what you or any of us think we're feeling is real? Freddie's messed with our minds good and proper.'

That applied to the way he felt about Josie, he

realised with a jolt. Could he be sure those emotions were real? They certainly *felt* real.

'I don't know,' said Diana. 'I'm not just upset about screwing things up for Harry and Josie. It's life in general. I'm single, jobless, talentless. I've worked so hard to get where I am, and now I've lost it all. My dad will feel completely vindicated when I tell him. He never thought I should go into the travel business.'

'Now that is ridiculous,' said Ant. 'From what I recall, your dad never understood how talented you are. Talented and gorgeous.'

He surprised himself by saying it, but he'd suddenly remembered how insecure Di had always been, and how little support her parents had given her. Somehow he felt he wanted to cheer her up...

'Do you really think so?' said Di, looking shy. 'But look at me. I'm unemployed, don't even own my own flat, *and* single.'

'Cheer up, worse things happen at sea,' said Ant.

'I doubt that somehow,' said Diana.

'Don't be too hard on yourself,' said Ant, putting his arms round her and giving her a hug. 'It's been a weird night, and quite frankly the way Josie's been banging on about the wedding, I'm not surprised Harry's been having second thoughts. That's not your fault.'

'She has been a bit hideous hasn't she?' Diana laughed.

They sat for a few moments, feeling the wind on their cheeks, and Ant felt something harmonious pass between them. Not that he wanted to

get back together, or anything, but at least it was a start to being friends again.

Night was passing and the moon was getting low in the sky.

'I'd almost forgotten you could be like this,' said Diana.

'Like what?'

'Nice,' said Diana, looking dreamy. 'Kind. You hide it well, but it's still there.'

'Thanks,' said Ant, 'you're not so bad yourself.'

He gave her a squeeze.

'Friends?' he said.

'Friends,' said Diana.

Friends. So much better than enemies.

Diana felt as if her heart was going to explode sitting next to Ant. It was as though the man she'd once known was just re-emerging; maybe he would reconnect with her, remember too what they'd had.

'Why did you stop being kind to people?' said Diana. 'Was it my fault?'

Ant didn't say anything, but continued to stare out to sea.

'Why didn't you give me a chance to explain?' he said.

The question hung between them. It was a fair point, and Di suddenly realised she'd been carrying her bitterness around with her for so long, it had never occurred to her she could have asked him his side of the story.

'What were you going to say that would have made a difference?' she said. 'I'd have thought it was obvious.'

'Not to me it wasn't,' said Ant. 'You spent weeks avoiding me, and then you disappeared one evening. I was frantic. I looked everywhere for you and no one knew where you'd gone.'

'Yeah, it looked like it,' said Diana, remembering the churning uncertainty of that night. 'I came back from hospital and you were in the bar all over Sian like a rash.'

'Sian was comforting me,' said Ant.

'Is that what you call it?' Old habits die hard, and she felt angry all over again.

'Yes,' said Ant. 'Di, listen, please.'

Something about the urgency in the way he spoke made her pause. It was time she heard him out.

'I genuinely thought you'd gone off me. You were always working shifts when I was free. Sian kept hinting that you were doing it deliberately, and even that you'd found someone else,' he said. 'I was worrying you were cheating on me.'

'Oh,' Diana wasn't sure whether to believe him. 'Did you believe her?'

'I didn't know what to think,' said Ant. 'I wanted to ask you but I didn't have the nerve, in case you told me we were finished. And then you ditched me in front of everyone.'

'But Sian knew,' said Diana. 'I told her about the miscarriage before I went to hospital. She was meant to tell you. Are you telling me she never did?'

'She never breathed a word,' said Ant. 'I know I'm a lot of things, but I would never have left you to go through that on your own. I am so sorry.'

Diana took a sharp intake of breath and blinked away the tears.

'All these years,' she said, 'and I blamed you. It's me who should be sorry.'

'I was a bit of a shit to you afterwards,' said Ant. 'I thought you didn't love me anymore. Sian was meant to be my consolation prize. God, she was a piece of work.'

'Wasn't she just?' said Diana.

'Why didn't you tell me you were pregnant?'

'I nearly did,' said Diana. 'It never felt like the right moment, and then I lost the baby, and you... We were so young, and I was frightened you wouldn't support me, and then it looked as if you wouldn't.'

'And I let you down,' said Ant. 'For what it's worth, I was devastated when I found out about the baby from the message on my answerphone. I wanted to go after you, but Sian said to leave it. I can't believe I was daft enough to listen. I'm sorry, Di. You deserved better. Much better.'

To her astonishment, there were tears in his eyes.

She stared into his eyes. This was her moment, it had to be.

Leaning forward, she kissed him on the lips.

Ant leapt back as if he'd been scalded.

'Di, I'm sorry, I didn't mean...' He let go of her hand, and got up. 'I'm sorry, Di, it's not you, it's me.'

And with that, he stumbled off into the dark, leaving Diana alone with her broken heart.

Harry stumbled through the darkness, calling

Josie's name. Where had she gone now? He had a feeling she wasn't going back home.

He felt wrecked from this evening. Utterly wrecked. He wished he'd never set eyes on bloody Diana for a start, or let himself get pushed into the whole engagement thing. He knew he wanted to spend the rest of his life with Josie, but the rest of his life was a long time. Marriage could wait. He wanted to have adventures with Josie, see the world before they settled down. If he hadn't been such an idiot and proposed when he had, they could be living happily together right now, without any of this pressure. Standing on this cliffedge looking out to sea, thinking about all the adventurers who'd left these shores in olden days, made him feel suddenly confined and restricted. He'd always played safe, been Mr Dependable. Now it was time to do something different, be someone different. And if Josie didn't want that person, so be it.

He found her on a small beach which led away from the cliff, to one side of the theatre. He remembered them picnicking here once. It had been a happy, relaxed day, early in their courtship. Maybe the fact that she was here was a good sign...

'Josie,' he said. She was sitting still on a rock, looking ghostly white in the pale moonlight, for all the world like an enchantress who'd just come out of the sea. She didn't say anything, so he hunkered down next to her.

'Look, I'm not going to beg, and I'm not going to plead, but hear me out, will you? I know things have gone wrong between us this weekend, but

292

you have to believe me. I love you more than anything else in the world, and I would never hurt you.'

'But not enough to marry me,' said Josie. 'And not enough not to cheat with my best friend.'

'I fell asleep and woke up to find Di beside me,' said Harry. 'I'm not remotely interested in Diana. You can believe that or not, but it's the truth. When have I ever lied to you?'

'When you asked me to marry you?' said Josie.

'Oh, that,' said Harry.

'Yes, *that*,' said Josie, looking angry.

'I do want to marry you,' said Harry. 'But not yet. I think we've rushed things. I know it's my fault, but there's a whole world out there. Come and see it with me, please. I want to travel, but not alone.'

Josie said nothing.

'That's it,' said Harry. 'That's all I have to say. I'm going back now. And in the morning I'm going home. Then I'm going to plan a world tour. I hope you'll be with me, but if not, I'm going anyway.'

Josie still didn't say anything, twisting her finger round and round, till eventually he realised what she was doing.

'No, Josie,' he said, tears choking him, 'no, please don't do this.'

'Sorry,' she said, crying too, as she handed him the ring, 'it's over.'

Harry took the ring without another word, and turned round to leave. There was nothing more to be said.

Josie sat back down on a rock after he'd gone, staring out to sea. Her thoughts were a mixed jumble. She'd been so excited about this weekend, excited to be marrying Harry, how could it all have gone so wrong?

He'd never said anything serious before about wanting adventures. Harry had on occasion mentioned going travelling, but in such a jokey way, Josie never thought he meant it. Why did he suddenly want to go travelling now? Unless it was another nonsensical thing that Freddie had put in his head.

What a night. What a bloody night.

She heard a shout from above, and then heard someone frantically scrambling down the path. It was Tatiana, looking somewhat dishevelled.

'Are you all right?' said Josie.

'All right? All right?' said Tatiana, spitting feathers. 'The man's gone completely mad.'

'Which man?'

'Mike,' said Tatiana. 'He tried – he tried to kiss me!'

She looked so indignant, Josie had to stifle a grin.

'I can't believe it. We were *acting*, and then he tried to kiss my arm. It was revolting. He called me – his little flower. Oh, God. Now I've probably lost the only chance of ever playing Titania. Why is life so unfair?'

'Where is he now?' asked Josie.

'I don't know,' moaned Tatiana, 'I pushed him over and ran down here.'

A tinkling of stones on the path above led to a panicked look on Tatiana's face.

'Hide me, please!' she said.

'There's a cave just there in the corner,' said Josie. 'Don't go too far in, it connects with the cove next door, and it's easy to get trapped by the sea. You have to know it's there. He won't find you, I promise.'

'You're an angel,' said Tatiana, and stumbled off towards the cave.

The sound of footsteps came nearer, and suddenly someone burst onto the beach.

Oh, shit now what should she do? Memories of Mike being very intense with every girlfriend he'd ever had, meant she knew how unlikely it was he was going to let Tatiana out of his sight.

But it wasn't Mike, it was Ant.

'Josie,' he said, 'are you okay? I just saw Harry. He said you'd given your ring back.'

'It was the right thing to do,' said Josie.

'And you're okay?' he said, 'you're really okay?'

'I will be,' said Josie, surprised. 'Since when did you care?'

In answer, Ant enveloped her in a big hug. It felt warm and comforting and secure.

'Oh, I've always cared,' said Ant. 'I just didn't realise how much, until tonight.'

Josie looked up into his eyes and suddenly everything made sense, the moon, and the stars, the lapping of the waves. She remembered how she'd felt as a student, when she'd longed and longed to know what it would feel like for Ant to kiss her.

2012: Tatiana

'Darling, Susan here. How are you?' Tatiana sighed. What did she want? It wouldn't be anything worth hearing. These days Susan rang rarely, and then it was mainly to remind her about tax issues.

'Fine,' said Tatiana. 'I know, I know, my tax return is due.'

'No, it's not that, darling,' said Susan. 'I have a possible opening.'

'Not Bournemouth Pier again?' said Tatiana. 'I think I'd rather starve.'

Particularly as she'd just read in the papers that Bron and Freddie were in talks about a new TV show. Something to do with hypnotism and English myths, she thought. Sounded like Freddie's usual bullshit. It made her a little sad to think Bron was still falling for it.

'No, no. It's a little more thrilling,' said Susan. 'It's Shakespeare. You've always wanted to do Shakespeare, haven't you, darling?'

'Oh my,' Tatiana could feel the excitement growing. 'Where? Is it rep, will it be going to the West End? What?'

'Calm down, darling, it's not that grand.' Susan instantly put a downer on it. 'It's a funny little place in Cornwall. A local theatre, trying to revive its fortunes. The producer is, er, let me look at my notes – a Mike Slowbotham, would you believe.'

'Cornwall? I'm not sure,' said Tatiana. 'Sounds muddy.'

'I'm sure it will be wonderful. There are opportunities for glamping. You can stay in a yurt. It's by the sea. The theatre's on a clifftop. It sounds heavenly. Darling, I'm sure you'd love it.'

'And the name of this idyll?'

'Tresgothen.'

Part Four

And All is Mended

'I will undo
This hateful imperfection of her eyes.
And, gentle Puck, take this transformed scalp
From off the head of this Athenian swain,
That he awaking when the other do,
May all to Athens back again repair,
And think no more of this night's accidents,
But as the fierce vexation of a dream.'
A Midsummer Night's Dream:
Act IV Scene 1

'Oh, go on then. Yes, I get a bit of a kick out of it.
Having people in the palm of my hand, persuading
them to do silly things. But no, I don't take advantage
of gullible people. That wouldn't be ethical. And
believe it or not, Piers, I do have a moral compass.'
Freddie Puck on *Piers Morgan's Life Stories*

Chapter Twenty-Eight

Diana had climbed back towards the Standing Stones. She didn't feel like going back to Josie's now. She couldn't face any of them: Josie, Harry, Ant. She'd never made such a spectacular fool of herself in her life. Oh, God. Even after their mutual soul-bearing, Ant had still rejected her. The look on his face had been horrendous to witness. He'd looked appalled. She felt sick to her stomach. The best thing she could do was keep out of everyone's way, Diana thought, so she might as well stay here till the sun rose. Then she would sneak back to the house, get her things and go and find a train. She had a feeling there might not be a train station in Tresgothen, but come hell or high water she was going to make her way home on her own. She had too much pride to go with Harry and Josie, and she certainly couldn't cope with Ant for four hours in a car in this raw state.

Looking over the sea, she became aware that the sky was becoming a tad lighter, deep blue giving way to steely grey. She watched as seagulls dipped down among the waves, and the light started to spread softly across the sky. After the excitements of the night, she wasn't sure she wanted to face what this new dawn was going to bring. All she knew was that nothing was ever going to be the same, and she wasn't sure if any of them were going to be able to come to terms with the consequences of what had happened tonight.

Harry stumbled back up the path, feeling completely heartbroken. He'd tried and he'd failed. Josie had given him back her engagement ring. She didn't want him any longer. Meeting Ant on the way, he'd sent him down to comfort Josie and then, not knowing what else to do, wandered back to the theatre, where he found a huge commotion going on.

'Where is she?' Mike Slowbotham was wailing. 'Where is she?' while M'stard and the rest of Tatiana's gang were holding him back. M'stard turned out to be stronger than he looked.

'Who?' asked Harry, intrigued. Yet another weird happening on this very strange night.

'Tatiana, of course,' boomed Mike. 'I love her, and she loves me. The little minx is only teasing me.'

'She doesn't love you,' said Gypsy. 'It's called acting.'

'Oh, woe is me,' declaimed Mike soulfully, 'my true love loves me not.'

'You, me both,' said Harry.

'Look, she's not your true love, and she doesn't love you,' said M'stard. 'I think you need to get home. Someone's had a teensy bit too much to drink.'

'Or he's been Freddieised,' said Harry with a sudden realisation. 'Didn't Freddie Puck hypnotise you, yesterday?' he said to Mike.

'Erm, I don't think so,' said Mike, looking confused.

'You stay here,' said Harry. 'I'm going to go and get Freddie. He's done a lot of damage tonight, and he's got a lot of making up to do.'

He left them to it. Mike was trying to break free again, so M'stard solved the problem by sitting on him, while the other two pinned him down. That was one way of doing things.

Harry walked with a renewed sense of purpose. It was time to tell Freddie Puck this damned experiment was at an end. He felt in his pocket and curled his hand round Josie's engagement ring. 'It's not over till the fat lady sings,' he muttered. Well, she'd better put off singing a little while longer.

Josie took a sudden step back. She'd been overpowered briefly by the moment.

'Sorry, Ant – I shouldn't have – this is just too soon,' she broke away from him, feeling raw and confused. 'Please don't expect anything.'

'It was my fault too,' said Ant. 'I'm sorry, Josie, I couldn't help it. You looked so sad and lonely. And I remember how I felt about you all those years ago.'

'That was then, this is now,' said Josie. 'And Freddie Puck's been messing with our heads. I don't know what's real anymore.'

'I'll give you as much time as you need,' said Ant, lacing his fingers over hers.

'I never knew you had such a sensitive side,' said Josie with a wry smile.

'I didn't either till this weekend,' said Ant. 'I'm so sorry about all of this.'

'It's not your fault,' said Josie.

'It is. You were right, and I was wrong about the hypnotism,' said Ant. 'I got totally carried away with seeing Freddie Puck. I thought it would be a bit of a laugh. I had no idea it would end up like this.'

'Does it have to?' said Josie. 'Maybe we should just go back and ask to get back to where we all were at the start.'

'I'm not exactly sure I want to,' said Ant. 'I think I've been a better person tonight than I have in a long time. And then there's you…'

Josie didn't answer him. She no longer knew what she wanted. But she'd give anything for none of this to have happened. The trouble was, could things ever be the same again? Even if they went back to their default positions, she now knew that Harry didn't want to marry her. And she had a feeling that no amount of hypnotism could make her forget that…

Ant was feeling hyper-aware of his surroundings as he walked back up the cliff path with Josie. She hadn't said yes, but she hadn't said no either. Maybe after all this was over and the dust had settled, they could work something out. Maybe…

They arrived back at the theatre to hear a debate going on.

'Do you think we should have tied him up? Isn't that like assault?'

'It was for his own good,' said another voice. 'He would have run after Tati, and then where would we be?'

'Where is she do you think?' a third voice fretted. 'I do hope she's okay.'

304

'It's okay,' said Josie, pushing the theatre gate open, where she found Tatiana's three companions holding down a very defiant Mike. 'She's safe.'

'Where is she?' wailed Mike. 'She must love me, she must. Why would she have met me here at midnight if not for love?'

'To get a part in your play, you silly little man,' said M'stard in exasperation. 'Why on earth would a goddess like Tati be interested in a mere mortal like you?'

'Why indeed?' whispered Ant, laughing. The one funny thing that had happened all night had been watching Mike Slowbotham getting carried away.

They heard more voices, and Auberon and Freddie appeared, Harry hard at their heels.

'This nonsense has gone on long enough,' said Bron, 'Poor Tati. What have we done?'

'I thought you wanted to punish her,' said Freddie.

'I did,' said Bron, 'but it turns out I didn't want to humiliate her after all. Where is she, by the way?'

'Down on the beach,' said Josie. 'I left her hiding in a cave.'

'Where? Can you show me?' said Bron.

'With pleasure,' Josie said, and took him down the cliff path, Ant following behind. The day was dawning, and white light was poking under grey clouds, so they got a clear view of the beach as they scrambled towards it. Ant suddenly realised the beach was much smaller than when they'd left.

'Hang on,' he said. 'What's happening? Is the tide coming in?'

'Oh no!' said Josie.

'What's the matter?' asked Bron.

'I forgot about the tide,' said Josie in a whisper; she'd gone deathly pale. 'It's going to block off the entrance to the cave and Tatiana's trapped inside.'

Chapter Twenty-Nine

Harry had only just about taken in the sight of Josie and Ant holding hands (it was so swift he thought he'd made it up) before they disappeared with Bron to show him where Tatiana had gone. He was going to ask Ant just what the hell he thought he was doing, but was stopped in his tracks by Josie bursting back up the track, shouting for help.

'What's going on?' said Harry, alert for an opportunity to redeem himself in Josie's eyes.

'It's Tatiana,' gasped Josie. 'She's stuck in a cave and the tide's coming in. Has anyone got a signal? We need to ring the coastguard.'

Several people tried and failed to get their phones working. Eventually Freddie managed to patch a call through, and was shouting rapid instructions to the person on the other end.

'Where are we again, Josie?'

'Tresgothen Cove,' she said, 'it's just beyond Torpoint.'

Freddie relayed the information. 'They said they know where to find us,' he said, putting his phone in his pocket.

'How long?' said Josie.

'Twenty minutes, they think,' said Freddie.

Josie looked anxious, gnawing her lip in a gesture Harry knew and loved.

'We may not have twenty minutes. We have to get Tatiana out of there. We need a rope, *now*.'

'What did you tie Mike up with?' said Harry with sudden inspiration.

'The belt from my kimono,' said M'stard. 'It's quite long and tough.'

He pointed at the obi belt Mike was tied up with, it was the kind Josie associated with sumo wrestlers and looked like it could do the job.

'You mean dressing gown,' said Freddie.

'It's better than nothing, and it's long enough,' said Harry. 'Untie Mike and give it to me.'

'What about Mike?'

Mike was huffing and puffing about the indignity of it all.

'Oh, leave it to me,' said Freddie, clicking his fingers, and instantly Mike fell into a deep snoring sleep.

Once the cord to the kimono – which luckily seemed quite strong – was removed, everyone hurried down to the beach where Bron was standing in a pool of water at the entrance of the cave, shouting encouragement to Tatiana. The sea was swirling dangerously round the entrance, and the beach was rapidly being eaten up. Tatiana's crew stood around helplessly wringing their hands.

'Right,' said Harry. 'It's not far to your yurt is it? One of you, go and get blankets, towels, a flask; anything that we might need. Someone needs to try and get into the cave and rescue Tatiana. If we tie the rope round that person's waist, and the rest of us form a human chain, we might be able to do it.'

'Me,' said Bron. 'I'll do it. Tati, darling, help is at hand. We'll have you out of there as soon as we can.'

Diana heard the shouting from the top of the cliff. She peered over the edge, and in the early morning gloom, could see a gaggle of people gathering on the beach. They seemed to be panicking. What on earth could be going on?

Curiosity pricked, Diana went back to the cliff path, and found her way down to the beach.

It was definitely getting lighter now. Diana glanced at her watch. Nearly 5a.m. The grey clouds were outweighing the black, the lightening of the sky heralding the arrival of the sun. It was still warm, but a light spray was coming off the sea as she scrambled down the rocky path to where everyone was standing.

'What's happening?' She spotted Josie looking worried.

'It's all my fault,' said Josie, wringing her hands. 'I told Tatiana to hide from Mike in the cave, but I forgot about the tide coming in, and now she's trapped. We've called the coastguard, but we're not sure when they're going to get here. Bron's insisting he's going in to get her.'

'Right.' Harry was at the cave's entrance, tying

308

a knot in a rope around Bron's waist.

'Are you sure you want to do this?' he said.

'Bring it on,' said Bron. 'Are you sure this knot is secure?'

'It should be, I was a boy scout,' said Harry, testing it to be sure. 'I'll double it to make sure.'

Happy that it was fine, Harry turned to everyone else. 'I'll hold the rope, and everyone form a chain behind me. Bron can then swim into the cave, and he should be able to get Tati.'

'Shouldn't we wait for the coastguard?' asked Diana. This seemed immensely risky to her, and she liked Bron. She didn't want anything happening to him.

'No time,' said Harry.

'And I owe Tati,' said Bron. 'Wish me luck.'

He started to wade towards the cave, the water soon up to his shoulders. 'Tati, I'm coming to get you,' he shouted, before he was lost in the swirling waters of the cave.

'Do you think they're going to be okay?' said Diana.

'I hope so.' Josie was looking sick. 'People have drowned in that cave before now.'

Harry was beginning to strain on the rope. 'Come on, I need a hand here,' he shouted.

Ant ran forward, and then Freddie, and one by one they formed a human chain. The sea was pounding hard at their heels now, and faintly from the cave Diana could make out a voice calling, 'Tati, Tati, I'm coming for you.'

She just hoped it wasn't too late.

Ant took his place in the line behind Harry,

feeling tense. God, they might both drown and he and Josie would be partly to blame. Josie had mentioned she was there, but they'd been so caught up in the moment, they'd completely forgotten about Tatiana. And now she was trapped.

'This is harder than it looks in the movies,' muttered Harry. 'I had no idea Bron would be this heavy.'

'Can you see anything?'

They peered into the darkness, and could just about make out Bron's head bouncing in the waves.

'Everything okay?' Harry called.

'I can see her…' said Bron.

'Keep going,' shouted Ant, 'you can do it!'

They felt the rope pull away from them and heard Bron shout, 'I've got her.'

'Brilliant,' said Harry. The rope went slack as Bron climbed up to the ledge where Tatiana was sheltering.

'Phew,' said Ant, 'thank God she's okay, I was beginning to feel guilty there.'

'Anything else you should be feeling guilty about, mate?' said Harry, with an emphasis on the *mate*.

'Sorry?' Ant didn't think he'd given anything away.

'You and Josie, you looked very cosy up there at the theatre.'

'I'm not sure I know what you mean,' bluffed Ant.

'Aren't you?' said Harry.

Ant was saved from having to answer by a tug

of the rope.

'I've got her,' shouted Bron. 'I'm coming out.'

Josie was at the back of the line, not sure what was happening till she heard Ant yell, 'He's got her!'

Tatiana's entourage burst into a round of spontaneous applause.

'I was so worried,' said M'stàrd, to no one in particular.

'We've still got to get them out,' Josie pointed out. 'The boys need all the help they can get.'

Harry and Ant had the rope now and were straining to pull it backwards.

'A bit of help here, please,' shouted Ant, and everyone resumed their positions. But this time, even at the end of the line, Josie could feel how much harder it was; everyone was stumbling and slipping on the pebbles. There were two people to get out of that cave and the waves were getting higher and stronger.

'Come on,' roared Harry, 'we can do this!'

Everyone pulled as hard as they could.

'I feel like that nursery story about the old man and the turnip,' muttered Josie, panting as she too felt the strain.

They tugged and pulled and the waves dragged the rope back and forth.

Then an excited, 'I can see them!' came from Harry, and they made one last pull, which caused them all to fall on top of each other higgledy-piggledy.

Harry was the first to stand up. He looked dazed, still holding onto one end of the rope. He pulled the other end, and it flew through the water into his hands.

'So much for scouts' knots,' muttered Ant.

The rope had come undone – and there was no sign of Tatiana and Bron.

Chapter Thirty

'Someone do something!' Harry heard Josie shout, and without thinking, he ripped off his shirt, kicked off his shoes and hurled himself into the water. It was freezing and the waves were crashing violently against the cave wall. But Harry was a strong swimmer and he confidently ploughed his way into the middle of the cave. Seconds later, he was aware that Ant was beside him.

'Can you see them?' shouted Ant above the waves.

He was going to reply in the negative, but then he caught sight of Bron, frantically bobbing about, trying to keep Tatiana's head out of the water.

'There!' he said, and swam towards them. It was confusing and dark in the cave and waves were coming in from the other side, which was making him disorientated. For every stroke forward, it felt as if he was being pushed two strokes back. But the adrenaline was pumping and kept him going.

Eventually he reached Bron and shouted,

'Here, let me help. I'll take Tatiana, and Ant will help you,' before realising that they were both stuck on a ridge, clinging to it for dear life.

'Tati's frightened,' said Bron, who looked worn out. 'I can't persuade her to come.'

'I can't swim,' wailed Tatiana.

'It's okay,' said Harry, 'I'm a trained lifeguard. Come on, I can help. We don't have much time.'

The waves were buffeting the rocks faster than ever, and water was pouring in from the other end of the cave at an alarming rate, making a broiling mass of wave, rock and seaweed.

'I can't!' screamed Tatiana.

'You can, or we're all going to bloody well drown,' said Harry with a decisiveness which took him by surprise. Taking her gently from Bron, and unpicking her fingers from where they were pinned against his shoulders, Harry got hold of her head, and began the slow swim on his back towards the mouth of the cave. It was hard going. The waves slapped in his face, and he was very aware of the ever-present threat of the rocks. But the first gleams of the sunrise were beginning to peek their way through and the cave entrance gradually grew nearer. Behind him, he could hear Ant muttering words of encouragement to Bron. They could and would do this, and Josie would be so proud.

'Oh my God, what has he done?' Josie pushed her way through the shocked throng, as she saw Harry dive into the thrashing water. It was bad enough Bron going in, but now Harry – and Ant, who followed in rapid succession. It was so stupid. They were all risking their lives. They were going to drown, and it was her fault. At this rate, by the time the coastguard arrived they'd be pulling four bodies out of the cave.

'They'll be okay,' said Diana, coming up to her and clutching her arm, 'they have to be.'

'I don't even know how well Harry can swim,' said Josie helplessly, 'he never shows much interest in the sea when we come down here.'

The sun was beginning to rise in earnest now, pink fingers spreading across the sky, making the sea appear both benign and friendly, and not the watery grave it threatened to be.

'The sea here can be so treacherous,' said Josie. 'Oh, why did I suggest Tatiana hide in the cave? I could kick myself.'

'Look, help's at hand.' Diana pointed as a boat rounded the cove and came speeding in their direction.

Thank God. Josie peered into the gloomy darkness of the cave; it was hard to see, but she thought she could make out figures battling their way through the water.

'Here! Over here!' She jumped up and down, waving to the coastguard. The boat was just puttering up to the cave entrance when Harry ploughed backwards through it, holding Tatiana. He looked magnificent, strong and brave, and Josie's heart leapt. He was okay. He was okay.

The men in the boat threw him a line, and picked Tatiana out of the water while Harry swam to shore. He was shivering, and Gypsy, who turned out to be surprisingly efficient, immediately threw the towels and blankets she'd

314

brought back from the yurt over him. 'Here, darling, you need to get as warm as possible,' she said.

'Have this,' said Freddie, giving him a nip of brandy. 'I brought it with me tonight to keep me going, didn't realise it was going to come in so handy.'

Tatiana was being given the once over by the men on the boat, who had wrapped her up in blankets, and seemed to be checking for hypothermia. By the sound of her loud complaining, she was recovering well, but there was still no sign of Ant or Bron.

'There!' Josie suddenly spotted them at the entrance of the cave. But then a wave went over their heads and they were lost from view.

'This was a bloody stupid idea,' had been Ant's first thought as he followed Harry into the water, but then there was no time for thought as he battled with spray, wind, waves and the cold. Time and time again the current dragged him towards the side of the cave, and he forced himself back on track. By the time he reached Bron, Harry was halfway back with Tatiana.

'Fancy a lift?' Ant said. 'Only you look a bit knackered.'

Bron was looking very cold, shivering violently.

'Come on, let's get you out of here,' said Ant.

Ant was strong, but he wasn't the greatest of swimmers. It took all his brute strength to get to the middle of the cave. The dark and the pounding of the waves disorientated him, and he had several panicky moments when he thought they might not make it. Then he became dimly aware that the entrance of the cave might not be too far away, and forced himself to power on. Bron seemed too worn out now to help, barely even kicking. It was like having a lead weight in his arms, and Ant was struggling to get him to the entrance, which was tantalisingly close. He tried not to think about the effect that age, and the water, would be having on Auberon's body. If he was finding it tough, Bron must be really struggling. Don't think about that, Ant admonished himself, otherwise we're both lost. One stroke at a time, he told himself, one stroke at a time. Then just as he was nearly there, a huge wave smashed over his head, and Bron moved suddenly out of his grasp. And then Bron was gone, and Ant was alone with the waves and the wind, in the darkness.

Seeing that Josie was still perched anxiously at the side of the cave, Diana went up to Harry.

'You okay?' she said.

'Fine,' said Harry. 'Bit chilly.'

'Have another blanket then,' she said. 'You need to keep huddled up, to avoid hypothermia.'

'She's right,' said M'stard, throwing another blanket over him. 'And here, have another nip of whisky.'

'I'm going to be paralytic if you're not careful,' said Harry. He stared nervously at the cave. 'Has anyone seen Ant yet? He's taking a long time.'

'Too long,' said Diana. She looked really worried. She followed Josie to the edge of the cave, where they both watched in silent horror as the coastguard's boat shone torches in the water, to see if they could spot anyone.

Diana felt a chill go down her spine. Ant. Not Ant. Whether he wanted her or not, now she'd met up with him again, she couldn't imagine a world without his big brash presence in it. Didn't want to.

She strained to see in the gloom of the cave. It was easy to detect movements that weren't there, but...

'Jose – can you see?' She clutched at Josie's arm as she saw a body moving in the water, no, two bodies, swimming side by side. The men in the boat saw them at the same time, and shouted rapid orders. Ropes flew into the water, and first Bron, and then Ant, were hauled to safety.

'Thank God,' said Josie, tears in her eyes, 'I thought I'd lost him.'

'Sorry?' said Diana.

'Ant,' said Josie, her eyes shining. 'I've been so blind. I'm in love with Ant.'

Now: Bron

He'd felt he was going to be a hero, seeing Tati like that, frightened and trapped in the cave. But he'd messed up and managed to lose the rope. He'd needed rescuing himself, and then had to be ignominiously hauled into the boat. Not only that, he'd spent the coldest, wettest, most terrifying hour of his life, only to end up looking like a prize idiot. Tati would laugh at him more than ever.

She was sitting, hair bedraggled, wrapped in blankets, holding court with the coastguards, most of whom appeared to be completely under her spell. Even soaking wet and blue with cold, she was beautiful to him. Not just beautiful, Tati looked magnificent, like a mermaid straight from the ocean. Whereas he...

Bron allowed himself to be examined by the experts, who checked his vital signs and insisted on making him drink some weak hot tea. He'd rather have had whisky, but it did make him feel better rapidly. True he'd got quite cold in the water, but surrounded by blankets he'd warmed up quickly. But he must look a right state. Unlike Ant, who was a vision of glowing young manhood. Bron felt quite jealous of the admiring looks Tatiana was casting him. She was barely sending any looks in his direction. Bron sighed heavily. He'd wanted to prove something to Tati today, and had only succeeded in looking like a fool. A stupid romantic old fool.

Chapter Thirty-One

'You love Ant?' her friend's shock was palpable. 'What about Harry? What about *me?*'

Oh God. In her moment of clarity, Josie had forgotten all about Diana's declaration of love to Ant.

'I'm sorry, Di,' said Josie, 'but it's just the way I feel. I can't help it.'

She walked away feeling she should care more, but somehow she didn't. She'd spent the whole night in turmoil. But now the sun was rising, and a new day was dawning and everything had become crystal clear. Harry was her past. Ant was her future and she'd nearly lost him. The sight of Ant fearlessly ploughing through the water was one she wouldn't forget in a while. Harry was heroic too, a little voice in her head said, but she ignored it. She was done with confusion and misery. Now she knew what she had to do.

'Do you think they're going to be all right?' Josie said, anxiously scanning the boat where Ant and the others were being checked over. She felt so responsible for what had happened. She should have remembered the danger of getting cut off in the cave. It was something that had happened to her several times in her teenage years, but never so dramatically as this.

After what seemed like forever, the boat putt-putted slowly to the shore, and the coastguards let everyone climb out.

'You've all been very lucky,' the captain said. 'Nothing worse than a dousing. But that was incredibly dangerous. You should never have attempted a rescue like that.'

'Sorry,' said Harry, 'that was my fault. We were worried you wouldn't get here in time.'

'As it happens, you got away with it,' the coastguard said, less sternly. 'Besides,' he added with a twinkle, 'it's not every day we get to rescue

319

celebrities. But don't do it again. That cave is notorious. Like I said, you were very lucky.'

Tatiana was looking slightly stunned, and her cavalcade rushed forward, making soothing noises, plying her with drinks, wrapping her up in so many layers she looked like a mummy, and generally behaving in the over-the-top manner Josie had come to expect.

'I'm so sorry, Tatiana,' said Josie, 'I was only trying to help. I'd completely forgotten the tide was coming in. It's all my fault.'

'Nonsense,' said Bron, briskly. 'If anyone's to blame it's me, for letting Freddie persuade me to go along with this hypnotism nonsense. It got out of hand, and we should have put a stop to it hours ago.'

'You?' Tatiana said. 'You had something to do with that – that idiot pursuing me?'

'Yes, and I'm sorry,' said Bron, 'but I can explain...'

'Forget it,' said Tatiana, delivering a ringing slap round his face. 'You and Freddie, same old, same old. And there I was, feeling grateful that you tried to rescue me. Come on, we're going back to the yurt.'

And with that, she and her cronies stormed off.

'I guess I deserved that,' said Bron with a sigh.

'Talking of Freddie,' Ant looked around, 'where is he?'

He'd been there when Harry and Ant had dived into the water, but he seemed conspicuously absent now. Having caused all this mayhem, he seemed to have done a runner with Will, who'd been filming the rescue. Light blue touch paper and retire...

'He might have gone back to the theatre to deal with Mike,' said Bron. 'If I know Freddie, he'll be getting him to sign all kinds of disclaimers.'

'Why are you still friends with him?' asked Ant curiously.

'Why is anyone friends with anyone?' said Bron. 'Habit, years of rubbing along together. Despite everything, we do make a good team.'

'Except when he ruins your love life,' said Ant.

'There is that,' said Bron.

Ant glanced at Harry, who was talking to the girls. He hadn't spoken to any of them since getting out of the water. He didn't like to go near Josie, because of what Harry had said earlier. He still wanted to be the decent friend. But something in what Bron said stirred up forgotten memories. Harry only knew Josie because of him. They'd come down here when they were at uni and he'd thought he was in with a chance, and then Harry, his mate, had stolen Josie from under his nose. Ant's indignation completely overrode his memories of having been distracted with Kerry – Kelly? He'd taken his eye off the prize and Harry had claimed it. And now Josie had chosen him again, and Harry had lost. It was the way of the world, and all was fair in love and war. He'd just nearly drowned. Life was too short to be noble; he wasn't going to pass up this opportunity. It might never come his way again.

Diana stood feeling miserable, trying to ignore

the fact that Ant was making puppy dog eyes at Josie, who was clearly itching to be alone with him. But Harry had cornered her, and was talking earnestly to her, so when Bron and Ant decided it was time to leave, Josie had no choice but to stay. Diana decided to follow them though she didn't quite know why. Nothing was ever going to bring him back to her. The whole thing was a total mess, and she couldn't think how they could remain friends after this.

'That was brave,' she said, as she caught up with Bron.

'Brave or stupid?' said Bron. 'Tati wasn't impressed, and without Ant coming to my rescue, it could have been a very different story.'

'It was nothing,' said Ant. 'It was pretty stupid of all of us to have gone in. The things we do for love, eh?'

'So you only went in to help to show off to Josie?' said Diana, feeling worse than ever. 'Ant, you're unbelievable. And there was me thinking you had a vulnerable side.'

'It wasn't just that,' protested Ant.

'It's all right,' Bron patted him on the shoulder, 'I did the same. Even if I still gained nothing from it.'

'You don't think she's going to forgive you, then?' said Diana.

'You saw her face,' said Bron, with a sigh. 'I don't think she'll ever forgive me.'

Harry felt hopeful when Diana left with Bron and Ant. Josie was staring out to sea, ominously silent.

'Well?' he said in the end, unable to stand the silence.

'Well, what?' said Josie.

'What's happening with us?' said Harry.

He thought again of having seen Josie and Ant holding hands earlier, and how Ant hadn't acknowledged his comment about it. A short stab of jealousy shot through him.

'I thought we'd established there *is* no more us,' said Josie, her gaze unblinking from the horizon. 'I'm sorry, Harry. It's over.'

'This is about Ant, isn't it?' said Harry. 'Josie, he's my best friend.'

'And Di's mine,' Josie shot back, 'but that didn't stop you snogging her.'

'I didn't snog her,' said Harry. 'She threw her arms round me.'

'And I found you asleep with your arms wrapped round her,' said Josie.

'Again, not guilty,' said Harry, 'Diana curled up next to me when I was already asleep.'

'Ant told me the way he feels, and I wasn't sure,' said Josie, 'but now I am. It's him I want, not you.'

Without looking at him, she turned away and headed up the cliff.

'It's not what you really feel,' Harry shouted into the wind. 'It's just Freddie screwing with your mind. And I'm going to prove it.'

Chapter Thirty-Two

Ant, Bron and Diana reached the theatre and pushed their way in. Freddie was sitting with a dazed looking Mike, saying, 'When you awake, none of this will have happened. You never met Tatiana Okeby here, you never agreed to produce her in *A Midsummer Night's Dream*. You have just been on an early morning stroll and had a little doze. When I count to three, you will fall into a deep sleep, and when you wake up you will have forgotten everything, three, two, one...'

And Mike slumped down.

'Perfect,' said Freddie, to Will. 'I think we can use that.'

'Do you really think that's a good idea?' said Bron. 'I don't think Tati will be happy to be shown up on camera.'

'It was your idea,' said Freddie.

'And I've changed my mind,' said Bron. 'Come on, I thought it was going to be funny, but it hasn't turned out that way.'

'Maybe you're right,' said Freddie. 'I think the words *sue*, and *you* may have been uttered as she left.'

'And what about us?' said Ant, 'I don't think your experiment has been entirely successful.'

He'd kept a careful distance from Diana since getting out of the water. He had been so stunned when she'd tried to kiss him earlier, he'd reacted

324

instantly. He knew he'd been cruel, and felt bad about it, but Diana wasn't for him, not any more. Not now he'd found Josie again. He didn't want to hurt her any more than he had to.

'You can say that again,' said Diana. 'I think I can count this as one of the most traumatic, upsetting and humiliating experiences of my life. So I don't want you showing any footage of it at all, thank you very much.'

'Oh,' said Freddie, looking a little discomfited. 'Has it really been that bad?'

'Bad? It's been worse than bad.' She gave Ant a knowing look. 'I've fallen in love and been re-jected, my best friend briefly chased me round this stage, and I've fallen out with all of the people I really care about. Tonight is the story of my life writ large. Everyone gets happy endings but me.'

'Do you really feel like that?' Ant was genuinely surprised. Despite her confidences in him earlier, Di had always seemed invulnerable to him, as if love didn't matter to her. He'd really thought the feelings she'd developed for him were skin-deep, brought about by the hypnotism; perhaps he'd been wrong.

'Not that you'd care,' snapped Diana. 'Because it looks like things have worked out for you.'

'What?' said Ant.

'She's coming up the path right now,' said Diana.

Ant turned as the gate creaked, and he saw Josie coming shyly towards him.

'I've made my decision,' she said shyly. 'And I choose you.'

And with that, she stood on tiptoes and kissed

325

him on the cheek.

Diana felt sick to the pit of her stomach when she saw Josie kiss Ant. It didn't seem fair. She had both Ant and Harry lapping out of her hands, and Di had no one, even if it was the hypnotism that had addled their brains, they'd still both chosen Josie. Diana knew it was mean-spirited of her, but she wanted just for once for Josie to know how it was when life didn't go the way you wanted. Let her feel rejection and disillusionment.

'So you haven't managed to sort things out with Ant, then?' said Bron, putting a sympathetic arm round her shoulder.

'I thought maybe I had,' said Diana, 'but looks like I was wrong.'

She stared gloomily at Ant and Josie, who seemed oblivious to everyone else.

'You're still in love with Ant?' Bron said perceptively.

'I don't know – yes – no, maybe,' said Diana. 'I'm feeling extremely confused right now. I'm not sure which of my feelings are real anymore.'

'I think you'd know,' said Bron. 'Just as I do about Tati.'

'Do you think she'll get over what you did to her tonight?'

'Somehow, no,' said Bron sadly. 'I think I might have finally nailed the coffin on our relationship.'

'And I think I'm destined to be a bitter old spinster,' said Diana. 'Quite frankly it wouldn't matter who I was in love with, being friends with Josie means that no one looks at me. They all flood to her.'

Diana had never thought about this before, but suddenly realised it was true. It hadn't mattered so much when she and Josie were both playing the field, and nothing was serious. But since Josie had met Harry it mattered very much. Very much indeed.

Harry sat down after Josie was gone.

Josie had got muddled up tonight. They all had. She didn't know what she was doing. He'd have to remind her of how she really felt. Harry got up and strode off. He was going to find Freddie Puck and sort this out once and for all. Ant had had his chance with Josie all those years ago, and blown it. Faint heart never won fair lady. Harry was damned if he was going to let her go so easily now.

He set off back up the cliff path, not quite sure what he was going to do. As he reached the theatre, he saw Mike Slowbotham stumble out, looking sleepy.

'Hello old boy,' he said. 'Seems to be a bit of a party going on in there. I must have had a hell of a night. I can't remember a thing.'

Maybe Freddie had put one thing right, thought Harry. Time for him to get everything else right too.

Josie was sitting on a hillock, holding Ant's hand in a happy daze, completely oblivious to everyone else. She felt otherworldly. A morning mist was creeping over the theatre, casting strange shapes and making her feel quite ethereal. She knew Diana was angry with her, but she couldn't mind somehow – though a bit of her thought she should – because sitting here, leaning against Ant, was making her feel sublimely happy. Happier then she'd ever felt in her life before.

They hadn't said much, but Josie felt as if they didn't need to. They could communicate through their minds, their senses; everything was accentuated. The sound of the sea, the soft summer breeze, the brush of his cheek against hers. Never had she felt like this. Never had she felt this dizzying rush of love and sweet desire. She wanted the moment to go on and on for ever.

'Good. I thought I'd find you here.' Tatiana swept in, with M'stard rushing behind her saying, 'Please, Tati, I think you should get back to the yurt, I'm not sure this will help.'

'I want to know what you did to me tonight, Freddie, you bastard. And I want any footage you've got of this evening, destroyed, *capisce?*'

Bron got up. 'Tati. Look, this was my fault. I thought I wanted to get back at you, and let Freddie persuade me it was a good idea. I realise now it wasn't.'

Tatiana looked sad suddenly.

'That's the trouble with you, Bron, isn't it?' she said. 'You've always let Freddie dictate to you. Even when it comes to us. *Especially* when it comes to us.'

'I know, and I'm sorry,' said Bron. 'You're right. Freddie, mate, I think this hypnosis thing has gone far enough. You need to sort things out.'

'If you absolutely insist,' said Freddie, 'but you have to admit, it has been such fun.'

'Not for me, it hasn't.' Josie turned to see Harry glowering fiercely at Freddie. She'd never seen him look so angry before.

'Oi, Ant,' he said. 'Leave my fiancée alone.'

Ant stood up. 'I'm sure we can sort this out in a civilized fashion...'Ant began, before Harry launched himself at him.

'I'm not,' said Harry. Josie screamed as he struck Ant on the nose, and knocked him to the ground.

Chapter Thirty-Three

Diana leapt to her feet, hand over her mouth as she watched Harry tackle Ant to the ground. 'Harry, no!' she screamed as Harry sat on Ant's stomach and pummelled his face, followed by, 'Please don't hurt him.' Not that he looked in danger of doing so. Ant being the stronger, he soon recovered from the element of surprise, and managed to push Harry off him.

'Come on, mate,' he said, 'we'll never solve anything like this.' But Harry just threw another blow at him. Ant ducked and Harry nearly tripped over.

'You bastard, Ant,' he panted, arms flailing wildly. 'You're not going to get away with this.'

He was bright red in the face from the exertion, and made a most unlikely boxer.

'You're mad,' said Ant, 'but if you really have to do this then–'

He struck, out and caught Harry a glancing blow on the cheek.

Harry appeared infuriated by this and charged

Ant, who pushed him away easily. The pair tussled to and fro for an instant, neither gaining much advantage, Josie shrieking helplessly, 'Stop! The both of you. Please.'

'You're never satisfied, are you?' spat Harry, as Ant managed to land another blow. 'You think you're so much better than everyone else, that you're entitled to take what you want. Well, you're not having Josie, do you hear?'

He hit out wildly, and managed a lucky blow in the stomach.

'Oof,' said Ant, before coming back at Harry with a huge shove, which made Harry fall over.

'It's not up to you, mate,' he said. 'Why don't you ask Josie?'

'What, so you can treat her like you did Di?' said Harry. 'Josie, you can't have forgotten that this is the man who left his girlfriend alone while she was having a miscarriage? Some romantic he is.'

'You bastard,' said Ant. 'It wasn't like that, and Di knows it.'

And with that, he was like a raging animal, raining blows down on Harry like a man possessed.

'Stop!' screamed Di. 'Both of you, please, just stop!'

Ant had never been so furious in his life. He couldn't think of anything but that he wanted to punish Harry, and pummel him half to death. How dare he say that about Diana? What did he bloody know about it?

Harry wasn't going to back down easily though. He might not be as strong as Ant, but he was good at ducking and diving, and hard as Ant tried, he wasn't connecting many punches. Ant was soon breathless from trying to keep up. He'd put on weight since he'd been home and Harry spent more time in the gym, which was giving him an advantage.

'And what about you?' he taunted. 'Some loyal fiancé you are. Not even prepared to follow through your promises. Josie's better off without you.'

'You!' Harry launched straight at him, forgetting to parry, so Ant managed to catch him in the stomach. Not so much of an advantage then. Ant had evidently spent more of his youth scrapping than Harry.

'Ugh,' Harry staggered backwards, but he soon steadied himself, and like the Duracell Bunny, he kept coming back for more. It seemed as if nothing was going to stop him.

'Don't you dare talk about Josie,' Harry said and he was off again, darting round Ant, throwing punches when he could.

Ant was beginning to tire. It had been a very long night. He was vaguely aware the girls were yelling at them to stop, but he found himself unable to step back. Harry had started and Ant was buggered if he was going to back out now.

'Can't you do something?' said Josie in desperation to Freddie, who looked like he was enjoying himself. 'They're going to kill each other.'

'I doubt that,' said Freddie. 'It's not like either of them is much cop.'

It was true that neither of them had really managed to inflict that much damage on the other, which was something, Josie thought. But they were beginning to tire now and were staggering round the theatre. Ant had a cut on his lip, and Harry had a bruised cheek. Josie couldn't bear that either of them was being hurt. She felt the first smidgeon of doubt about her behaviour. Had she done the right thing, choosing Ant? Maybe she'd have been better off choosing neither of them.

'This is all your fault, Freddie,' she said. 'We were fine till we met you.'

'You all agreed to be hypnotised,' shrugged Freddie, 'and the subconscious is a strange thing. You all appear to have acted out secret desires tonight.'

'Yes, but we didn't expect this,' said Josie. 'Di's barely speaking to me, the boys are fighting, I've no idea what I feel about anyone. You have to stop it.'

'She's right,' Bron said. 'Freddie, this has gone too far. What we did to Tati was bad enough. But this – you're playing with people's lives. It's not fair.'

'And so the lion eventually roars,' said Tatiana, looking slightly admiring.

'You still got something to give?' Ant taunted Harry, panting wildly. 'Come on then, come and get me!'

'I could keep this going all day,' said Harry savagely, and launched another attack.

Two of them fighting over her. Some other woman might be thrilled about that, but not Josie.

'Freddie, Bron's right, you need to do something now!'

Harry could barely stand. His ribs were aching, he had a huge stitch, his shirt was torn and his fists felt bruised. He hadn't had a physical fight with anyone since he was eight, when he'd punched Adam Fellows on the nose for saying Katrina Jones was a cow. Katrina had been his girlfriend at the time. Which just went to show chivalry wasn't dead.

Despite how rough he was feeling, Harry had no intention of backing down. Ant had crossed a line, and he was going to have to pay for it.

'Gentlemen, I think it's time to call it a day.' Harry was suddenly aware that Freddie Puck was standing in his way. 'This has gone far enough.'

Enraged that anyone would try to stop him now, and doubly enraged by all the trouble Freddie had wrought, Harry punched him on the nose.

'Ouch!' said Freddie, clutching his nose, which was pouring blood. 'There was no need for that!'

'Go, Harry,' said Tatiana. 'Team Harry for the win!'

'Not helping, Tati darling,' said Bron.

'Keep out of this,' said Harry to Freddie. 'It's my fight.'

He threw himself at Ant once more and soon they were rolling and scrapping on the grass like two street kids.

'Harry, stop it! You'll kill him!' He vaguely heard Josie's voice, which enraged him further. Harry fought like a madman, till he felt arms reaching from behind him and dragging him away from Ant. It was Bron.

'Enough, Harry, it's enough. This isn't going to

solve anything.'

Harry stood panting, his heart hammering. The fury started to drain away. He looked down at himself. What a state. 'I suppose,' he said.

Ant got up, looking rather sheepish, the cut on his lip still bleeding.

'Did I do that?' Harry was quite proud of himself. He'd never really considered fighting one of his life skills.

'Right,' said Bron. 'Let's be civilised about this.'

'So long as Ant says sorry,' said Harry.

'Sorry? You started it,' said Ant.

'If you can't keep your hands to yourself,' glared Harry.

'She was up for it,' taunted Ant. 'Let's face it, you lost her.'

'You...!' Harry threw a final enraged punch at Ant, which, catching him by surprise, caught him bang on the nose.

'Oh,' said Ant in surprise. He wobbled a bit, and unlike a Weeble, fell down.

'Ant!' there was a shriek from the girls.

'Oh, Harry,' said Josie. 'What have you done?'

Now: Bron

'My my, quite the hero tonight, aren't we?' Tatiana said.

Bron had taken Harry to one side and calmed him down while the girls were tending to Ant. Harry was sitting, looking genuinely stunned.

334

'I didn't mean to hit him that hard,' he kept saying, 'really I didn't.'

'I know old chap,' said Bron, patting him on the back. 'Heat of the moment, passions flying, and all that. If this were on the stage, it would make a great tragedy.'

'Thanks,' said Harry, 'but my life isn't normally this dramatic, and quite frankly, I prefer it like that.'

Bron paused from what he was doing and looked up at Tati.

'No,' he said, 'you know I'm not. I've never been the hero you deserved.'

This was an improvement. At least Tati was talking to him.

'You could always change that,' she said, a little smile playing on her lips.

Hang on, this was Tati warmer than he'd seen her towards him for years.

'Erm, how exactly?' he said, wondering if this were some kind of trick.

'By following it through.'

'What?'

'The standing up to Freddie thing,' she said. 'I rather like it.'

'Well, then, I shall do it some more,' said Bron. He strode over to Freddie, who was still nursing his sore nose.

'It hurts,' he complained. 'I should sue.'

'Stop being such a baby,' said Bron. 'It serves you right. You need to sort all of this out, right now.'

'Why should I?' said Freddie sulkily. 'They signed contracts. I never promised them they'd fall in love with the right people. Just that they'd plight their troth at midnight. Which they've all done. It will make great telly.'

'Great telly, my arse!' roared Bron. 'You've muddled these lovely people up enough, they deserve to be back together with the ones they love. Got it?'

'Got it,' said Freddie, completely taken aback.

'Ooh,' cooed Tati, 'I do love a masterful man.'

And Bron glowed with pride.

Chapter Thirty-Four

Ant came to in a daze. He didn't know where he was for a moment, then had a sudden rush to the head. He was lying in snow, next to Diana, giggling his head off.

'Di,' he said as her face swam into view, but then another face was looking over him anxiously. 'Where's Diana?' he said. 'I want Di.'

'It's Josie, Ant,' the face said. 'You've had a bang on the head.'

Ant felt his nose, which really hurt, and his stomach was aching.

'Josie?' he said tentatively. He wasn't lying in snow. Diana wasn't beside him, he was lying in dew-soaked grass on top of a cliff in Cornwall. And everything seemed to hurt.

'Are you all right?' said Josie. 'I was so worried.'

Josie was worried about *him*?

'I think so,' said Ant. He tried to sit up, but felt

a bit dizzy, and lay back down again. It was quite pleasant lying on the grass staring at the sky, relaxing. He had a feeling he had been under a lot of stress recently.

'Ant, Ant, talk to me,' Josie was rubbing his hands anxiously. Why was Josie rubbing his hands? Where was Diana?

'I'm fine really,' said Ant. 'Just give me a minute.'

'Yes, Josie, give him a minute,' he heard Diana say. 'Poor guy needs some air. Don't fuss so.'

'I'm not fussing,' said Josie.

'Here, this will help,' Diana produced something strong in a hip flask. 'It's brandy, I got it from Freddie.'

Ant took a sip and it nearly blew his head off.

Freddie? He felt more confused than ever. Then it all came flooding back. The hypnotism; the mix-ups, rescuing Tatiana, the fight.

He sat bolt upright, searching for Harry.

'You knocked me out,' Ant said indignantly.

Harry managed to look sheepish and defiant at the same time.

'You stole Josie from me.'

'You didn't want her,' said Ant.

'That's not true,' said Harry. 'I love Josie. I just don't want to get married ... yet. Maybe one day, but not now.'

They stared at each other, and for a moment Ant thought Harry might be about to kick off again, but then Ant burst out laughing.

'I guess none of us has behaved brilliantly tonight,' he said. 'Look at the state of us.'

He was aware that his nose was bleeding and his shirt was caked in blood, while Harry's was ripped at the collar. They were both covered in bruises, Harry sporting a particularly fine one on his cheek.

'It's not funny,' scolded Josie, applying a hankie to his nose. 'Harry could have really hurt you.'

'Here, let me,' said Diana. 'He needs his head held right back if that bleeding's ever going to stop.'

'Who do you think you are?' said Josie, clearly feeling she had the right to take charge. 'His mother?'

'Ladies, ladies, I'm quite capable of holding my own nose,' said Ant. 'Wonders'll never cease. Two women fighting over me. I could get used to this.'

He pinched his nose, tipped his head back, got up and limped over to Harry.

'No hard feelings, mate,' he said proffering his hand.

'None,' said Harry. 'Sorry about your nose.'

'Sorry about your shirt.'

They stood awkwardly for a minute before Ant said, 'Come here you stupid sod,' and enveloped him in a bear hug.

'Now what?' said Harry.

'Now Freddie is going to put things right,' said Bron.

Josie was seething. Diana had pushed her way over to Ant, as soon as he'd gone down, and was acting as if he were her property. Diana, who hadn't done anything but sneer and snipe at Ant all weekend. Diana, who'd spent half the weekend chasing after Harry, and the other half chasing Ant.

'What is it with you and men,' hissed Josie. 'Do

338

you always have to steal guys that belong to someone else?'

'Can't poor little Josie cope without her coterie of admirers?' sneered Diana. 'Are you going to add Freddie and Bron to the set? I bet Mike would happily join in too, given his recent disappointment.'

'What?' said Josie. 'I'm not the one who pursues other people's fiancés. Just because you can't get a man of your own doesn't mean you can steal mine.'

'You're the one who's spent the best part of the night pushing Harry away,' Diana said furiously. 'You know your trouble, Josie? You're spoilt rotten. With your big house, and your wealthy mummy and daddy who'll bail you out of the slightest crisis. You can't cope when things don't go your way. You're a spoilt little cow.'

'And you're a jealous bitch,' said Josie. 'I can't help it if you've had a crappy home life, you've lost your job, and screwed up your love life. You need to start taking responsibility for your own life. Not blaming other people for your mistakes.'

'You ... you... You have no idea what it's been like for me!' Diana looked angrier than Josie had ever seen her. 'How dare you say that?' She slapped Josie round the face.

Josie clutched her face, stunned.

'Oh, God,' said Diana, 'I'm so sorry – I didn't mean to...'

'Josie, are you okay?' Ant and Harry both sprang up like knights in shining armour.

'Great,' said Diana slumping down, defeated. 'Always the bridesmaid, never the sodding bride.'

'Blimey, a catfight,' said Ant, trying to make light of things. 'Did you have to stop?'

'Shut up, Ant. Josie, are you okay?' Harry said, putting his arm round her.

'Fine,' said Josie, shaking his arm off. She was still glaring at Diana, who was sitting down on the ground, the wind completely out of her sails.

'Are you sure?' Ant was over in a trice, trying to find a gap in her defences no doubt. She was fed up with the lot of them. Men were just too much trouble.

'Absolutely,' said Josie. 'I'm tired, fed up and I just want to go home.'

Harry came over to her again.

'Come on, Josie,' he said gently. 'It's been a mad night. We can sort this out, I'm sure.'

'Can we?' said Josie. 'I think my whole life has just fallen apart in front of me, and no,' – she could see that Ant was taking that as an invitation – 'I made a mistake earlier on. Being with you won't solve anything. I want to be alone, and this time I really mean it.'

And she got up and walked away.

Diana stood up too. 'I think I should go after her,' she said, her voice trailing off. 'I just said some unspeakable things.'

She felt sad and defeated. Josie was probably never going to speak to her again. Harry wasn't interested in her at all. The only thing she'd gained from this night was a truce with Ant.

'It might not do any good at the moment,' said Ant, squeezing her arm with surprising gentleness. 'I think we need to get back to where we were. Sorry I got us all into this. Truly I am.'

Ant saying sorry? Possibly the most surprising thing in a very surprising night? Diana raised a small smile.

'Since when did you start saying sorry?' she said.

'Since I realised what a pillock I was to you all those years ago, and how I've made it worse tonight,' said Ant. 'I can't be in love with Josie. It wouldn't work, and I'm sorry I hurt you by thinking I was. It's bad enough I hurt you before, I don't want to hurt you again.'

'I know,' said Diana, 'I'm not sure anything I've been feeling tonight is real. But I do know I've been carrying all that anger round with me for years. It hasn't done me much good. I can see now Sian had a lot to answer for; I should have given you the benefit of the doubt. I'm really sorry.'

'I'm glad we're friends,' said Ant. 'That's the only good thing that has come out of tonight.'

He kissed her on the cheek. Such a sweet tender kiss. And Diana felt something melt inside her. Ant. How very, very lovely he was. She wished he felt the same way about her.

'Come on, Freddie,' said Ant, 'time to get this show on the road.'

'You're all sure?' said Freddie.

'Absolutely,' said Diana. 'I'm fed up with feeling this miserable and confused. I'd rather wake up alone and never be in love again than feel like this.'

'And I just want Josie and me to be back the way we were,' said Harry.

'Ant, what about you?'

'Not to have to feel so responsible for every-one,' said Ant firmly. 'I prefer being a bastard. It's

341

much less hassle.'

'In that case,' said Freddie, 'when I click my fingers, you will think you've been having a strange dream, but everything else will be back to normal.'

'And Josie?'

'I'll go after her,' said Bron, 'persuade her to come back.'

'Right,' said Freddie. 'I'm going to click my fingers, three, two, one, and you're asleep...'

Diana felt herself yawning, overcome with weariness. Sleep seemed so welcome. Vaguely she was aware that Freddie was saying something about the Standing Stones, and then she remembered nothing more. She was fast asleep.

Chapter Thirty-Five

Josie was sitting down by the beach. It must be nearly 7am by now. She didn't know what had drawn her back, but the solitude, and the pounding of the waves as the sun rose higher in the sky, were having a calming effect on her shattered nerves.

She didn't know what she felt anymore. Couldn't untangle in her head whether she wanted to be with anyone, but going straight from Harry to Ant seemed like the worst idea she'd ever had. What had possessed her? It must have been the hypnotism, that or madness and moonlight.

Josie felt ashamed of the things she'd said to Diana. Diana was right, she *could* be spoilt sometimes, and she didn't know how the other half lived. She knew Diana's life had been much harder than her own. It had been cruel of her to say so. Diana's tough exterior hid a heart of gold, and she'd been a good friend to Josie, always there when she needed her. And without Diana's prompting Harry would probably never have moved in with her in the first place, or asked her to marry him.

Maybe Josie had been at fault for letting herself get caught up in the moment. She'd rushed headlong into this marriage thing without thinking it through. And she had got carried away. She could see that now. No wonder poor Harry had freaked. Another stab of remorse went through her. She'd been tough on him over Diana, and then fallen straight into Ant's arms, without considering his feelings. The one constant of the night, she realised, had been Harry's dogged persistence that he loved her. Maybe she should give him another chance. Not that he deserved it...

'Josie.' She looked up to see Bron standing there. 'I know tonight's been a disaster, but I've just about stopped Freddie from meddling and he's put the others back to sleep. When they wake up none of this will have happened. What do you think?'

'I think that's the best idea I've heard all night,' said Josie.

Ant was dreaming. He was eighteen again, and he and Diana were dancing in a sun-filled meadow. Which couldn't be right, because he'd met Diana in Switzerland. But that didn't matter in the dream. She looked beautiful. Her eyes sparkled and shone, and her titian hair flowed and danced down her back. She wore a simple white flowing dress, bare feet and had flowers in her hair. Rays of sunshine danced in the dew at their feet.

'It's the summer solstice,' she said, laughing. 'A time for rebirth and new beginnings.'

He whirled her round and round, their dance growing wilder and more heady. He was caught up in a whirlwind of dizzying intoxicating love and felt almost as if he were flying. He remembered this feeling. He remembered it so clearly, he felt he could reach out and touch it. This was once him. This was once Diana. This was what they'd shared and lost. How stupid, stupid, he'd been to let this go. It felt so perfect and right...

And suddenly the dream was fading and it felt like he was coming down to land. No! he wanted to cry, let me stay here with her, where I know and feel love. But nearer, nearer, the earth approached and suddenly he had tumbled down to earth once more. He sat up, staring into a glaring morning sun.

Ant felt bereft. The dream that held him had seemed so real. Of course it was obvious now. It was Diana he loved; had never stopped loving her. He'd hidden it in the recesses of his mind. He hoped that she could remember too, what they'd had once, because despite what he'd been pretending for years, what they'd had, had been very special.

Then he took in his surroundings. He was by the Standing Stones. How had he got here? The last thing he remembered was being at the theatre.

And then Ant saw her, curled up on a mound of grass, with flowers in her hair, looking for all the world like a sleeping angel.

Diana was dreaming that she was dancing across stepping stones. She was trying to reach someone. It was vital she found him. But the closer she came the further away he seemed. She ran lightly across the stones, barefoot, jumping from one to the other, yet not once did she slip and fall. The sound of the tinkling stream gave way to a louder sound and became a thundering roar, as she followed its path to a pool, where a waterfall gushed over the edge.

As she stared, a man emerged from the pool, a fine handsome figure with muscles to die for. He shook himself dry, and smiled at her, and her heart tumbled over itself as she remembered that she loved him, this man, whose name she had forgotten. Something had stopped them loving one another, but she couldn't think what. All she knew was that she longed for him now. So Diana ran as fast as she could towards him, her heart full of joy. But as she grew closer he faded away from her sight, until she woke up and found herself feeling a huge sense of regret and loss. The sun was getting quite bright in the sky. She shielded her eyes, as she became aware that someone was watching her.

She blushed as she realised who it was.

'Oh,' she blurted it out. 'I was just dreaming about you.'

'That's funny,' he said. 'I was dreaming about you too.'

There was a pause and Diana looked at him properly for the first time all weekend.

Suddenly she could see the young Ant, the Ant she'd fallen in love with.

'What was your dream about?' she said.

'We were dancing,' he said, 'and you were beautiful. You?'

Diana blushed again.

'You were swimming,' she said.

'And?'

'You were naked,' she admitted.

'Sounds like my kind of dream,' said Ant.

Diana blushed furiously.

'Come on, Di, don't be shy, it's not like we weren't close once,' said Ant, and presenting her with a bunch of Pansies, he added mischievously, 'Maybe it's time we were that close again.'

'Maybe,' said Diana, 'it is.'

Harry couldn't get comfortable. Something was poking him in the back and his head was leaning on something hard. He was dreaming that he was in a forest ablaze with colour. Only suddenly he realised it wasn't flowers and leaves as he'd at first thought, but a genuine fire, and Josie was trapped on the other side of it. He had to get her. He had to walk through fire to be worthy of her love.

'Harry! Harry!' he could hear her frantic calling. The flames looked fierce, but his love was stronger. Without a second thought he dived through them to reach her and was falling, falling, falling...

Harry woke up with a start. Pebbles were poking in his back and his head was perched awkwardly on a rock. But his arms were round a soft warm body. One he knew very well. His heart quickened with anticipation. What would she say when she knew it was him?

Josie turned round sleepily towards him.

'Oh, Harry,' she said. 'I was dreaming I'd lost you, but you were here all the time.'

'And I'll never go away again,' he said, kissing her softly on the lips, as the waves broke gently on the shore...

Chapter Thirty-Six

Ant couldn't believe it. He felt as if his eyes had been opened. As if he'd been washed clean and seen the world in a new light.

'Diana,' he said, hoping his voice was steadier than his unruly heart, which was beating at a rapid pace. 'I know this sounds mad, but I think I love you.'

Diana shook her head, and looked at him in a daze.

'It doesn't sound mad at all,' she said. 'In fact, I think it sounds perfect.'

'Are we sure this is real?' said Ant. 'It seems so sudden. The world feels so different.'

Diana pinched herself.

'Feels pretty real to me,' she said.

'But you hated me,' said Ant.

'And you hated *me*,' said Diana.

'I thought I did,' admitted Ant. 'But I was so

347

gutted when you ditched me, I just turned against you. I didn't know about the baby. If I had known the truth, things would have been different. When I did find out, I thought you'd kept me away deliberately, and it made me even angrier.'

'I know,' said Diana. 'If I hadn't been so hurt and angry myself, I'd have stopped and thought it through. I knew you'd never have left me without a good reason. But at the time I thought you'd abandoned me.'

'I could never have done that,' said Ant. 'You're the one person who's ever given meaning to my life. All I ever wanted was to look after you.'

'Oh, Ant,' said Diana, 'I wish I'd known.'

Ant paused, and then said, 'Did you ever know what it was? Boy or girl?'

Diana shook her head and looked sad.

'No, it was too early to tell,' she said. 'If it had lived it would have been seven by now. What a mad thought.'

Ant took her hand and locked it in his.

'I wasn't there for you then,' he said, 'but I promise I always will be from now on. Come on. We've wasted enough time. Let's not waste any more.'

'Harry? Oh Harry!' Josie snuggled up to him. 'I've been having terrible dreams, and I thought you'd left me. It feels like I've been walking through the woods for hours. I kept nearly catching you, and then you'd skip away from me. But here you were all the time.'

'And here I'll always be,' said Harry. 'I love you,

348

Josie, and always will. Without you my life would be meaningless.'

Josie felt her heart bursting with happiness. She felt as if she had been carrying around a great sadness, and now it was gone, to be replaced by a fizzing feeling of joy.

'I can barely remember anything about last night,' said Harry. 'Isn't that weird?'

'Me neither,' said Josie.

They lay watching the sea lap at the shore, feeling deeply content, and then Josie sat up suddenly.

'One thing I do remember,' she said urgently.

'Oh, what's that?' said Harry.

'Harry, do you truly in your heart of hearts want to marry me?' For some reason Josie knew she had to ask, even if she didn't like the answer.

Harry sat up too, and took her hand. He looked deep into her eyes, and kissed her.

'Josie, you have to know that I love you more than anything in the world. But I'm really sorry, I don't want to marry you – at least, not yet. I think, if I'm honest, we're rushing it.'

Josie took a deep breath.

'I think you're right,' she said simply. 'I got carried away with the ring and the big day. I'm sorry I've been such a nightmare about it. I didn't mean to be.'

'You were a bit,' said Harry, kissing her, 'but so long as I can still spend the rest of my life with you, I think I can forgive you.'

'So we are going to be together for ever?' said Josie, laughing.

'Most definitely,' said Harry. 'I couldn't imagine anyone else I'd rather be with.'

'Not even Diana?' said Josie.

'Especially not Diana,' he said kissing her on the lips.

'Come on,' said Josie, 'let's go home.'

Harry and Josie were coming down the path past the theatre, when they met Freddie and Bron.

'So how do you both feel?' said Freddie who looked unaccountably nervous.

'Great,' said Harry. 'I'm not sure if your hypnotism worked. Josie and I've been asleep all night.'

'Although I have been having some very weird dreams,' said Josie, 'and I can't work out how Harry's shirt got ripped, or he got that bruise on his cheek.'

'Maybe you elbowed him in your sleep,' said Bron.

'I'm sorry if we haven't given you any material to use,' said Harry.

'Oh, we got more than enough…' began Freddie, before Bron put in, 'I think we'll have to junk a lot of it, though. The quality wasn't that great.'

'Sorry it didn't work,' said Harry.

'Oh, I'm not sure about that,' said Freddie with a smile, looking past them. Harry and Josie turned round and to their astonishment, Diana and Ant were walking down the path wreathed in smiles, holding hands.

'What?' Harry and Josie both stood staring in disbelief.

'Guess what?' said Ant. 'The hypnotism worked. We've just plighted our troth to each other.'

'See, I told you,' said Freddie, smugly, 'I am the best.'

350

'Go on then,' said Ant, handing over twenty quid. 'Here's your money. You deserve it, mate.'

'You – really?' said Harry, gobsmacked. That was the last thing he'd been expecting. He was overcome with the urge to give his friend a huge bear hug. 'Well done, mate,' he said. 'What happened to your nose?'

'Don't know,' said Ant. 'I must have walked into one of those Stones in the dark. I've been having some very weird dreams.'

'So that's what I think I can call a success,' said Freddie. 'What about you two? Have you renewed your engagement?'

'Not exactly,' said Harry. 'We've decided to put off the wedding and go travelling for a bit. That is, as long as we still get our fee?'

Freddie was about to protest, but Bron nudged him, and he mumbled, 'Of course.'

'You two, travelling? Wow,' said Diana. 'That's amazing. Good luck with telling Josie's mum.'

'She can keep her hat for your wedding,' joshed Josie. 'I'm sure I can talk her round.'

'I do hope so,' said Harry, 'because I don't fancy having to kidnap you before our trip. Come on, let's go home, it's time to face the music.'

'Thanks,' said Diana to Freddie as they left. 'You've changed our lives for the better.'

Freddie bowed.

'Well, I'm glad to have been of service,' he said. 'I think the programme might need some fine tuning, but we can meet in the pub later and talk it all through.'

'What about you, Bron?' said Diana. 'What are

351

you going to do?' She had a funny feeling she owed him a great deal.

He nodded in the direction of the theatre.

'Tati's asleep in there. But when she wakes up, I'm going to do something I should have done a very long time ago.'

'Best of luck,' said Di, and she kissed him on the cheek. 'I don't know why, but I think you deserve it.'

They set off down the path to Josie's house.

'I'm so happy for you, Di,' said Josie, giving her a hug.

Diana felt emotional as she hugged her friend back.

'Are you sure you're okay about not marrying Harry?' she said.

'Fine,' said Josie, 'we're going to have so many adventures together. I can't wait.'

'I could eat a horse,' said Ant, 'I can't believe how hungry I am.'

'I ache all over,' said Josie. 'It's strange but I feel like I've been running a lot. Which is weird, because I'm sure Harry and I spent the whole night on the beach.'

'That's funny,' said Diana. 'My calves are really aching too.'

'And I've got bruises everywhere,' said Ant.

'Harry, I've only just noticed,' said Josie, 'your shirt's ripped. How did that happen?'

Diana had a sudden flashback to running around in the dark, trying to look for someone.

'You don't suppose...' she said slowly.

'What?' asked Ant.

'That there's something Freddie's not telling

us?' she said. 'How would we know if he'd hypnotised us and made us forget what happened?'

'That might explain why we're all aching so much,' said Josie.

'And why Ant and I have got bruises,' said Harry. 'If I didn't know any better, I'd think we'd been in a fight.'

'You two?' said Diana. 'Don't be so ridiculous.'

'Nah,' said Ant, shaking his head with conviction. 'That would be like us all having the same mad delusion. Don't believe it can be done.'

'Me neither,' said Josie. 'We must have strained ourselves from canoeing yesterday. Come on, race you home. If you're lucky, I might cook us eggs and bacon.'

And with that, the four friends ran laughing down the hill in the sunshine.

The world suddenly seemed a brighter, happier place. As if by magic.

Now: Bron and Tatiana

'Tati, darling.' He'd been sitting looking at her as she slept. She had never looked more beautiful to him.

'Mmm,' she said sleepily. She stirred and stretched with a yawn. 'I've been having the strangest dreams. You actually stood up to Freddie for once.'

'That was no dream,' said Bron. 'I did. He deserved it. I should have done it a long, long time ago.'

'Yes,' said Tati, looking at him levelly. 'You should have.'

Bron took his courage in both hands. It was now or never.

'Look, Tati, I know I let you down, over the abortion. God knows I wanted to have a baby with you. But I thought Freddie would replace you in the act if he found out you were pregnant. And I couldn't stand it. It was the worst mistake of my life, and I've been paying for it ever since. Can you ever forgive me?'

'Oh, darling Bron,' she said. 'I forgave you a long time ago. But pride, jealousy and the few shreds of dignity I had left stopped me from saying so. And I treated you pretty shabbily too.'

'No more than I deserved,' said Bron.

Tati took his hand, 'Oh, you dear, dear man. It was cruel and unkind of me to sell our story to the papers like that. Can *you* forgive *me?*'

Without hesitation, Bron leant over and kissed her. 'Nothing to forgive,' he said. 'Now, let's put the past behind us and get on with the rest of our lives.'

Epilogue: Three years later

'Now, until the break of day,
Through this house each fairy stray.
To the best bride-bed will we,
Which by us shall blessed be;
And the issue there create
Ever shall be fortunate.
So shall all the couples three
Ever true in loving be.'

A Midsummer Night's Dream:
Act V, Scene 1

'Dreams, Illusions, fancies. It's a bit of fun really.
Some mind trickery perhaps, but not to be taken too
seriously. I'm an entertainer, that's all. Mea culpa *if*
I've ever offended you. But come on, have I ... really?'

Freddie Puck: *The Art of Illusion*

'I'm so excited!' Diana was bouncing up and down like a two-year-old on speed. 'I can't wait to see them.'

'Me neither,' said Ant. 'Calm down. Their plane's only just landed. They'll be through soon.'

'I'll go and get us coffees,' said Diana. She went across to Costa Coffee. 'A latte and an Americano, please.'

'I don't believe it,' a familiar voice said behind her. 'Diana, is that you?'

'Bron!' said Diana. 'How fantastic to see you. What are you doing here?'

'Meeting Tati from New York,' he said. 'She's just been playing in *Cat on a Hot Tin Roof* on Broadway.'

'Oh yes, I saw that in the papers,' said Diana. 'So everything's going well, then.'

'Brilliant,' said Bron. 'You know we bought Tresgothen Manor, didn't you? You and Ant must come and see us.'

'That would be fantastic,' said Diana. 'I see Freddie has another series of *Let Me Hypnotise You* coming out.'

'He certainly does,' said Bron. 'It's amazing how successful that's been. People are starting to call for a revival of *Illusions,* so when Tati's had time to catch up, that's going to be our next project.'

'That's so brilliant,' said Diana. 'I'm really happy for you.'

357

'And you?'

'Ant and I are meeting Josie and Harry. They're finally coming home from their travels.'

'I can see congratulations are in order,' said Bron with a smile.

Diana blushed; it was hard to miss the enormous ring Ant had given her.

'Ant would insist on a rock,' she said. 'You and Tati should come to the wedding. Without you we might never have got together.'

'That would be lovely,' said Bron. He gave her a kiss. 'Tati's plane has just landed. I'd best be there or there'll be hell to pay.'

He slipped off out into the crowd, and Diana went back to find Ant.

'They're in baggage,' he said. 'Hopefully we don't need to wait much longer.'

'You'll never guess who I just met in Costa's,' said Di.

'Who?' said Ant.

'Only Bron,' said Diana.

'No! What's he doing here?' said Ant.

'Meeting Tati. You'll be pleased to know they're going to do a new series of *Illusions*.'

'Can't wait,' said Ant.

People had started to dribble through from customs. And they scoured the crowds, patiently until...

'There!' Ant pointed at Harry, who was pushing an enormous amount of luggage, with a fair-haired toddler sitting on the handlebars. Josie was following behind, pushing a six-month-old baby in a buggy.

Diana and Ant raced towards them, and soon

they were all hugging and laughing together.

'Let's see the ring,' demanded Josie. 'Wow, that's a monster. Trust Ant to be so ostentatious.'

'And these must be Tony and Di!' Diana said, as the little boy hid behind Harry's legs and the baby burbled happily in the pushchair. 'I can't believe you named them after us.'

'I can't believe you've managed to get her knocked up, not once, but twice since you've been away,' said Ant, before Diana dug him in the ribs.

'How old are they again?' said Di.

'Tony's eighteen months and Di's six months,' said Josie.

Ant whistled, 'That's going it some,' he said, 'well done, Harry!'

'Oh do shut up,' said Di, 'I think it's perfectly lovely. Parenthood suits you, you both look fantastic.'

They did. The pair of them were tanned, and glowing, and relaxed with the children.

'Fine,' said Harry. 'I've got enough material from our travels for my new book, about going round the world with small children in tow.'

'And we've decided we're going to settle down in Cornwall,' said Josie. 'We got fed up of big cities on our travels.'

'Well, I'm glad you made it back in time to be my bridesmaid,' said Di. 'I couldn't have done it without you.'

'And to think it was meant to be the other way round,' laughed Josie.

'You still not made an honest woman of her yet?' said Ant.

'Ah,' said Harry, 'we did have a wedding ceremony in Thailand, just us and the children on the beach. But I think now we're back...'

'Mum's been emailing me every day, asking whether we've fixed a date yet,' sighed Josie. 'I suppose I have kept her waiting a long time.'

'You are not going to steal our thunder, I hope,' said Ant.

'No chance,' said Josie, 'I have no intention walking up the aisle pregnant.'

'You're never–?' said Diana.

'Seem to be,' said Josie. 'It's so hard to sort out contraception when you're travelling.'

'Harry, old man,' said Ant, 'nice to see you're firing on all cylinders.'

'Now I know I'm home,' said Harry. 'I so haven't missed Ant being rude to me.'

'And we're glad to have you back,' said Diana. 'Now I can start planning my wedding in earnest.'

'So long as you aren't thinking of having fire-eaters,' said Josie.

'I wouldn't dream of it,' said Diana. 'It's going to be a small wedding...'

'...With only 150 guests,' whispered Ant.

'Shh,' said Diana, thumping him. 'And now you two are back, I just know it's going to be perfect.'

You want to know how it's done? I can't tell you that. Shh, or you'll spoil the magic.'
Freddie Puck: *The Art of Illusion*

Acknowledgements

This time around my first thanks have to be to the Bard, Ole Will himself, without whom I'd have never thought of – pinched – this idea. And also thanks to my parents Ann and Joseph Moffatt, who ignited my love of Shakespeare in the first place, and my two inspirational English teachers, Keith Ward and Sue Brown, who fanned the flames. Sue, I hope I've done justice to your favourite play!

At an early stage, I was inspired by the wonderful Pierces, whose song *You'll Be Mine* sends shivers up my spine and sparked an idea. I also delved deeply into Derren Brown's fascinating book *Tricks of the Mind* to get a proper understanding of how a real hypnotist works.

I am hugely grateful to the number of people on Twitter and Facebook who generously responded when I asked for experiences of hypnotism, and particularly to Clare Cody-Richardson, Rowan Coleman, Linda Green and Julie Mayhew, who generously shared their stories with me. And big thanks to my friend Rob Buckle for putting me right at the last minute on TV fees.

As ever, my thanks go to my wonderful agent Dot Lumley, who has always given me stonking support, and my editor Claire Bord and the brilliant team at Avon: Caroline Ridding, Claire Power, Cleo Little, Helen Bolton, Sammia Rafique and Becke Parker.

And finally, thanks to the people who read this in its earliest form: my twin sister Virginia Moffatt who is always my greatest cheerleader; the wonderful Rachael Lucas whose life is similar to mine, only with more children and pets; Sue Brown whose talk of Cornwall is always inspirational, Iris Rooney whose insights were incredibly valuable; and my lovely Twitter friends: Susan Creamer who taught me that procrastination is really processing, and Sarah Williams – I hope your wedding plans work out somewhat better then Josie and Harry's!

And finally a very special thank you to a wonderful couple, Laura and Iwan Griffith for allowing me to share in their special day and giving me an insight into the joys of Welsh weddings!

Afterword

Ideas come from all over the place for writers. And like the greedy magpies we are, we hone in on their shiny brightness and grab every trinket we can get. Often they begin small and burgeon into something as time goes on, and such was the case for me writing this book.

All I knew at the beginning was that my editor, Claire, wanted me to write a summery book. And for a long time I was completely devoid of ideas. Then I heard a song on the radio, and a nugget of an idea began to form. (The song was called *You'll be Mine* by the Pierces, and if you go to my website www.juliawilliamsauthor.com and look in the About section; you will find a list of the soundtracks to my books, and you can listen to it there.)

Music is fantastically important to me when I'm writing, and often forms the inspiration for stories, scenes and characters. This time around the song, which I find very haunting, made me think of enchantments and spells and falling in love. Unusually for me (I have terrible trouble with titles normally), the idea of calling a book *Midsummer Magic* tumbled into my head. I thought immediately of Cornwall, (a place I find both mysterious and fascinating), Standing Stones, and magic.

From there it wasn't too big a stretch to thinking about *A Midsummer Night's Dream*, and how I could write a modern take on it.

Initially, I thought this might be easy – after all, the plot's all there (thank you, Mr Shakespeare), but what works well in a play – an impish sprite dropping magical potion into people's eyes, seemed a bit more problematic in a novel. My first thought was to have my characters somehow take some hallucinogenic drugs, but that proved tricky, as it made my Puckish character seem rather sleazy, and Puck isn't a sleazy character...

In the end I hit on hypnotism as the key. I thought it could be a fun way of unlocking my characters' innermost desires in a way that perhaps they hadn't quite intended. I started to research the work of both Paul McKenna and Derren Brown for background and thus the characters of Freddie Puck, Auberon and Tatiana were born. I am indebted to Derren Brown's fascinating book, *Tricks of the Mind* for explaining the process of hypnotism to me and a lot else besides. If you're interested in mind games, it's well worth a read!

From then on in, I had my story, and though it has inevitably changed somewhat during the telling, the kernel of the original idea, which came from a simple song, remains. It's been a blast to write from start to finish. I hope you enjoyed reading it as much as I enjoyed writing it.

The publishers hope that this book has given you enjoyable reading. Large Print Books are especially designed to be as easy to see and hold as possible. If you wish a complete list of our books please ask at your local library or write directly to:

Magna Large Print Books
Magna House, Long Preston,
Skipton, North Yorkshire.
BD23 4ND

This Large Print Book for the partially sighted, who cannot read normal print, is published under the auspices of

THE ULVERSCROFT FOUNDATION